P9-BIX-211

ELECTORAL BEHAVIOR:

A Comparative Handbook

ELECTORAL BEHAVIOR:
A Comparative Handbook

EDITED BY **Richard Rose**

Secretary, Committee on Political Sociology

Professor of Politics, University of Strathclyde

 THE FREE PRESS

A Division of Macmillan Publishing Co., Inc.

NEW YORK

Collier Macmillan Publishers

LONDON

Copyright © 1974 by The Free Press
    A Division of Macmillan Publishing Co., Inc.

All rights reserved. No part of this book may be reproduced
or transmitted in any form or by any means, electronic or
mechanical, including photocopying, recording, or by any
information storage and retrieval system, without permission
in writing from the Publisher.

The Free Press
A Division of Macmillan Publishing Co., Inc.
866 Third Avenue, New York, N.Y. 10022

Collier–Macmillan Canada Ltd.

Library of Congress Catalog Card Number: 72–11285

Printed in the United States of America

printing number
1   2   3   4   5   6   7   8   9   10

Library of Congress Cataloging in Publication Data

Rose, Richard, 1933–
    Electoral behavior.

    Bibliography: p.
    1. Elections. 2. Political parties.
3. Political sociology. 4. Comparative government.
I. Title.
JF2011.R58.   301.5'92   72-11285
ISBN 0-02-926810-9

To STEIN   with whom there is no comparison

Contents

Acknowledgments

The editor of any book must first of all acknowledge the work of those who have contributed chapters to his volume. This is done with professional and personal pleasure. Professionally, the editor is most grateful to the contributors for adhering closely to the general outline prepared for the volume; this makes it possible for all who read and use it to have the advantage of easy comparison across chapters and, therefore, across nations. In addition, the editor appreciates the willingness of authors to revise their manuscript in response to editorial queries and comments, even when these invited them to depart from the initial outline. Personally, the editor has enjoyed both meetings and correspondence with a group of people who have proven as congenial as they are diverse in origins.

This book would never have been possible without the collaboration of colleagues in the Committee on Political Sociology. The initial research design was stimulated by discussions at a conference at Cambridge University, and carried forward at another conference at the University of Michigan. The first drafts of two papers in this volume were presented at a meeting at the Free University of Berlin, and others at the Loch Lomond conference on voting studies. The 1970 World Congress of the International Political Science Association in Munich also provided a useful opportunity for many contributors to meet as a group. Knowing the difficulties and drudgery of conference organization, the editor wishes to thank those who labored hard to provide the occasions upon which he and his collaborators might meet.

The dedication indicates the preeminent role of Stein Rokkan, the former secretary of the committee, in encouraging this volume and much else, in two decades of nonimperial but nonetheless effective voyaging from his Norse fastness in Bergen. In addition, continuing work in cross-national politics by S. M. Lipset, the former chairman of the committee, and Juan J. Linz, its current chairman, also requires a special acknowledgment. Each chapter comes with acknowledgments specific to it. A number of participants in the Loch Lomond conference contributed ideas to the initial planning of this volume and, upon occasion, useful machine-readable data and unpublished manuscripts. The confreres whose contributions are not otherwise apparent in this volume include D. E. Butler, Nuffield College, Oxford; Kevin Cox, Ohio State University; Hans Daudt and Frans Stokman, University of Amsterdam; Mattei Dogan, Centre National de la Recherche Scientifique, Paris; Klaus Liepelt, Institut für Angewandte Sozialwissenschaft, Bonn/Bad Godesberg; and Dr. Austin Mitchell, formerly of Nuffield College, Oxford and New Zealand, and now part of Anglo-Yorkshire television. The editor is particularly indebted to Klaus Liepelt for demonstrating the intricacies and potentialities of A.I.D. statistical analysis until his auditor got the point.

This book would never have seen the light of day without the assistance of grants from the Nuffield Foundation and the British Social Science Research Council. Mrs. R. West was especially competent in typing and retyping many manuscripts that the editor required. Mrs. K. M. E. Liston assisted greatly with the processing of complex galley and page proofs, and the staff of the Free Press labored long over the most complex manuscript that this editor has ever been responsible for.

Richard Rose
University of Strathclyde
Glasgow, Scotland

Contributors

DON AITKIN is Professor of Politics at Macquarie University, New South Wales. Born in Sydney, he attended the University of New England and received his Ph.D. from Australian National University. Professor Aitkin is the author of *The Country Party in New South Wales* and many articles on Australian politics.

SAMUEL H. BARNES attended Tulane University and received his Ph.D. from Duke University. He has held visiting Fulbright appointments in Paris, Florence, and Rome, and is now Professor of Political Science, University of Michigan, and program director of the Center for Political Studies there. He is the author of *Party Democracy: Politics in an Italian Socialist Federation* and articles on politics in many European countries.

WALTER DEAN BURNHAM received his M.A. and Ph.D. from Harvard University. Before becoming Professor of Political Science at Massachusetts Institute of Technology, he was on the faculty of Kenyon College, Haverford College, and Washington University. He compiled a basic text of 19th-century-America election data, *Presidential Ballots, 1836–1892,* and is the author of *Critical Elections and the Mainsprings of American Politics* and various articles on comparative electoral politics.

PHILIP E. CONVERSE is Professor of Political Science and Sociology and program director of the Center for Political Studies, University of Michigan. He received his Ph.D. from the University of Michigan and was a Fulbright Fellow in France. He is co-author of *The American Voter, Social Psychology,* and *Elections and the Political Order,* co-editor of *Human Meaning of Social Change,* and author of many articles on French and American electoral behavior.

KEITH HILL has been Lecturer in Politics, University of Strathclyde, Glasgow. He received his M.A. from Oxford University and was instructor at University of Leicester. He wrote the chapter on Belgium in *European Political Parties.*

MICHAEL KAHAN is Lecturer in Political Science at Tel-Aviv University, Israel. Born in Detroit, he received his B.A. from Wayne State University and his Ph.D. from University of Michigan. Professor Kahan has been an Assistant Study Director, Survey Research Center, University of Michigan and Nuffield College, Oxford University, and research fellow at Australian National University. He is the author of papers on British, Israeli, and Australian politics.

AREND LIJPHART received his M.A. and Ph.D. from Yale University and taught at the University of California, Berkeley. He is Professor of International Relations, University of Leiden. He is Editor of *European Journal for Political Research,* author of *The Trauma of Decolonialization: The Dutch and West New Guinea, The Politics of Accommodation: Pluralism and Democracy in the Netherlands,* and many articles on international relations and consociational democracy.

PERTTI PESONEN is Professor of Political Science, University of Helsinki and State University of New York at Stony Brook. He received his M.A. and Ph.D. from University of Helsinki and has been a Visiting Fellow, Institute for Social Research, University of Michigan. He was Professor, University of Tampere and Regular Visiting Distinguished Professor, State University of Iowa. He is Editor of *Politiika,* author of *An Election in Finland* and several books in Finnish about Finnish politics.

STEIN ROKKAN is Professor of Sociology at the University of Bergen, Director of Research at the Christian Michelsen Institute in Bergen, and Recurring Visiting Professor of Political Science at Yale University. He is an Honorary Doctor of Philosophy, University of Uppsala, and a Doctor of Politics, University of Helsinki. Professor Rokkan has been Vice-President of the International Sociological Association, President of the International Political Science Association, and Chairman of the European Consortium for Political Research. Among his publications are *Citizens, Elections, Parties; Party Systems and Voter Alignments; Comparative Survey Analysis* and *Mass Politics.*

RICHARD ROSE is Professor of Politics, University of Strathclyde, Glasgow. He received his D. Phil. from Oxford University. Professor Rose taught at the University of Manchester and has been a Visiting Fellow at the Institute of Political Studies at Stanford University. He is Secretary of the Committee on Political Sociology and a member of the United States–United Kingdom Fulbright Educational Commission. He is the author or co-author of *The British General Election of 1959, Must Labor Lose?, Politics in England, Influencing Voters, People in Politics* and *Governing Without Consensus: An Irish Perspective.* He is also the editor or co-editor of *Studies in British Politics, Policy-Making in Britain, European Politics,* and the *International Almanack of Electoral History.*

BO SÄRLVIK, is Docent in Political Science at the University of Goteborg, Sweden, where he received his Ph.D. He has been a visiting fellow at the Institute for Social Research, University of Michigan. Among his publications are *Electoral Behavior in the Swedish Multiparty System* and a number of articles in English and Swedish on Swedish electoral behavior.

MILDRED A. SCHWARTZ received her Ph.D. from Columbia University and is

Professor of Sociology at the University of Illinois at Chicago Circle. Formerly a research analyst for the Canadian Government, she has also been a study director of the National Opinion Research Center in Chicago as well as a visiting Professor at Harvard. She is a founder member of the Association for Canadian Studies in the United States, the author of *Public Opinion and Canadian Identity* and the co-author of *Political Parties and the Canadian Social Structure.*

DEREK W. URWIN is Docent in Comparative Politics at the University of Bergen, Norway. Born in England, he has been a Ford Fellow at Yale University, and formerly lectured in politics at the University of Strathclyde, Glasgow. He is the author of *Western Europe Since 1945,* the co-author of *Scottish Political Behavior,* and the author of many articles on comparative party politics.

HENRY VALEN is Professor of Political Science at the University of Oslo, Norway, where he received his M.A. and Ph.D. Formerly Research Director for the Institute of Social Research at Oslo, he has been Visiting Fellow at the Institute for Social Research at the University of Michigan and Visiting Professor at the Universities of Illinois, Iowa, Minnesota, and Wisconsin. He is co-author of *Political Parties in Norway,* and the author of various articles on Norwegian electoral behavior.

JOHN H. WHYTE is Reader in Political Science at Queens University in Belfast, Northern Ireland. Born in Malaya, he received his B.A. and B.Litt. from Oxford and his Ph.D. from Queen's University, Belfast. Formerly Lecturer in History at Makerere University, Uganda, Lecturer in Politics at University College, Dublin, and visiting fellow at the Center for International Studies, Harvard, he has authored *The Independent Irish Party, 1850–59, Church and State in Modern Ireland, 1923–70,* and various articles on Irish political history.

ELECTORAL BEHAVIOR:

A Comparative Handbook

1. COMPARABILITY IN ELECTORAL STUDIES

RICHARD ROSE

In the comparative study of politics every researcher faces a dilemma: whether to analyze only those countries he can know well at firsthand or whether to generalize about dozens of countries using data drawn from less familiar sources and contexts. Knowledge and ignorance are matters of degree: the student of local history may think that the historian of a nation is attempting an impossibly broad task, and the latter will think the former is confining himself to a dangerously parochial point of view. Similarly, the student of politics within one or two states may think that studies taking the whole world as a universe are broad to the point of emptiness. Reciprocally, those who take the globe as their territory, treating continents or states as the constituent units, may regard other researchers as lacking in perspective. Because these differences are matters of degree, there are many different ways one can combine generality and specific detail; the particular value placed upon either depends in part upon the problem at hand. It is in the nature of dilemmas that neither extreme is always the right one.

I

The case for the comparative study of electoral behavior rests upon strong substantive and methodological grounds. Only by comparisons across space and time can one learn under what circumstances and to what extent hypotheses hold true. Electoral behavior is particularly amenable to comparative analysis because it produces a large mass of quantitative data. Quantitative data is not only suitable for statistical analysis but also tends to present fewer difficulties in achieving conceptual equivalence cross-nationally. Voting is the chief form of mass political behavior in societies with competitive free elections. Whether individuals cast a vote because of traditional loyalties or conscious programmatic reasons, their choice can be significant as an affirmation of identity with a particular group, subculture, or *famille spirituelle* within the state. Votes also have consequences for government, as they strengthen or weaken the position of leaders of organized political groups bargaining about power.

Comparison makes no assumption that the countries compared are alike in every respect. Nor is it expected that they are unique in every respect. Total dissimilarity would be as surprising as total identity. To compare all is not to confound all. But to admit that countries differ in some respects is not to suggest that they differ in every respect, e.g., that in one country only working-class people vote socialist,

3

whereas in another only middle-class people vote socialist. Reciprocally, to advance universalistic propositions arguing the "essential" sameness of political behavior everywhere is to risk sacrificing much meaning by reductionism, or stretching definitions to embrace in a single category entities that are distinct from each other in many ways. To emphasize differences between countries stimulates the questions: different in what sense? under what circumstances? and to what degree?

The obstacles to cross-national comparison are formidable. They are not easily resolved by spending more and more money on data collection and bigger and better computers. They arise from the software that is part of the intellectual equipment of every social scientist. As a scholar spreads his interests more widely, he is likely to have less appreciation of the contextual and temporal limitations of his data. This sacrifice can be justified if comparison is motivated by a desire to test big ideas. While grand concepts and hypotheses can readily be stated, they are not easy to define in terms capable of reliable and valid application to dozens of different countries. For example, it is far easier to talk of "Left" and "Right" in the abstract than it is to decide whether many Western parties can be meaningfully described as either left- or right-wing on a simple one-dimensional scale. Difficulties in translating familiar ideas into precise measures are equally great when one seeks to analyze social structure empirically. How many social classes does a country have? Do differences in the number of classes arise from differences in sociological conventions or from differences intrinsic to social structure?

Given the intellectual as well as the practical difficulties involved in studying politics comparatively, it is not surprising that most scholars have moved cautiously in this area of research. A typical strategy has been to use an internationally recognized conceptual framework and techniques, but to apply it to data drawn from only a single country. American scholars writing about the United States provide numerous and brilliant examples of testing and generalizing ideas from knowledge of a single country. In the past two decades political sociologists have become increasingly ready to study a concept or the relationship between a pair of concepts by testing hypotheses wherever data could be found. At first this was usually in a single place, sometimes the community in which the scholar resided. Gradually scholars with similar interests in different places began to meet to compare ideas and exchange data. *Political Man* by S. M. Lipset (1960) was an early attempt to synthesize what could be said about an eclectic collection of data from a range of Western countries. Robert Alford's *Party and Society* (1963) was a landmark attempt to use survey data from four Western countries—America, Australia, Britain, and Canada—and, by re-analyzing it, produce results that went well beyond what had originally been published, both statistically and intellectually.

The technological revolution in the social sciences today has resulted in the intercontinental diffusion of quantifiable data about social structure and political behavior. New computers and new computing techniques have been developed to analyze this data with a speed that exceeds the calendar of quadrennial elections. The growing volume of electoral data has led to the foundation of archives to disseminate materials as well as to many conferences and working groups dedicated to the need to stand-ardize conventions and documentation concerning samples, interviewing techniques, formating data for computer input, and statistical analysis. The relative ease with which machine-readable quantitative data can be reproduced and transferred from university to university and country to country on magnetic tape now makes it practicable for scholars to order files of machine-readable materials from a data bank as they might order census volumes that are read much more slowly with the human eye. As yet, we have few guidelines about the extent to which specific indicators used in different national contexts can measure the same theorectically meaningful phenomena. Before people who are familiar with research problems in one country (or who are unfamiliar with them in any national context) begin to cast their nets more widely, it is desirable to take stock of what we already know about social structure and electoral behavior in Western nations.

II

The purpose of this volume is to provide a systematic and detailed introduction to the social structures, party systems, and electoral behavior of major Western nations. The tables provide information that can readily be compared from nation to nation. The text provides interpretations of tables and discusses contextual characteristics that may be unique to one land. The scope of what can be contained in a single volume is ultimately limited by a mixture of practical and theoretical considerations. The initial memorandum to contributors contained the following editorial injunction:

> Each chapter should be thought of as a basic guide for an intelligent social scientist unfamiliar with your country. The prime characteristic of such an introduction is that it clearly and carefully identifies fundamental intellectual issues and, where options are available in strategies of analysis, evaluates the practical consequences of alternative choices. Several books could be or have been written about the subjects to be covered in each chapter. Footnotes and bibliography should provide references to information and matters of controversy that cannot be covered within the compass of a single chapter.

Given such an introduction, a scholar seeking to do secondary analysis of a country would have sufficient initial background to begin work.

The universe of countries suitable for inclusion in this volume has been determined by several theoretical criteria. The first is the persistance of competitive free elections since 1945. Elections without free competition or the fair counting of votes may have some things in common with conventional Western ballots, but not sufficient to warrant comparison here. The second criteria is that a country ranks high in terms of conventional socioeconomic indicators of industrialization. Confining study to industrial-ized nations avoids problems of the comparability of literate and illiterate electors, or the validity of national elections without national media of communication.[1]

Before one begins to make comparisons across levels of socioeconomic development, it is well to consider whether there is such a thing as a single, homogeneous Western pattern of electoral behavior. Limiting study to countries with cultural origins in Christendom may seem a surprising condition to apply to countries that are often considered secular. The stipulation is necessary because research has repeatedly emphasized the importance in the development of party politics of divisions among nominally Christian groups and divisions between clerical and anticlerical groups. While the causes of these differences may now be matters of past history, the past can still persist into the present through political institutions and the intergenerational transmission of party identification. The principal countries excluded by this stipulation are Japan and Israel.

Using universalistic criteria to define a field of study is important for what it avoids as well as what it includes. This approach avoids examining only those countries that illustrate one's predetermined intellectual conclusions. It also avoids choosing countries on grounds of the convenience of data or of scholarly acquaintance. The size of a country is not presumed to determine its political significance. The smallest country included in this volume, the Republic of Ireland, is about one eighty-fifth the size of the largest, the United States. The chapter on the Netherlands illustrates that relatively small countries can still be great in their social and political complexity. Moreover, no assumptions are made about geographical determinism. Concentration upon modern societies originating in the Christian tradition inevitably assures a substantial representation of European countries. But it also embraces the Anglo-American societies of North America and Australasia. Bridging the Atlantic and the Pacific oceans is important in order to reduce the Eurocentrism of some comparative scholars, the insularity of some English scholars, and the All-American outlook of yet a third group of political scientists. Hypotheses about similarity are no more likely to be validated than dissimilarity hypotheses, for the countries have not been chosen because of the certain or assumed presence of particular conditions.

The table of contents makes evident that chapters could not be secured from every Western nation for publication in this volume. The reasons for this are familiar. In some countries there has still been no nationwide sample survey of voting behavior, nor has aggregate electoral data been intensively analyzed. Without some quantitative evidence about the relationship of social structure to voting behavior, a chapter could not contain sufficient comparable information to justify inclusion in this volume. In addition to quantitative data an editor must find a knowledgable scholar with the time to write a manuscript consistent with the aims of this book. Unfortunately, this is not always easily achieved, for knowledgable men have many demands made upon them, especially those engaged in comparative research. Faced with difficulties in obtaining manuscripts by an established deadline, an editor may delay publication or publish the chapters he has at hand. The editor has chosen the latter alternative, in the belief that the range as well as the quality of what follows is sufficient to cover all major types of Western nations in Continental Europe, Scandinavia, and the Anglo-American world. The alternative—to wait for the last chapter to be completed—was rejected as risking an indefinite or permanent delay.

Fortunately, a reader need not be solely dependent upon this book as his source of knowledge. It can be taken as an introduction in the belief that serious political sociologists will want to continue explorations after reading these pages. The detailed multilingual citations provide ample guides to further reading, and by their location in the text give easy reference on specific points of fact. Any reader wishing an introduction and bibliography to institutional information about European countries not included in this volume can find both in the compendious two-volume work of the Heidelberg *Instituts für Politische Wissenschaft, Die Wahl der Parlamente,* and in Stein Rokkan and Jean Meyriat, editors, *International Guide to Electoral Statistics.*[2] The bibliography of French electoral studies is lengthy, and substantial numbers of surveys have been undertaken and reported in greater or lesser detail.[3] Materials on Austria have been collected and published in a four-volume opus edited by Rodney Stiefbold and others, *Wahlen Und Parteien In Österreich.*[4] Detailed bibliographies of electoral research in all Scandinavian countries can be found in the successive annual volumes of *Scandinavian Political Studies,* first published in 1966.[5] This extremely useful book contains not only articles from research in progress about Scandinavia but also short notes written after each Scandinavian election. A major nationwide study of the Swiss electorate occurred in the autumn of 1971 under the joint auspices of the Universities of Geneva and Zurich. Bibliographies and articles on politics in Switzerland can also be found in the annual publication, *Annuaire Suisse de Science Politique/Schweizerisches Jahrbuch für Politische Wissenschaft.*[6] At the time this book was written New Zealand had not been the subject of a nationwide sample survey; community studies and ecological analysis have provided significant amounts of information about its electoral politics, although not in a format suitable for inclusion in this volume.[7]

The author of each national chapter was presented with a detailed draft outline, specifying topics to be noted, even if the only comment appropriate would be "not relevant here". Specimen draft chapters were provided.[8] By making explicit the questions that could and should be asked about electoral behavior, this volume avoids being a more-or-less random compendium of interesting facts that political sociologists think noteworthy about their country. The contributors have made a major commitment to comparison by casting their chapters in a framework permitting easy cross-reference. Any reader wishing to compare nations systematically gains enormously from this consistency. By using the index for quick cross-reference, a student of politics may readily learn what influence age or sex has upon party loyalty in many different countries. The two chapters about America are exceptional in that they do not follow exactly the general scheme. One reason for this is the existence of a large amount of literature in this field. Another is the ready accessibility of machine-readable data on American voting behavior through the Inter-University Consortium for Political Research of the University of Michigan. Findings from these surveys, commencing in 1948, are presented in *The American Voter* and *Elections and the Political Order.* Moreover, any attempt to summarize survey data about American elections is handicapped by the absence of any "normal" election since 1944, when Franklin D. Roosevelt was elected President with 53.4 percent of the popular vote.[9] Since then third-party candidates and deviations of voters from persisting party identifications have produced results considerably at variance with each other. The chapter by Philip Converse considers the extent to which social characteristics significant in American voting behavior can also be significant in other lands. W. Dean Burnham's chapter reviews at appropriate length characteristics of American electoral institutions that are often incapable of generalization to other countries.

An outline of topics might be based upon deductive or inductive reasoning. The former ensures that the parts specified have a logical structure, the latter that nothing is omitted that is regarded as intuitively or prima facie important. If research is conceived as a process of learning through time rather than a single act, the two approaches can be treated as complementary. Constructing a model free of empirical constraints will focus attention upon the connections between parts of the model, thus preventing the introduction of concepts in limbo. By trying to connect particulars one can avoid pandemonium. But unless one checks parts of the model against one or more countries, there is a danger of omitting many points of detail, cumulatively of considerable potential importance. Reciprocally, a content analysis of the literature about voting and elections would produce a long list of frequently discussed phenomena. But it would not indicate in what order, other than popularity, these phenomena might be discussed, nor would it indicate how one might relate information about social structure, electoral laws, and voting behavior. By seeking to apply general criteria to familiar contexts, one can find what has been left out; in the social sciences as in aerospace engineering, "what you leave out will kill you every time."

The basic assumption of the topical outline is simply stated: an election is a multivariate phenomenon. In other words, it is something more complicated than a simple summary of individual preferences for parties A and B, and it reflects a very wide range of influences. To understand how elections are won and lost, one must consider not only the influence social characteristics have on the individual voter, but also the roles played by such institutional arrangements as election laws—these also affect how many seats each party wins in its national parliament. The relationship between the multitude of influences is represented schematically in Figure 1. The entries above the line indicate influences upon individual voters: eligibility to vote rules, turnout considerations, party actions and political events, social characteristics, standing party identification, and issue predispositions. Many studies of voting terminate with statements about the preferences of individual voters. The most important political phenomena are not individual choices but the aggregate distribution of seats in the national parliament, affecting control of executive government. In a country with a simple two-party system the result is conceived as total victory or defeat; in a multiparty system in which coalition government is the norm there are complications in converting parliamentary seats into coalition shares.[10]

The information that authors provide in the chapters that follow concerns individual behavior, institutional arrangements, and aggregate election outcomes. Many details can be related to the entries in the flow chart because the entries are sufficiently abstract to accommodate phenomena from many different countries. The chief type

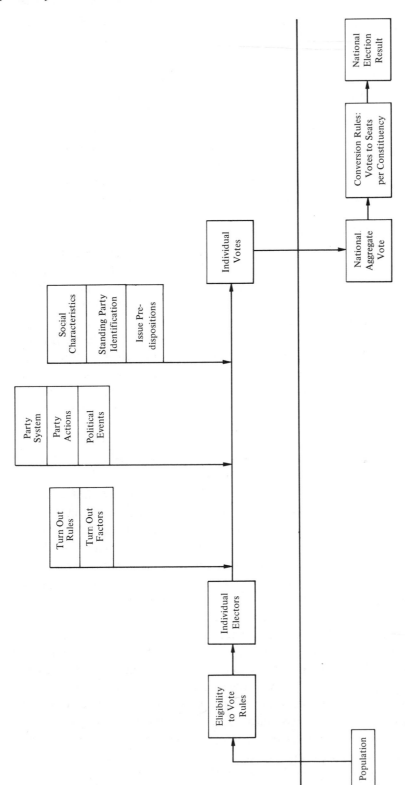

Figure 1: How an Election Result is Determined.

of information omitted concerns political events and issue predispositions: this is due to the fluid and sometimes idiosyncratic nature of such events within a country. To treat these topics properly would require a lengthy history of postwar events in each land. The flow chart is sufficiently "loose" in a logical sense so that additional influences can be entered. The only requirement is that the information added should be explicitly linked to other electoral phenomena. This flexibility is crucial, for it means the model can always be adapted to unusual but real political contexts; it is not confined, as are so many rational-deductive models, to the land of *Weissnichtwo*.

In a single country at a single point in time certain features of the model may be treated as constants: for instance, eligibility-to-vote rules and rules for converting votes to seats are likely to apply equally throughout the country. By contrast, political events will be highly variable. A change in the voting patterns or national election results in two successive elections in a country may reflect changes in the variables, e.g., new political events and/or changes in the relationships between these influences. For example, a particular event may cause some voters to deviate from their standing party identification because of special issue predispositions. In a lengthy period of time institutional features become variables too: franchise rules, eligibility-to-vote requirements, turnout rules, and the names and characters of parties may each alter. The rules for converting votes to seats can also change. Comparative analysis immediately turns many constants into variables. Institutional arrangements that must be the same within a country are unlikely to be identical between countries. For example, while "one man, one vote" is usually found in all Western societies today, this is not inevitably the case, as the campaign for federal voter-registration laws in America has demonstrated.

The social characteristics meriting political consideration here may be identified deductively or inductively. To proceed according to a single a priori theory is risky because of the problem of deciding which theory to adopt. Is everything of electoral significance to be reduced to economic categories? to social-psychological attitudes? to belief in one or none of the various Christian doctrines established by the Reformation? A great advantage of the approach of S. M. Lipset and Stein Rokkan is that it simultaneously considers the potential importance of different kinds of social influences, while economically confining attention to a few dimensions of social and political differentiation. The discussion by Lipset and Rokkan illustrates the difficulty of relating some theoretically important abstractions to empirical social phenomena. This problem is especially acute with regard to "center-periphery" differences, one of their crucial concepts. Are these differences to be conceived of as spatial distinctions between the capital city and the rest of a society? Or is a single region isolated from the cultural outlook general to a society? To what extent is the distinction one of language, national identity, or skin color—independent of territory? As Lipset and Rokkan provide no clear guidelines for the application of these concepts to survey data, and as the editor's experience indicates that these concepts are not easily applicable cross-nationally,[11] their approach is here treated as a suggestive but not an exhaustive catalog.

The social characteristics discussed in the chapters that follow were informed by theory but not determined by a single theory. All the survey measures deemed relevant to the Lipset-Rokkan approach are included, and then some. This strategy can be justified by the fact that the authors themselves allow for the emergence of new dimensions of political differentiation. Also, as Erik Allardt has noted, their analysis is not logically constrained to four categories.[12] This openness to additional data has proven useful because both age and sex differences have increasingly become subjects of political discussion since the initial conception of this volume. Moreover, this openness allows the author of an individual chapter to introduce any social characteristics he considers important in his own country, whether or not this importance is general. The limits upon the choice of social influences are practical. Standard demographic variables widely used in social research are obvious candidates for inclusion, and they are, by definition, normally available in surveys in every country included in this study. Such social characteristics are not always measured in identical form; for example, some surveys only ask about religious preference, whereas others also ask about church attendance. Because of this standard check list many social characteristics are explicitly documented as showing "no influence." So-called objective social attributes are here emphasized much more than subjective attitudes because the former are considered independent variables, and the latter, intervening variables. In the case of European countries there is also the danger that a subjective attitude such as party identification is not something independent of party preference, but merely another way of measuring a single phenomenon.[13] Additionally, there are problems of linguistic and conceptual equivalence in trying to apply measures of political attitudes in a cross-national context.[14] A separate volume would be required to work through all the problems involved at this level of analysis.

The authors of the chapters that follow were requested to be consistent in the presentation of tables of survey data to facilitate comparison and reanalysis. Prior to the presentation of each table about influences upon partisanship, there should be a discussion of how the social characteristic in question is measured in that particular country. For example, while years of schooling may always be represented by numbers, these figures may have different meaning, depending upon the year at which children start school and the minimum school-leaving age. The concept of a "minimum education" is theoretically clear. Nonetheless, readers will want to know whether this refers ten years or four years of schooling, or even illiteracy. Tables normally include a column showing the distribution of a given social characteristic within the society. The number of survey interviews upon which tables are based is given in the text or with each table. Thus an individual can calculate the number of cases in each cell in each table, and repercentage or recombine the data as he wishes, for use in other social-scientific contexts.

A major consideration in the analysis of social structure and voting is avoiding correlations that are in fact spurious. Nothing is more galling than to see a series of tables about the relationship of partisanship and age, sex, education, etc., with no indication of the extent to which apparently strong correlations are simply a function of the relationship of an omitted third influence, such as class. Each author was requested in presenting data to control consistently for the influence of one major determinant of partisanship. Only one control can normally be used if one is to avoid tables in which many cells are based upon statistically unreliable small numbers. Authors were not told which social characteristic should be regarded as most important in their national context. Where more than one might prima facie appear important, as is the case with class and religion in Germany and the Netherlands, each author has justified his choice of the key control and presented some tables showing what happens when an alternative is employed.

When survey data about the social determinants of partisanship are at hand, it is obscurantist and sterile to restrict oneself to purely verbal discussion about the relative importance of social influences upon party choice. A sense of magnitude and order can be gained by subjecting the data to multivariate statistical analysis in order to learn, with all the precision that statistics can supply, how much influence each of a number of social characteristics has. In the context of a single national study the choice of statistical techniques and of social characteristics employed as independent variables can proceed in a number of different ways. In comparative research it is important to use the same technique in every country. The multivariate statistical technique used here is that of A.I.D. (Automatic Interaction Detector), also known as tree analysis, because it produces a series of dichotomized groupings in a pattern that resembles the branches of a tree. The technique is thoroughly described in technical literature, and, following explorations by Klaus Liepelt in Germany and Austria and Bo Sarlvik in Sweden, it has become increasingly used in voting studies.[15] Tree analysis produces several statistics of interest in comparative research. It shows what social characteristics are most important in relation to partisanship, and how much of the total variance in partisanship is explained. In addition the terminal categories in the branches of the tree form recognizable and discrete groupings of people according to several social characteristics held in common; the size and exclusiveness of political partisanship of these end groups is itself important in characterizing the aggregate balance of social and political forces within a society.

The purpose of statistical analysis is not to maximize the amount of variance explained but to acquire knowledge of theoretical significance. If the former were the aim, then the more "contaminated" or tautological the relationship between two measures the better, for more variance would then be explained. In comparative analysis it is less important to strive for a total explanation of a single country than it is to consider countries in relation to each other. To make comparisons valid, it is particularly important that the variables used in each nation be the same insofar as possible. The contributors to this volume have responded nobly to the editor's request to include only the following social characteristics in their tree analysis: occupational class, trade-union membership, religious identification, church attendance, education, urban-rural residence, regional residence, linguistic differences (if relevant), age, and sex. When a good case appeared for employing additional social characteristics, these were included; inevitably, measures were occasionally omitted because of lack of data.

One can confidently compare the amount of variance explained by trees for different countries, because the same number and kind of independent variables were used.

A persistent problem in tree analysis is that the dependent variable must be stated in a dichotomous form. In a two-party system this can easily be done by excluding those who favor minor parties and those without any party preference, because they are a small proportion of the electorate. In a multiparty system it is not always simple to dichotomize the system. The problem is not confined to statistical analysis. It also arises in parliamentary votes, which reduce members of parliament to two categories: supporters and opponents of the government, with a small proportion of abstainers. The decision that each author makes about dichotomizing the party system is explained in the text, and itself is an important interpretive fact about the nation's party system. In countries in which more than one division of parties could be justified tree analyses were conducted with more than one set of dependent variables, and the results were compared in order to see which division of parties was most usefully associated with social divisions.

Every catalog of important political influences must have some limit. A single book, especially one that seeks to discuss many countries in detail, must necessarily have narrower confines than a volume with fewer themes or many themes discussed discursively and at a high level of generality. This volume excludes from consideration what happens within parliament and in the formation of a cabinet, except insofar as these institutions influence franchise laws or the nature of the party system. This focus in no sense implies that one area of political study is more important than another; it simply recognizes the necessity for the division of academic labor. The decision to draw the line at the "boundary" mechanism of converting parliamentary seats into control of the executive is particularly justifiable because of the large body of writings about coalition government.[16]

III

This volume presents the stuff of comparative analysis; no chapter is itself comparative, because of the need to know many details about national circumstances as a precondition of synthesis. The reader thus has an advantage denied each author: he can see how all the countries represented here compare. In this introduction only a few points of significance can be reviewed briefly.

The historical evolution of the countries studied reflects a number of common experiences: the formation of a state and the maintenance of its independence in war and peace; the transition from a primarily rural society to one in which industry and commerce are of major importance; and the resolution of differences among Christian churches and between clerical and anticlerical groups. There is no single way in which any of these problems has been resolved in all countries. In the shift from a rural to an industrial economy all nations have seen the size of their rural population decline.

But the decline of a smallholding peasantry is very different from the decline of the numbers employed in the large estates of the nobility. To note that each country has a unique history is not to say that its problems and alternatives for choice are unique, but that the sum total of past events is never exactly and entirely reproduced elsewhere.

The methods that social scientists can use to study elections are several and similar in all Western countries. Initially, scholars concentrated attention upon the analysis of election results in isolation. The analysis of election returns assures accuracy. This advantage is especially important in the study of the vote for small, regionally concentrated parties or for extremist parties such as the Communists, whose supporters may not readily identify themselves to survey interviewers.[17] It is a short step from noting peculiarities in electoral districts to seeking explanations in social differences, relying upon census data as well as impressionistic evidence to characterize these districts. The use of census data to characterize electoral districts is appropriate, insofar as community characteristics, e.g., the proportion of manual workers in an area, exercise an independent influence upon individual behavior. Ecological studies can be used less confidently as a source of information about the voting behavior of individuals, because ecological data do not take the individual as the basic unit of account. Sample surveys usually provide the most reliable and valid information about individual partisanship. The accuracy of sample surveys is likely to decline—assuming a constant sample size—when the number of parties rises, because the numbers of respondents supporting smaller parties in a multiparty system will be limited. National cross section samples are also unlikely to have substantial data about small subgroups in the population, whether they are distinctive in territorial or social terms. Survey and ecological methods for studying voting are not mutually exclusive; they can be profitably combined or alternated, according to the problem at hand.[18] In addition descriptive writings about elections can provide useful knowledge about the particular circumstances of a given general election. If one is seeking to test generalizations with data from a particular election, it is helpful to know whether the issues of the moment were likely to stimulate deviant voting by any groups within the electorate. The weakness of descriptive studies is that they are cast in a framework that does not permit easy comparison across time or space.[19]

The administration of elections reveals a limited number of differences in Western countries.[20] The character and status of officials chosen by ballot is the same in most lands: every country has nationwide popular elections to choose individuals to sit in at least one house of its national parliament. It is customary to have some form of local elections, but only in federal countries are lower-tier authorities likely to have substantial autonomous powers. This means that the typical citizen casts a ballot about once every four years for members of parliament, and perhaps one ballot in the interim for local representatives to a council with limited powers. In such circumstances it might be more reasonable if we did not refer to individuals as "voters," since this is a role they perform infrequently. Instead one might speak of "the behavior of ordinary individuals in electoral situations."[21] It is only in the United States that an individual has the opportunity to vote frequently, with ballots for a large number of administrative officials as well as legislators. It could be argued that the very infrequency of elections in many Western countries makes party choice more significant as an indicator of social rather than party loyalties, because social influences are continuing, whereas political campaign influences are infrequent.

By definition all the party systems considered here are multiparty systems, that is to say, more than one party contests national elections. Within political science two-party systems are conventionally treated as a special form of multiparty system, because of the presumed simplification of electoral choice that such a system offers between Ins and Outs. Any system with three or more parties is treated differently on the grounds that no one party need secure a government majority. The following chapters provide much evidence of the limitations of these distinctions. Few Western countries have a party system that matches the two-party ideal. The United States has seen third-party candidates appear in every political generation. Uncertainties of definition make it difficult to say whether Britain is a two-party system: the application of five different criteria show that it is a two-party system by some standards but not by others. If a two-party system is defined as one in which two and only two parties win votes, then no Western nation has a pure two-party system. If it is defined as one in which two and only two parties usually win seats in the national legislature, then America, Australia, and New Zealand can qualify for this distinction.

To note that most party systems consist of more than two parties is not to assert that they are all similar in any positive sense. It is even possible for a multiparty system to offer a clear-cut choice between Ins and Outs when one party consistently governs alone. In Ireland, for instance, the strength of *Fianna Fáil* has offered voters a choice between an interparty coalition government or a single-party *Fianna Fáil* government. By contrast the Netherlands has always been without a single dominant party; the multiplicity of parties winning seats there can fluctuate substantially. The chapters in this book emphasize that the relationships between parties in a single country cannot be reduced to simple questions of number.[22]

A comparison of the social structure of Western countries shows initially that characteristics treated as variables in some countries—e.g., language use—are constants in others. Language cannot be a source of division within the Netherlands or Germany because of linguistic unity, just as it has a high potential for political influence in a bilingual society such as Canada. Of the basic Lipset-Rokkan categories of differentiation, only industrial-class differences, regional, and urban-rural differences must occur in every land. There is no necessity for a society to be divided on religious, linguistic, or national identity terms. Frequently, differences in social structure are matters of degree. For example, Ireland has more farmers than Britain, Italy has more practicing Catholics than Australia or Sweden. When differences become great, as can occur with religion, one may treat them as if they were differences of kind, i.e., beyond a certain threshold, the whole of society may be affected by the weight of one part.

Efforts to compare within-nation religious differences illustrate how familiar concepts can have different meanings according to national contexts. In consequence we must rethink our idea of religion and recognize that differences can arise in more

than one dimension, even within a range of nominally Christian countries. One classification distinguishes denominations: conventionally, Catholics and Protestants are
each treated as homogeneous groups, though Protestant denominations may differ
substantially from each other.[23] Where free-thinking is organized or where religious
distinctions are clear, it can be meaningful to admit a third category, the confessedly
secular.[24] In classifying countries one might proceed by distinguishing between countries of homogeneous faith and those with divisions about faiths; additionally or alternatively, a simple index of proportion Catholic is sometimes used, given the historic
importance of Catholic-Protestant differences, and also, Catholic-anticlerical differences. Church attendance is also useful to identify persons most likely to be influenced
by religious organizations. Unfortunately, this measure creates difficulties because
the norm for Catholic churchgoing is much higher than that for Protestants. Hence,
regularity in attendance is not the same in both groups. Moreover, nonattendance may
signify mere indifference, or else the principled abstention of an anticleric. In no one
society are all of these differences simultaneously prominent: in the Netherlands and
Germany, however, religious differences are multidimensional rather than dichotomous in nature. Italy demonstrates that a dichotomous religious division between
practicing Catholics and anticlericals can polarize as well as simplify political choice.

Social characteristics are here important insofar as they affect the political behavior of individuals or the aggregate pattern of political divisions within a society.
Theories of social determinism imply that to a large extent social differences structure
party loyalties. Statistically, this means that social characteristics should explain a
large proportion of the variance in the tree analyses found in most chapters of this
book. By contrast, voluntaristic theories or theories stressing individual perception
and motivation imply that any multivariate statistical technique relying solely upon
social-structure characteristics would explain a relatively small proportion of the
variance in party loyalties. The use of virtually the same variables in the tree analyses
included here provides a straightforward test of these alternative hypotheses. Moreover,
the exclusion of persons without party preferences from analysis and the dichotomization of choice required by A.I.D. should raise the level of variance explained,
inasmuch as persons without party loyalties may be less susceptible to social influences;
in a complex multiparty system they may support several parties or simply veto one.

A comparison of the A.I.D. tree profiles for 15 Western countries (Table 1)
shows, first, that there is enormous variation in the structuring of the vote by social
influences. The Netherlands evinces the highest amount of variation explained;
Lijphart's careful analysis shows that this is not a transitory phenomenon, nor is it
dependent upon dichotomizing religious as against secular parties. The extent to which
social differences structure party loyalties is declining in the Netherlands, but it still
determines more than half the vote (infra, pp 259ff). The importance of social structure in the Netherlands arises from the phenomenon of *verzuiling*, which segments
groups within the national society. It is striking that Sweden, a country tied for third
in the degree of social structuring of the vote, is a society with a minimum of internal
divisions except occupational strata. The high level of industrialization and affluence

achieved in Sweden has not caused a decline in social determinism. This pattern is not unique to Sweden among Scandinavian countries; it equally affects Finland. In Norway occupational class, reinforced by regionalism and religion, structures partisanship to a high degree too. While Norway has had a long history of political differences about a variety of social questions,[25] it is noteworthy that occupational class and not other features of social structure account for most of the variance. Moreover Eckstein describes Norway as best characterized by egalitarianism rather than the hierarchical values of a *Standestaat*.[26] In Denmark economic influences similarly account for the bulk of the explained variance.

TABLE 1: **Comparative Effect of Social Structure upon Partisanship**

| | Variance Explained by | | | | |
	Occupation %	Religion %	Region %	Total %	Year
Netherlands	0	50.1	0.4	51.2	1968
Austria	12.0	30.3	2.9	46.0	1969
Sweden	32.0	0	0	37.9	1964
Norway	24.3	3.9	2.2	37.9	1965
Belgium	5.8	23.3	2.9	34.5	1970
France – 4th Republic	4.9	28.4	1.4	34.4	1956
– 5th Republic	2.4	11.2	4.4	18.7	1971
Finland	31.8	0	0	33.2	1966
Italy	0.3	21.9	1.5	28.3	1968
Denmark	19.4	n.a.	n.a.	27.7	1968
Germany	2.1	12.0	0	19.7	1967
Canada	1.7	8.0	2.9	15.0	1965
Australia	8.9	1.8	0	14.6	1967
U.S.A.	3.0	5.5	4.5	12.8	1952–64
Great Britain	3.3	0	0	12.0	1970
Ireland	0	0	0.5	3.1	1969

n.a. = not available
Sources as cited in chapters in this volume, except analysis by author of data from:
Austria: Institut fur Empirische Sozialforschung, Vienna.
France: 4th Republic, Institut National d'Etudes Demographiques, Paris; 5th Republic, SOFRES survey (February, 1971).
Denmark: Danish Marked Analyze, Copenhagen.
Canada: John Meisel et al. Canadian Election Study.
U.S.A.:   Secondary analysis by Klaus Liepelt of pooled presidential surveys, 1952–1964, by the University of Michigan.

The Scandinavian countries demonstrate that class differences may be important determinants of party loyalties without implying conflict at the level of the regime. This point is further emphasized by comparing them with Italy, where class differences are customarily considered great, and a multiplicity of Marxian parties seek votes to challenge the regime. Notwithstanding these institutional factors, partisanship is less structured by social differences in Italy than in Scandinavia. The same is also true of Belgium. Religion is the most important determinant of party preference in Italy, Belgium, and France, countries where regime challenges have been significant since the war. This variable not only reflects the role of the Church, but also the importance of anticlericalism in developing support for Communist or left-wing parties. In Germany too it is religion rather than class that is of greatest importance.

The freedom of Irish party loyalties from social determinants stands in extreme contrast to the Dutch picture. In Ireland people do not divide politically along class, religious, or regional lines. Party loyalty appears to derive from divisions originating in the civil war in Ireland after the 1921 Treaty with Britain. The position of other Anglo-American countries shows that social structure is of some importance in structuring party loyalties, but it does not account for a relatively large proportion of variance. In America, Britain, Canada, and Australia the proportion of variance explained is about one-third of that in Europe; moreover, it is much the same for each of the three countries. The British figure for the 1970 election reflects a decline in social structuring from the 1964 election, when 20.6 percent of total variance could be explained; but even this figure would not alter the foregoing generalization. The American figure, obtained by pooling surveys from the 1952, 1956, 1960, and 1964 presidential elections is likely to be unstable, but this instability itself reflects the weakness of social influences in structuring persisting party loyalties. The ability of the Liberal party to draw support from all social groups, including French-speaking Catholics, results in a low degree of social structuring of the vote in Canada.

The pattern of determinism displayed in Table 1 suggests that party systems in which two parties secure the great bulk of the vote tend to reflect social differences less than multiparty systems. The pressures to encompass large blocks of voters and the premium placed upon securing an absolute majority of seats to win control of government results in the major parties aggregating the views of voters inclusively, cutting across social distinctions. By contrast, in a multiparty system with proportional representation any single party may appeal to a narrow bloc of voters without jeopardizing its chances of participation in a coalition government. The findings for Germany reinforce this conclusion, for Germany is a country in which both religious and class differences have historically been very important, and its two major parties are confessional or socialist. Notwithstanding a social structure that, like the Netherlands, emphasizes both religion and class, Germany shows a limited degree of social structuring of the vote, presumably because of the desire of both the parties in a two-party system to attract support across lines of social division.

The emphasis placed upon class differences and, at times, religious and regional differences in theoretical studies of parties is only partly borne out by comparative statistical analysis. A.I.D. techniques credit the whole of the variance explained at any division to a single variable, "plumping" for the importance of a single influence. Occupation, religion, or region are shown to be of primary importance—depending upon the country. Table 1 is also noteworthy because of the relative importance of religious differences when they are present to compete with differences in occupational class. The degree of significance varies greatly from the Netherlands to Ireland. Only in the United States are all three social characteristics of approximately equal importance. The contrast between Southerners and those outside the South occurs as the first split in Liepelt's tree analysis of American voting; cumulatively, religion explains more variance than region because of the importance of religious differences outside the South. In Canada and Belgium, religion is also the most important influence; region and class are also significant but of lesser importance.

The extent to which social structure determines support for particular parties may also be assessed by examining the profile of support for each party. While at the national level one cannot say that social structure determines partisanship unless a large proportion of a group supports a single party, one can say that individual parties are based upon a social group if nearly all their supporters share a characteristic. For example, one cannot say that class determines an individual's decision to vote Communist, since most manual workers as well as most middle-class persons in most Western countries do not vote Communist. From a narrower perspective, one can say that a particular social characteristic is a precondition for supporting a given party, e.g., working-class identification may be a precondition for voting Communist.

Many parties described in the following chapters are cohesive in terms of a number of important social characteristics; some even draw their support from individuals who share two or more attributes in common. For example, Italian Communists are both working-class and anticlerical; the Canadian *Créditistes* are French-speaking and Catholic. A number of the largest parties are heterogeneous in their profile of support, that is, their voters tend to have no single social characteristic in common, except a party preference. In the case of the Canadian Liberals or the Australian Liberal-Country party, the ability to draw electoral support across major lines of social difference is an electoral asset. Yet the absence of a defined clientele can also be a token of electoral weakness; for example, the British Liberals get few votes because they lack a well-defined source of support within British society. They seek votes everywhere but the cross section that they draw is smaller than that of parties with more clearly, delimited clienteles. These facts are significant for both parties and party systems; they are explored elsewhere at length.[27]

Because parties may unite support on several grounds or none, party systems must be perceived in terms of multidimensional space, rather than along a simple Left-Right dimension. It is even possible to have a "no-dimension" party system, i.e., one in which no party can be placed on a social dimension because all are heterogeneous rather than cohesive in terms of major social characteristics.[28] Ireland and America here provide examples of the degree to which party systems are not aligned along any dimensions of social division. It does not follow from this that political differences are muted. The divisons in each of these party systems arose from the extreme conflict of civil war. Britain illustrates a second possibility: a party system in which one party can be classified as cohesively working-class even though its opponents cannot be classified as middle-class in the same schema, because they are not based upon a clientele that is equally and clearly homogeneous. The possibilities for complicated relationships are greatest in Canada; Mildred Schwartz's chapter shows how class, religion, language, and regional cohesion characterize some but not all Canadian parties. The number of dimensions in a party system and the number of points on which parties are relatively cohesive are thus variables to be examined by systematic comparison, rather than constants to be determined by a priori prescription.

Describing party systems in terms of the votes received by each party is much more nearly accurate in a proportional representation electoral system than in a single-member, simple-plurality electoral system. In the former the number of seats that a party wins is approximately proportionate to the number of votes it receives.[29] The relationship can be affected by the type of proportional system employed and by the strength of individual parties. Artificial or unintentional manipulation of parliamentary seats is not eliminated, as John Whyte's remarks on Ireland show (infra, pp. 629ff) but the effect is very much minimized. By contrast, the Anglo-American simple-plurality electoral system is a device for *dis*proportional representation. It gives larger parties a larger share of seats in parliament than their votes would entitle them to, if strict numerical proportionality were the ideal; reciprocally, smaller parties receive less than their share of seats. The justification is that the resulting tendency of groups to aggregate into a few or two parties offers voters a clear-cut choice of governments, in a way that is much less likely in a multiparty system sustained by proportional representation. America illustrates extreme contradictions in this respect. The United States Supreme Court has formally endorsed the view, stated by Chief Justice Warren, that "The weight of a citizen's vote cannot be made to depend on where he lives."[30] Yet this is just what happens in a simple-plurality electoral system for those who favor the second most popular candidate get no representation from their single-member constituency. The system is at its most extreme in the election of one man as President, for the second party has nothing to show for its tens of millions of votes. The simple-plurality electoral system has a minority appeal in a double sense. It makes it possible for a party with less than half the votes to win exclusive control of the executive branch of government. This regularly happens in Britain, and often happens in Canada and America. It is also of minority appeal—a majority of Western nations assign seats by proportional representation.

IV

The table of contents of this volume emphasizes how much it is a work of collaboration. An individual scholar who is an expert on a particular nation will always have an advantage in detailed knowledge, because there is not world enough and time for a single individual to become deeply expert about many countries. Expertise is not a matter of birth or residence. Seven of the chapters happen to be written by authors who are natives and now resident in the country they write about, but two are written by scholars who are neither natives nor resident in the country that they have learned to know well from travel and from reading. Each author has succeeded in combining the virtues of intimate knowledge of a single country with a readiness to communicate his knowledge in a framework explicitly designed for cross-national comparison.

Collaboration was possible across three continents because of the network of relationships developed by the body sponsoring this book, the Committee on Political Sociology. The committee was formed in 1960 as a research group of the International Sociological Association, with seventeen members from thirteen countries. Its first chairman was S. M. Lipset; Stein Rokkan was its first secretary. Prior to the foundation of the committee, both men had been active in encouraging the comparative analysis of social structure and political behavior, publishing major books and articles in the field.[31] The first priority of the committee was to encourage further study of social structure and party systems by bringing together political sociologists from a variety of Western countries to exchange ideas, thus stimulating comparative work by individuals and in collaboration. The scholars in the committee have had other interests too. Morris Janowitz's group in comparative military sociology grew so large that it became a separate ISA committee, as did a working group on comparative community politics under Terry Clark.[32] Other working groups have remained within the ambit of the committee, focusing on such topics as nation-building, the consolidation and breakdown of regimes, and comparative policy studies.[33]

The work of the Committee on Political Sociology has been advanced through a variety of channels, with formal conferences playing a significant part. The committee has been responsible for sessions at the quadrennial world congresses of the International Sociological Association since 1962, and since 1964 at the triennial congresses of the International Political Science Association, with which it is also formally linked. The committee has organized small round-table conferences of its own at a variety of sites since 1961. For example, the initial plans for this book were formulated at a conference held at Loch Lomond, Scotland, in July, 1968, and final arrangements were agreed at the IPSA Congress in Munich in 1970. Because of common interests and overlapping memberships, the committee has also collaborated with the International Social Science Council of UNESCO, and its work has been greatly assisted by meetings sponsored by the ISSC. Because membership has been flexible, with readiness to work a major requirement, committee members have been able to get together for discussions and progress on manuscripts in the course of travels that now seem one of the most demanding requirements of comparative research. In a decade in which getting research grants sometimes seemed more important than doing research, members of the committee have concentrated on the latter activity. Often, communication required little more than the facilities of the International Postal Union, with secretarial services borrowed from one of a number of obliging institutions.

Ultimately, the proof of a scholarly committee is its publications, not its travel log. Since formation the committee has sponsored a number of publications concerned primarily or exclusively with the interrelated question of social structure, party systems and voting alignments.[34] These include:

"Approaches to the Study of Political Participation," a special issue of *Acta Sociologica* VI: 1-2 (1962).

E. Allardt and Y. Littunen, editors, *Cleavages, Ideologies and Party Systems*. Helsinki: Westermarck Society, 1964.

S. M. Lipset and Stein Rokkan, eds., *Party Systems and Voter Alignments*. New York: Free Press, 1967.

Otto Stammer, ed., *Party Systems, Party Organizations and the Politics of New Masses*. Berlin: Free University, 1968.

Stein Rokkan et al., *Citizens, Elections, Parties*. Oslo: Universitetsforlaget; New York : D. McKay, (1970).

Richard Rose and Derek Urwin, eds., "Social Structure, Party Systems and Voting Behavior", a special issue of *Comparative Political Studies* II : 1 (1969).

Erik Allardt and Stein Rokkan, eds., *Mass Politics*. New York : Free Press, 1970.

In addition members of the committee have collaborated with other international research institutions in the preparation of the following related volumes :

Richard L. Merrit and S. Rokkan, eds., *Comparing Nations*. New Haven: Yale University Press, 1969.

Mattei Dogan and Stein Rokkan, eds., *Quantitative Ecological Analysis in the Social Sciences*. Cambridge, Mass. : MIT Press, 1969.

Stein Rokkan and Jean Meyriat, eds., *International Guide to Electoral Statistics*. The Hague & Paris : Mouton, 1969.

Stein Rokkan, Jean Viet, Sidney Verba, and Elina Almasy, *Comparative Survey Analysis*. The Hague & Paris: Mouton, 1969.

Particularly relevant to the genesis of this book are two journal articles by the editor, in collaboration with Derek Urwin. "Social Cohesion, Political Parties and Strains in Regimes" appeared in the special issue of *Comparative Political Studies* cited above. In advance of the collection of expertly vetted national profiles of social structure and political behavior, it showed what significant political conclusions might be drawn from a synthesis of such materials. This article will be drawn upon in a book to be published by the two authors as a sequel to this volume. Another article by Rose and Urwin—"Persistence and Change in Western Party Systems since 1945," *Political Studies* XVIII: 3 (1970)—examines dynamic properties of social structure and party systems; a further paper on interwar politics, "Persistence and Disruption in Western Party Systems between the Wars" by Urwin and Rose was presented to the World Congress of the International Sociological Association at Varna, Bulgaria, in 1970. It is hoped subsequently to extend this analysis well back into the nineteenth-century in order to analyze how the party systems of today developed from preindustrial and predemocratic origins. These volumes constitute part of the continuing work of the Committee on Political Sociology.

The committee in no sense encompasses the whole field of political sociology or the sociology of politics.[35] For example, it is complemented by studies in the field of national government organized by the Smaller European Democracies group, under the direction of Hans Daalder, Robert Dahl, Val Lorwin, and Stein Rokkan, as well as by the explicitly comparative work in which the directors are engaged.[36] Relevant studies of crucial problems defined within the context of a single nation include Arend

Lijphart's Dutch study, *The Politics of Accommodation*, and his writings on consociational democracy;[37] in a less cheering field there is Richard Rose's Northern Ireland study, *Governing without Consensus*.[38] A sample of a wide range of work on political sociology in the past decade can conveniently be found in an anthology edited by Mattei Dogan and Richard Rose, *European Politics*.[39] The committee has encouraged relatively little work outside Europe or Western nations. It has not needed to do so, in view of the great impetus given that field by the activities of the Committee on Comparative Politics of the American Social Science Research Council, under the leadership of Gabriel Almond, Lucian Pye, and others.[40] Survey studies of non-Western nations have been encouraged by Gabriel Almond, Sidney Verba, and a multinational group of scholars working in countries as far apart as Nigeria and India.[41] In America, Europe, and (increasingly) other continents scholars based in the Survey Research Centre of the University of Michigan, under the leadership of Angus Campbell, Philip Converse, Warren Miller, and Donald Stokes, have made major contributions to comparative politics by their writings and by the generous provision of research training and facilities.[42]

The chapters that follow are not a summary of the committee's findings; it would take more than a single volume to present this. While each chapter was specially written for this book, the surveys were not collected with committee funds. It is of the nature of collaborative work that individuals come together of their own accord, because they already share common interests notwithstanding disparate backgrounds. Collaborative and comparative research provides a setting in which unique abilities and historical conditions stand out. Cumulatively, it demonstrates the truth of the adage that the whole is greater than the sum of its parts.

Notes

1. See e.g., W. J. M. Mackenzie, "The Export of Electoral Systems," *Political Studies* V:3 (1957), and T. E. Smith, *Elections in Developing Countries* (London: Macmillan, 1960).
2. *Die Wahl Der Parlamente*, edited by Dolf Sternberger (Berlin: Walter de Gruyter & Co., 1969, two vols.); Stein Rokkan and Jean Meyriat, *International Guide to Electoral Statistics* (The Hague & Paris: Mouton, 1969).
3. For a review of particular electoral events in the period, see conveniently Philip M. Williams. *French Politicians & Elections, 1951-1969* (Cambridge: University Press, 1970), and, on institutions, Peter Campbell, *French Electoral Systems and Elections since 1789* (London: Faber, 1965).
4. (Vienna: Verlag für Jugend und Volk, 1966-68, four vols.).
5. (Oslo: Universitetsforlaget; New York & London: Columbia University Press, annually).
6. Published annually by the *Association suisse de science politique* through the *Institut de science politique*, Lausanne.
7. See e.g., R. M. Chapman, W. K. Jackson and A. V. Mitchell, *New Zealand Politics in Action* (London: Oxford University Press, 1962); R. S. Milne, *Political Parties in New Zealand* (Oxford: Clarendon Press, 1966); and Alan Robinson, "Class Voting in New Zealand," in S. M. Lipset and Stein Rokkan, eds., *Party Systems and Voter Alignments* (New York: Free Press, 1967).
8. The draft chapter on Britain by Richard Rose, using 1964 British election data, appears in Otto Stammer, ed., *Party Systems, Party Organizations and the Politics of New Masses* (Berlin: Institut für politische Wissenchaft an der Freien Universität, 1968).

9. On the "normal" vote, see Chapter 2 by Philip Converse in *Elections and the Political Order* (New York: Wiley, 1966).

10. See e.g., Eric Browne and Mark N. Franklin, "Aspects of Coalition Payoffs in European Parliamentary Democracies," *American Political Science Review* LXVII:2 (1973).

11. See S. M. Lipset and Stein Rokkan, "Introduction," in *Party Systems and Voter Alignments*. Cf Richard Rose and Derek Urwin, "Territorial Differentiation and Political Unity in Western Nations" (Lausanne: ISSC Conference on Indicators of National Development, duplicated, 1971).

12. See Erik Allardt, "Past and Emerging Political Cleavages," in Otto Stammer, ed., op. cit.

13. For a discussion of party identification in a European context, see Uwe Schleth and Erich Weede, "Causal Models on West German Voting Behavior," *Sozialwissenschaftliches Jahrbuch für Politik* (Munich-Vienna: Gunter Olzog, Band 2, 1970, pp. 73-97).

14. See e.g., Sidney Verba's contribution to Stein Rokkan et al., *Comparative Survey Analysis* (The Hague and Paris: Mouton, 1969).

15. See especially Klaus Liepelt, "The Infra-Structure of Party Support in Germany and Austria," reprinted in Mattei Dogan and Richard Rose, eds., *European Politics* (Boston: Little, Brown, 1971); Bo Sarlvik, "Socioeconomic Determinants of Voting Behavior in the Swedish Electorate," *Comparative Political Studies* II:1 (1969), and "Socioeconomic Position, Religious Behavior, and Voting in the Swedish Electorate," *Quality and Quantity* IV:1 (1970); and J. A. Sonquist and J. N. Morgan, *The Detection of Interaction Effects* (Ann Arbor, Mich.: Survey Research Center, Monograph No. 35, 1964).

16. For problems of cabinet formation where coalitions do not exist, see e.g., Richard Rose, "The Making of Cabinet Ministers," *British Journal of Political Science* I:3 (1971), and Laurin T. Henry, *Presidential Transitions* (Washington: Brookings Institution, 1960).

17. See e.g., Mattei Dogan, "Political Cleavage and Social Stratification in France and Italy," pp. 129ff, in S. M. Lipset and Stein Rokkan, eds., op. cit.

18. See e.g., Mattei Dogan and Stein Rokkan, eds., *Quantitative Ecological Analysis in the Social Sciences* (Cambridge, Mass.: MIT Press, 1969); and compare, Stein Rokkan et al., *Comparative Survey Analysis*.

19. In addition to Nuffield studies of British general elections by D. E. Butler and others, see also D. E. Butler, ed., *Elections Abroad* (London: Macmillan, 1959), and W. J. M. Mackenzie and K. E. Robinson, eds., *Five Elections in Africa* (Oxford: Clarendon Press, 1960).

20. For a general review see W. J. M. Mackenzie, *Free Elections* (London: Allen & Unwin, 1958).

21. Quoted from Richard Rose and Harve Mossawir, "Voting and Elections: a Functional Analysis," *Political Studies* XV:2 (1967), p. 193.

22. Jean Blondel's inductive classification schema attempts to encompass a variety of existing Western party systems without an explicit theoretical rationale. Hence it results in such types as a "two and one half" party system. See "Party Systems and Patterns of Government in Western Democracies," *Canadian Journal of Political Science* I:2 (1968).

23. See e.g., Charles Glock and Rodney Stark, *Religion and Society in Tension* (Chicago: Rand, McNally, 1965).

24. In a country such as Yugoslavia one would also have to allow for a substantial Moslem group. The Jews are nowhere sufficiently numerous to encourage separate analysis in nationwide surveys, outside Israel.

25. See e.g., Stein Rokkan, "Electoral Mobilization, Party Competition and National Integration" in J. LaPalombara and M. Weiner, eds., *Political Parties and Political Development* (Princeton: University Press, 1966), and Stein Rokkan and Henry Valen, "Regional Contrasts in Norwegian Politics," in Erik Allardt and Stein Rokkan, eds., *Mass Politics* (New York: Free Press, 1970).

26. Harry Eckstein, *Division and Cohesion in Democracy; A Study of Norway* (Princeton: University Press, 1966).

27. See Richard Rose and Derek Urwin, "Social Cohesion, Political Parties and Strains in Regimes," *Comparative Political Studies* II:1 (1969).

28. Ibid., pp. 32ff.

29. For details on the relations of seats to votes, see Douglas Rae, *The Political Consequences of Electoral Laws* (New Haven: Yale University Press, 1967). Cf. Enid Lakeman, *How Democracies Vote*, 3rd ed. (London: Faber, 1970).

30. Quoted from the decision in Reynolds vs. Sims (1964) in Gordon E. Baker, *The Reapportionment Revolution* (New York: Random House, 1966), pp. 184–93.

31. See e.g., the earliest articles reprinted in Stein Rokkan, *Citizens, Elections and Parties* (Oslo: Universitetsforlaget; New York: McKay, 1970); and S. M. Lipset, Paul F. Lazarsfeld, Allen Barton, and Juan Linz, "The Psychology of Voting" in G. Lindzey, ed., *Handbook of Social Psychology*, Vol. II (Cambridge, Mass.: Addison-Wesley, 1954).

32. See e.g., Jacques van Doorn, ed., *Armed Forces and Society* (The Hague: Mouton, 1968) and *Military Professions and Military Regimes* (The Hague: Mouton, 1969); Morris Janowitz and Jacques van Doorn, *On Military Regimes* (Rotterdam: University of Rotterdam Press, 1971, two vols.); Terry Clark, ed., "Comparative Research on Community Decision-Making," a special issue of *New Atlantis* II (Winter, 1970), and Terry Clark, ed., *Community Structure and Decision-Making* (San Francisco: Chandler, 1968).

33. For a history of the committee's work see Stein Rokkan, "International Co-operation in Political Sociology," in E. Allardt and S. Rokkan, eds., op. cit.

34. In addition to the above, the work done and stimulated by S. M. Lipset on the comparative study of students and politics should also be noted.

35. Cf. Giovanni Sartori, "From the Sociology of Politics to Political Sociology," in S. M. Lipset, ed., *Politics and the Social Sciences* (New York: Oxford University Press, 1969).

36. The first volume in the Smaller European Democracies series is Basil Chubb, *The Government and Politics of Ireland* (Stanford: University Press, 1970).

37. See e.g., "Typologies of Democratic Systems," *Comparative Political Studies* I:1 (1968) and "Consociational Democracy," *World Politics*, XXI:2 (1969).

38. *Governing Without Consensus: An Irish Perspective* (Boston: Beacon Press, 1971).

39. (Boston: Little, Brown, 1971).

40. Cf. Committee on Comparative Politics; *A Report on the Activities of the Committee, 1954–70* (New York: Social Science Research Council, 1971).

41. See e.g., G. A. Almond and Sidney Verba, *The Civic Culture* (Princeton: University Press, 1963), and the first of a forthcoming series of studies primarily in the non-Western world, Sidney Verba, Bashiruddin Ahmed, and Anil Bhatt, *Caste, Race and Politics* (Beverly Hills, Calif.: Sage, 1971).

42. For a detailed review of the significance of this work see Kenneth Prewitt and Norman Nie, "Election Studies of the Survey Research Center," *British Journal of Political Science* I:4 (1971).

Continental Europe

2. BELGIUM:
Political Change in a Segmented Society

KEITH HILL

I. The Development of the Belgian Political System

Belgium is virtually alone among advanced industrial democracies in its linguistic divisions. The last census to contain a question about language, in 1947, reported that 55 percent of the population normally spoke Dutch, 44 percent French, and 1 percent German (see Tables 1 & 2). Yet, for nearly all of Belgium's political history linguistic differences have been of little consequence for competition between parties.

TABLE 1: Total Population and Percentages of Regional Distribution, 1890-1961

	1890	1920	1947	1961
Flemish Region[1]	50.3	51.5	54.2	55.7
Walloon Region[2]	41.5	38.2	34.6	33.1
Brussels-Capital[3]	8.2	10.2	11.2	11.1
Belgium	6,069,321	7,405,569	8,512,195	9,189,741

Source: calculated from census data, Ministère de l'Intérieur etc.

[1]The Flemish region comprises the provinces of Antwerpen, Limburg, Oost—and Westvlaanderen, the *arrondissement* of Leuven in the province of Brabant, and the population of the Brussels *arrondissement* after subtracting the population of the communes of Brussels-Capital.

[2]The Walloon region comprises the provinces of Hainaut, Liège, Luxembourg, and Namur, and the *arrondissement* of Nivelles in the province of Brabant.

[3]Brussels-Capital comprises, at the first two time-points, the fourteen communes designated as components of the Brussels agglomeration in the 1910 and 1920 censuses: Anderlecht, Brussels, Etterbeek, Forest, Ixelles, Jette, Koekelberg, Laeken, Molenbeek-Saint-Jean, Saint-Gilles, Saint-Josse-ten-Noode, Schaerbeek, Uccle, Woluwe-Saint-Lambert, and, thereafter, the nineteen communes constituted by the addition of Auderghem, Berchem-Sainte-Agathe, Evére, Ganshoren, Watermael-Boitsfort, Woluwe-Saint-Pierre, and the suppression of the commune of Laeken.

I wish to thank Professor Richard Rose and Thomas T. Mackie of the University of Strathclyde for their encouragement and assistance in the writing of this chapter. Research in Belgium was financed in part by the Sir Ernest Cassel Educational Trust.

The two other countries in which linguistic diversity reaches comparable levels are Canada and Switzerland. Unlike Belgium, however, these states faced the problem of reconciling linguistic subcultures at the initial stage of state-formation and sought to manage it through the device of federalism. The process of political development was quite different in Belgium. Conflict about the linguistic character of the state was absent at the period of state-formation (from the secession of the southern provinces of the Kingdom of the Netherlands in 1830 to the international recognition of the new Belgian state in 1839). Moreover, it failed to emerge as an issue that could mobilize more than a minuscule segment of the electorate until after the institutionalization of religious and class cleavages in the party system.

The first election in which political parties articulating linguistic demands attracted measurable support was in 1919, when Flemish nationalist lists acquired 3 percent of the vote (see Appendix 1). In the interwar and postwar periods Flemish nationalism demonstrated its capacity to win an increasing share of the popular vote in Flanders. The emergence of the francophone parties in the mid-1960s gave parties challenging the unitary character of the Belgian state their greatest impetus. That mobilization reached a high point in 1971, when the linguistic parties gained 22 percent of the national vote.

TABLE 2: **Proportions of the population normally speaking the National Languages, 1920 and 1947, Regional and National**

	Dutch	French	German
Flemish Region			
1920	94.9	5.0	0.0
1947	94.0	5.4	0.2
Walloon Region			
1920	2.4	94.5	3.1
1947	2.1	95.1	2.4
Brussels-Capital			
1920	37.2	62.6	0.1
1947	24.6	72.7	0.4
Belgium			
1920	52.7	46.0	1.2
1947	54.8	43.7	1.0

Source: Calculated from census data, Ministère de l'Intérieur, etc.

It would be misleading to measure the impact of the language question simply in terms of the electoral support of the linguistic parties. In two periods, 1929-1939 and since 1962, the issues of cultural autonomy and administrative and economic decentralization have dominated the policy concerns of the Catholic, Socialist, and Liberal parties. Yet, for the so-called traditional parties language has remained only one among a series of programmatic concerns (G. Van de Put, 1966; W. Dewachter, 1966, 1969). If the Communist party is grouped with those parties whose policy and electoral appeal is organized around nonlinguistic issues, it is found that such parties still attracted 78 percent of the vote in 1971. Especially in the light of recent comparative developmental analysis, which has served to emphasize the historical precedence of conflict between central nation-building elites and culturally distinctive subject-populations (cf S. M. Lipset and S. Rokkan, 1967), two questions arise from the Belgian experience: Why did linguistic conflict develop so late? Why has its electoral impact remained relatively small? These questions constitute the underlying theme of the chapter.

A. Center and Periphery in Nineteenth-Century Belgium

One important condition for center-periphery conflict in the state-building phase of political development—the existence of a political elite culturally distinct from a part of the subject-population—was present in nineteenth-century Belgium. The first Belgian census in 1846 showed 57 percent of the population as Dutch-speaking and the remainder as French-speaking. However, the demographic preponderance of the Flemish was not reflected in the linguistic composition of elite groups. French was the language of the landed interest, of the industrial and commercial bourgeoisie, and of the hierarchy of the Roman Catholic Church. It was also the language of government. It was not until 1894 that a speech in Dutch was made in the Belgian parliament. Only in 1898 did Dutch become an official language, to be used in the promulgation of laws (P. Doms, 1965).

The hegemonic role of French was not the consequence of the political subjection of the Flemish region by the francophone part of the country. It was instead the result of a centuries-old cultural asimilation to French of the resident elites of the Flemish provinces. As early as the sixteenth-century French had become the common language of commerce in Flemish towns. Since then it had formed the essential means of communication between successive colonial rulers and the native administrative elites. Under the restricted franchise of the *régime censitaire* (1830-1893), the Flemish elite participated as equals with their Walloon counterparts: their language was naturally French. Thus for nearly the whole of the nineteenth-century, influential social groups in Flanders did not find their access to the sociopolitical elite frustrated by unfamiliarity with its language.

The absence of a peripheral Dutch-speaking elite concerned enough to campaign against the inferior status of the Flemish community does not mean that there were no opinion leaders among large sections of the Flemish population or that there was no sense of grievance about the position of the Flemish in the Belgian state. For most of the century the major structural feature of the Flemish region was its agrarian economy. Belgium experienced the industrial revolution early, but the first areas affected by industrialization were the Walloon provinces of Hainaut and Liège. By the last decade of the century about 40 percent of the total industrial work force was Flemish. Yet this group still composed only 30 percent of the working population of the Flemish region, which was almost the same as the size of the agrarian work force in the region (see Table 3). Flemish rural society was characterized by a high level of religious practice and a powerful attachment to the Catholic Church. Indeed, the Church was the overwhelming source of political authority in Flanders. It exercised its authority through the Dutch-speaking lower clergy.

TABLE 3:   The Economic Structure, 1890–1961, Regional and National

	PRIMARY SECTOR	SECONDARY SECTOR	TERTIARY SECTOR
1890			
Flemish Region	29.0	30.9	40.1
Walloon Region	16.1	43.9	40.0
Arrondissement of Brussels	15.0	35.8	49.2
Belgium	22.1	36.8	41.1
1920			
Flemish Region	24.2	46.0	29.9
Walloon Region	15.2	57.8	27.0
Arrondissement of Brussels	9.3	47.9	42.8
Belgium	18.4	50.9	30.6
1947			
Flemish Region	15.4	48.3	36.1
Walloon Region	12.0	54.1	33.9
Arrondissement of Brussels	5.4	40.1	54.5
Belgium	12.6	49.0	38.4
1961			
Flemish Region	8.5	49.9	41.6
Walloon Region	8.6	49.6	41.8
Arrondissement of Brussels	2.8	37.6	59.6
Belgium	7.5	47.7	44.8

Source: Calculated from census data, Ministère de l'Intérieur etc.

The political efficacy of the priests was to be demonstrated in the elections after the extension of the suffrage. In the period of universal suffrage with plural voting, 1894–1914, the Catholic party's average share of the Flemish vote was 64 percent. The role of the lower clergy in social mobilization was shown in the first three decades of the twentieth century. It was the priests who played the central role in the creation of both farmers' associations, which helped to preserve the historical preeminence of the Church in the countryside, and Catholic workers' organizations, which enabled the Church to resist in large measure the secular influences of industrialization and urbanization (S. H. Scholl, 1966).

Nevertheless there is enough evidence to suggest that the energies of many Flemish priests were not wholly absorbed by pastoral activities or by mobilizing support for the Catholic party. Many were strongly identified with the cause of the Dutch language in the Belgian state. The lower clergy provided some of the earliest leaders of the Flemish literary movement. For these priests concern for the language blended easily with Catholicism. As V. R. Lorwin (1966, p. 160) expresses it:

> The tide of godlessness which threatened pious Flanders was peculiarly associated with the French language and literature, which "oozed crime and demoralization." It was associated with the French nation, persecutor of the Church, with French-speaking Wallonia, where Flemish immigrants lost their faith and with the francophone . . . bourgeoisie of Flanders itself.

This combination of religious and linguistic activism has been a thread running through the work of the Flemish lower clergy until far into the twentieth-century (see A. Melot, 1933, p. 126).

Elsewhere in nineteenth-century Europe priests were the leaders of peasant movements against the oppression of landlords and the depredations of anticlerical regimes. Had the Flemish clergy been called upon to mobilize their followers against the political system, the resulting movements would probably have acquired the added dimension of a nationalist struggle. In any event neither challenge presented itself. The land question did not arise in an agrarian population composed of smallholders and tenants with reasonable security of tenure (Seebohm Rowntree, 1910). Moreover, the Catholic party emerged victorious from its parliamentary struggle with the anticlerical Liberals, which dominated Belgian politics for four decades from the middle of the nineteenth-century. The object of the Catholics was to defend a constitution that favored the Church. In this sense, therefore, the Flemish clergy was called upon to encourage the endorsement of the Belgian state and to defend its constitutional provisions against Liberal and, later, Socialist anticlericalism.

B. THE CLERICAL–ANTICLERICAL CLEAVAGE IN BELGIAN POLITICS

From 1830 until 1894 Belgian electoral politics was dominated by two political groupings, at first broadly and later more narrowly identifiable as the Catholic and Liberal parities. Electoral challenges to these parties were sporadic, and presented by individuals rather than organized political groups. In no election did the vote of the two parties fall below 97 percent. Nationally, electoral support for the parties was equally divided and fairly stable (as is shown by the national means and standard deviations from the mean in Table 4). However, support for the parties was not equally distributed at the regional level, with the Catholics dominant in Flanders and the Liberals as strong in Wallonia.

The tax qualification of the *régime censitaire* restricted the vote to at most 11 percent of the adult male population. Electoral support of both Catholic and Liberal parties was thus confined to the relatively wealthy sectors of society. Little else is definitely known about the social bases of party support in nineteenth-century Belgium. Historians of the period normally observe that the Liberal vote came mainly from the commerical and industrial bourgeoisie, while the Catholic party received the over-whelming support of the countryside and still retained a substantial urban vote. It seems reasonable to suppose that the Liberal vote became more exclusively that of non-Christians, and the Catholic vote more exclusively that of churchgoers, as the conflict between the parties shifted from the question of the public role of the Church to the question of the philosophical bases of private morality.

TABLE 4: **Means and Standard Deviations of Party Votes in Elections from 1848 to 1892, National and Regional**

	CATHOLIC PARTY		LIBERAL PARTY	
	Mean	SD	Mean	SD
Flemish Region	64.2	9.7	35.7	9.4
Walloon Region	35.4	7.0	64.4	7.2
Belgium	48.9	7.3	50.9	7.0

Source: Calculated from W. Moine, 1970

Belgian historiography has traditionally portrayed the constitution-makers as two sharply differentiated groups, Liberals on one side and Catholics on the other. Some historians have been tempted to link anticlericalism, which became a powerful current in the Liberal party from the mid-nineteenth century, with the political ideas of the Liberals of the 1830s. However, as the detailed study by Colette Lebas (1960) has emphasized, even if it is possible to detect broad tendencies among the parliamentarians of the early period of state-formation, it is extremely difficult to draw sharp distinctions at the individual level. Some defended the interests of the Church and others defended the interests of the state. Yet these positions did not necessarily correspond to religious differences: not all *political* Catholics were believers and very few *political* Liberals were antireligious.

The concern of the Liberals for constitutional and civil liberties complemented the concern of the Catholics to ensure the liberties of the Church. Since neither group wanted to impede religion in itself, the Church found itself greatly advantaged by the constitution of 1831. The Church was protected from any encroachment by the state in both its internal organization and its relations with the papacy. Its priests were to receive their salaries from the state. The guarantee of freedom of association (while not applying to workmen's associations) applied to religious orders. The guarantee of freedom of education allowed the founding of independent Catholic schools in communes in which Catholic teaching was not otherwise available. The advantage to the Church was reinforced by subsequent legislation that permitted communal councils to finance Catholic education from public funds.

In principle Catholic parliamentarians were forced to admit the incompatibility of current Catholic doctrine with the liberal aspects of the constitution. In practice they chose to live with the inconsistencies and to disregard the indictments of the liberal order that emanated from Rome in 1832 (*Mirari Vos*) and 1864 (*Quanta Cura*). Their consistent operational distinction between political questions and questions of faith was summarized by Dechamps in the parliamentary session of 1863-1864:

> In the sphere of faith and beliefs we are obedient to a religious authority . . . But in the political sphere we are answerable only to our reason. (Trans. from K. Van Isacker, 1955, p. 33.)

That reason, observing the advantages to the Church, led to an unfaltering and, as the evidence suggests, virtually unanimous endorsement of the liberal order among parliamentary Catholics throughout the nineteenth-century.

Acceptance of the liberal regime was not so complete in the nonparliamentary Catholic elite. Stimulated by the encyclical of 1864 and by the *Syllabus*, the Belgian form of Catholic integralism—*ultramontanism*—appears to have gained some support among intellectuals and the hierarchy in the 1870s. The extent of its influence in the Catholic population is less clear. Dr. Van Isacker, who has argued for the dominant hold of ultramontanism on Catholic opinion between 1870 and 1880, observes nonetheless that the mass of Catholics continued to believe in the "wisdom and necessity" of the liberal institutions. No upholder of the ultramontanist programme was ever elected to the Belgian parliament (see K. Van Isacker, 1955, pp. 238, 265). In sum, clerical-anticlerical conflict in Belgium was in no sense the result of a serious threat of the subjection of the state to the interests of the Church (cf. M. Claeys-Van Haegendoren, 1967; D. W. Urwin, 1970).

Nor, amidst the changing focus of the conflict between clericals and anticlericals, did the reverse threat of state control over the Church ever emerge. The subject of the conflict—the relationship of the Church to the state school system—remained constant. However, the substance of the opposition between defenders and attackers of the Church altered from debate about the proper spheres of the religious and secular powers to the question of religious truth. For the Liberal constitution-makers and their immediate successors, there was little doubt about religious truth, and less about the social value of religious education in the primary schools. The point was made by Fleussu:

> the morality of the poor is the safeguard of the power of the rich (Trans. from C. Lebas, 1960, p. 116).

The early Liberals came to fear not the influence of the Church on the poor, but its influence on those rich enough to be able to vote in the *régime censitaire*. Liberal suspicions of the long-term anticonstitutional aims of the Church were encouraged by events outside Belgium. The promulgation of *Mirari Vos* in 1832, and the Catholic Reaction, as it had manifested itself in the France of Charles X and in Spain, created doubts that the evident commitment of the Belgian parliamentary Catholics to the constitution could not allay. Moreover, there could be no question of the anti-Liberal attitudes of the Belgian hierarchy. In 1838 it published a pastoral letter indicting all Liberals as Freemasons and, thus, anti-Christians (see A. Simon, 1949, pp. 22-24).

The desire to develop a state school system in which Catholic political influence would be limited led the Liberals in 1846 to break away from their initial collaboration with the Catholics. In that year a congress of Liberal parliamentarians and the representatives of Liberal electoral associations met to create a national organization that would support a program aimed at the promotion of state education at all levels. The right of the Church to provide religious instruction in the state education system was accepted, but otherwise the Church was to enjoy no special privileges. This secular concept of education was the ongoing concern of the *doctrinaire* Liberals until they were succeeded by the explicitly antireligious *radical* Liberals as the dominant element in the party in the 1860s.

While the doctrinaire Liberals recognized the legitimacy of the Church's activities in the religious sphere and attacked its intervention in public affairs, the radical Liberals considered the Church's influence in every aspect of private and social life as pernicious. The Radicals rejected not only the political teaching of the Church but also the performance of such religious rites as baptisms, marriages, and funerals. They condemned the Church above all because it offended the new deity of Progress. As Pieter van Humbeeck announced in 1864:

> A corpse lies on the earth, barring the road to progress. This corpse of the past, to call it bluntly by its name. . . is catholicism (Trans. from T. Luyckx, 1969, p. 125).

Antagonism to Catholicism far outweighed electoral and social reform in the balance of radical Liberal policy concerns. After the partial election of 1878 produced a Liberal majority in parliament, the Radicals inaugurated a massive attack on the educational activities of the Church. The primary school law of 1879 proscribed communes from adopting and funding Church schools. It also effectively excluded Catholics from teaching in state schools by insisting that their teachers should hold state education diplomas. It further stipulated that every commune should establish a state school in which religious instruction should play no part. In 1881 a law prevented communes from supporting Catholic secondary schools.

The Catholic response to this attack was a rapid and extensive mobilization of the churchgoing population against the state education system. The historian Pirenne has estimated that within four months of the passage of the primary school law the state education system had lost 30 percent of its pupils and 20 percent of its teachers to the "free" Catholic schools (cited by V. Mallinson, 1963, p. 96). By the end of 1880 more than 60 percent of the schoolgoing population was enrolled in the Catholic schools (calculated from T. Luyckx, 1969, p. 177).

The crisis also provoked the permanent activation of the Catholic party's electoral machine. In 1879 existing electoral organizations were fused into a single Federation of Catholic Circles and Associations. When it met in congress in 1884, it brought together representatives from 800 local groups (see G. Guyot de Mishaegen, 1946, p. 182). The efficacy of the Catholic electoral machine, with the priests as its agents in the parishes, was demonstrated by the Catholic party's electoral victory of 1884, which ushered in thirty years of uninterrupted Catholic rule.One consequence of this Catholic political mobilization was that the Catholic party was electorally prepared for the challenge of universal suffrage.

The introduction of universal suffrage inaugurated a decline in Liberal party support that lasted until its resurrection as a nonconfessional party in the 1960s. However, during this period anticlericalism grew as an electoral force. Hostility to the Church, and specifically its educational activities, was associated with the Belgian Workers' Party from its creation in 1885. Anticlericalism and a shared desire for electoral reform enabled the Liberal and Socialist parties to form electoral cartels in several elections between 1894 and 1912. However, these parties never acquired the parliamentary majority they needed in order to relaunch the attack on the Catholic school system. During the interwar period, when it became possible to form Socialist–Liberal coalitions, the continuing saliency of the schools question for both parties could not compensate for their oppositions on social and economic questions.

After the end of the Second World War the political differences of the Socialist and Liberal parties had declined sufficiently to permit the emergence of the only Socialist–Liberal bipartite coalition in Belgian history. The main element of unity in the 1954–1958 coalition was its attack on state subsidies to Church schools (see T. Luyckx, 1969, pp. 435-37). This late apotheosis of ministerial anticlericalism led to a nemesis not at all dissimilar from that experienced seventy years earlier. Practicing Catholics returned to the Catholic party to give it its highest vote in any election since 1950. The defeat of the Socialist and Liberal parties led to their effective abandonment of anticlericalism, (the process was more rapid in the Liberal party). With the signing of the School Pact in 1958 by the Catholic, Socialist, and Liberal parties, the schools question was placed outside the arena of political conflict, where it has remained. But if clerical-anticlerical conflict has disappeared at the policy level, its residual effect is still strongly apparent in mass electoral behavior.

C. THE CLASS CLEAVAGE IN BELGIAN POLITICS

The founding of the Belgian Workers' Party in 1885 introduced class cleavage into the Belgian party system. The first object of the Socialists was to secure universal male suffrage. The pressure applied by the Socialists, in the form of a general strike in 1891, together with the parliamentary activities of radical Liberals and social Catholics, led to the introduction of universal male suffrage with plural voting in 1893. The first election under the extended franchise took place in 1894.

The electoral impact of the Socialist party was very different from region to region. In Brussels and Wallonia the Socialists emerged as a potent third force, largely at the expense of the Liberals. In Wallonia, though not in Brussels, the Socialists made consistent electoral progress throughout the period of the plural suffrage. In Flanders, on the other hand, their initial success was slight and their progress minimal (see Table 5). It is reasonable to suppose that the greater industrialization of Brussels and the

Walloon region allowed the Socialists to appeal to a larger working class than existed in the Flemish region. Yet this is not a total explanation of the unequal distribution of Socialist support. In 1890 there already existed a substantial secondary sector in Flanders. In the next thirty years it grew to encompass half the region's work force.

TABLE 5:   **Electoral Change, 1894-1961**

PARTY		FLEMISH REGION	WALLOON REGION	BRUSSELS REGION
1894–1912				
Catholic	M	64.9	38.0	42.5
	b	−0.176	0.089	−0.112
	r	−0.498	0.552	−0.212
Liberal	M	23.1	26.5	28.8
	b	0.364	−0.401	0.130
	r	0.532	−0.850	0.253
Socialist	M	6.8	34.5	22.7
	b	0.036	0.230	−0.024
	r	0.119	0.669	−0.069
1919–1939				
Catholic	M	43.0	27.0	26.8
	b	−0.321	−0.348	−0.272
	r	−0.632	−0.565	−0.365
Liberal	M	12.8	16.7	26.1
	b	−0.118	−0.142	−0.100
	r	−0.705	−0.385	−0.177
Socialist	M	27.0	46.8	30.2
	b	0.049	−0.572	−0.328
	r	0.187	−0.855	−0.502
1946–1961				
Catholic	M	55.1	30.8	30.3
	b	−0.308	0.217	−0.143
	r	−0.513	0.440	−0.222
Liberal	M	11.0	11.6	18.6
	b	0.097	−0.015	−0.013
	r	0.337	−0.056	−0.021
Socialist	M	27.3	43.7	39.3
	b	0.223	0.655	0.627
	r	0.596	0.730	0.617

Key M=average electoral vote.
  b=per annum change in percentage of the vote (positive or negative) over period.
  r=measure of consistency of trend indicated by b; the nearer to 1 or −1, the more consistent the trend.

The fact that the Socialist party averaged only 7 percent of the Flemish vote from 1894 to 1912 suggests that other explanations for its lack of success need to be adduced.

One explanation that would have sat well with the Socialists of the period is that the plural vote disadvantaged them by giving the wealthy extra votes to use in support of the Catholic and Liberal parties. Indeed, the removal of the plural vote was the major electoral change demanded by the party until 1919. Had this been the case, however, the regional distribution of the total vote would have changed after the abolition of plural voting. Yet the proportion of the total vote cast in those regions in which the non-Socialist parties were strongest did not decline. The Flemish and Brussels proportion of the total votes cast show little change from 1912 to 1919 (see Appendix 1): the changed shares of the Flemish and Brussels regions result from the addition of the Flemish communes of the Brussels *arrondissement* to the Flemish region for the post-1912 results. In 1919 the Flemish communes constituted 3 percent of the entire population. The reasonable inference, therefore, is that the Socialists were not strongly disadvantaged by the plural vote.

The fundamental explanation of the differential impact of the Socialist party both before and after the First World War is to be found in regional differences in religious practice. Although no data are available on church attendance before the 1950s (see Table 6), the modern figures probably reflect the historical patterns. In Brussels, and particularly in Wallonia, urbanization and industrialization had led to a fairly low level of religious practice by the last decade of the nineteenth-century. In Flanders, by contrast, churchgoing remained high and the Church militant in its response to the Liberal attack on religious education.

TABLE 6: **Religious Practice, Regional and National**

REGION	PRACTICING	NONPRACTICING
1950-1951		
Flemish	60.2	39.8
Walloon	40.7	59.3
Brussels*	34.9	65.1
Belgium	49.6	50.4
1968		
Flemish	73.9	26.1
Walloon	44.1	55.9
Brussels*	44.7	55.3
Belgium	58.9	44.1

Sources: 1950-51. Collard, 1952. The data were supplied by Church sources; the percentages are calculated on the basis of the population canonically bound to Mass attendance, estimated at 85 percent of parochial populations. For a critique of Collard's data see Deleeck, 1957.

1968. Delruelle, 1970. Respondents were asked if they were "practicing Catholics," defined as "some-one who goes to Mass regularly."

*The percentages are for the Brussels *arrondissement*. The 1968 survey found that 35.1 percent of the respondents in Brussels-Capital considered themselves to be practicers.

In the election of 1919, however, the Socialist vote increased sharply in all regions. Growth in support for parties of the Left was an international postwar phenomenon, but an additional factor in Belgium may have been the spectacular extension of Socialist influence in the population as a result of the growth of its social organizations during the preceding decade. In 1910 only 7 percent of the work force of the secondary and tertiary sectors of the economy belonged to trade unions.* By 1920 the level of unionization had risen to 30 percent and by 1930 to 35 percent. In the decade after 1910 membership in Socialist and Catholic friendly societies rose by more than half. Most of this growth occurred in Socialist organizations. In 1910 the Socialist share of trade-union membership stood at slightly less than 60 percent, but by 1920 it was as high as 80 percent. (By 1930 it had declined to 70 percent.) Before the war the Socialist share of friendly society memberships was about 45 percent, and after the war it was 70 percent. In all areas of social organization the major competitor of the Socialist party was the Catholic social complex. The popular impact of Liberal organization was negligible.

From the trade-union data it is clear that the Flemish provinces were more affected by the growth of sociopolitical organizations than the other regions. Before 1914 Catholic and Socialist trade unions competed equally for Flemish members. In 1910, when 9 percent of the nonagrarian work force belonged to trade unions, the Catholics had 49 percent and the Socialist 51 percent of the membership. By 1920 the Socialist share had probably increased considerably. The rate of unionization was higher in Flanders than elsewhere; by 1930 the proportion of the Flemish nonagrarian work force belonging to trade unions stood at 49 percent. At this date Catholic trade unions had recovered from the initial advance of the Socialists and had 46 percent of the members. The Catholic trade unions continued to increase their share of the organized work force in the 1930s and after the Second World War. In 1947, with 56 percent of the work force organized, the Catholic share had also reached 56 percent.

The pattern of organizational memberships was quite different in the Walloon provinces. The level of unionization was lower than in Flanders: 6 percent in 1910, 31 percent in 1930, and 35 percent in 1947. Competition between Catholic and Socialist unions was also lower, with the Socialists dominating trade-union organization throughout the period. Their share rose from 71 percent in 1910 to 91 percent in 1930. In 1947 it was 79 percent. Socialist trade unions have played a comparably important role in the Brussels area. From 58 percent of trade-union members in the province of Brabant in 1910, the Socialist share rose to 82 percent in 1930. In 1947 it was 67 percent. However, the level of unionization has remained low in Brabant (5, 17, and 20 percent at the three time points).

The political organization of occupational groups was not restricted to the industrial work force or to urban-industrial settings. In 1919 a Catholic middle-class

---

* The data presented here are calculated from the following sources: national trade-union and friendly-societo membership, M. P. Fogarty, 1957, p. 220; national and regional trade-union membership, J. Neuville, 1960, pp. 67-86; middle-class association membership L-E. Troclet, 1931, p. 15; farmers'-association membership, A. Varzim, 1934, pp. 92-101.

association was founded to articulate the interests of artisans and tradespeople (the *Christelijke Landsbond van den Middenstand van België/Alliance des classes moyennes chrétiennes*). By 1931 it included 25,000 members. The Catholic farmers' association, *Boerenbond*, probably encompassed 60 percent of the Flemish agrarian population by the early 1930s. Its francophone counterpart, *Alliance Agricole*, was founded only in 1930, and its influence was much smaller, probably limited to not more than 10 percent of the Walloon rural population in the 1930s.

These occupational organizations directly involved about 6 percent of the entire work force in 1910, 30 percent in 1930, and 35 percent in 1947. In the area dominated by Brussels their influence has been small, ranging from 3 percent of the work froce in 1910 to 10 percent in 1930 and 1947. In the Walloon region they have directly affected from 4 percent of the work force in 1910 to about 25 percent in 1930 and 1947. Their influence has been the greatest in the Flemish region, where the proportion of the work force directly involved in these sociopolitical organizations has risen from 10 percent in 1910 to 35 percent in 1930 to 40 percent in 1947. Since trade union memberships are generally lower than memberships in other types of social organizations, these percentages undoubtedly underestimate the extent of popular involvement in sociopolitical groups. They are nonetheless high, and have become higher in the post-1947 period: in 1967 the level of unionization in Belgium had reached 61 percent of the work force (R. Senelle, 1970, p. 68).

The peculiarly embracing character of sociopolitical organization in segmented societies such as Belgium, Austria, and the Netherlands has been noted by a number of writers (cf. A. Lijphart, 1969; L. Huyse, 1970; V. R. Lorwin, 1971). In such societies almost all the organized life of substantial sections of the urban working-class and rural populations, and of artisan and employers' groups, is contained within the framework of Socialist or politico-religious organizations. In Belgium the Socialist movement acquired the characteristics of "a state within a state" from the earliest years of its existence. Yet the conditions that were conducive to the development of highly introverted Socialist blocks—the *soziale Ghettoparteien* of countries like Austria and Germany—were absent in Belgium. Universal suffrage was conceded at an early stage, and there was no attempt by government to impede the growth of working-class organizations (see S. M. Lipset and S. Rokkan, 1967, p. 22). It is understandable that trade unions, cooperatives, friendly societies, savings banks, and a range of leisure associations should have had a distinctive political character because early socialists provided the organizational skills for their growth. Nevertheless, some further stimulus was probably required for these organizations to become agencies of social segregation. That stimulus was the challenge of social Catholicism for the allegiance of the working class. The need to maintain group solidarity against directly competitive institutions and ideologies produced that politicization of the Belgian social structure observed by Seebohm Rowntree as early as 1910:

> There is extraordinarily little social intercourse between Catholics and Liberals, and practically none between Catholics and Socialists. Politics enter into almost

every phase of social activity and philanthropic effort, and it is the exception rather than the rule for persons holding different political opinions to co-operate in any other matter. Thus in one town there will be a Catholic, a Liberal, and a Socialist trade union, a Catholic, a Liberal, and a Socialist co-operative bakery, a Catholic, a Liberal, and a Socialist thrift society, each catering for similar people, but each confining its attentions to members of its own political party. The separation extends to cafes, gymnasia, choral, and temperance, and literary societies; indeed, it cuts right through life. (Cited by R. C. K. Ensor, 1915.)

Although Seebohm Rowntree's description exaggerates the penetration of the Liberal organizations into the social structure, there is no reason to doubt the general tone of his observations for the period. Unfortunately, no individual-level investigations have been carried out subsequently to arrive at a closer appreciation of the social distance between members of different sociopolitical groups. Given the truth of the current assumption that the traditional ideological blocs are rapidly losing their influence in Belgian society (an electoral indicator of which is the decline of 21 percent in the combined Catholic and Socialist vote since 1961), it seems unlikely that a contemporary social survey would throw much light on the historical reality. The fact of continued segmentation of important social institutions in Belgium (see Table 7) may be reflective of organizational persistence rather than current social consciousness. On the other hand there is nothing to suggest that, for most of the twentieth-century, Belgium has not been marked by what Professor V. R. Lorwin (1971) has called "segmented pluralism." Moreover, the continuing high level of support for the Catholic and Socialist parties among the working class (the social group most affected by the sociopolitical complexes) suggests that membership in politicized social organizations still has important consequences for electoral behavior.

TABLE 7: **Political Segmentation of Social Activities in the 1960s**

ACTIVITIES	YEAR	CATHOLIC	SOCIALIST	LIBERAL	STATE/ OTHERS	SEGMENTED PORTION
1. Membership of farmers' unions	1963	c. 100.0	—	—	—	c. 100.0
2. Membership of trade unions	1968	47.2	42.0	6.4	4.4	95.6
3. Votes for parties	1968	31.8	28.0	20.9	19.3	80.7
4. Readership of newspapers	1969	52.2	8.9	19.4	19.5	80.5
5. Administration of social insurance	1963	41.0	32.0	—	27.0	73.0
6. Students in tertiary education	1965-66	61.4	—	—	38.6	61.4
7. Administration of sickbeds	1967	60.0	—	—	40.0	60.0
8. Pupils in primary/ secondary education	1965-66	57.6	—	--	42.4	57.6

Sources : 1 & 5 : A. Van Den Brande, 1963; 2 : *The Europa Year Book* 1968; 3 : N. Delruelle, 1970; 4: calculated from J. Gol, 1970; 6, 7 & 8: calculated from *Annuaire Statistique de la Belgique 1967* Institut National de Statistique, 1968.

While it is evident that the importance of the "organizational variable" (G. Sartori 1969) for Belgian political development can be confirmed only by ecological analysis, its attractiveness as an element of explanation is beyond question. The growth of Socialist organizations in the Flemish region from 1910 to 1920 offers the most likely explanation of the sudden rise in the Flemish Socialist vote from the election of 1912 to that of 1919. By the same token, the organizational response of the Catholics to this Socialist growth seems to account for the failure of the Socialist vote to increase more than marginally after 1919. More important, the response of the Catholics may explain why the working class in Flanders has exhibited such a high level of religious practice— in 1968 67 percent of the Flemish working class claimed regular attendance at Mass (calculated from Delruelle, 1970).

Continued adherence to the Church has had strong implications for the continued dominance of the Catholic party in the Flemish region. Indeed, reinforced by the wide extent of Catholic social organizations in both urban and rural areas, it may have created a loyalty to the Catholic party that impeded the electoral growth of the Flemish nationalist parties in the interwar years. If the joint influence of the schools question and class interest cemented the Flemish urban electorate to the Catholic party or the Socialist party, making it impenetrable for the Flemish nationalists, the strength of the Catholic farmers'-organization probably prevented their encroachment on the Flemish agricultural vote. Although Nationalist electoral strength in the interwar period was located in rural and semirural *arrondissements* it is unlikely that they drew their electoral support from an agrarian work force so tightly integrated in the Catholic bloc. In contrast the organizational weakness of the Catholics among francophone farmers may have facilitated the rapid mobilization of electoral support for the Rexist party in Walloon rural areas in 1936 (see R. De Smet, et al, 1958, p. 59). The generally lower level of sociopolitical organization in Walloon urban areas, by comparison with those of Flanders, may have permitted the growth of Communist support between 1936 and 1950.

A recent cross-national study of party systems in the interwar period places Belgium among the five countries displaying the least electoral change (D. W. Urwin and R. Rose, 1970). This is a significant finding for a country that experienced the centrifugal force of a peripheral nationalism in addition to economic depression and the destabilizing influence of communism and fascism. It is suggestive of a special element in Belgian electoral politics, the country's singularly politicized social structure that is the result, above all, of the competition between the Catholic and Socialist parties for the support of the industrial working class.

In Wallonia the Socialists emerged early as the dominant party. Its surge forward from 1894 until the 1920s was halted for two decades by the growth of the Communist party, which was particularly strong in the late 1940s. In the 1950s, however, the Socialist party overcame the Communist encroachment on its electorate and embarked on an upward electoral curve that was halted only by the emergence of the francophone parties. The strength of the Socialists reflects the electoral importance of class politics in the region. This factor has been less marked in the politics of the Brussels conurbation, where Catholics and Liberals have retained greater electoral support. It is in Flanders that the class cleavage has been of least influence in electoral behavior. There most of the working class has given its support to the Catholic party, as has most of the middle class and the farmers. In a region in which Catholic social organizations have articulated the interests of the working class as effectively as—and more extensively than—Socialist organizations, the primary characteristic of the Flemish Socialist electorate has been secularism rather than social class.

D. CENTER AND PERIPHERY IN TWENTIETH-CENTURY BELGIUM

The dominance of the Catholic party in Flanders and of the Socialist party in Wallonia have defined historically the political regions of Belgium. These distinctive patterns of regional electoral behavior arose from differences in the rate of industrialization and the level of adherence to the Church. The contribution of linguistic differences in establishing these patterns was minimal: the spread of anticlerical and socialist ideas may have been easier in a francophone population than in a population that, at the turn of the century, still spoke almost mutually incomprehensible Dutch dialects. During the interwar period the growth of support for the Flemish nationalist parties made the politics of the Flemish region increasingly different from those of the Walloon region and the Brussels conurbation. However, it is only since the election of 1965 that language has acquired a significance comparable to class and religiosity in distinguishing regional electoral behavior.

The spatial clustering of linguistic groups has allowed solutions for linguistic demands to be applied within physically limited areas. This clustering also allows the linguistic parties to adopt federalist positions. However, the relative importance of language and region has differed in the programs of the linguistic parties. The primary focus of the Flemish nationalist parties and of the Brussels francophone party (FDF) has been on linguistic rather than regional demands. Their main concern has been with the linguistic rights of individuals. This contrasts with the program of the francophone party of the Walloon region (RW), whose central concern is the economic rights of a community that is cohesive primarily on spatial, and only secondarily on linguistic, criteria.

The Flemish movement (comprising Flemish sympathizers within the traditional parties and the separate Nationalist parties) has sought to make the status and opportunities of all Dutch-speakers, irrespective of location, equal to those of French-speaking Belgians. The initial demands of the Flemish movement concentrated on the introduction of a unilingual Dutch regime in areas in which Dutch-speakers formed the overwhelming majority. The movement's implicit aim was to undermine the socio-economic hegemony of the resident francophone population of Flanders. At the end of the interwar period, with most of the movement's reforms achieved in the Flemish region, it was directing its attention increasingly to the situation of the Dutch-speaking minority in the Brussels conurbation. In Brussels the low ascriptive status of the Dutch language was leading to the acculturation of the Dutch-speaking population. The

Flemish movement's concern to prevent the absorption of the Dutch-speakers into the dominant francophone culture contributed ultimately to the language laws of 1963.

The official bilingual character of the capital city was reaffirmed in the 1963 measures. Indeed, from the recognition of Brussels as the bilingual capital of a bilingual country flowed certain linguistic arrangements highly deleterious to the capital's francophone majority. The Brussels statute required parity between Dutch- and French-speaking employees in all public services—in the administrations of the nineteen communes as well as in the postal, telecommunication, and transportation services, etc. The new statute of Brussels was not the only threat to the francophone population of Brussels in the 1963 linguistic package. The linguistic reorganization of the central civil service was also mandated. The introduction of linguistic parity in the national bureaucracy threatened the jobs of the heavily overrepresented francophone staff. The requirement of bilingualism in the upper echlons of the civil service blighted the career prospects of francophone bureaucrats (since the francophones have generally not cared to learn Dutch, bilingual positions are normally occupied by Flemings). Finally, the fixing of the linguistic frontier in 1963 faced actual and would-be residents of the new francophone suburbs in the peripheral communes of Brussels-Capital with the prospect of living in communes with permanent Dutch educational and administrative arrangements. These measures provided the stimulus for the creation of the FDF in 1964.

The FDF aspires to reverse or at least severely limit the provisions of the 1963 language laws. Its program is aimed, therefore, against the interests of both the resident Dutch-speaking population of the Brussels conurbation and the many thousands of Flemings who travel into Brussels daily to work. The FDF does not seek to defend the rights of a spatially or economically united community, but of a linguistically cohesive social group. In defending the prniciple of unilingualism in the public services and the national bureaucracy, it represents both the Brussels francophones and the francophones who work in Brussels but live in adjacent Walloon areas (notably the *arrondissements* of Nivelles and Charleroi). The FDF extends its support to francophone demands outside the Brussels area by endorsing the federalist aims of the RW and the popular francophone demand for the return of the communes of the Voeren/Fourons to the province of Liège. (In the 1963 changes in the linguistic frontier these six communes were incorporated in the province of Limburg. Their inhabitants, most of whom speak a species of low German, have expressed the constant wish to return to the francophone linguistic regime. They have given absolute electoral majorities to the list *Retour à Liège* in the elections of 1965 and 1968, and in the absence of the list in 1971 engaged in massive electoral abstention.) In the elections of 1968 and 1971 the FDF formed an electoral cartel with the RW in the Nivelles *arrondissement*.

While the RW offers reciprocal support for the linguistic aims of the FDF, its own program revolves around the attempt to stem the economic decline of the Walloon region. This decline, the result of an obsolescent heavy industrial structure, contrasts with the economic prosperity of the Flemish region. (P. Romus, 1967.) Not only has this contrast fed Walloon grievances, it is seen by the Walloon federalists as the inevitable consequence of Flemish political hegemony in the Belgian unitary state,

Flemish parliamentary dominance is considered to have led to disproportionate economic investment in the Flemish region. Federalism offers the possibility of regional economic development free of the competing demands of the Flemish economy. Short of federalism, the RW has advocated proportionate investment and credit budgets and the separate discussion of these budgets by regional parliamentarians sitting in economic councils.

The emergence of the francophone parties is attributable to the success of the Flemish movement. Yet there is a paradox in this success. In former times, when the inequalities suffered by the Flemish population were inestimably greater than in the period since the end of the Second World War, the electoral support of the Flemish nationalist parties was smaller. Furthermore, the period since the fulfilment of most of the formal demands of the movement in 1963 has seen the major growth of the postwar Flemish nationalist party (VU). Explanations of both phenomena are to be found in changes in the relationship between the political and social systems in Belgium. The proliferation of Catholic and Socialist sociopolitical organizations in the interwar period provided the institutions through which Flemish grievances could be redressed. Flemish Socialists saw in the extension of the Flemish education system a means of material and ideological emancipation for the Flemish population (see C-H. Hojer, 1946, p. 11). However, the movement was primarily Catholic. By the second election of the interwar period (1921), all Flemish Catholic parliamentarians subscribed to the "minimal program" of the major Flemish cultural organization, *Katholieke Vlaamsche Landsbond* (see F. Van Kalken, 1944, p. 57).

In 1925 the Socialist party and the Flemish Catholics formed a coalition on a joint program of economic and linguistic reform. Although the coalition lasted only eleven months, the fears of the Liberals and the conservative Catholic francophones that the experiment would be repeated gave the Flemish Catholics the role of arbiter in succeeding Catholic-Liberal coalitions. From this position the Flemish Catholics (with the parliamentary support of the Flemish Socialists) introduced the extensive program of linguistic reform of the 1930s, which almost completed the linguistic demands of the "minimal program" : unilingual tertiary education in Dutch (with the creation of the Flemish University of Gent in 1930), unilingual secondary education in the Flemish region (1932), unilingual local government (1932), the introduction of Dutch-speakers into the national civil service (1932), a unilingual judicial system (1935), and the creation of unilingual military units up to the divisional level (1938). Thus in the interwar period the major traditional parties acted as the chief agencies for the transmission of Flemish demands for social and cultural equality with francophone Belgians. The role of the Flemish nationalists was that of spur and threat : it became more critical as the "minimal program" neared completion and the commitment of the Flemish Socialists and Catholics to linguistic reform became less strong.

The linguistic reforms of the interwar period did much to raise the status of the Dutch-speaking community within the Flemish region. In the central administration and the capital city of the Belgian state, however, the equality of Dutch- and French-speakers was still not an effected norm. The wartime occupation of Belgium should have been only a parenthesis in the progress of Dutch-speakers to complete formal equality. Yet after the end of the Second World War the force of the Flemish movement was weakened and the achievement of its aims retarded.

The postwar prosecution and imprisonment as collaborators of a number of Flemish nationalists undermined the legitimacy of the movement and the effectiveness of the Nationalist party as a pressure group. The political arena was simultaneously filled by other major issues. From the Liberation, in 1944, until 1950 the royal question dominated Belgian politics. This crisis was succeeded by two lengthy conflicts that mobilized the Belgian electorate on religious and class lines: the schools question, which lasted from the early 1950s until its solution in the Schools Pact of 1958, and the economic question, which culminated in the strikes of the winter 1960-1961 (V. Feaux, 1963).

Francophone resistance to the Flemish movement also stiffened after the war. Within the traditional parties influential groups of francophone defense emerged, stimulated in part by the royal question, which appeared to many francophones as a guise for Flemish political aggression. Linked to this was the new situation of the Flemish Catholic party, which had been the main channel of Flemish demands. After the creation of the strongly centralized Christian Social party in 1945, Flemish Catholic parliamentarians no longer enjoyed their bargaining power of the interwar years.

The Catholic and Socialist parties regained their historical role as the mediators of Flemish interests in the early 1960s. A Catholic-Socialist coalition was responsible for the 1963 laws that extended Dutch-speakers' equality into those areas where earlier measures had proved ineffective. In common with the reforms of the interwar period the measures of the 1960s contributed to the status of Dutch-speakers in those social agencies directly amenable to governmental influence, such as local and national bureaucracies, the army, the diplomatic service, the school system. In improving the collective status of the Dutch-speaking community the state was simultaneously improving the occupational opportunities of individual Dutch-speakers in these agencies. Outside the institutions of the state, however, the middle-class Dutch-Speaker continued to find his career prospects limited by francophone control of many of the largest commercial and industrial undertakings of Flanders and Brussels.

The Catholic-Socialist coalition, 1961–1965, recognized this situation and made a limited attempt to extend the language laws into the private sector. Enterprises located in the Flemish region were instructed to produce Dutch-language versions of their public documents. Managements of public utilities and firms with state contracts in the Flemish region were directed to communicate with their employees in the language of the region. Although these requirements were met, extensive areas of private enterprise remained outside the purview of government. The admission of Dutch-speakers to managerial posts has been generally resisted. Some firms have relocated their headquarters in Brussels rather than submit to any change in their linguistic arrangements (J. Brazeau, 1966). No government since 1963 has demonstrated the will or the capacity to tackle the problem in depth, which has left the VU as the only party offering radical solutions to it. The electoral growth of the VU since the mid-1960s almost certainly results from a massive infusion of middle-class voters.

The two indicators of social class in Table 8 show that the VU draws disproportionate support from higher-status occupations and those regarding themselves as middle-class. The profile of VU support is closer to that of the Liberal party (PVV) than to those of the Catholic (CVP) and Socialist (BSP) parties in terms of social class in the Flemish region. VU support is also more like that of the PVV in religiosity than the support of the other two parties. Both VU and PVV draw more support from religious practicers than nonpracticers.

TABLE 8: **Party Profiles, 1968, Regional and National**

	CVP	BSP	PVV	VU	RW	FDF	PCB	%	N
Percent of sample	(39)	(28)	(18)	(9)	(3)	(2)	(1)		
Occupation									
Workers	34	61	19	29	30	17	60	38	905
Employees	26	24	26	28	30	43	20	26	618
Independents	15	8	21	19	17	13	16	14	341
Professionals	9	6	25	18	20	26	4	13	298
Farmers	16	2	9	6	2	—	—	9	206
Subjective Class Assessment									
Working-class	55	82	28	44	43	21	70	56	134
Middle-class	41	17	57	52	46	60	26	38	922
Bourgeoisie	4	1	15	4	10	19	4	6	136
Religiosity									
Practicing	87	24	48	74	43	24	7	58	142
Nonpracticing	13	76	52	26	57	76	93	42	104
Region									
Flanders	68	41	36	95	—	—	—	53	130
Wallonia	22	49	43	—	100	—	78	34	839
Brussels-Capital	10	10	21	5	—	100	22	13	335

TABLE 8A: **Brussels-Capital**

	CVP	BSP	PVV	FDF	VU	PC	%	N
Percent of sample	(28)	(21)	(29)	(18)	(3)	(2)		
Occupation								
Workers	25	38	13	17	26	30	23	141
Employees	35	38	32	43	37	20	36	221
Independents	22	13	21	14	10	40	18	114
Professionals	17	11	34	26	26	10	23	139
Subjective Class Assessment								
Working-class	37	67	15	22	30	33	34	221
Middle-class	46	27	60	60	45	50	49	321
Bourgeoisie	16	6	25	18	15	17	17	110
Religiosity								
Practicing	62	15	28	25	55	—	34	231
Nonpracticing	38	85	72	75	45	100	66	438

TABLE 8B: **Walloon Region**

	PSC	PSB	PLP	RW	PC	%	N
Percent of sample	(25)	(41)	(23)	(8)	(3)		
Occupation							
Workers	32	69	17	30	70	45	348
Employees	24	18	24	31	20	23	175
Independents	14	6	22	17	10	11	88
Professionals	9	5	24	20	—	12	94
Farmers	21	2	12	1	—	9	70
Subjective Class Assessment							
Working-class	48	83	26	43	82	58	466
Middle-class	47	16	62	46	18	37	297
Bourgeoisie	6	1	12	10	—	5	43
Religiosity							
Practicing	84	18	44	44	9	43	357
Nonpracticing	16	82	56	56	91	57	482

TABLE 8C: **Flemish Region**

	CVP	BSP	PVV	VU	%	N
Percent of sample	(50)	(22)	(12)	(16)		
Occupation						
Workers	36	57	24	29	38	488
Employees	25	27	25	27	26	331
Independents	14	9	18	19	14	182
Professionals	8	5	23	17	11	135
Farmers	16	2	9	7	11	138
Subjective Class Assessment						
Working-class	60	85	38	43	60	761
Middle-class	38	14	50	53	37	467
Bourgeoisie	2	1	11	4	3	38
Religiosity						
Practicing	92	35	65	75	73	956
Nonpracticing	8	65	35	25	27	346

Source: Delruelle, p. 49.

Table 9 indicates that many VU and PVV voters have shifted their electoral support to these parties from the CVP. The condition for this transfer of presumably churchgoing middle-class support from the Catholic party was the relaxation of the obligation to vote CVP that resulted from the signing of the Schools Pact in 1958. It was intrinsically more likely that the decline of religious conflict would affect the electoral attitudes of middle-class churchgoers than those of working-class churchgoers in the Flemish region. For working-class churchgoers the schools question was one among a range of interests that linked them to the Catholic party. Workers are closely

TABLE 9A: **Party Gains and Losses, 1961-1968, Flemish Region**

	CVP Gain from	CVP Loss to	BSP Gain from	BSP Loss to	PVV Gain from	PVV Loss to	VU Gain from	VU Loss to
CVP			4	2	20	3	42	
BSP	1	2			4	1	6	1
PVV	1	5	1	2			3	2
VU		12	1	4	1	6		
RW								
FDF								
CPB								
Others/Blank		2	1	4				
Total gain from other parties	2		7		25		53	
Total gain from new electors	13		10		22		25	
Total gain as % 1968 vote	15		17		47		78	
Total losses as % 1961 vote		21		12		10		3
1968 N	656		283		161		202	
1961 N		710		277		101		101

TABLE 9B: **Party Gains and Losses, 1961-1968, Walloon Region**

	PSC Gain from	PSC Loss to	PSB Gain from	PSB Loss to	PLP Gain from	PLP Loss to	RW Gain from	RW Loss to
PSC			2	1	15	2	8	
PSB	1	3			9	2	44	
PLP	1	13	1	5			11	
RW		2		9		7		
PC			1	1			5	
Others/Blank	1	5		2	1	2	3	
Total gain from other parties	3		4		25		71	
Total gain from new electors	18		11		22		30	
Total gain as % 1968 vote	21		15		47		100	
Total losses as % 1961 vote		23		18		13		
1968 N	213		340		196		69	
1961 N		223		347		120		

TABLE 9C: **Party Gains and Losses, 1961-1968, Brussels-Capital**

	CVP/PSC Gain from	CVP/PSC Loss to	BSP/PSB Gain from	BSP/PSB Loss to	PVV/PLP Gain from	PVV/PLP Loss to	VU Gain from	FDF Gain from
CVP/PSC			2	6	9	7	25	11
BSP/PSB	7	2			7	1		30
PVV/PLP	1	13	1	7			5	23
VU	1	4				1		
RW						1		
FDF		10		19		18		
PC								1
Others/Blank		1	1	4	1	1		3
Total gain from other parties	9		4		17		30	68
Total gain from new electors	35		10		26		50	32
Total gain as % 1968 vote	44		14		43		80	100
Total losses as % 1961 vote		30		36		28		
1968 N	186		141		192		20	118
1961 N		138		186		147		

Source: Delruelle, pp. 118–119.

integrated in the Catholic bloc through multiple memberships in its labor and welfare organizations, with the result that their support for the CVP is both effective and instrumental. This is not generally the case with middle-class churchgoers, whose socioeconomic position makes them less likely to be involved in the social organizations. Indeed, the increasing postwar influence of the Catholic social organizations in the policy-making councils of the party may have caused some middle-class alienation from the CVP.

In the election of 1965 both the PVV and the VU probably gained considerable electoral advantage as a result of middle-class disenchantment with the CVP. In the two succeeding elections the appeal of the PVV to middle-class Flemish voters has proved less strong. The electoral appeal of the PVV has been weakened by its association with the strongly francophone Liberals of Brussels and Wallonia. Moreover, its commitment to the unitary organization of the Belgian state has probably prevented it from achieving that combination of linguistic and class appeals which has attracted growing electoral support to the VU. The continued electoral growth of the VU in 1971 suggests that the CVP's middle-class support has been further eroded. One policy consequence of the CVP's loss of its middle-class electorate may be the increasing influence of the popular social organisations in the party.

The 1965 electoral success of the Liberal party in Flanders was repeated more dramatically in Wallonia and Brussels-Capital. The Liberal impetus was maintained in the Walloon region in 1968. As Table 9 indicates, this repeated success was largely at the expense of the Catholic party (PSC). The electoral decline of the Liberal party in 1971 was largely to the benefit of the RW (see p. 66). The acquisition of Liberal voters by the RW in 1971 has probably increased the disproportionate support from the middle-class that the RW had already manifested in 1968 (Table 8). The same increase in middle-class support is probably to be found in the support of the Brussels FDF. In 1968 the growth of FDF support was already attributable to its attraction of Liberal as well as Socialist Voters, as Table 9 shows. Indeed, the emergence of the FDF probably caused the decline in Liberal support in Brussels-Capital from 1965 to 1968. It is likely that the gains of the FDF in 1971 came very largely from the Liberal electorate.

The electoral behavior of the middle-class in Belgium has changed considerably between 1961 and 1971. In 1965 a large proportion of middle-class churchgoers transferred their votes from the Catholic party to the Liberal party. In the Flemish region a large proportion of middle-class churchgoers also transferred their support to the Flemish nationalist party. Since 1965 many middle-class Catholic and Liberal voters have shifted their electoral support to the linguistic parties.

Working-class electoral behavior has been more stable. The class has maintained its support for the Catholic and Socialist parties. Few important political issues divide these parties, while the linguistic cleavage has turned the Belgian middle-class increasingly into two competing political fractions. In Belgium, therefore, one might speak of an increasingly political unified working-class and an increasingly politically fragmented middle-class. In this respect Belgium is virtually alone among advanced industrial societies.

II.   The Electoral System Since 1894

Belgium has a bicameral legislature, comprised of the Chamber of Representatives and the Senate. All representatives are directly elected. Since 1894 their number has risen from 152 to 212. The number of directly elected senators is equal to half the number of representatives. A smaller group of senators is elected by the provincial councils. There are now forty-eight provincial senators. Since 1921 a further group of senators, half the number of provincial senators, is coopted by the Senate itself. The heir to the throne is an ex-officio member of the Senate from the age of eighteen. Since 1894 the number of senators has risen from 103 to 179. In the same period the functional role of the Senate has become increasingly similar to that of the Chamber (see W. Dewachter, 1967, p. 241). The minimal incidence of "split-ticket" voting between Chamber and Senate suggests that this functional identity is perceived by the electorate. Throughout this section discussion is confined to the Chamber as the larger elective assembly.

A.   THE ELECTORAL SYSTEM BEFORE 1894

Before the first legislative election based on universal male suffrage in 1894 the percentage of the adult male population with the right to vote in parliamentary elections had probably never exceeded 11 percent (calculated from J. Gilissen, 1958). Three qualifications were required of voters: that they be male, have attained the age of twenty-five, and have paid a stipulated amount of direct taxes in the year preceding an election. Between 1831 and 1848 the fiscal quota varied from town to country and from province to province. It was always lower in the countryside. In 1848, to forestall the possibility of revolutionary disorders in Belgian towns, a Liberal ministry introduced legislation standardizing the fiscal quota at the lowest level specified in the constitution. The enfranchised population was thus extended from about 46,000 to about 79,000, or 2 percent of the population.

In practice, however, the voting population was larger under the restricted franchise than these figures would suggest. In 1871 the tax qualification for voting in provincial and communal elections was made substantially lower than that for national elections; the result was that perhaps as much as 20 percent of the adult male population had the right to vote in provincial elections and 30 percent in communal elections. With the total removal of the tax qualification in 1883, when it was replaced by the requirement of primary education, the franchise for local government became almost that of universal suffrage (see J. Gilissen, 1958, p. 99).

B. THE ELECTORAL SYSTEM SINCE 1894

1. The Franchise

In 1893 universal male suffrage was enacted for national elections. The extension of the franchise was tempered by a system of plural voting. Although one vote was guaranteed to all Belgian males of twenty-five enjoying their civil rights, one voter could cast up to three votes in an election. An extra vote went to heads of families occupying houses on which they paid a personal tax of at least five francs, and/or to those owning property worth 2,000 francs or receiving rents or interest to the value of 1,000 francs. The possession of higher educational qualifications was worth two extra votes. The same rules applied for Senate elections except that the age minimum was raised to thirty years. As a result of the new electoral law the number of registered electors rose from 136,000 in 1892 to 1,354,000 in 1894. Of the latter figure about 850,000 electors disposed of one vote, 290,000 electors of two votes, and 220,000 of three (see J. Gilissen 1958, p. 125).

Plural voting lasted until 1919, when the qualification for voting in elections to both Chamber and Senate was fixed at one vote for all Belgian males of twenty-one who have resided for at least six months in the commune in which they cast their vote. In the following two years two measures incorporated women into the electorate. First, the mothers and widows of soldiers who had died in the war were allowed to vote in national elections; second, the female franchise was established for communal elections. It was not until 1948 that women acquired the same voting rights as men in national elections.

Not all Belgian residents of twenty-one are qualified to vote. Most of those excluded are non-Belgian nationals. In the election of 1961 4 percent of Belgian residents were not eligible to vote (see W. Dewachter, 1967, p. 70).

2. THE CONSTITUENCIES

Since 1831 the basic electoral unit, to which seats in the Chamber of Representatives are assigned, has been the electoral *arrondissement*. However, the method of allocating seats to votes has been changed. Until 1899 candidates continued to be elected on simple majorities. The tendency of majoritarian systems to distort the relationship between popular vote and parliamentary representation was exaggerated by another factor in Belgium. By the last decade of the nineteenth-century most electoral *arrondissements* had become multimember constituencies, and in those with ten or more seats list-voting had been introduced. The list that got the most votes was elected to the Chamber in its entirety.

In the first election under universal plural suffrage the Catholic party, with 50 percent of the vote, gained 68 percent of the seats in the Chamber, while the Liberal party, with 29 percent of the vote, gained only 13 percent of the seats. The Socialist party was probably not disadvantaged at all in this election, because its support was less dispersed than that of the Liberal party. For the non-Catholic parties the lesson of this and later partial elections was that the majoritarian system was likely to ensure Catholic dominance of the parliamentary scene. The Catholic party had some incentive to accede to their demands for a change in the electoral system. It hoped to reduce the number of seats gained by the Socialists in Walloon urban constituencies and to restore its own representation there by the introduction of proportional representation. In 1899 the majoritarian system was replaced by the d'Hondt system of proportional representation at the level of the *arrondissement*. The new system went a long way toward eliminating the discrepancy between popular votes and parliamentary representation. (In the general elections of 1900 and 1912 the Catholic share of seats in the Chamber exceeded its share of the vote by 8.6 and 3.3 percent, respectively; the Liberals and Socialists were together underrepresented by 4.2 and 2.8 percent, respectively.) Proportionality has been even more closely attained since the 1919 electoral law that included the redistribution of votes at the provincial level.

The boundaries of the thirty electoral *arrondissements* are determined by their relationship to the forty-four administrative *arrondissements*. Twenty electoral *arrondissements* are based directly on single administrative *arrondissements*, while the remaining ten are constituted by fusions of two or three of the administrative areas. Until 1965 the electoral law required that the ratio of representatives to residents should not exceed one to 40,000 (the new norm is one seat to 43,347 inhabitants). Administrative *arrondissements* are combined to attain the minimum population required for two seats. The result is that electoral *arrondissements* vary considerably in geographical extent and number of registered electors (in 1968 the largest electoral *arrondissements*, Brussels, had 1,008,920 registered electors, and the smallest, Neufchâteau-Virton, 62,038). Moreover, since the administrative system dates from the Napoleonic period, electoral boundaries do not correspond to contemporary demographic features, with resulting mixes of economic and, in the case of the Brussels *arrondissement*, linguistic characteristics (see W. Dewachter, 1969, pp. 23–26). By the same token, electoral boundaries are not susceptible to redrawing for partisan advantage.

3. THE DISTRIBUTION OF SEATS

The requirement of the electoral law that the seat-to-population ratio should not exceed one to 40,000 has necessitated a constant increase in the number of seats in the Chamber of Representatives. Since 1949 the number of seats has been fixed at 212. From 1919 the addition and redistribution of seats followed the decennial censuses with irregular lapses of time. In 1965, however, the electoral law was amended to provide for the redistribution of seats within three years of each census. At the time of the 1968 election the seat-to-population ratio stood at 1:45,280 over all *arrondissements*. The highest ratio was 1:52,697, the smallest 1:38,098, and the standard deviation from the mean 3,376. In fact, the average ratio was somewhat higher in the Flemish *arrondissements* and in Brussels than in the Walloon *arrondissements*. This gave the francophone region a slightly greater number of seats in the Chamber than its population warranted (see Table 10). But the regional maldistribution amounted to only two seats, and in the postwar period it has probably never risen to more than four.

A somewhat more significant level of maldistribution arises from the differential proportion of foreign residents in the linguistic regions. In Wallonia, where large numbers of foreign workers are employed in the coal mines and in the steel industry, foreign residents constitute 12 percent of the population as against 3 percent in Flanders. (In the Brussels *arrondissement* foreigners comprise 11 percent of the population.) The allocation of seats in terms of the distribution of Belgian citizens would lead to a considerable increase in the number of Flemish representatives in the

TABLE 10: **Actual and Proportionate Distribution of Seats by Region, 1968**

	ACTUAL SEAT DISTRIBUTION		SEAT DISTRIBUTION IN PROPORTION TO:							
			Population		Belgian Citizens		Registered Electors		1968 Voters	
	%	N	%	N	%	N	%	N	%	N
Flemish Region	50.5	107	50.9	108	53.1	112	51.1	108	51.8	110
Walloon Region	34.0	72	33.1	70	31.5	67	32.5	69	32.0	68
Brussels Arrondissement	15.6	33	16.0	34	15.4	33	16.3	35	16.2	34
Total N		212		9,605,601		8,939,955		6,170,167		5,554,642

Chamber. As Table 10 indicates, the representation of the Flemish region would rise from thirty-five to forty-five seats above that of the Walloon region. Demands are beginning to be heard among the more intransigeant exponents of the Flemish cause for just such a change in the electoral law. An argument could also be made for an increase in the representation of Flanders and Brussels at the expense of Wallonia in terms of the ratio of registered electors to number of seats. Such a redistribution would work to the advantage of Brussels, with its older population, more than the Flemish region, with its younger population.

4. THE NOMINATION OF CANDIDATES

There are four constitutional requirements of candidates for the Chamber of Representatives. Candidates must be Belgian citizens, in the full enjoyment of their civil and political rights, legally resident in Belgium, and twenty-five or older. The electoral law also stipulates that candidates be endorsed by the signatures of a certain number of registered electors in the *arrondissement* of candidature (500 in Brussels; 400 in Antwerpen, Gent, Charleroi, and Liège; 200 in the other *arrondissements*). There is no deposit requirement and no legal restriction on campaign expenditures of individual candidates or national parties.

The parties themselves lay down further criteria for candidature, such as party-membership for a minimum time period and an expression (sometimes written) of loyalty to the decisions of the directive organs of the party. Since 1965 the *Christelijke Volkspartij* (the Flemish wing of the Catholic party) has imposed an age limit of sixty-five on its candidates (see F. Swaelen, 1969, pp. 77–79). It has also proscribed its representatives from combining their parliamentary positions with office holding as mayors or aldermen in communes with more than 30,000 inhabitants. (This is a meaningful restriction in Belgium, where about 70 percent of the members of the Chamber in 1965 were also mayors, aldermen, or communal councillors [calculated from W. Dewachter, 1967, p. 201.])

It is in the Socialist party, however, that the most extensive range of qualifications is demanded of candidates. Of the eight Socialist federations examined by Wilfried Dewachter, the smallest list of qualifications required of candidates was five years' party membership, an expenditure of 7,000 francs at the Socialist cooperative, and the reading of a Socialist newspaper. The largest set of requirements he found was five years' membership in the party, a Socialist trade union, and a friendly society; five years' membership in a Socialist cooperative together with a personal account of 15,000 for a two-person household (plus 2,000 francs for any other member of the household); the reading of two Socialist newspapers; the wife's membership in the party and the Socialist womens' organization, the childrens' attendance at a state school and membership in the party youth organizations; and residence in the appropriate electoral *arrondissement* (see W. Dewachter, 1967, pp. 115–16).

Although there is no method of candidate selection prescribed in the constitution, a system of preelection polls among party members has evolved in the three traditional parties. The polls, comparable to the "closed" primaries in the United States, are used in all Socialist and Catholic *arrondissement* federations, but probably in only a minority of the Liberal federations. The limited data available suggest that the poll system plays the most important role in the selection of candidates in the Socialist party, and a less important role in the Catholic and Liberal parties.

Using the data assembled by Wilfried Dewachter for members of the Chamber in 1965, it is possible to make some estimates about the importance of the polls in their selection, as follows (the proportion of the group for which data were available is indicated in parentheses): Socialist group, 93 percent selected by polls (47 percent); Catholic group, 57 percent selected by polls (81 percent); Liberal group, 48 percent selected by polls (56 percent). In the Socialist and Catholic cases the residual percentages are made up of candidates added to party lists after the polls by the directive committees of the parties. In the Liberal case the residual percentage comprises candidates placed on lists by federation committees without recourse to the poll system. Dewachter observes that his data probably exaggerate the extent of selection by poll in the Socialist and Catholic parties. The data were collected from the larger federations in which the influence of elite groups is less marked than elsewhere (W. Dewachter, 1967, pp. 124, 138).

There are both formal and practical limits to the operation of "inner-party democracy" via the poll system. Wherever polls are employed, party leaderships retain the right to amend the lists of candidates selected in the polls. The national committee of the Catholic party and the *arrondissement* committees in the Socialist and Liberal parties may add or reject candidates and alter the order of lists presented in the elections (K. Hill, 1970). Moreover, it is likely that not more than half the members of any party participate in the polls. Even in the Socialist federations, where participation has been found to be highest, there is evidence to suggest that party members largely endorse the lists as they are presented by the leadership groups (J. Stengers and A. Phillippart, 1959). This may explain why it is in the Socialist party that the fewest candidates are appointed to electoral lists after the polls. The poll system is not used in the *Volksunie* or the Communist party, and apparently not, thus far, in the francophone parties.

5. THE COUNTING OF VOTES

The d'Hondt system of proportional representation with distribution at the provincial level proceeds in three stages. The initial stage involves the allocation of seats within the electoral *arrondissement*. The total number of valid votes cast is divided by the number of seats in the Chamber to which the *arrondissement* is entitled. The vote of each party list is then divided by the product of this calculation (called the *electoral divisor*), and the party acquires a seat for each whole number produced by this division. It is possible that, at this stage, every seat or no seat at all has been allocated. Typically, several seats remain to be allocated through the provincial distribution.

The next stage involves the calculation of how many of the residual seats are due to each party over the whole province. It is not the case that all parties may benefit from this second distribution. Since 1947 the electoral law has stipulated that a list must obtain a quorum of at least 66 percent of the electoral divisor in at least one *arrondissement* before it may go forward to the provincial distribution. At this stage each list's total vote in the province is divided in turn by 1, 2, 3, etc., *plus* the number of the seats it has already gained in the *arrondissement* allocations. The parties with the largest scores thus produced are accorded seats until all the seats remaining for distribution have been allocated.

In the third stage the residual seats are assigned to *arrondissement* lists. First, the *electoral quotient* of every party to be benefited is calculated in each *arrondissement*. The electoral quotient is the product of dividing the party's vote by the electoral divisor of the *arrondissement*. Second the electoral quotient is divided by 1 plus the number of seats already acquired by the party in the *arrondissement*—this yields the *local fraction*.

TABLE 11: **The d'Hondt System of Proportional Representation: The Case of Limburg Province in 1968**

STAGE I: *The* Arrondissement *Allocation of Seats to Party Lists*

Arrondissement *of Hasselt*

Party Lists	CVP	BSP	PVV	VU		Seats due: 6 Total: 4 lists
Votes	64,953	27,245	21,603	23,774		137,575 137,575 ÷ 6 = 22,919.17
Electoral Divisor						
Seats distributed	2	1	0	1		Total: 4 seats
Residual seats						2

Arrondissement *of Tongeren-Maaseik*

Party Lists	CVP	BSP	PVV	VU	RAL	Seats due: 7 Total: 5 lists
Votes	82,267	22,323	20,368	20,990	1,933	147,881 147,881 ÷ 7 = 21,125.86
Electoral Divisor						
Seats distributed	3	1	0	0	0	Total: 4 seats
Residual seats						3
Less than 66% of Electoral Divisor				✓		
Seats distributed based on Party Lists	5	2	0	1	0	

TABLE 11 (*Continued*)

STAGE II *The Provincial Distribution of Residual Seats to Party Lists.*

Province of Limburg

					Residual seats due: 5
Party Lists	CVP	BSP	PVV	VU	
Votes	147,220	49,568	41,971	44,764	
Seats gained *plus* 1,2,3, etc =	5+	2+	0+	1+	
Scores: 1			41,971		
2			20,985	22,382	
3		16,523*			
4					
5					
6	24,537				
7	21,031				
Provincial distribution of residual seats	2	0	2	1	

STAGE III *The Assignment of Seats to* Arrondissement *Lists*

Arrondissement of Hasselt

Party Lists	CVP	BSP	PVV	VU	
					Party Vote ÷ Electoral Divisor=
Electoral Quotient	2.8340		0.9425	1.0372	
					Electoral Quotient ÷ 1 + Seats Allocated=
Local fraction	0.9446		0.9425	0.5186*	
Rank order of local fraction	4		5	6	

Arrondissement of Tongeren-Maaseik

Party Lists	CVP	BSP	PVV	VU
Electoral Quotient	3.8941		0.9641	0.9935
Local fraction	0.9735		0.9641	0.9935
Rank order of local fraction	2		3	1

Results of the election

Party Lists	CVP	BSP	PVV	VU
Arrondissement *of Hasselt*	3	1	1	1
Arrondissement *of Tongeren-Maaseik*	4	1	1	1
Province of Limburg	7	2	2	2

*All 5 seats assigned to scores higher than this.

Local fractions are then compared and seats are assigned in the order of magnitude of the fractions until all parties have gained the number of seats to which they are entitled. The seats gained in the initial allocation and the final assignment are added together to give the total number of seats obtained by each list in each *arrondissement*.

The following example shows how this somewhat complex system worked in the province of Limburg in the election for the Chamber of May, 1968. Five parties were present: Catholic (CVP), Socialist (BSP), Liberal (PVV), Flemish nationalist (VU), and the party (RAL) demanding the return of the communes of the Voeren to the province of Liège (see above, p. 45).

6. PARTICIPATION IN ELECTIONS

Compulsory voting was introduced in 1893. Unexcused abstention was made punishable by admonitions, fines, and loss of political rights. Turnout in elections averaged 95 percent from 1894 to 1912, 93 percent from 1919 to 1939, and 92 percent from 1946 to 1971 (calculated from W. Moine, 1970; *Annuaire Statistique*, 1967; *Courrier Hebdomadaire*, 1971). The legal sanctions have not been widely used. Between 1946 and the period after the election of 1961 only 0.24 percent of all abstainers were prosecuted, and only 0.20 percent convicted (see W. Dewachter, 1967, pp. 282-83). Similar laxity was apparent in the interwar period (see H. Tingsten, 1963, pp. 189-92). Nonetheless, Belgian electors clearly perceive their legal obligation to vote. One corollary of this is the comparatively high level of blank and invalid votes cast in Belgian elections. In the interwar elections these averaged 5 percent, and since 1946, 6 percent. From 1965 there has been a distinct upward trend in the proportions of abstainers and those casting blank and invalid votes.

7. AGGREGATE ELECTION RESULTS

W. Moine (1970) provides *arrondissement* results for the period 1847-1914. R. De Smet, R. Evalenko, and W. Fraeys (1958, 1959, 1961) provide results for cantons, *arrondissements*, and provinces for the period 1919-1961. The Ministry of the Interior has published in mimeograph form the election results for cantons *arrondissements*, and provinces since 1961 (Ministère de l'Intérieur/Ministerie van, Binnenlandse Zaken, 1965, 1968).

III. The Party System Since 1894

There are few constraints on electoral competition in Belgium. The average number of lists in elections in the interwar period was twenty-five, and in the period 1946–1971, twenty. Wilfried Dewachter has distinguished three types of list: party lists, party dissidents, and limited candidatures (the last category groups eccentric and/or nonpolitical candidatures) (W. Dewachter, 1967, p. 188). Since 1946 no limited candidature has been successful, and only four dissident candidates have been elected, on the following lists: *Union democratique belge* (1946), *Rassemblement social-chrétien de la liberté* (1954), *Liste L'Allemand* (1961), and *Rassemblement national* (1961). It is not the number of competing lists that defines a party system, but the number and types of major parties.

A. THE NUMBER OF PARTIES

1. CANDIDATES NOMINATED

One definition of a major party is a party nominating candidates for more than half the seats in the legislature and thus having a chance to form a government. The concept of nomination for individual seats is somewhat difficult in an electoral system with multimember constituencies. Since parties normally include as many candidates on their lists as there are seats available, however, the presence of a party list in a constituency may be taken to constitute competition for all the seats.

On the criterion of having nominated candidates for more than half the seats, the Catholic, Liberal and Socialist are classified as major parties for the entire period 1894–1971. The Catholic party has competed in every constituency in every election. (In 1894 four Catholics were returned unopposed in two Flemish *arrondissements*; in the partial elections of 1896 and 1898 there were seven unopposed Catholic candidatures in three Flemish *arrondissements*. These are the only cases of uncontested elections in the period.) Since 1900, the Liberal party has also competed in all constituencies at every election. From 1894 to 1912 the Socialist party contested from 76 to 93 percent of the seats. After 1900 it contested all seats in the Brussels *arrondissement* and the Walloon region, but in the Flemish region it was reduced from contesting 85 percent of the seats in 1896–98 to contesting 63 percent in 1912. Since 1919, it has competed in all Flemish as well as in all Brussels and Walloon constituencies.

Two other parties have contested all seats in an election: the Rexist party in 1936 and 1939 and the Communist party in 1946, 1949, and 1950. At the first election in which it competed, the Communist party contested five out of 186 seats (1921). In the following election, in 1925, it contested 59 percent of the seats. With the exception of a single election since then, the Communist party has competed for at least 73 percent of the seats. The exception was the election of 1958, when it contested only 47 percent of the seats. (In that election it competed in only one Flemish *arrondissement*, that of Leuven. Only in the first three postwar elections has the party contested the provinces of Limburg and Luxembourg.)

A second problem in classifying parties in terms of the number of seats for which they nominate candidates is peculiar to Belgium. Linguistic parties contest seats in their appropriate linguistic regions, but not elsewhere. This produces a differential result in terms of the percentage of all seats contested, for in all elections the Flemish seats comprise more than 50 percent, and the Brussels and Walloon seats less than 50 percent of the total. Clearly, the possibility of forming a government is not open to parties contesting less than half the legislative seats. The number of candidates nominated is, however, not the only criterion of major-party status. In the case of the francophone parties, therefore, their claim to be considered major must rest on their electoral success. Nonetheless, even though the Brussels and Walloon francophone parties contested only 41 percent of all seats in the election of 1965 (all the Brussels seats and fifty-five of the seventy-two Walloon seats), in the following two elections the FDF and the RW attained major-party status in terms of seats contested. By contesting the Brussels seats and all the Walloon seats in 1968 they competed for 49.5 percent of all seats. In 1971, when a francophone list linked to the FDF was presented in the Leuven *arrondissement*, the francophone parties contested 53 percent of the seats. By contesting all Flemish seats and the Brussels seats after 1921, the Flemish nationalist parties acquired major-party status by competing in more than half the seats in the interwar period. In the election of 1949 the Flemish nationalist lists were present in 80 percent of the Flemish *arrondissements*. Since 1954 the *Volksunie* has contested all the Flemish and Brussels seats and thus about 65 percent of all seats. In the election of 1900 the Daensist party contested 61 percent of all seats.

2. VOTES RECEIVED

A second criterion of major party status is the prcentage of the votes acquired.

As Appendix 1A shows, in only two elections before 1968 (1936 and 1939) did the Catholic party poll less than a third of the votes. In 1971 the party's share of the vote dropped to 30 percent. In the first election in which it competed and in the partial elections of 1902–1904 the Socialist party gained less than 20 percent of the national vote. From 1906–1908 until 1968 the socialists only once gained less than 30 percent of the vote, in the election of 1949. In the elections of 1968 and 1971 it gained 28 and 27 percent of the votes cast. The Liberal party's share of the vote dropped below 10 percent in 1946, and rose slightly above 20 percent in 1965 and 1968. Three other parties have gained more than 10 percent of the national vote: the Rexist party in 1936, with 11.5 percent; the Communist party in 1946, with 12.7 percent; and the *Volksunie* in 1971, with 11.1 percent.

National percentages underestimate the regional strength of the linguistic parties. The regional profiles of party support present a quite different picture from analysis at the national level. In the Flemish region the picture is of the dominance of the Catholic party. In the elections under plural suffrage the party averaged 64 percent of the vote (see Table 5). Since 1919 the Catholic party's share of the vote has fallen below 40 percent in only four out of sixteen elections. The Socialist share of the vote in the same period has never exceeded 30 percent and never dropped below 24 percent. The Liberal party's share declined to less than 10 percent in 1946 and rose to 17 percent in 1965. The Flemish nationalist party polled a maximum of 15 percent in the interwar period (1939); since the end of the Second World War its maximum attainment has been 19 percent, in 1971.

One-party dominance is less marked in the Walloon region. In the elections of 1919 and 1925 the Socialist party won 51 percent of the vote, and has been within 3 percent of that score in three other elections. It has never gained less than 34 percent of the vote since 1919. The Catholic party has never gained more than 35 percent of the vote since 1919, and only once less than 20 percent (1936). From 1919 until 1965 the Liberals gained between 10 and 20 percent of the vote. In 1965 and 1968, however, they gained 25 and 27 percent. In 1971 their share of the poll dropped to 18 percent. In 1946 the Communist party gained more than 20 percent of the Walloon vote, as did the *Rassemblement Wallon* in 1971. In 1936 the Rexist party received 15 percent of the votes in the Walloon region.

It is in Brussels that party shares of the vote are most evenly divided and also most subject to disruption. Since 1919 the percentage of the vote gained by the Catholic party has varied between 19 and slightly less than 36 percent, that of the Socialist party between 20 and 45 percent, and that of the Liberal party between 13 and 33 percent. The Communist party gained almost 12 percent of the vote in 1936 and over 17 percent in 1946. In the election of 1936 the Rexist party received 18 percent of the votes cast. From 1965 to 1971 the share of the vote acquired by the FDF has risen from just under 11 to more than 33 percent.

A useful summary of the distribution of party support and the trends in party support over several time periods is offered by Rae's index of electoral fragmentation (D. Rae, 1967, pp. 53–58). The fractionalization measures indicate the extent to which party systems diverge from two-party equality. However, one-party dominance as well as two-party equality attains the index-rating of 0.5, and this accounts for the approach to that score found in the Flemish region from 1894 to 1912.

TABLE 12 : **Electoral Fractionalization, Four Time Periods, Regional and National**

	1894–1912	1919–1939	1946–1961	1965–1971
Flemish region	0.53	0.72	0.60	0.72
Walloon region	0.67	0.68	0.68	0.75
Brussels-Capital	0.68	0.76	0.71	0.77
Belgium	0.64	0.72	0.66	0.77

3. SEATS GAINED

A further means of defining a major party is parliamentary representation.

On the criterion of seats gained three parties have been of primary importance since 1894: the Catholic, Liberal, and Socialist parties. Before the introduction of proportional representation in 1900 the Catholic party enjoyed substantial parliamentary majorities, with 68 percent of the seats after 1894 (with 51 percent of the national vote) and 72 percent of the seats after the partial elections of 1896–1898 (with 48 percent of the vote). From 1900 until 1919, the Catholic party continued to enjoy a parliamentary majority, with about 55 percent of the seats. In only one parliament since 1919 has the Catholic party acquired a majority of the seats: from 1950 to 1954. In the elections of 1949 and 1958 however, it gained 49.5 and 49.1 percent of the seats respectively.

In the period of the plural suffrage only three seats were gained by minor parties: two by Daensist candidates and one by a dissident Flemish Catholic. In the period 1919–1940 and since 1944 the growth of the linguistic and the Communist parties has not seriously impaired the parliamentary domination of the traditional parties. In the interwar period these parties averaged 90 percent of seats gained, and in the postwar period 91 percent. Their minimum share of seats in the lower house in the interwar period was 77 percent (1936) and in the postwar period 76 percent (1971). Although the major part of this traditional party share of parliamentary seats went to the Catholic and Socialist parties (interwar 75 percent; postwar 77 percent), it is evident that the simple acquisition of parliamentary seats does not define a major party. While averaging only 15 percent of the seats from 1919 to 1940, the Liberal party was in the government for 95 percent of the period. With a similar average percentage of parliamentary seats since the end of the Second World War, the Liberal party has been in the government only 45 percent of the period. The Catholic party was in government permanently during the interwar period, and for 81 percent of the time since 1944. The Socialist party was in coalition for 48 percent of the interwar period and for 65 percent of the 1944–1971 period. On the criterion of coalition potential the Communist party must be included as a major party; it was in the government for twenty-six months between 1946 and 1949.

B. THE CHARACTERISTICS OF PARTIES

1. CHRISTELIJKE VOLKSPARTIJ/PARTI SOCIAL CHRETIEN

The party was founded in 1945. Before the First World War the Catholic party had no formal organization. From the turn of the century, however, competition for the placing of candidates on Catholic lists was growing between the older and conservative Catholic electoral associations and the newer popular Catholic organizations mainly grouped in the Belgian Democratic League. In 1921 the legitimacy of the various Catholic groups was recognized in the structure of the Catholic Union. The Union had no separate program but officially endorsed the programs of its four components: the Federation of Catholic Circles and Associations, the League of Christian Workers, the Flemish Farmers' Association (*Boerenbond*), and the League of the Middle Classes. The failure of the Catholic Union to handle the conflicts dividing Catholics over social and linguistic reform led to the reorganization of the Catholic party into the Bloc of Catholics of Belgium in 1936. The Bloc was officially divided into linguistic wings: the *Katholieke Vlaamsche Volkspartij*, in the Flemish region, and, the *Parti Catholique Social*, in francophone areas. By the end of the interwar period, however, it was evident that this attempt at centralization and standardization of policy had failed. The party founded in 1945 as a mass party with individual rather than group memberships has proved considerably more cohesive at both the programmatic and parliamentary levels.

In a cross-national perspective the CVP/PSC is a religious party. Its major appeal, in common with other national Catholic parties, has been based on the defense of Church interests, particularly in the educational field. On the peculiarly Belgian unitarist-federalist dimension the party has been unitarist. In the legislative elections of 1968 the party suffered a considerable split on linguistic lines. In Brussels the Catholic federation split between two lists, the francophone PSC list, which operated in the Brussels and Nivelles *arrondissements*, and the *Cartel Van Den Boeynants*, composed chiefly of strongly unitarist Flemings. In the 1971 elections the Brussels federation presented a united list. In each of the regions, however, the linguistic wings of the party campaigned on separate linguistic programs.

2. BELGISCHE SOCIALISTISCHE PARTIJ/PARTI SOCIALISTE BELGE

The party was founded in 1885 as the Belgian Workers party and changed its name in 1945. Until that year the party had an affiliated membership with various social organizations. Since then the party has had a mass organization based on individual memberships.

The party is a social-democratic party. Although it has retained its original program without modification, its political practice has been marked by considerable reformism. It is historically an anticlerical party and has not formally "deconfessionalized" itself. In 1969 its then secretary, Léo Collard, proposed the creation of a "progressive" party composed of workers irrespective of their confessional stance. The appeal has so far created few reverberations.

By comparison with the other traditional parties the BSP/PSB has weathered the linguistic storm successfully. An increased formal recognition of its linguistic components was made in 1971 with the creation of a dual presidency, occupied by the Flemish and Walloon leaders, Van Eynde and Leburton. The party has always been strongly unitarist. In 1968 its Brussels federation suffered a split on linguistic lines, when Flemish socialists presented a list called the *Rode Leeuwen* competing with the predominantly francophone PSB list. The separation was perpetuated in 1971.

3. Partij van de Vrijheid en Vooruitgang/Parti de la Liberte et du Progres

The old Liberal party was refashioned and renamed in 1961. The Liberal party, whose official founding date was 1847, was never a strong national organization; its strength was localized in the *arrondissements*. The regional Liberal organizations (the *Liberaal Vlaams Verbond*, the *Fédération Bruxelloise*, and the *Entente Libérale Wallonne*) were more important than the national party organization in the formation of policy. The attempt at centralization and policy standardization led by Omer Van Audenhove in 1961 did not succeed in eliminating the old cadre-type of party organization. The party's linguistic divisions have increased the influence of the local and regional organizations.

Until 1961 the Liberal party could be properly described as a liberal-secular-bourgeois party. However, the effective "deconfessionalization". of the party's program in that year and the increased emphasis on the party's conservative economic program justify its subsequent classification as a conservative-bourgeois party.

On the important domestic unitarist-federalist dimension the PVV/PLP's record has been mixed. In the elections of 1965 the party campaigned on the strongest unitarist platform. It maintained this position, though less unequivocally, in the following legislative elections. After the communal elections in 1970 Brussels Liberals formed coalitions with the FDF in a number of Brussels communes. In 1971 the party split three ways on the linguistic question in the Brussels *arrondissement*. The national list, the *Cartel Snyers-Boscour*, was composed of "moderate francophones" and Dutch-speaking Liberals from the Brussels *arrondissement* (the *Blaauwe Leeuwen*). A second list, the *PLP de la région bruxelloise*, was a francophone list with close FDF sympathies. The third list, Mundeleer's *LIB-LOB* list, comprised so-called independent Liberals. All three lists were officially recognized by the national party.

4. Communistische Partij van België/Parti Communiste de Belgique

The party was founded in 1921 by a group expelled from the Belgian Workers party. Before the 1965 elections it adopted a federalist position in relation to the language question. It also suffered a Maoist dissidence before 1965. The Maoists contested the elections of that year in Brussels as the *Parti Communiste Belge*, and in two Walloon provinces as the *Parti Communiste Wallon*. The party also presented lists in the following election in these regions and in the Flemish region, where it was called the *Vlaams Communistische Partij*. It did not contest the elections of 1971.

5. CHRISTELIJKE VLAAMSE VOLKSUNIE

The *Volksunie* was founded in 1953. Before 1919 occasional Flemish lists had been presented in elections, but they acquired only a minuscule proportion of the vote in the Flemish region. The first important Flemish nationalist formation was the *Frontpartij*, which gained five seats in the elections of 1919. In 1933 the *Frontpartij* merged with other nationalist groups to form the *Vlaams National Verbond*. They fought the 1936 elections under this title and the elections of 1939 as the *Vlaansche Nationale Blok*. A number of its leaders were involved in a measure of collaboration with the occupying forces during the war and were prosecuted and imprisoned after the Liberation. Weakened in this way and with the nationalist question temporarily overshadowed by other political issues, the Flemish nationalist movement developed slowly in the postwar period. In the 1949 elections a grouping of Flemish parties contested the elections as the *Vlaamse Concentratie*. No nationalist lists were presented in 1950, and although the *Volksunie* contested all Flemish seats and those of the Brussels *arrondissement*, its electoral significance remained small until 1965.

In cross-national terms the party must be classified as a nationalist party, and within Belgium it clearly operates at the federalist end of the unitarist-federalist spectrum. As its title clearly suggests, the party claims to be inspired by Christian principles. In the postwar period this has not been important politically or electorally. With the achievement of many of the formal aims of the Flemish movement in the late 1960s, the *Volksunie* has sought to reorient its program to a less restrictedly linguistic appeal. In its 1968 election program it demanded the nationalization of the energy sector of the economy, the strengthening of regional investment policies, and the establishment of development areas.

6. FRONT DEMOCRATIQUE DES FRANCOPHONES BRUXELLOIS

The FDF, founded in 1964, had no direct antecedents in the Brussels region. Francophones presented lists in four elections in the interwar period, but their maximum vote in the *arrondissement* was 0.6 percent. Francophone lists also appeared in 1949 and 1961, but their share of the vote was 0.3 and 0.2 percent, respectively. The language laws of 1963 caused activists to leave the Catholic, Socialist, and above all the Liberal parties in order to create a party of francophone defense in the Brussels agglomeration.

It is difficult to classify the FDF in cross-national terms. It is a party preoccupied with the problems of the francophone section of the population of Brussels. It rejects linguistic parity in the agglomeration and the extension of the Dutch language in education and communal government. It demands the attachement of the peripheral communes to the bilingual regime operating in Brussels-Capital and the establishment of an agglomeration council. It is nationalist insofar as it represents the interests of a specific ethnic group and federalist insofar as it accepts the program of the RW.

7. RASSEMBLEMENT WALLON

The RW was founded in 1967. The electoral antecedents of the Walloon separatist party date only from the last election of the interwar period, when a Walloon party competing in four *arrondissements* gained its highest vote in Charleroi, 3 percent. Sporadic Walloon lists appeared in the elections of 1946, 1949, 1958, and 1961. In the last election the highest share of the vote in an *arrondissement* gained by all these Walloon lists was the 1 percent of the *Parti d'Unité Wallonne* in Liège. The first important Walloon parties, those of the 1965 elections, did not spring primarily out of the long-standing separatist groups but out of the ranks of the Socialist party. It was from the *Mouvement Populaire Wallon*, founded after the general strike of 1961, that the founders of the *Front Wallon* (1964) and the *Parti Wallon des Traveilleurs* (1964) sprang. The *Front* absorbed the *Parti d'Unité Wallonne* and presented lists in five *arrondissements* in the province of Hainaut in 1965. The *Front Wallon* was subsequently merged into the RW. The other Walloon party of 1965, the PWT, was distinctly more socialist. In 1965 it formed a cartel list with the *Union de la Gauche Socialiste* in Hainaut and presented its own lists in the province of Liège. It was from the *arrondissement* of Liège that François Perin was elected as a PWT representative. When Perin became president of the RW in 1967, the PWT retained its separate identity and competed against the RW in Liège and Hainaut in 1968. The party did not contest the elections of 1971.

The RW can be classified as a nationalist party. It is aslo a federalist party. It has sought to present a centrist economic program. Given the economic difficulties of the Walloon region, the party inevitably favors governmental intervention in the economic sphere.

IV. The Act of Voting Today

A. ELECTIONS AND BALLOTS

Elections for all 212 seats in the Chamber of Representatives and for 106 of the 179 Senate seats take place simultaneously. Since the end of the First World War only four out of sixteen legislatures have actually lasted the maximum term of four years permitted by the constitution. The system of candidate-substitutes made it unnecessary to hold by-elections frequently during the interwar period (in fact, only seven occurred); parliamentary convention has discontinued by-elections since 1945. Legislative elections are the only nationwide elections in Belgium.

Historically, Belgian electors have participated in two types of subnational election: for provincial and communal councils. Since 1949 elections for the provincial councils have been held at the same time as the legislative elections. Beginning in the postwar period in 1946 communal elections take place at six-year intervals. Constitutional reforms introduced in 1971 have instituted two further types of elective assembly, the so-called agglomeration councils (for Brussels-Capital, Antwerpen, Liège, Gent, and Charleroi) and councils for federations of communes. A single referendum has been held in Belgium. In 1950 the impassioned political debate surrounding the war-time activities of Leopold III occasioned special legislation for a referendum about the resumption of his constitutional powers (Van Den Daele, 1950; Arango, 1963).

The Belgian voter receives two ballot sheets, one for the Chamber, the other for the Senate. On these sheets appear party lists, each headed by a number. The numbers of the party lists are chosen by lot at the Ministry of the Interior some weeks before the elections. Any party may choose to be included in this national selection and have its lists appear throughout the country in the order thus established. The additional ordering of party lists contesting only one or a very limited number of *arrondissements* is decided at the local level.

Party lists are composed of titular (or direct) candidates and their substitutes, though not necessarily in numbers identical to the number of seats to be distributed within the *arrondissement*. The order of names in each list is not alphabetical, but determined by a variety of intraparty mechanisms. A vote is cast by filling in a circle above a party list or at the side of a candidate's name. A variety of strategies is open to the voter. By filling in the circle at the top of the list, he casts a simple party vote endorsing the order of the candidates presented by the party. The voter is also able to indicate his preferences among the candidates. He may vote for either a titular candidate or a candidate-substitute, or for both a titular candidate and a substitute. All preferential votes count initially toward the total party vote, which determines the number of seats to be gained by the party. It is only after the seat distribution has been decided upon that preference votes become relevant for the selection of representatives or senators.

B. LEGAL CHARACTERISTICS OF VOTING

General supervision of the preparation and administration of the legislative elections is handled by the electoral affairs office of the Ministry of the Interior. At the local level *arrondissement* civil servants cooperate with communal authorities in the publication of lists of electors and in decisions about numbers and location of the polling stations (known as sections).

In each *arrondissement* voting and counting are organized through a three-tier system of administrators. The *arrondissement* has a principal election bureau composed of a president and four assessors. They are responsible for the supervision of preliminary arrangements for the election and for aggregating the votes counted at the cantonal level. The president of the principal bureau is either the president of the *arrondissement's* Court of First Instance or, where no such court exists, the justice of the peace in the chief commune of the province. The assessors, in this and the two subordinate election bureaus, are private citizens coopted for the specific task of administering the election.

The next tier down the line is the canton. The president of the cantonal bureau, normally a justice of the peace, is also aided by four assessors. The third and lowest level of electoral supervision is found within the individual polling section. The president of the section's bureau (again, normally a justice of the peace) is appointed by the president of the cantonal bureau. The four assessors and their substitutes are the eight youngest electors of thirty years or more on the section's electoral list. Members of the election bureaus receive no payment for their activities other than the reimbursement of their travel expenses. It is a singularity of Belgian legislative elections that about 50,000 citizens are involved in their administration as a civic obligation. Votes are counted first in the sections and then aggregated at the canton and *arrondissement* bureaus.

Legislative elections are held on Sundays, and voting takes place from 8 A.M. until 2 P.M. An elector normally votes within his commune of residence, except where a sparse population requires the grouping of two or three communes in order to achieve an electorate of at least 150. In such a case the electoral law stipulates that no elector should have to travel more than four kilometers from his commune to vote. One polling section is provided for communes with electorates not exceeding 800. Where the numbers on electoral lists are greater, sections are added. Except in *arrondissements* where ten or more representatives have to be elected, no section may have an electoral list with more than 800 or less than 150 names. In the former *arrondissements* sections are provided for not more than 600 electors. Such detailed specifications about polling stations arise from the need to accommodate an electorate legally obligated to vote.

Of the four electoral reforms first applied at the 1970 communal elections, only the law extending the franchise to eighteen-year-olds was not in force for the 1971 legislative elections. Conscript soldiers of voting age voted for the first time. They voted, however, on the Wednesday preceding the legislative elections in polling sections set up in the barracks. Election bureaus, composed mainly of soldiers, wore civilian clothes. The vote was compulsory except for those authorized to vote by proxy or by post, the other innovations of 1971. Proxy voting was designed for those electors whose professional activities kept them out of the country on voting day (diplomats, seamen, etc.,). Postal voting, on the other hand, was introduced for electors resident within the country but unable either to be moved or to leave their place of work in order to vote (the sick, nurses, bargees, etc). No analysis is yet available of the electoral significance of these innovations.

C. ELECTORAL LISTS

Lists of electors are published biennially by the communal authorities. The names of those who are twenty-one or more are taken from the registers of inhabitants maintained by the communes. Registration is legally mandatory. A legal obligation is also placed on those who move from one commune to another to provide their future addresses to their present communal authorities, who ensure the transfer of their names to the registers of the new communes of residence. There is ample time for the addition to the final electoral lists of those names incorrectly omitted from the preliminary lists of electors.

No detailed estimates have been made of the extent to which electoral lists are inaccurate. The difficulties faced by communal authorities in the Brussels area in keeping close check of their high-density populations presumably help to explain Delruelle's finding that the names of those deceased for several years were frequently included on electoral lists. Again, it was in Brussels, where residential mobility is high, that Delruelle noted a particularly high level of inaccuracy in electoral lists resulting from changes in address (1970, p. 36, note 11). It is reasonable to assume a fairly high level of accuracy in the initial compilation of electoral lists from the practical necessity for Belgians of producing identity cards issued by communes of residence in a range of normal social situations.

The biennial compilation of lists of electors normally leads to the exclusion of electors who become eligible to vote between the dates at which the lists are published. The fact that the lists are not issued definitively until December and that the terminal date for eligibility of twenty-one-year-olds is fully six months earlier makes it necessary for new electors to wait as long as two and a half years before becoming eligible to vote. As a result of the same technical requirements new residents in the commune may find themselves excluded from the electoral lists for up to the same period of time.

Belgian electoral registers have considerable value as aids to survey research. In addition to the names and addresses of electors, the lists provide dates of birth, communes of origin, and dates of settlement in the commune (Lindemans, 1968). They also give the occupations of electors. Coenen (1961, p. 31) warns, however, that the occupational descriptions are imprecise.

V. Data for Analysis

A. DATA SOURCES

A reliable nationwide survey relating voting preference to social structure was not carried out in Belgium until 1968* (Delruelle, 1970). Some of the published results of this survey, suitably reanalyzed, are presented below. From 1946 to 1960 the *Institut universitaire d'information sociale et économique* occasionally included findings on voting preference related to sex or age amongst the surveys published in its *Bulletin de L'INSOC* (G. Jacquemyns, 1946–1960). Although the presumption is that the surveys

* At least, no national survey intended for publication was carried out until this date. The political parties are reputed to have commissioned surveys in the 1960s, but their results have remained confidential.

were national, INSOC never provided information on the extent and size of its samples or on the sampling methods employed. The writer is informed that the INSOC data is not available for secondary analysis. The only other pre-1968 national survey known to the writer is the Belgian section of a Common Market study conducted by Gallup International in 1962. (Its publication is noted in the *Courrier Hebdomadaire du CRISP,* 187, and some of its results are printed in P. Luzzato Fegiz, 1966.) The survey (N=770) is badly skewed against the occupational category of workers. But even after the use of weighting techniques, Socialist voters remain so grossly undersampled as to render the survey worthless. Since January 1969 the survey organization International Research Associates Europa has been conducting polls on voting intention at approximately three-monthly intervals. Its national-level results (N=c.3,000), showing voting intention in relation to such variables as age, social class, level of education, and commune size, have been published from time to time in two daily newspapers, *Het Laatste Nieuws* and *Le Soir.*

Results are avilable for only one non-national survey specifically concerned with electoral behavior. In 1964-1965, Wilfried Dewachter conducted a postal survey in thirty-eight Flemish communes. The results of the survey (N=475) are published in *De wetgevende verkiezingen etc* (1967). Otherwise, several nonelectoral surveys (with N's of c. 500 and less) have provided incidental findings on voting preferences related to social and attitudinal characteristics in local populations. Three of these surveys have been broadly concerned with levels of political information and participation among Socialist voters in the Brussels *arrondissement* in 1958 (J. Stengers and A. Philippart, 1959); among those between eighteen and twenty-two years of age in 1963 (A. Philippart, 1964); and among a cross section of the populations of seven communes in the three regions in 1964 (L. Huyse, W. Hilgers, and C. Henryon, 1966; L. Huyse, 1969; L. Huyse, 1970). Data on voting preferences are also presented in a study of the political attitudes of workers in a Brussels commune (J. Coenen, 1961) and in an investigation into the social background of religious practice in three Flemish Communes (K. Dobbelaere, 1966). The two studies were carried out in 1958.

The late development of quantitative political science in Belgium, which the paucity of survey material suggests, is further demonstrated by the sparsity of ecological studies. Only two attempts have been made to relate aggregate data to national electoral behavior; each investigation has focused on the electoral behavior of a single social group, workers and salaried employees. The first (R. De Smet and R. Evalenko, 1956) uses simple correlation to test a set of propositions about the support of the working class for the Socialist party in the early 1950s. The study has been severely criticized for methodological and conceptual weaknesses as well as for the inadequacy of some of its data sources (H. Deleeck, 1957; J. Stengers, 1958; W. Dewachter, 1967). The second study (A.C.W., 1959) aims at quantifying the working class contribution to the Catholic party's electoral support in the 1950s. The study assumes that workers and employees not voting Socialist and all other occupational groups not voting Liberal give their support to the Catholic party; the proportion of both groups in the Catholic vote is arrived at after combining these residuals. A considerably more sophisticated ecological study has been conducted by M. Aiken and H. Van Hassel

(1970), who were concerned with political competition and stability in communal elections.

The initial problem to be faced in ecological analysis for national elections in Belgium is that of the "fit" between census tracts and electoral units. The smallest unit for which national election results are available, the electoral canton, is not an administrative unit. Census returns for communes composing the cantons will therefore need to be aggregated.

In a society in which levels of religious practice constitute the major explanatory variable in electoral behavior, the absence of information on churchgoing in official data sources comprises a considerable limitation for ecological analysis. In the post-1945 period, however, empirical investigation of religious practice at the parochial and diocesan level has been carried out in all parts of Belgium. These studies have been concerned with all types of communities and should allow at least ordinal-level inferences to all communes for use in ecological analysis. (See the reports of the Centre de recherches socio-religieuses and the Centrum voor socio-godsdienstig onderzoek, both now located in Leuven; J. Kerkhofs, 1954; J. Kerkhofs and J. Van Houtte, 1962; K. Dobbelaere, 1966).

A further difficulty arises in the classification of communes along an urban-rural dimension in a country in which it is common to travel considerable distances to work and in which there is great variation in the geographical extent of communes. A typology of communes according to their degree of urbanization in the interwar period is contained in the *Arrêté ministériel du 3 décembre 1938* (Ministère de l'Intérieur, 1938). Nonofficial typologies on the basis of the 1961 census are to be found in I. De Lanoo etc. (1963) and W. Van Waelvelde and H. Van Der Haegen (1967). (For a brief discussion of the question see W. Dewachter, 1970 [1], [2].)

Although no questions on language were included in the 1961 census, and such questions are now permanently discontinued, the inclusion of details on commune of birth in electoral lists enables inferences to be drawn about the language used in individual households. It is clear that the most important case for such analysis is Brussels-Capital; an attempt to estimate the distribution of linguistic groups in the nineteen communes, using 1967 electoral lists, has been made by L. Lindemans (1968).

National censuses have been carried out at roughly ten-year intervals since 1846. They present the normal range of findings (including language until 1947) for communes (c. 2500), administrative *arrondissements* (44), and provinces (9). The yearbooks of the Institut National de Statistique provide only limited demographic data at the sub-national level.

B. THE ELECTION SURVEY OF 1968

With one exception the contingency tables presented in this chapter are the results of a survey conducted by the Institut de Sociologie of the Université Libre de Bruxelles immediately after the Belgian legislative elections of March 31 1968. The full results are published in N. Delruelle, R. Evalenko, and W. Fraeys, *Le comportement politique des électeurs belges* (Editions de l'Institut de Sociologie de l'Université Libre de Bruxelles, Bruxelles, 1970). The survey was designed to examine the relationship between votes cast in 1968 and a number of social structural and attitudinal variables. The published results have been reanalyzed in order to exhibit the destinations of popular support for parties instead of the origins of party support normally presented in the study itself. Two categories of respondents have been omitted: those who returned blank voting forms and those whose preference was placed in the category "Others." In both cases the numbers of respondents were too small (1 and 2 percent, respectively) to permit meaningful analysis.

The survey is based on a nationwide systematic sample. Although 4,542 electors were interviewed, the usable number (N) is considerably smaller as a result of the refusal of 33 percent of the respondents to divulge their voting choice. A double weighting was given to the sample taken in the Brussels region. In the following tables the results for Halle-Vilvoorde (the predominantly Flemish part of the region) have been weighted down and merged with the results of the rest of Flanders. When results for Brussels-Capital are presented, the weighted survey N is retained. For the presentation of results at the national level, the Brussels-Capital results have been weighted down to their correct proportion in society.

1. QUESTIONNAIRE RESPONSE AND ACTUAL VOTE

At the national level the cumulative discrepancy between votes reported in the 1968 survey and votes cast in the preceding election reaches 14 percent. Almost all of the discrepancy would seem to be accounted for by the overreporting of votes for the Catholic party (+6.7 percent). Where census data permit comparison, the agreement of survey and census parameters suggests that there is no marked oversampling of social groups particularly predisposed toward the Catholic party (See Delruelle, 1970, pp. 181-9). Nor are there any indications that such groups were readier to reveal their voting choices (See Delruelle, 1970, p. 47). At 33 percent refusal to reveal voting choices is exceptionally high in Belgium—marginally higher than in Italy in the Almond and Verba Five-Nation study and considerably higher than in the other four countries (calculated from data in Five-Nation Code Book—ICPR, 1959)—but nonresponse tends to be greater in those social categories where Catholic voting is more common: females, the old, higher-status occupations, and religious practicers. While it is entirely possible that the Catholic disproportion is a random result in the survey, analysis of reported votes, within the three regions suggests that social conformism influenced responses to the questionnaire.

One aspect of conformism is the tendency to report support for traditionally dominant parties in the regions. In Flanders the reported vote for the Catholic party exceeds its electoral vote by 11 percent. In Wallonia reported Socialist voting exceeds the actual vote of the Socialist party by 5 percent. In Brussels-Capital, historically an area of Liberal strength, the reported level of Liberal support exceeds its electoral results by 1.5 percent: in the election of 1965 the Liberals acquired a sizable plurality, in 1968 and were beaten into second place by only 1 percent of the vote.

The national discrepancy between reported and actual votes results from more than the weight of the overestimated Catholic vote in the Flemish region. In Wallonia, too, the reported vote of the Catholic party exceeds its actual vote by 5 percent. Clearly a factor other than the dominant-party effect is present. The exaggerated support in the two major regions together with the differential between reported and actual voting for the other parties in the regions suggests that respondents tend to identify themselves as supporters of the more socially acceptable parties. This is a second aspect of conformism.

The least respectable party is the Communist party, which is underreported in all regions. With 1.4 percent of the vote in Flanders and 2.4 percent in Brussels-Capital, it is easy to see how Communist support in these two regions might be undersampled. In fact, no respondents claimed to have voted Communist in the Flemish region; only 1.8 percent of the Brussels-Capital sample identified themselves as Communist voters. In the Walloon region, where the Communist party acquired 7 percent of the actual vote, only 2.5 percent of respondents identified themselves as Communist voters.

In the emphatically Catholic milieu of Flanders support for the historically anti-clerical Liberal and Socialist parties evidently lacks social acceptability: support for the parties is equally underreported at 4 percent. There is much less reluctance to report support for the Flemish nationalist party, which has historically affirmed its Catholic character. Support for the party is underreported by one percent. In Brussels-Capital and Wallonia support for the linguistic parties is underreported by 1 percent and 2.5 percent respectively. (The discrepancy between reported and actual votes is lower in the capital than in the Flemish and Walloon regions. It is to be expected that pressures toward social conformism should be weaker in the context of a great urban region.)

2. THE STRENGTH OF PARTY IDENTIFICATION

The simultaneous election of the Chamber of Representatives and the Senate provides the opportunity for "split-ticket" voting in Belgian elections, but the practice has never become established. In the elections of the 1960s the average difference in party shares of the votes for the two houses was 0.2 percent in 1961, 0.1 percent in 1965, and 0.3 percent in 1968. There is a very slight tendency for voters to complete the ballot sheet for the Chamber of Representatives and to leave blank that of the Senate. In the 1960s nonvoting in the Senate elections was 0.01 percent higher than in the Chamber elections. The relatively small extent of voting changes between the two legislative bodies is reflected in the responses to the 1968 survey, in which only 4 percent of the respondents reported different votes for Chamber and Senate. The highest level of differential voting was reported by the supporters of the francophone party in the Walloon region (17 percent); the next highest level is found among Flemish nationalist voters in Brussels-Capital (8 percent).

The high degree of party loyalty suggested above is supported by the 1968 findings on long-term electoral behavior. As Table 13 indicates consistency in party choice is very high: of the voters in the election of 1961, 92 percent maintained their voting choice in 1965, 83 percent in 1968. Voting stability is higher in Belgium than in the comparably fragmented society of France (cf. D. MacRae, 1967, pp. 297-98) and considerably higher than in the United Kingdom (cf. D. Butler and D. Stokes, 1969, pp. 93-98). Table 13 reveals little volatility in party choice. Only in the case of the Flemish nationalist party (VU) in Flanders is there evidence of voters moving away from and then returning to the party in consecutive elections.

TABLE 13: **Percentage of Stability of Party Choice—1961, 1965, and 1968—Regional and National**

PARTY CHOICE 1961	PERCENTAGE 1961 VOTERS VOTING SAME PARTY 1965 AND 1968							
	Flemish region		Walloon region		Brussels-Capital		Belgium	
	1965	1968	1965	1968	1965	1968	1965	1968
CVP/PSC	92	81	90	81	83	72	91	80
BSP/PSB	96	90	94	84	88	66	94	85
PVV/PLP	92	89	96	90	90	76	93	87
CPB/PCB	—	—	91	68	*	*	91	70
VU	91	94	—	—	*	*	91	91
Average	93	84	93	84	87	69	92	83

*Communist (1 case) and VU (4 cases) voters excluded from Brussels-Capital columns but included in national analysis.

There is also relatively little circulation of voters between parties, such as has been observed in the United Kingdom (cf. Butler and Stokes, 1969, pp. 283-92). Movement away from the historically dominant Catholic party (CVP/PSC) and Socialist party (BSP/PSB), as shown in Tables 13 and 14, is uniform. It is the undirectionality of voting change and the impact of new voters (See Table 9) that account for the considerable electoral changes in Belgium in the 1960s. The intensity of party identification is predictable in a society characterized by high institutionalized political cleavages.

3. SECOND PREFERENCES

Information about second preferences in the 1968 survey (Table 15) suggests a number of measures of electoral behavior, one of which is the extent of strong party commitment in the electorates of the parties. Both the inability or unwillingness of party supporters to state a second preference and the choice of casting a blank ballot rather than a vote for another party indicate strong party commitment. It is reasonable to assume that the greater the proportion of party supporters in these categories (No Answer/Don't Know and Blank columns), the more stable the party's electoral support is likely to be in adverse electoral circumstances.

As Table 15 indicates, party commitment thus measured is higher among the supporters of the Catholic (CVP/PSC), Socialist (BSP/PSB), and Liberal (PVV/PLP) parties than among those who voted for the Flemish nationalist party (VU), the francophone parties (FDF-RW), and the Communist party (CPB/PCB). In all regions

TABLE 14: **Percentage Turnover in Party Choice, 1961-1968, Regional and National**

PARTY CHOICE 1961	PARTY CHOICE 1968						
	CVP/ PSC	BSP/ PSB	PVV/ PLP	VU	CPB/ PCB	FDF- RW	N
Flemish region							
CVP	81	2	5	12	—	—	663
BSP	2	90	2	5	—	—	251
PVV	3	1	89	7	—	—	90
VU	—	2	4	94	—	—	51
Walloon region							
PSC	81	3	14	—	—	2	209
PSB	1	84	5	—	1	9	344
PLP	2	3	90	—	—	6	115
PCB	—	16	—	—	68	16	19
*Brussels-Capital**							
CVP/PSC	72	3	12	4	—	9	74
BSP/PSB	6	66	8	—	—	20	92
PVV/PLP	1	1	76	1	—	20	70
Belgium							
CVP/PSC	80	2	7	9	—	1	911
BSP/PSB	2	85	4	2	1	6	642
PVV/PLP	2	2	87	3	—	6	242
VU	2	2	6	91	—	—	54
CPB/PCB	—	15	—	—	70	15	20

*1961 Communist (1 case) and VU (4 cases) voters excluded from the Brussels-Capital table but included in national table.

strong party commitment is more extensive among Catholic and Socialist voters than among Liberal voters. There are fewer strongly committed party supporters among Walloon voters for the Socialist and Liberal parties than among their Flemish counterparts. Liberal commitment is particularly low in Brussels-Capital. Strong party commitment among Catholic voters is also markedly lower in Brussels-Capital than elsewhere. (Voters for the two Catholic and Socialist lists in the Brussels electoral *arrondissement* have been grouped together, which accounts for same-party second preferences among Catholic and Socialist supporters in the Flemish region and Brussels-Capital. If same-party second preferences are added to those refusing to state a second preference and those preferring to cast a blank ballot, the percentage of strongly committed Catholic voters in Brussels-Capital is 48.) In the legislative elections of 1971, the heaviest electoral losses occurred in the Liberal vote in the Walloon region and in Brussels-Capital and in the Catholic vote in Brussels-Capital (see Appendix 1).

Supporters of the francophone parties will have voted for these parties in two elections at the most; the same is true of about two-thirds of the supporters of the Flemish nationalist party. It is likely that the relatively low level of strong party commitment among such voters reflects their susceptibility to cross-pressures in terms of personal voting histories and group voting norms. Strong party commitment is least extensive among Communist voters. The extent to which supporters of the

TABLE 15: **Party Choice and Second Preferences, in 1968, Regional and National, in Percentages**

PARTY CHOICE 1968	SECOND PREFERENCES								
	CVP/ PSC	BSP/ PSB	PVV/ PLP	VU	FDF- RW	CPB/ PCB	NA/DK	Blank	N
Flemish region									
CVP	1	13	10	23	—	0	37	16	658
BSP	21	—	3	9	—	5	37	19	281
PVV	30	14	—	6	—	1	32	17	158
VU	45	11	8	—	—	2	21	11	200
Walloon region									
PSC	—	8	30	—	7	1	37	17	211
PSB	18	—	12	—	15	9	27	19	338
PLP	28	13	—	—	20	1	23	15	195
FDF-RW	5	32	23	—	—	5	23	12	68
PCB	5	48	9	—	19	—	9	9	21
Brussels-Capital									
CVP/PSC	11	18	29	2	5	—	27	9	186
BSP/PSB	17	3	14	—	20	2	35	10	154
PVV/PLP	22	19	—	—	22	1	29	8	191
FDF	12	24	30	—	—	4	18	11	117
VU	35	20	10	—	—	5	15	15	20
CPB/PCB	—	33	8	—	8	—	42	8	12
Belgium									
CVP/PSC	2	12	16	16	2	0	36	16	962
BSP/PSB	19	0	11	4	10	3	32	18	696
PVV/PLP	28	11	—	2	15	1	27	14	450
VU	45	12	8	—	—	2	21	11	212
FDF-RW	8	28	27	—	—	4	21	12	127
CPB/PCB	4	43	11	—	18	—	14	11	28

Communist party are prepared to contemplate voting for other parties, together with the relatively high rate of turnover in its support (see Table 14), suggests that the Belgian Communist party receives disproportionate support from uncommitted or floating voters.

Strong party commitment, as defined above, probably implies a degree of hostility toward other parties; it does not measure the political distance between party supporters or indicate the extent of polarization in the party system. Some 55 percent of the respondents in 1968 were prepared to indicate a second preference. The extent to which these respondents selected as their second preferences parties occupying central or extreme positions on any salient cleavage dimension suggests the extent to which consensus or dissensus is present. The frequency with which party supporters select other parties indicates the political proximity or distance between electoral groups.

With the decline in saliency of the schools question, two dimensions of political cleavage dominated the electoral politics of Belgium in the late 1960s: economic decision-making associated with social class, and the organization of the state along more or less unitary lines. It is possible to identify the Catholic party as occupying the area nearest to the center on both dimensions (see Section III). It is at least suggestive of the relatively nonpolarized character of Belgian politics that the Catholic party is the major second preference of the supporters of all parties other than the francophone and Communist parties. In all three regions, it is the major second preference of Liberal voters, and in the Flemish and Walloon regions it is the major second preference of Socialist voters. Supporters of the Flemish nationalist party exhibit a very strong tendency to choose the Catholic party in both the Flemish region and Brussels-Capital.

A reciprocal tendency to prefer the traditional parties is to be observed amongst Catholic voters. In the Walloon region and in Brussels-Capital the major second preference of Catholic voters is the Liberal party. In all regions the second largest group of Catholic voters expressing a second preference selects the Socialist party. However, considerable distance exists between the supporters of the traditional class parties. In all regions the Liberal party is the choice of only the third largest group of Socialist voters expressing a second preference. Liberal voters evidently find themselves closer to the Socialist party than the latter's supporters to them. In the Flemish region and in Brussels-Capital the second largest group of Liberal voters selects the Socialist party as a second preference, although it is the choice of only the third largest group of Liberal voters in the Walloon region.

Some significant divergences are to be found in this pattern of shared preferences among the supporters of the traditional parties. In the Flemish region the largest group of Catholic voters expressing second preferences selects the Flemish nationalist party. In Brussels-Capital the largest proportion of second preferences among both Liberal and Socialist voters goes to the francophone party.

Second preferences may also provide the means of estimating the impact of the differential saliency of political cleavages on party support. On two assumptions—first, that voters are able to identify parties' distinctive positions in relation to major political cleavages; second, that all those respondents indicating a second preference will vote for the selected party when the cleavage is activated—it is possible to predict the maximum changes in electoral support to be anticipated in different electoral circumstances. In the light of the actual changes occurring between 1968 and 1971 it is possible to estimate the extent to which political cleavages affected electoral behavior. In the clerical-anticlerical cleavage the dominant poles of attraction are taken to be the Catholic and Socialist parties. In the class cleavage the Liberal party is taken to confront the Socialist party. In the linguistic cleavage the traditional unitary parties are taken to confront the federalist parties.

The estimates of change arrived at indicate the appropriate electoral strategies for the parties (Table 16). The Catholic party can only win on religion and can make large losses on class and language, especially in Flanders. The Socialist party is likely to make greater gains through the activation of the class cleavage than the religious cleavage, but it is likely to win on both. It is also likely to lose less on language than the Catholic party. The Liberals are likely to lose electoral support heavily with the activation of the religious cleavage, but to gain equally heavily on class. The Liberal

TABLE 16 : **Second Preferences as Predictors of Electoral Change, 1968-1971***

	MAJOR SALIENT CLEAVAGE			
	Religion	Class	Language	Actual Change
Flemish Region				
CVP	+11	− 9	− 9	− 1.2
BSP	+ 3	+ 8	− 2	− 1.4
PVV	− 7	+ 6	0	+ 0.1
VU	− 9	− 3	+14	+ 1.9
Walloon Region				
PSC	+ 7	− 8	− 1	− 0.5
PSB	+ 6	+ 5	− 5	0.0
PLP	−11	+ 9	− 5	− 9.1
FDF-RW	− 3	− 6	+13	+10.2
Brussels-Capital				
CVP/PSC	+11	−13	− 2	− 7.5
BSP/PSB	+12	+11	− 4	+ 0.7
PVV/PLP	−11	+16	− 5	−10.4
FDF	− 2	−10	+15	+14.9
VU	− 2	− 1	0	+ 1.4
Belgium				
CVP/PSC	+ 9	− 9	− 6	− 1.8
BSP/PSB	+ 4	+ 7	− 4	− 0.7
PVV/PLP	− 8	+ 8	− 3	− 4.2
FDF-RW	− 2	− 3	+ 6	+ 4.4
VU	− 7	− 2	+ 8	+ 1.2

*Maximum expected changes in party shares of the vote resulting from changes in issue saliency, with actual changes in party support.

party is likely to lose quite heavily on language in the Walloon region and in Brussels-Capital but not at all in the Flemish region. The linguistic parties gain on language but lose on religion and class. While the Flemish nationalist party is particularly susceptible to losses on religion, the francophone parties are more susceptible losses on class.

In the legislative elections of 1971 there was no political conflict on the religious cleavage. Although the class cleavage was activated through debate on budgetary and fiscal policies, the dominant cleavage was that of language. However, the impact of the linguistic question was more pronounced in the Walloon region and in Brussels than in the Flemish region (see Section I). The comparison between the predicted and actual electoral changes in the Flemish region confirms this (see Table 16). While the Socialist and Catholic parties seem to have lost on language, the Flemish nationalist party falls considerably short of its maximum possible gain on language. The Liberal party must be assumed to have gained on class.

The apparent predictive power of second preferences is supported in the Brussels-Capital and Walloon cases, where the maximum predicted gains of the parties benefiting from the language question are very close to the actual results. However, there is little relationship between the predicted and observed losses of the parties losing from the language cleavage. The losses of the Liberal party (which could have occurred only on the language cleavage) are much higher than predicted. Although it is possible that the Socialist party was gaining on class from the Catholic party particularly in Brussels-Capital while simultaneously losing to the francophone party on language, there is no such explanation available to account for its electoral stasis in the Walloon region. In short, second preferences have limited power as predictors of electoral change.

VI. Social Structure and Voting

A. THE CONTROL VARIABLES

Three social divisions have emerged as political cleavages in the Belgian party system: religiosity; social class; language. To facilitate cross-national comparison broad class categories have been established (see Table 27), but the class variable used in the tables is that of occupation. The 1968 survey did not contain a question on language. However, it can be safely assumed that respondents in the Walloon region are almost all francophone. No separate results are available for the German-speaking Eastern cantons, but germanophones comprise little more than 2 percent of the population of the Walloon region (see Table 2). It can also be assumed that virtually all of the respondents in the Flemish region are Dutch-speakers (the clear exceptions are the few FDF voters in Halle-Vilvoorde). Although it is reasonable to suppose that VU voters in Brussels-Capital are Dutch-speakers and FDF voters francophones, no other assumptions about language can be made for respondents in Brussels-Capital. It needs to be emphasized that the concept of region as it operates in this section for Brussels-Capital as well as the two other regions is spatial rather than linguistic. Language acquires a separate political significance in that it provides each linguistic group with a common set of cultural interests. These interests are essential for the emergence of explicitly linguistic parties, but they are also articulated by the linguistic wings of the traditional parties. If only for this reason, the nature of political debate within each linguistic community is irreducibly distinct from that of the others. Precisely because all political groups within the linguistic communities share the same linguistic concerns, the saliency of language as a divisive factor within the linguistic populations is reduced. Insofar as a regional effect is to be detected in electoral behavior, it is the product of the distinctive concatenation of structural variables influencing spatially concentrated populations.

Region is always used as a control in the following tables. Wherever possible religiosity is also controlled for (the constraint is in the data source). Occupation is used as a control where it seems appropriate.

B. CONVENTIONS

Party choice is shown for all major political parties in the legislative elections of 1968.

In Brussels-Capital both the Catholic and the Socialist federations split on the language question in the 1968 elections, and electoral lists were presented by the linguistic wings of both parties. Respondents voting for the predominantly Flemish Catholic list, the *Cartel Van Den Boeynants*, have been grouped with voters for the PSC. Similarly, those who voted for the Flemish Socialist list, the *Rode Leeuwen*, have been grouped with PSB voters.

Two statistics were computed for the tables. Using chi square, all tables were found to be significant at the .01 level. Tau betas are appended to the contingency tables.

C. RELIGIOSITY

Belgium is not a country divided in terms of religious affiliation. In the 1960s 85 percent of the population were affiliated at least nominally with the Roman Catholic Church (calculated from *Europa Year Book*, 1968). Of the remainder, probably not more than 1 percent belonged to the handful of Protestant churches. Although the Liberal and Socialist parties have until recently adopted strongly anticlerical positions, the ideology of *laicité* has not penetrated Belgian society at large. Most Belgians have participated in religious ceremonies such as baptisms, marriages, and funerals. Religious differentiation occurs in the degree to which voters are integrated into the activities of the Church. At high levels of integration (weekly or more frequent attendance at Mass, membership in Church organizations, etc.) voters give high priority to the political interests of the Church and vote overwhelmingly for the Catholic party (see K. Dobbelaere, 1966, pp. 146–60). The lowest levels of integration, however, do not necessarily imply a hostility to religious values as such, but rather a greater receptivity to other kinds of political appeals (see W. Dewachter, 1967, p. 327).

The question asked about churchgoing in the 1968 survey is probably a very weak measure of church attendance. As Table 6 indicates, the response to the 1968 survey suggests that religious practice was markedly higher in the late 1960s than in the early 1950s. Yet Collard as well as his critics considered that the earlier survey overestimated the normal level of regular Mass attendance. There are no grounds for believing that regular churchgoing has increased in the intervening period. Therefore, the survey almost certainly exaggerates the percentage of regular church attendance in the population, and specifically the percentage of churchgoers giving electoral support to parties other than the CVP/PSC.

As the findings in Table 17 show, the largest proportion of votes from church-goers goes to the CVP/PSC. The unidimensional religious appeal to the Catholic party helps to explain its failure to attract more nonpracticing voters. While the BSP/PSB emerges as a party whose support is sharply differentiated in terms of religiosity as a result of its traditional anticlericalism, its class role explains why its support among the indifferent is relatively less strong than that of the CVP/PSC among churchgoers. It would seem that the PVV/PLP's adoption of a nonconfessional electoral appeal in the early 1960s has given it fairly equal support among churchgoers and those indifferent to the Church.

TABLE 17: **Religiosity and Party Choice, Regional and National, in Percentages**

	CVP/PSC	BSP/PSB	PVV/PLP	VU	FDF-RW	CPB/PCB	N
Flemish region							
Practicers	63	10	11	15	0	—	984
Nonpracticers	14	56	16	12	1	1	354
							Tb=0.135
Walloon region							
Practicers	49	18	24	—	9	1	334
Nonpracticers	7	58	23	—	8	4	448
							Tb=0.114
Brussels-Capital							
Practicers	51	9	22	5	13	—	205
Nonpracticers	16	27	32	2	20	2	405
							Tb=0.049
Belgium							
Practicers	59	12	15	11	3	0	1427
Nonpracticers	12	50	22	5	8	2	1049
							Tb=0.126

Nationally, support for the linguistic parties is sharply distinguished, though regional analysis does not confirm this distinction. In the Flemish and Walloon regions regular and irregular churchgoers are about equally disposed to give support to the federalist parties, although in Brussels-Capital the FDF is clearly more attractive to the indifferent. The apparent national distinction is the result of the preponderance of churchgoers in the Flemish electorate and the higher percentage of the indifferent in the Walloon region. Regional analysis also indicates that while the PVV/PLP continues to attract more support among its traditional nonchurchgoing clientele than amongst churchgoers in the Flemish region and in Brussels-Capital, it has succeeded in collecting equal support among both groups in the Walloon region.

The Catholic party acquires a considerably larger share of the vote of churchgoers in the Flemish region than in the Walloon region or in Brussels-Capital. The settlement of the schools conflict in 1958 evidently relaxed the obligation felt by the devout to support the CVP, permitting the electoral advances of the PVV and the *Volksunie* in the elections of the 1960s. However, the distribution of electoral support changed less in Flanders in the elections of 1965 and 1968 than in the other regions. The activation of the class cleavage, as manifested in the canvassing of middle-class churchgoers by the PVV/PLP, has proved less effective in the Flemish than in the Walloon region; the impact of the language question has been less marked than in Brussels-Capital. The dominant influence in Flemish electoral behavior has remained religiosity.

The importance of class politics in the Walloon region probably accounts for the greater strength of the Socialist party among religious practicers than in other regions. In Brussels-Capital the saliency of linguistic politics probably explains the relatively high appeal of the CVP/PSC to the indifferent. In the elections of 1968 in Brussels the major Catholic list, headed by the retiring premier Van Den Boeynants, made a strong cross-cultural appeal on a unitary platform directed mainly against the FDF.

D. OCCUPATION

No standardized set of occupational categories has yet been developed for use in surveys in Belgium. The national census categories do not provide much useful guidance, limited as they are to four heterogeneous groups (employer/property-owners/farmers; salaried employees; workers; helpers) and have not been adopted in the few surveys carried out. The occupational categories used in the 1968 survey correspond to one scheme adopted by Dewachter (1967) and do not deviate substantially from those used by Huyse (1969). This classification, therefore, is in a fair way to becoming the standard survey grouping in Belgium. The only occupational group that presents problem for the purpose of cross-national comparison is the *independants*, the category grouping tradespeople and artisans. As an occuptional group such workers are probably most akin to salaried employees. However, on the behavioral variables of political choice and subjective class assessment, they have more in common with professionals. For this reason the independents have been placed in the middle-class group in the matrix (see p. 98). The category of *Farmers* is composed of proprietors. Farm laborers comprise less than one percent of the contemporary Belgian work force, and there is no evidence that many, if any at all, were interviewed in the 1968 survey.

The detailed components of the occupational categories used in the tables are as follows (the French terms are from the 1968 survey, the Dutch terms from Dewachter's 1964–1965 survey, and the translations are the writer's):

OCCUPATIONAL GROUP	FRENCH TITLE	DUTCH TITLE	COMPONENTS
Workers	*Ouvriers*	*Arbeiders*	Manual workers
Employees	*Employés*	*Bedienden*	White-collar workers, lower civil servants

Independents	*Commerçants, artisans*	*Middenstanders*	Tradespeople, craftsmen
Professionals	*Cadres*	*Patroons*	Managers, executives, higher civil servants, "liberal" professions
Farmers	*Agriculteurs*	*Boeren*	Smallholders, tenant farmers

The occupational category of respondents in the 1968 survey is determined by that of the head of the household, the former occupation of retired heads of household, and the former occupation of the husbands in the case of widows.

As the national level findings in Table 18 demonstrate, no strong relationship is to be observed between occupation and party choice. The most important reason for the weakness of the relationship is the consistently high support in all occupational

TABLE 18: **Occupation and Party Choice, Regional and National, in Percentages**

	CVP/ PSC	BSP/ PSB	PVV/ PLP	VU	FDF-RW	CPB/ PCB	N
Flemish region							
Workers	46	34	7	12	0	0	495
Employees	47	24	12	16	0	—	334
Independents	48	14	16	20	1	—	184
Professionals	40	11	27	20	2	1°	127
Farmers	74	4	12	10	—	—	198
							Tb=0.031
Walloon region							
Workers	18	63	9	—	6	4	346
Employees	27	33	26	—	13	2	175
Independents	28	19	41	—	10	2	100
Professionals	20	19	49	—	12	—	91
Farmers	59	9	31	—	1	—	70
							Tb=0.101
Brussels-Capital							
Workers	30	35	16	4	13	2	142
Employees	27	22	26	3	21	1	219
Independents	33	15	34	2	14	3	116
Professionals	22	11	42	4	21	1	133
							Tb=0.018
Belgium							
Workers	35	45	9	7	3	2	900
Employees	38	26	18	10	7	1	618
Independents	40	16	26	12	6	1	341
Professionals	28	12	37	13	9	0	298
Farmers	70	5	18	6	0	—	206
							Tb=0.055

groups for the Catholic party. It is highest amongst farmers, and only among professionals does support for the CVP/PSC noticeably decline. A clearer pattern of occupational support is found for the parties specifically competing on the dimension of the class cleavage. While support for the BSP/PSB declines with higher occupational status, that for the PVV/PLP increases. Support for the Flemish nationalist party shows pronounced increases in higher occupational groups, and there is a similar, if less strong, trend for the francophone parties.

It is in the Walloon region that the relationship between occupation and party choice is strongest. Support for the CVP/PSC is lower in all groups than the national average, but particularly low among professionals, because of the strength of the Liberal party in this category. A systematic relationship between higher occupational category and increased support for the PVV/PLP is to be observed. There is a very high concentration of support for the Socialist party among Walloon workers but a drastic reduction of support among salaried employees. However, the decline in the percentage voting for the BSP/PSB in the higher status urban occupations is not as great in the Walloon region as elsewhere: 19 percent of Walloon professionals vote for the Socialist party. There are two possible explanations of this phenomenon. A proportion of the professional category may be composed of the managerial element in the complex of Socialist social organizations in the Walloon region (see Section I). A further proportion of the category may comprise members of the bureaucracies of Socialist-controlled communes. Party affiliation is a normal condition of appointment to national and communal bureaucracies in Belgium (see J. Vandendries, 1958). Finally, the lower-than-national-average support for the CVP/PSC among Walloon farmers may be explained by the lower level of churchgoing and the relative weakness of Catholic agricultural organizations in Walloon rural areas.

In the Flemish region much higher support is found among all occupational categories for the CVP/PSC than in the Walloon region. Like their Walloon counterparts, Flemish professionals give less support to the Catholic party than the other occupational groups, but in the Flemish region professional support goes to the *Volksunie* as well as to the PVV/PLP. The VU clearly constitutes a pole of attraction for the higher occupational categories in the Flemish region. The Flemish nationalist party gains more support among Flemish independents and professionals than does the (newer) *Rassemblement Wallon* in these groups in the Walloon region. In all categories except the independents, however, the VU attracts less support than does the FDF in Brussels-Capital.

In Brussels-Capital the Liberal and francophone parties attract more support in the lower occupational categories than they do elsewhere. By comparison with the other regions, the PVV/PLP in Brussels-Capital competes for the support of the professional category as much with the linguistic party as any other party. The profile of occupational support for the Socialist party in Brussels-Capital is very similar to that of the Flemish region; with the exception of stronger support among workers, the sources of CVP/PSC support in the capital city are comparable to its support in the Walloon region.

The weakness of the relationship between occupation and party choice in Belgium results from the crosscutting influences of religious and linguistic appeals. The consistently high levels of support for the CVP/PSC indicate that religious practice is the more important intervening variable. It might be expected, however, that occupational status would be more strongly linked to party choice among nonchurchgoers for whom the attraction of the Catholic party is low and for whom the potential influence of class is higher.

TABLE 19: **Occupation and Party Choice by Religiosity, National, in Percentages**

	CVP/ PSC	BSP/ PSB	PVV/ PLP	VU	FDF- RW	CPB/ PCB	N
Practicing							
Workers	57	22	8	10	3	0	463
Employees	58	12	15	12	3	0	344
Independents	56	7	17	15	4	—	203
Professionals	46	4	34	11	6	—	169
Farmers	78	9	13	8	0	—	239
							Tb=0.035
Nonpracticing							
Workers	11	69	9	3	4	4	448
Employees	13	44	23	7	12	1	273
Independents	16	29	40	5	7	3	137
Professionals	5	28	43	8	15	2	116
Farmers	3	41	55	—	—	—	29
							Tb=0.075

Table 19 suggests that the relationship between occupation and party choice is little higher among the indifferent than among churchgoers. Nonpracticing workers vote very heavily for the Socialist party. However, support for the BSP/PSB is also very high among the nonchurchgoing middleclass groups. The appeal of the Socialist party to them may lie in its continued association with anticlericalism. In general, the relationship between occupational status and party choice is weaker at the higher levels. Although considerable support for the PVV/PLP is found higher in the occupational hierarchy, these groups are more susceptible to the appeals of the linguistic parties than are the nonpracticing workers. This is predictable in that the linguistic appeal is in many respects a veiled class appeal (see Section I), but support for the linguistic parties still falls into a category logically distinct from support for an explicitly class party.

In a complementary manner support for the Catholic party is dominant in all occupational categories of churchgoers. Although support for the *Volksunie* is fairly evenly distributed among the urban categories of practicers, this contrasts with the uneven distribution of support for the Liberal and Socialist parties. It appears from Table 19 that when churchgoers do vote for the PVV/PLP and the BSP/PSB, it is along class lines.

Table 20 examines in detail the influence of church attendance on the electoral behavior of occupational groups. Farmers, workers, and employees are the three groups in which religiosity has the strongest influence on party choice. In rural communities, where the influence of the Church is commonly said to be very strong, it is likely that nonpractice indicates a more definite ideological position than in urban society: hence, the very low level of support for the CVP/PSC among nonpracticing farmers. It is in rural communities and among workers and salaried employees that the interest groups and social organizations associated with the political parties are

TABLE 20: **Religiosity and Party Choice by Occupation, Regional, in Percentages**

		CVP/ PSC	BSP/ PSB	PVV/ PLP	VU	FDF- RW	CPB/ PCB	N
Flemish region								
Workers :	P	61	17	7	14	—	—	336
	N P	14	69	8	8	1	1	159 Tb=0.162
Employees :	P	62	11	10	17	—	—	227
	N P	16	52	15	16	1	—	107 Tb=0.115
Independents :	P	59	6	13	21	2	—	144
	N P	12	43	28	18	—	—	40 Tb=0.089
Professionals :	P	52	4	24	20	1	—	92
	N P	11	29	34	20	3	3	35 Tb=0.061
Farmers :	P	79	—	10	10	—	—	185
	N P	—	62	38	—	—	—	13 Tb=0.156
Walloon region								
Workers :	P	42	39	9	—	9	1	110
	N P	7	74	9	—	5	6	236 Tb=0.123
Employees :	P	55	13	21	—	9	1	75
	N P	6	47	29	—	15	3	100 Tb=0.117
Independents :	P	43	9	34	—	14	–	44
	N P	16	27	46	—	7	4	56 Tb=0.043
Professionals :	P	35	—	53	—	12	—	51
	N P	—	42	45	—	12	—	40 Tb=0.114
Farmers :	P	74	4	20	—	2	—	54
	N P	7	25	69	—	—	—	16 Tb=0.235
Brussels-Capital								
Workers :	P	61	8	14	6	11	—	36
	N P	20	44	17	3	13	3	106 Tb=0.074
Employees :	P	44	13	25	6	12	—	84
	N P	17	27	27	1	26	1	135 Tb=0.034
Independents :	P	63	6	9	6	17	—	35
	N P	20	19	44	—	12	5	81 Tb=0.094
Professionals :	P	48	6	32	2	12	—	50
	N P	6	13	48	5	26	1	83 Tb=0.047

P   = Practicing
N P = Nonpracticing

strongest (see Section I). It is a reasonable supposition that membership in each of the major sociopolitical complexes correlates quite highly with practice and nonpractice as well as with party choice. It is among workers in the Flemish region that the strength of the Catholic social organizations is greatest, and it is among Flemish workers that church attendance has the most influence. The lower level of Catholic social organization in the Walloon region probably contributes to the weaker relationship between religiosity and party choice among Walloon workers. Salaried employees are somewhat less involved in the sociopolitical organizations of the Catholic and Socialist parties, and in this group in all regions the relationship between religiosity and party choice is weaker than among workers. Both churchgoing and indifferent independents and professionals are relatively untouched by the politicized organizations; these groups show even less relationship between religiosity and political choice.

E. SUBJECTIVE CLASS ASSESSMENT

Individuals can be identified as belonging to social-classes according to such nonattitudinal criteria as income, occupation, residence, education, etc. They can also be grouped in terms of shared beliefs and life-styles. When respondents in a survey are asked to assess their class position, their answers will be influenced partly by the descriptive criteria of social class and partly by their attitude toward the group norms. The ability of the respondents to assess their social-class implies some awareness of shared class characteristics and probably some *positive* concept of the class to which they ascribe themselves.

In the 1968 survey respondents were asked to assign themselves to one of the following social classes: working-class (*la classe ouvrière*); middle-class (*les classes moyennes*); bourgeoisie (*la bourgeoisie*); others (*autres*). The last group (3 percent of the usable responses) is excluded from both Table 21, which presents the relationship

TABLE 21: Subjective Class Assessment and Party Choice, Regional and National, in Percentages

	CVP/ PSC	BSP/ PSB	PVV/ PLP	VU	FDF- RW	CPB/ PCB	N
Flemish region							
Working-Class	48	32	8	11	0	0	771
Middle-Class	52	9	17	22	1	—	466
Bourgeoisie	32	9	45	11	2	2	47
							Tb=0.034
Walloon region							
Working-Class	20	59	11	—	6	4	459
Middle-Class	27	17	46	—	9	1	327
Bourgeoisie	33	7	39	—	22	—	46
							Tb=0.113
Brussels-Capital							
Working-Class	30	41	12	3	12	2	220
Middle-Class	26	12	35	4	22	2	313
Bourgeoisie	27	8	43	3	17	2	104
							Tb=0.049
Belgium							
Working-Class	38	42	9	7	3	1	1,341
Middle-Class	41	12	27	12	7	1	922
Bourgeoisie	27	6	47	6	13	1	136
							Tb=0.052

between subjective class assessment and party choice at the regional and national levels, and Table 22, which examines this relationship controlling for occupation.

The stronger the differences in party choice between the self-assessed social classes, the more the *concept* of class can be assumed to act as determinant of party choice. One way of examining the relationship between the concept of class and party choice, while controlling for correct class identification on the nonattitudinal criteria, is to observe the political choices of those who fail to identify their correct social class. A convenient method of making operative the idea of *correct social class* is to take the subjective class assessment of the majority of an occupational category as the measure. On these criteria workers in all regions and employees in the Flemish region can be regarded as working-class; in all other regions employees, independents, and

TABLE 22: **Subjective Class Assessment and Percentage of Party Choice, by Occupation and Region**

		CVP/ PSC	BSP/ PSB	PVV/ PLP	VU	FDF- RW	CPB/ PCB	N	
Flemish region									
Workers	: W C	46	36	8	9	—	0	437	
	M C	39	15	13	30	2	—	46	Tb=0.035
Employees	: W C	46	34	7	12	1	—	179	
	M C	48	12	16	23	1	—	143	Tb=0.024
Independents	: W C	49	28	7	16	—	—	69	
	M C	50	6	21	23	—	—	105	Tb=0.026
Professionals	: M C	42	8	24	24	1	—	74	
	B	34	3	44	12	3	3	32	Tb=0.021
Farmers	: W C	73	4	13	9	—	—	45	
	M C	79	3	10	8	—	—	77	Tb=0.002
Walloon region									
Workers	: W C	18	66	7	—	5	4	311	
	M C	15	44	26	—	15	—	27	Tb=0.037
Employees	: W C	23	51	16	—	10	—	70	
	M C	26	22	34	—	15	3	88	Tb=0.043
Independents	: W C	19	38	19	—	19	4	26	
	M C	32	11	49	—	8	2	66	Tb=0.060
Professionals	: M C	22	22	41	—	16	—	51	
	B	12	4	65	—	19	—	26	Tb=0.038
Farmers	: W C	44	28	28	—	—	—	18	
	M C	57	2	40	—	—	—	42	Tb=0.042
Brussels-Capital									
Workers	: W C	27	42	10	4	14	2	106	
	M C	40	17	33	3	7	—	30	Tb=0.046
Employees	: W C	26	45	16	2	11	—	62	
	M C	26	13	27	5	27	2	130	Tb=0.045
	B	36	14	41	—	9	—	22	Tb=0.021
Independents	: W C	42	19	19	3	10	6	31	
	M C	26	8	48	—	17	1	65	Tb=0.042
Professionals	: M C	18	12	42	4	22	1	67	
	B	19	6	51	3	21	—	63	Tb=0.004

W C = Working Class
M C = Middle Class
 B = Bourgeoisie

professionals can be regarded as middle-class. These assumptions about correct class assessment will underly the following discussion.

At the national level there is no clear pattern of support for the Catholic party among self-assessed social classes (Table 21). Although increasing support for the CVP/PSC is found in the higher class groups in the Walloon region, this is not observed in Brussels-Capital and is somewhat reversed in the Flemish region. The relationship between subjective social-class and party choice is far clearer with the explicity class parties: there is a regular decline in support from working-class through middle-class to bourgeoisie in the case of the BSP/PSB in all regions, and, with the exception of the small Walloon bourgeois class, a corresponding increase in support for PVV/PLP. The decline in support for the Liberal party in the Walloon region among the self-assessed bourgeoisie is largely explained by the considerable preference of this group for the francophone party.

The fact that the level of support for the FDF-RW in the Walloon region is higher in the middle-class than in the working-class is contrasted strongly against the sources of support for the VU in the Flemish region and the FDF in Brussels-Capital. While it is not easy to explain the high level of support for the FDF-RW among the Walloon bourgeoisie, the contrasting lower levels of support for the linguistic parties in the other regions among this group may be explained by the political attitudes of what might be termed the *national bourgeoisie*. In the Flemish region the commercial and industrial elite has been and remains French-speaking and francophile (see Section I). It has no sympathy for either the linguistic or federalist aims of the *Volksunie*. It is likely that the similar group resident in Brussels-Capital, the proprietorial and decision-making elite of a national network of industrial and commercial concerns, is equally suspicious of the federalist aspirations of the FDF-RW.

Regional analysis of party choice among subjective social classes controlling for occupation(Table 22) confirms the general relationship between middle-class identification and support for the linguistic parties. In the Flemish region a significant difference in support for the VU is found between workers and employees identifying themselves (correctly) as working-class and those identifying themselves as middle-class. (Among the small number of VU voters in Brussels-Capital the pattern is inconsistent and even reversed.) With the exception of the independents, this pattern is confirmed for the FDF-RW in the Walloon region, as it is (with the exception of the workers category) for the francophone party in Brussels-Capital.

The Liberal party everywhere gains distinctly greater support from working-class groups identifying themselves as middle-class. Conversely, the BSP/PSB attracts more support from members of the middle-class who assess themselves as working-class than from correct middle-class identifiers. (In the Walloon region, however, Socialist voting is quite high among the small number of workers whose subjective class assessment is middle-class.) The Socialist party in the Flemish region is again stronger among correct than among incorrect working-class identifiers, but it is not as strong in the former group as the CVP/PSC. There is no consistent relationship between correct and incorrect self-identification of class in the support of the Catholic party:

the proportion choosing the party is fairly similar in both groups in all occupations. The concept of social-class is not an important determinant of support for the CVP/PSC.

F. COMMUNE SIZE

The published results of the 1968 survey contain no findings on the relationship between urban and rural residence and party choice. Sophisticated measures of urbanization have been developed in Belgium (see Section V), but they have not been used in electoral surveys. Commune size is not a surrogate for degree of urbanization. The territorial extent of communes varies widely between provinces, and this variation has some effect on their population sizes. (In the province of Hainaut in the Walloon region the territorial extent of communes is particularly small. The populations of these urban-industrial communes is comparable to those of the territorially extensive, but rural, communes of the province of Limburg.) National aggregations of communes by population size in relationship to party choice are, therefore, likely to be somewhat misleading. Nonetheless, in order to facilitate cross-national comparison, a national INRA survey is included, showing the relationship between commune size and voting intention in 1970 (Table 23).

TABLE 23: **Commune Size and Voting Intention, National, in Percentages**

	CVP/ PSC	BSP/ PSB	PVV/ PLP	VU	FDF- RW	CPB/ PCB	N
Less than 2,000	51	22	15	7	5	0	246
2,000-4,999	53	23	12	9	2	1	318
5,000-9,999	52	20	13	12	2	1	321
10,000-25,000	46	26	10	14	3	2	268
25,000 plus	35	28	15	19	2	1	182
5 major cities	33	30	21	8	7	1	489

Tb=0.015

Since churchgoing is higher in rural than in urban communities and the occupational interests of farmers are mainly articulated through pressure groups associated with the Catholic party, it is likely that support for the CVP/PSC will be very high in agrarian communes. However, the level of urbanization is unlikely to have much influence as a separate variable in voting behavior. The dense network of physical communications in the country and the extensive daily traveling to work experienced by a large proportion of the population militate against localistic patterns of political relationships.

The relationship between commune size and party preference is slight, as Table 23 reveals. The expected pattern of high CVP/PSC support in the least populated communes is confirmed. What is less expected is the even spread of Socialist support.

It is possible that the fairly high scores for the party in the communes with small populations result from the strength of the Socialist party in the Walloon region, where communes are smaller. The clear pattern of increasing support for the *Volksunie* in areas of higher population also results in part from the regional discrepancy in commune sizes, but it is also a reflection of the extent to which Flemish nationalism has been transformed into an urban phenomenon in the post-1945 period (see Section I). The sharp drop in support for the VU in the category of 5 *major cities* is explained by the fact that three of them are wholly or predominantly francophone, viz. Liège, Charleroi, and Brussels-Capital.

G. AGE

Table 24 presents the relationship between age and party choice at the regional and national levels. No strong overall relationship is found between age group and party choice, but a distinct pattern of support can be observed for the parties suffering

TABLE 24: **Age and Party Choice, Regional and National, in Percentages**

	CVP/ PSC	BSP/ PSB	PVV/ PLP	VU	FDF- RW	CPB/ PCB	N
Flemish region							
Less than 40	48	19	20	22	0	0	466
40 to 60	46	25	14	15	0	0	510
60 plus	57	23	11	8	—	0	385
							Tb=0.009
Walloon region							
Less than 40	17	34	33	—	13	4	259
40 to 60	29	40	21	—	8	2	327
60 plus	30	46	17	—	4	2	260
							Tb=0.015
Brussels-Capital							
Less than 40	26	18	30	3	20	3	180
40 to 60	29	18	30	3	18	1	286
60 plus	28	29	24	3	15	1	198
							Tb=0.005
Belgium							
Less than 40	36	23	20	13	6	2	815
40 to 60	37	29	19	8	5	1	981
60 plus	44	32	15	5	3	1	748
							Tb=0.005

electoral decline and those making electoral gains in the 1960s. The greatest support for the Catholic and Socialist parties is found in the older age groups, that of the Liberal and linguistic parties in the younger age groups.

The relationship between age and party choice is least weak in the Walloon region.

Although the Socialist party gains almost half the votes of those in the oldest age group, it competes with the Liberal party in the youngest. Support for the FDF-RW is markedly higher among the under-forties than in the older age groups. In the Flemish region the Flemish nationalist party attracts the support of the second largest group of voters under the age of forty years. The CVP/PSC remains dominant in this age group, however, with almost half the available votes.

A slight irregularity in the expected progression of support in the age groups is observed in the Catholic and Socialist parties in the Flemish region. Amongst those aged between forty and sixty, the CVP/PSC gains its lowest level of support and the BSP/PSB its highest. A plausible generational explanation for this phenomenon lies in the fairly rapid rate of electoral change occurring in the Flemish region in the 1930s, when many in this age group voted for the first time. Although the peak of Socialist electoral growth was reached in the mid-1920s, it continued to make slight electoral advances thereafter and was certainly a salient electoral force in a way it had not been before 1914. The elections of the 1930s also saw the major advances of the Flemish nationalist movement, and those advances occurred overwhelmingly at the expense of the Catholic party.

H. SEX

The common finding in Catholic countries that more women than men vote for the Catholic party receives prima facie confirmation in Table 25. The normal explanation for this is that women are more regular attenders at church than men. Table 26 confirms that in Belgium a greater proportion of women are practicers than men (60 percent vs. 53 percent) and that women are the greater proportion of practicers (55 percent). At the national level slightly more female practicers vote for the CVP/PSC than do male practicers, but this pattern is not consistently repeated within the regions. Only in the Flemish region are there more churchgoing women who vote for the Catholic party than churchgoing men. The weight of Flemish female churchgoers in the female sample (39 percent) clearly contributes to the national observation that women vote more for the Catholic party than men. However, that observation also results from the fact that in all regions more female nonchurchgoers vote for the CVP/PSC than male nonchurchgoers.

TABLE 25: **Sex and Party Choice, National, in Percentages**

	CVP/ PSC	BSP/ PSB	PVV/ PLP	VU	FDF- RW	CPB/ PCB	N
Men	35	29	17	10	7	2	1,223
Women	42	27	18	7	5	1	1,293
							Tb=0.002

A second common finding in all countries is that women vote less for the Left parties than men. This is true nationally and regionally, in all subgroups, for the support of the Belgian Communist party. However, at the national level, the reluctance of women to vote for the Socialist party is only slightly confirmed (Table 26). The expectation that churchgoing women are less inclined to vote for the BSP/PSB than churchgoing men is slightly substantiated in the Flemish region and in Brussels-Capital. In the Walloon region, however, more churchgoing women vote for the Socialist party than churchgoing men. Furthermore, in all regions the BSP/PSB receives more support among women indifferent to the Church than among nonchurchgoing men. Thus, in four of the six subgroups identified, women have a greater propensity to vote for the Socialist party than men.

TABLE 26 : **Sex and Party Choice by Religiosity, Regional and National, in Percentages**

		CVP/ PSC	BSP/ PSB	PVV/ PLP	VU	FDF- RW	CPB/ PCB	N	
Flemish region									
Practicing	: M	58	13	10	18	0	—	451	
	W	66	9	12	13	0	—	511	Tb=0.004
Nonpracticing :	M	15	53	14	17	1	1	197	
	W	15	56	18	9	1	1	160	Tb=0.003
Walloon region									
Practicing	: M	54	15	21	—	10	1	142	
	W	48	18	26	—	7	0	216	Tb=0.003
Nonpracticing :	M	6	53	25	—	10	6	266	
	W	12	60	20	—	6	2	223	Tb=0.006
Brussels-Capital									
Practicing	: M	52	12	25	5	6	—	95	
	W	48	8	23	4	18	—	128	Tb=0.005
Nonpracticing :	M	16	26	34	3	17	3	193	
	W	17	29	29	1	22	3	235	Tb=0.002
Belgium									
Practicing	: M	56	13	13	13	4	0	648	
	W	60	11	17	9	3	0	793	Tb=0.002
Nonpracticing :	M	11	47	22	6	11	3	575	
	W	14	51	21	3	8	2	500	Tb=0.002

The apparent contradiction that the Catholic and Socialist parties in Belgium draw more support from women than men in most of the important social subgroups can be resolved by comparing the two parties that have experienced a general electoral decline with the parties that have experienced general electoral growth. In the Flemish region the party exhibiting consistent rapid growth in the 1960s was the VU; in all subgroups the VU receives more support from men than women. This is also true of the party's support in Brussels-Capital. In the case of the Liberal party, whose growth in the Flemish region has been by no means as rapid, more women than men support it in all subgroups. In the Walloon region the growth of the francophone party has been rapid; it receives more support from men in all subgroups.

The PVV/PLP in the Walloon region maintained its electoral impetus of 1965 in the following election, and can therefore be identified as a party of electoral movement more clearly than its Flemish counterpart. The support of the Walloon Liberal party is mixed: it gains more support among churchgoing women than men, but in the larger group of nonchurchgoers it gains more support from men than women. In Brussels-Capital, where the PVV/PLP's share of the vote went up by 17 percent from 1961 to 1965 and down by 7 percent from 1965 to 1968, the party gains more support from men than women in all subgroups. The dichotomy between parties of electoral advance and those of electoral decline in explaining voting differences between the sexes only fails noticeably in the case of the francophone party in Brussels-Capital, which has the strongest record of rapid electoral growth. In the FDF in Brussels-Capital women in all subgroups contribute more support than men. Nonetheless, this finding does not detract substantially from the conclusion that in Belgium women are not more politically conservative but are more traditional in their voting behavior than men.

VII. Conclusions

A. THE BASIC EXPLANATORY VARIABLES

1. TREE ANALYSIS

A.I.D. is a useful technique for comparing the relationship between party choice and different social structure variables. Only four variables were directly available from the 1968 survey for use in A.I.D. analysis: party choice, religiosity, occupation, and region. In order to facilitate cross-national analysis, a fifth variable was constructed, that of social class. Workers, employees, and farmers were grouped together in the working-class category, and independants and professionals were grouped into the middle-class category.

The sample was dichotomized in turn between the voters of each of the major parties and all other party voters. (The supporters of the linguistic parties were also grouped against all other voters in order to see if a relationship other than region would distinguish these respondents; no split occurred.) With each major party, a single split occurred. In the cases of the Catholic and Socialist voters the amount of variance explained was quite high (23 and 18 percent). These results indicate the primacy of religion in Belgian electoral behavior. It was to be predicted that churchgoing would distinguish Catholic party voters from the supporters of other parties. Less predictable was the finding that nonchurchgoing, rather than class or occupation, was the major distinction between Socialist and other party voters (see also Appendix 2).

2. RELIGIOSITY, REGION, AND CLASS IN BELGIAN ELECTORAL BEHAVIOR

The measure used to test the relationship among religiosity, region, occupational class, and party choice was Tau beta. Simultaneously controlling for the effects of other variables, *Tb*s were obtained for each variable and party choice over all subgroups of the sample. These scores were then pooled according to a method suggested by

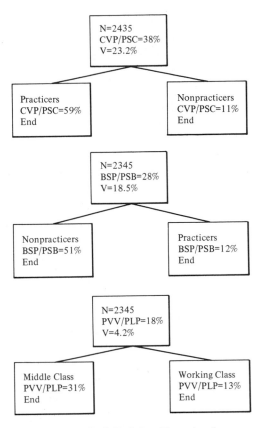

Figure 1: A Belgian Tree Analysis: Each Major Party vs. All Other Parties.

H. M. Blalock (1960, p. 239) in order to obtain a single measure of association between each variable and party choice, with the following results:

Religiosity and party choice : $Tb = 0.103$
Occupation and party choice: $Tb = 0.045$
Region and party choice   : $Tb = 0.038$

None of these results indicate a strong relationship at work. This is, however, to be anticipated in a political system in which voters are subjected to crosscutting pressures along three dimensions of party choice.

The general reliability of the relationships revealed by the Tau beta measure is indicated by the results of a stronger measure of association based on analysis of variance (M. N. Franklin, 1971). The relationship between religiosity, social class (*not* occupation), region, and party choice were as follows:

Religiosity and party choice   : $\Sigma^2 = 0.345$
Region and party choice   : $\Sigma^2 = 0.174$
Social class and party choice : $\Sigma^2 = 0.164$

Thus, by several different statistical measures religiosity emerges as by far the most important explanatory variable in Belgian electoral behavior, with region and class enjoying about the same lower explanatory power.

B. SUMMARIZING THE FINDINGS

Four social cleavages have been of primary importance in generating party competition and determining electoral behavior in Western Europe: center-periphery, religious, urban-rural, and class cleavages (S. M. Lipset and S. Rokkan, 1967). All of these cleavages are present in Belgian society, and party conflict has emerged explicitly on all but the urban-rural cleavage. In the present analysis, however, limitations in the survey data currently available have restricted the analysis to the relationship between religious and class cleavages and party choice.

The absence of detailed survey data on urban-rural differences is probably not a critical omission. It has been argued that a number of factors reduce the impact of such residential differences on electoral behavior in national elections in Belgium (see Section VI F). In the only rural group identifiable in the sample—the farmers—the distinctively high support given to the Catholic party is to be explained in terms of religiosity and, possibly, occupational factors rather than in terms of the urban-rural dichotomy (see Section VI C-D).

The more serious gap in the survey data concerns language. Linguistic interests have led to the emergence of linguistic parties in all three of Belgium's language groups.* The present importance of the language question suggests that language is as important as religiosity, region, and class in influencing current Belgian electoral behavior. Among a few social subgroups, indeed, language could prove to be the dominant influence in electoral choice. This seems likely among both Dutch-speakers and francophones in Brussels-Capital, and it could be the case among the francophone minority in the Flemish region.

Region is not a surrogate for language, although the high level of linguistic homogeneity of Flanders and Wallonia permits the use of these regions as a rough index of language. It is true that regional variations in the electoral behavior of linguistic groups

---

*   Under the terms of the Treaty of Versailles, 1920, Belgium gained from Germany three predominantly German-speaking cantons on its eastern border: Eupen, Malmédy, and Sankt-Vith. The cantons were incorporated into the province of Liège; their population has constituted less than one percent of the total population. In the election of 1929 a German irredentist list acquired 52 percent of the vote in the cantons. In the two other inter war elections, 1932 and 1939, in which such lists appeared, they gained 46 percent of the vote. In 1971, a Catholic dissident group composed of German-speakers the *Christliche Unabhängige Wählergemeinschaft*, gained 20 percent of the vote in the Eastern Cantons.

almost certainly contribute to the fairly high relationship observed above between region and party choice (see Section VII A). But the major factor at work in producing the regional effect on party choice is that set of systematic differences in psychological orientations between the residents of the different regions, resulting from contextual influences of which language is only one (see K. R. Cox, 1969, pp. 75ff). Clearly, region is a separate and important variable that needs to be included in any analysis of the relationship between social structure and party choice in Belgium.

A comprehensive analysis of social structure and voting in Belgium must be conducted in terms of the interaction of five basic variables: religiosity, class, language, region, and urban-rural residence. In order to observe the conjoint influence of these variables on party choice, it would be logically necessary to isolate no less than sixty subgroups in the population. The presence of all three linguistic groups in all regions and the nonapplicability of the urban-rural dichotomy in Brussels-Capital would produce a model of social cleavage in Belgium, including twenty-four subgroups in Flanders and Wallonia and twelve in Brussels-Capital. (If the largely German-speaking Eastern cantons were treated separately, the number of cells in the model would rise to eighty-four. However, the addition is not justified because the smallness of the population in these cantons would render the findings insignificant.)

Empirically, then umber of cells with measurable findings in a social survey would probably decline to forty-two. The number of German-speakers in Flanders and Brussels-Capital is so small as to produce negligible cell entries. It is also unlikely that more than minuscule numbers would be found for the categories of francophone workers in Flemish rural areas and for Dutch-speakers of both social classes in Walloon rural areas. The optimal grid of subgroups in the population would, therefore, comprise fourteen in the Flemish region, twenty in the Walloon region, and eight in Brussels-Capital.

In the present investigation limitations in survey data have confined the analysis to only twelve subgroups: those experiencing the interaction of the religious and class dichotomies in the three regions. In summarizing the findings, however, the class variables has been trichotomized in order to separate farmers from the working-class category. In occupational, residential, and religious terms farmers form a highly distinctive subgroup in the social structure. These social-structural characteristics combine with a singularly high level of political cohesiveness to justify the separate presentation of farmers. A sixteen-cell model of Belgian society is thus generated. The distribution of the sixteen subgroups in the population and the levels of party support within them are presented in matrix form in Table 27.

The matrix analysis demonstrates the extensive fragmentation of Belgian society. The largest subgroup, that of churchgoing Flemish workers, forms less than a quarter of the population, and only two other groups—nonpracticing workers in Flanders and Wallonia—constitute more than 10 percent. Although the interaction of religiosity, class, and region creates a pattern of small social groupings, only three subgroups include less than 2 percent of the population: middle-class churchgoers in Brussels-Capital and the two sets of nonpracticing farmers. The population is fairly evenly distributed among the remaining ten subgroups, whose average size is 5 percent.

The distribution of party support within the subgroups indicates the continuing primacy of religious and class interests in party choice of Belgian voters. In seven sub-

TABLE 27 : **Party Support (by Percentage) in Basic Social Groups**

	PRACTICERS			NONPRACTICERS		
	Flemish region			Flemish region		
	Middle Class	*Working Class*	*Farmers*	*Middle Class*	*Working Class*	*Farmers*
CVP	55	61	79	12	15	—
BSP	5	15	—	36	62	62
PVV	17	9	10	31	10	38
VU	20	15	10	19	11	—
FDF-RW	1	—	—	1	1	—
CPB	—	—	—	—	—	—
	(9.7)	(23.2)	(7.6)	(3.1)	(11.0)	(0.5)
	Walloon region			Walloon region		
	Middle Class	*Working Class*	*Farmers*	*Middle Class*	*Working Class*	*Farmers*
PSC	39	47	74	9	6	6
PSB	4	29	4	33	66	25
PLP	44	14	20	46	15	69
VU	—	—	—	—	—	—
FDF-RW	13	9	2	9	8	—
PCB	—	1	—	2	5	—
	(3.9)	(7.6)	(2.2)	(3.9)	(13.8)	(0.6)
	Brussels-Capital			Brussels-Capital		
	Middle Class	*Working Class*			*Middle Class*	*Working Class*
CVP/PSC	54	50			13	18
BSP/PSB	6	11			16	35
PVV/PLP	22	22			46	22
VU	3	6			2	2
FDF-RW	14	12			19	20
CPB/PCB	—	—			3	2
	(1.8)	(2.5)			(3.4)	(5.0)

Total party strengths in the sample : CVP/PSC, 39 percent; BSP/PSB, 28 percent; PVV/PLP, 18 percent; FDF-RW, 5 percent; VU, 8 percent; CPB/PCB, 1 percent. Percentages in parentheses indicate the proportion of the whole sample constituted by the social group in the cell.

groups (55 percent of the sample) the largest proportion of voters supports the Catholic party, and in the other nine subgroups the largest proportion of voters supports one or the other of the major class parties. Furthermore, the level of polarization around these class and religious parties is high: the average level of support for the dominant party in the subgroups is 57 percent, while the average level of support for the second largest party is only 19 percent. (The percentages used in this discussion are weighted averages.) It is the crosscutting influence of religiosity and social-class that prevents the translation of extreme social fragmentation into extreme political fractionalization in Belgium.

Religious interests are the most common unifying factor. Churchgoers form 59 percent of the population. Of the eight subgroups composed of churchgoers, only the Walloon middle-class exhibits greater support for a party other than the Catholic party (in this case, the PLP). The average level of support for the Catholic party among churchgoers stands at 59 percent. When churchgoers do not vote for the religious party, their preference is for parties articulating class rather than linguistic interests: 27 percent as against 14 percent. Even among nonchurchgoers, there is a higher level of support for the Catholic party (14 percent) than for the linguistic parties (13 percent). It is class interests that provide the major motivation for party choice in the nonpracticing 41 percent of the population. Among nonchurchgoers support for the major class parties averages 73 percent (51 percent Socialist and 22 percent Liberal).

The role of class and religion in linking social groups divided by linguistic differences is confirmed by the analysis of the second largest parties in the subgroups. In only two of the sixteen subgroups is the second largest percentage of votes given to a linguistic party rather than a religious or class party. Both groups are composed of middle-class voters—churchgoers in Flanders and nonchurchgoers in Brussels-Capital. Churchgoing workers and farmers in the Flemish region give equal support to linguistic and class parties in a low second place behind the Catholic party. Support for the linguistic parties is generally higher in the middle-class than in the working-class (17 percent as against 13 percent), and higher among religious practicers than nonpracticers (14 percent and 13 percent). It is highest of all among middle-class churchgoers (18 percent).

The differential distribution and saliency of linguistic parties in the regions, together with the preeminence of religious conflict in Flanders and class conflict in Wallonia, make region a significant influence in Belgian electoral behavior. Yet the influence of language is inferior to that of religiosity or class, and the contextual factors relating to the nature of conflict in the regions reflect the primacy of the religious and class variables. The high level of support for the Catholic party in all social classes of churchgoers weakens the relationship between class and party choice in Belgium. At the same time the relationship between religiosity and party choice is weakened by the preference of 41 percent of churchgoers for nonreligious parties. It is the competing attraction of three dimensions of political choice that reduces the impact of any one social-structural variable and produces the pattern of weak statistical relationships observed throughout the preceding analysis of social structure and party choice in Belgium.

C. THE COMPARABILITY OF BELGIUM

The division of the population into three language groups constitutes the most striking aspect of the Belgian social-structure and invites the readiest comparisons. Two other advanced industrial democracies exhibit a similar degree of linguistic heterogeneity, Canada and Switzerland. With its current linguistic tensions, Canada is the closer parallel. Despite the increasing saliency of language, religiosity and class remain the primary influences on electoral behavior in Belgium. Austria, France, and Italy are, like Belgium, predominantly Catholic countries, where the degree to which voters are integrated into the Church comprises a major explanatory variable in party choice. In these countries, as in Belgium, the parties to which nonchurchgoers give their votes have been associated historically with anticlericalism, but their sources of electoral support are largely determined by social-class.

The main tendencies in the Belgian party system are those of Christian democracy (the CVP/PSC), social democracy (the BSP/PSB), and liberalism (the PVV/PLP). Useful comparisons in terms of the distribution of party support among social groups can be made, therefore, between Belgium and a number of other Western European countries in which the same tendencies predominate: Austria, Germany, Luxembourg, the Netherlands, and Switzerland. The involvement of a considerable proportion of the Belgian population in highly politicized social institutions associated, above all, with the Catholic and Socialist parties points to the comparison of Belgium with other countries of the "segmented pluralist" type, notably Austria, the Netherlands, and Switzerland. While the Catholic–Socialist dualism makes Austria the most apt comparison, the most interesting comparison is the Netherlands: in both countries there is growing evidence of the disintegration of sociopolitical blocs and of a consequent long-term decline in electoral support for the traditionally dominant parties.

Appendix 1: Party Share of Valid Vote: 1894-1971

APPENDIX 1A: **Party Share of Valid Vote, National: 1894-1971**

	CATHO-LIC	LIBERAL	SOCIAL-IST	DAEN-SIST	FLEMISH NATION-ALIST	COMMU-NIST	REXIST	BRUS-SELS FRANCO-PHONE	WAL-LOON FRANCO-PHONE	OTHERS
1894	51.6	28.5*	17.4*	1.2	—	—	—	—	—	1.3
1896-8	50.7	22.2*	23.6*	1.9	—	—	—	—	—	1.6
1900	48.5	24.3	22.5	3.0	—	—	—	—	—	1.7
1902-4	49.8	25.3	20.6	2.2	—	—	—	—	—	2.1
1906-8	48.6	26.7*	21.5*	1.1	—	—	—	—	—	1.9
1912	51.0	25.1*	22.0*	1.5	—	—	—	—	—	0.3
1919	36.6	17.6	36.6	—	2.6	—	—	—	—	6.5
1921	37.0	17.8	34.8	—	3.0	0.1	—	—	—	7.3
1925	36.1	14.6	39.3	—	3.9	1.6	—	—	—	4.3
1929	35.4	16.6	36.0	—	6.3	1.9	—	—	—	3.8
1932	38.6	14.3	37.1	—	5.9	2.8	—	—	—	1.3
1936	27.7	12.4	32.1	—	7.1	6.1	11.5	—	—	3.2
1939	32.7	17.2	30.2	—	8.3	5.4	4.4	—	—	1.8
1946	42.5	9.6*	32.4*	—	—	12.7	—	—	—	2.7
1949	43.6	15.3	29.8	—	2.1	7.5	—	—	—	1.9
1950	47.7	12.1*	35.5*	—	—	4.7	—	—	—	0.1
1954	41.1	13.1*	38.5*	—	2.2	3.6	—	—	—	1.5
1958	46.5	12.0*	37.0*	—	2.0	1.9	—	—	—	0.7
1961	41.5	11.1	36.7	—	3.5	3.1	—	—	—	2.9
1965	34.5	21.6	28.3	—	6.8	4.6	—	1.3	1.1	1.8
1968	31.8	20.9	28.0	—	9.8	3.3	—	2.8*	3.2*	2.2
1971	30.0	16.7	27.3	—	11.1	3.1	—	4.8*	6.3*	0.5

APPENDIX 1B: **Party Share of Valid Vote, Brussels: 1894-1971**

	% TOTAL VOTE	CATHO-LIC	LIBERAL	SOCIAL-IST	DAEN-SIST	FLEMISH NATION-ALIST	COMMU-NIST	REXIST	BRUSSELS FRANCO-PHONE	OTHERS
1894	10.9	47.4	30.6	19.6	—	—	—	—	—	2.4
1896	11.6	43.4	29.8*	24.5*	—	—	—	—	—	2.2
1900	11.3	38.9	24.5	25.7	4.4	—	—	—	—	6.5
1902	11.2	40.4	24.6	23.6	4.9	—	—	—	—	6.5
1906	11.8	39.3	31.9	20.7	3.1	—	—	—	—	5.0
1912	13.1	45.5	31.6	22.1	0.8	—	—	—	—	—
1919	10.6	23.2	28.7	30.6	—	1.3	—	—	—	16.3
1921	11.0	28.0	28.1	28.4	—	1.5	—	—	—	14.0
1925	11.1	32.4	22.6	37.6	—	1.4	4.2	—	—	1.8
1929	11.3	33.4	26.8	31.8	—	2.3	3.8	—	—	1.9
1932	11.3	30.0	27.6	33.8	—	2.1	4.4	—	—	2.2
1936	11.3	18.9	18.4	25.9	—	2.8	11.8	18.5	—	3.7
1939	11.6	21.8	30.4	23.0	—	2.8	9.1	8.5	—	4.5
1946	11.7	30.2	13.4	35.4	—	—	17.4	—	—	3.6
1949	12.6	31.0	24.9	29.4	—	1.5	9.5	—	—	3.7
1950	12.7	34.7	18.4	41.4	—	—	5.5	—	—	—
1954	12.7	24.6	19.4	45.1	—	0.9	3.7	—	—	6.2
1958	12.6	33.5	18.2	42.9	—	1.1	2.7	—	—	1.6
1961	12.7	28.0	17.0	41.6	—	1.6	3.6	—	—	8.1
1965	12.7	19.6	33.5	26.3	—	2.9	4.1	—	10.6	3.1
1968	12.9	27.6	26.3	20.0	—	4.3	2.4	—	18.6	0.8
1971	12.7	20.1	15.9	20.7	—	5.7	2.8	—	33.5	0.2

Note : 1894–1912: *arrondissement* of Brussels; 1919 onward: Brussels-Capital.

APPENDIX IC: Party Share of Valid Vote, Walloon Region: 1894-1971

	% Total Vote	Catho-lic	Liberal	Social-ist	Commu-nist	Flemish Nation-alist	Rexist	Franco-phone	Others
1894	46.0	37.0	32.1*	29.4*	—	—	—	—	1.5
1896-8	49.7	37.8	27.2*	34.8*	—	—	—	—	0.1
1900	45.2	36.9	25.0	37.0	—	—	—	—	1.1
1902-4	45.8	39.7	26.6	32.8	—	—	—	—	0.9
1906-8	45.5	37.9	25.0*	35.9*	—	—	—	—	1.2
1912	42.6	38.7	23.0*	37.1*	—	—	—	—	1.1
1919	41.8	27.9	18.8	51.0	—	—	—	—	2.3
1921	41.5	30.9	19.3	48.0	0.1	—	—	—	1.8
1925	40.9	27.6	15.1	51.0	2.5	—	—	—	3.9
1929	40.1	30.8	17.1	48.1	2.6	0.1	—	—	1.6
1932	39.0	30.2	14.4	48.3	4.5	0.1	—	—	2.5
1936	38.5	17.9	12.2	41.0	9.3	—	15.3	—	4.4
1939	37.9	24.9	19.3	38.0	9.1	0.0	6.2	—	2.5
1946	36.3	27.0	10.0*	37.6*	21.4	—	—	—	0.4
1949	35.3	32.0	14.7	37.8	12.6	—	—	—	2.9
1950	35.4	33.8	12.6*	45.9*	7.8	—	—	—	—
1954	34.5	30.5	12.7*	49.4*	6.7	0.0	—	—	0.7
1958	33.3	35.1	11.4*	47.8*	4.5	—	—	—	1.3
1961	32.9	31.0	11.8	46.4	6.4	—	—	—	4.5
1965	32.7	24.6	25.4	35.2	9.5	—	—	3.3	2.0
1968	32.3	21.0	26.7	34.5	6.9	—	—	10.7	0.3
1971	32.3	20.5	17.6	34.5	5.9	—	—	20.9	0.7

APPENDIX ID: Party Share of Valid Vote, Flemish Region: 1894-1971

	% Total Vote	Catho-lic	Liberal	Social-ist	Daen-sist	Flemish Nation-alist	Commu-nist	Rexist	Franco-phone	Others
1894	43.1	67.9	24.1	4.4	2.7	—	—	—	—	0.8
1896-8	38.7	67.4	14.3	10.5*	4.5	—	—	—	—	3.2
1900	43.6	63.0	23.7	6.6	5.1	—	—	—	—	1.8
1902-4	43.0	63.1	24.1	6.8	3.8	—	—	—	—	2.2
1906-8	42.8	62.7	27.3*	6.4*	1.7	—	—	—	—	1.8
1912	44.3	65.6	25.4*	6.1*	2.2	—	—	—	—	0.7
1919	47.6	47.3	14.1	25.3	—	5.2	—	—	—	8.1
1921	47.6	44.5	14.1	24.8	—	6.1	—	—	—	10.6
1925	48.0	44.2	12.4	30.1	—	7.7	0.3	—	—	5.2
1929	48.6	39.6	13.7	27.1	—	11.7	0.9	—	—	7.0
1932	49.7	47.0	11.2	29.1	—	10.8	1.1	—	—	0.8
1936	50.2	37.2	11.2	26.7	—	13.6	2.3	7.0	—	2.1
1939	50.6	41.0	12.6	26.0	—	15.1	1.7	2.2	—	1.4
1946	52.0	56.2	8.4*	28.3*	—	—	5.5	—	—	1.7
1949	52.1	54.4	13.3	24.3	—	3.6	3.6	—	—	0.8
1950	52.0	60.4	10.2*	26.9*	—	—	2.5	—	—	0.1
1954	52.9	52.0	11.7*	30.0*	—	3.9	1.5	—	—	0.8
1958	54.1	56.5	10.8*	29.0*	—	3.4	0.1	—	—	0.1
1961	54.5	50.9	11.6	29.7	—	6.0	1.0	—	—	0.8
1965	54.6	43.8	16.6	24.6	—	11.6	1.7	—	0.2	1.2
1968	54.8	39.1	16.2	26.0	—	16.9	1.4	—	0.3	0.2
1971	55.0	37.9	16.3	24.6	—	18.8	1.6	—	0.4	0.5

Note : Flemish cantons of the *arrondissement* of Brussels excluded before 1919.

*Electoral cartels in operation. In estimating the distribution of cartel votes before 1919, parties have been awarded the mean of their share of the vote in preceding and succeeding non-cartel elections or their share of the vote in the closest election; for cartels since 1946 a simple division of the vote has been made.

Appendix 2: Voting Intention in Belgium: A Tree Analysis

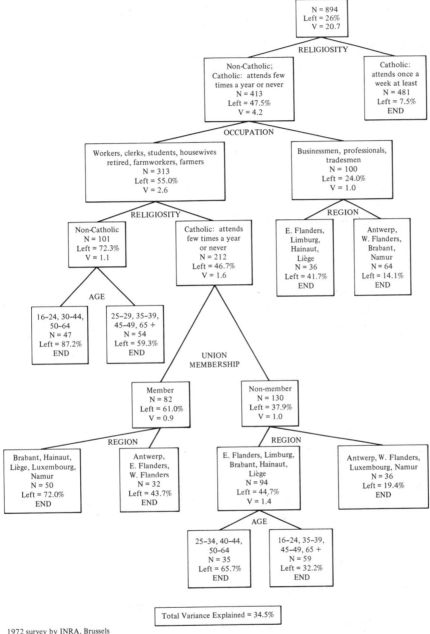

1972 survey by INRA, Brussels

The results of a second AID analysis appear here. The analysis was performed on the Belgian data-set from the *1970 European Communities Study*, carried out under the supervision of Ronald Inglehart of the University of Michigan. The dependent variable is Voting Intention, dichotomized between Left parties (i.e., Socialist and Communist) and all others. The independent variables used are church attendance (religiosity), occupation, province of residence (region), age, trade union membership, sex, commune-size, education, and language. The total variance explained is 34.5, of which religiosity comprises 23.3, occupation 4.2, region 2.9, age 2.5, and union membership 1.6. It is interesting to note that language does not emerge here as a significant element of differentiation. Otherwise, the results for religiosity and occupation virtually replicate the results of the first AID analysis, and reaffirm the primacy of the religious variable in Belgian electoral behaviour.

References

A.C.W. *De arbeiders en de politieke verkiezingen.* Brussel: A.C.W., 1959.

AIKEN, M., and VAN HASSEL, H. "De sociale struktuur en het politieke proces." *Res Publica* XII:3 (1970): 379-426.

ARANGO, E. R. *Leopold III and the Belgian Royal Question.* Baltimore: Johns Hopkins Press, 1963.

BLALOCK, H. M. *Social Statistics.* New York: McGraw-Hill, 1960.

BRAZEAU, J. and JONCKHEERE, J. *Essai sur la question linguistique en Belgique: Rapport à la Commission royale d'enquête sur le bilinguisme et le biculturisme.* Montreal: Institut de Recherches en Sciences Sociologiques, Inc., 1966.

BUTLER, D. and STOKES, D. *Political Change in Britain.* London: Macmillan, 1969.

CLAEYS-VAN HAEGENDOREN, M. *25 jaar belgisch socialisme.* Antwerpen: Standaard Wetenschappelijke Uitgeverij, 1967.

———. "Party and Opposition Formation in Belgium." *Res Publica* IX:3 (1967): 413-36.

COENEN, J. *Opinions politiques en milieu ouvrier.* Bruxelles: Institut Emile Vandervelde, 1961.

COLLARD, E. "Commentaire de la carte de la pratique dominicale en Belgique." *Lumen Vitae* VII (1952): 644-52.

COURRIER HEBDOMADAIRE. *Une étude d'opinion en belgique.* Bruxelles: Centre de Recherche et d'Information Socio-Politique, 1963, 187.

———. *Les élections legislatives du 7 novembre 1971.* Bruxelles: Centre de Recherche et d'Information Socio-Politique, 1971, 541-45.

COX, K. R. "On the Utility and Definition of Regions in Comparative Political Sociology." *Comparative Political Studies* 2, no. 1 (1969): 68-98.

DE LANOO, I., CLAEYS, U. and SANSEN, M. "De sociografische indeling van de Belgische gemeenten." *Politica* I (1963): 1-20.

DELEECK, H. "De belgische verkiezingsuitslagen." *De Gids op Maatschappelijk Gebied* III (1957): 179-207.

DELRUELLE, N., EVALENKO, R. and FRAEYS, W. *Le comportement politique des électeurs belges.* Bruxelles: Institut de Sociologie de l'Université Libre de Bruxelles, 1970.

DE SMET, R. E. and EVALENKO, R. *Les élections belges* plus *Annexes.* Bruxelles: Institut de Sociologie Solvay, 1956.

———, EVALENKO, R. and FRAEYS, W. *Atlas des élections belges, 1919-1954*, plus *Annexe Statistique.* Bruxelles: Institut de Sociologie Solvay, 1958. (Supplements with results of 1958 and 1961 elections published in 1959 and 1961, respectively.)

DEWACHTER, W. "De propaganda vertaalt de verkiezingsgestalte van 23 mei 1965." *Res Publica* VIII: 1 (1966): 106-27.

———. *De wetgevende verkiezingen als proces van machtsverwerving in het belgisch politiek bestel.* Antwerpen: Standaard Wetenschappelijke Uitgeverij, 1967.

———. *Politieke Kaart van België.* Antwerpen: Standaard Wetenschappelijke Uitgeverij, 1969.

———. "Elections communales et degré d'urbanisation en Belgique." Munich: IPSA VIII World Congress, 1970.

———. "Gemeenteraadsverkiezingen en verstedelijking." *Res Publica* XLI: 3 (1970): 289-310.

DOBBELAERE. K. *Sociologische analysevan de katholiciteit.* Antwerpen: Standaard. Wetenschappelijke Uitgeverij, 1966.

DOMS, P. "L'emploi des langues dans les chambres législatives en Belgique." *Res Publica* VII:2 (1965): 126-40.

ENSOR, R. C. K. *Belgium.* London: Williams and Norgate, 1915.

EUROPA YEARBOOK. *Vol. I. Part II: Europe.* London: Europa Publications, 1968.

FEAUX, V. *Cinq semaines de lutte sociale.* Bruxelles: Institut de Sociologie de l'Université Libre de Bruxelles, 1963.

FOGARTY, M. P. *Christian Democracy in Western Europe, 1820-1953.* London: Routledge & Kegan Paul, 1957.

FRANKLIN, M. N. "Measuring the Proportion of Variance Explained in a Contingency Table." Mimeographed. Glasgow: University of Strathclyde, 1971.

GILISSEN, J. *Le régime représentatif en Belgique depuis 1790.* Bruxelles: La Renaissance du Livre, 1958.

GOL, J. *Le monde de la presse en Belgique.* Bruxelles: Centre de Recherche et d'Information Socio-Politique, 1970.

GUYOT de MISHAEGEN, G. *Le parti catholique belge de 1830 à 1884.* Bruxelles: Maison Ferdinand Larcier, 1946.

HILL, K. "Belgium." In S. Henig and J. Pinder, eds. *European Political Parties.* London: Allen & Unwin, 1969.

HÖJER, C-H. *Le régime parlementaire belge de 1918 à 1940.* Uppsala: Almquist & Wiksells Boktryckeri, 1946.

HUYSE, L. *L'apathie politique.* Anvers: Editions Scientifiques Erasme, 1969.

———. *Passiviteit, pacificatie en verzuiling in de Belgische politiek.* Antwerpen: Standaard Wetenschappelijke Uitgeverij, 1970.

———, HILGERS, W. and HENRYON, C. *La participation politique en Belgique.* Louvain: Editions Nauwelaerts, 1966.

I. C. P. R. "Five-Nation Study June-July, 1959." Inter-university Consortium for Political Research. NORC 427, 1960.

Institut National de Statistique. *Annuaire Statistique de la Belgique.* Tome 88. Année 1967. Bruxelles: 1968.

JACQUEMYNS, G. *Bulletin de l'INSOC:* Bruxelles: Institut Universitaire d'Information Sociale et Economique, 1946-1960.

KERKHOFS. J. *Godsdienstpraktijk en sociaal milieu.* Bruxelles: Cahiers de *Lumen Vitae no. 5.*

———, and VAN HOUTE, J., eds. *De kerk in Vlaanderen.* Tielt: 1962.

LEBAS, C. *L'union des catholiques et des libéraux de 1839 à 1847.* Louvain: Editions Nauwelaerts, 1960.

LIJPHART, A. *The Politics of Accommodation.* Berkeley: Univ. of California Press, 1968.

LINDEMANS, L. *Huidige taalverhoudingen in de Brusselse agglomeratie.* Brussel: Uitgeverij Boekhandel Simonstevin, 1968.

LIPSET, S. M. and ROKKAN, S. "Cleavage Structures, Party Systems, and Voter Alignments: An Introduction." In Lipset and Rokkan, eds. *Party Systems and Voter Alignments: Cross-National Perspectives.* London: Collier Macmillan, 1967.

LORWIN, V. R. "Belgium: Religion, Class and Language in National Politics. In R. A. Dahl, ed. *Political Oppositions in Western Democracies.* New Haven: Yale Univ. Press, 1966.

———. "Segmented Pluralism: Ideological Cleavages and Political Cohesion in the Smaller European Democracies." *Comparative Politics* III: 2 (1971): 141-75.

LUYCKX, T. *Politieke geschiedenis van België van 1789 tot heden.* Amsterdam/Brussels: Elsevier, 1969.

LUZZATTO FEGIZ, P. *Il volto sconoscutio dell' Italia: seconda serie. 1956-1965.* Milano: Guiffré, 1966.

MACRAE, D. *Parliament, Parties, and Society in France, 1946-1958.* New York: St. Martin's Press, 1967.

MALLINSON, V. *Power and Politics in Belgian Education, 1815 to 1961.* London: Heinemann, 1963.

MELOT, A. *Le parti catholique en Belgique.* Louvain: Editions Rex, 1933.

MINISTERE DE L'INTERIEUR. *Recensement général du 31 décembre 1890.* Bruxelles: 1893.

———. *Recensement général du 31 décembre 1920.* Bruxelles: 1926.

——— *Arrétê ministériel du 3 décembre 1938.* Bruxelles: 1938.

———. *Recensement général du 31 décembre 1961.* Bruxelles : 1966.

———/Ministerie van Binnenlandse Zaken. *Elections législatives/Parlementsverkiezingen*, 1965, 1968. Mimeographed, n.d.

MINISTÉRE DES AFFAIRES ÉCONOMIQUES. *Recensement général da la population, de l'industrie et du commerce au 31 décembre 1947.* Bruxelles: 1949.

MOINE, W. *Résultats des élections belges entre 1847 et 1914.* Bruxelles: Institut Belge de Science Politique, 1970.

NEUVILLE, J. *La"représentativité" des syndicats.* Bruxelles: La Pensée Catholique, 1960.

PHILIPPART, A. "Une enquête sur l'information et les connaissances politiques des jeunes en Belgique. *Res Publica* VI:4 (1964): 383-96.

RAE, D. W. *The Political Consequences of Electoral Laws.* New Haven: Yale Univ. Press, 1967.

ROMUS, P. *La Wallonie dans la Communauté Européenne.* Bruxelles: Presses Universitaires de Bruxelles, 1967.

SARTORI, G. "From the Sociology of Politics to Political Sociology." In S. M. Lipset, ed. *Politics and the Social Sciences.* New York: Oxford Univ. Press, 1969.

SCHOLL, S. H., ed. *150 jaar katholieke arbeidersbeweging in België, 1789-1939.* 3 vols. Brussel: De Arbeiderspers, 1963, 1965, 1966.

SEEBOHM ROWNTREE, B. *Land and Labour: Lessons from Belgium.* London : Macmillan, 1910.

SENELLE, R. *Structures politiques, économiques et sociales de la Belgique.* Bruxelles: Ministère des Affaires Etrangères et du Commerce Extérieur, Textes et Documents: 257–59 (1970).

SIMON, A. *L'église catholique et les débuts de la Belgique indépendente.* Wetteren: Scaldis, 1949.

STENGERS, J. "Regards sur la sociologie électorale belge." *Revue de l'Université de Bruxelles* (janvier-mars, 1958): 122–74.

———and PHILIPPART, A. *Une expérience d'enquête électorale.* Bruxelles: Institut Universitaire d'Information Sociale et Politique, 1959.

SWAELEN, F. "De samenstelling der kandidatenlijsten in de Vlaamse CVP." *Res Publica* XI:1 (1969): 77–94.

TINGSTEN, H. *Political Behavior: Studies in Election Statistics. Totowa*, N. J.: Bedminster Press, 1963.

TROCLET, L-E. *Les partis politiques en Belgique.* Bruxelles: L'Eglantine, 1931.

URWIN, D. W. "Social Cleavages and Political Parties in Belgium: Problems of Institutionalization." *Political Studies* XVIII: 3(1970): 320–40.

———and ROSE, R. "Persistence and Disruption in Western Party Systems Between the Wars." Mimeographed. Varna, Bulgaria: World Congress of the International Sociological Association, 1970.

VAN DEN BRANDE, A. "Mogelijkheden van een sociologie der belgische conflicten na de Tweede Wereldoorlog, 1944–1961." *Sociologische Gids* X:1 (1963): 2–29.

VAN DEN DAELE, G. "Beschouwingen over de uitkomsten der volksraadpleging." *De Gids op Maatschappelijk Gebied* 2–3 (1950): 206–11.

VANDENDRIES, J. "L'influence de la politique dans la vie de l'administration en Belgique." *International Review of Administrative Sciences* XXIV (1958), 512–22.

VAN DE PUT, G., "Verkiezingsprogramma's." *Res Publica* VIII:1 (1966): 67–105.

VAN ISACKER, K. *Werkelijk en wettelijk land: De katholieke opinie tegenover de rechterzijde, 1863-1884.* Antwerpen: Standaard Boekhandel, 1955.

VAN KALKEN, F. *Entre deux guerres: Esquisse de la vie politique en Belgique de 1918 à 1940.* Bruxelles: Office de Publicité, 1944.

VAN WAELVELDE, W. and VAN DER HAEGEN, H. "Typologie des communes belges d'après le degré d'urbanisation au 31 décembre 1961." *Bulletin de Statistique* 9 (1967): 722–75.

VARZIM, A. *Le Boerenbond Belge.* Paris: Desclée de Brouwer et Cie., 1934.

3. GERMANY:
Continuity and Change in Electoral Politics
DEREK W. URWIN

The contemporary West German party system is the latest stage in a century of political development. While the Federal Republic has existed only since 1949, a German state has been in being since 1870 and German "society" or "societies" have existed for centuries. Historically there has always been a lack of coincidence between "political" Germany and areas of German national identity or of German-speaking people. The Federal Republic is of particular interest because, on the surface at least, severe political disjunctions exist between the past and the present: the party system of the Federal Republic, for example, is quite different from that of the earlier regimes of the Second Empire or the Weimar Republic. The abrupt changes of political regime and political style experienced by the country comprise the "jagged curve" of German history (Spiro, 1962, p. 470). Yet, while "Bonn is not Weimar" (Allemann, 1956), there has been considerable continuity in the structure of German society and politics: the past cannot be exorcised completely.

Any examination of the historical background of contemporary West German politics must take into consideration a number of important dates which delineate not only regime changes and distinct political styles, but also significant territorial changes. The answer to the question "What is Germany like?" is different depending upon the period used as the point of reference. A crucial political change occurred in 1870, when most of the German areas of Europe were united under Prussian leadership to form the Second German Empire. Previously, the geographic area of Europe where people spoke the German language had been divided politically into a multitude of kingdoms, principalities, and city states; before 1815 almost 400 independent political units existed within the area incorporated into the Empire. Until 1870 Germany did not exist as a state; it was no more than a geographic expression. The Second Empire was a union of twenty-six states. The political system of the Empire combined monarchical

The research has been supported by a grant from the British Social Science Research Council, and was partly written at Yale University under a Ford Foundation Fellowship. I wish to record my indebtedness to Klaus Liepelt, who not only provided the survey data, but also stimulated the intellectual framework of the chapter. I am also grateful to R. Rose, W. Paterson, and W. P. Shively, who offered valuable criticisms of earlier drafts.

109

authoritarian rule, buttressed by a strong civil service and army recruited primarily from the aristocracy and upper-classes, with the semblance of democratic politics. National unification and the formal adoption of universal manhood suffrage gave an increased impetus to the development of national political parties. Constitutional and institutional provisions prevented political parties from effective participation in governments and hindered the development of constructive legislative behavior: in effect, political parties were electoral groups without power in government.

The next important date is 1918, which marked Germany's defeat in the First World War. With the flight of the monarchy to the Netherlands, the imperial regime collapsed, leaving a governmental and institutional vacuum. In its place was created the Weimar Republic, with a popularly elected president and a government answerable to parliament. The suffrage was expanded to include all adults: in addition, the electoral system was changed to proportional representation. One major consequence of military defeat in 1918 was that Germany was forced to cede substantial territorial areas to the new Polish state (the Prussian provinces of Posen and West Prussia and part of Upper Silesia), to Denmark (North Schleswig), and to Belgium (the districts of Eupen and Malmedy), and to re-cede Alsace-Lorraine to France (see Figure 1). The large areas ceded in the east meant that the province of East Prussia was physically separated from the rest of the country by a Polish corridor, and Danzig became a free city.

The third important date is 1933, when the Weimar Republic fell before Adolf Hitler and the Nazi party. Competitive party politics came to an end as the Nazis established a one-party system. The new regime was termed the Third Reich, and became a prime example of totalitarian dictatorship. While the experience of the Third Reich had important consequences for the development of Germany, the absence of competitive party politics means that the main features of the period are outside the terms of reference of this chapter.

The final dates are 1945 and 1949. After six years of war the Third Reich was destroyed in 1945 by military defeat and occupation. One major consequence of defeat was an end to the short-lived unity of Germany. At the Potsdam Conference of 1945 the victorious Allies agreed that the territory east of the Oder and Neisse rivers (East Prusia, the rest of Silesia, and large areas of Brandenburg and Pomerania) should be placed temporarily under Polish administration pending a later peace conference that would determine the fate of the area. However, the expulsion of most of the pre-1945 German population and the international situation since 1945 make it unrealistic to consider the cession as anything else than permanent. For four years the remainder of the country was administered in separate zones by the four victorious allies. While the eastern provinces that formed the Soviet zone of occupation remained apart, eventually to become the Communist-ruled German Democratic Republic (Deutsche Demokratische Republik or DDR), the other three zones were gradually reintegrated socially, economically, and politically. In 1949 they were finally united as the German Federal Republic (Bundesrepublik Deutschland, or BRD).

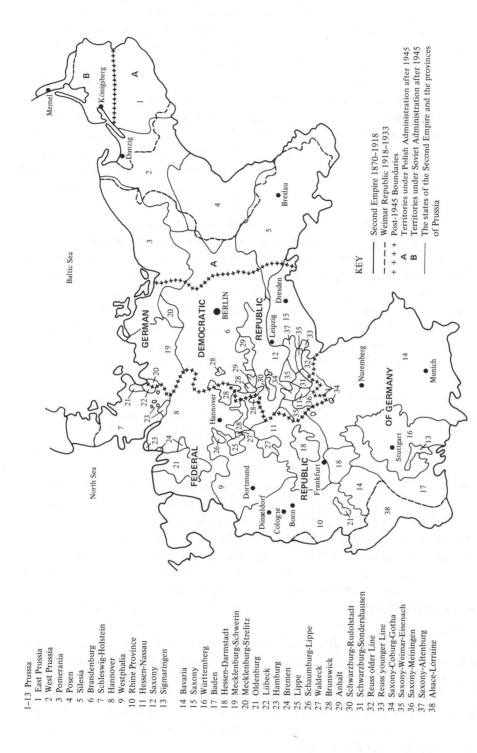

Figure 1: The boundaries of Germany since 1870

Despite the changes in regime and governmental structure and the removal of territory from German administration since 1870, there has been considerable political continuity from the Second Empire to the Federal Republic. For example, the institutional structure of the Weimar Republic, especially with regard to the relationship between the president and the chancellor, bore a striking resemblance to the dual-executive character and practices of its predecessor. The institutional structure of the Federal Republic also owes much to an interpretation and evaluation of institutional practices developed under the earlier regimes. Moreover, from the inception of the Second Empire to the Nazi dissolution of all parties except their own, the party system remained more or less unchanged insofar as the number and nature of *tendances* and ideologies are concerned. The fortunes of individual parties, however, fluctuated dramatically.

Sartori (1966) suggests that after the breakdown of monarchical rule in 1918 and the introduction of party government, the German party system displayed the features of polarized pluralism: that is, it possessed centrifugal drives, ideological rigidity, little elite consensus, no opportunities for practical alternative government, and the growth of irresponsible opposition (see also Stürmer, 1967). In the last "normal" Weimar election of 1928, before the startling rise of the Nazi party (NSDAP), no less than forty-one parties contested the election. The voting strength of the leading three parties was 56.1 percent (54.3 percent in the territory of the Federal Republic). Although fourteen parties contested the first Federal Republic election in 1949, the leading three parties garnered 72.1 percent in the valid votes cast. Sixteen years later their share of the vote had risen to 96.4 percent, despite the electoral presence of seven other parties. Thus there seems to have been after 1949 a radical coalescence of parties: only three of those that emerged or reemerged after 1945 remained by 1969 as serious contenders for parliamentary seats. Moreover, since 1960 only one new party, the National Democrats (NPD), has emerged as a serious challenger.

While pre-1870 data on social-structure and electoral politics are available for analysis, there are considerable problems of comparability. Here we shall follow the conventional practice of taking 1870 as the starting point of politics *in* Germany. Of the other cut-off points listed earlier, all are useful for analyses of some aspects of the development of German politics. However, because political behavior changed very little between the second Empire and the Weimar Republic, despite changes in governmental structure and territorial jurisdiction, it seems more convenient simply to consider pre-1933 Germany as a whole, before moving on to examine the Federal Republic.

The great geographical differences between pre-1933 Germany and the Federal Republic create problems in utilizing aggregate data and in terminology. In the following pages *Germany* or the *Reich* refer to the pre-1933 boundaries, while the post-1945 system is referred to as the *Federal Republic* or *West Germany*. Unless otherwise stipulated, pre-1918 data refer to all the territory administered by the Second Empire; 1918-1933 data to the territory of the Weimar Republic; post-1945 data refer only to the territory of the Federal Republic.

I. Germany Until 1933

A. SOCIAL-STRUCTURE, 1870–1933

It is necessary to concentrate on a selection of social-structure variables that, a priori, ought to be the major lines of partisan cleavage. The standard checklist of social indicators used here are: regional and cultural divisions; religious divisions; rural-urban divisions; and class divisions (Lipset and Rokkan, 1967, p. 9).

1. REGIONALISM

The regional particularism of preunification Germany remained even after the establishment of the Second Empire, especially in the south and west. Berlin never enjoyed the central position and strength of London or Paris: indeed, it was not until the nineteenth-century that Berlin succeeded in becoming the political center of Germany. While political power concentrated in the Prussian capital after 1870, administrative power tended to remain with the constituent states of the federation. Moreover, a substantial German minority remained outside the boundaries of the new state in the Austrian provinces, the Sudetenland, and other German-speaking parts of the Austro-Hungarian Empire. Many Germans still regarded the Hapsburg capital of Vienna as their cultural center. It should be noted that while the regions of the new state may have possessed different cultural traditions, they shared a common linguistic and ethnic background. Significant ethnic peripheries—Poles in West Prussia, Posen, and Upper Silesia, and French in Alsace-Lorraine—were present in the Second Empire, but these were mostly lost in the Treaty of Versailles. They were not salient in domestic politics, although they were sometimes important in foreign politics.

2. RELIGION

The Reformation divided the German people between Protestantism and Catholicism. The German Reich was predominantly Protestant in that Catholics comprised 33 percent of the population. This numerical weakness and the abortive Kulturkampf waged against them by Bismarck persuaded Catholics that they were an embattled minority, and so they decided to organize and reinforce their own social and political movements (see inter alia, Schmidt-Volkmar, 1962; Bachem, 1927; Bornkamm, 1952; Franz, 1954). The geographical distribution of religious strength was very uneven. Most Catholics were clustered in the south and west, while the north and east were overwhelmingly Protestant. This geographical distribution, created by the Reformation, remained basically unchanged over the centuries. Tiny enclaves of a particular religion, created by the choice of the local prelate or ruler during the sixteenth-century, survived intact despite being surrounded by a sea of the other religion (see Milatz, 1965, pp. 70-80).

3. URBAN-RURAL DIVISIONS

In common with other industrializing nations of the West, Germany experienced a great upsurge in population in the late nineteenth-century. Between 1830 and 1930 the aggregate population increase was 140 percent. The most significant population trend was growing urbanization. In 1871 64 percent of the population of the Reich resided in rural communities with less than 2,000 inhabitants. Within a single generation the rural sector dropped to under 40 percent (Table 1: see also Clapham, 1936, p. 278; Stolper, 1967, p. 15). The northeastern provinces of the Reich, including some of the heartlands of Prussia, did not participate in this transformation of society. As late as 1925 the provinces of East and West Prussia, Pomerania, Mecklenburg-Schwerin, and Mecklenburg-Strelitz all had over 50 percent of their population living in communities of under 2,000 inhabitants, with only one-fifth or less of their population employed in industry (see Raupach, 1967). Because place of residence does not always correspond to place and nature of work, an alternative measure of the urban-rural division is the proportion of the population dependent upon agriculture and related occupations. In 1882 42 percent of the Reich population was still employed in agriculture and forestry. By 1925 this figure had declined to 23 percent. The farming population was primarily concentrated in those communities with less than 10,000 inhabitants: there it consisted of 42 percent of the population (Milatz, 1965, pp. 80-81).

TABLE 1:   **Urbanization, 1871–1933**   (in Percentages)

	1871	1880	1890	1900	1910	1925	1933
Cities (100,000 and over)	5	7	12	16	21	27	30
Large towns (20,000-100,000)	8	9	10	13	13	14	14
Small towns (2,000-20,000)	24	25	25	25	25	24	24
Rural areas (under 2,000)	64	59	53	46	40	36	33

Source: *Statistisches Jahrbuch für das Deutsche Reich*

4. INDUSTRIALIZATION

The urbanization of the country was caused by its industrialization. The great upsurge in industrial expansion occurred only after 1871. By World War I the metamorphosis of Germany from a primarily agrarian to an industrial state was achieved (see Clapham, 1936; Stolper, 1967). By 1925 the proportion of people employed in industry and crafts had risen to 41 percent, while those engaged in trade and commerce had increased to 27 percent (Milatz, 1965, pp. 80-85).

In Germany industrialization failed to modify radically the traditional society, and Germany, especially Prussia, remained a country characterized by the values and rigidity of an estate society (*Ständestaat*). The new commercial middle-class did not become dominant socially or politically. The old status divisions were emphasized and formalized by a widespread use of titles within a status hierarchy headed by the military officer corps and the bureaucracy: recruitment to these two professions was overwhelmingly from the traditional aristocracy. Dahrendorf (1967,p. 58) describes the Second Empire as an "industrial feudal society" characterized by a "formalized status hierarchy of a system of social stratification modeled on military or bureaucratic orders of rank." While the fall of the monarchy in 1918 may have produced a constitutional revolution and a reduction in the influence of the aristocracy, it did not mean the disappearance of the *Ständestaat*.

B. CONSTITUTIONAL STRUCTURE AND ELECTORAL LAW

The political system of the Empire had several consequences for the German party system. The introduction of manhood suffrage permitted mass mobilization, but this existed alongside an authoritarian form of Government. The operation of the 1871 constitution revolved around the twin pivots of the emperor and the chancellor. The chancellor, the head of the government, was appointed by the emperor, who was also responsible for foreign and military affairs. The functioning of the federation was achieved through the upper chamber, the Bundesrat, which was composed of delegates from the constituent states. Prussia, because of its size, dominated this body, which deliberated in closed sessions. Within this nexus of power relationships, only the chancellor was responsible in any way to the popularly elected Reichstag; however, it could not directly appoint or remove him. Since electoral victory did not necessarily lead to participation in government, parties had neither opportunity nor incentive to moderate their views in the hope of gaining office.

The multiplication of parties was furthered by the two-ballot electoral system, since the availability of the runoff second ballot reduced the risks of multiparty competition on the first ballot. From 1871 to 1918 members of the Reichstag were elected from single-member constituencies by an absolute majority; if no such majority was obtained, a second or runoff ballot was held later, with only the two leading contenders from the first ballot standing. In 1873 397 electoral districts were established, with each district returning one deputy to the Reichstag. The constituencies were constructed so that, on average, one deputy would represent 100,000 people, with the proviso that each constituent state should have at least one representative. Universal, secret, and direct suffrage to all males aged twenty-five or over, first granted by Bismarck in the North German Confederation in 1867, was adopted (see Milatz, 1965, ch. 1). For a man of Bismarck's political philosophy the granting of universal manhood suffrage and the secret ballot might seem strange. However, he expected its impact to be muffled by the constitutional arrangement of the Empire's institutions and by the constitutional ban on deputies receiving salaries (see Eschenburg, 1959, pp. 53-59). A further barrier was that elections were held on working days. The introduction of the secret ballot did not mean an immediate end to the intimidation of voters (Rosenberg, 1958). To some extent the continuing existence of intimidation was aided by the fact that in the largest state, Prussia, open voting was retained in elections to the state assembly until 1918.

Despite the great increase in population and in geographical mobility, no revision of constituency boundaries was seriously considered until toward the end of World

War I. The collapse of the monarchy in 1918 meant that the proposed redistribution never took place. Thus a rural bias increasingly existed in the electoral system, for the electorate multiplied rapidly in the industrialized areas but remained static or declined in rural areas. This gave conservative parties a much greater advantage in winning seats. By the First World War constituencies ranged in size from 12,990 electors (Deutsch-Krone) to 338,800 (Teltow-Beskow-Storkow).

The elections to the parliaments of the various states were perhaps as important as those to the Reichstag, and none more so than elections to the Prussian parliament, because the Reich chancellor also headed the Prussian government. The Prussian electoral system, introduced in 1849, was based upon status and wealth. It divided the electorate into three categories, according to the taxes they paid. Each category elected one-third of the deputies. It was not a nationally uniform division, for the cutting points varied between constituencies. Thus the whole system was based upon local elites and status groups; in several instances Class I consisted of only one elector. The size of the three electoral groups relative to each other remained fairly constant. In 1913 the distribution of the Prussian electorate was as follows: Class I, 4 percent; Class II, 16 percent; Class III, 80 percent (Finer, 1949, p. 229). Thus, four-fifths of the electorate could elect only one-third of the deputies. Moreover, the system was indirect in that voting for electors took place in small electoral districts of about 750 people. These electors then selected the deputies for the Prussian chamber of deputies (Abge-ordnetenhaus). After 1860 the Prussian electoral law also failed to take population changes into account or to revise constituency boundaries. Stein Rokkan (1962, p. 76) has observed that "it would be difficult to devise an electoral measure more calculated to alienate the lower-classes from the national political system than the one promulgat-ed in Prussia in 1849." While turnout in the 1912 Reichstag election was 84.5 percent, in the 1912 Prussian election it was only 32.8 percent. Although Prussia retained this system until 1918, many of the other states introduced universal, secret, and direct suffrage; Württemberg even introduced proportional representation (Table 2: see also Anderson and Anderson, 1967, pp. 314ff; Gagel, 1958; Lowell, 1896, I, ch. 6; Warren, 1964, pp. 19-24).

The two institutional pivots of the Weimar Republic were the popularly elected Reichstag and the president. The cabinet was intended to be a link between these two bodies, but in practice became dependent upon them and unable to resist demands emanating from either. The presidency, which was given widespread emergency powers, was almost a monarchical surrogate, while the Reichstag, through its ability to appoint and dismiss governments, enjoyed power without responsibility. Neither had executive responsibility. Governments had to be coalitions. The negative orientation of many of the parties toward the regime meant that government were usually unable to exercise executive responsibility.

The particular electoral system introduced also did little to discourage small groups from seeking legislative representation. The Weimar Constitution established thirty-five multimember constituencies under the principal of proportional representation. The suffrage was extended to all adults over the age of twenty. In each constituency an elector could only cast a vote for a party list, without being able to indicate any preferences for individual candidates on that list. Seats in the constituencies were distributed among the parties more or less directly accordingly to the votes won by the party

TABLE 2: **The States in the Second Empire: Population and Franchise**

STATE*	PERCENT OF REICH POPULATION, 1910	FRANCHISE
Prussia (1-13)	61.9	Three-class system based on taxes: open; indirect.
Bavaria (14)	10.6	Secret; direct.
Saxony (15)	7.4	Plural (1 to 4 votes); secret; direct.
Württemberg (16)	3.8	Secret; direct. 69 deputies elected in constituencies; 23 elected by proportional representation.
Baden (17)	3.3	Secret; indirect.
Hessen-Darmstadt (18)	2.0	All taxpayers; secret; indirect.
Mecklenburg-Schwerin (19)	1.0	None. Two estates: knights; districts.
Mecklenburg-Strelitz (20)	0.2	None. Two estates: knights; districts.
Oldenburg (21)	0.7	All taxpayers; secret; indirect.
Lübeck (22)	0.2	Two-class property tax system.
Hamburg (23)	1.6	Eighty deputies elected by direct, secret suffrage; 40 by property owners; 40 by *Notabeln*.
Bremen (24)	0.2	Property-class system. Secret; direct.
Lippe (25)	0.2	Three-class tax system. Direct.
Schaumburg-Lippe (26)	0.1	Two deputies appointed by monarch; 1 elected by clergy; 1 by professors; 3 by cities; 7 by rural communities. Secret; direct.
Waldeck (27)	0.1	Secret; indirect.
Brunswick (28)	0.8	Fifteen deputies elected by cities; 15 by rural communities; 18 by special occupations. Secret; direct.
Anhalt (29)	0.5	Two deputies appointed by monarch; 8 elected by highest taxed landowners; 2 by highest taxed men of commerce and industry; 14 by cities; 10 by rural communities. Secret; indirect.
Schwarzburg-Rudolstadt (30)	0.2	Four deputies elected by highest taxpayers; 12 by universal, secret, direct suffrage.
Schwarzburg-Sondershausen (31)	0.1	Six deputies appointed by monarch; 6 elected by highest taxpayers; 6 by secret, indirect suffrage.
Reuss older Line (32)	0.1	Three deputies appointed by monarch; 2 elected directly by landowners; 7 by secret, indirect suffrage.
Reuss younger Line (33)	0.2	One hereditary deputy; 3 elected by highest taxpayers; 12 by all taxpayers. Secret; direct.
Saxony-Coburg-Gotha (34)	0.3	Secret; indirect.
Saxony-Weimar-Eisenach (35)	0.6	Five deputies elected by highest taxed landowners; 5 by other high taxed citizens; 23 by secret, indirect suffrage.
Saxony-Meiningen(36)	0.4	Four deputies elected by great landowners; 4 by other high taxpayers; 16 by all citizens. Secret; direct.
Saxony-Altenburg (37)	0.4	Nine deputies elected by highest taxpayers; 21 by three class tax system.

*Numbers in parentheses refer to the key in Figure 1.

lists (see Milatz, 1965, pp. 40-51; Ziegler, 1958). Under the Constitution all the constituent states (now called *Länder*) also introduced proportional representation by
party lists for elections to their legislatures, although the method of allocating seats
to party lists varied from *Land* to *Land*.

The method of allocating Reichstag seats to parties was to give each party list in
each constituency one seat for every 60,000 votes it polled; for the election to the
Constituent Assembly in 1919 the total number of seats and the number in each
constituency were predetermined—one seat per 150,000 voters. To deal with surplus
votes constituencies were placed in groups of two or three to constitute a *Wahlkreis-
verband* (constituency association). Excess votes in the constituencies were combined
at this level, and again seats were awarded to party lists for each 60,000 votes polled.
If excess votes still remained, they were combined in a national pool (*Reichsliste*)
where the allocation procedure was repeated; here, however, a final remainder of
30,000 votes would obtain a seat. With constituencies possessing such a large electoral
magnitude (see Rae, 1967), it was relatively easy for very small and new parties to win
their quota of Reichstag seats; normally a total of about 100,000 votes out of 30,000,000
could gain one or two seats for a party. The only restriction placed upon a party was
that it could not be awarded more seats from the *Reichsliste* than it had already won
in the constituencies and *Wahlkreisverbände*. Thus very small parties often failed
to acquire any parliamentary seats.

C. PARTIES AND SOCIAL STRUCTURE

Despite great economic change in the period the party system of 1871 remained set
in the same mold until 1933. At first sight the number and names of pre-1933 German
parties appear multitudinous and confusing. It therefore seems advisable to indicate
at this point those parties that were important in German electoral and governmental
politics. A simplified view of the German party system before 1933 would identify at
least four main groups of parties, each appealing to, and claiming to represent,
specific social groups and subcultures. These four groups are the conservatives,
liberals, Catholics, and socialists. It is important to note that each *tendance* contained,
at least for part of the period, more than one party. The conflict between parties
relatively similar in ideological and programmatic terms gave the party system its
complexity.

During the Second Empire there were two major conservative groups, distinctive
both in their attitude toward the regime and their regional and social support. The
German Conservative party remained fundamentally a party of the Prussian aristocracy in the rural eastern provinces. It was a firm supporter of the monarchy, although
it was hostile to the idea of parliamentary government. It naturally supported high
protective tariffs for agricultural products and was suspicious of industrial and commercial interests, although it accepted the military and colonial expansion that
industrial development had made possible. In addition, the party contained strong

anti-Semitic tendencies since it saw Jews figuring prominently within industry and commerce. Its conservative rival was the *German Reich party*, which found its support among the upper-middle classes, large industrial interests, and, in certain areas, the Catholic aristocracy. The Reich party was much less particularistic than the Conservatives. It originally separated from the Conservatives because of its more pronounced nationalism and its staunch support of Bismarck's policies. Throughout the period it could usually be regarded as a loyal supporter of the government. Several smaller conservative parties also emerged. These were primarily "special interests" parties, tending to promote or defend a specific policy. For example, the *Agrarian Union* (*Bund der Landwirte*) emphasized the protection of agriculture, and the *Economic Union* stressed the need for legislation that would benefit and protect small landowners, shopkeepers, traders, and artisans.

There were also two important liberal parties. The *National Liberals* were similar to the Reich party in their commitment to the national state and the economic and foreign policy of the government, and in their claim to represent large industrial and commercial interests. They emphasized nationalism, the need to subordinate special interests to the national welfare, and generally supported governmental centralization. It is more difficult to give the other liberal grouping a party label, for throughout the period it experienced several splits and mergers, producing new names and programs each time. Generally, however, its supporters may be described as *Progressives*. In their political principles the Progressives were similar to other nineteenth-century liberal parties in Western Europe. They were committed to parliamentary democracy and were opposed to the imperial regime because of its authoritarian nature. They demanded social and political equality, the introduction of direct elections and universal suffrage at both national and state elections, the removal of education from religious control, free trade, and that governments should be responsible to the Reichstag.

The remaining two *tendances* may be discussed more briefly. In 1871 the *Zentrumspartei* (Center party) was formed to protect the interests of the Catholic minority. The *Zentrum* was based on the Catholic religion: thus it sought to embrace all economic interests. Whenever Catholic interests conflicted with government policy, the party presented a united front to the outside world. However, it experienced internal tensions similar to those of other Christian democratic parties when it considered economic issues, which emphasized the differencies between its conservative and social democratic sections. The Socialist *tendance* was represented by the *Social Democratic party* (SPD); like other Marxist parties in Europe, it claimed to be the sole representative of the working-class and advocated nationalization of all means of production. The SPD was hostile to the imperial regime—until 1890 legislation had actively discriminated against the party—though it had never attempted to put its revolutionary precepts into practice. Throughout the regime the SPD also experienced internal tension between its more orthodox Marxist members who refused to cooperate with governments or other parties, and those who were willing to support any legislation that conformed with the party's own program. During the Second Empire there existed smaller parties, which were regionally particularistic or represented national minorities. In general these were hostile to the regime: the more important of these parties are discussed later.

Only two of the six major parties of the Weimar Republic were survivors of the Empire: the SPD and the *Zentrum*. Another, the *Communist* party (KPD), was the result of an ideological split within the SPD. The other three parties were the National People's party, the People's party, and the Democratic party. The *National People's party* (*Deutsch Nationale Volkspartei*, or DNVP) was a merger of the old conservative parties, which had suffered most from the collapse of the old regime. The Conservative party, the Reich party, and several smaller parties united in 1918 to form the DNVP, which also attracted some former National Liberals. The disparate background of its members and the trauma of defeat and the Treaty of Versailles meant that the party's cohesion was continually disturbed by a conflict between a chauvinistic nationalism and a more pragmatic conservatism. The *People's party* (*Deutsche Volkspartei*, or DVP) was based upon the National Liberals, while the *Democratic party* (*Deutsche Demokratische Partei*, or DDP) was the survivor of the Progressive groups. A union of the two liberal groupings was prevented by different programmatic bases and the personal antipathy of some leaders.

A simplified lineage of German parties is given in Figure 2. One outstanding feature of the German party system during the 1920s was the large number of very small and splinter parties that contested elections: some of these also had antecedents in the Second Empire. After 1928 nearly all of these small parties and the conservative and liberal parties declined as an electoral force, as the Nazi party rapidly grew from an insignificant group to become the largest German party (see Milatz, 1965, ch. 5–6).

All the parties described above claimed to represent specific social groups and subcultures. Some parties established subordinate organizations to mobilize more efficiently their potential supporters. The development of the SPD and the *Zentrum* suggest that economic class and religion have been two politically important dimensions of the social-structure. The existence of agrarian and regional-specific parties indicate that these dimensions were also significant influences on the party system.

1. RELIGION

The Catholic minority formed the *Zentrum* in 1871 in order to have a political organization that would protect its interests in what it conceived to be a hostile atmosphere. Under clerical supervision, strong laymen's associations were to provide the organizational underpinning for the Catholic population. Associations such as the *Zentralkomitee der deutschen Katholiken* (established in 1868) and the *Volksverein für das Katholische Deutschland* (1890) were agencies for integrating Catholics of all classes across a whole range of social activities. The Kulturkampf, a policy of active social discrimination waged against the Catholic Church and its members by the government, also gave impetus to the political mobilization of Catholics. While the Kulturkampf was, to all intents and purposes, abandoned by 1879, its cessation did little to diminish the Catholic sense of alienation. For the remainder of the Second Empire the *Zentrum* remained apart from governments and from other parties, tolerated but never playing a positive role.

After 1918 the Bavarian section of the *Zentrum* formed its own group, the Bavarian People's party (BVP), which often pursued distinct strategies and policies. In general the policies of the BVP were more conservative and more agrarian than those of the *Zentrum*. During the Weimar Republic the *Zentrum* participated in governments more often than any other party. Nevertheless, it still remained alienated to some extent from the other parties; Blankenburg (1967, p. 148) describes it as a "foreign body" (see also Morsey, 1960).

While a substantial Catholic vote was given to other parties, virtually all the *Zentrum* vote came from Catholics. The number of Catholics voting for the party tended to decline between the 1870s and the 1920s, probably because of secularization: it has been estimated that betwen 1871 and 1924 the number of Catholics voting for the *Zentrum* ranged from a high of 86.3 percent in 1881 to a low of 48.3 percent in May, 1924 (Schauff 1928, pp. 74, 128–32). The party fared particularly badly in industrial regions in the 1928 election, indicating increasing strains between the economic demands of the Catholic working-class and the cultural autonomy the party had originally been formed to protect. Overall, it seems that the electoral mobilization of Catholics by the *Zentrum* was more successful in those areas where they were the victims of discrimination. In overwhelmingly rural Catholic areas, especially Bavaria, the *Zentrum* and the BVP had to compete against particularistic regional sentiments.

2. ECONOMIC CLASS

The Social Democratic party was formed in 1875 by the merger of two working-class groups. Because of its comprehensive organizational structure and working-class reaction against governmental and administrative discrimination, the SPD's electoral fortunes improved dramatically after the repeal of the anti-Socialist laws in 1890. However, the class cleavage did not override all other cleavages in the party system. The SPD proved unable to establish itself in overwhelmingly Catholic areas or to bridge the gulf between industrial workers and agricultural laborers and peasants. Moreover, no single cohesive or coherent majoritarian-oriented middle-class grouping emerged. A marked emphasis upon status divisions was probably the major motive for the considerable number of middle- and upper-middle-class parties that emerged between 1871 and 1930. Each party tended to represent a particular status group— either national or regional—and developed a distinct program (see Neumann, 1932; Manning, 1949; Hartenstein, 1962; Booms, 1954; Liebe, 1956). Typical were the two liberal parties of the Second Empire, the National Liberal and the Progressives. Both had a very low level of organization, being little more than loose associations of notables. While there was party fragmentation everywhere outside the SPD and the *Zentrum*, none of these Protestant middle-class parties felt any great inclination for a rapprochement with either the Catholic or the laboring classes. Attempts by these parties to incorporate working-class support were sporadic, weak, and in vain (see, for example, Nipperdey, 1963, pp. 187–92). The most important attempt was made through the non-Socialist trade-union federation, *Hirsch-Dunkerschen Gewerkvereine*, founded in 1868. However, once the SPD and the *Zentrum* appeared to mobilize the working-classes politically and in trade unions, these unions were eventually eliminated as serious competitors (see Syrup and Neuloh, 1957). Economic developments did not have a significant effect on the formation of the party system. The Industrial Revolution failed to destroy the basic social-structure and values of preindustrial Germany. The party system, therefore, reflected older cleavages as well as the merging class interests.

3. URBAN-RURAL DIVISIONS

The decline of the agricultural sector of the economy after unification reduced the possibility of a significant farmers' party arising. Numerous rural parties did appear, but were either regionally particularistic or were also distinctive because of non-rural economic or "ideological" reasons. An example of the former is the Bavarian Farmers League (*Bayerischer Bauernbund*) and of the latter the conservative Agrarian Union (*Bund der Landwirte*) and the more liberal German Farmers League (*Deutschen Bauernbund*) during the Second Empire. Attempts to form a major agrarian party of the Scandinavian or East European type failed because of the strength of regional loyalties, the success of the *Zentrum* in mobilizing rural Catholics, and the ability of the conservative parties to win and retain rural support. For example, large land-owners, especially in the eastern regions of Prussia, proved successful in mobilizing their rural hinterland to defend both their economic position and traditional cultural values. The deepening agricultural crisis of 1880 and the subsequent introduction of protective tariffs strengthened the conservative position in rural areas. In the 1912 Reichstag election fifty-one of the fifty-five deputies of the German Conservative party came from Prussian constituencies, and of these, forty-five were Junker aristocrats from the eastern regions of Prussia (Schieder, 1962, p. 121). The conservative appeal to agrarian interests gave it an electoral base, but it was a base in constant decline relative to the total German electorate. Shut off from the mass of German voters, the leaders of the conservative party in the 1920s, the DNVP, thought they could use the popularity of the Nazis and their mass organization as a means of expanding their electoral base in the same way as they had attempted to use the Agrarian Union in rural areas during the last decades of the Second Empire.

In the 1920s rural discontent aided the emergence of several splinter parties and later benefited the NSDAP. There seemed to be a permanent agricultural crisis from the middle of the 1920s until the fall of the Weimar regime. Peasant discontent broke out into direct action in Holstein in 1926. Throughout the country peasant hostility toward the regime increased. There was also an organizational fragmentation of the peasantry: they were later absorbed by the Nazis. This pattern was particularly notice-able in Protestant rural areas. The Nazis were the first national party able to exploit the antiurban and anticapitalist sentiments of the German peasantry. In fact, Protestant peasants were voting for the party to such an extent that by 1930 the NSDAP's electoral clientele was predominantly rural even before the party turned its organizational attention in that direction (see, inter alia, Loomis and Beegle 1946, pp. 55-60; Milatz, 1965; Stoltenberg, 1962; O' Lessker, 1968; Heberle, 1963). The socialist parties played a very minor role in rural areas. The Social Democrats had little rural organization and, moreover, little inclination to attempt the political mobilization of rural areas.

Instead, they tended to regard all rural dwellers as petty bourgeoisie. This attitude contrasts very strongly, for example, with the active and pragmatic rural strategy of the Norwegian Labor party (Nilson, 1954).

4. REGIONALISM

All the parties were regional to some extent, depending upon the spatial distribution of the economic or cultural groups supporting them. In this sense some parties and groups—for example, the Socialists and Catholics—constituted social and political peripheries. The Conservative party, primarily the political spokesman of the Prussian aristocracy, was probably more concerned with the retention of its old ascriptive values and privileges, and hence often found itself in conflict with government policy. It was the Reich party and the liberal parties that supported unification and subsequent centralization measures most ardently. Before 1870 nationalism and the dream of unification had been strongly advocated by liberals. After unification German liberalism was weakened and fragmented by a conflict between its desire for national unity and its belief in a democratic parliamentary framework. The constitutional format of the Reich was one factor that helped weaken liberal unity. The Progressive groups, which suffered much fragmentation before 1918, supported national unity but were hostile to the imperial regime because of its authoritarian characteristics. It was the more conservative National Liberals, supported by the larger industrial and commercial interests of the western regions, who were probably closer than any other party to the political and constitutional spirit of the Reich. Although the National Liberals were the most powerful party in the postunification years, they declined as an electoral force after the 1870s.

The unification of the country under Prussian leadership meant that to some extent regional loyalties were translated into party divisions. Apart from ethnic minorities, e.g., the Poles of West Prussia and Upper Silesia and the French of Alsace-Lorraine, very few significant regional parties emerged. The most prominent and durable were the Bavarian Farmers League and the Guelph party in the Prussian province of Hanover; after 1918 the latter changed its name to the German Hanoverian party. A greater proliferation of regional-cum-splinter parties occurred during the mid-1920s, when such parties appeared in Schleswig-Holstein, Brunswick, Baden, Württemberg, Hesse, and Thuringia. These parties were supported in part by people who found it difficult to adjust to and accept a national system of party oppositions, and they were particularly prominent in rural areas. Their appearance, in fact, marked the fragmentation of the national party system, preceding its absorption by the Nazis.

D. PARTIES AND ELECTIONS

The federal system of the Second Empire, the electoral laws of many states (especially Prussia), and the absence of redistricting both in the Empire and in Prussia had consequences both for the governmental structure and the behavior of political parties (see Molt, 1963, pp. 76–78; Muncy, 1944, pp. 216–19). Popular participation was discouraged. Turnout in national elections remained below 70 percent until 1887. The range in turnout was from 51.8 percent in 1871 to 84.5 percent in 1912, with the median 65.7 percent. Predemocratic and Prussian values were superimposed upon the industrial society. The survival of these values prevented the development of a society in which a commercial and industrial middle-class and the working-class could play a positive role. The parties became encapsulated, tending to retreat back into themselves, emphasizing through ideology how different they were from each other. Roth (1963, pp. 12; 8) has commented that the attempt by the SPD to create a distinct, insulated subculture—where the party would be "home, fatherland, and religion"—was essentially an exercise in "negative integration." This could be said to have been the ideal of other parties also. Fraenkel (1958, p. 178) has suggested that the insulation and isolation of the SPD was in fact aided by the introduction of the secret ballot. However, only the SPD and the Catholic *Zentrum* approached this ideal of organizational self-sufficiency. Overall, to use Loewenberg's (1966, p. 12) summary, "the many-sided sectional, ideological, religious and economic differences in the incompletely unified nation gained full expression in the party system."

This polarized, fragmented, multiparty system survived the fall of the Second Empire virtually unscathed. While the *tendances* may have remained operative, however, each political strand tended to experience further fragmentation: the 1920's showed how parties may be agencies of disintegration rather than integration (this point is emphasized by Daalder, 1966, p. 66). This splintering was due in part to the constitutional provisions and to the adoption of proportional representation. Between 1919 and 1928 the number of parties contesting elections separately rose steadily. The number of splinter parties reached its peak in the 1928 election, which also saw the lowest turnout of the period. It was the non-Marxist, nonconfessional parties that suffered fragmentation and, eventually, virtual annihilation; these parties lacked the organizational cohesion of an encapsulated movement. The *Zentrum* suffered from the "marauding" of regional and rural groups, especially in Bavaria, while the SPD had to contend with the more radical KPD. The political strength of the working-class was further weakened in the 1920s by a decline in the membership of the trade unions of almost 50 percent (Hartwich, 1967, pp. 67–71). Nevertheless, the share of the vote polled by the two Catholic parties and the SPD remained relatively high, declining from 48.7 percent in 1920 to 40.5 percent in November, 1932, and to 37.1 percent in 1933.

The coalescence of splinter parties and of nonvoters was achieved in the 1930s by the NSDAP. Generally it seems that the Nazi penetration of the electorate was more successful in the more Protestant and more rural areas. By contrast, the Nazi appeal was weaker in overwhelmingly Catholic rural regions and in those urbanized areas with large numbers of industrial workers (see Bracher, 1964). In the November, 1932 election the combined vote for the Nazis and the National People's party by region was as follows: Berlin 31.3 percent; Federal Republic territory, 37.2 percent; DDR territory, 45.1 percent; and in areas now part of Poland and Russia, 51.6 percent. The overall share of the vote was 41.4 percent. While it is true that the NSDAP did benefit from new voters, the increase in turnout that occurred in the 1930s was by no means constant throughout the country. It seems safer to assume that the previous nonvoters who in the 1930s voted for the Nazis were primarily from the same social groups as those electors who were already voting for the party. In the 1920s turnout was higher in Catholic than in Protestant areas; turnout in Protestant rural areas was especially low. Patterns of electoral participation remained constant in most Catholic areas, but changed dramatically in most Protestant regions. Furthermore, in most rural districts, irrespective of religious denomination, the combined vote of the SPD and KPD remained fairly stable (see, for example, Bracher, 1964; Bracher et al., 1962; Franz, 1957; Hagmann, 1946). Following their successful absorption of the support of most of the smaller parties, the Nazis brought the polarized party system to an end by their dissolution of all political organizations bar their own.

There are several techniques for measuring trends and fluctuations in party strength (see Rose and Urwin, 1970). The results of the application of some of these techniques to the German parties before 1933 are presented in Table 3. The criteria for including a party are twofold. It must have contested at least three elections, as this is the minimum for which a meaningful regression line can be formed, and it must have received 5 percent of the vote at least once, since parties that never reach this level are limited in their potential to fluctuate. One simple measure of fluctuation in party support is the elasticity of voting strength, which can be indicated by the percentage difference between the largest and the least share of the vote a party obtained at elections in each period. In nearly every instance the elasticity of German parties is high. Only the *Zentrum*/Bavarian People's party during the Weimar Republic was inelastic. The high range in vote for the SPD before 1918 and the NSDAP in the Weimar Republic reflects growth from negligible proportions to become the largest party in the system. The elasticity measure may give a distorted picture of a party's electoral strength because of one extreme result. This can be controlled by referring to the normal variability of a party's vote, i.e., the standard deviation. The figures in Table 3 confirm the variability of the election results, particularly those of the Weimar Republic. Only four results are below 4 percent, those for the two conservative parties of the Second Empire and those for the *Zentrum* in each time period. The relative consistency of those four results emphasizes the limited but constant electoral base of these parties. The high figures for the pre-1918 SPD and the NSDAP again illustrate the rapid growth of these parties. An analysis of trends in party support slightly modifies the picture given by the earlier measures. Trends in party strength are indicated by regression lines showing both the magnitude of any trend and its direction. Trends are calculated on a per annum basis: the cumulative trend is simply the multiplication of the per annum rate of change by the electoral lifetime of the party. Change at the rate of 0.25 percent of the vote per annum is taken here as the minimum rate of meaningful change. Only two of the parties of the Second Empire change at a rate greater than this: the upward trend of the SPD is matched by the downward trend of the National Liberals. Once again the German Conservatives show the least amount of change, the SPD the greatest. In the Weimar period all the parties show meaningful rates of change. The NSDAP and the KPD show upward trends. Again the *Zentrum* displays the least amount of change, and the NSDAP the greatest. Overall, these simple measures indicate that the variability of party strength during the Weimar Republic was considerably greater than in the Second Empire.

TABLE 3:   **Trends and Fluctuations in the Party System, 1871-1933, in Percentages**

	RANGE OF VOTE			TREND		
	Highest	Lowest	Elasticity	Per Annum	Cumu-lative	Standard Deviation
Second Empire						
German Conservative party	16.3 (1881)	7.0 (1874)	9.3	—0.06	—2.5	2.8
Reich Party	13.6 (1878)	3.0 (1912)	10.6	—0.17	—7.0	2.9
Zentrum	27.9 (1874)	16.4 (1912)	11.5	—0.15	—6.1	3.3
National Liberal	29.7 (1874/7)	12.5 (1898)	17.2	—0.42	—17.2	6.8
Progressive*	23.2 (1881)	7.8 (1878)	15.4	—0.06	—2.5	4.6
Social Democrat	34.8 (1912)	3.0 (1871)	31.8	0.82	33.6	11.2
Weimar Republic						
National Socialist	43.9 (1933)	2.6 (1928)	41.3	4.13	37.2	17.4
National People's party	20.5 (Dec 1924)	5.9 (Jul 1932)	14.6	—0.62	—8.7	5.4
People's party	13.9 (1920)	1.1 (1933)	12.8	—0.62	—8.7	4.5
Zentrum/Bavarian People's party	19.7 (1919)	13.9 (1933)	5.8	—0.32	—4.5	1.8
Democratic party	18.5 (1919)	0.9 (1933)	17.6	—0.90	—12.6	5.5
Social Democrat	37.9 (1919)	18.3 (1933)	19.6	—0.65	—9.1	6.1
Independent Social Democrat	17.9 (1920)	0.1 (1928)	17.8	—1.59	—14.3	7.7
Communist	16.9 (Nov 1932)	2.1 (1920)	14.8	0.77	10.0	4.4

*Including all the various splinter parties that incorporated the terms "liberal" or "progressive" into their name.

II.   The Federal Republic

Immediately following the first election to the Bundestag in 1949, many observers believed that the old multiparty system was being reestablished. There were a large number of parties contesting the election, and they had social and programmatic bases apparently similar to those of the pre-Nazi parties. Such comments did not appreciate the social and political changes brought about by the Nazis and the reaction to Nazism. These developments have culminated in a predominantly two-party system, with one small party preventing the two major parties from holding all the parliamentary seats. The transformation of the party system is greater than that of the social-structure, although obviously the more beneficial contemporary economic climate detracts from the lure of radical politics. Moreover, since radical economic change after 1870 did not significantly affect the overall nature of the earlier Reich party system, it seems hardly likely that economic reasons alone can explain the divergence between the Weimar and Federal Republic party systems. Thus, it is advisable first to consider the political events of the post-1945 years as they influenced the development of the West German party system.

A. THE PARTY SYSTEM

Just as the political events of 1933 destroyed the old multiparty system, so the political events of the 1945–1949 period played a primary role in determining the nature of the postwar party system. The present-day party system is due in no small measure to the policies of the Military Occupation authorities (see Loewenberg, 1968). In all four Occupation zones four parties that applied for licenses to operate were permitted to organize and carry on political activities. Two were the old working-class parties, the Social Democrats (SPD) and the Communists (KPD), and two were new combinations. The Christian Democratic Union (CDU) was a union of practicing Catholics (mostly associated with the pre-1933 *Zentrum*) and Protestant Conservatives. The Bavarian wing retained a distinct organization and called itself the Christian Social Union (CSU), although for most purposes the two parties can be regarded as one; in the following pages the term CDU refers to both parties unless otherwise stipulated. The fourth licensed party was the Free Democratic party (FDP), which was a combination of the old liberal parties. Other "potential" parties were hindered by the different policies adopted by the Occupation authorities. The French, for example, refused to allow regional or minor parties to operate in their zone. All the Occupation authorities banned parties specifically appealing to refugees from the eastern territories. The potential for a successor party to the NSDAP was hindered by the disenfranchisement of former Nazis. This was partially lifted in 1948, though in any case such parties or groups were discriminated against, receiving permission to operate only in the British zone and a few areas in the American zone (on Allied policies see, inter alia, Zink, 1957; Willis, 1962; Ebsworth, 1960; Scammon, 1953).

The policies adopted by the Allies meant that only the original four licensed parties were in a position to contest the 1949 election in every *Land*. This Allied decision gave three of these parties an advantage over others that they never lost. The KPD's scope for expansion was increasingly limited by the new territorial-geographical cleavage between the Federal Republic and the Democratic Republic. The forced amalgamation of the KPD and SPD and the subordination of the remaining parties to Communist control in the Russian zone contributed to the steady decline of the KPD in West Germany (see Weber, 1970). Being able to operate in a political vacuum, the licensed parties were able to assimilate most of the political *tendances* that existed. Through their own organizational ability and the tendency of any working party system to produce its own inertia, they proved capable of resisting challenges from other parties once licensing had been abolished.

Several other factors have contributed to the development of the post war party system. Because of the Weimar experience the 1949 Basic Law permits declaring parties unconstitutional if they are deemed to be working for the overthrow of the "free and democratic order." Two parties, the KPD and the neo-Nazi Socialist Reich party (SRP), have been banned under this constitutional provision by the Federal Constitutional Court. The 5 percent clause in the electoral law has proved to be as efficient as a plurality system in raising the threshold of representation for the smaller parties (Rae, 1967, pp. 111-13). The Party Act of 1967 allows for supervision of party statutes and structures to ensure that they conform to a democratic framework: moreover, it allocates both state financial aid and broadcasting time to parties on a formula determined by their size. Finally, the political tactics and nature of the leading party, the CDU, must be taken into account. Adenauer's skill as a broker-politician, the economic revival that was attributed to Erhard, the successful techniques the party adopted for marketing its policies—all enabled the CDU to become the first democratic party to collect under one umbrella most of the weakly organized groups to the right of the SPD. It thus became a major nonsocialist, nonauthoritarian party on a nonconfessional basis. The original conception of a Protestant-Catholic union has also been maintained in the CDU; a major guiding principle of allocating positions within the party is that there should be proportionality between the two denominations (see Heidenheimer, 1960; Wieck, 1963; Merkl, 1962).

While the contemporary party system differs considerably from that of the 1920s, it has a genealogical descent from its predecessor. The lineage of the contemporary party system is illustrated in Figure 2. While aggregate voting figures must be treated with caution, it can be seen from Table 4 that there is a similarity between the voting strengths of the major groupings in the two periods. Analyses of change in both the interwar and the post-1945 periods in competitive party systems in Western Europe and Anglo-America emphasize that in both time periods the overall extent of change and fluctuations in both individual party strength and in party systems is limited (Rose and Urwin, 1970; Urwin and Rose, 1970). On nearly every indicator of change utilized in these analyses, the German party system shows greater change than the median in both time periods. France is the only other country to be similarly volatile.

The high rate of change in the Weimar Republic reflected a party system in the process of disintegration. By contrast, the high rate of change in the West German party system after 1949 reflects greater stability, that is the disappearance of smaller parties and the coalescence of supporters into the two biggest parties. No other party, apart from the FDP, has been able to survive nationally as a continuous electoral force

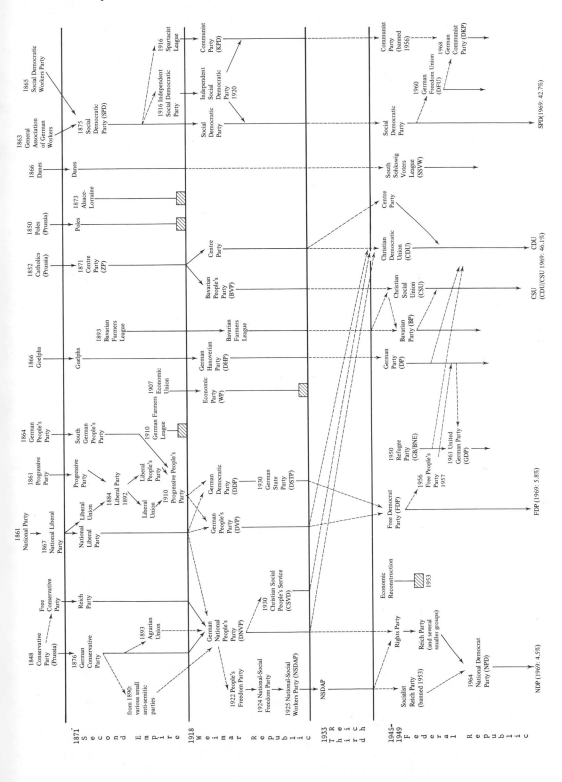

Figure 2: The Genealogy of German Parties

Source : Adapted from Faul, 1960, p. 116.

between 1949 and 1969 (on the smaller parties see Meyn, 1965; Lange, 1955). The
change has not abolished all differences in the social bases of support. The core areas
of CDU and SPD support tend to remain those where their Weimar predecessors had
their strongholds. In 1949 the CDU was still primarily a Catholic party: apart from
Schleswig-Holstein very few differences occur between the geographical distribution of

TABLE 4: **Electoral Strength of Party Groupings in the Weimar Republic (Federal
Republic Territory Only) and the Federal Republic (Selected Elections), in Percentages**

			1920	1928	1949	1961	1969
1.	Working-class parties						
	Social Democrats		21.1	26.9	29.2	36.2	42.7
	Communists		1.8	8.6	5.7	—	—
	Independent Social Democrats		13.8	—	—	—	—
	Others		—	—	—	1.9	0.6
		TOTAL	36.7	35.5	34.9	38.1	43.3
2.	Liberal middle-class parties						
	Peoples' Party (DVP)		12.4	8.7	—	—	—
	Democratic Party (DDP)		8.2	4.8	—	—	—
	Free Democrats (FDP)		—	—	11.9	12.8	5.8
		TOTAL	20.6	13.5	11.9	12.8	5.8
3.	Catholic conservative bloc						
	(a) Catholic parties						
	Zentrum		20.4	17.6	3.1	—	—
	Bavarian People's party (BVP)		7.6	5.6	—	—	—
	(b) Protestant National People's party (DNVP)		10.5	9.8	—	—	—
	conservative middle-class parties—small						
	parties		3.5	12.2	8.2	—	—
	(c) Christian Democratic Union/Christian Social						
	Union (CDU/CSU)		—	—	31.0	45.3	46.1
		TOTAL	42.0	45.2	42.3	45.3	46.1
4.	Extreme Right						
	National Socialists (NSDAP)		—	3.3	—	—	—
	Rights Party (DRP)		—	—	1.8	—	—
	Reich Party (DRP)		—	—	—	0.8	—
	National Democrats (NPD)		—	—	—	—	4.5
	Others		—	0.5	—	—	—
		TOTAL	—	3.8	1.8	0.8	4.5

its vote and that of the *Zentrum* in 1928. The geographical expansion of the CDU to
become a nationally competitive party did not occur until after the Federal Republic
has been established. The critical period for the realignment of the party system is not
the hiatus between 1933 and 1949, but the period between 1949 and 1953. In the 1960s
constituencies where the CDU tended to get its highest voting support were still predominantly Catholic rural areas. By contrast there were no overwhelmingly SPD areas,
and the party was exceptionally weak only in Catholic rural areas. SPD support has
tended to come more from those industrial areas that are less affected by other social
structure cleavages (on voting support in the 1950s see Linz, 1959; Hartenstein and
Liepelt, 1962; Heidenheimer, 1957; von der Heydte and Sacherl, 1955).

The expansion of the two major parties beyond their core groups means that they are less ideologically cohesive and less committed to a particular subculture. This has presented the parties with the problem of reconciling the interests of their central core with the need to cater to those new followers who may not be so intensely committed to the party. A lower level of partisan commitment can affect the electoral stability of a party; it has been suggested that the intensity of party identification decreased during the 1960s (see Wildenmann and Kaltefleiter, 1966, pp. 556-65; Wildenmann, 1968). Despite their search to attract and secure new followers, both parties have been constrained to ensure the retention of their traditional voting support. Parties like the CDU and SPD, which originated from clearly defined social groupings, are more likely to possess the necessary organizational self-sufficiency to achieve this with relatively little trouble, but only as long as no other party is associated with, or had traditionally been competing for, the support of the same social groups.

The problem of whether to concentrate its resources on its central core or on "floaters" has been more acute in the SPD than in the overtly confederal CDU. In the Weimar Republic the SPD had an advantage over most other parties in possessing a clearly defined electoral base. But the post-1949 challenge of the CDU, capable of reaching a majority, with its social, economic, and political bases of support becoming as prominent as the Christian element, has meant that electoral success can no longer be obtained merely by mobilizing core supporters. Hence the most serious problem for the SPD has been to extend its appeal to the middle-classes and Catholic workers who largely identified themselves with the CDU (see Linz, 1959, pp. 44-45). It should be remembered, however, that the SPD has probably never been so working-class as its popular image has suggested; Neumann (1932, pp. 28-29) claimed that even before 1933 the SPD gained 40 percent of its vote from the middle-classes. The steady growth of the SPD share of the vote from 29 percent in 1949 to nearly 43 percent in 1969 raises the question of whether the party is making inroads into the Catholic and middle-class electorate, and so becoming a major and enduring challenger to the CDU. The SPD believes that this is so, attributing success to such factors as the changed emphasis of the 1959 Bad Godesberg party program, the reversal of the party's foreign policy in 1960, the 1964 Concordat with the Catholic Church regulating education, and its participation in government after 1966.

In the late 1960s, however, each of the major parties evinced a concern with the electoral support of a new nationalist right-wing party, the National Democratic Party (NPD), founded in 1964. The significance of the NPD rests in part upon the volatile nature of the party system, and also upon its echoing of past social and political divisions and attitudes and their possible reemergence in the party system (see Liepelt, 1967). The National Democrats are the most serious neo-Nazi movement since the demise of the Socialist Reich party in 1952; they are also the only new challengers to the two major parties to emerge since the early 1950s. Between 1966 and 1968 the party enjoyed a significant but modest success in *Länder* elections. In the 1969 national election, however, the NPD failed to gain either 5 percent of the vote or any seats in the Bundestag. The party's performance in the late 1960s emphasized the resistance of the new party system to an outside challenge rather than the persistence of old ideologies.

B. SOCIAL STRUCTURE

1. Religion

The eastern territories of the Reich that became the German Democratic Republic or were ceded to Poland were overwhelmingly Protestant. In the territory of the Federal Republic the two religious confessions were more evenly balanced. In 1961 just over 50 percent of the West German population was formally classified as Protestant (mainly Lutheran), while nearly 46 percent was Roman Catholic. The high level of church membership is formal rather than significant: everyone must by law belong to a church. The procedure for opting out of church membership is cumbersome and is in any case disapproved of by the society. Separation of Church and state does not exist. By means of a 10 percent surcharge on income tax the churches are guranteed a regular and substantial income. Although church attendance remains fairly high, a greater degree of secularization has accompanied the establishment of numerical parity. Religious differences today do not have the same degree of bitterness and hostility as in Germany's past. The Christian Democratic Union has been able to appeal successfully to both Protestants and Catholics, while the percentage of SPD support that has come from Catholics has been quite substantial (see Hartenstein and Liepelt, 1962, p. 49; Rose and Urwin, 1969, p. 59). The geographical distribution of the two confessions remains basically unchanged from that of previous centuries (see Table 5). Most Catholics are clustered in the south and west; the northern regions remain overwhelmingly Protestant.

TABLE 5: **Religious Distribution of Population 1961, by Lander**

LAND	% PROTESTANT	% CATHOLIC
Schleswig-Holstein	88.2	5.6
Hamburg	76.6	7.4
Lower Saxony	76.9	18.8
Bremen	84.1	9.9
Hesse	63.4	32.1
North Rhine-Westphalia	43.5	52.1
Rhineland-Palatinate	41.9	56.2
Saar	24.8	73.3
Baden-Württemberg	48.9	46.8
Bavaria	26.5	71.2
Federal Republic Total	50.3	45.5

Source: Sänger and Liepelt, 1965.

2. Economic Class

From the ruin of 1945 the so-called West German "economic miracle" has made the Federal Republic one of the most economically prosperous nations in the world (see, inter alia, Wallich, 1955; Arndt, 1967). By the 1960s the Federal Republic had become the third largest industrial and the second largest trading nation in the world. This new affluence was achieved more rapidly and was distributed among the population more equitably than theretofore. It completed the modernization process begun in the nineteenth-century, which had progressed slowly and unevenly until greatly accelerated by the experiences of totalitarianism and war. Dahrendorf (1967) suggests that the industrial revolution did not succeed in modernizing Germany, but that the traditional social and political structures simply "absorbed" the economic changes. Modernization came about primarily because much of the traditional social-structure and value system was destroyed by the Nazis: the successful erosion of such practices was necessary if they wished to maximize their control of the country and stabilize their regime (see also Schoenbaum, 1966). Economic expansion after 1945 has afforded numerous opportunities for rapid social mobility and advancement.

While an emphasis upon status distinctions is still a feature of the contemporary West German society, the combination of rapid economic growth after 1945 and social mobility and advancement has given it a character different from that of its predecessors. This combination has helped to satisfy individual desires and has enabled the new constitutional system to consolidate itself and provide benefits for the various interests in the society. In 1961 the occupational structure of West Germany, in percentages of the total labor force, was: self-employed middle-class, 11 percent; farmers, 9 percent; salaried employees and officials, 30 percent; manual workers, 48 percent; farm laborers, 2 percent. The changed class structure means that no party can hope to enjoy electoral success without the support of a substantial part of the urban and industrial groups. On the other hand, workers of the type envisaged by Marx are not numerous enough for a straightforward class appeal to succeed: electorally, some recruitment from middle-class groups is essential. Yet the complex structure of rankings that still exists within the West German middle classes makes it difficult for one party to unite all the middle-class groups behind it.

3. URBAN-RURAL DIVISIONS

While population in West Germany has risen from 48 million in 1950 to 58 million in 1967, the rural population has declined still further. By 1967 only 21 percent of the population lived in communities with under 2,000 inhabitants. A 1964 survey showed that less than one-half of the residents of seven large urban centers had been born there (INFAS, 1964). Moreover, the growth of suburbs, dormitory areas, and improved transport facilities means that a considerable number of rural and semirural residents actually work in urban industrial environments. Inevitably, this has important consequences for the social-structure of these communities (see Dickinson, 1959). A higher rural birthrate does not counteract the migration, particularly of young people, to the cities and towns; indeed, a higher rural birthrate may even induce movement because of the lack of job opportunities in the countryside. The decline of agriculture since 1945 has accelerated even more rapidly. Its share of the labor force of the Federal Republic declined from 22 percent in 1950 to 11 percent in 1967. The rural sector is the only one that has not absorbed any part of the great population increase. On the contrary, it has always provided a labor reservoir for the expanding urban manufacturing and service industries (see, inter alia, Lütge, 1966; Franklin, 1969, ch. 2). The most important political consequence has been a reduction in the political influence of the farmer, although this influence has always been more significant than actual numbers have warranted.

4. REGIONALISM AND THE TERRITORIAL DIVISION OF THE REICH

Regional and local community ties were weakened by Nazi practices and by wholesale population movements during and after the war. The Allied governments dismantled the state of Prussia and created a new pattern of *Länder* a few of which, such as North-Rhine Westphalia, were completely artificial. Each of these *Länder* had elected a government and legislature before the establishment of the Federal Republic in 1949. The federal constitution of the new state has ensured the limited survival of regional loyalties and autonomy within a system that, in its broad outlines, is similar to the institutional pattern established by the Second Empire in 1871 (see, inter alia, Jacob, 1963; Loewenberg, 1966; Merkl, 1959; Cole, 1966). But the small regional parties that were prominent during the early years of the Federal Republic have faded into complete insignificance.

Before 1945 Berlin served as a center for the German Reich. But the postwar division of the old Reich and the geographical isolation of Berlin from the Federal Republic have meant that there is no undisputed metropolitan center to act as a political magnet. While central to the Federal Republic as a political issue, Berlin (including West Berlin) is now very much a periphery in the daily life of West Germany (see Merritt, 1966). The traditional pre-1871 pattern of "peripheries without a center" has reemerged, stimulated by formal constitutional and institutional arrangements, to produce what Edinger (1968, pp. 9–15) has called a "polycentric society."

Newspaper circulation provides a simple index of polycentrism. While ownership is concentrated, the majority of daily papers are local regional newspapers. In 1968 the total circulation of 603 daily newspapers was over 24 million, but only one, the *Bild Zeitung*, with a circulation of almost 5 million, could be called a national newspaper with a mass readership. Forty-four newspapers with a daily circulation of over 100,000 were published in no less than thirty-one cities. Transportation shows a similar picture. No single airport, for example, enjoys a predominance in commercial airline services; in 1969 the largest, Frankfurt, carried only 26 percent of all commercial flights and 36 percent of all passenger traffic. Finally, it should be noted that ethnic-linguistic homogeneity in the Federal Republic is even greater than in the old German Reich. Today, the only recognized ethnic minority among German citizens is the tiny Danish population in the north of Schleswig-Holstein. Furthermore, the prewar Jewish population of about 550,000 has virtually disappeared due to its systematic persecution during the Third Reich and to emigration after 1945 to Israel. In 1964, for example, only 20,000 Jews, mainly elderly, remained in West Germany: in the same year only 200 Jewish children were born (*Statistisches Jahrbuch*, 1964, p. 90).

The new territorial boundaries created by the imposed separation of the German Reich into two states after 1945, together with the forced cession of East Prussia, Pomerania, and Silesia to Poland, had a profound effect upon West German politics. The desire for reunification is something to which nearly every West German political leader pays lip service. The intensity of feeling remains at a very low level, and expectations of reunification have increasingly declined (see Edinger, 1968, pp. 88–93). In 1961 reunification was regarded as the most important issue by a majority of people; by 1969 it ranked no higher than eighth (*Die Zeit*, 1969). With the establishment of a rival German state, the German Democratic Republic, controlled by the Communist party, the social and ideological cleavage between the radical left of the Weimar Republic and other political forces has become complete. The adherence of West Germany to NATO and EEC, and of the DDR to the Warsaw Pact and Comecon, has removed the old cleavage to the sphere of international relations. A major consequence of the removal of the Communist "opposition of principle" (Kirchheimer, 1957) to a position outside the boundaries of the Federal Republic was a diminution in the salience of other social cleavages, because of the desire to present a united society. Moreover, the aggressive external opposition of the Communist party has led the SPD to deemphasize and then reject the common ideological heritage it shared with Communism.

The division of the Reich also created a new social group within the Federal Republic. Massive waves of refugees were ejected from or fled the once-German lands beyond the Oder-Neisse line that were placed under Polish and Russian jurisdiction. In 1939 nearly 10 million Germans lived in these regions: in 1957 the recognized German minority was given as only 65,000 (Dickinson, 1961, p. 96). A further 3.6 million refugees came from East Germany, and others from the Czechoslovakian Sudetenland. By 1962 one resident in five of the Federal Republic was not a native of West Germany. These refugees were originally settled in rural localities, the only areas with space to accommodate them. There was, however, no prospect of employment nor of easy assimilation into tightly knit rural communities. Movement to the urban areas for employment aided assimilation, as well as providing labor for the expanding West German industries (see *Demoskopie*, 1964; Lemberg and Edding, 1959). A further important factor was the Equalization of Burdens Law of 1952, which taxed all property that had escaped war damage up to 50 percent of its value. The money collected from this tax was to be redistributed to the refugees as compensation for losing their homes and property. Compensation was to be paid in installments spread over a period of thirty years.

In 1953 two related laws were enacted. The first was designed to ensure that no *Land* bore an unfair share of the burden of compensation. The other, the Expellees and Refugees Law, had three objectives; to unify *Länder* laws in this sphere; to give refugees from the German Democratic Republic equality with the refugees from Poland and Czechoslovakia; and to enable refugee farmers to be resettled on the land. Only the *Länder* of Schleswig-Holstein (32.1 percent) and Lower Saxony (29.6 per cent) now have refugee populations much higher than the national average of 21 percent, and only the small areas of the Saar (3.8 percent) and the Rhineland-Palatinate (11.8 percent) are noticeably below the average.

A desire by refugees to return to their homelands, as well as the danger of remaining as a discontented and unassimilated group, could have posed problems for West German politics. However, as early as 1956 a survey indicated that less than one-half of the expellees and refugees signified a willingness to return to the Oder-Neisse and Sudetenland territories, if this ever became possible (Kraus and Kurth, 1956, pp. 178–79, 204–05). A new political party, the GB/BHE, emerged in the early 1950s to represent the refugees and expellees; it could win votes from only one-quarter of its potential constituency at its best electoral performance in 1953. The GB/BHE was much more of a pressure group than a party: in this sense it was similar to many of the small splinter parties of the Weimar Republic (see Virchow, 1955).

C. THE ELECTORAL SYSTEM

The electoral system of the Federal Republic combines elements from its two predecessors: both single-member constituencies and proportional representation with party lists are used. Despite the combination of plurality and proportional methods, the electoral system of West Germany is essentially proportional. The existence of constituency-elected deputies is a technique for allocating to certain individuals some of the seats distributed to a party: this distribution is, overall, based upon proportional representation. Hence the popular term "personalized PR" is perhaps the most accurate description of the system.

The nature of the electoral law is not stipulated in the Basic Law, in order to permit flexibility and the opportunity for future parliaments to change it easily in order to penalize "undesirable" elements from gaining significant parliamentary representation. Since 1949 there have been three electoral laws. The first electoral law of 1949 was passed by the Parliamentary Council for the first general election only (see Pollock, 1952; Golay, 1958, pp. 138–47). Three-fifths of the deputies were to be elected in single-member constituencies by a simple majority. The remaining seats were filled by proportional representation from party lists. The PR allocation was made on a *Land* basis in such a way that it gave parties a proportional share of the total number of seats allotted to each *Land*; this was also done on a basis proportional to population. To prevent a great multiplicity of parties gaining seats, it was also stipulated that no party would be awarded any PR seats unless it won in that particular *Land* either one constituency seat or 5 percent of the valid votes cast.

Two subsequent electoral laws, a temporary one for the 1953 election and a more permanent one in 1956, modified the details of the original law, but accepted its general principles and framework. In 1949 each elector had only one vote, which was counted both for the constituency result and for the *Land* PR allocation among party lists. The major departure of the later laws was to give an elector two votes, one for a constituency candidate and one for a party list. In 1953 the number of list seats was made equal to the number of constituency seats. The splinter clause (*Sperrklausel*) was strengthened, in that parties now had to win either one constituency seat or 5 percent of the national valid vote in order to participate in the PR allocation of seats. The third electoral law of 1956 militated even further against minor parties. It amended the principle of allocating seats to parties to one solely of distribution on a national basis; to participate in the allocation of seats, parties must win either 5 percent of the national vote or three constituency seats. This rule does not apply to parties representing national minorities: so far the only party granted exemption has been the tiny *Südschleswig Wahlverband*, representing the small Danish population. The electoral law also applies to West Berlin. Because of the city's legal status, however, it may send only nonvoting representatives to the Bundestag. These representatives are elected by PR by its House of Representatives from among its party groups (see Plischke, 1965). Detailed accounts of particular general elections since 1949 can be found in Hirsch-Weber and Schütz, 1957; Kitzinger, 1960; Scheuch and Wildenmann, 1965; *Comparative Politics*, 1970.

The first electoral law left the determination of constituency boundaries to Landtag committees. It stipulated only how many of the total of 400 seats should be allotted to each *Land*, and that these should be divided between constituency and list seats in a 60:40 ratio. Given the impossibility of dividing most *Land* totals exactly, the final number of constituency seats was 242 instead of 240. In 1953 the determination of constituencies was handed to the federal administration, and in 1956 the task was passed to a permanent boundaries commission appointed by the federal president and consisting of the President of the Federal Statistical Bureau, one justice from the Federal Administrative Court, and five other appointees. The commission was bound to propose to the government any revisions within one year of the opening of each Bundestag; the government in turn must lay the proposal before the Bundestag without delay. The commission must obey the following precepts: each constituency must be a contiguous whole, a policy not always followed previously because of the patchwork pattern of traditional administrative areas; local administrative boundaries should be followed as far as possible; *Land* boundaries must be respected; and each constituency electorate must be within one-third of the average constituency electorate. However, the last precept has not always been followed. In a sense this is unimportant. Because of the essentially proportional nature of the system, which distributes seats on the basis of the total votes cast, the size of constituency is irrelevant. Nevertheless, it did permit the Christian Democrats to win a few excess seats in more sparsely populated areas. After the 1957 election, when the average constituency size was about 143,000 on a range from under 90,000 electors up to 265,000, the government ignored the boundary commission's recommendations. As a result the CDU won five extra seats in 1961. In 1963, however, the Federal Constitutional Court hinted that if redistribution did not take place, it might be forced to declare the subsequent general election void. Consequently, the commission's proposals were accepted, with a few modifications, by the Bundestag. In 1965 the average constituency size was about 155,000; the range was from 104,000 to 227,000.

The proportional allocation of seats is made by the d'Hondt (greatest average) system, the object of which is to ensure proportionality where the total number of seats, but not of votes, is already known (see Rae, 1967; Mackenzie, 1958). The d'Hondt method has proved popular in many countries because it is biased in favor of the larger parties. The total number of votes cast for each party is divided successively by the cardinal numbers 1, 2, 3, 4, 5, etc. The quotients obtained by this division are tabulated and ranked in order of their magnitude. Seats are awarded to parties by the descending magnitude of the tabulated quotients until the total number of seats to be filled has been distributed among the parties (see Table 6).

Until 1956 the d'Hondt calculations were made separately for each *Land*; thereafter the allocation of seats was made on the federal level. The system is, in fact, two-tier, for after the total number of seats won by each party has been determined, they are distributed among the *Länder* lists of that party according to the number of votes polled by each *Land* list, again by the d'Hondt method. Thus proportionality among the *Länder* is obtained as well as among the parties. Once the number of seats allotted to a party in any one *Land* is known, the number of constituency seats already won by the party in that *Land* is deducted from the total, and only the remaining difference is made up from the party lists. Overall, the system has rather peculiar consequences for a federal state in that it results in a bias in favor of the largest constituent state—the bias of the d'Hondt system is toward larger units. Yet the system is essentially proportional, for the total number of seats won by each party is determined by the d'Hondt method.

The constituency seats are not extra to or distinct from the proportional element; they are simply part of it. Adjustment among the *Länder* because of population changes is incorporated into the electoral system. The allocation is made, not upon the basis of *Länder* populations, but upon the number of valid votes cast for the parties. Abstentions, invalid votes, and votes for parties that fail to overcome the 5 percent barrier are ignored. Before 1956 the *Länder* distribution of seats was made on the basis of population distribution. It is possible for a party to win more constituency seats in a *Land* than the total number it is entitled to by the method of allocation outlined above. Superproportional seats (*Überhangsmandate*) are not taken away from a party, but it cannot obtain any list seats as it has more than filled its allotted quota. Instead, an equivalent number of seats is added to the *Bundestag* total, to be distributed among the other qualified party lists in that *Land*. Such excess seats had to be taken into consideration in 1949 (2 seats), 1953 (3), 1957 (3), and 1961 (5); with two exceptions, all these excess seats were won by the CDU in Schleswig-Holstein.

1. The Nomination of Candidates

The nomination of candidates is strictly regulated. The third electoral law distinguishes among three categories of candidates: those nominated by "established" parties; those nominated by other parties; and independents. Established parties are defined as those which have been continuously represented by at least five deputies in the Bundestag or a Landtag since the last election for that legislature. In this instance the nomination of constituency candidates needs only the signature of the party's *Land* executive committee. Other parties must demonstrate that they possess a written

---

TABLE 6: **Distribution of Seats by the d'Hondt method: Allocation of Bundestag Seats in 1965**

STAGE 1: VOTES WON BY THE PARTIES

Party	Votes Won
Social Democratic Party (SPD)	12,813,186
Christian Democratic Union (CDU)	12,387,562
Christian Social Union (CSU)	3,136,506
Free Democratic Party (FDP)	3,096,739

STAGE 2: CALCULATION AND TABULATION OF QUOTIENTS

Divisor	Quotients			
	SPD	*CDU*	*CSU*	*FDP*
1	12,813,186	12,387,562	3,136,506	3,096,739
2	6,406,593	6,193,781	1,568,253	1,548,369
3	4,271,062	4,129,187	1,045,502	1,032,246
4	3,203,296	3,096,890	784,126	774,185
5	2,562,637	2,477,512	627,311	619,348
300	42,711	41,292	10,455	10,322

STAGE 3: RANK-ORDERING OF QUOTIENTS BY MAGNITUDE AND DISTRIBUTION OF SEATS

Rank Order		Seats Awarded
Quotient	Party	
12,813,186	SPD	1
12,387,562	CDU	2
6,406,593	SPD	3
6,193,781	CDU	4
4,271,062	SPD	5
4,129,187	CDU	6
3,203,296	SPD	7
3,136,506	CSU	8
3,096,890	CDU	9
3,096,739	FDP	10
63,431	SPD	494
63,201	CDU	495
63,198	FDP	496

STAGE 4: TOTAL NUMBER OF SEATS WON BY EACH PARTY

Party	Number of Seats Won
SPD	202
CDU	196
CSU	49
FDP	49

Source: *Statistisches Bundesamt*, 1966

constitution and program and a democratically elected executive. They must inform the Federal Returning Office of their intention to participate in the election no later than the forty-seventh day before the election, and must have their status as a party certified by this official. And they must also collect 200 signatures from electors in each constituency where they wish to nominate a candidate and a list of one signature per 1,000 electors (up to a maximum of 2,000) in each *Land* in order to nominate a *Land* list. None of these requirements applies to parties representing national minorities. The same constituency requirements apply to independent candidates. The number of independent candidates has been increasingly negligible: only two stood in the 1965 general election.

The role of political parties in the nomination process is strictly supervised precisely because they occupy a privileged electoral position. Constituency candidates must be elected by a secret ballot of either all members of the constituency party or of a selection committee elected from among its members by the constituency party, not more than one year before the day of the election. The party's *Land* executive may object to and demand a reconsideration of a constituency nomination. If the original nominee is confirmed in a further secret ballot, however, his adoption is final. Such objections are rarely raised. Constituency parties enjoy considerable autonomy, partic- ularly if the seat is a safe one for the party. The minutes of the adoption meeting, including an attendance record and the full result of the ballot, must form part of the nomination papers presented to and examined by the constituency returning officer. Similarly, the *Land* returning officer must be satisfied that the compilation of a party's *Land* list, and the ordering of names on the list, have fulfilled the requirements of a secret ballot. The nature of the selection process for party lists varies both among parties and among *Land* sections of the same party. In compiling their *Länder* lists parties themselves may decide what type of majority—absolute or relative—is neces- sary for deciding the ordering of candidates. In all parties the selection of list candi- dates has often been influenced by the desire to produce a balanced list that would reflect all the important social groups in the *Land*. This quota system has been based upon such criteria as sex, age, interest groups, and religious denomination; it has also been regarded as important to produce a geographically balanced list that would include refugees.

2. The Electoral Machinery

Electoral administration is supervised by the federal returning officer (who is president of the Federal Statistical Bureau), who is appointed by the minister of the interior. Until the third electoral law changed the allocation of seats to a federal level, this official's functions were few, the bulk of the work being done by *Land* returning officers. Each *Land* and constituency also has a returning officer. These are appointed by the *Land* government or a delegated authority (for example, the *Land* minister of the interior). The *Land* returning officers are usually either senior officials in the *Land* Ministry or the heads of the *Land* statistical offices.

Constituencies are divided into wards sufficiently large to ensure the secrecy and anonymity of the ballot: there are over 50,000 wards. The polling stations are normally manned by local government officials. The casting of ballots must take place in private booths. Postal votes are regarded as a separate ward and are under the jurisdiction of different polling officials.

3. ELECTORAL REFORM

While there is a certain amount of pride (and surprise) in the success of the "personalized PR" system in combining satisfactorily two distinct electoral methods, the nature of the electoral system in West Germany remains open to debate (see Hennis, 1968). The combination of constituency seats and party lists was essentially a compromise adopted by the Parliamentary Council of 1948–1949. Parties differed about the type of electoral system that should be adopted: in particular, the CDU wished to adopt the single-member, simple majority system as used in Britain (see Merkl, 1963, pp. 82–89).

Throughout the 1950s the parties did not fundamentally revise their attitudes toward the electoral system. While the smaller parties remained firm protagonists of a proportional system with a lower or even no barrier clause, the CDU still hankered for the Anglo-American type system. It is not surprising that the party or individual CDU sympathizers were behind most of the proposals for reform that were made. With a majority of Bundestag seats, the CDU was in a position to change the law between 1953 and 1961, but preferred to continue as the leader of a government coalition with smaller parties, whose independent existence was ended by a more "natural" process of assimilation. Throughout the period of CDU government by coalition with smaller parties from 1949 to 1966, the possibility of electoral revision was used by the CDU as a weapon to retain the allegiance of their governmental partners.

The possibility of electoral reform increased in the late 1960s because of two factors: the rise of the NPD and the formation of a grand coalition between the CDU and SPD in December, 1966. The success of the NPD in *Länder* elections between 1966 and 1968, when it gained representation in eight *Länder* legislatures, made the two major parties consider the adoption of an Anglo-American electoral system as one way to debar the NPD from Bundestag representation. It seemed to some CDU leaders that the SPD within a grand coalition might be more inclined to support electoral reform: in this way the third party, the FDP, would also not be represented. Since the FDP's support was primarily middle-class, it was thought that the CDU would be able to inherit most of its electorate. But certain elements within the SPD saw a grand coalition primarily as a means of gaining respectability for the party in the eyes of middle-class voters. In fact, during the negotiations between the two parties about forming a grand coalition, it was indicated that electoral reform would occur, possibly even in time for the 1969 election.

Some SPD leaders believed that the party in the long run would benefit as much as, if not more than, the CDU from a "first-past-the-post" system. The question of reform had always divided the SPD, and its opponents were strengthened in 1968 by a report based on series of computer simulations. It predicted that because of the prevailing pattern of West German social-structure the SPD would be in danger of losing decisively rather than in a position of winning a majority should a plurality system be adopted (see INFAS, 1968: the analysis of social-structure upon which the exercise was based are in Liepelt, 1968; Liepelt and Mitscherlich, 1968). It should be noted that other computer simulations and interpretations of West German social-structure predicted a more favorable future for the SPD under different electoral systems (see Wildenmann et al., 1965; Wildenmann and Kaltefleiter, 1966; Wildenmann, 1968). Early in 1969 the SPD leader, Willy Brandt, whose own views were influenced by a desire to form a coalition with the FDP, declared that the party was no longer interested in changing the electoral law (see Conradt, 1970). Ironically, the SPD won 127 of the 248 constituencies in 1969, gaining a majority for the first time. The 1969 result indicated that the SPD may have fared even better under a plurality system.

D. THE ACT OF VOTING

1. THE LEGAL FACILITATION OF VOTING

Elections to the Bundestag are held every four years, unless exceptional circumstances force the federal president to dissolve it before a full term has expired: so far the president has never been required to end a Bundestag session prematurely.* The new election must take place during the last three months of the legislative term. Within this constitutional requirement, the actual date of the election is decided by the federal president, with the proviso that it must be a Sunday or a public holiday. By custom, he accepts the government's recommendation. An electoral register is compiled by the local authorities on the basis of the police registration of residence. No positive action is required of the elector. The electoral register is not published, but it is open for inspection for a period before polling day. An elector is normally notified of his inclusion in the register and, if his commune has been divided into more than one ward, of the place of polling. Since 1970 all citizens who are at least eighteen years of age have been entitled to vote: candidates must be at least twenty-one years of age. Before 1970 the minimum voting age was twenty-one, and that of eligibility for the Bundestag was twenty-five.

Since 1953 each elector has had two votes. He may, therefore, make a distinction between a party list and a candidate and his party. There is only one ballot paper for each elector. It consists of two columns: the left-hand column contains the names of the candidates standing for the constituency, while the right-hand column is for party lists. The name of each candidate in the constituency column must be followed by the name of his party. In the *Land* list column the names of the first five candidates on each party's list are given as well as the party name. There should therefore be no problem

---

* In 1972 the Bundestag session ended prematurely because of the erosion of the SPD/FDP majority over the Ostpolitik issue.

in identifying candidates with parties. The ordering of parties and candidates on the ballot form is determined by the number of national second (that is, list) votes received in the previous Bundestag election. New lists or candidates follow the established parties in alphabetical sequence by the names of the parties.

In 1949 a voter who expected to be away from his constituency on election day could apply for a certificate that would permit him to vote in any constituency of the same *Land*. In 1953 this right was extended to any constituency in the country. However, the objection was made that such a voter could not be aware of the local candidates or issues in a strange constituency, and, more serious, that parties might use this right to draft supporters into marginal constituencies that they were hoping to win; for example, it is claimed that the KPD tried to do this in Remscheid-Solingen in 1953. The third electoral law of 1956 scrapped this procedure and introduced the postal vote in its place. The certificate was retained, however, to prove the validity of the postal voter's ballot paper, and also to enable an elector to cast his ballot in any polling station of his own constituency. In 1957 the postal vote comprised 5 percent of the votes cast; in 1965 it rose to just over 7 percent. A majority of the postal votes are usually won by the CDU, with the FDP gaining a considerably higher percentage of the postal vote than among the electorate as a whole. In 1965 the CDU won 53 percent of the postal vote, and the FDP 11.5 percent.

2. TURNOUT

Electoral turnout in the Federal Republic is higher than in any previous period, being exceeded only by the 1933 figure. The range is from 78.5 percent in 1949 to 87.8 percent in 1957; the median is 86.8 percent. The comparative ease of voting does not seem sufficient to explain this high level of participation. A survey in 1959 indicated that this high level of participation has not necessarily been a reflection of a highly developed sense of political and partisan involvement. Most respondents believed that their vote was of little importance and influence, and were not unduly worried that this should be so. High turnout seems more a consequence of the belief that voting is the duty of every citizen (Verba, 1965, pp. 147–49; also Hartenstein and Schubert, 1961, pp. 36–37). The social characteristics of nonvoters, as suggested by numerous surveys, seem to be no different from those of nonvoters in other countries. Nonvoters are more likely to be women than men, young and old rather than middle-aged, less educated nonchurchgoers, and from low-income groups, and are less likely to belong to any organization or association.

A high level of voting has also been maintained in *Länder* elections: the range is from 59 percent (Baden-Württemberg in 1960) to 84 percent (Bremen in 1955); the median is 76.6 percent. The growing monopoly of the two major parties is also an outstanding feature of *Länder* elections. About five million electors who vote in national elections do not vote in *Länder* elections: this differential has been constant over the past two decades. The CDU, is apparently overrepresented among these 5 million voters. The drop in turnout leads to a greater SPD share of the vote and an increase in SPD representation in the *Länder* legislatures (see Figure 3). High turnout levels in

Länder elections may be attributed to the importance of the decisions made and the day-to-day administration carried out at this level of government. In addition, their importance is emphasized by the mass media as a measure of the current popularity of the parties. Certainly, because the President is elected indirectly, because the Bundestag serves for a fixed four-year period (apart from exceptional circumstances), and because there are no by-elections for Bundestag seats that become vacant (vacancies being filled from the remaining names in order on the list of the party whose deputy has vacated the seat), *Länder* elections are important to the parties as a guide to their future prospects on the national level. The high participation in these elections increases their value as a popularity index. One further important consequence of high turnout is that it reduces the possibility of sudden political change caused by fluctuating electoral participation.

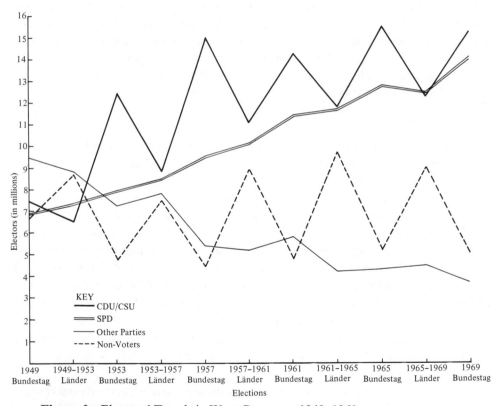

Figure 3: Electoral Trends in West Germany, 1949–1969.

6. Void Ballots and Split Tickets

The number of invalid votes in Bundestag elections increased from 3.1 percent to 4.0 percent between 1949 and 1961. This level is among the highest in Western nations today, and is also higher than in the Weimar Republic. The steady rise in the number of invalid votes suggested to many observers a possible disenchantment with the political and party system. In 1965, however, the level dropped to a new low of 2.4 percent. A study of invalid votes suggested that about 2 percent of the electorate deliberately spoiled their ballot papers as a form of protest (Stiefbold, 1965). But even here the protester seems to accept the social pressure to cast his vote as part of a citizen's duty rather than make his protest by not voting. It might be hypothesized that the elector who votes regularly in both Bundestag and Landtag elections in less likely to cast an invalid vote. Superficially, at least, this seems to be borne out by the evidence. The number of invalid votes cast in *Länder* elections is consistently lower than in Bundestag elections. In 1961 over 90 percent of invalid votes were classified as such because the ballot form had been returned blank or had been struck through. It is on evidence such as this that several commentators (for example, Barnes et al. 1962) have suggested that many electors are simply confused by the structure of the paper ballot and do not understand that they can cast two votes on the same form.

Most electors vote a straight ticket; that is, they cast their two votes for a constituency candidate and a list of the same party. The choice is determined primarily by party rather than by personality. Overall, the personality of constituency candidates is of little importance when compared to party identification and the personalities of the party leaders. By and large, both the CDU and the SPD receive a slightly larger share of first (constituency votes) than of second (list) votes, while the smaller parties, including the FDP, find the opposite to be true. In 1965, for example, the FDP received 1.6 percent more list than constituency votes. Generally, ticket splitting seems to have declined in recent elections along with the decrease in the number of significant parties contesting elections.

E. SOCIAL-STRUCTURE AND PARTY SUPPORT

The following section will discuss a number of social structural variables that can influence political behavior. Two themes will be considered: how each variable is measured, and its significance for party support. The data is drawn from interviews with 6,143 respondents gathered by INFAS (Institut für angewandte Sozialwissenschaft, Bonn/Bad Godesberg) in six national random surveys in 1967. The number of respondents who refused to state a party preference was 16 percent: a figure this high is a common feature of West German surveys. Moreover, the surveys were conducted in a nonelectoral period when the number of uncommitted persons might be expected to increase.

When those who refused to state a party preference are excluded, the distribution of party preferences corresponds to the distribution of votes at both the 1965 and 1969 elections. The two major parties are slightly overrepresented in the sample: 50 percent supported the CDU, which gained 47.6 percent of the vote in 1965 and 46.1 percent in 1969, while 44 percent supported the SPD, which gained 39.3 percent of the vote in 1965 and 42.7 percent in 1969. The FDP (9.5 percent of the vote in 1965 and 5.8 percent in 1969) and the NPD (2.0 percent in 1965 and 4.5 percent in 1969) are underrepresented: 4 percent of the sample supported the FDP and 2 percent the NPD.

The small number of FDP and NPD supporters inhibits any detailed study of their social characteristics. Strictly speaking, however, the analysis is not concerned with the level of support indicated for a particular party, but with differences in the distribution of partisan support by social and demographic groups. In analyzing party support, respondents are placed in four groups: CDU supporters; SPD supporters; FDP supporters; and all others. This last group consists of NPD supporters (who are too few to consider separately), those who named other parties, and those who did not state a party preference: the latter constitute the overwhelming majority in this category. The number of cases varies slightly from table to table because of refusals to answer, clerical omissions, or the inappropriateness of questions to some groups in society. Brackets around a figure in a table indicate that the number of respondents in that cell is less than fifty.

The development of the German party system has shown that class and religion have been the most durable and significant political divisions in German society. All earlier surveys and ecological analyses of West German politics confirm this (see, *inter alia*, Faul, 1960; Linz, 1959; Scheuch and Wildenmann, 1965; von der Heydte and Sacherl, 1955; Hirsch-Weber and Schütz, 1957). It would be meaningful, therefore, to employ controls for both class and religion for all data analyzed here. In order to facilitate comparisons with other countries, class will usually be employed as a control: religion will be controlled where it seems profitable to do so. The relative significance of these two variables will then be examined later by multivariate analysis.

1. CLASS

Class differences are customarily measured by occupational categories. Occupational class presents few difficulties in distinguishing between agricultural and non-agricultural occupations, and manual workers. Nonmanual workers are, however, a very heterogeneous group, differing in ways that historically have been related to political divisions. The social significance of inherited status and the widespread use of titles permit a status distinction between and within such groups as businessmen and industrialists, civil servants, professionals and other middle-class groups. Survey data, however, do not normally permit very sophisticated analyses of these smaller social strata; for example, the number of people with "old status," i.e., a title, is relatively small. Most official publications and surveys divide the middle-class into two groups— one consisting primarily of self-employed individuals, the other mainly of salaried employees. However, occupational groups are not always placed according to their mode of income. The most important exceptions are the so-called free professions; who are mainly salaried employees but who are always classified with the self-employed group because of their traditional ranking in the status order. The separation of workers and farmers presents fewer problems: both groups are distinctive in terms of both occupation and life-style. There is internal differentiation within the working-class between skilled and unskilled workers, although such distinctions may not be politically significant. Many surveys do not record farmers as a separate category, although they do not fit well into a system of categories derived from industrial society. In any case farmers form a very small part of the population in most surveys.

There are five occupational categories in the INFAS survey: (1) professional groups, self-employed businessmen, and farmers; (2) white-collar groups, combining public officials (*Beamte*) and salaried employees (*Angestellte*); (3) skilled workers; (4) unskilled workers; (5) a residual category of pensioners, people retired from active employment, and people with unearned income. The major drawback of the coding is that it is not possible to analyze separately how farmers vote, since they are in the same coding category as urban self-employed groups. In the following analysis skilled and unskilled manual workers have been merged, since there is no distinction between the number of skilled workers (50 percent) and unskilled workers (49 percent) who supported the SPD. The categories used in the analysis are: (1) *self-employed middle-class*, referring to the professional groups, self-employed businessmen, and farmers; (2) *salaried employees*, referring to the *Beamte* and *Angestellte*; (3) *workers*, comprising both skilled and unskilled workers; (4) a residual category of *pensioners*, with 64 percent of this group aged sixty-five or over, and a further 30 percent between fifty and sixty-five years of age.

Table 7 confirms the influence of occupational-class in West German politics. The higher one moves up the scale, the lower the SPD vote tends to be. The most homogeneous pattern of class voting is in the highest category, the self-employed middle-class: only 14 percent supported the SPD.

TABLE 7: **Occupation and Party Choice, 1967, in Percentages**

	CDU	SPD	FDP	NA*	GROUP % OF TOTAL
Self-employed middle-class	58	14	8	20	16
Salaried employees	45	34	4	17	28
Workers	33	49	1	16	37
Pensioners	45	36	2	17	19
					N = 6,023

* In this and the following tables the "not ascertainable" column also includes those who named other parties. Those who did not state a party preference constitute the overwhelming majority of cases in each instance.

2. RELIGION

There is little difficulty in measuring religion; the three conventional categories are Protestant, Catholic, and other or none. Very few surveys distinguish between Lutherans and other Protestant groups, although it has been suggested occasionally that their political behavior is distinctive. In 1967 only 4 percent of respondents were outside the major denominational categories: 50 percent said they were Protestants, 46 percent said they were Catholics. The CDU is supported by 54 percent of Catholics and 33 percent of Protestants. A plurality of Protestants—43 percent—favors the SPD, as do 30 percent of Catholics. Among the small group of respondents who professed a minor or no religion, 51 percent prefer the SPD. When occupational-class is controlled, differences in the party preferences of Catholics and Protestants are consistently found, with Catholics favoring the CDU more in all classes (Table 8). SPD support among the self-employed middle-class is exceptionally weak among Protestants as well as Catholics. Reciprocally, among Catholics the lower the class, the higher level of SPD support; a plurality of Catholic workers still supports the CDU.

TABLE 8:   **Occupation, Religion, and Party Choice, 1967, in Percentages**

OCCUPATION	RELIGION	CDU	SPD	FDP	NA	GROUP % OF TOTAL
Self-employed middle-class	Catholic	67	12	3	13	8
	Protestant	50	16	11	23	8
Salaried employees	Catholic	58	25	2	14	12
	Protestant	37	40	5	18	16
Workers	Catholic	44	41	1	14	18
	Protestant	22	57	2	18	18
Pensioners	Catholic	59	27	—	14	9
	Protestant	34	41	4	21	10

N = 5,773

Church attendance measures an individual's commitment to his church. However, problems occur in constructing a measure applicable to both Protestants and Catholics. Attending church at least once a month may be regarded as regular attendance by Protestants but as irregular by Catholics. The measurement of church attendance here is subjective: each respondent was asked to define himself as a regular churchgoer or otherwise. Church attendance appears to be as powerful a predictor of political choice as religious denomination within occupational categories (Table 9). In each

TABLE 9:   **Occupation, Churchgoing, and Party Choice, 1967, in Percentages**

OCCUPATION	CHURCHGOING	CDU	SPD	FDP	NA	GROUP % OF TOTAL
Self-employed middle-class	Churchgoing	71	8	3	18	8
	Nonchurchgoing	47	20	11	21	8
Salaried employees	Churchgoing	63	18	4	15	11
	Nonchurchgoing	36	43	4	17	17
Workers	Churchgoing	53	31	1	15	14
	Nonchurchgoing	22	60	2	16	23
Pensioners	Churchgoing	57	26	2	15	10
	Nonchurchgoing	33	45	2	20	9

N = 5,773

occupational category the difference between churchgoers and nonchurchgoers is greater than between Protestants and Catholics.

Differences also remain between the occupational groups. Because regularity of church attendance may be different for Protestants and Catholics, it is meaningful to introduce religion as a control. Two-thirds of Catholics defined themselves as regular churchgoers, as against one-fifth of Protestants. The CDU is preferred by two-thirds of churchgoing Catholics and by a plurality of churchgoing Protestants, while the SPD is favored by a plurality of nonchurchgoers of both denominations. When one controls for class, the CDU is preferred by all churchgoing occupational groups apart from Protestant workers (Table 10). By contrast, every nonchurchgoing category favored the SPD, with the exception of the self-employed middle-class of both denominations. Within each occupational category the difference between churchgoing and nonchurchgoing Catholics is greater than between churchgoing and nonchurchgoing Protestants. The table indicates that the inability of the SPD to win more working-class support is due to the strength of the CDU among Catholic workers who are regular churchgoers (11 percent of the population). The FDP does particularly well among the nonchurchgoing self-employed middle-class, being preferred by 10 percent of Catholics and 12 percent of Protestants.

TABLE 10:   **Occupation, Religion, Churchgoing, and Party Choice, 1967, in Percentages**

| | CATHOLIC | | | | | | | |
| | Churchgoing | | | | Nonchurchgoing | | | |
	CDU %	SPD %	Others %	Group % of Total	CDU %	SPD %	Others %	Group % of Total
Self-employed middle-class	75	6	19	6	40	30	30	2
Salaried employees	69	15	16	8	39	44	17	4
Workers	58	27	15	11	27	59	14	8
Pensioners	66	20	14	7	41	45	14	2

| | PROTESTANT | | | | | | | |
| | Churchgoing | | | | Nonchurchgoing | | | |
	CDU %	SPD %	Others %	Group % of Total	CDU %	SPD %	Others %	Group % of Total
Self-employed middle-class	53	14	33	2	49	17	34	6
Salaried employees	45	26	29	3	35	43	22	13
Workers	36	44	20	3	19	60	21	15
Pensioners	41	36	23	4	30	45	25	6

N = 5,773

Thus the historical patterns of German politics still remain. The present-day CDU and SPD rest mainly on those social groups that supported their predecessors. In addition, the CDU has attracted support from Protestant groups that before 1933 preferred one of the several middle-class parties that then existed. If the suggestion by Neumann (1932, pp. 28-29) about the voting clientele of the SPD during the Weimar Republic is correct, the SPD has not advanced significantly in its attempts to expand its working-class base. Comparing 1967 data with information gathered in 1953 (Linz, 1967, p. 302) can show whether the SPD has changed its profile of support in the interval. One problem with the 1953 data is the higher proportion of people who declined to indicate a party preference (24 percent). To make the comparison meaningful, only those respondents who indicated a party preference are considered. A comparison of the two sets of data suggests that very little change in the distribution of party support has occurred. A slight advance by the SPD among Catholic (from 38 to 47 percent) and Protestant (from 59 to 69 percent) workers is counteracted by similar CDU gains among these groups. Lesser parties have lost support to both. Among the self-employed middle-class the differential between the CDU and the SPD has increased, from 55 to 65 percent among Catholics and from 26 to 42 percent among Protestants. It seems that the SPD has advanced significantly only among Protestant salaried employees: among this group SPD support rose from 29 to 48 percent, whereas CDU support rose from 41 to 44 percent.

3. EDUCATION

Levels of education have tended to be lower in Germany than in many advanced industrialized societies, due to the pyramidal and highly selective nature of the educational system (see Scheuerl, 1968; Schultze and Führ, 1966; Führ, 1970). The length of education is determined by laws governing compulsory education. Since 1871 the field of education has always been controlled by the *Länder*, except during the Third Reich. The present degree of federal supervision and coordination is such that one can speak of a national system of education. Compulsory education begins at the age of six and continues to the age of fourteen or fifteen. This eight-year period can be defined operationally as a minimum education. Those pupils who attend school beyond this age can be said to receive a further education. Primary schools (*Grundschule*) accommodate pupils between the ages of six and ten. At the age of ten pupils must take an examination that determines both the kind and the length of their secondary education.

There are three kinds of secondary schools. Most pupils attend elementary or people's schools (*Volksschule*) for a further four or five years. The rest attend intermediate schools (*Mittel-* or *Realschule*) for five or six years or high schools (*Oberschule* or *Gymnasium*) for a period of seven to nine years. About four-fifths of the population receive only a minimum education. In the early 1960s only 18 percent of the fifteen-nineteen age group were full-time students (Ellwein, 1963, pp. 131-34). About 5 percent of nineteen-year-olds pass the *Abitur*, the examination that provides entry to universities and most other institutions of higher learning.

The content of learning is related to the length of education and the streaming process after the age of ten. After this age it is difficult to change from one type of secondary school to another, for the separate schools are designed to train the pupil for different futures. Generally, the more years a student spends in school, the more academic his education. Intermediate schools possess a more vocational character.

Denominational schools, which are state-supported, play an important role in the West German educational system. They are predominantly Catholic and are found at the primary level of education. Denominational schools dominate in the Catholic *Länder*. Elsewhere, primary schools are usually nondenominational: religious instruction is given separately to children of different confessions. The decision as to whether a community should have a denominational or nondenominational school usually belongs to a majority of the parents. Such schools may be politically important as it could be hypothesized that attendance at a denominational school would reinforce commitment to the church, and thus, indirectly, to the CDU.

The data only permit us to compare those who received a minimum elementary education with those who received further education. Education does not seem to be a strong independent influence upon partisanship, for it is closely correlated with occupation (Table 11). Within each occupational category there is little difference in party preference between those with a minimum and those with a further education. The major differences occur among the pensioners, but since this is an age group containing people who before their retirement were scattered among the other three occupational categories, these differences are not particularly meaningful. More interesting is the relatively high number of FDP supporters among the small number of the self-employed middle-class who have received more than an elementary education.

TABLE 11: **Occupation, Education, and Party Choice, 1967, in Percentages**

	LEVEL OF EDUCATION	CDU	SPD	FDP	NA	GROUP % OF TOTAL
Self-employed	Supraelementary	50	12	15	23	5
middle-class	Elementary	62	15	4	19	11
Salaried employees	Supraelementary	46	31	5	18	13
	Elementary	44	37	3	16	15
Workers	Supraelementary	33	47	2	18	2
	Elementary	32	50	1	16	35
Pensioners	Supraelementary	55	22	6	17	3
	Elementary	43	38	2	17	16
						N = 6,095

4. INCOME

Income, like education, is a variable that is usually associated with class. It is, however, more difficult to measure than either education or occupation. Survey questions concerning income normally relate to the regular income of the respondent, and this may not be an accurate measure of the wealth or total funds of the respondent or his family. Moreover, questions concerning income tend to have a high refusal rate or are deliberately answered incorrectly: 14 percent of the INFAS respondents refused to state to which income level they belonged. Wage increases and inflation mean that income measures defined in current money terms have a changing significance. The income categories in the 1967 survey rise, by steps of 200DM, from those with a monthly income of under 200DM to those with a monthly income of over 1,400DM: the official rate of exchange was then 4DM to one U.S. dollar. In the absence of any recognized convention these categories have been collapsed as indicated in Table 12. The most interesting finding is the stronger performance of the CDU among the lowest income groups. Overall, however, income does not seem to be a major explanatory variable in West German politics.

TABLE 12:   **Occupation, Income, and Party Choice, 1967, in Percentages**

	MONTHLY INCOME	CDU	SPD	FDP	NA	GROUP % OF TOTAL
Self-employed	1,200DM and over	61	15	12	11	5
middle-class	800–1,199DM	62	19	7	12	4
	400–799DM	58	16	1	25	3
	Under 400DM	(63)	(6)	(2)	(29)	1
Salaried employees	1,200DM and over	49	32	5	14	9
	800–1,199DM	43	39	3	15	13
	400–799DM	50	33	2	15	6
	Under 400DM	(56)	(19)	(—)	(25)	(0.3)
Workers	1,200DM and over	32	55	2	11	3
	800–1,199DM	33	53	2	12	14
	400–799DM	32	49	1	18	21
	Under 400DM	38	38	2	22	1
Pensioners	1,200DM and over	(39)	(39)	(6)	(15)	1
	800–1,199DM	45	38	6	11	2
	400–799DM	41	41	2	16	10
	Under 400DM	51	29	2	18	7

N = 5,282

In 1967–1DM = $ 0.25; $1 = 4DM

5. TRADE-UNION MEMBERSHIP

About one-third of the West German labor force is organized in trade unions. In place of the pre-Hitler situation, with several mutually antagonistic unions allied to different political parties, the post-1945 period saw the creation of a comprehensive and officially nonpartisan union federation, the DGB (*Deutscher Gewerkschaftsbund*). With a membership of 6.5 million, it is larger than any other West German organization apart from the churches. The DGB consists of sixteen individual unions and is primarily a federation of manual workers rather than white-collar employees. Its total domination of organized labor is prevented by two smaller white-collar associations, the Salaried Employees Union (485,000 members) and the Civil Servants Federation (650,000 members).

In 1967 34 percent of respondents said that they or someone in their family belonged to a trade-union. Trade-union membership or union ties appear to be a major influence upon party preference (Table 13). Within each occupational group union involvement leads to a higher level of SPD vote and a lower level of CDU vote. This is consistent in all four strata. Moreover, SPD support among salaried employees with union ties is greater than that among nonunionized workers. When the relationship between union membership and party preference is examined with religion controlled, 52 percent of the Catholic trade unionists prefer the SPD, while 33 percent support the CDU.

TABLE 13: **Occupation, Trade-Union Membership, and Party Choice, 1967, in Percentages**

	TRADE-UNION MEMBERSHIP	CDU	SPD	FDP	NA	GROUP % OF TOTAL
Self-employed middle-class	Member	(28)	(33)	(6)	(33)	(0.3)
	Relative is a member	(45)	(36)	(3)	(16)	1
	Non member	59	13	8	20	15
Salaried employees	Member	33	45	3	19	6
	Relative is a member	39	42	2	17	4
	Non member	51	28	4	16	17
Workers	Member	20	65	2	13	11
	Relative is a member	33	49	1	17	7
	Non member	40	40	1	18	18
Pensioners	Member	17	69	2	12	2
	Relative is a member	31	51	—	18	2
	Non member	51	29	3	18	15
						N = 6,023

6. URBAN-RURAL DIVISIONS

Because only 10 percent of the work force is employed in agriculture and related occupations, the political importance of the farm vote is limited. In 1965 the percentage of the population dependent on agriculture was higher than 30 percent in only two of the 248 constituencies, and above 20 percent in a further twenty-one: of these 23 constituencies, twelve were in Bavaria. The CDU won fifteen of these seats in 1949, and since 1953 has had comfortable majorities in all twenty-three in every election, except in one constituency in 1953 and 1957. The SPD has never won any of these farming constituencies. However, rural areas are not homogeneous in farm size or farming practices. Historically, differences have been associated with distinctive political behavior (see, for example, Heberle, 1963). The urban-rural division may be measured in two ways. Occupation provides one measure of a farming vote, but such an analysis is not possible here because farmers are not coded as a separate category. The other measure is the size of community of residence. This measure is used here. Size of community is not an ideal measure, however, for commuting has turned many rural areas into dormitory suburbs of neighboring towns, and some small towns have one or more factories. The four categories of community size employed here are those customarily used in demographic analyses of German society: communities with under 2,000 inhabitants; between 2,000 and 20,000; between 20,000 and 100,000; and those with 100,000 or more inhabitants.

When occupation is controlled, size of community consistently influences partisanship (Table 14). The CDU is strongest in the smallest communities, where many respondents are farmers. This is consistent with the historical weakness of the SPD in rural areas. Reciprocally, the larger the community, the greater the SPD support in each class. Overall, the CDU has a slight majority (51 percent) in the rural areas, while the SPD has a plurality of support (47 percent) in the largest cities. The data confirm figures available from published election results: they show a consistent and nontrivial relationship, with class controlled, between community size and party preference.

TABLE 14:   **Occupation, Size of Community, and Party Choice, 1967, in Percentages**

	SIZE OF COMMUNITY	CDU	SPD	FDP	NA	GROUP % OF TOTAL
Self-employed middle-class	100,000 and over	51	22	11	16	3
	20,000–99,999	51	16	14	19	2
	2,000–19,999	55	15	6	24	5
	Under 2,000	66	9	5	20	6
Salaried employees	100,000 and over	40	44	2	14	11
	20,000–99,999	48	30	6	16	5
	2,000–19,999	46	29	5	20	7
	Under 2,000	57	22	2	19	4
Workers	100,000 and over	24	61	1	14	9
	20,000–99,999	29	47	3	21	6
	2,000–19,999	35	49	1	15	11
	Under 2,000	40	42	1	17	11
Pensioners	100,000 and over	38	45	2	14	5
	20,000–99,999	42	34	4	20	3
	2,000–19,999	45	36	3	16	6
	Under 2,000	52	26	1	21	5

N = 6,023

7. REGION

There is no agreed classification of regions among students of German society. Most studies of political behavior tend to fit the ten *Länder* into two or three regional groupings along a north-south axis, giving a north-south dichotomy or a north-central-south trichotomy. Such arrangements usually show that there is little regional diversity in party preferences: variations between *Länder* in each region tend to be greater than differences between regions. There is much to be said, apart from the problem of the absence of any consensus on what constitutes a region, for taking regional boundaries from the institutional framework of the regime. It can be assumed

TABLE 15: Religion, Region and Party Choice, 1967, in Percentages

	CDU		SPD		FDP		NA		GROUP % OF TOTAL	
	Catholic	Protestant	Catholic	Protestant	Catholic	Protestant	Catholic	Protestant	Catholic	Protestant
Schleswig-Holstein	(40)	49	(40)	26	(5)	3	(15)	22	(0.3)	3
Hamburg	(62)	28	(25)	53	—	3	(12)	16	(0.1)	2
Lower Saxony	57	37	18	37	2	3	23	23	2	9
Bremen	(67)	36	(33)	47	—	3	—	14	(0.2)	1
North Rhine-Westphalia	54	31	31	48	1	5	14	16	14	14
Hesse	49	25	37	51	2	4	12	20	3	7
Rhineland-Palatinate	62	21	26	50	2	9	9	20	4	3
Saar	45	(14)	27	(64)	1	—	26	(21)	1	(0.2)
Baden-Württemberg	63	36	24	39	2	5	10	20	8	8
Bavaria	49	36	32	32	2	8	17	23	15	4

N=5,887

that these are politically meaningful, especially in West Germany, since it is a federal state. The regional units used here are the ten *Länder*. The value of using occupational-class as a control is weakened by the small numbers in several cells. Moreover, few meaningful differences appear within each occupational-class in the relationship between *Land* and party preferences: the major exceptions are the city *Länder* of Hamburg and Bremen, where a majority of salaried employees prefer the SPD. Religion would seem to be a more meaningful control because of the geographical difference in the two religions. No clear pattern emerges from Table 15. Overall, the differences in the party preferences of Catholics and Protestants remain, except in Bavaria and Schleswig-Holstein, where the CDU was favored by a plurality of Protestants. Catholics in the overwhelmingly Protestant areas in the north-Schleswig-Holstein, Hamburg, Lower Saxony, and Bremen—do not differ greatly in their party support from their coreligionists in some of the predominantly Catholic *Länder* in the south. Protestants in the two southernmost *Länder*, Bavaria and Baden-Württemberg, and in the most northerly *Land*, Schleswig-Holstein, support the SPD less than their coreligionists elsewhere. The differences that do exist between *Länder* when religion is controlled are determined by their different levels of industrialization and urbanization. Overall, region per se does not seem to be an important dimension of partisan division.

8. SEX

There are no difficulties in measuring sex per se. The figures in Table 16 confirm the cross-national phenomenon that women tend to be more conservative in their party choice than men. Within each occupational category, more women than men favor the CDU. However, class clearly remains a stronger influence on party preference

TABLE 16: **Occupation, Sex, and Party Choice, 1967, in Percentages**

	SEX	CDU	SPD	FDP	NA	GROUP % OF TOTAL
Self-employed middle-class	Men	55	15	10	20	8
	Women	61	14	5	20	8
Salaried employees	Men	41	37	5	17	13
	Women	49	32	3	17	15
Workers	Men	27	56	2	15	21
	Women	39	41	1	18	17
Pensioners	Men	40	44	2	14	7
	Women	48	30	2	19	11
					N = 6,022	

than sex. Differences between men and women may be less a function of biological distinctions than the product of other social characteristics differentially distributed between the sexes.

The most common assertion is that the greater conservatism of women is due to their greater religiosity. This is measured in Table 17 by introducing churchgoing as an intervening variable. While there remains a slight tendency for both female churchgoers and nonchurchgoers to favor the CDU more than their male counterparts, the difference between the sexes is due more to their different levels of churchgoing. There are as many churchgoers as nonchurchgoers among women, while among men, nonchurchgoers outnumber churchgoers by almost two to one. No further meaningful differences emerged when the relationship between sex and churchoging was examined with class controlled.

TABLE 17: **Sex, Church Attendance, and Party Choice, 1967, in Percentages**

	CHURCH ATTENDANCE	CDU	SPD	FDP	NA	GROUP % OF TOTAL
Men	Churchgoing	55	26	3	16	17
	Nonchurchgoing	29	50	5	16	31
Women	Churchgoing	63	20	2	16	26
	Nonchurchgoing	34	43	3	20	26
					N = 5,887	

9. AGE

Age is also easily measured, but political differences among age groups may be due to other characteristics: among middle-class groups, fore xample, age is generally associated with economic advancement. It might be expected that age groups would display significant differences in their political behavior because of different generational experiences caused by the political discontinuities Germany has experienced since 1918. Five generational groups have been formed here: (1) those born before 1903, socialized under the Second Empire; (2) those born between 1903 and 1917, socialized during the social and political instability of the Weimar Republic; (3) those born between 1918 and 1932, socialized during the Third Reich; (4) those born between 1933 and 1942; (5) after 1942, socialized during the postwar period of rising prosperity. These five generational groupings are summarized in tables as follows: (1) age 65 and over in 1967; (2) age 50–64 in 1967; (3) age 35–49 in 1967; (4) age 25–34 in 1967; (5) age under 25 in 1967. While generational and life-cycle differences do exit, they seem to have little effect upon the distribution of party preferences. There is no firm indication that older generations vote more for the CDU and younger generations more for the SPD (Table 18).

In view of the demonstrated importance of religiosity in determining party preference it will be meaningful to consider in West Germany the hypothesis that contemporary societies are undergoing a process of secularization. This would have important consequences for the future of West German party politics, since decreasing churchgoing rates would militate against the CDU. Limited support for the secularization hypothesis is found. The number of churchgoers in each group, as a percentage of that group, is as follows: 65 and over, 54 percent; 50–64, 49 percent; 35–49, 38 percent; 25–34, 37 percent; under 25, 37 percent. The marked difference in religiosity occurs between the over–50s and those born after 1917.

TABLE 18 :   Occupation, Age, and Party Choice, 1967, in Percentages

	AGE GROUP	CDU	SPD	FDP	NA	GROUP % OF TOTAL
Self-employed middle-class	65 and over	68	9	7	16	1
	50-64	57	15	6	22	5
	35-49	55	17	6	22	5
	25-34	63	10	10	17	3
	Under 25	56	13	13	18	1
Salaried employees	65 and over	(50)	(23)	(10)	(17)	(1)
	50-64	48	28	3	21	6
	35-49	44	36	4	16	10
	25-34	45	37	3	15	8
	Under 25	46	36	3	15	4
Workers	65 and over	(41)	(44)	—	(15)	(1)
	50-64	37	44	1	19	7
	35-49	32	51	2	16	13
	25-34	31	53	1	15	12
	Under 25	33	45	1	21	4
Pensioners	65 and over	48	33	2	17	12
	50-64	39	41	2	18	6
	35-49	37	41	4	18	1
	25-34	(43)	(29)	—	(29)	(0.1)
	Under 25	—	—	—	—	—
						N = 6,015

When the party preferences of the generational groups are examined with religiosity controlled, the difference in party preference within each age stratum is still affected by religiosity: in all age groups about three-fifths of churchgoers supports the CDU (Table 19). Age appears to be important only among the oldest nonchurchgoers. Religiosity rather than age is the important influence upon party preference: yet, because of this, the marked decline in churchgoing among the under–50s has major implications for future trends in West German politics.

F.   A TREE ANALYSIS OF WEST GERMAN ELECTORAL BEHAVIOR

The preceding discussion and analysis have emphasized the importance of class and religion in contemporary West German political behavior. The relationship is complex: neither major party is confined to a single religious or class group. When the social composition of each party is considered, we find that 59 percent of CDU supporters

are Catholics and 58 percent are regular churchgoers, while 37 percent of SPD supporters are Catholics and 25 percent claim to be regular churchgoers. Similarly,
occupational-class does not dichotomize the electorate into two unambiguous partisan
cohorts: workers contribute 61 percent of SPD support and 35 percent of CDU

TABLE 19:   **Church Attendance, Age, and Party Choice, 1967,**
in Percentages

	AGE GROUP	CDU	SPD	FDP	NA	GROUP % OF TOTAL
Churchgoing	65 and over	63	20	3	14	8
	50-64	59	21	2	17	12
	35-49	57	25	2	16	11
	25-34	60	23	2	15	9
	Under 25	60	20	3	16	3
Nonchurchgoing	65 and over	37	42	2	19	6
	50-64	32	43	4	21	13
	35-49	31	47	4	17	18
	25-34	28	51	4	16	15
	Under 25	30	47	4	19	5
						N=5,880

---

support. The relatively low working-class composition of the SPD makes it one of the
least working-class socialist or communist parties in Western Europe (see Rose and
Urwin, 1969, pp. 51–67).

Multivariate analysis offers a means of discovering which influences are the chief
determinants of electoral behavior. A.I.D. analysis can show the total configuration of
structural influences. Klaus Liepelt's work with this technique through the years has
offered valuable analyses of West German political behavior (see Liepelt, 1967;
Liepelt, 1968; Liepelt and Mitscherlich, 1968). The technique of tree analysis is
described in Sonquist and Morgan (1964). The analysis initially employed all those
social-structure variables used in the preceding section: occupational-class, religion,
churchgoing, education, income, trade-union membership, size of community of
residence, regionalism, age, and sex. The dependent variable is party choice, but since
the program can only dichotomize, the dependent variable is taken as the expression
of support for the SPD among respondents who expressed a preference for either the
CDU or the SPD.

The tree analysis (Figure 4) shows clearly that church attendance, rather than religion or socioeconomic status, is the most important single influence upon partisanship. Moreover, churchgoers are more strongly CDU than nonchurchgoers are
SPD. Churchgoing explains 11.1 percent of the total variance at the first branch.
Second in importance at this stage is trade-union ties; it explained 7.8 percent of the
variance. Religious denomination was third in importance (5.2 percent), and occupation fourth (4.8 percent). These influences in turn emerge at later stages of the branching of the tree. On both sides formed by the initial branch trade-union ties comes next

in influence. Among nonchurchgoers with trade-union ties, 74 percent favored the SPD; among churchgoers without union ties, only 21 percent were SPD. Together, these two further branches explain 5.6 percent of the variance. The two groups distinguished by union ties as well as church attendance could not be further subdivided. The unaffiliated group without church or union ties could be further subdivided along occupational lines, into an upper- and a lower-status group. In turn, the latter could be further subdivided to separate manual workers from pensioners and salaried employees. The churchgoers without union ties can be subdivided by their religious denomination, with 84 percent of the churchgoing Catholics outside unions favoring the CDU. The total reduction of the variance achieved is 19.7 percent. This is consistent with earlier tree analyses reported by Liepelt (1968), although his first branch is on union ties rather than religion. This branch accounts for only 6.4 percent of the variance, however, as against the 9.7 percent of variance explained by the two branches that follow according to religiosity.

The end groups obtained from the tree analysis are reproduced in Table 20 in descending order of the percentage of each group that supported the SPD. There are seven end groups, ranging in size from 24 percent of the total to 6 percent. These end groups cluster into three larger categories. One, which represents the "core" of the SPD, consists of 36 percent of those identifying with either of the two major parties: it is made up of nonchurchgoers with union ties and nonchurchgoing workers without union ties. A second group, also 36 percent of the total, forms the "core" support of the CDU: it contains all churchgoers without union ties and those in the self-employed middle-class who neither attend church nor have any kind of union ties. The balance in the middle (29 percent of the total) consists of two quite distinct groups, one that is not committed to either organizational network, and another (churchgoers with union ties) that is linked to both but cross-pressured by its attachments.

TABLE 20: **Principal Social Groups in West German Politics, 1967**

GROUP	N	% OF TOTAL	% SPD
A: Nonchurchgoers. Trade-union ties	1,148	24	74
B: Nonchurchgoers. No Trade-union ties Workers	561	12	65
C: Nonchurchgoers. No Trade-union ties Salaried employees and pensioners	806	17	49
D: Churchgoers. Trade-union ties	575	12	44
E: Churchgoers. No Trade-union ties Protestants	350	7	36
F: Nonchurchgoers. No Trade-union ties Self-employed middle-class	301	6	29
G: Churchgoers. No Trade-union ties Catholics	1,131	23	16
Total	4,872	100	48

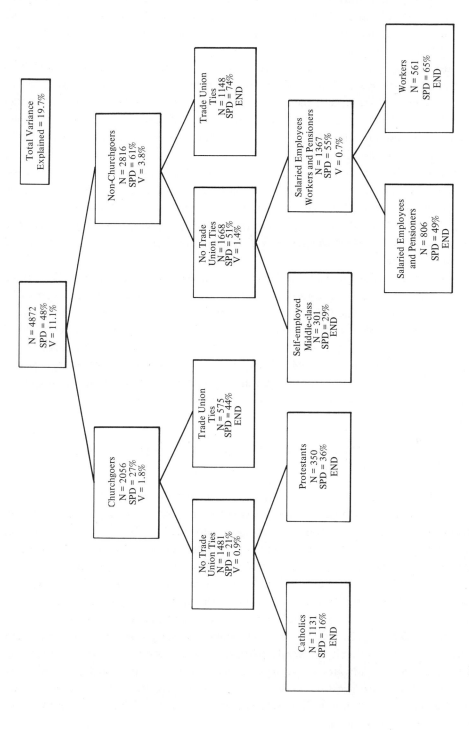

Figure 4: A Tree Analysis of West German Partisanship, 1967.

The tree analysis indicates that the most important influences on voting preference are organizational rather than subcultural ties. This is demonstrated by the emphasis on churchgoing rather than religious denomination and trade-union affiliation rather than occupational-class. Several differences discussed earlier, for example between the sexes and age groups and the patterns of regional distinctiveness, are omitted from the tree, while religion and occupational-class have a low explanatory value. The tree analysis thus confirms and refines historical interpretation. Churchgoing and trade-union ties are better measures of social-structure influence than religion or class because they indicate more clearly than denomination or occupation the *degree of commitment* of an individual to a class or religious subculture. Class, as indicated by occupational position, becomes important only for those occupational groups that do not possess a commitment to either class-based or religious organizations, as in the final branches among nonchurchgoers without unions ties. Distinctions between Protestants and Catholics emerge only within churchgoers without union ties, illustrating perhaps the different nature of individual commitment in the Protestant and Catholic churches.

The same conclusions may be drawn from an examination of the parties' social profiles. Table 21 gives the proportion of the total vote of each party that is formed by voters of each group. The CDU gains almost two-fifths of its followers from a single end group: 37 percent of CDU support comes from practicing Catholics without union ties. The SPD is in a similar situation; 38 percent of its support comes from nonchurchgoers with union ties. Moreover, these are the two largest end groups formed by the tree. These figures further emphasize the continuing importance of organizational and subcultural links in West German electoral politics.

G.   WEST GERMANY IN HISTORICAL AND COMPARATIVE PERSPECTIVE

Of all the political *tendances* significant in the development of the German party system in the nineteenth- and early twentieth-centuries, the two that have proved capable of surviving the several disjunctions experienced by Germany are those that from the outset were buttressed by cohesive and intense organizations that penetrated deeply specific elements of the society and were associated with or subordinated to a party organization. The strength of the *Zentrum* arose from its close relationship with the Catholic Church and the latter's influence over practicing Catholics. Similarly, the trade-union federation created and controlled by the SPD was probably the most important organizational network through which the party was able to establish and maintain a distinct subculture. While religious denomination may now be relatively unimportant as an indicator of voting behavior, while occupational-class may be important only among groups lacking close organizational ties, religiosity and trade-union connections continue to illustrate the enduring force of organizational links in determining partisan choice.

The disjunctions of German political history make comparison with other countries both difficult and interesting. Depending upon the aspect and period of German politics chosen, the researcher has a choice of comparable countries or situations: for example, Sartori (1966) has suggested that the party system of the Weimar Republic could be compared with those of post-1945 Italy, the Fourth French Republic, and perhaps the second Spanish Republic.

TABLE 21: **Social Profiles of the CDU and SPD, 1967, in Percentages**

Group*	CDU	SPD	Total
A	11	38	24
B	7	17	12
C	16	17	17
D	12	11	12
E	9	6	7
F	8	4	6
G	37	8	23
N=	2615	2257	4872

* The letters refer to the groups listed in Table 20.

Different comparisons are appropriate in the contemporary period. There are two distinct points to consider: similarity of social-structure (that is, the independent variable) and similarity of parties (the dependent variable). The most immediate comparison would seem to be with Austria, where occupational differences and religiosity are the most significant social-structure influences on party choice. Moreover, the party systems of the two countries are broadly similar in terms of the number, size, and nature of the political parties. Both countries possess two large parties, one socialist, the other conservative with a strong religious base; both countries also possess a small third party that is both middle-class and secular. Empirical comparisons between these two countries are aided by the fact that both possess the same language and similar cultural characteristics. Indeed, the similarities between West Germany and Austria are manifold: both countries have an antidemocratic past, and both have experienced in recent years a grand coalition of the two leading parties. It is worth noting that Liepelt (1968) has constructed trees for the two countries. His findings for West Germany were noted earlier. Religiosity also came out as the most important single influence upon partisanship in the Austrian tree: it was followed on both sides of the initial branch by readership of the party press. Thus in Austria as well as in West Germany the tree analysis emphasized institutional as against categorical (but unorganized) influences. West Germany acquired this kind of institutionalized party infrastructure only in the post-1949 period, whereas Austria had this kind of party politics in the 1920s, the time of the Weimar Republic.

Germany is not easily comparable in social-structure with those countries that have divisions along lines of language, national identity, center-periphery or region-alism, as well as class or religious cleavages. Hence comparisons with Belgium, Switzerland, Canada, the United States, and perhaps Norway are not appropriate. We may also omit from consideration those places—Scandinavia and Ireland—where agrarian parties have proved durable and enjoy significant support, or where farmers are still numerous.

Class and religion are both significant influences on French and Italian party politics, but in these two countries the working-class has been divided between com-munists and socialists. Moreover, in France, and perhaps also in Italy, the Right has also been fragmented politically. As we have suggested, the most appropriate German comparison in this respect would be the Weimar Republic, not the Federal Republic.

On the basis of the importance of class and religion in determining party choice, we could compare the CDU with the three major Dutch religious parties and the SPD with the Dutch secular, mainly working-class bloc. But this comparison shows that the degree of institutional strength in Germany today is much less than in the Nether-lands. The West German tree explains only 19.7 percent of the variance, whereas the Dutch tree in Lijphart's chapter explains about one-half of the variance.

Thus after Austria the most appropriate comparison would seem to be with Britain. Both countries have essentially a two-party system, with the socialist party based upon the working-class and the conservative party being catch-all in nature with heterogeneous support. The SPD has been more successful than the British Labour party in attracting a certain amount of middle-class support. While the CDU appeal to both Protestant and Catholic is especially successful among the middle-class, the party has nevertheless been successful in gaining significant support from all social groups. In this respect it is similar to the British Conservative party.

In some ways the dynamics of the West German party system are unique: the changes in the number, nature, and size of the various parties between 1949 and 1969 are nothing less than dramatic. They point to the substantial achievement of the West German nation in replacing within two decades a party situation of extreme disorder and fragmentation with one that is extremely orderly.

References

ALLEMANN, F. R. *Bonn ist nicht Weimar*. Cologne: Kiepenheuer & Witsch, 1956.

ANDERSON, E. N. and P. R. *Political Institutions and Social Change in Continental Europe in the Nineteenth Century*. Berkeley/Los Angeles: Univ. of California Press, 1967.

ARNDT, H. J. *West Germany: Politics of Non-Planning*. Syracuse: Syracuse Univ. Press, 1967.

BACHEM, K. *Vorgeschichte, Geschichte und Politik der deutschen Zentrumspartei*. Cologne: Bachem, 1927–1932.

BARNES, S. H., et. al. "The German Party System and the 1961 Federal Election." *American Political Science Review* 56 (1962): 899–914.

BLANKENBURG, E. *Kirchliche Bindung und Wahlverhalten.* Olten/Freiburg: Walter-Verlag, 1967.

BOOMS, H. *Die Deutsch-Konservative Partei: Preussischer Charakter, Reichsauffassung, Nationalbegriff.* Düsseldorf: Droste Verlag, 1954.

BORNKAMM, H. "Die Staatsidee im Kulturkampf." *Historische Zeitschrift* 52 (1952): 289–94.

BRACHER, K. D. *Die Auflösung der Weimarer Republik.* 4th ed. Villingen: Ring Verlag, 1964.

———, et al. *Die National-sozialistische Machtergreifung.* Cologne/Opladen: Westdeutscher Verlag, 1962.

CLAPHAM, J. H. *Economic Development of France and Germany 1815-1914.* 4th ed. Cambridge: Cambridge Univ. Press, 1936.

COLE, T. "New Dimensions in West German Federalism." In E. L. Pinney, ed. *Comparative Politics and Political Theory.* Chapel Hill: Univ. of North Carolina Press, 1966, pp. 99–122.

Comparative Politics 2 (1970), pp. 519–700 (special issue on the 1969 West German election).

CONRADT, D. P. "Electoral Law Politics in West Germany." *Political Studies* 18 (1970): 341–56.

DAALDER, H. "Parties, Elites, and Political Developments in Western Europe." In J. LaPalombara and M. M. Weiner, eds. *Political Parties and Political Development*, Princeton: Princeton Univ. Press, 1966, pp. 43–77.

DAHRENDORF, R. *Society and Democracy in Germany.* New York: Doubleday, 1967.

Demoskopie. Institut für Demoskopie: *Die Neubürger: Bericht über die Flüchtlinge und Heimatvertriebenen in der Bundesrepublik*, Allensbach: Demoskopie Verlag, 1964.

DICKINSON, R. E. *Germany: A General and Regional Geography.* London: Methuen 1961.

———."The Geography of Commuting in Western Germany." *Annals of the Association of American Geographers* 49 (1959): 443–56.

Die Zeit. 12 September 1969, p. 3. (The survey was conducted by the Institut für Demoskopie, Allensbach.)

EBSWORTH, R. *Restoring Democracy in Germany: The British Contribution.* London: Stevens, 1960.

EDINGER, L. J. *Politics in Germany.* Boston: Little, Brown, 1968.

ELLWEIN, T. *Politische Verhaltenslehre.* Frankfurt: Europäische Verlagsanstalt, 1963.

ESCHENBURG, T. *Der Sold der Politikers.* Stuttgart: Seewald Verlag, 1959.

FAUL, E., ed. *Wahlen und Wähler in Westdeutschland*, Villingen: Ring Verlag, 1960.

FINER, H. *Theory and Practice of Modern Government.* New York: Holt, 1949.

FRAENKEL, E. "Parlament und öffentliche Meinung." In *Zur Geschichte und Problematik der Demokratie: Festgabe für Hans Herzfeld.* Berlin: Duncker & Humblot, 1958.

FRANKLIN, S. H. *The European Peasantry.* London: Methuen, 1969.

FRANZ, G. *Die politischen Wahlen in Niedersachsen, 1867 bis 1949.* 3rd ed. Bremen: Walter Dorn Verlag, 1957.

———. *Kulturkampf: Staat und Katholische Kirche in Mitteleuropa.* Munich: Callweg, 1954.

FÜHR, C. *Zur Schulpolitik der Weimarer Republik.* Weinheim: Beltz, 1970.

GAGEL, W. *Die Wahlrechtsfrage in der Geschichte der deutschen liberalen Parteien 1848-1918.* Düsseldorf. Droste, 1958.

GOLAY, J. F. *The Founding of the Federal Republic of Germany.* Chicago: Univ. of Chicago Press, 1958.

HAGMANN, M. *Der Weg ins Verhängnis.* Munich: Bechstein Verlag, 1946.

HARTENSTEIN, W. *Die Anfänge der deutschen Volkspartei 1918-1920.* Düsseldorf: Droste, 1962.

———, and LIEPELT, K. "Party Members and Party Voters in West Germany." In S. Rokkan, ed. *Approaches to the Study of Political Participation.* Bergen: Chr. Michelsen Institute, 1962.

———, and SCHUBERT, G. *Mitlaufen oder Mitbestimmen: Untersuchung zum demokratischen Bewusstsein und zur politischen Tradition.* Frankfurt: Europäische Verlagsanstalt, 1961.

HARTWICH, H. *Arbeitsmarkt, Verbände und Staat 1918-1933.* Berlin: Colloquium, 1967.

HEBERLE, R. *Landbevölkerung und Nationalsozialismus.* Stuttgart: Deutsche Verlags-Anstalt, (1963). [An earlier, shorter English version was published as *From Democracy to Nazism* (Baton Rouge: Louisiana State Univ. Press, 1945).]

HEIDENHEIMER, A. J. *Adenauer and the CDU.* The Hague: Nijhoff, 1960.

———. "La structure confessionelle, sociale et régionale de la CDU." *Revue française de science politique* 7 (1957): 626–45.

HENNIS, W. *Grosse Koalition ohne Ende?* Munich: Piper Verlag, 1968.

HIRSCH-WEBER, W., and SCHUTZ, K., eds. *Wähler und Gewählte: Eine Undersuchung der Bundestagswahlen 1953.* Berlin: Vahlen, 1957.

INFAS. (Institut für angewandte Sozialwissenschaft). "Wählerstimmen und Mandate: Ergebnisse einer Wahlrechtsstudie," *Politogramm* (March, 1968); and "Wählerstimmen und Mandate: Dreier und Viererwahlkreise." *Politogramm* (August, 1968), Bad Godesberg.

———.(Institut für angewandte Sozialwissenschaft), *Ifas Report: Sonderheft Kassel* Bad Godesberg: 1964.

JACOB, H. *German Administration Since Bismarck.* New Haven: Yale Univ. Press, 1963.

KIRCHHEIMER, O. "The Waning of Oppositions in Parliamentary Regimes." *Social Research* 24 (1957): 127–56.

KITZINGER, U. W. *German Electoral Politics.* Oxford: Clarendon Press, 1960.

KRAUS, H., and KURTH, K. *Deutschlands Ostproblem: Eine Untersuchung der Beziehungen des deutschen Volkes zu seinen östlichen Nachbarn.* Würzburg: Holzner Verlag, 1957.

LANGE, M. G., et al *Parteien in der Bundesrepublik: Studien zur Entwicklung der deutschen Parteien bis zur Bundestagswahl 1953.* Stuttgart: Ring Verlag, 1955.

LEMBERG, E., and EDDING, F. *Die Vertriebenen in Westdeutschland.* Kiel: Hirt Verlag, 1959.

LIEBE, W. *Die Deutschnationale Volkspartei 1918-1924.* Düsseldorf: Droste, 1956.

LIEPELT, K. "Esquisse d'une typologie des électeurs allemands et autrichiens." *Revue française de sociologie* 9 (1968): 13–32.

———."Anhänger der neuen Rechtspartei: Ein Beitrag zur Diskussion über das Wähler-reservoir der NPD." *Politische Vierteljahresschrift* 8 (1967): 237–71.

———, and MITSCHERLICH, A. *Thesen zur Wählerfluktuation.* Frankfurt: Europäische Verlagsanstalt, 1968.

LINZ, J. J. "Cleavage and Consensus in West German Politics; The Early Fifties." In S. M. Lipset & S. Rokkan, eds. *Party Systems and Voter Alignments.* New York: Free Press, pp. 283–321.

———."The Social Bases of West German Politics." Ph.D. dissertation, Columbia University, 1959.

LIPSET, S. M., and ROKKAN, S., eds. Introduction to *Party Systems and Voter Alignments.* New York: Free Press, 1967: pp. 3–64.

LOEWENBERG, G. "The Remaking of the German Party System." *Polity* 1 (1968): 86–113.

———. *Parliament in the German Political System.* Ithaca: Cornell Univ. Press, 1966.

LOOMIS, C. P., and BEEGLE, J. A. "The Spread of German Nazism in Rural Areas." *American Sociological Review* 11 (1946): 724–34.

LOWELL, A. L. *Governments and Parties in Continental Europe* 2 vols. Boston: Houghton Mifflin, 1896.

LÜTGE, F. *Deutsch Sozial-und Wirtschaftsgeschichte*, 3rd ed. Berlin: Springer Verlag, 1966.

MACKENZIE, W. J. M. *Free Elections.* London: Allen & Unwin, 1958.

MANNING, P. W. *Rehearsal for Destruction: Political Anti-Semitism in Imperial Germany.* New York: Harper, 1949.

MERKL, P. H. *The Origins of the West German Republic.* New York: Oxford Univ. Press, 1963.

———. "Equilibrium, Structures of Interest and Leadership: Adenauer's Survival as Chancellor." *American Political Science Review* 56 (1962): 634–50.

———. "Executive-Legislative Federalism in West Germany", *American Political Science Review* 53 (1959): 732–41.

MERRITT, R. L. "West Berlin—Center or Periphery?" In R. L. Merritt and S. Rokkan, eds. *Comparing Nations.* New Haven: Yale Univ. Press, pp. 321–36.

MEYN, H. *Die deutsche Partei.* Düsseldorf: Droste, 1965.

MILATZ, A. *Wähler und Wahlen in der Weimarer Republik.* Bonn: Schriftenreihe der Bundeszentrale für politische Bildung, 1965.

MOLT, P. *Der Reichstag vor der improvisierte Revolution.* Cologne/Opladen: Westdeutscher Verlag, 1963.

MORSEY, R. "Die deutsche Zentrumspartei." In E. Mathias & R. Morsey, eds. *Das Ende der Parteien 1933*. Düsseldorf: Droste, 1960.

MUNCY, L. W. *The Junker in the Prussian Administration under William II.* (Providence: Brown Univ. Press, 1944.

NEUMANN, S. *Die deutschen Parteien: Wesen und Wandel nach dem Kriege*. Berlin: Junker and Dunnhaupt, 1932.

NILSON, S. S. "Wahlsoziologische Probleme des Nationalsozialismus." *Zeitschrift für die gesamte Staatswissenschaft* 110 (1954): 279–311.

NIPPERDEY, T. *Die Organisation der deutschen Parteien vor 1918*. Düsseldorf: Droste, 1961.

O'LESSKER, K. "Who Voted for Hitler? A New Look at the Class Basis of Nazism," *American Journal of Sociology* 74 (1968): 63–69.

PLISCHKE, E. "Integrating Berlin and the Federal Republic of Germany." *Journal of Politics* 27 (1965): 41–50.

POLLOCK, J. K. "The Electoral System of the Federal Republic of Germany." *American Political Science Review* 46 (1952): 1056–68.

RAE, D. W. *The Political Consequences of Electoral Laws*. New Haven: Yale Univ. Press, 1967.

RAUPACH, H. "Der interregionale Wohlfahrtsausgleich als Problem der Politik des Deutschen Reiches." In W. Conze & H. Raupach, eds. *Die Staats—und Wirtschaftskrise des Deutschen Reiches 1929/33*. Stuttgart: Klett, 1967, pp. 13–34.

ROKKAN, S. "The Comparative Study of Political Participation: Notes Toward a Perspective on Current Research." In A. Ranney, ed. *Essays on the Behavioral Study of Politics*. Urbana: Univ. of Illinois Press, pp. 47–90.

———, and MEYRIAT, J., eds. *International Guide to Electoral Statistics: National Elections in Western Europe*. Paris: Mouton, 1969.

ROSE, R., and URWIN, D. W. "Persistence and Change in Western Party Systems since 1945." *Political Studies* 18 (1970): 287–319.

———. "Social Cohesion, Political Parties and Strains in Regimes." *Comparative Political Studies* 2 (1969): 7–67.

ROSENBERG, H. "Die Demokratisierung der Rittergutsbesitzerklasse." In *Zur Geschichte und Problematik der Demokratie: Festschrift für Hans Herzfeld*, Berlin: Duncker and Humblot, 1958.

ROTH, G. *The Social Democrats in Imperial Germany*. Totowa, New Jersey: Bedminster Press, 1963.

SÄNGER, F., and LIEPELT, K., eds. *Wahlhandbuch 1965*. Frankfurt: Europäische Verlagsanstalt, 1965.

SARTORI, G. "European Political Parties: The Case of Polarized Pluralism." In J. LaPalombara and M. Weiner, eds. *Political Parties and Political Development*, Princeton: Princeton Univ. Press, 1966, pp. 137–76.

SCAMMON, R. M. "Political Parties." In E. H. Litchfield, ed. *Governing Postwar Germany*, Ithaca: Cornell Univ. Press, 1953.

SCHAUFF, J. *Die deutschen Katholiken und die Zentrumspartei*. Cologne: Bachem, 1928.

SCHEUERL, H. *Die Gliederung des deutschen Schulwesens.* Stuttgart: Klett, 1968.

SCHEUCH, E., and WILDENMANN, R., eds. *Zur Sociologie der Wahl.* Cologne/Opladen: Westdeutscher Verlag, 1965.

SCHIEDER, T. *The State and Society in Our Times.* London: Nelson, 1962.

SCHMIDT-VOLKMAR, E. *Der Kulturkampf in Deutschland 1871-1890.* Göttingen: Musterschmidt, 1962.

SCHOENBAUM, D. *Hitler's Social Revolution: Class and Status in Nazi Germany, 1933–1939.* New York: Doubleday, 1966.

SCHULTZE, W., and FÜHR, C. *Das Schulwesen in der Bundesrepublik.* Weinheim: Beltz, 1966.

SONQUIST, J. A., and MORGAN, J. N. *The Detection of Interaction Effects.* Monograph 35, Institute for Social Research. Ann Arbor: Univ. of Michigan, 1964.

SPIRO, H. "The German Political System." In S. H. Beer and A. B. Ulam, eds. *Patterns of Government*, 2nd ed. New York: Random House, 1962.

Statistisches Bundesamt. Bevölkerung und Kultur: Wahl zum 5. Deutschen Bundestag am 19 September 1965. (Series 8, No. 6), 1966.

Statistisches Jahrbuch für das Deutsche Reich. (Annual.)

Statistisches Jahrbuch für die Bundesrepublik Deutschland. (Annual.)

STIEFBOLD, R. P. "The Significance of Void Ballots in West German Elections." *American Political Science Review*—59 (1965): 391–407.

STOLPER, G., HAUSER, K., and BORCHARDT, K. *The German Economy: 1870 to the Present.* London: Weidenfeld and Nicolson, 1967.

STOLTENBERG, G. *Politische Strömungen im schleswig-holsteinischen Landvolk 1918–1933.* Düsseldorf: Droste, 1962.

STRIEFLER, H. *Deutsche Wahlen in Bildern und Zahlen: Eine so ziografische Studie über die Reichstagswahlen der Weimarer Republik.* Düsseldorf: Hagemann, 1946.

STÜRMER, M. *Koalition und Opposition in der Weimarer Republik 1924–1928.* Düsseldorf: Droste, 1967.

SYRUP, F., and NEULOH, O. *Hundert Jahre staatliche Sozialpolitik.* Stuttgart: Kohlhammer 1957.

URWIN, D. W., and ROSE, R. "Persistence and Disruption in Western Party Systems between the Wars." Paper presented to the World Congress of the International Sociological Association, Varna, Bulgaria: September 14–19, 1970.

VERBA, S. "Germany: The Remaking of Political Culture." In L. W. Pye and S. Verba, eds. *Political Culture and Political Development*, Princeton: Princeton Univ. Press, 1965, pp. 130–70.

VIRCHOW, M. "Der GB/BHE, ein neuer Partein typ?" In M. G. Lange et al. *Parteien in der Bundesrepublik: Studien zur Entwicklung der deutschen Parteien bis zur Bundestagswahl 1953.* Stuttgart: Ring Verlag, 1955, pp. 450–67.

VON DER HEYDTE, F. A., and SACHERL, K. *Soziologie der deutschen Parteien.* Munich: Isar Verlag, 1955.

WALLICH, H. *Mainsprings of the German Revival.* New Haven: Yale Univ. Press, 1955.

WARREN, D., JR. *The Red Kingdom of Saxony: Lobbying Grounds for Gustav Strese-mann*, Hague: Nijhoff, 1964.

WEBER, H. *Die Wandlung des deutschen Kommunismus.* Frankfurt: Europäische Verlagsanstalt, 1970.

WIECK, H. G. *Die Entstehung der CDU und die Wiedergründung des Zentrums.* Düsseldorf: Droste, 1953.

WILDENMANN, R. "Parteien-Identifikation in der Bundesrepublik." In O. Stammer ed. *Party Systems, Party Organizations, and the Politics of the New Masses*, Berlin: Institut für politische Wissenschaft an der Freien Universität Berlin, 1968, pp. 234–69.

———, and KALTEFLEITER, W. "Voraussetzungen zur Erörterung der Auswirkungen von Wahlsystemen, Eine Entgegnung," *Politische Vierteljahresschrift* 7 (1966): 556–73.

———, et al. "Auswirkungen von Wahlsystemen auf das Parteien- und Regierungs-system der Bundesrepublik." In E. Scheuch and R. Wildenmann, eds. *Zur Soziolo-gie der Wahl.* Cologne/Opladen: Westdeutscher Verlag, 1965, pp. 74–112.

WILLIS, F. R. *The French in Germany 1945-1949.* Stanford: Stanford Univ. Press, 1962.

ZIEGLER, D. J. *Prelude to Democracy: A Study of Proportional Representation and the Heritage of Weimar Germany 1871-1920.* University of Nebraska Studies: New Series, No. 20, 1958.

ZINK, H. *The United States in Germany 1944-55.* Princeton: Princeton Univ. Press, 1957.

4. ITALY:
Religion and Class in Electoral Behavior

SAMUEL H. BARNES

The fundamental political divisions of Italy have existed in their present mold for at least a half century. Their origins are even more remote, for the social cleavages of an industrial society are superimposed on previous lines of stratification; religion blurs further the political impact of class. Only recently has the impact of industrialization begun to erode premodern fissures, hence their traces are likely to linger into the future. The result is a series of cleavages that originate in different ages and lead to contemporary structures of political conflict that sometimes seem to contradict and sometimes to confirm the conventional wisdom about political behavior.

Thus according to the conventional wisdom Italy is badly fragmented politically. Cited as evidence is the existence of the largest nonruling Communist party in the world, a small neofascist movement, and a ruling Christian Democratic party that is based on religious values in an increasingly secular age and society. Italy also has Monarchist, Republican, Liberal and, as of 1970, three Socialist parties represented in parliament. Political fragmentation and polarization coexist with low levels of mass education, slight interest in politics and one of the highest rates of electoral turnout in the world.

Italy is also considered to be poorly integrated socially. Class divisions are sharp, differences between North and South remain highly salient, and the religious question divides otherwise similar groups. The Italian citizen is viewed as alienated and despairing, the government perpetually on the verge of collapse, and the administration chaotic.

But Italy is also a European, industrial, parliamentary democracy. Compared with the universe of polities existing today it ranks very high on indices of political and economic development. It is only when compared with the countries of northern Europe and North America that it appears behind in industrialization and in achieving a secularization of politics, national integration, and a homogeneous national political culture. Contemporary politics still reflect regional, religious, social, and cultural differences of the past to a remarkable degree. This is of course true of all polities, but they are probably quantitatively somewhat more significant in Italy than in the other countries considered in this volume. Certainly the conventional wisdom suggests this. Our goal in this chapter is to subject the conventional wisdom concerning Italian politics to a critical analysis in the light of empirical research. We will be concerned in particular with assessing the impact of religion and class on contemporary political attitudes and behavior.

I. Historical Background

In determining what is the proper historical perspective needed for an analysis of contemporary Italian politics it is necessary to keep a number of dates in mind, for they serve as alternative cutoff points for different kinds of analyses. The first important date is when modern Italy begins—1861 (or, for some purposes, 1870, when Rome was incorporated). The next date of great significance for political behavior is the achievement of universal manhood suffrage in 1919. The third is the March on Rome on October 28, 1922. The final date is 1943, when military defeat and partisan activity led to the overthrow of fascism. Each of these dates is useful for some analyses and not for others.

For most purposes, social scientists concerned with the political and especially electoral behavior of modern Italy will begin with 1861 or later. While statistical and other records exist for most of the states that were joined to form Italy, problems of access and comparability render them difficult to use; in general, records since unification have been excellent. In 1870 Rome was incorporated into the new kingdom and made its capital. Territorial changes since that date have been marginal; the principal administrative subdivisions of the country have also not changed greatly.

There has been considerable political continuity since unification, despite the change in regime and the experience of fascism. However, the strength of different political forces in the country has altered greatly. During the late nineteenth-century the polity was dominated by the politics of *trasformismo*. This was the practice of putting together a government by dealing on an individual basis with members of parliament, securing their support by favors provided them and their constituents. Parties in the modern sense did not exist; factions developed around personalities and, to a lesser extent, vague ideological tendencies. In present-day political terms these elites were on the whole liberal in the European sense. Catholics were forbidden by the papal *Non expedit* (1874) to participate in politics because the Papal States were incorporated into Italy against the objections of the pope; he in turn refused to cooperate with the new regime. In this heavily Catholic country the pope's actions deprived the system of legitimacy in the eyes of many of its citizens, including groups that could have been very important for its stability.

Socialism and its rival, anarchism, became important in the later years of the century. The development of unity on the left then as now was difficult to achieve, with the socialist tendency finally dominating over anarchism. The Italian Socialist party was founded in 1892, and even with the electorate restricted by property and educational qualifications, socialists began to be elected to the lower house. As the electorate gradually expanded due to relaxation of franchise requirements as well as the growing ability of the electorate to meet them, the prospects of socialist electoral success led first to an easing of the papal ban against Catholic political activity and then to its repeal by the time universal manhood suffrage was achieved in 1919.

The 1919 elections were the first in which all adult males voted without property, educational, or age restrictions. It was also the first year in which the clear outlines of the present party system are visible. Italian socialism was badly divided by the Russian Revolution. A general strike in Italy failed to bring down the government, and the party was gravely weakened. It was further damaged in 1921 when its revolutionary wing broke away to form the Italian Communist party. The Popular party, the forerunner of the present Christian Democratic party, was a potential source of support for stability and democratic reforms, but it was ambivalent about cooperating with the Socialists, and governments remained weak and unstable. Although the Fascists had had only modest electoral success, Mussolini was invited to form a government following the March on Rome on October 28, 1922. (Mussolini arrived by train!)

The first Fascist government was a coalition, but the members of other parties were soon weeded out and opposition parties largely destroyed. The dictatorship was established in 1925. Whatever measure of broad support that Fascism received in its early years seems to have disappeared in the 1930s; though internal opposition was never very effective, fascism could not survive the war. Mussolini had been appointed head of the government by the king and he was dismissed by the king in 1943, after the Fascist Grand Council had voted to oust him. Arrested, he was freed by the Germans and set up a fascist republic under their close control. When they retreated from Italy, he was caught and executed by a partisan band.

The Italians rejected the monarchy in a referendum in 1946 and at the same time elected a constituent assembly that drew up a new constitution. It is the basic document that governs Italy today.

A. SOCIAL STRUCTURE SINCE 1861

The four gross indicators of the social environment of the political system used in this analysis are the size and distribution of the population, employment in industry, urbanization, and literacy.

The population of Italy (using its present borders) almost doubled between 1861 and 1961, from 25,756,000 to 49,877,000. In addition, between 1869 and 1962 more than 24,000,000 people emigrated to the United States, Canada, Australia, Argentina, and other countries, and at least 8,000,000 of these never returned (Ciaurro, 1968, p. 297). Moreover, internal migration has been very great, and the gross changes in population of various parts of the country often mask even larger shifts in population. The mortality and birthrates today vary greatly from one region to another. The national average birthrate, for example, was 37 per 1,000 in 1871 and 18.4 in 1961; Piedmont and Calabria had rates of 36.5 and 36.7 per 1,000 in 1871 and 13.4 and 24.1 in 1961 (*Annuario Statistico*, 1878, p. 45; 1962, p. 28). Nevertheless, the overall portion of the population living in the south has declined slightly, from 39 percent in 1860 to 36.1 percent in 1967 (Tarrow, 1967, p. 41; *Annuario dell Economia, della Politica, della Coltura*, 1968, p. 103).

A distinctive feature of Italian history has been its late and incomplete industrialization. Modern methods of manufacturing came relatively late to this cradle of the joint stock company, modern banking, and superb craftsmanship. Although some pockets of industry are long-established, at the time of unification the population was 68.6 percent agricultural; in 1950 the agricultural sector comprised 42.4 percent and in 1964 24.3 percent of the population. But even within the modern sector much of the activity was in fact that of artisans; small family-oriented manufacturing firms were still very important in the postwar period despite the existence of some very large companies.

Italy has always been an urban civilization; its Renaissance cities elevated local particularism to a very high level in art and politics. Relatively few people live in the countryside, and villages are often without many of the amenities of urban life. According to the census of 1961 only 174,996 Italians lived in communes with less than 500 persons, 765,850 lived in the 501 to 1,000 category, and 2,717,080 in the 1,001-2,000 category. The total living in communes with fewer than 5,000 people (12,292,371) was similar to the number in communes above 100,000 (12,530,221) (*Annuario Statistico Italiano*, 1962, pp. 26-27).

Illiteracy has been extensive in Italy relative to northern European countries. In 1871 72.9 percent of the population was illiterate. In the postwar period the percentage has declined from 14.1 percent in 1951 to 8.4 percent in 1961, and is today disappearing. Functional illiteracy, however, is more serious than these figures indicate.

B. THE ELECTORAL SYSTEM IN THE TWENTIETH-CENTURY

From unification until 1882 the Italian electorate was extremely restricted. The average number of votes needed to elect a deputy was 500, and sometimes slightly more than 100 sufficed (Capecchi et al., 1968, p. 23). From 1882 until 1919 the electorate was gradually expanded to include the entire adult male population. Literacy and property requirements for men thirty and over were dropped in 1913; universal manhood suffrage for men over twenty-one was adopted for the 1919 elections; women first voted in national elections in 1946.

Until 1882 the single-member district system was used; from 1882 until 1892 a multimember system was in effect; for the period 1892-1913 the single-member district system was again utilized. Proportional representation was adopted in 1919 and today seems to be firmly installed as the system that divides Italians least. There is no weighty section of opinion, as exists in France and Germany, that advocates switching to a single-member system. Attempts to tamper with the proportional features of the law in order to ensure a working majority in parliament, as with the so-called "swindle law" of 1953, offer excellent ammunition to the opposition. Adopted for the elections of that year, this law would have guaranteed a comfortable absolute majority to the party or parties that secured 50 percent plus one of the votes. Memories of a somewhat comparable Fascist electoral law were called up in opposition, and when the DC coalition failed by a fraction to achieve 50 percent, the law was quietly repealed. Because of such experiences democracy and the present form of proportional representation tend to be equated in Italy, at least at the national level and for the Chamber of Deputies.

In the half-century following unification elections were won by careful tending of the small electorate, intimidation, governmental interference when necessary, and other practices so corrupt that the minister responsible was labeled by Gaetano Salvemini the "Minister of Evil." These practices declined with the rise of mass parties, except for their extensive use by the Fascists in the last elections under the monarchy. Postwar elections have been free of irregularities. The secrecy of the ballot is assured by the constitution (Article 48) and by practice.

Since women acquired the franchise for the 1946 elections, all adults have been able to vote except for the usual restrictions relating to felons, and so on. Voting age differs, however, for the two houses: it is twenty-one for the Chamber and twenty-five for the Senate. Voting is defined as a "civic duty" and nonvoters with inadequate explanations have the fact stamped on their identity papers. Although civic duty is seldom a principal determinant of political behavior in Italy, turnout is high. Voting has become an established norm of the culture, and great efforts are made to comply with the norm. The competitiveness of the party system, the effortless registration, the financial inducements in the form of reduced fares on trains, and the holiday atmosphere of a Sunday ballot combine to ensure a high turnout.

Registration is easy. The authorities keep records of inhabitants; when one reaches voting age, he is added to the rolls automatically and before an election is sent a certificate. He remains on the rolls until he is removed by death or by acquiring residences elsewhere. Fascist laws that long remained in force made it difficult to change one's legal residence, so that voters returned to their "home" commune to vote. The law has been declared unconstitutional and the practice is now breaking down, but the large number of people who live and work in one commune while maintaining their legal and hence voting residence in another remains large, though declining. This has been a serious handicap for survey research in the past, as electoral rolls are used for sampling. Such voters are difficult to trace, unfortunately, because they are also likely to be emigrants of possible unusual electoral volatility. Today, however, the numbers involved are small.

Election to the Chamber is by party list in constituencies ranging from four to forty-seven seats. These constituencies generally group together the provinces of a small region or a part of a large region. They follow closely the administrative divisions of the country. However, the constituencies themselves seldom reflect fully the structure of normal party organization, which is largely by province, so that drawing up the list and managing the campaign in the constituency often present problems of coordination between coequal party units. In practice there is often a pragmatic partitioning of the constituency; candidates may campaign in only part of the area and in fact may feel that their "real" constituency is a limited part of the whole.

The election of senators is also in fact largely by proportional representation, in the following manner: each region of Italy is allotted a number of senators proportional to its population, with a minimum of seven except for the sparsely populated regions of Molise and Valle d'Aosta, which are guaranteed minimums of two and one senators. Each region is then divided into a number of districts of roughly similar size equal to the number of senators to be elected. Each party runs one candidate in each district. Anyone with 65 percent of the vote in that district is declared elected. Otherwise, the votes for all candidates of a party or group of parties in the region are pooled and seats are assigned by proportional representation to the parties and then to the candidates who received the highest percentage of votes within their individual districts. This system permits parties to draw up joint regional lists. Thus the Social Proletarians and the Communists might agree that in District X the latter would put up no candidate while the former would run none in another district. In this manner the Social Proletarians could obtain representation in the Senate and the Communists would be assured of additional votes in the region. This practice is of marginal importance. Most senators are elected by proportional representation with the region as the constituency; for example, in 1968 only two were elected by receiving 65 percent of the vote—one from the Christian Democratic party and one from the *Südtiroler Volkspartei*.

The Chamber and the Senate have similar powers and are elected at the same time, so that not surprisingly they virtually duplicate one another. As one is elected by party lists in large constituencies and the other in single-member districts—at least ostensibly —it may be tempting to use the Senate returns so as to have units comparable to British or American constituencies. For most purposes this would be unwise. The voting age differs for the two. And despite their constitutional equality, the Chamber is of greater political importance than the Senate. Most party leaders sit there and most ministers are chosen from the Chamber. The Chamber also receives more attention in elections. And most senators are in fact elected by proportional representation.

The 1948 constitution provided for one deputy for every 80,000 electors. The number of seats in the Chamber consequently fluctuated upward—574 in 1948, 590 in 1953, 596 in 1958. The number was permanently fixed at 630 for the Chamber and 315 for the Senate by constitutional amendment in 1963. The number to be elected in each constituency is adjusted for every election according to the latest population figures, so it is thus not necessary to redraw the constituency boundaries.

The major parties present lists throughout the country. This is not the same thing as mounting effective campaigns, and the smaller parties, especially the Monarchists and Republicans, often are barely visible outside of their areas of concentrated strength. The nomination of candidates is a party matter, unregulated by law and unstudied by scholars. Technical problems of securing signatures make it difficult for casual lists to get on the ballot, but the sixteen parties on the Roman ballot in 1968 (including the Pensioners' party, dissident leftists, local lists, etc.) suggest that the difficulties are not overwhelming.

The counting of votes involves a discussion of the system of preference votes (D'Amato, 1964). The elector votes for the party and may, if he wishes, list particular preferences. In constituencies electing fewer than sixteen he may mark up to three; in others, four. The number of candidates elected on a list depends on the total vote for that list, while the particular candidates elected are determined by the number of preference votes received. Thus position on the list means little. There are great differences in the extent to which the right to express a preference is exercised. Overall, for example, the rate varied in 1958 from 13.97 percent in the constituency of Milan to 51.04 percent in that of Palermo (Schepis, 1963, Table 26). But this masks considerable differences among the parties and it also means different things in different areas and parties. In much of the south, for example, the local organizations of the Right and Center parties, including the Christian Democratic, make arrangements with candidates to deliver to them a certain number of preference votes. In this case the large number of preference votes cast reflects not only the greater personalization of politics but also the clientelistic nature of party organization. Certainly the politics of preference votes is an inadequately studied subject in Italy.

In distributing votes among the party lists a quotient is established for the constituency by dividing total vote by seats to be filled plus two. Seats are assigned to parties that meet multiples of the quotient. If this process would result in more deputies being seated than have been allotted the constituency, the quotient is computed again on the number of seats plus one, then plus none, until seats are assigned. Votes that do not contribute to the election of a candidate are transferred to the national electoral office, if the party received 300,000 votes nationally and elected at least one candidate in a constituency. Likewise, seats not distributed even with the quotient of the number of seats plus two are transferred to the national electoral office. A national quotient is then established and parties are assigned the remaining seats. However, there is no nationalist. Instead, parties rank unsuccessful candidates according to their number of preference votes. Thus a candidate who receives a large number of preference votes but is not elected on the constituency list still has a chance of being elected by the national college. Moreover, candidates who were elected in two constituencies, or to both the Senate and the Chamber, must opt for one or the other (they can run in up to three Chamber constituencies); the candidate with the next highest number of preference votes on the vacated list is then declared elected. Subsequent vacancies are filled in a similar fashion, avoiding by-elections. In the Valle d'Aosta, if no one receives a majority in the competition for the single Chamber seat, a runoff election is held two weeks later between the two leading candidates. For the Valle d'Aosta Senate seat a plurality suffices.

Participation as a percentage of those eligible to vote varied between 45.5 percent in 1870 and 65 percent in 1909 in the period of restricted suffrage (Capecchi et al., 1968, p. 23). With the suffrage extended, in the hotly contested election of 1919 only 56.6 percent of those eligible to vote did so; this rose only to 60.9 percent in 1921. Under the republic it has been consistently high:

1946	1948	1953	1958	1963	1968
89.1%	92.2%	93.8%	93.8%	92.9%	93%

The true rate of participation is actually higher because these figures are based on the total electoral rolls. In order to vote, electors must have certificates that are delivered to them by municipal authorities. The percentage not delivered because the elector could not be found is revealing concerning the turnout rate (the certificates not delivered are retained by the authorities until the polls close). In 1946 the certificates not delivered were 5.4 percent of the total; in 1948, 3.5 percent; in 1953; 2.7 percent; in 1958, 2.7 percent; in 1963, 3.0 percent. Regional differences are significant: the rate in Abruzzo in 1963 was 8.3 percent; in Molise in the same year it reached 14.9 percent. These are regions of heavy emigration, suggesting that many voters simply are no longer resident there and, further, that the lists are inadequately updated. Thus the rate of participation for Abruzzo goes from 86.5 percent to 94.8 percent and Molise from 79.5 percent to 94.4 percent if it is computed on the basis of electoral certificates delivered (Capecchi et al., 1968, pp. 69-70). Scholars analyzing turnout in Italy must take such factors into account. The phenomenon of the nonresident voter will not be as important in the future, but it will remain. Those who emigrate abroad to work will be carried on the rolls; indeed, many of them will return to vote.

Blank ballots and invalid ballots are of some importance in the final results. Between 1948 and 1963 blank ballots varied between .6 percent and 1.8 percent of the total; during the same period invalid ballots ranged from 1.3 percent to 2.0 percent of the votes cast. (For an analysis of the correlates of blank ballots and invalid ballots see Capecchi et al., 1968 pp. 71-72.)

Complete electoral returns are published in several volumes by the Ministry of the Interior. They are not commercially available and hence are difficult to obtain. More limited but still useful sources are the *Annuario Parlamentare* and, for elections since 1963, the *Annuario Politico*. Neither of these is truly satisfactory, nor is any other single source available.

C. THE PARTY SYSTEM IN THE TWENTIETH – CENTURY

A simplified overview of the Italian party system in this century would identify at least four principal historical *tendances*—the secular bourgeois tradition, the leftist tradition, the Catholic tradition, and the fascist tradition—with each supported by particular social groups and subcultures. These are not always represented by single parties, however, and the overlapping and exchanges through time between parties appealing to the same groups and subcultures provide much of the dynamics of the Italian party system.

The formation of modern Italy was the achievement of secular elites who came to terms in a highly selective fashion with many traditional regional elites. They were actively opposed by Catholic elites, however, who were forbidden by the Church to participate in the affairs of the new state that had been formed in part at the expense of the papacy. The Catholic masses were unmobilized; the emerging urban proletariat, attracted by anarchism and denied the vote, was not an important political force until late in the century. In the absence of Catholic and leftist participation the restricted electoral system left politics in the hands of the liberal elite. With the extension of the suffrage, however, the rise in votes for the Left led to a strategy of incorporating the

Catholic masses into the system as a conservative force. But the Italian party system was denied the stabilizing influence of the Church, and the liberal politicians were unable to incorporate the new voters into their system of mutual favoritism. The result was a long-term decline in their electoral strength and the rise of two mass movements, one socialist and one Catholic.

The Catholics began to organize prior to the First World War, and combined for the 1919 elections to form the *Partito Popolare*, which received the second highest number of votes and seats. This party, greatly expanded in conception and support, formed the basis for the Christian Democratic party after the Second World War. The socialist movement has chronically suffered from disunity and frequently from disarray as well. It has always contained a wide spread of opinion ranging from reformist to revolutionary, and this opinion has usually found political expression in at least two parties. Thus prior to the rise of fascism there were sporadically at least two socialist parties and in the 1920s a communist party as well. However, they all shared a common subculture, and the socialist tradition is remarkably durable.

The fourth tradition is the fascist. Fascism is an Italian invention, and its "real" meaning continues to be the subject of analysis and research in Italy and abroad. Within the context of a discussion of the party system, it is sufficient to note that it was a movement that secured the support of a number of elite groups and at the same time was able to mobilize, or simulate the mobilization of, a substantial mass following. As a result of its years in power there has been a blurring of distinctions between who had and who had not been a Fascist, with only the peasantry, the working-class and its leaders, and some Catholic elements largely free of contamination. This fact had considerable ramifications for the party system after 1945.

There is another well-established political practice in Italy that merits attention, though it is not an organized point of view as much as it is a state of mind, or, more properly, a set of behaviors. That is clientelism, in which local notables construct a network of followers through mutual favoritism, pork-barrel politics, and intimidation. It is sometimes said to antedate even the classical Greek and Roman political traditions of the peninsula. The nineteenth-century party system relied almost exclusively on these practices to the neglect of party organization and ideology. As an organizational segment of the party system it is no longer of significance, but as a source of votes and as an explanatory variable it still retains considerable importance. The Christian Democratic party, the Liberals, and the Monarchists rely heavily on these methods, especially in the south, and it is an important element in all parties. But it is today a technique for getting votes, not a separate tradition.

It is only with the rise of the leftist parties that parties as organizations acquired meaning in Italy. The previous parties were aggregations of notables, each of whom tended his own fences with the assistance on a personal basis of the prime minister and cabinet. Cabinets were formed on the basis of these personal arrangements (*trasformismo*) with few considerations of ideology or party organizational needs. It was a system that worked well only with a restricted electorate, so that the rise of the Left and subsequent emergence of the Popular party left the notables without a mass following. This weakness added to the attractions of fascism for the traditional political elites of the country, and it also contributed to the discrediting of many of them at the end of the Second World War.

These traditions were all represented in the last elections before the rise of fascism, and they were also present at its downfall. They thus provide a background for the analysis of the party system since 1945. The Italian party system as of 1970 has at least nine parties that can claim realistically to be national parties. These are the following, as conventionally listed from the Left to the Right:

ITALIAN POLITICAL PARTIES IN 1970

PCI	*Partito Comunista Italiano*—Italian Communist party
PSIUP	*Partito Socialista Italiano di Unità Proletaria*—Italian Socialist party of Proletarian Unity
*PSI	*Partito Socialista Italiano*—Italian Socialist party
*PSU	*Partito Socialista Unitario*—Unitary Socialist party
PRI	*Partito Repubblicano Italiano*—Italian Republican party
DC	*Democrazia Cristiana*—Christian Democratic party
PLI	*Partito Liberale Italiano*—Italian Liberal party
PDIUM	*Partito Democratico Italiano di Unità Monarchica*—Monarchist party
MSI	*Movimento Sociale Italiano*—Italian Social Movement (Neofascist party)

*These two formed a single party in 1968, the Italian Socialist party—Italian Social Democratic party (PSI-PSDI).

Each of these parties runs candidates in all the thirty-two constituencies. In the Valle d'Aosta the single-member system leads to two competitive coalitions. In addition to these national parties there are three major regional parties, the Sardinian Action party, the *Union Valdostaine*, and the *Südtiroler Volkspartei*. Moreover, there is a third category of party that sometimes assumes marginal significance—this includes dissident socialist groups, non-Marxist radical lists, protest groups such as the pensioners, etc. Their importance is limited to certain elections and constituencies in which they have had a marginal impact on seats assigned to particular parties.

The list of major parties on the ballot has varied little since 1946. The MSI and others absorbed votes that went to the "Everyman's Party" in 1946; the Monarchists have split and reunited during the interim; the socialists have split, merged (with a faction refusing to merge), and split again, so that in 1969 there were three major socialist parties in addition to the PCI. The actual number of parties on the ballot in a constituency varies from election to election and from constituency to constituency. However, the national nature of the major parties and their near monopoly of votes mean that for practical purposes the party system is remarkably stable and national.

Electoral returns reinforce the contention that Italy is a system of "Polarized Pluralism" (Sartori, 1966). The two largest parties have received at least 62 percent of the vote between them since 1953. In 1946 the Christian Democrats received 35.2 percent, the Socialists 20.7 percent, and the Communists 18.9 percent. In 1948 the Socialists and Communists supported a joint list, which received 31 percent of the vote;

however, more Communists than Socialists were elected. Since that time the Communists have been the number-two party and the PSI third. The vote of other parties has been fragmented, with the PSDI's 7.1 percent in 1948 and the PLI's 7 percent in 1963 being the highest levels reached by fourth parties during the postwar period. What has shifted, however, is the vote for parties within these categories. The Communists have received an increasing percentage of the leftist portion, and the extreme Right has declined in favor of the moderate Right of Christian Democrats and Liberals.

Taking changes of name, mergers, and splits into account, there has been little change in the party system. The nine parties listed above (along with their predecessors) accounted for 97.7 percent of the votes in 1948 and 98.6 percent in 1968. The only other parties of importance were those representing ethnic minorities and particular regions. Although each parliament lists a few independents, almost all were elected on a party list and subsequently broke with the party. Few of these are reelected, unless they join a party.

The fragmentation of the vote gives rise to the perpetual problem of a majority in the parliament. The electoral system reproduces quite faithfully in the parliament the division of the vote, with only a slight tendency to favor the larger parties through the distribution of remainders. The location of the Christian Democratic party near the center helps it to dominate all governments, as it has since 1946, but the importance of marginal deputies to a cabinet gives smaller parties such as the Republicans and, formerly, the Social Democrats a crucial role in the parliamentary system despite their meager representation.

The historically important *tendances* in Italian political parties have been previously described as secular bourgeois, leftist, Catholic, and fascist. Richard Rose has suggested that the following groupings seem relevant in a European context: conservative-bourgeois, religious, liberal-secular-bourgeois, socialist, communist, nationalist, fasicst, agrarian, and protest. All of these forms have been of significance in Italy, and most of them are still represented in the party system. One must point out however, that parties are usually both more and less than is suggested by the label of the *tendance*. The PCI, for example, is the largest communist party in the world after the Chinese and Russian. Yet if the Chinese and Russian parties represent the ideal type, then the PCI might better be placed in the socialist category. If we accept the attitudes and expectations of most of its leaders, militants, and voters as expressed in interviews, it has little in common with these two ruling communist parties. Italy has a strong socialist tradition: the socialist *tendance* is the first in voting strength and in organizational effectiveness in the country. The strongest organizational base within that *tendance* is occupied by the PCI, which is also the largest in electoral strength. It is important in understanding Italian communism that it be viewed as a part of the socialist *tendance* rather than as merely the clever and cynical agent of a foreign power.

The Republicans are more difficult to classify. They are a part of the left, and many of them are perhaps non-Marxian socialists. At the same time they are also secular and bourgeois. Only in the Romagna do they have a mass following. The PRI fits poorly in contemporary schemes of classification.

The Christian Democratic party is obviously a religious party, but is so much more than that. As the party of order and continuity in Italy as well as the governing party, it attracts many followers for nonreligious reasons. In fact, it attracts different groups for different reasons. However, the Christian Democratic party is first and above all else the party of the Church and thus must be classified as a religious party. The Liberal party was traditionally a liberal-secular-bourgeois party, but in the postwar period it has become increasingly the party of constitutional conservatism. The PLI could perhaps equally well today be labeled a conservative-bourgeois party. The Monarchists are a traditionalist–clientelistic party that fits none of the categories. Although most of its strength—which is in severe decline—was southern and rural, it is not an agrarian party. It is the dying representative of a type of party now extinct in most of Europe. It does, however, have characteristics that are common to other Italian parties of the Right and Center as well as to parties in other countries. The MSI is a fascist-nationalist party, with perhaps a greater emphasis on the second than the first. It is also in practice a protest party in its appeal to the dissatisfied. Single-theme protest parties such as the pensioners exist but without electoral success. The *Südtiroler Volkspartei* is the party of German-speaking particularists; in its socioeconomic outlook it is a conservative-bourgeois party.

An analysis based on *tendances* thus must carefully specify the dimensions involved (see Barnes, 1970a). The major historical dimensions are Left and Right, but this is a complex issue involving socioeconomic, religious, and other dimensions. On most of these the Communists, Socialists, and Republicans are on one side and the rest on the other. The major political dimensions relevant to early postwar cabinet formation would be Left, Right, and Center, with the Christian Democrats divided between Center and Right and the rest Left or Right. In cabinet formation in the late 1960s the relevant divisions would be Left, Center-Left, and Right. Thus in making the leap from historical *tendance* to cabinet formation care must be taken to sketch in the connections.

Indeed, conventional notions of Left and Right are useful for some but not all aspects of contemporary political analysis. There is a strong association between party identification and Left-Right self-placement and between party identification and an index of programmatic position. The tau beta correlation for the former is .63, for the latter .40 (Barnes, 1970a). Much of the Christian Democratic vote is leftist on socioeconomic issues, however, and that party has seemingly moved to the Left in recent years. This ability to cover both its flanks has been a constant source of strength for the DC. But it also is the cause of much of its internal factionalism and the increasingly difficult task of putting together a government.

D. COMPETITION FOR SEATS

Italian parties are highly articulated by American or even British standards, and the multimember constituency, preference votes, and control over the composition of the lists place the party in virtually complete control over who is and who is not elected.

While the role of the party apparatus is crucial in all of the parties, it varies according to the strength of the central bureaucracy.

In the PCI, for example, the party organization nominates what is in effect a "balanced ticket," assuring representation to relevant territorial and socioeconomic categories. Party militants are then instructed as to whom to give their preference votes, and voters are encouraged to vote for the party rather than to express preferences. Although selection of the persons actually elected is greatly influenced by the organization, it cannot, of course, control the total number of votes received. Thus it is only the marginal candidate, the nth one in the party's scale of importance, who cannot be certain of election. For the rest, once they have been nominated, election is no surprise. The national leaders receive many preference votes; others have only a small spread between them.

The same system works, though less effectively, within the socialist parties. The better-known party officials are usually assured the preference votes of the militants, whereas the candidates on the list who have no close organizational ties have little chance of election. The Christian Democratic party works somewhat the same way throughout most of Italy, though there are party notables who possess such a strong local, clientelistic, or affiliated organizational base that they are not effectively controlled by the organization. The Liberals and Monarchists are much more parties of notables, and the role of the organization is limited or nil. Little has been written of a scholarly nature about the organization and selection of candidates in the MSI.

In a system such as the Italian there is little competition between individual candidates of different parties. It is the party that counts, and the parties that are closest together in subcultural networks and policy preferences are the ones that compete most in elections. Within parties there is a subtle competition for preference votes, but the process has not been studied. Turnover of personnel between one parliament and the other thus represents different things in different parties. For the Communists it generally represents a deliberate attempt to keep the delegation young and representative of the diverse groups within the party. In the socialist parties it more likely represents the shifting prestige of leaders within local and national party organs. In the DC it represents a combination of these factors plus some particularly Christian Democratic considerations. What it does not usually represent—in comparison with, for example, the United States—is the rejection by the public of particular individuals. It is true that important public figures are sometimes not reelected, but the reasons are likely to be found in intraparty politics; the most important party figures can be assured of election by being placed on the ballot in constituencies in which the party is very strong and by being guaranteed the preference votes of the party militants.

E. CONTINUITIES AND DISCONTINUITIES

In comparing electoral returns for Italy in the twentieth-century it is important to consider the effects of the twenty years of fascism. Optimists view this as a parenthesis in the democratic evolution of the country; pessimists suggest that it was the necessary culmination of tendencies within the prefascist regime. Political tendencies within Italy have been remarkably constant throughout this century. Labels, personnel, and situations, however, have changed so much between prefascist and postfascist Italy that the utility of general comparisons between the party and electoral systems of the two is open to question. On the other hand there are important continuities, such as the persistence of radicalism in certain areas, the continuing relationship between the strength of the church and of the Popular and Christian Democratic parties in some areas, the traditionalism in parts of the south, and so on. The postwar period forms a natural unit of analysis. Extending the analysis further into the past requires particular attention to definition of concepts, variables, and units of analysis.

II. The Act of Voting Today

A. ELECTIONS AND BALLOTS

There are two major types of elections in Italy, the national parliamentary balloting, called *elezioni politiche*, or political elections, and local elections, labeled *elezioni amministrative*, or administrative elections. In the former, citizens vote for lists and express preferences among candidates for the Chamber of Deputies and for a single candidate for the Senate. In the latter, representatives to the communal and provincial councils are chosen. Citizens of the five special regions (Sicily, Sardinia, Valle d'Aosta, Trentino-Alto Adige, and Friuli-Venezia Giulia) have been voting for representatives to the regional assemblies as well; the other regions elected regional representatives for the first time in 1970. Although referenda are provided for in the constitution, parliamentary elections are the only national elections that have been held under the 1948 constitution. A referendum on the monarchy was carried out before the constitution took effect. This constitution gave the Chamber a five-year term and the Senate a six-year term, but permitted the dissolution of either house under certain conditions. In practice the Senate has always been dissolved with the Chamber, so that both have been replaced in the same elections. A constitutional amendment has regularized this practice by establishing a maximum five-year term for both. All parliaments to date have lasted the full five years. The actual date of the election, however, is set only at the time of dissolution and can fluctuate over a period of several months, a practice that can be frustrating to scholars planning surveys.

The ballot for a parliamentary election contains the symbol or symbol and name of each party presenting a list in the constituency. The party's position on the ballot in each constituency is determined by the date of filing its list in that constituency. Parties that have difficulty in agreeing on a list thus are penalized by being lower on the ballot, though the importance of position is unknown. The ranking of names on the list is determined by the party. Often a well-known national leader or two will head the list with others following in alphabetical order, but this is at the discretion of the party. Although the lists are widely publicized, the ballot itself contains only the party symbol or symbol and name. Preferences must be written in; one technique is to provide voters with a tiny stencil containing the name; the candidate's number on the list may be used instead of his name.

B. THE LEGAL FACILITATION OF VOTING

Elections are administered by the Ministry of the Interior. Voting is from 6:00 A.M. to 10:00 P.M. on Sunday and from 7:00 A.M. to 2:00 P.M. on Monday. These are legal holidays, and reduced fares facilitate travel. Voting booths are widespread and access is seldom a problem.

There are no provisions for absentee voting, a factor that causes considerable disruption to those Swiss, German, and other foreign industries that employ large numbers of Italian workers. Special polling booths are set up in hospitals and rest homes, and servicemen and sailors may vote in communes other than those of their legal residence.

C. ELECTIONS SINCE THE FALL OF FASCISM

In a political system that dates only from 1943 it is not easy to determine which political situations are normal and which are not. However, changes from election to election are very slight, and the current voting patterns show no signs of altering dramatically in any five-year period. Longer-range trends are another matter.

There are several aspects of the elections in the postwar period that should be clarified, if only to make reading of the overall returns more meaningful. The first is the stability of the leftist vote combined with the great changes that took place in its distribution in the first three elections. In the elections to the Constituent Assembly that drew up the new constitution the Socialists outpolled the Communists. The former party soon split, however, and the majority faction entered into an electoral alliance with the Communists for the 1948 election in which far more Communists than Socialists were elected from the joint list. By 1953 the PCI was much stronger than the PSI and larger than the two socialist parties combined, and that relationship has been maintained. On the extreme right the attitudes expressed by the *Uomo Qua-l'unque* ("Everyman's" party) were absorbed by the MSI, though the former was perhaps more Poujadist than fascist.

The first two elections for parliament were held under conditions of extreme tension. The 1948 campaign was one in which the Christian Democratic party and the Church utilized a fiercely anticommunist rhetoric and the atmosphere was of impending revolution. The 1953 campaign was similarly bitter due to the "swindle law" that promised a bonus in seats to the party or group of parties with an absolute majority. Thus in the first few elections an atmosphere of impending doom appeared to be the norm. The last three, however, have been quite mild in tone and, in comparison, not very exciting. It is difficult to argue that the strident tones of the earlier campaigns made a great deal of difference in the outcome, unless it is that the Christian Democrats secured additional anticommunist votes that might otherwise have gone to the right-wing parties. The recent elections were dominated by the theme of the Opening to the Left. There has been nothing in Italian elections comparable to the special features of several recent French elections. Party identification is very strong in Italy. In the CISER 1968 survey almost 80 percent of the respondents claimed to have always voted for the same party. Thus shifts from election to election seem to be small.

The concept of a normal vote for Italy has received little attention. The long-term trends seem to point away from equilibrium in the distribution of votes *within* the Right and Left and stability between the Right and Left, with perhaps slow and gradual increase in the Left. The PCI share has grown steadily while the extreme Right has declined, due mainly to the disintegration of the Monarchists. These general trends mask a number of contradictory trends in particular regions of the country. An analysis using aggregate ecological and electoral data uses the concept of a party's normal expected vote in a province based on socioeconomic correlates of its vote on the national level (Capecchi et al., 1968, pp. 307ff.). This demonstrates that both the PCI and DC receive far more votes than predicted in their areas of core strength. That is, organizational and subcultural variables are needed in addition to socioeconomic ones. And of course in some areas these parties receive fewer votes than predicted, indicating that the potential of further gains for them is real, though there seem to be identifiable outer limits. To pursue this point further requires a discussion of the data available for analysis.

III. Data for Analysis

There are numerous bibliographies of Italian politics. Especially recommended among those dealing with electoral behavior are the ones by Sivini (1967, 1968) and Passigli (1962).

A. SAMPLE SURVEYS

National surveys have been undertaken on a regular basis in Italy since 1946, when Pierpaolo Luzzatto Fegiz, now professor of statistics in the University of Rome, founded DOXA (via G. Mameli, 10, Milan) as a private market-research organization. It is the Italian affiliate of the Gallup group. Another major organization is CISER (via Paganini, 7, Rome), which merged in 1969 with DEMOSKOPEA to form DEMOSKOPEA/CISER. Both DOXA and CISER have done extensive political polling for Italian parties and government agencies, and some of these data have found their way into private academic archives. There are several other market-research organizations, but their involvement with political surveys is limited and noncumulative. Luzzatto Fegiz has published two massive volumes containing a thorough profile of the work of DOXA over a twenty-year period (Luzzatto Fegiz, 1957; 1966).

DOXA conducts regular surveys containing a wide range of questions. Most DOXA and CISER surveys use national probability samples utilizing the random selection of names from lists of inhabitants of communes that are themselves randomly selected after stratification by section of the country and size of commune. Quota samples are sometimes used for inquiries concerning specific populations, for example, immigrant workers in industrial areas. Area sampling of households is not used. Sample size is usually between 1,500 and 3,000. The large number of parties makes larger samples desirable for political surveys.

There have been few academic surveys on the national level. The *Civic Culture* Italian survey with 995 respondents is a useful exception. *How Nations See Each Other* reports the results of a 1948 survey executed by DOXA (Buchanan, 1953). As part of the University of Michigan program in comparative representation studies CISER executed a national survey for Samuel H. Barnes with 2,500 interviews following the 1968 parliamentary elections. For reviews of other national and local surveys see Sivini (1967, 1968) and Passigli (1962).

B. SECONDARY ANALYSES

The most useful general secondary analysis of Italian survey data for introductory purposes is by Gianfranco Poggi. He used DOXA data from the 1958 and 1963 electoral studies and CISER data for 1963 to construct a profile of Italian political preferences, paying special attention to class and occupation (Poggi, 1968). A relevant study devoted to Italian youth is LaPalombara and Walters (1961). The *Civic Culture* data are available for secondary analysis, and studies are beginning to appear.

C. ECOLOGICAL ANALYSES

Ecological analyses along with electoral geography have been the most extensively employed methods for investigating Italian voting behavior. These studies are greatly facilitated by the coincidence of electoral and administrative subdivisions and by the ample socioeconomic data collected by the census and other governmental sources. Excellent data are readily available at the provincial level. The problem is more complicated at the communal level due to the reticence of Italian officialdom to make readily available to scholars many kinds of data that are in fact public property and not confidential. This is especially true of data that are not regularly published on a systematic basis, such as financial materials; while these can often be obtained at the communal level, collecting them sometimes proves to be impractical and securing them from the relevant ministry in Rome problematical. It is consequently impossible to say in general terms what is and what is not potentially available for ecological analysis.

There have been numerous analyses of electoral results correlated with a wide variety of variables. The most impressive of these is a major study by a group at the Istituto Carlo Cattaneo in Bologna published with the title *Il Comportamento Elettorale in Italia* (Capecchi et al., 1968). This is the most ambitious undertaking of its kind in Italy and merits a brief description. It is based on data for 7,144 communes and the ninety-two provinces of Italy. National electoral results for 1946, 1948, 1953, 1958, and 1963 were used. The referendum on the republic in 1946 was used as indicative of subcultural cleavages. Many demographic variables from the 1951 and 1961 censuses were used, as well as data on radio and television ownership in 1957 and 1962. Data on membership in the PCI and DC, the daily circulation of the PCI newspaper, and per capita income were available also, but only at the provincial level. These data were employed in numerous static and dynamic analyses of Italian electoral behavior. In appendices Vittorio Capecchi discusses "The Possibilities and Limits of Research on Electoral Behavior based on Ecological Data," and Giordano Sivini reviews previous electoral research in Italy. These data are all on tape at the Istituto Carlo Cattaneo (via Santo Stefano, 6, Bologna).

There are dozens of local studies and other analyses that pay particular attention to certain groups such as immigrants and residents of land-reform areas, regions of rapid industrialization, and so on.

D. NONVOTING AND ITS MEASUREMENT

The electoral rolls are based on legal residence and do not take into account employment and actual residence elsewhere; many nonvoters are in fact nonresidents as well. Therefore the extent of the danger of sampling from the lists is difficult to estimate. Public servants understandably ascribe great accuracy to the electoral rolls; indeed, there is no evidence that the rolls are not adequately maintained *within the limits of administrative procedures.* The problem is that in the past it was difficult to change legal residence, and the extent to which that mentality still operates is unknown. The result is that some people simply do not live in their commune of legal residence, may or may not return there to vote, and are almost certain not to be there when the interviewer calls. Experience with a national sample of 3,000 in 1968, of whom 2,500 were interviewed, suggests that this probably is no longer a serious problem.

In addition to the electoral rolls authorities have basic data on every individual in the commune; this facilitates interviewing subjects under twenty-one. A problem with both sets of names is access. Legally they are public property. However, it is not always easy for the researcher to gain access to these data. It is wise to view access to a sampling frame as a separate problem that must be consciously confronted and resolved. As indicated, voting rates are very high, even when based on electoral rolls rather than certificates delivered. To date there have been no extensive scholarly analyses of nonvoting in Italy.

E. VOTING AND ITS MEASUREMENT

There are a number of cleavages that crosscut Italian parties and render difficult the discovery of "the" explanatory variable. Occupational class, however measured, is important in Italy as elsewhere, but it is in turn affected by religion and other variables. Religion is of primary importance. As we will see, it is as much a psychological variable as a sociological one: most Italians are nominally Catholic, so it is the level of identification with the church that makes a difference. Region may not be as important as it is thought to be in the conventional wisdom, once proper controls are instituted, but it is still highly relevant especially if we expand the concept to include the areas that are heavily dominated by one subculture. There are also marked sex differences in voting. Thus occupational-class, religion, region, and sex merit particular attention.

The measure of partisan voting is a very important aspect of political survey work; unfortunately, in Italy it is the most difficult to obtain. The problem results from the refusal of many respondents to state a partisan preference. These respondents are concentrated in the parties of the Left, especially the PCI. The result is that every political survey taken greatly underrepresents the size of the Communist vote. The vote for the Christian Democratic party is always equaled or exceeded in the sample, and the votes for minor parties vary around an acceptable mean. The PCI voter remains elusive.

Several strategies are available for coping with this problem. One is to deal only with respondents who claim to be PCI supporters. Unfortunately, one does not know whether those who readily admit their PCI preferences are similar to those who do not. There is no reason to believe that they are. Another strategy is to employ one or several questions that give the researchers strong indications of the way the respondent leans even if he does not respond to the question directly. Still a third is to partition out the nonrespondents on the partisanship question among the parties on the basis of probable voting derived from socioeconomic characteristics. Each of these methods has its drawbacks. The first, in addition to giving possibly biased characteristics of PCI supporters, leaves one with an N too small for many kinds of analyses. The second, which is probably the best solution, still leaves a great deal to be assumed. The third, which may be acceptable under some circumstances, tends to assume what needs to be demonstrated; that is, that respondents' socioeconomic characteristics correlate strongly with vote. A related problem is that the vote for the DC tends to be inflated to varying degrees, and one does not know which respondents to filter out. In analyzing party preferences for most purposes it is necessary to use all of the major parties. Only in a few cases is it possible to group parties.

TABLE 1:   Religion, Class, and Urban-Rural Residence in
Italian Partisan Identification, 1968

	Urban		Rural	
	N	%	N	%
REGULAR CHURCH ATTENDANCE				
Working-class				
PCI	26	5	6	3
PSIUP	5	1	2	(1)
PSI-PSDI	42	8	23	11
PRI	3	(1)	1	(0)
DC	311	61	135	68
PLI	3	(1)	0	(0)
MON	2	(0)	0	(0)
MSI	5	1	2	(1)
Don't know	112	22	32	16
	509	100	201	100
Middle-class				
PCI	2	(0)	0	(0)
PSIUP	2	(0)	1	(1)
PSI-PSDI	33	9	5	7
PRI	6	2	1	(1)
DC	203	54	51	69
PLI	25	7	1	(1)
MON	3	(1)	0	(0)
MSI	8	2	3	(4)
Don't know	94	25	13	17
	376	100	75	100
NONREGULAR CHURCH ATTENDANCE				
Working-class				
PCI	174	24	39	20
PSIUP	25	4	8	4
PSI-PSDI	146	21	29	15
PRI	6	1	0	(0)
DC	157	22	54	28
PLI	5	1	3	(2)
MON	5	1	0	(0)
MSI	11	2	6	3
Don't know	173	24	52	28
	702	100	191	100
Middle-class				
PCI	23	7	3	(5)
PSIUP	7	2	0	(0)
PSI-PSDI	68	22	17	26
PRI	12	4	0	(0)
DC	86	28	22	33
PLI	15	5	3	(5)
MON	4	(1)	0	(0)
MSI	10	3	2	(3)
Don't know	84	28	18	28
	309	100	65	100

( ) = less than 5 cases.   Source: Barnes-CISER, 1968

Most surveys are based on samples covering the entire territory. Some leave out peripheral units such as the Valle d'Aosta or Alto Adige because of differences in parties. The Barnes-CISER data refer to the entire territory. Because of their limited population, however, omission of these peripheral areas would not greatly distort the results.

IV. Social Structure and Voting

The analysis that follows will concentrate on describing how a number of social-structural variables are measured and how they are distributed within the Italian electorate. Table 1 exhibits the impact of several of these variables. A dynamic analysis of their interrelationships will be presented in Section VI.

A. SEX

Sex differences are important in Italian politics for two reasons: the first is that women are more often churchgoers and hence more likely to vote Christian Democratic than men; the second is that there are far more women than men in the electorate.

The importance of the female vote for the DC is well-established. Writing of the 1958 elections, Mattei Dogan concluded, "Regardless of the possible margin of error, one can say without fear of error that, if only men had voted, the PCI and PSI would have obtained more votes than the DC, whose electoral strength is superior to that of these two parties together only thanks to the women's vote." (Dogan, 1963, p. 478). Dogan estimates that in 1958 60 percent of the electorate of the PCI and PSI was male while 63 percent of the DC vote was female, which is, in turn, 51 percent of the total female vote. Dogan suggests further that it is the very old and very young women, the unmarried or widowed, who contribute most heavily to the DC; married women are more likely to follow the choices of their husbands (ibid., pp. 482-86). The following table shows the distribution of admitted tendencies by sex as obtained by Barnes-CISER in 1968.

B. AGE

Generational groupings in Italy reflect the discontinuities of the country in this century. Those born before 1905 would have had some experience with party politics and free elections before the rise of fascism, as well as the experiences of the First World War and the unrest that followed it. Those born between 1905 and 1925 were greatly affected by the fascist experience and their reaction to it. Those born after 1925 have reached maturity since the fall of Mussolini. These dates are somewhat arbitrary, for it is difficult to assess the importance of different school-leaving ages, diverse experiences under fascism, the impact of the war, and so on. The importance of the fascist experience for fixing the attitudes of those who reached maturity in the early

TABLE 2:   Partisan Identification, by Sex, 1968, in Percentages

	% of Total Sample	% Male	% Female
PCI	12.4	60	40
PSIUP	2.0	70	30
PSI-PSDI	15.9	67	33
PRI	1.2	69	31
DC	42.6	38	62
PLI	2.9	57	43
MON	.6	21	79
MSI	1.9	70	30
Don't know	20.7	50	50

Source: Barnes-CISER, 1968

1940s is considerable, however—and this is the age cohort that presently predominates among the national elite. At the mass level differences are not as apparent, as is indicated by Table 3 (for an extensive analysis of generational differences see Barnes 1970b).

While differences in the Italian life cycle seem to be considerable, it is difficult to separate them from generational differences. This problem seems especially salient in

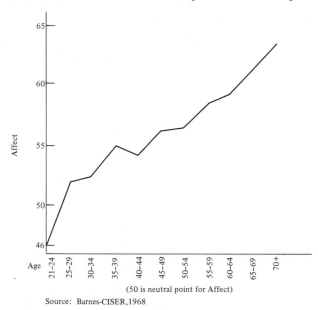

(50 is neutral point for Affect)

Source: Barnes-CISER, 1968

Figure 1: Italian Sympathy for Clerics in 1968, by Age.

the light of the discontinuities of twentieth-century Italian political life. Illustrative of this problem is the decline in affection for the clergy among the young. This is of great political significance, for it promises to disadvantage the Christian Democrats in the future. However, it is not possible with the data at hand to separate the life-cycle effect from true generational differences. Moreover, the political impact of these differences in attitudes toward the clergy is partially offset by the excess of women in the older age groups. Older women in general tend to favor the Christian Democrats. Within the working-class older men are more likely than the young to support the DC. The Communists are especially strong among the young, while Socialists are more popular with the middle group. (See Table 3 and Figure 1.)

TABLE 3: **Age and Party Preference in 1968, by Occupational Class in Percentages**

	AGE	DC	PCI	PSI-PSDI	OTHER PARTIES	N=
Middle-class	Under 40	43	8	19	31	413
	40-60	45	4	17	33	342
	60+	43	4	11	42	153
Working-class	Under 40	32	22	18	27	350
	40-60	33	17	21	29	391
	60+	45	13	15	27	269
Other (housewives,	Under 40	45	15	9	31	222
students, unemployed)	40-60	50	14	13	22	205
	60+	68	9	7	16	140

Source: Barnes-CISER, 1968

It is probable that both life-cycle and generational differences contribute to these findings, but they cannot presently be separated.

C. EDUCATION

For most Italians education begins at the age of six and continues through the age of eleven, or the end of elementary school. Compulsory education ends with the beginning of the *liceo*, or high school. In the past, at the end of elementary school children were forced into tracks that prepared them for eventual university study or for termination either at age 14, which is the end of the junior high, or at age 15, the end of technical school. The classical *liceo* prepared students for all university faculties. The scientific *liceo* (or program, as both classical and scientific courses usually exist in the same school) permitted entrance to most but not all higher education. The business high school permitted one to enter only the faculty of economics and commerce. For students not attending the university education was more specialized, but the availability of business and technical training varied greatly from area to area. Indeed, the possibility of education of any kind beyond the elementary level was limited in many areas. And for many even elementary schooling represented little more than sporadic attendance at poorly equipped schools and indifferently taught classes. Many older people today are functionally illiterate. This varies greatly from region to region, but is particulary acute in the South and Islands. This situation has been vastly improved in the postwar period, and all children today learn to read and write. Furthermore, recent reforms in the examination system and in the post-elementary-school level promise to push to a later age the crucial decision for or against a university preparatory course. The content of education in Italy varies considerably. The distinction between the scientific and humanistic program in the secondary schools is not of great importance, but the difference between these two, on the one hand, and the business and technical, on the other, is considerable. Most graduates of the former continue on to the university. In 1970 Italian universities granted only one degree, the *laurea*, and all university graduates use the title doctor.

Most Italian schools are government-supported and regulated in their curricula and standards. Religious schools are important, especially at the elementary level, but their programs differ little from those of the public schools. Furthermore, public schools give religious training. In the 1968 Barnes-CISER sample 86 percent attended public schools, 4 percent religious schools, 1 percent private but nonreligious schools, 2 percent mixtures of these, 1 percent don't-know and 6 percent never attended school. Using ecological data, Capecchi and his colleagues found a constant correlation between elementary education and DC vote, while higher education correlated negatively with the DC vote. They speculate that the chief explanation for this is the religious atmosphere and training in the elementary schools. Illiteracy in general correlates positively with the PCI vote. However, there are numerous regional and other particular exceptions, and these findings merit considerable refinement (Capecchi et al., 1968, pp. 169–204).

Length of education seems to have an important but complicated impact on the political preferences of Italians. As previously mentioned, illiteracy is correlated positively with the Communist vote and negatively with the vote of the non-Communist Left (Capecchi et al., 1968, pp. 170–88). Elementary education seems to favor the Christian Democrats. Education beyond that level favors the PCI and, to an even more marked degree, the non-Communist Left (Capecchi et al., 1968, pp. 190–91). The Right likewise benefits from higher education. These general tendencies thus suggest that higher education, in effect, benefits the smaller parties: the non-Communist Left improves at the expense of the Communists and the Right gains from the Christian Democrats. Only limited conclusions can be drawn from this level of analysis, however, whereas survey data permit a greater refinement.

According to Poggi's analysis of CISER and DOXA data, within each occupational-class similar dynamics are at work. Better-educated workers tend to vote less for the PCI and also less for the DC (Poggi, 1968, pp. 26–27). Artisans and white-collar workers also vote less heavily Communist with increasing education.

However, in this case the vote for the DC and for the PLI increases with education, and the PSDI vote increases while the PSI vote declines. The chief exception to these generalizations concerns what Poggi calls the "borghesia," composed of professional people, higher civil servants, entrepreneurs, managers, and so on. In this group the Liberal vote is high for both educational categories, but the PCI vote increases while the PSI, PSDI, and DC vote all decline with the higher educational category. Moreover, the percentage of those refusing to divulge party preference increases. The percentage voting for the Left is virtually similar in both groups—29 percent versus 30 percent—but the PCI share jumps from 3 percent to 18 percent. This is perhaps comparable to Rose's finding that the British group with the highest education was less conservative than the intermediate group (see p. 506).

D. RELIGION

Italy is overwhelmingly Catholic in the nominal religious identification of its population. Church attendance, however, is more indicative of religious commitment, and church attendance is highly correlated with the DC vote. In the mid-1950s 80 percent of the women and 57 percent of the men claimed to have attended church in the previous seven days. Table 4 indicates the differences among the parties on this variable. The DOXA surveys suggest that social-class differences are without importance (Luzzatto Fegiz, 1966, p. 1287). Not surprisingly, the frequency of attendance

TABLE 4A: Attended Church in Previous Seven Days, 1956, By Party, in Percentages

	PCI	PSI	PSDI	DC	PLI	MON	MSI
Yes	29	41	69	86	75	77	56
No	71	59	31	14	25	23	44
	100%	100%	100%	100%	100%	100%	100%

Source: Luzzatto Fegiz, 1966, p. 1285

TABLE 4B: Frequency of Church Attendance in 1968, By Party, in Percentages

	PCI	PSIUP	PSI-PSDI	PRI	DC	PLI	MON	MSI
At least once a week	12	20	29	39	69	53	37	39
Often during the year	16	22	28	17	16	16	21	21
Sometimes	24	30	25	17	10	20	21	30
Rarely	24	16	12	10	4	9	7	6
Never	24	12	6	17	1	2	14	4
	100%	100%	100%	100%	100%	100%	100%	100%
N=	279	50	369	29	1,048	56	14	47

Source: Barnes-CISER, 1968

varied from a high in Sardinia of 63 percent, to the Veneto, Sicily, and Campania, all with 58 percent, to Tuscany and Emilia with 42 percent. The former four are areas of Christian Democratic strength; the latter two are Left strongholds (Luzzatto Fegiz, 1966, p. 1289). The data confirm what is widely known: a major cleavage in Italian politics is along the dimension of the closeness of attachment to the Church. This will be explored in greater detail in the final section.

E. ETHNO-LINGUISTIC DIFFERENCES

Race and ethnicity are not meaningful variables in Italian politics. There are only three significant minority groups within the country, and their distinctiveness is linguistic and cultural. These are the French-speaking citizens of the Valle d'Aosta, the German-speaking inhabitants of Alto-Adige, and the Slavic minorities along the Yugoslav border. The first two have well-organized political forces; the third is less well articulated.

Cultural and linguistic differences among the various regions have been considerable but should not be overemphasized. Italians do have a strong sense of geographical as well as social place. Regional nuances are important. The regions are historic units and are useful for many analytical purposes. Except for those established under special statute, however, they did not have an administrative existence of their own until 1970. Before then they were used as units for electing the Senate, although creation of the regions as an intermediate level of government was anticipated by the constitution and strongly favored by the Left. Fear on the part of the Christian Democrats that they would merely reinforce the Left in several parts of the country delayed the enactment of enabling legislation.

The regions with strong ethnic minorities are of special interest. The Valle d'Aosta and Alto-Adige support separate parties. Alto-Adige has been a troublesome member of the Italian Republic. The letter but not the spirit of an agreement to give special status to its inhabitants was lived up to with the creation of Trentino-Alto-Adige as a special region. The latter, which was predominantly German-speaking, was joined with the overwhelmingly Italian Trento, with a result that the minority is not in control of its own special region. Taking into account the special problems of these regions, especially the existence of sui generis political parties and their small populations, it is sometimes useful to omit them from analysis of national politics.

Language differences are of declining importance in Italy. Italian, the Tuscan dialect that became first the literary language of the country and then the national language, is taught everywhere; in general, the more education a person has the more likely he is to speak fluent Italian. Regional dialects remain important, however, and some of these are mutually incomprehensible. This reinforces the localism so important in Italian politics. Only in the Valle d'Aosta and Alto-Adige do non-Italian languages have a special status; those areas are bilingual in their schools and governmental operations.

Psychological identification is closely related to the current migrations. Italians historically have a strong attachment to their city or village (*campanilismo*). The very particularism of their attachments makes the growth of larger identification difficult. The national minorities, especially the Germans, think of themselves in particularistic terms. There is also a certain amount of regional identification, but its depth and range have not been adequately charted. There are great regional differences in the support received by different parties, and they remain even after socioeconomic differences are controlled. The Left has long had regional strongholds; the DC receives more votes in some areas than others; some parties such as the Monarchists and Republicans are largely limited to a few areas of the country. The analysis below will show the way in which region assumes importance as an explanatory variable, but mainly for those not caught up in the organizational networks of the Left or the Church.

The only nationalist parties extolling a particularistic nationalism are the *Union Valdotaine* and the *Südtiroler Volkspartei*. The latter party has a German-speaking clientele that is unsympathetic to incorporation into the Italian republic, and it receives virtually the entire vote of those whose first language is German. These minorities are not important in the total national vote; the problem of Alto-Adige, however, is a recurring concern to Italy. Agreements reached in late 1969 promised to bring agitation and terrorism to an end.

F. REGION

Before 1970 Italy was divided administratively into provinces and communes with only five regions established; four of these predate the 1948 constitution that authorizes the division of the entire country into regions. The regions are almost universally used as convenient units of analysis, however, and no disagreement about their boundaries exists. These are the legal and historic regions. Also widely used is the division of the country into geographical areas that contain several of the historic regions of Italy within them, and on this criterion of division there is little agreement. The most common, though not the most useful, line of demarcation is north, center, and south. Another familiar division further distinguishes between the south and the islands and between northwest Italy, which is industrial and leftist in its culture, and northeast Italy, which is agricultural and Catholic. But the latter area sometimes includes Emilia-Romagna, which is leftist and sometimes does not. A more complete breakdown places Lombardy in a category by itself, because of its size and distinctive political coloration. And sometimes Sicily and Sardinia are considered separately. This confusion should cause no difficulty as long as it is remembered that some divisions are more appropriate than others for certain analyses, and that the relationship being examined can be strengthened or weakened by the choice of division used.

Continental Europe

G. URBAN-RURAL RESIDENCE

The relationship between urban-rural residence and the vote is complicated by regional differences in agriculture as well as in the significance of the size of communes. Italy has several dominant patterns of land tenure. Much of the south has been characterized by the latifundia system, in which land is divided into large estates and farmed by day laborers or rented to peasants. Although a peasant may own land, rent land, or work as a day laborer, what has been most salient traditionally is the precariousness of his existence and his domination by poverty and the local elites. The peasant usually lived in villages and took advantage of whatever economic opportunities were available in the neighboring fields. These villages can reach populations of more than 50,000 inhabitants without acquiring the social and economic structure of a city. In these areas politics tend to be clientelistic and archaic. Land reform, which is only a partial solution to these social problems, was designed to encourage a class of conservative owner-farmers; it has been only a modest success.

Central Italy was characterized by the *mezzadria*, or sharecropper system that is now disappearing. The *mezzadro* had legal protection and privileges not common in the south. These peasants, however, provided and continue to provide a strong base for the Left in the Red Belt across Central Italy. Owners, on the other hand, are strongly Christian Democratic and rightist. Northern Italy contains several agricultural zones. The northeast is dominated by conservative Christian Democratic owner-operators. The Po Valley contains many large farms with wage laborers, who are somewhat more secure and better off than the southern peasants. In declining agricultural regions some marginal land has been abandoned or taken over by southern migrants.

This brief introduction to the problem of Italian agriculture should suggest several problems of analysis. One is the great regional differences in the nature of agricultural employment and hence in the political ramifications of "rural" status. Another is the poor fit between size of commune and true urbanization: many "cities" are smaller than some agrotowns that are in fact merely overgrown villages of agricultural workers. Nevertheless, a few generalizations are possible. The most important single point to be emphasized is the class division of the agricultural vote. Independent farmers vote overwhelmingly for the center and right-wing parties. Landowners may vote for the Liberals or Monarchists, but the small owner-operators are heavily Christian Democratic. Farm laborers and sharecroppers, on the other hand, tend to be leftist, especially outside the South. These tendencies are even more pronounced in areas of concentrated Christian Democratic or Communist strength (See Capecchi et al., 1968, pp. 119–30).

Urbanization is itself associated with some important differences among the parties. The Christian Democratic party is much stronger in the smaller communes, and its strength declines regularly with increasing size of commune. The PCI is the party of large and, especially, middle-size communes. The non-Communist Left has declined less in the larger communes than the smaller. The Right has altered its image due to the decline of the small-town Monarchist group and the gain in the urban Liberal party.

H. RESIDENTIAL MOBILITY

Both internal and external migration has been heavy in Italy during the past generation; though fewer people now go to North and South America, many work in Switzerland, Germany, and other European countries. And the movement into the cities in all regions and from the south to the north has been dramatic. The changes implicit in these moves go far beyond simply changing residence, however, and hence residential mobility is not an adequate measure. A vast literature is accumulating concerning the political ramifications of these changes. (For a beginning see Ciaurro, 1968; and Passigli, 1969.)

I. MASS MEDIA

Compared with other Europeans Italians are relatively unconcerned with the mass media (see Almond and Verba, 1963, p. 94). The most important differences between Italy and other countries are to be found among those with little formal education; the better-educated are similar to their peers. The result is that the mass media, and particularly the press, are oriented toward the elite. There are several types of newspapers, and some description is necessary. The prestige papers are independent of party ties, but they are centrist in their orientations with, for example, *Il Corriere della Sera* of Milan being somewhat to the right of *La Stampa* of Turin. Each is sold throughout the country, often with special local pages. In addition smaller cities have local newspapers that are often the political vehicles of a local notable or clique. Thus the nonparty press cannot be considered to be politically independent.

There are two types of party press. The mass-circulation papers are either Communist (*Unità*) or Communist-oriented (*Paese Sera*). The other party papers have a small readership and great financial problems (for example, *Avanti!*—Socialist—and *La Voce Republicana*—Republican). Many of the local papers are pro-Christian Democratic, though not party-owned. Circulation figures are carefully guarded, but reliable figures were computed by Ignazio Weiss (1963) using data on newsprint consumption; Weiss also analyzed the ownership patterns of the Italian press.

Radio and television are state monopolies. They are operated independently of the government, but it is difficult to maintain that their coverage of political news is completely nonpartisan. Political programs are arranged to provide free time to all parties and to favor the larger parties. The television network covered the country very quickly and has a wide reception (see Luzzatto Fegiz, 1966, pp. 1371–1423). It is not easy to assess its political impact. The programs tend to favor the government in various ways. However, a study of the relationship between the diffusion of television sets and voting indicates a strong correlation between Communist voting and set ownership and a consistently negative correlation for the Christian Democrats (Capecchi et al., 1968, pp. 267–68). While this is true for all parts of the country, there are many third variables to take into account, so the presumed relationship requires further investigation. Advertising, but not political party commercials, is permitted on radio and television.

J. ORGANIZATIONAL MEMBERSHIPS

The Istituto Carlo Cattaneo studies have examined many aspects of organizationa and party membership in Italy in great detail (see Manoukian et al., 1968, and Poggi et al., 1968). They are summarized in Galli and Prandi (1970).

A discussion of organizational memberships in Italy cannot be as straightforward as one considering, for example, those in the United States. It must begin by noting the fragmented nature of the political culture and the tendency for individuals to be bound up in a particular political subculture for a major part of their public activities. Although there are several subcultures, the most important numerically are the Christian Democratic-Catholic and the leftist, which is Communist dominated. Each of these has a full complement of organizations to encompass the total organizational life of the individual. But what is even more striking about organizational ties in Italy is the large number of people who are not organizationally tied in with any subculture.

Almond and Verba found that membership in voluntary associations was lower by a substantial amount in Italy than in the other countries with the exception of Mexico. Reported trade-union membership was under 6 percent—about one-fourth that of the United Kingdom (22 percent) (ICPR, 1968, p. 109). Reported union membership in Italy in the Barnes-CISER 1968 study, however, was 13 percent. Italy thus seems much more similar to northern European countries than indicated by *The Civic Culture*.

Two considerations are important: first, union membership has political party implications and is subject to the same response problems encountered in that sensitive area; second, membership is not as significant as union identification, which is also difficult to measure. Identification is a sliding concept ranging from dues-paying activism to irregular financial contributions to voting for a particular slate in plant representation elections to joining in a strike called by a particular union. Unions representing the separate subcultures exist side by side in most large plants, and in recent years cooperation among them has improved greatly. The differences between *The Civic Culture* and the 1968 findings undoubtedly reflect in part real changes in the penetration of the unions between 1959 and 1968.

The largest percentage in the Almond-Verba study claiming organizational memberships was in charitable organizations, a category in which Italians led the five countries. The next highest was in civic and political organizations, in which Italy trailed only the United States; trade unions and religious organizations were next, followed by business organizations, a category in which Italy led the group. In fact, Italy's low ranking is almost solely the result of its ranking on trade-union membership and affiliation with social organizations. Thus the Barnes-CISER data greatly alter the Italian standing vis-à-vis other countries as reported in *The Civic Culture*.

Formal party membership becomes less meaningful as one moves from left to right along the party spectrum. In the PCI a vast and—at least relative to the other parties—efficient organization maintains membership rolls and collects dues. Although membership in the PCI today may not represent the level of commitment that it once did, it still involves activity on behalf of the party. The socialist parties are mass-membership parties but are not as effective as the PCI in collecting dues. The Christian Democratic party is also a mass party, but membership does not have the same importance in the party as it does in the leftist parties. The MSI is likewise a membership party; the Liberals and Monarchists seem to place little emphasis on membership.

Survey research on party membership must deal in an exaggerated form with the problem encountered in dealing with party preferences. Consequently, it is difficult to determine where the truth lies in the discrepancy between party claims and survey results. Party membership is not generally asked on Italian surveys, even those concerned most directly with electoral behavior.

TABLE 5: **Party Memberships, in Percentage of Total Sample Claiming Membership in Each Party**

ALMOND-VERBA		1968 BARNES-CISER	
PCI	.4%	PCI	2.3%
PSI	.5	PSIUP	.2
PSDI	.0	PSI-PSDI	1.1
PRI	.1	PRI	.2
DC	1.1	DC	3.0
PLI	.1	PLI	.2
MON	.0	MON	.0
MSI	.7	MSI	.8

The network of organizations tying people into particular subcultures in Italy might seem to be much less impressive than expected by some observers. It is probable that tradition and atmosphere are more important in the process than are formal organizational memberships.

K. OCCUPATIONAL CLASS

Occupational class presents no particular difficulties in analyzing Italian data if the categories employed first permit a distinction between white-collar and blue-collar occupations and second separate agricultural and nonagricultural occupations. As all of the Italian sources permit this, the chief problem encountered is likely to be in adapting categories designed for other countries to the Italian social system. Despite a declining agricultural population, that segment is still quite important; furthermore, there are sharp distinctions in some parts of the country between the voting patterns of independent farmers and those of farm workers. The "other" category includes owners and sharecroppers; the former are strongly DC in orientation.

Converting occupational class into social class creates no particular problems. The fit between education and occupation is very close. Although the sharply stratified class system of Italy based on education is altering slowly, it is still not common to find discrepancies between occupation and education. A university degree, for example, is a requisite for almost all upper- and upper-middle-class occupations; and the middle- and lower-middle-classes are dominated by those with more than an elementary education.

TABLE 6: **Political Preferences of Farm Population in 1958 (Males Only) in Percentages**

	WORKERS	OTHERS
PCI	19	6
PSI	25	11
PSDI	7	5
PRI	2	2
DC	26	43
PLI	1	3
MON	1	4
MSI	2	3
Don't know	17	24
	100%	101%

Source: Poggi, 1967, p. 27

The social significance of titles and inherited status and the clear distinctions within the middle-class have caused scholars to use a more complex system of classification than is common elsewhere. The upper-middle, middle, and lower-middle classes are often distinguished, for example, and the lower-class is sometimes divided into two. Great wealth or inherited wealth and status are necessary for the upper-class. The upper-middle-class is composed of professional people, managers, and industrialists. The middle-class includes many white-collar workers, owners of some businesses, highly skilled technicians, schoolteachers, and bureaucrats. The lower-middle-class is composed of some white-collar workers, some small businessmen, artisans, and some skilled workers. Unlike the United States, however, the distinction in life-style between white-collar and blue-collar workers remains considerable, though declining. It is consequently unwise to base social-class on income alone.

The agricultural population fits uneasily into the social-class categories of an industrial society. Most people in the agricultural sector can somewhat arbitrarily be placed in the lower-class unless they have considerable education. Much of Italian agriculture remains preindustrial in its methods and social structure. A rural middle-class of farmer-owners utilizing modern methods of producing for a market economy has recently begun to develop, but it is important only in scattered areas.

Having complicated the discussion by pointing out the fine distinctions made among middle-class and upper-class groups, it should be noted that the small size of the middle-class renders these refinements of marginal utility in dealing with a national sample, though they remain important for elite analysis. One useful breakdown is middle-class and above, lower-middle, and lower. Professionals, managers, and industrialists fit in the first category; small businessmen, artisans, and white-collar

TABLE 7: Classification of Occupations in Italy

CIVIC CULTURE (RESPONDENT OR SPOUSE)			DOXA	
Name	N	%		%
Professional 28 + 7	35	3.5	Prof., managers, industrialists, big business	5
Higher manager, Big business 4+5	9	.9	Farm owners, tenants	17
			Farm workers	8
Small business 53+25	78	7.8	Artisans	4
White-collar worker 104+48	152	15.3	Skilled workers	8
Skilled worker, artisan 109+49	158	15.9	Unskilled workers, domestic servants	11
Domestic servant 13+1	14	1.4	White-collar workers	7
Farm worker, tenant 51+51	102	10.3	Housewives, students, unemployed	40
Unskilled 120+103	223	22.4		
Farm owner 37+14	51	5.1		100%
Unclassified 173	173	17.4		
	995	100%		

(In analyses housewives are categorized by occupation of husband, but it is impossible to reconstruct this from Luzzatto Fegiz, 1956 or 1966, or from Poggi, 1968.)

Source : ICPR, 1968 — Source : Luzzatto Fegiz, 1956, XXV

CISER (Males only) 1963			Barnes-CISER (1968) (Respondent or spouse where applicable)		
	N	%		N	%
Prof., managers	74	5	Professional, managerial industrialist, etc.	127	5
Higher white-collar occupations	194	13	White-collar worker	492	20
Esercenti	132	9	Small businessman, artisan, shopkeeper	292	12
Artisans	155	10	Farm owner	182	7
Lower white-collar	91	6	Farm laborer	393	15
Farm owners	247	16	Skilled laborer	528	21
Workers	513	32	Unskilled laborer	381	16
Farm workers	131	9	Housewives, students, unemployed	105	4
	1,537	100%		2,500	100%

Source: Poggi, 1968

workers are in the second; workers, all farmers, and most others are in the third category (see Poggi, 1968). Even with this breakdown the middle-class would comprise only about 5 percent of the population, the lower-middle class about 25 percent, and the lower class all the rest. Complications arise with the division of the white-collar group into two segments (Poggi, 1968) and with the classification of unemployed persons, students, pensioners, and housewives. For most analyses middle- and lower-class categories are sufficient.

The governmental categories used for the census and other reports reflect economic activity but do not distinguish the type of work done. Professional personnel are listed in one category and administrative and technical people in another, but skilled and unskilled workers, farm owners and laborers, are grouped together.

L. INCOME

Income is an extremely delicate subject in Italian surveys. Initial suspicion that the interviewer is really a government investigator tends to be reinforced by questions concerning income. A method that seems to allay these fears is to present a card with wide income categories and to request that the respondent choose one of them (Luzzatto Fegiz, 1956, pp. 1134 ff. and 1966, pp. 1616 ff.; Barnes-CISER, 1968). Income is not a major explanatory variable due to the interclass nature of the DC. However, there are substantial differences among the income groups in the support given to various parties. (See Table 8.)

TABLE 8:   **Income and Party Preferences in 1968, in Percentages**

MONTHLY INCOME LEVEL IN 000 LIRE	-50	50-100	100-150	150-200	200-250	250-300	300-350	350+	Don't know	Ref-used to Answer
PCI	15	18	10	6	5	0	5	0	8	4
PSIUP	2	2	2	1	0	5	5	0	2	2
PSI-PSDI	13	16	22	17	14	15	21	23	7	13
PRI	1	1	1	3	0	7	11	0	1	0
DC	48	41	44	45	51	37	27	27	41	32
PLI	2	2	2	6	7	17	26	14	2	1
MON	1	0	1	0	1	0	0	5	0	0
MSI	1	2	2	3	3	2	0	4	1	1
Don't know	17	18	16	19	19	17	5	27	38	47
	100%	100%	100%	100%	100%	100%	100%	100%	100%	100%
N=	469	843	498	205	87	41	19	22	128	188

Source : Barnes-CISER, 1968

M. CONSUMPTION PATTERNS AND LIFE-STYLES

Little attention has been devoted to the problem of measuring differences in life-style in Italy, but it is evident that they are widespread and politically important. The gaps between north and south and between industrial and agricultural sectors are well known. Moving from one to the other involves for many the trauma of the entire modernization process. The television network is national, however, and almost everyone has access to a set in a bar, party or church hall, or home. Continued exposure to life-styles depicted on television must have a considerable impact on viewers in less-developed areas, but its political significance is unknown. Likewise, great differences exist in the life-styles of the ideological subcultures, especially the leftist and the Catholic ones, but they have not been analyzed systematically.

Telephone ownership is expanding but is not widespread. Italy is undergoing a roadbuilding and automobile explosion of enormous proportions; this is one of the most tangible bits of evidence of the economic boom. But the political implications of these by-products of development have not been investigated.

N. CONDITIONS OF EMPLOYMENT

There seems to be no simple association between work conditions and type of industry, on the one hand, and party preference on the other. One could doubtless find concentrations of high levels of support in particular industries for particular parties, but the industrial factor is difficult to separate from the general cultural factor and from the impact of local conditions. Industrial workers in the Red Belt may be heavily Communist, for example, but Communists are weak in some of the very largest industries of the country. It is sometimes suggested that the small, family-oriented industry that is still typical of much of Italy has a political impact through the mediation of paternalistic work relationships. But these are characteristic of much of Italian industry whether large or small. The necessary empirical links between politics and the structure of industry have not been documented.

A study of a Socialist party provincial federation by Barnes suggests that the complications of getting along with people of diverse party loyalties induces many people to separate politics and work. Certainly the decline in the importance of party cells at places of work within the PCI suggests this (Barnes, 1967, pp. 144-47).

O. SUBJECTIVE CLASS ASSESSMENT

Subjective class assessment is associated with party identification as in most countries, but it is only important for people who are in the lower-class on the basis of occupation. Among people who are middle-class in occupation it makes no difference whether or not they consider themselves middle- or lower-class. But among those in the lower occupational class there is a strong tendency to favor the Left among those who identify themselves as of the working class (*operaia*). (See Table 9.)

TABLE 9: Party Identification in 1968, by Occupational Class and Subjective Social Class, in Percentages

OCCUPA-TIONAL CLASS	SUBJECTIVE SOCIAL CLASS	PCI	PSIUP	PSI-PSDI	PRI	DC	PLI	MON	MSI	OTHER
Middle	Middle	6	1	16	3	43	5	1	3	21
	Working	5	1	17	1	45	4	1	2	23
Working	Middle	13	3	15	1	42	1	*	2	23
	Working	22	3	21	1	32	2	*	1	19

Source : Barnes-CISER, 1968

V. Social Psychological Influences

For the social scientist interested in cross-national comparisons, the study of social psychological influences on Italian political behavior offers great challenges and promises great reward. There is little work on a national scale in this area, and the analyses that exist merely suggest the rich vein to be tapped. Italy is a modern country that contains strongly traditional areas and subcultures; it thus offers a wide range of socioeconomic conditions for scholarly exploration. Technical facilities exist for most types of research, yet many fields of study are just now opening up.

Respondents often exhibit marked internal contradictions in their attitude structures, and one might argue that entire subcultures reveal these incompatibilities. Almond and Verba noted that the followers of the PCI, which is conventionally viewed as a totalitarian party, exhibit open democratic attitudes, while the DC supporters are mainly traditionalists and conservatives with fundamentally non-democratic attitudes (p. 160). Similar results are reported from a study of the socialization of Italian youth by Timothy Hennessey (1969). Almond and Verba also note that of the five countries studied Italy was the most polarized politically, with a "psychological clean break" between Left and Right (p. 132). Such attitudes are obviously the product of differences in life experiences, processes of political socialization, belief systems, and organizational attachments. They are thus a mixture of many different causes and of mutually reinforcing feedback. In this section we can only point out some of the pitfalls the researcher is likely to encounter and report some very preliminary findings that in turn suggest further analyses and research.

An initial admonition concerns the applicability of measuring instruments. A number of researchers in Italy have utilized measures of sense of efficacy, identification with politicians and parties, pessimism-optimism, and others. This demonstrates that it is possible in Italy to administer such questionnaires on a national scale. What has not yet been demonstrated is the utility and feasibility of much of this research. The first reservation to be encountered is the suitability for quite different cultures of measures developed in the American context. These measures are obviously measuring something, for the levels of association are quite high between attitudes and the expected demographic variables. What is missing is extensive methodological work that validates scales and indices. (For a sobering review of the methodological inadequacies of many of these in contemporary social science see Robinson, Rusk and Head, 1968.) For example, some items commonly used in the construction of scales of efficacy seem to be limited in their cross-cultural capacity to differentiate among respondents (see Mokken).

Another reservation stems from the range of variation in life-style and subculture to be found within an Italian sample. Of course, this is a problem of all national samples everywhere: questions designed for one educational level and cultural grouping may have slightly different meanings for another set of respondents. But when the culture is relatively homogeneous, the impact of this problem is minimized. And while Italy is homogeneous ethnically and in other ways, on this point it is much more varied than, say, the United States or any of the northern European countries. And these are the areas that have produced most of the measuring instruments.

Differences in educational levels are among the most important sources of difficulties. Many common questions are not very meaningful to a person of little or no education living a life of social and political isolation. Such people exist in all countries and simply become one code category among others. The difference between Italy and the United States, for example, lies in the number of Italians who are functionally semiliterate and socially isolated. Many women fall into this category, as do many inhabitants of rural areas. Questions designed to tap the political sophistication and knowledge of urban middle-class Italians do not adapt equally well to peasant women. Surveys tend to report large numbers of don't knows and nonresponses. Perhaps some of this can be remedied by improved interviewing techniques, but most is probably due to a genuine inapplicability of the questions to the life experiences of many of the respondents. In the absence of a great fund of experience with subnational samples it is not possible to clarify this point. For the present we must live with poor information concerning many respondents, especially in the area of attitudes.

The foregoing discussion is not intended to discourage survey research in Italy but rather exactly the opposite. Researchers in Italy face the same problems as elsewhere, though in a somewhat more serious form; and as national survey are extended to less-developed countries, the problem will become still more serious. Italy is thus a fine site for methodological experimentation. The important point of this warning is to avoid the hazard of making unwarranted assumptions concerning what is being measured.

A. POLITICAL EFFICACY

Sense of political efficacy in Italy is low as measured by the percentage that agreed with the statement, "Politics and government sometimes seem so complicated that people like me can't really understand what is going on." As Table 10 indicates, the differences among the parties are not very great. The PLI supporters are more efficacious within the middle-class. Somewhat surprising are the low scores of PSIUP lower-class supporters. The unclassified category—which is dominated by respondents whose occupations are unknown—is, as expected, quite low. In *The Civic Culture* Italians ranked lowest of all in levels of subjective civic competence, suggesting that the low sense of efficacy has behavioral consequences (Almond and Verba, p. 186).

TABLE 10: Sense of Efficacy in Percent of Each Party's Identifiers Indicating Efficacious Answer, 1968, by Occupational Class

	PARTY								
	PCI	PSIUP	PSI-PSDI	PRI	DC	PLI	MON	MSI	Other
Middle	28	*	28	*	26	42	*	21	22
	(53)		(152)		(399)	(45)		(24)	(201)
Working	18	6	13	*	14	*	*	*	6
	(182)	(31)	(188)		(365)				(212)
Unclassified	8	*	0	*	7	*	*	*	5
	(75)		(57)		(300)				(104)
Party mean	17	12	17	21	16	29	*	19	12
	(310)	(50)	(397)	(29)	(1064)	(72)	(14)	(47)	(517)

Figure in parentheses is N on which percentage is computed.
*Fewer than 20 cases.

Source : Barnes-CISER, 1968

B. INTEREST IN POLITICS

Italians also exhibit a low interest in politics. Table 11 presents the responses to the question, "Are you interested in politics?", in which the respondent chose among "very much," "more or less," "a little," and "not at all." The "very much" and "more or less" categories are combined. The DC middle-class supporters are low in interest in politics compared with the supporters of other parties. Within the lower class PCI supporters stand out as high in interest in politics. The low interest of those not classifiable by occupational class is apparent.

C. RELIGIOUS INFLUENCES

Another important dimension is religion, and any analysis of Italian political behavior must come to terms with its impact. The Italian population is overwhelmingly Catholic; 95 percent of the respondents in the 1968 Barnes-CISER survey claimed to be Catholic, and only 6 percent of the total claimed never to attend church. The important dimension in politics, however, is not religious preference as such but rather closeness to the church. Poggi has created an index of clericalism based on answers to several questions concerning the right and duty of the Church and its agents to intervene in public life, and this index shows a fine capacity to discriminate. Dichotomizing the index shows that 54 percent of the men and 27 percent of the women rank low on clericalism. The index demonstrates clearly that high scores on clericalism are associated with voting for the Christian Democratic party and low scores with support for the PCI.

TABLE 11: **Interest in Politics in 1968—"Very much" and "More or less" Combined, in Percentages, by Occupational Class and Party**

	PCI	PSIUP	PSI-PSDI	PRI	DC	PLI	MON	MSI	Other
					PARTY				
Middle	21 (53)	*	18 (152)	*	10 (399)	27 (45)	*	17 (24)	9 (201)
Working	18 (182)	6 (31)	8 (188)	*	7 (365)	*	*	*	4 (212)
Unclassified	1 (75)	*	2 (57)	*	2 (300)	*	*	*	2 (104)
Party Mean	15 (310)	12 (50)	11 (397)	14 (29)	7 (1003)	19 (72)	14 (14)	13 (47)	6 (517)

Figure in parentheses is N on which percentage is computed.
*Fewer than 20 cases.

Source : Barnes-CISER, 1968

These differences are even more significant within the working-class than Table 12 suggests. Limiting the analysis to the working-class as an occupational

TABLE 12: **DC and PCI Vote in 1958, by Clericalism and Socioeconomic Status, in Percentages**

Score on Clericalism Index	Middle	Lower-Middle	Lower
	SOCIOECONOMIC STATUS		
	Percent Voting DC		
Low	9	9	10
High	50	39	14
	Percent Voting PCI		
Low	18	20	31
High	0	3	5

Source : Poggi, 1967, p. 34

category and controlling for social class as attributed by the interviewer, the relationship between voting and orientation toward the church is even more dramatically revealed, especially pushing lower-middle- and middle-class workers toward either the PCI or DC.

TABLE 13: **Political Preferences of Workers in 1958, by Score on Clericalism Index and Socioeconomic Status, in Percentages**

Score on Clericalism Index		PCI	PSI	PSDI	PRI	DC	PLI	MON	MSI	Don't know	Total
						PARTY PREFERENCE					
					Middle-Class						
0-6	(22)	17	29	4	4	9	4	0	4	30	101
7-14	(20)	0	15	10	0	50	0	0	0	25	100
					Lower middle-class						
0-3	(47)	26	28	6	4	7	2	2	4	21	100
4-6	(39)	8	31	13	0	10	0	0	10	28	100
7-9	(30)	7	13	7	0	23	3	0	7	40	100
10-14	(27)	0	3	14	0	52	0	1	10	20	100
					Lower-Class						
0-6	(39)	32	21	11	3	10	0	0	5	17	99
7-14	(22)	4	9	22	0	13	0	0	13	39	100

Source : Poggi, 1967, p. 34

Clericalism, like efficacy, seems to be a product of a continuing socialization process with multiple sources. For many, support of the church's intervention in public life is an ideological position deriving from a commitment to integral Catholicism: for others, however, it is an affirmation of conservatism or, rather, traditionalism. It is support for doing things the way they have always been done. It is not necessarily the result of a specifically Catholic point of view (see Dogan, 1963, pp. 475-94). For this reason the leap from attitudes to belief systems must be taken with care in the analysis of Italian data (see Barnes, 1966a). A dynamic model of political behavior below will point out some of the nuances of the interpenetration of several variables.

VI. A Tree Analysis of Determinants of Italian Partisan Choice

A. SOME CONTRADICTIONS IN ITALIAN POLITICAL BEHAVIOR

Much has been written concerning the determinants of Italian political behavior. The complexities of the system encourage and facilitate the proliferation of explanations. Furthermore, few of the explanations are completely without merit. One can demonstrate, for example, that Italy is badly fragmented along a number of dimensions of political conflict. One cannot err by emphasizing the importance of social class in Italian politics. It is obvious that the country exhibits differences among social classes that are probably greater than those that exist in the other countries discussed in this volume. The differences reside in such dimensions as educational levels, life-styles, income, and possession of authority. It is equally obvious that these differences have political consequences and that the strength of the Left in general and the Communists in particular is greatly affected by the system of social stratification.

There are also great differences in political behavior between geographical areas, despite the tendency of these differences to be attenuated greatly when controls are added. At the same time over controlling may be a problem, as the differences in occupational structure, educational levels, and urbanization may be precisely the reasons for the political differences between the two parts of the country. In other words, the fact that people with the same characteristics are similar in their political behavior in different parts of the country may not be as important for national politics as the fact that the profiles of the populations still differ considerably even today. Individual similarities do not add up to regional similarities.

The preceding analysis has pointed out the importance of sex differences in Italian political choice, with women being much more favorable to the Christian Democratic party and men favoring the Left. This variable also needs much greater refinement than we have been able to achieve with the simple techniques of data manipulation utilized above.

Class, region, and sex are very simple variables that are of great importance in Italian politics. But we know that the largest Italian party is a multi class party, which means that the Left has no monopoly on working-class votes. We have mentioned that regional differences tend to disappear when controls are instituted. Finally, it is also obvious that despite the sex differential in party choice it is not possible simply to attribute the heavy female vote for the DC to sex alone. The analysis that follows provides a method for refining these crude associations and, in part, resolving some of the contradictions.

The tree analysis will also, in an indirect way, throw light on the role of ideology in Italian politics. Ideology is a topic that is much too involved to occupy us here. Without getting into an extended discussion, the analysis suggests that a further consideration of the role of ideology in Italian politics should not neglect the interaction of ideology and organization, for it demonstrates the importance of the latter in mediating between ideology and political partisan choice (see Barnes, 1966a). Specifically, it shows that the two strongest divisions within the country—those between Catholic and Marxist—have firm structural bases. And to anticipate further, the analysis shows that the variables of class, region, and sex are important in partisan choice in Italy, but much more so for those categories of individuals that are left out of the organizational networks of the two major subcultures than for others.

B. TREE ANALYSIS AND THE VARIABLES EMPLOYED

Tree analyses are increasingly familiar in social science, and no extensive description is necessary here (see Liepelt, 1968; Sarlvik, 1969, and the citations therein). The object of tree analysis is to explain as much of the variance in the dependent variable as possible through repeated bifurcation of the branches into categories based on the independent variables. The particular variety of tree analysis used here is that of DATUM-INFAS, which is in turn similar to the program described in John A. Sonquist and James N. Morgan (1964), with one important difference: the Sonquist-Morgan program automatically chooses the variables and dichotomization of the variables that explain the greatest portion of the total variance, while the DATUM-INFAS program permits the analyst to select the division at each branch that seems most relevant theoretically. For example, in the analysis that follows this option was used once—in selecting geographical subdivisions. Northeast Italy, northwest Italy, and central Italy formed a unit, while southern Italy and the islands *plus* Lombardy, which is treated as a separate geographical area, formed another unit, with this arrangement explaining 1.7 percent of the total variance. However, by taking the division with the second greatest explanatory power, which was similar to the above with the exception that Lombardy was in the northern rather than southern category, the total variance explained was 1.5 percent, which is not a great cost to pay in explanatory power considering the theoretical simplicity it brings to the analysis.

The present analysis is limited to socioeconomic variables. A large number were used, including occupation, union membership, strike behavior, social class, education, type of school attended, sex, marital status, age, length of residence, size of city, father's occupation, living standards of parents, father's political preference, income, region, organization memberships, and church attendance. The dependent variable—the one that is being "explained"—is identification with leftist parties (PCI, PSI-PSDI, PSIUP, PRI) as declared by the respondent.

A note of caution is necessary because of the severe underrepresentation of the PCI identifiers. Of the total sample, 20.7 percent did not express a preference for any party. Only 12.4 percent listed the PCI, although that party received 26.9 percent of the 1968 vote. An incomplete analysis of the nonidentifiers suggests that the PCI portion of this group is somewhat greater than its portion of the total vote; but it also demonstrates that the remaining PCI identifiers are in fact hidden in the vote for other parties as well. If true, this would attenuate the strength of the findings, so that better identification of the PCI voters should greatly increase the explanatory power of the variables included.

A further explanatory note is needed concerning what emerges as the very important variable of church attendance. This might be considered as a sociopsychological variable. That is, it may be measuring behavior (church attendance) or it may be measuring psychological identification with the Catholic subculture (giving what in the subculture is the "right" answer concerning church attendance). The percentage claiming weekly church attendance may seem high, but it is similar to findings reported by Almond and Verba and DOXA. In the Five-Nation Study 57 percent claimed weekly church attendance (ICPR Codebook, p. 111); DOXA reported 69 percent (Luzzatto Fegiz, 1966, p. 1283). Local studies of church attendance based on parish head counts suggest that these figures may be inflated. Nevertheless, in the absence of more compelling evidence we will interpret weekly church attendance as indicating deep involvement in the organizational network of the Catholic subculture.

C. THE TREE ANALYSIS

Figure 2 details the findings of the tree analysis. As we are concerned only with those who expressed a party identification, the total N is reduced to 1,983, 38 percent of whom preferred parties of the Left. The first bifurcation resulted in two almost equal groups: those who claimed to attend church weekly and those who did not. Of the former, 17 percent voted for the Left; of the latter, 58 percent. The portion of the total variance explained by this dichotomized variable is 18.1 percent, which is extraordinarily large compared with the portion explained by single variables utilized for similar analyses in other countries. This dramatically confirms that religion is of prime importance in the political divisions of Italy. And if weekly church attendance is interpreted as meaning above all else membership in the Catholic organizational network, then the importance of organization and subculture is dramatically illustrated.

Another organizational variable appears as the next branch in the tree—the presence of CGIL (the Communist-Socialist-oriented trade union) ties in the family as measured by membership claimed either by the respondent or claimed for the head of the family by the respondent. This variable emerged empirically as the next most important one in both branches of the tree. Among those with regular church attendance only twenty-seven claimed CGIL members in the family, and 70 percent of this group identified with Leftist parties. Among nonregular churchgoers the leftist identifiers rose to 93 percent of those with CGIL ties in the family. Within the latter group frequency of church attendance again assumes importance, this time separating those who sometimes attend church from those who never attend. The former in turn divide again between those with fathers who were workers or peasants and those with middle-class parents. Among those who sometimes attend church the final split is between residence in the north and in the south.

Among regular churchgoers without CGIL ties the next split is between working-class and non-working-class (i.e., working-class vs. middle-class and agricultural respondents). Only the former can be split further, this time into men and women. Table 14 shows the number in each category, the percentage of that category that identifies with the Left, and the percentage that category is of the total. The total variance reduced by these seven variables (or six, if the two different splits on the variable of church attendance are treated as a single one) is 28.3 percent.

D. AN INTERPRETATION

In Table 14 the nine categories into which the tree analysis has divided the sample are listed in order of the declining portion of that category that identifies with the Left. With the aid of the tree analysis and the groups that it has defined empirically we are able to place the importance of several prominent socioeconomic variables in perspective.

The most important finding is that organizational and subcultural ties are more important than the commonly emphasized variables of social status, region, and sex.

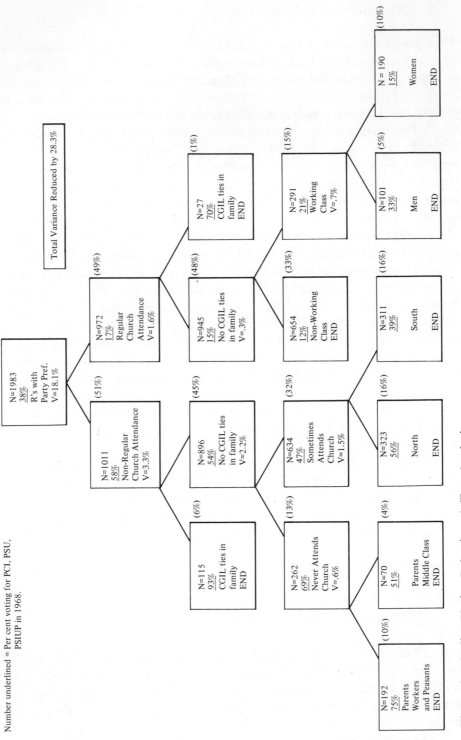

Number underlined = Per cent voting for PCI, PSU,
PSIUP in 1968.

Total Variance Reduced by 28.3%

N=1983
38%
R's with
Party Pref.
V=18.1%

(51%)
N=1011
58%
Non-Regular
Church Attendance
V=3.3%

(49%)
N=972
17%
Regular
Church
Attendance
V=1.6%

(6%)
N=115
93%
CGIL ties in
family
END

(45%)
N=896
54%
No CGIL ties
in family
V=2.2%

(48%)
N=945
15%
No CGIL ties
in family
V=.3%

(1%)
N=27
70%
CGIL ties in
family
END

(13%)
N=262
69%
Never Attends
Church
V=.6%

(32%)
N=634
47%
Sometimes
Attends
Church
V=1.5%

(33%)
N=654
12%
Non-Working
Class
END

(15%)
N=291
21%
Working
Class
V=.7%

(10%)
N=192
75%
Parents
Workers
and Peasants
END

(4%)
N=70
51%
Parents
Middle Class
END

(16%)
N=323
56%
North
END

(16%)
N=311
39%
South
END

(5%)
N=101
33%
Men
END

(10%)
N=190
15%
Women
END

Figure 2: Italian Voting Behavior: A Tree Analysis

The largest single bloc is the active Catholic non-working-class population, which comprises fully one-third of those identifying with a party. It is important that this group does not decompose into subgroups with much explanatory power. It is a conservative bloc that seemingly rejects strongly the appeal of the Left. This group of middle-class and peasant Catholics forms the largest bloc; it is larger still when active Catholic working-class women are added to it. This latter group is quite similar to the non-working-class active Catholic bloc. To say the same thing in different words, active Catholic women are strongly nonleftist in their preferences regardless of social

TABLE 14: **Italian Political Behavioral Groups in 1968**

	N	% IDENTI-FIERS	% LEFT
A. Nonregular church attendance CGIL ties in family	115	6	93
B. No church ties No CGIL ties in family Social origin: worker or peasant	192	10	75
C. Regular church attendance CGIL ties in family	27	1	70
D. Loose church ties No CGIL ties in family North	323	16	56
E. No church ties No CGIL ties in family Social origin: middle-class	70	3	51
F. Loose church ties No CGIL ties South	311	16	39
G. Active Catholic Working-class male	101	5	33
H. Active Catholic Working-class female	190	10	15
I. Active Catholic Non-working-class	654	33	12
TOTALS	1,983	100%	

class, while almost three times the portion of active Catholic working-class men support the Left than non-working-class active Catholic men and women. Thus sex turns out to be an important variable, especially for the 10 percent of the population classified as active Catholic working-class female. When this group is added to the 33 percent of the active Catholic non-working-class population, there is a formidable conservative bloc comprising 43 percent of the identifiers that gives its vote overwhelmingly to parties of the Center and Right.

The Left has a similar substantial hard-core bloc in the CGIL-affiliated respondents, but it is not comparable in size to the active Catholic bloc. Even if all of the unidentified Communist voters were to turn out to belong to this category—and there is no reason to assume that most of them would—the Left core would still be much smaller than that of the Center and Right.

Neither bloc, however, constitutes a majority of the population. Consequently, the one-third of the population that is not caught up closely in either of the organizational and subcultural networks holds the balance in the system. It is within this bloc that substantial differences emerge between north and south; in the north 56 percent of those with loose church ties—that is, those who attend church irregularly—support leftist parties, while in the south only 39 percent do so. As 32 percent of the population falls into these two categories, the differences between north and south in support for the Left are of prime political importance. And it must be underlined that this emerges inductively from the tree analysis as one of the powerful explanatory variables

Social class, which is widely viewed as a major explanatory variable in political behavior, likewise emerges as important in Italy. But this is true only within a particular socioeconomic category. Among people who are not at all tied up in the structures of the two major subcultures (who have no church or union ties) the difference between the portion coming from middle-class backgrounds identifying with the Left (51 percent) and those of worker and peasant background doing so (75 percent) is substantial. It seems that interest, as measured by class background, emerges as a separate important explanatory variable only when organizational and subcultural ties are minimized.

The above has enabled us to identify several bahavioral categories based on a tree analysis of the vote for the Left. We now turn to an examination of how the party vote differs within these categories.

E. BEHAVIORAL GROUP PARTISAN PREFERENCES

All of the groups identified by the tree analysis divide their vote among virtually all the parties, but the wide spread in the portion going to particular parties identifies the central tendencies of the group in question. Table 15 gives the party division of the vote of each group, while Table 16 gives the portion that voters from each group form of the total vote of each party.

Several preliminary generalizations are in order. The first is that it is much easier for the groups that attend church to show support for the PSI-PSDI than the PCI. Another is that—at least as measured in terms of declared party preference—the DC receives a higher percentage of support than the PCI in every group except the first three, the ones that have the highest identification with the Left. Support for the PSI-PSDI, on the other hand, does not vary nearly as much from one group to another. Only in the active Catholic working-class female and non-working-class groups does the PSI-PSDI following decline substantially. And it receives its peak support from the northern loose-church-ties—no-CGIL-ties—group and the no-church-ties—no-CGIL-ties—middle-class groups. Because of size and lack of strong organizational ties the loose-church-ties groups, north and south, are pivotal. The PCI, surprisingly, is more successful with this group in the south than in the north, while the PSI-PSDI portion is much larger in the north. And perhaps most important of all is the great appeal of the DC to the southern uncommitted group.

TABLE 15: **Division of Group Vote, by Party, in Percentages**

	TOTAL SAMPLE	BEHAVIORAL GROUP (Letters refer to group identified in Table 14)								
		A	B	C	D	E	F	G	H	I
PCI	12	58	37	34	9	13	12	7	1	3
PSIUP	2	6	4	9	3	1	2	0	1	1
PSI-PSDI	16	20	18	16	29	25	16	22	10	7
PRI	1	1	2	0	1	4	1	0	0	1
DC	42	4	16	19	28	24	36	55	64	63
PLI	3	0	0	3	3	7	3	1	1	4
MON	1	1	1	0	0	0	2	0	1	0
MSI	2	1	1	3	2	2	4	0	2	2
NA	21	9	21	16	25	24	24	15	20	19
	100%	100%	100%	100%	100%	100%	100%	100%	100%	100%
N=	2,500	127	244	32	433	92	408	119	238	807

There are few surprises in the group composition of the vote for individual parties. The proportion of the party's identifiers coming from a particular group is greatly limited by that group's proportion of the total sample, so that it is not the percentage as such that merits attention but rather the percentage in respect to the percentage of the total sample in that group. The first column in Table 16 contains this latter information, while the other columns relate the percentage of each party's identifiers contributed by the category.

Discovering the undeclared PCI identifiers from the breakdown by group is not easy. Apart from an expected tendency to concentrate somewhat in the groups without strong organizational commitments, the respondents who would not or could not identify with a party are spread over all of the groups. Only the no church-attendance-CGIL-ties group falls far below the all-group mean. This is understandable; having acknowledged CGIL ties, little additional risk is incurred in acknowledging a preference for the PCI or other left-wing parties. The dependence of the DC and PLI and to a lesser extent the PRI, Monarchists, and MSI on the non-working-class regular church attenders is apparent, as is the importance to the Monarchists and MSI of the uncommitted southern vote.

What emerges most clearly is the extent to which organizational and sub-cultural ties restrict the additional explanatory power of social-class, region, and sex. The analysis confirms that these variables are independently important, but primarily for individuals not caught up in the Church or union network.

VII. Conclusions

A. VARIABLES OF COMPARATIVE SIGNIFICANCE

Education is emerging as a variable of universal significance and often even quite similar impacts in different countries. Certainly people of similar education in diverse countries seem to be remarkably alike on many dimensions, at least in the Western

TABLE 16: **Division of Party Vote, by Group, in Percentages**

GROUP	TOTAL SAMPLE	PCI	PSIUP	PSI-PSDI	PRI	DC	PLI	MON	MSI	NA
A	5	23	16	6	3	0	0	7	2	5
B	10	29	20	11	14	4	1	14	4	10
C	1	4	6	1	0	1	2	0	2	1
D	17	13	28	32	14	11	15	0	17	21
E	4	4	2	6	14	2	8	0	4	4
F	16	16	14	17	17	14	20	43	34	19
G	5	3	0	7	0	6	1	0	0	4
H	10	1	4	6	0	14	4	7	9	9
I	32	7	10	14	38	48	49	29	28	30
	100%	100%	100%	100%	100%	100%	100%	100%	100%	100%
N=	2500	310	50	397	29	1064	72	14	47	517

industrialized democracies. Few difficulties should arise in including Italy in the comparative analysis of education and politics. And despite the importance of the secular-clerical conflict, it is of minimal importance in the educational system. That is, most Italians are educated in schools that are public but also in some respects religious. Although other types of schools exist, they enroll a small segment of the population and do not appear to be politically significant. This anomaly of the Italian political scene permits comparisons with systems that do have as well as do not have religiously divided school systems. It suggests that religious education in elementary school is no bar to a strong Marxist movement and that a largely secular system of higher education is compatible with the continuance of strong religious influences in politics.

Ethnicity is not an important variable. Neither is *religious* identification. But clericalism or closeness to the church has been demonstrated to have great explanatory power.

The analysis of *organizational* memberships is limited somewhat in its comparative potential by two considerations: the first is the subcultural separatism that leads to a proliferation of similar organizations with quite different clienteles; the second is the low organizational involvement of the mass of the population. The 1968 Barnes-CISER research, however, suggests that Italian rates may be more similar to those of other European countries than was indicated in the Almond-Verba Five-Nation Study.

Occupational class differences in partisan identification are of course important in Italy, but their impact is filtered through the variable of subcultural identification so that care must be exercised in cross-national comparisons.

The study of *involvement* in politics is a promising focus for comparative work because as a concept it is quite broad and thus permits the precise nature of the involvement to vary from system to system. It is especially important in Italy because the more usual indicators of involvement such as organizational ties and interest in politics and elections may miss a great deal that is significant concerning the ties of Italians to their polity. Fear of partisan reprisals, culturally derived masks of cynicism, and the importance of face-to-face relationships complicate the analysis of political involvement in Italy, but these factors should not be permitted to prevent cross-national comparisons.

Beneath the ideological and subcultural differences that separate Italian parties and the electorate there are real *issue* differences. However, these are not always what they seem. The distribution of issue preferences within the population reflects only in part their distribution within the parties; to some extent the existence of factions within most of the parties is an acknowledgement of this. The reason is that the strength of subcultural ties and group-relevant issues such as the role of the Church in public life are often more salient than socioeconomic issues. Thus the fit between issue preferences and party identification is not a perfect one (see Barnes and Pierce, 1970). This complicates comparison but also enriches it.

One of the most striking features of a country that is developing rapidly is the difference from one *generation* to another in life-style, occupation, and even region of residence. Political preferences, however, seem to be remarkably consistent, at least in terms of broad tendencies (see Barnes, 1970c). Nothing stands in the way of comparative analysis of these intergenerational influences. Moreover, the study of political socialization in Italy is both promising and largely unexplored.

Italy offers a fine example of a country with important *regional* differences. As such it is an excellent unit to compare with other countries in which regionalism has political significance.

B. COUNTRIES APPROXIMATELY COMPARED

The Italian electoral system facilitates comparison with other multiparty systems with proportional representation. Indeed, the electoral system as such does not prohibit fruitful juxtaposition of Italy to countries with two-party systems. The adoption of single-member districts by Italy would undoubtedly result in the disappearance of most of the minor parties and the emergence of a rather unseemly two-party system based on the Christian Democrats and Communists.

The Italian party system does render comparison more difficult. Its fragmentation and uniqueness cannot be ignored. The Left now has the PCI plus three socialist parties. Within limits, these can be treated as a single *tendance*, but the utility of doing so is quickly reduced by the differences in ideology and clientele. Perhaps only France provides an example of a similar range of alternatives on the Left, and even there the choice is not as wide. The Center and Right are somewhat more similar to the parties of other continental countries. Italian Christian Democracy shares many similarities with its counterparts in other countries; the German CDU/CSU in particular provides a good comparison. The Italian Liberals likewise have their counterparts in other countries. The other minor parties, however, are sui generis. The Republicans, Monarchists, and Neofascists have no counterparts in other national parliaments, though the NPD in Germany may provide a useful comparison for the MSI. Even if the Christian Democrats and Communists both appeal to diverse groups, their ideological and organizational bases render them quite different from the "catch-all" parties of the Anglo-American democracies. Catholicism and Marxism presently set limits on the flexibility and comparability of these two parties.

If it seems true that Italian parties differ so much from those of other countries that comparison is difficult, it remains possible nevertheless to compare the Italian electorate to that of other countries. The motivations of those who vote for the PCI and DC, for example, may not differ greatly from the considerations behind voting for socialist and conservative parties in other countries. Undoubtedly the ideological concerns of party elites are shared by some of the electorate, but it also seems highly probable that they are not the primary motivations of the mass of the voters. Issues of policy and interest can form as useful a conceptual apparatus as ideology for studying Italian parties and their supporters. The PCI and DC are, respectively, parties of change and conservatism and hence can be fruitfully compared with similar parties in other countries. But it should be remembered that they are considerably more than that; similarities should not be pushed to the point that they obscure real and fundamental differences.

Postscript

An Italian general election was held in May 1972, one year ahead of schedule. This was the first republican parliament that did not complete its full term. Prior to the election the PSU, which was the title assumed by the smaller of the two socialist parties when the unified party split, had assumed its old title of PSDI; and the Monarchists had merged with the MSI in the National Right (*Destra Nazionale*). The PSIUP failed to elect any deputies and dissolved following the election, with most of its leaders joining the PCI. The vote in the 1972 elections for the Chamber was as follows:

PCI	PSIUP	PSI	PSDI	PRI	DC	PLI	MSI	Other Parties
27.2%	1.9%	9.6%	5.1%	2.9%	38.8%	3.9%	8.7%	1.9%

The existence of several extremist parties on the Left and the renewed vigor of the MSI, combined with violence, economic distress and the emergence of law and order as an issue, threatened the stability of the system. However, the stability of the votes of the major parties demonstrated that the analysis offered in this chapter remains unaltered by the 1972 election. Samuel H. Barnes and Giacomo Sani carried out a national survey following the election, executed by Fieldwork, s.a. of Milan (viale Regina Margherita, 28), and various publications are forthcoming.

References

ABRAMSON, PAUL R. "The Changing Role of Social Class in Western European Politics." Paper presented to 1970 APSA convention. Los Angeles, 1970.

ADAMS, JOHN C., and BARILE, PAOLO. *The Government of Republican Italy.* Boston: Houghton Mifflin, 1966.

ALASIA, F., and MONTALDI, D. *Milano Corea: Inchiesta sugli immigrati.* Milano: Feltrinelli, 1960.

ALBERONI, FRANCESCO; CAPECCHI, V.; MANOUKIAN, A.; OLIVETTI, F.; and TOSI, A. *L' Attivista di partito.* Bologna: Il Mulino, 1967.

ALMOND, GABRIEL. *The Appeals of Communism.* Princeton: Princeton Univ. Press, 1954.

———,and VERBA, SIDNEY. *The Civic Culture.* Princeton: Princeton Univ. Press, 1963.

AMMASSARI, PAOLO. "Opinione politica e scelta elettorale." In Alberto Spreafico and Joseph LaPalombara, eds. *Elezioni e comportamento politico in Italia.* Milano: Comunità, 1963, pp. 733-99.

ARDIGO, ARCHILLE. "Indagine sul comportamento elettorale a Bologna." *Il Mulino* 8 (April, 1958): 207-16.

BANFIELD, EDWARD. *The Moral Basis of a Backward Society.* Glencoe: Free Press, 1958.

BARNES, SAMUEL H. "Ideology and the Organization of Conflict: On the Relationship of Political Thought and Behavior." *Journal of Politics* 28 (August, 1966a): 513-30.

———. "Italy: Oppositions on Left, Right and Center." In Robert A. Dahl, ed. *Political Opposition in Western Democracies.* New Haven: Yale University Press, 1966b, pp. 303-31.

————. "Left, Right, and the Italian Voter." Paper presented to the IPSA Congress. Munich: 1970a.

————. "The Legacy of Fascism: Generational Differences in Italian Political Attitudes and Behavior." Unpublished manuscript, ISR. Ann Arbor: 1970b.

————. *Party Democracy: Politics in an Italian Socialist Federation.* New Haven: Yale University Press, 1967.

————, and PIERCE, ROY. "Public Opinion and Political Preferences in France and Italy." Paper presented to APSA convention. Los Angeles: 1970c.

BLACKMER, DONALD L. M. *Unity in Diversity: Italian Communism and the World.* Cambridge: M.I.T. Press, 1968.

BRAGA, GIORGIO, *Il Comunismo fra gli Italiani.* Milano: Comunità, 1956.

————. *Sociologia elettorale della Toscana.* Roma: 5 Lune, 1963.

BUCHANAN, WILLIAM, and CANTRIL, HADLEY. *How Nations See Each Other.* Urbana: Univ. of Illinois Press, 1953.

CANTRIL, HADLEY. *The Politics of Despair.* New York: Basic Books, 1958.

CAPECCHI, VITTORIO; CIONI POLACCHINI, V.; GALLI, G.; SIVINI G. *Il comportamento elettorale in Italia.* Bologna: Il Mulino, 1968.

CAVALLI, L. *Gli immigrati meridionali e la società ligure.* Milano: F. Angeli, 1964.

CAZZOLA, FRANCO. *Carisma e democrazia nel socialismo italiano.* Roma: Istituto Luigi Sturzo, 1967, biblio. pp. 63–121.

CIAURRO, GIAN FRANCO. "Movimenti migratori e scelte politiche." In Mattei Dogan and Orazio Maria Petracca, ed. *Partiti politici e strutture sociali in Italia.* Milano: Comunità, 1968, pp. 275–351.

C.I.R.D. *Annuario Politico.* Milano: Comunità, 1963.

COMPAGNA, F. and DECAPRARIIS, V. *Geografia delle elezioni italiane dal 1946 al 1953.* Bologna: Il Mulino, 1954.

D'AMATO, LUIGI. *Il voto di preferenza in Italia.* Milano: Giuffrè, 1964.

DENNIS, JACK; LINDBERG, LEON; MCCRONE, DONALD; STIEFBOLD, RODNEY. "Political Socialization to Democratic Orientations in Four Western Systems." *Comparative Political Studies* 1 (April, 1968): 71–101.

DICAPUA, GIOVANNI. "La scelta dei candidati." In Mattei Dogan and Orazio Maria Petracca, eds. *Partiti politici e strutture sociali in Italia.* Milano: Comunità, 1968, pp. 579–608.

DIRENZO, GORDON J. *Personalità e potere politico: una indagine sui parlamentari italiani.* Bologna: Il Mulino, 1967.

DOGAN, MATTEI. "Le donne italiane tra il cattolicesimo e il marxismo." In Alberto Spreafico and Joseph LaPalombara, eds. *Elezioni e comportamento politico in Italia.* Milano: Comunità, 1963, pp. 475–494.

————, and PETRACCA, ORAZIO MARIA eds. *Partiti politici e strutture sociali in India* Milano: Comunità, 1968.

————. "Le comportement politique des Italiens." *Revue française de science politique.* June, 1959, pp. 383–409.

———. "Political Cleavage and Social Stratification in France and Italy." In S.M. Lipset and S. Rokkan, eds. *Party Systems and Voter Alignments.* New York: Free Press, 1967, pp. 129–195.

RAE, DOUGLAS. "A Note on the Fractionalization of Some European Party Systems." *Comparative Political Studies* 1 (October, 1968): 413–18.

EINAUDI, MARIO, and GOGUEL, F. *Christian Democracy in Italy and France.* Notre Dame: Univ. of Notre Dame Press, 1952.

EDELMAN, MURRAY. "Causes of Fluctuations in Popular Support of the Italian Communist Party Since 1946." *Journal of Politics* 20 (August, 1958): 535–53.

EVANS, ROBERT H. *Coexistence: Communism and Its Practice in Bologna, 1945-1965.* Notre Dame: Univ. of Notre Dame Press, 1967.

FALCONI, C. *La chiesa e le organizzazioni cattoliche in Italia (1945-1955).* Torino: Einaudi, 1956.

FREE, LLOYD A. *Six Allies and a Neutral.* Glencoe: Free Press, 1959.

FRIED, R. C. *The Italian Prefects.* New Haven: Yale University Press, 1963.

GALLI, GIORGIO, *Il bipartitismo imperfetto.* Bologna: Il Mulino, 1966.

———. *Storia del partito comunista italiano.* Milano: Schwarz, 1958.

———, and PRANDI, ALFONSO. *Patterns of Political Participation in Italy.* New Haven: Yale Univ. Press, 1970.

GERMINO, DANTE, and PASSIGLI, STEFANO. *The Government and Politics of Contemporary Italy.* New York: Harper & Row, 1968.

GHENI, CELSO, *Le elezioni in Italia (1946-1968).* Milano: Edizioni del Calendario, 1968.

HAZELRIGG, LAWRENCE E. "Religious and Class Bases of Political Conflict in Italy." *American Journal of Sociology* 75 (January, 1970): 496–511.

HENNESSEY, TIMOTHY M. "Democratic Attitudinal Configurations Among Italian Youth." *Midwest Journal of Political Science* 13 (May, 1969): 167–93.

I deputati e senatori del quinto parlamento republicano. Roma: La Navicella, 1969.

Inter-university Consortium for Political Research. *The Five Nation Study.* Ann Arbor: ICPR, 1968.

KOGAN, NORMAN. *A Political History of Postwar Italy.* New York: Praeger, 1966.

———.*The Government of Italy.* New York: Crowell, 1966.

LANDOLFI, A. *Il partito socialista oggi e domani.* Milano: Edizioni Azione Comune, 1963.

LASSWELL, HAROLD D., and SERENO, RENZO. "The Fascists: The Changing Italian Elite." Reprinted in Harold D. Lasswell and Daniel Lerner, eds. *World Revolutionary Elites.* Cambridge: M.I.T. Press, 1966, pp. 179–93.

LAPALOMBARA, JOSEPH. *Interest Groups in Italian Politics.* Princeton: Princeton Univ. Press, 1964.

———. "The Italian Elections and the Problem of Representation." *American Political Science Review* 47 (September, 1953): 676–703.

———. "Italy: Fragmentation, Isolation, and Alienation." In L. Pye and S. Verba, eds. *Political Culture and Political Development.* Princeton: Princeton Univ. Press, 1965, pp. 282–329.

———. "Political Party Systems and Crisis Government: French and Italian Contrasts." *Midwest Journal of Political Science* 2 (May, 1958): 117–42.

———, and WALTERS, J. B. "Values, Expectations, and Political Predispositions of Italian Youth." *Midwest Journal of Political Science* 5 (February, 1961): 39–58.

Le elites politiche. Bari: Laterza, 1961. Atti del IV Congresso mondiale di sociologia.

LEONI, A. *Sociologia e geografia religiosa di una diocesi, saggi sulla pratica religiosa nella diocesi di Mantova.* Roma: Università Gregoriana, 1952.

LIEPELT, KLAUS. "Esquisse d' une typologie des electeurs allemands et autrichiens." *Revue française de sociologie* 9 (1968): pp. 13–32.

LUZZATTO FEGIZ, PIERPAOLO. *Il volto sconsciuto dell' Italia, 1943-1953.* Milano: Giuffrè, 1957.

———. *Il volto sconosciuto dell' Italia, seconda serie, 1956-1965.* Milano: Giuffrè, 1966.

MACK SMITH, DENIS. *Italy: A Modern History.* Ann Arbor: University of Michigan Press, 1959.

MAMMARELLA, GIUSEPPE. *Italy After Fascism.* Notre Dame: University of Notre Dame Press, 1966.

MANOUKIAN, AGOPIK; BRUNELLI, L.; CANULLO, U.; DEGLI ESPOSTI, G.; GALLI, G.; PEPA, L.; PICCHI, A.; PRANDI, A.; ROSSI, A. M.; SCATASSA, B.; CAVAZZANI, A. SIVINI; and TURCO, L. *La presenza sociale del PCI e della DC.* Bologna: Il Mulino, 1968.

MAZZAFERRO, LUCIANO. *Elezioni politiche in una zona di riforma e di emigrazione.* Bologna: Il Mulino, 1959.

MELOTTI, UMBERTO. *Coltura e partecipazione sociale nella città in transformazione.* Milano: La Culturale, 1966.

MEYNAUD, JEAN. *Rapporto sulla classe dirigente italiana.* Milano: Giuffrè, 1966.

MOKKEN, ROBERT J. "Dutch-American Comparisons of the 'Sense of Political Efficacy'." *Quality and Quantity* forthcoming.

PASSIGLI, STEFANO. *Emigrazione e comportamento politico.* Bologna: Il Mulino, 1969.

———. "Gli studi di sociologia elettorale in Italia." in Alberto Spreafico and Joseph LaPalombara eds. *Elezioni e comportamento politico in Italia.* Milano: Comunità, 1963, pp. 973–988.

PIZZORNO, ALESSANDRO. *Comunità e razionalizzazione.* Torino: Einaudi, 1960.

POGGI, GIANFRANCO. *Il clero di riserva.* Milano: Feltrinelli, 1963.

———. *Le preferenze politiche degli italiani: analisi di alcuni sondaggi pre-elettorali.* Bologna: Il Mulino, 1968. Appendix lists major political surveys in Italy from 1946 to 1967.

———; CANTELLI, F. CERVELLATI; POLACCHINI, V. CIONI; PISCICELLI, P. DE VITO; CAPPELLO, S. GUARINO; SANI, G.; SIVINI, G.; CAVAZZANI, A. SIVINI. *L'organizzazione partitica del PCI e della DC.* Bologna: Il Mulino, 1968.

PRYCE, ROY. *The Italian Local Elections, 1956.* New York: St. Martin's Press, 1957.

ROBINSON, JOHN P.; RUSK, JERROLD G.; and HEAD, KENDRA, B. *Measures of Political Attitudes.* Ann Arbor: Institute for Social Research, 1968.

SARLVIK, BO. "Socioeconomic Determinants of Voting Behavior in the Swedish Electorate." *Comparative Political Studies* 2 (April, 1969): 99–135.

SARTORI, GIOVANNI. "European Political Parties: The Case of Polarized Pluralism." In Joseph LaPalombara and Myron Weiner, eds. *Political Parties and Political Development*. Princeton: Princeton Univ. Press, 1966, pp. 137–76.

SARTORI, GIOVANNI, et al. *Il parlamento italiano, 1946-1963*. Napoli: ESI, 1963.

SCHEPIS, GIOVANNI. "Analisi statistica dei risultati." In Alberto Spreafico and Joseph LaPalombara, eds. *Elezioni e comportamento politico in Italia*. Milano: Comunità, 1963, pp. 329–406.

Segretariato generale della camera dei deputati, *Annuario Parlamentare* Rome.

SIVINI, GIORDANO (a cura di). *Il comportamento elettorale: Bibliografia internazionale di studi e ricerche sociologiche*. Bologna: Il Mulino, 1967.

SIVINI, GIORDANO. "Studi e ricerche sul comportamento elettorale in Italia." Appendice B, di Vittorio Capecchi, et al., *Il comportamento elettorale in Italia*. Bologna: Il Mulino, 1968, pp. 401–17.

SONQUIST, JOHN A., and MORGAN, JAMES N. *The Detection of Interaction Effects*. SRC, 1964.

SPREAFICO, ALBERTO. "Il senato della republica: composizione politica e stratificazione sociali." In Mattei Dogan and Orazio Maria Petracca, eds. *Partiti politici e strutture sociali in Italia*. Milano: Comunità, 1968, pp. 609–43.

———. "Le previsioni electorali." In Mattei Dogan and Orazio Maria Petracca, eds· *Partiti politici e strutture sociali in Italia*. Milano: Comunità, 1968, pp. 121–61.

———. "Orientamento politico e identificazione partitica." In Spreafico and Joseph LaPalombara, eds. *Elezioni e comportamento politico in Italia*. Milano: Comunità, 1963, pp. 689–731.

TARROW, SIDNEY. "Economic Development and the Transformation of the Italian Party System." *Comparative Politics* 1 (January, 1969): 161–183.

———. *Peasant Communism in Southern Italy*. New Haven: Yale Univ. Press, 1967.

VISENTINI, L. "I dirigenti sindacali nel processo di sviluppo del Mezzogiorno." *Tempi moderni* 23, 25, pp. 21–48, 39–58.

WEISS, IGNAZIO. "La stampa quotidiana." In Alberto Spreafico and Joseph LaPalombara, eds. *Elezioni e comportamento politico in Italia*. Milano: Comunità, 1963, pp. 299–328.

———. *Politica dell' informazione*. Milano: Comunità, 1961.

ZARISKI, R. "The Italian Socialist Party: A Case Study in Factional Conflict." *American Political Science Review* 56 (June, 1962): 372–90.

5. THE NETHERLANDS:
Continuity and Change in Voting Behavior
AREND LIJPHART

I. Historical Background

A. SOCIAL STRUCTURE SINCE 1900

The Dutch Central Bureau of Statistics was founded in 1899, marking the beginning of large-scale, systematic collection of data about social-structure (Centraal Bureau voor de Statistiek, 1959, p. 3). The year 1900 is also a useful starting point because it marks the year by which the oldest generation of voters in the 1950s and 1960s had reached adulthood.

The total *population* of the Netherlands has more than doubled in this century, from slightly over 5 million inhabitants in 1900 to approximately 13 million in 1971. In terms of population Holland is the largest of the smaller European democracies, following immediately after the four major democratic states, Italy, Britain, West Germany, and France. Holland's* territory is, however, very small. Its population density is the highest in the world: almost 400 inhabitants per square kilometer, or approximately 1,000 per square mile.

After a relatively late and slow start—Holland's industrial revolution occurred later than the industrial revolutions in all of the neighboring countries—the country has become highly industrialized. The pace of industrialization may be measured in terms of the percentage of workers employed in the different sectors of the economy. By 1900 the number of workers employed in manufacturing, mining, and industry, 33 percent, was only slightly greater than the number of workers in agriculture, 30 percent. All other occupations (trade, transport, banking, insurance, professional and

I should like to express my gratitude to Theo Z. van der Net and Philip C. Stouthard for their assistance in designing the "trees" presented in Section VI, and to Attwood Statistics, the Netherlands Institute of Public Opinion, and the Steinmetz Institute, whose survey data constitute the empirical basis of Sections IV and VI. I am also grateful to Peter R. Baehr, Hans Daalder, Felix J. Heunks, Galen A. Irwin, Val R. Lorwin, Richard Rose, Jerrold G. Rusk, and Frans Stokman for their helpful comments and suggestions on the first draft of this chapter.

* The terms "the Netherlands" and "Holland" will be used here interchangeably, even though the latter term literally refers to only two of the eleven provinces of the Netherlands.

public employment, and domestic services) accounted for 38 percent of total employ-ment in 1900. The number of people in agriculture decreased to 23 percent in 1920, to 20 percent in 1947, and to 11 percent in 1960. (The figures reported here are for census years. Normally, censuses occur once every ten years, but the outbreak of the Second World War prevented the census of 1940. Instead, a census was taken in 1947.)

Urbanization has also proceeded rapidly. The number of people living in rural municipalities (those with a population of less than 20,000 inhabitants) was 63 percent of the total population in 1900. This percentage decreased to 54 percent in 1920, 44 percent in 1947, and 40 percent in 1960. At the same time the percentage of the total population living in towns and cities with more than 100,000 inhabitants grew from 23 percent in 1900 and 24 percent in 1920 to 30 percent in 1947 and 33 percent in 1960.

A very important structural factor with regard to political behavior in the Nether-lands is religion. Table 1 shows trends in the strengths of the different religions from 1899 until the decennial census of 1960. The Dutch Reformed Church (*Nederlands Hervormd*) is the most important Protestant denomination in the Netherlands. The Orthodox Reformed (*Gereformeerd*) churches are offshoots of the Dutch Reformed Church and have experienced further fragmentation within their own ranks. They are

TABLE 1: Numerical Strength of Religious Groups, 1899-1960, in Percentages

	CATHOLIC	DUTCH REFORMED	ORTHODOX REFORMED	OTHER	NONE	TOTAL
1899	35.1	48.6	8.2	5.8	2.3	100%
1909	35.0	44.3	9.4	6.3	5.0	100%
1920	35.6	41.3	9.1	6.2	7.8	100%
1930	36.4	34.5	8.7	6.0	14.4	100%
1947	38.5	31.1	9.7	3.7	17.0	100%
1960	40.4	28.3	9.3	3.6	18.4	100%

Source: Centraal Bureau voor de Statistiek, 1959, p. 26; and Centraal Bureau voor de Statistiek, 1963a, p. 8.

characterized by strict adherence to orthodox Calvinist doctrines. The "other religions" category consists of a number of smaller religious groups such as Lutherans, Mennonites, and Jews. The most outstanding change in the religious composition of the Dutch population during the twentieth century has been the loss of strength of the Dutch Reformed Church: almost one-half of the total population belonged to this church in 1899, but only 28 percent in 1960. To a large extent this decrease is accounted for by the increase in the percentage of people without religious affiliation. Catholics have made relatively small but steady gains and Orthodox Reformed adherents small but less steady gains, primarily as a result of the comparatively high birthrates of these two religious groups.

The different religious affiliations correspond to a large extent, but not entirely, with the distinct and deep subcultural cleavages in Dutch society. The Catholic subculture consists of virtually all members of the Roman Catholic Church with the exception of a relatively small number of liberal or nonpracticing members. The Calvinist subculture consists of the members of the Orthodox Reformed churches and that third of the members of the Dutch Reformed Church who constitute the orthodox wing of that church. All others—those not affiliated with any church, liberal and nonpracticing Catholics and Dutch Reformed people, and members of small churches —can be classified as secular. This secular group is divided ideologically into a socialist and a liberal subculture. Virtually all social and political organizations are rigidly bounded by these subcultural cleavages.

In the years around 1900 the subcultures were involved in a bitter and protracted political conflict. The main issues were the extension of the suffrage and state aid to religious schools. When the struggle reached a critical stage, the leaders of the political parties representing the four subcultures peacefully settled these issues by an agreement formally adopted in 1917. This settlement was based on the principle of proportionality: proportional allocation of public funds to all schools, both public and private, the latter mainly Catholic and Protestant, and universal suffrage on the basis of proportional representation.

From then on, Dutch politics became a politics of accommodation—fitting the general pattern of "consociational democracy"—which leaned heavily on both the substance and the method of the precedent established in 1917. Proportionality became the undisputed standard for the allocation of government funds among the subcultures, for the appointment of civil servants, and also for the division of network time on the state-owned radio and television stations among the broadcasting organizations of the subcultures. The method of the 1917 settlement—negotiations among the top leaders of all of the subcultures, i.e., an informal "grand coalition" of the subcultural elites—became more and more institutionalized, especially in the social and economic realms. The leaders of the political parties continued to meet unforeseen crises by means of summit conferences, but never completely applied the consociational principle to the day-to-day operation of the national government. Although Dutch cabinets have usually been broad coalitions, at least one of the major parties has always been in the opposition. (See Lijphart, 1968, esp. pp. 16–70, 103–38; Lijphart, 1969a, pp. 207–25.)

The consociational pattern began to break down in the 1960s. As religion and ideology gradually lost their political salience, the internal cohesion of the various subcultural organizations was weakened, and support for the traditional major parties declined drastically: together they received 91.5 percent of the total vote in 1956, but their combined vote declined to 78.7 percent in 1967 and 71.7 percent in 1971. At the same time their willingness to engage in the traditional methods of settling disagreements also decreased. and a government vs. opposition pattern began to replace consociationalism: in the 1971 parliamentary election campaign the left-wing opposition parties announced the formation of a "shadow cabinet" as an alternative to the governing coalition. (See Daalder, 1968, pp. 71–90; Lijphart, 1969b, pp. 231–47.)

B. ELECTORAL SYSTEMS SINCE 1849

A systematic survey of the provisions governing elections to the Second Chamber (lower house) since 1815 is provided in the chapter on the Netherlands in the *International Guide to Electoral Statistics* (Scholten and Ringnalda, 1969, pp. 232–60; see also Albrecht, 1960; van den Bergh, 1946; Geismann, 1964, esp. pp. 31–40; Nohlen, 1969, pp. 857-90; van Raalte, 1959, pp. 80–93). The politically less important First Chamber (upper house) is elected indirectly by the provincial legislatures. All elections to the Second Chamber have been direct elections since 1849. As the Second Chamber elections have been the only national popular elections in the Netherlands since 1849, they will be the sole concern here.

The extension of the franchise was hotly contested in Dutch politics in the late nineteenth and early twentieth centuries. For the first direct elections to the Second Chamber the franchise was extremely restricted; only those meeting rigid property qualifications had the right to vote. In 1800 the electorate constituted only 12 percent of the adult male population—approximately the same percentage as in England before the Reform Act of 1832. In 1887 the franchise was extended for the first time, and by 1890 the electorate was 27 percent of the adult male population. A second extension of the franchise in 1896 increased this proportion to 49 percent in 1900 and 63 percent in 1910. Universal male suffrage was adopted in 1917, and universal suffrage for both men and women in 1919. (Centraal Bureau voor de Statistiek, 1963b, p.8.)

The age requirement for voting in elections from 1849 to 1894 was twenty-three. The minimum age was increased to twenty-five for the last six elections held under the majority-plurality electoral system (1897–1917) and continued for the first six elections conducted under proportional representation (1918-1937). After the Second World War the minimum voting age was lowered to twenty-three, and in the 1967 and 1971 elections all citizens of twenty-one years and older were eligible to vote. A constitutional amendment passed after the 1971 elections lowered the voting age to eighteen.

Since 1849 the maximum term of office of members of the Second Chamber has been four years. In general this has also meant that elections have been held once every four years, although the frequency of elections has been increased occasionally by dissolutions of the Second Chamber before the end of its four-year term. In the 1849–1887 period, however, elections were held every two years, with one-half of the seats in the Second Chamber at stake in each of these elections.

The number of seats in the Second Chamber fluctuated slightly in the 1849–1887 period, for the basis of representation was one member for 45,000 inhabitants. The Second Chamber consisted of eighty-six members by 1886. The number was fixed at 100 from 1888 until 1956; then the size of the Second Chamber was increased to 150 members.

The great divide in the history of the Dutch electoral system occurred in 1917, when a constitutional amendment was passed that changed the majority-plurality system to the system of proportional representation. The first PR election was held in 1918. The basic rule of the *majority-plurality system* (1849–1917) was that an absolute majority was required for election on the first ballot; if no candidate attained an absolute majority, a second election was held between the two candidates who had received the highest numbers of votes in the first round. The number of constituencies and the number of representatives per constituency underwent a number of important changes. From 1849 to 1887 members of the Second Chamber were generally elected in two-member constituencies; every two years one of the members was elected for a four-year term. From 1888 to 1894 the country was divided into single-member constituencies except in the big cities, where larger multimember constituencies were retained. Finally, from 1897 to 1917 the entire country was divided into 100 single-member constituencies.

The electoral system since 1918 has been the *list system of proportional representation*. For all practical purposes the entire country forms a single constituency, although there are eighteen districts for administrative purposes. The principal changes that have occurred within this system are changes with regard to (1) the system of allocating the "surplus" seats according to the method of largest remainders or the method of largest averages, and (2) the electoral threshold. These two provisions of the electoral system are primarily important to the smaller parties, because they benefit from the largest-remainders method of allocating seats and from a low threshold. Overall, proportionality is not much affected by these provisions.

From 1918 to 1933 the rule of allocating seats according to the highest remainder was in effect. After 1937 the method of highest averages (the d'Hondt method) has been applied in all elections.

The electoral threshold is the minimum number of votes that a party has to get in order to be entitled to representation. In the first election held under the new system, in 1918, the threshold was fixed at 50 percent of the electoral quotient (i.e., the total number of valid votes divided by the number of seats). Since 100 seats were at stake, this meant that a small party was guaranteed at least one seat if its votes exceeded 1 percent of the total number of votes cast (the electoral quotient); it could, however, obtain a surplus seat with at least 0.5 percent of the total vote. For the second election in 1922 the threshold was increased from 50 to 75 percent of the electoral quotient (i.e., from 0.5 to 0.75 of the total vote). From 1937 on the threshold has equaled the electoral quotient. However, as a result of the expansion of the Second Chamber to 150 members in 1956, the electoral quotient and thus the electoral threshold were lowered to 0.67 percent.

Holland's pre-1956 system of proportional representation based on a single nationwide constituency with a threshold as low as 1 percent was the world's most extreme P.R. system. For a while Holland had to share its first place in this respect with Israel—the Knesset's 120 members are also elected in a single nationwide constituency with a 1 percent threshold—but Holland regained undisputed first place when the threshold was lowered to 0.67 percent after 1956.

C. THE PARTY SYSTEM IN THE 20TH CENTURY

The Dutch party system has shown remarkable continuity since the turn of the century. As far as the number of parties is concerned, it has always been a multiparty system, regardless of whether one counts all parties contesting elections, all parties actually elected to the Second Chamber, or only the larger and politically significant parties. From 1901 on there were seven important parties in the Second Chamber: the Catholics, two Calvinist parties (the Anti-Revolutionary party and a group of former Anti-Revolutionaries which in 1908 became the Christian Historical Union), the Socialists, and three Liberal parties. As a result of mergers the number of Liberal parties was reduced to two after the First World War and to a single Liberal party after the Second World War. In 1967 a new party emerged which should also be classified as a significant larger party: Democrats '66. and in 1971 another new major party entered the Second Chamber: Democratic Socialists '70.

In classifying the above parties as "large" or "major" parties, both a numerical criterion and the criterion of "coalition potential" was used (see Sartori, 1970, pp. 324–26). Thus the Communist party is classified as a "minor" party, although it received more votes in the 1946 election than the Christian Historical Union and the Liberal party. Also, Democrats '66 is classified as a "major" party because it is regarded as a possible partner in a future cabinet coalition, but it received fewer votes in 1967 than the "minor" Farmers party. Similarly, Democratic Socialists '70 was immediately regarded as a likely coalition partner after the 1971 elections. According to Sartori's counting rules, even the minuscule Radical party may have to be included among the major parties, because it joined with the Labor party and D'66 in setting up a "shadow cabinet" prior to the elections. To sum up: the Dutch multiparty system was a seven-party system until the First World War, a six-party system during the interwar years, a five-party system between the Second World War and 1967, a six-party system from 1967 to 1971, and a seven-party or eight-party system following the 1971 election.

In addition to these major parties there have been a large number of smaller parties, particularly after the introduction of proportional representation in 1917. Table 2 lists the numbers of parties participating in the parliamentary elections and the numbers of parties gaining representation in the Second Chamber. It also presents the numbers of minor parties and the percentages of the total vote obtained by them. For the purposes of this table the Radical party is regarded as a minor party.

Five main political *tendances* can be discerned in the Dutch party system. Until recently all of the smaller parties could also be classified according to the same *tendances*. In general they represented the extreme fringes within each *tendance*. The five principal *tendances* are: (1) the Catholic parties, representing the Roman Catholic subculture; (2) the Anti-Revolutionary Party and other Protestant fundamentalist parties, supported by members of the Orthodox Reformed churches; (3) the Christian Historical Union, supported by the conservative wing of the Dutch Reformed Church;

(4) the Socialist parties, representing various shades of left-wing opinion in the Socialist subculture; and (5) the Liberal parties and other secular bourgeois groups. The second and third of these *tendances* jointly represent the Calvinist subculture.

TABLE 2: **Numbers of Parties Contesting Elections and Winning Seats, and Percentages of the Total Vote Received by the "Minor" Parties, 1918-1967**

	Parties Contesting Elections	Parties Winning Seats	Minor Parties Contesting Elections	Percentage of Votes Obtained by Minor Parties
1918	32	17	26	12.8
1922	48	10	42	12.2
1925	32	11	26	11.6
1929	36	12	30	10.9
1933	54	14	48	16.1
1937	20	10	14	15.4
1946	10	7	5	13.8
1948	12	8	7	13.0
1952	13	8	8	13.3
1956	10	7	5	8.5
1959	13	8	8	8.4
1963	18	10	13	12.5
1967	23	11	17	16.8
1971	28	14	21	16.2

Sources: Adapted from Daalder, 1965-66, pp. 177, 178; Centraal Bureau voor de Statistiek, 1967, pp. 7, 38-39; *NRC-Handelsblad*, April 29, 1971.

II. The Act of Voting Today

A. ELECTIONS AND BALLOTS

The elections of members of the Second Chamber are the only nationwide elections. They usually occur at four-year intervals. The other direct elections in the Netherlands are the elections of the municipal councils and provincial legislatures; in some parts of the country there are regional councils, too. The municipal elections take place on the same day throughout the country, as do the provincial elections. They also occur once every four years. Municipal elections cannot be compared easily with parliamentary elections, because there are usually many specifically local groups that contest these elections in addition to or instead of the national parties. The provincial elections are more easily comparable with parliamentary contests, because the national parties are usually dominant at the provincial level. Furthermore, the provincial elections are indirectly of national significance because the provincial legislatures elect the seventy-five members of the First Chamber.

The ballot contains the lists of candidates nominated by the parties. The order of the lists is generally determined by the results of the previous election: the largest party is assigned the first list on the ballot, etc. The order in which the candidates appear on each list is determined by the parties themselves. The voter can mark the name of only one candidate on the ballot. Most voters—usually more than 90 percent—cast their vote for the first candidate of their party, which is in effect a vote for the entire list (Nohlen, 1969, p. 882). They can also cast a preferential vote for a candidate lower on the list, but such a candidate has to receive a great many votes in order to be elected before someone higher on the list: he needs at least one-half of the total vote cast for the list divided by the number of seats allocated to it. When a candidate receives insufficient preferential votes to be elected, these votes revert to the first candidate on the list and are redistributed, if necessary, according to the order in which candidates are ranked on the list.

B. THE LEGAL FACILITATION OF VOTING

All Dutch citizens who reside in the Netherlands and who are at least eighteen years old have the right to vote, with the exception of people excluded because of criminal convictions, mental illness, etc. Registration is automatic: the authorities compile the electoral registers from the municipal population registers. Several days before an election, every elector receives a notice giving the date of the election, the location of the polling station, the hours of polling, and the lists of candidates.

There are no absentee ballots. However, a voter may receive permission to vote in a municipality other than the one in which he resides. He may also vote by proxy. A number of voters without a fixed residence (e.g., people living on ships used in inland navigation) are registered in a special electoral register and are permitted to cast their vote anywhere in the Netherlands.

C. TODAY'S POLITICAL PARTIES

There have been five major parties since the Second World War. These parties are:
KVP (*Katholieke Volkspartij*), Catholic People's party
ARP (*Anti-Revolutionaire Partij*), Anti-Revolutionary party
CHU (*Christelijk Historische Unie*), Christian Historical Union
PvdA (*Partij van de Arbeid*), Labor party
VVD (*Volkspartij voor Vrijheid en Democratie*), People's Party for Freedom and Democracy—this is the Liberal party.

The new parties that may also be regarded as "major" parties according to the criteria discussed in Section I are:
——D'66 (*Democraten '66*), Democrats' 66. This party was founded in 1966 and received 4.5 percent of the votes in the 1967 parliamentary election. In the election of

1971 its support increased to 6.8 percent. It is an antiestablishment party, in the sense that it strives for a fundamental realignment of the parties on pragmatic bases instead of the old ideological and religious bases, which it considers irrelevant for contemporary problems. It also favors basic constitutional reform designed to give the voters greater political influence and to bring the voters and their representatives closer to each other. To this end, D'66 proposes the direct election of the prime minister (which in effect means the introduction of a presidential system) and the adoption of a majority electoral system in small districts instead of proportional representation. These proposals for constitutional and party reform constitute the most distinctive and original part of the program of D'66. On social and economic issues it takes a middle-of-the-road position. (see Gruijters, 1967.)

_____DS'70 (*Democratische Socialisten '70*), Democratic Socialists '70. This group seceded from the Labor party (PvdA) in 1970, in opposition to the influence of the New Left movement in the Labor party. Under the leadership of W. Drees, the son of the popular Socialist prime minister from 1948 to 1958, the new party achieved a remarkable success in the 1971 election by capturing 5.3 percent of the vote, eight seats in the Second Chamber, and two seats in the five-party coalition cabinet formed after the election.

_____PPR (*Politieke Partij Radikalen*), Radical party. This new party, founded in 1968, is a left-wing offshoot of the Catholic party (KVP). Initially, it had three seats in the Second Chamber as three elected members seceded from the KVP delegation in the Chamber. In the 1971 election it received only 1.8 percent of the vote and two seats.

The smaller parties that have been in existence for many years are:

_____CPN (*Communistische Partij Nederland*), Communist party of the Netherlands. The Communists have been represented continuously in the Second Chamber since 1918.

_____SGP (*Staatkundig Gereformeerde Partij*), Political Reformed party. Founded in 1918 and represented in the Second Chamber from 1922, this party is a fundamentalist Calvinist party, supported by adherents of some small Orthodox Reformed sects.

_____GPV (*Gereformeerd Politiek Verbond*), Reformed Political league. An even smaller fundamentalist Calvinist party, supported by adherents of a different Orthodox Reformed sect, this party was founded in 1948 but did not enter the Second Chamber until 1963.

_____PSP (*Pacifistisch Socialistische Partij*), Pacifist Socialist party. This is a radical left-wing party that is both pacifist and socialist in the doctrinaire sense. It was founded in 1957 and entered the Second Chamber in 1959 (see van der Land, 1962).

Finally, there are a number of small parties that have come into existence only recently, exemplifying—together with D'66, DS'70, and PPR—the fissiparous tendencies of the Dutch party system in the 1960s and early 1970s:

_____BP (*Boerenpartij*), Farmers party. This party, founded in 1958, made the first significant inroads into the strength of the establishment parties. It won three seats in the 1963 election and seven in 1967. During the 1967–1971 parliamentary period, however, it broke into four feuding groups. All four participated in the 1971 election, but only the BP itself managed to win a seat; its three offshoots were defeated. The BP can be described as a Poujadist party of protest against high taxes, bureaucratic power etc. Its support has by no means been restricted to farmers and rural areas.

——NMP (*Nederlanse Middenstands Partij*), Retailers party. The first election this special-interest party contested was in 1971; it won two seats then.

Eleven other parties, not listed above, participated unsuccessfully in the 1971 election.

In order to clarify the principal political patterns into which this great number and variety of parties can fit, the parties may be classified according to three political dimensions. These classifications will also be used in the analysis of the social-structure of the parties in Section IV.

The first important dimension is the religious-secular dimension. The large Catholic and Protestant parties (KVP, ARP, CHU), as well as the two fundamentalist Calvinist parties (SGP and GPV), can be classified without difficulty as religious parties. The Labor and Liberal parties (PvdA and VVD), D'66, DS'70, and the small left-wing parties (CPN and PSP) are clearly secular parties. But where do the Farmers party (BP) and the Radicals (PPR) belong?

In the Second Chamber, where the religious parties traditionally sit to the right and the secular parties to the left of the rostrum, the members of BP (and its seceded splinters) have sat with the religious parties on the right. On the basis of their party platform they should also be classified as a religious party (Lipschits, 1969, pp. 87–104, 139–40). On the other hand, the seven Farmers elected in 1967 had a heterogeneous religious background: two were Catholics, three belonged to the orthodox wing of the Dutch Reformed Church, and two were not members of any church (Daalder and Hubée-Boonzaaijer, 1970, p. 324). Frans Stokman also classifies the BP as a non-religious party (1968, p. 15). This example will be followed in this chapter. The Radicals (PPR) are not a religious party according to their own program (Lipschits, 1969, pp. 139–40). But various statements by leading Radicals have indicated that they do not regard themselves as a strictly secular party. Because it seceded from the Catholic party (KVP) and because of the Catholic background of the leadership, the Radicals will be classified as a religious party.

The secular parties can be further differentiated on the socialist-nonsocialist dimension. Socialist parties are the PvdA, PSP, CPN, and DS'70. Nonsocialist parties are the VVD, BP, and D'66.

A third significant dimension has appeared in the 1960s: the establishment-nonestablishment dimension. The establishment parties are the large parties that have jointly ruled the country in different coalitions since the First World War: KVP, PvdA, VVD, ARP, and CHU. The most forthrightly antiestablishment parties are D'66 and BP. The other small parties can also be classified as nonestablishment, if not so clearly antiestablishment. The only exception is DS'70, which cannot easily be placed in either category. (More detailed discussions of the Dutch parties may be found in Baehr, 1969, pp. 256–81; Bone, 1962, pp. 23–49; de Bruyn, 1971a, pp. 189–97; de Bruyn, 1971b, pp. 38–57; Daalder, 1955, pp. 1–16; Daalder, 1958, pp. 217–32; Daalder, 1966, pp. 188–236; Daudt, 1968, pp. 291–304; Geismann, 1964, esp. pp. 55–83; Goudsblom, 1967, pp. 82–94; Hoekstra, 1968; Lijphart, 1968, pp. 23–36, 167–70; Verkade 1965, pp. 37–55, 107–21, 225–46.)

D. "NORMAL" ELECTIONS SINCE 1945

The first five elections after the Second World War (1946–1959) showed a remarkably steady pattern of support for the major parties. The normal election outcome during this period was approximately 30 percent of the vote each for KVP and PvdA and approximately 10 percent each for ARP, CHU, and VVD. In these five elections the KVP and PvdA averaged 30.8 and 29.2 percent of the vote, respectively, and the other three parties 11.3 percent, 8.5 percent, and 8.8 percent respectively. The 1963 election already showed some erosion in the joint strength of the major parties, but it was still within this pattern. Table 3 shows the results of the 1967 and 1971 elections

TABLE 3: **Results of the Second Chamber Elections, 1956, 1967, and 1971, in Percentages**

	1956	1967	1971
PvdA	32.7	23.5	24.6
KVP	31.7	26.5	21.9
ARP	9.9	9.9	8.6
VVD	8.8	10.7	10.3
CHU	8.4	8.1	6.3
CPN	4.8	3.6	3.9
SGP	2.3	2.0	2.4
GPV	0.6	0.9	1.6
BP	—	4.7	1.1
D'66	—	4.5	6.8
PSP	—	2.9	1.4
DS'70	—	—	5.3
PPR	—	—	1.8
NMP	—	—	1.5
Other	0.8	2.7	2.5
Total	100%	100%	100%

Sources: Adapted from Centraal Bureau voor de Statistiek, 1957, p. 31; Centraal Bureau voor de Statistiek, 1967, pp. 38-39; *NRC-Handelsblad*, April 29, 1971.

and, for purposes of comparison, the "normal" election of 1956. The Liberal party (VVD) and the Anti-Revolutionary party remained close to their norms, but the two biggest parties and the Christian Historical Union suffered considerable losses. Together, the five establishment parties fell from 91.5 percent of the vote in 1956 to

71.7 percent in 1971. These trends in party support are not an isolated phenomenon; they from one aspect of the breakdown of consociational politics in the Netherlands since the middle of the 1960s.

III. Data for Analysis

A. SAMPLE SURVEYS

Three large nationwide election surveys have been conducted in the Netherlands. The first was conducted by the department of political science of the Free University of Amsterdam at the time of the Second Chamber elections of 1967 (N=4,292). A preliminary report of the principal findings has been published (Sociaal-Wetenschappelijk Instituut van de Vrije Universiteit, 1967) as well as an article based on some of the data (Hoogerwerf, 1966–67, pp. 297–330). The data will become available for secondary analysis upon publication of the main report of the survey. A smaller survey of the 1967 election is reported in Gruijters, Schermer, and Slootman, 1967). The second major survey was conducted at the time of the 1970 provincial elections by researchers at the Catholic University of Tilburg (N=1,838). The principal findings have been published in a short preliminary report (Stouthard, 1971, pp. 18–28). The third large-scale nationwide election survey concerned the Second Chamber elections in 1971. This was a joint project of the political science departments of the Dutch universities. The intention is to repeat these surveys for future Second Chamber elections and to make the data available to all scientific investigators immediately after collection (see de Hoog, Mokken, Roschar, and Stokman, 1971, pp. 29–44).

Several local and regional election surveys have been conducted in recent years. The first of these surveys was a panel study of Nieuwer-Amstel, a suburb of Amsterdam (van der Land et al., 1963; van der Land et al., 1964). More recent surveys of this kind are the survey held in the mining region of Limburg during the provincial elections of 1966 (Instituut voor Toegepaste Sociologie, 1966; de Bruyn and Nelissen, 1966), surveys in Amsterdam during the provincial elections of 1966 (Gruijters, 1966–67, pp. 3–28) and the elections for the municipal council in the same year (van der Maesen, 1966–67, pp. 169–200), a survey in Nijmegen at the time of Second Chamber elections of 1967 (Instituut voor Toegepaste Sociologie, 1967), and a survey in Utrecht at the same time (van Dam en Beishuizen, 1967).

The first important nationwide nonelection survey with material relevant to the study of voting was conducted by the Netherlands Institute of Public Opinion for a governmental advisory commission in 1954. Some of the principal findings were published (Nederlands Instituut voor de Publieke Opinie, 1956), but unfortunately the cards of this valuable study have been lost. Other nationwide nonelection surveys were held in May 1964 (Daudt and Lange, 1964), in November 1964 (Lijphart, 1968), and in

April 1965 (Daudt and Stapel, 1965–1966). Local and regional nonelection surveys with data relevant to voting behavior were conducted in Delft in 1962 (Hoogerwerf, 1964) and in rural areas near Wageningen in 1966 (Nooij, 1966, pp. 353–67).

B. ECOLOGICAL ANALYSIS

No substantial ecological analysis of national election results has been published so far. A few small-scale ecological studies of the big cities—Amsterdam, Rotterdam, and The Hague—are cited and summarized in Scholten and Ringnalda, 1969, pp. 255–56. Similar studies at the national level are Kusters, 1963, pp. 226—38, and Gadourek, 1967, pp. 117–32. Philip C. Stouthard of the University of Tilburg has collected ecological data for the Second Chamber elections of 1959, 1963, and 1967. The department of political science of the University of Leiden has collected similar data for the municipal elections of 1962 and 1966, for the municipal elections in municipalities with more than 20,000 inhabitants since 1933, for the Second Chamber elections of 1963 and 1967 and the provincial elections of 1966, organized by province and six urban-rural categories, and for the Second Chamber elections from 1888 to 1913. Most of these data are stored on IBM cards and are available for secondary analysis. (See Stokman, 1968, pp. 10–11.)

C. SECONDARY ANALYSIS OF SURVEY DATA

Because of the relative paucity of survey data on Dutch voting behavior and also because several studies have not become available pending completion of the primary analysis, there have not been many opportunities for secondary analysis. An exception is a survey conducted by the Netherlands Institute of Public Opinion in 1956, which has been used for secondary analysis a number of times (de Jong, 1956, pp. 171–215; Lipset, 1960, Chapter 7; see also Lipset and Rokkan, 1967, pp. 16–17). These data will also be used in Section IV. Another example is Stokman's secondary analysis of data collected by Attwood Statistics in 1966 (Stokman, 1966, pp. 12–33; see also de Bruyn, 1969, pp. 74–98).

Finally, there have been many essentially nonpolitical surveys that nevertheless contain data relevant for the analysis of voting behavior. The weekly polls of the Netherlands Institute of Public Opinion are particularly important in this respect. The Steinmetz Institute in Amsterdam has collected all NIPO surveys containing data on voting behavior and party affiliation since 1964. Several other essential nonpolitical surveys of this nature are also stored at the Steinmetz Institute. Moreover, most of the surveys mentioned in this section are already available or will eventually be available there.

D. NONVOTING AND ITS MEASUREMENT

When proportional representation was introduced in 1917, compulsory voting was also enacted. It remained in effect until 1970. (The term "compulsory voting" is not entirely correct, because the obligation consisted merely of presenting oneself at the polling station.) To a large extent because of this, voting turnout has always been very high. In the Second Chamber elections from 1925 to 1967 the turnout was always

TABLE 4: **Voting Turnout in Second Chamber Elections, 1925–1967, in Percentages**

	Turnout
1925	91.4
1929	92.7
1933	94.5
1937	94.4
1946	93.1
1948	93.7
1952	95.0
1956	95.5
1959	95.6
1963	95.1
1967	94.9
1971	78.5

Source: Centraal Bureau voor de Statistiek, 1967, p.11; *NRC-Handelsblad,* April 29, 1971.

higher than 90 percent (see Table 4). In the first election after the abolition of compulsory voting—the provincial elections of 1970—the turnout immediately fell to 68.9 percent. But in the Second Chamber elections of 1971 the turnout was 78.5 percent. Because of the consistently high turnout in the elections prior to 1970, nonvoting has not been a popular subject for investigation in the Netherlands. This will undoubtedly change, however, in the wake of the abolition of compulsory voting and the consequent dramatic increase in the number of nonvoters.

E. VOTING AND ITS MEASUREMENT

Most surveys attempt to discover the respondents' voting behavior by one or more of the following items: intended vote, recalled vote, and general party preference. The last item has generally been the most successful in obtaining a large response. However, no systematic studies have been undertaken concerning the relative reliability of the various methods of probing for voting behavior.

The 1967 election survey by the Free University included a question concerning the second preferences of the respondents. Seventy percent were willing to indicate a second choice: 59 percent mentioned one of the major parties and 11 percent one of the minor parties. The second choices were distributed rather unevenly among the major parties: Democrats '66 received the highest proportion (15 percent), followed by PvdA, ARP, and CHU (11 percent each), VVD (7 percent), and KVP (4 percent).

Table 5 cross-tabulates the respondents' second preferences with their vote in the 1967 elections. (Because the second preferences are cross-tabulated with the recalled vote and not with first preferences, the second preferences coincide with actual party choice in some cases.) Some interesting patterns emerge. Those who voted for one of

TABLE 5: **Party Choice in the 1967 Elections and Second Preferences, in Percentages**

				SECOND PREFERENCES						
	KVP	ARP	CHU	PvdA	VVD	D'66	Other	None/DK	Totals %	N
Party choice										
KVP	2	14	6	22	8	13	6	29	100	(1,045)
ARP	2	2	55	6	8	6	9	12	100	(397)
CHU	0	46	4	9	10	4	6	21	100	(334)
PvdA	5	5	7	4	3	28	20	28	100	(1,001)
VVD	7	13	17	6	5	23	7	22	100	(487)
D'66	10	5	1	19	23	8	11	23	100	(257)
Other	4	6	6	10	4	6	12	52	100	(771)
Total	4	11	11	11	7	15	11	30	100	(4,292)

Source: Adapted from Hoogerwerf, 1966-67, p. 300.

the Protestant parties (ARP, CHU, and the two small orthodox Calvinist parties, SGP and GPV, which are not shown separately in the table), also tended to indicate one of these parties as their second preference: 61 percent of the ARP supporters did, along with 49 percent of the CHU, 61 percent of the SGP, and 62 percent of the GVP. Hardly any of the adherents of the Protestant parties indicated the Catholic party (KVP) as their second choice. On the other hand, 20 percent of those who voted KVP gave their second vote to the ARP or the CHU. But more than twice as many KVP voters mentioned one of the major secular parties (PvdA, VVD, and D'66). Among those who supported the Labor party (PvdA) in the 1967 elections, D'66 and PSP were mentioned most often as second choices. The supporters of the two other socialist parties (CPN and PSP) mentioned the PvdA most often as their second choice (25 and 29 percent, respectively), followed by D'66 (11 and 13 percent), and PSP (10 percent of the CPN voters) and CPN (8 percent of the PSP voters). The supporters of the VVD most often indicated D'66 as their second choice, although remarkably high percentages also selected the CHU and ARP. Conversely, for the respondents who voted D'66 in the elections, the VVD was the most frequent second preference, followed by PvdA and KVP. (See Hoogerwerf, 1966–67, pp. 298–302.)

IV. Social-Structure and Voting

In order to analyze the relationships between social-structural variables and voting both during the period of "normal" elections (1946–1959) and in the recent years of political transition, it was decided to subject two surveys to secondary analysis: one that was held during the period of "normal" elections and one conducted as recently as possible. An important requirement was that both surveys contain the basic independent variables (in particular, class, religion, and religiosity). The earliest suitable survey that could be found is a survey conducted by the Netherlands Institute of Public Opinion in April and May, 1956 (N=1,226). This survey has already been used for purposes of secondary analysis by other investigators (de Jong, 1956; Lipset, 1960). The most recent suitable survey available for secondary analysis is a survey conducted by Attwood Statistics in May and June of 1968. Its original N is 1,285; its weighted N is 2,457. The weighting of the sample was necessary because of the overrepresentation of members of the Reformed Church in the original sample (Noordhof, 1969, pp. 267–73). In general, the two surveys are sufficiently similar to be analyzed comparatively. The principal difference between the two is that the 1956 sample is a sample of the adult population whereas the 1968 sample excludes respondents of sixty-five years of age and older. In order to make the two samples comparable in this respect, this age category was also eliminated from the 1956 sample, causing a 10.7 percent reduction in the sample size.

In both surveys "voting" is measured by a question about general party preference. Only those who indicated a party preference are included in the analysis; the "don't-knows" and "no-answers" are not considered. This category comprised only 8.6 percent of the 1956 sample, but no less than 38.4 percent in the 1968 sample, including 25.0 percent who stated explicitly that they did not have a preference for *any* party. This is in itself a telling indicator of the momentous changes in Dutch politics in recent years. Another possible explanation is that the 1956 survey was held shortly before a Second Chamber election, whereas the 1968 survey was conducted in a nonelection period.

In the tables that follow, the major religious parties (KVP, ARP, and CHU) always precede the secular parties (PvdA, VVD, and D'66). In order to keep the tables within manageable proportions, the smaller parties are not presented individually. They are either grouped together in the category of "other parties," or together with the major parties in the general classes of religious secular, socialist, nonsocialist, and nonestablishment parties. (The only exception is that the SGP and GPV could not be included in the category of religious parties because they were not listed separately in the 1968 survey. In order to maximize the comparability of the samples, these two small Protestant parties were also omitted from the religious-secular dichotomy of the 1956 sample.)

A. SOCIAL-CLASS

Because the two most prominent divisions of the Dutch party system are the religious-secular and the socialist-nonsocialist dimensions, one would expect these to be reflected in Dutch voting behavior. Of the various social-structural variables, religion (church affiliation and church attendance) and social-class should therefore be the best predictors of party preference. Social-class—as well as the closely related variable of education—will be examined first.

Table 6 presents the relationships between party preference and social-class in 1956 and 1968. The operational definition of social-class position is the interviewer's assessment of the respondent's socio-economic status. Both the 1956 and the 1968 surveys used a fourfold classification, here labeled A to D, with A representing the highest socioeconomic category and D the lowest. The distribution of the respondents among

TABLE 6 : **Class and Party Preference, 1956 and 1968, in Percentages**

	KVP	ARP	CHU	PvdA	VVD	D'66	OTHER	TOTALS %	N
1956									
A (High)	39	7	6	24	18	—	6	100	(67)
B	30	14	15	22	15	—	4	100	(278)
C	31	13	10	35	4	—	6	100	(356)
D (Low)	27	14	6	41	1	—	10	100	(293)
Total	30	14	10	32	7	—	7	100	(994)
1968									
A (High)	22	10	9	14	23	18	3	100	(181)
B	17	16	11	22	14	12	8	100	(510)
C	25	10	7	37	4	8	10	100	(672)
D (Low)	27	13	5	38	4	5	8	100	(150)
Total	22	12	9	29	9	10	8	100	(1,513)

the four categories is not even: in the 1956 survey the highest category (A) contains relatively few respondents, as do both the highest and the lowest categories (A and D) of the 1968 survey.

With only a few relatively small exceptions the major religious parties (KVP, ARP, CHU) receive their support about equally from the different socioeconomic categories. These parties do not have a clear class basis. On the other hand, social-class position is an important differentiator as far as the major secular parties are concerned. As socioeconomic status decreases, support for the PvdA steadily increases and support for the VVD—and for D'66 in 1968—steadily decreases. The pattern of support for VVD and

D'66 is generally similar in the 1968 survey, although it should be noted that the VVD has a more pronounced social-class basis than D'66.

Table 7 shows the relationships between social-class and support for the secular parties; only those respondents who indicated a preference for one of the secular parties are included in the table. The overall support for the nonsocialist parties increased considerably from 1956 to 1968 due to the growth of the VVD, which was

TABLE 7: **Class and Party Preference (Socialist vs. Nonsocialist Secular Parties), 1956 and 1968, in Percentages**

	1956				1968			
	Socialist	Non-socialist	%	Total	Socialist	Non-socialist	%	Total
A (High)	57	43	100	(28)	28	72	100	(101)
B	60	40	100	(103)	48	52	100	(259)
C	89	11	100	(141)	75	25	100	(365)
D (Low)	97	3	100	(135)	82	18	100	(79)
Total	82	18	100	(407)	61	39	100	(804)

Supporters of religious parties are excluded from this table.

the only nonsocialist secular party in 1956, and the emergence of two new nonsocialist parties, D'66 and BP. The distribution of the "secular votes" between the socialist and nonsocialist parties in the Second Chamber elections of 1956 and 1967 was 81-19 in 1956 and 60-40 in 1967, corresponding closely to the total percentages for 1956 and 1968 in Table 7. Apart from this overall change, however, the relationships between

TABLE 8: **Class, Education, and Party Preference (Religious vs. Secular Parties), 1956 and 1968, in Percentages**

	1956				1968			
	Religious	Secular	Totals %	N	Religious	Secular	Totals %	N
Middle-class (A,B)								
More than primary	59	41	100	(229)	41	59	100	(436)
Primary only	62	38	100	(92)	57	43	100	(237)
Lower-class (C,D)								
More than primary	56	44	100	(217)	42	58	100	(177)
Primary only	54	46	100	(378)	46	54	100	(629)
Total	57	43	100	(916)	46	54	100	(1,479)

social-class and party preference are very similar in the two years. The higher socio-economic categories tend to support the nonsocialist parties and the lower categories the socialist parties.

B. EDUCATION

Tables 8 and 9 present the relationships between education and party preference while class is held constant. The dividing line for education is between respondents with primary education only ending at about age thirteen, and those with more than primary education. Class is dichotomized into middle-class (status group A and B) and lower-class (status group C and D). In the 1956 survey, there are no significant differences among the class and educational categories in their support of the religious or secular parties, except that middle-class respondents with only primary education favor the religious parties to a somewhat greater extent than all other respondents. This tendency is much clearer in the 1968 survey: a clear majority of the less-educated middle-class people favor the religious parties, whereas the reverse is true for the others.

The differences among the class and educational categories are much greater in terms of support for the socialist or nonsocialist parties (Table 9). In the 1956 survey there is no relationship between party preference and education among lower-class

TABLE 9: Class, Education, and Party Preference (Socialist vs. Nonsocialist Secular Parties), 1956 and 1968, in Percentages

	1956				1968			
	Socialist	*Non-socialist*	*Totals* %	*N*	*Socialist*	*Non-socialist*	*Totals* %	*N*
Middle-class (A,B)								
More than primary	56	44	100	(94)	36	64	100	(259)
Primary only	71	29	100	(35)	60	40	100	(101)
Lower-class (C,D)								
More than primary	92	8	100	(95)	61	39	100	(103)
Primary only	95	5	100	(174)	80	20	100	(341)
Total	83	17	100	(398)	61	39	100	(804)

Supporters of religious parties are excluded from this table.

respondents; among middle-class respondents, however, those with more education tend to support the nonsocialists to a greater extent. But class remains the stronger predictor of party preference. In 1968 class and education are equally powerful predictors. When class is controlled, there are significant differences between the educational categories. Conversely, when education is controlled, the influence of class on party preference remains strong.

C. CHURCH AFFILIATION AND ATTENDANCE

As Table 10 shows, there is a very strong relationship between church affiliation and party preference. Catholics support the KVP in overwhelming numbers;

members of the Orthodox Reformed churches show an about equally strong preference for the ARP; and almost all respondents without church affiliation support the secular parties. These tendencies were much stronger in 1956 than in 1968. Members of the Dutch Reformed Church tend to divide their votes between the Protestant parties— particularly the CHU—and the secular parties. On the whole the distribution of party preferences in this religious group in 1956 is remarkably similar to the 1968 distribution.

TABLE 10: **Church Affiliation and Party Preference, 1956 and 1968, in Percentages**

	KVP	ARP	CHU	PvdA	VVD	D'66	Other	Totals %	N
1956									
Catholic	90	1	0	5	1	—	3	100	(326)
Dutch Ref.	0	10	29	41	13	—	7	100	(321)
Orth. Ref.	0	85	3	6	0	—	6	100	(114)
None	1	1	1	72	12	—	14	100	(194)
Other/DK/NA	8	5	5	69	10	—	3	100	(39)
Total	30	14	10	32	7	—	7	100	(994)
1968									
Catholic	68	0	0	7	6	11	8	100	(478)
Dutch Ref.	1	9	31	36	13	6	5	100	(366)
Orth. Ref.	0	73	2	8	2	4	12	100	(197)
None	2	1	2	55	13	16	11	100	(440)
Other/DK/NA	0	6	6	56	25	6	0	100	(32)
Total	22	12	9	29	9	10	8	100	(1,513)

The influence of the religious factor on party preference becomes even clearer when church attendance is also taken into consideration. Frequency of church attendance can be used as an indicator of the degree of religiosity. The questions concerning church attendance in the 1956 and 1968 surveys are not exactly the same. In 1956 the respondents were asked: "Did you attend church during the past week?" In 1968 the questions was: "Do you attend church or religious meetings regularly, occasionally, or never?" These different wordings should be kept in mind in interpreting the tables, particularly because the terms "regular" and "occasional" church attendance do not carry the same meaning for Protestants and Catholics—attending church twice a month is more likely to be considered "regular" attendance by a Protestant than by a Catholic.

Table 11 shows that in the 1956 survey support for the KVP is particularly strong among practicing Catholics (i.e., those who attended church during the week preceding the interview) and considerably weaker among nonpracticing Catholics. The same applies to the support of the ARP by members of the Orthodox Reformed churches. Church attendance serves as an even more important differentiator in the party preferences of members of the Dutch Reformed Church. Almost one-half of the practicing members support the CHU and more than two-thirds support the three Protestant parties (CHU, ARP, and SGP), whereas only about one-fourth of the nonpracticing members support the Protestant parties. The same relationships appear in the 1968 survey. As frequency of church attendance decreases, support for the KVP, CHU, and ARP by Catholics, Dutch Reformed, and Orthodox Reformed people decreases sharply.

TABLE 11: **Church Affiliation, Church Attendance, and Party Preference, 1956 and 1968, in Percentages**

	KVP	ARP	CHU	PvdA	VVD	D'66	Other	Totals %	N
1956									
Catholic									
Pract.	95	0	0	2	0	—	3	100	(295)
Nonpract.	50	7	0	30	10	—	3	100	(30)
Dutch Ref.									
Pract.	0	18	45	23	5	—	9	100	(121)
Nonpract.	0	6	19	52	18	—	6	100	(200)
Orth. Ref.									
Pract.	0	90	3	1	0	—	5	100	(93)
Nonpract.	0	62	0	29	0	—	10	100	(21)
None	1	1	1	72	12	—	14	100	(194)
Total	31	14	10	31	7	—	7	100	(954)
1968									
Catholic									
Regular	77	1	1	5	2	9	5	100	(380)
Occasional	43	0	0	7	20	13	17	100	(60)
Never	16	0	0	26	21	21	16	100	(38)
Dutch Ref.									
Regular	0	20	52	15	5	2	7	100	(122)
Occasional	2	5	31	27	22	5	7	100	(110)
Never	0	3	12	61	12	10	1	100	(134)
Orth. Ref.									
Regular	0	80	2	2	2	2	13	100	(166)
Occas./Never	0	39	3	39	0	13	6	100	(31)
None	2	1	2	55	13	16	11	100	(440)
Total	23	12	9	28	9	10	8	100	(1,481)

In the 1968 survey religiosity was also measured by means of the question, "Does religion play an important role in your life, a not very important role, or no role at all?" Church attendance turns out to give a slightly more sensitive prediction than this alternative indicator of religiosity (see Table 13), but the overall pattern is very similar: as "religiosity" (in terms of this indicator) decreases from high to low, support by the three religious groupings for their "own" political parties decreases, and support for the secular parties increases.

Table 13 summarizes the relationships among church affiliation, church attendance, and party preference. Church attendance in 1968 in dichotomized by combining
those who attend regularly and who attend occasionally into a single category of
"practicing" church members. Because of the different operational definitions of

TABLE 12 : Church Affiliation, "Religiosity" and Party Preference, 1968, in Percentages

	KVP	ARP	CHU	PvdA	VVD	D'66	OTHER	TOTALS %	N
Catholic									
High	79	1	0	3	2	8	8	100	(310)
Middle	49	0	1	14	13	14	7	100	(138)
Low	40	0	0	20	13	20	7	100	(30)
Dutch Ref.									
High	1	16	51	19	7	2	4	100	(180)
Middle	0	3	13	47	20	11	6	100	(140)
Low	0	4	9	65	13	4	4	100	(46)
Orth. Ref.									
High	0	77	2	3	2	2	13	100	(172)
Middle/Low	0	48	0	40	0	12	0	100	(25)
None									
High/Middle	9	0	6	27	36	18	3	100	(66)
Low	1	1	1	60	9	16	12	100	(374)
Total	23	12	9	28	9	10	8	100	(1,481)

church attendance in the two surveys and because of the relatively small numbers of
nonpracticing Catholic and Orthodox Reformed respondents, one has to be cautious

TABLE 13 : Church Affiliation, Church Attendance, and Party Preference (Religious vs. Secular Parties), 1956 and 1968, in Percentages

	1956				1968			
	Rel.	*Sec.*	*Totals* %	*N*	*Rel.*	*Sec.*	*Totals* %	*N*
Catholic								
Practicing	97	3	100	(288)	78	22	100	(440)
Nonpracticing	59	41	100	(29)	16	84	100	(38)
Dutch Ref.								
Practicing	69	31	100	(110)	59	41	100	(222)
Nonpracticing	26	74	100	(188)	15	85	100	(134)
Orth. Ref.								
Practicing	99	1	100	(88)	88	12	100	(167)
Nonpracticing	68	32	100	(19)	33	67	100	(12)
None	2	98	100	(179)	5	95	100	(434)
Total	58	42	100	(901)	46	54	100	(1,447)

in making comparisons between the two surveys. Nevertheless, it is clear that church attendance is an extraordinarily powerful predictor. And in predicting party preference for religious or for secular parties it is a stronger factor than church affiliation.

Tables 14 and 15 explore the relationships between church attendance and party preference with social-class as the control variable. As far as the choice between the religious and the secular parties is concerned, the influence of church attendance is not affected by social-class. The only slight exception is that in the 1968 survey the tendency

TABLE 14: Class, Church Attendance, and Party Preference (Religious vs. Secular Parties), 1956 and 1968, in Percentages

	1956				1968			
	Rel.	*Sec.*	*Totals* %	*N*	*Rel.*	*Sec.*	*Totals* %	*N*
Middle-class (A, B)								
Practicing	92	8	100	(187)	70	30	100	(418)
Nonpracticing	19	81	100	(144)	8	92	100	(255)
Lower-class (C, D)								
Practicing	91	9	100	(306)	76	24	100	(433)
Nonpracticing	18	82	100	(300)	9	91	100	(373)
Total	57	43	100	(937)	46	54	100	(1,479)

of practicing church members to support the religious parties is somewhat stronger among lower-class than among middle-class respondents (see Table 14). As far as the choice between the socialist and the nonsocialist parties is concerned, however, social class is a more powerful predictor, especially in the 1956 survey. In this survey there is no relationship between church attendance and socialist/nonsocialist party preference

TABLE 15: Class, Church Attendance, and Party Preference (Socialist vs. Nonsocialist Secular Parties), 1956 and 1968, in Percentages

	1956				1968			
	Soc.	*Non-Soc.*	*Totals* %	*N*	*Soc.*	*Non-Soc.*	*Totals* %	*N*
Middle-class (A, B)								
Practicing	67	33	100	(15)	28	72	100	(125)
Nonpracticing	59	41	100	(116)	50	50	100	(235)
Lower-class (C, D)								
Practicing	93	7	100	(29)	64	36	100	(103)
Nonpracticing	93	7	100	(245)	79	21	100	(341)
Total	82	18	100	(405)	61	39	100	(804)

Supporters of religious parties are excluded from this table.

among lower-class respondents and only a weak relationship among middle-class respondents: practicing church members have a greater tendency to support the socialist parties than the nonpracticing respondents. In the 1968 survey this relationship is reversed, and it is also stronger than in 1956: in both the middle- and the lower-classes practicing church members have a greater tendency to support the nonsocialist parties than do nonpracticing respondents. Social-class is still the stronger factor (see Table 15).

D. RURAL OR URBAN RESIDENCE

Table 16 presents the results of the Second Chamber elections of 1967 classified accordingly to the degree of urbanization. The urbanization scale is the carefully designed classification, based on the 1960 census, of the Central Bureau of Statistics. (Unfortunately, no similar cross-tabulation is available for the 1956 election.) In general all of the religious parties are stronger in the rural areas than in the urban areas, and the secular parties are stronger in the urban than in the rural areas. The only exception is the Farmers Party (BP), which, as its name suggests, has its principal strength in the rural areas. But it is by no means exclusively a rural party: in the 1967 elections it won more than 4 percent of the vote in the towns and larger cities, only slightly less than its percentage of the total nationwide vote.

TABLE 16: Rural-Urban Residence and Party Preference in the Second Chamber Elections, 1967, in Percentages

	KVP	ARP	CHU	PvdA	VVD	D'66	OTHER	TOTAL
Rural municipalities	29.3	13.5	11.5	18.9	9.1	2.3	15.4	100%
Larger rural municipalities	36.2	9.5	8.8	18.1	7.2	3.1	17.1	100%
Suburbs	24.6	10.9	8.6	19.1	19.0	5.8	12.0	100%
Towns	26.2	9.5	8.1	26.4	10.2	4.4	15.2	100%
Large cities	20.2	7.7	5.3	28.5	12.2	6.5	19.6	100%
Total	26.5	9.9	8.1	23.5	10.7	4.5	16.8	100%

Source: Adapted from Centraal Bureau voor de Statistiek, 1967, pp. 18–19.

Rural-urban differences also appear clearly in the 1956 and 1968 surveys, as Table 17 shows. As urbanization increases, support decreases for the religious parties and increases for the secular parties. The table also shows, however, that the influence of rural-urban differences disappears to a large extent when church attendance is controlled. But in the 1968 survey the influence of urban-rural residence remains relatively strong among practicing church members: this group still tends to support the religious parties (although less so than in 1956), especially in rural areas.

TABLE 17: **Rural-Urban Residence, Church Attendance, and Party Preference (Religious vs. Secular Parties), 1956 and 1968, in Percentages**

	1956				1968			
	Rel.	*Sec.*	*Totals*		*Rel.*	*Sec.*	*Totals*	
			%	N			%	N
Total sample								
Large cities	37	63	100	(175)	29	71	100	(313)
Smaller towns	56	44	100	(495)	43	57	100	(739)
Rural areas	70	30	100	(269)	63	37	100	(427)
Practicing								
Large cities	89	11	100	(57)	61	39	100	(118)
Smaller towns	87	13	100	(261)	70	30	100	(416)
Rural areas	97	3	100	(175)	82	18	100	(317)
Nonpracticing								
Large cities	12	88	100	(117)	9	91	100	(195)
Smaller towns	22	78	100	(233)	9	91	100	(323)
Rural areas	19	81	100	(94)	5	95	100	(110)

TABLE 18: **Province of Residence and Party Preference in the Second Chamber Elections, 1956 and 1967, in Percentages**

	KVP	ARP	CHU	PvdA	VVD	D'66	OTHER	TOTAL
1956								
Groningen	5.9	17.3	9.6	42.3	12.9	—	12.0	100
Friesland	6.9	22.1	16.0	40.9	8.4	—	5.7	100
Drente	6.9	15.7	12.2	44.5	15.2	—	5.5	100
Overijsel	28.0	10.1	13.1	31.8	7.6	—	9.4	100
Gelderland	32.2	9.3	13.1	31.3	7.9	—	6.2	100
Utrecht	25.8	12.9	11.1	32.6	9.3	—	8.3	100
North Holland	23.7	8.2	5.1	37.4	11.8	—	13.8	100
South Holland	18.7	12.3	9.4	37.8	11.3	—	10.5	100
Zealand	20.9	12.8	15.4	32.0	8.1	—	10.8	100
North Brabant	74.8	2.7	2.3	16.4	2.0	—	1.8	100
Limburg	78.5	0.8	0.6	17.5	0.9	—	1.7	100
Total	31.7	9.9	8.4	32.7	8.8	—	8.5	100
1967								
Groningen	5.5	16.7	9.7	33.2	12.0	2.7	20.2	100
Friesland	6.5	22.8	15.3	31.6	8.1	2.4	13.3	100
Drente	7.0	15.1	11.4	35.5	14.0	2.1	14.9	100
Overijsel	25.6	10.5	12.7	23.1	8.1	2.7	17.3	100
Gelderland	27.2	9.5	11.8	22.9	9.7	3.4	15.5	100
Utrecht	21.5	12.2	11.0	22.7	13.1	4.5	15.0	100
North Holland	19.8	8.4	5.2	24.7	13.1	6.9	21.9	100
South Holland	15.8	11.7	9.2	29.3	12.9	5.0	16.1	100
Zealand	17.6	12.6	15.0	24.3	10.4	2.2	17.9	100
North Brabant	56.6	4.1	2.5	10.5	7.5	4.8	14.0	100
Limburg	63.7	1.9	1.0	11.8	5.1	3.1	13.4	100
Total	26.5	9.9	8.1	23.5	10.7	4.5	16.8	100

Source: Adapted from Centraal Bureau voor de Statistiek, 1957, pp. 30–31; Centraal Bureau voor de Statistiek, 1967, pp. 36–39.

E. PROVINCE OF RESIDENCE

Table 18 presents the results of the 1956 and 1967 elections in Holland's eleven provinces. The most striking regional variation is the great strength of the KVP in the two southern provinces (North Brabant and Limburg) and its weakness in the three northern provinces (Groningen, Friesland, and Drente). The reverse applies to the other major parties with the exception of D'66, which is relatively strong in the south (especially in North Brabant) and weak in the northern provinces.

The regional distribution of the KVP's strength corresponds with the regional distribution of the Roman Catholic segment of the population. It is important, therefore, to analyze the relationship between province of residence and party preference while church affiliation is held constant. This is done in Table 19. The KVP is contrasted with all other parties combined; Catholics are contrasted with all other church members and those without church affiliation; and the provinces are grouped together in three classes, south, north, and the rest of the country. In the 1956 survey regional

TABLE 19: **Province of Residence, Church Affiliation, and Party Preference (KVP vs. Other Parties), 1956 and 1968, in Percentages**

	1956				1968			
	KVP	OTHER PARTIES	TOTALS %	N	KVP	OTHER PARTIES	TOTALS %	N
Catholic								
South	89	11	100	(185)	78	22	100	(238)
North	86	14	100	(7)	50	50	100	(8)
Rest	92	8	100	(134)	58	42	100	(232)
Other & No Rel.								
South	4	96	100	(25)	14	86	100	(29)
North	1	99	100	(106)	0	100	100	(165)
Rest	1	99	100	(537)	1	99	100	(841)
Total	30	70	100	(994)	22	78	100	(1,513)

differences in KVP support disappear when church affiliation is controlled. But regional variation is maintained when this control is introduced in the 1968 survey: Catholics living in the southern provinces have a stronger tendency to support the KVP than Catholics in the rest of the country.

F. AGE

The relationship between age and party preference is presented in Table 20. Respondents over sixty-five years of age in the 1956 sample were omitted from all previous tables in order to make the 1956 sample comparable with the 1968 sample, but they are included in Table 20 (and in Tables 21-23). In the 1956 survey age does not turn out to be an important factor affecting party preference, with the slight exception of the relatively strong support for the KVP among the twenty-one to thirty-four age group

TABLE 20: **Age and Party Preference, 1956 and 1968, in Percentages**

	KVP	ARP	CHU	PvdA	VVD	D'66	OTHER	TOTALS %	N
1956									
21—34	37	12	9	30	6	—	6	100	(363)
35—49	24	15	9	36	9	—	8	100	(411)
50—64	30	13	13	30	7	—	7	100	(220)
65+	27	9	10	40	10	—	3	100	(127)
Total	30	13	10	33	8	—	6	100	(1,121)
1968									
21—34	19	16	7	24	8	17	10	100	(512)
35—49	19	12	10	31	11	10	7	100	(568)
50—64	30	9	10	33	10	3	7	100	(433)
Total	22	12	9	29	9	10	8	100	(1,513)

and the weakness of this party among the thirty-five to forty-nine group. However, age is a factor of considerable importance in the 1968 survey. The main strength of the KVP is in the fifty to sixty-four age group—rather surprisingly, because this group corresponds to the thirty-five to forty-nine age group in the 1956 survey among whom preference for the KVP was low. There is one party for which age is a highly important factor: D'66. Approximately one-sixth of the youngest group supports this party compared with an insignificant percentage of the oldest group. In general the younger

TABLE 21: **Age, Church Attendance, and Party Preference (Religious vs. Secular Parties), 1956 and 1968, in Percentages**

	1956				1968			
	Rel.	Sec.	Totals %	N	Rel.	Sec.	Totals %	N
Total sample								
21—34	61	39	100	(344)	43	57	100	(504)
35—49	51	49	100	(385)	44	56	100	(560)
50—64	59	41	100	(210)	51	49	100	(415)
65+	47	53	100	(125)	—	—		
Practicing								
21—34	92	8	100	(197)	70	30	100	(287)
35—49	87	13	100	(181)	70	30	100	(322)
50—64	95	5	100	(115)	82	18	100	(242)
65+	82	18	100	(56)	—	—		
Nonpracticing								
21—34	20	80	100	(147)	8	92	100	(217)
35—49	19	81	100	(203)	9	91	100	(238)
50—64	16	84	100	(94)	8	92	100	(173)
65+	19	81	100	(69)	—	—		

respondents prefer the secular to the religious parties, the nonsocialist to the socialist parties, and the nonestablishment to the establishment parties. It is especially note-worthy that younger people tend to be antiestablishment rather than "left" in the sense of the established PvdA.

Table 21 shows that the preference of the younger generations for the secular parties in the 1968 survey cannot be explained by their lower degree of religiosity. Among the nonpracticing respondents there is no relationship between age and party preference, but among the practicing church members the oldest group supports the religious parties more strongly than the younger groups. Table 22 shows the clear relationship between age and preference for the socialist/nonsocialist parties in the 1968 survey (in contrast to the 1956 survey, in which these variables are not related at

TABLE 22: Age, Class, and Party Preference (Socialist vs. Nonsocialist Secular Parties), 1956 and 1968, in Percentages

	1956				1968			
	Soc.	Non-Soc.	Totals %	N	Soc.	Non-Soc.	Totals %	N
Total sample								
21—34	83	17	100	(133)	52	48	100	(285)
35—49	81	19	100	(188)	61	39	100	(315)
50—64	83	17	100	(86)	74	26	100	(204)
65+	80	20	100	(66)	—	—		
Middle-class (A,-B)								
21—34	56	44	100	(45)	36	64	100	(127)
35—49	57	43	100	(63)	42	58	100	(152)
50—64	74	26	100	(23)	53	47	100	(81)
65+	36	64	100	(11)	—	—		
Lower-class (C,-D)								
21—34	98	2	100	(88)	65	35	100	(158)
35—49	94	6	100	(125)	78	22	100	(163)
50—64	86	14	100	(63)	87	13	100	(123)
65+	89	11	100	(55)	—	—		

Supporters of religious parties are excluded from this table.

all), and the fact that the relationship remains strong when social-class is introduced as a control. Among both middle-class and lower-class respondents, support for the nonsocialist parties increases as age decreases.

A similar pattern emerges when the relationship between age and support for the establishment or nonestablishment parties is examined (Table 23). In the 1956 survey there is no relationship between these two variables. In the 1968 survey, however, support for the establishment parties increases steadily with age, and this relationship remains strong when church attendance is controlled. Especially among young non-practicing respondents, the preference for the nonestablishment parties—primarily D'66—is strikingly high.

TABLE 23: Age, Church Attendance, and Party Preference (Establishment vs. Nonestablishment Parties), 1956 and 1968, in Percentages

	Estab.	Non-estab.	Totals %	N	Estab.	Non-estab.	Totals %	N
			1956				1968	
Total sample								
21—34	94	6	100	(363)	73	27	100	(512)
35—49	92	8	100	(411)	83	17	100	(568)
50—64	93	7	100	(220)	90	10	100	(433)
65+	97	3	100	(127)	—	—		
Practicing								
21—34	96	4	100	(205)	80	20	100	(295)
35—49	94	6	100	(192)	85	25	100	(328)
50—64	95	5	100	(121)	92	8	100	(256)
65+	98	2	100	(57)	—	—		
Nonpracticing								
21—34	92	8	100	(158)	64	36	100	(217)
35—49	91	9	100	(218)	80	20	100	(240)
50—64	92	8	100	(97)	88	12	100	(177)
65+	96	4	100	(70)	—	—		

G. SEX

Table 24 presents the relationships between sex and party preference. In general women support religious parties more strongly than men; the only minor exception is the stronger male support of the CHU in 1956. The differences between the party preferences of men and women are greater in 1968 than in 1956. A likely explanation of these differences is that religion tends to be a more important factor for women than for men. This hypothesis is tested in Table 25. When church attendance is controlled in the 1956 survey, the relationship between sex and party preference virtually disappears. In the 1968 survey this relationship becomes weaker but does not disappear when church attendance is controlled.

TABLE 24: Sex and Party Preference, 1956 and 1968, in Percentages

	KVP	ARP	CHU	PvdA	VVD	D'66	OTHER	TOTAL %	N
1956									
Men	27	13	11	34	9	—	7	100	(500)
Women	34	14	9	31	5	—	7	100	(494)
Total	30	14	10	32	7	—	7	100	(994)
1968									
Men	16	10	8	33	10	12	10	100	(697)
Women	27	14	9	26	9	8	7	100	(816)
Total	22	12	9	29	9	10	8	100	(1,513)

TABLE 25: Sex, Church Attendance, and Party Preference (Religious vs. Secular Parties), 1956 and 1968, in Percentages

| | 1956 | | | | 1968 | | | |
| | Rel. | Sec. | Totals | | Rel. | Sec. | Totals | |
			%	N			%	N
Total sample								
Men	53	47	100	(475)	37	63	100	(685)
Women	60	40	100	(464)	53	47	100	(794)
Practicing								
Men	91	9	100	(233)	67	33	100	(355)
Women	91	9	100	(260)	78	22	100	(496)
Nonpracticing								
Men	17	83	100	(242)	5	95	100	(330)
Women	21	79	100	(202)	12	88	100	(298)

H. LABOR-UNION MEMBERSHIP

Labor-union membership and party preference are closely related, reflecting the close formal and informal ties between the PvdA and the Socialist labor-union

TABLE 26: Labor-Union Membership and Party Preference, 1956, in Percentages

| | KVP | ARP | CHU | PvdA | VVD | Other | Totals | |
							%	N
NVV (Socialist)	1	1	1	90	1	5	100	(145)
KAB/NKV (Catholic)	94	0	0	4	0	2	100	(107)
CNV (Protestant)	0	56	26	14	0	4	100	(90)
Total	30	15	7	43	1	4	100	(342)

federation (NVV), between the KVP and the Catholic federation (KAB, renamed NKV in the early 1960s), and between ARP and CHU and the Protestant labor federation (CNV). Table 26 presents the results for 1956. No question on labor-union membership was included in the 1968 survey.

I. SOCIAL-PSYCHOLOGICAL INFLUENCES

The relationship between social-psychological variables (such as interest and involvement in politics, intensity of partisanship, etc.) and voting in the Netherlands has not yet received systematic scholarly attention. The only exception is a study of political efficacy, in which a relationship was found between low efficacy and voting for the Communists (CPN), Pacifists (PSP), Farmers Party (BP), and other nonestablishment parties (Daudt, van der Maesen, and Mokken, 1968, pp. 298–301; see also Mokken, 1969, pp. 425–48).

V. Social Profiles and Party Profiles

Of the variables discussed in Section IV, three stand out as the most important determinants of party preference: church affiliation, church attendance, and social class. This applies both to the 1956 survey and to the 1968 survey. In the 1956 survey education, rural-urban residence, province of residence, age, and sex are of very minor or no importance when the basic three variables are controlled. But in 1968 they are related to party preference even when the basic three variables are controlled; these basic variables, however, are still stronger determinants of party preference.

When we compare the relative predictive powers of church affiliation, church attendance, and social-class, the most important variable is church attendance because it differentiates very well between the religious and the secular parties. In order to differentiate further among the religious parties, church affiliation is the crucial variable. And in order to differentiate among the secular parties, social-class is the most helpful predictor. This may be summarized as follows:

Practicing	⎰ Roman Catholic ⎱ Dutch Reformed ⎰ Orthodox Reformed	KVP CHU ARP
Nonpracticing	⎰ Lower-class ⎱ Middle-class	PvdA VVD and D'66

Table 27 presents the relationships between these five groups and party preference. The percentages that are correctly predicted according to the above fivefold predictive scheme have been italicized. The scheme works particularly well in predicting the party preferences of practicing Catholics and practicing members of the Orthodox Reformed churches. It works much less well for secular members of the middle-class: in the 1956 survey more respondents belonging in this category support the PvdA than the VVD, and in the 1968 survey the combined preference for VVD and D'66 exceeds the preference for the PvdA only slightly. But in both years support for the VVD (and D' 66 in 1968) is much greater and support for the PvdA much smaller in the secular middle-class group than in the secular lower-class group. In all probability the difference in party preference would be greater if a sharper operational measure of class divisions were used.

It should also be noted that the predictive scheme works considerably less well for the 1968 than for the 1956 data—a clear indication of the declining predictability of political allegiances in recent years. This affects the practicing church members and the religious parties in particular.

The data of Table 27 can be percentaged by column instead of by row in order to show the social composition of the parties instead of the party preferences of social

TABLE 27: Party Preferences of Five Groups, Classified According to Church Attendance and Church Affiliation or Class, 1956 and 1968, in Percentages

	KVP	ARP	CHU	PvDA	VVD	D'66	OTHER	TOTALS %	N
1956									
Cath. -Pract.	*95*	0	0	2	0	—	3	100	(295)
Dutch Ref.-Pract.	0	18	*45*	23	5	—	9	100	(121)
Orth.Ref. -Pract.	0	*90*	3	1	0	—	5	100	(93)
Secular-L.C.	4	6	7	*68*	5	—	10	100	(321)
Secular-M.C.	3	4	12	44	*32*	—	6	100	(152)
Total	30	13	10	33	7	—	7	100	(982)
1968									
Cath.-Pract.	*72*	0	0	5	5	10	7	100	(440)
Dutch Ref.-Pract.	1	13	*42*	21	13	3	7	100	(232)
Orth. Ref.-Pract.	0	*76*	2	5	2	3	12	100	(185)
Secular-L.C.	3	2	4	*65*	5	11	10	100	(373)
Secular-M.C.	2	2	4	40	*25*	*20*	8	100	(261)
Total	23	12	9	29	9	10	8	100	(1,491)

Italic numbers indicate correct predictions.

groups. This is done in Table 28 for the six major parties. Without exception, the largest segment of the support of each party is derived from the expected group in the fivefold predictive scheme. A comparison of the 1956 and 1968 surveys shows that

TABLE 28: Composition of the Clienteles of the Major Parties, 1956 and 1968, in Percentages

	1956					1968					
	KVP	ARP	CHU	PvDA	VVD	KVP	ARP	CHU	PvDA	VVD	D'66
Cath.-Pract.	*94*	0	0	2	1	*95*	1	2	6	14	29
Dutch Ref.-Pract.	0	17	*56*	9	8	1	16	*77*	11	21	5
Orth. Ref.-Pract.	0	*64*	3	0	0	0	*77*	2	2	2	4
Secular-L.C.	4	15	23	*68*	24	4	3	11	*57*	14	28
Secular-M.C.	1	5	19	21	*67*	1	3	9	24	*47*	*34*
Total %	100%	100%	100%	100%	100%	100%	100%	100%	100%	100%	100%
N	(296)	(132)	(97)	(320)	(72)	(336)	(184)	(128)	(428)	(139)	(151)

the general loss of support by the religious parties has not diminished their social homogeneity. In fact, the two Protestant parties seem to have increased their homogeneity, but this is almost entirely due to the stricter definition of frequency of church attendance in the 1956 survey. The secular parties have become more heterogeneous in social composition from 1956 to 1968. This is only partly accounted for by the less strict standard of church attendance in the 1968 survey. D'66 is the least homogeneous of all major parties—at least in terms of class and religious criteria. As indicated earlier, D'66 is much more homogeneous than the other parties as far as its age composition is concerned.

Another way of summarizing the relative predictive powers of the variables discussed in Section IV is to present the results of a tree analysis. Figures 1 and 2 show the trees for the 1956 and 1968 data. (The computer program used for this purpose was the program developed by Philip C. Stouthard; see Stouthard, 1969, pp. 60–73.)

The political parties were dichotomized into religious and secular parties. The first box of Figures 1 and 2 gives the total number of respondents expressing a party preference and the percentage supporting the religious parties. Each of the lower boxes gives the same information concerning each division or subdivision of the original sample. The reduction of the initial variance resulting from each division or subdivision is also indicated.

The trees confirm that the basic independent variables—particularly church attendance and church affiliation—are indeed excellent predictors. The total variance explained is unusually high: 63.3 percent for 1956 and 51.2 precent for 1968. Moreover, an extremely high proportion of the reduction of the variance is produced by the very first division according to church attendance: 53.4 percent (1956) and 44.1 percent (1968). The next step in each case is a division of the subgroups according to church affiliation. These subdivisions explain a further 7.7 percent (1956) and 4.2 percent (1968) of the variance. The only additional step in the 1956 tree is another subdivision according to church affiliation. This means that the 1956 tree contains *only* the religious variables as explanatory factors. In the 1968 tree two other variables appear; province of residence and education. Together, however, they explain only 1.0 percent of the variance.

The political parties can alternatively be dichotomized into socialist and other (religious plus secular nonsocialist) parties. These tree analyses were also performed on the 1956 and 1968 data. The general patterns of these trees are not very different from those in Figures 1 and 2, although both the percentage of the variance explained by church attendance and the total reduction of the variance are smaller than when the religious-secular difference is used to dichotomize the parties. The total variance explained is 51.0 percent in 1956 and 36.6 percent in 1968. The first division, which is according to church attendance, reduces the variance by 38.3 percent (1956) and 27.5 percent (1968). Church attendance and church affiliation together account for 46.6 percent (1956) and 30.9 percent (1968) of the variance. Class and education also enter the picture, but compared with the overwhelming strength of the religious variables, they have only a very modest degree of influence: they reduce the variance by 4.4 percent in 1956 and 5.1 percent in 1968. A residual 0.7 percent of the variance is explained by province of residence in 1968.

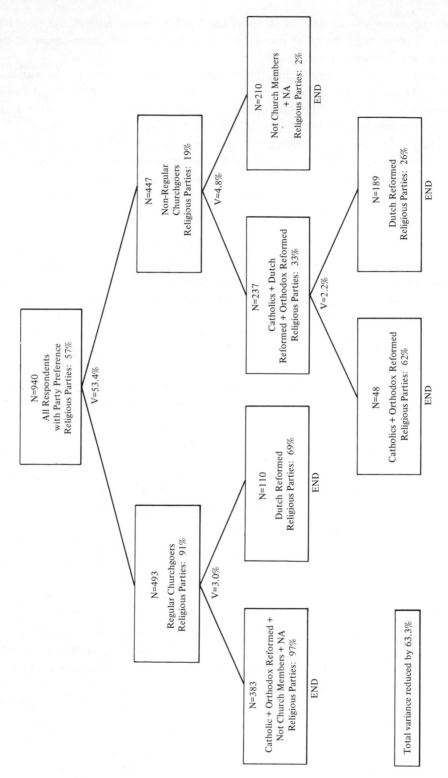

Figure 1: A Dutch Tree Analysis: Religious *vs.* Secular Parties, 1956.

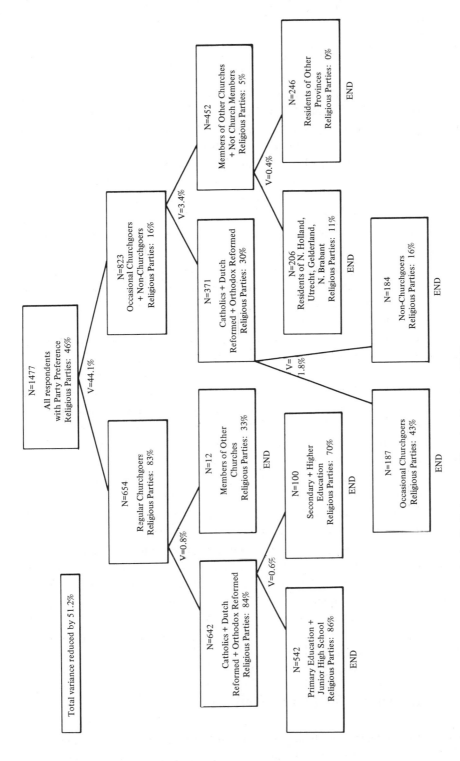

Figure 2: A Dutch Tree Analysis: Religious *vs.* Secular Parties, 1968.

VI. Conclusions

A. VARIABLES OF COMPARATIVE SIGNIFICANCE

In order to compare the influence of the various social-structural variables on voting behavior in the Netherlands with that in other democratic countries, we have to examine whether these variables can be used fruitfully in comparative analysis. Of the three basic variables affecting Dutch voting behavior, social class is a universal feature of industrialized nations. For comparative purposes, however, it is advisable to use a different indicator of class than the interviewer's rating of socioeconomic status which is used in Section IV of this chapter. These ratings can differ a great deal from country to country and are therefore not reliable for comparative analysis. A preferable indicator of social class in comparative studies is occupation or education.

The two other basic variables, religion and religiosity, can be used in comparative analysis without major difficulties. Frequency of church attendance, which is used as the indicator of religiosity in Section IV, is a straightforward measure that is eminently suitable for comparative work, and it has already been used in surveys in many countries (see Lijphart, 1971a). As far as religion is concerned, Holland is characterized by a number of special features not often found elsewhere. It is almost evenly divided between Protestants and Catholics—a situation existing elsewhere only in West Germany and Switzerland. A unique feature of the religious composition of the Dutch population is the very high percentage of people who do not belong to any church at all, close to 20 percent according to the 1960 census (see Table 1). This may be a troublesome factor in comparative studies of the influence of church affiliation on political behavior.

Most of the other social-structural variables—rural-urban residence, age, and sex—should not give rise to major problems in comparative research. Careful attention should be paid to equivalence of categories, of course, particularly as far as rural-urban residence is concerned, but also with regard to age. Regional variations are often the most distinctive characteristics of countries and are consequently difficult to analyze comparatively. In Section IV province of residence is used to analyze regional variations. This is not an altogether satisfactory measure for comparative purposes or even for the analysis of regional differences in Holland. Holland's most strikingly special region is the Roman Catholic south of the country, which coincides largely but not completely with the two southern provinces: the southern part of the province of Gelderland should also be included.

B. DUTCH PARTIES IN COMPARATIVE PERSPECTIVE

The nature of Holland's political parties presents serious obstacles to comparative research in a number of respects. In the first place the party system is an extreme multiparty system: fourteen different parties were elected to the Second Chamber in 1971 (see also Table 2). Holland's extreme system of proportional representation is the most important reason for the electoral successes of the many splinter parties. Some of the minor parties have equivalents elsewhere. Communist parties akin to the Dutch CPN exist in almost all democracies. Left-wing socialist parties like the PSP are not uncommon either. The Farmers party (BP) is unique, but may be compared to the French Poujadists. It is not similar to the Agrarian or Center parties of Scandinavia or to the Swiss Farmers party. Finally, the SPG, GPV, and PPR do not have any equivalents elsewhere.

The importance of the minor parties should not be overrated, however; together they receive only a small percentage of the total vote. In order to place the Dutch party system in comparative perspective it is more important to focus on the major parties. The existence of two significant Protestant parties is a truly unique phenomenon. Catholic parties exist in many countries, but Protestant parties are rare indeed. The only party that is somewhat similar to the ARP and CHU is the Christian People's party in Norway. On the other hand, the two Dutch Protestant parties may be considered to form a kind of Christian Democratic grouping of parties together with the KVP. All three parties belong to the European federation of Christian democratic parties, and their representatives in the European parliament in Strasbourg are members of the Christian democratic parliamentary group. In the local and provincial elections of 1970 these three parties participated in some areas as a single electoral list, usually called the CCP (Combination of Christian Parties), and they issued a joint election manifesto in 1971.

The PvdA and VVD present few problems: they are comparable to other socialist and liberal parties on the continent of Europe. DS'70 is also a socialist party, albeit a rather conservative one. D'66 is an unusual but not really a unique phenomenon. It may be considered a left-wing liberal party, similar in many respects to the interwar left-wing liberal VDB (*Vrijzinnig Democratische Bond*, Liberal Democratic party). Its platform of constitutional and electoral reform may be regarded as an extension of the basic political tenets of liberalism. The social composition of the supporters of D'66 resembles that of the VVD more closely than that of any of the other major parties (see Table 28). And the two parties also form a kind of "mutual admiration society" as far as their supporters' second preferences are concerned (see Table 5). Goals similar to those of D'66 are pursued by movements under the leadership of Ralf Dahrendorf in Germany and Jean-Jacques Servan-Schreiber in France within the organizational context of the liberal parties of their countries: the German Free Democrats and the French Radicals.

On the basis of the parallels presented above, the Dutch party system may be considered to consist of three basic groupings of major parties: Christian democratic (KVP, ARP, and CHU), socialist (PvdA and DS' 70), and liberal (VVD and D'66). There are a number of continental European countries with similar party systems: West Germany, Belgium, Luxembourg, Switzerland, and Austria. Therefore, comparisons of voting behavior in the Netherlands with voting behavior in these countries may lead to the most interesting and fruitful results. West Germany is particularly suitable for this type of comparative analysis, because of its religious division between Catholics and Protestants. Switzerland is less suitable, because its religious party is exclusively Catholic and not a joint Catholic-Protestant party like the German CDU.

On the basis of a different set of criteria Israeli politics and voting behavior offer a number of interesting opportunities for comparison. The substantive ideological content of Israel's parties differs from that of the Dutch parties—although *Mapai* may be likened to the PvdA—but both countries have party systems with a clearly ideological bent. They both have extreme systems of proportional representation, extreme multiparty systems, and a tradition of multiparty coalition governments. Finally, the religious-secular dimensions is an equally prominent feature of the party systems of both Israel and the Netherlands.

Postscript

The Second Chamber election of November, 1972, occasioned by the collapse of the coalition cabinet formed after the 1971 election, confirmed the pattern of accelerating change in Dutch voting behavior. The voting turnout was relatively high: 82.9 percent of all eligible voters, including for the first time the 18–21 year age group. Twenty parties contested the election, and fourteen were successful in winning one or more seats in the Second Chamber. Compared with the 1971 election results, the alliance of left-wing parties (PvdA, PPR, and the increasingly left-oriented D'66), which again formed a "shadow cabinet" before the election, improved its position: the PvdA received 27.4 percent of the vote and the PPR 4.8 percent, but D'66 declined to 4.2 percent. Of the other major parties, the VVD and ARP were winners (14.4 and 8.8 percent, respectively) and the KVP, CHU, and DS'70 losers (17.7, 4.8, and 4.1 percent, respectively). The minor parties together received 13.8 percent of the total vote. From a long-term perspective, the losses suffered by the KVP and CHU are particularly significant. These two religious parties have both lost more than 40 percent of the average support they had in the "normal" elections of the 1946–58 period. The nationwide election surveys conducted in 1971 and 1972 show that church affiliation and church attendance are still powerful predictors of party choice, but also that their influence continues to decrease (see Werkgroep Nationaal Verkiezingsonderzoek 1971, 1972; Werkgroep Nationaal Verkiezingsonderzoek 1972, 1973).

References

ALBRECHT, M. *De invloed van het kiesstelsel op de samenstelling van de volksvertegen-woordiging en op de vorming van de regering*. Amsterdam: Arbeiderspers, 1960.
BAEHR, PETER R. "The Netherlands." In Stanley Henig and John Pinder, eds. *European Political Parties*. London: Allen & Unwin, 1969.

BARENTS, J., and DE JONG, J. J. "Partis politiques et classes sociales aux Pays-Bas." Mimeographed. Paris: IPSA Congress, 1955.

BERGH, G. VAN DEN. *Eenheid in verscheidenheid: Een systematisch-critisch overzicht van alle kiesstelsels.* Alphen aan den Rijn: Samsom, 1946.

BONE, ROBERT, C. "The Dynamics of Dutch Politics." *Journal of Politics* XXIV: 1 (February, 1962).

BRUYN, L. P. J. de. "Partijen: Verbonden delen." *Politiek* XXIII: 3 (March, 1969).

———. "Partijen en partijstelsels." In A. Hoogerwerf, ed., *Verkenningen in de politiek*, vol. 1. Alphen aan den Rijn: Samsom, 1971.

———. "Confessionele politieke stromingen." In A. Hoogerwerf, ed. ibid., vol. 2.

———, and NELISSEN P. L. C. "Onbehaaglijke stemming: Resultaten van een kiezers-onderzoek. *Sociologische Gids* XIII: 6 (November-December, 1966).

Centraal Bureau voor de Statistiek. *Statistiek der verkiezingen 1956: Tweede Kamer der Staten-Generaal, 13 juni.* Zeist: De Haan, 1957.

———. *Zestig jaren statistiek in tijdreeksen: 1899-1959.* Zeist: De Haan, 1959.

———. *13e Algemene Volkstelling, 31 mei 1960: Deel 7. Kerkelijkegezindte, B. Voornaamste cijfers per gemeente.* Zeist: De Haan, 1963.

———. *Statistiek der verkiezingen 1963: Tweede Kamer der Staten-Generaal, 15 mei.* The Hague: Staatsuitgeverij, 1963.

———. *Statistiek der verkiezingen, 1967: Tweede Kamer der Staten-Generaal, 15 februari.* The Hague: Staatsuitgeverij, 1967.

DAALDER, HANS. "Parties and Politics in the Netherlands." *Political Studies* III: 1 (February, 1955).

———. "Nationale politieke stelsels: Nederland." In L. van der Land, ed. *Repertorium van de sociale wetenschappen: Politiek.* Amsterdam: Elsevier, 1958.

———. "De kleine politieke partijen: Een voorlopige poging tot inventarisatie." *Acta Politica* I: 1–4 (1965–1966).

———. "The Netherlands: Opposition in a Segmented Society." In Robert A. Dahl, ed. *Political Oppositions in Western Democracies.* New Haven: Yale Univ. Press, 1966.

———. "Politiek bestel en sociale realiteiten." In H. Brugmans, et al. *Welvaart en Democratie.* Tilburg: Gianotten, 1968.

———, and HUBÉE-BOONZAAIJER, S. "Sociale herkomst en politieke recrutering van Nederlandse Kamerleden in 1968, I." *Acta Politica* V: 3 (April, 1970).

DAM, M. P. A. VAN, and BEISHUIZEN, J. *Kijk op de kiezer: Feiten, cijfers en perspectieven op basis van het Utrechtse kiezersonderzoek van 15 februari 1967.* Amsterdam: Parool, 1967.

DAUDT, HANS. "Party-System and Voters' Influence in the Netherlands." In Otto Stammer, ed. *Party Systems, Party Organizations, and the Politics of New Masses.* Berlin: Institut für-Politische Wissenschaft an der Freien Universität Berlin, 1968.

———. "Verkiezingsonderzoek in Nederland." *Acta Politica* III: 1 (October, 1967).

———, and LANGE, HENK. "Youth and Politics in the Netherlands." Mimeographed. Geneva: IPSA Congress, 1946.

————, and STAPEL, J. "Parlement, politiek en kiezer: Verslag van een opinie-onderzoek." *Acta Politica* I.1–4 (1955-1956).

————; MAESEN, CONSTANCE E. VAN DER; and MOKKEN, R. J. "Political Efficacy: A Further Exploration." *Acta Politica* III: 4 (July, 1968).

EEKEREN, W. A. M. VAN. "The Catholic People's Party in the Netherlands." PhD. dissertation. Georgetown University, 1956.

GADOUREK, I. "Political Radicalism and Social Change." *Mens en Maatschappij.* XLII: 2 (March-April, 1967).

GEISMANN, GEORG. *Politische Struktur und Regierungssystem in den Niederlanden.* Kölner Schriften zur Politische Wissenschaft, vol 4. Frankfurt am Main and Bonn: Athenäum Verlag, 1964.

GOUDSBLOM, JOHAN. *Dutch Society.* New York: Random House, 1967.

GRUIJTERS, J. P. A. " 'Wisselende kiezers' bij de verkiezingen van 23 maart 1966: Enige gegevens uit een Amsterdams onderzoek." *Acta Politica* II: 1 (1966–1967).

————. *Daarom D'66.* Amsterdam: Bezige Bij, 1967.

————; SCHERMER, K.; and SLOOTMAN, K. *Experimenten in democratie.* Amsterdam: Bezige Bij, 1967.

HOEKSTRA, D. J. *Partijvernieuwing in politiek Nederland: Samenvatting en commentaar.* Alphen aan den Rijn: Samsom, 1968.

HOOG, R. de; MOKKEN, R. J.; ROSCHAR, F. M.; and STOKMAN, F. N. "Nationaal verkiezingsonderzoek." *Acta Politica* VI: 1 (January, 1971).

HOOGERWERF, A. *Protestantisme en progressiviteit: Een politicologisch onderzoek naar opvattingen van Nederlandse protestanten over verandering en gelijkheid.* Meppel: Boom, 1964.

————. "De Nederlandse kiezers en het partijstelsel: Verbondenheid, weerstand en voorstelling." *Acta Politica* II: 4 (1966–1967).

Instituut voor toegepaste sociologie. *Achtergronden van stemgedrag: Een sociologisch onderzoek naar de achtergronden van het stemgedrag bij de verkiezingen voor de Provinciale Staten 1966 in de Limburgse Mijnstreek.* Nijmegen: 1966.

————. *In het spoor van de kiezer: Bliksemonderzoek naar het stemgedrag in Nijmegen bij de verkiezingen voor de Tweede Kamer.* Nijmegen: 1967.

JONG, J. J. de. "The Role of Women in Dutch Politics." Mimeographed. The Hague: IPSA Congress, 1952.

————. *Overheid en onderdaan.* Wageningen: Zomer en Keunings, 1956.

KOOL, FRITS. "Communism in Holland: A Study in Futility." *Problems of Communism* IX: 5 (September-October, 1960).

KUSTERS, W. J. J. "Stembusgedrag en maatschappijstructuur." *Sociologische Gids* X: 5 (September-October, 1963).

KUYPERS, G., et al. "The Dutch Voters in 1967." Mimeographed. Brussels: IPSA Congress, 1967.

LAND, L. VAN DER. *Het ontstaan van de Pacifistisch Socialistische Partij.* Amsterdam: Bezige Bij, 1962.

————, et al. Kiezer en verkiezing: *Verslag van een onderzoek met betrekking tot de verkiezingen van 1956 in Nieuwer-Amstel voor de Tweede Kamer der Staten Generaal.* Mimeographed. Amsterdam: Nederlandse Kring voor Weterchap der Politiek, 1963.

————, et al. "Voting in the Netherlands: A Panel Study in an Amsterdam Suburb." Mimeographed. Geneva: IPSA Congress, 1964.

LIJPHART, AREND. *The Politics of Accommodation: Pluralism and Democracy in the Netherlands.* Berkeley: Univ. of California Press, 1968.

————. "Consociational Democracy." *World Politics* XXI: 2 (January, 1969).

————. Kentering in de Nederlandse Politiek." *Acta Politica* IV: 3 (April, 1969).

————. "Class Voting and Religious Voting in the European Democracies: A Preliminary Report." Occasional paper no. 8, Survey Research Centre, University of Strathclyde, 1971.

————. "Verzuiling." In A. Hoogerwerf, ed. *Verkenningen in de politiek.* vol. 2. Alphen aan den Rijn: Samsom, 1971.

LIPSCHITS, I. *Links en rechts in de politiek.* Meppel: Boom, 1969.

LIPSET, SEYMOUR MARTIN. *Political Man: The Social Bases of Politics.* Garden City, N.Y.: Doubleday, 1960.

————, and ROKKAN, STEIN. "Cleavage Structures, Party Systems, and Voter Alignments: An Introduction." In Lipset and Rokkan, eds. *Party Systems and Voter Alignments: Cross-National Perspectives.* New York: Free Press, 1967.

MAESEN, CONSTANCE E. VAN DER. "Kiezers op drift: Voorlopige analyse van de Amsterdamse gemeenteraadsverkiezingen 1966." *Acta Politica* II: 3 (1966–1967).

MOKKEN, R. J. "Dutch-American Comparisons of the 'Sense of Political Efficacy.'" *Acta Politica* IV: 4 (July, 1969).

Nederlands Instituut voor de Publieke Opinie. *De Nederlandse Kiezer: Een onderzoek naar zijn gedragingen en opvattingen.* The Hague: Staatsdrukkerij en uitgeverijbedrijf, 1956.

————. *Zo zijn wij: De eerste vijfentwintig jaar NIPO-onderzoek.* Amsterdam: Agon Elsevier, 1970.

NIEZING, J. "Dekleine partij: Enkele hypothesen." *Sociologische Gids.* X: 5 (September-October, 1963).

NOHLEN, DIETER. "Niederlande." In Dolf Sternberger and Bernhard Vogel. eds. *Die Wahl der Parlamente und anderer Staatsorgane: Ein Handbuch.* Bank I: Europa. Berlin: De Gruyter, 1969.

NOOIJ, A. T. J. "Boerenpartij en radicalisme." *Sociologische Gids* XIII: 6 (November-December, 1966).

NOORDHOFF, J. D. *Sex in Nederland.* Utrecht: Spectrum, 1969.

RAALTE, E. VAN. *The Parliament of the Kingdom of the Netherlands.* London: Hansard Society, 1959.

SARTORI, GIOVANNI. "The Typology of Party Systems—Proposals for Improvement." In Erik Allardt and Stein Rokkan, eds. *Mass Politics: Studies in Political Sociology.* New York: Free Press, 1970.

SCHOLTEN, G. H., and RINGNALDA, G. "Netherlands." In Stein Rokkan and Jean Meyriat, eds. *International Guide to Electoral Statistics*. Vol. 1: *National Elections in Western Europe*. Paris and The Hague: Mouton, 1969.

Sociaal-Wetenschappelijk Instituut van de Vrije Universiteit. *De Nederlandse kiezers in 1967: Enkele eerste resultaten van een landelijke enquête*. Amsterdam: Agon Elsevier, 1967.

STOKMAN, FRANS N. "Election Studies and Voting in the Netherlands." Mimeographed. Loch Lomond Voting Conference, Scotland, 1968.

STOUTHARD, PH.C. "Analysis by Means of Sequential Contrasting Groups: A Computer Algorithm." *Sociologia Neerlandica* V:1 (Spring, 1969).

———. "De verkiezingen van maart 1970." *Acta Politica* VI:1 (January, 1971).

VERKADE, WILLEM. *Democratic Parties in the Low Countries and Germany: Origins and Historical Developments*. Leiden: Universitaire Pers, 1965.

WEIL, GORDON L. *The Benelux Nations: The Politics of Small-Country Democracies*. New York: Holt, Rinechart & Winston, 1970.

WERKGROEP NATIONAAL VERKIEZINGSONDERZOEK 1971. *De Nederlandse kiezer '71*. Meppel: Boom, 1972.

WERKGROEP NATIONAAL VERKIEZINGSONDERZOEK 1972. *De Nederlandse kiezer '72*. Alphen aan den Rijn: Samsom, 1973.

Scandinavia

6. FINLAND:
Party Support in a Fragmented System
PERTTI PESONEN

Historically and in the present Finland is a border between Western and Slavic Europe. For six centuries it was a part of the territory of the Swedish crown. The Swedish era rooted Western culture firmly in Finland, and the Swedish instrument of government of 1772, with the modifications of 1789, was the fundamental law of the land until 1919. Yet from the days of the Napoleonic War until the 1917 Russian Revolution, Finland was a part of the czarist Russian empire. The 1905 revolutionary ferment in Russia was followed by the passage of a new electoral law for Finland and its promulgation by the czar, acting as grand duke of Finland. The Russian Revolution of October, 1917, was followed four weeks later by the Finnish parliament declaring its national independence on December 6, 1917. Finland's trade and culture are largely West-oriented. This has not altered facts of geography: Helsinki, the capital, lies almost equidistant between Leningrad and Stockholm.

I. The Historical Evolution of Party Divisions

When Alexander I, czar of Russia, received an oath of allegiance in 1809 from the Diet of four estates representing the Finnish people, he also solemnly pledged to respect the religion, fundamental laws, and legal order of the country. The new grand duchy thus had the status of an autonomous state. The government was "representative" only in the national sense; it was composed of Finns. The assembly of the estates (the Lantdag) was not summoned again until 1863. The traditional Diet of four estates then functioned actively for four decades, and political parties began to form. In 1906 the present parliament (Eduskunta) of 200 members was established with universal adult suffrage, including women, thus reducing the number of legislative chambers from four to one and increasing the size of the electorate by ten times (the male electorate by five times). Modern Finnish politics dates from this reform.

The first party division arose from nationalist agitation about the language issue in the 1860s and 1870s. The great bulk of the population customarily spoke Finnish, a distinctive language unrelated to either Russian or Swedish or to other Indo-European languages. It was akin only to Estonian and Hungarian. The Finnish party demanded increased educational and other rights for the Finnish-speaking majority; the Swedish party emerged as a counterforce. Both parties generally dominated two estates in the Diet: the Finnish, composed of the clergy and the peasants' estates, and the Swedish, including the nobility and the burgesses. The second major division concerned Finland's relations with Russia. This became highly salient when Russia launched its unconstitutional Russification program in 1899. The constitutionalist position was championed in Finland by the Swedish party and by the Young Finnish party, a group that broke off from the Finnish party and formed a party of its own in 1904. The Old Finns adopted a tactic of compliance and compromise; although this was not a rigid stance, it was also far from a mood of capitualation. Social problems, linked with socialist ideologies, provided the third political front of great importance. However, due to the limited franchise the Diet did not pay adequate attention to these pressing problems. The strongest advocate of social reforms was the Finnish Labor party, founded in 1899, and since 1903 called the Social Democratic party of Finland. It began to organize mainly among the industrial workers, tenant farmers, and farm laborers who were not eligible to vote before 1906.

The first election with a democratic franchise was held in March, 1907. The Social Democratic party (SDP) capitalized on its mass organization and experience in agitation, winning eighty of the 200 seats in parliament, with 37 percent of the vote. The only other party to win as much as one-quarter of the vote was the nonsocialist Old Finnish party. Despite its newness, the SDP had become one of the strongest socialist parties in the world. Its vote was still far less than that of the previously unrepresented 80 percent of the population to whom the party had appealed; it was also below the 62.4 percent estimated to constitute Finland's "unprivileged" population (Gylling, 1907). Obviously there were several political dimensions cutting across the class cleavage in Finnish society. In 1907 there was the competing radicalism of the Finnish party, the appeal of the new agrarian parties to the poor rural classes, the unpopularity of the SDP's antireligious attitude, and possibly the political inactivity of the "unprivileged" electors. The Swedish party changed its name in 1906 to the Swedish People's party in order to make a new kind of mass appeal to all segments of the socially heterogeneous Swedish-language group. The Christian Workers League, with a religious orientation, received only 1.6 percent of the vote and disappeared from the scene after the First World War. The fairly modest beginning of agrarian parties led to more success. The two agrarian party groups founded in 1906 were fused in 1908 into the Agrarian Union, which established its prominence in the first elections in independent Finland in March 1919. Despite their remarkable initial success, the Social Democrats gained a majority of parliamentary seats only once (in 1916); subsequently, the SDP has never reached the status of its counterparts in Sweden and Norway.

Finland's independence was declared in December, 1917. The war of independence was simultaneously a civil war between the socialist Reds and the bourgeois Whites; it was fought from late January to early May in 1918. The party system then underwent a major restructuring. The SDP was reorganized under the leadership of moderate party members who had not played an active role in the rebellious movement. In the election of March, 1919, the SDP elected eighty members to parliament, the same number as in 1907. Red leaders who had fled to Russia founded the Finnish Communist Party (*Suomen Kommunistinen Puolue*) in Moscow in August, 1918. It sought votes in Finnish elections in the 1920s under the banners of the Socialist Workers party and the Workers and Small Farmers party, gaining a maximum of 14.8 percent of the vote in 1922. Communist activity was outlawed in 1930. The Finnish and Young Finnish parties had served their purpose by 1918, and their place in the party system was taken by two new nonsocialist parties in November, 1918. The dividing issue now concerned the constitution of independent Finland. The founders of the conservative National Coalition party (since 1951 called the National Coalition) favored the monarchist tradition, whereas the National Progressive party was founded as the party of the republicans. It was quite clear after the elections of 1919 that the monarchist cause was lost. The parliament elected that year passed the Constitution Act (Form of Government), which established the Republic of Finland; it has been continuously effective to the present day. In the 1930s an extreme right-wing group, the Patriotic People's Movement, emerged as a political force; its maximum electoral vote was 8.3 percent at the 1936 general election.

The Second World War was a trying time for a border land, but Finland managed to avoid occupation by any foreign power. In November, 1939, Russian troops invaded Finland. The Finns fought a long winter war, ending in March, 1940, with the cession of 32,000 square miles to the Soviet Union. After the German attack upon the U.S.S.R. in June, 1941, Finland again became engaged in fighting against Russia. An armistice was signed in Moscow in September, 1944, confirming the cession of additional territory to Russia and incorporating terms of reparations. Communist political activity was now made legal, and the right-wing groups, such as the Patriotic People's Movement, banned. The Finnish People's Democratic Union (FPDU) became the vehicle for Communist electoral appeals; it gained 23.5 percent of the vote in the March 1945, election, an election unusual because it occurred just before the end of the Second World War.

Since 1945 Finland has been indubitably a multiparty system, with the most successful party at a general election never winning more than 27.2 percent of the vote (see Table 1). The two major left-wing parties—the FPDU and the SDP—together poll between 40 and 50 percent of the vote; when the vote for the SDP left-wing splinter group, the Social Democratic League, is included, the three parties achieved a majority of the vote in 1966, and of parliamentary seats in 1958 and 1966. Because the two major left-wing groups have had much the same electoral strength, divisions within the Left have been persistently important. In the 1970 election the FPDU vote declined markedly, and the Social Democratic League, with Communist electoral cooperation withdrawn, lost seven seats. The National Progressive party, the successor to the Young Finnish party after 1918, was transformed into the Finnish People's party in 1951; then, by merging with another successor of the progressives, the Liberal Union, combined to found the Liberal People's party. The Agrarian Union remained for a long time the strongest nonsocialist party and was, at times, the leading political power in the country. In 1965 it followed the Swedish and Norwegian examples and changed its name to Center party. It suffered a considerable decline in 1970, when a small-holders' party, the Rural party of Finland, gained eighteen seats in a surprise election victory. The support of the Conservatives has remained rather stable; in 1970 the Conservatives did so well that they became, for the first time, the second largest party

TABLE 1: Parliamentary Elections in Finland from 1945 to 1972

	FPDU	SDL	SDP	SFP/ FRP	AGR/ CENT	LPP	CONS	SPP	Other
				VOTE (IN PERCENTAGES)					
1945	23.5	.	25.1	1.2	21.3	5.2	15.0	7.9	0.8
1948	20.0	.	26.3	0.3	24.2	3.9	17.1	7.7	0.5
1951	21.6	.	26.5	0.3	23.2	5.7	14.6	7.6	0.5
1954	21.6	.	26.2	.	24.1	7.9	12.8	7.0	0.4
1958	23.2	1.7	23.2	.	23.1	5.9	15.3	6.7	0.9
1962	22.0	4.4	19.5	2.2	23.0	6.3	15.0	6.4	1.2
1966	21.2	2.6	27.2	1.0	21.2	6.5	13.8	6.0	0.5
1970	16.6	1.4	23.4	10.5	17.1	6.0	18.0	5.7	1.3
1972	17.0	1.0	25.8	9.2	16.4	5.1	17.6	5.4	2.5
				ELECTED MEMBERS					
1945	49	.	50	—	49	9	28	14	1
1948	38	.	54	—	56	5	33	14	—
1951	43	.	53	—	51	10	28	15	—
1954	43	.	54	.	53	13	24	13	—
1958	50	3	48	.	48	8	29	14	—
1962	47	2	38	—	53	13	32	14	1
1966	41	7	55	1	49	9	26	12	—
1970	36	—	52	18	36	8	37	12	1
1972	37	—	55	18	35	7	34	10	4

FPDU = Finnish People's Democratic Union (1944–; *Suomen kansan demokraattinen liitto*, SKDL); includes the Finnish Communist Party.
SDL = Social Democratic Opposition in 1958; since 1959 Social Democratic League of Workers and Smallholders (*Työväen ja Pienviljelijäin Sosialidemokraattinen Liitto*, TPSL).
SDP = Social Democratic Party of Finland (1899–).
SFP = Small Farmers' Party(1929–51); Small Farmers' party of Finland (1962–).
FRP = Former SFP, since 1966 Finnish Rural party.
AGR = Agrarian Union (1906–1965).
CENT = Center party (former AGR, name changed in 1965).
LPP = National Progressive party (1918–51), Finnish People's party (1951–65), and Liberal People's party (1965–).
CONS = National Coalition (Conservatives) (1918–).
SPP = Swedish People's Party (1906–).
Included in "Other" are the Swedish Left (one member in 1945), the Liberal Union (one member in 1962), and the Christian League (1.1 percent and one member in 1970; 2.5 percent and 4 members in 1972).

in Finland. The Swedish People's party has maintained its distinctive role in Finnish politics, despite the slow decline of its vote since 1936. Another recent element in the Finnish party system is the Christian League; it contested the 1970 election and succeeded in electing one man to Parliament; it elected four Members in 1972. (For party descriptions see Pesonen, 1968, Chap. 1, and Nousiainen, 1971, ch. 2 and 6). After the

1972 election the Finnish Parliament had an eight-party system, with the SDP holding fifty-five seats, and the Conservatives, the Center (ex-Agrarian), and, the FPDU parties each having from thirty-four to thirty-seven seats in a 200-member parliament.

Parliament passed the first legislative act pertaining to parties in 1969. The act was necessitated by state subsidies paid to party organizations since 1967, it also attempted to prevent further splintering of parties. It provided that after the 1970 election only registered political parties would be allowed to nominate candidates in parliamentary elections. The parties mentioned above are now listed in the official party register of the Ministry of Justice; any party failing to have one member elected in two successive elections will lose its party status, unless it can produce a petition signed by 5,000 enfranchised persons who declare themselves supporters of that party. A similar petition of 5,000 people will be needed before any new party can be officially recognized and have the right to nominate candidates in the future.[1] It is unlikely to affect the persisting fractionalization of party strength, a characteristic that has made Finland a "truly" multiparty system, with no single party dominating it, except in 1916-1917.

II. The Electoral System and the Electorate

Finland is governed by a system that combines a strong elected president and a parliamentary form of government, with a prime minister and cabinet responsible to the parliament (Eduskunta). The constitutional structure thus has similarities with the Fifth French Republic. The governing cabinet is almost always a coalition of several parties (see Törnudd, 1969), thus providing a similarity with the Fourth French Republic. The unicameral parliament of 200 members has been elected twenty-six times since 1907. Details of the results of all elections from 1907 to 1962, with a bibliographical guide, can be found in Rantala (1969).

The universal franchise law adopted in 1906 created an electorate of 1,272,000; by 1970 the number of eligible electors had grown to 3,094,000. The gradual increase during the period has been the result of population growth and two decisions to lower the voting age: from twenty-four to twenty-one in 1944, and to twenty in 1969. During the fall session of 1971 the constitutional committee of the parliament again considered proposals to lower the voting age to eighteen years. With few exceptions, such as high court judges and regular-army soldiers, every elector has also been legally eligible for election to parliament. Of the new members of Parliament elected in 1970, three men were so young that they had to be granted a leave of absence from parliamentary duties in order to do their compulsory military service.

One can assert a comparative generalization that newly enfranchised electors only gradually make active use of their right to vote. Finland provided a temporary exception to this general rule, because of the high degree of electoral mobilization immediately after universal suffrage was introduced. In the parliamentary election of March, 1907, 71 percent of the electorate voted, and a 69 percent turnout was also recorded in he exciting election of 1917. But immediately after the initial enthusiasm of 1907 the turnout dropped down to as low as 51 percent in 1913. The turnout was between 56 and 58 percent during the 1920s; 63 to 67 percent in the 1930s; and 75 to 80 percent in the 1940s and 1950s. In the 1960s the turnout continued to rise, reaching a peak of 85 percent in 1962. The increasing mobilization of the electorate has largely diminished sex differences in turnout: the male lead was 10.5 percent in 1911 and 8.9 percent in 1939, but the difference was only 1.9 percent in 1962 and 1970 (Table 2). Age differen-

TABLE 2: **Electorate and Voter Turnout in Parliamentary Elections, 1945 to 1972**

	ELECTORATE	VOTERS	TURNOUT	(IN PERCENTAGES)	
			All	Men	Women
1945	2,284,200	1,710,300	74.9	77.5	72.7
1948	2,420,300	1,893,800	78.2	81.0	75.9
1951	2,448,200	1,825,800	74.6	78.4	71.4
1954	2,527,000	2,019,000	79.9	82.9	77.4
1958	2,606,300	1,954,400	75.0	78.3	72.1
1962	2,714,800	2,310,100	85.1	86.1	84.2
1966	2,800,500	2,378,700	84.9	86.1	83.9
1970	3,094,400	2,544,500	82.2	83.2	81.3
1972	3,178,000	2,587,100	81.4	81.9	80.9

ces in voting turnout show a familiar pattern in Finland: young age groups vote less frequently than the middle-aged. This is consistent within the idea of a gradual politicization of new electors. But here too there seems to be one exception: the very youngest age group is relatively active immediately after the voting age has been lowered (Martikainen and Sänkiaho, 1969). Unusual publicity about the lowering of the voting age apparently activates the "newsworthy" age groups.

The turnout of voters for the choice of 300 electors to choose a president, once every six years, has shown extreme fluctuations. In the first presidential election, in 1925, it was 39.7 percent; in 1962 it was 81.5 percent. In local government elections national turnout has also shown a regular increase, from figures between 42 and 48 percent in the 1930s to a level of at least 75 percent since 1960, with a peak of 79.4 percent in 1964.

Voting is not compulsory in Finland, but social pressures encourage a high voter turnout. Many administrative arrangements attempt to make participation as easy as possible. These include balloting on two successive days (a Sunday and a Monday, from 9 A.M. to 8 P.M.), automatic registration, and a large number of polling stations. In 1970 the voting districts numbered 5,311, thus averaging only 582 electors per district: 1,324 in urban communes, 366 in rural ones. In addition it is possible to vote in hospitals, in Finnish embassies and consulates abroad, and on Finnish ships. The old practice of voting with previously obtained absentee ballots on election-days was altered in 1970 to voting in advance by post. This arrangement was used by 6.7 percent of voters at the 1970 election.

The task of the Finnish voter is to choose one candidate nominated in his constituency, and to write on a small ballot paper the number assigned to his chosen candidate. This gives the voter a multitude of persons to choose from. Finnish constituencies are fairly large—the average "district magnitude" is 13.3 seats per constituency—and the parties are allowed to nominate as many candidates as there are seats to be filled in the constituency. For example, Helsinki with twenty-two seats was the largest constituency in 1970. There were six full lists of twenty-two candidates, nominated by five parties alone and by one two-party electoral alliance; another list of nineteen candidates—a total of 156 nominated candidates. In the smallest multi-member constituency, North Karelia, six parties or party alliances put up eight candidates each, giving the voters a total of 48 persons to choose from.

The ballots serve a dual purpose. First, they support the candidate's party list. The number of seats won by each party (or electoral alliance) is determined through d'Hondt's "highest average" system of proportional representation (see Pesonen, 1968. pp. 7ff.). Secondly, the individual votes also rank order the candidates within the party lists; seats are assigned to candidates within a party according to their position in the rank order. Until 1966 one person could be nominated as a candidate in several constituencies; this possibility was not used frequently. Since 1970 a person can be a parliamentary candidate in only one constituency. Because of this, plus the unpredictability of the intraparty distribution of individual votes, Finnish political parties can hardly guarantee in advance that even their most important leaders will get elected.

There are minor exceptions to the proportional-representation system in Finland. The Aaland Islands have been a single-member constituency since 1948, and there was also a single-member constituency in Lapland from 1907 to 1938. Otherwise the country is divided into fourteen multimember constituencies. Some redistricting took place before the elections of 1939, 1948, 1954, and 1962, but the changes in district boundaries were not made for the sake of increased proportionality in representation. The 199 seats are allocated among the constituencies before each election in relation to their number of inhabitants. This procedure gradually moves seats from the less advanced toward the rapidly growing regions. When Helsinki became a constituency by itself in 1954, it elected nineteen members; in 1970 and 1972, the number was twenty-two. Its surrounding constituency, Uusimaa, elected fifteen members in 1954 and twenty-one in 1972. What distorts proportionality slightly is the fact that the allocation of seats is based on total population and not on the number of adult electors. There were 17,407 electors for each member elected in Helsinki in 1970, but only 13,990 electors per member in the constituencies of Oulu and Lapland.

III. Voting and Its Study

The study of voting behavior began in Finland by the use of ecological techniques of analysis, relating statistics about the social and economic characteristics of communes to their turnout differences and party preferences (e.g., Allardt, 1956; Nousiainen, 1956). In addition, such explicitly political variables as "the rate of Reds killed in the civil war of 1918" were also soon employed. The ecological analyses were done separately for the south and west and for the north and east. Given the significance of regional variations, not least in the support for the Communist party, the findings merited considerable interest and interpretation (see for example, Allardt, 1964; Allardt and Pesonen, 1967, pp. 350 ff.).

Surveys of Finnish public opinion began in 1945, when the Finnish Gallup Institute was founded. In its early research, however, this company tended to avoid political questions and dealt with various journalistic feature topics. By 1971 the Finnish Association of Market Research Institutes had sixteen members; some corporations and advertising agencies also had research units. Surveys have been organized by universities and individual scholars. Finnish television audiences have been studied since 1960, and the first large readership study in 1964 comprised seventy-four daily newspapers and periodicals, and more than 10,000 interviews (Hellevuo, 1971).

The first Finnish panel study of voting behavior dealt with the presidential election of 1956 (see Pesonen, 1971a.). Election forecasts and other voter surveys based on national probability samples were rare in Finland until the mid-1960s, but, especially since 1966, information has been collected increasingly about the electorate, sometimes primarily for newspaper articles, sometimes in connection with interviews performed mainly for a nonpolitical scholarly purpose. The analysis that follows does not intend to summarize Finnish surveys. The intention is to present original analysis of survey data collected soon after the parliamentary election of 1966, by a nationwide random sample of 1,263 complete interviews.[2] The main problem areas covered by this questionnaire were the electors' interest in the campaign and the basis of their party choice.

It has been customary in Finland to define a person's party affiliation in terms of the party whose candidate the person votes for. Oftentimes political parties are said to have as many supporters as they receive votes. Questions of the Michigan type, concerning party identification, have been considered too difficult to administer in mass surveys. Often the party affiliation question is of the following type: "Should we have parliament elections tomorrow, which party's candidate would you probably vote for?" Consequently, it has been customary, both in scientific discussions and in everyday usage, to combine two different concepts: on the one hand, there is the common tendency of the electors to rank one political party above the others; on the other hand, there is the actual behavior of the electors in marking the ballot on election day.

Nevertheless, party affiliation and the party choice that is carried into effect on voting days are two different concepts. The mass support of political parties extends outside their group of voters. Nonvoting electors include people with party preferences; these can be considered the parties' "voter reserve." Some youths who are not yet enfranchised may also have a party affiliation. Political parties sometimes receive votes from people who are not their consistent supporters. For example, the Swedish

People's party in some Finnish constituencies has individual supporters who, of necessity, need to vote for an "alien" party, because their own party does not nominate candidates there. Some voters are unattached to any party. Individual candidates can also have personal electoral followings. An elector may decide to vote for a party other than his own. This has been quite frequent in two kinds of Finnish elections—in those of the president's electoral college and in local elections—although, voters appear increasingly bound by party considerations in both kinds of elections.

The party choice of most voters is determined by their standing party affiliation. In the survey of April, 1966, respondents were first asked about their party choice. ("Which party's candidate did you vote for?" or "Supposing you had voted, which party's candidate would you probably have voted for?") After this another question concerned the certainty of their choice. ("Would you say that this is your sure position, or is it somewhat uncertain?") According to the responses the party choice of 86 percent of the voters, and of 75 percent of the non-voters, coincided with their sure party affiliation. If we consider such persons as affiliated partisans, about 2,250,000 of Finland's 2,800,000 electors had an affiliation at the time of the 1966 election.

By combining election statistics and survey data, one can estimate both the "reserve vote" and the success that parties had among uncertain voters. The Finnish electorate was divided in 1966 into the following groups by their voting turnout and party support:

	Voters	*Nonvoters*	*Total*
Party supporters	2,040,000	210,000	2,250,000
Uncertain preferences	330,000	70,000	400,000
No party choice	9,000	141,000	150,000
TOTAL	2,379,000	421,000	2,800,000

These estimates are approximations only. For example, all the disqualified ballot papers (0.3 percent) are counted as voters with "no party choice," although not all disqualified ballots are destroyed on purpose. The cells illustrate how analysts of party support can differently operationalize party affiliation. In aggregate studies based on election statistics the unit of analysis embraces certain and uncertain voters. Analysis of the strength of party identification is not possible without survey data. Yet the 2,379,000 party choices realised with ballots in 1966 included an estimated 330,000 votes that were not inspired by the voter's party affiliation (as defined above). Only about 2,040,000 electors (73 percent of the electorate) were simultaneously voters and actual supporters of the parties. In the following analysis the term "party supporters" usually refers to all electors who said they had voted for a party, or would be likely to vote for it. Defined so broadly, the party supporters comprised an estimated 94 percent of the 1966 electorate. The grouping provides comparability with observations based on election statistics because they also count each vote as equal without regard to whether the voting choice was based on a firm conviction or an a temporary mood.

Table 3 permits a comparison between the un nobilized "reserve vote" of the parties and their success outside the ranks of affiliated supporters. It seems that the reserve vote was best mobilized by the FPDU, Center, and Conservatives in 1966, whereas the SDP might have had a reserve vote that did not aid its election success. Such conclusions must be drawn with caution, however, because these survey responses could have reflected the post election mood rather than the situation at election time. The average immobilized potential of the parties was 12 percent.

TABLE 3: **Votes Cast for the Parties in 1966, and the Voters and Nonvoting Supporters of the Parties by Certainty of Party Choice**

	Votes	Percent of Voters		Percent of Nonvoters	
		Certain	Uncertain	Certain	Uncertain
FPDU	502,635	91	9	6	2
SDL	61,274	87	13	10	7
SDP	645,339	90	10	12	3
CENT	503,047	88	12	8	1
LPP	153,259	65	35	10	4
CONS	326,928	77	23	7	3
SPP	138,690	89	11	10	4
Others	38,874	90	10	—	5
Total	2,370,046	86	14	9	3

The choice of one of the two socialist parties was relatively often based on the voter's strong party identification. On the other hand, the Conservatives were successful as a specifically election party in gaining votes from uncertain electors. Liberal voters included a third who were not actual party supporters. Earlier studies have shown that the individual Conservative candidates attracted relatively many votes for their party. The organization and party identification of the Liberals has been found weak in Finland. Moreover, having been founded very recently, the LPP had to fight in 1966 mainly as an election combination with very little opportunity to function in any other capacity before the parliament dissolved in December, 1965.

IV. The Constancy of Party Support

Election results indicate that the Finnish electorate consists of fairly stable groups of party supporters. For example, a comparison of 17 Western democracies showed that between the two world wars, Finland was one of the five countries that had "static party systems"; a similar study of trends since 1945 found Finland one of the three most static systems among 19 nations (see Rose and Urwin, 1970; Urwin and Rose, 1970). A post war example of the "rigidity" of the Finnish electorate was the election of 1954. As no parliamentary government could be negotiated to solve a cabinet crisis, President J. K. Paasikivi dissolved the parliament to see what direction the negotiations to form a new cabinet coalition should take. The result was an almost exact copy of the preceding election outcome; the mean change in the party's share of vote was 0.8 percent. Only six seats changed hands, and the total net turnover of vote distribution amounted to 3.1 percent.

The net vote of the SDP grew 7.7 percentage points from February, 1962, to March, 1966; this was lost by the SDL, CENT, CONS, SFP, FPDU, SPP, and "others" (see Table 1). However, 29 percent of those who voted in 1966 said that they had decided on their party choice either in 1965 or in 1966. It would be possible to explain the net change without any individual party conversions through the renewal of the electorate and through changing levels of turnout among the supporters of different parties, but these are not sufficient to explain the reported 29 percent of late deciders. For example, in 1966 the Conservatives received 20,000 fewer votes than in 1962. However, the estimates shown in Table 4 indicate that they actually lost about 2.6 percent of the voters to five different parties and won about 1.5 percent from the same five parties. From one election to the next the gross exchange of voters between the Conservatives and the five other parties was 4.1 percent (or 96,000 voters), leaving them with a net loss of 0.9 percent. In addition, Table 4 estimates that the Conservatives obtained more than 40,000 new voters from the youngest age groups and the previous nonvoters. The FPDU provides an example of very few conversions. According to Table 4 the gross exchange of this party, 1.0 percent (21,000 voters), included 0.4 percent lost to SDP and 0.5 percent gained from it, and 0.1 percent new voters won from the Center. Altogether, the total FPDU vote included in 1966 (according to Table 4) 391,000 constant and 15,000 converted voters plus 37,000 first-time electors

TABLE 4: **Party Choice of Voters in 1966 Related to Their Voting Behavior in the Parliamentary Election of 1962, in Percentages**

1962 Vote	EPDU	SDL	SDP	CENT	LPP	CONS	SPP	Others	1962 Total
				1966 Party Choice					
Nonvoters, NA	2.5	0.2	3.8	1.0	0.6	0.9	0.7	—	9.7
Age 21–24	1.6	0.1	2.0	1.5	0.4	0.8	0.6	—	7.0
FPDU	16.5	—	0.4	—	—	—	—	—	16.9
SDL	—	2.0	0.2	—	0.1	0.1	—	—	2.4
SDP	0.5	0.2	19.0	0.4	0.4	0.3	—	0.3	21.1
CENT	0.1	—	1.0	17.5	0.6	0.7	—	0.1	20.0
LPP	—	—	0.4	0.2	3.1	0.3	0.1	0.1	4.2
CONS	—	0.1	0.5	0.6	1.3	10.6	0.1	—	13.2
SPP	—	—	0.1	—	—	0.1	4.1	—	4.3
Others	—	—	—	—	—	—	0.1	1.1	1.2
1966 Total	21.2	2.6	27.4	21.2	6.5	13.8	5.7	1.6	100.0
(N)	(185)	(35)	(427)	(272)	(86)	(196)	(65)	(18)	

In preparing the table, the actual number of votes cast for each party in 1966 was distributed in relation to the survey responses recalling the behavior in 1962; this was done separately for two regions that are combined in this table. Those 1962 voters who subsequently died and 1966 nonvoters are excluded.

and 59,000 voters who either had not participated in 1962 or did not reveal their party choice in that election.

When looking at the details of Table 4 one should of course remember at least two obvious sources of error: sampling fluctuations and potential inaccuracies of recollections of the respondents. The interview question was as follows: "Previous parliamentary elections were held in February, 1962. Did you happen to vote then, or did you for some reason fail to participate?" Then, "Which party did you vote for?" The replies would not reflect any temporary defection from party ranks, followed by a return "home" as the general election neared. The results of the local elections of 1964 indicated that there were a substantial number of temporary defection between 1962 and 1966. Overall, Table 4 is best interpreted as showing clearly the general direction of gross and net changes between parties, while perhaps underestimating the actual volume of movement.

The estimated number of voters who floated between parties between two elections was 11 percent of the electorate. In a system of seven parties there are six possible directions in which a voter can move when he leaves his former party in search of another. As movement can occur in two directions, this yields a total of forty-two possible shifts, excluding the effect of abstention and of new voters. If the line between a pair of parties is considered a border that can be crossed in either direction, then we can interpret Table 4 as showing that fourteen out of twenty-one possible party borders were crossed in the period 1962–1966: ten in both directions and four others in one direction. Should we count the group "others" (including mainly voters of SFP-FRP) as the eighth party, there were twenty-eight party borders, and Table 4 shows traffic across eighteen of them. All the conversions and their net effects can be estimated as follows:

	Gross Exchange		Net Exchange	
Between socialist parties	30,700	(1.3%)	4,900	(0.1%)
Between nonsocialist parties	101,500	(4.6%)	44,500	(1.9%)
Between socialist and nonsocialist parties	86,100	(3.8%)	35,100	(1.4%)
	218,300	(9.7%)	84,500	(3.4%)

Three-fifths of the gross and net exchange involved no crossing of the line between socialist and nonsocialist parties. Because individual changes in party choice to some extent cancel out, an examination based on election statistics cannot offer much information about party conversions on the individual level. However, the changes in 1962–1966 between the Liberals and Conservatives and those between the Center and the Conservatives were also seen in an ecological study of five regions of the country (Sänkiaho, ch. 7 in Pesonen, 1971b).

Political loyalties not only persist between elections but also between generations. The effect of preadult political socialization within the family is significant in Finland.

Table 5 shows the pattern of parental party identification, as recalled by Finnish electors interviewed in April, 1966.

TABLE 5: Party Preference in 1966 Related to Father's Party, in Percent of Total Electorate with Party Preference

| FATHER'S PARTY | RESPONDENT'S PARTY | | | | | | | | TOTAL |
	FPDU	SDL	SDP	CENT	LPP	CONS	SPP	Others	
FPDU	7.6	0.2	1.7	0.3	0.1	0.1	—	—	10.0
SDL	0.1	0.2	0.1	0.2	—	—	—	—	0.6
SDP	3.2	1.0	12.2	1.4	1.1	1.3	—	0.1	20.3
CENT/AGR	2.6	0.5	4.6	12.9	1.6	1.8	0.1	0.7	25.0
LPP	0.1	0.1	0.2	0.2	0.5	1.1	—	—	2.2
CONS	0.2	0.1	0.9	1.2	0.9	5.5	0.1	—	8.9
SPP	0.1	—	0.4	—	0.1	0.3	3.6	—	4.5
Others	—	—	0.2	—	—	0.4	0.2	0.1	0.9
Don't Know	5.8	0.6	8.1	4.4	2.2	3.1	1.8	0.5	26.5
Refusals	0.8	—	0.1	0.2	0.1	0.1	—	—	1.3
Total	20.5	2.7	28.5	20.8	6.6	13.7	5.8	1.4	100.0
(N)	(203)	(37)	(477)	(290)	(91)	(209)	(73)	(20)	

The survey responses have been weighted according to the actual number of votes received by each party in 1966; nonvoters with a party preference are included in this table.

Three-quarters of those interviewed could recall their father's party, notwithstanding the disturbances caused by the banning of parties in the 1930s and 1940s. Of those who could recall their father's party, 59 percent voted for the same party and 41 percent supported a different party. The group of voters who were constant between generations falls to 39 percent, however, if one calculates it as a proportion of all persons interviewed, whether or not they can recall their father's partisanship. Similarly, the proportion that knowingly votes differently from the fathers falls to 27 percent if calculated against the total sample. The net effect of the shifts between generations is limited, because some movements cancel out. This is summarized in Table 6.

TABLE 6: Gross and Net Effect of Intergenerational Changes in Partisanship (cf. Table 5)

	LOST	WON	GROSS EXCHANGE	(%)	NET EFFECT	(%)
FPDU	67,000	166,000	233,000	(8.7)	+99,000	(+3.9)
SDL	9,000	48,000	57,000	(2.3)	+39,000	(+1.5)
SDP	213,000	215,000	428,000	(16.2)	+2,000	(0)
CENT/AGR	310,000	87,000	397,000	(15.2)	−223,000	(−8.6)
LPP	44,000	101,000	145,000	(5.5)	+57,000	(+2.1)
CONS	88,000	131,000	219,000	(8.4)	+43,000	(+1.6)
SPP	26,000	8,000	34,000	(1.3)	−18,000	(−0.5)
Others	20,000	21,000	41,000	(1.6)	+1,000	(0)
Total	777,000	777,000	1,554,000	(2×29.6)	±241,000	(±9.1)

The two generations were in disagreement in both directions along fifteen party borders; nine additional party borders were crossed in one direction. Consequently, in the system of twenty-eight borders only four two-party borders remained uncrossed, according to this survey sample. During the change of generations, the Agrarian and Social democratic parties lost the most supporters. However, the SDP compensated for its losses by winning support, especially from families affiliated to the Agrarian Union. The net impact of the exchanges was beneficial to the leftist block:

Changes among socialist parties	20%
Changes among nonsocialist parties . . .	30
From the Left to the nonsocialist	16
From the nonsocialist to the Left	34
	100% (N=413)

These figures also show that the cleavage between the political left and the nonsocialist parties did not close the party system into two "blocks" when the generations changed, as 50 percent of the disagreements across the generations were across the cleavage. On the other hand, of the 218,000 changes between the parties from 1962 to 1966, 39 percent were across the socialist/nonsocialist divide and 61 percent inside the party blocks (see Table 4).

We might summarize the combined effect of intergenerational and interelection change by looking at those party borders where movement was frequent in either Table 4 or 5 in both tables.

Party Borders	Changes in Choice, 1962 to 1966		Disagreement Between Generations	
	N	(%)	N	(%)
LPP/CONS	37,000	(1.6)	45,000	(2.0)
SDP/CENT	32,400	(1.4)	156,000	(6.0)
CENT/CONS	31,000	(1.3)	89,000	(3.0)
FPDU/SDP	20,700	(0.9)	134,000	(4.9)
SDP/LPP	19,000	(0.8)	34,000	(1.3)
SDP/CONS	18,200	(0.8)	56,000	(2.1)
CENT/LPP	17,000	(0.8)	48,000	(1.8)
SDL/SDP	10,000	(0.4)	29,000	(1.1)

With few exceptions the "low fences" of the Finnish party system seemed to be the same, whether one compares the conversions of individual voters or disagreements of the two generations. The line between FPDU/Center, which ranked fourth (76,000 changes, 2.8 percent) in the frequency of intergenerational change, was almost blocked by the time of the legislative term 1962–66. Other party borders that had included significant crossing over the long run but had become seemingly less open included the SDP loss to the FPDU and the advantageous exchanges of the SDP with the Center party.

The influence of family is also shown by the fact that 90 percent of those who reported the same party preference as their fathers were certain party supporters; among those whose choice conflicts with their fathers, 82 percent had a "sure" preference, with the proportion falling to 68 percent among those who claim no recollection of their father's party. Similarly, when one examines the time at which an individual reported deciding which party to vote for, those who made a choice in harmony with their fathers' were most likely to have made their voting decision before the year of the election: 84 percent were in this category. Among those changing from the parental party, 67 percent made up their minds in advance. Among those with no family preference to anchor their views, the proportion making up their mind before election year fell to 58 percent.

Newly converted voters also are slow to make certain their new party affiliation. In 1966 90 percent of those with a choice consistent with their 1962 preference (N= 1008) were certain supporters of their party. By comparison, 70 percent of those who had changed their party choice (N=134) were certain supporters. Thus it is easier and surer for a party to win new voters than seek to enlarge its certain support.

V. Distances and Dimensions Within the Party System

The political elite tends to think of Finland's parties along a continuum of political and strategic positions, from the extreme left-wing Communists to the right-wing of the Conservative party. One constant reminder of this unidimensional model of the party system is the parliament's seating arrangement, where members are seated by party from the left to the right. (By contrast, in Sweden members of Parliament are seated by constituency.) The one exception in Finland is the Swedish People's party, which for practical reasons is seated farthest to the right, although it is considered to have a "strategic" location close to the center. The same unidimensional model seems to influence the formation of government coalitions in Finland, and it is repeatedly referred to in political speeches and manifestos.

However, the Left-Right dimension offers only a partial picture of how the multiple political parties are positioned vis-à-vis each other. The correlation matrices in Table 7 offer one empirical example of parliamentary party similarities. We find in legislative voting a general tendency to conform to the Left-Right dimension, and the three leftist parties, FPDU, SDL, and SDP, differ from the nonsocialist grouping, CONS, SPP, LPP, and CENT. But there are many exceptions to the general tendency. For example, the parties usually considered most distant in the system, FPDU and Conservatives, were so only during one of the three governments reviewed here. Furthermore, the SDP had positive correlations with the Conservatives during the nonparty government and with Finnish People's party and the Liberal Union during the latter coalition government. The grouping of the parties into government and opposition had an independent effect on party distances. The small Liberal Union, which was not in the nonsocialist coalitions in 1962-66, was the least conforming legislative partner. Ties were also looser during the nonpartisan caretaker cabinet of Reino Lehto than they were during the parliamentary coalitions headed by prime ministers Ahti Karjalainen and Johannes Virolainen.

TABLE 7: **Correlation of Legislative Voting by the Eight Parliament Groups Elected in 1962***

| | A. Karjalainen (Agr, Cons, Fpp, Spp, and Trade Unions) | | | | | | |
	FPDU	SDL	SDP	AGR	FPP	LIB	CONS
SDL	.83						
SDP	.21	.35					
AGR	−.41	−.42	−.18				
FPP	−.40	−.24	.07	.28			
LIB	−.50	−.37	.04	.18	.32		
CONS	−.78	−.61	−.14	.59	.46	.51	
SPP	−.71	−.60	−.20	.56	.43	.45	.86
	B. Lehto (Nonparty Government)						
	FPDU	SDL	SDP	AGR	FPP	LIB	CONS
SDL	.48						
SDP	.06	.31					
AGR	−.14	−.30	−.12				
FPP	−.61	−.39	−.07	−.04			
LIB	−.23	−.11	−.01	.20	.39		
CONS	−.50	−.30	.11	.20	.39	.31	
SPP	−.42	−.40	−.09	.38	.34	.56	.56
	C. Virolainen (Agr/Cent, Cons, Fpp/Lpp, and Spp)						
	FPDU	SDL	SDP	AGR/ CENT	FPP/ LPP	LIB	CONS
SDL	.83						
SDP	.58	.65					
AGR/CENT	−.52	−.41	−.23				
FPP/LPP	−.34	−.23	−.18	.64			
LIB	−.33	−.24	−.03	.26	.25		
CONS	−.48	−.38	−.19	.68	.60	.23	
SPP	−.34	−.34	−.27	.50	.69	.21	.74

*Adopted from Risto Sänkiaho, *Eduskunnan äänestysdimensiosta vaalikaudella 1962–1966* (On Voting Dimensions in the Parliament during the Electoral Period 1962–1966), Institute of Political Science, University of Helsinki, Research Reports N 17/1969, Table 14.

Data are for the periods during the Cabinets of (a) Ahti Karjalainen, Apr. 1962, to Dec., 1963; (b) R. H. Lehto, Dec., 1963, to Sept., 1964; and (c) Johannes Virolainen, Sept., 1964, to May, 1966. The correlations are based on samples of 100 votes taken during each Cabinet.

The general picture of the party system as perceived by the electors can be studied by asking survey respondents to rank-order all or as many of the parties as they can. Such responses are useful for drawing conclusions on three different levels: (1) they tell about the shape and scope of the political world of the individual electors and about probable and improbable directions of individual change; (2) on the group level they tell about cohesion of the groups of party supporters and their internal cleavages; (3) they tell about the political system as a whole, insofar as one can deduce from individual responses how distant parties are from one another and what political dimensions exist in the party system.

The following question was put to those who revealed their party choice in April 1966: "Which other party would you have possibly voted for?" Everybody was also asked "Are there parties in this list that you would not have voted for under any circumstances? Any other such parties?" The following percentages of the sample answered the questions:

(Own party choice	. . . . . .	90%)
Second party	. . . . . .	56%
	* * * * * *	
Last party	. . . . . .	80%
Second last party	. . . . . .	60%
Third last party	. . . . . .	40%
Fourth last party	. . . . . .	26%
Fifth last party	. . . . . .	16%

These percentages show that a majority of electors could be positioned in relation to four different parties: their own party; the most disliked party; the second most rejected party; and a second-choice positive preference.

Table 8 shows the distribution of second choices by first-party preference. The supporters of the two largest parties, the SDP and Center, found it most difficult to think about any alternative to their own party, whereas the supporters of the Liberals and the Social Democratic League found it most natural to consider alternatives. The supporters of the SDL leaned toward their "mother" party, the SDP, and the supporters of the FPDU leaned towards other left-wing parties. The supporters of all other parties were mutually inconsistent. Therefore, political parties not only divide the electorate into supporting groups but also have their supporter groups internally divided into wings with different second choice parties. The most popular second party in the spring of 1966, the SDP, was agreeable to the extreme Left as well as to the nonsocialist parties, illustrating again that the Finnish party system does not have any sharp cleavage between the leftist and the nonsocialist blocks. Of the SDP's own supporters, 19 percent looked to the FPDU and SDL, and 36 percent in the nonsocialist direction.

The political party for which the electors would not have voted under any circumstances was usually the FPDU. The cleavage between the Communists and non-Communists was deeper in the spring of 1966 than it had appeared to be eight years earlier (Pesonen, 1968, pp. 141, 161). Anticommunism seemed such an obvious attitude for the CONS and LPP supporters that they found it easiest to name the impossible party choice. The Center and the SDP supporters were generally against FPDU. Only the supporters of the SDL were divided into two groups; they were equally antagonistic toward their alliance partner, the FPDU, and toward nonsocialist parties. The picture of party dislikes is more comprehensive when the second-last parties are also included. The opponents of the FPDU had a negative attitude toward the SDL. The SDL thus became the second least liked party. But the socialist vs. nonsocialist cleavage also enters the picture, for the party that the SDP is second readiest to reject is the Conservatives, followed by the Center party; SDL supporters also show the same preference ordering. Neither regards the other as a bitter enemy because proximate.

TABLE 8: **Party Preference in 1966 Related to Second Party Choice, "Most Impossible" Choice, and the two "Most Impossible" Choices, in Percentages**

| | PARTY PREFERENCE IN 1966 | | | | | | | | | |
	FPDU	SDL	SDP	CENT	LPP	CONS	SPP	Others	Non-P	Total
SECOND PARTY										
FPDU	.	13	11	0	—	—	—	—	1	4
SDL	18	.	8	—	—	1	—	—	1	5
SDP	38	67	.	16	31	19	23	25	3	16
CENT	2	3	10	.	19	15	16	35	1	8
LPP	—	3	15	9	.	31	6	15	2	11
CONS	1	3	6	24	28	.	8	10	—	9
SPP	—	—	2	—	—	5	.	—	—	1
Others	3	—	3	3	1	—	7	5	2	2
No other	27	8	34	31	5	21	23	—	19	26
DK	4	—	9	14	15	6	15	10	55	10
Refusals	7	3	2	3	1	2	2	—	17	8
Total	100%	100%	100%	100%	100%	100%	100%	100%	100%	100%
LAST PARTY										
FPDU	.	38	49	65	82	84	49	70	17	49
SDL	5	.	2	1	3	1	3	—	1	2
SDP	3	5	.	2	2	1	—	5	—	1
CENT	23	11	10	.	—	3	4	—	1	7
LPP	9	—	3	1	.	—	6	10	3	3
CONS	38	24	12	6	3	.	1	5	3	11
SPP	6	8	7	4	1	3	.	—	4	5
Others	1	—	1	3	2	1	1	—	3	2
No Answer	15	14	16	18	7	7	36	10	68	20
Total	100%	100%	100%	100%	100%	100%	100%	100%	100%	100%
TWO LAST PARTIES										
FPDU	.	49	53	69	87	86	54	70	17	52
SDL	5	.	19	38	46	53	21	25	3	25
SDP	8	10	.	5	2	4	3	10	—	3
CENT	35	33	22	.	10	9	14	15	2	15
LPP	25	8	9	4	.	1	6	10	4	8
CONS	55	35	28	8	9	.	2	30	7	20
SPP	22	19	11	7	13	8	.	10	9	13
Others	3	5	4	3	5	5	5	—	5	4
NA	47	41	48	65	28	34	95	30	153	60
Total	200%	200%	200%	200%	200%	200%	200%	200%	200%	200%
(N)	(203)	(37)	(477)	(290)	(91)	(209)	(73)	(20)	(150)	(1,550)

A useful measure of the psychological distances between the parties can be obtained when one combines on each party border the conceptions of the supporter groups of each party about the other. Table 9 is the summary of Table 8 so calculated.

Its measure of mutual attractions is the sum of these percentages of second rankings. For instance, when 18 percent of the supporters of the FPDU ranked the SDL second and 13 percent of the SDL supporters ranked the FPDU second, the mutual attraction of these parties is shown in Table 9A by the figure 18+13=31. According to Table 9A mutual attraction was strongest on the following five party borders: SDL/SDP, LPP/CONS, FPDU/SDP, SDP/LPP, and CENT/CONS. All these borders had also been among the eight crossed most frequently between the elections of 1962 and 1966.

TABLE 9: **Summary of the Mutual Distances Between Party Supporter Groups (Table 8) as Measured by Totals of Second Choice Percentages, Second Minus Last Choices, and Second Minus Two Last Choices**

A. SECOND PARTY CHOICES

	FPDU	SDL	SDP	CENT	LPP	CONS	SPP
FPDU	.						
SDL	+ 31	.					
SDP	+ 49	+ 75	.				
CENT	+ 2	+ 3	+ 26	.			
LPP	0	+ 3	+ 46	+ 28	.		
CONS	+ 1	+ 4	+ 25	+ 39	+ 59	.	
SPP	0	0	+ 25	+ 16	+ 6	+ 13	.
Others	+ 3	0	+ 28	+ 38	+ 16	+ 10	+ 7

B. SECOND MINUS LAST CHOICES

	FPDU	SDL	SDP	CENT	LPP	CONS	SPP
FPDU	.						
SDL	− 12	.					
SDP	− 3	+ 68	.				
CENT	− 86	− 9	+ 14	.			
LPP	− 91	0	+ 41	+ 27	.		
CONS	− 121	− 21	+ 12	+ 30	+ 56	.	
SPP	− 55	− 11	+ 18	+ 8	− 1	+ 9	.
Others	− 68	0	+ 22	+ 35	+ 4	+ 4	+ 7

C. SECOND MINUS TWO LAST CHOICES

	FPDU	SDL	SDP	CENT	LPP	CONS	SPP
FPDU	.						
SDL	− 23	.					
SDP	− 12	+ 46	.				
CENT	− 102	− 68	− 1	.			
LPP	− 112	− 51	+ 35	+ 14	.		
CONS	− 140	− 84	− 7	+ 22	+ 49	.	
SPP	− 76	− 40	+ 11	− 5	− 13	+ 3	.
Others	− 70	− 30	+ 14	+ 20	+ 1	− 25	− 8

It would seem most appropriate to measure party distances by means of all four choices which together pinpointed how a majority of the electors were related to the parties. Table 9B shows what remains of the attractions indexes of Table 9A when a similar index value of dislikes is deducted. Here we find that the distance between the FPDU and the gets a negative value because the mutual attraction on this border was mainly caused by the Communists and is now balanced by the dislike of the FPDU among the Social Democrats. Finally, Table 9C takes into account the second last parties. Now we see very few positive party distances remaining.

The combinations of likes and dislikes in Table 9 make it easy to place the four major parties in relation to each other, along the dimension FPDU..SDP..Center.. Conservative. The two left-wing parties are relatively close to each other, but contrary to expectation the SDP is also close to the two right-wing parties. The supporters of the Swedish People's party tend to fall in about the middle of this order, as do those who are classified as favoring other parties. The remaining parties do not fit so neatly into a unidimensional rank-ordering scheme. In part this may be because of distortions of sampling error, but it may also indicate genuine political differences. The evidence of Tables 8 and 9 would seem to suggest that on the level of the electorate the Finnish party system reflected at least seven different political dimensions (Pesonen, 1971b, chap. 14). These can be named as follows:

the Left—the Right

producers and agriculture—consumers and urban industries

the established parties—temporary small parties

recognized and noted centers—"the forgotten people"

communism—anti communism

Finnish—Swedish

victorious—losing

We might add that following this survey the emergence of the Christian League seems to express yet another political dimension in the Finnish multi party system.

VI. The Changing Social-Structure

The development of modern Finnish society has followed a familiar course, from that of a society greatly dependent upon agriculture and, in Finland's case, forestry, to one in which industry and commerce is dominant. In Finland, however, the change has taken place later and more slowly than in most other Western European countries except Ireland. The proportion of workers in agriculture and forestry has declined from 77 percent in 1880 to 31 percent in 1960, but the primary economy remained the largest category of employment until as late as 1960 (see Table 10); it has been continuously decreasing since then.

The shift from a rural to an industrial society has brought increasing prosperity, an increase that has been far greater in each of the last two decades than in the twenty years preceding. Taking the net national product (market value) per capita for 1926 as 100, and controlling for inflation, we get the following "income per capita" indexes:[3]

Years:	1926	1936	1946	1956	1966
Income:	100	131	128	239	378

Between 1948 and 1965 the annual growth rate was often as high as 5 percent. In cross-national comparisons of per capita income Finland has ranked approximately on a par with the Benelux countries and higher than Austria but somewhat lower than West Germany and other Scandinavian countries (Waris, 1968, p. 66; SYF 1970, table 441).

TABLE 10:   **Population of Finland by Industry, 1880-1970, in Percentages**

	1880	1900	1920	1940	1960	1970
Agriculture and Forestry	77	68	64	51	31	18
Industry and Construction	6	11	15	21	30	33
Commerce	1	2	3	5	9	14
Transport and Communication	2	3	3	5	7	8
Services	3	3	3	6	11	16
Other	11	13	12	12	12	11
Total	100	100	100	100	100	100
Population in Millions	2.0	2.6	3.1	3.7	4.4	4.6

Adopted from Waris, 1968, p. 22.   The data for 1970 is preliminary.

The decline in the number of farmers in the period 1940–1960 has been matched by a decline in workers too, both in absolute numbers and in percentages. This in turn has been complemented by a rise in the middle-class. Rauhala (1964, p. 1010) calculates that in a socioeconomic classification of Finland's economically active population the workers declined from 62 percent in 1940 to 51 percent in 1960 and the farmers from 24 to 16 percent, whereas the middle-class rose from 11 percent in 1940 to 30 percent in 1960, with the small upper-class (3 percent) remaining constant in size. A long-term influence upon the proportion of farmers in Finnish society has been the effect of population growth and the mechanization of agriculture. In the nineteenth century "peace, potatoes, and vaccination" increased Finland's population, mainly the rural proletariat. In 1901 only 33 percent of the agricultural population worked on farms of their own (Waris, 1968, p. 22). Because of settlement policies and the mechanization of agriculture, only 19 percent of the active agricultural population (7 percent of all economically active persons in Finland) were classified as farm labor in 1960 (SYF, 1970, table 24).

The movement from the farms took many Finns to the cities. In 1900 only 12.5 percent of the population lived in urban communes, in a country with a total population of 2,655,000. By 1968 48.8 percent of the population lived in urban communes, in a society with nearly 4.7 million people. The rate of urbanization is expanding rapidly, for an additional 10.4 percent became urbanites in the period 1960–1968. The proportion living in an urban environment is, moreover, higher than the proportion living in areas administratively described as urban communes.

In the 1960s migration of Finns to Sweden in search of work rose to such a level that the growth of Finland's resident population was halted. Internal migration has transferred population from the "peripheries" of Finnish economy to the advanced southern regions of the country. For example, the combined parliamentary representation of five constituencies in central Finland has decreased from 64 members in 1962 to 57 members in 1972.

The range of conditions affected by industrialization and urbanization can aptly be described by factor analysis of ecological aggregate data. Two such studies show how family structure and migration are best understood as single components of the one and all-embracing social dimension of the twentieth-century, called alternatively industrialization or modernization. In a factor analysis of regional differentiation that dealt with thirty carefully selected variables and used the 548 communes as the unit of analysis, the division-of-labor factor emerged as the most common dimension of regional differentiation. The variables with the highest loadings included the proportion of the population working in industry, construction, and services; population density; per capita income; and the percentages of rented dwellings, of population aged fifteen to sixty-four, of electrified dwellings, of female population, of population born outside the commune, of those completing middleschool, of divorced population, of one-person households, etc. Three other dimensions of regional differentiation identified as of about 1950 were labeled the "propensity for economic disturbance," the "changes in per capita income," and "social disengagement" (Riihinen, 1965, pp. 268–73). A developmental factor analysis of more than 100 time-series data from 1911 to 1961 shows the great preponderance of one general line of social change, corresponding to common notions of industrialization and modernization. That study also indicates the increasing speed of Finland's social change since World War II (Seppänen, 1965). One analyst has concluded that the six general characteristics that best describe the continuously industrializing Finnish society in the 1960s were its mechanization, wealth, urbanization, leisure time, social security, and internationalization (Waris, 1968, p. 139).

Finland is also a modern society in that its politics are largely secular, without popular divisions concerning the official state church, the Evangelical Lutheran church. (The Greek Orthodox church is also a state church, because of the Russian heritage, but its membership comprises only 1.3 percent of the population.) Finland is homogeneous in its nominal religious identification in that 92.7 percent of the population belonged to the Lutheran state church in 1968. Less than 1 percent belonged to other churches, and only 5.3 percent of the population refused to have any nominal religion, placing their names instead on the civil register (SYF, 1970, table 20). Church attendance is almost as low as nominal membership is high. Only about 3 percent of parish membership attended Sunday services in the 1950s; however, broadcast religious services are among the most popular radio programs in Finland. On the level of political elites church membership and the position of state churches constitute both a kind of ideological cleavage and a current issue in Finland. For example, demands for a complete separation of state and church were expressed by the SDP in 1971, and many labor leaders have traditionally abstained from church membership.

Early migration from Sweden and centuries of rule by the Swedish crown have left a large-enough Swedish population in Finland's southern and western coastal regions to make the country bilingual. By virtue of decisions made according to the language law after the 1960 census, Finland's 518 communes include forty-one where Swedish is the only official language during the ten-year period 1963–1972. In addition thirty-two communes are officially bilingual with a Swedish-speaking majority and forty-four are bilingual with a Finnish majority (SYF, 1970, table 22). The number of Swedish-speaking Finns has remained virtually constant between 1900 and 1960. The growth of the Finnish majority has gradually decreased the Swedish-speaking population from 12.9 percent at the turn of the century to 7.4 percent in 1960.

VII. Social-Structure and Party Support

Persons who have the same family name are alphabetized in Finnish telephone directories by their first name and not by their occupation, as they would be in Sweden and Denmark. Yet it is essential to remember the "occupation or title" of a person in Finland, too, in order to identify him both officially and socially. It would be unusual and generally improper to address a male as *herra* X, if his true identity is farmer X, truck driver X, postal clerk X, opera singer X, plumber X, fireman X, pensioneer X, or master of philosophy X. This applies to politicians as well. In parliamentary elections the ballots present the name, occupation, place of residence, and list number of each nominated candidate, in addition to affiliating him with a given party or electoral alliance. In order to appeal to their voters, some established professional politicians maintain their original occupational identity all through their political careers.

In survey research the occupations of the respondents or those of the head of their household are easy to obtain. They are then generally grouped into five classes. About one-half of the population belongs to the workers. That group is largely comparable to the manual workers of studies in other countries. As applied in Finland (and first institutionalized by the Finnish Gallup Institute), however, the terms manual or blue-collar may be occasionally misleading, because several service occupations, such as sales, are included in the Finnish worker group. The other class of workers, the farm laborer, has been decreasing in size. Although politically interesting, this class tends to be too small to be usefully studied in most survey samples. The farm laborer is usually combined with other workers. The farmers cover one-quarter of the Finnish population. Especially before the recent mechanization of forestry, many persons in this category were wage workers in the forests during several winter months each year. They are often called small farmers or small peasants rather than farmers or peasants; sometimes the size of holdings is used as an objective criterion to differentiate further the farmer class. Also included in this grouping are fishermen and some foremen etc. in forestry and farming. The remaining one-quarter of the population is employed in the white-collar occupations. A further differentiation gives two classes, the middle-class and the executive class. The latter is a broad grouping comprising not only managerial positions but also independent small entrepreneurs, artists, etc., and all university graduates.

Table 11 relates the occupation of Finnish electors to their party preference. The table omits the 10 percent of the sample who did not have or reveal any party preference; it includes both the voters and the nonvoters of the 1966 parliamentary election. A comparison of the occupational profiles shows how each party tends to anchor its support on one occupational group. The support for the Center party and "Others" (mainly the Small Farmers party) came largely from the farmers. Each party of the Left was primarily supported by the workers, while the Conservatives and the Liberals received most of their support from the white-collar groups. On the other hand, we find that the farmers made up a cohesive occupational group politically: a clear majority of them supported the Center, the former Agrarian Union. Also, about one-half of the electors in executive positions supported the Conservatives, whereas the lower-middle-class divided its support among the SDP and the Conservatives, with the Liberals ranking third in popularity. Of the two worker groupings, the nonpartisans excluded, 79 percent supported either the FPDU, SDL, or SDP. Of people in the other occupations, in turn, only 24 percent supported one of the three socialist parties. The "index of class voting" is 55, considerably higher than any recorded by Robert R. Alford (1963, p. 102) for the four Anglo-American democracies.

Because the workers are the largest occupational group, even a small fraction of labor support might be significant for the occupational background of a small party. This is seen in Table 11. To illustrate the point further, we can convert the percentages into estimated absolute numbers as follows:

TABLE 11: **Party Preference by Occupation and Occupation by Party Preference in Finland, 1966, in Percentages***

	PARTY PREFERENCE								
	FPDU	SDL	SDP	CENT	LPP	CONS	SPP	OHTERS	TOTAL (N)
(a)									
Farmer	9	—	8	60	2	7	10	4	100 (348)
Farm Labor	25	—	45	24	6	—	—	—	100 (34)
Worker	34	4	42	6	5	6	3	0	100 (669)
Middle-Class	6	3	29	8	15	28	9	2	100 (223)
Executive	4	1	10	9	15	53	8	—	100 (126)
Total Sample	20	3	29	21	7	13	6	1	100 (1,399)
(b)									
Farmer	11	—	7	72	7	12	43	70	25
Farm Labor	3	—	4	3	2	—	—	—	2
Worker	79	81	70	15	35	20	22	10	48
Middle-Class	5	16	16	6	36	33	23	20	16
Executive	2	3	3	4	20	35	12	—	9
TOTAL	100	100	100	100	100	100	100	100	100
(N)	(203)	(37)	(477)	(290)	(91)	(209)	(73)	(20)	(1,550)

*Occupational grouping by head of household; respondents without party preference omitted; survey data weighted according to the actual vote distribution.

	Farmers	*Workers*	*White Collar*
FPDU	61,000	442,000	37,000
SDL	—	57,000	13,000
SDP	52,000	554,000	147,000
CENT	396,000	96,000	55,000
LPP	11,000	65,000	98,000
CONS	63,000	71,000	246,000
SPP	65,000	34,000	55,000
Others	27,000	4,000	8,000
Total	675,000	1,323,000	659,000

Although the SDL received four-fifths of its support from the workers, it ranked only sixth among the parties in that occupational group. The farmers supporting SDP and middle-classes in favor of Center were as numerous as were workers supporting SDL. On the other hand, the Center party had as wide a worker support as the Liberals had a white-collar support, but only the latter characterized the popular base of the party. Four of the above entries are large enough to account alone for 10–20 percent of the Finnish electorate: the workers supporting the SDP, those in favor of FPDU, the farmers supporting the Center, and the middle-classes in favor of the Conservatives. This characterizes the social base of the four largest parties, but it does not account for the political split of the workers between social democracy and communism.

A comparison of Table 11 with information gathered in 1948 (Rantala, 1956) shows that the percentage of workers in the FPDU and SDP groups had changed very little in eighteen years. On the other hand, the percentage of farmers among the supporters of the Center (Agrarian Union) had decreased from 90 in 1948 to 72 in 1966, while the share of the white-collar groups in Conservative support had increased from 48 to 68 percent. Obviously both changes have been caused by the decrease in Finland's farming population. In 1971 the occupational profiles of the parties did not differ much from those in 1966 (Gallup in *Apu*, 1971: 44).

The following review of how some social characteristics relate to party support will apply the three broad occupational groupings as the basic control variable. One-half of the Finnish population belongs to the workers, including farm labor. We also need to separate the farming quarter from the middle-classes.

PLACE OF RESIDENCE AND REGIONALISM

The distribution of votes cast in 1966 (Table 1) is broken in Table 12 by rural and urban residence and by region. Table 13 contains comparable survey data on the ecology of the electorate.

As was to be expected from the occupational structure of party support, the Center party has the most rural following in Finland. The Agrarians', since 1965 the Center's, first serious attempt to enter the cities raised the party's urban percentage,

but only from 3.7 in 1962 to 4.6 in 1966. (Slow progress continued between 1966 and
1970: while the rural votes for the Center decreased from 35.8 to 29.2 percent, the
urban vote rose from 4.6 to 5.4 percent.) The "others" (mainly small farmers) are also
a rural group. The most urban counterpole is the Liberal People's party. Its predecessor, the National Progressive party, had begun to lose its original rural base as
early as in the beginning of the 1920s. The voter base of the SDP is considerably more
urban than that of the FPDU.

TABLE 12: Party Vote by Rural/Urban Residence and by Region, Parliamentary
Election of 1966, in Percentages

	FPDU	SDL	SDP	CENT	LPP	CONS	SPP	OTH-ER	PERCENT OF TOTAL
Rural voters	20.2	2.1	21.4	35.8	3.5	9.5	5.3	2.2	44.3
Urban voters	22.7	3.2	34.3	4.6	9.7	17.9	6.8	0.8	38.3
Commune unknown*	15.1	1.2	20.9	16.5	10.7	29.9	4.2	1.4	2.1
Votes in S/W	20.4	2.5	32.3	13.3	8.1	16.0	6.4	1.0	48.5
Votes in C.F.	19.1	3.0	22.0	29.6	3.2	12.2	8.1	2.8	21.3
Votes in N/E	27.3	2.1	18.5	36.0	5.9	9.1	—	1.2	14.6
Rural in S/W	17.9	2.4	27.3	29.9	4.6	11.7	4.8	1.4	19.9
in C.F.	18.0	2.3	18.2	38.9	1.9	8.9	8.5	3.3	14.6
in N/E	28.3	1.1	14.5	44.3	3.7	5.9	—	2.2	9.7
Urban in S/W	21.5	3.1	36.3	2.7	10.2	18.3	7.4	0.5	28.2
in C.F.	23.7	4.8	30.8	8.5	6.0	18.0	7.1	1.1	6.2
in N/E	31.7	1.6	26.8	12.1	12.1	15.2	—	0.5	3.7

The 14 multimember constituencies have been grouped into three regions as follows: S/W—Helsinki,
Uusimaa, Turku South and North, Häme South and North, Kymi; C.F. —Mikkeli, Kuopio, Central
Finland, Vaasa; N/E—North Karelia, Oulu, and Lapland. Aaland is excluded.
Data Source: *Official Statistics of Finland XXIX*, A: 29. Percentages are of actual votes; the percent-
ages of total (in parenthesis) are of the total electorate.
*Absentee ballots which were counted on constituency-level only.

The survey evidence in Table 13 concerns urban/rural residence, urban/rural place
of birth, and internal migration during the four years preceding the election. We find
that the rural base of the Center party was not entirely due to its agricultural character.
In rural communes the party was also favored by one out of eight workers and one out
of six middle-class persons, although it was almost neglected by the urban workers and
the urban middle-class. The general urban/rural difference of the FPDU and the SDP
was actually concentrated in their worker support.

A large majority of the Finnish electorate was born in rural communes. Their
political division is not unlike that of all the electorate. On the other hand, those born
in cities lean toward the urban parties—the Conservatives, Liberals, and SDP—and
avoid the Center. When occupation is controlled for, urban birth and urban residence
seem politically similar. During the past four years one elector out of seven had moved

TABLE 13: **Ecological Comparisons of Party Preferences in 1966, with Controls for Occupation, in Percentages**

	FPDU	SDL	SDP	CENT	LPP	CONS	SPP	OTHER	PERCENT OF TOTAL
Rural electors	20	2	23	34	4	9	6	2	57.9
Urban electors	21	4	36	3	10	21	5	0	42.1
Stable	21	3	28	22	6	12	7	2	85.6
Moved in 1961–65	19	1	31	13	12	23	1	0	14.4
Born in									
Rural communes	21	3	27	26	5	11	5	2	76.1
Urban communes	18	3	33	5	11	22	7	1	23.1
Born abroad	—	—	32	19	—	17	32	—	0.8
Electors in S/W	19	3	34	15	8	16	4	1	52.9
Electors in C.F.	21	4	23	23	4	11	11	3	32.8
Electors in N/E	27	—	22	35	6	9	—	1	14.3
F Rural	9	—	8	61	2	6	10	4	24.1
Urban	27	—	8	29	—	36	—	—	0.8
W Rural	35	3	38	12	4	5	3	0	25.9
Urban	31	5	47	2	6	6	3	0	24.2
MC Rural	6	3	22	17	13	31	5	3	8.0
Urban	5	2	23	4	16	40	10	—	17.0
F Stable	9	—	8	59	2	7	11	4	24.1
Mobile	12	—	—	58	—	30	—	—	0.8
W Stable	34	5	42	7	4	5	3	0	42.6
Mobile	27	2	44	10	9	7	—	1	7.5
MC Stable	4	2	24	8	14	36	10	2	18.9
Mobile	12	1	18	9	18	39	3	—	6.1
F Born rural	9	—	8	62	1	7	10	3	23.7
Born urban	25	—	10	35	12	—	—	18	1.2
W Born rural	35	4	40	9	5	4	3	0	38.0
Born urban	29	6	47	1	6	9	2	—	11.8
MC Born rural	6	3	25	10	14	35	5	2	14.4
Born urban	5	1	20	4	17	41	12	—	10.1
F in S/W	2	—	10	71	2	10	3	3	9.4
in C.F.	13	—	6	47	1	6	20	7	10.7
in N/E	15	—	10	70	3	3	—	—	4.8
W in S/W	31	5	47	4	6	6	1	—	28.1
in C.F.	34	6	38	9	3	4	6	—	15.4
in N/E	39	—	30	18	6	5	—	2	6.7
MC in S/W	5	1	25	2	17	40	10	—	15.4
in C.F.	1	4	17	20	14	35	9	—	6.7
in N/E	16	—	21	14	10	30	—	9	2.8

F = Farmer   W = Working-Class   MC = Middle-Class

to a new commune. The mobile electors tended to favor the Conservatives and Liberals and supported only seldom the Center and the Swedish People's party. Absentee ballots (Table 12) are another indicator of the unusual mobility of the Conservatives and the Liberals. But we find also that the differences in occupational structure account for the different mobility rates. Only the Swedish-speakers avoid internal migration. Furthermore, there is an unusual dualism in the Swedish ecology. For example 49 percent of the SPP supporters lived in the least industrialized (0 to 29 percent) communes and 25 percent in the capital, while the corresponding percentages of all electors were only 20 and 11.

The concentration of the Swedish People's party along the southern and western coast is the most obvious example of political regionalism in Finland. The Swedes dominate the single-member constituency of Aaland, and the SPP ranks second in Vaasa, second or third in Uusimaa, fourth in Helsinki, and sixth or seventh in the southern Turku constituency. In Finland as a whole multipartyism persists, although no constituency is itself so highly fragmented. The two most northern ones (Lapland and Oulu) approach a two-party system, as the combined vote for the FPDU and Center was about 70 percent in 1966. In two others (Mikkeli and North Karelia) the Center and the SDP together received more than 60 percent, and in the northern Häme constituency the SDP and the FPDU had more than 60 percent; in all other constituencies two parties suffice for a majority of the voters.

For Tables 12 and 13 the fourteen multimember constituencies were grouped into the northeast (electing thirty-seven members in 1966), central Finland (fifty-three members), and the economically more developed remainder of the country, the southwest (109 members). The northeastern "two-party system" is most prevalent in the rural communes but also influences the urban vote there. While the Center and the FPDU are relatively strongest in the peripheries, the regional base of the SDP, Liberals, and Conservatives is relatively sturdier in the growing southwest. The regional political climates are reflected inside the occupational groupings too. Among the workers, about one-half support the SDP in the southwest but less than one-third in the northeast, where the FPDU in turn gets two-fifths and the Center one-fifth of labor support. The farmer wing of the FPDU is also strongest in the peripheral regions. The Swedish People's party gets its largest farmer support in central Finland (west coast), and the Conservative farmers are in the southwest.

ECONOMIC STATUS

Table 14 adds the electors' subjective class identification and their father's occupation to the basic control variable, occupation. Table 15 measures wealth by family income and telephone ownership.

The subjective class identification of Finnish electors tends to coincide with their objective occupational grouping. However, two aspects of the subjective class distribution are worth noting. Many farmers (11 percent of the electorate in Table 14A) view themselves as small farmers rather than regular farmers or peasants. It is difficult to draw an exact line between these two classes with objective economic measures, but the difference is a real one, economically and psychologically as well as in the sphere of the farmers' interest organizations. On the other hand, our "executive" group, which is defined by both work and education, seems a fairly technical grouping without much corresponding psychological content. Most people who are classified in this

TABLE 14: **Party Preference by Subjective Class Identification and Father's Occupational Grouping, with Controls for Occupation, in Percentages**

		FPDU	SDL	SDP	CENT	LPP	CONS	SPP	OTHER	PERCENT OF TOTAL
A. *Subjective Class*										
Farmers		1	—	4	75	3	8	9	—	13.2
Small farmers		18	—	15	46	1	3	9	8	10.6
Workers		35	5	44	6	2	4	3	1	49.0
Lower-middle-class		3	0	20	9	22	38	7	1	23.0
Executive		—	—	12	14	4	58	12	—	2.0
All farmers		8	—	9	62	2	6	9	4	23.8
All middle-class		3	0	19	10	20	39	8	1	25.0
B. *Father's Occupation*										
Farmer		13	2	20	40	5	10	8	2	44.8
Farm labor		36	5	39	7	3	1	3	6	5.2
Worker		33	3	41	4	6	11	2	—	34.8
Lower-middle-class		7	4	27	7	11	37	6	1	7.0
Executive		—	—	17	1	21	49	12	—	5.8
All workers		33	4	40	4	6	10	2	1	40.0
All middle-class		4	2	22	5	15	42	9	1	12.8
(a) (F)	Farmer	1	—	3	75	3	8	10	—	12.7
	Small farmer	14	—	14	52	—	2	8	10	8.5
	Worker	30	—	16	18	—	6	24	6	2.3
	Middle-class	—	—	—	51	—	35	14	—	0.6
(W)	Small farmer	34	—	17	27	7	—	15	—	2.1
	Worker	38	5	45	4	2	3	2	1	41.3
	Middle-class	4	—	31	11	27	25	1	1	5.3
(MC)	Worker	15	7	46	12	4	11	2	3	5.2
	Middle-class	3	0	17	8	18	44	9	1	18.8
(b) (F)	Farmer	8	—	7	64	1	5	12	3	21.4
	Worker	25	—	13	38	—	11	—	13	2.8
(W)	Farmer	26	3	39	17	5	5	4	1	16.0
	Worker	40	4	44	2	5	4	1	—	29.3
	Middle-class	16	9	37	5	7	24	—	2	3.2
(MC)	Farmer	3	4	13	20	17	32	7	4	7.5
	Worker	13	3	36	2	11	30	5	—	8.3
	Middle-class	—	—	17	5	16	50	12	—	8.9

F=Farmer   W=Working class   MC=Middle-class

occupational group identify with the middle-class and not with the executive class. When combining the occupations and the subjective classes into their three basic types, we find the two groupings coinciding for 81 percent of the electors. Only 16 percent viewed themselves differently from the occupational grouping. Such electors include the workers who identify themselves with the middle-class or the small farmers, and the middle-class-persons and the farmers who identify with the workers.

The subjective identification with small farmers has considerable political relevance. Only those farmers who called themselves "small farmers" supported the Left or the "others" (Small Farmers' party), and those workers who identified with small farmers tended to be not only leftist but also Communist. In the occupational farmer group one-half of the small-farmer identifiers but three-quarters of the regular farmer identifiers supported the Center party. Among the workers, only those identifying with the middle-class gave considerable support to the Liberals and the Conservatives. An identification with either the workers or the middle-class also divides the occupational middle-class into two fairly different political tendencies: the former mainly leftist, the latter Conservative and Liberal. When viewed separately, the occupational group and the subjective class give a fairly similar prediction of the electors' party choice, but simultaneously these two independent variables provide many additional observations about class and party.

The total percentages in Table 14B illustrate Finland's social change. During one generation the farming population has decreased from one-half to one-quarter while the workers have increased from one-third to one-half and the middle-classes from 13 percent to one-quarter. However, 60 percent of the electors stayed in their father's occupational grouping while 38 percent moved socially. The latter group includes workers and middle-class with a farmer background (18 and 8 percent) and middle-class with a worker background (8 percent).

Table 14B reflects the importance of family in political socialization. The most leftist workers came from worker homes, the Center-oriented farmers had farming fathers, and the most Conservative middle-class electors came from middle-class families. Correspondingly, only the workers with a middle-class background had some tendency to support Conservatism, farmers and middle-class with a worker background to support socialism or communism, and workers and middle-class coming from farming families some tendency to support the Center party.

According to our 1966 data the median family income was 7,700 marks per annum. This varied by occupational grouping as follows:

Farmers   5,200
Farm labor   4,800
Workers   7,700
Lower-middle-class .   10,800
Executive position . .   14,700

It seems that the data concerning the incomes are not consistent enough to be quite comparable. Some respondents may have felt that the interview concerned monetary wages and salaries only, and this, in turn, may have decreased the income reported by the farmers. This is suggested by another question: "Are you employed so that you get a money income?" An affirmative answer was given by 58 percent of all respondents but only by 28 percent of the farmers (and their family members). The corresponding percentage among the Center supporters was 34 and among the "others" 50, but it varied between 62 and 68 percent among the FPDU, SDP, LPP, Conservative, and SPP supporters.

Even with this reservation in mind, it is important to relate party and income. The income profiles of the eight party groups was the following (quartile distribution in marks per annum):

	Q_1	Median	Q_8
FPDU	3,700	6,300	10,200
SDL	4,700	9,100	11,800
SDP	3,600	8,800	12,200
CENT	2,800	3,500	8,300
LPP	7,200	10,800	14,700
CONS	7,100	11,600	17,300
SPP	4,600	7,600	13,200
Others	1,700	6,200	10,200
Total	4,300	7,700	11,900

Thus, the lowest reported income was earned by the supporters of the Center party and the highest income by the predominantly middle-class parties, LPP and Conservatives. On the Left we find the reported median income of the SDP supporters higher than that of the FPDU supporters. Also, the SDP group has more variance while the FPDU tends toward more cohesiveness in internal income distribution.

In Table 15 the annual family income is dichotomized, with 8,000 marks as the "cutting point." This defines 52 percent of the electorate as the low-income and 48 percent as the high-income group. The party distribution of these two groups differs in a way that is consistent with the income profiles of the parties. The impact of income also penetrates through the three broad occupational groupings. Among the workers we see the tendency of the high-earning half to support the SDP, while the low-income half divides its support evenly among the FPDU and the SDP, and even has some tendency to favor the Center. The high-income quarter of the farmers contains hardly any Social Democrats, and only the low-income quarter of the middle-class has a relatively noteworthy minority of Center and FPDU supporters.

Television and telephone ownership were used as indicators of wealth in the 1966 study. Radio could not be used because it was in practically every home (96 percent). Television was getting more widely diffused in 1966, when 64 percent of the electors reported that they could watch TV programs at home. Interestingly, television ownership appeared unrelated to party preference, except for the relative infrequency of TV ownership among the supporters of the Swedish People's party. On the other hand, telephones had a strong relationship with party preference. Of all electors, 41 percent had a telephone at home. The Center supporters had almost the same frequency (42 percent). The corresponding percentage was only 17 among the FPDU and 33 among the SDP supporters but rose to 60 among the Liberals and Swedes and to 73 percent among the Conservatives. Table 16 shows the percentages counted the other way. Like income, this measure of wealth had some independent impact on party preference. True, the Center was popular among the farmers and the SDP

TABLE 15: **Party Preference by Income and Telephone Ownership, with Controls for Occupation, in Percentages**

		FPDU	SDL	SDP	CENT	LPP	CONS	SPP	OTHER	PERCENT OF TOTAL
	Low income	24	2	25	39	4	8	6	2	51.8
	High income	16	3	33	12	10	20	5	1	48.2
	Telephone	8	2	24	21	10	25	9	1	40.3
	No telephone	29	3	32	20	4	6	4	2	59.7
F	Low income	10	—	10	58	2	7	9	4	19.0
	High income	7	—	1	64	2	8	16	2	5.9
W	Low income	37	3	37	11	4	4	4	—	26.5
	High income	29	5	48	3	6	7	1	1	23.6
MC	Low income	10	2	20	18	11	30	9	—	6.3
	High income	4	2	23	5	16	40	8	2	18.7
F	Telephone	3	—	5	65	2	11	13	1	9.9
	No telephone	14	—	10	58	1	3	8	6	14.9
W	Telephone	18	4	47	9	8	10	3	1	13.1
	No telephone	39	4	40	6	4	4	2	0	37.0
MC	Telephone	4	2	16	7	16	43	11	1	17.2
	No telephone	9	3	36	12	12	23	3	2	7.8

Low Income=Annual family income less than 8,000 marks.
F=Farmer   W=Worker   MC=Middle-class.

popular among the workers whether or not they had a telephone, but we notice also the concentration of FPDU support among the nonowning workers, that of SDP support among the nonowning middle-class, and of Conservative support among the telephone owners in the middle-class.

Although this review concerns structural variables, one should also keep in mind the psychological correlates of party affiliation. In an earlier comparison of the urban supporters of the FPDU, the Social Democrats, and the nonsocialists, two factors were noted to have an impact on party preference independent of actual earned income. One was satisfaction with living standards. Satisfaction increased with higher incomes, but also, independent of their actual incomes, the FPDU supporters were the least satisfied and the nonsocialist supporters the most satisfied. Insecurity of income as experienced through current or former unemployment was an equally radicalizing factor. (Pesonen, 1968, pp. 99–103.)

SOCIAL ACTIVITY

Table 16 contains information about citizen participation in civic associations, emphasizing membership in trade unions and religious associations. Table 17 has data on newspaper readership.

TABLE 16: Party Preference by Association Memberships, with Controls for Occupation, in Percentages

	FPDU	SDL	SDP	CENT	LPP	CONS	SPP	OTHER	PERCENT OF TOTAL
One or no type of association	21	2	31	20	6	13	5	2	72.8
Two or More	18	3	23	23	7	18	8	0	27.2
Trade union	31	4	34	6	7	14	3	1	28.3
Nonunionized	16	2	26	27	6	14	7	2	71.7
Religious assn.	9	—	26	31	8	19	4	3	5.4
No rel. assn.	21	3	29	20	6	14	6	1	94.6
F 0-1 Assn.	13	—	9	59	—	5	8	6	17.8
2- Assns.	—	—	5	65	6	9	14	—	7.1
W 0-1 Assn.	32	4	43	8	5	5	3	0	38.3
2- Assns.	36	7	39	6	3	8	1	0	11.8
MC 0-1 Assn.	5	2	26	7	16	35	7	2	16.7
2- Assns.	6	3	15	10	13	41	12	—	8.3
F Union	37	—	9	31	—	5	18	—	1.4
No union	8	—	8	62	2	7	9	4	23.5
W Union	42	5	41	3	4	3	1	1	18.4
No union	28	4	43	10	5	7	3	—	31.7
MC Union	6	3	23	7	15	39	7	—	8.5
No union	5	2	23	9	15	36	9	2	16.5
F Religious assn.	—	—	—	81	—	9	—	10	1.4
No rel. assn.	10	—	8	58	2	9	10	3	23.5
W Religious assn.	13	—	54	9	9	8	7	—	2.4
No rel. assn.	34	5	42	7	5	5	2	0	47.7
MC Religious assn.	12	—	7	18	14	44	5	—	1.6
No rel. assn.	5	2	23	8	15	37	9	1	23.4

F= Farmer   W= Worker   MC= Middle-class

In order to become legal entities in Finland, civic associations must be officially registered by the Ministry of Justice. The register contains now about 100,000 associations (there were only 45,000 in 1947). According to a 1954 Gallup survey 70 percent of all adult men and 52 percent of the women belonged to some organization. Nowadays both the sports associations and the cooperatives count a total of over 1,900,000 memberships, a number close to the economically active population in the country (Waris, 1968, pp. 106–08).

In the 1966 study the following question was asked about participation in associations: "This is a list of different associations.[4] Does it include such types that you belong to? Are there others?"
A total of 62 percent of the respondents mentioned that they belonged to some association; 27 percent took part in two or more and 11 percent in three or more different types. Nine percent reported membership in political parties and 26 percent in trade unions. Other popular types of associations include the sports clubs (13 percent), women's organizations (9 percent), producers' organizations (8 percent), and youth organizations (8 percent). These percentages include only those types the active respondents mentioned first or second.

According to Table 16 the partisan differences in the number of associations are not large. Yet there is some tendency among the supporters of the Left not to belong to more than one type of civic association, while the nonsocialists are more prone to take part in a variety of associations. The control for occupation seems to add two exceptions to this general finding. The socially inactive farmers tended to support not only the Left but also the party of "the forgotten people," the Small Farmers' party. Within the worker grouping the extreme Left may have been more active in associations than the Social Democrats.

The total membership of Finnish labor unions was 768,000 in 1968. Of those, 272,000 were counted in the four central federations of white-collar-organizations and 496,000 were in the primarily blue-collar oriented trade unions (298,000 in the Finnish Central Trades Union; 95,000 in the Finnish Trade Union Federation; and 103,000 in the independent unions). (SYF, 1970, table 305.) According to the 1966 survey data the percentage of unionization (26 percent of total electorate) varies considerably by party. The most unionized group of supporters is the FPDU (43 percent), followed by the SDL (36), SDP (34), Liberals (31), and Conservatives (29 percent); the latter two obviously belonging mainly to the white-collar unions.

The unorganized groups of Table 16 are the supporters of the Center and the Swedish People's party. Their compensation for nonunionization is membership in the producers' organizations (Center 24, SPP 21 percent). The table does not show data on public offices. Let us mention, however, that municipal positions of trust were (with the exception of the SDL, 19 percent) relatively more frequent among the nonsocialists (Center 17, LPP 12, Conservatives and SPP 10 percent) than they were among the socialists (FPDU 9, SDP 6 percent). The larger number of municipal offices in rural than in urban communes accounts largely for these differences.

As has been noted above, there is no clash of competing religions in Finnish society. But religiosity is by itself one dimension in the political system and it has even caused the advent of the Christian League as a new minor party. The 1966 data do not have a good measure of religious activity. We might, however, juxtapose those 5 percent who reported membership in religious associations and the rest of the electorate. According to Table 16 the religiously active group contains very few supporters of the FPDU and has relatively many nonsocialists. Among the workers the Social Democrats are closer to religious activity than the supporters of the extreme Left, although the reverse might be true of those middle-class people who support the socialist parties.

One function of the church for centuries was to provide the basic mass education in Finland. Illiteracy became rare long before compulsory education was legislated in 1910 and fully implemented in 1921. During the 1960s there has been a great increase in enrollment in secondary education and in the universities, as well as in vocational and technical training. The party political impact of education has been found similar to that of occupation (Pesonen 1968, p. 93). Unfortunately, our present data do not have information on education, nor is it possible here to analyze to what extent the political impact of education might be independent of that of occupation.

TABLE 17: Party Preference by Newspaper Readership, with Controls for Occupation, in Percentages

	FPDU	SDL	SDP	CENT	LPP	CONS	SPP	OTHER	% OF TOTAL
One or no daily newspaper	23	2	32	18	7	11	5	2	64.2
Two or more	16	3	22	26	5	20	7	1	35.8
Socialist paper	49	4	33	4	2	6	2	—	14.7
Non soc. paper	16	2	28	24	7	16	7	—	85.3
F 0–1 Newspaper	12	—	8	56	2	6	10	6	13.9
2– Newspapers	6	—	8	66	1	8	10	1	11.0
W 0–1 Newspaper	34	3	43	6	6	5	3	—	36.0
2– Newspapers	32	8	39	9	4	6	1	1	14.1
MC 0–1 Newspaper	5	3	28	8	17	32	5	2	14.3
2– Newspapers	7	1	15	8	12	44	13	—	10.7
F Socialist paper	93	—	7	—	—	—	—	—	0.9
Non soc. paper	6	—	8	61	2	8	11	4	24.0
W Socialist paper	52	4	36	4	2	2	—	—	10.6
Non Soc. paper	28	5	44	8	6	6	3	0	39.5
MC Socialist paper	28	5	30	2	2	23	10	—	3.2
Non soc. paper	2	2	22	9	17	39	8	1	21.8

F=Farmer   W=Worker   MC=Middle-class

In 1969 the total daily circulation of newspapers in Finland was 1,863,000, i.e. 396 copies per 1,000 population (SYF, 1969, table 363). According to our 1966 survey 95 percent of the electors read a newspaper regularly and 35 percent read two or more papers. The mean was 1.4 daily newspapers per person. This figure varied somewhat by party: readership was below the mean among the "others" (1.2) and the FPDU (1.3) and above the mean in the Center and Swedish (1.5) and the Conservative (1.6) groups. Correspondingly, Table 17 shows the tendency of the electors reading several newspapers to support the nonsocialist parties. Noteworthy details in Table 17 include the tendency among the farmers of both the FPDU group and the "others" (small farmers) to read one paper only; among the workers, the relatively many papers of the SDL and Center supporters; and in the middle-class, the high readership of the Conservatives and the Swedes.

Finland has an established tradition of party affiliated newspapers. As in many other countries, the socialist press gets fewer readers than one might expect on the basis of the socialist vote. In 1965 the total circulation of Finland's ninety-one newspapers could be summarized as follows (Nousiainen, 1971, p. 133):

Conservative, Center, and SPP press .	42 %
Nonsocialist independent papers . .	29
FPDU, SDP, and SDL press . . .	14
Independent and nonpartisan papers .	15
	100 %

As could be expected, the choice of daily newspapers is often political in Finland (Pesonen, 1968, pp. 49–51). No less than 89 percent of the consumption of the socialist press was concentrated among the Left party supporters in 1966, as 73 percent (N=119) of the FPDU paper readers were FPDU supporters and 58 percent (N=76) of the readership of the SDP press were Social Democrats. On the other hand, only 39 percent (N=390) of the Center press readership supported the Center party, and 28 percent (N=378) of the Conservative paper readers supported the Conservative party. According to Table 17 only 15 percent of the electorate read some socialist paper. In all the occupational groupings the readers of the socialist press had a strong tendency to support the FPDU, and in the middle-class the readership of a socialist newspaper also pointed toward a tendency to lean toward the SDP.

LANGUAGE, SEX, AND AGE

Finally, the party preference of the Finnish electors is compared in Table 18 with three additional socially dividing characteristics: mother tongue, sex, and age.

Almost three-quarters of the Swedish-speaking electors support the Swedish People's party. The most loyal to their ethnic party are the Swedes of the middle-class. About one-fifth of the Swedish-speaking farmers and one-half of the Swedish workers have slipped to the Left. Thus a total of 23 percent of the Swedes supported the FPDU or the SDP in 1966. This increased the total Left support by 4 percent, theoretically enough to elect three or four members to the parliament. That has also been the actual scope of Swedish-language representation in the parliament's socialist party groups. On the other hand, we may speculate that the SPP support among Swedish workers is worth two seats in the parliament. That was enough to tilt the parliamentary majority from socialist to nonsocialist in the 1945 election.

TABLE 18: **Party Preference by Language, Sex, and Age with Controls for Occupation, in Percentages**

		FPDU	SDL	SDP	CENT	LPP	CONS	SPP	OTHER	% OF TOTAL
Finnish-speaking		21	3	30	22	7	15	0	2	91.1a
Swedish-speaking		13	—	11	2	—	2	72	1	7.7
Women		20	3	28	20	7	15	5	2	51.5
Men		21	3	29	22	5	12	7	1	48.5
21–28 years		18	2	35	16	7	17	5	0	19.3
29–50 years		23	3	28	20	6	13	5	2	44.3
51 or more years		18	3	26	25	6	13	7	2	36.4
F	Finnish	9	—	8	69	2	8	—	4	21.1
	Swedish	12	—	7	4	—	—	75	2	3.3
W	Finnish	34	5	43	7	5	5	1	0	47.3
	Swedish	27	—	25	—	—	—	48	—	2.2
MC	Finnish	6	2	25	9	16	41	0	1	22.6
	Swedish	—	—	3	—	—	6	91	—	2.2
F	Women	12	—	9	56	1	8	8	6	12.6
	Men	7	—	8	64	2	5	12	2	12.3
W	Women	31	5	41	7	7	6	3	0	26.5
	Men	36	4	43	8	3	4	2	0	23.6
MC	Women	5	1	20	10	16	42	5	1	12.6
	Men	6	3	25	6	14	33	12	1	12.4
F	21–28	17	—	8	53	—	9	13	—	3.0
	29–50	8	—	7	61	1	7	10	6	10.0
	51–	9	—	9	61	2	6	9	4	11.9
W	21–28	28	2	50	8	5	6	2	1	10.2
	29–50	38	5	37	7	5	6	2	0	23.1
	51–	31	5	44	7	5	4	4	—	16.8
MC	21–28	2	1	24	11	15	39	8	—	6.1
	29–50	7	1	29	8	15	32	7	1	11.2
	51–	7	4	11	7	14	43	12	2	7.7

a No information or other, 1.2 percent.

Of the two sexes boys are the majority of very young Finns. Because their mean life expectancy is low—in 1961–1965 only 65.4 years while that of women was 72.6 years—the females constitute the majority in the total population. In 1966 Finland had 1,070 females per 1,000 males (1,156 in the urban and 1,003 in the rural communes).

The ratio was naturally higher among the enfranchised population (urban 1,254, rural 1,052). Despite their lower voter turnout the women have also been the majority of the voters since the election of 1927. For example, in 1966 the percentage of females among the voters was 52.7 and among all the electors, 53.4. But of the 200 candidates who gained election to the parliament only 16.5 percent were women.

Some studies have shown the conservative tendency of the women in Finland (Pesonen, 1958, p. 104; Pesonen, 1968, pp. 37–40, 54, 106). In our 1966 data the expected differences are quite weak. Yet we see in Table 18 some tendency of the men to favor the socialist parties and of the women to support the Conservatives and the Liberals. These differences are more pronounced in the worker and middle-class subgroups; the picture of the farmers is confused, possibly due to the attraction of the Center party.

In order to observe age differences, the respondents are classified in Table 18 in three political generations: those eligible to vote for the first time in 1962 or 1966, those enfranchised in 1945–1958, and those who could vote in 1939 or before. The Center and the SDP seem to have reverse tendencies: the former losing and the latter gaining relative support with the renewal of the electorate. The FPDU was popular in the postwar generation. The Conservatives had special popularity among the youngest, and the SPP among the oldest generation. Inside the occupational groupings we note the perhaps unexpected Communist tendency of the young farmers and the appeal of the Small Farmers' party to the oldest age group. Among the workers the postwar generation was even more pro-Communist than pro-SDP, but the new voters have quite different preferences. In the middle-classes one generational difference is of special interest. The prewar generation found the Social Democrats distasteful, whereas the postwar generations no longer equate white-collars and a bourgeois party choice.

The comparison of age and party could also be made via the age profiles of the parties. The following figures list the quartile age distributions:

	Q_1	Median	Q_3
FPDU	31	41	54
SDL	37	46	56
SDP	29	40	55
CENT	34	47	59
LPP	31	40	55
CONS	29	42	55
SPP	35	48	61
Others	37	45	53
No Party	32	43	53
All	31	43	56

Thus each of the quartiles varied within the range of eight years, e.g., the median from the forty years of the SDP and the Liberals up to the forty-seven years of the Center and the forty-eight years of the Swedish People's party. The youngest quarter contained only 21–29-year-olds among the Social Democrats and the Conservatives, but 21–34-year-olds among the supporter group of the Center and 21–37-year-olds among that of SDL and the Small Farmers' party.

VIII. Conclusion

In the foregoing presentation of social-structure and party support the dependent variable was defined as either the choice of political party reported by voters when interviewed after the parliamentary election of 1966, or alternatively, as the choice the nonvoters considered a likely one. Both certain and uncertain supporters of the parties are thus included. Excluded are those 10 percent who did not express any preference.

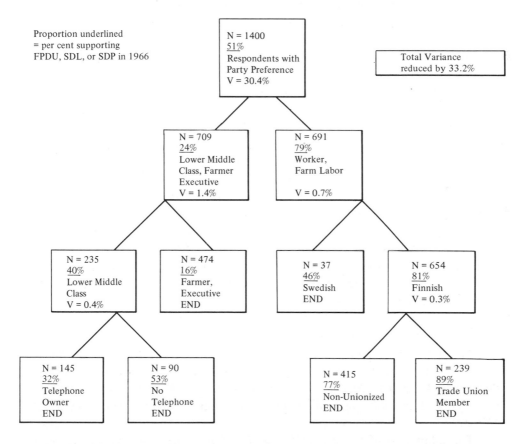

Figure 1: A Tree Analysis of the Choice Between Socialist and Nonsocialist Parties in Finland.

When Finland's eight-party system was reduced to the socialist/nonsocialist dichotomy and when the occupational structure was viewed as the simple worker/nonworker cleavage, an usually high "index of class voting" (55) was noted. Similarly, a tree analysis using the A.I.D. program indicates the importance of occupation as a central predictor of party support in Finland. The following eleven independent variables were used in our A.I.D. analysis: occupation, rural/urban residence and region, income and telephone ownership, trade-union membership and membership in religious associations, sex, age, language, and television ownership. Figure 1 summarizes the results.

The first split of the sample reduces total variance by 30.4 percent. The importance of occupation continues even further on the nonworker side, where the lower-middle-class tends more toward the Left than do the farmers and the electors in executive positions. Telephone ownership, a measure of both wealth and communicability, creates the end groups of the lower-middle-class branch of the Finntree. Among workers language is second in importance (Swedish-speaking workers are less likely to vote Left). Union membership then comes next in importance among Finnish-speaking workers. In all, four of the eleven social influences entered in the program are employed in differentiating voters: occupation, language, union membership, and telephone ownership.

Another analysis was also made in order to find out what readership of a socialist newspaper (Table 17) as a twelfth independent variables does to the Finntree. It did not affect the workers, but it was the strongest variable on the nonworker side (readers 69 percent, N=45). Only subsequently were the nonreaders split into the lower-middle-class and the farmer/executive grouping. Furthermore, in this case it is age and not the ownership of a telephone that divides the lower-middle-class into the two end groups.

Although the political borderline between the Left and the nonsocialists is closely connected to social differences, it is by no means uncrossable. Moreover, that political dichotomy represents only one aspect of Finnish party competition. The dependent variable of this analysis consists of three socialist and five nonsocialist parties. Therefore the tree analysis simplifies the problem. It does not differentiate the farmers who support the Center from the middle-class electors who support the Conservatives, and it stops short of indicating anything about the Communist/non-Communist cleavage among the workers.

Let us summarize Table 11–18 in order to present typical profiles of the supporter groups. First, the five nonsocialist parties:
——The social base of the *Swedish People's party* is easy to define: it is the Swedish minority in Finland. The party's support occurs where Swedes live along the coast; they are, as a group, internally differentiated into rural and urban elements. They tend to be old and immobile, read many newspapers, but in 1966 had comparatively few TV sets.
——The main base of the *National Coalition (Conservatives)* is among the middle-classes, especially the executives. The party's support is heaviest in the developed regions, where it also appeals to the farmers. Its worker support tends to come from

middle-class families. The Conservatives are mobile and have the highest income, telephone ownership, and newspaper readership. They were popular among the women and the youngest age groups in 1966.

——The *Liberal People's party* is Finland's most urban party, with a second-generation urban tradition. Like the Conservatives, the LPP supporters tend to live in the Southwest, be mobile, have high incomes and telephone service, and are favored by women. In addition they appeal to workers who identify with the middle-class.

——The base of the *Center party* is quite solidly rural and mainly agricultural. Its typical supporters are geographically immobile, identify with the regular rather than the small farmers, are active in the producers' organizations, read many newspapers, and are religious, old, and male.

——The *Small Farmers' party* was typically based in 1966 on socially inactive and religious small farmers in central Finland. Its supporters tended to be old and did not read many newspapers.

Three nonsocialist parties (SPP, CENT, SFP) thus have distinct support profiles; the Conservative and Liberal parties are more like each other but even they are not without mutual differences. As regards the Left, the following characteristics occur:

——The *Social Democratic party* is primarily urban and also has relatively many city-born supporters. It is regionally biased to the southwest, possibly more liked by men, popular among the young in 1966, but it does not appeal to the older generation of middle-class electors.

——The *Finnish People's Democratic Union* is strongest among that generation who became new electors after the Second World War. Its vote is predominantly male. Supporters read few newspapers and seldom have telephones, but participate actively in the trade unions.

When comparing the SDP and the FPDU supporters, we find that the FPDU group tends to be more rural and more peripherally located, with somewhat less income, less religious activity, and more interest in the socialist press. The FPDU gets little middle-class support from the low-income group, while the SDP competes evenly with the Conservatives for the support of the lower-middle-class.

——The *Social Democratic League* of Workers and Smallholders began as the Social Democratic Opposition in 1958. In 1966 its base seemed similar to that of the SDP, but the SDL supporters tended to be older and read more newspapers. Our data contain no farmers at all with an SDL preference.

The workers remain the most typical base of popular support for all leftist parties, but the middle-classes will be an obvious target for future Left/nonsocialist competition. Until the Second World War the Red/White cleavage that had been expressed dramatically in the civil war of 1918 tended to keep middle-class persons from looking leftward. Such is not the case among the younger white-collar groups today.

Generally speaking the distribution of party support has been more stable in Finland than the structure of the society. Only the Swedish People's party provides an example of close dependence on one social group, the relative decline of which has decreased the party accordingly (12.4 percent in 1922, but 5.4 percent in 1972). The

Agrarian-Center heyday continued through the 1960s despite the decrease in agricultural population. The party was successful both in mobilizing its basic support and in appealing to new occupational groups, although the city gates did not open widely. The Conservatives compensate for their declining farmer wing among the growing middle-classes. Some social change may alienate groups and lead to protest-type political movements. Such was the rise of backwoods Communism after World War II, a movement unlike industrial Communism because it could not be traced to socialist traditions (Allardt, 1970). In 1970 the Small Farmers-Rural party championed a populist movement that was also based on social alienation (Helander, 1971; Paakkinen, 1972).

Finnish political parties have their internal cleavages too. Although the parties are eight in number, the need to adjust to several political dimensions may create internal tensions. There have been bitter intra-Communist animosities since 1968; tensions somewhat flavored by generational cleavages appear between the moderate and the radical Social Democrats; and soon after the unsuccessful election of 1970 a peripheral opposition forced the Center party to reemphasize its traditional farmer base.

Notes

1. The SDL thus lost its party status after the election of 1972 (see Table 1); but it soon collected the 5,000 signatures required for a reentry to the party register.
2. The sample was taken in three stages: (1) the communes were grouped according to their relative industrialization; (2) a total of 215 voting districts were drawn at random from the five strata of communes; and (3) seven names were taken at random from each of the 215 registers (except one, which was received too late). The field work was done by the Finnish Gallup Institute. Of the 1,498 attempted interviews 1,263 were completed (50 persons had died or were ill, 43 had moved, 84 could not be reached, 40 refused, 9 were too late). In communes from 0 to 39 percent industrialized the sampling ratio was one-half of the rest of the country, and their 287 cases were duplicated, giving the total of 1,550 cases in the analysis.
3. Calculated from Seppänen, 1971, p. lxxiv, variable 280.
4. Mentioned were: a youth association, sports club, temperance society, trade union, producers' association, party association, womens' association, religious association, community club, national defence association, other.

References

ALFORD ROBERT R. *Party and Society: The Anglo-American Democracies.* Chicago: Rand McNally, 1963.

ALLARDT, ERIK. *Social struktur och politisk aktivitet.* Borgå: Söderström & Co., 1956.

———. "Social Sources of Finnish Communism: Traditional and Emerging Radicalism." *International Journal of Comparative Sociology* V. (1964): 49–72.

————. "Types of Protest and Alienation." In E. Allardt and S. Rokkan, eds. *Mass Politics: Studies in Political Sociology*. New York: Free Press, 1970, pp. 45–63.

————, and PESONEN, PERTTI. "Cleavages in Finnish Politics." In S. M. Lipset and S. Rokkan, eds. *Party Systems and Voter Alignments*. New York: Free Press, 1967, pp. 325–66.

GYLLING, EDVARD. "Katsaus viime eduskuntavaaleihin." In *Työväen kalenteri 1908*. Helsinki: 1907.

HELANDER, VOITTO, ed. *Vennamolaisuus populistisena joukkoliikkeenä*. Hämeenlinna: Arvi A. Karisto, 1971.

HELLEVUO, TAUNO. "A Review of Market Research Developments in Finland." *Mainosuutiset—The Finnish Magazine of Advertising* (1971): 20–22.

MARTIKAINEN, TUOMO, and SÄNKIAHO, RISTO. *Äänestysaktiivisuus v. 1968 kunnallisvaaleissa I*. University of Helsinki, Institute of Political Science, Research Reports N 16/1969.

NOUSIAINEN, JAAKKO. *Kommunismi Kuopion läänissä*. Joensuu: Pohjois-Karjalan Kirjapaino, 1956.

————. *The Finnish Political System*. Cambridge: Harvard University Press, 1971.

NYHOLM, PEKKA. *Parliament, Government and Multi-Dimensional Party Relations in Finland*. Helsinki: Societas Scientiarum Fennica, 1972.

Official Statistics of Finland, XXIX A:29, 31. Parliamentary Elections 1966 and *1970*. Helsinki: Valtion painatuskeskus, 1966, 1970.

PAAKKINEN, LILJA. "Jatkuvuuden murtuminen valitsijamiesten vaaleissa." In P. Pesonen, ed. *Protestivaalit, nuorisovaalit*. 1972, pp. 180–214.

PESONEN, PERTTI. *An Election in Finland: Party Activities and Voter Reactions*. New Haven: Yale University Press, 1968.

————. "Picturing Elections Abroad: A Study in Finnish Politics." In Oliver Walter, ed. *Political Scientists at Work*. Belmont, Calif.: Duxbury Press, 1971, pp. 106–24.

————, ed. *Protestivaalit, nuorisovaalit: Tutkielmia kansanedustajien vaaleista 1966, 1970 ja 1972*. Helsinki: Ylioppilastuki, 1972.

RANTALA, ONNI. "Finland." In S. Rokkan and J. Meyriat, eds. *International Guide to Electoral Statistics: National Elections in Western Europe, Vol. 1*. The Hague: Mouton, 1969.

RANTALA, ONNI. *Suomen poliittiset alueet I. Poliittisten aatteitten levinneisyys 1907–1958*. Turku: 1970.

RIIHINEN, OLAVI. *Teollistuvan yhteiskunnan alueellinen erilaistuneisuus* (Summary: "Regional Differentiation of Industrial Society"). Porvoo-Helsinki: Werner Söderström, 1965.

SEPPANEN, PAAVO. "Muuttuva yhteiskunta," *Sosiologia* 2 (1965): 73–89.

————. *Suomalainen yhteiskunta (Sosiaalinen muutos aikasarjoina)*. University of Helsinki, Institute of Sociology, Research Reports No: 166, 1971.

Statistical Yearbook of Finland, Year 1969. Helsinki: Central Statistical Office, 1970. (Abbr. SYF 1970.)

Suomi käsikirja. Helsinki: Otava, 1968.

SÄNKIAHO, RISTO. "A Model of the Rise of Populism and Support for the Finnish Rural Party." In E. Rasmussen, ed. *Scandinavian Political Studies Volume 6/1971.* New York: Columbia Univ. Press, 1971.

TARKIAINEN, TUTTU, and RANTALA, ONNI. *Eduskunnan valitseminen 1907–1963. Suomen kansanedustuslaitoksen historia IX.* Helsinki: Eduskunnan historia-komitea, 1971.

TÖRNUDD, KLAUS. *The Electoral System of Finland.* London: Hugh Evelyn, 1968.

WARIS, HEIKKI. *Muuttuva suomalainen yhteiskunta.* Porvoo: Werner Söderström OY, 1968.

7. NORWAY:
Conflict Structure and Mass Politics
in a European Periphery

HENRY VALEN and STEIN ROKKAN

Norway lies at the northwestern periphery of the continental landmass of Europe: a long stretch of land from the North Sea to the Arctic, much of it too mountainous for regular settlement, a country marked by geographical barriers and contrasts in ecological conditions.

What sort of politics would you expect in such a territory? Obviously geography alone could not account for the structure of alignments that emerged in Norway during the early phases of mass politics. Norway is not the only mountainous territory in the world, not the only territory markedly divided by geography and ecology—just think of Scotland, Spain, Switzerland and Austria, of Canada and New Zealand, of the Andean states of Latin America. But all these territories clearly differ in the character of their mass politics. To understand the peculiarities of the developments in Norway we have to analyze a series of complex processes of interaction over time: we have to look at the processes of *center formation* and territorial consolidation, we have to study the variations in the *cultural reach* of the centers and the difficulties of standardization, and we have to find out about differences in the character of the *economic linkages* among the centers and between the centers and the countryside.

Norway in European Geopolitical Space

Let us first place our country within an overall *conceptual map* of the sources of variations within Europe:[1]

This typological–topological map groups the territories of sixteenth–seventeenth century Western Europe on two dimensions: one cultural, the other economic. The north–south axis sorts out the territories by the outcome of the great religious wars: to

---

The authors are indebted to Ragnar Waldahl, who did the computational work, and Sigmund Gronmo, who read the manuscript and made valuable suggestions. But the authors take the full responsibility for the contents.

the north the incorporation of the Church within the growing apparatus of the bureau-cratic nation-states, to the south the cultural dominance of the transterritorial Roman Catholic Church. The economic axis groups the territories to the west and to the east of the great trade route belt of city-states and confederal structures from Venice and Genoa to Amsterdam and Hamburg: to the west the growing political centers allied to the interests of the urban commercial and industrial bourgeoisie, to the east the emerging agrarian bureaucracies deriving their resources from alliances between

Economic Integration of Nation-State

		Seaward Peripheries	Seaward Empire-Nations	City-State Europe	Landward Empire-Nations	Landward Peripheries
	Political Centers:	Weak	Strong	Weak	Strong	Weak
	City Network:	Weak	Strong	Strong	Weak	Weak
Protestant		Iceland				Finland
			← Norway			
			Denmark		Sweden	
			← Scotland			
			England	Northwest Germany	Prussia	Baltic territories
Mixed				Netherlands Rhineland Switzerland		
Catholic		Ireland	France	Belgium Italy	Bavaria	Poland
			Spain Portugal	Catalonia	Austria	Hungary

Cultural Integration of Nation-State — High / Low

the military and the landowners, on both sides and at one remove the peripheries that failed to develop strong enough centers of their own until the nineteenth-century.

Within this schematic map of sixteenth-seventeenth-century Europe Norway will be found in the far northwestern corner: Protestant but on the margin between the "seaward empire-nations" and the "seaward peripheries." Lying beyond the domain of the Roman Empire and for a long time also beyond the reach of the Roman church, Norway was able to build up a distinctive political system of its own quite early in the Middle Ages: on top of the local and the regional institutions of the judicial-legislative *ting* assemblies of free peasants was built a national dynasty and a growing number of territory-wide institutions for defense and taxation. This early state-building phase culminated in the thirteenth-century, the great period of Norwegian imperial dominance across the North Sea and beyond. This medieval state proved short-lived, however, the central structure and its resource base was too weak to overcome the ravages of the Black Death, and the territory succumbed to control from outside. By the sixteenth-century Norway had been integrated in a joint political system with Denmark. The center of this system was Copenhagen: the capital where the great decisions were taken, where the Bible and the other books were printed, where the officials were educated.

In terms of our conceptual map Norway moved into the "seaward periphery" cell of the map during the sixteenth-century: it was a territory without a strong political center of its own. But the move was not complete. By northern European standards Norway still had strong cities closely linked with the European commercial network: politically it was a colony under Denmark but economically it held its own. This economic independence did not create any drive toward cultural autonomy. The two countries had both been Lutheranized after 1536, and the urban bourgeoisie in Norway found no difficulties in accepting the Danish orthographic standards in their writing even though their oral language differed considerably from the Danish.

This situation at the margin goes far to explain the peculiarities of Norwegian mass politics after the establishment of domestic sovereignty under the union with Sweden in 1814: (1) a long tradition of bureaucratic rule and internal order under the absolutist reign of the Danish kings and their officials; (2) a strong urban patriciate, partly of foreign origin, well integrated into the European commercial network; (3) hardly any aristocracy and only few large landowners but a large number of freehold peasants, most of them strongly tied to the local economy and most of them, particularly in the peripheries, still operating at subsistence level, at a low level of monetization.

The constitution of 1814 was essentially a product of a coalition between the territorial bureaucracy and elements of the urban patriciate. But these statemakers also had to rebuild a nation, so they strengthened the new administrative structure by bringing in the independent Norwegian peasantry. The result was the most democratic suffrage provision in Europe at the time: all freehold peasants were given the vote. This set a time bomb ticking: how long would it take for the peasantry to actively make use of these rights and overpower the coalition of officials and patricians?[2]

The peasantry was still highly localized. Only a small proportion had entered into the money economy, and there were only a few traces of cultural mobilization through sectarian movements. The first thrusts of political mobilization came in the 1830s: these were essentially directed against local officials and culminated in the establishment of a law institutionalizing communal self-government in 1837. The decisive thrust came in the 1860s and 1870s through the cumulative impact of several waves of mobilization: first, through rapidly increasing urbanization and the consequent growth of a radical bourgeoisie; secondly, through the spread of religious and other cultural movements across the countryside; finally, through the establishment of campaign organizations at the local level to mobilize voters in elections. These successive waves of mobilization culminated in 1879–82: the result was a decisive coalition in parliament between the urban radicals and large sections of the peasant representatives against the defenders of the king and his officials. This was the beginning of Norwegian mass politics: the party of opposition on the Left (*Venstre*) established itself as a nationwide organization in 1883, and was quickly followed by a parallel organization on the Right (*Hoire*). The original constellation was one of two-party competition, but this did not last long. Once it had won through, the Left was split up again and again, first toward the Right, later toward the Left. To understand these splits and the resulting party system we have to go back to our conceptual map and to our analysis of the crucial phases of political development.

A Model of the Norwegian Conflict System

Norway had its state-building phase during the Middle Ages and during the period of Danish rule. There was a well-established apparatus of extraction and control; the territory had been largely penetrated from the center. But this system was not of the Prussian type: it was kept in check by the patriciates of the different cities and by the large but still inert mass of independent peasants. There was a state but no distinctive national culture. The Reformation had left the heritage of a state church and had prepared the ground for the early introduction of compulsory mass education, but these crucial institutions of nation-building were still dominated by standards set in Copenhagen. As a result the early periods of mass politics were at the same time periods of intensive struggle over issues of nation-building. The Danish standards set during the centuries of political subjection were increasingly rejected, but the new national center was not strong enough or united enough to be able to impose a new set of standards before the decisive waves of peasant mobilization. The result was a protracted battle over the control of the crucial agencies of nation-building: literature, education, religion. The initial battle pitted the nationalist urban intelligentsia and the awakening peasantry against the conservative defenders of the continuities with Danish culture, but this battle over the control of the central legitimizing symbols of the system was crosscut by conflicts over economic issues, first between the urban and the rural economies and later between the privileged owners of businesses or land and the swelling proletariat of rural labor, fishermen, smallholders, and industrial workers.

The struggle over the control of the nation-building process took place during a period of rapid growth of the cities and of accelerated monetization of exchanges between the urban and the rural economies. Thus tensions increased between the bourgeoisie and the peasantry over policies of taxation and resource allocation, and eventually this generated a deep split in the opposition front of the Left. These processes of rapid economic development at the same time deepened the class cleavage in the system, both in the primary economy and in the industrializing communities.

The ancien régime was overthrown by a coalition of the central radicals and the rising peasantry of the peripheries but this victorious initial coalition split up over a succession of issues: (1) *control of the nation-building agencies, the schools and the Church;* (2) protection of the *market for primary economy commodities* against pressures from the industrial and the urban sectors and from abroad; (3) the fight for the interests of the finally enfranchised *rural and urban proletariats of smallholders, fishermen, and workers.*

These three sets of issues produced a complex history of alignments and realignments. In our efforts to analyze these complexities we have found it useful to spell out the relationships between the underlying cleavage and the resulting party fronts in a two-dimensional diagram (Fig. 1) initially inspired by Parson's A–G–I–L paradigm.[3] This paradigm posits three phases of party development: (1) the bipolar

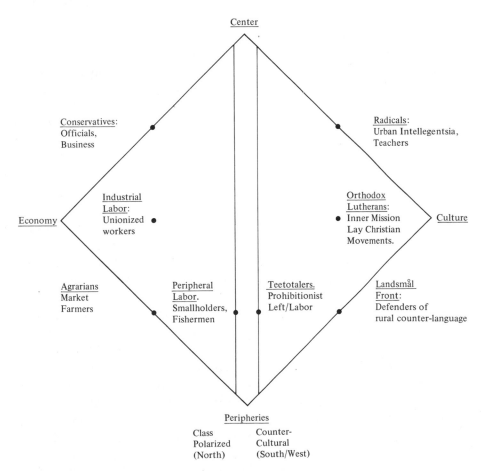

Figure 1: A Model of the Norwegian Cleavage System

Left-Right phase; (2) the phase of successive splitups of the Left coalition; (3) the emergence of the labor coalition of the peripheral rural proletariat and the increasingly mobilized industrial working-class.

The first split in the initial Left opposition came in 1888, when the orthodox fundamentalists of the south and west opposed against the secularized radicals of the center. This division lost in importance after the extension of the suffrage to all men in 1898 and the dissolution of the union with Sweden in 1905. The old Left was again consolidated as the great champion of the counterculture: it allied forces in defense of the rural language *landsmål*, it fought for the democratization of church governance, and it favored strict legislation for the protection of the young against the evils of alcohol. These are still the three crucial variables on the cultural side of Norwegian politics: the position taken for or against the urban vs. the rural linguistic standard, the stand taken on the prohibition issue, the degree of identification with the orthodox wing of the Lutheran church. These variables do not necessarily pull in the same direction in all regions, but they all help to explain variations in electoral behavior within the broad "counter-central" front in Norway.

These three movements pulled together for a generation or so, but with the continuing urbanization and the spread of secularizing ideologies the strains within this large aggregate proved too strong for the party leadership, especially after the introduction of proportional representation in 1920.

Of the three cultural variables the first, the language posture, tended to divide the party the least: the *Venstre* leaders and their followers did not all use *landsmål* themselves, but they identified with the cause and generally offered strong support for the demands for parity for this counter-language. The two other variables proved much more divisive for the old party: the Left was deeply split over the issue of the recognition of the orthodox faculty of theology established in 1906 in protest against the liberal-latitudinarian doctrines of the State University and was even further split in the 'twenties over the prohibition issue. The party was nevertheless able to maintain a show of unity at the polls until 1933, when the first steps were taken toward the establishment of a splinter party on the orthodox wing. This was the *Christian People's party*, first entrenched in the west but from 1945 onward a nationwide movement on a par with the mother party.

The splits along the economic axis began to appear shortly after the introduction of manhood suffrage and the appearance of a socialist workers' party. There was first a split toward the Right: a *National Liberal* party broke off in 1906 and allied itself with the conservatives in an effort to broaden the basis for a united front against the socialists. Very much as in England, the remaining "true Left" was increasingly tempted to mobilize support from the enfranchised urban and rural working-class. In the economically highly divided areas of eastern Norway these efforts led to a split in a socialist direction: a splinter party, the *Worker Democrats*, established itself in some of the provinces of the East and accelerated the decline of the old party in that region of Norway. This process of regional differentiation went even further with the establishment of a distinctive *Agrarian* party during the First World War: this party had its greatest initial successes in the areas with the most market-oriented agriculture in the east and the Tröndelag, but found it much more difficult to compete with the old *Venstre* in the south and the west. This party changed its name in the 'fifties and has now also begun to compete in some urban areas as the *Center* party.

These differentiations all took place within what we have called the "established bloc" of the electorate: the strata already enfranchised at the time of the decisive party-forming struggles of the 1880s. Four of the six parties generated through this process proved viable: the old "Left"—now better translated as the Liberals—the Christians, the Agrarians, and the Conservatives still make up the "bourgeois" bloc of the Norwegian party system. The Worker Democrats disappeared as a distinctive force during the 1930s, and the National Liberals were gradually absorbed by the Conservatives.

The "bloc of the underprivileged" was also divided by geography and ideology. The first electoral successes of the Socialist party came in the northern periphery, the first industrial successes of the union movement in the industrialized east. Much like the *Venstre*, the Socialists were torn between center and periphery. The great struggle over the control of the party after the Russian Revolution was not so much over issues of doctrine as over differences in organizational structure: the winning coalition on the left essentially derived its strength from the peripheries, while the minority wing of Social Democrats found most of its strength in the areas of early industrialization near the center.[4] Much like the old Left the Labor party of the peripheries—particularly in the east and in the Tröndelag and less so up north—derived great strength from the teetotalist movement: alcohol was seen as the great danger to the dignity of the worker and was fought as the symbol of the evils of the threatening urban and foreign capitalist forces. This radicalization of the peripheral proletariat produced an initial alliance with the Comintern in 1918, but this proved short-lived: there was a further split in 1923, this time on the Communist left, and then a merger of the main party with the Social Democrats in 1927.

These developments produced the six-party system of the first period of stable politics after World War II: a *Communist* party, strong in 1945 but seriously weakened after the 1948 *coup* in Czechoslovakia, a dominant Labor party, and then the four parties of the *"established bloc."* The struggle over foreign policy in the early 'sixties brought in a seventh parliamentary party: a splitoff to the left of the governing Labor party. This Socialist People's party held two of the 150 seats in Parliament from 1961 to 1969 and played an important part in the deadlock between Labor and the "bourgeois" bloc in 1963-65. It was deeply split in 1968-69 between a pragmatic-populist and a revolutionary Marxist-Leninist wing; this far-left wing, the youth movement SUF, dramatically left the party that winter. At the 1969 parliamentary election the party suffered a serious loss, but has since then proved able to consolidate itself and must now definitely be counted as an important element in the Norwegian political landscape.

Mass Strength and Parliamentary Power

Figure 2 summarizes the long story of party development in statistical detail. To bring out the decisive contrasts, all except the smallest ephemeral parties have been ordered on an approximate linear dimension and grouped in two opposing blocs: before 1927 the graph gives the balance of strength between the descendants of the original Left and the alliances on the Right; from 1927 onward the graph describes the changes in the balance between the rising "bloc of the underprivileged" and the receding but still very vigorous "established bloc". To make it easier to gauge the strength of the successive blocs on either side of the spectrum we have traced *majority lines* to the left and to the right: the movements of the percentage bars back and forth across these lines tell the story of the succession of equilibria and periods of disruption in Norwegian politics.

Figure 3 illustrates the consequences of these electoral alignments and realignments for the majority-minority balance in parliament and for the party composition of the cabinet. The movements across the majority lines were clearly much more marked at the parliamentary than the electoral level in the early periods of mass politics. As in so many other countries of the West, the extension of the suffrage and the organization of mass parties triggered a series of changes in the electoral institutions. In the ancien régime the elections were decided in two steps: the registered citizens first chose a set of electors for their district and these came together within larger constituencies to choose the members of the Storting. At both stages there were several positions to be filled within each territorial unit, and the decision was by plurality: the candidates gathering the largest numbers of votes were elected. With the rise of mass parties these procedures proved increasingly cumbersome and in many cases also led to arbitrary results. The first reform came six years after the introduction of manhood suffrage: from 1906 onward the members of parliament were elected in single-member constituencies without intermediaries. By contrast to the Swedes and the Finns the Norwegian leaders rejected proportional representation at that stage: the struggle over the breakup of the union with Sweden had produced a brief spell of "centrist" politics and a great deal of assistance to the recognition of parties as permanent elements of the political landscape. For twelve years the elections in Norway were run on the French model: absolute majority required in the first *tour*, a runoff if no candidate reached this level. This system no doubt accelerated the fragmentation of the party system: it encouraged local deals and accentuated regional contrasts in alignments. It also increased quite markedly the threshold against the emerging working-class party: as the graphs show the Labor party reached near-equality in votes with the old Left in 1915 (32.1 vs. 33.1 percent) and surpassed it in 1918 (31.6 vs. 28.3 percent) but still gained much fewer seats, largely because of countercoalition in the second *tour* (1915: 19 Labor vs. 74 Left; 1918: 18 vs. 51). The Labor party pressed forward demands for electoral reform, and the established parties gave way: the first election under proportional representation took place in 1921. The crucial factor in this decision was the conflict within the established bloc: the Left as well as the Right

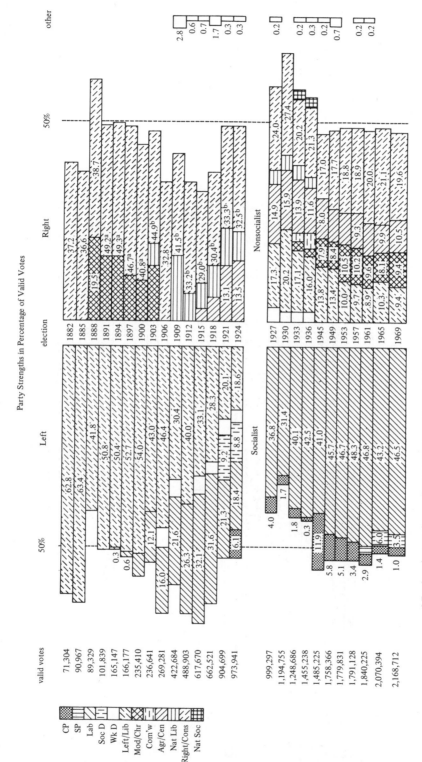

Figure 2: The Voting Strength of the Norwegian Parties, 1882–1969

[a] For these elections, the statistics do not distinguish Moderate and Right votes.

[b] For these elections, the statistics do not distinguish National Liberal and Right votes.

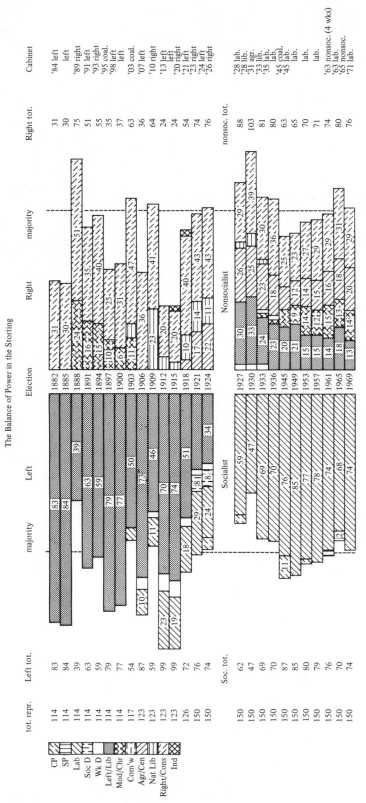

Figure 3: The Political Composition of Parliaments and Cabinets in Norway, 1882–1969

feared the rising strength of the Labor party and knew that it might quickly reach a majority position once it crossed the threshold. But they were unwilling to merge in a broad national coalition against Labor: they preferred the safer strategy of proportionalization.

The procedure introduced in 1921 was the d'Hondt list system. This favoured the leading Labor party, but the three nonsocialist parties were able in 1930 to force a revision that allowed them to establish local list alliances to offset this effect without forcing full mergers. This did not stop the advance of the Labor party toward the majority point: 42.5 percent of the votes and seventy seats in 1936; 41 percent and seventy-six of the 150 seats in 1945. With this slight majority in hand the party proceeded to abolish the list-alliance rule and then demonstrated the importance of this brake on overrepresentation at the election of 1949: they gained 45.7 percent of the votes and as many as eighty-five of the 150 seats. This set the stage for the great compromise of 1952: the Labor party reduced the level of overrepresentation by switching from d'Hondt to the Sainte-Laguë procedure but gained an important advantage through the merger of urban with rural constituencies. The system established in 1952 is still valid: this groups the country in as many multimember constituencies as there are *fylker* (provinces) and assigns the seats among the party lists by dividing the votes cast for each successively by 1.4, 3, 5, 7 and the further odd numbers. The initial devisor of 1.4 still sets a high threshold for smaller parties and produces some overrepresentation of the medium-sized and the larger parties. There is still no complete proportionality, and a variety of schemes have been proposed to tighten the fit between voting strength and shares of seats: the most popular ones call for proportionalizing mandates-at-large of the Danish and the Swedish type.[5]

Notes to Figs. 2 and 3

Norwegian name	*Elections*	*English translation*	*Abbreviation*
Norges Kommunistiske Parti	1924–	Communist Party	CP
Sosialistisk Folkeparti	1961	Socialist People's Party	SP
Det Norske Arbeiderparti	1894–	Labor Party	Lab.
Norges Socialdemokratiske Arbeiderparti	1921–24	Social Democrats	Soc. D.
Arbeiderdemokratene	1906–18	Worker Democrats	Wk. D.
Radikale Folkeparti	1921–36		
Venstre		Left 1882–1924	Left.
	1882–	Liberals 1924–	Lib.
Moderate	1888–03	Moderates	Mod.
Kristelig Folkeparti	1933–	Christian People's Party	Chr.
Samfunnspartiet	1933–49	Commonwealth Party	Com'w.
Landmandsforbundet	1915–18		
Bondepartiet	1921–53	Agrarians/Centre	Agr./Cen.
Senterpartiet	1957–		
Frisinnede Venstre	1909–30		
Frisinnede Folkeparti	1933–36	National Liberals	Nat. Lib.
		Right 1882–1924	Right
Høire (Høyre)	1882–	Conservatives 1927–	Cons.
Nasjonal Samling	1933–36	National Socialists	Nat. Soc.

This ordering of the parties from a working-class left to a nationalist-elitist extreme right is not based on any detailed analysis of the dimensions of policy disagreements and the likelihood of coalitions. In its basic structure this ordering has been confirmed through analyses of differences in attitudes toward Labor policies, but the placement of some of the minor parties in the middle range of the spectrum is questionable and should not be interpreted to reflect detailed research on the "dimensionalities" of Norwegian politics.

Separate figures for the votes cast for the Moderates and Right have only been established for 1888, see *Indstilling S.XX* (1890). For subsequent elections through 1903 the combined percentage strength of the two groups has been entered under "Right" in Figure 2 and only approximate distributions have been indicated on the basis of the known ratios of seats.

Separate figures for the National Liberals and the Right are not given in the statistics from 1909 to 1924. In Figure 2 the percentages given for the Right therefore refer to the totals for these two parties.

The Seven Dimensions and the Five Parties

These changes in the conditions of electoral action only marginally affected the fundamentals of the national system of conflict alignments: in fact, it may be argued that the changes in the electoral arrangements were direct products of the processes of conflict articulation and conflict aggregation triggered by the waves of mobilization since the 1880s.

In our reading of the history of Norwegian mass politics seven dimensions of cleavage stand out as crucial in the structuring of alternatives and in the alignments of the electorate.

First, *geography*: the contrast between the eastern center and the two peripheries, the countercultural southwest and the class-polarized north.

Secondly, the three *cultural* dimensions: (1) the conflict over *linguistic* policy, between the defenders of the established central standard *riksmål* and the protagonists of the rural counter-language, now officially called *nynorsk* (New Norwegian); (2) the conflict over *moral* legislation, quite particularly the control over the production and consumption of *alcohol*; (3) the conflict over the control of the *church*, now largely a contrast between the active Christians, mostly Orthodox Lutherans closely attached to lay religious bodies, and the substantive majority of religiously indifferent citizens, most of them (95 percent) members of the state church but taking very little part in services beyond the rituals of baptism, marriage, and funerals.

Thirdly, three *economic* dimensions: (1) *the rural-urban conflict in the commodity market*—the battle between market farmers and the various urban interests over the control of prices and subsidies; (2) the *rural class struggle* of laborers, smallholders and fishermen against their local superiors and the urban establishment; (3) the *industrial class struggle* of the unionized working-class against owners and employers and their corporate organizations.

These seven sets of dimensions combined to produce the system of five major parties of the 'fifties:

These are the seven dimensions and the five parties we shall focus on in our analysis. We shall also on occasion give the breakdowns for the two minor parties on the Left, the CP and Socialist People's party, but none of the seven dimensions can be said to have any decisive weight in accounting for the differences between their electorates and that of the Labor party. The split offs toward the socialist Left can to some extent be explained in center-periphery terms: the CP established strongholds in the forestry areas of the east and in the far north, and the Socialist People's party established an interesting alliance between an intellectual stronghold in the capital and a series of concentration points in the peripheral north. But the crucial dimensions of cleavage were in both cases at the interelite and the intersystem level: the two parties rejected the policies of the majority faction within Labor not only in the domestic arena but also in foreign affairs, the CP allying itself with the Soviet Union, the Socialist People's party violently opposing both the Atlantic alliance and the European Economic Community.

Our developmental analysis of the party system suggests that the electoral alternatives were generated through the interaction over time of these basic dimensions of cleavage. But are there still the dimensions that count for the rank-and-file of the electorate? This is the first of the questions we shall try to tackle in our analysis of data

Dimension	Party: LABOR	LEFT – LIB.	CHR.	AGR.	CONS.
Geography					
S/W Opposition to Center		Opp→Opp	Opp		Def
North vs. Center	Opp				(Def)
Culture					
Language Opposition		Opp→Opp			Def
Teetotaler Opposition	(Opp)	Opp——————→Opp split			Def
Religious Opposition		Opp——————→Opp			Def
Economy					
Rural Opposition to Urban Interests		Opp————————————→Opp split			Def
Rural Class Opposition	Opp			Def	(Def)
Industrial Class Opposition	Opp				Def

Note: Opp = alignment in opposition to dominant elite on given dimension.
Def = defensive alignment.
(Opp) or (Def) = contributory element in the electoral aggregate.

on electoral behavior in Norway. In earlier writings we have made extensive use of *ecological* data in analyzing the dimensions of electoral behavior in Norway.[6] In this chapter we shall focus our analysis on data from *sample surveys:* we carried out one nationwide and one local sample survey during the very calm election of 1957[7] and organized further nationwide surveys in the realigning election of 1965 and in the "ins-outs" confrontation of 1969.[8] Most of the analyses in this chapter will bear on data from the interviews collected before and after the election of 1965.

We shall first use the data to review the evidence for the weight of the seven dimensions taken one by one. We shall next combine a number of these dimensions in an overall sociocultural matrix for Norway and discuss the evidence cell by cell. We shall then offer a detailed analysis of the interaction of some of these variables and try to pin down the configurations that help to account for the greatest portions of the variance in electoral behavior. We shall finally ask questions about the stability of our findings and discuss possible sources of change in the alignments we have analyzed.

Inherited Identities and Current Electoral Alignments

Let us now review a series of tables from the 1965 sample survey for evidence of the continuing impact of the historical dimensions of cleavage.

We shall specify for each of the historical dimensions the variables or combinations of variables we have used as indicators. In each of the tables the dependent variables will be the party choice of the survey respondent as reported in the post-election interview: the respondents checked off as nonvoters in the electoral registers have not been included in these tables.

GEOGRAPHY

To bring out the essential features of Norwegian electoral geography we have combined two of the dimensions in our original paradigm: the center-periphery dimension and the urban-rural dimension (see Table 1).

The data tells us a great deal about the continuing importance of the inherited alignments:

Party	Strongholds	Weakest support
Conservatives	Urban areas of the east, particularly Oslofjord	All rural areas
Agrarians/Center	All rural areas: no regional differentiation	All urban areas
Christians	Rural areas of south/west	Rural areas outside south/west
Liberals	Rural *and urban* areas of south/west	Other regions: no difference between urban and rural areas.
Labor	Rural areas in east, both urban and rural areas in north	Rural areas in south/west
Socialist People's party	Urban areas in east and north	South/west

These patterns of territorial differentiation are consistent with findings from a number of earlier elections.[9] In fact, the territorial variations show remarkable stability over time. The question is to what extent are these variations due to differential geographical distributions on variables reflecting one or more of the other conflict dimensions? This question will be a major concern in the subsequent section.

CULTURE

Tables 2-4 offer evidence of the impact of the three cultural dimensions on voter alignments: the position on the language issue, the attitude to alcohol, the level of religious activity.

All three middle parties have positive values on these difference scores: they recruit more voters within each of the countercultural movements. But there are important differences among the three middle parties. The Liberal party, the residual of the old Left, gains most on the language dimension but little on the religious score. The Christian People's party is most distinctive on the religious score but gains heavily on the

TABLE 1: **Electoral Behavior by Region and Urbanization, 1965 Survey, in Percentages**

	SPARSELY POPULATED			DENSELY POPULATED		
	East	*South/ West*	*Middle/ North*	*East*	*South/ West*	*Middle/ North*
Comm.	0	0	1	2	1	1
Soc. PP	4	2	2	8	3	10
Labor	54	30	51	45	46	54
Liberal	6	19	8	6	23	8
Christian	1	14	1	6	8	9
Center	22	22	24	1	2	6
Conser.	13	13	13	32	17	12
Total	100	100	100	100	100	100
N	305	263	199	424	178	113

Densely populated areas consist of cities, towns, and rural communes in which at least 75 percent of the population live in agglomerations; all other communes are classed as sparsely populated.

teetotalist dimension as well. The Center party is much less of a countercultural party: it is essentially the political wing of an economic interest group but gains its votes in rural areas moderate to strong in countercultural opposition.

The two parties opposing each other at the economic end of our basic paradigm (Fig. 1) both score negatively on these cultural dimensions. The Labor party never actively opposed the rural counter-language *nynorsk* but clearly attracts fewer voters within that camp than among the less activist of the *riksmål* users (26 percent vs. 55 percent). The Conservative party was always a strong champion of the standard urban language, even though it has had to adjust to local majorities in the south/west: this party has the strongest support among the *riksmål* activists and is very weak on the *nynorsk* side (36 percent vs. 8 percent). There is a similar pattern for teetotalism: the Labor party is strong among the indifferent groups in the middle (48 percent and 55 percent vs. 34 percent and 31 percent at the teetotalist and the proalcohol extremes) while the Conservative party is very weak (8 percent) among active teetotalers and remarkably strong (41 percent) within the group rejecting the current alcohol restrictions. The tendency is the opposite direction on the third of our cultural variables, religious activity. On this score the differential for Labor is particularly strong (50 percent for the religiously inactive and the low scorers, only 21 percent for members of religious organizations) while quite weak for the Conservative party (24 percent vs. 14 percent).

The three cultural variables are clearly highly intercorrelated and generally tend to work in the same directions in political terms. But there are nevertheless striking differences among the three: this goes for the three countercultural parties in the

TABLE 2: **Electoral Behavior by Language Preference, 1965 Survey, in Percentages**

	LANGUAGE PREFERENCE			
	Nynorsk, active	Nynorsk, inactive	Riksmål, inactive	Riksmål, active
Comm.	0	0	1	1
Soc. PP	1	3	7	2
Labor	26	44	55	33
Liberal	26	14	8	11
Christian	13	16	3	6
Center	24	16	12	11
Conser.	10	7	14	36
Total	100	100	100	100
N	113	148	816	401

The respondents were asked: "Which form of the Norwegian language do you prefer to use when you are writing, *nynorsk* (New Norwegian) or *bokmål/riksmål* (Classical Norwegian)?" and "How strongly are you interested in the language question; would you say you are very interested, somewhat interested, or not much interested?" Interested and somewhat interested replies have been combined as "active".

TABLE 3: **Electoral Behavior by Teetotalist Activity, 1965 Survey, in Percentages**

	Teetotaler, active	Teetotaler, inactive	Nonteetotaler, accepts alcohol policies	Nonteetotaler, rejects alchohol policies
Comm.	0	1	1	1
Soc. PP	2	4	5	8
Labor	34	48	55	31
Liberal	18	8	9	11
Christian	23	4	1	0
Center	15	15	14	8
Conser.	8	20	15	41
Total	100	100	100	100
N	323	75	798	280

The respondents were asked: "Do you consider yourself to be a teetotaler, or do you happen to take a drink from time to time?" If teetotaler: "How strongly are you interested in the question of total abstinence; would you say you are strongly interested, somewhat interested, or not much interested?" For nonteetotalers: "As you know, in this country government has put into effect many measures regulating the use of alcohol. What do you think of these rules: do you think the rules are too strict or too lenient?"

middle of the spectrum no less than for the two class-polarized parties at each end. This must be due partly to interactive affects among the three variables themselves and partly to differences in their political weight within different geographical and socio-

TABLE 4: Electoral Behavior by Level of Religious Activity, 1965 Survey, in Percentages

	RELIGIOUS ACTIVITY			
	None	*Low*	*Middle*	*High: member of religious organizations*
Comm.	1	1	0	0
Soc. PP	8	4	2	1
Labor	48	53	47	21
Liberal	10	9	13	14
Christian	0	2	7	35
Center	9	14	17	15
Conser.	24	17	14	14
Total	100	100	100	100
N	617	373	323	160

Religious activity score	*Attendance in previous month:*		
	Religious meetings/ services	Religious programs on radio or television	Membership in religious organizations
None	0 and/or	0—1	0
Low	1—2 and/or	2	0
Middle	3 or more and/or	3 or more	0
High	Any value	Any value	1 or more

These three variables clearly bring out the countercultural character of the three middle parties, the offshoots of the old Left:

	Percentage differences in electoral strength between highest and lowest category for each cultural variable		
	Language	Teetotalism	Religious activity
Labor	−29	−21	−32
Middle parties			
Liberal	+18	+10	+ 4
Christian	+13	+23	+35
Center	+13	+ 7	+ 6
Conser.	−29	—33	−10

economic environments. Before we analyze such multivariate effects we shall, however, first have to present a few straightforward breakdowns by occupation and education.

ECONOMY

In our basic model of the Norwegian cleavage system we posited three basic economic dimensions: (1) the conflict between the *rural and the urban economies*; (2) the *class* struggle in the *primary* economy; (3) the *class* struggle in the *secondary/tertiary* sectors.

These three oppositions can be graphically represented in a simple triangle of electoral fronts[10] as follows:

In this model the system is given three distinct economic poles: labor, business, and the farm interest. Each pole has found expression in a set of articulate economic organizations, and each of these is reflected in one dominant political party. The electoral fronts fall largely between the three poles. Between poles L and B Labor and other socialist parties compete with the Conservative, Liberal, and Christian parties for the votes of the new middle-class. Between poles B and F the four nonsocialist parties keep on struggling for the votes of the petty bourgeoisie and the economically independent, particularly the citizens who have moved from the farms into urban occupations. Between poles L and F Labor competes with the Center, Liberal, and Christian parties for the votes of smallholders and fishermen.

In terms of our original paradigm the electoral fronts between F and B and between F and L express conflicts in the *commodity* market: fights over prices and subsidies between the producers and the consumers of food and other primary economy commodities. By contrast the F–L and the B–L fronts reflect conflicts in the market for *labor*: fights over the wages and the status of economically dependent workers and employees. The F–L front represents the dimension of *rural* class cleavage in our paradigm, the B–L front the *urban–industrial* class cleavage. This set of correspondences helps to pin down an important dilemma of aggregation: the Labor party aggregates on the L–B front by attracting the new middle-class of better-educated salaried employees but risks conflicts within its own ranks over the price-salary balance by maintaining its strong wing in the primary sector. In fact there is a significant asymmetry in the triangle: the Labor party is engaged in a double price-wage struggle on the F–L front (better prices for primary products, particularly fish, better wages for workers and other "have-nots" in the primary economy), while the Conservatives fight different parties in the two markets: the Agrarians on the B–F front and the Labor party on the B–L front. This asymmetry goes far to account for the difficulties of the Labor party in the great controversy over Norway's entry into the Common Market although the likely effects of membership are disputed, a great number of leaders and voters hold the opinion that this would favor the industrial labor market, which it has generally, but would also bring about greater hardships for the primary economy.

In our attempts to translate this model into a set of survey tabulations we have depended essentially on two variables: occupation and education.

Table 5 presents the distributions of party choices by major occupational groups. The occupations have been roughly categorized in terms of the poles and the interfaces in Figure 4: workers at Pole L; higher private employees, independent professionals, self-employed and employers at Pole B; farmers and forest owners at Pole F; a variety

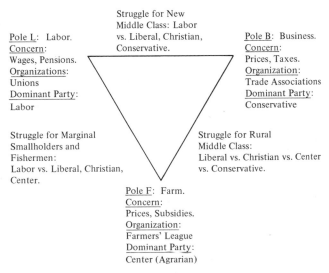

Figure 4: A Model of the Electoral "Fronts" in
Norway: The Functional-Economic Dimensions

of intermediary categories at the L–B and the L–F interfaces (the number of respondents in occupational categories at the B–F interface is too small for a sample of this size).

The tables show clearly that the occupations placed at the three poles offer high levels of support to their distinctive parties:

Pole *L*: 68 percent for Labor, 76 percent for the three socialist parties
Pole *B*: 51–62 percent for the Conservative party
Pole *F*: 64 percent for the Center party

At the L–B interface the party divisions vary markedly by occupational status as well by the type of employer. We find 55 percent for Labor among the lower-middle-class personnel in the public sector and 43 percent for the same category in private employment as against only 25 percent among higher-level employees in the public sector. We find roughly inverse differentiation for the Conservative party: 18, 24, and 35 percent. The public-private contrast is no longer as strong as it once was,[11] but is still of some importance in differentiating between Liberals and Conservatives. The Liberals were traditionally stronger at the lower ranks of public service. This can still be seen in the difference for lower clerical-technical personnel: 16 percent Liberal vs. 18 percent Conservative in the public sector, 14 percent vs. 24 percent in private employment. The Liberals have retained a strong hold on artisans and other self-employed citizens who do not hire any help: in this category we find 37 percent Labor, 20 percent Liberal, and 28 percent Conservative as against 9, 16, and 62 percent for employers.

TABLE 5:   **Electoral Choice by Major Occupational Categories, in Percentages**

POLE OR INTERFACE IN FIG. 4:

	L		L—B			B		L—F	F
	Workers	Clerical and technical personnel, public employment	Clerical, sales and technical personnel, private	Independents, without hired help	Higher-salaried employee, public	Higher-salaried employees, private	Independents, with hired help and professionals	Small-holders, fishermen	Farmers, forest owners
Comm.	1	0	1	2	1	1	0	0	1
Soc. PP	7	4	9	3	3	3	1	2	0
Labor	68	55	43	37	25	22	9	39	10
Liberal	8	16	14	20	16	13	16	11	7
Christian	6	4	4	3	10	7	7	4	9
Center	4	3	5	7	10	3	5	30	64
Conser.	6	18	24	28	35	51	62	14	9
TOTAL	100	100	100	100	100	100	100	100	100
N	634	68	109	76	122	121	60	150	122

Respondents classified either by own occupation or by occupation of head of household.

The sample allows less differentiation at the L–F front. The figure for small holders and fishermen confirms their intermediary position: 39 percent for Labor at this interface as against 68 percent at the L pole and 10 percent at the F pole. By contrast to the situation at the L–B interface, the major competitor for votes at this front is the Center party: the Liberals and the Conservatives count very little in this struggle.

Summarizing the evidence in Table 5 we might say that status differences weigh heavily in the urban sector, most markedly for Labor (maximum percentage-point difference by status, 59) and the Conservatives (max., 56), much less for the two counter cultural parties (Liberals, 12; Christians, 6). In the rural sector the politics of class struggle do not come out so clearly in the aggregate: a percentage-point difference of 29 for Labor vs. 34 for the Center party. These figures might have been higher if we had included the primary economy workers at the L–F interface, but there are too few of these, and in a sample of this size there seemed to be little sense in recategorizing a minor group just for the sake of symmetry. In any case other tables show enormous variations by type of locality in the electoral choices of the rural proletariat: there is little point, therefore, in differentiating further at the level of the total nationwide sample.

Table 6 adds further evidence of the importance of social status in determining electoral choice. For the parties at the ends of the L–B poles in our diagram there are near-linear regressions by educational level: for Labor the percentages are 62, 41 and 25; for the Conservatives there is a reverse series—6, 19 and 41. The progression for

TABLE 6 : **Electoral Behavior by Years of Formal Education, 1965 Survey, in Percentages**

	Elementary education only	*Further education: less than 3½ years*	*Further education: more than 3½ years*
Comm.	1	*	1
Soc. PP	6	4	4
Labor	62	41	25
Liberal	8	12	15
Christian	5	8	5
Center	12	16	9
Conser.	6	19	41
Total	100	100	100
N	615	540	327

*Less than 0.5 percent

the Liberals is much less marked, and the figures for the Christians show no significant differences by educational level : this corresponds roughly to the results for this party in the table for occupational differences. The most striking difference between Table 5 and 6 bears on the Center party, generally a party of the "haves" in the local community, but few with much education beyond the primary school and various vocational courses. The educational variable essentially helps to measure status within the mobile urban population: school certificates count throughout the territory; land counts mainly in your local community.

So much for each of the seven dimensions one by one. But how do these variables interact in producing votes for the different parties? This is the question we shall proceed to examine on the next pages.

A Sociocultural Matrix for the Analysis of Norwegian Politics

Our basic findings so far suggest a two fold configuration: a set of territorial cultural variables seems to count most in differentiating the parties of the middle from those of the Left and of the Right; a set of functional-economic variables helps to contrast the socialists from the conservatives. Let us now look at the possible combinations of these economic variables with the cultural ones.

With the sample at hand we cannot combine in one matrix all the cultural variables with all the economic ones: this would produce many cells with too few cases for analysis. We have therefore chosen to group the cases by region, type of locality, and occupational status and to dichotomize each of the resulting 2 x 2 x 2 cells by one cultural variable at the time.

The dichotomies have been chosen to maximize the differentiations by party:

For region we have contrasted the countercultural south/west with the aggregate of all the other territories.

For type of locality we have contrasted all communes with more than 75 percent of the population in agglomerations with all the others.

For occupational status we have grouped workers, smallholders, and fishermen in a "*low*" category and scored all the others "high."

Figures 5 – 7 give the resulting sociocultural matrixes. On the language dimension we have dichotomized between *nynorsk* and *riksmål/bokmål* users: this gives a

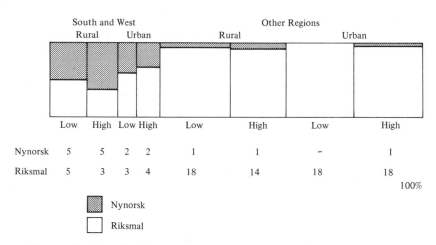

	South and West				Other Regions			
	Rural		Urban		Rural		Urban	
	Low	High	Low	High	Low	High	Low	High
Nynorsk	5	5	2	2	1	1	–	1
Riksmal	5	3	3	4	18	14	18	18

100%

▨ Nynorsk
☐ Riksmal

Figure 5: Distribution of Language: By Region, Urbanization, and Occupational Status (Total area=100 percent)

breakdown for the entire sample of 17 vs. 83 percent, but the cut will be seen to vary enormously with region and type of locality. The other dichotomies are a bit more even: 27 percent are reported teetotalers, and 32 percent can be scored high on religious activity. In all the three cases the rural areas of the south/west differ markedly from the rest of the territory: these areas constitute the strongholds of the countercultural movements. It is clear that a great deal of the variance by region can be explained by this concentration on the three cultural variables. The urbanized areas of the south/west differ less markedly from the rest of the country: the difference is most marked for language and religion, least for teetotalism within the urban working-class.

There is no similar effect for occupational status: in the great majority of cases the control for occupational status does not reduce the variance in countercultural posture.

The only major difference by status is found on the teetotalism dimension (Fig. 6). There is a higher teetotalist score in the middle-class than in the working-class in the urban areas of the south/west, while there is a difference in the reverse direction both in the rural and in the urban areas of the other regions. On the religious score there is

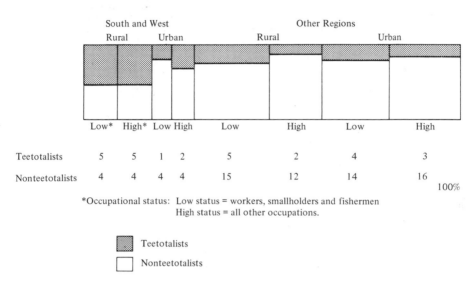

*Occupational status: Low status = workers, smallholders and fishermen
High status = all other occupations.

| | Teetotalists |
| | Nonteetotalists |

Figure 6: Distribution of Teetotalism: By Region, Urbanization, and Occupational Status (Total area = 100 percent)

a similar but less pronounced contrast between the regions, this time only in the rural areas: higher religiosity in the upper status categories than in the lower in the south/west, slightly higher scores for the lower than the higher status in the other regions.

The message of the three graphs is clear: the rural south/west owes most of its political distinctiveness to its countercentral culture. Once we control for the cultural dimensions there is not much left to explain in terms of sheer geography. In the appendix we have presented three detailed tables for the party distributions within the 2 x 2 x 2 x 2 electorates: the first shows the impact of the *language* position on political choice in each group, the second the impact of *teetotalism*, and the third of *religious* activity. These tables are hard to read: we have included them for the benefit of readers who wish to pursue the multivariate analysis further. To simplify the presentation we have extracted from these basic tables a few summaries by region and type of community and given difference scores (see Tables 7 – 14).

Let us first look at the joint rates for the three *socialist* parties: there are differences among these on some of the background variables, but with a sample of this size we cannot go far in the analysis of the small parties to the left of the Labor party. We have already established that the three cultural variables tend to reduce the pull of the socialist parties. We also know that the socialist vote is strongly dependent on class position. Our question is, what is the impact of the cultural variables when we control for class position?

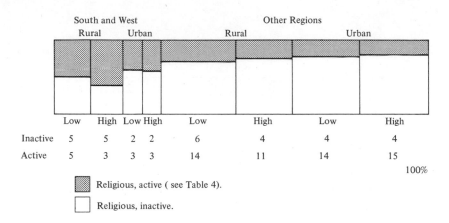

	Low	High	Low	High	Low	High	Low	High
Inactive	5	5	2	2	6	4	4	4
Active	5	3	3	3	14	11	14	15

Religious, active (see Table 4).

Religious, inactive.

Figure 7. Distribution of Religious Fundamentalism: By Region, Urbanization, and Occupational Status (Total area = 100 percent)

Tables A, B, and C demonstrate that citizens of low occupational status are far more inclined to vote socialist than those of higher status. And the tendency is consistent when we control for region and urbanization. A comparison of the socialist propensities of low-versus high-status citizens by their position on the three cultural variables reveals quite marked differences between regions.

Let us first look at the data for the south/west in Table 7.

Practically without exception, the countercultural electorates are less inclined than the others to vote socialist. However, the countercultures make markedly greater inroads on the socialist vote in the lower-than in higher-status groups. This tendency is consistent for all cultural variables in the south/west region.

The rural working-class, the smallholders, and the fishermen are clearly much more sensitive to countercultural pressures than their counterparts in the urban areas. Evidence from other analyses suggests that this in itself is an effect of social-structure: the rural south/west tends to have smaller holdings and is on the whole more egalitarian in structure. As a result the occupational status distinctions do not count as heavily in determining the vote: this leaves much more room for the purely cultural influences on politics.

The general conclusions are clear :

1. The countercultures have built up the greatest pressures on political alignments in the areas where they command local majorities: there is a much stronger spillover effect to politics wherever they have been able to build up strong community pressures.

2.   They have created much more efficient barriers against the spread of socialist politics in the *rural* areas and have their greatest impact on the politics of the *lower strata* of these communities: there is simply less leeway for such effects among the farmers and the rural middle-class.

TABLE 7: **Proportions Voting Socialist in the South/West: By Urbanization, Occupational Status, and Position on Three Cultural Variables**

| | RURAL | | URBAN | |
	Low Status	*High Status*	*Low Status*	*High Status*
Language:				
Riksmål	55	14	78	34
Nynorsk	37	20	50	44
Difference	− 18	+ 6	− 28	+ 10
Nonteetotalist	70	20	73	42
Teetotalist	26	15	46	27
Difference	− 44	− 5	− 27	− 15
Religious Activity:				
Inactive	63	26	78	33
Active	29	11	50	40
Difference	− 34	− 15	− 28	+ 7

3.   In the areas of maximal strength the counterculture even affects the voting of citizens beyond the immediate organizational reach: Table 8 shows lower proportions voting socialist in the south/west even among those who do *not* identify with the movements.

In the other regions (Table 8) the cultural dimensions carry less weight and do not affect voting the same way in all cells. The language issue affects such a low proportion of the electorates outside the south/west that we cannot give reliable figures for a small sample such as this. The other two dimensions produce their strongest impact within the *urban working-class:* this is the reverse of the finding for the south/west. Within the higher status groups there is a clear difference between the influence of the stand on alcoholism and the influence of religion. Within the better-off stratum in the countryside teetotalism does make some difference: the differential is 16. But there is no effect of religion. There is a tendency in the reverse direction in the urban areas: teetotalism makes much less of a difference than religion within both occupational strata. These differences cannot be explained at the individual level of analysis: the south/west differs from the other regions not only in the strength of the countercultural movements but also in the character of the rural and the urban class oppositions and in the party alternatives open to the citizens in their localities.

To get closer to an understanding of these contrasts we shall first look at variations in Conservative strength: Table 9 gives the variations in votes for this party by geography and cultural identity for the higher strata of voters.

The urban-rural differences turn out to be much less marked in the south/west than in the other regions. The Conservatives are weak both in the urban and in the rural areas of the south/west. In the other regions they score roughly twice as many votes in the urban areas as in the rural: this is the case whatever the cultural identity.

TABLE 8: **Proportions Voting Socialist in Rural Areas: By Occupational Status and Region**

| | LOW STATUS | | | HIGH STATUS | | |
	South/ West	Other Regions	Diff.	South/ West	Other Regions	Diff.
Language:						
Riksmål	55	74	− 19	14	34	− 20
Nynorsk	37	75	− 38	20	20	0
Difference	− 18	+ 1		+ 6	− 14	
Nonteetotalists	70	74	− 4	20	36	− 10
Teetotalists	26	76	− 50	15	20	− 5
Difference	− 44	+ 2		− 5	− 16	
Religious Activity:						
Inactive	63	75	− 12	26	33	− 7
Active	29	69	− 40	11	33	− 22
Difference	− 34	− 6		− 15	0	

In the urban south/west the Conservative party loses on all the three cultural dimensions, quite particularly on the language issue (31 percent Conservative among *riksmål* voters, 3 percent among *nynorsk*). In the urban areas of the other regions

TABLE 9: **Proportions Voting Conservative within Higher Status Groups: By Region and Urbanization**

| | SOUTH AND WEST | | | OTHER REGIONS | | |
	Urban	Rural	Difference	Urban	Rural	Difference
Language:						
Riksmål	34	26	+ 8	48	23	+ 25
Nynorsk	3	15	− 12	*	7	(− 7)
Difference	− 31	− 11		(− 48)	− 16	
Nonteetotalist	28	27	+ 1	50	24	+ 26
Teetotalist	17	12	+ 5	34	8	+ 26
Difference	− 11	− 15		− 16	− 16	
Religious Activity:						
Inactive	29	24	+ 5	48	27	+ 21
Active	20	16	+ 4	45	8	+ 37
Difference	− 9	− 8		− 3	− 19	

*No Cases.

there are marked differences for language (differential 48) and teetotalism (16), but hardly any on religion (3): the urban bourgeoisie in these areas is much more conformist in religious matters while overwhelmingly liberal in its posture on alcohol legislation and of course very much against the rural counterlanguage.

The *Center* party, the old Agrarians, is much less affected by the countercultures (see Table 10). The party gains most of its votes among the better-off farmers and is

TABLE 10: **Proportions Voting for the Center Party in Rural Areas: By Region and Occupational Status**

	LOW STATUS			HIGH STATUS		
	South/ West	Other Regions	Difference	South/ West	Other Regions	Difference
Language:						
Nynorsk	17	14	3	34	46	− 12
Riksmål	12	12	0	22	34	− 12
Difference	+ 5	+ 2		+ 12	+ 12	
Teetotalist	16	16	0	27	44	− 17
Nonteetotalist	13	13	0	32	33	− 1
Difference	− 3	− 3		− 5	+ 11	
Religious Activity:						
Active	15	15	0	31	40	− 9
Inactive	14	14	1	28	33	− 5
Difference	+ 1	+ 1		+ 3	+ 7	

strongest in the more class-polarized areas outside the south/west. Within the south/west the party gains most on the language dimension (differential 12), and very little on the other dimensions (religion: 3; teetotalism: –5). In the other regions there are slight gains on all three counts but the dominant factor is clearly economic position (differentials roughly twice those for the south/west).

The findings for the Conservatives and for the Center party tell us more about the character of the contrasts in political structure between the regions. In the south/west the Center faces real competition for the rural votes both from the Liberals and the Christians. In the other regions the main competitors are the Labor party and, in the north, the Conservatives. In the urban areas the Conservatives face one type of opposition in the south/west, a very different one in the other regions. In the cities of the south/west the Conservatives have to fight not only the Labor party but must compete with the Christians for votes in the lower-middle-class and with the Liberals in the better-off strata. The countercultures affect not only the overall position of the Labor party but also the character of the struggle within the established urban strata. In the other regions there are much stronger tendencies toward polarization: Labor vs. Center in the typically agricultural areas, Labor vs. Conservatives in the cities.

To clarify these differences let us look at the Christian and the Liberal parties in their old stronghold, the south/west. Table 11 gives details for the Christian party, Table 12 for the Liberals.

The Christian party could hardly fail to gain most on the religious dimension. It is interesting, however, to see that the differential is almost equally high for

TABLE 11: Proportions Voting Christian in the South/West: By Urbanization and Occupational Status

| | RURAL | | | | URBAN | |
	Low Status	High Status	Difference	Low Status	High Status	Difference
Language:						
Nynorsk	17	18	− 1	25	3	+ 22
Riksmål	6	14	− 8	2	5	− 3
Difference	+ 11	+ 4		+ 23	− 2	
Teetotalist	19	30	− 11	41	10	31
Nonteetotalist	3	2	+ 1	2	2	0
Difference	+ 16	+ 28		+ 39	+ 8	
Religious Activity:						
Active	23	26	− 3	28	8	+ 20
Inactive	0	4	− 4	0	2	− 2
Difference	+ 23	+ 22		+ 28	+ 6	

teetotalism. The differentials are much less pronounced on the language dimension: the votes of the secular *nynorsk* identifiers tend to go to the Center party in the rural

TABLE 12: Proportions Voting Liberal in the South/West: By Urbanization and Occupational Status

| | RURAL | | | | URBAN | |
	Low Status	High Status	Difference	Low Status	High Status	Difference
Language:						
Nynorsk	20	13	− 7	19	43	− 24
Riksmål	21	24	− 3	10	27	− 17
Difference	− 1	− 11		+ 9	+ 16	
Teetotalist	34	16	18	9	46	− 37
Nonteetotalist	5	19	− 14	16	25	− 9
Difference	+ 29	− 3		− 7	+ 21	
Relgious Activity:						
Active	27	16	11	16	30	− 14
Inactive	14	18	− 4	12	34	− 22
Difference	+ 13	− 2		+ 4	− 4	

areas (differential 12 for the high-status group vs. 4 for the Christian) and to the Liberals in the cities (differential 16 for the high-status groups as against — 2 for the Christians).

In the south/west generally the Christian party tends to be a cross-class movement in the rural areas and much more of a lower-class countercultural movement in the cities: it clearly feeds very much on in-migrant families of rural origin maintaining their cultural identities within strong network of religious and teetotalist organizations.

The Liberal party offers an interesting contrast. The party has a strong position within the countercultural lower-class in the rural areas but is much more of a middle-class party in cities. There are some interesting differences among the three cultural dimensions, however. It is easiest to summarize these in a table of rank orders in differentials:

	RANK ORDER OF DIFFERENTIALS: SOUTH/WEST			
	Liberals		*Christians*	
Language	Urban High:	16	Rural Low:	11
	Urban Low:	9	Rural High:	4
	Rural Low:	— 1	Urban Low:	4
	Rural High:	— 11	Urban High:	— 2
Teetotalism	Rural Low:	29	Urban Low:	39
	Urban High:	21	Rural High:	28
	Rural High:	— 3	Rural Low:	16
	Urban Low:	— 7	Urban High:	8
Religion	Rural Low:	13	Urban Low:	28
	Urban Low:	4	Rural Low:	23
	Rural High:	— 2	Rural High:	22
	Urban High:	— 4	Urban High:	6

We can summarize this account of the south/west as follows:

1. The Liberals are still strong within the teetotalist lower-class in the countryside but have their major basis within the middle-class of the urban areas, particularly among teetotalers and *nynorsk* identifiers.

2. The Christians have much more hold on the better-off stratum in the countercultural rural areas but represent a lower stratum of culturally more *verzuild* voters in the cities.

The Liberals and the Christians are weaker outside the south/west and do not aggregate their votes quite in the same way. Table 13 gives details for the other regions.

The Christians mobilize practically all their votes among the teetotalers and the active members of religious organizations: this is the case across all the regions. But the Christian party is much more of a middle-class party outside the south/west. It makes particularly heavy inroads among the teetotalers in the urban higher-status groups (differential 30). Interestingly, the effect is not so strong for religion: on this score the party does better within the working-class than within the middle-class.

The Liberal party gains very little on the cultural dimensions outside the south/ west. In the rural areas it does gain slightly among teetotalers and the religiously active in higher strata, but the most of its votes are mobilized outside these countercultures. The party is in any case very weak in these areas. In the cities the party tends to be stronger outside than inside the countercultures: this is the direct reverse of the finding for the south/west. This contrast between a "west-country" wing and an "Oslo" wing of the Liberal party is a well-known feature of the political landscape. In a sense this is a late residual of the initial "Left" alliance between the urban radicals and the mobilizing peasantry, but the character of this joint alignment obviously changed, first with the Agrarian splitoff, later with the establishment of the Christian People's party. These developments made inroads into the old "Left" in the south/west countryside and made the postwar Liberal party much more of an urban party even there. The contrast between the two wings still remains, however: the eastern wing is weaker and much more secularized, while the south/west wing, even though still tied to the counter-cultures, tends to be closer to the urban bourgeois establishments.

We may conveniently summarize these various findings in a schematic review of the structural strongholds of each of the parties and a rank-ordering of the effects of the three countercultures on the behaviour of voters within each such stronghold:

	Region	Structural strongholds			Effects of countercultural dimensions					
		Type of Commune	Stratum		Strongest				Weakest	
Soc.	SW	U	L		Lang.	−28	Rel.	−28	Teet.	−27
				RL:	Teet.	−44	Rel.	−34	Lang.	−18
	Oth.	R	L		Rel.	− 6	*Lang.*	*+ 1*	Teet.	+ 2
		U	L		Rel.	−24	Teet.	−15	Lang.	N.A.
Lib.	SW	R	L		Teet.	+29	Rel.	+13	*Lang.*	*− 1*
		U	H		Teet.	+21	Lang.	+16	*Rel.*	*− 4*
	Oth.	None		RH	Lang.	+13	Teet.	+ 7	Rel.	+ 6
				UH	*Rel.*	*− 2*	*Teet.*	*− 5*		
Chr.	SW	R	H		Teet.	+28	Rel.	+22	Lang.	− 4
		U	L		Teet.	+39	Rel.	+28	Lang.	+23
	Oth.	None		RH	Teet.	+14	Rel.	+ 6	Lang.	+ 5
				UL	Rel.	+27	Teet.	+22	Lang.	N.A.
				UH	Teet.	+30	Rel.	+16	Lang.	N.A.
Cen.	SW	R	H		Lang.	+12	Rel.	+ 3	*Teet.*	*− 5*
	Oth.	R	H		Lang.	+12	Teet.	+11	Rel.	+ 7
Cons.	SW	U	H		Lang.	−29	Teet.	−11	Rel.	− 9
				RH	Teet.	−15	Lang.	−11	Rel.	− 8
	Oth.	U	H		Lang.	−48	Teet.	−16	Rel.	− 3
				RH	Rel.	−19	Lang.	−16	Teet.	−16

Differences between the countercultural identifiers (*nynorsk* identifiers, teetotalers, high scorers on religiosity) have also been given for one or two of the other structural categories (RL, RH, UL, or UH) within which the party has a high proportion of voters. The *underlined* difference scores are those deviating most from the regional pattern for the given party. Given the very small number of *nynorsk* identifiers in the cities outside the south/west, no reliable estimates of differences for this dimension can be given for these categories except for the Conservatives (other regions: UH).

This scheme obviously does not allow any weighting of effects across all the variables. Nor does it give any indications of the extent of interaction among the variables. To get closer to estimates of the joint impact of various combinations of our basic variable we shall proceed to a series of "tree analyses" of the data from the same survey.

TABLE 13: **Differences in Liberal and Christian Strength in the Regions Outside the South/West.**

| | RURAL | | | | | | URBAN | | | | | |
| | Lower Status | | Higher Status | | Difference | | Lower Status | | Higher Status | | Difference | |
	L	C	L	C	L	C	L	C	L	C	L	C
Teetotalers	3	2	14	14	−11	−12	2	23	5	32	−3	−9
Nonteetotalist	6	0	7	0	−1	0	4	1	10	2	−6	−1
Difference	−3	+2	+7	+14			−2	+22	−5	+30		
Religious Activity:												
Active	6	1	12	7	−6	−6	2	27	8	19	−6	+8
Inactive	6	0	6	1	0	−1	4	0	10	3	−6	+3
Difference	0	+1	+6	+6			−2	+27	−2	+16		

The Interaction of Geography, Culture, and Economic Class

Analyses using the Sonquist-Morgan Automatic Interaction Detection algorithm have been undertaken on a great number of sample surveys in Europe.[12] The results have in some cases proved difficult to interpret, particularly when several closely correlated variables have been entered into the analysis. To facilitate interpretation we have chosen to restrict our "trees" to the seven dimensions singled out as the fundamental ones in our historical analysis of the development of mass politics in Norway. To establish our basic sociocultural matrix we had to reduce all our survey variables to dichotomies. The A.I.D. program allows us to enter much more differentiated variables for testing against the political criterion. Our seven predictor variables distinguish these categories:

GEOGRAPHY
1 Oslofjord
2 East Inland
3 South
4 West
5 Middle: Trondelag
6 North

URBANIZATION
1 Less than 14 percent of inhabitants of the commune living in agglomerations
2 15–74 percent
3 75–100 percent: includes all smaller cities
4 The four largest cities.

EDUCATION
0 Elementary school only
1 Less than 1½ years beyond elementary school

2 $1\frac{1}{2}$–$2\frac{1}{2}$ years beyond elementary school
3 $2\frac{1}{2}$–$3\frac{1}{2}$ years beyond elementary school
4 $3\frac{1}{2}$–$4\frac{1}{2}$ years beyond elementary school
5 $4\frac{1}{2}$–$5\frac{1}{2}$ years beyond elementary school
6 $5\frac{1}{2}$–$6\frac{1}{2}$ years beyond elementary school
7 $6\frac{1}{2}$–$7\frac{1}{2}$ years beyond elementary school
8 More than $7\frac{1}{2}$ years beyond elementary school

OCCUPATION
1 Manual worker
2 Clerical and technical, public
3 Clerical and technical, private
4 Higher-salaried, public
5 Higher-salaried, private
6 Self-employed, with hired help
7 Self-employed, no hired help
8 Farmer
9 Smallholder, fisherman

LANGUAGE
1 *Nynorsk*, active
2 *Nynorsk*, inactive
3 *Riksmål*, inactive
4 *Riksmål*, active

TEETOTALISM
1 Teetotaler, active
2 Teetotaler, inactive
3 Nonteetotaler, inactive
4 Nonteetotaler, active

RELIGION
1 No activity
2 Low
3 Medium
4 High (member of religious organization)

Our criterion variables are five: the proportions voting or not voting for one of the five party alternatives distinguished in our earlier analysis. In our analysis of socialist voting (CP, Soc., and Labor) we were able to use the entire sample: only those registered as nonvoters are excluded. The mean proportions voting for the four parties of the "established bloc" are too small to permit analysis by the A.I.D. procedure: in these cases we have restricted our comparisons to the nonsocialist sector of the sample. An equivalent procedure could not be used on the socialist side: the CP and the Socialist People's party simply account for too small proportions even of this aggregate.

Let us now look at each of the five trees in succession and then proceed to a comparison of the proportions of variance explained by this procedure across all the parties.

1. SOCIALISTS VS. NONSOCIALISTS

Figure 8 gives the tree solution for the division between socialist voters and voters for the four parties to the right on the political spectrum.

The seven variables account for 37.9 percent of the variance. As we might have expected, the socioeconomic variables turn out to count heaviest in the reduction of variance: the first split is by occupation. Interestingly the split cuts through the middle-class: the lower clerical and technical employees fall in with the workers as particularly prone to vote socialist.

What is even more important is that this worker–lower-middle-class half of the sample is at the same time much more affected by cultural influences than is the other half. The next split for the worker–lower-middle-class group is by *religion*. The religiously organized voters within this group are much less inclined to vote socialist, particularly in the south/west: again a confirmation of findings in earlier tables. The religiously less active divide further by the level of education. Within each of these groups culture and geography again come out heavily: language in the case of the more educated, region for the least educated. But the language variable does not contrast the two subcultures: it splitsoff the subculturally *active* from the more indifferent. This is an important finding: the socialists have always tried to take an intermediary, if not neutral, position on the language issue and have in fact lost out on both sides, both within the active *nynorsk* culture and, even more, within the *riksmål* movement. The figures for the party choices of the two terminal groups confirm this:

	Soc.	Lab.	Lib.	Cons.
Group 18	2	35	25	30
Group 19	11	61	7	16

By contrast, the politics of the other half of the initial sample appears to sort itself out largely by status variables: this is an economically and educationally highly diverse group, and the cultural variables simply do not have as much of a chance to come through. The dichotomization procedures in fact produce quite diverse groups: at both educational levels the farmers and the employers are splitoff as the least prone to vote socialist (2.1 and 29.4 percent), but the contrasting group of smallholders, fishermen, self-employed without hired help, and (quite unexpectedly) higher-salaried employees is difficult to disentangle. The fact that a group of such heterogeneous structure can be splitoff on this one political criterion tells us something important about the cross-cutting character of the Labor party. It not only attracts votes within the rural proletariat and among the smaller independents in the urban areas but has also established itself within the upper reaches of the municipal and the national bureaucracy: the party has been in or close to power for more than a generation and has been able to attract quite a few supporters in the high echelons of the public sector.

Only one of these highly heterogeneous groups turns out to split significantly on a cultural variable: the better-educated group splits on the language question but not on a straight *nynorsk–riksmål* line. The underlying factor is again clearly occupational

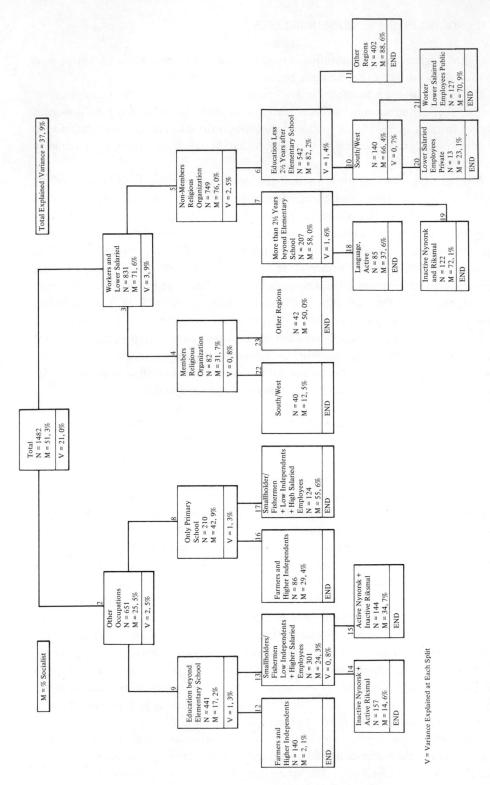

Total Explained Variance = 37, 9%

M = % Socialist

V = Variance Explained at Each Split

Figure 8: A Norwegian Tree Analysis: Socialist *vs.* Nonsocialist Voting

differentiation: the higher-salaried employees in this group (No. 13) are clearly more likely to be active *riksmål* advocates and consequently to vote Conservative while the farmers, fishermen, and self-employed will vary much more in their language posture and spread their votes much more evenly among the different parties. A check for the party choices within these two terminal groups confirms this:

> Group 14: 51 percent Cons., Cons.-Nonsoc. ratio .60
> Group 15: 30 percent Cons., Cons.-Nonsoc. ratio .45

Obviously, with a larger sample groups of this structure could easily be split up on further variables. Unfortunately the 1965 sample survey was too small to allow further splits. We have had access to a larger file of pooled Gallup data for Norway and have carried out tree analyses on these, but the variables in these surveys allow much fewer differentiations and therefore do not help us in sorting out terminal groups of the type we have brought out in our analyses of the 1965 data.

To sum up, occupation and education clearly count most in explaining variance in socialist votes. The urban-rural dimension never comes out directly: the voters in the rural areas are either grouped with the employers in the other sectors of the economy or in that incongruous category of "smallholders, fishermen, self-employed, and higher-salaried employees". Of the cultural dimensions only religion and language come out independently: the correlation between religiosity and teetotalism is too high to allow both to produce splits in an A.I.D. tree. Region dichotomizes just as in our initial matrix but only in two terminal splits within the worker–lower-middle-class group: the south/west produces a much lower socialist vote among the religious activists (Group 22: 12.5 percent) and among the less educated of the less religious (Group 10: 66.4 percent). No regional variables come through in the other half of the tree: as we showed in our analysis of the basic matrix, the south/west is much more distinctive at the lower-status level than at the higher.

Once we carry out separate tree analyses by region, the teetotalist dimension turns out to have some weight of its own. Thus in the tree for the south/west (total variance explained: 35 percent) all the three cultural variables produce successive splits within the lower stratum outside the primary economy: first religion, then teetotalism, and finally the level of linguistic identity. Similarly in the tree for the other regions (total variance explained: 41 percent) two of the cultural variables count for the working-class–lower-middle-class group: religion for the less educated, language for the more educated. And there is a similar tendency for the higher status-cum-primary splitoff: for the less educated among those there is first a splitoff on teetotalist activity (the active teetotalist score lower on socialist voting) and then a split on religiosity among those outside the inner teetotalist subculture; for the more educated language again turns out to be the most important cultural variable.

2. THE CONSERVATIVE SHARE OF THE NONSOCIALIST VOTE

Figure 9 gives the tree solution for the Conservatives. In this analysis all the socialists have been taken out of the sample: most of the working-class and quite a

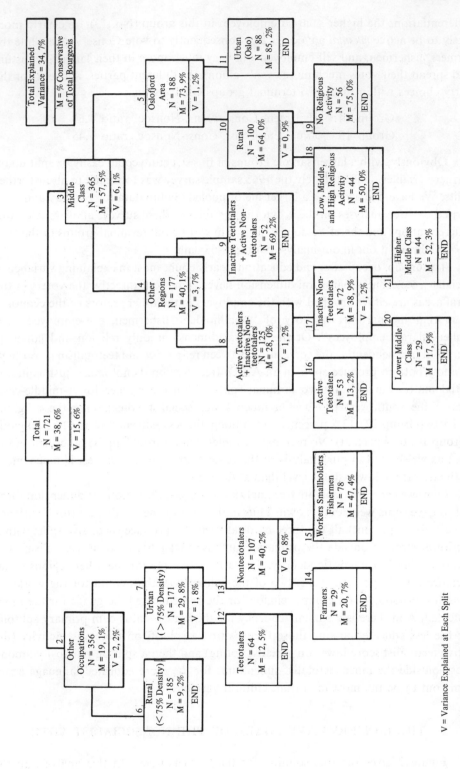

V = Variance Explained at Each Split

Figure 9 : A Norwegian Tree Analysis: Conservative vs. Other Nonsocialist Parties

chunk of the lower-middle-class is no longer there to affect the succession of splits. There is still enough status differentiation left to produce clear socioeconomic splits for the Conservatives, however. In fact, occupation turns out to be the dominant variable in the tree. The first split is very much as expected: the higher urban occupations are more likely to support the Conservatives than the lower and the rural. The further splits force us to consider regional differentiations. The rural splitoff goes counter to the established rule: the lower-status smallholders and fishermen turn out to vote Conservative in greater proportion than the farmers and the owners of forests. This reflects regional contrast: in the coastal economy of the north the fishermen and the smallholders who vote against the socialists are much more likely to vote Conservative, in the other regions the Center party is apt to dominate in the rural areas.

Generally, region and type of community account for much of the variance in the strength of the Conservatives. The party has its strongholds in the cities and is particularly strong in the center of the nation: in the capital the party in fact collects 85 percent of all the nonsocialist votes.

Of the three cultural variables teetotalism counts most for the strength of the Conservatives: three of the four cultural splits are on this variable. The party recruits quite heavily among the active opponents of the restrictive alcohol policies maintained by a coalition of Labor and middle-party forces. The only other cultural variable to come out in the tree is religion: the Conservatives are weaker among the active fundamentalists. But much of the effect of religion is washed out by the other variables. This is also the case for the language variable: the Conservatives are known to attract a high share of the votes of the active *riksmål* identifiers, but once the effects of class, urbanization, and region have been taken out, there is little left to explain for the variable.

3. THE CENTER PARTY SHARE OF THE NONSOCIALIST VOTE

Figure 10 gives the tree for the Center party. This is still largely a single-interest movement: the first split sets the independents in the primary economy apart from all the other occupational groups and accounts for almost 30 percent of the total variance within the nonsocialist bloc. Interestingly, the further splits are either geographical or cultural. The primary-economy sector first splits on the strength of teetotalist–antiteetotalist identification, then on language on the one side and on the urbanization level on the other. The status between smallholders, fishermen, and farmers comes last in the succession: it counts only within one small heterogeneous group (no. 11) almost evenly divided among the four nonsocialist parties. The terminal split between farmers on the one hand and smallholders/fishermen on the other in fact reflects a regional contrast: the actively antiteetotalist fishermen and smallholders of the north tend to prefer *riksmål* and vote Conservative, while the Center party derives considerable strength from active teetotalers and *nynorsk* identifiers.

Outside the group of economically independent farmers, smallholders, and fishermen, the Center party gains most of its support in the rural areas outside the south/

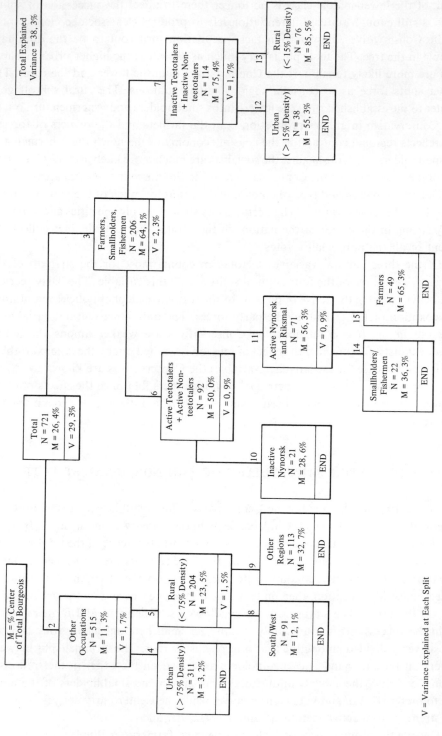

V = Variance Explained at Each Split

Figure 10 : A Norwegian Tree Analysis: Center Party vs. Other Nonsocialists

west : these voters tend to be agricultural workers, service employees, and independents in commerce and transportation closely tied in with the primary economy. In the south/west the competition for the rural votes outside the strict farm households is vigorous: the Liberals and the Christians have a much stronger hold on the rural population in this region than elsewhere in the country.

4. THE CHRISTIAN PARTY SHARE

Figure 11 gives a tree solution for the Christians. Again the proportion of variance accounted for is quite high: 36 percent. This is the countercultural party par excellence: the two first splits are on teetotalism and religious activity: there is hardly anyone voting for the Christian party outside the teetotalist counterculture (group 2 : 3 percent of the nonsocialists), while more than half of the active teetotaler members of religious organizations vote with the Christians if they vote on the nonsocialist side. The further splits vary in character. Among the teetotaler members of religious organizations the lowest proportion of Christian votes is found among farmers, smallholders, and fishermen (group 6: 37 percent), the highest proportion in the urban occupations (group 11 : 87 percent). This reflects the structure of alternatives: in the rural areas the three middle parties all appeal to the religious vote; in the urban areas the Liberals and the Conservatives offer very little opposition in these circles. The other side of the tree presents less obvious findings. Among the active teetotalers outside the religious organizations there is a marked regional differential, a most unusual one: the two peripheries of the south/west and the north split off against the east and the middle. The splitoff group (no. 9) is small, and the difference may be due to sampling error, but the message seems interpretable: in the south/west and the north the decisive frontline seems to run between the religiously organized and the others; in the other regions even voters outside these organizations are likely to vote Christian if they are active teetotalers. Even in the south/west and the north, however, attendance at services and meetings does count: there is quite a high proportion voting Christian at the middle level of religiosity, most markedly so in the cities (group 15 : 36 percent).

5. THE LIBERALS AND THEIR SHARE

Figure 12 gives the tree solution for the Liberals, the residual legatees of the grand old Left opposition. As expected, our battery of variables explains very little (only 17 percent) of the variance in their share of the nonsocialist vote. The tree is in fact very difficult to interpret: the Liberals collect votes in all sorts of quarters but have not been able to retain any clear-cut niches in the sociocultural structure.

By contrast to all the other parties the Liberals first split on geography: the party is markedly stronger in the south/west than elsewhere, and this traditional contrast cannot be entirely reduced to differences in the strength of the countercultures.

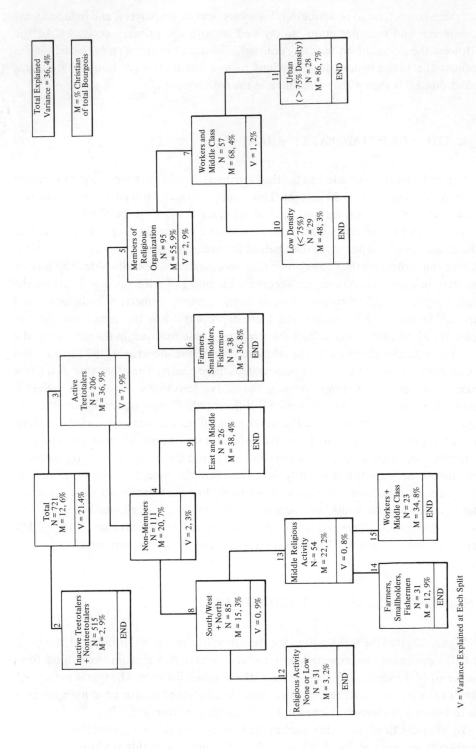

Figure 11: A Norwegian Tree Analysis: Christian People's party *vs.* Other Nonsocialists

V = Variance Explained at Each Split

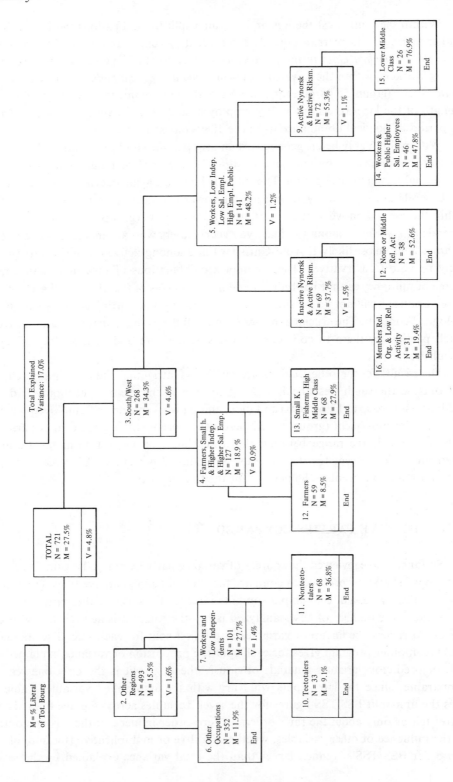

Figure 12: A Norwegian Tree Analysis: Liberal vs. Other Bourgeois parties

Within the south/west there is an intriguing split by occupation: the Liberals are weaker among the farmers (group 12: 8.5 percent), stronger among smallholders *and the better-off middle class in the private sector* (group 13: 28 percent), and strongest among workers, within the lower-middle-class *and among the higher employees in the public sector* (group 5: 48 percent). We have already commented on the traditional strength of the Liberals among public employees and officials, which is a legacy from the period of political dominance from the 1880s onward.

Within this highly heterogeneous urban group in the south/west (no. 5: 141 cases) there are further splits by language posture, by the level of religious activity, and, interestingly, even by occupation. The splits by language again cuts across subcultures: the Liberals are particularly strong among lower-middle-class voters either actively within the *nynorsk* movement or indifferent *riksmål* users (group 15: 77 percent). The Liberals are weakest among the inactive *nynorsk* users who are members of religious organizations (most likely to vote Christian) and among active *riksmål* voters (more likely to vote Conservative). These complex combinations of inherited culture and degree of militancy cannot be studied in detail in samples of this size: a full account of these variations will not be possible without a large sample cutting across a variety of ecological contexts. The crucial consideration in all this is the structure of alternatives: which parties are there to compete for votes at the core and at the edges of each subculture?

The results for the other regions are much less intriguing: the tree simply tells us that outside the south/west the Liberals gain least in the primary economy and the middle-class (group 6: 12 percent) and most among workers and self-employed outside the teetotaler movement (group 11: 37 percent). There is still a great deal of variance to be explained: the range between the lowest and the highest terminal group is 9 percent vs. 77 percent for the Liberals, as against 3 percent vs. 87 percent for the Christians, and 3 percent vs. 86 percent for the Center party.

6. THE FIVE PARTIES COMPARED

So far we have reviewed the sources of variance party by party. To gain some perspective we shall now proceed to compare the evidence across all five trees. Obviously we cannot carry out a direct comparison of the tree for the socialist alternative with the four others: the number of cases analyzed is not the same. It is nevertheless of great interest to review the lineup of variables at the first split for each tree. The standard A.I.D. computer program gives for each split the proportion of variance explained by each of predictor variables entered: obviously the first split is the only one readily comparable, since the later splits will vary with the first-ranked variable. Table 14 gives the first-split BSS/TSS figures for the seven variables across the five trees. These figures tell us only about the rank-orders of zero-order influences: there is no control for the influence of other variables, whether additive or multiplicative (the sum of the zero-order BSS/TSS's is much larger than the total variance explained by the seven variables conjointly). The table is nevertheless of great interest: it tells us about the rank-orders of direct influences and shows which predictor variables compete for first place.

TABLE 14: **Percentage of Initial Variance Explained by Background Variables**

	ALL VOTERS		NONSOCIALISTS ONLY		
Background variables	*Socialist proportion*	*Conser.*	*Center*	*Christian*	*Liberal*
	(BSS/TSS % before First Split)				
Occupation	20.9	15.6	29.3	3.4	4.5
Education	7.3	7.2	5.3	0.7	0.9
Religious activity	4.6	7.5	2.1	19.7	0.3
Teetotalism	4.9	12.2	3.4	21.4	0.6
Language	6.8	7.6	2.5	3.1	1.4
Region	2.5	9.8	2.8	4.3	4.8
Density of population	2.5	10.9	18.6	0.7	1.3

The table confirms our basic interpretation of the party system:

	Urban *and* rural	Urban	Rural
Class parties	*Labor* (and other socialists) All regions	*Conservatives* South/West only	*Center*
Countercultural parties	*Christians*	*Liberals*	

These positions in sociocultural territorial space are confirmed by the rank-orders of the sources of variance.

	Class	*Urbanization*	*Culture*	*Region*
Socialist	*First* (20.9)	Last (2.5)	Low: language max. (6.8)	Last (2.5)
Conservative	*First* (15.6)	Third (10.9)	High: teetotalism max. (12.2)	Fourth (9.8)
Center	*First* (29.3)	Second (18.6)	Low: teetotalism max. (3.4)	Low (2.8)
Christian	Low (3.4)	Low (0.7)	*First:* teetotalism (21.4) Second: religion (19.7)	Med. (4.3)
Liberal	Second (4.5)	Low (1.3)	Low: language max. (1.4)	*First* (4.8)

This map of the sources of variance gives us in a nutshell the results of the splitoffs from old Left opposition:

1. An *economic* splitoff, the transformation of a rural interest group into an independent party, the Agrarians, currently the Center party.

2. A *countercultural* splitoff, the transformation of the fundamentalist movement into an independent party, the Christians.

3. A *territorial residual*, the transformation of the old catch-all opposition party of the Left into a regional establishment with a variety of alliances with radical-centrist groups in other parts of the country, particularly the Oslofjord area.

The map is not very much altered when we control for multiple influences and interactions: this is done in Table 15. In this table the total proportions of variance

TABLE 15: Percentages of Variance Explained in the Tree Analysis by Types of Background Variables

	ALL VOTERS		NONSOCIALISTS ONLY		
	Socialist	*Cons.*	*Center*	*Christian*	*Liberal*
Socioeconomic variables	29.3	17.6	30.2	3.7	8.2
Cultural variables	6.3	7.6	3.2	30.2	4.1
Territorial variables	2.2	9.5	4.9	2.5	4.8
Total variance explained*	37.9	34.7	38.3	36.4	17.0

*Because of rounding errors the partial variance does not always add up exactly to the total amount of variance explained.

explained is broken down into the three crucial categories of sources: socioeconomic, cultural, territorial. The main point to note is the change in the rank-order of sources of variance for the Liberals: the socioeconomic variables turn out to weigh much heavier than the territorial. But the overall structure remains the same:

Rank-order for Proportions of Total Variance					
Socioeconomic var.	Cen.	Soc.	Cons.	*Lib.*	Chr.
	(78%)	(77%)	(52%)	(48%)	(10%)
Cultural var.	Chr.	*Lib.*	Cons.	Soc.	Cen.
	(83%)	(24%)	(21%)	(17%)	(8%)
Territorial var.	*Lib.*	Cons.	Cen.	Chr.	Soc.
	(28%)	(27%)	(10%)	(7%)	(6%)

METHODOLOGICAL NOTE: DIFFICULTIES IN THE COMPARISON OF TREES

Our 1965 sample was reinterviewed at the 1969 election, and tree analyses were carried out for both elections. The trees prove remarkably similar, with only minor changes occurring. Thus in 1969 the Liberals split first on occupation and next on region: the rank-order from 1965 was reversed. The 1969 election brought a heavy loss to the party in the south/west, while it maintained its position much better in other regions. [13] Consequently the regional variations in the Liberal vote declined between 1965 and 1969: this was reflected in the split. But in general the structure has remained remarkably stable.

One objection may be raised against both these tree analyses: the samples are too small. How would the solutions have been if the number of cases had been large enough to permit more splits?

An attempt has been made to answer this question. We have been given access to pooled Gallup data for the two-year period from October, 1969, to September, 1971. The Norwegian Gallup Institute interviews a nationwide sample of some 1,500 respondents every month. Our material consists of some 29,000 cases. The dependent variables were operationalized exactly as in the 1965 analysis: socialist versus nonsocialist preference, and each nonsocialist party versus all the other ones.[41] The background variables entered were the same in both studies, but in the Gallup data there are fewer differentiations. Thus the cultural variables are all dichotomized: *nynorsk* versus *riksmål*, teetotalers versus nonteetotalers, devout Christians versus less committed (self-classification). Similarly the urbanization variable is highly simplified: urban versus rural residence. Finally, in the Gallup data occupation is classified in only four categories: workers, salaried employees, independents, and farmers/fishermen.

By and large the pooled Gallup data produced trees of about the same structure as our 1965 study, but the splits are fewer. The most important difference is that the total variance explained is much lower in the Gallup data.

TABLE 16: **Percentage of Variance Explained: A Comparison Between the 1965 Survey and Pooled Gallup Data from 1969-71**

	ALL VOTERS		NONSOCIALISTS ONLY		
	Percent Socialist	*Proportion Conservative*	*Proportion Center*	*Proportion Christian*	*Proportion Liberal*
1965 survey	37.9	34.7	38.3	36.4	17.0
Pooled Gallup data	22.3	21.8	32.7	28.5	3.8
Difference	15.6	12.9	5.6	7.9	13.2

As Table 16 indicates the discrepancies are largest for the Socialist, the Conservative, and the Liberal vote. The results for the two data sets are most similar for the Center party and for the Christian People's party, both in terms of explained variance and in the structure of the trees.

The result of the comparison is rather surprising. We had expected to find that the greater the number of cases, the more splits there would be and the more of the variance would be explained. In fact the reverse was true. Why? There are three possibilities: first, a difference in sampling procedures between the two studies; second, differences in the structure of the predictor variables; third, the low stability of the terminal groups in samples as small as the one interviewed in 1965.

Both studies are based upon nationwide stratified random samples. The 1965 survey was based on a master sample stratified by region, the level of urbanization, and the occupational composition of communities. The primary sampling units (PSUs) were drawn randomly from within the established strata of communities. And within each PSU the respondents were drawn randomly from the public election register.[15] The Norwegian Gallup Institute uses a master sample stratified along the same lines as the election survey. The interviewer is given a list of initial addresses within each PSU and is then required to draw the respondents according to specified rules. Provided these rules were followed there should be no reason to doubt that every citizen within the PSU rated the same probability of selection.

In an effort to test the impact of possible differences in sampling the seven predictor variables in the 1965 survey were recoded to conform exactly to the structure of the Gallup data. A tree was then run to determine the sources of variance in socialist/nonsocialist voting. Using this procedure on the 1965 data, 31.7 percent of the total variance was explained: this is some 9 percent higher than in the pooled Gallup data, but 6 percent lower than in the differentiated 1965 analysis. The fact that the result of this rerun still differs from the Gallup analysis suggests a difference in sampling procedure. However, the difference might also be due to lower reliability in the collection and coding of data: in a commercial poll errors of fieldwork and response classification might be more frequent. We are not in a position to decide which factors have been at work.

It might be objected that the political situations were not the same in the two cases: this, rather than differences in sampling, might explain the gap between the figure of 31.7 percent for the academic survey and 22.3 percent for the pooled Gallup data. Our comparison between the trees for our own two surveys, the first in 1965 and the next in 1969, suggests very little change during the four-year period. It is of course possible that the change in the regional distinctiveness of the Liberals might explain the drastic reduction in the proportion of explained variance in the Gallup data: 17.0 percent in the 1965 data, only 3.8 percent in the pooled data for 1969–70. But it is hard to see how this one change could have brought about a 9 percent reduction in the proportion of explained variance for the socialists: it seems more likely that this discrepancy must be due to differences in sampling procedures, in field work, or in both.

On the other hand, our rerun of the tree for the 1965 survey produces a reduction of 6 percent in the proportion of variance explained: the simplification of the structure of the predictor variables decreases their explanatory power. It is easy to see how this comes about. If we look at the original tree for the socialist voting (Figure 8), we see that the lower-salaried employees are grouped with the workers in the first split. In the Gallup tree the split was between workers and the rest: there is no separate occupational code for lower-salaried employees. This obviously reduces the possibility of accounting for variance on the basis of occupation.

Generally we conclude that the more detailed the articulation of the predictor variables, the greater the proportion of variance likely to be explained. This means that we should be wary of drawing conclusions from cross-national differences in the proportions of variance explained: the differences *need* not tell us anything about the impact of the national social-structure on voter alignments but may simply reflect differences in coding. The first thing to check, therefore, in evaluating cross-national collections of A.I.D. trees is the actual categorization of the predictor variables!

Obviously there is always the danger that the differentiations introduce new dimensions of variation. We have been made very much aware of this danger in our analysis of the influence of our cultural variables in party choice. At least two of the cultural variables are two-dimensional: language and teetotalism. The four-point codes for these variables in fact link up two different dimensions of cultural identity: the purely structural fact of the *socially inherited and/or reinforced membership* of the subculture vs. the *intensity of the identification*, the personally motivated willingness to invest one's energy into the maintenance of a distinctive culture. This is very much parallel to the Marxist distinction in the analyses of class consciousness: the objectively given *Klasse an sich* vs. the subjectively realized *Klasse für sich*. What is interesting is how rarely membership per se turns out to reduce variance: in the majority of cases membership interacts with intensity on both or on the one side of the cultural divide.

Theoretically the 2×2 attribute space allows seven dichotomous splits: one pure membership split, one pure intensity split, one diagonal split (high-central plus low-countercentral vs. low central plus high countercentral), and altogether four unilateral splits (one cell split off from the other three). Reviewing the five trees in Figures 8–12 we found these actual splits:

	Language	*Teetotalers*
Straight membership splits (c. vs. cc)		Cons. gr. 12-13 Lib. gr. 10-11
Straight intensity splits (h vs. l)	Soc. gr. 18-19	Center gr. 6-7
Diagonal splits (hc+lcc vs. lc+hcc)	Soc. gr. 14-15 Lib. gr. 8-9	Cons. gr. 8-9 (group 8 split up in next run)
Single-cell splits		
hc vs. others	*No cases*	
lc vs. others	*No cases*	
hcc vs. others		Chr. gr. 2-3
lcc vs. others	Center gr. 10-11	

Of a total number of nine splits on these two cultural variables, only two contrast the members of one subculture against the other: the other splits are by intensity or by some combination of intensity and membership. This is no accident: the intensity measure is conceptually closer to the dependent variable than the pure membership. In fact, we have on occasion questioned whether we ought to include these intensity variables on the structural side of the "tree equation": the act of standing up for your language or for your position on the use of alcohol is already in itself a political act. We nevertheless decided to keep the two cultural variables two-dimensional: there is no one-to-one relation between intensity and voting and the conditions for a politicization of such activity into one particular party channel might come out with greater clarity if we included the two dimensions in the tree analysis.

The Resulting Party Profiles

So far we have analyzed the successes of the different parties in mobilizing support from the different cells of the sociocultural-territorial matrix: our dependent variables have been the percentage strength of each party in each cell.

But parties also have a structure: they are made up of leaders and members recruited from different quarters of the social systems, and they soon establish images of themselves as collectivities of particular types. To map differences in the structure of parties we can proceed in several directions. In this section we shall concentrate on the composition of each party at the mass level; we shall present differences in the percentage strength of major sociocultural categories within each party. We shall in fact proceed by percentaging in the other direction: our 100 percent total is no longer the sociocultural category but the entire party electorate. There is an obvious interrelation between the two enterprises: if a party succeeds equally well in all sociocultural categories, it will represent a mirror image of the total electorate; if it succeeds only in one, it will be entirely dominated by those voters. But there are interesting variations that deserve study. To allow comparison we can measure the *distinctiveness of each party:* the discrepancy scores simply measure in each case the percentage-point distance from the average for the entire nationwide sample. We can group the parties in a two-dimensional space on the basis of their distinctiveness score X.

	Cultural Distinctiveness (sum of scores)			
	Highest			*Lowest*
Socioeconomic distinctiveness: scores for occup. + educ.				
High: 30+		Cons. (65)	Agr. (33)	Lab. (29)
Med.: 21-30		SPP (65)	Lib. (33)	
Low: −20	*Chr.* (142)			

The position of the SPP in this matrix is an interesting one. The Socialist Left is as distinctive as the Conservative party in their rejection of the countercentral culture, but the scores differ in political significance from one variable to another: on religion and on teetotalism the party tends to reject the established policies and to opt for secularization and permissiveness, on language the great majority identify with *riksmål* but do not want to make a political issue of this question. Equally interesting is the low level of distinctiveness on education: the SPP is much less distinctive on education than on occupation. In practice this means that it has so far attracted more of the better educated workers in addition to its middle-class sector. The sample is too small to pursue this analysis in further detail: we can only refer to the painstaking analysis of Gallup data for the SPP to be published in a dissertation by Ingemar Glans of the University of Lund.

Let us finally attempt a series of *summarizing portraits* of each of the six parties:

1. The average *Laborite* comes from the working-class or may be a smallholder/fisherman or of the urban lower-middle-class. He or she tends to have had very little schooling beyond primary education. Although most are not against drinking and speak *riksmål*, they are inclined to be less active on both these issues. The Labor voters are most unlikely to be members of religious organizations, but otherwise their reli-

gious behavior comes pretty close to the average. Laborites are about equally likely to live in urban as in rural areas. They are slightly less to live likely in the south/west than in other regions.

2. Our profile of the supporter of the *Socialist People's party* is less definite. Politically these voters stand to the left of Labor. Like the Laborites they tend to come from the working-class or from the lower-middle-class, but fewer hail from rural occupations. They tend to be more educated than Laborites. The SPP supporters are most likely to live in a city or some other urbanized area outside the south/west region. They tend to be negative toward the church and are often actively against alcohol restrictions. Usually they speak *riksmål* but are not much interested in the language conflict.

3. The supporters of the *Center party* are most frequently farmers and their families, living mostly at some distance from areas of urbanization. In religious posture they tend to resemble the average Norwegian, but fewer of them score "no" on such activity. Similarly, they represent the average tendency on teetotalism but are not often against alcohol restrictions. In language preference they lean in the *nynorsk* direction but are not very distinctive in this respect.

4. The *Conservative* voters tend to belong to the upper-middle-class and are on average well educated. They tend to live in urban areas and are heavily represented in the region around the Oslofjord. They speak *riksmål* and feel strongly committed to protecting this language. They are unlikely to be teetotalers and generally take a liberal stand on alcohol policies. In religious matters the Conservative voter tends to conform to the traditional state church, but is otherwise religiously passive.

5. The *Christian* voters are most likely to be fundamentalist members of some religious lay organization. They are almost all active teetotalers. They are less distinctive on language preference but on the whole lean in the direction of *nynorsk*. They are heavily represented in the south/west region and can be found with equal frequency in urban and rural communities. Voters for the Christian People's party outside the south/west region are much more likely to live in urban areas.

6. The *Liberal* voter has a less distinctive profile than the supporters of any other party. The Liberal party is a typical middle party on almost all dimensions. Only on the language issue does the party veer off to an extreme position: it gathers more active *nynorsk* supporters than the other parties. This is particularly true of voters in rural areas. But in some parts of the country, especially in the Oslo area, the party has a substantial proportion of active *riksmål* supporters as well. There are a number of such contrasts in the party, but these tend to cancel each other out on national averages. The Liberals have always been particularly strong in the south/west region and differ considerably in profile between this region and the east. In the south/west the Liberal supporter is more likely to be an active teetotaler, while in other regions he is more likely to take a passive posture on the other side. There is a similar contrast for religion. There is also a difference in socioeconomic composition. In the south/west the Liberal party is an alliance of the rural lower-class and the urban middle-class. In the rest of the country the average Liberal is much more thoroughly middle-class, although generally alienated from the Conservative bourgeoisie on one score or another.

TABLE 17: **Rank Order of Party Distinctiveness from National Average for Seven Structural Variables: Highest Discrepancy Score on any Value of the Variable**

	SocPP		Labor		Liberal		Christian		Center		Conser.	
Highest	Rel.:	27	Occ.:	21	Reg.:	27	Teet.:	62	Occ.:	40	Occ.:	34
	Lang.:	23	Ed.:	14	Lang.:	14	Rel.:	54	Urb.:	39	Ed.:	31
	Urb.:	22	Teet.:	12	Ed.:	13	Lang.:	26	Rel.:	13	Lang.:	25
	Occ.:	21	Lang.:	11	Teet.:	13	Reg.:	26	Ed.:	12	Teet.:	24
	Reg.:	15	Reg.:	6	Occ.:	12	Occ.:	7	Reg.:	5	Urb.:	19
	Teet.:	15	Rel.:	6	Rel.:	6	Ed.:	7	Teet.:	8	Reg.:	18
Lowest	Ed.:	7	Urb.	4	Urb.:	3	Urb.:	4	Lang.:	7	Rel.:	12

A Concluding Comment

We started out by identifying seven historical cleavage dimensions in Norwegian mass politics. We proceeded to single out seven operationally defined variables measuring these dimensions either directly or in some combination. We then reviewed data from a sample survey carried out in 1965 for evidence of the continuing weight of these variables in the alignment of voters among party alternatives. We have stuck closely to this design and have obviously missed a lot of information in doing so: there are no tables for sex, age, marital status, trade-union membership, home ownership, or possession of other material goods in this chapter. We do not say that these variables are without importance: we simply decided to stick to the variables closest to our model of the development of Norwegian mass politics. Sex and age did not count directly in the structuring of our party system: the system remained very much the same after the women were given the vote, and the only evidence for a decisive structuring of politics by age can be found in the history of movements on the far Left and in the conflicts since the late 1960s between youth groups and mother parties over the entry into the EEC. We know that trade-union membership helps to explain the variance in voting, but practically all of this variance can also be accounted for by variables of occupation and education: the same goes for income and home ownership. We found it useful to include in our measure of class both a variable for occupation and one for education, but we did not judge it necessary to add further indicators of this dimension of our cleavage model. We did not choose our initial variables on the basis of any overall mapping of the total range of possible variables but derived them from a general developmental model built up to account for macrovariations in the systems of mass politics in Europe.

We did find that those seven variables accounted for a remarkable proportion of the variance in voting. But does this prove definitively that the position in sociocultural-territorial structure determines the choice of party? Is there a definite causal structure in our data? We do not think it possible to interpret our findings in strict terms of causality: we have to recognize possibilities of interaction, of positive or negative feedback. We have already discussed this in our analysis of the membership vs. intensity dimensions of cultural identity. The close correlations there might reflect long feedback loops: identification with one or the other culture may have led to identification with a party defending that culture and the social pressures existing within the party context may in their turn have reinforced and intensified the initial identification. Much depends on the closeness of the organizational ties between the culture and the party. In the case of the Christian People's party these are very tight ties indeed: the party tends to monopolize the political representation of the lay movements close to the orthodox wing of the state church. For most members of these movements the vote for the Christian party is part of an overall syndrome of expressive behaviors. What we have established statistically is the rough equivalent of an interitem correlation in a scale. Similar ties can be seen between the *nynorsk* movement and the Liberals and between the broad culture of urban business and professional networks and the Conservatives, but in these cases there are wider margins of variation, greater tolerance of dissonance. There are obvious circuits of reinforcement linking the stand taken on the language issue and the rejection of restrictive alcohol policies to the identification with the Conservative party: again it makes sense to view these postures as so many expressions of a syndrome. But there are other parties competing for votes within the broad majority of *riksmål* users, and the acceptance of social drinking goes far beyond the circles of business and the professions. These are cases where multivariate analysis is essential: we may not be able to establish strict causal relationships but we may be able to determine some of the parameters of political choice in particular sociocultural contexts.

This line of reasoning could be extended to all our variables: we could distinguish for each of them between what we call an "inherited-membership" dimension and an "active-advocacy" dimension. You may have been born in a particular region and still live there but may not think of yourself politically in such terms: territorial membership may be important statistically but need not be salient to the voter. Similarly for the urban-rural dimension: "rurality" may or may not be a salient dimension of politics. The same goes for occupational-educational status: the distinction between objective vs. subjective class is too well known to require further comment. We have no independent data on the intensity of regionality and rurality, but we do know that it is easier to predict party choice from subjective than from objective class.[16] We could have included this variable of subjective class in our battery but considered this ill-advised: we found the variable to be too close to our party choice criterion and feared that the first splits on subjective class would vitiate the further analysis of interactions. We may not have been consistent on this point. We should perhaps have entered both "membership" and "advocacy" variables on all our dimensions.

Generally, we have not here considered systematically, the possible variations in the *saliency* of the different cleavage dimensions. Our original model posited a sequence of oppositions within the system: first, a diffuse center-periphery contrast; later, a conflict over cultural standards; later again, a struggle over economic stakes between the rural and the urban economies and between workers and employers.

The model specified a process over time but also spelled out a *structure of inherited contrasts*. Our analyses of data for 1965 suggest that most of these dimensions are still important for party choice, but this says little about the subjective saliency of the variables for the individual voter. The Converse-Valen analysis of preference orderings and transition matrices shows that class and religion were the most salient dimensions to the voters of the mid-60s:[17] the other issues had lost in importance. Our analyses show that the other dimensions—region, the rural-urban contrast, the language issue— still count in conditioning the choice of party, but there are clearly differences over time and across sociocultural contexts in the subjective salience of the different dimensions: some were highly salient at the time of the "freezing" of major alignments but have since lost in importance; some have stayed latent for some time but have suddenly become salient again under the impact of new constellations at the macro-level.

The struggle from 1970 onward over the entry into the European Common Market has clearly restructured the saliency of the different dimensions. The coalition of the four nonsocialist parties broke up in 1971, when there was a marked reversal in the organization of the conflict dimensions: the center-periphery opposition and the conflict between the primary and the urban economy emerged as most salient, while the earlier conflict over class issues receded in importance. As a result we experienced a rapprochement between Labor and the Conservatives in an alliance against the defenders of the periphery: the broad antimarket coalition was made up of the Socialist Left, the Center party, and large chunks of the Liberal and the Christian parties. A similar restructuring took place in the months before de Gaulle's famous *non* of Jan. 14, 1963.[18] In some sense this issue brings out into the open again all the old dimensions of the Norwegian experience of mass politics: the opposition to the bureaucracy at the center; the struggle against the culture of the cities and the influences from abroad; the fight for the protection of the fisheries and of agriculture; and the fear of foreign capitalist forces.

TABLE A: **Electoral Behavior and Language; by Region, Occupation and Urbanization, in Percentages**

	RURAL								URBAN							
Occupation	Low				High				Low				High			
Region	*South/West*		*Other Regions*		*South/West*		*Other Regions*		*South/West*		*Other Regions*		*South/West*		*Other Regions*	
Language	Riks-mal	Ny-norsk	Riks-mal	Ny-norsk	Riks-mal	Ny-norsk	Riks-mal	Ny-norsk	Riks-mal	Ny-norsk	Riks-mal	Ny-norsk	Riks-mal	Ny-norsk	Riks-mal	Ny-norsk
Comm.	0	0	0	0	0	0	0	0	0	0	2		2	0	2	
Soc. P P	4	1	4	0	2	0	3	0	5	6	11		1	0	5	
Labor	51	36	70	75	12	20	31	20	73	44	69		31	44	25	
Liberal	21	20	5	5	24	13	7	20	10	19	4		27	43	9	
Christian	6	17	0	0	14	18	2	7	2	25	6		5	3	6	
Center	12	17	14	15	22	34	34	46	0	3	0		0	7	5	
Conser.	6	9	7	5	26	15	23	7	10	3	8		34	3	48	
Total	100															
N	67	70	257	20	50	76	200	15	41	36	257	6	62	30	264	7

TABLE B: Electoral Behavior and Teetotalism, by Region, Occupation, and Urbanization, in Percentages

	RURAL								URBAN							
Occupation	Low				High				Low				High			
Region	South/West		Other Regions		South/West		Other Regions		South/West		Other Regions		South/West		Other Regions	
Teetotalism	teetotalist	not teetotalist	tee-total.	not teetot.	tee-total.	not teetot.	tee-total.	not teetot.	tee-total.	not teetot.	tee-total.	not teetot.	tee-total.	not teetot.	tee-total.	not teetot.
Comm.	0	0	0	1	0	0	0	0	0	0	2	2	0	2	2	1
Soc. P P	3 {26}	3 {70}	2 {76}	4 {73}	0	2	0	4	0 {46}	7 {73}	9	12	0 {27}	2 {40}	0	6
Labor	23	67	74	69	15	18	20	32	46	66	59	71	27	38	25	26
Liberal	34	5	3	6	16	19	14	7	9	16	2	4	46	25	5	10
Christian	19	3	2	0	30	2	14	0	41	2	23	1	10	2	32	2
Center	16	13	16	13	27	32	44	33	4	0	0	1	0	3	2	5
Conser.	5	9	3	7	12	27	8	24	0	9	5	9	17	28	34	50
Total	100															
N	74	63	61	217	67	59	36	180	22	56	56	207	30	63	41	230

TABLE C: Electoral Behavior and Religion, by Region, Occupation and Urbanization, in Percentages

	RURAL								URBAN							
Occupation	Low				High				Low				High			
Region	*South/West*		*Other regions*		*South/West*		*Other regions*		*South/West*		*Other regions*		*South/West*		*Other regions*	
Religion	low	high	low	high	low	high	low	high	low	high	low	high	low	high	low	high
Comm.	0	0	1	0	0	0	0	0	0	0	2	0	2	0	2	0
Soc. P P	4	1	3	2	2	0	4	0	7	3	13	6	2	0	6	0
Labor	59	28	71	67	24	11	29	33	71	47	72	57	29	40	27	21
Liberal	14	27	6	6	18	16	6	12	12	16	4	2	34	30	10	8
Christian	0	23	0	1	4	26	1	7	0	28	0	27	2	8	3	19
Center	14	15	13	15	28	31	33	40	0	3	0	2	2	2	4	7
Conser.	9	6	6	9	24	16	27	8	10	3	9	6	29	20	48	45
Total	100															
N	66	71	196	81	50	74	153	60	42	36	209	54	52	40	211	58

Notes

1. For details of this typology of early polity-building characteristics and its use in the explanation of variations in the structuring of mass politics, see S. Rokkan, "Dimensions of State Formation and Nation-Building," in C. Tilly, ed., *The Building of States in Western Europe* (Princeton: Princeton University Press, 1972). This scheme represents a further development of the model first proposed in S. M. Lipset and S. Rokkan, eds., *Party Systems and Voter Alignments* (New York: Free Press, 1967) and later expanded by S. Rokkan in *Citizens, Elections, Parties* (New York: McKay, 1970).

2. These developments have been described in further detail in S. Rokkan, "Norway, Numerical Democracy and Corporate Pluralism," in R. A. Dahl., ed., *Political Oppositions in W. Democracies* (New Haven: Yale University Press, 1966) and in "Geography, Religion and Social Class," in S. M. Lipset and S. Rokkan, op. cit.

3. For further details see the Introduction to Lipset and Rokkan, op. cit.

4. For a detailed comparison of Norway, Denmark, and Sweden on this point, see W. Lafferty, *Economic Development and the Response of Labor in Scandinavia* (Oslo : Univ. Forl., 1971).

5. A detailed account of changes in the Norwegian electoral system is given in B. Kristvik and S. Rokkan, "Valgordningen" [The Electoral System] in *Politiske valg i Norge* (Oslo, Universitetsforlaget, 1966). For a quick overview of Norwegian developments in a comparative perspective see S. Rokkan, "Electoral Systems," *Int. Ency. Soc. Sci.* 1968, repr. in *Citizens, Elections, Parties*, op. cit., ch. 4.

6. See especially S. Rokkan and H. Valen, "Regional Contrasts in Norwegian Politics," in E. Allardt and S. Rokkan, eds., *Mass Politics* (New York: Basic Books, 1970). The archive of aggregate data by commune now runs from the "prepolitical" elections of the 1860s down to the present. For details see S. Rokkan and H. Aarebrot, "The Norwegian Archive of Historical Ecological Data," *Soc. Sci. Info* 8(1) 1969: 77–84, and *European Political Data*, the Newsletter of the ECPR Data Information Service.

7. For a full report see H. Valen and D. Katz, *Political Parties in Norway* (Oslo: Universitetsforlaget, 1964). Details of the nationwide survey are given in S. Rokkan, *Citizens*, op. cit., ch. 10-12.

8. A detailed analysis of the data for 1965 and 1969 is given in H. Valen and W. Martinussen, *Velgere og politiske frontlinjer* (Oslo: Gyldendal, 1972). Of particular importance for the argument of this chapter is the analysis of the dimensionalities of voting in 1965 presented in P. E. Converse and H. Valen, "Dimensions of Cleavage and Perceived Party Distances in Norwegian Voting," *Scand. Pol. Studies* 6, 1971: 107–152.

9. For a review of data on the electoral geography of Norway, see S. Rokkan and H. Valen, "Regional Contrasts in Norwegian Politics," in E. Allardt and S. Rokkan, eds., *Mass Politics* op. cit.

10. This figure was first presented by S. Rokkan in his article "Norway: Numerical Democracy and Corporate Pluralism," in R. A. Dahl, ed., *Political Oppositions in Western Democracies* (New Haven: Yale University Press, 1966) p. 93.

11. For a discussion of evidence for 1917, see S. Rokkan, ibid.

12. For an early example see Klaus Liepelt, "The Infra-Structure of Party Support in Germany and Austria," in M. Dogan and R. Rose, eds., *European Politics, A Reader* (Boston : Little Brown, 1971), pp. 183–202. Liepelt also carried out, with Henry Valen, the first A.I.D.-type analysis of Norwegian survey data.

13. For further details see Valen and Martinussen, op. cit. and S. Rokkan and H. Valen, "The Election to the Norwegian Storting in Sept. 1969," *Scand. Pol. Studies* vol. 5 (1970): 287–300.

14. Our analysis of socialist versus nonsocialist voting is based upon data from October, 1969–June, 1970 altogether 12,564 cases. For the other parties the material for the whole period has been used.

15. For a description of sampling procedures in the election survey see H. Valen and W. Martinussen, *Velgere og politiske frontlinjer*, op. cit., appendix 1.

16. See Valen-Katz, *Political Parties in Norway*, op. cit., ch. 9.

17. Converse-Valen "Dimensions of Cleavage and Party Distances." op. cit.

18. For details see the final section of Rokkan-Valen, "Regional contrasts . . . " op. cit.

8. SWEDEN:
The Social Bases of the Parties in a Developmental Perspective

BO SÄRLVIK

As in several other countries in Western Europe, in Sweden the 1920s were the formative years of the present party system. At the end of World War I Liberals and Social Democrats had gained sufficient strength to press through a sequence of constitutional reform bills, enacted in 1918–1921. Shaken by the political turbulences in postwar Europe, the Conservatives bowed to the inevitable. Henceforth, democratic representation and parliamentary government were fully established, and the party system became adapted to the new democratic order. This process of adaptation involved images and strategies as well as the social bases of parties and the division of voting strength among major political groupings. From these alterations emerged the five-party system and the political alignment of social groups that will be explored in this chapter.

It must be said that the Swedish five-party system grew out of political oppositions that in many ways were older than the 1920s. In the preceding decades boundaries of lasting significance for the social bases of the main parties had been drawn. The party system has certainly also undergone significant changes since. An important shift in the center of gravity of political power occurred as a consequence of the continued Social Democratic growth through the 1930s, just as the style of Swedish parliamentarism was reshaped from 1932 onward because of the Social Democrats' long-lasting role as the major governmental party. In spite of the multiparty situation Swedish parliamentarism came to bear much resemblance to the government-opposition duality in two-party systems. Even more pervasive, of course, is the transformation of the issues of party competition, which reflects social change; modern highly industrialized and urbanized Sweden is, indeed, vastly different from the still semiagricultural country of the 1920.

This chapter will present data and analyses to map the relationships between political behavior and social characteristics within the electorate of today's Sweden. First, however, we shall attempt to place that cross section in a time perspective by a retrospective exposition of the genesis of the party system and its stabilization during the country's first decade of democratic government. We will then employ aggregate population and election statistics as well a sequence of interview surveys to explore those developmental trends within the modern party system.

A Retrospective Overview: The Emergence of a Multiparty System

The party system formed by the end of the First World War represented political dividing lines in a society that had undergone profound structural change during a time span of about half a century. The crucial phase in this development had occurred before the war. We must go back to the decades preceding the 1911 election—the country's first election with general suffrage for men—to see the significance of the new constitutional reform after the war.

Compared with most other countries in Western Europe Sweden had been relatively late in industrialization, but in the late nineteenth-century economic development accelerated, resulting in tremendous industrial expansion. Export industries like sawmills, paper and paper pulp production, steel and engineering manufacturing, and ore mining expanded, along with domestic industries such as textiles. Another major feature of the period was large-scale emigration; from 1870 to 1910 the net emigration exceeded 850,000 persons. Each of these processes absorbed a large share of the rural population, especially the agricultural laborers. Furthermore, the emigration put a ceiling on population increase and helped to prevent the growth of an underemployed proletariat. From 1870 to 1910 the agricultural sector's share of the economically active population fell from 72 percent to 50 percent. The stagnant agricultural society was broken up. The farm laborers, the crofters, and the sons and daughters of farmers had got new options (see Table 1. A-C).

Political modernization came late to Sweden, too. It was not until 1866 that a new parliamentary order replaced the old four-estate Riksdag (nobility, clergy, bourgeoisie, and farmers) with a two-chamber Riksdag. It was a constitutional reform with strong conservative guarantees, however. The new First Chamber was elected by county councils and the councils of certain cities; these in turn were chosen in elections in which the voting right was steeply graded according to tax assessment (i.e., with increasing tax followed the right to cast an increasing number of ballots). Furthermore, strict income and property qualifications for eligibility made certain that the First Chamber would represent the upper classes. Even for the Second Chamber income and property qualifications were set so as to provide a quite limited electorate. Actually the Second Chamber electorate included only about half as large a proportion of the population as the county and city council electorate. In parliamentary elections, however, no voter could cast more than one ballot. In the countryside the regular farmers in general retained the voting right they had previously had as the electors of the old farmer estate. (In this regard the Swedish constitution has had for centuries, a broader popular base than most preindustrial societies in Europe.) In the towns the reform changed the composition of the electorate to some extent. But it did not—and was not intended to—result in a democratized suffrage.[1] Almost four-fifths of the male population above the age of twenty-one were without the franchise when the first Second Chamber election took place in 1866 (see Table 2).

This constitutional arrangement institutionalized one politically significant cleavage in the preindustrial society, that between the higher bureaucracy and the landed proprietors, on the one hand, and farm owners on the other. The two chambers were devised so as to prevent the former from being overwhelmed by the voting strength of the latter; it was intended to establish a balance of interests, but most of the time it resulted in stalemate.

In the First Chamber the higher bureaucracy made up about 40 percent of the membership until 1910, while about one-third of the members may be classed as estate owners; socially the two categories were indeed not very distinct from each other, and a sizable proportion of both belonged to the old nobility. A contingent of industrialists and commercial enterprisers represented the nonagricultural sector in this conservative chamber (about one-fifth of the membership). In the Second Chamber the farm owners'

TABLE 1: **Economic Change and Population Change: A Retrospective Overview of Trends**

A. ECONOMICALLY ACTIVE POPULATION BY BRANCH OF ECONOMY [1]

Percentage of Economically Active Population in:	1965	1960	1950	1940	1930	1920	1910	1870
Agriculture, forestry, fishing	10	13	20	29	38	43	50	72
Manufacturing, mining, construction	44	45	41	35	32	31	26	11
Commerce, transport, public administration, other services	46	42	39	36	30	26	24	17
Total percent	100	100	100	100	100	100	100	100

B. ECONOMICALLY ACTIVE POPULATION BY OCCUPATIONAL STATUS [2]

Percentage of economically active population:	(1965*)	1960	1950	1940	1930	1920	1910	1870
Agriculture								
Entrepreneurs (farm owners)	(5*)	7	10	12	11	12	15	18
Family members working on family farm	—	2	3	6	10	12	14	17
Farm workers	—	3	5	9	13	17	19	36
Other Sectors of the Economy								
Entrepreneurs	—	6	8	8	7	5	6	4
Salaried employees	—	35	28	20	14	12	9	4
Workers	—	47	46	45	45	42	37	21
Total percent	*	100	100	100	100	100	100	100

* Only the percentage for entrepreneurs in agriculture is given here, because comparable census data cannot be obtained for the entire classification.

C. PROPORTION OF THE POPULATION LIVING IN BUILT-UP (DENSELY POPULATED) AREAS [3]

	1965	1960	1950	1940	1930	1920	1910	
Percentage of the population living in built-up areas	77	73	66	56	48	45	34	
	1970	1960	1950	1940	1930	1920	1910	1870
Total population *in millions*	8.0	7.5	7.0	6.4	6.2	5.9	5.5	4.2

[1] Data for 1940-1965 are based on *Historisk statistik för Sverige. Del 1. Befolkning*, Andra uppl. 1720-1967, Statistiska centralbyrån, Stockholm 1969, p. 83. Data from preceding years are drawn from Sten Carlsson, "Den sociala omgrupperingen i Sverige efter 1866", *Samhälle och riksdag*, vol. I, (Uppsala; Almquist & Wicksell, 1966), 2. 281. All of the data reported in this table are based on population censuses. Over the years various changes have been made in the classification criteria. In *Historisk statistik för Sverige* as well as in Sten Carlsson's work, previously published data have been adjusted for the sake of comparability over time, but some discrepencies are likely to remain.

[2] The category of "Family members working on family farm" is comprised of sons, daughters, siblings, etc. who are working on the family's farm while the "farm workers" category consists of wage earners and others who are usually considered as hired labor; this category also comprises crofters. It should also be noted that a small proportion of farm inspectors and foremen (less than 1 percent) actually are included in the "salaried employee" category in the lower part of Table 1.B. The table has been adapted from Sten Carlsson, op. cit., p. 295. It should be noted that in this table the "Agriculture" category does *not* include forestry and fishing.

[3] Built up (densely populated) areas are defined as a clusters of dwelling houses with at least 200 inhabitants. To clarify the significance of this definition of "built up areas," it should be noted that the agrarian settlement on the rural countryside typically has not the "farm village" form that is more usual on the European continent. Actually, the old "farm villages" disappeared in Sweden in the early nineteenth century as a consequence of a large-scale land reform. Data from: *Historisk Statistik för Sverige*, I, p. 66.

interests were voiced through the majority Farmers' party; farm owners and a small group of estate owners formed a majority in the chamber until the turn of the century (52 percent in 1897).[2] Although it eventually developed into a conservative party, the old Farmers party was thus formed as an opposition party encompassing both narrow group interests (e.g., in regard to old inequities in land property taxation) and currents of agrarian liberalism as well as a more populist resentment against the ambitions of the bureaucratic and military elites.[3]

In the 1880s the coming of neoprotectionism created an issue that transgressed established political cleavages.[4] As in Germany, whose lead Sweden was to follow, protectionism had its roots in an agrarian crisis as well as in a nationalistic effort to support domestic industries. On this issue a protectionistic coalition consisting of majorities in both of the chambers could be formed.

The clashing of interests over the change from free trade to protectionism mobilized popular political engagement to a hitherto unseen extent. Nationwide organizations for propaganda and electioneering came into being for the first time. Furthermore, food tariffs so clearly affected the interests of the disfranchised strata that opposition to protectionism almost inevitably became an impetus to widen the demand for a suffrage reform.

The latter was articulated through enfranchisement organizations, which temporarily grew into a mass movement in the ensuing decades. At the same time the temperance movement raised political interest and provided opportunities to acquire organizational skills within the lower-middle-class and the working-class; around the turn of the century the movement counted more than 200,000 members. Within the same strata the new "free churches" (Protestant fundamentalists like the Baptists) questioned the authority of the state church and, in effect, estranged most of its membership from political traditionalism. Thus the foundation was laid for a liberal party with both town and small farmer support. In 1900 these groups coalesced in the new Liberal parliamentary party (see Chart 1). While the enfranchisement movement had petered out, a Liberal party organization was built up (1901) and reached a membership of more than 40,000 in 1910.[5]

CHART 1. The Parties

CONSERVATIVE PARTY *Moderata Samlingspartiet* (Moderate Coalition Party). Party name changed in 1968; previously: *Högerpartiet* (the Right party)	The modern parliamentary Conservative (Right) party grew out of several agrarian, protectionist, and generally conservative parties that existed in the chambers from the very beginning of the two-chamber system. In each of the chambers they were reorganized as unified conservative parties in 1912. From 1935, the Conservatives like the other parties organized themselves in a joint parliamentary party. A *national party organization* was formed in 1904.
PEOPLE'S PARTY (LIBERALS) *Folkpartiet*	A Liberal parliamentary party was formed in 1900 and was then joined both by an existing People's party and a substantial number of previously unaffiliated liberal Members. A *national party organization* was formed in 1902. After a party split in 1923-1934 the two fractions reunited under the present party name.
SOCIAL DEMOCRATIC LABOR PARTY *Sveriges Socialdemokratiska Arbetareparti*	The *party organization* was formed in 1889, without any representation in the Riksdag. Obtaining only a few seats before the 1907-1909 Suffrage reform, it was not until 1906 that the Social Democrats formally organized themselves as a parliamentary party.
COMMUNIST PARTY *Vänsterpartiet Kommunisterna*	In 1917 a Left Socialist party split off from the Social Democrats. After a split in 1921 a Communist party was formed. The dissenting Left Socialists soon returned to the Social Democrats.
CENTER PARTY *Centerpartiet* Party name changed in 1957; previously: Agrarian party, *i.e. Landsbygdspartiet Bondeförbundet*	The Agrarian party was formed in 1921 through the merger of two farmers' parties which had been formed as *national voters' organizations* in 1913 and 1917, the two parties had elected their first Members in 1917.

The mainstream within the Farmers' party concurrently moved toward the Right. In the new context a suffrage reform might become a threat to the farm owners' economic interests as well as their political influence. Thus protectionism and reluctance to extend the suffrage merged into a conservative outlook. In the 1910s was added to this, an entirely new element namely a broad movement of national opinion to support the strengthening of the country's military forces. This became the third main component of the conservative outlook.[6] The emergence of a modern party system with supporting mass organizations was also to encompass the political right: A national conservative organization was formed in 1904 to challenge the liberal group.[7] The old Farmers party—which had existed only as a parliamentary party— disintegrated in the midst of the renewal of the party system that was thus taking place. For some years after the turn of the century there was actually one rural and one urban conservative fraction in the Second Chamber, although they both maintained connections with the same national mass organization.[8]

Parallel to this development, from the 1890s the Social Democrats and the trade unions began to gain strength among industrial workers in the towns as well as in the industries in the countryside. By the first decade of the new century the trade unions had become an impressive mass movement (although there was a temporary setback after the general strike in 1909).[9] The Social Democratic party and its associated organizations grew together with the unions; in 1912 the party membership was about 65,000. The political significance of the labor movement was furthermore heightened when an increasing number of workers passed the income qualifications for suffrage; in 1905 thirteen Social Democrats were elected to the Second Chamber, and in 1908 the parliamentary party increased its membership to thirty-four.

The decades from 1870 to 1910 were also a period of tremendous growth of communication—in both senses of the word. About 12,000 kilometers of railways— almost the entire modern railway network—were constructed during these years. At the same time the communication of ideas was stimulated by an almost explosive growth in the number of newspapers and of newspaper circulation, especially during the later part of the period.

In Table 2 we have brought together a selection of indicators of social modernization and political mobilization that accompanied the breakthrough of industrialization. As compared to the drastic rates of increase for communication and transportation shown in the table, the rate of urbanization may appear moderate, but it really reflects the fact that important sectors of the industry were located in the countryside. Organization growth is, of course, only partially indicated by the trade-union statistics. If temperance organizations, national party organizations, consumers' cooperatives (above 70,000 in 1910), and free churches are taken into account, one may estimate that considerably more than half a million people must have been drawn into the new popular movements.

The table also shows that the relative size of the electorate was growing, although the legal franchise requirements remained unchanged. This was the effect of an increasing income level, especially in the towns. Most of this enlargement of the electorate occurred from 1890 to 1908. The average annual income of male industrial and mining workers was about doubled from the 1860s to 1910–1913; since franchise requirements were not changed it is of course the nominal income and not the "real income" that is relevant in this case.[10] The rise in electoral participation within the

TABLE 2: Political Mobilization and Modernization in the Decade before the Suffrage Reform

	PROPORTION OF MEN ABOVE AGE 21 ENFRANCHISED			PROPORTION PARTICIPATING IN ELECTION AMONG ENFRANCHISED POPULATION			TRANSPORTATION AND COMMUNICATION			URBANIZATION: PROPORTION LIVING IN TOWNS AND BOROUGHS	ORGANIZATION: THOUSANDS OF MEMBERS OF LABOR UNIONS
	Towns	Country side	Total	Towns	Country side	Total	Railways: MILLIONS OF "PASSENGER KILOMETERS"	Mail: MILLIONS OF UNITS SENT	Mass Media: NEWSPAPER CIRCULATION, THOUSAND OF COPIES		
									(1865 ca) 100		
Election 1872/ c:a 1870, resp.	21%	22%	22%	41%	16%	19%	98	58	(1884 ca) 500	13%	(1886 ca) 8
Election 1908/ c:a 1910, resp.	45%	31%	35%	70%	57%	61%	1426	394	(1912) 1.786	30%	(1909) 148

Data for electoral participation pertain to the elections in 1872 and 1908, respectively.

Other indicators refer to the beginning and the end of the 1870-1910 period, although with some deviations as explained in the notes.

ENFRANCHISEMENT AND TURNOUT: *Historisk statistik för Sverige. Statistiska översiktstabeller utöver i del I och II publicerade*, Statistiska centralbyrån (Stockholm: 1960). See also: Andrén, *Tvåkammarsystemets tillkomst och utveckling. Sveriges Riksdag*, vol. IX (Stockholm: 1937). It should be noted that *indirect elections* were quite usual in the *countryside* in the early part of the period. In 1872 participation was 22 percent in the sixty countryside constituencies that held direct elections, and 12 percent in the seventy-eight constituencies where "elections of electors" were held. Only two town constituencies (out of thirty-six) had indirect elections; if they are excluded, the participation rate increases only with .5 percentage units. In 1908 *all but one of the constituencies held direct elections.*

RAILWAYS: Annual average for 1866-1970 and data for 1910, resp. MAIL: Annual average for 1876-1880 and data for 1910, resp. Incl. printed matter, etc. For *letter and postcard* mail only, the corresponding data are 33 and 172 millions, respectively. Source: *Historisk statistik för Sverige. Statistiska översiktstabeller* etc.

URBANIZATION: data from *Historisk statistik för Sverige*, Del I, Befolkning.

ORGANIZATION: Very approximate data from 1886. The later data pertain to 1909, when the union membership had become drastically reduced due to a general strike. In 1908 the membership had been about 213,000, while it fell even below the 1909 figure in 1910. By the end of World War I the labor unions had regained their strength of before the general strike. Source: Westerståhl. *Svensk fackföreningsrörelse* (Stockholm: 1945).

NEWSPAPER CIRCULATION: Data for 1865 and 1884 are approximations given in: Gunnar Wallin: *Valrörelser och valresultat. Andrakammarvalen i Sverige 1866-1884;* (Stockholm: 1961).

Data for 1912 are based on an estimate reported in *TS-Boken*, 1969.

enfranchised population was, indeed, spectacular. Especially in the countryside, this trend was to some extent linked to another politicization phenomenon, the disappearance of indirect Second Chamber elections in the constituencies (see note to the table).

A new political culture had emerged. It required a reshaping of the constitutional framework. The demand for democratic representation could no longer be effectively resisted, but it could be delayed, as it was, until the end of the First World War.

The new Liberal party became the largest in the Second Chamber almost immediately after its formation, and from 1905 Liberals and the small Social Democratic group together had a majority in that chamber. The Liberals were nevertheless unable to carry through the suffrage reform they had sought for so long, principally because of the resistance of the compact conservative majority in the First Chamber. The necessary compromise was finally reached under a conservative government in 1907 and enacted as a law in 1909 (constitutional amendments require decisions by two parliamentary sessions with a general election in between). The reform granted, almost without restriction, the voting right to all male citizens; minor restrictions remained until the second constitutional reform. In order to prevent a complete predominance of the Left in the Second Chamber, proportional representation in multimember constituencies was introduced in place of the old single-member-simple-majority election system. The basis of the First Chamber was also partially democratized by limiting the number of ballots a voter could cast in local government elections to a maximum of forty.

The effect of the reform on the First Chamber (after its complete renewal in 1910 by councils chosen in accordance with the new rules) is shown in Table 3. As seen in the table, the First Chamber lost its almost homogeneously conservative composition. Yet, the income-graded suffrage guaranteed a conservative majority until the final democratization of the constitution.

In the Second Chamber and its electorate the Conservative-Liberal balance that had prevailed from around 1900 was succeeded by a *tripartite* division (see Tables 3–4). The conservative share of the vote, of course, shrank over the entire country until it became a party about the same size as the Social Democrats. What remained of the old Farmers' party joined a unified Conservative party formed in the Second Chamber immediately after the election.. The Liberal party, with 40 percent of the vote, retained its parliamentary strength, but its electoral base shifted. In the new electorate it drew the major part of its support from the rural countryside. In the cities and, to an even more marked extent in densely populated nonurban areas (i.e., "industrial villages") the Social Democrats became the largest of the parties. Ecological analyses suggest that the Social Democrats, indeed, won most of the industrial workers vote in his first election with extended suffrage.[11]

The Liberal predominance in a tripartite grouping was dissolved almost as swiftly as it appeared. The Liberals got involved in an agitated controversy about the country's military defense. This estranged a large part of its middle-class and farmer support and at the same time polarized the political climate to the advantage of the Social

Sweden   379

TABLE 3: Political Change after the Constitutional Reforms in 1907-1909 and in 1918-1921

PARTY STRENGTH IN THE RIKSDAG

	Number of Members of First Chamber		Number of Members of Second Chamber		Number of Members of First Chamber		Number of Members of Second Chamber	
	1911	**1912**	**1911**	**1912**	**1918**	**1919**	**1921***	**1922******
Conservative parties	128	86	84	64	88	38	71	62
Agrarian parties	—	—	—	—	—	19	30	21
Liberals	15	52	98	102	45	41	47	41
Social Democrats (incl. Left Socialists)	2	12	35	64	17	52	80	99
Communists	—	—	—	—	—	—	2	7
Others	5	—	13	—	—	—	—	—
TOTAL	150	150	230	230	150	150	230	230

*Elected in 1920.

**Elected after dissolution 1921.

Table 3 shows distributions of seats in the parliamentary sessions immediately before and after the first election to be held according to the new electoral rules enacted through the two suffrage reforms.

The changes in the party composition of the two chambers were not entirely the results of the suffrage reforms. They certainly also reflect shifts in voting behavior among those whose right to vote was not directly affected.

Sources: Edvard Thermaenius, *Sveriges Riksdag,* vol. IX (Stockholm: 1935). *Historisk statistik för Sverige. Statistiska översiktstabeller,* Statistiska centralbyrån; (Stockholm: 1960). A few members who were not formally party-affiliated have been included in the figure for the party they were closest to. Of the thirteen nonaffiliated Second Chamber members in 1911, eight may be considered as Conservatives and five as Liberals.

Democrats. By 1914 the Liberal party had lost enough to become the smallest of the three parties. In that year's elections the Social Democrats also had their breakthrough in northern Sweden (Norrland), an area that used to be strongly dominated by radical liberalism; some northern areas with continuing free-church traditions still remain as Liberal strongholds.

TABLE 4:   **Electoral Participation and Party Division of the Vote, 1911–1970**

		TURNOUT	PARTY DIVISION OF THE VOTE PERCENTAGE						
		Percen-tage	Commu-nist party	Social Dem. party	Center (Agra-rian) party	People's Party (Liber-als)	Christian Dem. Coal.	Locald Bourg. Coal.	Conser-vative party
1970	P	88.3	5.2a	45.3	19.9	16.2	1.8	—	11.5
1968	P	89.3	3.0	50.1	16.1	15.0	1.5	0.4	13.9
1966	L	82.8	6.4	42.2	13.7	16.7	1.8	4.3	14.7
1964	P	83.9	5.2	47.3	13.4	17.1	1.8	1.5	13.7
1962	L	81.0	3.8	50.5	13.1	17.1	.	.	15.5
1960	P	85.9	4.5	47.8	13.6	17.5	.	.	16.5
1958	L	79.2	4.0	46.8	13.1	15.6	.	.	20.4
1958	P	77.4	3.4	46.2	12.7	18.2	.	.	19.5
1956	P	79.8	5.0	44.6	9.4	23.8	.	.	17.1
1954	L	79.1	4.8	47.4	10.3	21.7	.	.	15.7
1952	P	79.1	4.3	46.1	10.7	24.4	.	.	14.4
1950	L	80.5	4.9	48.6	12.3	21.7	.	.	12.3
1948	P	82.7	6.3	46.1	12.4	22.8	.	.	12.3
1946	L	72.0	11.2	44.4	13.6	15.6	.	.	14.9
1936	P	74.5	7.7a	45.9	14.3	12.9	.	.	17.6
1932	P	68.6	8.3a	41.7	14.1	11.7c	.	.	23.5
1921	P	54.2	4.6	39.4b	11.1	19.1	.	.	25.8
1911	P	57.0	.	28.5	.	40.2	.	.	31.2

aIncluding a splitoff "Marxist Leninist" party in 1970; in the 1930s the Communists were divided into two parties.

bIncluding the Left Socialist party.

cTotal for the two liberal parties which existed during the party split 1923-1934.

dVotes for coalition ballots that could not be attributed to national parties.

Table 4 displays turnout and vote distributions for the postwar elections as well as some preceding elections of particular political importance. The 1911 *election* was the first to be held with *general suffrage for men;* at the same time *P.R. in multimember constituencies* was introduced. The first parliamentary election after the *enfranchisement of women* was held in *1921.*

National *parliamentary* elections (Second Chamber before 1970) are indicated by a *P* after the election year in the table. *L* indicates elections of county councils and city councils of cities not included in any county. Percentages in the vote distributions are based on the total number of votes cast, but they do not add up to 100 because of the exclusion of a slight proportion of "Others" (c. 1 percent in most cases).

After the end of the war and the postwar constitutional reform a new shift occurred. The Conservatives lost their last extra-democratic lever to political influence when the constitutional reform did away with their First Chamber majority (see Table 3). Among the farmers new political movements had been formed for the purpose of voicing specific agrarian demands more effectively. In 1917 they first won their parliamentary representation and in 1921 they merged under the Agrarian party label (see Chart 1). Unlike concurrent party formations on the Left, the new party was not a result of party splitting; almost all the new Agrarian members were men without any previous parliamentary careers. The main part of its voting support must have been drawn from the old agrarian component of the Conservative party, but there was also a substantial outflow of earlier Liberal voters.

The Liberals entered the liberal-socialist coalition government in 1917, having kept 28 percent of the vote in that year's election. But the decline continued; in 1921 the party had reached 19 percent on its downhill way (see Table 4). What remained of the party's voting support consisted primarily of a core of voters with attachments to the free churches or the temperance movement. A fraction with roots in the old urban liberalism actually broke off to form its own party in 1923, and this split remained until 1934, when the two fractions merged to form the *People's Party*. P R—to which the Liberal Party once had been bitterly opposed—rescued it from total elimination just as it made possible the emergence of the Agrarian party.

The Social Democrats experienced the splitoff of a Left-socialist fraction in 1917 but regained most of that loss in 1921, when the Left-socialist fraction itself split through the formation of a Communist party. After their period of growth the Social Democrats (including the Left socialists) reached 39 percent of the electorate in 1917. For a decade the Social Democrats were stagnated at about that level in parliamentary elections with a small Communist party (4 to 6 percent) on its left flank.

The multiparty system had emerged and become stabilized.

The Modern Party System: Developmental Trends

THE PARLIAMENTARY BASES OF GOVERNMENTS: PARTIES AND COALITIONS

In its first decade of existence, the 1920s, modern parliamentary government could be described as a search for temporary majorities. After the end of the Liberal-socialist coalition none of the parties attained a majority of its own, while at the same time the possibility of forming governmental coalitions was precluded by the Liberals' determination to stay out of any collaboration with the Left as well as with the Right. Hence a sequence of minority governments was formed by the Social Democrats, the Conservatives, and—quite successfully—the small and split Liberal center. Each of these governments could survive only as long as it secured additional support for its legislative program. In this game the Liberals were favored because when in government they could let the Right and the Left alternate in the supporting role, and when in opposition they could decide the fate of the government.

From 1932 parliamentary government came to mean Social Democrats in the government position, either alone or as a dominant part of a coalition. There were two circumstances that brought about this new setting for parliamentary politics. After the stagnation during the 1920s a moderate but politically significant increase in the socialist share of the vote occurred in the 1930s. The great economic depression, provides the backdrop for this shift to the left in the electorate. In 1932 Social Democrats and Communists thus attained 50 percent of the vote. This has been the baseline for the strength of the socialist vote: sometimes it has been exceeded by a few percentage points and occasionally it has been barely missed (see Table 4). Although the Social Democrats' own share of the vote has hovered around the 46–47 percent level, this balance of strength has, in effect, precluded the formation of a "bourgeois" (i.e., nonsocialist) parliamentary Government during subsequent decades.[12]

The other of the two circumstances that reshaped preconditions for parliamentary government consisted of a change in the party constellation, which broke up the previous deadlock in coalition formation. Until the early 1930s the Agrarian party had been a party of the political right, and thus the Liberals had been in a position to block the formation of a majority coalition. The economic hardships of the farmers in the depression led the Agrarian party to enter an agreement with the Social Democratic minority government, which had been formed after the 1932 election. Furthermore, this collaboration led to a formal coalition government that lasted until the outbreak of World War II.[13] (It is noteworthy that the same kind of coalitions were formed in Norway and Finland during this period.) Through the war the country was governed by a grand coalition.

The years after the war have been a period of Social Democratic government, interrupted only by a Social Democratic-Agrarian coalition government, 1951–1957. Although that coalition secured an impressive governmental majority, it did not improve the two parties' electoral fortunes: both of them suffered serious setbacks at the polls. In a sense both of the parties were rescued from the coalition by a major conflict over a pension reform, which finally was carried through by the Social Democrats against the opposition of all the nonsocialist parties. The Agrarian party —now appearing under the new Center party label—returned to opposition and managed to attract substantial new voting support from outside the shrinking agrarian population, ending up with a much enlarged base. At the same time the Social Democrats also gained increased strength from the pension conflict and thus consolidated their governmental position through the 1960s.

In retrospect the significance of the attempt to revive the prewar farmer– labor coalition lies indeed not in its formation but in the fact that it failed. The multiparty system has stiffened in a "Bourgeois-Social Democrat" *two-bloc* formation.

The 1965 division of seats in the two chambers shown in Table 5 presents the balance of party strength that has prevailed during most of the postwar decades. In the Second Chamber the Social Democrats and the Communists have formed a majority when counted together, except for some years in the 1950s. Although the Communists cannot unequivocally be included in the parliamentary base of a Social Democratic government, it clearly meant that the bourgeois parties were unable to form a majority coalition during most of the period. In the First Chamber the Social Democrats have continuously held the majority, which sometimes has been of crucial importance because financial matters have been decided by the total (i.e. added) distribution of votes in the two Chambers in instances when they have come to differing decisions. The 1969 division really reflects the result of an election in which the Social Democrats

TABLE 5: **Balance of Party Strength in the Riksdag, 1965–1971**

	1971 session (*unicameral*)	1969 session First Chamber	1969 session Second Chamber	1965 session First Chamber	1965 session Second Chamber
Communists	17	1	3	2	8
Social Democrats	163	79	125	78	113
Center party	71	21	39	19	35
People's party	58	27	34	26	43
Conservatives	41	23	32	26	33
Total	350	151	233	151	233*a*

*a*Including one Member who was elected on a Bourgeois coalition ballot but did not join any parliamentary party.

THE ELECTORAL ORDER BEFORE AND AFTER THE 1969 CONSTITUTIONAL REFORM. In the two-chamber *Riksdag* that existed until the end of 1970, the First Chamber was elected by members of county councils and city councils of cities not included in any county. The election period was eight years, and one-eight of the chamber was renewed each year. County councils as well as city councils had four-year election periods. This election system gave some overrepresentation to large parties. The Second Chamber was elected every fourth year in twenty-eight multimember constituencies. The proportional system was devised so as to disfavor very small parties. This had a ceiling effect on the Communist representation and entirely excluded the Christian Democrats.

The new unicameral Riksdag is elected every third year in general elections when the communal and county councils are also elected. Of its 350 seats 310 are distributed over the twenty-eight constituencies. These are allocated to parties under the application of a proportional system within each of the constituencies. The remaining forty seats are then allocated to constituency parties so as to attain full proportionality (with some restrictions) between national voting strength and size of parliamentary representation. The restriction in proportionality pertains to parties that obtain *less than 4 percent* of the national vote. Such parties are entirely excluded from representation unless they obtain at least 12-percent of the vote in at least one constituency. In the latter case a party obtains only the seats it is entitled to within those constituencies where the share of the vote reaches the 12-percent level, and it cannot obtain any of the seats in the "national pool." In 1970 the regular Communist party barely exceeded the 4-percent limit and thus secured proportional representation, while the Christian Democrats were still excluded.

The *voting age* has been lowered repeatedly; the citizen now obtains the right to vote in the calendar year when he reaches the age of twenty.

gained support considerably above their normal level. In general, thus, the party's governmental position has had a much more precarious parliamentary base than its long-lastingness might suggest.[14]

A new parliamentary framework has been created through the introduction of the unicameral Riksdag in 1971 (see under Table 5). The party balance that resulted from the 1970 election is also shown in Table 5. Aside from the weakening of the Social Democratic party, which may (or may not) be a temporary phenomenon, the parliamentary situation appearing in this first session of the new Riksdag contains features that will clearly be of lasting significance.

As is seen in the table the Center party is at present the largest of the opposition parties. This is, of course, not an unchangeable state though it is a result of a profound change in the party's general appearance that is likely to be irreversible: the Center party no longer represents a homogeneous agrarian section of the electorate. "The logic of the situation" at present seems to require the Center party to seek political power through the building of either a majority coalition or a centrist bloc of bourgeois parties.

The constitutional reform has also made the Social Democrats' position much more vulnerable. The party's perennial First Chamber majority, which was at least partly due to an overrepresentation effect of the election system, has been eliminated. A Social Democratic government can thus no longer rely upon a "reserve power" to bloc an alternative coalition formation after a defeat in a parliamentary election. Furthermore, the almost complete proportionality built into the new election system will probably eliminate the previous systematic underrepresentation of the Communist. It is true that the bourgeois parties used to gain about as much as the Social Democrats from that underrepresentation effect, so the balance between them should not be significantly affected by the new election system. It remains to see, however, if the sheer size effect of a larger Communist party in the Riksdag will be entirely negligible.

Party Organizations

FINANCE

Party resources depend upon party financing. This is a somewhat opaque sector of party activities; we will not even attempt to estimate the total costs involved. The trade-union movement publicly contributes very large sums to the Social Democratic party, both nationally and locally. The Conservative party—and earlier also the People's party—has received contributions from private enterprises that seem to match the trade-union contributions reasonably well, at least as long as one is calculating in terms of magnitudes. Unfortunately, there are only partial data available as to the financing arrangements of private enterprises.[15]

The most noteworthy feature in Swedish party financing is the extent to which the parties now depend on *grants from national and local government sources*. This is a new phenomenon, brought about by legislation enacted in the late 1960s. A national party-support scheme provides state grants to national party organizations that have obtained parliamentary representation. The size of the grant to each party is proportional to its parliamentary strength. The new legislation has furthermore authorized communal and country councils to support lower-tier party organizations too. Party subsidies have consequently been introduced all over Sweden.

As the system is new, its consequences are somewhat uncertain. It has for example been argued that the public grants may make individuals and organizations less willing to support political parties financially. In a sense it was also the purpose of the public-financing scheme to make the parties less dependent upon private sources of economic support. Another reason was that the Social Democrats and the trade-union movement were in serious financial trouble because of the great and increasing deficits shown by the Social Democratic newspapers, which are owned mainly by the labor unions.

The size of the public party support is quite impressive, as is demonstrated by the following figures for 1970.[16]

	Grants to political parties
State grants	24.5 million SwCr
County grants	9.4 million SwCr
Communal grants	27.9 million SwCr
Total, approx.	61.8 million SwCr
(Total, approx. = U.S. $ 12 million)	

We are not in a position to estimate how large a portion of the parties' total cost is covered by grants from public funds. It is obvious that the public support must greatly exceed the total amount of regular membership dues paid by individually affiliated party members. As an illustrative figure, the People's party reports that about half of the total cost of its national organization during the 1970 election year was covered by state grants; this budget does not include activities on the constituency and local level. It is certain that both the Conservatives and the Social Democrats—which are generally better off financially—derive a larger proportion of their means from other sources. But public funding has profoundly changed the preconditions for party financing.

THE PARTIES' ORGANIZATIONAL RESOURCES

All of the Swedish parties have a nationwide voter organization. The local organizations found in almost every commune are in general federated on the county level to form the parties' parliamentary constituency organizations. The constituency organizations usually work through annual district conferences and through some type of executive committee with a small permanent staff. Although election campaigns are generally planned and monitored by the national party organizations, the constituency and local organizations play a significant role in electioneering and—perhaps even more—in the parties' continuous study groups and external propaganda activities. The most important function of the constituency organizations is to arrange the candidate nominations for parliamentary elections. The influence that national party organizations can exert on the constituency nominations is generally considered to be quite limited.

The constituency parties thus compose the parliamentary election ballots. The ordering of the candidates on the ballot determines the order in which they can be elected in multimember constituencies; if a ballot obtains enough votes for two seats,

number one and number two on the list will be elected, etc. The voters can strike out
particular names on such a ballot, but the effect of such changes is normally negligible.
More important is the provision that a party can present more than one name list under
its common party label; these lists are then considered to form an electoral cartel. The
nonsocialist parties usually present at least two party ballots in each constituency,
while the Social Democrats have done so only in a few instances. Such alternative
party ballots are often designed for different parts of the constituency, for example
one for the countryside and another for the cities. Being mostly designed to implement
a calculated campaign strategy, such alternative party ballots very seldom give rise to
internal factional feuds.[17]

At the national level the organization structures comprise national congresses,
various types of national party councils, and fairly well-staffed permanent party offices.
Financing and fund-raising are generally in the hands of the national voter organizations rather than the parliamentary parties. The party leader is almost invariably the
chairman of both the national organization and the parliamentary party.

Within the national party framework there exist a variety of subsidiary organizations; for example, occupational groups and women have their own organizations. The
political organizations for youth are usually more loosely affiliated to the parties. Since
the beginning of the century a large workers' educational association has organized
study activities in close cooperation with the Social Democratic party and the labor
unions. More recently similar organizations have been formed by nonsocialist parties.

The parties' internal power structures have not been too extensively researched.[18]
It is quite apparent, however, that policies and strategies are mostly decided by the
parliamentary parties and their leaderships. In general, conflicts between parliamentary
parties and national organizations are not to be discerned. Such dissension is not very
likely to occur because of the joint chairmanship held by the party leaders and because
a sizable portion of the national party council also holds membership in the parliamentary party. As the control over the parliamentary nominations remains in the
constituency organizations, there is still room for a continuous and significant influence
from local party organizations on national politics. In other words, the parties' policy-
making centralized, but the recruiting of the policy-makers is decentralized.

On the basis of the parties' reported membership figures one can calculate that
about one-fourth of the adult population holds party membership. These figures (which
do not include youth organizations or educational side organizations) are shown in the
Table below. In a sense this estimate is somewhat inflated because of the peculiar structure of the Social Democratic party, which allows union locals to register their members
collectively as party members. As a result about 70 percent of the Social Democratic
membership consists of collectively affiliated union members.

One can compare the figures cited with an estimate based on survey data. According to the latter, only about 16 percent of the enfranchised electorate are members of
the parties or their youth organizations. Most of the difference can be attributed to the
Social Democratic union membership, since the estimates obtained for other parties
coincide fairly well with their reported membership figures. It seems that a large ma-

jority of those collectively affiliated through the unions do not actually think of themselves as party members and, consequently, are not registered as such in an interview survey. Instead of almost 40 percent (as membership statistics would indicate), only about 15 percent of the Social Democratic voters say they are party members (see the percentaged survey data included with the party-membership statistics). Both the Conservatives and the Center party appear in the survey data to have a larger proportion of

Party Organizations

	Reported memberships[a] *(Thousands of persons)*	*Election Survey 1968: Interview Data[b] Proportion party members of each party's voters, percent*
Communist party	15	(15)
Social Democratic party[c]	890	15
Center party	182	20
People's party	76	12
Conservative party	136	21

[a]Membership statistics pertain to 1970.

[b]Entries in this column show the percentage of each party's voters in the interview sample who reported that they were members of that party. (A small number of respondents were actually members of party other than the one they voted for.)

[c]The number of individually affiliated members of the Social Democratic party can be estimated to about 267,000.

organized members in their voting support. In terms of numbers the Social Democratic party organization is nevertheless larger than that of any other party, even if we take only the individually affiliated membership into account. In reality the organizational strength of the party is even greater than these data would suggest, because it has also access to most of the labor unions' organizational resources—beneficial during election campaigns. To some, but clearly a lesser extent the Center party is advantaged by its close connection with the various farmers' organizations.

If it is difficult to estimate even the organizational strength of the parties, it may appear that the voters' *affective attachment to political parties* must be an even less tangible phenomenon. However, we have measured the strength of the voters' psychological party attachments in a sequence of election studies and have found some proportions and relationship that show a remarkable degree of stability over time. The data in Table 6 present the essentials of the picture formed by these measurements. The upper part of the table is based on an adaption of the well-known party identification measure to the Swedish party system. As is seen in the table, the proportion of "strong party identifiers" is considerably larger in the Social Democratic voting support than among the nonsocialist voters.[19] The People's party can obviously count upon that kind of attachment to a much lesser extent than the other major parties. If we disregard the Communist party (whose voting support shows a remarkably high turnover rate from election to election), the strength of the voters' partisan engagement seems to form a U-shaped curve over the Left-Right arraying in the party system.[20] The pattern does indeed suggest a comparison with an attitude scale on which one expects the intensity of attitudes to increase toward both extreme ends. There are concurrent and competing explanations of this pattern which can be substantiated by our data. Thus the perpetual competition that goes on between the nonsocialist parties is accompanied by a continuous exchange of voters among these parties; it is not suprising that one then finds a fairly sizable category of voters who are consistently nonsocialist but who do not have a strong sense of attachment to any particular party.[21] We have also found that the attachment to the party among Social Democratic voters is strengthened by supporting group membership, like trade-union affiliation. It is noteworthy that the latter phenomenon also appears within a part of the Center party. Among the Center party voters who are farmers, as many as 54 percent consider themselves "strongly convinced adherents" of their party. Weak partisanship, however, is shown by the party's newly acquired nonagrarian support; only 19 percent of these voters are "strong identifiers" according to our criterion.

The lower part of Table 6 captions the result of measuring voters' expectations before the 1968 election concerning the consequences of a possible change to a nonsocialist government. We can conceive of this, too, as a measure of partisanship. These data thus substantiate the impression that a strong sense of partisanship is most widespread among the Social Democratic voters. We cannot really explore the import of this

TABLE 6: Aspects of Partisan Engagement

	PARTY VOTE IN 1968				
	Communist party	Social Democr. party	Center party	People's party	Conservative party
Proportion of voters with *strong party identification* in agreement with actual party vote	23% (39)	51% (1.458)	29% (469)	19% (370)	37% (286)
Proportion of voters who feel strong *concern about government change*	55% (20)	57% (668)	26% (225)	34% (185)	40% (131)

Source: Election Survey, 1968.

In the upper part of the table we employ a measure of *party identification* which shows the proportion of voters who were "strongly convinced adherents" of the party they voted for. This is our operational definition for a strong party identification in agreement with actual party vote.

The lower part of the table shows the proportion of each party's voters who thought that a change to a nonsocialist government would lead to a "very great" or "rather great" change in the conditions in the country. These have been categorized as people with a strong sense of *concern about governmental change*. The complementary response alternatives were: "not a particularly great change" and "no change at all". This question was asked only in preelection interviews with half of the total sample.

Percentage bases are indicated within parentheses.

"partisanship" in the present inquiry. Suffice it, therefore, to state that it appears to involve both a sense of being personally affected by the kinds of policies that are pursued in the country and a conviction that it matters which party is in power.

MASS-MEDIA RESOURCES

The five major parties have equal access to free television and radio time in election campaigns through the Swedish Radio, which is a public corporation with legal monopoly over broadcasting and television. This is of course especially important for the parties with weak newspaper support. The press resources are, indeed, quite unevenly divided among the parties as is shown below from with data on newspaper circulation. The People's party in particular has a strong source of support in the liberal press, which controls about half of the total newspaper circulation. Quite recently a new scheme that gives financial support to weak newspapers has been introduced. In view of the press situation this scheme can be considered as a complementary form of party support; about half the state-subsidized newspapers are Social Democratic. The effect of this scheme will hardly be to change the present balance in the daily press; at most, it may help to save a number of papers with strong local competitors. To some extent—it should also be noted—the predominance of the liberal press is balanced by the trade-union weeklies, which cover most of the LO membership and generally support the Social Democrats.

The Daily Press

	Number of newspapers	Proportion of total weekday net circulation for each newspaper category.
Communist party	1	.1
Social Democratic party	24	21.0
Center party and Independent Liberal	13	3.0
People's party	47	49.8
Conservative party	43	17.8
Nonaffiliated and others	21	4.3
TOTAL	149	100.0%
		N= 5 million copies

ource: *TS-Boken 1970.*

A CHANGING ELECTORATE

Long-term economic and population changes in Sweden were followed by a recasting of the entire political framework, and a multiparty system adapted to this new framework emerged around 1920. In quantitative terms subsequent changes in the economic system have been no less impressive. In the 1920s about 40 percent of the economically active population was engaged in agricultural work; this sector had shrunk to about 20 percent by 1950 and to about 10 percent by the mid 1960s. The trends appearing in the table also reflect the increasing importance of those branches of the economy that deal with distribution and services rather than manufacturing of goods (Table 1A). The tremendous technological development that has occurred through these decades is not directly registered in our statistical array, but it is one component of the structural change that becomes visible in a gross enlargement of the share of the labor force engaged in nonmanual work (viz. the "salaried employee" category in Table 1B). Economic change has been accompanied by an immense growth of the allocative and regulative *capabilities* of government. From 1920 to the late 1960s public expenditure's share of the GNP expanded from about 13 percent to about 45 percent.

Yet the party system may appear to have remained very much the same through these decades, with the significant exception, of course, that the balance of strength shifted in favor of the Social Democrats in the 1930s. The party system, then, has remained the same—if we describe it broadly as being composed of a big labor party, sided by a radical wing on the Left and by three parties largely based on the urban and rural middle-class on the Right. We shall now attempt to delineate some developmental trends that can clarify how the social bases of the parties were indeed adjusted to the changing composition of the electorate. In the following section we shall then describe in much more detail the social profiles of the Swedish parties at the time of the 1964-1968 elections.

It is beyond the scope of this inquiry to explore the dynamic relationship that connects changes in the voting support of parties with the policy strategies adopted by their leaderships. Much of the changes we will deal with, however, are not to be understood as merely mechanical reflections of population changes. Party elites do indeed make policy choices that affect both the size and the composition of their voting support. That relationship exists even when the parties—as has been the case in Sweden—largely retain their positioning within a Left-Right spectrum.

One aspect of long-term change is illuminated by Table 7, which shows the development of electoral participation within main social strata during the period 1921-1948. From the baseline in 1921 the turnout has risen to its present level in distinct steps with intervening periods of stagnation; such distinct rises occurred at the three elections included in the table, 1928, 1936, and 1948. The later elections are not included in the table because quite comparable data are lacking. The picture becomes complete, however, if one adds the new rise in turnout rate that occurred in the late 1960s. In the latter phase the participation differences among main occupational strata were almost eliminated; the vestiges can indeed be considered politically insignificant. (See turnout rates in Table 4 and group data in Table 11A.) As is seen from Table 7 this was certainly not true for the earlier decades. Differences among social strata were quite considerable, and they come forth at least as sharply among men as among the newly enfranchised women. As the differences among social strata were slowly reduced, the working class's share of the *voting* electorate slightly increased through the 1920s and 1930s.[22]

TABLE 7: **The Rise of Electoral Turnout, 1921-1948**

	"Upper Socioeconomic Strata" (Social Group I)		"Middle Socioeconomic Strata" (Incl. Farm Owners) (Social Group II)		"Workers" (Incl. Farm workers) (Social Group III)	
	Men	*Women*	*Men*	*Women*	*Men*	*Women*
1921	66.7	60.2	65.7	49.3	58.4	43.5
1928	84.7	83.4	75.7	66.9	69.4	58.1
1936	85.5	85.3	80.6	72.8	76.8	67.9
1948	93.3	92.3	87.7	84.0	82.2	77.7

The tables include the 1921 election as a baseline and then the four elections when major increases in the turnout rate occurred (cf. Table 4).

The table shows participation rates within the "*social group*" classification that for a long time was used in official election statistics. Because of the nature of the classification the relative size of these "social groups" remained fairly the same over the entire period: in round figures they comprised about 5, 40, and 55 percent of the population, respectively. The classification and the data in Table 1 are more suitable than the "social-group" classification for the purpose of describing structural socioeconomic changes. Data for 1921–1936 are based on the entire electorate, while the 1948 data are based on a 10 percent sample.

Data Source: *Riksdagsmannavalen åren 1945–1948, Sveriges Officiella statistik. Allmänna val.*

In general the rate of political mobilization appears quite inert until the end of the 1920s. This is also brought out by a comparison with an even earlier baseline for men, the 1911 election. At that time the turnout rates were 68, 61, and 52 percent in the upper middle, and working-classes, respectively. After a temporary rise in 1914–1917, the turnout then dropped a bit and stagnated till 1928.

As Table 7 does not account for the agrarian population separately, it needs to be said that the farm owners consistently showed a somewhat higher turnout than the total rate for the middle-class stratum in which they are included. The farm and lumbering workers contrarywise showed a participation rate distinctly lower than the working-class turnout. It is indeed one of the significant features of the upsurge at the 1936 election that it involved a marked mobilization of the rural workers, even though they still lagged behind the working-class at large.

In general the trends and the social differentiation described here coincide with those appearing in several European countries. It is noteworthy, however, that the level of electoral participation was clearly higher in several comparable countries (e.g., 80.7 percent in Denmark and 84.1 percent in Norway in 1936, as compared to 74.5 percent in Sweden the same year).[23]

As the shift from farm work to other sectors of the economy has been so sweeping, we may first ask how it has affected the parties' voting support, especially that of the Agrarian (Center) party. When estimating these effects, one has to take into account the important fact that the electoral base of the Agrarian party did not include the entire agrarian population. The core of its voting support consisted from its very emergence of the farm owners and their families. The same was generally true of the rural voting support received by the People's party and—even more so—of the Conservative farm vote. As is seen from Table 1B, the size of the farm-owner group did not decline very much from, say, 1920 to 1950. The dropout from the agrarian sector consisted, up to that time, mainly of the farmers' sons and daughters, and in a large reduction of the number of hired farm workers. Thus, even though the farmers' family members were quite likely to vote for the political party of their parents, the real shrinkage of the Agrarian party's potential electoral base for a large part of the period was much more limited than the total decrease of the agrarian population. With the aid of ecological data one can calculate that the Agrarian party already in its early stage won about two-fifths of the farm-owning stratum (i.e., farm-owners and their families).[24] From such calculations as well as through inspection of the vote distributions in rural areas one can furthermore conclude with a fair amount of certainty that this share was increased up to a "saturation level" of around 65 percent of the farm vote (with the narrower definition given above) in the 1930s. Most of this gain must have come from the Conservative party, which lost heavily in the countryside. It is worth noting that the 1930 was also a period of intensive organization-building among the farmers. By the end of the decade almost all aspects of farming had become included in powerful economic cooperative organizations, which were even entrusted with the implementation of some of the government's most important agricultural policies. At the same time the great majority of the farmers joined a more general-interest organization, the RLF, which contributed to the development of a strong spirit of group solidarity of a kind that previously had existed only in the trade unions. To an increasing extent Agrarian party members took over the leadership of this organizational network.[25] At the local level in particular this was facilitated by the existence of a strong Agrarian party organization. It is a safe conjecture that the Agrarian party benefited from this development. Again it is worth noting that the Agrarian party never won the complete predominance among the farmers that the socialist parties did among industrial workers; there still remain areas where, in particular, the Conservatives retain a substantial farmer support.

To sum up: the diminishing of the farm-owning stratum did indeed reduce a heavily nonsocialist section of the electorate. This of course lowered the ceiling for the "vote potential" of the Agrarian party. But by enlarging its following within the farm-owners stratum, the Agrarian party could nevertheless for a long time preserve its share of the vote fairly well.

After the war even the farm-owner stratum has diminished at an accelerating rate. It was in this situation that the renamed Center party succeeded in finding new sources of voting support within both the middle-class and the working-class. The development of the party's social base up to the present situation is delineated in Table 8A. (The survey data base is described in the ensuing section.) The time series in the table starts with the 1956 election, when the party was still restricted to its traditional voting support. We have furthermore included the "pension referendum" in 1957, which really constituted the turning point. The subsequent broadening of the party's support is reflected in the decreasing share that comes from the farm vote. The Center party is still very much a countryside party, however. As is shown in the lower part of the table, it is also still a farmer's party in the sense that it has largely retained its predominant share of the farm vote. (The 1956 proportion is probably abnormally low. It seems to reflect a loss in the farm vote because of discontent over the party's coalition with the Social Democrats.)

The growing socioeconomic sector of the electorate was largely "non-working-class" and urban in its composition as is shown in Table 1B–C. The salaried-employee category in Table 1B–C includes all kinds of employees not considered workers, which is to say that it is comprised of clerical employees as well as engineers and personnel in qualified administrative positions. The proportion of the gainfully employed population included in these occupational strata was more than doubled (from 12 to 28 percent) in the years from 1920 to 1950, and by 1960 it had almost tripled (it was up to 35 percent). As the three nonsocialist parties, taken together, have drawn the predominant proportion of their support from the salaried employees and enterprisers as well as from the farm-owner stratum in the countryside, it becomes clear that the relative size of this social base has not been diminished because of the shift from the agricultural sector.

TABLE 8 A: Development of the Center (Agrarian) Party, 1956-1968

	Proportion of farmers of the total Center (Agrarian) party voting support	Center (Agrarian) party's proportion of total farmer vote
Election 1956	77%	48%
Referendum 1957 (refers to the voting support for the referendum proposal espoused by the Agrarian party)	(44%)	56%
Election 1960	57%	69%
Election 1964	48%	64%
Election 1968	29%	61%

Note: The farmer category here includes also farmers' wives as well as other family members engaged in work on family-owned farms. Hired farmworkers are not included.
Data Source: Election Survey 1956, Referendum Survey 1957, Election Survey 1964, Election Survey 1968.

The population change has become clearly reflected in the composition of the People's party voting support. Its main source of voting support has been moved from the countryside to the cities. The definite shift, which is strikingly apparent in Table 8B, occurred at the 1948 election, when it coincided with a large electoral success for the People's party. From then on the party has received its strongest support from the big-city electorate.

We can also look at the shift of the Liberal vote in an even longer time perspective, through an ecological study by Carl-Gunnar Janson in which the main parties' voting support at the 1948 election has been correlated with their electoral strength in 1911. The Conservative party, which had lost heavily over the entire country, nevertheless retained much the same geographical distribution of its voting strength: in 1948 it was *relatively* strong in the same areas that had been its strongholds in 1911, just as its weaker areas were very much the same. For the People's party, on the other hand, the correlation is virtually nil. The explanation is that in 1948 the People's party had become dependent upon an urban middle-class stratum that had grown from relative insignificance to a major component of the electorate. (It may be conjectured that the difference between the Conservatives and the People's party was partly evened out in some later elections when the former party increasingly gained new support.) For the Social Democrats the corresponding correlation is moderate. One can safely infer that this is mainly the effect of a continued spread of industrialization, strengthening the party in regions where it was still comparatively weak in 1911.

TABLE 8 B: **Voting Support of the People's (Liberal) Party: The Shift from the Countryside to the Cities**

	1921	1932a	1936	1944	1948
The People's party (Liberal) proportion of the vote:					
Countryside	21.1%	13.3%	12.7%	12.1%	18.6%
Cities	13.8%	10.0%	13.2%	13.8%	27.0%
Difference: countryside percent *minus* urban percent	+7.3	+3.3	−0.5	−1.7	−8.4
aTwo liberal parties combined					

Note: As distinguished from the classification in *Table 1C*, the city areas are defined here on the basis of the administrative nature of each commune.
Data Source: Official election statistics.

In the same ecological study the proportions of voters in different occupational groups within the constituencies were also employed as the independent variables in multiple-regression analyses, with each party's share of the vote as the dependent variable. When the expected values thus obtained for the socialist parties in the 1948 election were correlated with the actual constituency outcomes, a correlation coefficient of .81 was obtained. (The correlation coefficient is, of course, a measure of the fit between observed data and the regression hyperplane.) As very similar results were obtained for the entire 1944–1960 period covered by the study, we may conclude that the constituency variance in the "Bourgeois–Socialist" division of the vote is mainly due to the socioeconomic differences among various parts of the country. The perseverance of this connection between socialist voting and the size of the industrial sector is further substantiated by the finding that already in 1911 the ecological correlation between the socialist vote in the constituencies and the proportion of nonagricultural workers amounted to .74.

	Conservative Party	People's Party	Social Democrats & Communists combined
Correlation between 1911 and 1948 shares of the vote in the constituencies	.798	.004	.619

Source: Carl-Gunnar Janson, *Mandattilldelning och regional röstfördelning.* (Stockholm: 1961).

We shall not follow the vote development for the three nonsocialist parties in any more detail here. To a large extent shifts in their relative strength show a complementary pattern; increases for one of the three parties have most often been offset by decreases for one or both of the others. In terms of party strategies the three nonsocialist parties have thus been as much involved in a mutual competition for the middle-class vote as in a competition with the Social Democrats for the electoral majority.[26]

The bulk of the voting support for the Socialist parties, especially the Social Democrats, must have come from industrial workers and other nonagricultural workers through the entire period. Table 1 B makes it clear, however, that the socialist vote would have stagnated considerably below the 53–54 percent level attained in the 1930s if substantial support had not also been drawn from other social strata. We encounter two problems here: one is to appraise the contribution of the farm workers' vote and the effect of the shrinking of that stratum; the other problem is to arrive at some estimate of the size of the middle-class support.

We have to be content with aggregate data if we wish to map the size and location of the socialist support in the decades between the wars. We can gain some insight about the composition of the early socialist voting support by means of simple calculations, if we are willing to determine some parameters with the aid of recent survey data. Thus for the sake of calculating magnitudes we may assume that as much as 80 percent of the nonagricultural workers' votes went to the socialist parties in the 1920s and that the only additional support consisted of about 60 percent of the votes cast by farm and lumbering voters. As these values are probably on the high side, we could alternately set them to, say, 70 and 40 percent, respectively. Let us denote the first of these parameter value pairs as alternative A and the latter as B. If we take into account the fact that the participation rates in the working-class strata were somewhat lower than the average, we would expect for the 1920s a socialist vote of about 40 percent under alternative A and about 35 percent under alternative B, rather than the 44 percent that was the normal socialist share of the vote at parliamentary elections in that decade. For the 1936 election the discrepancy would widen even under our most extreme assumptions about the workers' vote (alternative A): in that case the socialist proportion would have become about 41 percent instead of the actual 53.6 percent. As is brought out in Table 10A, the parameter values posited in these calculations deviate only modestly from the proportions observed in our later election interview surveys. Although we have very little additional evidence to rely on, it seems likely that the parameter values in our alternative B are closest to the 1920 reality, while the later development brought about a voting pattern more similar to alternative A. Thus the socialist parties were already very predominant within the working-class in the early 1920s, yet, managed to increase somewhat in these strata. By this reasoning we arrive at the conclusion that the middle-class proportion approached one-fifth of the socialist vote in the 1920s and later grew to about one-fourth.[27]

In order to evaluate the impact of the rural workers' vote we can also rely on a previous ecological analysis which suggests that the Social Democrats were not able to mobilize these workers to any great extent until a comparatively late stage.[28] That inference is substantiated by their low participation rate as well as by the weakness of the farm workers' unions until the 1930s. It is furthermore noteworthy that the Social Democrats obtained a remarkably large gain in the rural areas at the very moment of their decisive electoral success in 1936; the total socialist vote increased by 4.8 percent in the countryside as compared with 1.2 percent in the cities. Available data do not allow us to account with certainty for the changes that compensated for the shrinking of the rural workers' stratum in the subsequent period. We can register only a very modest increase of the "other workers" share of the population. The effect of that increase was enlarged in the voting electorate, however, because of the higher turnout among the nonagricultural voters. If this addition was also more homogeneously social-ist, it could be sufficient to sustain the total working-class share of the socialist vote.

The shift away from farming and countryside also affected the electoral base of the Social Democrats in another way. Large numbers of sons and daughters of farmers have become workers during this period. This raises the question about how completely the inflow from the agrarian strata was won by the socialist parties. We have presented in Table 9 an analysis of data from an election survey in 1964 that answers the question in a summary way. In the table the 1964 working-class voters have been divided accord-ing to their fathers' occupational status. We have also subdivided the present workers, first into substrata within the working-class and second with respect to trade-union membership. The first-mentioned subdivision has been made so as to distinguish farm workers as well as a somewhat heterogeneous category of workers in transportation, services, etc., from the manual workers engaged in industrial and construction work. We can see in the table that urban middle-class or farmer parental background is indeed a factor that helps to "explain" nonsocialist voting within the working-class. We can also see that union membership contributes to the spreading of political group norms within the working-class. The same is true for employment in industrial and construction work where the work group is particularly likely to be socially homo-geneous. As to the subcategories with farmer or urban middle-class background, we find strong socialist majorities, though not quite as strong as among those with working-class parents. The only deviations appear in two exceptional categories; that is, farmers' children who have become farm workers or who are nonunionized workers. To appreciate the significance of these data, of course, one must keep in mind that the agrarian inflow came from an environment where nonsocialist voting traditions had prevailed. We feel warranted to infer from these data that the proportion of the "inflow" that went to the socialist parties was at least sufficiently strong to allow the socialist share of the working-class vote to be maintained. If we think of the table as representing a time slice at the end of a process in which the proportion of workers with working-class parents has grown successively, we can see that the total socialist share can even have increased over time even if the voting patterns within the sub-categories had remained constant through the process.[29]

We can map the development through the last decade with much more certainty than we could for the previous period, because sample survey data are available from election studies undertaken at each of the parliamentary elections in 1956, 1960, 1964,

TABLE 9: **Relation of Father's Occupation to Party Choice Within the Working-Class**

WORKING-CLASS VOTERS, 1964	FATHER'S OCCUPATION			
	Farmer	*Middle-class (excl. Farmers)*	*Working-Class*	*All*
Occupational subcategory				
Workers in manufacturing and construction Industries	70% (175)	81% (101)	90% (352)	83% (628)
Other nonagricultural workers	62% (131)	68% (93)	79% (233)	72% (457)
Farm and lumbering workers	45% (60)	63% (16)	64% (66)	56% (142)
Trade-Union membership				
Member	70% (237)	78% (147)	87% (468)	81% (852)
Nonmember	50% (129)	63% (63)	76% (183)	65% (375)
All	63% (366)	74% (210)	84% (651)	

The table shows the combined *Social Democratic – Communist proportion of the vote in each subcategory*. Percentage bases are indicated within parentheses.

Note: The socioeconomic (occupational) classification is applied so as to include the entire occupation; viz., retired persons are classed according to previous occupations, housewives according to husbands' occupations, etc. This particular analysis differs from those appearing in following tables, however, in that all wives have been included in their husbands' occupational categories even if they are gainfully employed themselves. In the lower part of the table working-class voters have been classified according to complementary criterion, i.e., trade-union membership. In this case wives have been classified as "members" if either the wife or her husband belongs to a trade union.

Source: Election Survey, 1964.

and 1968. The composition of the Social Democratic vote as well as the size of the socialist vote within different social strata is displayed in Table 10A–B.

About three-quarters of the Social Democratic vote was drawn from the working-class in 1956. In spite of the large population shifts that had occurred, the social composition of the Social Democratic voting support was thus quite similar to what it is likely to have been twenty years earlier, at the 1936 election. It is not to be wondered that a lively debate was going on within the Social Democratic party at that time about the possible ways to win support from the growing numbers of employees in non-manual work. At the 1960 election one could discern a socialist rise within the middle-class (see Table 10B). The shift then appeared in a more substantial way in the 1964 and 1968 elections. At the latter elections the working-class share of the Social Democratic vote also shows signs of shrinking a bit below its previous level. We can see, however, in the lower part of Table 10A that the socialist proportion of the working-class vote remained fairly stable. As all of the differences appearing in the table are either just barely or not quite significant at a conventional confidence level, they are certainly not suited to be used as the ground for extrapolation of trends. What we can safely infer is,

TABLE 10A: **Working - Class Vote, 1956–1968**

THE WORKING-CLASS PROPORTION OF THE TOTAL SOCIAL
DEMOCRATIC VOTING SUPPORT
(*Percentage bases are indicated within parentheses*)

Election 1956	75% (458)
Election 1960	74% (663)
Election 1964	69% (1,248)
Election 1968	66% (1,458)

THE SOCIAL DEMOCRATIC AND COMMUNIST PROPORTION
OF THE WORKING-CLASS VOTE AND OF THE VOTES CAST BY FARM &
LUMBERING WORKERS AND OTHER WORKERS, RESPECTIVELY

	Total Working-Class Vote	Farm & Lumbering Workers	All Other Workers
Election 1956	73% (483)	a)	a)
Election 1960	78% (653)	58% (64)	81% (589)
Election 1964	75% (1,211)	55% (140)	78% (1,211)
Election 1968	75% (1,305)	57% (119)	77% (1,186)

*a*Appropriate subclassification not available.

Source: Election Surveys, 1956, 1960, 1964, 1968.

The occupational classification employed in Table 10A-B will be described in connection with Table 11 in the following section. The Social Democratic–Communist proportions of the vote within different social strata shown in this table should be compared with the corresponding proportions of the total vote in each of the interview surveys. These are given here together with the actual percentages in the electorate as a whole: *1956: 49% (49.6%); 1960: 52% (52.3%); 1964: 53% (52.5%); 1968: 54% (53.9%).*

first, that the Social Democrats have maintained their working-class electoral base. The population shift has been favorable to the Social Democrats to the extent that it has diminished the stratum where its support was particularly weak, that is, the farm owners. Within the growing middle-class strata the Social Democrats, at least in the

TABLE 10B: **The Middle-Class Vote, 1956–1968**

THE SOCIAL DEMOCRATIC AND COMMUNIST PROPORTION OF THE VOTE
WITHIN MIDDLE-CLASS STRATA
(PERCENTAGE BASES ARE INDICATED WITHIN PARENTHESES.)

	Salaried Employees*a*	Enterprisers & other self-employed (excl. Farmers)	Farmers
Election 1956	32% (297)	17% (97)	13% (134)
Election 1960	39% (353)	17% (147)	7% (160)
Election 1964	42% (768)	23% (236)	7% (270)
Election 1968	47% (900)	28% (247)	6% (222)

*a*Includes also shop assistants.

Source: Election Surveys, 1956, 1960, 1964, and 1968.

1960s, have gathered sufficient support to stay at about the total electoral strength the party has had since the mid-1930s. Other things being equal, it would furthermore require only a very modest increase of the salaried-employee support to sustain the total socialist share of the vote at a potential majority level even if the manual workers' proportion of the population continues to decline a bit. Needless to say this would require the strong socialist majority among the manual workers to be maintained. We shall not engage in further speculations along these lines. The important conclusion is that in the foreseeable future the electoral balance will be decided by political rather than by population trends.

The Social Bases of the Parties: A Cross-Sectional Overview

We have seen that social change has altered the social bases of parties, yet left intact the main features of social differentiation within the Swedish multiparty system. The social differentiation among the parties is accompanied by a gradation in their orientations toward welfare policies, social equalization, and the role of private enterprise. This can be well represented as a Left-Center-Right ordering within the party system. If anything is to be stated as a functional characteristic of Swedish party politics, it should be the relative absence of political conflict cutting across this major axis of the party system.

We must add one qualification, however. Swedish politics encompasses rural interests that have consistently put some stress on the simple unidimensionality of the party system. As we have seen, this has in the past led the former Agrarian party to transgress the "Bourgeois–Socialist" boundary that otherwise makes the multiparty system function very much as a two-bloc system. At present Agrarian demands tend to become merged with more widespread discontents in peripheral countryside and small-town areas, which are experiencing an increasing degree of concentration of economic growth to main industrial centers. Modern economic change has thus created social tensions that are being channeled through new support for the Center party: as the periphery has become less agricultural in its composition, so has the Center party.

While in the preceding parts of this chapter we have attempted to explore processes of change over time, we shall now take a cross-sectional view of the party division in the electorate at one point in time, the later elections of the 1960s. This describes a situation that is no more likely to form a stable state than were the foregoing phases in the party system's development. On the other hand, it is also no more likely to undergo any fast transition. A slight modification of a social pattern can constitute a politically significant shift, however, as was proved by the 1970 election when the Social Democrats lost the electoral majority position they had attained in 1968.

The survey has been built through a series of nationwide election studies by the Institute of Political Science, University of Göteborg, in cooperation with the Swedish Central Bureau of Statistics.[30] Most of the tables display data from the 1968 election survey, a part of a three-election panel study; some multivariate analyses have been done on data from the 1964 election interviews with the same panel sample.

A comprehensive picture of the present social differentiation within the party system is given in Tables 11A–B. We have used there a conventional social-status classification that defines strata on the basis of occupational criteria.[31] The classification scheme has been applied so as to include the entire population–retired persons have been classified according to their previous occupations, while housewives and other household members not gainfully employed have mostly been included in the occupational category of the head of the household. This is actually the same classification that was employed in some foregoing tables where we distinguished between middle-class and working-class social groups. As operationalized in the present study, the working-class includes the two occupational categories of workers that appear in these tables. As always, there is a certain amount of arbitrariness involved in both the choice of strata-defining criteria and—perhaps even more—in our way of collapsing strata into broad "social classes." For example, one might argue that the "shop assistants" should more appropriately be included in a working-class than in a middle-class substratum. For that reason it may be mentioned that this group consistently makes up about half of the "foremen and shop assistant" stratum, and that the two components of this stratum are quite similar to each other in their voting behavior. As to the distinction between "salaried employees" and "workers," it has for a long time been a comparatively unambiguous occupational status criterion, and our experience with occupational self-rating in interview surveys proves that it is also remarkably salient to most people. Furthermore, it constitutes a sharp boundary between different types of unions on the labor market. By way of contrast the distinction between "skilled" and "unskilled" workers that is often included in social classifications proves to be almost inapplicable in the Swedish context. Again, this has to do with labor market conditions, since the labor unions have tended to be organized as industry unions including all categories of workers.

We see from Table 11A that while the Social Democrats receive a very strong majority of the votes cast by the large stratum of workers outside the agricultural sector as well as in the bordering middle-class stratum of foremen and shop assistants, the party's majority position is somewhat less pronounced among farm workers and lumbering workers. In the 1968 election—when the party's share of the total vote was exceptionally large—it received more votes than any other party in most of the remaining strata; the exceptions are our upper-class stratum of large entrepreneurs and salaried employees in higher positions together with the farmers. This is, of course, also the effect of the influx of Center party support in the urban middle-class strata; the bourgeois majority that actually prevails in these strata is now split among three parties of substantial size.

The resulting dispersion of each party's votes across social strata is brought out by Table 11B. We may summarize these distributions into two quantities that really decide the balance of party strength in the electorate. The Social Democrats draw about one-third of their votes from the middle-class (or a little less if the borderline

TABLE 11A: **Voting Within Social Strata: Party Division and Turnout Rates**

	Communist party	Social Democr. party	Center party	People's party	Christian Democr. Coal.	Local Bourg. Coal.	Conservative party	DK/NA	Total percent	Turnout percent	Number of cases
Large entrepreneurs, professionals, executives, and other salaried employees in higher positions	0%	14	16	27	1	1	39	2	100	97	180
Small businessmen and entrepreneurs	0%	31	24	22	2	—	16	5	100	94	230
Salaried employees in lower positions (excl. foremen, etc.)	1%	43	14	24	1	1	15	1	100	91	601
Foremen in industry, shop assistants	2%	71	7	11	0	—	6	3	100	94	222
Workers (excl. farm workers, etc.)	2%	75	10	7	2	0	3	1	100	93	1,281
Farmers	0%	6	61	9	3	0	19	2	100	93	238
Workers in agriculture and foresting	1%	56	27	8	1	—	6	1	100	90	132
Students and others not included in any occupational stratum	(6%)	(30)	(13)	(32)	(—)	(2)	(13)	(4)	100	(90)	59
Total interview survey sample	1%	53	17	14	1	1	11	2	100	93	2,943
TOTAL ELECTORATE	3%	50	16	15	2	0	14	—	100	89	

Source: Election Survey, 1968

category of shop assistants is transferred to the working-class). At the same time the bourgeois parties draw about one-quarter of their total voting support from the workers' strata.

TABLE 11B: **Social Composition of the Major Parties' Voting Support and of the "Nonvote", in Percentages**

	Social Democr. party	Center party	People's party	Conservative party	Non-voters	Total interview survey sample
Large entrepreneurs, professionals, executives, and other salaried employees in higher positions	2%	6%	13%	24%	2%	6%
Small businessmen and entrepreneurs	4	11	13	12	7	8
Salaried employees in lower positions (excl. foremen, etc.)	16	17	35	28	24	20
Foremen in industry, shop assistants	10	3	6	4	6	8
Workers (excl. farm workers, etc.)	61	26	21	12	44	44
Farmers	1	29	5	15	8	8
Workers in agriculture and foresting	5	7	· 3	2	6	4
Students and others not included in any occupational stratum	1	1	4	3	3	2
Total	100	100	100	100	100	100
Number of cases	1,458	469	370	286	214	2,943

Source: Election Survey, 1968

The division of the nonsocialist vote is also bound up with social stratification. The Center party thus relies less on support from the urban middle-class than do the two other bourgeois parties. We also find that although both the People's party and the Conservatives obtain the largest portions of their votes from the lower-middle-class (salaried employees and small entrepreneur strata), their vote distributions are differently skewed. Big entrepreneurs and employees in high-status positions make up a conspicuously large portion of the Conservative vote; in combination with a still substantial farm wing this affords a distinctive social profile to the Conservative party. The People's party gathers most of its complementary support from the working-class. One result of the recent increment of the Center party's strength in the worker strata is actually that the Left-Right ordering in which the parties appear in the tables now corresponds entirely to the relative importance of each of the parties' working-class support.

It is evident that even in a multiparty system so conspicuously oriented to the representation of group interests as in Sweden, none of the parties stands exclusively for a socially homogeneous segment of the electorate. When we speak of the social bases of parties, this should therefore be understood as a way of locating the social mode of the dispersion of a party's voting support across social strata. This is partly so because the group interests of the real world are less distinctly fenced than are the occupational categories in our tables. It is also so because individuals form party attachments that often survive changes in their social situation. As the formation of such attachments is very much a process of socialization, the social experiences of a previous generation can furthermore put their mark on current behavior in a very different social context. A "social" description of the party system also needs qualification on another ground. Parties do not entirely stand for conceptions of group interests, they stand concurrently for generalized conceptions of the goals and means of politics.[32]

At present we will not go beyond this general characterization of the parties' ideological orientations, but rather attempt to specify our mapping of the social determinants of voting behavior.[33]

When one is exploring the social antecedents of political behavior with the aid of a social stratum scheme, he is employing a research tool that embraces a range of implicit status and context factors tied to the individuals' occupational roles. One is income, another is education, and a third may be membership in an organized interest group. Among the environmental conditions there are some that are not necessarily reflected in the individual's occupation but nonetheless influence his social situation. The degree of urbanization and industrialization of the individuals' residence areas are obviously relevant indicators of such influences.

We will treat some of these factors separately in the form of a brief exposition. Our main purpose will then be to highlight—rather than inquire into—the nature of the social processes that connect individuals' political behavior with "social antecedents." In a subsequent section we will show how a computerized analysis mode—the tree analysis—can be employed to select an "optimal" combination of social characteristics, if one's main purpose is to predict political behavior.

The school system is one of the society's most important means of providing for the recruitment of occupational roles. This is so obvious that education is often treated as a supplementary social-status criterion. As education furthermore involves socialization, the educational differentiation is also accompanied by a differentiation in regard to the kind of political norms the individuals are exposed to in their environment during their years of schooling. This differential influence was perhaps even more significant under the old noncomprehensive school system, which all generations of voters except the very youngest one have experienced.

The overall relationship between education and party choice is displayed in Table 12A. Recent gross changes in the school system have made it necessary to combine comparable levels in very different school types. In general it should be clear that the classification distinguishes between three levels of general education, with subcategories representing increasingly extended and/or theoretically oriented schooling.

A large majority of the voters has no formal schooling other than six or seven years of grade school. It is only in the youngest age groups of the electorate that the

TABLE 12 A: Relation of Education to Party Vote and Electoral Participation, in Percentages

	Communist party	Social Democr. party	Center party	People's party	Christian Democr. Coal.	Local Bourg. Coal.	Conservative party	DK/NA	Total percent	Turnout percent	Number of cases
Primary education in grade school (less than 9 years):[a]											
1. No further school	1	63	18	9	2	0	5	2	100	92	1,737
2. Vocational school for industrial work	2	74	11	9	—	—	2	2	100	91	139
3. Other secondary education (but not gymnasium)	1	48	15	21	—	1	11	3	100	95	284
Extended primary education and/or at most two years of general secondary education[b]											
4. At most two years of completing schooling on secondary-education level	2	39	21	15	1	1	20	1	100	94	368
5. More than two years of completing secondary education and/or non-university education beyond the secondary level	2	33	16	24	1	1	20	3	100	93	151
Completed secondary education in gymnasium:											
6. At most two years of education after gymnasium	1	24	16	32	1	1	25	—	100	95	138
7. Academic and comparable education	3	18	13	25	1	3	34	3	100	95	126

[a] E.g, Technical or commercial school.
[b] Secondary education on an intermediary (i.e., nongymnasium) level in the earlier school system. Completing secondary education refers to various kinds of nonacademic education, usually technical, clerical, or commercial.
Source: Election Survey, 1968.

extended compulsory school (now nine years) and the vast expansion of the secondary and higher school system has yet brought about an entirely different picture.

The latter observation may naturally lead one to speculate how the future party division will be affected by the presence of a much enlarged proportion of voters with more than elementary education and—presumably—employment in nonmanual work. Table 12B contains some relevant data. In this table we have cross-classified the

TABLE 12B: **Education, Age, and Voting**

	AGE		
	21–30	**31–50**	**over 50**
Education Categories 1-2	71% (241)	68% (571)	61% (908)
Education Categories 3-4	59% (187)	39% (238)	37% (192)
Education Categories 5-7	33% (164)	22% (137)	24% (91)

Voters have been classified according to level of school education and age so as to create a ninefold property space. For each of the cells in this space the table shows the Socialist (Social Democratic and Communist) proportion of the total vote. Category numbers for school education refer to the classification in Table 12A. Numbers of cases are given within parentheses.
Source: Election Survey, 1968.

electorate according to both age and education (note that the absolute cell frequences reflect the educational change referred to above). As is seen in the table, the proportion of socialist voters decreases with increasing education in all age categories. But we also see that on each educational level the socialist proportion is larger among voters up to the age of thirty than among older voters (see also the age sections of Reference tables I–II at the end of this chapter). One possible explanation may be that the Social Democrats have been more successful in gaining new middle-class support among the younger voters. The data in Table 12C suggest that another process is also at work.

TABLE 12C: **Relation of Party Choice to Type of Education and Father's Occupation Among Young Voters (Aged 21–25 in 1968)**

FATHER'S OCCUPATION	EDUCATION CATEGORIES		
	1–2	**3–4**	**5–7**
Entrepreneur, salaried employee etc., Farmer	54% (48)	40% (57)	31% (74)
Worker	86% (59)	78% (54)	55% (22)

The table shows the Social Democratic & Communist proportion of the vote within each of the categories.
(Percentage bases are indicated within parentheses.)
Source: Election Survey, 1968.

In this case we have investigated the voting behavior of the very youngest age cohorts (those coming of enfranchisement age in 1966 or 1968) and undertaken a classification according to their education as well as their fathers' occupations. The party division is entered for each of the cells of the resulting property space. While the general relationship between education and party choice appears again in this table, we also find a marked relationship between the young voters' party choices and their fathers' occupations. To the extent that this relationship persists, it would mean that an increasingly large proportion of the group with more than elementary education (and nonmanual occupations) will consist of voters with parental working-class background who retain a socialist party attachment. Thus it may be one of the consequences of a heightened rate of social mobility to widen the socialist support outside its traditional base.

We will illuminate the connection between voters' partisan attachments and their membership in organizations for *interest articulation* merely with one simple tabulation.[34] In Table 13 we have classified salaried employees and wage earners according to their union membership. Furthermore, the table includes also occupationally active people who were not union members classified according to their self-rated status as salaried employees or workers. Among the union federations appearing in the table, LO is the main federation of manual workers' trade unions. The LO also includes some borderline groups, e.g., state and municipal workers is lower grades. TCO comprises large white-collar unions, including employees in private enterprises as well as in public services. The industrial foremens' organization is also affiliated to this federation. SACO is primarily a federation of unions for salaried employees with university education, embracing the higher echelons of state and municipal administration, the school system (above the elementary level), the hospital system, the ministry of the state church, the court system, and, as a final example, the fire brigades. It has been combined in the Table with the SR, which is a small federation of civil servants unions including the office of foreign affairs and the state transportation system and the officers of the army (lower-grade military personnel belong to TCO). As a general rule these unions have bargaining and strike rights, although the latter were, in effect, abrogated in a recent case when the SACO–SR groups were involved in a salary conflict with the government that could not be mediated. The membership figures for the major federations as well as for some other important interest groups are displayed in the box below Table 13. It is worth noting that the large majority of the unionized employees are engaged in enterprises affiliated to one large employers' confederation. In the agricultural sector of the economy the organization coverage is almost complete; the import of the membership statistics is really that almost every enterpriser in farming or ancillary occupations is affiliated to at least one part of this organization network.

Given the coincidence of organizations and social strata, it is not surprising that the party divisions displayed in Table 13 are also very similar to those that appeared in our occupational strata classification (Table 11A). Among workers, however, one finds a distinct relationship between party choice and organization membership when comparing unionized and nonunionized workers. The whole of that difference cannot be attributed to organization membership as such; nonunionized employees who class

TABLE 13: **Union Membership and Voting, in Percentages**

	Communist party	Social Democr. party	Center party	People's party	Christ. Democr. Coal.	Local Bourg. Coal.	Conservative party	DK/NA	Total percent	Number of cases
Members of LO	2	81	8	5	1	0	2	1	100	655
Nonunion members who consider themselves workers	1	60	18	11	2	—	7	1	100	276
Members of TCO	1	46	14	21	1	2	13	2	100	328
Members of SACO or SR	(4)	(17)	(14)	(25)	—	—	(40)	—	100	48
Nonunion members who consider themselves salaried employees	2	34	15	28	0	0	19	2	100	183

The table contains only gainfully employed voters. For comparison, two nonmember categories have also been included. These consist of voters who are neither members of an union nor of an entrepreneurs', farmers', or professional organization and do not consider themselves self-employed. These voters have been classified according to self-rated status as "worker" or "salaried employee" (a small number of people not giving any self-rating is included). Source: Election Survey, 1968.

MAJOR ECONOMIC INTEREST GROUPS

	Membership: thousands of members
LO, The Swedish Federation of Trade Unions	1,680
TCO, The Central Organization of Salaried Employees	719
SACO, The Swedish Confederation of Professional Associations	115
SAF, The Swedish Employers' Federation; *number of employees in affiliated enterprises*	1,269
LRF, National Federation of Farmers; *Members of local unions* (The LRF includes two parallel types of organizations: the local unions and the cooperative organizations. The total number of memberships in the cooperative organizations amounts to 902,000; most farmers hold multiple memberships in such organizations.)	133

Note : According to tax-assessment statistics for 1969, the total number of gainfully employed persons was 4.2 million, of whom 3.9 million were salaried employees or wage earners. *Organization data pertain to 1970.*

themselves as workers are much less likely than the organized to be engaged in industrial work and much more likely to have various types of service occupations. Even so, it is warranted to consider the overwhelming homogeneity of the union vote as an indicator of trade unions' political influence within those occupational categories where they include almost all of the wage earners. As to the two other organizational groups neither could be considered allied to any political party. The TCO shows a quite even split between socialist and bourgeois voting. In general the nonunionized salaried employees are somewhat more likely to vote for a bourgeois party than are the TCO members. The significance of the status difference that exists between the membership of TCO and SACO–SR deserves to be noted; the size of the Conservative vote in SACO–SR is, indeed, almost as large as the socialist support in the TCO.

When we conceive of class cleavages or of a social stratification in a society, we are referring not only to occupational differences but also to differentiation with regard to value allocations—especially in the form of income inequality—that prevails in that society. It is also true of the socioeconomic classification used in this inquiry that the various categories can be grouped together so as to form broader strata with differing modal incomes. Thus the income level of the "top stratum" of large entrepreneurs and salaried employees is distinctly higher than that of the lower-middle-class strata, which consists of small entrepreneurs and salaried employees in lower positions: the modal income of the latter is furthermore somewhat higher than the typical worker income. But the coincidence between strata boundaries and income classes is far from complete. A sizable proportion of the salaried employees and entrepreneurs earn about the same as–or less than–a large portion of the worker stratum. As to the farmers, their average taxable earnings fall below the average for manual workers' incomes.

Our data on the relationship between voting and income affords partial support to the expectation that the bourgeois–socialist cleavage should correspond to a social division between high- and low-income earners (see *Reference Table II*, at the end of the chapter.) There is certainly an income level above which the socialist proportion of the vote declines quite sharply. Below that level, however, there is a slight trend in the opposite direction; the Social Democratic share of the vote increases with increasing income. A more searching analysis has actually shown that the latter trend goes through all income classes among the workers, while the trend in the table presented here remains among salaried employees.[35] Moreover, it was found that differences among occupational strata in regard to the socialist share of the vote persist on all income levels. It is especially noteworthy that workers are much more likely than salaried employees to vote for a socialist party even if they are in the same income bracket. We cannot present here a full investigation of the group and organization differences that underlie this pattern. Suffice it to state that working and employment conditions as well as organization membership turn out to be politically more significant than income differences among low- and medium-income earners.

The voters' distribution over areas with differing density of population is shown in Appendix Table I (section: Place of residence). The area unit is the parish, which is the smallest unit for which population census data are available (there are more than

2,500 parishes in the country). The parishes are classed with regard to the proportion of the population that lives in builtup (densely populated) neighborhoods. The party division of the vote within each of these parish categories is given in Reference Table II. We find that the Center party obtains 41 percent of its total vote from the two least urbanized parish categories, where only 20 percent of the electorate have their residence, and we also see that the party's support amounts to 47 percent of the total vote in the most rural of these categories.

The location of the Center party's nonfarmer support can be specified with the aid of our sample data. For that purpose we have calculated the Center party share of the votes cast by people who do not belong to the farmer category in our occupational classification (note that this includes also housewives and family members engaged in farm work) for each of the parish categories. As is demonstrated by the results displayed below, the more rural the area, the more likely that voters who are not themselves farmers will support the Center party.

	PROPORTION OF PARISH POPULATION LIVING IN BUILTUP AREA			
	90% or more	50-89.9%	10-49.9%	Less than 10%
Center party proportion of the "nonfarmer vote"	9%	17%	19%	37%
Number of cases	(1,585)	(520)	(246)	(152)

We can then gauge the impact of the economic structure of the individuals' residence area directly in Table 14. Here we have combined two criteria in order to classify voters according to their own occupations as well as the occupational composition of the population in the areas where they live.[36] The party division within each of the resulting categories is displayed in compressed form by the indication of the socialist and the Center party proportions of the vote. The bottom section of the table shows these parties' proportions of the total vote within each of the parish categories. It is apparent from these data that the socialist proportion of the vote declines with a decreasing degree of industrialization. This is mainly the effect of the consequently smaller proportion of workers up to the point in our areal classification where at least 10 percent of the population is engaged in agriculture. In the most rural categories, however, we find that the Center party vote goes up appreciably among workers as well as among salaried employees and entrepreneurs. As these areas, on the other hand, make up a fairly small part of the total electorate, the weaker support that the party obtains from urbanized and industrial areas is by no means insignificant. To get the complete picture one must include the fact that about one-third of the Center party vote actually was drawn from parish areas where less than 10 percent of the population is in agriculture. But it is clearly in the less urbanized—economically "peripheral"—areas that the Center party is most likely to attract workers and salaried employees as well as entrepreneurs other than the farmers.

TABLE 14: Voting by Areal Economic Characteristics and Occupational Status

Occupation Category/Party Vote	AREAL ECONOMIC CHARACTERISTICS				
	Less than 10% in agriculture etc.:			10–40% in agriculture, foresting, etc.	More than 40% in agriculture, foresting, etc.
	60% or more in industry	40–59% in industry	Less than 40% in industry		
Workers					
Socialist parties	82%	81%	82%	74%	56%
Center party	5%	6%	6%	16%	27%
Salaried Employees and Entrepreneurs (excl. farmers)					
Socialist parties	48%	40%	39%	40%	23%
Center Party	12%	14%	11%	24%	40%
Farmers					
Socialist parties	..	..	..	5%	4%
Center party	..	..	..	63%	63%
Total: All Occupations					
Socialist parties	69%	60%	56%	52%	33%
Center party	9%	10%	9%	26%	40%
Total number of cases	246	832	651	668	324

Areal Economic Characteristics: The areal units, the parishes, are classified according to the occupational composition of the population. This classification takes into account the proportions engaged in: (*a*) agriculture and ancillary occupations like foresting; (*b*) industrial production; (*c*) other branches of the economy, e.g. commerce and transportation.

Occupational status: Respondents in each parish category are classified according to occupational status as specified in the table; housewives have been classified according to their husbands' occupations. The *Total* section of the table includes also respondents who could not be included in any occupational category.

Voting: Table entries show the proportions of socialist (Social Democratic and Communist) and Center party votes within each of the property space cells. A double point (..) indicates that category size is smaller than 20 in the sample and no percentage is given.

Source: Election Survey, 1968; parish classification: 1965 Population Census

A COMPUTERIZED TECHNIQUE TO LOCATE THE SOCIAL DETERMINANTS OF VOTING—TREE ANALYSIS

We have seen how the relation between the individuals' party affiliations and their social positions can be described either in broad socioeconomic strata or by specifying social roles and status positions by such indicators as income or education. The latter can mostly be considered as components or correlates of our social stratum classification. When we employ a large set of indicators, we are in a sense locating individuals in a multidimensional property space in which each of the indicators forms a dimension. If we think of the indicator classes as defining rows and columns of such a space, it becomes clear that by the intersections we obtain subcategories representing all the possible attribute combinations. A social strata classification is a way of imposing a more parsimonious set of concepts (and corresponding operational criteria) over such a multidimensional social property space. The effect is to subsume groups of subcategories that are considered to mean the same under common labels.[37]

We will now demonstrate that one can attain a similar kind of reduction of a large attribute space in an inductive fashion by making use of the computerized analysis technique of tree analysis. We will treat the voters' choice between socialist and bourgeois voting as a dichotomous dependent variable.

While the tree analysis can be used for several analytic objectives, we will here be interested in its capacity to construct a composite classification in which a large number of "predictor classes" are combined in an optimal way. The criterion of optimality is that the total sample of respondents shall be partitioned into a classification that is as parsimonious as possible in terms of the explanatory factors and as exhaustive as possible in its capacity to account for the variance in the dependent variable. The program arrives at that end through a sequence of binary splits. At each step it thus creates a new pair of categories defined by a unique combination of characteristics (the one that caused the split *plus* all those used to define all previous splits in the same branch of the tree). The splitting of a given group comes to a stop when none of the classifications the analyst has included in his "predictor list" can create subcategories that differ with regard to their means on the dependent variate.[38] The "trees" in Figures 1–2 show how the sequential splitting proceeds and how each of the branches ends with a pair of final categories. It is in each case, these final categories that form the overall classification that has been generated by the analysis.

Technology should not lead one to believe that the resulting mapping of social realities should be independent of the analyst's theoretical preconceptions. The analyst determines the "predictor list" employed by the program. He can also define the statistical rules for category splitting. We shall demonstrate this by the two analyses displayed in the subsequent charts.

In the first of these analyses (Figure 1) we have entered a list of predictors that includes not only indicators of the individual's present social status but also an indicator of upward social mobility. We have furthermore let the analysis comprise the social status of the present voters' fathers. The data are drawn from our aforementioned interview study of the 1964 election.[39]

In the tree analysis displayed in Figure 1 we let the computer apply extremely lenient rules for category splitting; that new subcategories are allowed to form even when they contribute very little to the overall predictive capacity of the final classification. This is not a preferable strategy if one aims at parsimony. But in this case it has the virtue, as an inspection of the tree will substantiate, of allowing us to trace the effects of almost all types of social antecedents through a diversity of attribute combinations. It becomes clear that these factors appear mostly in an additive fashion; the more factors predisposing for bourgeois voting that are heaped upon each other in a category definition, the larger is the proportion of bourgeois voters in that category, and vice versa. Some factors substitute for each other in different parts of the tree. Thus salaried employees cannot differ on the labor-union criterion but do differ with regard to education, and the latter factor gives rise to politically different subcategories. In this context the education criterion seems mainly to discriminate between occupational status levels among the salaried employees.

A much simplified classification is presented in Figure 2, which shows an alternative tree analysis applied to the same data. We have changed the set of explanatory factors that could be used only by excluding the fathers' social status from the list. A causal analysis has proved that the relationship between the present voters' party affiliations and their fathers' occupations is mainly the result of a network of relationships between the fathers' social status and various aspects of the voters' past and present social positions. We therefore preferred not to include intergenerational social mobility as a criterion in our classification but rather to treat it as a preceding condition in a causal sequence. The statistical model was also changed in Fig. 2, in that we now chose a split criterion that would allow new subcategories to be split off only if they would lead to significant increments to the predictive power of the final classification. The main difference between the two trees is thus that in the latter one we sacrificed detailed information in the interest of parsimony. On the other hand, we sacrificed very little in "predictive power." That capacity can be gauged with the aid of conventional one-way analysis of variance for each of the two classifications; it is found that the correlation ratio for Figure 1 was .38, while it was .35 for the classification in Figure 2. This is to say that the second classification accounts for 35 percent of the variance in the dependent variate in our sample data. The usefulness of the classification is perhaps even better indexed by a different statistic, which tells us that 84 percent of all voters has been placed in categories in which one of the two blocs has a majority exceeding 70 percent. This proportion should be compared to the 54–46 percent division in the sample as a whole.

It is worthwhile comparing the classification generated in Figure 1 with the conventional social stratum scheme. The two schemes bear a very close resemblance to each other. Neither forms an unambiguous status hierarchy. This is true of the conventional classification both because it has really been fashioned in a somewhat heuristic way (rather than on the basis of any empirical measurements of status rankings) and because it comprises parallel stratifications for urban and rural occupations. The tree analysis classification is theoretically not intended to generate a status hierarchy. Certain deviations from such a hierarchy are quite obvious. For instance, one would not on any ground consider unionized workers to form a lower (or higher) stratum than the non unionized workers. The theoretical distinction that comes to mind is rather that between workers who are class-conscious and those who are not. Such

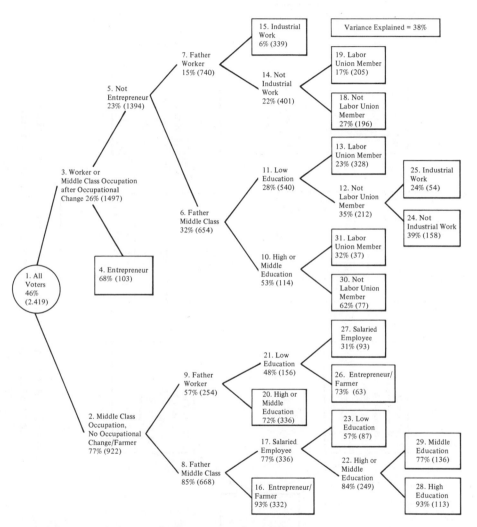

Figure 1: Social Antecedents of the "Two-Bloc" Party Choice in Sweden (Outcome of a tree analysis applying a very lenient "split criterion" for the forming of new subcategories)

Percent entries show the nonsocialist proportion of the vote in each of the categories. The number of cases in each group is given within parentheses. *Final groups* are indicated by being put into boxes.

Source : Election Survey 1964.

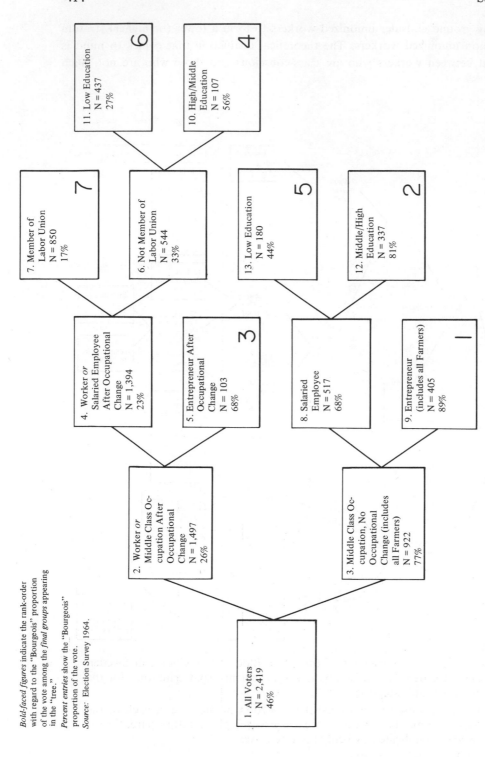

Bold-faced figures indicate the rank-order with regard to the "Bourgeois" proportion of the vote among the final groups appearing in the "tree."

Percent entries show the "Bourgeois" proportion of the vote.

Source: Election Survey 1964.

Figure 2: Relation of Socioeconomic Characteristics to "Two-Bloc" Party Choice in Sweden (An optimal combination of characteristics generated by the A.I.D. program)

1. All Voters
N = 2,419
46%

2. Worker or Middle Class Occupation After Occupational Change
N = 1,497
26%

3. Middle Class Occupation, No Occupational Change (includes all Farmers)
N = 922
77%

4. Worker or Salaried Employee After Occupational Change
N = 1,394
23%

5. Entrepreneur After Occupational Change
N = 103
68%

3

8. Salaried Employee
N = 517
68%

9. Entrepreneur (includes all Farmers)
N = 405
89%

1

7. Member of Labor Union
N = 850
17%

7

6. Not Member of Labor Union
N = 544
33%

13. Low Education
N = 180
44%

5

12. Middle/High Education
N = 337
81%

2

11. Low Education
N = 437
27%

6

10. High/Middle Education
N = 107
56%

4

qualifications stress the need for further research both about the class structure of the society and about the consequences of that structure for political behavior. By and large, the tree analysis corroborates the mapping of the social determinants of voting that we obtained by describing the parties' social bases within various social strata.

LEGEND TO FIGS. 1.& 2.

This is a listing of brief operational definitions for the classifications employed as predicators in the tree analyses displayed in the figures.

1. Occupational status: The classification is comprised of "Workers", "Salaried employees", "Entrepreneurs and other self-employed," and "Farmers." The "Farmer" category is defined on the basis of farm ownership etc. Other respondents were classed in the appropriate status category on the basis of their self-rated occupational status. — The classification is applied so that retired persons are classed according to their previous occupations; housewives who were not presently gainfully employed were classified according to their husbands' occupations.

2. Occupational Mobility: This classification pertains to upward social mobility and it discriminates, essentially, between individuals in "urban middle class" occupations. These are divided into two groups: "Middle class occupation without previous occupational change from worker status" and "Middle class occupation after occupational change." Actually, the classification comprises also a complementary criterion labelled "Mixed social status": this criterion applies to cases when a married woman had a middle class occupation, while the husband was a worker or *vice versa.* As this criterion is applicable only to a fairly small category, it does not appear as an independent criterion in the tree. It has in effect been combined with the "occupational change criterion." — Finally the classification includes two "rest categories,"namely "Workers" and "Farmers".

3. Education: A trichotomy comprised of "Low," "Middle" and "High" education.

4. Labor Union Membership: This dichotomy separates members of workers' trade unions from all others of whom some are thus members of, e.g., salaried employee organizations. Married women whose husbands were members of labor unions have been classed in the "member" category.

5. Manual work in manufacturing, mining or construction industries vs "all others": This dichotomy separates a sub-category within the working class.

6. Fathers' socioeconomic status: A trichotomy consisting of "upper class," "middle class" (including farmers) and "working class." This criterion was excluded by the analyst's decision from the tree analysis presented in *Figure 2.*

An *income* classification was entered in the tree analyses but was never employed as a group defining criterion on the ground that other "predictors" consistently turned out to discriminate better. The same was true for a farmer-nonfarmer dichotomy; hence the farmers' category is always included in the appropriate "Entrepreneur" or "Middle class" category in the trees.

RELIGIOUS BEHAVIOR AND VOTING

Even factors that are not primary determinants of a party system may have a subsidiary influence upon the formation of party affiliations in the electorate. Although religion is not a central issue in Swedish politics, there exists a traditional linkage between religion and politics such that the bourgeois parties, in general, are likely to choose pro-church and pro-christian standpoints when such matters cause any visible dissension. Likewise, it is usual for non socialist parties—but not for the socialist parties—to include some references to the importance of Christian beliefs in statements of their policy goals.

There also exist more specific linkages between party politics and religious affiliation. This has to do, primarily, with the existence of "free churches" (Protestant sects) at the side of the Lutheran Swedish church. The latter is most often denoted as the state church because of its constitutional status. Almost the entire population (96 percent) is affiliated to the state church in a legal sense. This is also true of most adherents of the free churches, whose total reported membership amounts to around 300,000. Non-Protestant religious denominations, of course, exist, but they lack political significance due to the smallness of their followings.

The People's (Liberal) party has since the very time of its formation maintained a strong support among the adherents of the free churches, while the Conservative party has been closer to the state church. The People's party has traditionally included a "cultural-radical," nonreligious wing of adherents, especially within the big-city upper and middle-classes. Fairly recently an expressly Christian splinter party (the Christian Democratic Union) was formed, and has got scattered representation in local government councils.

When one wishes to inquire into the import of individual religious orientations, he needs a measure of attachments to religious beliefs or to a church as a social reference group.[40] We will employ here the individual's self-reported regularity in attending religious service. We also conceive of church attendance as a measure of the degree of centrality that church-espoused beliefs have. We have also collected data on individual church affiliations.

The overall relationship between churchgoing and voting is shown in Tables 15A–B. In the upper part of Table 15A there appears a distinctive increment in the likelihood of casting a nonsocialist vote with increasing frequency in churchgoing. When reading the table, one should also keep an eye on the percentage basis for each category. The lower part of Table 15A shows the party divisions among voters categorized according to their religious denominations. In general the free-church adherents are obviously much less socialist than the large mass of voters who attend the state church. As shown by the data displayed below, the two types of churchgoers also differ with regard to frequency in church attendance. As much as 53 percent of the free-church adherents say they attend a religious service "at least once a month," while the corresponding figure for those who go to the State Church is only 12 percent. No significant difference appears between the denominations when we compare individuals whose churchgoing habits are similar. The political significance of the free churches is heightened by the comparatively strong church attachment shown by their members.

The resulting composition of each party's voting support is displayed in Table 15B. We can see that all four of the major parties recruit about half of their support from among the two categories that might be labeled as conventional—rather than practicing—church adherents. The three nonsocialist parties, however, draw about one-fifth or one-fourth of their votes from more diligent worshippers, while that

TABLE 15A: Churchgoing, Church Affiliation, and Party Choice, in Percentages

	Communist party	Social Democr. party	Center party	People's party	Christ. Democr. Coal	Local Bourg. Coal	Conservative party	Total* percent	Number of cases
Churchgoing									
At least once a month	—	26	25	25	9	0	16	100	384
Several times a year	1	51	23	11	0	1	13	100	782
More seldom	1	63	15	12	0	0	9	100	1,086
Never	5	67	8	13	—	1	5	100	361
Church Affiliation (For people who didn't say they never attend religious service)									
State church	1	54	19	13	0	0	13	100	1,907
Attend state and free church alternately	—	57	25	12	1	—	5	100	77
Free church	1	38	20	23	13	1	4	100	258

Interview Question: "How often do you attend religious service in state church or in some free church? Do you attend religious service (1) at least once a month, (2) several times a year, (3) more seldom, or (4) never?" If response is alternative 1–3: "Do you usually go to state church or to some free church?"

*Voters who failed to indicate their party choice are not included in this table.

Source: 1968 Election Survey.

category makes up only 7 percent of the Social Democratic vote. We can also see that the People's party still retains a comparatively strong support among the free-church adherents, though by no means does it maintain any predominating position among these voters. The very peculiar profile of the Christian Democrats comes forth in these tables: more than four-fifths of its voting support consists of free-church adherents, drawing about 13 percent of the votes cast by the free-church adherents. Though the party itself may be considered as a negligible quantity, it has actually made a quite important inroad into one of the traditional strongholds of the People's party.

Church attendance is somewhat more frequent within the middle-class strata than in the working-class. A part of the relationship between religious and political behavior that appears in the foregoing tables is therefore an expression of social strata differences that embrace both of these types of behavior. In order to appraise the import of religion on political behavior we need to control for occupational effects. We will do so with the aid of the socioeconomic classification generated by the tree

TABLE 15B: **Churchgoing and Church Affiliation: The Composition of Party Support, in Percentages**

	Commu- nist party	Social Democr. party	Center party	People's party	Christ. Democr. Coal.	Conser- vative party	Total interview- survey sample*
Churchgoing							
At least once a month	—	7	20	26	87	22	15
Several times a year	15	28	39	25	3	37	29
More seldom	36	48	34	36	10	34	41
Never	49	17	7	13	—	7	15
Total percent	100	100	100	100	100	100	100
Church Affiliation							
State church	44	73	78	69	15	87	72
State church & free church alternately	—	3	4	2	2	2	3
Free church	7	7	11	16	83	4	10
Never attending religious service	49	17	7	13	—	7	15
Total percent	100	100	100	100	100	100	100

*Including also categories not accounted for separately in this table.
Source: 1968 Election Survey.

analysis in Chart III. This classification lends itself very well to a grouping of three main categories (of about equal size), which differ distinctly in respect to the socio-economic predispositioning of the voters' party choices.

Individual church attachment makes little difference to voting behavior when the socioeconomic predisposition is strongly one-sided, that is, within two socioeconomic categories in Table 16 that together comprise about two-thirds of the sample. In the case of the category with a strong nonsocialist predisposition, the data reveal a saturation phenomenon: only a complete withdrawal from conventional church attendance goes together with a reduced propensity to conform to the bourgeois political group norm. But as soon as one has passed the step to at least a conventional religious observance, the additional political effect of a stronger church attachment does not seem to add much to an already massive motivation for a bourgeois voting. In the working-class context, one may, instead, speak of a threshold phenomenon. As life experience an environmental influences weigh heavily in favor of socialist voting, it takes an unusually strong attachment to a church community with opposing political norms to increase the propensity to vote for a nonsocialist party. Typically, this is associated with free-church membership. In the remaining third of the voting electorate —where no one-sided political predisposition prevails—we find contrariwise that the effect of differing degrees of church attachment is quite striking. Most of this gray zone is composed of subcategories that could be labeled as urban lower middle-classes.

Percent entries below show the socialist (Social Democratic & Communist) proportion of the vote within each of the subcategories obtained by classifying voters according to churchgoing frequency as well as denominational affiliation. Percentage bases are given within parentheses.

	Regularity in Church Attendance		
Church Affiliation	At least once a month	Several times a year	More seldom
State church	28 (232)	51 (681)	63 (994)
Free church	25 (142)	51 (59)	60 (57)

Note: Those who "never" attend religious service are of course not included in this table. We have also excluded the small category of people who attend both state church and free church.

Source: Election Survey, 1968.

One way to summarize the political importance of religion is to ascertain how much more we can explain of the variance in the two-bloc vote (treated as a dichotomous variable) if we add our measure of religious attachment to the socioeconomic classification generated by the tree analysis. It is then found that the socioeconomic antecedents alone account for about 35 percent of the variance in the sample. If we take account also of the effect of church attendance, that proportion increases to 39 percent.[41]

We thus feel warranted to infer from the data that the individual's religious outlook normally does not influence his political preferences in a way that runs counter to conceptions of those social group interests that are strongly established in his environment. Rather, a religious motive for party choice seems to obtain significance when that kind of group influence is lacking. Hence, the distinctive political alignment of social groups in the Swedish electorate reduces the role of religion to that of a subsidiary factor also in the determination of individual electoral behavior.

The Positioning of Parties

In our exposition of the modern party system we have consistently relied upon the conception of a main political axis that allows us to array the parties in a Left-Right ordering. One can find empiric ground for such a mapping of the parties' political positioning in the contents of their public statements of policy goals as well as in cross-section survey measurements of the attitudinal differentiation that prevails in the mass electorate. As to the particular ordering that appears in our tables, it deserves to be qualified only in respect of the placing of the two centrist parties. The ideological shading in this part of the party spectrum are really too diffuse to justify the locating of the Center party "to the left" of the People's party on the ground of any distinctive

TABLE 16: Relationship Between Churchgoing and Two-Bloc Vote Within Socioeconomic Categories

	REGULARITY IN CHURCH ATTENDANCE				
	At least once a month	Several times a year	More seldom	Never	Total
Socioeconomic categories with extremely strong bourgeois pre-dominance*a*	7 (191)	13 (265)	17 (229)	36 (56)	14 (741)
Intermediate categories*b*	37 (142)	56 (246)	69 (329)	75 (108)	60 (825)
Socioeconomic category with extremely strong socialist pre-dominance*c*	59 (80)	83 (241)	87 (386)	89 (139)	83 (846)

Entries indicate the Social Democratic and Communist proportion of the vote in each category. Percentage bases are indicated within parantheses.
*a*Final groups with rank order numbers 1-2 in the *Tree Chart* III. *b*Final groups with rank order numbers 3-6. *c*Final group with rank order number 7.
Source: Election Survey 1964.

ideological separation between them. Nonetheless, the Center party has obviously been more likely than the People's party to choose policy standpoints that allow collaboration with the Social Democrats. As will be seen, the Center party's placing also corresponds well to the cognitions of the party system that are most generally held in the electorate. Through the last decade the two centrist parties have been engaged in collaboration that has brought them very close to each other; without question they both represent a more liberal outlook than does the Conservative party.

To illustrate the kind of opinion differentiation over social-welfare policies that often appears in the electorate, we have brought together survey data in Table 17. As we have deliberately selected these data from interview measurements that uncover a

Left-Right ordering among the parties, the reader should be cautioned that one does not find an equally clear pattern in all measurement instances.

Respondents were asked whether they agreed or disagreed (wholly or in part) with the contents of "ideology-loaded" statements presented to them on printed cards. In the table we have compressed the data obtained from three of these queries by indicating only the proportions of each party's voters that expressed a "leftist" view about their contents, i.e. the proportions agreeing with a "leftist" statement or, in the opposite case, disagreeing.[42]

TABLE 17: **Attitudinal Differentiation in the Electorate, Percentages Agreeing with a Leftist View**

Statements	Commu-nist party	Social Democr. party	Center party	People's party	Conservative party
"Leaders of banks and industries get too much influence if the state doesn't have the capacity to control the private enterprise." (*Agree*)	82	79	53	49	28
"There will be less risk of unemployment if the state gets more influence over banks and business enterprises." (*Agree*)	86	74	31	28	13
"Social reforms have gone so far in this country that in the future the state should rather diminish than increase benefits and subsidies to the citizens." (*Disagree*)	77	73	38	39	24

As explained in the text, *percent entries show the proportions of each party's voters who took a "leftist" stand* on the views listed in the table above. With little variation among the parties, 8-15 percent of the respondents gave ambiguous answers about the various statements, while the remainder expressed a "rightist" opinion.
Source: Election Survey, 1968.

We have selected policy statements of the kind that frequently appear in public argument between spokesmen for socialist and nonsocialist views. One can see from the data that there is a substantial amount of within-party variance in the voters' responses to such views. Although these phrases bear a conspicuous ideological coloring, they do not automatically call forth partisan responses. In respect of the opinion modes of their voters, however, the parties differ along the Left-Right dimension of the party system. There is a wide discrepancy in this regard between socialist and conservative voters, while the supporters of the centrist parties—as expected—occupy an intermediary position.

One may also map the position of the parties by dealing directly with the voters' cognitions of distances among the party standpoints. In the 1968 election survey, the measure consisted of a series of queries in which respondents were asked, for each of the five major parties in turn, to indicate which of the four remaining parties they considered as "closest," "second closest," and "furthest away" from their particular party.[43]

The voters' judgments on the distances among the parties are displayed in a compact form in Table 18. For each of the parties the table shows which party was most frequently considered "closest," as "second closest," and "furthest away." The proportion of all respondents who have agreed on each particular judgment is also indicated in the form of a percentage. In some instances—when less than 70 percent of the respondents hold a common view—the table indicates two different parties in a given position as well as the corresponding percent proportions. Not all respondents were really able to complete the task of constructing five different rank-orders.

We can infer from these data that there is a widespread common understanding in the electorate about the main features of the parties' positioning in the party system. About 70 percent agree that the two centrist parties are closest to each other, irrespective of which of them is taken as the reference point. When judging the distances from the Conservative party, the same or larger proportions of the respondents consider the People's party as closest, the Center party as second closest, the communists as furthest away, and—implicitly—the Social Democrats as positioned somewhere between the Center party and the Communists. Almost the same amount of agreement endorses the judgments about the distances from the People's party: the Center party is closest and the Conservatives are second closest.

A large part of the judgments suggest that the Center party must be located somewhere between the People's party and the Social Democrats. There is less consensus about its precise placing. The most frequent response pattern implies that the Center party is closer to the Conservatives than to the Social Democrats, but there is a sizable minority who thinks, the opposite is the case. Likewise, there is a moderate majority for the judgment that, taking the Social Democrats as the reference point, the distance from the Social Democrats to the Communists is the shortest one. On the other hand, quite a large proportion would instead think of the Center party as being closest to the Social Democrats. Further analyses of complementary data have revealed that this particular ambiguity must be bound up with a peculiar uncertainty about which criteria to apply when making judgments on the relationship between the two socialist parties. For instances, when asked which party they "liked second best," a majority of the Social Democrats mentioned the Center party rather than the Communists. It seems that Social Democratic voters would consider the Communists as closest to the Social Democrats in a "factual sense"—because of their common socialist labeling —but nevertheless think of the Center party as closest in an "evaluative sense."

Most of this variation is captioned in Table 19 where the same data are presented in the form of average distances from each of the parties. As distinguished from the foregoing table, these averages are based only upon judgments made by the people who actually voted for the party that serves as the reference point in the respective column. In this case the distance from the Social Democrats to the Center party appears to be

TABLE 18: **Voters' Views About the Distances Among the Parties**

PARTY FROM WHICH DISTANCES WERE JUDGED

	Communist party	Social Democr. party	Center party	People's party	Conservative party
Closest party	Soc. Democr.: 81%	Communists: 54% Center: 30%	People's: 73%	Center: 72% Conserv.: 20%	People's: 74%
Second closest party	Center: 54% People's: 20%	Center: 47% People's: 26%	Conserv.: 52% Soc. Democr.: 21%	Conserv.: 59% Center: 20%	Center: 73%
Most distant party	Conserv.: 77%	Conserv.: 78%	Communists: 79%	Communists: 79%	Communists: 79%

Interview Question: "One often thinks that certain parties are comparatively close to each other in regard to the policies they want to pursue. Also, one may consider that other parties are further apart from each other. I have here some cards with the names of the larger parties, and I would like to ask you to compare the party that is listed first with the others on the various cards. (*For each card with one of the parties placed at the top.*) Which of the parties do you think is closest to....? Which of the parties do you think is second closest to....? Which of the parties do you think stands furthest away from....?"

The table shows which party was most often mentioned in each particular position and the percentage of all respondents who gave that answer. In some instances, when a sizable minority disagreed with the majority view, two parties (and two percentages) are indicated.

Abbreviations: Communist party, *Communists*; Social Democratic party, *Soc. Democr.*; Center party, *Center*; People's party, *People's*; Conservative party, *Conserv.*

smaller than the distance from the SDP to the Communists. The explanation of this seeming contradiction is that some Social Democrats consider the Communists to be "furthest away," while this was almost never said about the Center party. It is the only instance where the averages deviate from the data in the foregoing table. Out of well over 12,000 complete individual rank-orders contained in the data material, less than twenty percent imply any reversals of the parties' relative placing within this Left-Right ordering.

As touched upon previously, various techniques for nonmetric dimensional analysis can be applied to this kind of data. In a nontechnical fashion these can be summarized in the two alternative geometric representations given in the frame below. The upper version is based strictly on the most frequent distance judgments that appear in our data. (In technical language we have treated these data as forming a conditional proximity matrix. The unidimensional representation is then obtained by unfolding the stimulus I-scales that can be derived from the row-wise rank-ordering of the proximity measures.) The other has been constructed on the ground of nonrigid, heuristic criteria. We have then taken into account the variation in the data and modified the picture so that three distances have obtained equal length, namely those from the Communists to the Social Democrats, from the Social Democrats to the Center party, and from the Center party to the Conservatives.

TABLE 19: Voters' Cognitions of Distances from Their Own Parties to Other Parties

Average proximity score given to:	VOTER'S PARTY				
	Communist party	Social Democr. party	Center party	People's party	Conservartive party
Communist party	—	3.09	1.16	1.12	1.06
Social Democrats	3.84	—	2.35	2.08	1.98
Center party	2.84	3.22	—	3.86	3.17
People's party	2.19	2.43	3.81	—	3.76
Conservatives	1.11	1.20	2.67	2.92	—
Number of cases on which average is based	37	1,347	448	356	275

For the purpose of summarizing the data, simple integer scores have been given to each possible response: score 4 to "closest party," score 3 to "second closest party," score 1 to "most-distant party"; if a party has not been mentioned it has been given score 2. Respondents who could not at all rank-order distances from their own party have been excluded. When the rank-orders were incomplete, each of the parties not mentioned has been given score 2. *Entries* are *averages* of the scores thus given to the parties.
Source: Election Survey, 1968.

The overall inference to be drawn from the data is that in the electorate the prevalent views of the party system varies around these two pictures. A word of caution is in order here: the data do not prove that all the individuals who see the party system in this way must also have distinctly ideological political attitudes. Rather, we find evidence in the cross-section data that the Left-Right ordering of the parties serves as a frame of reference also for citizens whose political opinions otherwise show very little of ideological consistency.[44]

Our double picture of the party system, finally, serves to illuminate crucial preconditions for party competition as well as coalition formation in the Swedish multiparty system.[45] We can see why the Left-Right ordering may result in a Social Democratic—Bourgeois two-bloc formation, when a three-party bourgeois collaboration appears to be a requirement for a nonsocialist "minimum winning coalition". On the other hand, it is not surprising that there have been situation when Social Democrats and the Center party have joined their strengths. In particular this has happened when the Social Democrats have been comparatively weak, yet the eventuality of a nonsocialist majority formation has seemed precluded. The distances among the non-

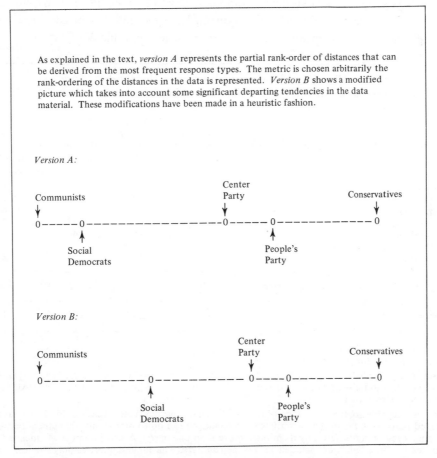

As explained in the text, *version A* represents the partial rank-order of distances that can be derived from the most frequent response types. The metric is chosen arbitrarily the rank-ordering of the distances in the data is represented. *Version B* shows a modified picture which takes into account some significant departing tendencies in the data material. These modifications have been made in a heuristic fashion.

Figure 3: Geometric Representation of Interparty Distances

socialist parties also clarify why the bourgeois bloc is affected by tensions that some-times give rise to a three-bloc formation. At last it becomes apparent that the Social Democrats cannot engage in any close collaboration with the Communists without taking the risk of estranging voters who really think the two parties should be far apart from each other.

We are fortunately in a position to confront this theoretical reasoning about party strategies with empirical data that gauge the voters' preferences in respect of party collaboration in one concrete situation. In interviews during the weeks before the 1968 election a cross section of voters was asked which parties they wished to see represented in the government. The interview query was framed so as to invite the respondent not only to mention the party he intended to vote for but to compose a coalition of parties, if he was not decidedly against such collaboration. (See the question text found in Table 20, where the data are summarized.) When asking a question like this, one cannot expect that all respondents will be familiar with the parliamentary rules of the game. Hence it is not surprising that some people suggested very broad coalitions, while others suggested a government composition with an unrealistically narrow base. Such responses were not disturbingly frequent, however, and do not have any appre-ciable effect on the response patterns that are reflected in Table 20.

TABLE 20: **An Alternative Measure of Interparty Distances:**
Voters' Preferences About the Composition of the Government in 1968

	VOTER'S PARTY			
Party that should be included in government	*Social Democr.*	*Center party*	*People's party*	*Conservative party*
Communists	9	0	1	1
Social Democrats	87	20	15	7
Center party	23	79	78	76
People's party	11	65	87	84
Conservatives	5	41	46	89
"Centrist parties" or "bourgeois parties" without specification	0	5	4	8
"All parties," don't know, not ascertained	10	11	7	4
Number of cases	666	226	185	131

Source: Election Survey, 1968.

Interview question (in pre-election interview):

"Which party or parties would you most prefer to have included in the Government?—[*Probes:*] Would you like to have any other party in the Government?—Which party or parties?" All parties mentioned are recorded.

Entries in the table are the percentage of each of the major parties' voters that would like to have the indicated party included in the Government. Percentages add up to more than 100 percent because a great many respondents naturally mentioned more than one party. A small number of unclassifiable responses are, in effect, not included in any percentages. The table comprises only the four major parties' voters.

The picture of the electorate formed by these data is strikingly concordant with prevailing party strategies. Most Social Democrats really prefer their party to form a government alone. Among those who would add one or more of the other parties, most would prefer the Center party. It is noteworthy that this finding is in agreement with our aforementioned measurement of the Social Democrats "second party preferences," while it is at least partially at variance with the "party distance" data. The supporters of the Center party and the People's party are mostly in favor of including also the other of these centrist parties in a government. But a large part of these parties' voting support would clearly wish to see all the three nonsocialist parties in a government coalition. One could add that this finding is substantiated by a complementary measurement which proved that about the same proportion of the centrist voters were really in favor of the idea that the three parties should merge so as to form a joint bourgeois party. That view was also supported by a large majority of the Conservative voters.[46] The Conservative voters obviously realize that their preferred party can enter a government only in a coalition with the two centrist parties: A large majority of the Conservative voters wanted a three-party bourgeois coalition. An equally overwhelming majority of the Conservative voters did indeed wish that the nonsocialist parties would unite into one party.

These data are not evidence that party strategies are unilaterally governed by voter opinions. For instance, the recent rapprochement between the two centrist parties was accomplished by deliberate measures taken by the two parties' leaderships after the obliteration of the Agrarian party's coalition with the Social Democrats. What is manifest in the data—in that particular case—is that the centrist collaboration has been met with widespread approval within the voting support of the two parties. Even so, the data suggest that party strategies cannot develop over the heads of the people, because party standpoints are bound to influence ideas in the heads of people. When large masses of voters have adopted views about the grounds for political collaboration among different parties, such expectations will impose lasting restrictions upon the possibilities for displacements of party positions. The lastingness of such preconditions for the positioning in the party system is bound up with the social differentiation among the parties, which we have described in the previous sections in this chapter. These factors determine the working of the Swedish multiparty system.

APPENDIX TABLE I: **Social Composition of Electoral Groups,**
in Percentages

	Social Democr. party	Center party	People's party	Conservative party	Non-voters	Total interview survey sample
Age						
21–30	22	19	25	19	39	23
31–40	16	19	15	18	11	16
41–50	18	19	19	19	13	18
51–60	20	20	20	17	11	19
61–84	24	23	21	27	26	24
Total	100	100	100	100	100	100
Sex						
Percent men	52	57	49	47	43	51
Marital status						
Married	72	75	66	61	46	69
Widowed/Divorced	12	8	9	15	19	12
Not married	16	17	25	24	35	19
Total	100	100	100	100	100	100
Family income a						
(Sw Cr)						
0–4,999	9	10	11	11	22	11
5,000–9,999	11	12	10	13	17	12
10,000–19,999	24	33	20	20	34	25
20,000–29,999	30	23	19	15	16	25
30,000–39,999	16	9	18	8	6	13
40,000 or more	10	13	22	33	5	14
Total	100	100	100	100	100	100
Place of Residence:						
Density of population b						
(Proportion of parish population living in builtup area):						
90% or more	65	31	69	57	59	59
50–89.9%	21	28	18	21	16	21
10–49.9%	9	18	8	13	12	11
Less than 10%	5	23	5	9	13	9
Total	100	100	100	100	100	100
Number of cases	1,458	469	370	286	214	2,943

Source: Election Survey, 1968.

a Income data have been drawn from the tax-assessment registers. The family income equals the sum of the two spouses' incomes for married people, while for unmarried people it is, of course, identical with the person's own income.

b The parish classification has been obtained from the 1965 population census.

APPENDIX TABLE II: Voting in Population Groups, in Percentages

	Communist party	Social Democr. party	Center party	People's party	Christian Democr. Coal.	Local Bourg. Coal.	Conservative party	DK/NA	Total	Turnout percent	Number of cases
Age											
21–30	2	55	15	16	1	1	9	1	100	88	674
31–40	1	53	20	12	1	0	12	1	100	95	466
41–50	2	53	18	14	1	0	11	1	100	95	532
51–60	1	53	18	14	1	1	9	3	100	96	562
61–84	1	54	16	12	3	0	12	2	100	92	709
Sex & Marital Status											
Men	2	54	19	13	1	0	9	2	100	94	1,517
Thereof: Married	2	54	20	13	2	0	8	1	100	96	1,065
Not married	3	51	17	13	1	0	13	2	100	88	452
Women	1	53	15	14	2	1	12	2	100	92	1,426
Thereof: Married	1	54	17	13	2	1	10	2	100	94	961
Not married	1	51	12	18	1	1	14	2	100	87	465
Family Income (Sw Cr)											
0–4,999	3	48	17	15	2	0	11	4	100	85	320
5,000–9,999	1	54	19	12	1	0	12	1	100	89	340
10,000–19,999	2	51	23	11	2	1	9	2	100	90	745
20,000–29,999	1	63	15	11	2	1	6	1	100	96	727
30,000–39,999	2	61	11	17	1	0	6	2	100	97	398
40,000 or more	1	36	16	20	1	0	24	2	100	97	409
Place of Residence: *Density of Population* (Proportion of parish population living in builtup area):											
90% or more	2	59	9	16	1	1	10	2	100	93	1,728
50–89.9%	1	52	22	12	2	0	10	1	100	95	621
10–49.9%	1	45	27	9	2	—	12	4	100	92	337
Less than 10%	—	30	47	8	1	0	12	2	100	89	257

Source: Election Survey, 1968.

Notes

1. Georg Andrén, *Tvåkammarsystemets tillkomst och utveckling, Sveriges Riksdag*, vol. IX (Stockholm: 1937). This is the main study of political representation in Sweden from 1866. The literature on the subject covered in this overview section is rich. However, only a few general references to the major studies will be given in the footnotes here; the reader is referred to these works for exhaustive bibliographies. Good overviews of the parliamentary parties in the Riksdag as well as the national party organizations are found in Edvard Thermaenius, *Riksdagspartierna, Sveriges Riksdag*, vol. XVII (Stockholm: 1935), and in: Pär-Erik Back, *Det svenska partiväsendet*, in: *Sämhalle och Riksdag*, vol. II, (Uppsala: 1966).

2. Edvard Thermaenius. *Lantmannapartiet. Dess uppkomst, organisation och tidigare utveckling* (Uppsala: 1928).

3. Lars Sköld, Arne Halvarson, *Riksdagens sociala sammansättning under hundra år. Samhälle och riksdag*, vol. I (Uppsala : 1966).

4. Gunnar Wallin, *Valrörelser och valresultat. Andrakammarvalen i Sverige*, 1866-1884, (Stockholm: 1961). Torbjörn Vallinder: *I kamp för demokratien, Rösträttsrörelsen i Sverige* 1886-1890 (Stockholm: 1962).

5. Hans-krister Rönnblom, *Frisinnade landsföreningen* 1902-1927. *Skildringar ur den liberala organisationsrörelsens historia i vårt land* (Stockholm: 1929).

6. Up to 1905 the conservative outlook included another nationalistic theme, namely, hostility toward Norway's separation from the union with Sweden. The emergence of the modern Conservative outlook is outlined in Nils Elvander, *Harald Hjärne och konservatismen. Konservativ idédebatt i Sverige* 1865 - 1922 (Uppsala : 1961). The interrelationships between ideological orientations, party strategies, and standpoints in the union controversy are investigated in Evert Vedung, *Unionsdebatten 1905. En jämförelse mellan argumenteringen i Sverige och Norge*, (Kristianstad: 1971).

7. See Arne Wåhlstrand, *Allmänna Valmansförbundets tillkomst* (Uppsala : 1946).

8. Edvard Thermaenius, op cit, esp. pp. 179ff.

9. Jörgen Westerståhl, *Svensk fackföreningsrörelse. Organisationsproblem. Verksamhetsformer. Förhållande till staten* (Stockholm: 1945).

10. G. Bagge, E. Lundberg, I. Svennilson, *Wages in Sweden 1860-1930*, vol. I, (London: 1933).

11. Olle Johansson, "Socialdemokratins väljare 1911 och 1914," *Historisk Tidskrift*, 1967. See also, Gösta Carlsson, "Partiförskjutningar som tillväxtprocesser," *Statsvetenskaplig Tidskrift*, 1963.

12. The boundaries indicated above for the Social Democrats and for the socialist total vote were transgressed during the World War II: In the first part of the war the Social Democratic support swelled beyond its normal level. Later the Communist party showed an upsruge. We have disregarded these "deviating" election outcomes in the above overview on the ground that they so obviously reflect the impact of very temporary and peculiar circumstances.

13. This phase of Swedish parliamentarism has been treated in a monograph by Olle Nyman, *Svensk parlamentarism 1932-1936. Från minoritetsparlamentarism till majoritetskoalition* (Uppsala: 1947).

14. Electoral trends in the postwar period and their relationships to party strategies are treated more extensively in three articles published by this author in *Scandinavian Political Studies:* "Political Stability and Change in the Swedish Electorate", vol. 1 (1966); "Party Politics and Electoral Opinion Formation: A Study of Issues in Swedish Politics 1956-1960", vol. 2 (1967), and "Voting Behavior in Shifting 'Elections Winds', An Overview of Swedish Elections 1964-1968" vol. 5 (1970). A study of opinion formation at the national referendum on the pension question is presented in Bo Särlvik, *Opinionsbildningen vid folkomröstningen 1957* (Stockholm: 1959). The shaping of party strategies in this conflict is studied in: Björn Molin; *Tjänstepensionsfrågan. En studie i svensk partipolitik* (Göteborg. 1965). A comprehensive study of the forming of Governments and coalitions through the postwar period is presented in Olof Ruin, *Mellan samlingsregering och tvåpartisystem* (Stockholm: 1968).

15. In the early 1950s a governmental investigation committee published summary party budgets for the years 1948–1949. Unfortunately, these data must now be considered as entirely outdated. See *Om offentlig redovisning av den politiska propagandans finansiering. Partifinansieringssakkunnigas betänkande*. Statens offentliga utredningar 1951:56; (Stockholm: 1951). In 1966 the total expenditures of the national organizations were estimated to about 40 million SwCr, according to an investigation carried out by a newspaper; see Nils Andrén, "State Support for Political Parties," *Scandinavian Political Studies*, 3, 1968.

16. Data concerning county and communal party support are drawn from Iris Nilsson, *Om lag om kommunalt partistöd*, Seminar paper, Socialhögskolan (Stockholm: 1971), mimeo. A report on

community party support is to be found in *Utredningen om den kommunala democratin* (Statens offentliga utredningar 1972 : 52).

17. The parties' parliamentary nomination procedures have been investigated in Lars Sköld, *Kandidatnominering vid andrakammarval. Författningsutredningen: I* (Stockholm: 1958). A study of the party nominations at a communal election is presented in Bengt Barkfeldt et al., *Partierna nominerar. Den kommunala självstyrelsen*, 3 (Uppsala: 1971).

18. A good overview is given in Pär-Erik Back: *Det svenska partiväsendet*, in: *Samhälle och riksdag* II (Uppsala: 1966).

19. The party identification concept has been introduced in the writings of Angus Campbell and his collaborators, see, e.g., Campbell, Converse, Miller, Stokes, *The American Voter*, (New York: 1960).

20. This type of relationship between intensity in political engagement and positioning on the predominant attitudinal dimension of a party system was first suggested and substantiated with cross-national survey data in an article by Angus Campbell: "A la recherche d'un modèle en psychologie électorale comparative", *Revue franc. Sociol.*, VII (1966).

21. This material has been drawn from the author's article, "Voting Behavior in Shifting 'Election Winds.' An Overview of the Swedish Elections 1964-1968," *Scandinavian Political Studies*, 5 (1970). A more exhaustive analysis is contained in the author's forthcoming study: *Electoral Behavior in the Swedish Multiparty system*.

22. See Gösta Carlsson: "Partiförskjutningar som tillväxtprocesser," *Statsvetenskaplig Tidskrift* 1963.

23. Herbert Tingsten: *Political Behavior* (Stockholm: 1937).

24. See Gösta Carlsson, "Partiförskjutningar som tillväxtprocesser", *Statsvetenskaplig Tidskrift* (1963).

25. Detailed data on the party composition of the leadership of the farmers' interest organizations in 1950-51 are given in Gunnar Hellström, *Föreningsdemokrati och förtroendemannakår* (Halmstad 1964).

26. For a more detailed analysis see the author's article on "Political Stability and Change in the Swedish Electorate," *Scandinavian Political Studies*, vol. 1 (1966).

27. Although our calculations have proceeded in a fashion somewhat different from that chosen by Gösta Carlsson, op. cit., it should be noted that we have taken advantage of his calculations. It should furthermore be noted that a more sophisticated analysis of aggregate data has recently been presented in Leif Lewin, Bo Jansson, and Dag Sörbom, *The Swedish Electorate 1887-1968* (Uppsala : 1972). As a matter of course such an analysis can provide ground for more specific estimates than the ones presented above.

28. See Gösta Carlsson, op. cit.

29. The table is actually drawn from an extensive analysis of generational change. In this we have also looked into the vote division within different age groups. There is some evidence in the data that the younger workers with a middle-class background were less likely than the older to vote for a socialist party; the trend in the summary table remains, however.

30. This research program includes surveys at the parliamentary elections in 1956, 1960, 1964, 1968, and 1970, and also a survey at the pension referendum in 1957. Descriptions of study designs and samples are to be found in this author's reports for the official election statistics; see: *Riksdagsmannavalen 1959-1960*, II, (Stockholm: 1961), *Riksdagsmannavalen 1961-1964*, II (Stockholm 1965), and *Riksdagsmannavalen 1965-1968*, II (Stockholm: 1970). All of these reports are published in the series *Sveriges officiella statistik* by the Swedish Central Bureau of Statistics. See also other publications by this author cited in the footnotes of this chapter.

31. The socioeconomic classification scheme was originally constructed by the Central Bureau of Statistics for its election-participation statistics. For the purpose of the interview surveys we have constructed a somewhat modified version of this classification. The strata appearing in the tables have been formed by collapsing a large number of subcategories used in the coding process.

32. The main themes in recent ideological controversies among the parties are outlined in a study by Leif Lewin, *Planhushållningsdebatten* (Uppsala: 1967).

33. The attitudinal contents of voters' party affiliations are treated in the author's study of "Electoral Behavior in the Swedish Multiparty System" (mimeo., forthcoming in print).

34. A comprehensive treatment of the political functions of the interest organizations can be found in Nils Elvander: *Intresseorganisationerna i dagens Sverige* (Lund: 1969), (2d ed.)

35. More specified tabulations are to be found in this author's chapter in *Riksdagsmannavalen 1965-1968*, Statistiska Centralbyrån (Stockholm: 1970). The trends mentioned above have proved to be persistent over time through our sequence of election studies.

36. The data presented here are all drawn from the interview sample survey at the 1968 election in order to facilitate direct comparisons with our other data analyses. Corresponding aggregate data

are also available, however, and are published in *Riksdagsmannavalen 1965-1968, II*; interview sample and aggregate data show a very good agreement.

37. The concepts of "attribute space" and "attribute space reduction" have been introduced in the writings of Barton and Lazarsfeld. See, e.g., Paul F. Lazarsfeld and Allen H. Barton, "Qualitative Measurement in the Social Sciences. Classification, Typologies, and Indices," in Lerner and Lasswell, eds, *The Policy Sciences* (Standford: 1951).

38. This computer program is also known as the *Automatic Interaction Detector A.I.D.*), The original version of the program is fully described in John A. Sonquist and James Morgan, *The Detection of Interaction Effects, Survey Research Center Monograph No. 36, Institute for Social Research* (Ann Arbor: 1964). Further research on the underlying analysis model and recent program development are presented in John A. Sonquist, *Multivariate Model Building. The Validation of a Search Strategy* (Ann Arbor: 1970); John A. Sonquist Elisabeth Laugh Baker, James N. Morgan, *Searching for Structure. (Alias - AID - III.)* (Ann Arbor: 1971).

39. These tree analyses are fully described in two articles by this author: "Socioeconomic Determinants of Voting Behavior in the Swedish Electorate," *Comparative Political Studies*, II (1969). "Socioeconomic Position, Religious Behavior, and Voting in the Swedish Electorate," *Quality and Quantity*, IV (1970).

40. This section contains materials drawn from the author's article "Socioeconomic Position, Religious Behavior, and Voting in the Swedish Electorate," *Quality and Quantity*, IV (1970).

41. Both of these proportions of "explained variance" are correlation ratios for sample data. The latter one has been obtained by a one-way analysis of variance over the full set of twenty-eight categories formed by the combination of the socioeconomic and the church attendance classifications.

42. A technical note may be in order. When using this kind of measure, one normally obtains a somewhat oversized proportion of agreeing answers because of a phenomenon known as "response aquiescence." This effect becomes evened out over a full set of measures, but it may give the reader a too "leftist" overall impression of the response distributions shown in the table here. With the aid of scaling and dimensional analysis techniques one can relate the separate measurement to underlying attitude dimensions, but it goes beyond the scope of the present chapter to present such exhaustive analyses.

43. Methodologically this is known as a version of the "cartwheel technique" for collecting stimulus comparison data. The data theory and appropriate analysis techniques are treated in Clyde H. Coombs: *A Theory of Data* (New York: 1964).

44. The material presented here is drawn from a study preparation that comprises a set of different similarity and preference order measures. A part of this material has previously been published in the author's article in *Scandinavian Political Studies*, 5 (1970), op. cit.
    The percentages in Table 19 differ slightly from those appearing in that article, because we have now excluded a small category of persons who were, in effect, not able to answer the appropriate questions. See also this author's previously published study of party change as a measure of distances and dimensions in the Swedish party system: "Partibyten som mått på avstånd och dimensioner i partisystemet," *Sociologisk forskning* (1968).

45. With a different methodological approach these preconditions have been analyzed in Olof Ruin, *Mellan samlingsregering och tvåpartisystem. Den svenska regeringsfrågan 1945-1966.* (Stockholm 1968).

46. Detailed data are given in the author's article in *Scandinavian Political Studies* 5, (1970), op. cit.

References

Following are works quoted in the text as well as some additional articles and books treating the party system and parliamentary government in Sweden. For some of the latter, the fact that they are written in English has been an additional reason for their inclusion. Of the works quoted in the chapter, those that primarily treat social and economic conditions, the politics of other countries, etc. are omitted from the bibliography. Election Statistics Reports of the Swedish Central Bureau of Statistics

Sweden 433

are not listed in this bibliography. An annotated bibliography on Swedish election statistics has been prepared by Esbjörn Janson (see citation below).

ANDREN, GEORG. *Tvåkammarsystemets tillkomst och utveckling. Sveriges Riksdag*, vol. IX. Stockholm: 1937.

ANDREN, NILS. "State Support for Political Parties." *Scandinavian Political Studies* 3 (1968).

BACK, PÄR-ERIK. "Det sevenska partiväsendet." In: *Samhälle och riksdag*, vol. II. Uppsala: 1966.

BARKFELDT, BENGT; BRÄNDSTRÖM, DAN; SIMM, UNO; and ZANDERIN, LARS. *Partierna nominerar. Den kommunala självstyrelsen*, vol. 3. Uppsala: 1971.

CARLSSON, GÖSTA. "Partiförskjutningar som tillväxtprocesser." *Statsvetenskaplig Tidskrift* (1963).

ELVANDER, NILS. *Harald Hjärne och konservatismen. Konservativ idédebatt i Sverige 1865–1922*. Uppsala: 1961.

———. *Intresseorganisationerna i dagens Sverige*, 2nd ed. Lund: 1969.

GERDNER, GUNNAR, *Det svenska regeringsproblemet 1917–1920. Från majoritetskoalition till minoritetsparlamentarism*. Uppsala: 1946.

———. *Parlamentarismens kris i Sverige vid 1920-talets början*. Uppsala: 1954.

JANSON, CARL-GUNNAR. *Mandattilldelning och regional röstfördelning*. Stockholm: 1961.

JANSON, ESBJÖRN. "Sweden." In Stein Rokkan and Jean Meyriat, eds. *International Guide to Electoral Statistics*. Paris: 1969.

JOHANSSON, OLLE. "Socialdemokratins väljare 1911 och 1914." *Historisk Tidskrift* (1967).

LEWIN, LEIF. *Planhushöllningsdebatten*. Uppsala: 1967.

MOLIN, BJÖRN. *Tjånstepensionsfrågan. En studie i svensk partipolitik*. Göteborg: 1965.

———. "Swedish Party Politics: A Case Study." *Scandinavian Political Studies* 1 (1966).

NYMAN, OLLE, *Svensk parlamentarism 1932-1936. Från minoritets-parlamentarism till majoritetskoalition*. Uppsala: 1947.

———. *Tvåkammarsystemets omvandling. Från privilegierätt till demokrati, Samhälle och riksdag*, vol. III. Uppsala: 1966.

RÖNNBLOM, HANS-KRISTER, *Frisinnade landsföreningen 1902-1927. Skildringar ur den liberala organisationsrörelsens historia i vårt land*. Stockholm: 1929.

RUIN, OLOF. *Mellan samlingsregering och tvåpartisystem. Den svenska regeringsfrågan 1945–1960*. Stockholm 1968.

———. "Patterns of Government Composition in Multi-Party Systems: The Case of Sweden." *Scandinavian Political Studies* 4 (1969).

RUSTOW, D. A. *The Politics of Compromise*. Princeton: Princeton Univ. Press, 1955.

SÄRLVIK, BO. *Opinionsbildningen vid folkomröstningen 1957*. Stockholm: 1959.

———. "Political Stability and Change in the Swedish Electorate." *Scandinavian Political Studies* 1:1966.

————. "Party Politics and Electoral Opinion Formation. A Study of Issues in Swedish Politics 1956–1960." *Scandinavian Political Studies* 4 (1967).

————. "Partibyten som mått på avstånd och dimensioner i partisystemet." *Sociologisk forskning* (1968).

————. "Socioeconomic Determinants of Voting Behavior in the Swedish Electorate." *Comparative Political Studies* II (1969).

————. "Socioeconomic Position, Religious Behavior, and Voting in the Swedish Electorate." *Quality and Quantity* IV (1970).

————. "Voting Behavior in Shifting 'Election Winds'—An Overview of Swedish Elections 1964–1968." *Scandinavian Political Studies* 5 (1970).

SJÖDEN, RUNE. *Sveriges första TV-val. En studie i radions och televisionens roll som propagandamedier under 1960 års valkampanj.* Uddevalla: 1962.

SKÖLD, LARS, *Kandidatnominering vid andrakammarval.* Stockholm: 1958.

————, and HALVARSSON, ARNE. "Riksdagens sociala sammansättning under hundra år." In *Samhälle och riksdag*, vol I. Uppsala: 1966.

STJERNQUIST, NILS. "Sweden: Stability or Deadlock?" In Dahl, ed., *Political Oppositions in Western Democracies.* New Haven: Yale Univ. Press, 1966.

THERMAENIUS, EDVARD. *Lantmannapartiet. Dess uppkomst, organisation och tidigare utveckling.* Uppsala: 1928.

————. *Riksdagspartierna, Sveriges Riksdag*, vol. XVII. Stockholm: 1935.

VALLINDER, TORBJÖRN. *I kamp för demokratin. Rösträttsrörelsen i Sverige 1886–1890.* Stockholm: 1962.

VEDUNG, EVERT. *Unionsdebatten 1905. En jämförelse mellan argumenteringen i Sverige och Norge.* Kristianstad: 1971.

VERNEY, D. *Parliamentary Reform in Sweden.* Oxford: 1957.

WÄHLSTRAND, ARNE. *Allmänna valmansförbundets tillkomst.* Uppsala: 1964.

WALLIN, GUNNAR. *Valrörelser och valresultat. Andrakammarvalen i Sverige 1866–1884.* Stockholm: 1961.

Anglo-America

9. AUSTRALIA:
Class Politics in the New World
DON AITKIN AND MICHAEL KAHAN

I. Historical Background

White Australia began as a penal colony, a dumping ground for those sentenced by English courts to transportation. Before the American War of Independence such convicts were shipped to Virginia and other plantation colonies; during and after it they were confined to hulks until their number grew intolerably large. On January 26, 1788 more than a thousand convicts and their attendant warders disembarked in Sydney Cove. By the time transportation ended in 1868, more than 150,000 felons had followed them.

When their terms of imprisonment were over, most convicts stayed in the new land, where for many years they formed the bulk of the working-class. Since a substantial proportion of the convicts were from Ireland, Australia had from the beginning a much higher proportion of Roman Catholics than England. Early in the nineteenth-century explorers noted the suitability of inland Australia for the grazing of sheep for wool. There followed the exploration of the back country, the settlement of much of it by willing immigrants from the British Isles, and the gradual conversion of the penal colony into a collection of commercial enclaves whose residents began to demand institutions of government they had been familiar with at home. In this process a basic division hardened between the largely ex-convict working-class, containing most of the Irish and Catholics, and the landowning middle-class, containing most of the Scottish Presbyterians and the respectable English. Although there has been much change in the succeeding century, these early equations were slow to break down, and are the basis of the modern Australian party system.

Until the First World War immigration helped to reinforce these divisions. The great majority of the immigrants came from the British Isles, and these included a substantial minority of Roman Catholic Irish. The hostility of the Australian-Irish community for England was aggravated both by the movement for home rule in

The work on which this chapter is based was carried out when both authors were members of the department of political science, Research School of Social Sciences, Australian National University, Canberra. We should also like to thank Sue Fraser for her patient and careful research assistance. The survey data on which this chapter is based have been deposited with the Inter-University Consortium for Political Research, Ann Arbor, Michigan, USA.

Ireland and by the Catholic Church's policy of recruiting many of its priests for Australia from Ireland and training its native-born priests in Ireland or at the Irish College in Rome (Murtagh, 1959). These tensions reached their point of greatest strain in 1916, when the Irish, led by the Roman Catholic Archbishop of Melbourne, Dr. Daniel Mannix, reacted to the English suppression of the Dublin uprising of 1916 by opposing the conscription of Australians to fight an "English" war; the proposal was defeated at two national plebiscites. In this struggle the Labor, Irish, and Catholic grouping within Australia was ranged against the Liberal, English, and Protestant grouping in a fashion that has had no subsequent parallel (O'Farrell, 1968). Immigration from Ireland has greatly diminished in the twentieth-century, and although the Catholic-Protestant cleavage has remained important, the end of Anglo-Irish fighting in 1921 removed the chief cause of nationalistic controversy. The post-1945 immigration of Catholics from continental Europe, especially from Italy, has further reduced the significance of an Irish-oriented sectarianism. Despite the flood of immigrants, the population is strikingly homogeneous: 81 percent in 1966 were native-born and overwhelmingly descendants of earlier migrants from the British Isles, 8 percent had been born in the British Isles, 2 percent in Italy, and 6 percent elsewhere in Europe.

If religion has been one of the great underlying dimensions of Australian politics, the pattern of settlement has been another. Each of the six colonies began as a seaboard settlement, from which explorers and, in their wake, pastoralists, farmers, and prospectors pushed out in search of inland seas and eldorados. As each colony grew in prosperity so did its principal town; and since the interior ("the bush") was of little use save for large-scale agriculture and grazing, these towns had no serious inland rivals. Before the end of the nineteenth-century the rural areas began to lose part of their natural increase to the cities, while immigrants have traditionally preferred the city to the bush. The paradoxical consequence is that Australia's 3,000,000 square miles accommodate the world's most urbanized society: in 1966 58 percent lived in metropolitan areas and another 25 percent in nonmetropolitan cities and towns; 41 percent of the entire population lived in two cities, Sydney and Melbourne.

The concentration of population has been reinforced by a structural change in the economy. The Australian colonies of the nineteenth-century were pastoral dominions exporting wool and, later, wheat, meat, and dairy products to England and Europe. Since the federation of the colonies in 1900 Australia has become progressively more industrialized; in 1966 the distribution of its work force among the primary, secondary, and tertiary sectors of the economy was comparable with that of the United States. As a result Australia is less dependent on primary production, although this area still contributes about half the nation's export earnings.

Federation itself was an example of concentration of political power. The essential homogeneity of the populations of the colonies, the sheer logic of their situation, burgeoning Australian nationalism in the latter part of the nineteenth-century, and anxiety about colonial defense all made federation possible. But political centralization did not stop with federation—in the last seventy years the center of gravity in Australian politics has shifted decisively to Canberra, since 1927 the seat of the national parliament and a major city. National personalities and policies now dominate the media, a change in emphasis that occurred during the depression of the 1930s and has accelerated since.

"The outstanding characteristic of Australian electoral systems is probably complexity" (Rydon, 1969, p. 119). Experimentation accompanies complexity, for in electing their legislatures Australians have tried most of the systems used elsewhere. The liberalization of the forms of voting came early, and one of them, the secret ballot, was introduced in the 1850s—early enough to be known elsewhere as "the Australian ballot" (Crisp. 1965; Fredman, 1967). Manhood suffrage for the lower house of parliament was widespread by 1860, and women were first enfranchised in 1894 in South Australia. By 1906 the last vestiges of plural voting for the lower house were removed, and two years later all the states and the Commonwealth had universal adult suffrage.

Complexity has been in part a by-product of the nation's federal structure. In 1901 the six states and the Commonwealth each had a bicameral legislative body: a house of representatives and a senate (the "upper house") at the federal level and a legislative assembly (or house of assembly) plus an "upper" legislative council in each of the states. Sometimes the electoral systems returning members to these houses of parliament have differed from state to state, and within each state from house to house. In general, changes in the suffrage for the upper house followed those for the lower, but Queensland abolished its legislative council in 1921 and New South Wales converted its council in 1933 from a nominee house to one elected by an electoral college of members of both houses. There are still small property qualifications attached to the franchise for the South Australian Legislative Council.

For most of the twentieth-century voters in the various states and the Commonwealth have elected their members of parliament from single-member seats, initially using simple-majority, then preferential voting. But proportional representation in multimember constituencies has been used in Tasmania for state elections since 1907, in New South Wales for state elections between 1920 and 1927, and in elections for the Commonwealth Senate since 1949. The Tasmanian experience suggests that PR does not always lead to fragmented party systems and weak governments: a Labor government in that state faced a Liberal opposition from 1934 to 1969, when the positions were reversed. However, the application of PR to Senate elections has converted the Senate into a safe harbor for the nominees of the two major party machines; since each state becomes an electorate electing five members, only the fifth seat is ever in doubt. A major split in the Labor party in 1955 led to the creation of a splinter group, the Democratic Labor party, to which PR has given the balance of power in the Senate.

Compulsory preferential voting has become pervasive. The colony of Queensland experimented with a form of optional preferential voting as early as 1892. Victoria and Western Australia adopted it in 1911, the Commonwealth in 1918. (Federal electoral laws and regulations are made by the federal parliament, not by the states.) It became universal in 1962. Under this system the voter numbers the candidates in the order of his preference for them. Should no candidate receive an absolute majority (50 percent

+1 vote) of the formal votes cast, the primary votes (=*first* preference votes) of the candidate receiving least support are excluded and recounted, each vote now being distributed to the candidate who received the voter's *second* preference. The process is repeated until one candidate possesses an absolute majority.

Preferential voting has become an important element in the tactics of Australian electoral politics. It allows factional disputes within a party to be fought out electorally with a minimum risk of presenting the seat to the other side; it allows the major non-Labor parties, the Liberal and Country parties, to engage in side competition for seats while presenting a relatively united front to Labor; it also allows the DLP, a break-away Labor group, to direct second preferences away from Labor. Because Australians possess strong party loyalties, and because preferential voting complicates the ballot, a party supporter faced with the problem of allocating preferences among six or seven candidates for a House of Representatives seat (let alone among twenty or more for a Senate list) will turn gratefully to his party's official "how to vote" card, which he can bring with him into the polling booth. It is common for the flow of preferences between Liberal and Country party candidates to exceed 90 percent, i.e., more than 90 percent of Liberal voters will give the Country party candidate their second preference.

Queensland introduced compulsory voting in 1914 with a maximum penalty of £2 for failure to vote; the Commonwealth followed in 1924, and the practice was universal by 1942. The measure was introduced by the political parties in their own interests. Compulsory voting obviates the need to get out the vote, reduces the need for a large corps of workers (approximately one Australian voter in twenty belongs formally to a political party branch, compared with perhaps one in eight in Britain), and increases informal voting (that is, the casting of ballots that are invalid because they do not give a complete list of the voter's preferences or for some other technical reason), especially for the Senate, where the combination of uncaring voters, large ballot papers, and the compulsory ordering of preferences can produce informal voting as high as 10 percent. Compulsory voting has also brought about the phenomenon of the "donkey voter," the elector who numbers the candidates from top to bottom (or, on the Senate ballot paper, form left to right), thus benefiting the candidate whose alphabetic preeminence placed him at the head of the paper (Rydon, 1961 and 1968; APSA, 1963; Masterman, 1964). Compulsion denies political scientists the intellectual pleasure of analyzing turnout variations; on the other hand, it does somewhat simplify the analysis of election results.

Although "one man, one vote" was enshrined very early, "one vote, one value" has never won complete acceptance. Each party when in power has tried its hand at juggling the electoral system to maximize its own representation in parliament. The characteristic device, known as "vote-weighting," has been the creation of separate quotas for city and country seats, whereby country seats contain on average a smaller number of voters. The disparities have sometimes been grotesque in state politics—in 1968 the largest Assembly seat in South Australia, urban, contained 45,000 voters, while the smallest, rural, had only 5,000—but in federal redistributions the seats have been kept at approximately equal size; even after some tendentious amendments to the

Commonwealth Electoral Act in 1965 urban seats contained only 7 percent more voters than rural seats (Aitkin, 1968). In general the weighting of rural votes has operated to the disadvantage of the Labor party, which draws much of its support from the cities. Labor is also disadvantaged in that its supporters tend to be disproportionately concentrated residentially.

In consequence, Labor is generally underrepresented in parliament in terms of the share of the vote won by its candidates. In the four postwar elections to 1954 the differences were slight. The Liberal party won on average the same proportion of votes as of seats (38 percent), the Labor party was slightly disadvantaged (votes, 48 percent; seats, 47 percent), and the Country party greatly favored (votes, 10 percent; seats, 15 percent). Independent and minor party candidates won no seats. In the six elections since 1955 the DLP, which has averaged 7 percent of the vote but won no seats, has helped to keep the ratios for the other parties reasonably close. But the margin for the Country party is favorable (votes, 9 percent; seats, 16 percent), the Liberal party is advantaged (votes, 37 percent; seats, 43 percent), and the Labor party further disadvantaged (votes, 45 percent; seats, 41 pecent). The Country party's imbalance derives in part, however, from a strategy of contesting only those seats it is likely to win. These general comments apply with much the same force to the various state electoral systems, save that vote-weighting has been more extensively practiced in the states, though not in Tasmania, which uses its five federal constituencies as seven-member state constituencies.

The pattern of geographical concentrations of industrial workers, farmers, and middle-class has one other consequence for the electoral system. The majority of seats do not change hands in elections—about three-quarters of all the seats in the House of Representatives are safe for the parties whose members hold them. Between 1951 and 1969 an average of ten seats in a House of 122 to 125 members changed hands at each election: the lowest was five seats in 1958, the highest sixteen in 1961. Only a minority of voters can genuinely play a part in determining the result of an election.

The first federal House of Representatives contained seventy-five members. The constitution requires the Senate to give equal representation to all states and fixes the number of seats in the House at ("as nearly as practicable") twice the number of senators. In 1970 the Senate contained sixty members and the House 125; the principal increase occurred in 1949. The bare bones of the electoral framework are set out in Table 1.

During the colonial era parliamentary politics was characterized by shifting personal alliances and the absence of stable ideological or interest cleavages (Loveday and Martin, 1966). The first mass party to emerge was the Australian Labor party, born of the maritime and shearers' strikes in 1890. Nine years later Queensland experienced the rule of Australia's first short-lived Labor government; in 1904 the first federal Labor government took office. Labor's immediate electoral successes and its strong mass organization caused major reorganization in the camps of its rivals. At the beginning of the twentieth-century the formal division in politics turned on attitudes to tariffs. By 1910 the free-trade and protectionist groups had merged into an anti-

TABLE 1: Australia—Parliaments, Populations, and Electorates

	Population[1]	%	Seats in Federal Parliament		Electors[2]	Seats in State Parliament	
			House of Representatives	Senate		Legislative[3] Assembly	Legislative Council
New South Wales	4,623,900	36.4	45	10	2,438,667	96	60
Victoria	3,480,800	27.4	34	10	1,809,549	73	35
Queensland	1,820,000	14.3	18	10	953,564	78	
South Australia	1,177,800	9.2	12	10	624,626	47	20
Western Australia	1,001,300	7.9	9	10	484,128	51	30
Tasmania	395,600	3.1	5	10	211,220	35	19
Australian Capital Territory	139,800	1.1	1	none	63,293	(none)	
Northern Territory	74,100	0.6	1	none	21,186	(none)	
Commonwealth	12,713,300	100.0	125	60	6,606,233	—	—

[1]Estimated population, December 31,1970.

[2]At House of Representatives elections, October 25,1969. State rolls for lower house elections are similar, save in Western Australia where the minimum voting age is eighteen.

[3]House of Assembly in South Australia and Tasmania.

socialist Liberal party, and for a decade Australia enjoyed its only taste of a straight two-party system. In 1919 farmers' and graziers' organizations set up their own political group, the Country party, which restricted its territorial ambitions to the representation of all those electorates outside the major cities (Graham, 1966). The Country party's breakthrough was enhanced by the introduction of preferential voting, but it would have occurred even had there been no change in the electoral system. This threefold division continued until 1955, when a dissident Labor group broke away from the ALP to form the Democratic Labor party, vociferously anticommunist in attitude and enjoying the support of some sections of the Roman Catholic Church, (Murray, 1970; Rawson, 1969; Duffy, 1969). In 1970 the DLP secured five of the sixty seats in the federal Senate, though its electoral support was too diffuse to allow it to win any seats in the lower houses of the federal or state parliaments. Most elections have seen at least one minor group seeking a place in the sun. The Communist party has generally secured about 1 percent of the votes; it rarely contests more than a quarter of the seats.

The two principal parties have shown a pervasive tendency to split and regroup. The federal Labor government fell apart during the First World War because of the conscription issue: Prime Minister W. M. Hughes and most of his cabinet regrouped with their former opposition as the National party, favoring conscription. During the depression the federal Labor government broke up over the best means of dealing with the budgetary crisis and unemployment; a senior Labor minister, J. A. Lyons, became the nucleus around which his own followers and the opposition reformed in 1931 as the United Australia party. The UAP soon took office and held it for ten years. The confused 1955 split occurred because of the Labor party's attitude to Communist activity within trade unions, and took place while the party was in opposition. Each of these three splits set back the ALP electorally for some years; in the 1930s the Labor movement experienced in addition a succession of internal conflicts fought out at state and federal elections. Mainly owing to these splits, the non-Labor parties have controlled the federal government three-quarters of the time since 1910. The Liberal party has been less prone to fission, but very ready to change its name and to some extent its stance in order to profit from the errors of its principal rival. Nonetheless, the UAP collapsed both in parliament and outside during the Second World War, and was replaced in due course by a new Liberal party, much more strongly based organizationally than its predecessors and more long-lived than any of them (West, 1965).

Australia's party system has been variously described as "two-party", "two and half-party", "three-party", "four-party", and "multi-party". Each description has some force, according to the arena being studied: parliamentary alignments are typically bipolar, but the electoral situation is much more competitive. Rae's fractionalization index (Rae, 1967, pp. 53–58), which ranges from 0.00 (a one-party state) through 0.50 (pure two-party) to something approaching 1.00 (a multiplicity of parties), provides a measure of party competitiveness over time. In Australia since federation the mean fractionalization index for federal elections is 0.64, but there is considerable variation from period to period (Table 2).

At the same time the persistent dimension in party conflict has been that of Labor versus non-Labor, the latter force now including three parties. Moreover, the Labor party and the Liberal party (including its antecedents) have customarily taken the lion's share of the vote since 1910 (Table 3). The data illustrate the general stability of party voting over more than sixty years, and demonstrate also that the two major parties have generally polled more than eighty percent of the first-preference votes. As with votes so—to some extent—with seats. The Country party has been able to keep a steady hold on some 16 percent of the seats in the House of Representatives because of the

TABLE 2:   The Changing Competitiveness of the Australian Party System, 1901-1969

Period*		Description	Average Fractionalisation Score (Rae's index)
1901–1906	Early 3-party:	Labor vs. Free Trade vs. Protection	0.69
1910–1917	Pure 2-party:	Labor vs. Liberal	0.53
1919–1929	Stable 3-party:	Labor vs. National vs. Country	0.63
1931–1943	The Era of Splits:	(Labor vs. Labor) vs. UAP vs. Country)	0.71
1946–1954	Stable 3-party:	Labor vs. Liberal vs. Country	0.61
1955–1969	Stable 4-party:	Labor vs. Liberal vs. Country vs. DLP	0.65

*The terminal year for each period is that of federal elections for the House of Representatives.

TABLE 3:   Party Shares of the Formal First Preference* Vote, Elections for the House of Representatives, 1910-1969, in Percentages

	Labor	Liberal	Country party	DLP	Others
1910	50	45 (Liberal)	—	—	5
1913	48	49	—	—	3
1914	51	47	—	—	2
1917	44	54 (Nat.)	—	—	2
1919	42	45	9	—	4
1922	42	40	13	—	5
1925	45	42	11	—	2
1928	45	39	12	—	4
1929	49	34	11	—	6
1931	38 (two groups)	42 (UAP)	12	—	8
1934	41	37	13	—	9
1937	43	34	16	—	7
1940	48 (three groups)	30	14	—	8
1943	50	21 (various groups)	12	—	17
1946	50	33 (Liberal)	11	—	6
1949	46	39	11	—	4
1951	48	40	10	—	2
1954	50	39	8	—	3
1955	45	40	8	5	2
1958	43	37	9	9	2
1961	48	34	8	9	1
1963	45	37	9	7	2
1966	40	40	10	7	3
1969	47	35	8	6	4

*From 1910 to 1917 simple majority counting was in force; thereafter, preferential voting.

residential concentration of its supporters; the two major parties have shared the remainder between them, roughly in accordance with their respective shares of the vote. In terms of seats contested, however, the DLP is a national party while the Country party is not: in 1969, for example, Labor contested 124 of the 125 seats, the DLP 109, the Liberal party 105, the Country party 25, the Communist party 7, and miscellaneous independent and minor party candidates 76 seats. This pattern is a typical one.

To describe these parties in simple ideological or *tendance* terms is not an easy task. All Australian parties share a general belief (resigned or enthusiastic, according to the case) in the need for government intervention in the economy and in society; this attitude has existed since colonial days. Similarly, each partakes of an old-established radical, egalitarian tradition that awards high status to few, denies the virtues of birth, and desires to cut the pompous and vain down to size. Within these bounds the Liberal party represents a conservative, private-enterprise point of view (it resembles the British Conservative party rather than its namesake), and the Labor party a radical but usually nonsocialist working-class ideology. The Country party combines free enterprise orthodoxy with an agrarian socialist disposition: as expressed in one bon mot, farmers like to "capitalize their gains and socialize their losses." In social matters it is probably the most conservative of the four. The DLP reflects a Catholic antipathy toward communism and anything connected with it, but in regard to many economic subjects it bears traces of its Labor origins (Overacker, 1952 and 1968; Jupp, 1968; Miller, 1964).

The normal alliance patterns have been Liberal + Country vs. Labor; since 1955 the DLP has also been against Labor, though not formally allied with the two non-Labor parties. There have been some variations at the state level. The Labor party supported a minority Country party government in Victoria for many years, while in Queensland the Country party is the senior partner in the coalition, not the junior as elsewhere. In South Australia the two parties have been fused as one—the Liberal Country League—since the early 1930s, and in Tasmania the Country party is known as the Australian Center party (Tas.), the result of a merger between a dissident Liberal state member and a Country party organization that lacked an M.P.; there is no Center party in any other state, or federally. The steady growth of Australia's urban population and the proportionate decline in country electorates has caused a decline in the Country party's share of the vote. An amalgamation of the ALP and DLP is not impossible, but decreasingly likely: the DLP is no longer, in attitude or in the character of its supporters, a breakaway splinter of the ALP.

II. Voting

Australians are practiced voters. With compulsory voting operating in some states for all three tiers of government—federal, state, and local—and triennial elections almost everywhere, most Australian electors will cast a vote once a year. In addition they may be called upon to vote in referenda or plebiscites, the first concerning proposed alterations to the federal or state constitutions, the second matters of public importance at the state level (typically the hours at which drinking places may remain open: such plebiscites are not required by law but can have a formidable de facto significance). Similar party alignments exist at both state and federal levels, but except in the capitals and the larger cities local government elections are not fought on formal party lines. Even in the cities the non-Labor parties generally support the dictum that "party politics should be kept out of local government," and non-Labor candidates for municipal office campaign under such labels as Citizens' Municipal Organization. The Labor party, on the other hand, regards city government as just one more political arena.

The fact of multiple electoral arenas makes it difficult to measure the extent to which the electorate has become nationalized. State issues can intrude into federal elections, and the reverse has also been true. Most voters maintain a single party loyalty in both state and federal politics; only 6 percent of the respondents in a 1967 national survey professed separate loyalties in state and federal politics, and only 2 percent appeared to have voted systematically for different parties at the two levels. The greater apparent variation is probably due both to electoral boundary differences (which alter the pattern of candidature presented to each voter) and to the greater importance of local issues and candidates in state politics (Rydon, 1969). However, there have been some persistent differences. For example, from 1937 to 1963 the average vote for Liberal and Country League candidates at federal elections to the House of Representatives in South Australia was 44 percent; in the period 1938 to 1962 its share of the vote in state elections to the Assembly was 38 percent.

For purposes of international comparison the election to study is that for the federal parliament—elections to the House of Representatives are the traditional measure of party standing. Senate elections are in some ways the best guide to party preferences, since each state votes as one electorate, the influence of personalities is much reduced, voters can choose among all parties, and, when Senate elections are held separately from those for the House (as they have been since 1963), the fate of the government is not at stake. On the other hand, Senate elections attract donkey voting and higher than usual informal voting. It is manifestly unwise to assume that House and Senate elections provide the same information. Between 1955 and 1969 the average share of the vote won by the Liberal and Country parties was 2 percent less at Senate elections than in elections for the House of Representatives, and that of the DLP was 2 percent greater; the ALP share was the same.

The ballot for House of Representatives elections contains in alphabetical order by surname the full names of the candidates. In Senate ballots candidates may be grouped in any order desired by them, and the groups are then placed from left to right in an order determined by lot. Candidate's addresses and occupations are not given: these are published in the list of nominations some weeks before the poll. Party affiliations are not listed, perhaps because no party, when in power, has been confident that such a change would not benefit opponents.

The conduct of federal elections is entrusted to the chief electoral officer and his staff, and similar arrangements exist in each of the states. The chief electoral officer, who is formally responsible to the minister for the interior, also plays an important part in federal electoral boundary redistributions. Electoral regulations reflect a compromise between the traditional view that parties do not exist and subtle partisan finagling. The regulations controlling postal and absentee votes have been a favorite target in both state and federal politics, as have those concerning the dissemination and nature of political propaganda.

Voting takes place on a Saturday between 8 A.M. and 8 P.M. No special provision is made to allow those at work to vote, since Saturday is not a working day for most voters. A voter may vote at any polling place within the subdivision in which he is enrolled (each constituency is divided into a number of subdivisions), or may cast an absentee vote in any other subdivision or constituency within his state. He may also cast a postal vote by prior application, if more than five miles from a polling place, out of state, seriously ill or infirm, traveling, or prevented by religious principles from voting on polling day. Polling places are very widely distributed, and only in remote country areas are many voters distant from one. Postal and absentee votes generally comprise between 8 and 10 percent of all votes cast; their distribution appears strikingly to favor the non-Labor parties (Aitkin and Morgan, 1971), and can be the difference between victory and defeat in close contests. As in Britain, the most likely causes of this bias are the greater familarity of the middle-class with filling in forms and the more extensive and efficient organization of the Liberal and Country parties.

Compulsory voting ensures that between 91 and 96 percent of the enrolled electorate actually vote. Of the balance, some are deliberate nonvoters, and others are involuntary or forgetful; error in the electoral rolls also makes some contribution. As each voter accepts a ballot his name is crossed off the electoral roll by a polling clerk; those whose names have not been crossed off are pursued by the divisional returning officer, who sends an inquiring letter (known popularly as a "please explain"); those who cannot provide satisfactory explanations (in practice any plausible reason apart from sheer forgetfulness or preoccupation with other matters) have the option of accepting a small fine ($2) at the hands of the commonwealth electoral officer in their state or of contesting the matter in court. The vast majority of those receiving "please explain" have the luck or the wit to be able to provide "valid and sufficient reasons." Court actions are uncommon.

The rolls are continuously maintained by an electoral officer in each federal division (i.e., constituency); rolls are reprinted regularly, and a supplementary roll is printed for each election. The general accuracy of the roll is impressive (Kahan and Aitkin, 1968), and the probity of the electoral officers unquestioned: there is no evidence that electoral malpractices occur on other than a trivial scale. Less than 1 percent of respondents to the 1967 survey declared that were an election held tomorrow they would not vote.

Converse's ingenious attempt to establish a baseline division of the vote for each party with "normal" and "deviating" components (Converse, 1966) has not been followed in Australia; it is likely, however, that the "normal" support for the major parties would appear higher in Australia than is the case in America, partly because of the lack of the nonvoting alternative, and because of the difficulty that voters have in regarding either the Country party or the DLP as a halfway house. The best that can be done here is to provide average party votes in elections for the House of Representatives. From 1946 to 1954 these are: Liberal, 37.9 percent; Country party, 10.0 percent; Labor, 48.3 percent. The averages since the entry of the DLP (1955–1969) have been: Liberal, 37.1 percent; Country party, 8.8 percent; Labor, 44.6 percent; DLP, 7.3 percent. The entry of the DLP has been principally at the expense of the ALP. The deviations from these means have been slight, but there have been larger variations in voting from one state to another. A study of the components of variance in national voting from 1913 to 1966 showed a long-term tendency toward the nationalization of the vote, ruptured by the entry of the DLP, whose electoral support varies markedly from state to state. In the recent period 1955–66 state and local forces appeared to account for 18 percent and 44 percent of the interelection variance respectively (Aitkin, 1968).

Of all the elections since 1946 only that of 1955 could be described as a realigning election in Key's sense; previous such elections have been those of 1917, 1931, and 1943 (Key, 1955; Rydon, 1969; Blewett, 1971). The movement in votes between elections can be simply illustrated by expressing each party's vote at a given election as a percentage of its vote at the immediately preceding election (see Table 4).

TABLE 4 : **Changes in Major Party Shares of the National Vote, 1946–69**

		LIBERAL AND COUNTRY PARTIES		LABOR	
Election	*Type*	+ *Ratio*	*Vote Change*	+ *Ratio*	*Vote Change*
		%	%	%	%
1946	Maintaining	132	+10.5	99	−0.2
1949	Deviating	115	+ 6.6	92	−3.7
1951	Maintaining	100	+ 0.8	104	+1.7
1954	Maintaining	94	− 3.3	105	+2.4
1955	Realigning	101	+ 0.6	89	−5.4
1958	Maintaining	98	− 1.1	96	−1.8
1961	Maintaining	90	− 4.4	112	+5.1
1963	Maintaining	109	+ 3.9	95	−2.4
1966	Maintaining	109	+ 4.0	88	−5.5
1969		87	− 6.7	117	+7.0

The Liberal and Country parties are placed together for the purposes of this exercise because they have been in a stable coalition since 1949; results would have been very similar had the Liberal party been treated on its own. As in the British case the progress of the two groups has not been wholly symmetrical. Both increased their share of the vote in 1951 and saw it reduced in 1958; the coalition did not benefit directly to any great extent from the realignment of the Labor vote in 1955. The progress of the DLP is of interest here, as its share of the vote seems to have been set in a slow negative trend since 1958: 1955, 5.2 percent; 1958, 9.4 percent; 1961, 8.7 percent; 1963, 7.4 percent; 1966, 7.3 percent; 1969, 6.0 percent; 1972, 5.2 percent.

III. Data for Analysis

Nationwide polling of voting intention began in 1943; the polling organization, Australian Public Opinion Polls, undertook its first survey in October, 1941. Because of APOP's affiliation with the Gallup organization, its questionnaires follow a familiar pattern, and this has facilitated both secondary analysis within Australia and international comparative studies (Goot, 1969; Alford, 1964; Rokkan et al., 1969, contains an extensive relevant bibliography). There is no other nationally organized commercial polling organization, but the Commonwealth Bureau of Census and Statistics maintains a large and efficient survey group to staff its work force and population surveys, which study a rotating 1 percent sample of Australian households. The Australian Broadcasting Commission also operates an efficient survey branch that is national in scope. Several market-research organizations operate in Sydney and Melbourne; their services, along with those of APOP, have been utilized in the past by academic researchers.

APOP sample sizes have varied between 1,500 and 2,500. In 1964 it changed from quota sampling to what it called "probability sampling," a form of area sampling using quota controls; statistical sampling errors cannot be computed for APOP data. Nonetheless, APOP predictions of Australian election and referendum results have been impressively accurate over the whole of the organization's existence, and its findings have gained a wide acceptance as meaningful contemporary measurements of opinion (Goot, 1969; Aitkin, 1969). There is an index covering the subjects dealt with in APOP surveys between 1941 and 1968 (Goot and Ilbery, 1969).

While academic workers and journalists have used APOP data from the beginning, academics have been slow to design and administer their own surveys. The best known cover a Sydney constituency in 1958 (Rawson, 1961), a Melbourne constituency in 1960 (Burns, 1961), a Sydney state constituency in 1965 (Power, 1968), and three Brisbane state constituencies in 1963 and 1966 (Hughes, 1969). Aitkin and Kahan at the Australian National University began a nationwide panel survey of political attitudes in 1967, using techniques developed at the University of Michigan's Survey Research Center. For the ANU survey a random sample of 2,054 voters was interviewed in 1967 and as many as possible were reinterviewed in 1969. A report describing the sample has been published (Kahan and Aitkin, 1968), as has a short paper (Aitkin, Kahan, and Barnes, 1970); other papers have circulated in cyclostyled form, and a lengthy report is in preparation.

Not all political surveys have been conducted at election times. Alan Hughes has pursued authoritarianism and other psychological dispositions in samples of Sydney and Melbourne voters (A. Hughes, 1970). Davies, who took part in the 1960 La Trobe survey, reinterviewed some respondents as part of a study of political attitudes in the new suburban areas (Davies, 1962), and reinterviewed them again to obtain their images of class and its relation to politics (Davies, 1967). Western and Hughes have studied the political content of the mass media and what voters make of it (1967). The same authors have also investigated the effects of exposure to a telecast of a party leader's opening speech (Hughes and Western, 1966).

There have been two other quasi-national surveys carried out by members of the Australian National University: the first concerned aspects of social stratification (Broom et al., 1968), the second religious behavior (Mol, 1971). Both surveys investigated the correlates of political behavior but as a secondary interest. The Bureau of Census and Statistics has obtained much information of interest to social scientists, although it has avoided matters with any partisan content. It is also slow in publishing its findings.

Ecological analysis has been a popular journalistic occupation in Australia because votes are initially counted by polling place. A representative example of academic work in this genre is Connell and Gould's investigation of the nature of Liberal support within one electorate (1967). In state elections the returns are published by polling place, but in federal elections they are aggregated first into subdivisions, which may contain up to 10,000 votes; unofficial polling-place figures for federal elections can usually be obtained. A major difficulty has been the lack of fit between census and electoral boundaries, remedied very recently by the reconstruction of federal electorates in the 1966 census by the Bureau of Census and Statistics; thus far no analyses have been published. A close examination of polling-place data demonstrated the basis of electoral support for the Country party (Aitkin, 1965). Hughes and Graham (1968) have summarized federal and state electoral statistics since 1890; their handbook is an indispensable resource for those interested in Australian electoral politics and representative government; it also lists all ministries—colonial, state, and federal—since 1890.

The principal published work involving secondary analysis is Goot's study of the congruence between attitude and vote (Goot, 1969). Alford's pioneering comparative study of the relationship between class and politics (Alford, 1964) made extensive use of APOP data. The national surveys of politics, class, and religion already referred to are not yet available for reanalysis. There is a continuing archive of APOP cards in the department of sociology, Research School of Social Sciences, Australian National University, Canberra, and in America at the Roper Center Williamstown, Massachusetts.

The remainder of this chapter explores data collected in the ANU 1967 national survey of political attitude (N=2,054). The respondents were drawn from eighty of the 122 federal electoral divisions, randomly selected with probability proportionate to size. The two federal territories—the Australian Capital Territory (Canberra and its hinterland) and the Northern Territory, which together contain approximately 2 percent of the electorate—were excluded from the sample. Voting preference, as distinguished from party identification, was obtained in answer to the question, "If a federal election were held tomorrow, which party would you vote for?" Ninety-one percent of the respondents gave a specific answer to this question: Liberal, 42 percent; Labor, 40 percent; Country party, 6 percent; DLP, 3 percent; other, 1 percent. This group provided the data for analysis. Of the remainder, 8.5 percent did not know for which party they would vote, and .5 percent said they would not vote.

Respondents have been grouped into Liberal+Country party, Labor party, and DLP, a set that includes all but 1 percent of those stating a party preference. The Country party voters resembled their Liberal counterparts in most ways, but were rather more conservative on social and economic questions (Aitkin, 1972). They are merged here to simplify data presentation. The DLP voters, a still smaller group, justify separate presentation because they cannot sensibly be merged with another group.

Party identification, i.e., an abiding personal attachment to one party rather than another (Campbell et al., 1960) has not been much investigated and is not a standard survey question. But it is an important phenomenon nonetheless. In 1967 87 percent of the respondents readily attached a party label to themselves, and another 5 percent did so in response to further questions. Party identification is not identical to party voting, but the overlap is very large (Table 5).

TABLE 5 : **Party Identification and Party Preference, in Percentages**

| | | PREFERENCES | | |
Total	Party Identification	LIB-CP	LAB	DLP
41	Liberal	94	6	*
38	Labor	6	94	*
7	Country Party	95	5	*
3	DLP	4	4	92
11	None	49	47	4
100				

(N=2,001)
* less than 0.5 percent

The pattern of Table 5 is virtually identical when the data are controlled for occupational class. Variations in the strength of party identification are significantly related to voting preferences, and controlling for class makes no difference in figures (Table 6). Comparison of these data with their American and British equivalents (Campbell et al., 1960; Butler and Stokes, 1969) suggests that party identification in Australia has a relationship to voting more like the British than the American example; identification and actual vote are very close, in a complementary fashion. When there was a pronounced swing to the Liberal and Country parties in 1966, the movement was proportionately greatest among those who had no party identification or declared that it was not very strong.

TABLE 6 :   **Strength of Party Identification and Party Preference, in Percentages**

		PREFERENCES		
Total	*Strength of Identification*	LIB-CP	LAB	DLP
14	Very strong Liberal or Country party	98	2	0
24	Fairly strong Liberal or Country party	96	3	1
11	Not very strong Liberal or Country party	85	14	1
11	None	49	47	4
8	Not very strong Labor	13	87	0
16	Fairly strong Labor	4	96	0
16	Very strong Labor	1	99	0
100				

(N=1,758)
(DLP identifiers were too few to subdivide.)

Some 8 percent of Australian voters reject any particular party label. Another 21 percent had changed their identification at least once since they first formed likes and dislikes about the parties, two-thirds of them from Labor to Liberal identification. Non-Labor voters have demonstrated a long-standing recourse to independent candidates when their own party is in disfavor, but there is no strong tradition of the independent voter, he who puts "measures before men" (a colonial tag) or who "votes for the man, not for the party." In this respect, too, the Australian party system cleaves to the British rather than to the American model.

The result of Australian elections often hangs on the distribution of voters' second and later preferences (Hughes and Graham, 1968). The frequency of preference counts enables reliable estimates to be made of the general level of second preferences within the party system, save for Labor voters, whose primary votes are rarely counted again, since Labor candidates are rarely pushed into third place. The 1967 survey provided an additional measure of voters' second preferences and of their last preferences, a measure of antipathy obtained by asking "And which party would you put last?" Table 7 summarizes these data for the four major groups of voters.

The ability of the Liberal and Country parties to maximize their support through preferences is strikingly demonstrated. Also notable is the preference of Labor voters for the Liberal party rather than the DLP or Communist party, and the general antipathy toward these two latter parties. Too much should not be read into these preference lists, however. While Country party voters see the Liberal party as a preferred non-Labor alternative—since the Liberal party competes in rural constituencies —the Country party is much less salient to urban Liberals, as it does not contest city seats. Similarly, Communist candidates are very rare in the country, which helps to explain why Country party voters are less likely than Liberals to place the Communist party last; Liberals more frequently have the opportunity to make real choices between

Communist, Labor, and DLP candidates. Patterns of candidature play some part in determining the model of the party system that voters possess.

TABLE 7 : **Second and Last Preferences, by First Preferences, in Percentages**

	SECOND PREFERENCES					
First Preference	Liberal	Labor	Country party	DLP	Other*	Total
Liberal	–	29	41	17	12	100
Labor	44	–	19	17	19	100
Country party	78	15	–	3	4	100
DLP	64	16	11	–	9	100

	LAST PREFERENCES					
First Preference	Liberal	Labor	Country party	DLP	Com-munist	Other*	Total
Liberal	–	25	4	19	36	16	100
Labor	19	–	7	31	37	16	100
Country party	4	30	–	30	24	12	100
DLP	7	29	10	–	39	15	100

*Includes "don't-know" answers

IV. Social Structure and Voting

In the following discussion each characteristic is considered twice, first in terms of the problems it raises as a variable, second in terms of its significance for party preference.

A. CLASS

Occupational class in Australia has not received much academic study as a political influence, although it is universally recognized as the principal cleavage in party politics and the most important determinant of party preference. The principal studies are those of Davies (1967), Alford (1964), and Encel (1970). Congalton (1969) established ratings of occupational prestige, but his samples were not representative. APOP classifies its respondents by occupation, and Broom and Hill (1965) developed a simple threefold class schema from APOP data that correlated well with self-perceived class.

Class distribution depends ultimately on the decision of the investigator as to the location of such ambiguous groups as white-collar workers and farmers. The two following lists give some indication of the spread of occupations. Both lists contain the same proportion of farm owners, and in both manual workers make up 50 percent of the sample. The differences between the proportions for other groups reflect the difficulty involved in allocating to categories such occupations as teachers, public servants, and law clerks, or assessing by interview a manual worker's skill. A complex scale distinguishing supervisory from nonsupervisory in the white-collar group can easily be constructed from survey data, but analysis so far has not found such elaboration to be of much value in explaining party preference.

APOP 1969/70		ANU 1967	
(based on the average of ten national samples in 1969/70)			
Category	Percent	Category	Percent
Professional, managers, owners, small		Professional	7
businessmen	12	Managers, proprietors, skilled	
Farm owners	9	nonmanual	17
White-collar workers	25	Farm owners	9
Skilled workers	26	White-collar workers	14
Semiskilled and unskilled workers and		Skilled workers	18
farm workers	24	Semiskilled and unskilled and	
Other/NA	4	farm workers	32
		Other/NA	3
	100		100

The great majority of respondents placed themselves either in the middle or the working-class. Though Davies (1967) and Hammond (1954) found that Australians commonly use tripartite schemes (top–middle–bottom or upper–middle–working), respondents willing to place *themselves* in an upper-class are thin on the ground (only eight in 2,054 in the ANU survey). For all practical purposes of analysis a simple dichotomy of middle–working (for self-perception) or nonmanual–manual (for objective grading) seems most sensible. But the two dichotomies measure different attributes, and accordingly their relationship to party preference is different (Table 8). One sees the tension between subjective and objective social class emerges strongly. For those for whom the two measures are incongruent the pull of the non-Labor parties is stronger. Where the two measures are congruent the contribution of class to voting is strongest. Yet in both strata one in four of those whose subjective and objective class placements are in harmony vote for the party of the other class. Class does not explain everything.

In the remaining analysis all data are presented with controls for class, using the nonmanual/manual division. Farmers and graziers[1] are treated as nonmanual because of their status as owners and employers, though most are accustomed to physical work on their farms and properties.

TABLE 8 : **Self–Perceived Class, Occupational Class, and Party Preference, in Percentages**

TOTAL		LIB-CP	LAB	DLP
	Nonmanual			
	See self as:			
34	Middle-class	73	24	3
12	Working-class	52	44	4
	Manual			
	See self as:			
21	Middle-class	56	42	2
33	Working-class	26	70	4
100				
(n=1,631)				

B. INCOME

Income is difficult to use as a variable: it is heavily dependent on occupation; it may not be an accurate measure of funds at the disposal of the household; and respondents do not always answer questions about income accurately. Nearly 13 percent of the sample refused to answer the question or said they did not know what the breadwinner's income was.

TABLE 9: **Annual Income, Class and Party Preference, in Percentages**

Total		LIB-CP	LAB	DLP
	Nonmanual: $A			
13	$6,251 or more	75	23	2
8	$4,251 to $6,250	71	22	7
18	$2,251 to $4,250	67	30	3
6	$ 751 to $2,250	60	37	3
2	less than $ 750	43	52	6
	Manual: $A			
6	More than $6,251	65	29	6
4	$4,251 to $6,250	52	43	5
25	$2,251 to $4,250	36	61	3
13	$ 751 to $2,250	35	62	3
4	less than $750	31	66	3
100%				

(n=1,736)
A$1.00=US$1.42 and British £0.57

In both strata the proportion preferring the non-Labor parties rises with income. The lowest-income group consists predominantly of pensioners, whose preference for the Labor party may reflect their perception of Labor as the party most likely to increase pensions.

By international standards incomes in Australia are spread narrowly, and there are few indices of consumption that discriminate well. Cars, radios, and television sets are almost universal household possessions. Extra family income, brought about by two or more members of a family working, makes little difference to party preference. In the nonmanual stratum it is simply irrelevant; among manuals Labor voting is 8 percent higher where there is more than one breadwinner. This may simply demonstrate that in the poorest households wives and children go to work of necessity.

An index of composite socioeconomic status can be formed by dichotomizing education, income, subjective class, trade-union membership, and house ownership. The index runs from "working-class" on all five items to "middle-class" on all five (Table 10).

TABLE 10: Composite Socioeconomic Status, Class, and Proportion Voting Labor

Total		Non-Manual	Manual	
2	Working-class on all five variables	*	73	(N=30)
16	Working-class on four variables middle-class on one	50	82	
24	Working-class on three variables, middle-class on two	45	70	
24	Working-class on two variables, middle-class on three	37	40	
22	Working-class on one variable middle-class on four	25	46	
12	Middle-class on all five variables	23	11	
100%	(N = 1,244) *Sample too small			

Although there is overall a steady increase in the disposition to vote Labor as composite socioeconomic status declines, the probability of those with nonmanual occupations voting Labor never rises above .50. Among manual workers an increase in working-class attributes is associated with a steeper rise in Labor voting. By comparison with Britain (Rose, 1968) middle-class characteristics are more widely distributed among the Australian working-class: 34 percent of a British sample of manual workers lacked two or more characteristics of the "ideal-type worker," while in Australia the proportion is greater than 70 percent. While cross-national differences in class criteria account for some of this variation, the Australian working-class is undoubtedly more heterogeneous than the British.

C. CONDITIONS OF EMPLOYMENT

Miners are distinctive among manual workers because of their geographical separateness and the interrelation of their work, community, and social lives. Miners provided one of the industrial bases of the Labor party, and fourteen of the fifteen miners in the sample were Labor voters. But the increasing mechanization of the mining industry has made miners a negligible fraction of the manual stratum, despite the great increase in mineral output during the 1960s. Most other manual workers live in suburbia or country towns (Table 11).

TABLE 11: **Occupational Groups Within the Manual Stratum, and Party Preference, in Percentages**

Total		LIB-CP	LAB	DLP
	Type of Work			
21	Transport	32	64	4
17	Factory	34	63	3
13	Building & Construction	39	59	2
24	Other Secondary	39	57	4
20	Tertiary (Service Industry)	44	54	2
6	Rural	48	48	4
100%	(N = 911)			

Among rural workers only the shearers are unionized; the remainder (the great majority) typically work as the sole employees of farmers or graziers, and share many of their values (Aitkin, 1972). Labor voting is highest in the transport industry and factories, where unions have traditionally been strong, the level of skill required low, and working conditions generally inferior.

D. SEX

Since women as a group live longer, receive less education, work less, and earn less than men, differences between the sexes in their partisan preferences are likely to be greatly influenced by these secondary differences (Table 12). The figures illustrate the familiar pattern of the greater preference of women for conservative parties, although class is manifestly a stronger influence than sex. APOP findings over the years confirm that this disparity is an abiding one; the differences have been sufficient to support the claim that the Liberal and Country parties owed their victory in 1961 to the support of women voters. Other analysis indicates that wives tend to follow their husbands in voting preference; where they differ, the wife is likely to be the Liberal, the husband the Labor supporter.

TABLE 12:   Sex, Class, and Party Preference, in Percentages

Total		LIB-CP	LAB	DLP
	Non Manual			
24	Men	63	33	4
23	Women	74	23	3
	Manual			
28	Men	33	64	3
25	Women	43	54	3
100%	(N=1,773)			

E. AGE

Age is a similarly complicated variable, with at least two important ingredients: the effects of having been born at a certain time (generation), and life-cycle effects. Five generations have been proposed for native-born Australian voters (Aitkin, Kahan, and Barnes, 1970):

Generation	Proportion of sample %	Born in the period	First Voted during the period	Age in 1967
I	18	1874–1908	1901–1929	59–93
II	12	1909–1916	1930–1937	51–58
III	14	1917–1925	1938–1946	42–50
IV	14	1926–1933	1947–1954	34–41
V	27	1934–1945	1955–1967	21–33

(These generations exclude immigrants, who form another 15 percent of the voting population.) Generation II came to maturity during the depression, Generation III during the Second World War and Labor's hegemony, Generation IV in the early years of the postwar non-Labor governments, and Generation V since the entry of the DLP. Generation I, because of its span, is largely residual. No life-cycle measures have yet been developed, and there are no data available. Most survey data on party preference (little of it specifically directed to this point, however) suggest that generational influences are the stronger ones.

Table 13 shows that there were marked generational differences in the direction of the first vote (note that the class control also is different). In the 1930s and 1940s Labor pulled disproportionately from the pool of the new voters. Since the early 1950s, on the other hand, the balance has swung the other way (Table 14).

Time has eroded generational distinctiveness. In both class groups the youngest generation (V) is the least disposed to vote Labor, but the older generations have begun to resemble one another in the pattern of their voting. The picture of a generation gap is hard to support with these data (see also Aitkin, Kahan, and Barnes, 1970). The

TABLE 13: **Generation, Parents' Class, and First Vote, in Percentages**

Total			LIB-CP	LAB	DLP
	Middle-Class Parents				
9	Generation	I	76	24	—
6		II	65	35	—
5		III	64	36	—
6		IV	67	32	—
11	(Youngest)	V	70	26	4
	Working-Class Parents				
12	Generation	I	24	76	—
9		II	21	79	—
11		III	22	78	—
11		IV	30	70	—
20	(Youngest)	V	44	52	4
100	(N=1,357)				

Parents' class when respondent was growing up, as reported by respondent.

shift to the non-Labor parties among those with working-class parents is in part a function of upward mobility among native-born Australians: 61 percent of the sample

TABLE 14: **Generation, Parents' Class, and Party Preference, 1967, in Percentages**

Total			LIB-CP	LAB	DLP
	Middle-Class Parents				
9	Generation	I	74	24	1
6		II	63	35	2
5		III	71	25	4
6		IV	66	29	5
11	(Youngest)	V	69	25	6
	Working-Class Parents				
12	Generation	I	35	60	5
8		II	39	58	3
11		III	38	62	0
11		IV	42	56	2
21	(Youngest)	V	46	50	4
100	(N=1,434)				

say they had working-class parents, but only 46 percent now place themselves in the
working-class.

F. EDUCATION

The length of education of most Australians is determined by varying state laws
governing compulsory schooling. In general education begins at age five and continues to age fifteen; the legal minimum school leaving age in Tasmania is sixteen.
The educational background of the electorate in 1967 was: primary school or less,
33 percent; minimum secondary, 31 percent; full secondary, 17 percent; secondary
plus technical college, 13 percent; university, 6 percent. Primary school typically
consists of six grades from age six (from ages five to six children are in kindergarten),
secondary school of a further six grades, broken by an examination at the end of the
fourth grade. University admission depends upon attaining minimum standards at
a further examination at the end of sixth grade (Partridge, 1968). Length of
education appears to have only a slight effect on voting, and that runs counter to
class (Table 15).

TABLE 15: Education, Class, and Party Preference, in Percentages

Total		LIB-CP	LAB	DLP
	Nonmanual			
5	Tertiary	64	32	4
31	Secondary	68	28	4
11	Primary	71	27	2
	Manual			
1	Tertiary (N=9)	56	33	11
30	Secondary	41	56	3
22	Primary	33	64	3
100	(N=1,763)			

In the nonmanual stratum a tertiary education lowers the tendency to vote Liberal
or Country party, but it should be noted that the primary and secondary groups include
most of the strongly non-Labor farmers and graziers. In the manual stratum the more
education, the more non-Labor. The notion of the university as a political catalyst,
radicalizing the middle-class and socializing the working-class into middle-class
attitudes, is an intriguing one. But most of the surveys of student opinion in the late
1960s suggested that students as a group were not different from the rest of their
generation in their preference for non-Labor parties (Aitkin, 1970).

In general the longer the attendance the more academic the content of education.
However, this is not so for those who pursue technical college diplomas, commonly

as part of an apprenticeship. The last two years of high school are notably academic in content. The new colleges of advanced education are endeavoring to provide tertiary education that emphasizes the "applied" or "practical" as distinct from the "theoretical" bias traditional in universities. Information as to content is hard to obtain quickly, and is not collected in surveys.

The character of schools is important. Some 72 percent of the sample attended state-run secular schools throughout their formal education, while 16 percent attended church schools and 12 percent experienced both state and church education. The church schools are predominantly Roman Catholic. Protestant schools cater to the children of farmers and graziers and to the urban middle-class. Liberal MPs are disproportionately drawn from their ex-pupils. Mol (1971) demonstrated that Catholics educated in Catholic schools were "better" Catholics (and more conservative politically) than those who were not. The Protestant schools appear to support the values of the traditional Britain-oriented elite.

G. RELIGION

Australia is apparently religious: only 11 percent were prepared to label themselves "no religion" in the 1966 census, or to skip the question altogether, an option permitted in the census schedule. The survey sample proved even more willing to give a religious affiliation, dividing as follows: Anglican, 37 percent; Roman Catholic, 25 per-

TABLE 16 : **Religion, Class, and Party Preference, in Percentages**

Total		LIB-CP	LAB	DLP
	Nonmanual			
17	Anglican	74	26	—
11	Catholic	52	34	14
16	Nonconformist	74	25	1
2	Other religions	79	21	—
1	No Religon (N=23)	39	61	—
	Manual			
20	Anglican	37	62	1
15	Catholic	28	63	9
15	Nonconformist	49	50	1
2	Other religions	46	54	—
1	No Religion (N=26)	27	69	4
100	(N=1,755)			

cent; Nonconformist, 31 percent; other religions, 4 percent; no religion, 3 percent. Reported church attendance among these groups suggests that Catholics form the largest single group of churchgoers in Australia; the great majority of Anglicans do not attend church regularly, and many do not attend at all. Nonconformists (mostly Presbyterians and Methodists) occupy a half way position (Table 16).

For those in the nonmanual stratum religion seems to act as a conserving influence for the non-Labor parties, while the DLP serves as an alternative for Catholics, but for no one else. The strong pull of the non-Labor parties for Nonconformists and those confessing other religions (principally Greek Orthodox, Russian Orthodox, and Jews) holds also in the manual stratum, where there is very nearly an even split between the major parties. The strong Catholic support for the ALP—despite the existence of the rival DLP—is also clear (see also Alford, 1963).

These contrasts are sharpened if we control for church attendance as well as class. Regular churchgoers are defined as those who attend church once a month or more frequently.

TABLE 17 : **Church Attendance, Class, and Party Preference, in Percentages**

		NONMANUAL			MANUAL		
Total		LIB	LAB	DLP	LIB	LAB	DLP
	Regular						
7	Anglican	81	19	—	46	54	—
16	Catholic	52	29	18	28	55	17
13	Non conformist	80	18	2	60	40	—
1	Other	79	21	—	45	55	—
	Irregular						
22	Anglican	76	24	—	38	62	1
7	Catholic	52	45	3	28	70	2
15	Nonconformist	73	27	—	47	50	3
2	Other	83	17	—	47	53	—
	Never						
9	Anglican	61	39	—	31	68	1
3	Catholic	44	56	—	26	74	—
5	Nonconformist	61	39	—	30	70	—
*	Other	[Sample too small]			[Sample too small]		
100	(N=1,692) * less than 0.5 percent						

Support for the DLP is greatly affected by churchgoing but hardly at all by class; among nonchurchgoing Catholics the ALP is the preferred party. Table 17 also makes clear that churchgoing adds to the conserving effect of religion: a sizable majority of *manual* Nonconformist church attenders preferred the non-Labor parties, and a majority of *nonmanual* "nominal" Catholics preferred the ALP—two rare Australian examples of class taking second place to another demographic influence.

H. NATIONAL ORIGIN

Less than 1 percent of Australians are of aboriginal descent, and the great majority of the 19 percent of Australian residents who were born outside Australia emigrated from the United Kingdom and Europe. Australia is thus racially homogenous. There are, however, differences between the native-born and immigrants and between English speaking immigrants and non-English-speaking immigrants (Table 18).

TABLE 18 : **National Origin, Class, and Party Preference, in Percentages**

Total		LIB-CP	LAB	DLP
	Nonmanual			
40	Native-born	67	29	4
5	Born UK or New Zealand	70	28	2
3	Other Immigrant	75	21	4
	Manual			
40	Native-born	37	61	2
6	Born UK or New Zealand	38	59	3
6	Other Immigrant	45	45	10
100	(N=1,742)			

Non-British immigrants are unenthusiastic about the ALP. British migrants are much like the native-born in their party preferences. The support for the DLP among non-British working-class immigrants is quite striking; it is almost entirely confined to Roman Catholics, most of them from Italy.

I. REGIONALISM

Australia's six states and two territories provide well-defined geographical units with their own political systems, all very similar. The various states have all been credited in folklore with their own styles of life and values (thus Queensland is "easygoing," South Australia "staid," Western Australia "hospitable," and so on). Similar labels are applied to the capital cities in each state (Sydney is "American" or "vulgar," Melbourne "dreary"). Such descriptions are inherently difficult to substantiate, as is the more sophisticated comment that the flavor of New South Wales politics is "pragmatic" while that of Victoria is "ideological."

Table 19 suggests that, apart from the relative strength of the DLP in Victoria, where the party was founded, there is little to distinguish the states in terms of party preference. The pattern of voting in Victoria suggests that in the nonmanual stratum

TABLE 19 :   **State, Class, and Party Preference, in Percentages**

Total		LIB-CP	LAB	DLP
	Nonmanual			
15	New South Wales	70	29	1
15	Victoria	64	28	8
6	Queensland	67	32	1
5	South Australia	72	28	0
7	Western Australia and Tasmania	74	24	2
	Manual			
18	New South Wales	39	60	1
14	Victoria	39	54	7
8	Queensland	41	58	1
6	South Australia	35	64	1
6	Western Australia and Tasmania	33	63	4
	(N=1,767)			
100				

The Western Australia and Tasmania samples have been amalgamated to increase sample sizes.

the DLP has profited at the expense of the Liberal party, whereas among manual workers it has profited at the expense of the ALP.

J. URBAN/RURAL

An English traveller in the 1930s wrote that "there are two Australias, town and country; and the first starves the second" (Wood, 1934, p. 20). The sentiment is shared by all those who support the Country party and many who do not (Aitkin, 1971). The "country" can be defined as everywhere outside the capital cities, or everywhere outside cities of a certain size or the "purely rural" areas, i.e., farming areas and their service townships. In Table 20 the first definition is employed, as antiurbanism in Australia has essentially expressed itself as a distrust of the metropolis (Aitkin, 1972).

TABLE 20 :   **Urban/Rural, Class, and Party Preference, in Percentages**

Total		LIB-CP	LAB	DLP
	Nonmanual			
26	Urban	64	33	3
21	Rural	74	22	4
	Manual			
30	Urban	36	60	4
23	Rural	45	53	2
100	(N=1,767)			

Support for the Labor party is lower among rural voters in both strata (Table 20). The greater enthusiasm of country people for the non-Labor parties is not simply a function of the number of farmers and graziers outside the cities. Comparable differences occur in New South Wales, Victoria, South Australia, and Western Australia. In Queensland, where the state capital, Brisbane, holds a smaller proportion of the state's population than is the case in any other state, and where there are several provincial cities, these differences in party preference are negligible. (The Tasmanian sample is too small to be divided.) The rural industries employ some 10 percent of the work force and are concentrated in a minority of the constituencies. The partisan volatility of wheat farmers has been a phenomenon of Australian politics, but since 1949 their loyalties have been solidly non-Labor. Graziers and dairy farmers, the other two sizable groups within the rural sector, have never supported the Labor party in any number. The pattern of party preference within the capital cities is much the same. This is to be expected: the cities serve much the same collection of functions, and stand in much the same relation to their rural hinterlands.

K. RESIDENTIAL MOBILITY

Australians are a highly mobile people; of the sample less than 10 percent of those older than 50 had never moved, and address-changing is as rapid as in the United

TABLE 21 : **Age, Residential Mobility, Class and Party Preference, in Percentages**

LENGTH OF RESIDENCE	NONMANUAL			MANUAL		
	LIB-CP	LAB	DLP	LIB-CP	LAB	DLP
			Age 21–30 years			
0–2 years	72	22	6	53	47	0
3–10 years	73	25	2	42	55	3
11 years or more	65	30	5	34	56	10
			Age 31–50 years			
0–2 years	73	24	3	42	53	5
3–10 years	68	27	5	34	63	3
11 years or more	66	29	5	35	62	3
			Age 51 years or more			
0–2 years	77	23	0	[Sample too small]		
3–10 years	74	25	1	44	55	1
11 years or more	61	35	4	39	58	3

States, greater than 20 percent per annum (Kahan and Aitkin, 1968). There has been little study of the political consequences of mobility, though some of its macropolitical effects—the erosion of the base of the Country party because of the drift to the city, the growth of the suburbs as a new political arena—are obvious. Respondents were asked how long they had "lived in this area", a phrase used to avoid simple changes in address from one house to another in the same street. Since the young are more likely to move than the old, and are more Liberal, a further control was added—age. Occupational class has only the slightest effect upon the propensity to move, the middle-class being marginally more mobile than the working-class in each age group. Age is much more important: one-third of the youngest group had moved in the previous two years, but only 12 percent of the thirty-one to fifty age group had done so. Seventy percent of the oldest group had not moved for at least ten years, compared with 50 percent of the middle group and one-third of the youngest. Table 21 suggests that the frequent movers are less likely to be Labor voters in all age groups and both classes. The differences are not large but they are consistent in direction.

L. HOME-OWNERSHIP

Although there are state housing commissions providing cheap rental accommo-dation and there is much private renting, three Australian families in every four own their own home or are in process of buying it. Housing commission areas, in common with council house estates in England, have a working-class flavor, but few of them

TABLE 22 : **Home-Ownership, Class, and Party Preference, in Percentages**

Total		LIB-CP	LAB	DLP
	Nonmanual			
23	Own	70	26	4
15	Buying	68	29	3
7	Renting	63	34	3
1	Housing commission (N=24)	50	50	0
	Manual			
20	Own	46	51	3
20	Buying	39	57	4
10	Renting	32	65	3
4	Housing commission	13	87	0
100	(N=1,672)			

are large enough to form distinct communities. The pattern of party preference is symmetrical in both classes (Table 22). The lesser tendency to vote Labor among manual home-owners might suggest that home-owning produces a more conservative attitude among manual workers, but a number of other hypotheses have equal face validity; housing differences may, for example, reflect income differences.

M. MASS MEDIA

The Australian mass media are strikingly decentralized. Only the radio-broadcasting system of the Australian Broadcasting Commission has nationwide coverage, but its program schedules and the contents of news broadcasts differ from state to state. Of the daily newspapers only *The Australian* aims at a national readership, principally in the capital cities. Other major newspapers circulate mainly within the boundaries of one state. Television channels are even more decentralized, though the ABC is building up a national network.

There are no daily newspapers owned by any political party. The principal metropolitan dailies are generally anti-Labor in editorial policy, although the *Sydney Morning Herald* has supported the ALP on at least one occasion, and *The Australian* is erratically radical in attitude. In radio and television private enterprise competes with the ABC, which is modeled in part on the BBC. State and federal laws control political advertising at the time of elections. The ABC makes radio and television time available free to the major parties during election campaigns, and provides a regular and impartial coverage of public affairs.

The fifteen capital-city dailies have a circulation equal to about one-third of the whole population; since these papers are sold chiefly in the capital cities, their coverage there may be as much as twice as high. There are more than 200 suburban give away newspapers, more than 300 country newspapers, only a minority of which are dailies, and a number of Sunday newspapers, none of which in 1970 had a national readership (Mayer, 1964; Western and Hughes, 1967). Two newcomers in 1971, the *Sunday Australian* and the *National Times*, both have national circulation ambitions. Only 6 percent of the sample claimed *not* to read any newspaper regularly, 23 percent only one, 39 percent two, 20 percent three, and 12 percent four or more. A 1966 survey (Western and Hughes, 1967) found that 84 percent of a national sample took at least one newspaper a day, and 26 percent two or more; virtually all households possessed both radio and television. Four major groups own most of the metropolitan dailies (and most of the metropolitan commercial TV stations as well), but there is no consistent style and no editorial uniformity apart from opposition to Labor. In general it is class that appears to determine readership patterns. The readers of the "quality" papers (the *Sydney Morning Herald*, the Melbourne *Age*, and *The Australian*) are disproportionately from the nonmanual stratum; nonmanual readers prefer lighter fare—and less politics. When newspaper reading is controlled for class, variations in party preference disappear.

N. ORGANIZATIONAL MEMBERSHIPS

Trade-union membership is not known precisely; in 1969 it was estimated by the Commonwealth Bureau of Census and Statistics at 2,239,000, i.e., approximately 50 percent of wage and salary earners (*Quarterly Summary of Australian Statistics,*

September, 1970). Trade-union membership was reported in 39 percent of households of the sample.

The positive relationship between union membership and Labor preference is clear. Since party preference is much affected by the circumstances of birth and education, trade union membership is unlikely to be a principal cause of party preference. If anything, party identification may encourage union membership. Those respondents who were compulsorily members of unions (64 percent of the unionists in the sample) were asked whether they would have joined the union had this been a

TABLE 23 : Trade-Union Membership, Class, and Party Preference, in Percentages

Total		LIB-CP	LAB	DLP
	Nonmanual			
35	Not a union member	72	26	2
11	Union member	49	45	6
	Manual			
25	Not a union member	44	53	3
29	Union member	26	71	3
100	(N=930)			

matter of choice (Table 24). Although four of these cells are small, there is a strong suggestion that attitudes to union membership among employees are at least in part a product of party loyalty, independent of class.

TABLE 24 : Class, Party Preference, and Voluntary Union Membership, in Percentages

Total		Would have joined union	Would have Not joined union
	Nonmanual		
8	LIB-CP voters (N=24)	50	50
7	LAB voters (N=21)	76	24
	Manual		
22	LIB-CP voters	53	47
62	LAB voters	74	26
100	(N= 286)		

DLP respondents were too few to permit cross-tabulation.

Political party membership involves the payment of a subscription, but accurate figures for party membership are impossible to obtain, since parties do not keep membership lists with an auditor's accuracy. Furthermore, Australian parties are reluctant to disclose membership details. Membership figures are therefore estimates and greatly overstate the number of party activists. A 1967 estimate (Nelson and Watson, 1969) put total party membership exclusive of trade-union affiliation to the ALP at 269,000, or 2 percent of the population and 4 percent of the electorate. Liberal party total membership was estimated at 127,000, the Country party at 81,000, the ALP at 42,700 and the D.L.P. at 18,300. Less than 5 percent in the ANU survey claimed to have paid a party subscription in the past year. Compulsory voting removes the need for a large corps of party workers, and only the Country party (which charges its members a minimum of $A5 a year) makes a steady drive for members. Most unions are affiliated with the ALP but their members have no consequent rights to participate in the life of the party. The union is entitled to send delegates to ALP state conferences, but these delegates must be party members in their own right.

Membership in voluntary organizations in Australia is high: 47 percent claimed to belong to one organization, exclusive of trade unions, political parties, or churches, and 24 percent to two or more. Membership in two or more voluntary associations correlates highly with interest in politics. There has been little study of voluntary organizations in Australia, and there is little idea of their number or interrelation. One official census in 1969 found more than 500 churches, committees, clubs, and societies in Canberra (population 125,000). Of those reporting organizational membership 71 percent claimed to be active in at least one group. The great majority of the organizations mentioned were sporting clubs, parent-school associations and community service clubs, such as Rotary.

Joining is more a middle-class than a working-class phenomenon: 33 percent of the nonmanual stratum, but only 16 percent of the manual stratum, belonged to two or more organizations. Joiners in both classes were more likely to prefer the non-Labor parties (Table 25).

TABLE 25 : **Organization Memberships, Class, and Party Preference, in Percentages**

Total		LIB-CP	LAB	DLP
	Nonmanual			
15	Two or more	75	23	2
12	One	65	30	5
20	None	65	32	3
	Manual			
9	Two or more	47	51	2
12	One	41	57	2
32	None	35	61	4
100	(N=1,767)			

V. Social Psychological Influences

A. FAMILY INFLUENCES

The intergenerational persistence of party identification, important in maintaining stable party systems, is most simply indexed by comparing parents' identification reported by the respondent with the respondent's own partisanship. Father's preference is used as the independent variable in the following analysis; very similar patterns

TABLE 26 : **Father's Party Identification, Respondent's Class, and Party Preference, in Percentages**

Total		LIB-CP	LAB	DLP
	Nonmanual			
18	Liberal-Country party	81	17	2
2	None	67	29	5
6	Father not in Australia	71	26	3
6	Don't know	77	20	3
15	Labor	50	45	5
	Manual			
10	Liberal-Country party	71	28	1
2	None	34	66	0
9	Father not in Australia	38	56	6
8	Don't know	39	56	5
24	Labor	24	74	2
100	(N=1,705)			

Eight respondents had fathers with DLP identification

result if mother's preference is chosen instead. Table 26 implies that parental influence is stronger than class when the two are in conflict, especially in the manual stratum, where offspring of Liberal or Country party supporters are themselves overwhelmingly non-Labor. Among nonmanuals with Labor parents, however, the opposite pulls of class and partisan inheritance lead to a more even division in party preference. Where there is no tradition of family partisanship, where it was not known, or where the respondent is a migrant, occupational class operates in the fashion familiar from earlier tables.

B. PARTY COMPETENCE

The popular view that parties differ in their ability to deal with certain problems may help to explain both stability and change in party preference. For example, those in the older age groups who think pensions are important are more likely to prefer Labor than those who do not: the correlation is suggestive but not conclusive, since most persons dependent solely on a pension are retired manual workers.

Respondents were asked to name the most important problems that the federal government should do something about, and to nominate the party or parties most likely to do what they (the respondents) wanted with respect to each problem. Table 27 summarizes the nominations of parties for the range of problems cited. The first row, for example, sets out the party preferences of those who thought that only the Liberal and/or Country parties were most likely to do what they wanted with respect to the problems they had mentioned.

TABLE 27 : Party Competence, Class, and Party Preference, in Percentages

Total		LIB-CP	LAB	DLP
	Nonmanual			
15	Liberal-CP	95	3	2
6	No difference between the parties	78	21	1
6	Liberal-CP for one problem; Labor for another	69	29	2
10	DLP; other combinations	69	21	10
12	Labor	25	74	1
	Manual			
10	Liberal-CP	81	17	2
6	No difference between the parties	47	48	5
4	Liberal-CP for one problem; Labor for another	52	48	0
7	DLP; other combinations	42	54	13
24	Labor	9	90	1
100	(N=1,392)			

The majority mentioned only one party as competent and indicated in overwhelming proportions their intention to vote for it, whatever their occupational class. But 39 percent said there would be no difference between the parties, or nominated different parties for different problems. Within the manual stratum such respondents divided evenly between the major parties; within the nonmanual stratum they showed a marked preference for the non-Labor parties. Non-Labor supporters in both classes were much more likely to nominate the Labor party, or to say that there was no difference between the parties, than were Labor supporters to return the compliment. A chicken-and-egg conundrum stares out from the data. Do manual workers who see no difference between the parties drift to support the non-Labor parties, or does their perception serve as post hoc rationalization of a party preference whose origins lie elsewhere?

In theory the extent to which a party system is polarized ought to have an important bearing on the stability of voting. The greater the perceived "distance" between the parties the harder it ought to be, *ceteris paribus*, for a voter to depart from his current voting preference. The difficulty of measuring party distance has been demonstrated by Converse (1966). We can gain some insight into these perceptions by studying the distribution of answers (Table 28) to the question, "In general, would you say that there is a *good deal* of difference between the parties, *some* difference, or *not much* difference?"

This attitude overlaps to some extent with intensity of party identification. Those who see little difference between the parties include many with only lukewarm party identification or none at all. Its effect is slight and appears to work in opposite directions in the two strata.

TABLE 28 : **Party Difference, Class, and Party Preference, in Percentages**

Total		LIB-CP	LAB	DLP
	Nonmanual			
19	Good deal	71	25	4
13	Some	71	27	2
18	Not much	63	33	4
	Manual			
16	Good deal	46	51	3
11	Some	42	56	2
23	Not much	33	65	2
100	(N=1,581)			

C. INTEREST IN POLITICS

Interest in politics has been shown to correlate positively with turnout. Since turnout in Australia is compulsory, attention shifts to the relationship of interest in politics to party preference (Table 29).

TABLE 29 : **Interest in Politics, Class, and Party Preference, in Percentages**

Total		LIB-CP	LAB	DLP
	Nonmanual			
11	Good deal	62	36	6
21	Some	71	27	2
13	Not much	72	24	4
3	None	50	46	4
	Manual			
7	Good deal	30	66	4
18	Some	42	55	3
20	Not much	40	57	3
7	None	30	66	4
100	(N=1,761)			

Labor-voting is related to both the highest and lowest levels of interest in politics; a medium degree of interest in politics has no effect on party preference.

D. FEELING OF PROSPERITY

J. B. Chifley, prime minister from 1945 to 1949, coined the term "hip-pocket nerve" to describe why voters turn against parties in power in times of economic difficulties. Politicians can also be heard to complain that there is no offsetting "gratitude nerve", rewarding parties when times are good. The calculus of prosperity was explored by asking, "Are you and your family better off now than you were three or four years ago, are you worse off, or have you stayed the same?"

Gratitude seems present, if at all, only among better-off manual workers, who disproportionately favor the governing Liberal–Country group. The patterns no

TABLE 30 : **Present Prosperity, Class, and Party Preference, in Percentages**

Total		LIB-CP	LAB	DLP
	Nonmanual			
23	Better off	71	25	4
18	Same	66	31	3
9	Worse off	67	32	1
	Manual			
16	Better off	48	49	3
23	Same	33	64	4
11	Worse	30	66	4
100	(N=1,651)			

doubt depend a lot upon the party in power at the time, and might look very different in other circumstances. Nonetheless it is a striking comment on the strength of party attachment that nearly a third of those manual workers who felt worse off now than three years ago were intending to vote for parties that had been in power throughout that time.

VI.   Tree Analysis of Australian Electoral Behavior

Tree analysis is a multivariate statistical technique enabling one to assess the pattern of influence of the variables discussed above.[2] The analysis employed the following social-structure variables: region (i.e., state); urban or rural residence; occupational class; religion; regularity of church attendance; age; income; sex; trade-union membership; education; and national origin. The analysis included all respondents who expressed a clear party preference with regard to an election in 1967.

Figure 1 illustrates the results. The first split into occupational groups of almost equal size explains 8.9 percent of the total variance. Class-related variables remain

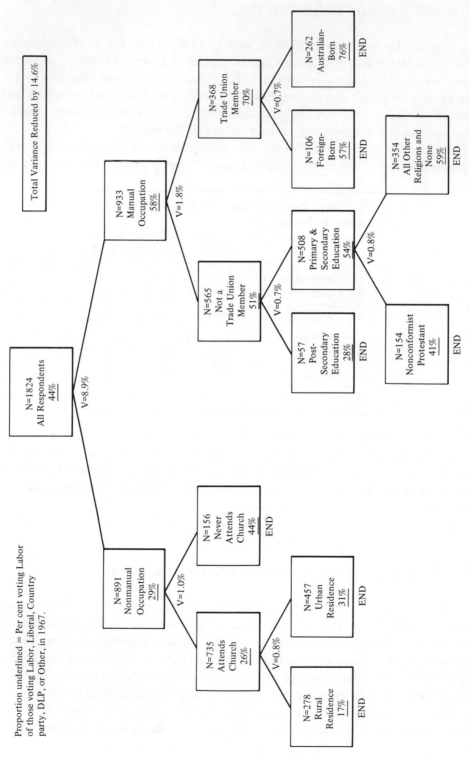

Total Variance Reduced by 14.6%

Proportion underlined = Per cent voting Labor of those voting Labor, Liberal, Country party, DLP, or Other, in 1967.

Figure 1: A Tree Analysis of Australian Electoral Behavior

important for those with manual occupations, who divide next by trade-union membership. The latter group is then split by education, those with post secondary education displaying a marked preference for the non-Labor parties. Those with less education divide by religion into Nonconformists and others. The trade-union members divide by nationality, the Australian-born forming the group most likely to vote Labor; neither group can be split further. The nonmanual branch of the tree is shorter. The second split divides churchgoers from nonchurchgoers, who cannot be further divided; the churchgoers, however, are split once more, into those in rural areas (the group least likely to vote Labor), and urban-dwellers.

The tree's branches in Figure 1 are of two kinds: the main ones have to do with occupation or class, and they support the minor branches, which display noneconomic characteristics. Moreover, none of these latter variables is to be found in both halves of the tree: national origin, education, and religion are important only for those with manual occupations, while churchgoing and urban/rural residence make a difference only for those with nonmanual occupations. The application of the A.I.D. program to different and larger sets of variables, including social-psychological measures, did not alter this general finding, although it produced larger and more complex trees. Class, whether objectively or subjectively defined, remained the most powerful predictor of vote; churchgoing and religious denomination were the most important noneconomic variables; and income, itself highly correlated with occupational class, occasionally emerged as significant.

In short, Australia is an homogenous polity, whose principal division—though not a strong one—is occupational class and what goes with it. It seems eminently reasonable to adapt Rose's argument (1968) about class in Britain and suggest that in Australia class occupies its dominant position because of the absence of any other powerful cleavages. The circumstances of the country's settlement and history have produced a close-knit society largely free of ethnic, religious, or ancestry cleavages: occupational class, or more crudely, wealth, fills the vacuum.

The battle lines of Australian electoral politics are summarized in Table 31, which ranks the end groups of Figure 1 in descending order of their support for the Labor party.

Facing one another across a wide middle ground stand the faithful partisans of either side. Group A, Australian-born trade unionists in manual occupations, comprises 14 percent of the sample, and more than three in four of them vote Labor. Group H is the solid, God-fearing, rural middle-class, 15 percent of the sample, whose members are even more united in their rejection of the Labor party. Each of these solid groups is flanked by a larger body of somewhat less dependable supporters. On the Labor side these consist of poorly educated manual workers who are not trade unionists and foreign-born manual workers who are. On the non-Labor side there is the mass of the urban church-attending middle-class together with a small group of qualified tradesmen. In the center of the field are two strongly cross-pressured groups whose political loyalties are evenly divided: those of the middle-class who never go to church, and poorly educated manual workers who come from Nonconformist homes and do not

TABLE 31 :   **The Principal Groups in Australian Electoral Behavior, 1967**

		N	Proportion of the Sample %	Proportion Voting Labor %
A	Australian-born manual workers who belong to trade unions	262	14	76
B	Manual workers, not trade unionists, and not Nonconformists, who have only primary or secondary education	354	19	59
C	Foreign-born manual workers who belong to trade unions	106	6	57
D	Workers in nonmanual occupations who never go to church	156	9	44
E	Nonconformist manual workers, not trade unionists, who had only primary or secondary education	154	9	41
F	Urban church attenders with nonmanual occupations	457	25	31
G	Manual workers, not trade unionists, with postsecondary education	57	3	28
H	Rural church-attenders with nonmanual occupations	278	15	17
		1,824	100%	(44%)

Wives have been grouped according to the occupations of their husbands.

belong to trade unions. These cross-pressured voters make up nearly a fifth of the sample. Their number, and the fact that even among the polar groups significant minorities vote for the other side, make it clear that Australian electoral behavior is not simply an artifact of the country's social structure. Party histories, personalities, issues, and policies of the moment, and voters' perceptions of them, must form an indispensable part of any general explanation of electoral behavior.

VII.   Conclusion

In the nineteenth-century Australia's new settlers brought with them British political institutions, a store of common experiences and traditions, a general dislike of the aristocratic basis of English society, and a determination to build something better in the Antipodes. The first seventy years of the twentieth century have seen the establishment of an independent federal state, the inflow of more than a million non-English immigrants, and a great weakening of formal and informal ties with the mother country. Yet patterns of electoral behavior are astonishingly like those of Great Britain. The resemblance is even closer in the sister Dominion of New Zealand, which has both a unitary constitutional structure and almost undiluted British immigrant stock (Robinson, 1967). It is true that neither colonial offshoot maintains an equivalent of the British Liberal party — in Australia the battle to determine the principal non-Labor party was fought decisively in the first decade of the twentieth-century — but each has its own sports: Social Credit in New Zealand, and the Democratic Labor and Country parties in Australia. Yet the primacy of occupational class as the rock on which the party system rests and as the major influence upon electoral behavior, is firmly established in all three. For this reason it is more sensible to compare Australia with Great Britain, New Zealand, and the class-oriented polities of the Scandinavian countries than with Canada or the United States, despite its sharing, with these latter nations, a federal structure and a settler foundation.

Postscript

In elections held on December 2, 1971, the Labor party won a small majority of seats and returned to power after a period in Opposition of 23 years. Party shares of the vote were as follows: Labor, 50 percent; Liberal, 32 percent; Country party, 9 percent; DLP, 5 percent; others, 4 percent. The swing to Labor continued a trend that began in 1969. Australia now possesses a second national polling organization, ANOP, an offshoot of Britain's NOP. In sympathy with an apparent worldwide trend, the voting age in Australia has been reduced from 21 to 18 years.

Notes

1. An Australian term, roughly similar to rancher, for one who raises sheep.
2. The program used in this instance was the A.I.D. (Automatic Interaction Detector) program developed by Sonquist and Morgan of the University of Michigan (1964) and supplied as part of the OSIRIS social-science package by the Inter-University Consortium for Political Research, Ann Arbor, Michigan.

References

AITKIN, DON. *The Country Party in New South Wales: Membership and Electoral Support.* APSA monograph no. 8. Canberra: APSA, 1965.

————"Electoral Forces in Federal Politics." Paper delivered to the Tenth Annual Conference of the Australian Political Studies Association. Hobart: 1968.

————"Political Review." *The Australian Quarterly*. XLI: 2 (March, 1969).

————"A Sample of Surveys." *Politics* V: 1, (May, 1970).

————*The Country Party in New South Wales. A Study of Organisation and Survival.* Canberra: Australian National Univ. Press, 1972.

————, and MORGAN, KIM. "Postal and Absent Voting: A Democratic Dilemma." *Australian Quarterly*, XLIII: 3 (September, 1971).

————, KAHAN, MICHAEL; and BARNES, SUE. "What Happened to the Depression Generation?" In Robert Cooksey ed. *The Great Depression in Australia.* Canberra: Society for the Study of Labour History, 1970.

ALFORD, ROBERT R. *Party and Society. The Anglo-American Democracies.* London: John Murray, 1964.

APSA (Australasian Political Studies Association). *The 'Donkey Vote' for the House of Representatives.* Sydney: APSA, 1963.

BLEWETT, NEAL. "A Classification of Australian Elections: Preliminary Notes." *Politics* VI: 1 (May, 1971).

BROOM, L., and HILL, R. J. "Opinion Polls and Social Rank in Australia: Method and First Findings." *Australian and New Zealand Journal of Sociology* I (1965).

————; JONES F. L.; and ZUBRZYCKI, G. "Social Stratification in Australia." In J. A. Jackson, ed. *Social Stratification.* Cambridge: Cambridge Univ. Press, 1968.

BURNS, CREIGHTON. *Parties and People.* Melbourne: Melbourne Univ. Press, 1961.

CAMPBELL, A. et al. *The American Voter.* New York: Wiley, 1960.

CONGALTON, A. A. *Status and Prestige in Australia.* Melbourne: Cheshire, 1969.

CONNELL, R. W., and GOULD, FLORENCE. *Politics of the Extreme Right: Warringah 1966.* Sydney: Sydney Univ. Press, 1967.

CONVERSE, PHILLIP E. "The Concept of a Normal Vote." In A. Campbell et al. *Elections and the Political Order.* New York: Wiley, 1966.

————, "The Problem of Party Distance in Models of Voting Change." In M. Kent Jennings and L. Harmon Ziegler, eds. *The Electoral Process.* Englewood Cliffs, Prentice-Hall, 1966.

CRISP, L. F. *Australian National Government.* Melbourne: Longmans, 1965.

DAVIES, A. F. "Politics in the New Suburb." *Australian Journal of Politics and History* VIII: 2 (November, 1962).

————, *Images of Class.* Sydney: Sydney Univ. Press, 1967.

DUFFY, PAUL J. "The Democratic Labor Party: Profile and Prospects." In H. Mayer ed. *Australian Politics—A Second Reader.* Melbourne: Cheshire, 1969.

ENCEL, S. *Equality and Authority.* Melbourne: Cheshire, 1970.

FREDMAN, L. E. "The Introduction of the Australian Ballot in the United States." *Australian Journal of Politics and History* XIII: 2 (August, 1967).

GOOT, MURRAY. *Policies and Partisans. Australian Electoral Opinion 1941 to 1968.* Occasional monograph no. 1, Department of Government. University of Sydney, 1969.

————, and ILBERY, JAKI. *Australian Public Opinion Polls. Index 1941-1968.* Occasional monograph no. 2, Department of Government. University of Sydney, 1969.

GRAHAM, B. D. *The Formation of the Australian Country Parties.* Canberra: Australian National Univ. Press, 1966.

HAMMOND, S. B. *Social Structure and Personality in a City.* London: Routledge, 1954.

HUGHES, ALAN. "Psychological Dispositions and Political Attitudes." Doctoral thesis. Australian National University, 1970.

HUGHES, COLIN A., *Images and Issues.* Canberra: Australian National Univ. Press, 1969.

————, and WESTERN, JOHN S. *The Prime Minister's Policy Speech.* Canberra: Australian National Univ. Press, 1966.

————, and GRAHAM, B. D. *A Handbook of Australian Government and Politics.* Canberra: Australian National Univ. Press, 1968.

KAHAN, MICHAEL, and AITKIN, DON. *Drawing a Sample of the Australian Electorate.* Occasional paper no. 3, Department of Political Science, Research School of Social Sciences. Australian National University, 1968.

KEY, V. O. "A Theory of Critical Elections." *Journal of Politics* XVII:1 (1955).

JUPP, JAMES. *Australian Party Politics.* Melbourne: Melbourne Univ. Press, 1968.

LOVEDAY, P., and MARTIN, A. W. *Parliament Factions and Parties.* Melbourne: Melbourne Univ. Press, 1966.

MASTERMAN, C. J. "A Note on the Effect of the Donkey Vote for the House of Representatives." *Australian Journal of Politics and History* X:2 (August, 1964).

MAYER, HENRY. *The Press in Australia.* Melbourne: Lansdowne, 1964.

————, *Australian Politics—A Second Reader.* Melbourne: Cheshire, 1969.

MOL, HANS. *Religion in Australia.* Melbourne: Nelson, 1971.

MILLER, J. D. B. *Australian Government and Politics.* Lodon: Duckworth, 1964.

MURRAY, ROBERT. *The Split: Australian Labor in the Fifties.* Melbourne: Cheshire, 1970.

MURTAGH, JAMES G. *Australia: The Catholic Chapter.* Sydney: Angus and Robertson, 1959.

NELSON, HELEN and WATSON, LEX. "Party Organisation." In H. Mayer, ed. *Australian Politics—A Second Reader.* Melbourne: Cheshire, 1969.

O'FARRELL, PATRICK. *The Catholic Church in Australia. A Short History: 1788-1967.* Melbourne: Nelson, 1968.

OVERACKER, LOUISE. *The Australian Party System.* New Haven: Yale Univ. Press, 1952.

————, *Australian Parties in a Changing Society: 1945-67.* Melbourne: Cheshire, 1968.

PARTRIDGE, P.H. *Society, Schools and Progress in Australia.* Oxford: Pergamon, 1968.

POWER, JOHN, ed. *Politics in a Suburban Community.* Sydney: Sydney Univ. Press, 1968.

RAE, DOUGLAS. *The Political Consequences of Electoral Laws.* New Haven: Yale Univ. Press, 1967.

RAWSON, D. W. *Australia Votes.* Melbourne: Melbourne Univ. Press, 1961.

————, "The D. L. P.—'Get On', 'Get Out' or Neither?" In H. Mayer, ed. *Australian Politics—A Second Reader.* Melbourne: Cheshire, 1969.

ROBINSON, ALAN D. "Class Voting in New Zealand." In Lipset Seyman M. and Rokkan, Stein eds. *Party Systems and Voter Alignments: Cross-National Perspectives.* New York: Free Press, 1967.

ROKKEN, STEIN, et al. *Comparative Survey Analysis.* The Hague: Mouton, 1969.

ROSE, RICHARD. "Class and Party Divisions: Britain as a Test Case." *Sociology,* 2 (1968).

RYDON, JOAN. "The Electorate." In John Wilkes, ed. *Forces in Australian Politics.* Sydney: Angus and Robertson, 1968.

————, "The Electoral System." In H. Mayer, ed. *Australian Politics—A Second Reader.* Melbourne: Cheshire, 1969.

SONQUIST, JOHN and MORGAN J. N. "The Detection of Interaction Effects." Ann Arbor: Survey Research Center, 1964.

WEST, KATHARINE. *Power in the Liberal Party.* Melbourne: Cheshire, 1965.

WESTERN, J. S. and HUGHES, COLIN A. "The Mass Media: A Preliminary Report." *Politics* II: 2 (November, 1967).

WOOD, THOMAS. *Cobbers.* Lobdon: Oxford Univ. Press, 1961.

10. BRITAIN:
Simple Abstractions and Complex Realities

The most familiar model of electoral behavior postulates a two-party system, with the parties divided on class lines and control of government regularly alternating between them. Britain is usually cited as the best example of this ideal-type electoral system. Yet because this ideal-type model is an abstraction, it is both necessary and desirable to analyze British politics rigorously to see how closely complex realities match the abstract ideal. One must review the evolution of electoral politics, the character of contemporary elections, and the extent to which class loyalties translate into votes and seats for the two major parties.

I. Historical Background

Britain is often considered prototypical because it led the world in industrialization in the second half of the eighteenth-century. The number of workers employed in manufacturing, mining, and industry surpassed the numbers in agriculture as early as 1821; by repealing the Corn Laws in 1846, Britain became committed to a policy that made agriculture decline, with industrial development paying for imported food.

A much earlier draft of this paper, based on analysis of 1964 British election data, was presented to a Conference of the Committee on Political Sociology at the Free University of Berlin in January, 1968. It is reprinted under the title "Party Systems, Social Structure and Voter Alignments in Britain" in Otto Stammer, editor, *Party Systems, Party Organizations, and the Politics of New Masses* (Berlin: *Institüt fur politische Wissenschaft*, 1968).

In revising the draft printed here I have benefited first of all by the Gallup Poll Ltd. making available survey data initially collected for the *Daily Telegraph*. Helpful comments suggesting alteration or clarification of the manuscript were received from D. E. Butler, G. D. M. Block, J. M. Bochel, F. W. S. Craig, J. A. T. Douglas, James Hutchison, D. A. Kavanagh and W. L. Miller. Miss Mary Dickie and T. T. Mackie provided research assistance, under a grant from the British Social Science Research Council, and Mrs. R. West retyped the manuscript again and again.

Urbanization also came early in Britain. By 1851 half the population lived in cities, and many nominally rural areas included mining villages and cotton or woolen mills. By 1885 suburbanization was beginning, with important implications for party organization (Cornford, 1963). The majority of the population became literate by about 1840, and virtually complete literacy was achieved by 1885. No formal requirement of literacy ever entered the franchise laws. Only in Ireland was there ever a noticeable minority of illiterate voters. A variety of criteria of socioeconomic development converge in classifying Britain as a "developed" or "modern" society by 1850 (Rose, 1965, pp. 86–88). Moreover, from 1801 to 1901 the population of the United Kingdom grew from 11,944,000 to 38,237,000, thus giving it size as well as skills. These social changes created substantial and unanticipated pressures upon the traditional electoral systems and the values that justified it (cf. Birch, 1964).

The rationalization of the electoral system began generations after the commencement of industrialization, and took more than a century to accomplish. Until 1949 certain electoral practices could be traced back to the fifteenth century (Anson, 1911, pp. 101ff). In the delimitation of constituencies practices have not yet been fully rationalized. The Reform Act of 1832 routed the defenders of the traditional electoral system known as Old Corruption, which had prevailed with little alteration from the seventeenth century (cf. Grego, 1886; Gwyn, 1962). The 1832 Reform Act sought to bring consistency into the procedure by which individuals could qualify for voting; it did not greatly extend the franchise. The numbers eligible to vote increased by one-half, but accounted for less than one-fifth of the total adult male population (see Butler and Cornford, 1969, p. 333). A second reform was the abolition of a number of virtually uninhabited constituencies and the creation of new constituencies in populous urban areas. Third, a registration procedure was established, since individual electors now had a formal rather than a traditional claim to the vote. In practice the requirement of registration became an obstacle to voting for some nominally qualified subjects (Seymour, 1915, chs. 5–6). The Reform Act of 1867 substantially expanded the number of urban workers eligible to vote. The ballot was made secret by Act of Parliament in 1872, and legislation against corrupt and illegal practices begun to take effect with the Act of 1883 (O'Leary, 1962). These two reforms meant that substantial numbers of voters were no longer intimidated or bribed before casting their ballot. The Reform Act of 1884 enfranchised about 88 percent of adult males, but there still remained seven different types of franchise qualifications, and plural voting was permitted for persons with more than one qualification, about 7 percent of registered voters. Because registration put the burden for claiming the franchise upon the individual, as in America today, about one-third of the population eligible to vote failed to register. By 1911 an estimated 59 percent of the adult male population successfully claimed the franchise (Blewett, 1965, p. 31). Party organization was important for registering qualified supporters and challenging persons registered by the other side. Seymour succinctly notes that nineteenth-century electoral reform was the product of parliamentary bargaining and ad hoc responses to events; it did not endorse "a uniform doctrinaire principle... [such as] the innate voting rights of man" (1915, p. 488).

The Representation of the People Act, 1918, was the first to rationalize previous centuries of electoral practice by introducing a new principle, a vote for every adult male. Owners of commercial and business property, as well as university graduates, were allowed additional votes, the latter in twelve special university seats. (See Butler, 1963, pp. 146–53). The Act radically reformed the method of registration, making local government officials effectively responsible for listing all persons legally qualified to vote. Women aged thirty and above were also enfranchised in 1918; all women twenty-one or above were given the vote by an Act of 1928. Since 1918, and only since 1918, the electorate has come near to equaling the adult population.[1]

The continuity of British elections and the constant use of the single-ballot, simple-plurality method of voting make it deceptively easy to produce election results for periods back to 1832. Election results by constituency from 1832 until 1910 are available in McCalmont's *Poll Book* (1910), and for the period from 1885 until 1939 in successive annual editions of the *Constitutional Year Book*. A prose discussion of constituencies for the period 1885–1910 is found in Pelling (1967), and a set of maps and tables for elections since 1885 has been prepared by Kinnear (1968). An analysis of national election results and trends, 1868–1900, is found in Dunbabin (1966), and for 1885–1910 in Cornford (1970). The definitive text for election results by constituency since 1918 is that of F. W. S. Craig (vol. I, 1969; vol. II, 1971a). The definitive source of national vote totals and of much other incidental electoral information since 1918 has also been provided by Craig (1971, 2nd ed.). Craig's figures are used in all election calculations in this study, unless otherwise signified. Official publications of returns, although issued since 1857, are virtually useless because no indication is given of the party affiliation of the candidates.

Election results for the period before 1885 must be treated very cautiously because, in Hanham's apt phrase, (1959, p. 191) "General elections were not general," i.e., local factors greatly affected the pattern of competition between candidates. In many constituencies seats were uncontested because of the expense of parliamentary electioneering. At the closely fought general election of 1885, only 6 percent of seats were uncontested; in the period 1885–1910, however, the average number of uncontested seats was 21 percent (Lloyd, 1965). Since 1922 the number of uncontested seats has always been less than 11 percent of the total, and since 1945 it has been less than 1 percent. The fall in uncontested seats after 1885 reflects the desire of party managers to make general elections nationwide contests, and the significance of issues salient throughout the United Kingdom. Stokes (1967, p. 192) has shown that the swing in the vote in British constituencies, 1892–1895, was about half that found in the United States in the 1950s; this indicates the extent of homogeneity already achieved in the electorate. Stokes could calculate meaningful swing figures for about three-quarters of the American Congressional contests in the 1950s, but for only 46 percent of the British contests. In the majority of United Kingdom seats at that time, changing patterns of contest including "no contest" not only vitiate the calculation of swing but also reduce the comparability of national vote totals, because all parties did not fight in the same constituencies.

Since 1885 it has been meaningful to speak of a British, i.e., a nationwide, party system. Yet it is important to note that since that date at least *three* different party systems can be distinguished (Table 1):

TABLE 1 : The Party Systems of Britain, 1885–1970

	Votes Mean%	Votes S.D.%	Seats Mean N	Seats S.D.	Elections Contested
1885–1910					
Conservatives	47.5	2.9	266	67	8
Liberal Unionists	*a*	*a*	50	22	7
Liberals	45.3	1.8	259	72	8
Irish Nationalists	3.6*b*	2.3	83	2	8
Labour	4.6	4.0	24	24	6
1918–1935					
Conservatives	44.8	9.0	372	94	7
Liberals	19.9	9.6	85	60	7
Labour	31.5	5.7	148	80	7
Others	3.8	5.0	23	36	7
1945–1970					
Conservatives	45.2	3.7	303	50	8
Liberals	7.1	3.1	8	3	8
Labour	46.1	2.2	313	45	8
Others	1.6	1.0	5	8	8

a Liberal Unionist votes included with Conservative votes in source.

b Includes both pro and anti-Parnellites. Vote percentage low because many seats were won uncontested and no vote was therefore recorded.

S.D. = Standard deviation

Sources: 1885-1910, Kinnear (1968); 1918-1970, Craig, (1971 pp. 21,22)

1. A multiparty system existed from 1885 to the outbreak of the First World War; six of the eight general elections of the period did not produce government by a single party. When in office, the Conservatives relied upon support by the Liberal Unionists of Joseph Chamberlain, who had left the Liberal party because of a proposal to give Ireland home rule. Reciprocally, the Liberal governments were usually dependent upon parliamentary support from Irish Nationalists. In this period Labour emerged as the fifth party in the multiparty system.

2. The period 1914–1945 is best labeled a coalition party system. The dominant pattern of government was not that of two large parties with one a majority, but coalition between two or three parties. This occurred in wartime, 1915–1918 and 1940–1945, in postwar conditions of 1918–1922, and in the aftermath of the 1931 economic depression, 1931–35. For sixteen years in this period Conservative, Liberal, and Labour MPs sat in cabinet together. In addition Britain was governed by minority Labour governments in 1924 and 1929–1931; on both occasions support by a substantial number of Liberal MPs was a necessary condition of Labour holding office. Of the

seven general elections in the period, only 1924 resulted in government by a single majority party. The instability of the party system in the period is emphasized by the replacement of the Liberals by Labour as the second party in the two-party system and by the calling of six general elections between 1918 and 1931. It is also indicated by the qualifications that candidates used for their party labels, especially in 1918, 1922, and 1931; in these three elections it is difficult to produce a meaningful national total of Conservative or Liberal votes (cf. Craig, 1971, pp. 1–4, 8–9).

3. The idea of a two-party system originated when the two parties were Conservatives and Liberals; it survives today with Labour and Conservatives as the two parties. The collapse of the Liberal party was not brought about by gradual electoral decline but by the disruption of the Liberal parliamentary party and by subsequent splits at constituency level during and after in the First World War (cf. Clarke, 1971; Wilson, 1966; Kinnear, 1968, section III). Similarly, the emergence of the Conservative party as the sole anti-Labour party was contingent, not inevitable, in the very fluid political situation that followed the coalition of some Conservatives and some Liberals under Lloyd George from 1918 to 1922 (cf. Cowling, 1971). In the last general election before the political disruption of the First World War the Labour party nominated but fifty-six candidates for the 670 parliamentary seats. Only *after* the breakup of the Liberal party in Parliament did Labour begin to contest a majority of parliamentary seats. Labour did not establish a clear preeminence over the Liberals in parliamentary seats until 1924, nor did it establish preeminence in terms of votes until 1931. In experiencing a major disruption and realignment between the two wars, Britain is identical with every other Anglo-American nation (cf. Urwin and Rose, 1970).

II. The Party System Today

Whether Britain is considered a two-party system today depends upon the way in which the terms is defined. Only if terms are defined in a clear and theoretically meaningful way can one then determine whether or to what extent two parties, and only two, monopolize electoral politics.

In terms of control of government Britain has been a one-party system since 1945, for at each general election a single party has gained a parliamentary majority and thus monopolized control of the executive. Because the Conservatives and Labour have each won majorities in this period, one can say that two and only two parties have been in charge of government since 1945. Majority government can rest on slim margins. In 1950 Labour governed with 315 MPs in a House of Commons of 625, and the following year the Conservatives won office with 321 MPs. In 1964 Labour governed with 317 MPs in a House of 630. When majority government can rest on such margins, one might hesitate in asserting that majority rule represents the workings of an inevitable law. There is also no mechanical, pendulumlike swing assuring the regular alternation of a pair of majority parties in government; the governing party has secured reelection in four of the seven postwar contests. Any alternation of parties in office is also not an inevitable consequence of British electoral institutions. In elections to the devolved Northern Ireland Parliament, conducted by British-type procedures, the Unionists won every election from the first in 1921 to the last in 1969.

The Conservative and Labour parties have tended to have a duopoly of seats in the House of Commons, winning an average of 97.8 percent of all seats in general elections since 1945. The best showing by a third party occurred when the Liberals elected twelve MPs in 1966. The two major parties have not, however, enjoyed so great a duopoly of votes, averaging 91.3 percent of the vote at general elections since 1945. The two-party share of the poll has ranged from 96.8 percent in 1951 to 87.5 percent in 1964. At no general election since 1935 has the winning party taken as much as 50 percent of the vote. The Conservative poll of 49.7 percent in the 1955 election is the best postwar showing by any party.

Measures of vote fractionalization also demonstrate a tendency to duopoly in British party politics. A value of 0.50 on Rae's index represents a perfectly competitive two-party system, with votes shared equally between the parties: as the score rises above 0.50 duopolistic competition declines (Rae, 1967, pp. 53ff). The average value for postwar British elections is 0.58, ranging from 0.53 at the 1951 election to 0.60 in the 1945 and 1964 contests. While Britain has a much lower fractionalization score than countries with proportional-representation election systems (mean index: 0.73), it is less close to the pure two-party standard than the average country with a British-type plurality-electoral system (mean index: 0.54) (Rae, 1967, pp. 98ff). The two-party tendency in British elections is not intrinsic to the conditions of the society. It is to a substantial extent "manufactured" by the mechanics of the electoral system. The simple plurality system used in Britain tends to give a disproportionate bonus of seats to the strongest parties (Table 2).

TABLE 2 : **The Relationship of Seats to Votes in the United Kingdom, 1970**

	Candi-dates	MPs	MPs %	Votes (000)	Votes %	Votes per MP
Conservatives	628	330	52.3	13,145	46.4	39,834
Labour	625	288	45.7	12,208	43.1	42,839
Liberal	332	6	1.0	2,117	7.5	352,839
Scottish National	65	1	0.2	306	1.1	306,802
Plaid Cymru	36	0	0	175	0.6	—
Communist	58	0	0	37	0.1	—
Others*	93	5	0.8	354	1.2	70,818

Source: Craig, 1971, p. 20
*Principally Northern Ireland votes, both Protestant and Catholic.

The British party system is not equally a two-party system in all four parts of the United Kingdom. Duopoly competition is greatest in England, the largest part of the United Kingdom (Table 3).

TABLE 3 : **Duopoly in Voting Within the United Kingdom, 1970**

	England %	Wales %	Scotland %	N. Ireland %
Conservative	48.3	27.7	38.0	54.2
Labour	43.4	51.6	44.5	12.6
Two-party	(91.7)	(79.3)	(82.5)	(66.8)
Liberals	7.9	6.8	5.5	1.5
Nationalist	—	11.5	11.4	24.5
Other	0.4	2.4	0.6	7.2
Votes (000)	23,360	1,516	2,688	779

Source: Craig, 1971, p. 20

In the United Kingdom ten of the twelve seats won by lesser parties in 1970 were taken in the 119 seats outside England. In the period 1964–1970 it might be better to speak of an *English* rather than a British two-party system. The system is weakest in Northern Ireland, the most un-English part of the United Kingdom (see Rose, 1971, ch. 8).

If a two-party system is defined as one in which only candidates from two parties contest elections, then Britain has never had a two-party system. In the period since 1945 the average number of candidates contesting a constituency has varied from 2.2 in 1951 and 1955 to 3.0 in 1950 (see Craig, 1971, p. 21). In five of the eight contests since 1945 a majority of the seats had three or more candidates. In 1970 only 185 of the 630 constituencies saw a straight fight between Conservative and Labour party candidates. In three-cornered contests the victorious candidate need not win 50.1 percent of the vote in his constituency. In 1970 20 percent of successful candidates won with less than half the vote; since 1945 an average of 21.2 percent of the seats has been won by a minority vote (cf. Craig, 1971, p. 74). The winning poll in such circumstances is usually above 40 percent; only eighteen constituencies have been won since 1945 by a candidate polling less than this (Pulzer, 1967, p. 55).

At any general election the majority of candidates will be defeated. While a major-party candidate may face a hopeless task in his own constituency, nationally his party has a chance of victory. A defining characteristic of a minor party might be that the party nominates insufficient candidates to have a theoretical chance of winning a majority in the House of Commons. By this standard only the Liberals have some claim to be a third major party in Britain. The Liberals have nominated candidates for more than half the seats at three of the eight elections to the Commons since 1945. The number of candidates has fluctuated with the party's internal conditions and supporters' hopes, ranging from 475 in a disastrous 1950 election to 109 in 1951. Nationalist parties might claim that within their own nation–Wales, Scotland, or Northern Ireland—they are a major party. *Plaid Cymru* has fought a majority of seats in Wales at each parliamentary election since 1959; the Scottish National Party did so in Scotland in 1970. In Northern Ireland Nationalist or Republican candidates have fought a majority of Westminster seats at each election since 1955 (cf. Craig, 1971, pp. 62–63). All other groupings, except for Communists, have nominated derisory numbers of candidates at post–1945 elections. The Communists fielded 100 candidates in 1950, but their numbers fell to a low of ten in 1951; Communist candidates have won one-eighth of a constituency's vote only six times since 1950 (Craig, 1971, p. 61).

The British party system is competitive inasmuch as the margin in votes—if not in seats—between the winner and runner-up is usually small. The biggest gap between the two parties occurred in 1945, when Labour led the Conservatives by 8.4 percent. The closest race in terms of votes was in 1951, when Labour secured 0.8 percent more of the vote than the Conservatives; the latter won a majority of seats in the House of Commons. The average margin of the winning party has been 3.6 percent of the vote, i.e., about a million votes. The even strength of the parties nationally is not reflected at the constituency level. The national picture is a consequence of large Labour and large Conservative constituency majorities tending to balance out in aggregate. At any one election the number of seats that changes hands is a small fraction of the total. Boundary changes make it difficult to give exact figures for constituencies changing hands at every election since 1945. On average, since 1951 about fifty of 630 seats have changed hands at a British general election (Craig, 1971, p. 53). The reciprocal of this is that the great majority of seats do not change hands, and incumbent MPs are usually safe from threatened defeat for decades. In the 1955–1970 period 470 of the 630 seats in the House of Commons remained in the control of one party (cf. Jones, 1964; Rasmussen, 1966).

From the point of view of a politician any change in votes, however small, is significant if it tips the balance of power in the Commons from one party to another. In Britain a very small change in vote will produce disproportionately large changes in seats. For example, a swing of one vote in one hundred from Conservative to Labour or vice versa will cause approximately fifteen seats to change hands between the two parties.[2] This will in turn alter the balance of power in the Commons by thirty seats; a swing of 2 percent would alter it by about sixty seats. Thus a small swing in votes can have a disproportionate political effect, easily overturning a parliamentary majority or creating a landslide in terms of parliamentary majorities, though not in terms of votes.

When the voting strength of the parties is reviewed by absolute and comparative standards, postwar British elections are remarkable for the absence of major trends or realignments (cf. Rose and Urwin, 1970). In fact the typology of maintaining, realigning or deviating elections can hardly be applied. In eight postwar elections the balance of the two parties has been very even, equally important, the range in vote has been limited. The extremes in Labour's vote have been only 5.7 percent apart in a quarter of a century; in the same period the Conservatives have been 10.1 percent apart, from the nadir of 1945 to a peak in 1955. The Liberal vote has ranged less in absolute terms but more proportionately; the Liberal vote per candidate has fluctuated from 11.8 percent in 1950 to 18.6 percent in 1945. The freedom of the prime minister to determine the date of the next election at any time within five years from the preceding election is not, in practice, a means for a governing party to maximize its vote by calling a snap election. In their election timing prime ministers seek to minimize the risk of defeat. Yet in four of the seven postwar elections the governing party has had its vote fall. Only two elections have been held in abnormal circumstances. In 1945 the election occurred between the end of the war in Europe and in Japan. In 1951 the election was held shortly after a major split in the Labour cabinet, while there was war in Korea and the threat of war in the Persian Gulf.

The conventional way to measure the aggregate change of vote is in terms of swing, i.e., the average of the gain in votes by one party and the loss by another. The concept is thus an attempt to summarize the *net* effect of a large number of changes in voting behavior between elections, including movement to and from the ranks of non-voters. The measure was developed by D. E. Butler during the late 1940s and early 1950s, when two-party competition was at its highest (cf. McCallum and Readman, 1947, appendix III). Swings have been very low. Since 1945 the median swing, i.e., the average of the votes gained by one major party and lost by the other, has been 2.7 percent, and the mean has been 2.5 percent, calculating swing from aggregate national vote totals (Craig, 1971, p. 22). The concept of swing is convenient for summarizing findings from opinion polls, by-elections, or general elections, and relating them to parliamentary seats won and lost (Butler, 1947). The Butler method for calculating swing declines in utility, however, as third parties gain votes: they need not even gain seats to spoil the logical symmetry of the formulation. In the 1960s alternative measures of swing have been put forward (cf. Berrington, 1965; Steed, 1965; Rasmussen and Butler, 1965). All the revisions suffer from a common disadvantage, the assumption that only two parties have votes worth noting. Miller (1972) has proposed as an alternative the use of a transition matrix to summarize voting shifts between any number of parties and abstention; it can even accommodate changes in the number of parties fighting successive elections. The value of thinking of the movement of voters between more than two categories is emphasized by the asymmetrical way in which Conservative and Labour voting strength has altered since 1945. In a pure two-party system one party's gain would equal the other party's loss. Yet in two of the seven post-1945 elections, 1951 and 1959, both parties have seen their vote move in the same direction. In the remaining five contests the average differences between the shifts in vote for the two parties was 2.3 percent. In the extreme instance of 1964 the Labour party won sweeping gains even though its vote rose by only 0.2 percent. It did this because the Conservative vote fell by 5.9 percent. If changes in vote are calculated in relation to movements within the total electorate, thus including abstainers, these asymmetries could be greater.

The persistence of party loyalties at a regional as well as United Kingdom level can simply be demonstrated by correlating the vote of the parties in the regions of

Britain for all pairs of elections since 1918. Great Britain is here divided into eleven regions, following the standard regional boundaries defined by the Central Statistical Office, except that the old London County Council area is abstracted from the southeast and treated as a separate "inner London" region (see *Abstract of Regional Statistics*, 1970, p. 49). The higher the correlation, the greater the nationwide consistency in the relative strength of a party between two elections. In other words the correlation matrix controls for the effect of a national trend; as long as the change up or down occurs evenly in each region, the correlation remains high. If there is a major change in the spatial distribution of a party's vote, however, the correlation will fall or become negative. As voters are not randomly distributed throughout a country, any large-scale change in a party's electoral support is likely to be reflected in regional voting and thus lead to lower correlations. It is also possible for election results to show a higher level of correlation between pairs of elections distant in time than between successive elections. This happens in America because some issue-dimensions are important sporadically rather than persistently (see Pomper, 1967; Burnham, 1968; Converse, 1969).

TABLE 4:   **Regional Correlations in Conservative Vote, 1918–1970**

	1918	1922	1923	1924	1929	1931	1935	1945	1950	1951	1955	1959	1964	1966
1922	.94													
1923	.86	.90												
1924	.91	.93	.98											
1929	.96	.93	.95	.98										
1931	.86	.86	.90	.94	.94									
1935	.87	.89	.95	.98	.97	.96								
1945	.78	.72	.85	.87	.88	.89	.91							
1950	.85	.73	.82	.86	.90	.87	.87	.96						
1951	.82	.75	.86	.88	.90	.88	.89	.98	.98					
1955	.83	.75	.87	.89	.91	.91	.91	.99	.98	.99				
1959	.85	.81	.93	.94	.94	.95	.95	.97	.96	.97	.98			
1964	.75	.80	.95	.94	.90	.91	.96	.92	.85	.90	.91	.95		
1966	.76	.83	.96	.94	.89	.89	.94	.90	.83	.90	.90	.93	.93	
1970	.75	.85	.96	.93	.87	.90	.93	.86	.77	.84	.85	.91	.97	.98

The pattern in Table 4 shows an extremely high degree of persistence in voting, not only between successive pairs of elections, but also at points distant in time. The median correlation among the 105 values in the matrix is above 0.90, and none falls below 0.72. Even though the first election in the period, 1918, is the most atypical, the regional Conservative vote of 1918 correlates with that for 1970 at a level of 0.75. Since 1945 two-thirds of all correlations have been higher than 0.90. The matrix for Labour voting shows a similarly high degree of persistence. In the period 1918-1945 Labour was first becoming established as a national party; it did not contest all seats in any region until the 1929 general election, and it contested all seats in a region in only 7 per-cent of its opportunities in the period. This accounts in part for substantial fluctuations in the correlation of its vote; the median value is nonetheless high, falling between

.80 and .90. In the post-1945 period the Labour party has consistently fought nation-wide in Great Britain; the correlation of its vote has always been 0.90 or higher. The Liberal party has had its national vote totals fluctuate greatly in the half-century, from a British low of 2.6 percent in 1951 to a high of 30.1 percent in 1923. This in turn is reflected in a much greater inconsistency in regional voting strength; the median correlation falls between .60 and .70 for the half-century and between .70 and .80 for the period since 1945. The persistence in the pattern is not dependent upon the size of the regions. If one takes the subdivision of the electorate of Britain into twenty-five regions, as in the Nuffield election studies, 1950-1966, a similar pattern emerges: ten of the fifteen Conservative correlations are 0.90 or higher, and the lowest is .80; the "lowest" Labour correlation of the fifteen in the matrix is .95.

III. Voting and Its Study

The last and least of the major statutory reforms of electoral law occurred with the passing of the Representation of the People Act, 1949. This provides the framework for British general elections today. It removed anachronisms that tended to favor the Conservatives, such as plural voting. The main positive feature of reform was the provision for recurring redistribution of seats, in accordance with population changes (cf. Butler, 1959). Hence constituency boundaries that had been redrawn only once between 1885 and 1945 have been altered three times since. After several years of committee consideration a Representation of the People Act was also passed in 1969. Its chief features were lowering the voting age from twenty-one to eighteen and a provision for description of the candidates on ballot papers. (For full legal details see Wollaston, 1970; an excellent nontechnical outline is in Leonard, 1968. Cf. Cmnd. 3550, 1968.)

By contrast with an American, a British elector has very few chances to cast a vote. The only nationwide election is the choice of one Member of Parliament from each of 630 constituencies. In addition to voting for a single MP, a British elector will also have a local-government vote—or two votes if he lives in a two-tier local authority area. Local elections differ greatly from parliamentary contests because of the lesser significance of the offices at stake, the lower frequency of contested seats, the presence of party groups not represented in parliamentary elections, and, not least, the much lower turnout of voters (cf. Sharpe, 1962; Fletcher, 1967; Stanyer, 1970). The only other ballots sanctioned by law concern local matters such as the conditions for the sale of drink in Wales and Scotland. Elections for the Northern Ireland Parliament at Stormont are not fought on United Kingdom constituency boundaries or British party lines (see Rose, 1971, ch. 8). If a member of the House of Commons dies or retires outside the time span of an election, the voters of his constituency will elect a replacement in a by-election. An average of eleven by-elections have been held annually since 1945, nearly half the result of the death of a sitting member. By-election results usually show a swing of votes against the government of the day, because of differential abstention rates, support for "third" parties, and some voters changing sides (see Craig, 1971, pp. 42–43; cf. King, 1968).

The procedure for nominating candidates is simple. A candidate must secure signatures from ten electors in the constituency and post a £150 ($375) deposit; the deposit is forfeited if the candidate fails to secure more than one-eighth of the vote. The measure was introduced to bar frivolous candidatures. It also places a financial burden upon Liberal and Nationalist candidates, the ones most likely to lose deposits. Legally, a candidate is not a party nominee, nor does a generic party label appear on the ballot paper. The absence of party labels seems to have had little effect on voters' choice as between candidates listed top or bottom in alphabetical ordering (cf. Bagley, 1966). The 1969 Act permits every candidate to describe himself with a phrase of up to six words; many candidates use terms such as "Conservative" or "the Labour party candidate." The Act was intentionally drafted to avoid the problem of registering parties centrally (Wollaston, 1970, pp. 133–34). In practice "breakaway" candidates rarely run against official nominees. The simplicity of the single-ballot, simple-plurality electoral system makes marking and counting votes much easier than in a land with proportional representation. Only a trivial number of ballots—one-seventh of 1 percent in 1970—are declared invalid (Craig, 1971, p. 75).

No electoral reform has ever sought to recast all the constituencies in Britain in order to maximize one set of conditions or a single principle (see Butler, 1955; Starzinger, 1965). Instead, claims to representation based originally on medieval titles have been periodically reviewed, revised, and updated since the 1832 Reform Act. In 1944 boundary commissions were established by statute for each of the four parts of the United Kingdom. Statutes now require the commissions to report every ten to fifteen years on findings from a general review of constituency sizes and boundaries. The commissions are expected to give consideration to factors other than numerical equality. Within each nation local government boundaries are usually respected. The determination of parliamentary representation for the four parts of the kingdom, independently of simple population considerations, results in national quotas favoring Scotland and Wales as against England and Northern Ireland. At the 1970 general election the average constituency in England had 64,064 electors; in Wales, 54,410 electors; in Scotland, 51,112 electors; in Northern Ireland, 85,766.

Northern Ireland is underrepresented at Westminster in proportion to its population because of the substantial powers delegated to its own parliament. Overrepresentation of Wales and Scotland arises from a desire to have a fixed national quota of MPs for these two nations, without regard to any change in the distribution of population within the United Kingdom. Scotland has had seventy-one MPs since 1918 and Northern Ireland twelve. Wales went from thirty-five to thirty-six MPs in 1950. Marginal adjustments in the size of the House of Commons primarily involve adjustments for population growth in English constituencies. In addition the Scottish Highlands enjoys a persisting benefit because the boundary commissioners dislike creating constituencies large in land area; the Highlands constituencies tend to be among the smallest in electors (cf. Starzinger, 1965). Underpopulated constituencies are also found in major cities, including London, where slum clearance and change of land use have caused a decline in once-crowded urban neighbourhoods. Abnormally large constituencies are usually found in suburban areas, where those who leave city centers have found homes. As the time since redistribution increases, the disparities in constituency size increase. In 1970, fifteen years since the last redistribution, the standard deviation in the size of English constituencies was 15,897; ten had more than 100,000 electors and four had less than 30,000. The failure of the Labour government to enact new constituency boundaries prior to the 1970 general election, notwithstanding the presentation of recommendations from boundary commissioners, brought a charge of gerrymandering. The best estimate is that the changes recommended by the nonpartisan boundary commissioners would have increased the Conservative majority by eleven, had they been put into effect before the 1970 general election. (See Steed, 1971, p. 415; Cf. Rose, 1967, p. 206.)

The responsibility for seeing that every person eligible to vote is duly registered rests with local government officials, working under the supervision of the Home Office (Leonard, 1968, pp. 12ff). The registration officers annually circularize every household in October, requesting a household member to return a registration form on behalf of every person there. Deletions and additions are then checked officially, and there are opportunities for the public to inspect and amend the register. The new register comes into effect in mid-February for a twelve-month period. Government studies estimate that about 4 percent of persons technically eligible have their name omitted from the register. This group includes a disproportionate number of persons recently of voting age, those who have moved during the year, lodgers, and immigrants. After the lowering of the voting age to eighteen in 1969, from one-third to two-fifths of eligible young voters were not registered in 1970 because of unfamiliarity with the new law (Butler and Pinto-Duschinsky, 1971, p. 263). There is no persisting discrimination; an individual unregistered at one election is unlikely to remain off the register for a period of years (cf. Gray & Gee, 1967). About 1 percent of the electorate is registered to vote at more than one address: it is illegal for such persons to vote more than once.

Election day is not a legal holiday, nor does the law guarantee employed persons time off to vote. The polls are open from 7 A.M. until 10 P.M. Polling stations are numerous; given the high degree of urbanization in Britain, distance from a polling booth is no problem to the overwhelming mass of electors. Persons unable to vote in person may claim a postal or proxy ballot if they are servicemen, employed away from home, have moved, or are ill. At the 1970 general election 2.1 percent of the total vote was cast by post. This vote favors the Conservatives, since their middle-class supporters are more amenable to filling in forms to claim a vote, and Conservative party organizers are more efficient in encouraging individuals to claim a postal ballot. The Conservatives usually hold six to a dozen seats in the Commons by virtue of their superiority in organizing the postal vote (cf. Butler and Pinto-Duschinsky, 1971, pp. 331–32).

Measurement of turnout at a general election is complicated by the inevitable aging of the electoral register during each year. Death removes some voters. The movement of population within and between cities creates difficulties in voting for some electors.

Moreover, persons on holiday are not authorized to claim a postal vote. The register issued in mid-February is already four and one-half months out of date from the time of compilation in October, and it continues to decline in accuracy. It is estimated that by the time it is replaced about 11 percent of persons named will have moved within or outside the constituency (Gray and Gee, 1967). It follows from this that the official count of the number of electors can be reduced by about .67 percent per month, starting from October in the year before an election is held, in order to produce the best adjusted estimate of turnout. The mean unadjusted turnout in eight post-war elections is 78.1 percent; the mean adjusted turnout is 82.4 percent (Craig, 1971, p. 47-48). Turnout has varied from a high adjusted figure of 88.4 percent in 1951 to 75.1 percent in 1970.

TABLE 5: **Turnout at General Elections, 1950–1970**

Election	Unadjusted %	Adjusted %
1950	83.9	83.9
1951	82.6	88.4
1955	76.8	83.2
1959	78.7	85.0
1964	77.1	83.3
1966	75.8	77.4
1970	72.0	75.1

Adjusted turnout = Unadjusted turnout divided by the sum of $100\% + 3.4\%$ (not registered) $- 1.0\%$ (registered twice) $- 0.15$m (effect of death) $- 0.67$m (removals); m=months from the date of compilation of the register, as reported in Craig, 1971, p. 47.

The distinctive British contribution to the literature of electoral behavior is the study of election campaigns by a mixture of firsthand observation, interviews with campaigners, institutional analysis, and the use of descriptive statistics to analyze constituency results. Since 1945 a study of each general election has been prepared at Nuffield College, Oxford (see McCallum and Readman, 1947; H. G. Nicholas, 1951; D. E. Butler, 1952 et seq.). David Butler has been associated with the research since its inception (cf. Butler, 1968; Rose, 1966). These eclectic studies conveniently provide information about single elections as seen through the eyes of contemporary participants and observers; the appendices provide more detailed analyses of results. No attempt has been made to cumulate the findings of these single-election studies. The technique has been adapted to many countries outside the Western world as well as within (cf. Butler, 1959; Mackenzie and Robinson, 1960). The word "psephology" has been coined to describe these studies (Butler, 1952, p. 1). The term "psephos" refers to the study of aggregate election results. It is derived from the Greek word for pebble (the Greeks voted by dropping pebbles in an urn), and remains the most characteristic form of studying electoral behavior in Britain. (For a full bibliography see Rose, 1969, pp.415–20; Butler and Cornford, 1969 and the references to this chapter.)

The ecological study of election results has been handicapped in Britain by the aggregation of votes from a number of polling districts into a single constituency return. This practice was introduced in the nineteenth-century to increase confidence in the secrecy of the ballot at a time when electorates were much smaller. A second limitation is the lack of fit between constituency boundaries and units for which census data are reported. In response to requests from political and academic groups 1966 census tables were published for each constituency (*Census 1966*, 1969). This material has begun to be used for multivariate aggregate analysis of the 1970 election results (see, e.g., Crewe and Payne, 1971). Aggregate analysis of electoral data is possible for earlier general elections: problems of fitting boundaries for election and census data can be overcome with specialist knowledge (see, e.g., Cox, 1967; Cox, 1970). In the period before the secret ballot was introduced poll books were published for a number of constituencies, showing how each voter cast his ballot (cf. Vincent, 1967).

Nationwide sample surveys of voting preferences have been undertaken by public-opinion polls in Britain since the foundation of the Gallup Poll in 1938. The largest single repository of survey data on British voting is the Gallup file at the Roper Center for Opinion Research, Williamstown, Massachusetts (cf. Alford, 1963). Other organizations regularly publishing opinion polls in the national press include National Opinion Polls, begun in 1959, Opinion Research Center, beginning in 1965; and Louis Harris Research, since 1969. Marplan conducted quarterly surveys for *The Times* in the period up to the 1970 general election. In addition Research Services has intermittently published surveys of political attitudes for two decades. Surveys usually involve from 1,000 to 2,500 interviews; some organizations use quota samples, others use random samples, and some use both methods alternatively. All surveys but Marplan take Great Britain as their universe; Northern Ireland is excluded because of its distinctive political situation.

The 1970 British general election was a setback for the polls because four of the five published polls incorrectly predicted a Labour victory. The average error in estimating the margin between the two parties was 6.7 percent. In the three previous elections the average error of the polls in estimating the gap was 1.4 percent, with no error in naming the victor. By comparison, postelection academic surveys by Butler and Stokes have had errors in estimating the gap of 3.0 percent in 1964 and 4.8 percent in 1966 (see Rose, 1970, pp. 60ff). While the degree of error involved in a sample survey may be crucial in forecasting which party wins a highly competitive British election, it is of very limited concern in an analysis of major social characteristics of voters.

The only nationwide voting survey undertaken by university-based researchers has been the joint Nuffield College-University of Michigan panel survey of British voters, directed by D. E. Butler and Donald Stokes, involving interviews with a panel of voters in 1963, 1964, 1966, 1969 and 1970. The principal publication is *Political Change in Britain* (1969). Data from the first three surveys are available in machine-readable form to members of the Inter-University Consortium for Political Research, Ann Arbor, Michigan. In 1966 a nationwide survey of MPs' and candidates' views of electioneering was conducted by Richard Rose and Dennis Kavanagh (see Kavanagh, 1970). Other nationwide surveys with materials especially relevant to electoral studies include *The Civic Culture* study in 1959 by Almond and Verba (1963) and W.G. Runciman's study of social stratification (1966). Special studies of middle-class voters (Bonham, 1954) and working-class voters (Rose, 1968) involved secondary analysis of nationwide samples, as did a study of young voters by Abrams and Little (1965) and a pioneering comparative study by Alford (1963). In addition special studies of working-class voters, based upon samples from a few areas, have been undertaken by McKenzie and Silver (1968); Nordlinger (1967); and Goldthorpe, Lockwood et al. (1968). A study by Rose & Mossawir (1967) examined attitudes toward voting and elections of respondents in a single constituency. Constituency surveys have been published in book-length or journal-article form for every election but one since 1950. Especially noteworthy are studies concentrating upon the effect of television (Trenaman and McQuail, 1961; Blumler and McQuail, 1968) and a panel study of voting change between 1959 and 1964 (Benewick et al., 1969). Goodhart and Bhansali (1970) have related results from monthly opinion polls to aggregate economic data in order to develop a model of the political consequences of fluctuations in the economy.

Party preference is measured by asking an individual how he intends to vote at the next election, or if a general election occurred tomorrow. Voting intentions are subject to substantial fluctuations between election campaigns. For instance the proportion stating an intention to vote Labour fluctuated between 55.0 and 31.5 percent in NOP monthly surveys between the 1966 and 1970 elections, and between 53.5 and 28.0 percent in Gallup monthly surveys. These fluctuations are also borne out by the discrepancy between by-election and local-election votes and general-election results (cf. Craig, 1971, p. 43; Rose, 1970). The reasons for these fluctuations are explicable (see, e.g., King, 1968; Goodhart and Bhansali, 1970). This does nevertheless mean that a survey in an interelection period is likely to give a profile of partisanship somewhat different from the pattern prevailing at general elections. For example, the 1963 Butler-Stokes survey found Conservative strength 6.0 percent below that shown at the general election the following year.

Measuring voting by asking a respondent what he did at the last election held is less subject to fluctuation. For example, Gallup Poll questions put shortly before the 1970 general election showed a recalled 1966 preference deviating only 1.2 percent and 3.8 percent, respectively, from the true Conservative and Labour totals. Butler and Stokes found that in aggregate the recalled 1959 preferences of respondents interviewed in 1963 deviated an average of 2.9 percent from the true result. Reliance upon reported past voting has two weaknesses: it does not give evidence about persons who have entered the electorate since the previous election, and there is a tendency for some voters to alter their recollected vote. Efforts to measure partisanship by asking individuals the party they identify with have proven of little use in Britain. The simplicity of party and electoral systems means there is virtually no distinction between party identification and voting preference. In 1964 92 percent of persons identifying with the Conservative party voted for it, 5 percent voted Liberal, and 2 percent voted Labour. Among Labour identifiers 93 percent voted Labour, 4 percent Liberal, and 2 percent Conservative (Butler-Stokes, 1964).[3]

It is difficult to locate and analyze Liberal supporters by means of nationwide surveys. The proportion of Liberals in the electorate is limited in number, yielding relatively few cases even in a large sample. For example only seventy-five of the 2,009 persons interviewed in the 1963 Butler-Stokes study identified themselves as Liberals, though the party was relatively popular at this time. Problems of definition and measurement are also substantial. Because the Liberals are imperfectly national, contesting only about half the constituencies, one may define an individual as a Liberal if he actually casts a ballot for a Liberal candidate or if he states a desire to do so if the Liberals field a candidate in his constituency. No firm statement can be made about the proportion of the electorate that will have a chance to vote Liberal at a general election until nominations close ten days before the ballot. The attractive power of the Liberal party also depends in part upon the pattern of contest in a constituency. Liberal candidates appear to draw strength disproportionately from persons who would otherwise support the weaker of the two major parties. In Labour seats they thus draw disproportionate support from the Conservatives, and vice versa. In addition some who regard the Liberals as their first choice might vote for one of the two major parties rather than "waste" their vote where a Liberal has not chance of election.

There is considerable movement in and out of the category of Liberal supporters. The 1970 Gallup studies found that nearly half of 288 persons who reported a Liberal vote in 1966 intended to support another party in 1970, a rate of defection three times that of Labour and nine times that of the Conservatives. Reciprocally, of the 410 persons who reported a Liberal preference in 1970, only 36 percent said that they had voted Liberal in 1966—19 percent had supported Labour, and 11 percent the Conservatives. The remainder came from the ranks of young voters or former nonvoters. When Liberal supporters were asked what they would do if forced to make a choice between Conservative and Labour candidates (which would happen in the absence of a Liberal candidate), 34 percent said they would vote Conservative and 34 percent Labour; the rest would not vote. There is no certainty, however, that this pattern is consistent. In 1964 Butler and Stokes (1969, p. 333) found that the majority of Liberals with a second preference favored the Conservatives, and in 1966, Labour. The substantive consequence of these fluctuations is limited by the slight importance of Liberal seats in the House of Commons. Their potential for parliamentary strength under a proportional-representation or single-transferable vote form of election would be much greater (cf. Williams, 1967; Butler, Stevens, and Stokes, 1969).

Floating voters, the complement of loyal partisans, can be defined by more than one form of movement from the ranks of a loyal partisan (cf. Miller, 1972; Milne and Mackenzie, 1969). If floating means no more than failure to turn out and vote for the party favored, then loyalty is measured by readiness to vote as well as by party preference. At the other extreme an individual might be characterized as a floating voter only if he crossed lines and voted Labour if previously Conservative, or Conservative if previously Labour. This would assume that an individual temporarily moving to the Liberal party was as likely to return to his party of origin as to continue to lapse, a not unjustifiable assumption (Butler and Stokes, 1969, pp. 337-38). A significant number cannot be consistent in their behavior; these are persons coming of age and voters dying between any pair of elections. According to Butler and Stokes (1969, tables 12.6 and 12.7) less than two-thirds of the electorate votes (or abstains) in an identical way in successive general elections.

Probably the simplest criterion to use in assessing floating voters is to consider whether an individual has moved from one major party to another between two general elections. Notwithstanding the large turnover in seats between the 1966 and 1970 general elections, only a small fraction of individuals—7.1 percent—switched their votes between major parties (Table 6). Yet relatively small changes in votes can have major political consequences. In 1970 most of the Conservative gain in votes from 1966 was netted by the conversion of voters from Labour to Conservative ranks. What Labour gained in support among younger voters was offset by the lesser readiness of 1966 Labour supporters to turn out to vote for that party again. The sense of individual continuity is strong throughout a political lifetime. In a 1963 survey 75 percent *claimed* that they had always voted for the same party (Butler and Stokes, 1964).

TABLE 6: **Movement of Votes Between the Parties, 1966–70, in Percentages**

	(1966 Vote)		
	Con.	Lab.	Lib.
(1970 Vote)			
Conservative	95.1	12.4	25.8
Labour	3.6	85.3	20.5
Liberals	1.4	2.3	53.7

Source: 1970 Gallup survey.

The definition and location of nonvoters in sample surveys also present difficulties. A disproportionate number of nonvoters are persons who have moved after the electoral register was compiled, or are persons whose names have been omitted from the register (cf. Gray and Gee, 1967; Gray, 1970). Moreover, some persons who do not vote are likely to state an intention to vote in advance of polling day, or claim they have done so afterward. In 1970 75 percent of Gallup Poll respondents stated that they definitely would vote and another 11 percent stated that they probably would vote. Only 5 percent stated that they definitely would not vote. There appears to be no consistent party bias in nonvoting. According to postelection surveys in 1964 and 1970, nonvoters were most likely to be Labour sympathizers; in 1966, it was Conservatives (cf. Rose, 1970, pp. 29, 36; Butler and Stokes, 1969, pp. 289-90). In each instance differential turnout created an advantage of about 1 percent for the favored party.

The proportion of British people who refuse to state a party preference is extremely low. In 1970 95.3 percent of persons questioned by the Gallup Poll stated a party preference or inclination. In addition another 2.3 percent were honest don't-knows, for they readily volunteered a description of what they had done at the 1966 general election; another 2.0 percent can be considered persistent nonvoters, for they reported abstaining in 1966 too. Only 0.3 percent gave a pair of evasive answers, stating they could not remember how they voted in 1966 and could give no preference for the 1970 general election.

The principal survey data used in this study of British voting consist of four large nationwide samples by the Gallup Poll in the four weeks before the 1970 general election. As is customary in British samples, Northern Ireland was excluded. The four samples aggregated here were stratified by region, constituency type, and percentage Labour majority, with quotas for respondents set within each constituency on the basis of sex, age, and occupation (cf. *Election 70*, 1970, pp. 25-27; Bluff, 1971). While quota samples do not conform to requirements for statistical significance tests, they do avoid the difficulties arising from substantial nonresponse rates, problems that have marred several major British surveys, (cf. Almond and Verba, 1963, p. 518). The Gallup surveys combine a questionnaire that is broad in scope, containing measures of nearly all social characteristics of theoretical interest here, with a size—9,634 cases— that permits multivariate statistical tests far more elaborate than would be possible with sample sizes conventionally employed in academic studies. A similar analysis of 1964 Gallup data from two random samples provides a basis for cross-checking, as do results from 1966 Gallup surveys (cf. Rose, 1968a; *Election 70*, 1970, pp. 27-39; Gallup Poll, 1969). The ready availability in published form of a variety of constituency surveys and of the Butler and Stokes study makes it unnecessary to collate in the following pages the findings of many different studies.

In analyzing the 1970 Gallup surveys respondents have been divided into three groups—Conservatives, Labour, and Others—depending upon their answers to the question, "If you vote, which candidate will you support?" In response to this question 88.5 percent immediately volunteered a party preference, and after one probe an additional 6.8 percent named a party that they were inclined to support; these two groups have been combined to identify partisans. Of those in the Other category, 43 percent indicated Liberal sympathies and another 47 percent were don't-knows. Because the Other sympathizers are heterogeneous they will not be intensively analyzed. The characteristics of Liberals and don't-knows are presented so that one can see to what extent a change in support for one of the major parties is asymmetrical, i.e., does not create a complementary change in the other major party but a shift in the ranks of the Other voters. The four aggregated 1970 Gallup surveys place Labour ahead by 4.5 percent in Great Britain. There is no evidence that the persons who swung to the Conservatives at the last minute of the 1970 campaign so differed from a cross section of the electorate as to affect conclusions about continuing relationships between social structure and party loyalties (cf. Rose, 1970). Hence the data have been weighted so that the proportions of Conservative, Labour, and Other voters exactly reproduce those given by the 1970 election results. The weights used were: Conservatives, 1.09; Labour, 0.94; Others, 0.89. The tables reported here from the 1970 Gallup surveys are thus based upon a total weighted number of 9,611 cases.

IV. Social Structure and Voting

The familiar statement, "Class is the basis of British party politics; all else is embellishment and detail" (Pulzer, 1967, p. 98), argues the importance of controlling for class in any analysis of voting behavior. Yet one must still consider how classes are defined, how many classes exist in Britain, and how strong an influence class is upon voting behavior. Prima facie, class is not totally deterministic, because Labour, the party of the majority class, the manual workers, has failed to win a majority of the elections it contests. The proposition also leaves unclear whether class is the only ascertainable influence upon voting, or whether it is the most important among several influences.

Class is usually defined in Britain by a single attribute—the occupation of the head of the household in which a respondent lives, whether the head is the individual himself or a relative. If a person is retired, then the former occupation of the head of the household is used. The use of a single measure avoids the problems of weighting arising from attempts to devise a composite status measure employing several social and economic indicators. Moreover, comparison is facilitated between surveys because most British researchers seek to stratify people in terms of the same attribute, occupation. The basic class distinction is between manual workers, i.e., the working-class, and nonmanual workers, i.e., the middle-class. The number of people who are upper-class, i.e., rentiers living on income and/or persons with inherited titles, is too few to show significant numbers in a nationwide sample—though sufficiently prominent historically to merit separate analysis in studies of political recruitment (cf. Guttsman, 1963). Because agriculture is unimportant in a society as industrialized as Britain, there is no need to provide a separate classification for farmers. Farm owners or managers can be assigned to the middle-class, and farm laborers to the working-class.

Any discussion of systems of classification inevitably stresses the complexities of the operation and the difficulty of resolving questions about marginal cases. Given the interest of sociologists in the nuances of class structure in England, a large literature has arisen about criteria for assigning people to different occupational categories (see, e.g., Runciman, 1966; Stacey et al., 1969). What is striking is the extent to which differently labeled schema converge in their findings: about one-third of the population is assigned to the middle-class and two-thirds to the working-class, after a handful of unclassifiable individuals are excluded. Differences between the proportions placed in these two categories in nationwide surveys are usually no greater than what one would expect from sampling fluctuation (cf. Rose, 1968a, table 17). A survey undertaken in a single constituency or community may differ from this national average because of local and regional variations in occupational structure.

In addition to dichotomizing the population between manual and nonmanual occupations, every stratification scheme also differentiates occupational categories within the middle-class and the working-class. Probably the most widely used classification scheme, that of the Institute of Practitioners of Advertising (cf. Market Research Society, 1963), divides the population into three middle-class and three working-class strata:

Middle-Class	A:	Professional, higher managerial, or administrative workers.
	B:	Intermediate managerial, administrative, or professional workers.
	C1:	Clerical, supervisors and junior managerial, administrative, or professional workers.
Working-Class	C2:	Skilled manual workers.
	D:	Semiskilled and unskilled manual workers.
	E:	Casual workers; persons dependent on welfare payments; pensioners.

The labels admit ambiguity in the intermediate categories of clerical workers (C1) and skilled manual workers (C2). Butler and Stokes found a paradox among their stratum analogous to C1 respondents, a category they labeled routine nonmanual workers. Although 68 percent of these respondents identified themselves as working-class, 61 percent also stated that they favored the Conservatives (1969, Tables 4.3, 4.8). In a study of political behavior it would seem most reasonable to resolve ambiguities by assigning such a doubtful group to the same stratum as supervisory nonmanual workers because of a similarity of party preference. Instead, without further discussion this group was assigned to the working-class. As it forms but one-tenth of the sample, this only marginally affects the subsequent analysis. In this chapter all analyses of Butler-Stokes data have assigned this marginal group to the middle-class.

The object in any scheme of classification is to elaborate categories in which important attributes tend to be similar for all within the group and different from those in other groups. Hence the number of classes used for intensive analysis here is determined by party sympathies in the six strata reported in Gallup surveys (see Table 7).

The analysis employs two groups within the middle-class, an upper-middle-class category of professional and businessmen, where Conservative sympathies are very strong, and a lower-middle-class category in which Conservative supporters are a majority, but not an overwhelming majority. By contrast none of the three working-class groups differs substantially from each other. Labour enjoys majority support in each category, and there is a clear-cut division between the party preferences of the lower-middle-class and the stratum immediately below, the skilled working-class. Because of the size of the surveys for analysis, each of the three class groups is large; the smallest, the upper-middle-class category, contains 1,419 respondents.

Table 7 confirms, as has every previous nationwide survey in Britain, the relationship between occupational class and party preference. But three important qualifications must be made. The first is that a proportion of the electorate has no party preference or a Liberal preference. A partially misleading picture of the political profile of a class can be given if only supporters of the two major parties are considered (cf. Butler and Stokes, 1969, e.g., table 4.8). Within the working-class this group of nonaligned voters almost prevents Labour from being the party of a majority of

TABLE 7 : Occupational Class and Partisanship, in Percentages

Totals			Con	Lab	Other	Difference Con–Lab
	Upper-Middle-Class					
2	A :	Professional	76	18	6	+58
13	B :	Businessmen	69	23	8	+46
		Total	70	22	8	+48
	Lower-Middle-Class					
22	Cl :	Office workers	54	37	9	+17
	Working-Class					
32	C2:	Skilled	40	50	10	−10
24	D :	Semi and unskilled	35	54	11	−19
7	E :	Welfare recipients	36	51	13	−15
			38	51	11	−13

workers. As it is, Labour's relative advantage over the Conservatives does not make it absolutely strong. The second qualification is that the relationship between class and party preference is asymmetrical. The middle-class is more strongly Conservative than the working-class is Labour; the most homogeneous occupational category is also the highest ranking. A third qualification follows from this: the relationship between class and party is partial rather than complete.

One way to resolve the problem of categorizing people by social classes is to ask individuals to assess their class subjectively. The Gallup survey did this by asking, "If you had to say which social-class you belong to, what would you say?" The five alternatives listed in Table 8 were then read out to each respondent. The use of this forced-choice response to a question from a stranger has substantial theoretical justification, if class is defined in terms of individual status in interpersonal relations (cf. Marshall, 1950, p. 92). In all, 52 percent of the respondents described themselves as working-class, 48 percent in one of three middle-class categories, and 0.4 percent as upper-class. The Butler-Stokes study produced a substantially higher estimate of subjective working-class identification (1969, ch. 4). This is apparently a consequence of the question used; it has not been replicated by other surveys measuring subjective class assessment in Britain (cf. Rose, 1965a, p. 73; Runciman, 1966). Two-thirds of those placed in the working-class by virtue of their occupaton also placed themselves there; similarly, two-thirds, of lower-middle-class respondents gave themselves a middle-class status, as did 87 percent of those in the upper-middle-class. There were more working-class people who upgraded themselves than middle-class people who downgraded themselves. In all, 30 percent of respondents showed inconsistencies cutting across the manual/nonmanual line between objective and subjective classifications.

TABLE 8 : **Subjective Class* and Partisanship, in Percentages**

	Con	Lab	Other	Total
Upper-Middle-Class				
Upper-middle	81	13	6	2
Middle	72	20	4	9
Lower-middle	66	24	9	2
Working	53	38	9	2
Lower-Middle-Class				
Upper-middle	62	28	10	1
Middle	64	27	9	9
Lower-middle	55	34	10	5
Working	39	52	9	7
Working-Class				
Upper-middle	63	28	9	1
Middle	53	38	9	13
Lower-middle	49	39	12	7
Working	31	58	11	43

* Upper-class responses omitted because of the paucity of cases.

The relationship between objective and subjective class meets expectations. Persons who are consistently manual or nonmanual in both schema are more likely to support the class-typical party. The higher the self-rating a person gives himself, e.g., upper-middle-class rather than middle-class, the more likely he is to favor the Conservatives. Notwithstanding the consistent rise in Conservative support within the strata of the middle-class, there are always bigger differences between those in the lowest category of the subjective middle-class and people who think of themselves as workers, than there are between those in the bottom and top of middle-class subjective rankings. With subjective class, as with occupational class rankings, there is an asymmetry of influence. Those who identify with the middle-class are more likely to favor the Conservatives than those who identify with the working-class are to favor Labour.

The imperfect correlation of occupational class and partisanship could occur if occupation is not the best economic measure of class. For example, income might be a better measure of social position. While Gallup surveys do not record income figures, such data are available in a variety of political studies of the 1960s. All confirm that there is no consistent tendency within a class for partisanship to alter with rising income (cf. Runciman, 1966, p. 172; Goldthorpe, Lockwood et al., 1967; Nordlinger, 1967, pp. 153ff; McKenzie and Silver, 1968, p. 84; Butler-Stokes, 1964; Bechhofer, 1971).

One difficulty in measuring class by income is that family needs differ greatly according to the size of a family and its stage in the life cycle. A family with young children will have to make its income cover more needs than a working couple without children or with one or two children at work. The use to which respondents choose to put what income they have is an indication of life-style opportunities and preferences. Hence differences in consumption patterns within classes may be a better predictor of voting than income differences. Because of the saturation coverage of British households by television this is not a discriminating influence. But automobiles and telephones are not pervasive goods in Britain. Owning a car may be considered a sign of affluence; a vehicle also makes an individual independent of collective forms of public transport and enables him to explore environments apart from his immediate face-to-face neighborhood (M. Abrams, 1959). Having a telephone indicates that an individual relates easily to others at a distance; he is not confined in a network of face-to-face relationships. In both cases increasing independence of face-to-face ties would be expected to weaken class influences upon voting, especially in the working-class, where a substantial degree of face-to-face communal solidarity is often considered a precondition for strong Labour support.

A consistent relationship between consumption patterns and party preferences appears in Table 9. Within each class families with more consumer goods are more conservative. In three out of four possible comparisons the better-off group in a lower-class is likely to be more conservative than the less prosperous group in the class immediately above it. The finding is not unique to the 1970 general election. It also held true in 1964 (cf. Rose, 1968a, table 18). In other words voters with more consumer goods tend toward the Conservatives, whether or not they are in government at the time (cf. Goodhart and Bhansali, 1970, p. 79). It is not clear from the data if this relationship reflects the material prosperity of these with more consumption goods, or whether a more individualistic and less collectivistic outlook leads individuals to favor more consumer goods and the more "individualistic" Conservative party. (Cf. Runciman, 1966, ch. 2, on egoistic and fraternalistic values.) Theoretically, the finding is also important because it questions the assertion of Goldthorpe, Lockwood et al. (1968) that affluent workers remain pro-Labour because of status differences with the middle-class. Given the small size of the Goldthorpe, Lockwood sample (*ibid.*, pp. 4-5, 84-86) of affluent workers (N=229), the Gallup findings are more reliable.

Education is another social characteristic often considered an important correlate of class (Converse, 1973, pp. 730f). Some sociologists might argue that it is the chief determinant of class position and thus, indirectly, of party preference. Moreover, insofar as education is influenced by parent's class, it is possible for intergenerational influences upon education also to affect party preferences. In Britain compulsory schooling stopped at age eleven before 1918, at age fourteen until 1945, and then at age fifteen.[4] Hence there is a substantial difference between the minimum the state requires and the maximum obtainable at a university. A minimum education may be defined as any education ending at age fourteen until 1945 and at age fifteen thereafter. Youths staying on at school usually sit one examination at age sixteen, with a portion then leaving school. Others will continue to work for university entrance qualifications.

TABLE 9 : **Consumption Styles and Partisanship, in Percentages**

	Con	Lab	Other	Total
CAR OWNERSHIP				
Upper-middle-class				
Two cars	81	12	7	3
One car	71	22	7	9
No car	57	33	11	3
Lower-middle-class				
Two cars	68	23	9	2
One car	55	35	10	12
No car	49	42	9	8
Working-class				
Two cars	45	43	11	2
One car	44	46	10	27
No car	33	56	11	35
TELEPHONE				
Upper-middle-class				
Yes	76	18	6	10
No	58	31	11	5
Lower-middle-class				
Yes	63	29	7	13
No	48	42	10	9
Working-Class				
Yes	55	36	9	11
No	35	54	11	53

Those who succeed will remain in further education until the age of twenty-one. Only about five percent of the electorate has continued into university education or its equivalent. The content of education is directly related to length of attendance; the longer the time an adult has spent at school, the more academic his education will be (cf. Weinberg, 1969). The proportion of the electorate attending university or public schools (i.e., fee-paying private secondary schools) is so limited that significant numbers are rarely found in national sample surveys. Nevertheless, this group is disproportionately prominent within the House of Commons (cf. Rose, 1968, p. 154). Changes in the structure of secondary education introduced in 1965 affect a limited but increasing proportion of youths (cf. Tapper, 1971). It will of course take decades before the youths affected by the reform of secondary education constitute a majority of the electorate.

Because more education implies a higher social status, one might expect that within each class more education would increase the probability of a person favoring the Conservative party. However, some people experience inconsistency between their educational background and their current occupational status: they may be middle-class yet without further education, or working-class with education "above" their occupational standing. In either or both situation one might expect individuals to react distinctively, with downwordly mobile persons becoming more Labour and up-wardly mobile middle-class people more Tory than those for whom education and occupation are consistent. The data in Table 10 do not support these hypotheses. In all three strata there is a consistent tendency for those with the least education to be the

TABLE 10 : Education and Partisanship, in Percentages

	Con	Lab	Other	Total
Upper-Middle-class				
Further	71	20	8	6
Intermediate	72	21	7	5
Minimum	66	27	8	4
Lower-Middle-Class				
Further	58	34	8	5
Intermediate	59	31	9	7
Minimum	48	42	10	10
Working-Class				
Further	53	34	13	4
Intermediate	44	46	9	14
Minimum	35	54	11	46

Further education=At school age seventeen or above; minimum=left school age fourteen or younger before 1945, and age fifteen from 1945 onwards. Intermediate education is that received by those age sixteen or fifteen to sixteen, depending upon year of birth.

most likely to favor Labour. The most educated middle-class voters, however, are slightly less likely to favor the Conservatives than are those with an intermediate qua-lification. While the percentage differences are small, they are consistent with other research findings (cf. Rose, 1965a, p. 69; Rose, 1968a, Table 7; Butler-Stokes, 1964). Higher education, unlike intermediate education, involves a greater break from the home environment, placing young people in a more cosmopolitan educational milieu, where a wide variety of political outlooks are discussed and considered acceptable.

This influence would work in opposite directions upon children from middle-class and working-class homes (cf. Jackson & Marsden, 1962, p. 174).

Trade-union membership is another correlate of class, both in social theory and in the ideology of the Labour movement. In the picturesque phrase of the late Ernest Bevin, a leading trade unionist and cabinet minister, the Labour party grew out of the bowels of the trade-union movement. In 1970 the Trades Union Congress reported a membership of 10 million members, approximately 40 percent of the total labor force. About three-fifths of this membership are formally affiliated by union headquarters as members of the Labour party. In survey research respondents are frequently asked whether they or the head of their household is a member of a union, in order to avoid treating housewives whose husbands belong to unions as if they were remote from this part of the Labour movement. In 1970 Gallup surveys estimated that 40 percent of the population was in a family with at least one trade-union member.

There is a consistent tendency within each class for individuals belonging to a trade union to favor the Labour party (Table 11). Unionized lower-middle-class voters are as likely to be Labour as Conservative; reciprocally, among manual workers nonunionists are as likely to be Conservative as Labour. Personal involvement in

TABLE 11 : **Trade-Union Membership and Partisanship, in Percentages**

	Con	Lab	Other	Total
Upper-Middle-Class				
Member	58	32	10	3
Nonmember	73	20	7	12
Lower-Middle-Class				
Member	45	46	9	6
Nonmember	57	33	10	16
Working-Class				
Member	31	60	9	31
Nonmember	44	44	12	33

union activities at a place of work is not required for union membership to be influential. Within a given class wives of union members are much more likely to favor Labour than are the wives of men who are not in unions. In short, union membership is an indicator that a family is inclined to be a Labour household. Butler and Stokes argue (1969, pp. 151ff) that there is a reciprocal influence between union membership and Labour party sympathies. Some people join unions, they suggest, because they come from Labour families; it is family partisanship that makes them prounion and not vice versa. The proportion of manual workers who have the option whether or not to join a union is, however, greatly limited by the spread of compulsory union membership agreements. Moreover, as unionization in Britain antedates the development of the Labour party by about two generations, the causal connection is most likely to be historically from union membership—whether voluntary or compulsory—to Labour sympathy, and not vice versa. Notwithstanding this, nearly one-third of working-class trade unionists support the Conservatives.

The significance of organization membership independent of class is difficult to assess because of the relative size and strength of trade unions as organizations. Politically, the most important point to note is that the strength of trade unions and, formerly, of retail cooperative societies provides an opportunity for manual workers almost everywhere in Britain to join and become active in organizations that are specifically for their class. As these organizations are linked to the Labour party locally as well as at the national level, this encourages the diffusion of pro-Labour views through extra party channels. Concurrently, arrangements for sponsoring candidatures by unions and cooperative societies provide more than a hundred safe seats in the House of Commons for working-class candidates (cf. Harrison, 1960).

Party membership figures are difficult to evaluate because party membership is not defined as clearly in practice as it is in theory. Only 2 percent report themselves active campaign workers for a political party, and 14 percent as dues-paying members (cf. Butler and Stokes, 1969, pp. 25, 421; see also Butler and Pinto-Duschinsky, 1971, ch. 11). The chief source of data about membership in organizations other than unions, churches, and parties is that collected in *The Civic Culture* survey of Britain in 1959 (Almond and Verba, 1963, ch. 11). Reanalysis of these data shows that organizational members—47 percent of those interviewed—differed little from nonmembers in their partisanship. A total of 57 percent of middle-class members were Conservatives and 64 percent of nonmembers. In the working-class 54 percent of members were Labour and 49 percent of nonmembers.

The press is difficult to treat as an independent influence because of the correlation between class and newspaper readership. Do individuals choose newspapers because they accord with their prior political outlook, or do they take their political preferences from the papers that they read? A third alternative is that party preferences are independent of media preferences, with class differences in newspaper readership causing spurious correlations between partisanship and readership. The concentration of daily newspaper circulation in four popular and four quality dailies circulating nationwide in about four-fifths of British homes limits the field requiring analysis. While each of these papers tends to favor one of the two major parties, this support is by no means consistent or unequivocal; none is owned by a political party. (Cf. Seymour-Ure, 1968; Butler and Freeman, 1969.)

The pattern of replies in Table 11 shows marked within-class differences in partisanship between readers of pro-Conservative papers (*Telegraph*, *Mail*, and *Express*) and pro-Labour papers (*Mirror* and *Sun*). Those who read no paper approximate the profile of party loyalties that would be expected of their class. The relationship is consistent in all classes; it is sufficiently strong to give a Conservative majority among the working-class readers of three pro-Conservative papers, and a Labour majority among middle-class readers of the two Labour papers. The numbers of readers of three quality papers are too small to permit presentation in Table 12. Readers of the Liberal-Labour *Guardian* disproportionately favor Labour; however, readers of *The Times*, an "Establishment" paper, do not favor the Conservatives more than is usual within the middle-class. Butler and Stokes have presented evidence to support the proposition that newspaper choice greatly reflects social values formed early in life, values that also affect party loyalties. In other words the correlation of newspaper readership and partisanship results from a common prior influence. At most the partisanship of the press may reinforce attitudes. This influence by no means favors one party. Similarly, studies of the effect of television upon political outlooks have concluded that viewing politics on television does little to alter basic party loyalties, although it may affect a few more transitory attitudes. (Cf. Trenaman and McQuail, 1961; Blumler and McQuail, 1968; BBC Audience Research, 1970.)

TABLE 12 :   **Readership of the National Daily Press and Partisanship, in Percentages**

	Con	Lab	Other	Total
Upper-Middle-Class				
Telegraph	82	13	6	4
Mail	78	15	7	2
Express	77	16	6	5
Mirror	52	40	7	2
Sun	40	53	7	1
None	62	25	13	1
Lower-Middle-Class				
Telegraph	71	21	8	3
Mail	68	24	8	3
Express	64	27	9	6
Mirror	34	55	11	5
Sun	30	63	7	2
None	52	35	13	3
Working-Class				
Telegraph	73	17	9	2
Mail	57	34	8	6
Express	51	40	9	14
Mirror	27	64	9	24
Sun	23	68	9	8
None	37	47	16	10

The multiplicity of indicators of class, each correlating to some extent with party preference, suggests considering the composite effect of all these indicators. This can be done in a theoretically meaningful way by trying to give empirical content to those ideal-type constructs, the middle-class and working-class voter. An ideal-type worker in Britain would be expected to have a manual occupation and a minimum education, to be in a trade union family, to live in a state-owned council house, and to think of himself as working-class. Reciprocally, a middle-class person would be expected to have more than a minimum of education, not to belong to a union, to live in his own house or a privately rented house, and to think of himself as middle-class. People who have all these ideal characteristics should reflect the maximum influence of class conditions upon party preference.

Because the ideal worker and middle-class voter are theoretical constructs, it is first necessary to consider to what extent individuals in the electorate conform to these stereotypes. In all, a fifth of the Gallup sample conforms to ideal-type figures; of these, 12 percent are pure middle-class as against 9 percent who are pure working-class (Table 13). In other words nearly one-third of the middle-class conforms to a sociological stereotype, but only one-seventh of British manual workers does so. The median

TABLE 13 : **Ideal-Type Class Characteristics and Partisanship, in Percentages**

	Con	Lab	Other	Total
Upper-Middle-Class				
Middle-class characteristics :				
Four	78	15	6	7
Three	67	25	8	5
Two	59	30	10	2
One	40	47	13	0.5
None	—	—	—	—
Lower-Middle-Class				
Middle-class characteristics :				
Four	69	22	9	5
Three	59	31	10	7
Two	47	43	10	6
One	35	57	8	3
None	21	69	10	1
Working-Class				
Working-class characteristics :				
Four	19	73	8	9
Three	29	60	11	21
Two	42	47	11	20
One	59	30	11	10
None	67	21	11	3

manual worker is likely to have only two of the four expected attributes of a worker, whereas the median lower or upper-middle-class person will have three attributes; 46 percent of upper-middle-class people will have all four. Ideal-type manual workers are almost as strongly Labour as their middle-class counterparts are Conservative (Table

13). Greater conformity to stereotype helps explain the consistently greater support for the Conservatives in the middle-class, as compared to Labour support among workers. Reciprocally, it emphasizes the importance of intermediate social groupings. The median British voter has two middle-class characteristics as well as two working-class characteristics besides occupation; this group constitutes 28 percent of the total electorate. In addition another 17 percent has one or no class characteristics that would correlate with their occupation. Together, these cross-pressured or deviant categories constitute nearly half the total electorate.

Community environment may be related to political behavior in two important but different ways. In some situations the environment may create a distinctive influence independent of class. For instance, people living in Scotland or Wales may see British politics differently from persons in England. Alternatively, environment can be important insofar as people with a particular characteristic cluster together, intensifying or otherwise altering individual political behavior. For example, Scots or Welshmen living in England may have a different attitude toward their nationality than if in Scotland or Wales. Such influences can operate independently of class, or where class-related influences are concentrated in one place, the ecological effect may strengthen them.

Because agriculture is of little importance in twentieth-century Britain, there are few constituencies in which the agricultural vote per se could determine election results (cf. Self and Storing, 1962; Howarth, 1969). Moreover, the character of rural areas is not homogeneous in terms of land tenure; factory farming, feudally derived tenancies, and marginal hill farms can all be found within Britain. There is often a difference in character as well as size, however, between rural areas and large cities. In rural areas small communities have centuries of preindustrial history and have been least affected by great population changes consequent to industrialization. "Traditional" values have a greater chance to survive in the countryside, even though some people may be working in a modern environment. (Cf. Stacey, 1960.)

Defining a rural area is difficult because of obsolete administrative boundaries separating otherwise homogeneous clusters of people living in urban-type environments. Administratively defined urban and rural areas can create erroneous classifications because these boundaries were established in the late nineteenth-century, and suburban developments as well as the growth of new urban centers have altered the character of many local authorities. Moreover, the dispersion of industry in Britain is not confined to large cities; for example, coal tends to be mined in villages. The safest practice is to separate out rural areas, the most distinctive part of Britain. The division of towns from cities above 50,000 population in Table 14 is intended to provide an intermediate classification between two polar extremes. The data show that 78 percent of the population are urban dwellers and 59 percent live in larger cities. There is a consistent tendency in each class for rural residents to be more conservative. But rural voters are too few in aggregate and too much like their urban neighbors to form a distinctive voting bloc in Britain.

TABLE 14 :   **Urban/Rural Divisions and Partisanship, in Percentages**

	Con	Lab	Other	Total
Upper-Middle-Class				
Cities above 50,000	68	25	7	9
Cities under 50,000	68	23	9	3
Rural areas	77	15	7	3
Lower-Middle-Class				
Cities above 50,000	51	39	10	13
Cities under 50,000	51	37	12	4
Rural areas	63	30	7	5
Working-Class				
Cities above 50,000	38	53	10	37
Cities under 50,000	37	50	13	13
Rural areas	40	50	10	14

Housing in Britain defines face-to-face communities in a peculiarly distinctive fashion, because one-third of all families are tenants in municipally owned council houses. Council houses are usually grouped together in substantial numbers, thus creating neighborhoods that are readily identifiable as working-class. In 1970, 79 percent of council house tenants were working-class, 17 percent lower-middle-class, and 4 percent upper-middle-class. The political salience of council house tenancy is strength-

---

TABLE 15 :   **Housing and Partisanship, in Percentages**

	Con	Lab	Other	Total
Upper-Middle-Class				
Homeowners	74	19	7	11
Private tenants	55	39	6	2
Council tenants	55	31	13	1
Lower-Middle-Class				
Homeowners	63	29	8	12
Private tenants	48	40	12	4
Council tenants	39	51	10	6
Working-Class				
Homeowners	50	40	10	24
Private tenants	38	50	10	13
Council tenants	27	63	11	26

ened by the fact that tenants have enjoyed subsidized rents. For such tenants an election may be seen as a ballot for Conservative or Labour landlords. The Labour party has hsitorically been identified as favoring low council house rents. Reciprocally, the Conservative party has historically been identified as the party favouring home-ownership.

A clear relationship exists between housing and party preference. A majority of working-class home-owners favor the Conservatives, just as working-class council tenants are the most strongly Labour group. It would be wrong to infer from this that working-class home-owners inevitably live in middle-class surroundings. In parts of England small nineteenth-century terrace houses, sometimes scheduled for slum clearance, may be owned by the manual workers who live in them.

Another indicator of the social character of an area is the political inclination of the constituency. While parliamentary constituencies need not be "natural" social units, it would be rare for a safe Conservative or Labour seat to constitute anything other than a relatively homogeneous middle-class or working-class environment. Reciprocally, marginal seats will be socially mixed. The definition of marginality or safeness of a seat is not rigid (cf. Rasmussen, 1966). Hence the classification used here is a relatively simple one: sets held by less than a 10 percent majority before the 1970 election are considered marginal, and those by greater shares of the vote are considered safe.

The concentration of partisans in a constituency consistently gives the stronger party an extra advantage within all classes (Table 16). The effect of clustering is greatest in the working-class; 40 percent of workers vote Labour where most of their neighbors are Conservative, but 63 percent vote Labour where most of their neighbors are Labour. The effect is also strong among lower-middle-class voters. By contrast, upper-middle-class voters are almost impervious to local influences; even in safe Labour seats two-thirds still vote Conservative. The relationship is not unique to the 1970 British general election and can be validated by the ecological analysis of census data as well as by survey data (cf. Butler and Stokes, 1969, pp. 144ff; Miller, 1972).

Ecological differences may also be found at a regional level. No agreed classification of regions exists among British social scientists or government departments; many differently bounded areas are used for purposes of regional studies (cf. Smith, 1964). The most familiar regional classification scheme is the New Standard Regions of the Registrar General's office, as revised in 1966 for economic-planning purposes (*Abstract of Regional Statistics, 1969*, appendices I-II). The instability of regional boundaries indicates uncertainty about the theoretical rationale of analyzing voting in regional terms within England.

By controlling for class one can eliminate the effect of variations from region to region in the proportion of manual and middle-class voters. There is a tendency for the northernmost regions to be more Labour and for the southern regions, excluding London itself, to show Conservative inclinations (see Table 17 and Butler and Stokes, 1969, pp. 135ff). The degree of regional distinctiveness in part reflects ecological

TABLE 16: **Constituency Partisanship and Individual Partisanship, in Percentages**

	Con	Lab	Other	Total*
Upper-Middle-Class				
Safe Conservative	73	19	8	4
Conservative marginal	75	17	8	2
Labour marginal	68	27	5	3
Safe Labour	67	25	9	4
Lower-Middle-Class				
Safe Conservative	64	25	10	4
Marginal Conservative	55	37	8	4
Marginal Labour	53	37	10	5
Safe Labour	43	48	9	6
Working Class				
Safe Conservative	47	40	13	12
Marginal Conservative	42	46	12	11
Marginal Labour	41	49	10	15
Safe Labour	29	63	9	21

*Excludes Liberal and other constituencies.

effects illustrated in Table 16. The differences in Table 17 are also explicable in terms of contrasting historical traditions, such as the strength of the Conservative organization in the West Midlands, a radical Liberal tradition in East Anglia, and the early rise of the Labour party in parts of London and in northern England.

Differences between England, Scotland, Wales, and Northern Ireland are national rather than regional, for distinctive political institutions exist for aspects of government in the three non-English parts of the United Kingdom. The institutional distinctiveness is greatest in Northern Ireland and least in Wales. Psychological identification with symbols of Englishness, Scottishness, Welshness, or Irishness is one means of measuring national identity. Surveys have shown that these nations, rather than Britain, are the primary identification of the majority of people in non-English parts of the United Kingdom (see Rose, 1970a, table 5). This is not, however, translated into identification with a nationalist party. The multinational character of the United Kingdom coexists with major parties drawing support across national lines. Only in Northern Ireland, where national identity is itself a subject of dispute, is there substantial support for "independence" parties of Protestants or Catholics (cf. Rose, 1971, ch. 6-7). Language differences are no source of national divisiveness because of the pervasiveness of English, even in Scotland and Northern Ireland, where Gaelic was once an indigenous language. In Wales an estimated 26 percent of the population speaks Welsh, but only 1 percent is Welsh monoglot. This makes language divisive *within*

Wales, separating the more populous industrial south from rural and remote parts of north and west Wales, where Welsh is still widely spoken (Cox, 1970). Scotland is also divided between a populous industrial central belt and the Highlands area. While large in terms of acreage the Highlands has only 5 percent of the Scottish population. Hence the distinctive partisanship of the Highlands is of little significance within Scottish or United Kingdom politics (cf. Rose, 1968, table 7).

TABLE 17: **English Regional Differences and Partisanship, in Percentages**

Total		UPPER-MIDDLE-CLASS			LOWER-MIDDLE-CLASS			WORKING-CLASS		
		Con	Lab	Other	Con	Lab	Other	Con	Lab	Other
6	North	74	22	4	49	48	2	29	66	5
9	Yorks and Humber	67	26	8	54	39	7	38	54	8
14	Northwest	69	24	7	55	38	6	39	54	7
8	East Midlands	80	13	6	59	37	4	37	53	10
9	West Midlands	80	15	5	59	31	10	45	46	10
4	East Anglia	74	20	6	56	28	17	47	40	14
21	London	60	31	9	49	40	11	34	54	12
13	Southeast	71	23	5	55	34	11	45	43	12
7	Southern	77	13	10	62	26	12	47	40	13
7	Southwest	79	15	6	65	24	11	38	47	18

(English N=8,217)

In surveys covering the whole of Great Britain the number of Scottish and Welsh nationalist respondents is too small to permit analysis. Surveys taken in 1968, when nationalist sympathies were strong, provide an indication of the extent to which support for Nationalist parties is independent of class (Table 18).

Nationalist support is found at virtually the same level in the middle-class and working-class within each of the three nations. The principal differences in nationalist vote occur among the three nations.

Alternatively, national differences may influence support for the two major parties within the middle-class or the working-class. The historical strength of the Liberal and Labour parties in Scotland and Wales gives grounds for expecting differences to persist (cf. Morgan, 1963; Kellas, 1968), and this is indeed the case (Table 19). Support for major parties varies consistently among the three nations of Great Britain. Wales is the most pro-Labour within each of the three classes, and England the most pro-Conservative. The tendency is not unique to the 1970 general election; it was also found in 1963–1966, when the Nationalist parties had not yet become prominent (Butler and Stokes, 1969, pp. 140–41). National differences are stronger in the middle-class than in the working-class. Labour strength in the working-class differs more between English regions than between nations. (Cf. Tables 19 and 17.)

Migration across national boundaries within the United Kingdom is unlikely to affect the aggregate partisanship of its different parts. This is because few Englishmen move into non-English areas and while substantial proportions of Scots, Welsh, and

TABLE 18 : **Nationalist Parties support and Class, 1968, in Percentages**

	Con	Lab	Nat	Lib	Other
Wales					
Middle class	50	24	8	12	7
Working class	26	47	9	7	10
Scotland					
Middle class	50	13	27	5	5
Working class	26	33	30	5	7
Northern Ireland*					
Middle class	57	10	21	— 12 —	
Working class	43	23	22	— 12 —	

* In Ulster party labels are not exactly comparable to those in other parts of the United Kingdom, and have altered since 1968.
Sources : Gallup Poll, 1968, Wales (N=657) and Scotland (N=667); Northern Ireland (N=1,291) Rose, 1971.

Irish move to industrial areas of England, their numbers relative to that of the receiving English population are insufficient to distort the native English pattern. If one assumed that the least nationalistic migrate, their departure would make the non-English nations more distinctive.

TABLE 19 : **National Differences in Support for Major Parties, in Percentages**

	Con	Lab	Other	Total
Upper-Middle Class				
England	70	22	7	13
Scotland	71	19	10	1
Wales	54	32	14	1
Lower-Middle Class				
England	55	36	9	19
Scotland	47	40	13	2
Wales	37	51	12	1
Working Class				
England	39	50	11	54
Scotland	29	58	12	6
Wales	32	60	8	4

Britain has a very high degree of racial homogeneity—if race is defined as biological difference in skin colour. Even with continuous immigration of colored Commonwealth citizens in the past decade the country is still about 98 percent white. In colloquial English "race" is often used to refer to groups of immigrants with distinctive cultural habits, e.g., Cypriots or Italians are said to belong to a different race, as well as Africans and Pakistanis. Neither surveys nor census figures conventionally distinguish individuals by skin color. Instead the euphemism "Commonwealth-born" is employed. While persons born in the nonwhite nations of the Commonwealth are usually not white, they may be the offspring of English parents who were serving in the colonies. For example, both Hugh Gaitskell and R.A. Butler were born in India. All Commonwealth citizens are eligible to vote or stand for Parliament upon taking up residence in Britain. In 1964 ecological evidence suggested that in some West Midlands areas a small but crucial number of white voters switched their party allegiance to anti-immigrant candidates standing as Conservatives. This pattern was neither general nor persisting. By 1970 election results indicated that Labour did better than average in areas of high colored immigration; its gain in colored votes more than offset any additional "anticolored" vote that it lost (cf. Deakin, 1965; Deakin and Bourne, 1970; Steed, 1971, pp. 405-408). The 1970 Gallup survey found that among middle-class Commonwealth-born respondents (N=39) 51 percent favored Labour and 38 percent the Conservatives; among working-class respondents (N=52) 65 percent favored Labour and 24 percent the Conservatives.

Historically, religion has distinguished Conservative and Liberal supporters independently of class and in ways that overlapped with national differences. The Church of England is the established state church, but only in one nation of the kingdom. The established Church of Scotland is Presbyterian, and in Wales Nonconformist Protestants were sufficiently strong and divided among themselves to disestablish the state church and prevent the establishment of any church. Northern Ireland too is without a state church, although its politics are hardly nonsectarian: Catholics tend to identify themselves as Irish and reject the ruling Unionist party. The majority party, the Unionists, has maintained a monopoly in cabinet for Protestants (cf. Rose, 1971).

In terms of nominal identification, Britain is overwhelmingly a Christian and Protestant society. In 1970 only 7 percent of persons interviewed said that they had no religion (Table 20). But there are variations in institutional loyalties. A total of 61 percent identify with the established Church of England, and another 8 percent with the established (Presbyterian) Church of Scotland. Roman Catholics claim 8 percent of religious adherents as do Nonconformist Protestants, historically against both the Established Church and Roman Catholicism. Within each class, Anglicans are more pro-Conservative than persons of any other denomination. Those who state no religion or are non-Christians (whether Hindu immigrants or British Jews) are consistently more pro-Labour than Protestant denominations. This does not mean that the Labour party is anticlerical, but rather that the Conservatives are seen as favoring a single established church to which this minority does not belong. The position of Catholics is more complex. They are the most pro-Labour of all denominations in the working and lower-middle-class. This allegiance is primarily ethnic. Most Catholics in Britain are of Irish descent and have developed a strong antipathy to the party opposed to home rule for Ireland. Upper-middle-class Catholics are unlikely to be of recent Irish migration; some will be from old English Catholic families, and others will be well-to-do converts. This Catholic group appears better able to adapt to upper-middle-class norms than Nonconformist Protestants, at least insofar as party loyalties are concerned. In favoring the Conservatives, moreover, they are consistent with the Catholic Church's traditional antipathy to socialism (cf. Clarke, 1971, pp. 254-59).

Because the Church of England and the Church of Scotland are state churches, they are often the religious identification of people who never, in fact, attend religious services. Hence it is desirable to control for church attendance within classes. Unfortunately this question was not asked in the Gallup surveys, and the Butler-Stokes surveys do not have sufficiently large numbers to generalize with great confidence from an intensive breakdown of their respondents. The findings that they report do indicate a small but consistent relationship between church attendance and favoring the Conservatives in both the middle and working-classes (1969, pp. 125ff; cf. Bochel

TABLE 20 : Religion and Partisanship, in Percentages

	Con	Lab	Other	Total
Upper-Middle Class				
Church of England	75	18	6	9
Church of Scotland	73	18	9	1
Protestant Nonconformist	59	33	8	1
Roman Catholic	69	26	5	1
Other/None	55	34	12	2
Lower-Middle Class				
Church of England	59	33	8	13
Church of Scotland	52	35	12	2
Protestant Nonconformist	49	39	11	2
Roman Catholic	44	48	9	2
Other/None	41	44	15	0
Working Class				
Church of England	41	50	9	39
Church of Scotland	35	54	12	5
Protestant Nonconformist	39	48	13	5
Roman Catholic	30	62	8	8
Other/None	32	51	17	7

and Denver, 1970). The aggregate effect of this influence is limited because only 26 percent of the population reports going to church as much as once a month. For the most part the British people today are nominally Christian or apathetically secular. They are not anticlerical by conviction.

Just as parents may pass on a nominal religious identification to their children, so too they may pass on identification with a political party. This thesis implies that party strength is highly inelastic from generation to generation, affected chiefly by differential birth rates and death rates. When the thesis is applied to studies of political attitudes as well as party loyalties (Abrams and Little, 1965), the implications for stability become even greater.

Yet the conditions that must be met for an individual to maintain the same party loyalty as his parents are multiple and contingent. The Butler and Stokes study (1969, ch. 3) focuses primarily upon a conditional influence: if parents are united in party loyalty, their children are likely to follow their course as adults. But this begs the prior question, what proportion of British voters come from homes where both parents are known to have had the same party identification? The answer is less than half.

	Percentage
Both parents same party identification	40
One parent's identification known, other parent's identification not recalled	30
Both parents conflicting identifications	6
Neither parent's identification recalled	24

Source: Butler-Stokes, 1963

In three-tenths of all cases the party preference of one parent was recalled, but the respondent had no memory of how the other parent, usually the mother, voted. In another three-tenths of all cases freedom from parental determinism is indicated inasmuch as the party choice of neither parent is recalled, or they are positively in conflict. In short, a simple theory of intergenerational determinism fails because a substantial portion of the adult electorate was not subjected to a consistent push toward a single party by their parents. Among those who have been subjected to a Conservative or Labour influence, there is of course a tendency to follow parents. A total of 80 percent had an initial party preference identical to that of their parents, and 78 percent claimed the same party identification in 1963; in this interelection period 72 percent stated that they had the same voting intention as their parents.

The most important political point is not the intergenerational persistence of partisanship among one-third or less of the electorate, but the proportion of a party's support that is *not*, as it were, delivered by the obstetrician. An analysis of individuals who identified with the Conservative or Labour parties at the time of the 1963 Butler-Stokes survey shows that only half the support for each party could be said to be delivered by the family, with both parents positively identifying with the same party as the respondent himself, or with one parent positively identifying and the other without identification with any party (Table 21).

The bulk of the supporters who were changers were not converts from the other major party; they were adults who had grown up in a family where there was either no clear cue for party loyalties or there was a conflict. In some cases a conflict might arise in adult life between parental Liberalism and the absence of a Liberal candidate in the voter's constituency. The high proportion of voters who are not delivered at birth gives each party an incentive to seek recruits and, once they are gained, not to take them for granted as inevitably lifelong supporters.

TABLE 21 : **A Profile of Intergenerational Support for Parties, 1963, in Percentages**

	Conservative Voters	Labour Voters
Both parents, same party	35	30
One parent pro, one neutral	17	20
One parent pro, one other party	6	3
Both parents, no party identification	18	25
Parents Liberals	13	9
Parents other major party*	10	13
	99	100

* 2 percent of Labour respondents with mixed Con-Lib parents included here, as well as 1 percent of Conservative respondents with mixed Lab-Lib parents.
Source : Butler-Stokes, 1963.

Generational differences can be of importance because older people initially formed party allegiances in very different historical circumstances from those known to younger British voters. Labour did not unambiguously supplant the Liberals as one of the two major parties until 1935. In the period 1922-1931 Labour was usually stronger than the Liberals, but before that the Liberals were one of the two established parties and Labour was not. The Liberal party eventually forced one-time supporters to choose between its opponents by failing to nominate candidates for three-fourths of constituencies in elections in the 1930s. In trying to measure generational differences in Britain there are historical landmarks besides the transformation of the party system. The most important are the post-1955 prosperity, the Second World War, the interwar depression, and the end of an era of Victorianism in the First World War. It is less easy to fix precisely the age crucial for the formation of party loyalties. Here the electorate is divided into age cohorts on the assumption that the critical period for forming partisan allegiance will be in adolescence. The exact age of each respondent is not recorded in Gallup surveys; respondents are assigned to age groups. Hence the generational groupings employed here approximate a definition stipulating that the formative years for political awareness are after age fourteen. The oldest respondents in 1970 reached their formative years before or during the First World War; the youngest became politically aware about 1966.

The party preferences in Table 20 show the extent to which older voters in Britain tend to be Conservatives and younger voters are Labours. The effect of age appears more pronounced in the middle-class than in the working-class. This may reflect the likelihood that voting Labour became accepted by manual workers or their parents a decade or more before it became accepted in middle-class families. The steadiness in the change in position between the two parties argues against any shift arising from a single dramatic historical event. For example, a Labour government was in office at the time of the world depression; thus, it was not an unambiguous stimulus to the Left. Age-related differences in partisanship are also a function of the decline of the Liberal party and the gradual dying off of those raised in families in which Labour was not perceived as a major party (see Butler and Stokes, 1969, ch. 3).

TABLE 22 : **Generational Effects upon Partisanship, in Percentages (Age in 1970 in brackets)**

	Con	Lab	Other	Total	Difference Con–Lab
Upper-Middle Class					
New voters (18-24)	50	40	10	1	10
Prosperity (25-34)	63	28	9	2	25
Wartime (35-49)	70	22	7	6	49
Depression (50-64)	78	15	7	4	63
Pre-Great War (65+)	80	14	6	1	66
Lower-Middle Class					
New voters	40	49	11	5	–9
Prosperity	53	36	10	4	17
Wartime	55	35	9	6	20
Depression	65	28	7	5	37
Pre-Great War	60	32	8	2	28
Working Class					
New voters	33	52	15	10	–19
Prosperity	37	53	11	11	–16
Wartime	37	54	9	18	–17
Depression	40	52	9	15	–12
Pre-Great War	43	46	11	10	–3

The aggregate effect of greater Labour support in younger age groups can cumulatively alter the balance of power between the parties. As the cohorts of voters die who were raised before Labour became a major party, Labour's strength among the elderly rises. Moreover, class differences in family size give another advantage to Labour, the party of larger working-class families. While the proportionate effect of each advantage is small, the parties are so closely matched in aggregate strength that small differences can be important electorally. The advantages are not so great as to be deterministic. The Conservatives, after all, won the 1970 British general election, notwithstanding demographic trends favoring Labour (cf. Butler and Stokes, 1969).

The party preferences of men and women differ in total (Table 23). Because the two parties are so closely matched it is technically correct to suggest that an exclusively male franchise would give Labour a victory at nearly every British general election and an exclusively female franchise would give the Conservatives recurring victories

(Gallup, 1969, p. 168). The apparent Conservative advantage among women is, however, partly a function of the longer life of women and the tendency of older people, at this particular point in history, to favor the Conservatives. Women constitute 59 percent of the over-sixty-five voters, and 51 percent favored the Conservatives in 1970, as against 37 percent Labour; by comparison, among elderly men, 46 percent were Conservative and the same proportion Labour. Sex differences appear stronger in the working-class, but this is because the category also includes a disproportionate number of elderly women living on pensions.

TABLE 23 : Sex and Partisanship, in Percentages

	Con	Lab	Other	Total
Upper-Middle Class				
Men	70	23	7	9
Women	71	21	8	6
Lower-Middle Class				
Men	53	40	7	9
Women	54	34	11	13
Working Class				
Men	35	56	10	30
Women	41	48	11	34

Any treatment of intending Liberal voters must proceed cautiously because of problems presented by the pattern of candidacies (*supra*, pp. 497). This difficulty is partly offset by the fact that the 1970 Gallup surveys identify a relatively large number of Liberal supporters (N=410). A study of their social characteristics shows that in class terms Liberals differ from Conservative and Labour supporters, because they are almost an exact cross section of the national population in class terms, whereas the latter are not (Table 24).

TABLE 24: Class and Liberal Partisanship, in Percentages

	Con	Lab	Non Voters	Lib	Total
Upper-middle class	22	7	10	13	15
Lower-middle class	25	18	18	24	22
Working class	52	74	72	63	64

The mean difference between party strength within a class and the national proportion in each class is not high (7 percent) for either of the two major parties because their supporters contribute substantially to the national totals. The possibility for deviation is much higher among Liberals and nonvoters. Yet the mean difference of Liberals from national figures is 2 percent, for non-voters, 6 percent. The third electoral party in Britain is not a deviant social group but one that tends to be almost exactly representative of the whole society. The Liberals' electoral weakness suggests that some bias in class support is desirable in order to maintain a large and stable vote.

V.   Conjoint Social Influences

Carefully anatomizing parts of society complements but cannot substitute for the consideration of society in the aggregate. The political importance of the combinations of social characteristics that constitute British society today may be studied deductively or inductively. One may start with a theoretically meaningful and clearly stated set of assumptions and see to what extent these are relevant and powerful in the determination of partisanship. Alternatively, one may inductively seek to establish by multivariate statistical techniques the number and relative strengths of many social influences for which data is available. In this section both approaches will be employed.

The Lipset–Rokkan (1967) analysis of party systems in Western nations emphasizes the a priori importance of a small cluster of social-structural conditions: urban-rural differences, industrial-class differences, religious differences, and variations between "central" and "peripheral" groups, whether resting on racial, linguistic, regional, or national-identity distinctions. In applying this theoretical framework to Britain the first point that one notes is the virtual absence of racial and linguistic divisions. The colored population is less than 2 percent of the total and only began to arrive in the late 1950s; it is not yet accepted as a permanent part of society. Hence while race relations present substantial political problems in Britain, these problems are not electoral because of the overwhelming numerical preponderance of the white population (cf. E. J. B. Rose et al., 1960). The second point is the degree to which Britain is a unilingual society. While distinctive languages are found among the indigenous populations in parts of Wales and the Scottish Highlands, together these groups constitute less than 2 percent of the population; nearly all Welsh and Gaelic–speakers are also competent in English. Hence the major social dimensions of political differentiation are urban vs. rural residence, middle-class vs. working-class, Protestant vs. Catholic, and English vs. Scottish and Welsh residence. Collectively, they provide sixteen different social groupings that can potentially influence the structure of party loyalties.

This matrix analysis emphasizes the high degree of concentration of the population into two groups: 37 percent of the population is English, Protestant, urban, and of the working-class, and 22 percent shares all these characteristics, except that they are of the middle-class (Table 25). Given the proximity of rural areas to urban industrial centers in Britain and the penetration of industry into nominally rural areas, it is relevant to note that an additional 18 percent in rural areas are also English and Protestant, differing only in their occupational class. In aggregate, two of the sixteen groups embrace 58 percent of the population, and four groups collectively include 76 percent of the population, Stated negatively, eight of the sixteen theoretically possible groupings contain in total only 5.6 percent of the population; moreover, only one of the eight non-English categories, the Protestant urban-working-class of Scotland and Wales, constitutes more than 2 percent of the population of Britain. National identity and religion are the most important characteristics in which there may be complete consensus (cf. Rose, 1971, ch. 14). Britain is very nearly homogeneous on both dimensions.

In theory, the even balance between the Conservative and Labour parties might result from one of two diametrically opposite conditions. On the one hand, each social group identified in Table 25 might be highly polarized, i.e., nearly everyone in it would support one party. In such circumstances the overall balance in strength between the two parties would only be an artifact of extreme divisions canceling out in the process of aggregation. Alternatively, party preferences might be completely independent of these major social characteristics. In such circumstances the overall balance of the two parties would be identical with the division in each part of society. Britain does not consistently approximate either of these two ideal-types. Some groups divide fairly evenly in their partisanship, whereas in others one party enjoys a very high degree of support. Generally the largest groups are the least polarized. This is most noteworthy in the two groups forming 48 percent of the electorate: English Protestant workers. Where Labour might be expected to be very strong, it has a plurality but not a majority of support. Reciprocally, the greatest Labour predominance is found among Catholic urban workers outside of England. They give Labour an advantage of 57 percent over the Conservatives, but collectively constitute only 1.2 percent of the British population. The weakness of the Labour party in the working-class is made more significant by the relatively greater strength of the Conservatives in the Protestant middle-class.

The pattern of party support shown in Table 25 leads to a complex conclusion: middle-class rather than working-class voters show the greater tendency to "polarize" politics by homogeneously supporting a single party. There are circumstances in which nonclass factors, e.g., religion and national identity, may also be important. But the theoretical importance of these influences is counteracted by the small proportion of non-English and/or Catholic voters within British society. Ironically, if Britain were less dominated by England in population terms, then its politics would appear more "class conscious" (cf. Rose, 1971, pp. 42, 71-73).

Given the existing composition of British society, one can turn to the use of tree analysis, i.e., the Automatic Interaction Detector algorithm (Sonquist & Morgan, 1964) to consider the total amount of variation in partisanship that can be explained by existing social-structural characteristics. The characteristics included here have been reviewed in the preceding section—occupational class, trade-union affiliation type of tenancy, education, car ownership, telephone, religion, urban-rural differences, region and nation, constituency partisanship, age, and sex. Unless otherwise specified, only Conservative and Labour supporters are included in the tree analysis; the proportion of respondents excluded is small. In seeking to identify the things that differentiate Labour from Conservative supporters, one can say that the greater the proportion of variation that can be explained, then the more structured are party alignments; the less the variation, the more dispersed or open is the relationship between social-structure and party strength.

TABLE 25 :   The Size and Partisanship of Basic Social Groups, in Percentages

	MIDDLE CLASS					WORKING CLASS			
	England					England			
	Protestant		Catholic			Protestant		Catholic	
	Urban	**Rural**	**Urban**	**Rural**		**Urban**	**Rural**	**Urban**	**Rural**
Conservative	60	69	53	71	Conservative	40	41	32	34
Labour	31	24	40	28	Labour	49	49	60	58
Other	9	7	7	2	Other	11	11	8	9
Total	(21.6%)	(6.7%)	(2.6%)	(0.5%)	Total	(36.8%)	(11.1%)	(5.1%)	(1.1%)
	Scotland & Wales					Scotland & Wales			
	Protestant		Catholic			Protestant		Catholic	
	Urban	**Rural**	**Urban**	**Rural**		**Urban**	**Rural**	**Urban**	**Rural**
Conservative	53	67	31	—	Conservative	32	36	16	—
Labour	34	25	56	—	Labour	57	56	73	—
Other	13	8	13	—	Other	11	8	11	—
Total	(3.7%)	(0.7%)	(0.5%)	(0.0%)	Total	(6.8%)	(1.6%)	(1.2%)	(0.0%)

Total party strengths: Conservatives, 46 percent; Labour, 44 percent; Others, 10 percent. Weighted N=9,610. Percentages in parentheses refer to the proportion that each cell contributes to the total society.

Analysis of British voting at the 1970 general election shows a surprising degree of openness : the total variation explained in party preference is 12.0 percent. This means that the relationship between social-structure and party preference is much less in Britain than in the Netherlands or the Scandinavian countries. A second feature of the tree in Figure 1 is that occupational class is not the most important influence upon party preference. Instead, home ownership accounts for 7.1 percent of variation in party preference. By comparison occupational class would have accounted for 5.3 percent of the variation among all respondents. Affiliation to a trade union is the second most important influence, both among tenants and home-owners. Among nonunion members ownership of a telephone further discriminates partisans: persons with a telephone are much more likely to vote Conservative than those without. Ownership of a telephone is itself not likely to cause party preference, but rather indicates that a person is not only of a reasonable income but also in a social network extending beyond immediate face-to-face contacts characteristic of the old industrial working-class (cf. Bott. 1957). Home-owners without a union affiliation can also be further divided on the basis of their use of a telephone; the more middle-class group is

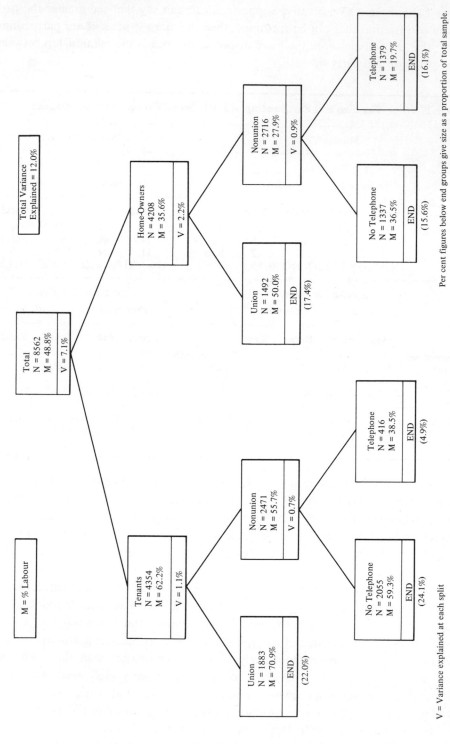

Total Variance
Explained = 12.0%

M = % Labour

Total
N = 8562
M = 48.8%
V = 7.1%

Home-Owners
N = 4208
M = 35.6%
V = 2.2%

Tenants
N = 4354
M = 62.2%
V = 1.1%

Nonunion
N = 2716
M = 27.9%
V = 0.9%

Union
N = 1492
M = 50.0%
END
(17.4%)

Union
N = 1883
M = 70.9%
END
(22.0%)

Nonunion
N = 2471
M = 55.7%
V = 0.7%

Telephone
N = 1379
M = 19.7%
END
(16.1%)

No Telephone
N = 1337
M = 36.5%
END
(15.6%)

No Telephone
N = 2055
M = 59.3%
END
(24.1%)

Telephone
N = 416
M = 38.5%
END
(4.9%)

Per cent figures below end groups give size as a proportion of total sample.

V = Variance explained at each split

Figure 1:   A Tree Analysis of British Voting, 1970

80 percent Conservative, and the less fully middle-class group is 63 percent Conservative. The limited structuring of partisanship by social influence is shown by the restricted number of branches in the tree and by the limited polarization in most of the end groups. The largest—nonunion tenants without telephones—divides less than six to four Labour, and the third largest, home-owning families with trade-union affiliations divides exactly evenly between the two parties.

An alternative or supplementary theory of influence posits that an individual's involvement in politics is likely to be important, independently of his social characteristics or as an intervening variable. The 1970 Gallup survey has four questions that can be used to measure political involvement. In ascending order of the proportion involved they are: interest in the election; perceived difference between the parties; concern about election result; and how likely the respondent is to vote.[5] A tree analysis combining these influences, plus the social-structural characteristics listed above, found that only one of these indicators of involvement—interest in the election—could explain as much as 1.6 percent of the variance in the total universe, prior to the first branch (the most interested were the most likely to favor the Conservatives). Viewed in relation to social-structure, however, measures of involvement were of relatively slight influence; seven social characteristics were more important. Moreover, only one of these involvement measures—concern with who won the election—entered at any point in the subsequent branching of the tree, explaining 1.0 percent of the variance but not altering the general picture given in Figure 1.

Conscious class loyalties are another form of potentially important psychological involvement. If class consciousness is an important influence, one would expect a tree analysis including subjective class identification to show a major increase in the structuring of partisanship, i.e., in the total variance explained. Subjective class identification explains 8.8 percent of the total variance at the initial split, and the whole tree 14.7 percent. This is but slightly more than can be explained without allowing for any subjective factor. Moreover, at the second and third level of branching home-ownership and trade-union membership reappear as the most important influences, thus reemphasizing points stressed previously (Figure 1).

The absence of a stronger relationship between working-class occupation and Labour sympathies has been noted by many writers, usually in a context far broader than that of voting behavior. It can be argued that working-class Conservative sympathies—in association with or independent of party choice—betoken a deferential outlook toward persons of higher status. The existence of deference is then said to be of great importance in the political culture and, by extension, in the government of Britain (cf. Nordlinger, 1967; Parkin, 1967; McKenzie and Silver, 1968). The existence or significance of deferential attitudes or deferential subjects in Britain is a topic outside the scope of this study. Kavanagh (1971) has thoroughly summarized the literature and shown that not only are there conceptual and empirical weaknesses in discussions of the concept but also that deferentials are a small proportion of the electorate by almost any measure of deference (1971, table 1). In this chapter it is more appropriate to define the problem as one of deviation from class-typical patterns of party loyalties and to examine *both* middle-class *and* working-class voters. Given the preponderance of support for a party within a class, why do some individuals cleave to a party that is not endorsed by the majority of their class?

It is most appropriate to ask this question about middle-class voters, inasmuch as this group has a more sharply defined class preference. A priori, one might expect that the minority who vote Labour in the middle-class might be a particularly distinctive group, in order to withstand relatively pronounced class norms. They might be distinctive socially, or by being more involved in politics and better insulated against class influences because they become more knowledgeable. A. I. D. analysis, using the same independent variables as employed above, shows that home ownership is the most important influence differentiating middle-class voters, explaining 5.5 percent of total variance; youth is second in importance; placement in the upper- or lower-middle-class is the third most important variable differentiating the middle-class. Within the middle-class there is a wide variety of social characteristics influencing party preferences: eight different characteristics show up at least once in the tree, and twenty-three end groups result. The total variance explained by social differences within the middle-class is 12.7 percent. When measures of involvement are added, the total variance explained is 14.4 percent; of this, involvement measures contribute 2.0 percent. These findings indicate that the propensity of middle-class people to favor the Conservatives is much more a function of position in society than involvement in politics.

Within the working-class there are two alternative sets of expectations about Conservative voters. They may be considered the least politically involved *lumpenproletariat*. Alternatively McKenzie and Silver have argued that working-class Conservative voters are at least as politically involved as Labour voters (1968). Parkin (1967) suggests that it is precisely because of political awareness that some working-class voters favor the party of the "dominant" class, the Conservatives. Alternatively neither social characteristics nor attitudes may be important. Since working-class Conservative votes are 41 percent of major party voters among the Gallup sample, they might be a cross section of the working-class rather than a distinct deviant group.

Tree analysis supports the thesis that working-class Conservative voters tend to be a cross section of their class rather than an isolated social group. The total variance explained by social and involvement measures is 8.6 percent, two-fifths less than in the middle-class. The primary division within the working-class is between tenants and home-owners; this explains 4.5 percent of the within-class variance. The involvement measure of most importance is interest in the election, but it explains only 0.5 percent of the total variance in the working-class. The other influences are union affiliation and constituency strength. This pattern rejects both the *lumpenproletariat* and hyperinvolvement hypotheses. One might conclude that it is misleading to write about working-class Conservatives, because Conservative partisanship is not a substantive characteristic isolating persons within the working-class. Instead, one should speak of working-class people who, in an electoral role, favor the Conservative party.

Deference could be more important as a source of respect for political authority, especially the authority of leaders of a party that one votes against. The theory postulates that respect for high-status Conservative leaders among manual workers in Britain helps to sustain political stability, with the majority of the population working-class and the government usually Conservative (cf. Nordlinger, 1967). The theory cannot be fully tested here, but one crucial factual assumption may be examined : the presumed respect of manual workers for Conservative leadership. The 1970 Gallup survey provides a measure of this in the question : Which party has the best leaders? Asking this at the time of a Labour government gave the working-class party whatever advantage accrues to the party in office. Moreover, Harold Wilson had cultivated the image of Labour as a party of government, as well as emphasizing its freedom from upper-class social connections. Reciprocally, the Conservatives remained the high-status party, with Edward Heath presenting an image of upper-class Conservatism with all the care that might be expected from someone who was, contrary to appearances, of much more humble origin.

TABLE 26 : **Leadership Attitudes and Partisanship, in Percentages**

| | | Best Leaders Are: | | |
		Con	Lab	Other %
Upper-Middle Class				
Con. voters		62	20	18
Lab. voters		4	86	10
Others		11	31	58
	Total..	45	36	19
Lower-Middle Class				
Con. voters		57	19	24
Lab. voters		4	83	13
Others		9	31	60
	Total..	33	44	23
Working Class				
Con. voters		61	17	22
Lab. voters		2	84	14
Others		8	25	67
	Total..	38	51	11
Total: Best Leaders		30	48	22

Contrary to theoretical assumptions, a substantial plurality of British voters in 1970 thought that the best leaders were found in the Labour party and not the Conservative party. The class showing the greatest regard for the Conservative leadership was the upper-middle-class; manual workers and lower-middle-class respondents preferred Labour leadership (Table 26). This pattern is clear and consistent: it suggests that respect for leadership is not a function of deference (or inverted snobbery) between distant social classes, but arises from similarities between leaders and led. Manual workers have more confidence in a party that they expect will include working-class politicians in its ranks, and Conservatives have confidence in the party of upper and upper-middle-class politicians. The greater respect for Labour leadership is not simply a function of the numerical strength of the working-class. Table 26 demonstrates that a small but noteworthy minority of Conservative voters in every class in 1970 preferred Labour's leaders to the leadership of the party they voted for. By contrast, only an insignificant proportion of Labour voters preferred Conservative leaders, contrary to one variant of the deference hypothesis. (To attempt to explain this by saying that Conservative voters are deferential to anyone in authority, including a Labour cabinet, might also imply a hypothesis that the data rejects, namely, that Labour voters are inclined to reject leadership, including that of their own party.) The favor shown Labour's leadership in 1970 is best interpreted as evidence of an instrumental rather than an expressive and deferential orientation toward political leadership. At the time of the interviews Labour politicians—partly by virtue of holding office and partly by the demonstration of political skills—were often considered more competent than their Conservative counterparts by political journalists. This was particularly true in the comparison of Harold Wilson and Edward Heath, and was not wholly dependent upon party loyalties (Butler and Pinto-Duschinsky, 1971, p. 64). Given a different set of political leaders or a different political situation, these evaluations could alter (cf. Rose, 1968b), since traditional social status is no longer sufficient to gain an individual politician respect in Britain.

Examination of the multiplicity of social influences sustaining the Liberal party provides a further test of the importance of class. An A.I.D. analysis juxtaposing Liberal voters against Conservative and Labour voters emphasizes how Liberal support is dispersed throughout society. Only two characteristics discriminate Liberals to any extent: residence in a relatively Conservative or Liberal constituency, and/or being Nonconformist or non-Christian in religion. No social characteristic explains as much as 1 percent of the variance in voting; collectively, these two divisions produce three end groups in tree analysis and explain only 1.2 percent of the total variance. The addition of four measures of political involvement does not create more end groups, though it raises the proportion of variance explained to 2.0 percent; in the first split persons who do not think it matters which of the two major party wins appear more Liberal. The Liberal party is so variegated in its social sources of support and its policies that it cannot meaningfully be regarded as a radical party of the Right or the Left. A comparison of Liberal voters with nonvoters emphasizes that the Liberals are not opting out of political involvement by supporting a third party, for involvement measures clearly distinguish Liberals from nonvoters. The most important influences differentiating the two groups are, in order; likelihood of voting ; interest in the election; education; and concern with which party wins—33.7 percent of the variance between Liberals and nonvoters can be explained.

Conventionally, theories of class determinism have emphasized the primacy of occupation as the chief or sole determinant of an individual's weltanschauung, including his party loyalty. The foregoing analysis shows that this approach is inappropriate to contemporary British politics. First, occupational position fails to determine or correlate with many other characteristics regarded as defining a working-class or a middle-class milieu (see Table 13). Moreover, Labour support within the working-class is not as strong as Conservative support within the middle-class. Support for both Conservative and Labour parties is widely dispersed through many formal and informal groups in society; Liberal support, while small, is even more diffuse. Insofar as homogeneous groups can be found, these are more likely to be middle-class than working-class. Home ownership and trade-union membership appear more important than occupation in explaining British partisanship in 1970.

To emphasize the limited importance of occupational class is not to assert the unimportance of socioeconomic characteristics in the determination of party loyalties.[6] Home ownership and trade-union membership are indicators of social position just as much conditioned by economic influences as is occupation. The relative importance of economic conditions is also underscored by the persistent failure of religion, nationality, or regional differences to appear in the tree analyses. Home ownership and union membership differ from occupational class, however, in that the latter is more often considered a lifetime status. A man may change his job, but with a given level and type of skill he is less likely to change his class standing; this will increasingly be the case insofar as educational qualifications acquired in youth become a precondition for adult social mobility. To note this is not to suggest that he need remain stationary in every economic sense. The gradual expansion of national income provides an opportunity, directly or indirectly, for individual economic circumstances to change. Economic interests remain even though structures change, for there is no certainty that all socioeconomic groups will be equally advantaged. On balance, change means greater prosperity. In the period 1959-1970, when the British economy was subject to major difficulties, the median wage earner saw his net real income rise by 19 percent (Turner and Wilkinson, 1971). This rise means greater discretionary income and thus greater scope for voluntary choice. The social characteristic most emphasized here—home ownership—can be conceived as an alternative chosen by a substantial proportion of the population, as against renting from the council or a private landlord. Having a telephone is even more a matter of voluntary choice. Butler and Stokes have also noted the political importance of individual choice of membership in a trade-union (1969, ch. 7). In such circumstances the limited influence of occupation upon voting can be interpreted as a sign of the increasing importance of voluntary choice in lifestyles. This not only affects politically unimportant consumer purchases, but also facilitates changes in partisanship.

The effect of fluctuating market influences upon partisanship is further emphasized by an intensive aggregate analysis of the political consequences of economic changes in the 1950s and 1960s, undertaken by C. A. E. Goodhart and R. J. Bhansali (1970). These authors correlated party preference, as reflected in monthly opinion polls, with a number of major macroeconomic measures such as shifts in unemployment, price rises, changes in personal income, and alterations in the balance of payments position

of the pound. Two of these measures—changes in unemployment six months previously and price inflation—correlated strongly with changes in party popularity. It is particularly noteworthy that the number of persons who changed party preference was
much greater than the number put out of work. In other words, fear of unemployment
spreads disillusion with the governing party among some still in work (Ibid., pp.81-86).
Butler and Stokes report findings from survey data consistant with this (1969, ch.18).
Few influences could be more crudely "economic" than prices and unemployment
levels. Unlike occupational class, these conditions are not durable attributes of individual voters, but are relatively unstable attributes of the macroeconomy.These levels
may arise or fall, relative to desires and expectations, within a matter of months, thus
accounting for substantial between-elections swings in the popularity of the major
parties. While these macroeconomic conditions are customarily more amenable to
central-government influence than is social mobility, it is no easy task for the governing
party to manage the economy to assure electoral success. Conventional economic
theories assume that measures taken to reduce unemployment are likely to make
prices rise, or vice versa. But in 1970 both unemployment and prices were rising. The
Labour government was defeated at a general election because it could not successfully
time a preelection economic boom. The coefficient of relationship between economic
conditions and partisanship may also change through time. For example, in a period of
abnormally high unemployment in 1970-1971, the decline in Conservative support was
less great, in proportion to the rise in unemployment, than Goodhart and Bhansali's
earlier analysis would have predicted.

A comparison of A. I. D. analyses of party preference in the general elections of
1959, 1964, 1966, and 1970 does indicate one secular trend: a decline in the ability of
social characteristics to structure partisanship. An A. I. D. analysis of Gallup respondents interviewed in 1964 could then explain 21.9 percent of the variance in their 1959
voting and 20.6 percent of 1964 partisanship. An analysis of the 1966 preferences of
1970 Gallup respondents explains 16.8 percent of the variance, 4.8 percent more than
that achieved in examining the respondents' current preferences. The 1970 decline in
the influence of social-structure, by comparison with the two previous elections, is
associated with a decline in the working-class preference for Labour rather than a fall
in the middle-class preference of Conservatives. While it would be premature to interpret any such trend as inevitable, it is, at a minimum, evidence of the potential "loose-
ness of fit" of social-structure and partisanship in Britain. In addition the tree analyses
demonstrate that politically important socioeconomic influences are the same from
election to election, whatever their conjoint strength. In 1964 occupational class
appeared in the first branch of the tree, followed by tenancy and trade-union membership, the only other variables to enter the tree. In 1966 tenancy and then trade-union
membership came first, as in the 1970 analysis.

Both inductive and deductive analysis show that the role of class in British party
politics is more complex and different than is often assumed. The middle-class is more
subject to influence than is the working-class. Moreover, occupation is not necessarily
the best indicator of an individual's position in a network of social and political loyal-

ties. The economic influences that have affected British voters in the period 1964-1970 are much more fluid than those associated with a person's life chances in work. The swing from Conservative to Labour in 1966 and from Labour to the Conservatives in 1970 emphasizes the speed with which crucial changes in power can occur within a two party system as evenly balanced as in Britain. The balance is also evidence that British voters, choosing free of social-structural pressures, will more often depart from a working-class Labour norm than from a middle-class Conservative norm.

VI. The Comparability of Britain

The relation of Britain to other Western nations may be considered in two very different ways. One might ask to what extent its social-structure and party system is similar to that of other countries. Alternatively, one might ask to what extent its prominence rests upon rare or unique characteristics, or even upon the accident that much research material is available in English, the chief international language of social scientists.

In comparing British social-structure with that of other Western countries it is important to consider the extent to which they also concentrate population into two urban industrial classes, homogeneous in terms of religion and national identity. For example, Switzerland is not comparable to Britain in social-structure because one would require several times more cells to identify basic social groups in Switzerland, due to its religious and linguistic complexities. In Ireland, which is also homogeneous in religion, albeit the religion is Catholicism, the different balance of rural to urban residents makes social-structure not exactly comparable. Australia and New Zealand appear most similar to Britain in their high degree of homogeniety on all but industrial class lines. Among Scandinavian countries Sweden matches Britain in religious and linguistic homogeniety, although it has a larger rural population. In continental Europe Germany has shown signs of approaching a party system divided on occupational grounds, but religion has by no means lost all its former importance.

A pioneering study by Robert Alford of the relationship of social-structure to party loyalty concluded that Britain has a "high level of class voting" (1963, p. 168). The judgment was based upon a comparison with two other countries where class must compete with other major influences—Canada and America—as well as with Australia. The evidence was derived from an index of class voting that measured the relationship between party support across middle-class and working-class groups. Ironically, in view of the concern of social scientists with working-class political behavior, Britain's "high level" of class voting occurred through a low number of middle-class people voting Labour rather than because of working-class solidarity. Multivariate statistics provide a more precise way to consider the importance of both class and nonclass influences. This shows that Britain approximates Australia in the extent to which class is related to party preference; the greater variance in partisanship explained in Australia results from the prominence there of extra-economic influences, e.g., church attendance and migration. Party loyalties in Britain are much less structured by class and economic factors than in Sweden; in this Scandinavian country they explain 35.4 percent of the variance as between labour and bourgeois parties. Britain differs from Germany and Austria, two continental societies where a socialist and a non-socialist party are preeminent, because religion enters very prominently in explaining party loyalties, and party loyalties are more structured there.

The electoral system used to determine each party's share of representation in Parliament is common in its fundamentals in the Anglo-American world except for the Republic of Ireland. It is not common in continental Europe or Scandinavia, where proportional-representation systems are customary. Differences in electoral systems are not a major obstacle in the comparison of Britain and other European countries. There is no sociological evidence to suggest that introducing a proportional-representation system in Britain would increase the number of parties seeking votes (of. Tables 2 and 3); the existence of several small nationalist parties plus the survival of the Liberal party mars the symmetry of a nominally two-party system. In a pure proportional-representation electoral system the parliamentary strength of these parties would be greater, but there is no evidence that they would approximate the Conservatives or Labour in size. The chief likely consequence would be that government could not be carried on by a single party because of the absence of an overall majority; instead, bargaining about parliamentary coalitions would become the rule, albeit the partners would bargain from positions of unequal strength.

If two-party systems are defined as systems in which two parties regularly poll at least nine-tenths of the vote, then Britain belongs to a small group of Western countries that have reduced electoral choice to two major alternatives. Three other Anglo-American countries belong to this group—Australia, New Zealand, and the United States—along with Germany and Austria. The evolution of the British party system in the twentieth-century is a reminder, however, that the number and the names of parties are not proof against change. This is a major inhibition in making comparisons across the decades, except in Australia and New Zealand, which also experienced major upheavals in their party systems between the wars.

As a member of the Socialist International the Labour party might appropriately be compared to other members of this body, whether called labour or socialist, in nearly every Western nation except the United States. The U. S. Democratic party may be compared to the Labour party only on the negative grounds that it is "less dissimilar" than the Republican party. Within the universe of the Socialist International, there are parties that are electorally very weak, e.g., in Ireland and Canada. Moreover, there are socialist parties—in the singular or plural—in continental Europe that owe their strength as much to anti-clerical feeling as to working-class sympathies. This has been especially true in France. In France, Italy, and Finland, parties of the Socialist International compete vigorously and not always successfully for votes against Communist parties. Britain has had neither a successful Communist party nor a breakaway left-wing socialist party since the departure of the Independent Labour party from its Labour alliance in 1932.

The Conservative party, unlike Labour and the Liberals (cf. MacCallum Scott, 1967), has no formal institutional ties with parties outside the United Kingdom. It can best be characterized by a series of negatives: it is not socialist nor is it clerically inclined. The party represents no linguistic or cultural group, nor does it owe its past or present existence to a single outstanding leader, as does the French Gaullist party. Its status as a successful catch-all party with heterogeneous support would make it comparable to the Australian Liberal-Country party, the Canadian Liberals, the German CDU, the Irish parties (especially *Fianna Fail*), the New Zealand National party, and the American Democrats and Republicans (cf. Rose and Urwin, 1969, table 2). The question of affinity between the British Conservatives and European parties has become of practical significance as Britain joins the European Common Market. The party now faces three or four alternatives in selecting a cross-national party group within the European parliament : the Christian Democratic group, the group of Liberals and Associates, a European Democratic Union consisting solely of French Gaullists, or constituting a fourth group on its own. (Forsyth, 1969, pp. 479-80).

Given the efforts of both Conservative and Labour parties to enter the European Common Market in the 1960s, it is ironic that these Common Market countries are those with which the party system of Britain has least in common. This is not of itself an argument against association, for the Anglo-American world is also heterogeneous in its party systems and social-structures. Among those nations Britain might be closely compared with Australia and New Zealand. A case might also be made for comparison with Sweden.

In the relative simplicity of its party system and the concentration of its population into two major urban groupings, Britain has characteristics found in idealized models of party systems. But this is not to say that models of two-party class politics fit Britain—or any other country—in every respect. The analysis of social-structure and party loyalties emphasizes the weakness rather than the strength of class influence upon party loyalties in Britain today.

Notes

1. A convenient catalog of statutes concerning electoral law since 1696 is contained in Gwyn (1962, pp. 255-56). For reforms see Seymour (1915) for the period 1832–1885; Blewett (1965) and Morris (1921) for the period 1885–1918; and since 1918, Butler (1963). For the local government franchise see Keith-Lucas (1952).
2. The number of seats changing hands is not a constant for each percent of swing. It is a function of the direction of swing and the distribution of votes in marginal seats at the preceding election, as well as of the evenness of swing in all constituencies. There can be considerable variations around the approximate figure of fifteen seats.

3. Citations to Butler–Stokes, 1964 refer to data obtained by this author from analyzing the machine-readable file of survey responses to the 1964 panel study reported in Butler and Stokes, 1969. The file was obtained from the Inter-University Consortium for Political Research, Ann Arbor, Michigan.
4. The school-leaving age was raised to 16 in 1972.
5. The validity of these items as indicators of political involvement is shown by the fact that when nonvoters are compared with supporters of the Conservative and Labour parties, these are the only influences to emerge in the branches of the tree analysis.
6. Moreover, occupational stratification may remain important in industrial contexts, such as wage disputes (Goldthorpe, 1969).

References

ABRAMS, Mark. "The Home-centred Society." *The Listener*, (November 26, 1959).

ABRAMS, P., AND LITTLE, Alan. "The Young Voter in British Politics." *British Journal of Sociology* XVI:2 (1965).

ABSTRACT OF REGIONAL STATISTICS 1969. London: Her Majesty's Stationery Office, 1969, 1970.

ALFORD, Robert. *Party and Society*. Chicago: Rand, McNally 1963.

ALMOND, G. A., AND VERBA, S. *The Civic Culture*. Princeton: Princeton Univ. Press, 1963.

ANSON, Sir William. *The Law and Custom of the Constitution*. Vol. 1, 4th ed. Oxford: Clarendon Press, 1911.

BAGLEY, Christopher R. "Does Candidates' Position on the Ballot Paper Influence Voters' Choice?" *Parliamentary Affairs* XIX:2 (1966).

BBC AUDIENCE RESEARCH. "The 1970 General Election on Television." London: BBC, 1970.

BECHHOFER, Frank. "A Sociological portrait: Income." *New Society*, (October 14, 1971).

BENEWICK, R., BIRCH, A.H., BLUMLER, J. G., AND EWBANK, A. "The Floating Voter and the Liberal View of Representation." *Political Studies* XVII:2 (1969).

BERRINGTON, Hugh. "The General Election of 1964." *Journal of the Royal Statistical Society Series A* (General) CXXVIII:1 (1965).

BIRCH, A. H., *Representative and Responsible Government*. London: Allen & Unwin, 1964.

BLEWETT, Neal. "The Franchise in the United Kingdom, 1885-1918." *Past and Present* No. 34, 1965.

BLUFF, J. P. *British Opinion Polling Before the 1970 General Election*. Master's thesis. Glasgow: University of Strathclyde, 1971.

BLUMLER, J. G. AND McQUAIL, D. *Television in Politics*. London: Faber, 1968.

BOCHEL, J. M., AND DENVER, D. J. "Religion and Voting." *Political Studies* XVIII:2 (1970).

BONHAM, John, *The Middle-Class Vote*. London: Faber, 1954.

BOTT, Elizabeth. *Family and Social Network*. London: Tavistock, 1957.

BURNHAM, W. Dean. "American Voting Behavior and the 1964 Election." *Midwest Journal of Political Science* XII:1 (1968).

BUTLER, D. E. "The Relation of Seats to Votes." In McCallum, R. B. and Readman, A. q.v. 1947.

———. "The Redistribution of Seats." *Public Administration* XXXIII:2 (1955).

———. *The Electoral System in Britain Since 1918*. Oxford: Clarendon Press, 2nd edition, 1963.

———. "Instant History." *New Zealand Journal of History* II:2 (1968).

———. *The British General Election of 1951*. London: Macmillan, 1952; *of 1955* (1955); *of 1959* (1960 with Rose, Richard); *of 1964* (1965, with King, A.S.); *of 1966* (1966, with King, A. S.); *of 1970* (1971) with M. Pinto-Duschinsky.

———, ed., *Elections Abroad*. London: Macmillan, 1959.

———, AND CORNFORD, J. "The United Kingdom." In S. Rokkan & J. Meyriat, *International Guide to Electoral Statistics*. Hague: Mouton, 1969.

———, AND FREEMAN, J. *British Political Facts, 1900-1968*. London: Macmillan, 1969.

———, STEVENS, A., AND STOKES, D. "The Strength of the Liberals under Different Electoral Systems." *Parliamentary Affairs* XXII: 1 (1969).

———, AND STOKES, Donald. *Political Change in Britain*. London: Macmillan, 1969.

CENSUS 1966. *United Kingdom General and Parliamentary Constituency Tables*. London: Her Majesty's Stationery Office, 1969.

CLARKE, P. F. *Lancashire and the new Liberalism*. Cambridge: University Press, 1971.

CMND. 3550, *Conference on Electoral Law*. London: Her Majesty's Stationery Office, 1968.

CONVERSE, P. E. "Survey Research and the Decoding of Patterns in Ecological Data." In M. Dogan and S. Rokkan, ed., *Quantitative Ecological Analysis in the Social Sciences*. Cambridge: MIT Press, 1969.

———. "Some Priority Variables in Comparative Electoral Research." (*Infra, pp. 727-45*).

CORNFORD, James. "The Transformation of Conservatism in the Late Nineteenth-Century." *Victorian Studies* VII:1 (1963).

———. "Aggregate Election Data and British Party Alignments, 1885-1910." In E. Allardt & S. Rokkan, eds. *Mass Politics*. New York: Free Press, 1970.

COX, Kevin. "Regional Anomalies in the Voting Behavior of the Population of England and Wales: 1921-1951." Ph.D. dissertation, University of Illinois, 1967.

———. "Geography, Social Contexts and Voting Behavior in Wales, 1861-1951." In E. Allardt and S. Rokkan, eds. *Mass Politics*. New York: Free Press, 1970.

COWLING, Maurice. *The Impact of Labour 1920-1924*. Cambridge: University Press, 1971.

CRAIG, F. W. S. *British Parliamentary Election Results, 1918-1949*. Glasgow: Political Reference Publications, 1969.

————. *British Parliamentary Election Statistics, 1918-1970.* Chichester, Sussex: Political Reference Publications, 2nd edition, 1971.

————. *British Parliamentary Election Results, 1950-1970.* Chichester: Political Reference Publications, 1971a.

CREWE, Ivor and PAYNE, Clive "Analysing the Census Data." In Butler, D. E. and Pinto-Duschinsky, M. 1971 *q.v.*

DEAKIN, Nicholas. *Colour and the British Electorate.* London: Pall Mall, 1965.

————, AND BOURNE, JENNY. "Powell, the Minorities and the 1970 Elections." *Political Quarterly* XLI:4 (1970).

DUNBABIN, J. P. "Parlimentary Elections in Great Britain, 1868-1900: A Psephological Note" in *English Historical Review* LXXXI: 1 (1966).

ELECTION 70. *Pre-Election Handbook* London: Gallup Poll, 1970.

FLETCHER, Peter. "The Results Analysed." In L. J. Sharpe, editor, *Voting in Cities: the 1964 Borough Elections,* London: Macmillan, 1967.

FORSYTH, M. "European Assemblies." In Henig, S. and Pinder, J., *European Political Parties.* London: Allen and Unwin, 1969.

GALLUP POLL "Voting Behaviour in Britain, 1945-66." In Rose, Richard, 1969, *q.v.*

GOLDTHORPE, John. "Social Inequality and Social Integration in Modern Britain." *Advancement of Science* (December, 1969).

————. LOCKWOOD, David et al. "The Affluent Worker and the Thesis of Embourheoi-sement." *Sociology* I:1 (1967).

————. LOCKWOOD, David, et al. *The Affluent Worker:Political Attitudes and Behaviour* Cambridge: University Press, 1968.

GOODHART, C.A.E., AND BHANSALI, R. J. "Political Economy." *Political Studies* XVIII:1 (1970).

GRAY, P. G., AND GEE, F. A. *Electoral Registration for Parliamentary Elections.* London: Government Social Survey, 1967.

GRAY, S. *The Electoral Register. Practical Information for use when Drawing Samples both for Interview & Postal Survey.* London: Government Social Survey, 1970.

GREGO, Joseph. *A History of Parliamentary Elections and Electioneering in the Old Days.* London: Chatto and Windus, 1886.

GUTTSMAN, W. L. *The British Political Elite.* London: MacGibbon & Kee, 1963.

GWYN, W. B. *Democracy and the Cost of Politics.* London: University of London Press, 1962.

HANHAM, H. J. *Elections and Party Management.* London, Longmans, 1959.

HARRISON, Martin. *Trade Unions and the Labour Party Since 1945.* London: Allen and Unwin, 1960.

HOWARTH, Richard W. "The Political Strength of British Agriculture." *Political Studies* XVII:4 (1969).

JACKSON, B. AND MARSDEN, D. *Education and the Working-Class.* London: Routledge & Kegan Paul, 1962.

JONES, C. O. "Inter-Party Competition in Britain—1950-1959." *Parliamentary Affairs* XVII:1 (1964).

KAVANAGH, Dennis. *Constituency Electioneering in Britain.* London: Longmans, 1970.

————. "The Deferential English: A Comparative Critique." *Government and Opposition* VI: 3 (1971).

KEITH-LUCAS, B. *The English Local Government Franchise.* Oxford: Basil Blackwell, 1952.

KELLAS, J. A. *Modern Scotland.* London: Pall Mall, 1968.

KING, Anthony. "Why All Governments Lose By-Elections." *New Society.* (March 21, 1968.)

KINNEAR, Michael. *The British Voter: an Atlas and Survey since 1885.* London: Batsford, 1968.

LEONARD, R. L. *Elections in Britain.* Princeton: Van Nostrand, 1968.

LIPSET, S. M. AND ROKKAN, S. "Introduction." In S. M. Lipset and S. Rokkan, eds. *Party Systems and Voter Alignments.* New York: Free Press, 1971.

LLOYD, Trevor. "Uncontested Seats in British General Elections, 1852-1910." *The Historical Journal* XVII: 2 (1965).

MCCALLUM, R. B., AND READMAN, A. *The British General Election of 1945.* London: Oxford University Press, 1947.

MACCALLUM SCOTT, J. H. *Experiment in Internationalism.* London: Allen and Unwin, 1967.

MCCALMONT, F. H. *The Parliamentary Poll Book.* London: Stanford, 1910.

MCKENZIE, R. T. AND SILVER, Allan. *Angels in Marble.* London: Heinemann, 1968.

MACKENZIE, W.J.M., AND ROBINSON, K.E. *Five Elections in Africa.* Oxford: Clarendon Press, 1960.

MARKET RESEARCH SOCIETY. *Social Class Definition in Market Research.* London: Market Research Society, 1963.

MARSHALL, T. H. *Citizenship and Social Class.* Cambridge: University Press, 1950.

MILLER, W. L. "Measures of Electoral Change using Aggregate Data." *Journal of the Royal Statistical Society. Series A* CXXXV: 1 (1972).

MILNE, R., AND MACKENZIE, H. C. "The Floating Vote." Reprinted in R. Rose, ed. 1969, *q.v.*

MORGAN, R. "Is Wales a Region?" *Parliamentary Affairs* XVIII: 4 (1963).

MORRIS, H. L. *Parliamentary Franchise Reform in England from 1885 to 1918.* New York: Columbia University: Studies in History, Economics and Public Law XCVI: 2 (1921).

NICHOLAS, H. G. *The British General Election of 1950.* London: Macmillan, 1951.

NORDLINGER, Eric. *The Working-Class Tories.* London: MacGibbon & Kee, 1967.

O'LEARY, Cornelius. *The Elimination of Corrupt Practices in British Elections, 1868-1911.* Oxford: Clarendon Press, 1962.

PARKIN, Frank. "Working-class Conservatives." *British Journal of Sociology* XVIII:3 (1967).

PELLING, Henry. *Social Geography of British Elections 1885-1910.* London: Macmillan, 1967.

POMPER, Gerald. "Classification of Presidential Elections." *Journal of Politics* XXIX:3 (1967).

PULZER, Peter. *Political Representation and Elections in Britain.* London: Allen and Unwin, 1967.

RAE, Douglas. *The Political Consequences of Electoral Laws.* New Haven: Yale University Press, 1967.

RASMUSSEN, Jorgen. "The Implications of Safe Seats for British Democracy." *Western Political Quarterly* XIX:3 (1966).

RASMUSSEN, J., BUTLER, D. E. Rasmussen—"The Disutility of the Swing Concept in British Psephology."; Butler—"A Comment on Professor Rasmussen's Article." *Parliamentary Affairs* XVIII:4 (1965).

ROSE, E. J. B., et al. *Colour and Citizenship.* London: Oxford University Press, 1969.

ROSE, Richard. "England: a Traditionally Modern Culture." In L.W. Pye and S. Verba, eds. *Political Culture and Political Development.* Princeton: University Press, 1965.

———. *Politics in England.* London: Faber, 1965a.

———. "The Nuffield Election Studies Come of Age." *The Times* (October 2, 1966).

———. *Influencing Voters: a study of Campaign Rationality.* London: Faber, 1967.

———. "Class and Party Divisions: Britain as a Test Case." *Sociology* II:2 (1968).

———. "Party Systems, Social-Structure and Voter Alignments in Britain." In Otto Stammer, ed. *Party Systems, Party Organizations and the Politics of New Masses.* Berlin: *Institut für politische Wissenschaft*, Free University, 1968a.

———. "Voters show their Scepticism of Politicians." *The Times* (April 9, 1968b).

———. *Studies in British Politics.* 2nd rev. ed. London: Macmillan, 1969.

———. *The Polls and the 1970 Election.* Glasgow: Occasional Paper No. 7, University of Strathclyde Survey Research Centre, 1970.

———. *The United Kingdom as a Multi-National State*, Glasgow: Occasional Paper No. 6, University of Strathclyde Survey Research Centre, 1970a.

———. *Governing Without Consensus.* London: Faber, 1971.

———, AND MOSSAWIR, Harvé. "Voting and Elections, a Functional Analysis." *Political Studies* XV: 2 (1967).

———, AND URWIN, D. W. "Social Cohesion, Political Parties and Strains in Regimes." *Comparative Political Studies* II:1 (1969).

———, AND URWIN, D. W. "Persistence and Change in Western Party Systems since 1945." *Political Studies* XVIII:3 (1970).

RUNCIMAN, W. G. *Relative Deprivation and Social Justice.* London: Routledge, 1966.

SELF, PETER and STORING, Herbert. *The State and the Farmer.* London: Allen and Unwin, 1962.

SEYMOUR, Charles. *Electoral Reform in England and Wales, 1832–1885.* New Haven: Yale University Press, 1915.

SEYMOUR-URE, Colin. *The Press, Politics and the Public.* London: Methuen, 1968.

SHARPE, L. J. *A Metropolis Votes.* London: School of Economics Greater London Papers No. 8, 1962.

SMITH, B. C. *Regionalism in England: Regional Institutions—a Guide*. London: Acton Society, 1964.

SONQUIST, J. A. T., and MORGAN, J. N. *The Detection of Interaction Effects*. Ann Arbor: Monograph No. 35, Survey Research Centre, 1964.

STACEY, Margaret. *Tradition and Change, a study of Banbury*. London: Oxford University Press, 1960.

———. ed. et al. *Comparability in Social Research*. London: Heinemann, 1969.

STANYER, Jeffrey. "Electoral Behaviour in Local Government: a Model of a Two-Party System." *Political Studies* XVIII:2 (1970).

STARZINGER, Vincent. "The British Pattern of Apportionment." *Virginia Quarterly Review* XLI:3 (1965).

STEED, Michael. "The Results Analysed." In Butler, D. E. and King, A. S., *q.v.* 1965.

———. "The Results Analysed." In Butler, D. E. and Pinto-Duschinsky, M., *q.v.* 1971.

STOKES, Donald. "Parties and the Nationalization of Electoral Forces." In W. N. Chambers & W. D. Burnham, *The American Party Systems*. New York: Oxford University Press, 1967.

TAPPER, Ted. *Young People and Society*. London: Faber, 1971.

TRENAMAN, J., and McQUAIL, D. *Television and the Political Image*. London: Methuen, 1961.

TURNER, H. A., and WILKINSON, F. "Real Net Incomes and the Wage Explosion." *New Society*. (February 25, 1971).

URWIN, D. W., and ROSE, Richard. "Persistence and Disruption in Western Party Systems Between the Wars." (Varna, Bulgaria; World Congress of the International Sociological Association), 1970.

VINCENT, John. *Pollbooks: How Victorians Voted*. Cambridge: University Press, 1967.

WEINBERG, Aubrey. "Education." In Stacey, Margaret, ed. *q.v.* 1969.

WILSON, Trevor. *The Downfall of the Liberal Party, 1914–1935* London: Collins, 1966.

WILLIAMS, Philip. "Two Notes on the British Electoral System." *Parliamentary Affairs* XX: 1 (1967).

WOLLASTON, H. W. ed. *Parker's Conduct of Parliament Elections*. London: Charles Knight, 1970.

11. CANADIAN VOTING BEHAVIOR

MILDRED A. SCHWARTZ

I. Historical Background

A. THE NATURE OF CANADIAN SOCIETY

There are two wellsprings of Canada's origin: one French and the other British. The French is earliest, stretching back to 1535, when Jacques Cartier explored the St. Lawrence River; the first permanent settlement was established in 1608, New France, from then to its cession to Britain in 1763, reflected the royal authority of France, becoming a "closely controlled projection of a highly centralized regime" (McRae, 1964, p. 222). New France was primarily a trade center and military outpost, not a haven for settlement. It is estimated that during the whole period of French rule no more than 10,000 people migrated to Canada. Relatively meager contacts with the homeland, a style of life not conducive to vast differences in social privilege, and peace and prosperity all helped the development of a distinctive colonial culture. Hence the first half of the eighteenth-century saw a growing gap between the French in Canada and in France (Lanctôt, 1963–1965). General Wolfe secured England's dominion over French Canada in the Battle of the Plains of Abraham in 1759. To the French Canadians, the English victory was a blow from which they have yet to recover. While the Treaty of Paris permitted them to return to France, this was not a viable alternative for most. It was mainly the representatives of officialdom who left. One consequence of the British conquest was a new role for the Roman Catholic Church as guardian and protector of its communicants.

> Throughout the French regime the Church, while independent in doctrinal matters, had been subject to stringent control by the state, but this relationship broke down under British rule, and once certain unfamiliar problems such as episcopal consecration has been settled the church enjoyed a far greater degree of independence than ever before. It is scarcely surprising that the episcopacy became one of the strongest supports of the new regime. . . . Beyond its religious functions, the church acquired a special significance as a rallying point for the defence of French Catholic culture. (McRae, 1964, p. 231.)

The English-speaking merchants who soon came to Quebec were in favor of repressive measures, but a more conciliatory approach was advocated by the first British governors. The latter policy was the one established, finding expression in the

Quebec Act of 1774, which guaranteed the free practice of the Catholic religion and the continuity of French civil law and seigneurial tenure. At the same time it denied the calling of a representative assembly. Altogether, these measures and procedures helped ensure a loyal, docile population in a traditionalistic society. The loyalty of the Church leaders to their new rulers and their protective role vis à vis their flock was thus gained at a price.

Traditionalism has been the dominant theme in the history of Quebec, but not the only one. The roots of disaffection with authority go back to the days of New France, where, as an early intendant observed, the habitants were "naturellement indociles." With the coming of the British, there were even more reasons for tension. The American Revolution and the French Revolution, for example, did not pass unnoticed nor unsupported in Quebec (Wade, 1968, pp. 76–80). The most serious challenge to the status quo came later in the 1840s with the appearance of Louis Joseph Papineau's Rouge movement. Papineau himself was both a nationalist, in the sense of wanting full rights for French-speaking Canadians, and a radical, advocating more political democracy (Wade, 1968, pp. 152–95, 341–82). Only the first of these themes, an inward-looking nationalism but without Papineau's anticlericalism, has characterized the majority of Quebec's subsequent movements of protest, pronouncements of politicians, and writings of intellectuals (Wade, 1968; Irving, 1963; Cook, 1966; Cook, 1967). But the other theme has been present as well, emerging at various times to express a wider view of Canadian nationhood and a more positive assessment of the role of representative government.[1]

During the years of French rule the British were expanding their possessions in North America. From the early seventeenth-century the British had harried the French in what was to be Nova Scotia, with the French colony of Acadia the main political football. Acadia was finally surrendered through the Treaty of Utrecht, and English-speaking settlers began to move into Nova Scotia in sizable numbers—especially after Quebec was ceded. At this time there was not much movement into Quebec, but that changed after the American Revolution. Just who these settlers were is of interest not only to the historian, but also to the student searching for the ideological roots of Canadian politics. In the United States those who left were called Tories, in Canada they and their descendants are still honored as "United Empire Loyalists." Those who take this characterization seriously are inclined to argue that it was this wave of settlement that was to set the conservative, royalist, and even elitist tone of Canadian politics for generations to come. Yet many respected historians and political scientists find this too simple a generalization. Some settlers were in this sense Tories, but only some of them. Indeed, as the political scientist McRae argues, it was as exiles in a new land that many of the Loyalists discovered their liberalism, for what they found was a strong executive and a weak legislature (McRae, 1964, p. 237). Against the power of entrenched oligarchy, the Chateau Clique and Family Compact, there were those in both English- and French-speaking Canada who directed the fight for responsible government. In 1837-1838 the struggle took the form of outright rebellion.

Meanwhile, the colonies themselves were changing, as large numbers of English-speaking settlers came from both the United States and Britain. New political arrangements were explored, including responsible government, but none of them was really satisfactory in dealing with innumerable problems of which two are sufficient to note: relations between French- and English-speaking inhabitants, and stimulation of a backward economy.

The existing colonies represented economic and social interests not only diverse but in overt opposition to each other. The magnitude of these differences may be appreciated when we note how regional differences remain as the prime cleavage in Canadian society a hundred years later. Yet the men who have been immortalized as the Fathers of Confederation were able to bring together a workable plan of union. It was enacted by the British Parliament as the British North America Act, July 1, 1867. But not all the colonies found union at this time attractive, and Newfoundland did not join until 1949 (Waite, 1962).

Canada has a written constitution, based mainly upon the British North America Act. The BNA Act provided the basis for a federal government in Canada, dividing the responsibilities and powers between the federal and provincial levels of government and protecting certain basic rights. The framers of the Act felt they were making their intentions crystal clear; but changed circumstances and other factors have called these into question. For example, it is generally accepted, at least by English-speaking commentators, that the Fathers of Confederation leaned toward a unitary system, and while this seemed impossible to achieve because of the existence of divergent interests in different parts of the country, the compromise favored a strong central government. The example of the United States, torn by civil war, gave strong impetus to this view. The nature of the federation was specified through the list of powers assigned to each of the levels of government, with the federal government also given the authority to legislate "for peace, order, and good government." But as an act of the British Parliament, interpretations of the BNA Act faced their highest tribunal in the Judicial Committee of the Privy Council in London. These Privy Councilors had the disconcerting inclination to interpret the Act in quite the opposite direction—they gave increased authority to the provincial governments. The gradual, though still incomplete repatriation of the constitution has not existed for a sufficiently long time to examine the trends of the Supreme Court of Canada, which now, in any case, faces new problems growing from the demands for a special status for Quebec. (Russell, 1962; Gérin-Lajoie, 1950; Laskin, 1960; Cook, 1966, pp. 62–78; Meekison, 1968.)

The BNA Act gave both levels of government power to raise revenues, although the provinces had much more limited capacities. From the outset of confederation this distribution of powers ran into trouble. Certain provincial responsibilities, such as highways and education, can use almost unlimited funds. Certain provinces, either through industrial wealth or natural resources, have increased their economic differential from other provinces. Various means to equalize these differences and to take into account soaring costs of modern life have been attempted. A major royal commission

(Report, 1940) and regular federal-provincial conferences bring adjustments in financial arrangements, but we can anticipate that these will probably never be satisfactorily resolved.[2]

The BNA Act clearly defines education as within the jurisdiction of the provinces. This has been an important guarantee of the autonomy of the school system in Quebec. But in special circumstances the federal government may intervene, for instance, if the provincial legislature proposes to interfere in the rights of denominational schools existing at the time of entry into confederation. In time the courts have become the guardians of such sectarian rights. But the sections of the BNA Act specifying the federal government's rights were the occasion of serious political conflict. This occurred at the time that Manitoba became a province and moved to abolish public support for denominational schools, although such support had been enjoyed while Manitoba was a territory. The attempt of the Conservative government in Ottawa to block this change brought about some major realignments in Canadian politics, including the first shift to the Liberal party in Quebec. Some Quebeckers were more concerned by the movement of the federal government into the sacrosanct arena of provincial rights than they were by denominational schools per se. In recent years the separation of powers generally has produced a dilemma for those who wish to finance the soaring costs of education without sacrificing complete provincial autonomy.

Since 1871 a full census of the population has been taken every ten years. Since then, the population has increased fivefold in the last hundred years, to over 20 million. Expansion has been accompanied by shifts in the distribution of people from east to west, and from farm and country to the city. An example of such a change is the share of the population held by the eastern provinces. After confederation Prince Edward, New Brunswick, and Nova Scotia had about one-quarter of the total populations. In 1961 these provinces were augmented by Newfoundland to make up the Atlantic provinces, yet together they now had but 10 percent of the total population. Another example of change is the proportion living in large metropolitan areas. In 1871 there were no metropolitan centers of 100,000 population. In 1968 there were nineteen, with just under 50 percent of all Canadians.

One remarkable feature of the Canadian population is the demographic tenacity of the French, whose *revanche des berceuses* has kept the percentage of French origin hovering around 30 percent of the total population. Most are concentrated in Quebec, but all provinces have some residents who affirm an identification with their French origin. Relations between English- and French-speaking Canadians, both within and outside of Quebec, have been a pressing problem in the 1960s, as illustrated by the publication of research reports and papers presented to the Royal Commission on Bilingualism and Biculturalism and the commissioners reports (Report, 1967; 1968; 1969; 1969a).

Historically, there have been much greater variations in the proportion and distribution of those who are of neither British nor French origin.[3] At the first census after confederation those of other origins constituted 7 percent of the population: at the

1961 census they were 26 percent. As the west opened to settlement, it became a home to people from all parts of the world, including Americans and Canadians. But it was largely European peasants who flocked to the prairie farmlands, and today, they and their children, along with settlers from other parts of the world, make up one-half of the population of the three prairie provinces. Large-scale European migration since World War II has not affected this area as much as did previous waves of immigrants. The majority of these recent migrants have gone to Ontario, and about another one-quarter to Quebec and British Columbia. The results have been an appreciable change in the ethnic composition only of Ontario and British Columbia. In 1941 18 percent of the Ontario population was neither British nor French; in 1961, it was 30 percent. During the same time span British Columbia changed from 27 to 37 percent other origins. The Royal Commission on Bilingualism and Biculturalism, while primarily set up to deal with the problems between the two founding groups, was not able to ignore these other ethnic groups. The melting pot has simmered gently in Canada, and all ethnic groups have retained a considerable degree of politically relevant identity (Vallee, Schwartz, Darknell, 1957, pp. 540–49; Schwartz, 1964, 253–71; Leslie, 1969, pp. 419–33).

The industrial revolution was several decades old when Canada reached nationhood, and some aspects of it had already begun to take hold. That concomitant of early industrialization, the railroad, was an important means of welding together the far-flung settlements making up the new nation. But Canada's early attractions lay in its resources, and the bulk of its wealth was the product of such commodities. To a considerable extent a reliance on the exploitation of resource wealth has not ceased, as a series of staples continue to dominate Canada's economic development, although industrialization has certainly occurred. The process of industrialization, however, has been highly uneven (Howland, 1958; Wilson, Gordon, Judek, 1965), as have been most other important demographic and economic trends (see Table 6).

If we need a summary way to characterize the end results of the formative influences on Canada's development it lies in the concept of regional heterogeneity. Geographically, economically, and demographically, Canada is a set of separate units. Politics have brought the units together but have also kept them apart. The remainder of this chapter will examine some of the results of this heterogeneity on political behavior (Cornell, Hamelin, Ouellet, Trudel, 1968; Warkentin, 1968; Schwartz, 1973).

B. ELECTORAL SYSTEM

1. POLITICAL CHARACTER

Canada's basic political characteristics are a federal structure of government, with an elected House of Commons[4] an appointed Senate at the national level, and elected legislatures in each of the provinces (Dawson, 1964). Only Quebec has had a bicameral system, with the second chamber appointed, but this was abolished in 1969

(Orban, 1967; Orban, 1969). Other functions of government are carried out by an appointed judiciary (Fox, 1966, pp. 246–62) and an administrative machinery (Cole, 1949; Cole, 1966; Report, 1962–1963). The federal government bureaucracy is filled through competitive examination, although the administrative heads—deputy ministers or their equivalent—can be recruited from outside the civil service. Political appointees consequently still have a role in a government bureaucracy otherwise run by more universalistic criteria. Reasonably equal chances of recruitment for personnel at all levels, regardless of characteristics such as ethnic origin, are possible, assuming equality of educational opportunity and of language use. These chances are not distributed independently of other characteristics, however, and this has been a sore point, particularly among the French-speaking (Vallee, Schwartz, Darknell, 1957, p. 545; Porter, 1965). Controversy over the place of bilingualism in the federal civil service has made this issue especially pertinent in recent years (Fox, 1966, pp. 59–61, 238–42; Report, 1969). At the provincial level the bureaucracy has been run with less concern for hiring and promoting on the basis of merit, but this is changing with the increased importance of technical qualifications.

Perhaps the most notable feature of government in Canada is its federal structure. Some reference has already been made to the kinds of tensions that existed from the outset of confederation in allocating powers between the two levels of government. (We need not consider here the conflicts between the municipal and provincial levels.) Instead of abating, these tensions have increased in magnitude.

> Provincial functions have grown in importance relative to the functions of the central government: expenditures upon education and health, upon roads and urban development, have multiplied.... With these changes, the fiscal power of the provinces has increased relative to that of the federal government, this being the result not only of higher provincial and municipal taxes but also of the very large fiscal transfers from the federal to provincial governments. (Johnson, 1968, pp. 22–23.)

It may be no accident that provincial governments have grown in strength and viability just at a time when federal governments struggled to carry on with weak or nonexistent parliamentary majorities. In the past 100 years Canada has not worked out an agreed form of federalism (Wheare, 1953; Crepeau and Macpherson, 1965; Mallory, 1954; Fox, 1966, pp. 75–112; Smiley, 1967; Scott, 1959; Johnson, 1968; Meekison, 1968; Cotnam, 1967; Trudeau, 1967). In the east the Maritime provinces have considered political union, in which Nova Scotia, New Brunswick, and Prince Edward Island would form a single province (Maritime Union Study, 1970). Although unattractive to political leaders in Alberta, a similar union for the three prairie provinces has also been broached.

2. The System of Voting

The right to vote has been variously defined through the years; virtual universal suffrage has been enjoyed since 1920. To vote in a federal election one must be eighteen, a Canadian citizen, resident in Canada for a year before the election, and resident in the constituency on the day of the election writ. Among those disqualified are the chief and assistant chief electoral officers, the returning officer in each constituency (although he can cast a tie-breaking vote), and inmates of penal and mental institutions. At times various ethnic and racial groups have been excluded, but these restrictions have finally eroded. As of 1960, for example all Canadian Indians were able to vote. The student of provincial elections must also take into account the possibility that provinces may have different qualifications (Dawson, 1964, pp. 349–53; Ward, 1963, pp. 226–30; Qualter, 1970, pp. 4–18).

Prior to each federal election an enumeration of voters is prepared, as set forth in the Dominions Elections Act, 1938 (Canada, Representation Commissioner, 1968). As soon as possible after an election is called the returning officer for each constituency appoints two enumerators for each urban polling division and one for each rural polling division. Enumerators are selected on the recommendation of the candidate who won the previous election, and in the case of urban constituencies, also by the candidate for the party that came second. In other words, both the winning and the second-voting party in urban constituencies participate in enumeration. As Qualter notes,

> The right to nominate enumerators, who are then paid by the state, is an important source of minor patronage to the two largest parties and is of great assistance in recruiting compaign workers. (Qualter, 1970, p. 23.)

Enumerators visit each home in their area, inquiring who is entitled to vote. Voters who come into the polling station are presented with a ballot that lists, in alphabetical order, the names, occupations, and home addresses of the candidates seeking to represent that constituency in the federal house. There has been no mention of party affiliation on federal ballots and those of most provinces, but the Election Act of 1970 promises to change this. Normally a voter may select only one candidate, but in two instances in Halifax and Prince Edward Island there were formerly two-member constituencies. The redistribution of seats prior to the 1968 federal election abolished these two-member seats. Provincially, there are still a number of such constituencies. (Engelmann and Schwartz, 1967, p. 122.)

Constituency boundaries are drawn separately for municipal, provincial, and federal elections. The party in office has an important advantage in setting these boundaries, even when members of other parties are represented on a redistribution board. At the federal level such redistribution may take place after the decennial census, which helps determine the population bases for each province's share of seats. In 1964 a federal statute transferred the drawing of boundaries to ten provincial commissions, whose activities are apparently much more closely geared to population-related criteria. The 1968 election was based on these new constituencies. The major effect has been to give better representation to urban residents, although still not with full weight given to their share of the voting population. (Qualter, 1970, pp. 81–128). The example of the federal government has led to the establishment of nonpartisan redistribution commissions at the provincial level. That a serious need exists is indicated by the even greater weight given to constituencies outside the big cities (for example, Long, 1969).

Seats in the House of Commons are allocated on the basis of both province and population. At confederation there were 181 seats. This rose to 265, 1953-1965; now there are 264.

The calling of elections at all levels of government is the responsibility of the governing party. This is a distinct advantage, allowing the governing party maneuverability. The maximum life of a federal house is five years, and normally an election is called before the expiration date. Similar procedures are followed in the provinces. The timing of federal and provincial elections is quite independent. The nomination of candidates is primarily the task of the party at the constituency level. Independent candidates without party support are increasingly rare in modern times. Some control from party headquarters is exerted over nominations, but this is not usually overt. Open participation of party headquarters or the party leader occurs when it is necessary to find a seat for a particular individual—sometimes the leader himself or one designated for a cabinet position. The amount of participation of rank-and-file party members in the nomination procedure varies with the party and the constituency. (Engelmann and Schwartz, 1967, pp. 162-67; Meisel, 1962; Perlin, 1964; Scarrow, 1964; Land, 1965.)

C. PARTY SYSTEM

1. HISTORY

One essential feature of the history of parties in Canada is the dominance of two parties, the Liberal and Conservative. The other is the strong provincial effect on party fortunes and on the fragmentation of the two-party system.

There have been twenty-five general elections between 1878 and 1970, the last in 1968. Up until 1917 there were occasional third-party candidates as well as independents; together, the Liberals and Conservatives won well over 90 percent of the popular vote and of the seats in the House of Commons. The election of 1917 was special in many respects, and a turning point in Canadian politics. Conscription to obtain sufficient troops for overseas duty was adopted in that year, as was the only federal coalition government in Canada's history. The coalition did not last long, but the effects of its policies were far-reaching. One was an almost lethal blow to the Conservative party in Quebec. While some Liberals had participated in the union government, the Quebec contingent had remained aloof under the leadership of Sir Wilfrid Laurier (Graham, 1960; Dawson, 1958; Skelton, 1921). Following the dislocations of the war and growing industrialization, agrarian protest parties were formed, mainly in western Canada. These were the provincial United Farmers parties and the related Progressive party, which contested the federal election of 1921. The Progressives were for the most part soon incorporated into the Liberal party, but the issues they fought and the interests they represented were of longer duration (Morton, 1967). Western radicalism had a new political expression in Social Credit and the Cooperative Commonwealth Federation (CCF) (Lipset, 1950; Engelmann and Schwartz, 1967; McHenry, 1950; Irving, 1959; Macpherson, 1953). Agrarian protest was not, of course, to be the sole theme; either separately or in conjunction with farmers, labor parties of different hues arose (Beck and Dooley, 1960; Horowitz, 1968; Robin, 1968). In Quebec, meanwhile, protest was taking a more "nationalistic" direction, making serious inroads into traditional party support. For example, wartime issues again brought forth dissension, and in the election of 1945, 34 percent of the popular vote went to third parties. Out of this, 13 percent was received by *Bloc Populaire Canadien,* a nationalist party opposed to the way the Liberals had handled conscription in 1944 and advocating a kind of left-wing syndicalism. More recently Social Credit has become in important electoral force in Quebec. In the elections of 1962 and 1963 this party obtained 26 and 27 percent of the provisional vote; this declined to 18 percent in 1965 and 16 percent in 1968 (see Pinard, 1971).

A detailed examination of party fortunes in federal elections since World War II shows how the relative strength of the two-party system is regionally circumscribed (see Table 1). In the four Atlantic provinces the Conservatives and Liberals normally

TABLE 1: **Percentage of Popular Vote Won by Two Major Parties, Canada and Provinces, 1945-1968**

	GENERAL ELECTIONS								
	1945	1949	1953	1957	1958	1962	1963	1965	1968
Newfoundland	—	—	100	95	99	95	95	97	96
Prince Edward Is.	96	97	99	99	100	95	98	98	97
Nova Scotia	83	90	93	95	95	89	94	91	93
New Brunswick	88	93	95	97	97	91	88	90	94
Quebec	59	85	90	89	96	70	65	77	75
Ontario	83	83	87	86	89	81	82	78	79
Manitoba	60	70	67	62	79	72	76	72	73
Saskatchewan	52	58	50	53	71	73	78	72	64
Alberta	41	52	60	56	74	62	67	69	86
British Columbia	58	65	45	54	65	54	56	49	61
Canada	69	79	80	80	87	75	74	73	77

gain over 90 percent of the popular vote. With only Quebec out of order, the average percentage of the vote won by the two major parties declines as we move westward. Over the nine elections British Columbia gave an average of 56 percent of its popular vote to the two older parties. In Saskatchewan and Alberta, both of which have strong ties with third parties, the traditional two-party system was most strongly upheld during the period of Conservative party ascendance. Third parties are often of short-lived duration and challenge the two older parties only in certain geographic areas (Beck, 1968).

Third parties have found their greatest scope in provincial politics. Farmer and Labor parties have both been more numerous and relatively more successful at the provincial level, especially in Quebec and the western provinces (Robin, 1972). *Union Nationale* became the governing party in Quebec in 1936, organizationally replacing the Conservatives in that province. Since that time it has exchanged government and opposition with the Liberals (Quinn, 1963; Lemieux, 1969a). Less potent but still noteworthy is the proliferation of independent and other minor party candidates, running strong in one or two elections but soon disappearing, only to be replaced by other special-interest groups. In Alberta and British Columbia the strength of the major parties has been seriously undermined. In Alberta opposition to the governing party has all but disappeared, giving virtually one-party government. The CCF has been a strong contender in British Columbia since the 1930s, and since 1952 the official opposition to the Social Credit government.

Canada has provided fertile ground for third parties because of a combination of social and political factors (Engelmann and Schwartz, 1967, pp. 52-53). The west is the frontier. Today it has new attractions, as witnessed by the burgeoning population of British Columbia and Alberta, and these attractions are quite distinct from the rest of Canada. The frontier, as we know, is always a place for innovation, and for suspicion of the established order. The frontier then is often associated with new forms of political expression. In addition we have in such new places of settlement a concern with economic exploitation. Certainly economic grievances exist elsewhere. But in the Atlantic provinces the disgruntled have worked through the two old parties, attempting to persuade governments to improve their economic conditions. Complaints of economic domination by English-speaking Canada have frequently been voiced in Quebec, but when these find expression in protest parties, the economic theme is subordinated to the "nationalistic" message. But all the splinter parties in the west have had a dominant conviction that eastern business interests were treating them unfairly, and that existing political parties were similarly exploitative.

In western Canada it is still possible to be regaled by stories of how, during the drought and depression of the 1930s, farms were foreclosed by eastern banks and farm machinery manufactured in the east sold more cheaply in Europe than in the west. We have here a form of "internal colonialism" that extends beyond the conflict between urban and rural interests. In an economy dominated by agriculture, as the west was, all residents were affected by serious dislocations, regardless of their own occupation.

Another factor is the extent the political culture involves values upholding a two-party system. In the Canadian general elections of 1958 and 1962 the two-party system was even the subject of campaign appeals. The real question is, how much does it concern the ordinary voter? In a survey conducted immediately after the 1965 general election respondents were asked for their views of majority government. Voters had absorbed the rhetoric about majority government, but saw little applicability to their own voting habits. Least importance was attached to it in Quebec and the west (Schwartz, 1973, ch. 8). The two-party system has been weakest in those areas where the proportions of British origin have been lowest.

Lipset has argued that, paradoxically, the very demands for caucus solidarity that give parliamentary government its strength also reduce its potency in Canada (Lipset, 1954, pp. 175-77, 196-98). Whenever individuals or groups find themselves at variance with the stance of the parliamentary party, there is little alternative but to form new political groupings better expressing the dissident views. In some cases opposition within the major parties has led to the formation of splinter parties. In others, as with farmers, dissent from the established political organizations has been from the outside. This suggests that caucus solidarity in Canada, unlike Britain, has been less able to contain the diversity and intensity of interests represented.

Given the political situation, the permanence of third parties has gained statutory recognition. In 1963 parties with more than eleven seats in parliament could claim an extra allowance of $ 4,000 for their leaders. In itself this recognition is not likely to be a centrifugal force. Yet it is of some note that not long after its institution, Réal Caouette, the leader of the Quebec wing of Social Credit, broke with his party and took his following into a new splinter party, *Le Ralliement des Créditistes.*

There is evidence that third parties have been more likely to emerge in those places that have a history of one-party dominance. Maurice Pinard has presented this argument with particular cogency. In general, he argues, where the second major party is traditionally weak, those opposed to the status quo represented by the party in office have little alternative. They can present their differences within the governing party, but this is hardly likely to bring about large-scale changes. Working or voting for the old opposition does not do much good, or is unattractive for a variety of reasons. With the existing political channels either unappealing or too weak to be effective, the pressure is very strong to create a new party. Pinard presents detailed evidence of this pattern for Quebec in the elections of 1958 and 1962, and also, though in less detail, elsewhere in Canada (Pinard, 1967; 1971).

These points suggest the inevitability of third parties, given the cleavages in Canadian society and the channels for their expression. But just as important is the evidence that these third parties have only limited potential on the national scene. Their greatest strength continues to lie at the provincial level and in those locations never fully integrated into the mainstream.

2. PARTY DIFFERENCES

Drawing distinctions among political parties is no easy task. One complication stems from the fact that parties with the same name, but separated by provincial boundaries or by federal or provincial spheres of influence, can be quite distinct. This is augmented by the different problems handled by the two spheres of government, the strongly regional nature of the country, and organizational separation, whether partial or total, between federal and provincial wings of the party. This latter leads to what one commentator calls "federal-provincial schizophrenia" (Black, 1967). (Another complication arises from the passage of time, as party stances become transformed through changing circumstances, not the least of which is finding effective means for winning elections. We might expect to find such shifts most commonly in the older parties, whom their critics in any case find as alike as Tweedledum and Tweedledee. It is hence illuminating to look at the more overtly ideological third parties. Social Credit, for example, grew from its first leaders' convictions that Major Douglas's principles of social credit contained the key to social and economic well-being (Macpherson, 1953; Irving, 1959). Yet party platforms in recent years show no trace of these principles. The CCF began with a vow to abolish capitalism. At the Winnipeg convention in 1956 this goal may still have been present, but it received no mention (Engelmann and Schwartz, 1967, p. 227).

Despite the difficulties of characterizing Canadian parties, some guidelines do exist. Scarrow takes as his starting point the question of whether the Conservative and Liberal parties in Canada are comparable to the Republican and Democratic parties in the United States. His answer is in the negative. Based on a review of existing literature and an examination of Canadian Gallup Poll data, he concludes that interparty differences are considerably more blurred in Canada than in the United States. The traits he isolates as particularly important in making for this relative lack of differentiation in Canada are "the absence of party conflict, the nonpartisan posture of organized interest groups, the dominance of noneconomic correlates of partisan preference, low image differential, low party identification, low policy polarization among respective supporters, and wide swings of the electoral pendulum" (Scarrow, 1965, p. 76).

In a highly imaginative paper Meisel categorizes parties in terms of six attributes: ideology, locus of power, structure, basis of support, personnel, and modus operandi. The resulting scheme is too complex to duplicate here, but a few examples should illustrate the key differences. One important aspect of the orientation of any party is its conception of the nature of Canada. The crucial questions, according to Meisel, are whether Canada "is a British country, a partnership between the two founding groups, or a multiethnic, pluralistic state like the United States of America, dedicated to the idea of creating a 'melting pot' " (Meisel, 1967, p 42). He characterizes the Liberal party as committed to "dualism–pluralism," the Conservative to "British connection–pluralism," and the NDP to "dualism-strong centralism." This evaluation is derived from a review of the statements of leaders and major spokesmen. It also has considerable affinity to the views of rank-and-file party supporters (Schwartz, 1967). Another dimension of party ideology is concerned with "whether a party assigns the state a socialist-welfare-state function, or it leans more to what used to be called laissez-faire. This division indicates whether a party is on the left or the right, in the sense in which these terms are usually employed." All three parties are what Meisel calls "welfare-statist" in orientation, but the Liberals are also oriented to business, the Conservatives to business and farm interests, and the NDP to a more socialist perspective.

A more direct approach to the role of ideology in Canadian parties is made by Gad Horowitz. Like Scarrow, his approach is inherently comparative, asking why "In the United States, organized socialism is dead; in Canada, socialism, though far from national power is a significant political force" (Horowitz, 1966, p. 143). His explanation for this difference encompasses the relative strength of toryism in both countries, and the position and character of liberalism. The basis of his argument is derived from Hartz (Hartz 1955; Hartz, 1964). The thesis is that the new societies founded by Europeans were fragments thrown off from Europe, and as such, lost "the stimulus to change that the whole provides" (Hartz, 1964, p. 3). To have the full ideological spectrum from feudal or tory through liberal whig to liberal democrat to socialist requires that each of the elements be in interaction with each other.

Horowitz lists those characteristics of English Canadian society that are related to the presence of toryism. Pointedly, he terms these "un-American." They are:

(a) the presence of tory ideology in the founding of English Canada by the Loyalists,...
(b) the persistent power of whiggery or right-wing liberalism in Canada (the Family Compacts) as contrasted with the rapid and easy victory of liberal democracy (Jefferson, Jackson) in the United States;
(c) the ambivalent centrist character of left-wing liberalism in Canada as contrasted with the unambiguously leftist position of left-wing liberalism in the United States;
(d) the presence of an influential and legitimate socialist movement in English Canada as contrasted with the illegitimacy and early death of American socialism;
(e) the failure of English Canadian liberalism to develop into the one true myth, the nationalist cult, and the parallel failure to exclude toryism and socialism as "un-Canadian"; in other words, the legitimacy of ideological diversity in English Canada. (p. 150)

The major political carrier of toryism has been the Conservative party. Horowitz draws some important distinctions between U.S. Republicans and Canadian Conservatives, deriving from the later's affinities with the British Conservatives.

It's not simply their emphasis on loyalty to the crown and the British connection, but a touch of the authentic tory aura—traditionalism, elitism, the strong state, and so on. The Canadian Conservatives lack the American aura of rugged individualism. Theirs is not the characteristically American conservatism which conserves only *liberal* values. (p. 157)

Another point of difference between the neighboring countries is the existence of the red tory. Horowitz uses this term to cover two different political types: the Conservative with affinities for the CCF/NDP but not the Liberals, and the socialist with a preference for the Conservatives but not the Liberals. The second type is probably more accurately conceptualized as a tory socialist. The sources of this affinity have already been suggested in the parallel views of society as an organic whole. The nature of socialism differs between the two countries. "In Canada, socialism is British, non-Marxist, and worldly; in the United States it is German, Marxist, and other-worldly" (159). Marxist socialism has not been absent in Canada; it finds expression in the Communist party, among other places, but it has not been a dominant ideology in the CCF or NDP.[5]

Finally the character of liberalism too differs in Canada because of its contacts with toryism and socialism. According to Horowitz, "The key to understanding the Liberal party in Canada is to see it as a *centre* party, with *influential* enemies on both right and left" (162). By contrast, he considers liberal Democrats in America to be on the left (169).

While some disagree with Hartz's analysis of "fragment" societies, and others might well question Horowitz's distinctions between political ideologies in the United States and Canada, he has drawn attention to important if subtle details of difference. These are among the distinguishing marks of Canadian nationhood—neither British nor American but uniquely affected by both.

Our own approach to Canadian parties has differed from all of the analyses presented above (Engelmann and Schwartz, 1967, pp. 3-14). Our focus has been comparative, but not necessarily in terms of the United States or Britain. We have used four dimensions of analysis: the breadth of party support; the nature of its organization and leadership; the focus of appeal; and the relation to government. Each dimension is dichotomized, distinguishing first of all between parties with a broad social base and those with a restricted one.

The paradigm resulting from this scheme contains sixteen categories. In Canada only five types were found (Engelmann and Schwartz, 1967, p. 248). Two party types predominate: broad-based, cadre parties of electoral success with governmental experience—the Liberals, the Conservatives, *Union Nationale* in Quebec, and Social Credit in the west—and mass parties of principle with restricted bases and no federal governmental experience—the CCF and the New Democratic Party.

Rose and Urwin classify the Liberals and the NDP as heterogeneous parties that bring together voters of diverse social characteristics. In this regard the NDP is a special case for a socialist party, resembling only the unsuccessful experiences of the Irish Labor party and the old Italian PSDI (Rose and Urwin, 1969, p. 16). Despite the evidence we provide of the lack of social cohesiveness among party supporters, we would qualify this classification. On the basis of the support it currently attracts the NDP is far from being a single-class party. But its regional heterogeneity is limited by its weak appeal in the Atlantic provinces and even Quebec. In this regard it has some affinities with the remaining parties, which Rose and Urwin classify as cohesive because they manifest mutually reinforcing loyalties. In the case of the Conservatives this is reflected by their preponderance of English-speaking, Protestant supporters. This is true as well for Social Credit, augmented by its regional concentration in the west, though broad definitions of language and religion obscure the importance of non-British as well as non-French origins and non-Establishment Protestant faiths for Social Credit. Most cohesive of all are the *Créditistes* of Quebec, whose language, religion, social class, and region are all mutually reinforcing.

From this analysis we see how Canadian parties reflect the diverse tensions of Canadian society. Cohesive class parties are absent, but the presence of parties differentiated by religion, language, and region means that the political stress level is kept high, and augmented by regionally linked economic problems. The ability of the Liberal party to attract a broad spectrum of support, and particularly to incorporate Quebec support, has eased tensions considerably. Today the greatest danger for the Liberal party, and perhaps for Canada, would arise if it lost its strength in Quebec. Then there would be no party with support integrating Canadians who differed in many fundamental social characteristics. Canadian diversity refutes an expected pattern of regularity in electoral systems. Rae states the hypothesis thus: "Plurality formulae cause two-party systems" (1967, p. 93). Ninety percent of his cross-national tests result as expected. But all the Canadian elections Rae tests between 1945 and 1963 reject the hypothesis. As the previous description of party history indicated, this was a period of considerable electoral instability, in which three elections resulted in minority governments. Rae is sufficiently persuaded by the Canadian examples (as well as the Austrian exceptions) to alter his hypothesis (95).

Cairns examines the Canadian situation in much more detail, taking into account elections from 1921 to 1965 (1968, pp. 55-80). He asserts: "The electoral system has consistently exaggerated the significance of cleavages demarcated by sectional/provincial boundaries and has thus tended to transform contests between parties into contests between sections/provinces" (62).

He bases this conclusion upon the fact that the majority party has generally won a greater proportion of seats than votes. This has aggravated the tendency of the major parties to concentrate their appeal in those areas where they are confident of gaining support. The Conservatives have not compaigned vigorously in Quebec nor have the Liberals in Alberta. At the same time a minor party with a sectional stronghold has generally been rewarded with more seats than its share of the vote, while minor parties without a regional locus have had difficulty in surviving.[6] Cairns suggests that perhaps the peculiar problems of Canada could be helped by a system of proportional representation,[7] which he feels would force parties to seek votes in all areas of the country, and hence would lead to greater national integration (Cairns, 1968, p. 80).

II. The Act of Voting Today

A. TURNOUT

Voting is not an automatic act. Although it is relatively easy in Canada both to qualify and to vote, there is considerable variation in voting rates. Scarrow has compared turnout figures from 1921 to 1958, using two separate sets of figures for computing percentages (1967, pp. 104-14). These are numbers on the voter lists and the population aged twenty-one and over. Turnout is about 6 percent lower when the total adult population is used as the base as against voter lists. This may not be due to errors and omissions on the part of enumerators but because the total population contains approximately that percentage who are ineligible to vote by reason of lack of citizenship or insufficient length of residence in their constituency.

Scarrow's paper on turnout remains the most thorough analysis of this subject in Canada, although his data end at 1958. Turnout in federal elections since 1921 has been over 60 percent in three elections in the 1920s, and over 70 percent every election since then, with but two exceptions. What is of particular interest is variations in levels of turnout by province. Table 2 contains turnout data from 1921 to 1965 (Courtney, 1967). Turnout is unusually high in Prince Edward Island and Saskatchewan, unusually low in Alberta and Newfoundland. In the two latter provinces we are undoubtedly seeing the effects of the lack of a competitive party structure. In the two former areas high turnout is achieved by the existence of a highly politicized environment, encouraged in Prince Edward Island by almost the highest per capita circulation of newspapers in the country and in Saskatchewan by the continuing effects of the CCF's stimulation of grass roots political involvement as a solution to local problems (Lipset, 1950). Moreover, both provinces have been the scene of highly competitive electoral contests.

TABLE 2: **Percentage of Average Voter Turnout in Provinces, Canadian Federal Elections, 1921-1965**

Provinces	Turnout
Prince Edward Is.	83
Saskatchewan	77
Nova Scotia	77
New Brunswick	76
British Columbia	74
Quebec	73
Manitoba	73
Ontario	72
Alberta	68
Newfoundland	65

Source: Data from Courtney, 1967, pp. 200–201.

Some information is available on correlates of turnout. Scarrow has examined the relation between urban and rural residence and the likelihood of voting. Rural turnout was higher in eight out of ten elections between 1925 and 1958. The difference has varied from 14 percent to less than 2 percent. The measure of urban and rural used, however, presents some problems. The chief electoral officer has defined as "urban" all polling districts in an incorporated municipality of at least 5,000 population. This differs from the current census definition, which considers any municipality of at least 1,000 population as urban. It could be argued that the larger unit is more likely to be urban, yet the exclusion of unincorporated municipalities frequently omits distinctly urban areas, such as the suburbs of some cities. Scarrow's response to these complexities was to make additional comparisons in Ontario and Quebec, using only the most clearly rural and urban constituencies. In each of the five elections examined turnout was distinctly higher in rural ridings. This was especially so in Quebec.

Laponce found parallel differences in estimating turnout in British Columbia for the 1963 election (Laponce, 1967, p. 80). Yet Laponce also sounds some cautionary notes on the accuracy of these aggregate findings. These arise from an exceedingly detailed survey conducted in one constituency in Vancouver, where the sampled population could be checked against voter lists. His conclusions are that under-representation of voters is minimal, not much more than 1 percent in the riding studied. Instead, there is considerable *over* enumeration. This does not seem to arise from the excessive enthusiasm of enumerators, eager for the extra money that each name brings, but the procedures do contribute to inflated lists, since enumerators may collect information from third parties and are not required to challenge self-reported eligibility. This results in the listing of persons unable or highly unlikely to vote—noncitizens, the deceased, critically ill, those moved from the district or away on prolonged trips. Some of these, of course, are still eligible to vote, even though they will not. But Laponce estimates that all such persons enumerated in the riding studied made up almost 7 percent of the sample. If these enumeration practices are common, then it is possible that turnout is actually higher in urban areas than normally calculated. The reference is only to urban constituencies, since it is presumed that people know more about their neighbors in rural areas. At the moment, however, this must remain as a generalization based on one sample.

Laponce's article is more concerned, in any event, with determining how many eligible voters are voluntary abstainers and for what reasons. In his sample he isolated 16 percent who did not vote in the 1963 election, although they were not prevented from doing so by physical or other disability. They were divided into five main types: boycotters, retired electors, barbarians (those with least political knowledge), poorly informed spectators (moderately informed but lacking involvement), and well-informed spectators. Of the voluntary nonvoters, barbarians made up the largest category (45 percent), and poorly informed spectators the next (23 percent). At the moment we do not know to what extent Laponce's findings are applicable to the remainder of the country. That voluntary nonvoters are mainly undereducated, poorly informed, and little interested in politics is probably general, however.

We turn again to Scarrow for an analysis of voting in provincial elections. Unlike the United States, where turnout in off-year state elections is always lower than in presidential election years, there is no comparable trend in Canada. For the six provinces where data were available, turnout was compared with that in the immediately preceding federal election. Higher turnout in provincial elections occurs in Alberta, Nova Scotia, and Quebec, and lower turnout occurs in Manitoba, Ontario, and British Columbia. Most of these trends may be attributed to the relative competitiveness of the different elections. For example, Quebec provincial elections are closely fought contests between the Liberals and *Union Nationale*, but at the federal level the Liberals normally have such a strong position that competition is minimal. The higher rate of turnout in Alberta is almost all accounted for by early responses to the emergence of Social Credit. Since then turnout has declined, and Alberta in general is a province with low participation rates.

B. VOTING

1. STABILITY OF CHOICE

Although the life of a federal parliament is five years, there have been six elections between 1957 (the beginning of a Conservative upsurge) and the election in 1968. Four of these elections resulted in minority governments. It is worth considering how partisan choice is affected during such a period of governmental change and instability.

The stability of partisan attachments is revealed to some extent by aggregate electoral statistics. For example, in six general elections between 1953 and 1965, 25 percent of the 265 constituencies gave the same party a plurality at each election. Twenty-nine percent switched once, 35 percent twice, 9 percent three times, and only 2 percent four times (Courtney, 1967, pp. 204-206). That is, the change from a Liberal government in 1953 to a minority and then a strong Conservative government and finally to a series of minority governments came about through an alteration in the voting patterns of probably less than half the constituencies at any one election. These data themselves suggest much less than a massive alteration in the voting habits of Canadians. Yet one is inclined to think that major realignments must be taking place among the electorate during a period of political change and instability. In a nation-wide survey conducted after the 1965 election[8], 14 percent of the respondents said that they had not voted in 1965. Another 6 percent would not report on the party they had voted for, either because of forgetfulness or unwillingness to share this kind of inform-ation. Our hunch is that most of these probably did not vote, since it is not likely that the lapse of a few months would be a major cause of not remembering how one voted. In addition a turnout rate of 80 percent seems more reasonable, compared to the general electorate. In a preceding question respondents were asked if they voted in the 1963 election, and if so, for which party. Thirteen percent reported not voting, and another 10 percent could not remember or refused. In this instance there were probably some who quite legitimately forgot what they had done two years earlier. In considering the stability of partisan choice, however, we can only take into account those respondents who gave an explicit party choice for each of the elections. If we use as our base the 80 percent of the respondents we feel quite sure voted in 1963, then 71 percent of these reported voting for the same party in the two past federal elections. If we consider only those we are quite certain voted in both elections, then those choosing the same party twice rises to 83 percent. The stability of party preference among regular voters, even in a time of political volatility, is very high.

In Table 3 we have the percentages who voted for the same party twice according to region and party. Bases for the percentages are those with a known party choice in 1965. There are two major findings from this table—confirmed, we might add, by other measures of partisan stability used in the survey. One is the larger pool of loyal electors among supporters of the major parties, and second is the greater loyalty of voters to their party in the older regions of Canada. The extent of party differences is even more sharply revealed if we consider the percentage that did not vote or gave no answer on their 1963 vote: this was 11 percent for those who voted Conservative in 1965, 16 percent for Liberals, 16 percent for NDP, 24 percent for Social Credit, and 15 percent for Créditistes. For known voters among the two older parties, no more than 10 percent switched from one party to another in the two elections. Variations by region are due both to lower turnout in the earlier election or to vote switching. For example, in the prairie provinces 22 percent of those who voted Liberal in 1965 did not vote or did not report this in 1963. In addition 15 percent had previously voted Conservative. The parties that benefit also vary by region. For example, of current NDP voters in Quebec, 6 percent had voted Conservative in 1963 and 29 percent Liberal. In the prairies, however, NDP switchers were evenly divided between former Conservatives and Liberals.

TABLE 3: **Percentage Voting for Same Party in 1963 and 1965 Federal Elections, by Region and Past Vote, 1965 Vote**

	Liberal	Conservative	NDP	Social Credit
Atlantic	85	83	(25)[b]	—
	(100)	(83)	(8)	
Quebec	80	74	33	69
	(357)	(97)	(70)	(65)
Ontario	14	82	61	—
	(424)	(311)	(132)	
Prairies	57	76	55	46
	(89)	(125)	(56)	(37)
British Columbia	72	76	77	38
	(78)	(58)	(62)	(26)
Total	74	79	56	40
	(1,048)	(674)	(328)	(67)[a]

Figures in parentheses are base Ns.

[a] The total for Social Credit includes four cases in the Atlantic provinces and Ontario. The Quebec *Créditistes* are not included.

[b] Too few cases to percentage.

Source: Schwartz, 1973, ch. 6.

On the basis of these two elections—and no argument can be made for their typicality—vote switching was done mainly by the supporters of minor parties, parties still sufficiently new not to have built up the solid support of the major ones, and by new voters. It seems that at this period a good deal of the change that did occur was a result of the behavior of those who had not previously voted, or if they had, they did not have firm enough ties with a party to recall its name. Some of the nonvoters were not eligible to vote in the previous election, but others are periodic voters, casting their ballot when issues, candidates, and interest have some special, personal appeal.

Further comparisons of party stability have been made by Laponce (1969, pp.136-64), in which two samples of the constituency of Vancouver-Burrard were interviewed prior to the elections of 1963 and 1965. Data are presented in Table 4, along with comparative figures for national samples in four elections. Results differ from our own for the 1965 election. It should be noted that the index used by Laponce was computed using the previous (1963) election as the base, and our survey used a more reliable form of sample than did the Canadian Institute of Public Opinion.

TABLE 4: Index of Party Stability, 1957-1968

	Canada 1957 (CIPO)	Canada 1958 (CIPO)	Canada 1963 (CIPO)	Canada 1965 (CIPO)	Canada 1968 (CIPO)	Burrard 1963 (Laponce)	Burrard 1965 (Laponce)
NDP	80	66	74	79	80	96	92
Liberal	83	78	87	81	83	87	81
Conservative	93	94	72	78	70	66	73
Social Credit	77	32	78	62	56	75	69

Index=y/x × 100. x is number who supported the party in the previous election and y is the number who still support the party in the election studied.
Source: Laponce, 1969, pp. 141, 206.

Additional information on the stability of partisan choice is available from other subnational samples (Regenstreif, 1965, pp. 117, 123, 137, 139). Stability between 1958 and 1962 is treated in detail by Pinard, whose principal concern is with the sources of Social Credit support in Quebec (Pinard, 1968, pp. 50-53). His analysis is of a contextual nature, taking into account the ecological character of constituencies and the individual character of voter choice. Constituencies are classified according to their political fortunes in the federal elections of 1957 and 1958 (the latter year being one of a large-scale Conservative sweep to victory), and also by the judgment of informants on the strength of party organization. Those few districts that had Conservative members in 1957 and 1958 are classified as strong Conservative; those that switched from Liberal to Conservative as intermediate Conservative; and those that remained Liberal in both elections as weak Conservative. Pinard's conclusion is that the weaker the Conservative party in a district, the more likely that the 1958 Conservative voters would switch to Social Credit in 1962.

These data provide some of the empirical support for Pinard's thesis, already referred to, on the absence of a viable opposition and the rise of protest parties. It is a thesis, however, that has not gone unchallenged. Lemieux, for example, examining the electoral history of the Quebec constituency of Lévis, comes up with quite opposite conclusions. He believes that Social Credit won support in 1962 largely from those who had voted Conservative in 1958, and moreover, from those centers where the Conservatives had been most successful in 1958. Liberals also lost proportionately more supporters in those areas where they had remained strong in 1958. (Lemieux, 1964, pp. 46-50.) Pinard disputes these points, attributing them to an ecological correlation that would not hold up under individual analysis. Yet Pinard's argument seems much less clear-cut when we examine his data in detail. Pinard presents his data with the vote in the 1958 election as the independent variable. In weak, intermediate, and strong Conservative districts, respectively, the percent of former Conservatives who voted Social Credit in 1962 was 46, 29, and 4. The stronger the Conservative constituency, the greater likelihood there was a stable Conservative vote across the two elections (Pinard, 1968, p. 51). If the data are run with 1962 vote as the independent variable, however, the results are more equivocal. Again going from weak to strong Conservative districts, the percentage of those voting Social Credit in 1962, but Conservative in 1958, is 42, 64, and 41. At both extremes Social Credit picked up relatively more support from former Liberal voters. Remembering that Lemieux considered Conservative strength only in terms of 1958 performance (more likely to be in Pinard's intermediate category), Pinard's transposed findings conform exactly to Lemieux's generalizations. Before leaving these data, two important items of information must now be disclosed. One is that the sample of Social Credit voters was actually largest in the *weak* Conservative districts, in confirmation of Pinard's basic hypothesis. Second is the fact that some of these generalizations are based on quite small case bases. The sample, for example, picked up only twenty-two 1962 Social Credit voters in "intermediate" districts.

Additional evidence on the relation between behavior in two elections based on surveys comes from a study done by Regenstreif. Prior to the 1965 election 1,001 interviews were conducted in Vancouver, Sault Ste. Marie, Toronto, and Hamilton. Data are presented in aggregate form, and from what we already know about regional effects this may well be troublesome. The base variable in 1963 vote—70 percent of the Liberals, 66 percent of the Conservatives, and 89 percent of the NDP indicated that they would again vote for these parties in 1965 (Gagne and Regenstreif, 1967, p. 543). Whatever stock we wish to place on these absolute figures, we do know at least that in the two provinces where interviewing was conducted, the NDP did have a more stable base of support in federal elections than elsewhere in Canada.

In the United States students of voting behavior have found it useful to differentiate between those who vote for a party in a single election and those who identify themselves in general terms as partisan supporters. The latter are, for example, more consistent in their political attitudes if they are strong rather than weak identifiers (Campbell et al., 1960, pp. 120-45). In his four-city study, Regenstreif also considered identification. He found that NDP identifiers were more likely to vote for their party than identifiers with the two older parties. The percentages were 92 for the NDP, 76 for the Liberals, and 68 for the Conservatives. This range of difference was not so great when identifiers were distinguished according to the strength of their attachment. Very strong identifiers indicated that they would vote for their party in the coming election in the case of 100 percent of the NDP, 86 percent of the Liberals, and 92 percent of the Conservatives (Gagne and Regenstreif, 1967, pp. 541-42).

Further study on the importance of party identification remains to be done. On the basis of preliminary analysis of national samples after the 1965 and 1968 election it has been suggested that identification has no greater stability in Canada than does party preference in a particular election (Meisel, 1970, p. 5). It is not clear, however, whether we should consider either of these measures as distinctly volatile or not. It appears that in any election we can anticipate a "normal" shift of about one-quarter of the electorate who had previously voted.

2. SECOND CHOICE

An electoral system based on single-member constituencies can be used as a rough measure of public opinion only in the sense of indicating winners and losers. Where there are more than two candidates in a constituency, wins and losses are an even less effective measure of the way in which the public assesses the parties. One way to compensate for the deficiencies of electoral data is through information on party images. For example, Meisel has used the semantic differential technique to evaluate images of all national parties and has also traced shifts in these images from 1965 to 1968. Among the interesting findings are the improvement in the image of the Liberals and the decline in image for the NDP. The relation between these images and party preference remains to be analyzed (Meisel, 1970). A sample of voters in two constituencies in Quebec provided Lemieux with information on party images along eight dimensions, including issue stands and various forms of leadership. He uncovered two basic factors differentiating the four parties. The first produced a ranking of NDP–Liberal–Conservative–*Ralliement des Créditistes*, conforming to what would be conventionally understood as an economic Left-Right dimension. On the second factor parties ranked Créditiste-Liberal-Conservative-NDP, apparently tapping an ethnic dimensions, ranging from the most to the least French (Lemieux, 1969).

Most relevant are data on second-choice parties (Schwartz, 1973, ch. 8). Unfortunately, because of confusion in the administration of our 1965 questionnaire, the resulting data can only be used to indicate some general tendencies. Insofar as we can determine, the second choice of most party supporters was one of the two major parties. Liberal and Conservative voters who chose NDP as an alternative did so with about half the frequency with which they chose the other major party. Only the *Créditistes* considered a minor party, the NDP, as a significant alternative.

Eighty-one percent of our sample replied that there was some party that they currently would not vote for, with not much difference among partisan supporters. In all instances the excluded parties were mainly the minor ones. Most objectionable was *Le Ralliement des Créditistes*, singled out by 45 percent of those who first indicated that they would exclude some party from the realm of choice. Social Credit and NDP were mentioned next in frequency, by 19 and 14 percent, respectively, of the relevant population.

A more accurate assessment of second-choice parties comes from an examination of those few constituencies that have been represented by two members. Ward has compiled data on ten constituencies of this sort in federal elections between 1887 and 1945 (Ward, 1967, pp. 125–29). Some split-ticket voting was apparent, but without any patterns, and these electoral data cannot in themselves be interpreted without considerably more information about individual constituencies. One of the two-member districts in existence until the redistribution after the 1965 election was Halifax. It has been studied by Davis in three elections, using both total electoral results and samples of ballots (Davis, 1964, pp. 19–32; Davis, 1966, pp. 366–71). The amount of difference estimated between straight–and split-party choices varies with the procedure used, but at the highest level, based on a sample of ballots, the ratio of split to straight ballots was .171 in 1962, .132 in 1963, and .084 in 1965. In the 1962 election the ratio was higher for Conservatives compared to Liberals, .163 to .147. In 1963 and 1965 the ratios are lower and almost identical. Although two NDP candidates also ran, they were much less likely than the older parties to receive consistent support. In the three elections studied the ratio of split to straight ballots for the NDP was .435, .638, and .431, respectively. However imperfectly, as the author concludes, these data indicate that "other than partisan impulses" operate in the act of voting.

3. FEDERAL-PROVINCIAL VOTING PATTERNS

In a federal system of government, where the two levels have different responsibilities and face different problems, and where elections for the two legislatures are not held simultaneously, it would not be surprising if individual voting behavior varied with the election in question. The apparent tendency for the party in power federally to be out of power in the majority of the provincial legislatures has been attributed by some commentators to a conscious effort on the part of voters to achieve a balance of power (Underhill, 1955, pp. 27–46; Wrong, 1957, pp. 252–64). No evidence has ever been presented for this motivational theory, nor does it even seem plausible in the light of what is known about cognitive bases of voting behavior generally. Generalizations about voting behavior that derive from aggregate results of federal and provincial elections are an example of fallacious reasoning based on presumed ecological correlations. It is appropriate to ask, "What is the relation between federal and provincial voting?", not to state, "Here is a relationship and let us now deduce some explanations."

We have two bodies of data to bring to this issue, although neither is really complete. The first of these is an examination of federal and provincial electoral trends by Scarrow, unfortunately ending at 1957 (Scarrow, 1960, pp. 289–98). At the very least the data are historically relevant. From 1930 to 1957 there were 104 federal and provincial elections; in sixteen of these the party victorious at the provincial level was different from the party in power at the federal level. Compared to other federal systems in a comparable time period, this turns out to be quite a low level of party alternation. During presidential years in the United States a party split between the governor and president occurred in 29 percent of the states. In Australia 35 percent of the elections were of an alternating character. Scarrow concluded that "the available evidence demonstrates not only that the Canadian electorate is not unique in its voting pattern, but that it appears to be a relatively poor example of the alternating voting habit" (Scarrow, 1960, p. 293). Scarrow is also intrigued by the possible effects of differential rates of turnout in federal and provincial elections. He found, for example, in some areas where turnout was higher in federal elections, that the Liberal vote was most affected, suggesting that there may be a pool of federally oriented Liberals who do not vote in provincial elections (Scarrow, 1960, p. 295; Scarrow, 1967, p. 113). This has also been found by Wilson and Hoffman (1970) in Ontario.

The most effective means for examining the relation between federal and provincial voting behavior is through the appropriate survey data. Our survey provides such information for a limited time span: vote in the 1965 election compared to that in the most immediately past provincial election. The time of the latter would vary from province to province. Table 5 documents those who voted for the same party in the two elections. What is most striking about these data is the vast amount of inter-regional variation in the stability of partisan choice except for the more localized Social Credit.

TABLE 5: Percentage Voting for Same Party in Both Last Provincial and Federal Election, 1965 Vote by Region and Past Federal Vote

	Liberal	Conservative	NDP	Social Credit
Atlantic	86	93	(12)[b]	
	(100)	(83)	(8)	—
Quebec	79	61	10	
	(357)	(97)	(70)	—
Ontario	53	82	46	
	(424)	(311)	(132)	—
Prairies	58	43	54	84
	(89)	(125)	(56)	(37)
British Columbia	38	28	71	92
	(78)	(58)	(62)	(26)
Total	64	68	44	82
	(1,048)	(674)	(328)	(67)[a]

Figures in parentheses are base Ns.
a The total for Social Credit includes four cases in the Atlantic provinces and Ontario.
b Too few cases to percentage.
Source: Schwartz, 1973, ch. 6.

At both levels of government the two major parties are strong in the Atlantic provinces, except in Newfoundland, where the Liberals had almost total ascendancy until the Conservative upset of 1968 (Beck, 1968, p. 410). Concomitantly, minor parties are weak. There are, then, two solid bodies of support for the Liberals and Conservatives. Relatively, Liberals are somewhat more likely to switch in provincial elections, when they vote Conservative.

Provincially, there has been strong two-party government in Quebec, where power alternated between the Liberals and *Union Nationale*. Federally, however, the Liberals traditionally have greatest power, challenged mainly by third parties rather than by the Conservatives. The one exception to this pattern in recent years was the election of 1958. We see these political realities revealed in the responses of voters, with a high degree of consistency only among Liberal voters. In the 1962 provincial election federal Conservatives reportedly voted for the same party in 61 percent of the cases. No Conservative candidates ran, but this represents the link with *Union Nationale*. NDP support has been very weak at the provincial level, and about 60 percent of these voters reportedly cast their provincial ballot for the Liberals. *Créditiste* voters are not shown on the table since at this time their party was not a contender on the provincial scene; provincially, about one-third voted Liberal, one-quarter *Union Nationale*, and one-quarter would not report their choice. A comparison between the 1968 federal and the 1970 provincial elections, where the separatist *Parti Québécois* and the *Créditistes* both ran, would undoubtedly produce quite different results.

In Ontario the Conservative party is strong provincially, and 82 percent of those who voted for the party in the federal election did so as well in the provincial one. Where a provincial choice is known for Liberals, more than half went to the same party and one-quarter to the Conservatives. Interestingly, about two and one half times as many federal NDP voters had previously voted for the provincial Conservatives as for the Liberals. Some of this pattern is probably attributable to what we have previously discussed as the tory socialist, but it is also the case that the greater strength of the Conservatives in Ontario is the source of a strong electoral pull generally (Wilson and Hoffman, 1970, 1971).

In the two elections considered the Atlantic provinces provided a milieu for stable major party support. This was also true for the Liberals in Quebec and the Conservatives in Ontario. But in the western provinces the major parties have lost their appeal at the provincial level. Federal Liberals are drawn to Social Credit and half as frequently, to the Conservatives. Federal Conservatives are pulled to Social Credit. There is also some attraction from the provincial NDP, largely in Saskatchewan, where there is a strong Liberal party, able to command allegiance at both levels of government. The Conservatives, however, are weak. While there is some independent evidence of tory socialism and its counterpart, the kinds of alternatives available clearly affect voters' choices. Social Credit may draw support from the older parties in provincial elections, but NDP supporters are almost immune to its appeals. When they did not vote for the NDP, they chose instead one of the major parties.

Finally, in British Columbia, where at the provincial level the traditional parties have been eclipsed, considerably less than half of the federal voters stick with the same party provincially. Social Credit obtains the bulk of the votes of both federal Liberals and Conservatives. Social Credit even picks up votes here from federal NDPers. In this province alone we find evidence of stable party support across types of elections for the minor parties. These results are supported by Laponce's study of a single constituency (Laponce, 1969, pp. 168–74).

We have been able to document a kind of split-ticket voting by the individual voter, independently of aggregate results. We need to know more about these voters, in particular, what motivates their choices (Courtney and Smith, 1966). At the structural level there are a good number of reasons that can be suggested for their existence.

These include the special interests of each province, arising from a unique configuration of demographic and economic factors. Such local concerns have much more opportunity for incorporation into campaign themes and programs at provincial than at federal elections. Moreover, the division of powers between the two levels of government means that their responsibilities differ and the consequent issues they bring before the public may be quite distinct. The fact that elections fall at different time periods accentuates these possible differences, since an issue troublesome at one time may be insignificant at another. Some of these factors have also contributed to differences in political traditions among the provinces, in particular the emergence of third parties and their differential strength in provincial legislatures. In some areas, then, voters are faced with quite different electoral choices. Even where the party names are the same federally and provincially, the programs, policies, and personnel can be quite different.

C. ELECTORAL TRENDS

An attempt to summarize electoral trends at both the federal and provincial levels has been made by Rasmussen (1967, pp. 98–106), following procedures outlined by Schlesinger for determining the competitiveness of a party system (Schlesinger, 1955, pp. 1120–1128). Schlesinger uses as his measures each state's popular vote for governor and president. Data for Canada are popular vote for the winning party in provincial and federal legislatures, covering the period between 1920 and 1964. Competitiveness is measured along two dimensions: the percentage of elections in which the leading party changed, and the percentage in which the dominant party won the greatest share of the popular vote. Schlesinger defines five categories of party competitiveness, all of which are exemplified in Canada. Rasmussen's generalizations about party systems, to be understood as empirical types and not as legally defined systems, compare Canada with the United States. While illuminating, there is probably greater utility in his classification of party systems found in each of the ten provinces. For example, in competitive systems, parties have relatively equal probability of winning elections, with no single winner exceeding 65 percent of the elections. Moreover, there is rather frequent alternation of the party in office, such that in at least 40 percent of the elections the incumbent party is replaced. Such systems have operated in Manitoba and British Columbia at the provincial levels. Federally, they are exemplified by two clear cases, Ontario and British Columbia, and by two marginal cases, Saskatchewan and Alberta. The usefulness of this scheme is dependent on a careful scrutiny of the data on which it is based, since the time spanned is comparatively short and the limits set for determining competitiveness are somewhat arbitrary. There are at least two other efforts to describe electoral trends. In one case Pinard has considered electoral contests in order to predict the circumstances leading to the emergence of third parties (Pinard, 1967). Schwartz has sought to provide the structural context for predicting the extent of partisan attachment (1973, ch. 6).

Quite a different perspective on electoral trends comes from recent work by Rose and Urwin. They look at election results for nineteen countries since 1945 in order to examine the level of party stability in these societies and to account for variations. The authors note that the mean "elasticity" of party support, by which they mean variations in electoral strength over time, is 7.0 for ninety-two parties; the Conservatives in Canada were second only to the Gaullists in their high level of elasticity, with an average of 26.2 percent (Rose and Urwin, 1970, pp. 292–93). In addition the persistence of party support, measured by the standard error from the trend line, can be used to indicate whether changes in support are cumulative over time. This tends to be high in both the United States and Canada. In Canada wide swings in party support are indicated by a standard error of 5.5 percent for the Liberals and 8.4 percent for the Conservatives (Rose and Urwin, 1970, p. 294).

III. Data for Analysis

A. SAMPLE SURVEYS

Until as recently as five years ago there were no major Canadian surveys conducted under academic auspices. The first of these, done shortly after the 1965 election, provides the bulk of data for this chapter. The study was designed by John Meisel, Philip Converse, Maurice Pinard, Peter Regenstreif, and this writer, and supported by the Canada Council and the Committee on Election Expenses. Over 2,000 respondents, selected through a multistage probability sample, were interviewed in either one of the official languages. Since more sparsely populated areas were oversampled, weighting procedures were then used to adjust for actual population distribution. Sample sizes reported were first weighted and then reduced to approximate real values. The only serious discrepancy occurs in British Columbia, where the sample is half that reported in the tables. Cautious interpretations should be made in this area, particularly when dealing with provincial subsamples. (Meisel and Van Loon, 1966; Schwartz, 1973, ch. 4). Data are already available for secondary analysis at the Institute for Behavioral Research at York University, Toronto, Ontario, and the ICPR at the University of Michigan.

The major variable analysed here is the vote in the past election. Since the survey used was conducted only several months after the 1965 election, we are satisfied that this question is an adequate measure of partisanship. We also asked about voting in the preceding (1963) election, usual vote, and partisan identification. Less detailed questions were also included about provincial voting habits. The 1965 election study has since been followed by one after the 1968 election, this the sole responsibility of John Meisel (Meisel, 1970).

The Royal Commission on Bilingualism and Biculturalism gave impetus to the most extensive range of behavioral science research in Canada.[9] The commissioners' reports include their assessment of the situation and their recommendations to the government, in many instances based on specially commissioned research (Report, 1967; 1968; 1969; 1969a). The research reports are of particular interest to anyone who wishes to understand ethnic cleavages in Canadian society (Johnstone, 1969; McRae, 1969; Lalande, 1970). One major national survey was conducted for the Commission by the Groupe de Recherches Sociales. Access to the survey and to all the reports, including those that will not be published, has yet to be negotiated.

Good province-wide studies are becoming more readily available, including two done in Quebec (Groupe de Recherches Sociales, 1962, 1964; Pinard, 1969, 1969a, 1971). Access to the data themselves, however, still remains to be arranged. A data archive and survey research center has recently been set up at the University of Montreal. Two studies have been done in Ontario under the auspices of the Institute for Behavioral Research at York University. Information about these can be obtained from the Institute, which in general will provide the simplest access point for surveys already completed. These include the growing number of constituency studies authors have placed on deposit in the data archives at York University.

B. SECONDARY SOURCES

The most readily available survey data, and those that have been most widely used for the analysis of voting behavior, have been collected by the Canadian affiliate of the Gallup organization, the Canadian Institute of Public Opinion Research (CIPO), which has been in operation since 1941. Most of the early CIPO material on cards has been destroyed, though newspaper releases remain. Extant material includes several surveys conducted in 1945, 1949, and 1951, and everything since 1953. These are deposited at the Roper Center for Public Opinion Research in Williamstown, Massachusetts; the Institute for Behavioral Research at York University, Toronto, Ontario; and the Social Science Data Archives at Carleton University, Ottawa, Ontario.

A sample designed primarily to satisfy the needs of commercial polling presents special problems of analysis. For example, CIPO normally uses quota sampling techniques, although in recent years these have been adapted to produce surprisingly reliable samples. But as sampling techniques have improved, sample sizes have declined. There are adequate samples for analyses of nationwide patterns and for some subgroups, but others are difficult or impossible to obtain. This includes the inability to consider the Atlantic provinces individually.

The usual question asked by CIPO is vote intention, but from time to time past vote is also queried. In the case of future vote we have to consider the relation between intention and actual behavior at another point in time, and in the case of past vote, the relation between memory and past behavior. The closest relationship between questionnaire response and actual vote is obtained from surveys taken immediately before or after elections, and Alford, in all of his studies, relies most heavily on these (Alford, 1963; 1964; 1967). Yet a close reading of his data indicates that at times he has also relied on recollection of past vote, in one case at least, of several years.

Two other works have relied heavily on CIPO data, one by Regenstreif and one by the present author (Regenstreif, 1965; Schwartz, 1967). Of the three, it would appear that Alford is most affected by the accuracy of the measure of voting, since his concern is with the relation between social class and voting behavior. Yet he is clearly on firm ground in the generalizations he makes because there is enough stability between what people say prior to an election and what they do (or what they say they do) to trace consistent patterns of behavior. Regenstreif, who seeks an explanation for the rise and fall of Diefenbaker Conservatism, uses the data in a more descriptive fashion. Moreover, since he is looking for predictors of the rise and fall of Conservative success, vote intention is generally a superior measure. In the Schwartz study of public opinion there was no particular concern with voting per se, but rather with partisan inclination, and this was adequately measured by expected voting behavior.

C. ELECTORAL DATA

Data on all federal elections may be obtained from the reports of the chief electoral officer, published after each election. We find them in even more convenient form in Scarrow's compendium, *Canada Votes*, which also contains less accessible data on provincial voting. Scarrow's data end at 1962, but more recent results are available in other publications (Courtney, 1967; Thorburn, 1967; Beck, 1968). The researcher who wishes to examine electoral results in more detail—that is, through the smallest subdivision, the poll—must go directly to the electoral reports. These do not indicate the boundaries of the polling stations, however, and for these we must obtain "notices of grant of poll." Notices have an unfortunate habit of disappearing after elections, but the political science department of the University of Waterloo now has them for every urban constituency from 1953 on. Some provinces keep similar records. The University of Waterloo has detailed election reports for Ontario prior to 1900, since 1928 for British Columbia, and since 1935 for Quebec. Alberta began publishing such results in 1959.

IV. Social Structure and Voting

A. THE BASIC DIFFERENTIATORS

1. REGION

It is impossible to understand Canadian social structure without understanding the primary formative and continuing influences of territorial divisions. The physical aspects of territory have attained their social significance from the fact that each region has become associated with particular settlement groups facing common problems. Both problems and solutions are to a large extent conditioned by what is physically at hand.

TABLE 6:   Selected Indicators of Regional Disparities, 1960s

	Population Distribution[1]	French Origin[2]	Urban Pop.[3]	Personal Income[4]	Unemployment Rate[5]	Industrial Output[6]	Average schooling[7]
Newfoundland			50.7	59			
Nova Scotia			54.3	75			
Prince Edward Island			32.4	69			
New Brunswick			46.5	69			
Atlantic Provinces	10.2	18	49.5	—	6.4	593	9.3
Quebec	29.0	81	74.3	88	4.7	1022	8.7
Ontario	34.5	10	77.3	115	2.5	1445	9.9
Manitoba			63.9	97			
Saskatchewan			43.0	99			
Alberta			63.3	99			
Prairie Provinces	17.2	7	57.6	—	2.1	1373	9.7
British Columbia	9.2	4	72.6	115	4.5	1335	10.5
CANADA	100.0	30	69.7	—	3.6	1121	9.6

[1] Population estimates, June, 1965. Source: Canada, 1967, p. 273.

[2] Population reporting French origin, 1961. Source: 1961 Census of Canada.

[3] Percent of population urban, 1961. An urban area is a densely settled locality containing at least 1,000 persons. Total for Atlantic Provinces excludes Newfoundland. Source: Stone, 1967, p. 29.

[4] Personal income expressed as percent of Canadian average, 1965. Source: Brewis, 1969, p. 17.

[5] Average unemployment rates for 1966. Source: Ostry, 1968, p. 26.

[6] Net value added by agriculture, forestry, fishing, and trapping; mining, construction, and electric power; manufacturing. Expressed in dollars per capita, 1963. Source: Brewis, 1969, p. 31.

[7] Average years of schooling of labor force, 1966. Source: Economic Council, 1969, p. 130.

Some indication of the ways in which the regions of Canada vary is given in Table 6. One of the crucial features of life in Canada is the stability of regional differences. For example, no matter how rates of employment fluctuate for the country as a whole, with few exceptions the relative position of provinces remains the same (Ostry, 1968, p. 27). The same is true for trends in per capita income (Chernick, 1966). Analyses of the economy indicate that, regardless of its level of expansiveness, serious regional disparities remain and will continue unless there are concentrated efforts at amelioration (Economic Council of Canada, 1966; 1968; 1969; Green, 1969). Some population differences have been more volatile. These include an increase in those of non-French, non-British origin in Ontario and British Columbia; changes in educational achievement in all provinces; and trends in urbanization. Yet most of such changes as well have served to sustain or augment regional differences.

Canada is divided into ten provinces, plus the northern area of the Yukon and Northwest Territories. Usually these units or some variant of them form the basis for distinguishing regions. The most common grouping adds together Newfoundland, New Brunswick, Nova Scotia, and Prince Edward Island for the Atlantic provinces and Manitoba, Saskatchewan, and Alberta for the prairie provinces. This is not to say that the provinces included in the two groups are perfectly homogeneous, but only that, relative to the remainder of the country, their composition and problems are sufficiently similar to speak of each grouping as a distinct region. This usage has long precedent in the work of economists and geographers (Caves and Holton, 1959; Putnam, 1954; Camu, Weeks, Sametz, 1964; Wilson, Gordon, Judek, 1965). The remaining three provinces, Quebec, Ontario, and British Columbia, are usually treated separately, giving a total of five regions. The north, which is sparsely settled would be dealt with only under special circumstances. For most of the data to be reported here the fivefold grouping of regions will be used.

Electoral rather than survey data will generally prove most useful in establishing connections between region and voting behavior. As an illustration, Table 7 demonstrates the fluctuating fortunes of the governing party in elections between 1921 and 1968. Quebec and the Atlantic provinces have most often produced majorities for the governing party. Such support, in contrast, has been most deficient in the west. In other words the party in office can expect to govern with a mandate that only poorly reflects the regional makeup of the nation. Regions in turn vary in the extent to which they have full claim on the government, and hence in their relative power (Schwartz, 1973, ch. 3). For the remainder of this chapter little more will be said about the electoral history of regions. Our concern will be with a number of variables important for the study of voting behavior. Each variable will be approached through a critical assessment of the

TABLE 7: **Percentage of Popular Vote for Governing Party, 1921-1968**

Election	Governing Party	Atlantic	Quebec	Ontario	Prairies	British Columbia	Canada
1921	Liberal	50.6	70.2	29.8	16.3	29.8	40.7
1925	Liberal*	42.5	59.3	31.0	30.6	34.7	39.8
1926	Liberal	45.6	62.3	38.9	42.1	37.0	46.1
1930	Conservative	54.7	44.7	54.4	40.0	49.3	48.7
1935	Liberal	54.5	54.4	42.7	35.3	31.8	44.9
1940	Liberal	52.5	63.3	50.8	43.1	37.4	51.5
1945	Liberal	47.5	50.8	41.1	30.0	27.5	41.1
1949	Liberal	55.4	60.4	45.7	41.9	36.7	49.5
1953	Liberal	54.9	61.0	46.9	37.5	30.9	48.9
1957	Conservative	48.6	31.1	48.8	28.6	32.6	38.9
1958	Conservative	54.5	49.6	56.4	56.2	49.4	53.6
1962	Conservative	45.4	29.6	39.3	44.9	27.3	37.3
1963	Liberal	49.9	45.6	36.3	26.1	32.3	41.7
1965	Liberal	47.4	45.6	43.6	25.4	30.0	40.2
1968	Liberal	41.4	53.6	46.6	34.8	41.8	45.5

* The election of 1925 resulted in two governments, the first Liberal and the second Conservative.

ways in which it is measured, and a summary of the evidence will be related to voting behavior. To begin with, origin and class, as they interact with region, have been selected as principal differentiators of voting behavior.

2. ORIGIN

Origin is a catch-all term in many ways, and its significance to the individual and to his society may vary according to how it is measured. Four indicators are relevant to Canadians: language, place of birth, national origin or ethnicity, and religion. Since not even this listing is unequivocal, each indicator will be discussed in turn, with emphasis on the ways it has been defined. We will then be able to review research findings on the role of origin in political behavior, taking into account the measures used.

LANGUAGE   In our national survey language was determined by response to the question, "What language do you speak most often in the home?" Sixty-seven percent reported that this was English, 29 percent French, and 4 percent other languages. If other questions are used, as in the census of Canada or by CIPO, different results are produced. For example, the census asks about both mother tongue—language first spoken as a child and still understood—and official language—i.e., French, English, or both. CIPO leans to official language but confuses the issue by sometimes permitting three categories of answer and sometimes two. A review of opinion trends on political issues indicated that the bilingual were much like the French-speaking but not identical to them (Schwartz, 1967, pp. 165–66). Evidence of social and personality factors associated with bilingualism in Canada (Johnstone, 1969; McRae, 1969; Lalande, 1970; Gardner and Lambert, 1959, pp. 266–72; Lieberson, 1965, 1970), and the government's current concern with fostering bilingualism (Report, 1967; 1968; 1969; 1969a) certainly suggest that more care should be taken to acquire information on this point (Lieberson, 1966).

From the question we did use, we could determine the distribution of users of the two official languages among party supporters. Data are presented in Table 8. The most extreme party is the *Créditiste*, which is almost totally French-speaking. Our data also confirm the strong attraction of the Liberal Party for the French-speaking, an attraction shared by no other national party. The Conservatives were not only low on support by francophones, but also by those of other language groups. In contrast Social Credit, with its strong representation in western Canada, was most likely to be supported by those who did not ordinarily speak either of the official languages. Regional differences do not add much to this summary. We find that the tendency for the French-speaking to vote Liberal is true in all regions. But one regional difference does appear, and that is the appeal of the Liberals and NDP for the foreign-speaking in Ontario. Six percent of all respondents in our Ontario sample said that they spoke a language other than French or English in the home, while 8 percent of the Liberals and 10 percent of the NDP were of these other linguistic groups. Conservatives were almost solely English-speaking. In the prairie provinces, with a sample total of 7 percent, foreign-speaking, Conservatives, Liberals, and NDP each attracted about 6 percent, but Social Credit supporters consisted of 13 percent foreign-speaking.

TABLE 8: Language Most Often Used in the Home, and Vote in 1965, in Percentages

	Liberal	Conservative	NDP	Social Credit	Créd.	Total[a]
English	61	84	74	84	3	67
French	34	13	20	2	97	29
Other	4	3	6	14	—	4
Total	(1,048)	(674)	(328)	(67)	(65)	(2,727)

a Includes other parties, don't-knows, etc.

BIRTHPLACE In 1961, 84 percent of the Canadian population was native-born. Our sample found a slighter lower percentage, 82, either as an artifact of sampling variation or the consequence of increased immigration in the intervening years. Table 9 describes the composition of each party's supporters according to their place of birth. It is apparent that language and birthplace tap different dimensions of origin. Most notably, while language is a good indicator of French origin, birthplace is most obviously not, since most of those who identify themselves as French-speaking are from the original settlement groups. The only country whose natives show up in significant numbers in our sample is the British Isles. The British contribute about 11 percent to the Conservatives and NDP, but only 5 percent to the Liberals, perhaps reflecting a habit shaped in the homeland. All other Europeans gravitated, in varying degrees, to the Liberals.

TABLE 9: Country of Birth and Vote in 1965

	Liberal	Conservative	NDP	Social Credit	Créd.	Total[a]
Canada	84	80	75	71	97	82
British Isles	5	11	12	9	—	7
Poland	2	1	1	—	—	1
Italy	2	*	1	—	—	1
Germany	1	1	3	4	—	1
Russia	*	*	2	6	—	1
Netherlands	*	1	1	2	—	1
Hungary	*	*	1	—	—	*
Other European	3	1	4	4	3	2
United States	1	2	1	2	—	2
All other	1	2	1	2	—	1
Total	(1,048)	(676)	(328)	(67)	(65)	(2,727)

* less than 1 percent
a Includes other parties, etc.

Table 10 looks at the regional distribution of the native-born. If nothing else, it indicates the heterogeneity of each party's supporters according to their place of birth. For example, east of Ontario almost all Liberal supporters were born in Canada; in British Columbia, over one-half were. This reflects, of course, the differential distribution of the native-born across Canada. Also worth noting then are those instances in which a party within a region has an unrepresentative proportion of native-born among its supporters. Such is the case of the Conservatives and NDP in Quebec. The Conservatives are, of all parties, most attractive to the British-born, while the NDP numbers relatively more other Europeans among its supporters. Foreign-born support for the Liberals is highly diverse, but it is largely British for the NDP.

TABLE 10:   **Percentage Canadian Born, 1965 Vote, by Region and Past Vote**

	Liberal	Conservative	NDP	Social Credit	Totala
Atlantic	95	90	[100]c		93
	(100)	(83)	(8)	—	(229)
Quebec	95	89	89	97	93
	(352)	(92)	(70)	(65)	(793)
Ontario	75	83	71		76
	(424)	(311)	(132)	—	(1,054)
Prairies	81	71	70	81	76
	(89)	(125)	(56)	(37)	(395)
British Columbia	59	38	61	61	56
	(78)	(58)	(62)	(26)	(256)
Total	84	80	75	71	82
	(1,048)	(674)	(328)	(67)b	(2,727)

Figures in parentheses are base Ns.
a Column totals include other parties, don't-knows, etc.
b The total for Social Credit includes four cases in the Atlantic provinces and Ontario. The Quebec *Créditistes* are not included.
c Too few to percentage

Looking at our data with birthplace as the independent variable, we find that in Ontario the largest number of British-born voted Liberal, approximately one-third of those in the Ontario sample. Owing to the diversity of that party's supporters, however, they do not have the same impact as they do in either the Conservative or New Democratic parties. In the prairies it is the NDP and Conservative party that draw disproportionately on foreign-born voters. In both parties these were largely British. Finally, in British Columbia, where 25 percent of the sample was born in Britain, the Conservatives drew the largest number of the British-born, who in fact made up the largest group of Conservative voters, exceeding the Canadian-born by 3 percent. Social Credit, whose supporters make up only a small subsample, was also most diverse. The other remaining parties each had about one-quarter of their supporters of British origin.

The Canadian population that is foreign-born arrived in Canada mainly during two periods. The first was prior to 1921, accounting for 27 percent of the foreign-born;

the second was between the intercensal period, 1951–1961, when 42 percent of the immigrants arrived. Since some assumptions have been made about the political behavior of immigrants according to the time of their arrival (Schwartz, 1964), our questionnaire also obtained this information, although with less fine distinctions than made by the census. Our major time periods are pre-1939 and between 1946 and 1960. Although the bulk of the foreign-born in our sample were pre-World War II arrivals, their distribution by region and party gives us very small subsamples. Even so we can detect two tendencies. These are the differential attraction of all immigrants to regions, with the Atlantic provinces and Quebec being especially low in this regard, and the differential attraction of postwar immigrants to regions, with the western provinces particularly low here. The first of these tendencies, demonstrated in Table 10, resulted in parties with a large part of their social base in the eastern part of the country having the bulk of their supporters from among the native-born. The opposite was true of the minor parties, traditionally centered in the west, which consequently had a proportionately larger share of foreign-born supporters. One pertinent contrast is the smaller proportion of early arrivals among Liberals compared to other parties. This holds true in every region other than the Atlantic, where in any event cases are exceedingly few. This suggests that the Liberals had devised an effective form of appeal to recent immigrants, to some extent independent of the effects of their region of residence (cf. Schwartz, 1967, 170). For Social Credit, appeal was largely to early arrivals, while the remaining parties show greatest fluctuation according to region.

ETHNICITY   For a variety of reasons, including the lack of an official assimilationist ideology, the hyphenated Canadian has been a pervasive fact of life (Vallee, Schwartz, Darknell, 1957, pp. 540–49). How one goes about measuring the salience of this form of ethnic identity is not so clear. Our questionnaire asked, "Please tell me from what country most of your ancestors came?" In recent years the census of Canada has asked, "To what ethnic or cultural group did you or your ancestor (on the male side) belong on coming to this continent?" In Quebec the Montreal-based Groupe de Recherches Sociales has asked, "Do you consider yourself a French Canadian, an English Canadian, a Jewish Canadian, or a Canadian of another nationality?" Since Jews make up a mere 1.4 percent of the Canadian population, this seems a puzzling approach. Jews, however, are a rather visible 5 percent of Montreal, where ethnic lines for all groups have been reinforced by residential segregation (Keyfitz, 1963, Lieberson, 1970). The question used reflects a situation peculiar to Montreal and a way of thinking fairly general among the French-speaking in Quebec (Groupe de Recherches Sociales, 1960; 1962; Pinard, 1971). The 1961 census found that 44 percent of the population identified themselves as British, 30 percent as French, 6 percent as German, and approximately 2 percent as either Ukrainian, Italian, Dutch, Scandinavian, or Polish. Jews could identify themselves in ethnic as well as religious terms, and those who responded in ethnic terms comprised 1 percent of the total. Those of Indian and Eskimo origin and those either not stated or not covered by the existing categories combined each account for slightly over 1 percent of the total.

Our survey found some difficulties in assigning national origins (see Table 11). Of the total sample, 8 percent said they had North American ancestry and over 2 percent "other," i.e., neither European, Asiatic, nor North American. (Africans and Latin Americans are inconsequential in Canada.) Noticeable numbers have emigrated from the United States at various times, although such a background would not constitute ancestry in our sense. Moreover, since both of the puzzling categories turn up more often in the Atlantic provinces and Quebec, this suggests they were frequently used by persons whose families had long been resident in Canada. If this is the case, then we certainly should have used another form for our question, one that would have better permitted persons to identify themselves with a salient foreign ancestry. In that sense perhaps some variant of the Groupe de Recherches' question would have been more appropriate.

TABLE 11: **Ancestral Origin and Vote in 1965**

	Liberal	Conservative	NDP	Social Credit	Crédit	Totala
British	41	65	48	56	1	46
French	29	12	16	—	79	24
German	3	4	6	11	—	4
Ukrainian/ Russian	2	4	7	12	—	3
Polish	3	1	3	—	—	2
Italian	3	1	1		—	2
Scandinavian	1	2	3	9	—	2
Dutch	1	1	2	4	—	1
Hungarian	1	*	1	—	—	1
Other European	4	3	3	—	3	4
Asian	*	*	*	—	—	*
North American	8	5	6	8	11	8
Other	3	1	2	—	6	2
Base N	(1,048)	(676)	(328)	(67)	(65)	(2,727)

a includes other parties, etc.
* Less than 1 percent

Examining Table 11 for details on the social bases of each of the parties, we find the Conservative party is most British; with the exception of support from Germans, Ukrainians and Russians, and Scandinavians, it is poorly representative of the ethnic diversity of Canada. The Liberals, in contrast, reflect the ethnic makeup of Canada almost perfectly. Proportionately, the NDP has heavy support from ethnic groups other than French or British. The French were significantly underrepresented in the NDP and were totally absent from our Social Credit sample. Instead, the composition of that party was largely British, with strong additions from those ethnic groups that are major settlers of the western provinces. *Le Ralliement des Créditistes* was largely French in origin. But, as we saw in Table 8, it was likely to be even more French than our question suggests. That is, in Table 8, 97 percent of the *Créditiste* supporters were French-speaking, while here only 79 percent said they were of French origin. This would suggest that most of those who gave their origin as "North American" or "other" understood this to mean Canadian, incorporating with this for their Original French ancestry.

Data are available on ancestry and past vote for each of the regions, but in view of the problems of interpreting the residual categories of origin, it hardly seems worthwhile recording these here. We can report that inspection of these tables reveals that the overall generalizations made in Table 11 recur regionally. The proportions in question vary from region to region, but everywhere the Conservatives tend to be more British than the regional norm. This is most apparent in Ontario, where 80 percent of the Conservatives were British, compared to 64 percent in the province as a whole. The Liberals everywhere tend to attract slightly more than their share of French supporters, if we use as a standard of comparison the proportion of French ancestry in the region, and they also reflect each region's ethnic diversity.

An as yet unpublished work by John Meisel and Philip Converse relates language, ancestry, and region in an attempt to isolate "purer" instances of origin, particularly for the French. Their results have not been correlated with party preference, but they do show that their more refined categories of origin are associated with behavioral differences. One of these is the inclination of those of pure French origin—i.e., French-speaking, of French ancestry, and living in Quebec—to be less likely to reveal their past vote than other Canadians. Similar dispositions were found with respect to party identification, attachment to a single party, and the significance of party as against candidates or leaders in voting choice. This suggested that the "pure" French gave less importance to party ties than did other Canadians, but instead were inclined to attach more significance to "personality cults." This should alert us to the possibility that different groups of origin may not share the same basic political orientations. We already, know, for example, that the French-speaking generally avoid giving opinions on political issues (Alford, 1964, p. 228; Schwartz, 1967, pp. 223-26).

RELIGION   Of all the indicators of origin in our survey, religion is the greatest source of polarization for political parties. The two most sharply differentiated parties are related ones: Social Credit and the *Créditistes*. The national party had almost no Catholic supporters but had instead an unusually high proportion of persons identified in Table 12 as "other Protestants".

These are mainly fundamentalist and dissident sects whose members, or their fore-fathers, settled in the west to find a haven for free religious expression (Clark, 1948). Anglicans, whose church is one with high prestige and who are mainly of English origin, also have a disproportionately high representation among Social Credit supporters. In contrast, the *Créditistes* are entirely Catholic, reflecting the narrowness of their appeal even in Quebec.

The preceding attempt to interpret the nature of Social Credit support was based largely on a connection between religion and national origin. Such an argument would seen plausible for the other parties as well, indicating that it is really ethnicity that is the crucial variable. This is mainly due to the historical connection between French origin and the Catholic religion. While numerically less important, we have similar connections between other European origins and Lutherans and Anabaptist sects prevalent in western Canada. But if we take those who usually speak French as a good indicator of French origin, then a comparison of the percent of French-speaking in each of the parties with the percent of Catholic shows that the latter is always greater. This is admittedly a crude way of examining independence, but it is sufficient to indicate that religion has a connection with political behavior distinct from that of

TABLE 12: **Religion and Vote in 1965, in Percentages**

	Liberal	Conser-vative	NDP	Social Credit	Crédit.	Totala
Roman Catholic	57	22	31	6	100	43
Ukrainian Catholic	1	2	3	—	—	1
United Church	17	35	24	26	—	22
Anglican	10	18	13	21	—	12
Presbyterian	3	9	3	9	—	5
Baptist	3	3	2	—	—	3
Lutheran	1	3	3	11	—	3
Greek Orthodox	*	*	1	4	—	*
Other Protestant	3	5	4	20	—	4
Jewish	2	*	3	—	—	2
None	2	3	5	2	—	3
Base N	(1,048)	(676)	(328)	(67)	(65)	(2,727)

* Less than 1 percent
a Includes other parties, don't-knows, etc.

ethnic origin. For example, in a study of class-based voting in Canada based on CIPO data, Alford had no indicator of origin other than religion. But his findings that Catholics outside of Quebec were more likely to vote for the Liberal party and that, in 1962, religious-based cleavages were strongest in Ontario suggest that there are distinctly religious roots to this behavior (Alford, 1963, 1964, p. 215; Engelmann and Schwartz, 1967, p. 48). Even more persuasive is Anderson's work, although it is confined to one constituency in Ontario. She found that religion was not only the most important variable associated with voting, but that its effect was distinct from that of ethnicity. While some of the subsamples were very small—for example, thirteen Irish Canadians—results were consistent. For each ethnic group she found that the majority of Catholics planned to vote Liberal immediately before the 1962 election (Anderson, 1966, pp. 27-37).

From our national survey we can examine the Catholic vote in each region. Table 13 confirms what has already been suggested. Region by region, proportionately more Catholics supported the Liberal party than they did any other. The one exception was the *Créditistes* in Quebec. Most striking is the low appeal of the Conservatives to Catholics in Ontario. In 1965 as much as in 1962, when Alford examined voting, Ontario was sharply divided along religious lines. This is particularly important since here we are speaking primarily of the major parties, not minor parties that can be assumed to have a particularistic focus of appeal and consequently a restricted social base. Outside of British Columbia the NDP tends to have low support from Catholics compared to their place in the population. It is difficult to say how relevant this is, but in past years there was some concern by the more conservative elements of the Catholic clergy that the CCF, the precursor of the NDP, was a representative of godless socialism. In at least one constituency the NDP has obtained strong support from working-class Catholics (Wilson, 1968).

TABLE 13:   **Percentage Roman Catholic Vote, 1965, by Region and Past Vote**

	Liberal	Conservative	NDP	Social Credit	Total[a]
Atlantic	47	28	[25][c]		38
	(100)	(83)	(8)	—	(229)
Quebec	87	83	77	100	86
	(357)	(97)	(70)	(65)	(793)
Ontario	43	6	19		25
	(424)	(311)	(132)	—	(1,054)
Prairies	27	14	12	8	18
	(89)	(125)	(56)	(37)	(395)
British Columbia	15	10	13	0	13
	(78)	(58)	(62)	(26)	(256)
Total	57	22	31	6	43
	(1,048)	(674)	(328)	(67)[b]	(2,727)

Figures in parentheses are base Ns.
a Column totals include other parties, don't-knows, etc.
b The total for Social includes four cases in the Atlantic provinces and Ontario. The Quebec Créditistes are not included.
c Too few to percentage.

Why does the religious factor continue to be so prominent in Canadian politics? There has been no specifically religious party in Canada, nor one dominated by anti-religious orientations. There are two near exceptions to this generalization, both concerning minor parties. *Le Parti Rouge*, in the days before confederation, had close affinities with European revolutionary movements and, like them, was outspokenly anticlerical. But pressure from the Catholic Church and Wilfrid Laurier's later efforts from within the Liberal party in urging his compatriots to tone down this theme were both, in their ways, successful. That is, anticlericalism as a significant electoral appeal pretty well disappeared from the scene, at least until recently. The other near exception is that in the early days of the Social Credit party, it achieved much success because of religious connections. William Aberhart, the first leader of Social Credit and the premier of Alberta, was also a lay preacher for the Calgary Bible Institute, and the evangelical fervor of his message helped to obscure the line between politics and religion. While Aberhart's successor, Ernest Manning, inherited both of his mentor's mantles, more sophisticated audiences today do see the distinction. The cases of *Les Rouges* and Social Credit do not contribute much to accounting for the continuing importance of religion in Canadian politics. The more persuasive reasons also lie back in Canada's early history, but their significance appears in their connection with the major parties.

The tie-in between religious issues and the major parties was in some sense adventitious. The Catholic Church attained new power after the British conquest, and as the principal spokesman for the interests of the French-speaking, its political involvement was inevitable. Settlement by English-speaking people, accustomed to privileges for the Anglican Church, led to their concern with politics in order to continue exiting advantages, especially in view of rights given to Catholics. The channel for expressing these contrary political interests was the precursor of the present-day Conservative party, which was able to fulfil these apparently contradictory roles by the separation of the relevant populations into upper and lower Canada (Ontario and Quebec). But many Protestants objected to the political power of the Anglicans, and one of the sources of bitterness reflected in the rebellion of Upper Canada in 1837 was the disposition of crown lands for the support of the clergy. *Les Rouges*, as we have already mentioned, had an important anticlerial theme. Hence the ancestor of the Liberal party has at its roots opposition to both the Anglican and Catholic churches' involvement in politics.

One finding that is particularly sharp in all the surveys mentioned is the connection between Catholicism and voting Liberal. This realignment of the Catholic vote took place early in this century. One important impetus to the change was the Liberal party leaderhip of Sir Wilfrid Laurier, a French-speaking Catholic who was an appealing orator and an imaginative leader. To those of French origin, he was almost irresistible. The Catholic clergy in French Canada were much slower to change their view, and they were for many years disturbed by the possibility that the Canadian Liberals were really first cousins to the revolutionary, anticlerical liberals of the continent (Wade, 1968, p. 359). But the historic affinity between the Catholic Church and the Conservative party existed not only in Quebec. In a survey done in Kingston, Ontario, after the 1953 federal and 1955 provincial elections, Meisel had in his sample a number of respondents who were in religious orders and who had voted Conservative in the provincial election. These people indicated their satisfaction with the provincial Conservative government, particularly on the issue of "separate schools," that is, Catholic schools. Meisel was intrigued by this finding and attempted to examine its implications more closely through an ecological analysis of voting returns for those elections. He selected four polling units—one a convent, the other a hospital and home for the aged run by a Catholic order, and two units with majorities of Catholic voters. While the evidence is not as representative as we would like, it does indicate that those "closest to the Church" were more likely to vote Conservative than rank-and-file Catholics[10] (Meisel, 1956, pp. 481–96).

However, there have been a number of situation that have served to turn the average Catholic voter away from the Conservatives as much as to attract them to the Liberals. In some instances these were issues that affected voters at least as much because of their French origin as their religion. Here we would include the Manitoba school question; the treatment of Louis Riel, executed after leading two uprisings in western Canada (Wade, 1968, pp. 393-446; Stanley, 1961); and the conscription crisis of the Boer War and two world wars (Wade, 1968, pp. 447-535, 708-80; Laurendeau, 1962; Dawson, 1961).

Some issues were directly relevant to voters as Catholics, regardless of origin. For example, in the 1920s the Ku Klux Klan was active in Canada with a violently anti-Catholic program. In Saskatchewan the Klan gave its support to the Conservatives, who, whether they liked it or not, never openly repudiated it. In Ontario the Loyal Orange Order was vociferous in its anti-Catholicism, and its members were staunch supporters of the Conservatives.

Some of these examples hardly suggest deliberate attempts by Conservatives to alienate Catholic support, yet deliberate or not, the end result has been the same. It might be predicted that, with the secularization of the world, such religious-based political cleavages will one day lose their strength (Engelmann and Schwartz, 1967, pp. 228-31). Perhaps portending such a decline is a study done in the constituency of Middlesex East, Ontario, after the 1965 federal election. Using a multiple-regression analysis of ecological data, it was found that religion, measured by the percent Roman Catholic in each poll, was quite weak in explaining political behavior (Simmons, 1967, pp. 389-400). Yet some doubt remains that secularization will have major impact on the connection between religion and voting in Canada. Even Catholic support for the Liberals has no theological sanction, but arises from perceived social interests. In a random sample of Ontario voters interviewed in June, 1968, Lynn MacDonald confirmed the usual association between Liberals and Catholics and between Conservatives and Protestants (MacDonald, 1969). In probing for the current sources of this association MacDonald considered three possibilities. No contribution seemed to have come from issues with a religious content, nor from the religion of candidates. Most effect could be attributed to "social involvement in the religious community," confirmation of Meisel's earlier findings in Kingston.

The student of Canadian political life must take into account the deeply rooted cleavages related to the diversity of origin. French-speaking alignments are crucial, and to a large extent these are duplicated in divisions between Quebec and the rest of Canada. But to end with these would be to ignore the extent to which other origins and other regions contribute to the fragmented nature of Canadian society. Moreover, there is no one indicator of origin that encompasses all the significant aspects of politically related behavior. Whenever possible, then, measures of each aspect of origin should be used.

3. Social Class

occupation Depending on one's theoritical or ideological orientation, various ways have been used to measure social class. The most common, and generally the most convenient, is occupation of the household head. Information on occupation is readily available from CIPO surveys using fairly standard categories. The distribution of occupational categories in our national survey according to vote in 1965 is given in Table 14. The purest example of a party with a diverse social class makeup is the Liberal.

TABLE 14: Occupation of Household Head and Past Vote, in Percentages, 1965

Occupation of Main Earner	Liberal	Conserv.	NDP	Social Credit	Créd.	Totala
Professional, owner, manager	21	18	21	15	8	20
Sales, clerical	16	17	13	9	9	15
Manual	40	30	47	43	61	39
Service	4	5	7	7	6	5
Farmer	5	12	5	9	5	7
Not in the labor forceb	13	18	7	16	12	13
Not stated	*	*	–	–	–	*
N	(1,048)	(676)	(328)	(67)	(65)	(2,727)

a Includes other parties, don't-knows, etc.
b Includes retired, unemployed, unemployed female heads of households, and military personnel.
* Less than 1 percent.

Alford's analysis of social class and voting supports two hypotheses: (1) there is a low level of class-based voting in Canada and (2) there is a diversion of class-related behavior by the strength of regional interests. Alford's index of class voting is computed as follows: "Subtract the percentage of persons in nonmanual occupations voting for Left parties from the percentage of persons in manual occupations voting for Left parties" (Alford, 1963, pp. 79-80). This index easily fits Britain, Australia, and the United States, where parties of the Left can be defined with little difficulty. In Canada it is not as easy to do this. In *Party and Society* Alford combined votes for the Liberals and CCF as representing votes for the Left. This procedure aroused some criticism, since the Liberals are not clearly a left-wing party. The very fact that at different times and in different regions various parties may attract a greater share of working-class support can be interpreted to confirm Alford's conclusion that class-based voting is low in Canada. We will also use this procedure here and differentiate between Liberal and NDP votes, as Alford does in more recent work (Alford, 1967, pp. 84-86).

Alford locates Canada at the bottom of class voting scale in comparison with three other Anglo-American democracies. His index of class voting between 1952 and 1962 averaged 40 in Britain, 33 in Australia, 16 in the United States, but only 8 in Canada (Alford, 1963, p. 102). A followup study of these countries establishes the same rank-order and no sign of increased class voting in Canada (Alford, 1967, p. 85). In attempting to account for these national differences Alford placed great emphasis on regional cleavages in Canada, which prevent the emergence of nationally oriented class interests. Whatever class voting did occur tended to emerge within certain regions, but not always in a consistent fashion.

Ontario has the highest level of class voting in six of the ten surveys here reported; British Columbia is second-highest in five of them. The Atlantic provinces vacillate considerably, being highest in two and lowest in three. Quebec is almost consistently low, as are the Prairie provinces. (Alford, 1963, pp. 263, 266)

Since this time period there has been no appreciable increase in class voting for the country as a whole. On the basis of a 1965 CIPO survey Alford found an index of $+6$; our survey taken several months later gives an index of $+1$. Looking only at the one explicitly working-class party still gave an index of only $+8$ or $+4$, depending on the survey. Table 15 presents indices of class voting for each of the regions in 1965, using both Alford's and our own data. In some respects Alford's data display more of the expected patterns, especially the low level of class voting in the Atlantic provinces and the high level in British Columbia. But before placing too much emphasis on such discrepancies, it should be pointed out that Alford found similar fluctuations in his indices within short periods of time. For example, a survey conducted in January, 1961, gave an index of class voting of $+28$ in the prairies, but ten months later the index in that region was -20 (Alford, 1963, p. 265). Alford's solution was to ignore such short-run changes in favor of long-run stabilities, and we will be guided by this.

TABLE 15: **Index of Class Voting for Regions, 1965**

	Liberal	*NDP*	*Total*
Atlantic provinces	-2	$+4$	$+2$
Quebec	0	$+2$	$+2$
Ontario	-4	$+10$	$+6$
Prairie provinces	-8	$+9$	$+1$
British Columbia	-8	$+30$	$+22$
Canada	-2	$+8$	$+6$

Source: Alford, 1967, p. 86.

	Liberal	*NDP*	*Total*
Atlantic provinces	$+22$	$+1$	$+23$
Quebec	-7	-4	-11
Ontario	$+1$	$+13$	$+14$
Prairie provinces	-5	$+3$	-2
British Columbia	-17	$+12$	-5
Canada	-3	$+4$	$+1$

Source: 1965 Election Study.

In the past, class voting in Ontario was moderately high, ranging from $+9$ to $+27$ and averaging about $+17$ in the ten surveys between 1945 and 1961. In 1965 it is closer to this level in our survey than in Alford's, but in both there is a similar pattern, that is, the major part of the class voting found in Ontario is attributable to the attraction of working-class voters to the NDP. The Liberals, in contrast, have almost none of this class base. Here we have an instance, then, where the combination of Liberal and NDP votes enhances the general level of class voting found in the area, perhaps giving it an importance that its connection with a minor party would not otherwise suggest. At the same time it indicates that Ontario is one of two provinces where the NDP can be regarded as an unequivocally working-class party (Wilson and Hoffman, 1971).

British Columbia has usually been next to Ontario in the level of class voting. In 1965 it was first in Alford's survey but ranked fourth in our own. This was due to two contrary tendencies: an unusually small proportion of working-class voters among the Liberals—considerably less than in Alford's sample—and a smaller proportion of working-class voters among the NDP than was true in Alford's sample. This is due in our case to the attraction of the working-class to Social Credit. The ratio of non-manual to manual workers is 2.2 in the Liberal, .9 in the NDP, and .5 in the Social Credit. In this situation class voting is a feature only of the two minor parties. We must be cautious in these interpretations, however, because of the small subsamples in British Columbia.

The unusually high measure of class voting in the Atlantic provinces has been found in some of Alford's earlier work. In addition his 1965 index is also similar to ones found at other times. In other words the Atlantic provinces have not displayed any consistent pattern of class voting. When class issues are stressed, as apparently they were at the time of our survey, then they are clearly manifested, since there are no significant third parties to deflect them. This is one area where the Liberal party can and occasionally does play the role of class party.[11]

There is generally little sign of class voting in the prairie provinces, and our data support this. But this is the area of greatest strength for the minor parties, at least on the provincial level, and one should anticipate some carryover of a protest orientation to federal politics. This shows up only faintly for the NDP, however, partially due to the exclusion from our index of farmers, who were an important source of loyal support for the CCF in Saskatchewan and, to a lesser extent, for the federal NDP. Yet if we look at the full spectrum of competing parties, the expected role of the minor parties does emerge. At least we may draw such an interpretation from the ratio of nonmanual to manual workers in each of the parties. It is 1.2 in the Conservative, 1.1 in the Liberal, .8 in the NDP, and .5 in the Social Credit. The two newer parties obtain support from a relatively larger working-class base than do the older ones. Again we have proportionately strong support from the working-class for Social Credit.

Class position and partisan alignments in Quebec are unique compared to the rest of Canada. The Liberal party is almost perfectly representative of the occupational structure of the province. It has no particular class character; the ratio of nonmanual to manual workers among its 1965 supporters was 1.1. In each of the other regions non-manual have always outnumbered manual supporters of the Conservatives, even if not by a great deal. In Quebec, however, the opposite is the case. Of Conservative support-ers, 21 percent are nonmanual, 49 percent manual, and 19 percent are not in the labor force. Disregarding the latter group and the farmers, the ratio of nonmanual to manual is .4. This may be attributed to the exceedingly weak electoral position of the Conservatives, who attract older, marginally integrated voters.

Data in Table 16 should make us wonder about the Conservatives in general. If we look at two other indicators of class position, subjective class identification and medium income, the Conservatives are not so distinctive in Quebec. On subjective class position, for example, identical proportions (52 percent) selected the working-class in Quebec and the prairies; only in British Columbia was a strong working-class identification missing. Conservatives are below Liberals in median income, with the greatest difference one of $1,200 in Ontario and British Columbia. These income differentials are partly attributable to the high proportion of Conservative supporters outside the labor force. Other data from our survey on satisfaction with the current financial situation and with prospects for the future indicate a fairly high frequency of pessimism among Conservatives (Schwartz, 1973, ch. 5). Unless we wish to believe that feelings of dissatisfaction are independent of political behavior, it is necessary to reconsider the importance of party ideology or official stands expressed by party leadership. We would argue that parties of protest are not only those that are so labeled on the basis of ideology. Parties of protest may simply be ones that frequently play an opposition role, often as the only viable alternative, particularly for voters who are too tradition-bound to choose third parties. These have often been characteristics of the Conservative party nationally. We should also not overlook the status components of political protest. When the usual high-status ethnic and religious groups have their leadership role challenged (Breton and Roseborough, 1968, pp. 604-35), members who are not themselves in privileged positions may be strongly attracted by parties known for the appropriate ethnic character. Hence the British origin of Conservative party leadership would enhance its position for attracting protest votes from those cramped by economic conditions and crowded by what they see as the achievements of other ethnic groups. Some confirmation of the varied nature of protest parties comes from Pinard's research on *Union Nationale* support in the 1962 Quebec provincial election (Pinard, 1969; 1970). A lack of class-based voting in Quebec was attributable to extensive working-class support for the *Union Nationale*. Yet, despite its conservative image this party has been a party of protest, especially to those whose status interests were ethnic as well as economic. The fact that party elites did not translate this protest into terms that would be of advantage to the working-class is almost irrelevant.

> In other words, the workers did not turn to the National Union because of its ideology—although it was reformist in the early phases—but rather because it was a movement well suited for the mobilization of social unrest born from serious economic adversities (Pinard, 1970, p. 104).

The situation of the two remaining parties in Quebec is quite distinctive. In the 1965 election the NDP received strong support from professionals in Montreal and Quebec City, resulting in a nonmanual-to-manual ratio of 1.4. Farmers and those outside of the labor force were almost totally absent from NDP voters. The *Créditistes*, however, continued to play their role as a party of protest, essentially of economic protest (Pinard, 1971). Their support was largely from the working-class, giving a ratio of nonmanual to manual of .25.

TABLE 16: Comparison of Liberal and Conservative Voters on Two Indicators of Social Class, 1965, by Region

	PERCENT WORKING-CLASS IDENTIFIERS		MEDIAN INCOME	
	Liberal	*Conservative*	*Liberal*	*Conservative*
Atlantic provinces	56	48	$3,500	$3,800
	(100)	(83)	(97)	(82)
Quebec	37	52	$5,000	$4,500
	(357)	(97)	(335)	(87)
Ontario	43	42	$6,700	$5,500
	(424)	(311)	(417)	(301)
Prairies	44	52	$5,700	$5,000
	(89)	(125)	(87)	(120)
British Columbia	28	21	$6,100	$4,900
	(78)	(58)	(76)	(58)
Canada	42	45	$5,500	$4,900
	(1,048)	(674)	(1,012)	(648)

Figures in parentheses are Ns.
Median income is calculated only for those who indicated some income.
Income figures are rounded to the nearest $100.

One question that needs to be raised with respect to these findings concerns the kind of occupational distinctions used. How valid is it to work with a simple manual/nonmanual division? Regardless of the theoretical assumptions, the fact that many have found consistent empirical correlations between occupation and other variables bespeaks its value. Alford himself has found the division meaningful in countries other than Canada. We should then assume that even such a gross measure of occupational class should have the same validity in Canada as it does in other industrial societies. But some nagging doubts remain. A study of occupational prestige, in which prestige is considered one of the components of the class hierarchy, augments our suspicions. In a replication of a 1963 study of occupational prestige Pineo and Porter document the similarities between Canadians and Americans in the degree of prestige assigned to a variety of occupations. Similarities are very great. But some differences also exist —between the United States and Canada, between English- and French-speaking citizens, and when the analysis is completed, probably among regions. The report of these findings in an initial one. At the moment, however, we can observe a considerable overlap in prestige ratings, between manual and nonmanual occupations, particularly clerical and sales as compared to skilled positions (Pineo and Porter, 1967, pp. 24-40). Further support for the imprecision of traditional manual/nonmanual distinctions comes from Blishen's work. Using census data from 1951 he constructed a class scale combining occupation, years of schooling, and income (Blishen, 1958, pp. 519-31).

More recently he has developed a scale, following the model of Duncan (Duncan, 1961, pp. 109-38, 139-61), in which he uses income, education, and prestige as measured by the Pineo-Porter scale (Blishen, 1967, pp. 41-53). In both cases, while there is a scale suggesting a class hierarchy, there are no natural cutting points. However the cutting points are made, there does not appear to be any relation to class theories that presume discontinuities between manual and nonmanual workers.

We are left with a dilemma. Perhaps it is because such crude indicators of class have been used that we found so little class-based voting. Yet, even allowing for the imprecision of the dichotomy, why does it work in other countries and not in Canada? One way out of the dilemma would be to use a number of different measures of class, including more refined occupational categories, and relate these to voting behavior. We also need to include farmers in some way, since they still make up a sizable share of the work force in some regions. Their exclusion often seems based on a variety of ideological premises, including the belief that they cannot be "true socialists" (Bell, 1967, p. 93).

Granted the crudeness of our occupational categories, what is open to much greater question is the class orientation attributed to various parties. That is, one of the reasons that Alford and our own work find so little class-based voting in Canada is because there is no one or even two parties that almost invariably attract disproportionate support from only one class. Hence we saw areas in 1965 where the Conservatives had more of a working-class base than the Liberals. This was also found at the time of the 1962 election (Engelmann and Schwartz, 1967, pp. 47-49; Alford, 1964, pp. 203-34). The fact that parties with the same name may differ in social composition across provincial lines, as well as in specific or general policies, style of politics, or ideological orientation (Engelmann and Schwartz, 1967, pp. 50-52). stems largely from the nature of Canadian society, in which regional factors condition both the nature of the political setting and the contemporary problems. For example, if we were to use income as a measure of social class we would have to take into account significant interregional income differentials, still not fully explained by economists (Denton, 1966). In a different sense, however, class-based voting exists; it is consistent class-based parties that are missing.

EDUCATION Another frequently used indicator of social class is education. In Canada educational quality differs from region to region, and the educational achievement of residents varies as well. At the time of the 1961 census 3.0 percent of the population had a university degree. The range was from 1.7 in the Altantic provinces, 2.6 in the prairies, 3.0 in Quebec, 3.3 in British Columbia, to 3.4 in Ontario. Quality indicators such as expenditure per pupil, median salary of teachers, and the retentiveness of the school system also show strong interregional variation. (Nash, 1961, pp. 118-29; Cheal, 1962, 120-26). There have been dramatic moves in the past decade to raise the level of education and to remove regional disparities, but the latter still persist to a significant degree (Economic Council of Canada, 1969, pp. 123-38).

This variability helps explain some of the occupational differences across regions as well as differences in income, in the sense that education is both cause and effect of the opportunity structure. But in addition, differences in quality make it difficult to compare regions in terms of the educational achievement of their residents. This is aggravated by the fact that provinces differ in the way in which they organize education. For example, school attendance is compulsory from the ages of six to sixteen in most parts of Canada but may end at fourteen in Quebec, fifteen in Newfoundland, and extend from seven to fourteen in rural Nova Scotia (Katz, 1961). Ontario has offered thirteen years of precollege education for many years, with Grade 13 made compulsory for admission to the University of Toronto in 1931. Recently there has been a move in Ontario to confine secondary education to four years (Harris, 1967). In Quebec, meanwhile, where many have been generally unhappy with the competitive position of French-speaking Quebeckers, particularly the large numbers who have not completed their formal schooling, the move has been to change the educational system radically. The results of the 1966 provincial election, in which *Union Nationale* defeated the Liberals, were partly attributed to the concern that changes proposed were too sweeping (Dion, 1967), but no government is able fully to stem the pressure to change.

Because provinces vary in the number of years they require for elementary and secondary schooling, the social significance of a given number of years of school is not the same in all parts of Canada. How, then, should we measure education in a national survey, especially as educational standards and requirements are in flux? If possible, we need to know the number of years of schooling completed, where respondents attended school, and the stage reached. In none of the surveys reviewed here were all of these kinds of questions asked. On CIPO surveys there is some variability; respondents are generally asked for the last type of school they attended, whether public (elementary), high, technical, or university. When grade categories are used, these are inclined to be determined by the organization of education in Ontario. In our own survey we asked only years of schooling, thereby losing the means for assigning respondents to different educational levels or stages. Table 17 provides these data for

TABLE 17: **Distribution of Party Supporters, 1965, by Level of Education, in Percentages**

Years of Schooling	Liberal	Conservative	NDP	Social Credit	Crédit	Total[a]
0–5	10	6	5	1	21	9
6–8	24	25	24	29	44	26
9–11	30	33	41	33	27	33
12–13	19	20	15	29	3	19
14–16	11	10	5	8	3	9
17 plus	5	5	9	—	3	5
N	(1,048)	(676)	(328)	(67)	(65)	(2,727)

[a]Includes other parties, don't-knows, etc.

party, revealing that, with the exception of *Créditistes*, there was little overall difference in years of schooling for party supporters. Focusing on those who can be presumed to have at least some postsecondary education in Table 18 reveals both regional differences and party consistency. For example, the Liberals tend to have more of the

TABLE 18: **Percentage with 14 or More Years of Schooling, 1965, by Region and Past Vote**

	Liberal	Conservative	NDP	Social Credit	Total[a]
Atlantic	13 (100)	6 (83)	[14][c] (8)	—	8 (229)
Quebec	15 (357)	12 (97)	24 (70)	6 (65)	13 (793)
Ontario	18 (424)	18 (311)	9 (132)	—	15 (1,054)
Prairies	11 (89)	11 (125)	16 (56)	13 (37)	13 (395)
British Columbia	20 (78)	24 (58)	10 (62)	0 (26)	14 (256)
Total	(1,048)	(674)	(328)	(67)[b]	(2,727)

[a]Column totals include other parties, don't knows, etc.
[b]The total for Social Credit includes four cases in the Atlantic provinces and Ontario. The Quebec: *Créditistes* are not included.
[c]Too few to percentage.
[d]Figures in parentheses are base Ns.

best-educated supporters everywhere, except in the prairies. NDP supporters were especially well-educated in Quebec and the prairies. A low level of advanced schooling was characteristic of Social Credit in British Columbia and Quebec. Alford studied the 1962 election and found a similar pattern (Alford, 1964, p. 219).

Regenstreif presents CIPO trend data on education and party preference but without taking into account regional differences. He notes, for example, a curvilinear relationship between university education and support for the Liberals and Conservatives. In 1953, when the Liberals were in the ascendancy, 51 percent of the university-educated voters planned to vote Liberal, and 36 percent Conservative. In 1957 the Liberals were on the decline, giving way to a minority Conservative government. At that time, 36 percent of the university-educated favored the Liberals and 49 percent the Conservatives. By 1958, when the Conservatives achieved a sweeping victory, 30 percent of the college-educated intended to vote Liberal and 61 percent Conservative. By 1962, although they were still able to hold on to a minority government, the Conservatives lost a large share of their support. Prior to that election vote intention of the university-educated was 46 percent Liberal and 39 percent Conservative. A similar political situation existed in 1963, at which time 50 percent of the university-educated planned to note Liberal and 31 percent Conservative. (Regenstreif, 1965, p. 47). In other words the party preferences of the university-educated have fluctuated with party fortunes. In one sense, of course, this is to be expected, since the ascendancy of a party is determined by its attraction of electoral support. Yet this support need not come from all segments of the population, and what is interesting about the party preferences of the university-educated is that they reflect or even exaggerate the ebb and flow of party fortunes. This was not true to nearly the same extent of the two other educational categories, those with high school and elementary education. In both latter groups a majority did not expect to vote Conservative until 1958, when the tide had turned and the Conservatives were poised for a sweeping victory. Nor did the bulk of each group switch to the Liberals until 1963, when the move against the Conservatives was already under way.

4. RELATIONS AMONG VARIABLES

Occupational class turns out to be a poor predictor of class-based voting in Canada for a variety of reasons. One is the lack of a nationally based class structure, due to the uneven process of industrialization. Moreover, the salience of class is strongly reduced by alternative cleavages, particularly those related to region and origin. None of this, however, means that class cleavages, at least in the sense of economic differences, are not important. It is rather that they are not consistently manifested through political behavior. Economic factors, for example, are clearly operative in the responses of westerners, vulnerable as they have been through their reliance on single crops. Politically this has been translated into a number of channels, the most important of which are the CCF/NDP and Social Credit. Yet unlike the NDP or its predecessor, Social Credit is normally not perceived as a class party. This is partly due to the lack of class-based appeals from the party hierarchy, or at least the lack of appeals to the working-class. Rather it seems that, with the emphasis now on free enterprise, the appeal is to the businessman, especially the small businessman. This does not alter the fact that in certain times and places—in 1965 this was true in British Columbia and Quebec—the working-class does find Social Credit an appealing party. We have no doubt, if only from Pinard's work, that Social Credit in Quebec represents an important form of economic protest. Yet elsewhere as well, Social Credit's appeal to the working-class still has some significance, despite the growing prosperity of those provinces where the party has achieved power. That is, we must not be misled by the characteristic of an aggregate, the wealth of British Columbia and Alberta under Social Credit governments, to deny that individual members of that aggregate, residents of these provinces who vote Social Credit, may have motivations and interests seemingly at odds with those of the organization to which they give their support. In other instances voters may support the major parties despite their class interest. But we had evidence again, that regardless of the official position of the Conservative party, a number of its supporters see it as a vehicle for their economic protest. This seems especially plausible where ethnic interests would appear to reinforce economic ones. Class interests are not absent in Canada. Rather, there is no single avenue for their political expression, mainly a result of the regional fragmentation of the country.

Given the confused place of class in Canadian voting behavior, is it really worth the effort to continue to analyze voting data along this dimension? The answer is decidedly yes, and for several reasons. We obviously need data for comparative purposes. Some predict, not without an air of wishful thinking, an increase in class-based voting (Horowitz, 1966a, pp. 3–10; Wilson, 1967). But more important are the possible interaction effects between province, origin, and class. For example, Alford found Protestants more likely to vote along class lines than Catholics. But comparing Catholics in Quebec and Ontario, those in Ontario were more likely to vote according to their class position (Alford, 1963, p. 272). In the four cities studied by Regenstreif, religion emerged as the dominant variable, but again there were some interaction effects, although regional factors could not be considered.

> Those people voting Conservative tend to follow religious lines, whereas those voting NDP tend to follow class lines. Liberals are being cross-pressured with some following class lines and others religious lines. Voting along religious lines is definitely stronger within the working-class than within the middle-class, but is favorable only to the Liberals and the Conservatives. (Gagne and Regenstreif, 1967, p. 537.)

Wilson's survey in Waterloo-South lends further support to this relationship, where, for example, working-class Catholics gave strong support to the NDP (Wilson, 1968). This does not, however, mean that the influence of origin will soon disappear from Canadian voting habits, at least not as long as the NDP remains a minor party.

While one can construct profiles of the Canadian electorate (for example, Laponce, 1969, pp. 60–70), it has not yet been possible to decide on the *relative* importance of each variable. Laponce's effort with his Vancouver sample did allow him to refine the demographic character of each party, with the result that he described only a small proportion of supporters (Laponce, 1969, pp. 181–89). A tree analysis of our 1965 survey in which the focus is on Liberal supporters also does not add much to our knowledge, at least partly because of the heterogenous nature of the social base of that party. It is the contrast with each of the other parties that points up the importance of origin, particularly religion, the influences of region, and the lesser, though still potent, relationship between voting and social class.

B. SECONDARY SOURCES OF VOTER ALIGNMENT

1. COMMUNITY OF RESIDENCE

There has been a steady growth of urbanization in Canada: at the time of the 1961 census, 70 percent of the population was living in urban communities. The three most highly urbanized provinces are Ontario, Quebec, and British Columbia, in that order. Each has a larger share living in urban areas than the Canadian average. The Atlantic provinces are still largely rural, although by 1961 the three Maritime (excluding Newfoundland) provinces had 50 percent of their population urban. The prairies too were largely rural, but the trend to increasing urbanization began after World War II, and in 1961, almost two-thirds of the population was in urban areas (Stone, 1967).

There is no generally agreed-on definition of "urban." Official definitions in Canada have varied, and trend analyses of urbanization need to make appropriate adjustments. Data reported above are based on the 1961 census definition, in which urban areas are included in one of the following: (1) incorporated cities, towns and villages of at least 1,000 population; (2) unincorporated agglomerations (generally considered towns or villages) of at least 1,000 population; (3) builtup fringes of incorporated cities, towns, and villages of at least 5,000 population, with a population density of at least 1,000 persons per square mile (Stone, 1967, p. 5).

Such definitions may not capture the full extent of urbanization with regard to participation in big-city life, but big cities certainly exist. At the 1961 census enumeration there were fifteen metropolitan areas of more than 100,000 population. These were unevenly distributed regionally. Ontario had seven such urban areas, and there were two each in British Columbia, Quebec, and Alberta. The remaining two were in Manitoba and Nova Scotia. Everywhere except in the Atlantic provinces approximately two-thirds of the urban population resides within the confines of these metropolitan areas. City life is increasing in numerical importance, but it is unevenly distributed both among regions and within them.

The relation between community of residence and party fortunes is available from electoral results. As previously noted, the Reports of the chief electoral officer classify polling stations by a criterion of urbanization different from that of the census. If necessary, the two procedures could be made to coincide in most instances. That is, polling stations could be reclassified in conformity with the census definition. But whether using one or another definition of urbanization, there is no published record of trends in voting behavior relating party fortunes to the character of particular constituencies. Yet we do know that in recent years the Conservatives have had most of their strength in rural areas and small towns and that the NDP has become an increasingly urban party. The *Créditistes* had a base of support similar to the Conservatives, but confined to Quebec. The Liberals have been more varied in the areas where they have done best, but the tendency has been to more urban strength. For the 1962 federal election Meisel has related party strength to type of community and concluded that the Conservatives did better in rural areas, the NDP in urban ones; there was no relation between community type and Liberal strength. (Meisel, 1964, pp. 280–81). An examination of seats in the Ontario legislature indicates that "safe seats—those that stay with one party for prolonged periods—are mainly rural." Urban constituencies, however, fluctuate more among the contending parties (Grossman, 1967, pp. 99–103). The most thorough use of aggregate data is by Pinard, in tracing the growth of Social Credit in Quebec. He uses size of community as an indicator of social integration, assuming that the smaller the community, the more integrated its members. Size of community was also related to the existence of social strain, measured by the extent of out-migration. Both of these measures were then related to the strength of Social Credit. Pinard's findings are placed in the context of a general model of the rise of political movements in mass societies.

> At the beginning, when there are no strains, the movement is more successful among less integrated communities, as predicted by mass theorists; but it remains weak. On the other hand, if the strains are severe, at that stage, integrated communities appear as more conducive grounds for the diffusion of the movement, contrary to the claims of the mass theorists. Only later [that is, when the movement has become successful] do larger communities regain their greater conduciveness (Pinard, 1968, p. 342).

While electoral data would seem to be most useful in making generalizations about voting behavior and community type, there is also a place for survey data. For one thing they are convenient to use. Since survey data usually tell us much more about voters than just their place of residence, they can be related to characteristics of voters and to opinion climates. Survey data on community and voting are available from Regenstreif (1965, pp. 14, 33, 37, 38), Alford (1964, p. 225), and Engelmann and Schwartz (1967, p. 61).

Using CIPO data, some distinctions can be made among communities of varying sizes. Alford, for example, makes a threefold distinction between rural communities, small cities with populations up to 30,000, and large cities with populations above 30,000. Alford also shows how generalizations about parties at the national level need not hold up when we examine individual provinces. For example, using more refined categories of community size, the 1962 survey results indicated a steady progression in Conservative support from urban to rural. The larger the city, the fewer the respondents who gave a Conservative voting preference (Alford, 1964, p. 212). However, "The Conservatives were only stronger in the rural-areas [as compared to cities] in New Brunswick, Ontario, and Manitoba; there were no rural-urban differences in Conservative support in Quebec, Saskatchewan, and British Columbia" (Alford, 1964, p. 226). In the three types of communities used for analyzing provincial results, only in New Brunswick, Ontario, and Manitoba did a larger proportion of those living in rural communities say they would vote Conservative as compared to either of the two urban communities. This does not mean, of course, that the social base of Conservative support was mainly rural in these provinces and not in others. Within each province the nature of party support is at least partially determined by the character of the total population. For example, in Ontario 47 percent of those in rural communities intended to vote Conservative. A similar proportion had the same voting intentions in smaller cities, while in larger ones only 35 percent planned to vote for the Conservatives. But Ontario is also the most urbanized province. Hence the social base of Conservative support was 49 percent from large cities, 23 percent from smaller ones, and 28 percent from rural communities. We may contrast this distribution of support with that in Saskatchewan. There was no difference among the three types of communities in party preference, where about half those in rural communities and both small and large cities planned to vote Conservative. At the same time,

Saskatchewan is the most rural province, and the bulk of Conservative supporters (as well as those of other parties) are resident in rural communities.

Looking at national results again, on the basis of the 1962 survey as well as the election, the Liberals tended to do best in larger cities. But on the basis of how residents in the three types of communities planned to vote in each of the provinces, this pattern did not necessarily hold up. It was true in two provinces, New Brunswick and Alberta. In New Brunswick 59 percent of large-city voters expressed a Liberal preference, compared to 26 percent in rural areas. Thirty percent in large cities planned to vote Liberal in Alberta, compared to 17 percent in rural areas. In both provinces urban voters predominated among Liberal supporters. On the basis of vote intention of community residents Alford also observes that there were no urban-rural differences in Ontario, Saskatchewan, and British Columbia. But as far as the nature of the party was concerned, the majority of supporters in Ontario and British Columbia lived in large cities, while those in Saskatchewan were in rural communities.

By treating party as both independent and dependent variable several often contrary tendencies are illuminated. First we have the differential attraction to parties of residents in different types of communities. Focusing on province (or region) reveals again a differential attraction, but not necessarily of the same general pattern as the country as a whole. Then, since provinces vary greatly in their degree of urbanization, the same party in different provinces will normally have a varying social base. Finally, parties may still differ in their appeal to residents of different types of communities within a province.

While the absolute number of large cities is much smaller in Canada than in the United States, the neighboring countries share a characteristic growth since World War II, not in the central cities, but in the suburbs (Keyfitz, 1964, pp. 35–36). The political effect of moving to the suburbs has been the subject of considerable speculation and somewhat less research in the United States, with the assumption, not always confirmed, that movement is associated with political change (Wallace, 1964; Wood, 1958). No research in Canada has been specifically directed to the phenomenon of suburbanization and its political implications. Clark, however, has suggested that suburban residents are of particular interest because residential movement has helped free them from traditional group bonds and made them vulnerable to the appeal of new social movements. Clark interprets Diefenbaker's early appeal in these terms. While the Conservatives had long been identified with British origin, Protestant religion, and middle-class status, and suburbanites were largely of these characteristics, Diefenbaker's appeal was unique in breaking away from the traditional image of the party. (Beck and Dooley, 1963, p. 36; Newman, 1963, pp. 71–75.) Clark argues:

> If the suburban residents who voted for Mr. Diefenbaker had any one set of social characteristics in common it was that they were almost all young, had only recently become home-owners and settled members of a community, and many were being called upon to vote in 1957 and 1958 for the first time in their lives.... Voters such as these did not have many group interests of an ethnic, religious, or social class sort to protect. What they were seeking was a meaning or purpose

in their lives, a sense of social belonging or mission, and this they found in identification with the movement Mr. Diefenbaker headed up and in the campaign to defeat the Liberal Government (Clark, 1963, p. 74).

2. AGE

The move to collect information on age by recording actual years is particularly useful, as survey data accumulate, for long-term studies of generational effects. In a single survey it is not likely that the investigator will want to take into account each individual year, but by having them he can establish whatever cutting points are meaningful to his research interests. We followed this procedure in our 1965 national survey.

Data on the relation between age and party preference nationally are included in the works of Alford and Regenstreif. Regenstreif, for example, presents data for the elections of 1953, 1958, 1962, and 1963 (Regenstreif, 1965, pp. 14, 33, 37, 38). During this time the most consistent associations were between older age and support for the Conservatives and younger age and support for Social Credit. The Liberals and CCF either did not have a consistently greater appeal to any age group or attracted fairly uniform support from all. The 1958 election was the first sweeping victory for the Conservatives in many years. The new dynamism of the party was reflected to some extent in the national figures, in the sense that there was added support from those under fifty. In western Canada, where Diefenbaker's message found an especially responsive audience, the Conservatives attracted new support from all ages, particularly those under thirty (Regenstreif, 1965, p. 138). By 1962, however, nationally at least, the Conservatives were no longer communicating so well to the young. Regenstreif attributes some of the attraction of older voters to the Conservatives to specific policies. Prior to the 1957 election the Liberal government had raised the old-age pension by only six dollars. The Conservatives condemned this, not as an undesirable form of state intervention, but as niggardly, and subsequently took more generous action. But Regenstreif also points out that differential support from age groups is confounded by two other factors. These are the greater success of Conservatives in rural areas and in the prairies and Maritimes, all places where there is an older-than-average population base.

Regenstreif's final observation raises an interesting question, even though he does not consider all the empirical evidence that he himself presents. The behavior of those fifty and older is something of a dilemma. It is this segment of the electorate that came to maturity in the thirties during the depression and under the Conservative adminis- tration of R. B. Bennett. Accordingly, it continued to have an image of the Conservative party as the "party of hard times." That this often articulated perception of the Tories by the electorate could be overcome is a tribute to the impact of Diefenbaker himself (Regenstreif, 1965, p. 87). The dilemma of why older voters, directly experiencing the connection between the depression and Conservatism, should still vote Conservative is actually more far-reaching than Regenstreif suggests. For one thing it was not a pattern of voting behavior unique to the 1962 election. It is rather a more general tendency, obscured only during those times when the Conservatives could extend their appeal to a broad spectrum of voters. In 1962, for example, and possibly using the same data, Alford found that in Saskatchewan and Alberta, where Conservative appeal was strong for all sectors of the population, there was no tendency for those over fifty to prefer the Conservatives with any greater frequency than other age groups (Alford, 1964, pp. 223–24). In our 1965 election study Conservative supporters were, on the average, older than the other voters in their region. We may, however, partially discount as sampling fluctuation the extraordinarily large sample of older Conservatives that we happened to select in British Columbia (Table 19). Voting studies generally have established that political attachments become more stable with age. This means that new parties, with the notable exception of those with a special platform for the aged, have a much more difficult time gaining support from older voters than they do from younger ones. This would account for the more youthful appeal of Social Credit and, to some extent, the NDP. But it still does not tell us why older people less frequently vote Liberal. An interpretation of the possible meaning of these trends is also handicapped by the lack of finer age breaks. A single age category, grouping those fifty and over, includes persons at quite different stages of the life cycle, from those in the prime of life and at the peak of their careers to those retired and infirm, spending their last years on a fixed pension.

TABLE 19: **Percentage of Respondents Fifty Years of Age and Older, 1965 Vote, by Region and Past Vote**

	Liberal	Conservative	NDP	Social Credit	Total[a]
Atlantic	34	39	[43][c]	—	38
	(100)	(83)	(8)		(229)
Quebec	39	39	14	23	34
	(357)	(97)	(70)	(65)	(793)
Ontario	30	37	35	—	32
	(424)	(311)	(132)		(1,054)
Prairies	31	37	43	24	34
	(89)	(125)	(56)	(37)	(395)
British Columbia	38	65	33	38	40
	(78)	(58)	(62)	(26)	(256)
Total	34	39	32	32	34
	(1,048)	(674)	(328)	(67)[b]	(2,727)

Figures in parentheses are base Ns.
[a]Column totals include other parties, don't-knows, etc.
[b]The total for Social Credit includes four cases in the Atlantic provinces and Ontario. The Quebec *Créditistes* are not included.
[c]Too few to percentage.

As in other countries young people in Canada have been attracted to new political movements. For example, by 1960 people were beginning to grow dissatisfied with the unfulfilled promise of change and progress that the 1958 Conservative victory had been intended to herald. Two by-elections were held in Ontario in 1960, at which time a sample of voters was surveyed with a mailed questionnaire (Scarrow, 1961, pp. 79–91). This was a period when the CCF was undergoing its transformation, but before the New Democratic party had yet been officially organized. For the purpose of these two elections interim local organizations were formed, auspiciously and simply called the New party. In one of the by-elections the New party candidate was successful. The survey evidence showed that the young voted New party to a disproportionately high degree (Jewett, 1967, pp. 54–55). In our survey, however, we found that the NDP was attracting more than its share of older voters in its traditional home in the prairies.

Social Credit in Quebec also has had a differential attraction for the young. Using for comparison the two extreme categories of those twenty-four or younger and those sixty or older, Pinard found

> Social Credit obtained 24 percent more votes among the younger age group (voting for the first time in a federal election) than it did among the oldest age group. Indeed, this is one of the very strong relationships observed in the present study (Pinard, 1968, pp. 270–271).

Young people's voting behavior in Quebec was also related to a more general unrest and dissatisfaction with traditional ways. For example, a survey by the Groupe de Récherches Sociales in 1963 found the youngest most in favor of Quebec's separation from the rest of Canada (Gzowski, 1963, pp. 13–18). The 1970 provincial election in Quebec also found the separatist *Parti Québécois* drawing disproportionate support from the young (Regenstreif, 1970; Désjardins, 1970). The 1965 election survey found that *Créditiste* and especially NDP voters were preponderantly young. In the country as a whole the trend in political opinions for those under thirty has been consistently in the direction of greater nationalism. This has been true of the youthful supporters of all parties, possible anticipating eventual changes in public policies (Schwartz, 1967, pp. 192–193).

3. SEX

Sex differences in Canadian political behavior are similar to those reported for other countries. For example, Regenstreif reports on the lower level of interest in politics and the less likelihood of voting among women in the 1963 election. He does not present supportive data for his other generalizations, but these include the lower frequency of voting for new parties. Regenstreif, who appears to have had difficulty with interviewing women, suggests that they are more prone than men to reverse their intentions. He suggests that this is because, just before the election, they are persuaded to vote for their husbands' party. Disparities in political involvement are less among university-educated women, the younger, those living in the suburbs, and the English-speaking (Regenstreif, 1965, pp. 96–97).

Alford did an analysis of sex differences in the 1962 election and found few. He concluded that while there may be "some distinctive values or perspectives which produce particular political attitudes" associated with sex within some provinces or religious groups, these were not manifested in a consistent partisan direction (Alford,

1964, 225). Among young people greater generational conflict among women in French Canada is a significant indication of where social changes are occurring (Johnstone, 1970).

4. MEMBERSHIPS

TRADE UNIONS are the one and generally the only kind of membership asked about in most surveys. More accurately, in CIPO surveys the question is whether any member of the household is a union member. An association with organized labor is obviously a concomitant of social class, but not all members of the working-class are union members and those excluded are frequently the economically most disadvantaged. Conversely, not all union members can be characterized as working-class, notably those in clerical and professional occupations, although they may have an ambiguous sense of identification with that class. In the 1962 election there were no differences nationally in the extent to which those in union households compared to nonunion households supported either the Liberal or Social Credit parties. Twenty-six percent of those in union households planned to vote Conservative, contrasted with 40 percent in nonunion. The reverse was true with respect to support for the NDP: 22 percent in union households were for the NDP as compared to 8 percent in nonunion (Alford, 1964, p. 211). Regenstreif found similar types of differences, though not necessarily percentages, prior to the elections of 1953, 1958, 1962, and 1963 (Regenstreif, 1965, pp. 13, 33, 37, 38).

What is the effect of region on patterns of union partisanship? Data from Alford's analysis, although often based on few cases, suggest that only some provinces followed the national pattern: Manitoba, Ontario, Saskatchewan, and to some extent British Columbia. In the remaining provinces the differential strength of third parties was related to the attraction of trade-union support.

> ...where there were two parties, the Liberals usually benefited from trade-union support. Where there were more than two parties, the third party (whether New Democratic or Social Credit) usually drew off trade-union support from the Conservatives, rather than from the Liberals. Whether the endorsements by labour of various parties or the association of a party with economic liberalism in certain provinces and not in others accounted for these patterns could be discovered by analysis of party and interest group strategy in the various provinces (Alford, 1964, p. 223).

From national data Regenstreif points up an interesting contrast in party choice, taking into account level of skill, union affiliation, and language spoken. In 1953 at least three patterns are worth noting. One was the greater likelihood of those in union households who were unskilled to be stronger supporters of the CCF than were the skilled, who instead were more inclined to vote Liberal or Conservative. Second was the tendency of those in working-class occupations who were not unionized, regardless of skill level, to be more likely than their unionized counterparts to vote Conservative. The unskilled nonunionized were also more likely to vote CCF than the skilled. Finally, the French-speaking, regardless of skill level or union affiliation, rarely planned to vote CCF, but were most strongly attached to the Liberals. In 1963 the same analysis produced one major change: the new attraction of the French-speaking away from the Liberals and to Social Credit. During this time span unskilled unionized workers had increased their support for the Conservatives, and the skilled, both in and out of union households, had done so for the NDP (Regenstreif, 1965, pp. 101–102).

Pinard notes that when union leaders recognized how well Social Credit was doing in the 1962 election, they denounced the party to their members. They argued for union opposition on the grounds that the party stood for everything that was contrary to union interests. This had little avail, as survey and voting results indicate. Pinard attributes this to the low level of ideological sophistication of rank-and-file members and the cleavage between central and local union leaders, with the latter leaning to Social Credit (Pinard, 1968, p. 354). Ultimately the reason for the switch from Liberal to Social Credit stemmed from the extent of economic dissatisfaction in Quebec, a situation from which, for various reasons, the NDP was not able to achieve any advantage. With the Conservatives a weak alternative, membership in trade unions actually provided a channel for workers to direct their protest into the new party.

Given the low level of class voting in Canada we would not anticipate a strong association between trade-union affiliation and voting behavior. Yet the crucial participation of the trade-union movement in the formation of the NDP might be assumed to herald at least a closer tie between that party and organized labor (Horowitz, 1968; Young, 1969). Yet there still exist some factors which would appear to inhibit these developments. For example, from 1948 to 1962 CIPO surveys asked for opinions on the formation of a political party supported by organized labor. Those living in trade-union households were more inclined than the remainder to approve of such action, but they did not express overwhelming approval. By 1962 the NDP had already been created, yet 48 percent of those in union households—the largest percentage expressing a single opinion—still disapproved of a labor party (Schwartz, 1967, pp. 89–91). In addition to the factors indicating a low level of class voting in Canada, those specific to the conditions of unionism are also important (Jamieson, 1957, pp. 93–100; Crispo, 1966; Engelmann and Schwartz, 1967, pp. 57–58; Horowitz, 1968, pp. 234–52). Canada's economy is highly vulnerable to fluctuations in world markets and seasonally determined employment, leaving the worker in a relatively weak bargaining position. The working-class itself, only recently urbanized and with many recent immigrants, does not always look with favor on trade-union activities.

Federal jurisdiction on matters pertaining to labor has been limited through constitutional interpretations, permitting the perpetuation of pronounced regional differences in working conditions. Labor unity has never been strong, a consequence of the regional nature of economic interests and problems. Regional differences in outlook are accentuated in Quebec by the existence of a Catholic labor movement, only recently secularized. Trade unionism is a "foreign" import, brought to Canada from Britain and the United States. For many Canadian unions affiliated with the AFL-CIO policy-making autonomy is limited, and both formal and informal pressures exist against political participation. Trade unions themselves, tied to the feelings of members that politics should be an individual rather than a group act, have often been reluctant to engage directly in political action. Before the merger of the Trades and Labor Congress with the Canadian Congress of Labour in 1956 there were direct ties between the CCL and the CCF, but the TLC remained politically independent, despite the actions of some of its member unions. The formation of the united TLC-CCL did not lead to open support for the CCF, and the creation of the NDP with trade union assistance still leaves unions at any organizational level the option of not supporting the NDP. For these varied reasons, then, we can see why the tie between organized labor and a workers' party is not stronger in Canada.

PARTIES   This review of voting behavior appropriately ends with its association with one kind of organizational membership central to politics, that of political parties. What we know can be summed up very quickly. As our earlier characterization of parties indicated, both major parties are cadre ones, and hence we cannot expect much in the way of formal membership. Our 1965 election survey found that less than 5 percent of a national sample were currently dues-paying members of a party (Meisel and VanLoon, 1966). Particularly for the older parties, the payment of dues comes to a peak at election times, since the designation of local candidates is generally the job of members of the constituency organization. After the election, however, membership and interest drops off (Dawson, 1964, pp. 473–513; Meisel, 1962). To some extent the same state of affairs exists in the minor parties as well. This is especially the case as these parties age and lose their early missionary zeal (Zakuta, 1964; Engelmann, 1956, pp. 161–173; Irving, 1959).

A mailed survey of party members, or at least those on party lists, was done by Regenstreif in 1960 (Regenstreif, 1963, pp. 59–74). With a return rate of only 18 percent, nothing can be said for the representativeness of the sample. But the paper is instructive for its anticipation of some general findings—for example, the close connection between federal and provincial voting habits in the Atlantic provinces and the stronger emphasis on the person of the leader among those of French origin. A detailed study of party activists at all levels of party organization is underway in Winnipeg and Vancouver. In addition to providing the first body of comprehensive information on this subject, the study also provides a comparative perspective through similar interviews in Seattle and Minneapolis (Smith, Kornberg, Bromley, 1968; Kornberg, Smith, Bromley, 1969; Kornberg, Smith, Clark, 1970).

V.   Social-Psychological Influences

The stress in this chapter has been on structural factors influencing voting behavior. Normally, these assume greatest significance in any discussion of a mass electorate. There will be no attempt to review the whole field of social-psychological influences, one that we know can be immese (Lipset et al., 1954), though it has been only weakly explored in Canada. Some social-psychological influences have already been mentioned—for example, the perceptions of party differences, attachments to parties, and factors associated with the act of voting and partisan choice. Here we will mention a limited number of social-psychological themes that appear particularly pertinent in the Canadian context, indicating examples of research already done and avenues that might be explored.

Research on personality factors in political behavior ought to emphasize their importance in affecting meaningful choices among a limited number of alternatives. The variables considered should have some predictive value in determining such matters as choices among parties, leaders, or issues. For example, research by Smith et al. (1957) on the relation between personality and opinions did not reveal much association. This was because the issues studied were highly salient at the time of the study to the bulk of the public, while possible responses to the issues were narrowly constrained. In other words the structural context in which the individual voter operates largely conditions the responses he can make, regardless of personality dispositions. In much the same fashion Laponce's study of Vancouver–Burrard did not uncover startling findings about the relation between authoritarianism and reactions to political issues (Laponce, 1969, pp. 105–10). Research on personality must therefore to be concerned with factors that matter politically: for example, does reaction to authority affect the likelihood of voting for the NDP or the Liberals or to having the same party preference as one's father? Little is to be gained from a search for idiosyncratic or neurotic personality factors.

One reason for an interest in socialization lies in the importance of formative experiences for different personality types. Socialization is an area in which there is growing interest in Canada, although as yet there is not much published research. The most comprehensive study is by Johnstone (1969). He distinguishes differences, for example, in attachments to Canada and in attitudes to the ethnic makeup of the country according to age, language used in the home, and region of the country. Some followup, focusing on French-English differences, has been done by Lamy (1970), but he, like Johnstone, does not tell us what in the environment of these young people has brought about such differing perspectives. The socializing experiences themselves and their political implications remain to be explored.

The most comprehensive effort to treat the formal efforts of the school system to communicate the content and values of citizenship has been made by Hodgetts (1968). Although he collected impressive quantities of data from across Canada through observations, self-administered questionnaires to students and teachers, and interviews with teachers, Hodgetts' analysis of his data are quite sparing and do little to get to the heart of the social-psychological processes involved. However, his conclusions that history and social studies are taught from two perspectives in English and French Canada, by teachers often ill-informed and hostile to their subject, to indifferent students, raises serious questions about the nature of political socialization in Canada.

Something of the socializing experiences of a quite specialized group, that of party activists, is presented in the work of Kornberg and Smith (Smith, Kornberg & Bromley, 1968; Kornberg, Smith & Bromley, 1969).

One approach to the study of values comes from Lipset's work, comparing the United States and Canada (Lipset, 1963; 1964). This delineation of basic value patterns still needs empirical validation. Further comparison between the two countries is forthcoming from the 1965 election study, where replications were done of the Survey Research Center's questions on efficacy and cynicism. Canadians revealed a lower sense of efficacy and a greater degree of cynicism about their government. Even more noteworthy within the Canadian context are differences by region, party, and, less striking, by age and education. For example, the most consistently efficacious in their self-assessments are Liberal supporters and residents of Ontario (Schwartz, 1973; Rojecki, 1970).

The relation between attitudinal dispositions and possible political action has been explored through a survey in one community in Alberta, where small businessmen were compared with branch managers. The small businessmen were higher on measures of conservatism, political intolerance, authoritarianism, and alienation, all considered to be predisposing factors to right-wing extremism (Nolan and Schneck, 1969).

Given the obvious political content of issues, candidates, and party leaders, it is little wonder that these three continue to receive attention, regardless of disciplinary perspective. One interest in Canadian research has been the association between issue stands or attitudes toward candidates, specific population groups, and party choice (Schwartz, 1967; Regenstreif, 1965, pp. 48–51, 68–83; Laponce, 1969, pp. 77–104, 111–35).

The way in which presumed characteristics of candidates bears on voters' choices was investigated by Kamin through a survey in Kingston and Cornwall, Ontario, prior to the 1957 election. He found that English and French origin respondents underchose names of candidates that could be presumed to be of the opposite origin. When the party affiliation of candidates was added, however, then ethnicity faded as the crucial variable (Kamin, 1958).

Another focus of interest concerns the relative importance of issues, candidates, and leaders in bringing about changes in voting patterns (Sears, 1969, pp. 354–69). This is illustrated in Canada by a survey in three federal constituencies in Hamilton, Ontario, immediately before the 1968 election. At a time when many were commenting on the phenomenon of "Trudeaumania," the researchers found that Mr. Trudeau did indeed have a highly favorable image among almost all population subgroups. Moreover, they found that perceptions of the party leader had some independent influence on voting behavior, especially for those without firm attachments to a party (Winham and Cunningham, 1970).

Reference-group theory, among other sources, has taught us to look at the existence of group identity as a precondition of group-related action. In the political context this means that self-identification in group terms, the awareness of group interests, and the ability to make comparisons with other groups all contribute to the likelihood of political mobilization. How such group consciousness arises and which group identities are salient under what circumstances suggest areas of research that could have important results for understanding the dynamics of political action.

One particular form of group identification, that of class consciousness, is already a familiar theme. For example, the 1965 election study found that normally those who identify themselves as working-class are more likely to vote NDP, regardless of objective class characteristics. Unskilled workers and farmers, however, were more likely to support the NDP if they saw themselves as middle-class (Gagne, 1969).

The significance of regionalism in Canadian political life has also been explored in terms of group consciousness. It is hypothesized that political behavior reflecting regional concerns will more likely occur where there is an awareness of regional interests and identification in terms of a territorial locus (Schwartz, 1973).

Origin remains a salient characteristic in many modern, industrial societies and continues to provoke strong tensions. For the student of politics this means that the social psychologists' concerns with intergroup relations need to be translated and extended to cover more overtly political situations (Blalock, 1967). Questions on relations among groups, as this relates to perceptions of the distribution of power and justice in the allocation of rewards, illustrate issues that reflect on the political structure of the society. The most pertinent studies of this sort have been done for the Royal Commission on Bilingualism and Biculturalism (Breton and Roseborough, 1968).

For most students of social movements, particular stress is placed on the conditions for their emergence, the character of their leadership, and the kinds of people they are likely to attract (Toch, 1965). More narrowly, political concerns also have a place in the analysis of social movements. These include the impact that social movements may have on existing political institutions, the conditions under which they become transformed into traditional political parties, and the consequences of their development for the attraction of support. Considering the number of political movements that have emerged in Canada, this has not been a particularly popular approach. A social-movement approach has, however, been used for the study of the CCF and Social Credit (Zakuta, 1964; Irving, 1959).

VI. The Study of Voting Behavior in Canada

Notwithstanding some continuities with Britain and France, cultural influences have not been adopted without alteration; for example, in no sense is Canada a simple extension of Britain. The student of Canadian politics must also consider how the roots in Britain and France continue to be sources of *tension* within Canadian society.

Considering its importance, very little has been said about United States influence on life in Canada. Yet from the outset of Canadian nationhood and even earlier, an often unspoken dialogue with American institutions, ambitions, and people has permeated Canadian society. "How the Americans do it," even when not made explicit, is a critical theme. This is not to say that there is either blind borrowing from the United States or, conversely, that everything made in the U.S.A. is denigrated. But we must be constantly aware of the latent, and sometimes manifest, tension of being neighbor to an economic, military, and demographic giant. Sharing the same language, those who speak English can hardly be immunized against its cultural onslaught. And being North American, regardless of origin or language, the attractions of a high standard of living and a mass culture can hardly be resisted.

The pervasiveness of American institutions extends even to the political sphere. Despite a system of government that is one of the most obvious points of difference between the two countries, the example of the United States is thought to affect not only the issues that the Canadian government must face, but even the way government and politics are conducted. Laponce is one of the few political scientists who has recognized that Canadians, at least in a symbolic sense, participate in U.S. elections as they do in federal, provincial, and local ones. Moreover, interest in American elections is not a reflection of indifference to Canadian politics but is tied in with a generally high level of political interest (Laponce, 1969, pp. 164–67).

American influence is not wholly benign, and from time to time political elites argue against American penetration. Currently most objection to American influence comes from the young and those in professional occupations. Politically it is more likely to be expressed by NDP voters (Laponce, pp. 96–101), a reflection of strenuous criticism from at least the left wing of the NDP leadership. For example, Melville Watkins, an active member of the NDP and former head of the Royal Commission on the Foreign Ownership of the Canadian Economy, has been a particularly sharp critic of American economic penetration (Watkins, 1969, pp. 97–102). Just what the future of anti-Americanism as a political theme might be is difficult to predict, but *le fait Americain* is a pervasive element of Canadian existence.

At a time of growing nationalism it will also be important to watch for the political significance of ties with Britain (Engelmann and Schwartz, 1967, pp. 61–67). The place of pan-Gallicism also needs continued scrutiny as a possible counter to British and American influences for those in French Canada, or as an attempt to revive ties that were served not only by the British conquest, but also by the social and political changes of the French Revolution. For example, a review of public-opinion data indicates that 1960 was a turning point for French Canada. Among other things, the creation of French-speaking states in the Third World accompanied a new interest in international affairs in Quebec (Gow, 1970).

If one crucial area for the understanding of Canadian political life is the influence from other countries, notably Britain and the United States, the other is the contrast between Canada and other countries. For example, there is the common-sense notion that Canada is merely an extension of Great Britain or a variation of the United States. Efforts of Canadians to establish a unique identity are often couched in terms of differentiation from these similar nations. But does anyone ever consider Quebec as merely an extension of France? In the sense that they do not, they are more perceptive about the interaction of formative influences and historical developments than those who refer to the intrinsic oneness of Canada and other English-speaking nations. Here of course we enter an area where nationalistic sensibilities are easily offended. At the same time the question raised both by growing nationalism and the views of casual, outside observers has great relevance to sociological studies. The most primitive question at issue here is how one differentiates among units. That is, to what extent is Canada like other countries and to what extent is it different? The most valuable comparative studies that have included Canada as one of their cases have been those that dealt with similar countries. These include Alford's work on social class and voting behavior and Lipset's on value orientations (Lipset, 1963, pp. 226–33, 284–312; Lipset, 1964, pp. 173–92).

Comparative studies using Canada can be approached as a way of better describing and more completely understanding the nature of Canadian society itself. At the same time our comparative efforts should be adding data to testable and generalizable propositions about macrosociological problems. For example, Canada would be a useful sampling unit in studies of polyethnic strains or of regional cleavages. Comparisons can, of course, be made within nations as well as among nations. Attempts to incorporate both levels of differentiation in the same study, as Allardt (1966) suggests, may be most useful of all.

Postscript

This review was completed in the fall of 1970. As a result, we missed from our purview the 1972 general election, held under new electoral arrangements which included the enfranchisement of eighteen-year-olds, an election in which the Liberals slipped from a clear majority to the weakest minority government in Canadian history. Significant provincial changes included the election of an NDP government in British Columbia in 1972, adding to the NDP governments currently in Saskatchewan and Manitoba. In 1971, breaking thirty-six years of Social Credit government in Alberta, the Conservatives came from an extremely weak position to capture the legislature. Reference was made in the text to the Liberal victory in Quebec in 1970, but omitted were shifts in strength for other parties, fortunately discussed in Vincent Lemieux's article in the Robin (1972) volume. Also omitted were such details of the Quebec situation as would anticipate the terrorist-inspired crisis in October, 1970. For information about these events, as well as details of new data sources and new analyses of Canadian politics, we direct the reader to the 1973 edition of Engelmann and Schwartz.

Notes

1. The positions taken by *Cité Libre* would exemplify this (Carrier, 1968).
2. It can also be argued more broadly that "In a federal system,....conflict is inevitable" (Caplan,. 1970, p. 50; Caplan, 1969).

3. British includes English, Scottish, Welsh, and Northern Irish. Since the 1951 census immigrants and their descendants from Eire have been included with "other Europeans," a relatively small residual category.

4. The federal House has been studied by Ward and Kornberg, the latter through interviews, while Porter has singled out the political elite (Ward, 1963; Kornberg, 1968; Porter, 1965, pp. 386–416). Life histories of all Members of Parliament and Senators from 1867 to the present are available on IBM cards at Carleton University's data archives. Similar data are stored for provincial legislators from all provinces except Newfoundland and Prince Edward Island.

5. Criticisms of current NDP ideology are growing, both from within and outside the party, from those who advocate more radical positions (Thompson, 1969; Dumas and Smith, 1969).

6. A mathematical treatment of the relation between votes and seats is provided by Qualter (1968). He concludes that there is a reasonably good fit between the two.

7. A scheme for adapting a form of proportional representation to Canada, based on the 1953 Bonn arrangements, has been prepared by Schindler (1968).

8. This survey provides the major part of the data included in this chapter. Details are included in Section III, Data for Analysis, and in Schwartz, 1973.

9. There has been some dissatisfaction, however, with the way in which the problems have been conceptualized (Porter, 1969; Rocher, 1969).

10. A study of Baptist clergymen indicated some relationship between theological and political conservatism (Schindler and Hoffman, 1968).

11. We would consider our sample in the Atlantic provinces to be more reliable than what is usual for CIPO.

References

ALFORD, ROBERT R. *Party and Society: The Anglo-American Democracies.* Chicago: Rand, McNally 1963.

———. "The Social Bases of Political Cleavage in 1962." In J. Meisel, ed. *Papers on the 1962 Election.* Toronto: Univ. of Toronto Press, 1964.

———. "Class Voting in the Anglo-American Political Systems." In Seymour M. Lipset and Stein Rokkan, eds. *Party Systems and Voter Alignments.* New York: Free Press, 1967.

ALLARDT, ERIK. "Implications of Within-Nation Variations and Regional Imbalance for Cross-National Research." In Richard L. Merritt and Stein Rokkan, eds. *Comparing Nations.* New Haven: Yale Univ. Press, 1966.

ANDERSON, GRACE M. "Voting Behaviour and the Ethnic-Religious Variable: A Study of a Federal Election in Hamilton, Ontario." *Canadian Journal of Economics and Political Science* 32 (February, 1966): 27–37.

BECK, J. M., and DOOLEY, D. J. "Labour Parties New and Old." *Dalhousie Review* 40 (1960): 323–28.

———. "Party Images in Canada." In Hugh G. Thorburn, ed. *Party Politics in Canada* 2nd ed. Toronto: Prentice-Hall of Canada, 1967.

BECK, J. MURRAY. *Pendulum of Power.* Scarborough: Prentice-Hall of Canada, 1968.

BELL, DANIEL. *Marxian Socialism in the United States.* Princeton: Princeton Univ. Press, 1967.

BLACK, EDWIN R. "Federal Strains Within a Canadian party." In Hugh G. Thorburn, ed. *Party Politics in Canada*, 2nd ed. Scarborough: Prentice-Hall of Canada, 1967.

BLALOCK, H. M. Jr. *Toward a Theory of Minority Group Relations*. New York: Wiley, 1967.

BLISHEN, BERNARD R. "The Construction and Use of an Occupational Class Scale." *Canadian Journal of Economics and Political Science* 24 (November, 1958): 519–31.

BLISHEN, BERNARD R. "A Socio-economic Index for Occupations in Canada." *Canadian Review of Sociology and Anthropology* 4 (February, 1967): 41–53.

BRETON, RAYMOND, and ROSEBOROUGH, HOWARD. "Perceptions of the Relative Economic and Political Advantages of Ethnic Groups in Canada." In Bernard Blishen et al. *Canadian Society*, 3rd ed. Toronto: Macmillan of Canada, 1968.

BREWIS, T. N. *Regional Economic Policies in Canada*. Toronto: Macmillan of Canada, 1969.

CAIRNS, ALAN C. "The Electoral System and the Party System in Canada, 1921–1965." *Canadian Journal of Political Science* 1 (March, 1968): 55–80.

CAMPBELL, ANGUS, et al. *The American Voter*. New York: Wiley, 1960.

CAMU, P.; WEEKS, E. P.; and SAMETZ, Z. W.; *Economic Geography of Canada*. Toronto: Macmillan, 1964.

CANADA. Dominion Bureau of Statistics. 1961 Census of Canada. Ottawa: Queen's Printer, 1962–1963.

CANADA. *One Hundred: 1867-1967*. Ottawa: Queen's Printer, 1967.

CANADA, Representation Commissioner. *Report on Methods of Registration of Electors and Absentee Voting*. Ottawa: Queen's Printer, 1968.

CAPLAN, NEIL. "Some Factors Affecting the Resolution of a Federal–Provincial Conflict." *Canadian Journal of Political Science* 2 (June, 1969): 173–86.

———. "Offshore Mineral Rights: Anatomy of a Federal–Provincial Conflict." *Journal of Canadian Studies* 5 (February, 1970): 50–61.

CARRIER, ANDRE. "L'idéologie politique de la révue *Cité Libre*." *Canadian Journal of Political Science* 1 (December, 1968): 414–28.

CAVES, RICHARD E., and HOLTON, RICHARD H. *The Canadian Economy*. Cambridge: Harvard Univ. Press, 1959.

CHEAL, JOHN E. "Factors Related to Educational Output Differences Among the Canadian Provinces." *Comparative Education Review* 6 (October, 1962): 120–25.

CLARK, S. D. *Church and Sect in Canada*. Toronto: Univ. of Toronto Press, 1948.

———. "Group Interests in Canadian Politics." In J. H. Aitchison, ed. *The Political Process in Canada*. Toronto: Univ. of Toronto Press, 1963.

COLE, TAYLOR. *The Canadian Bureaucracy, 1939–1947*. Durham: Duke Univ. Press, 1949.

———. *The Canadian Bureaucracy and Federalism, 1947–1965*. Denver: Univ. of Denver Press, 1966.

COOK, RAMSAY. *Canada and the French-Canadian Question*. Toronto: Macmillan, 1966.

———. "French Canadian Interpretation of Canadian History." *Journal of Canadian Studies* 2 (May, 1967): 3–17.

CORNELL, PAUL G.; HAMELIN, JEAN; OUELLET, FERNAND; TRUDEL, MARCEL. *Canada: Unity in Diversity.* Toronto: Holt, Rinehart, Winston, 1968.

COTNAM, JACQUES. *Faut-il inventer un nouveau Canada?* Montréal: Fides, 1967.

COURTNEY, JOHN C., and SMITH, DAVID E. "Voting in a Provincial General Election and a Federal By-Election: A Constituency Study of Saskatoon City." *Canadian Journal of Economics and Political Science* 33 (August, 1966): 338–53.

COURTNEY, JOHN C., ed. *Voting in Canada.* Scarborough: Prentice-Hall of Canada, 1967.

CREPEAU, P. A., and MACPHERSON, C. B., eds. *The Future of Canadian Federalism; l'Avenir du Fédéralisme Canadien.* Toronto: Univ: of Toronto Press, Montréal: l'Univ. de Montréal, 1965.

CRISPO, JOHN H. G. *International Unionism in Canada: A Canadian-American Experiment.* Toronto: McGraw-Hill of Canada, 1966.

DAVIS, MORRIS. "Did They Vote for Candidate or Party in Halifax?" In John Meisel, ed. *Papers on the 1962 Election.* Toronto: Univ. of Toronto Press, 1964.

_____. "A Last Look at Ballot Behaviour in the Dual Constituency of Halifax." *Canadian Journal of Economics and Political Science* 32 (August, 1966): 366–71.

DAWSON, ROBERT MACGREGOR. *William Lyon Mackenzie King: A Political Biography I: 1874–1923.* Toronto: Univ. of Toronto Press, 1958.

_____. *The Conscription Crisis of 1944.* Toronto: Univ. of Toronto Press, 1961.

_____. *The Government of Canada*, 4th ed. revised by Norman Ward. Toronto: Univ. of Toronto Press, 1964.

DENTON, FRANK T. *An Analysis of Interregional Differences in Manpower Utilization and Earnings.* Ottawa: Economic Council of Canada, 1966.

DESJARDINS, MARCEL. "Les Libéraux et les 'Québécois' recrutent leur clientèle dans les mêmes milieux." Montréal: La Presse 18 avril, 1970.

DION, LEON. *Le Bill 60 et la société québécoise.* Montréal: HMH, 1967.

DUMAS, EVELYN, and ED SMITH. "The NDP Since its Founding." *Our Generation* 6 (June, 1969): 74–80.

DUNCAN, OTIS DUDLEY. "A Socio-economic Index for All Occupations." In Albert J. Reiss, ed. *Occupations and Social Status.* New York: Free Press, 1961.

ECONOMIC COUNCIL OF CANADA. *Second Annual Review: Towards Sustained and Balanced Economic Growth.* Ottawa: Queen's Printer, 1965.

_____. *Fifth Annual Review: The Challenge of Growth and Change.* Ottawa: Queen's Printer, 1968.

_____. *Sixth Annual Review: Perspective 1975.* Ottawa: Queen's Printer, 1969.

ENGELMANN, FREDERICK C. "Membership Participation in Policy Making in the C.C.F." *Canadian Journal of Economics and Political Science* 22 (1956): 161–73.

_____, and SCHWARTZ, MILDRED A. *Political Parties and the Canadian Social Structure.* Scarborough: Prentice-Hall of Canada, 1967.

FOX, PAUL, ed. *Politics: Canada*, 2nd ed. Toronto: McGraw-Hill of Canada, 1966.

GAGNE, WALLACE. "Class Voting in Canada." Doctoral dissertation, Department of Political Science, Univ. of Rochester, 1969.

_____, and REGENSTREIF, PETER. "Some Aspects of New Democratic Party Urban Support in 1965." *Canadian Journal of Economics and Political Science* 33 (November, 1967): 529–50.

GARDNER, R. C., and LAMBERT, W. E. "Motivational Variables in Second Language Acquisition." *Canadian Journal of Psychology* 13 (1959): 266–72.

GERIN-LAJOIE, P. *Constitutional Amendment in Canada.* Toronto: Univ. of Toronto Press, 1950.

GOW, J. I. "Les Québécois, la guerre et la paix, 1945–60." *Canadian Journal of Political Science* 3 (1970): 88–122.

GRAHAM, ROGER. *Arthur Meighen. I: The Door of Opportunity.* Toronto: Clarke, Irwin, 1960.

GREEN, ALAN G. "Regional Inequality, Structural Change, and Economic Growth in Canada—1890–1956." *Economic Development and Cultural Change* 4 (July, 1969): 567–83.

GROSSMAN, LAWRENCE S. " 'Safe' Seats: the Rural–Urban Pattern in Ontario." In John C. Courtney, ed. *Voting in Canada.* Scarborough: Prentice-Hall of Canada, 1967.

GROUPE DE RÉCHERCHES SOCIALES. *Les Electeurs québécois: Attitudes et opinions á la veille de l' élection de 1960.* Montréal: Groupe de Récherches Sociales, 1960.

_____. *Les Préférences politiques des électeurs québécois en 1962,* Montréal: Groupe de Récherches Sociales, 1964.

GZOWSKI, PETER. "This is the True Strength of Separatism." *Maclean's* (November 2, 1963): 13–18.

HARRIS, ROBIN S. *Quiet Revolution, A Study of the Educational System of Ontario.* Toronto: Univ. of Toronto Press, 1967.

HARTZ, LOUIS. *The Liberal Tradition in America.* New York: Harcourt, Brace, 1955.

_____. *The Founding of New Societies.* New York: Harcourt, Brace, 1964.

HODGETTS, A. B. *What Culture? What Heritage? A Study of Civic Education in Canada.* Toronto: Ontario Institute for Studies in Education, 1968.

HOROWITZ, GAD. "Conservatism, Liberalism, and Socialism, in Canada: An Interpretation." *The Canadian Journal of Economics and Political Science* 32 (1966): 143–71.

_____. "Toward the Democratic Class Struggle." *Journal of Canadian Studies* 1 (November, 1966a): 3–10.

_____. *Canadian Labour in Politics.* Toronto: Univ. of Toronto Press, 1968.

HOWLAND, R. D. *Some Regional Aspects of Canada's Economic Development.* Royal Commission on Canada's Economic Prospects. Ottawa: Queen's Printer, 1958.

IRVING, JOHN A. *The Social Credit Movement in Alberta.* Toronto: Univ. of Toronto Press, 1959.

JAMIESON, STUART. *Industrial Relations in Canada.* Toronto: Macmillan of Canada, 1957.

JEWETT, PAULINE. "Voting in the 1960 Federal By-elections at Peterborough and Niagara Falls: Who Voted New Party and Why?" In John C. Courtney, ed. *Voting in Canada.* Scarborough: Prentice-Hall of Canada, 1967.

JOHNSON, A. W. "The Dynamics of Federalism in Canada." *Canadian Journal of Political Science* 1 (March, 1968): 18–39.

JOHNSTONE, JOHN W. C. *Young People's Images of Canadian Society.* Ottawa: Queen's Printer, 1969.

JOHNSTONE, JOHN W. C. "The Problem of Generations in English and French Canada." Paper presented to the Illinois Sociological Association Workshop; Univ. of Illinois at Chicago Circle: April 4, 1970.

KAMIN, LEON J. "Ethnic and Party Affiliations of Candidates as Determinants of Voting." *Canadian Journal of Psychology* 12 (December 1958): 205–12.

KATZ, JOSEPH. *Elementary Education in Canada.* Toronto: McGraw-Hill of Canada, 1961.

KEYFITZ, NATHAN. "Canadians and Canadiens." *Queen's Quarterly* 70 (Summer, 1963); 163–82.

———. "The Changing Canadian Population." In Bernard R. Blishen et al., eds. *Canadian Society*, 2nd ed. Toronto: Macmillan, 1964.

KORNBERG, ALLAN. *Canadian Legislative Behaviour: A Study of the 25th Parliament.* New York: Holt, Rinehart, Winston, 1967.

——— ; SMITH, JOEL; and BROMLEY, DAVID. "Some Differences in the Political Socialization Patterns of Canadian and American Party Officials: A Preliminary Report." *Canadian Journal of Political Science* 2 (March, 1969): 63–88.

——— ; SMITH, JOEL; and CLARK, HAROLD. "Semi-Careers in Political Work: The Dilemma of Party Organizations." Paper prepared for the annual meeting of the Canadian Sociology and Anthropology Association: May 29–31, 1970.

LALANDE, GILLES. *The Department of External Affairs and Biculturalism: Diplomatic Personnel and Language Use.* Ottawa: Queen's Printer, 1970.

LAMY, PAUL G. "Political Socialization of French and English Canadian Youth: Socialization into Discord." Paper presented to the annual meeting of the Canadian Association of Sociology and Anthropology. Winnipeg: May 29–31, 1970.

LANCTOT, GUSTAVE. *History of Canada.* 3 volumes. Cambridge: Harvard Univ. Press, 1963–1965.

LAND, BRIAN. *Eglinton.* Toronto: Peter Martin Associates, 1965.

LAPONCE, J. A. "Nonvoting and Nonvoters: A Typology." *The Canadian Journal of Economics and Political Science* 33 (February 1967): 75–87.

———, *People vs. Politics. A Study of Opinions, Attitudes, and Perceptions in Vancouver –Burrard 1963–1965.* Toronto: Univ. of Toronto Press, 1969.

LASKIN, BORA. *Canadian Constitutional Law: Cases, Text and Notes on Distribution of Legislative Power.* Toronto: Carswell, 1960.

LAURENDEAU, ANDRE. *La Crise de la conscription.* Montréal: Editions du jour, 1962.

LEMIEUX, VINCENT. "The Election in the Constituency of Lévis." In John Meisel, ed. *Papers on the 1962 Election.* Toronto: Univ. of Toronto Press, 1964.

———, "La Composition des préférences partisanes." *Canadian Journal of Political Science* 2 (December, 1969): 397–418.

———, ed. *Quatre élections provinciales au Québec, 1956–1966.* Québec: Les Presses de l'Université Laval, 1969.

LESLIE, PETER M. "The Role of Political Parties in Promoting the Interests of Ethnic Minorities." *Canadian Journal of Political Science* 2 (December, 1969): 419–33.

LIEBERSON, STANLEY. "Bilingualism in Montreal." *American Journal of Sociology* 71 (July, 1965): 10–55.

———. "Language questions in censuses." *Sociological Inquiry* 36 (Spring, 1966): 262–79.

———. *Language and Ethnic Relations in Canada.* New York: Wiley, 1970.

LIPSET, SEYMOUR M. *Agrarian Socialism.* Berkeley: Univ. of California Press, 1950.

———. "Democracy in Alberta." *Canadian Forum* 34 (1954): 175–77, 196–98.

———. *The First New Nation.* New York: Basic Books, 1963.

———. "Canada and the United States—A Comparative View." *Canadian Review of Sociology and Anthropology* 1 (1964): 173–92.

———; LAZARSFELD, PAUL F.; BARTON, ALLEN H.; and LINZ, JUAN J. "The Psychology of Voting: An Analysis of Political Behavior." In Gardner Lindzey, ed. *Handbook of Social Psychology.* II. Cambridge: Addison-Wesley, 1954, pp. 1124–1175.

LONG, JOHN ANTHONY. "Maldistribution in Western Provincial Legislatures: The Case of Alberta." *Canadian Journal of Political Science* 2 (September, 1969): 345–55.

MACDONALD, LYNN. "Religion and Voting: A Study of the 1968 Canadian Federal Election in Ontario." *Canadian Review of Sociology and Anthropology* 6 (August, 1969): 129–44.

MACPHERSON, C. B. *Democracy in Alberta: The Theory and Practice of a Quasi-Party System.* Toronto: Univ. of Toronto Press, 1953.

MACQUARRIE, HEALTH N. "The Formation of Borden's first Cabinet." *Canadian Journal of Economics and Political Science* 23 (February, 1957): 90–104.

MAGNUSON, ROGER. *Education in the Province of Quebec.* Washington: U.S. Government Printing Office, 1969.

MALLORY, J. R. *Social Credit and the Federal Power in Canada.* Toronto: Univ. of Toronto Press, 1954.

MARITIME UNION STUDY. *The Report on Maritime Union Commissioned by the Governments of Nova Scotia, New Brunswick and Prince Edward Island.* Fredericton: Queen's Printer, 1970.

MCHENRY, DEAN E. *The Third Force in Canada: The Cooperative Commonwealth Federation, 1932–1948.* Berkeley: Univ. of California Press, 1950.

MCRAE, K. D. "The Structure of Canadian History." In L. Hartz, ed. *The Founding of New Societies.* Toronto: Longmans, 1964.

———. *The Federal Capital.* Ottawa: Queen's Printer, 1969.

MEEKISON, J. PETER. *Canadian Federalism: Myth or Reality.* Toronto: Methuen, 1968.

MEISEL, JOHN. "Religious Affiliation and Electoral Behavior." *Canadian Journal of Economics and Political Science* 22 (1956): 481–96.

_____. *The Canadian General Election of 1957*. Toronto: Univ. of Toronto Press, 1962.

_____. "The Stalled Omnibus: Canadian Parties in the 1960s." *Social Research* 30 (Autumn, 1963): 367–90.

_____. "Recent Changes in Canadian Parties." In Hugh G. Thorburn, ed. *Party Politics in Canada*, 2nd ed. Scarborough: Prentice-Hall of Canada, 1967.

_____. "Party Images in Canada: A Report on Work in Progress." Paper presented to the forty-second annual meeting of the Canadian Political Science Association. Winnipeg: 1970.

_____., and VANLOON, RICHARD. "Canadian Attitudes to Election Expenses 1965–1966." In Committee on Election Expenses. *Studies in Canadian Party Finance*. Ottawa: Queen's Printer, 1966, pp. 32–41.

MORTON, W. L. *The Progressive Party in Canada*. Toronto: Univ. of Toronto Press, 1967.

NASH, PAUL. "Quality and Equality in Canadian Education" *Comparative Education Review* 4 (October, 1961): 118–29.

NEWMAN, PETER C. *Renegade in Power, the Diefenbaker Years*. Toronto: McClelland and Stewart, 1963.

NOLAN, RICHARD L., and SCHNECK, RODNEY E. "Small Businessmen, Branch Managers, and Their Relative Susceptibility to Right-wing Extremism: An Empirical Test." *Canadian Journal of Political Science* 2 (March, 1969): 89–102.

ORBAN, EDMOND. *Le Conseil législatif de Québec, 1867-1967*. Montréal: Bellarmin, 1967.

_____. "La Fin du bicaméralisme au Québec." *Canadian Journal of Political Science* 2 (September 1969): 312–26.

OSTRY, SYLVIA. *Unemployment in Canada*. Ottawa: Queen's Printer, 1968.

PERLIN, GEORGE. "St. John's West." In John Meisel, ed. *Papers on the 1962 Election*. Toronto: Univ. of Toronto Press, 1964.

PICKERSGILL, JOHN W. *The Liberal Party*. Toronto: McClelland and Stewart, 1962.

PINARD, MAURICE. "One-Party Dominance and Third Parties." *Canadian Journal of Economics and Political Science* 33 (August, 1967): 358–73.

_____. "The Rise of a Third Party." Doctoral dissertation, Department of Social Relations, Johns Hopkins University, 1968.

_____. "Classes sociales et comportement électoral." In Vincent Lemieux, ed. *Quatre élections provinciales au Québec*. Québec: l'Université Laval, 1969.

_____. "La Rationalité de l'électorat: le cas de 1962." In Vincent Lemieux, ed. *Quatre élections provinciales au Québec*. Québec: l'Université Laval, 1969.

_____. "Working Class Politics: An Interpretation of the Québec Case." *Canadian Review of Sociology and Anthropology* 7 (May, 1970): 87–109.

_____. *The Rise of a Third Party: A Study in Crisis Politics*. Englewood Cliffs: Prentice-Hall, 1971.

PINEO, PETER C., and PORTER, JOHN. "Occupational Prestige in Canada." *Canadian Review of Anthropology and Sociology* 4 (February 1967): 24–40.

PORTER, JOHN. *The Vertical Mosaic*. Toronto: Univ. of Toronto Press, 1956.

_____. "Bilingualism and the Myths of Culture." *Canadian Review of Sociology and Anthropology* 6 (May, 1969): 111–19.

PUTNAM, DONALD F. ed. *Canadian Regions*, 2nd. ed. Toronto: Dent, 1954.

QUALTER, TERENCE H. "Seats and Votes: An Application of the Cube Law to the Canadian Electoral System." *Canadian Journal of Political Science* 1 (September, 1968): 336–44.

_____. *The Election Process in Canada*. Toronto: McGraw-Hill, 1970.

QUÉBEC. *Le Rapport de la commission royale d'enquête sur l'enseignement*. 3 volumes. Québec: Queen's Printer, 1963–1966.

QUINN, HERBERT F. *The Union Nationale: A Study in Québec Nationalism*. Toronto: Univ. of Toronto Press, 1963.

RAE, DOUGLAS. *The Political Consequences of Electoral Laws*. New Haven: Yale Univ. Press, 1967.

RASMUSSEN, JORGEN. "A Research Note on Canadian Party Systems." *Canadian Journal of Economics and Political Science* 33 (February, 1967): 98–106.

REGENSTREIF, S. P. "Some Aspects of National Party Support in Canada." *Canadian Journal of Economics and Political Science* 29 (February, 1963): 59–74.

_____. *The Diefenbaker Interlude: Parties and Voting in Canada, An Interpretation*. Toronto: Longmans, 1965.

_____. "Liberals Just as Lucky Winning as They Were Unlucky in 1966." *Toronto Daily Star*. April 30, 1970.

Report of the Royal Commission on Dominion-Provincial Relations. Ottawa: King's Printer, 1940.

Report of the Royal Commission on Government Organization. 5 Volumes. Ottawa: Queen's Printer, 1962–3.

Report of the Royal Commission on Bilingualism and Biculturalism. Ottawa: Queen's Printer. *I. The Official Languages*. 1967. *II. Education*. 1968. *III. The Work World*. 1969. *IV. The Cultural Contribution of the Other Ethnic Groups*. 1969a.

ROBIN, MARTIN. *Radical Politics and Canadian Labour, 1880-1930*. Queen's University: Industrial Relations Centre, 1968.

_____. ed. *Canadian Provincial Politics*. Scarborough: Prentice-Hall of Canada, 1972.

ROCHER, GUY. "Le Canada: un pays à rebâtir?" *Canadian Review of Sociology and Anthropology* 6 (May, 1969): 119–25.

ROJECKI, ANDREW. "Political Powerlessness and Attitudes Toward Government: The Canadian Context." Master's thesis, Department of Sociology, University of Illinois at Chicago Circle, 1970.

ROSE RICHARD, and URWIN, DEREK. "Social Cohesion, Political Parties and Strains in Regime." *Comparative Political Studies* 2 (April, 1969): 7–67.

_____. "Persistence and Change in Western Party Systems Since 1945." *Political Studies* 18 (September, 1970): 287–319.

RUSSELL, PETER H. "The Supreme Court's Interpretation of the Constitution Since 1949." In Paul Fox, ed. *Politics: Canada*. Toronto: McGraw-Hill of Canada, 1962.

SCARROW, HOWARD A. "Federal–Provincial Voting Patterns in Canada." *Canadian Journal of Economics and Political Science* 26 (1960): 289–98.

_____. "By-elections and Public Opinion in Canada." *Public Opinion Quarterly* 25 (1961): 79–91.

_____. *Canada Votes.* New Orleans: Hauser, 1962.

_____. "Distinguishing Between Political Parties—The Case of Canada." *Midwest Journal of Political Science* 9 (February, 1965): 61–76.

_____. "Patterns of Voter Turnout in Canada." In John C. Courtney, ed. *Voting in Canada.* Scarborough: Prentice-Hall of Canada, 1967.

SCHINDELER, FRED. "One Man One Vote: One Vote One Value." *Journal of Canadian Studies* 3 (February, 1968): 13–20.

_____, and HOFFMAN, DAVID. "Theological and Political Conservatism." *Canadian Journal of Political Science* 1 (December, 1968): 429–41.

SCHLESINGER, JOSEPH. "A Two-Dimensional Scheme for Classifying the States According to Degree of Inter-party Competition." *American Political Science Review* 49 (December, 1955): 1120–1128.

SCHWARTZ, MILDRED A. "Political Behavior and Ethnic Origin." In John Meisel, ed. *Papers on the 1962 Election.* Toronto: Univ. of Toronto Press, 1964.

_____. *Public Opinion and Canadian Identity.* Berkeley: Univ. of California Press, 1967.

_____. *Politics and Territory: The Sociology of Regional Persistence in Canada.* Montréal: McGill Univ. Press, 1973.

SCOTT, F. R. *Civil Liberties and Canadian Federalism.* Toronto: Univ. of Toronto Press, 1959.

SEARS, DAVID O. "Political Behavior." In Gardner Lindzey and Elliot Aronson, eds. *The Handbook of Social Psychology*, 2nd ed. V. Reading: Addison-Wesley, 1969, pp. 315–458.

SIMMONS, JAMES W. "Voting Behavior and Socioeconomic Characteristics." *Canadian Journal of Economics and Political Science* 33 (August, 1967): 389–400.

SKELTON, O. D. *Life and Letters of Sir Wilfrid Laurier.* London: Century, 1921.

SMILEY, DONALD V. *The Canadian Political Nationality.* Toronto: Methuen, 1967.

SMITH, JOEL; KORNBERG, ALLAN; and BROMLEY, DAVID. "Patterns of Early Political Socialization and Adult Party Affiliation." *Canadian Review of Sociology and Anthropology* 5 (August, 1968): 123–55.

SMITH, M. BREWSTER; BRUNER, J. S.; and WHITE, R. W. *Opinions and Personality.* New York: Wiley, 1957.

STANLEY, G. F. G. *The Birth of Western Canada: A History of the Riel Rebellions.* Toronto: Univ. of Toronto Press, 1961.

STONE, LEROY O. *Urban Development in Canada: An Introduction to the Demographic Aspects.* Ottawa: Dominion Bureau of Statistics, 1967.

THOMPSON, RICHARD. "Socialism and the NDP." *Our Generation* 6 (June, 1969): 65–73.

THORBURN, HUGH G. *Party Politics in Canada*, 2nd ed. Scarborough: Prentice-Hall of Canada, 1967.

Toch, Hans. *The Social Psychology of Social Movements*. Indianapolis: Bobbs-Merrill, 1965.

Trudeau, Pierre Elliott. Le Fédéralisme et la société canadienne-françiase. Montréal: HMH, 1967.

Underhill, Frank H. "Canadian Liberal Democracy in 1955." In G. Ferguson and F. H. Underhill. *Press and Party in Canada*. Toronto: Ryerson, 1955.

Vallee, Frank G.; Schwartz, Mildred; and Darknell, Frank. "Ethnic Assimilation and Differentiation in Canada." *Canadian Journal of Economics and Political Science* 23 (1957): 540-49.

Wade, Mason. *The French Canadians, 1760-1967*. Toronto: Macmillan, 1968.

Waite, P. B. *The Life and Times of Confederation, 1864-1867*. Toronto: Univ. of Toronto Press, 1962.

Wallace, David. *First Tuesday*. Garden City: Doubleday, 1964.

Ward, Norman. *The Public Purse: A Study in Canadian Democracy*. Toronto: Univ. of Toronto Press, 1962.

_____. *The Canadian House of Commons:* Representation, 2nd ed. Toronto: Univ. of Toronto Press, 1963.

_____. "Voting in Canadian Two-Member Constituencies." In John C. Courtney, ed. *Voting in Canada*. Scarborough: Prentice-Hall of Canada, 1967.

Warkentin, John, ed. *Canada, A Geographical Interpretation*. Toronto: Methuen, 1968.

Watkins, Melville. "The Multi-national Corporation and Canada." *Our Generation* 4 (Spring: 1969): 97-102.

Wheare, K. C. *Federal Government*, 3rd ed. London: Oxford Univ. Press, 1953.

Wilson, George W., et al. *Canada: An Appraisal of Its Needs and Resources*. Toronto: Univ. of Toronto Press, 1965.

Wilson, John. "Politics and Social Class in Canada: the Case of Waterloo South." *Canadian Journal of Political Science* 1 (September, 1968): 288-309.

_____, and Hoffman, David. "The Liberal Party in Contemporary Ontario Politics." *Canadian Journal of Political Science* 3 (June, 1970): 177-204.

_____, and Hoffman, David. "Ontario: A Three-Party System in Transition." In Martin Robin, ed. *Canadian Provincial Politics*. Scarborough: Prentice-Hall of Canada, 1972.

Winham, Gilbert R., and Cunningham, Robert B. "Party Leader Images in the 1968 Federal Election." *Canadian Journal of Political Science* 3 (March, 1970): 37-55.

Wood, Robert C. *Suburbia: Its People and Their Politics*. Boston: Houghton Mifflin, 1958.

Wrong, Dennis H. "The Pattern of Party Voting in Canada." *Public Opinion Quarterly* 21 (Summer, 1957): 252-64.

Young, Walter D. *The Anatomy of a Party: The National CCF, 1932-61*. Toronto: Univ. of Toronto Press, 1969.

Zakuta, Leo. *A Protest Movement Becalmed: A Study of Change in the CCF*. Toronto: Univ. of Toronto Press, 1964.

12. IRELAND:
Politics Without Social Bases

J. H. WHYTE

I. Historical Background

At the beginning of the twentieth-century Ireland was an integral part of the United Kingdom of Great Britain and Ireland. It was administered by the same government and subject to the same parliament as England, Scotland and Wales. Its MPs sat at Westminster on the same terms as those from other parts of the United Kingdom. The union, however, had long been an uneasy one. The majority of Irishmen differed in important ways from other citizens of the United Kingdom: they were Roman Catholics, not Protestants; their cultural tradition was Celtic, not Anglo-Saxon; their economy was agricultural, not industrial; they had a lower standard of living than the rest of the United Kingdom. These differences produced a sense of alienation, and before the end of the nineteenth-century an Irish Nationalist party had grown up, dedicated to securing home rule, i.e., autonomy for Ireland, within the United Kingdom. From 1885 onward Irish Nationalists controlled four-fifths of the Irish seats in the House of Commons at Westminster. The experience of this party provided further cause for discontent; though its objective was limited and its methods strictly constitutional, the Nationalists proved unable, in thirty years of agitation, to secure any form of home rule for Ireland. An abortive rising in 1916 marked the beginning of a new phase, in which Irishmen were prepared to use arms to seek complete independence. The change of mood was seen at the United Kingdom general election of 1918, in which the Irish Nationalist party lost almost all its seats and was replaced in most of Ireland by a new party, *Sinn Féin* (an Irish language phrase meaning "ourselves"), which refused to take its seats at Westminster and instead organized an alternative government in Ireland. Three years of guerrilla warfare followed, brought to an end by the Anglo-Irish treaty of December, 1921.

In this treaty the Irish negotiators made two important concessions: they abandoned their claim to an independent republic, and they acquiesced in the six north-eastern counties, which taken as a unit had a Protestant and pro-British majority, remaining part of the United Kingdom under the name of Northern Ireland—a status those counties have retained ever since. In return the British conceded to the remaining

I am grateful to Mr. Brian Farrell of University College, Dublin, for suggesting improvements in an earlier draft of this chapter.

twenty-six counties of Ireland the status of a dominion, under the title of the Irish Free State. Since that time the area has undergone further constitutional evolution. In 1937 a new constitution was adopted, which provided for an elected president and virtually repudiated dominion status; in 1949 the connection with the British Commonwealth was formally broken and a republic proclaimed. Neither of these developments, however, involved any change in the electoral or party systems. From the standpoint of electoral behavior the crucial year is 1921, the year in which Irish self-government was internationally recognized and the boundary of the State established. It is the year that will be taken as the starting point in the rest of this discussion.

The party system of the new state soon underwent violent change. At the time of the treaty *Sinn Féin* was the dominant political grouping, holding all the seats in the clandestine parliament which had been operating since 1919. It might have been expected to remain the dominant party in independent Ireland in much the same way as, more recently, Congress has remained the most important party in independent India. However, the treaty provisions immediately provoked a rupture between the more moderate elements in the party, who accepted it as the best settlement that could be obtained, and the intransigents, who regarded the abandonment of a republic as a betrayal. Disagreement soon led to violence, and a bitter civil war was fought in 1922-1923. In this war the supporters of the treaty were victorious. They formed a political party, *Cumann na nGaedheal* (Society of the Irish), which lasted until 1933; it then merged with certain other groups to form a new party, *Fine Gael* (Family of the Irish). *Fine Gael* is still one of the two largest parties in Irish politics. The defeated opponents of the treaty regrouped to continue the struggle for a republic by constitutional means. In 1926 a new party was formed, *Fianna Fáil* (Warriors of Destiny), which soon attracted the bulk of the republican or antitreaty vote: it has ever since been the second major Irish party. The split over the treaty of 1921 thus remains the basis of the Irish party system.

Disregarding ephemeral groups or those that never won parliamentary seats, minor parties can be grouped in three categories. First, there is the Irish Labour party. This is the oldest party in the country, having been founded in 1912, and has had continuous representation in parliament since 1922. In 1944 the National Labour party split off from it, and continued a separate existence until reunited with Irish Labour in 1950.

Second, there have been parties designed to defend agrarian interests. A Farmers' party was founded in 1922 and continued a separate existence until 1932, though it became more and more closely identified with *Cumann na nGaedheal* in its later years. *Clann na Talmhan* (Children of the Land) was founded in 1938 and had representatives in parliament continuously from 1943 to 1965. It was largely confined to Connacht, and its electoral support seems to have been inherited mainly by *Fine Gael*.

Third, there are extreme republicans—those who refused to follow *Fianna Fáil* in seeking to obtain their objectives through the existing political system after 1926. They cling to the original title of *Sinn Féin*, and occasionally contest elections; their greatest success was at the general election of 1957, when they won four seats. More attention has been gained by their militant allies, the Irish Republican Army, who have several times attempted to secure the reunification of Ireland by force, and who have been prepared on occasion to use violence within the republic as well as in Northern Ireland (Coogan, 1970; Bell, 1970). Republicans made their greatest electoral impact after 1946, when some founded *Clann na Poblachta* (Children of the Republic), a party with a radical social program. Begun at a time when there was widespread disillusionment with all the established parties, *Clann na Poblachta* quickly gained support from many who had never been republicans, and there was a moment when it seemed as if the Irish party system might be transformed. But at the general election of 1948 it gained only ten seats. Thereafter its support dwindled; in 1965 the party dissolved.

Another feature of the Irish parliamentary scene has been the strong showing of independent deputies (Chubb, 1957). Their number was as high as seventeen in 1923, and has averaged nine in the seventeen general elections since 1922. This is largely due to the Irish electoral system, which makes it possible for a candidate with a personal following in a particular area to win enough votes to gain a seat in a multimember constituency. Only recently has the number of independents declined. In the general election of 1965 they gained two seats, and in the general election of 1969 one.

The electoral history of Ireland since the Anglo-Irish treaty can be divided into four periods:

1921-1932

A multiparty system with no dominant party. During these years *Cumann na nGaedheal* was the largest single party and formed the government. But at no time did it have an absolute majority of seats. Until 1927 its parliamentary majority was secure because the largest opposition group, the republicans, refused to take their seats. In 1927 *Fianna Fáil* entered parliament, and thereafter the *Cuman na nGaedheal* government led a precarious existence, relying on the uncertain support of Labour and independents.

1932-1948

A multiparty system with a dominant party, *Fianna Fáil*, which overtook *Cumann na nGaedheal* as the largest single party in 1932, and formed the administration for the next sixteen years. For most of this period (1933-1937, 1938-1943, 1944-1948) it had an absolute majority. Its electoral strength, which in the twenties had been concentrated in the western seaboard counties, extended until it achieved a plurality in all areas of the country. For the other parties these were years of confusion and discouragement. *Fine Gael* appeared to be in full decline by the mid-forties. Labour was damaged by a split in 1944. Other parties were ephemeral or sectional. Fragmentation reached its peak at the general election of 1948, in which *Fianna Fáil* faced no fewer than five opposition parties (*Fine Gael*, Labour, National Labour, *Clann na Talmhan*, and *Clann na Poblachta*) as well as the usual quota of independents. However, that election marked the beginning of a new phase.

1948-1957

Competition between two evenly matched groupings. At the general election of 1948 *Fianna Fáil* lost its overall majority. The prospect of power after sixteen years in opposition had an emollient effect on the differences between the opposition groups: they combined to turn out the *Fianna Fáil* government, and formed an administration of their own termed the "interparty government", under the leadership of a *Fine Gael* deputy, John A. Costello. For the next nine years the Irish electorate had a choice between two competing teams: *Fianna Fáil* and an interparty alliance comprising all other parties. Governmental instability was relatively great: there were changes of government every three years. Instability was caused mainly by the economic difficulties Ireland was enduring at this period. Successive governments had to take drastic economic measures, lost popularity as a result, and found their majorities eroded at the ensuing general election. Mr. Costello's first government held office in 1948-1951; *Fianna Fáil* returned to office in 1951-1954; Mr. Costello's team had a second turn in 1954-1957; *Fianna Fáil* returned to power again in 1957. This period came to an end when the interparty coalition broke up. The party that appeared to derive most advantage was *Fine Gael*. It provided the prime minister and the largest number of other ministers, and its electoral fortunes revived after 1948. In 1957 the Labour party, dissatisfied with its achievements in coalition with *Fine Gael*, resumed its freedom of action.

1957-

A multiparty system with a dominant party, *Fianna Fáil*. In some ways this era has been a repetition of the second period, 1932-1948. The opposition parties have again lost their cohesion, and *Fianna Fáil* has been able to govern without interruption, even though it has not always had an absolute majority. The position is not entirely the same, however, for there has been a great simplification of the situation on the opposition side. Independents have been almost wiped out, and a number of minor parties have disappeared, leaving only *Fine Gael* and Labour, both with reasonably strong nation wide organizations, to face *Fianna Fáil*. Moreover, Labour has shifted to a new geographical base. From the foundation of the state up to the general election of 1961, the main strength of the Labour party lay not, as one might have expected, in the Dublin area, but in a belt of rural constituencies across the south and east. Its deputies probably owed their success as much to their reputation for constituency work as to their party's political program. A change first became evident at the general election of 1965, in which Labour, for the first time won a substantial footing (six seats out of its total of twenty-two) in the Dublin area, while retaining its strength in the southeastern rural belt. At the general election of 1969 this change continued; Labour made more gains in the Dublin area (where it now held ten seats out of its total of eighteen), while losing ground heavily in its traditional rural strongholds. It now appears for the first time to be a predominantly urban party. (For fuller accounts of the Irish party system see Moss, 1933; McCracken, 1958; O'Leary, 1961; Chubb, 1969; Chubb, 1970; O'Connor Lysaght, 1970; Busteed and Mason, 1970; Farrell, 1970; Ayearst, 1971; and Manning, 1972.)

In social-structure Ireland stands out in several ways among the countries treated in this book. It has the lowest per capita gross national product ($ 1,532 in 1971), the lowest degree of urbanization, and the highest emigration rate. The last ten or fifteen years, however, have seen considerable social change.

Urbanization and industrialization have both increased. Whereas in 1926 (the date of the first census after the establishment of the state) 32 percent of the population lived in towns with a population of more than 1,500, in 1966 (the date of the most recent census for which figures are available) the proportion was 49 percent. In 1926 51 percent of the labor force was engaged in agriculture; in 1966 the figure had dropped to 31 percent. The industrial sector accounted for 13 percent of the labor force in 1926 and 26 percent in 1966.

Irish demography has also been changing. Taking the period since independence as a whole, the picture has been one of high emigration and falling population. At the census of 1966 the population of 2,884,000 was actually 88,000 lower than it had been in 1926. Net emigration for the forty years 1926-1966 was calculated at 963,000, a prodigious figure for so small a country. But these global figures mask striking changes in recent years. With a stable and high birth rate and a falling death rate, the natural increase of the Irish people has been rising since the middle 'forties. During the 'fifties this was offset by the fact that emigration was then at its highest. But in the 'sixties, with increasing prosperity at home, emigration dropped markedly, and the resident population has begun again to rise. This may have important effects on Irish political culture. For decades observers have been struck by the conservatism, almost the fatalism, of Irish society. One explanation might be that emigration has siphoned off the most vigorous people from the country. If there is any truth in this, we may expect Irish politics to become more lively now that more young people are staying home.

One other feature of Irish society is worth mentioning: Ireland is surprisingly advanced educationally for a country of relative poverty. Illiteracy was almost stamped out in British times. The census of 1851 showed a literacy rate of 53 percent; by 1911 it had risen to 88 percent, and since then the census commissioners have found it unnecessary to ask questions on this point. Since Independence, and particularly since the end of the 'fifties, educational progress has been shown most clearly by the rising number of students going on to secondary and university education. The number of secondary-school children, which in 1921-1922 was 21,000, reached 151,000 in 1970-1971. The number of university students, which in 1922-1923 was 3,400, reached 16,900 in 1968-1969.

II. The Electoral System

The electoral system for the lower and more powerful house of parliament, the Dáil, has throughout the period since 1921 been proportional representation under the single-transferable-vote system. (For a description of how the system operates see

Chubb, 1970, Appendix E.) The total number of members has varied only slightly: 128 in 1921–1923, 153 in 1923–1937, 138 in 1937–1948, 147 in 1948–1961, 144 since 1961. Members are elected in multimember constituencies containing three or more seats. Before 1937 there were two university constituencies: one for the National University of Ireland and one for Dublin University. Since then university representation has been transferred to the Senate, and all Dáil constituencies have been territorial.

As a rule all constituencies are contested. Eight (including one university constituency) were left uncontested in the general election of 1922, but since then the only exceptions have been Dublin University in the general elections of September 1927 and 1933, Donegal West and Kerry South in the general election of 1938, and Donegal West again in the general election of 1943. Voting is not compulsory. Participation has varied from a low of 61 percent in 1923 to a high of 81 percent in 1933. The average turnout in the sixteen general elections since 1923 has been 73 percent. (For figures see Chubb, 1970, p. 332; Farrell, 1970, p. 483.)

The Irish Free State was set up with the same franchise as existed in Great Britain at that point: universal suffrage for men over twenty-one and women over thirty, with second votes for university graduates and the owners of certain business premises. However, this franchise remained in force only for the first general election of the new state in 1922. Ireland then moved quickly to complete universal suffrage. In 1923 women between twenty-one and thirty were enfranchised and plural voting was abolished. While qualified electors were still entitled to vote in respect of business premises or as graduates in university constituencies, they had to choose whether to cast a vote in this manner or to cast it from their place of residence. University constituencies disappeared in 1937, and the business vote was abolished (for parliamentary though not for local elections) in 1963. Registration has been automatic throughout the history of the state; it is carried out by local government officials.

Legislation on corrupt practices and election expenditure was substantially the same in Ireland as Britain until the Electoral Act of 1963. That measure, by agreement between the parties, removed the legal limits on election expenditure. In practice this has made little difference: the political parties are all too poor to take much advantage of their formal right to spend as much as they please on promoting their candidates.

Procedures concerning nomination have not been the subject of much legislation. As in Britain, frivolous candidates have been deterred by requiring a cash deposit from all candidates. The sum required was fixed at £100 in 1923; it is forfeited if the candidate has secured less than one-third of a quota at the time of his election. Since then the only important development has been a clause in the Electoral Act of 1963 giving candidates the right to have their party affiliation printed on the ballot paper alongside their name. This has entailed the establishment of a Register of Political Parties; only candidates belonging to a party whose name appears on this register are entitled to have their affiliation printed on the ballot. The Registrar of Political Parties (who is the Clerk of the Dáil) has interpreted his duties strictly, and will not include a group on the register unless he is satisfied that it is a genuine political party. He has already refused registration to two small groups on the ground that they failed to meet this condition.

The upper house of parliament, or Senate, is a weak body, being entitled to delay money bills for twenty-one days and non money bills for ninety days. From 1922 to 1936 it was constituted under a variety of franchises (O'Sullivan, 1940); after a brief period of single-chamber rule it was reconstituted in 1938, and its composition has remained stable since then. Its sixty members are chosen in three ways: (1) eleven members are nominated by the prime minister of the day at the beginning of each parliament; (2) six members are elected by university graduates—three by those of the National University of Ireland, three by those of Dublin University; (3) the remaining forty-three members are elected by a constituency consisting of local government councilors, members of the Dáil, and outgoing senators, a total of about 900 people. In theory these electors are supposed to have regard to the candidates' qualifications in a variety of vocations—for instance, five are elected to represent cultural and educational interests, eleven to represent agricultural interests, and so on. In practice these qualifications are almost ignored, and candidates are elected mainly on a party basis (Chubb, 1954, Garvin, 1969).

There are four circumstances in which an Irish elector may be entitled to cast a vote. First, there is the election of members of the Dáil. The maximum term of a parliament is five years; as in Britain, a prime minister may recommend the head of state to dissolve parliament earlier if he thinks it to his party's advantage. Only one parliament (that of 1938–1943) has run its full term; on average, parliaments between 1922 and 1969 lasted two years and ten months. Second, there is the election of the President of Ireland. This office was established in 1938, and its holder is directly elected by the people for a seven-year term. So far there have been contested elections in 1945, 1959, and 1966, with *Fianna Fáil* and *Fine Gael* putting up candidates in each; in 1945 an independent also stood. Third, there are elections for local authorities. These take place in principle every five years, though the set due in 1965 was postponed for two years, with the consent of all parties, so as not to clash with the general election of 1965 or the presidential election of 1966. Fourth, electors may vote in a referendum. The 1937 constitution lays down that all constitutional amendments must be, and certain other legislation may be, put to the people in a referendum. So far referenda have been held in 1959 and 1968 on constitutional amendments proposed by *Fianna Fáil* to alter the electoral system. In 1959 the proposal was made to abolish the single-transferable-vote system and replace it by a plurality vote in single-member seats, as in Britain. In 1968 the same proposal was put forward again; it was coupled with another, whereby greater variations in the ratio of seats to votes in different parts of the country would be permitted. On both occasions the amendments were rejected.

The ballot lists candidates in alphabetical order. As in Britain, there is some advantage to a candidate's appearing early in the alphabetical list. There is no academic writing on this point, but an article demonstrating the fact was published in the *Sunday Independent* (Dublin) on July 6, 1969. Parties are free to nominate as many candidates as they wish, and there are advantages in nominating as many candidates as there are seats to be filled in a constituency: each candidate is likely to have a personal following that will help to swell the party's poll. The interests of the candidates, however, pull in the opposite direction: the more who stand in a multimember constituency, the less chance there is for each individually. Generally the parties compromise by nominating more candidates than they can reasonably hope to elect, but not so many that they cover all the seats. In 1969 for 144 seats in the Dáil *Fianna Fáil* nominated 122 candidates; *Fine Gael*, 125; Labour, 99, and others, 27. (Figures for earlier elections, differing slightly, are in Chubb, 1970, p. 333, and Farrell, 1970, p. 483. Farrell appears the more accurate.)

The single-transferable-vote system gives the elector considerable scope. He can express preferences not just between parties but between the individual candidates of a given party: an Irish election combines the functions that in the United States are divided between a primary and a general election. Cross-voting between parties is not common except with the voters' lower preferences: election returns indicate that more than 80 percent of voters who give their first preference to a *Fianna Fáil* or *Fine Gael* candidate give their second preference to a candidate of the same party (Chubb, 1970, p. 157). But what can be important is the order in which the electors place the candidates of their favored party. This is a power they exercise with discrimination, and a deputy who heads the list for his party at one election is by no means certain to lead it at the next (Chubb, 1970, p. 158); indeed, he may be defeated by another candidate of the same party. In the general election of 1965 (the last at which precise comparisons can be made, since boundary changes make accurate comparisons of the pre- and post-1969 election positions impracticable) twenty-three sitting deputies were defeated at the polls. Of these, thirteen were unseated by candidates of other parties and ten by candidates of their own party. In short, an Irish deputy is in almost as much danger from his ostensible colleagues as he is from his opponents.

The division and distribution of constituencies can be an important consideration in Irish elections. The successive acts redistributing seats have each been drawn up by the government of the day, and passage through parliament has been secured by its party majority: there is no provision for an impartial boundary commission such as exists in the United Kingdom. The 1937 constitution sets some limits on a government's discretion: the minimum number of seats in a constituency must be three, and the ratio between the number of members in a constituency and the population of each constituency "shall, so far as it is practicable, be the same throughout the country." This provision acts as a real constraint: in 1961 the High Court invalidated a redistribution act passed two years earlier on the ground that the ratio between seats and votes showed unnecessary discrepancies between constituencies. Within these bounds it is remarkable what can be done by a ruling party anxious to maximize its strength. There is no obligation on the framers of redistribution acts to respect local government areas, and although in earlier redistributions the framers attempted to respect county boundaries, in more recent redistributions these boundaries have been cut across with great freedom.

The following axioms can be laid down for a ruling party anxious to redistribute seats to favor itself as much as possible:

First, in areas where the party is strong three-seat constituencies give the best results. Here the party should win two seats out of three. The criterion whereby the party judges itself to be strong may vary with the political situation. With all opposition supporters voting solidly against the ruling party and giving all their lower preferences to other opposition groups, the ruling party can still expect to pick up two seats out of three if it wins more than 50 percent of the first-preference votes. In practice the opposition vote is unlikely to be as solid as this, and the ruling party's candidates should pick up some lower preferences from some opposition voters. In these circumstances the ruling party can expect to win two seats out of three even if its first-preference vote falls to about 46 percent.

Second, in areas where the party is weaker four-seat constituencies will be more advantageous. If the opposition vote is solid against the ruling party, the latter can still expect to win two seats out of four even if its first-preference vote is barely over 40 percent. If the opposition vote is not solid, the ruling party should pick up two seats out of four with a first-preference vote as low as about 37 percent.

Third, five-seat constituencies have no merits and should be eliminated. The party would have to be extraordinarily strong in the area—67 percent if the opposition is solid, above 60 percent even if the opposition is not solid—to win four seats out of five. In practice the best result it could hope for is three seats out of five; this is a less favorable ratio than would be obtained from three-seat constituencies. If the party is rather weak in the area, it is likely to obtain only two seats out of five, a less favorable ratio than it would obtain from four-seat constituencies.

Fourth, the objections to five-seat constituencies apply a fortiori to constituencies with more than five seats.

It is interesting to note how *Fianna Fáil* governments, which have been responsible for the last four redistributions of seats, have conformed more and more rigorously to these axioms. Constituencies with more than five seats have disappeared since 1948. Five-member constituencies have now almost disappeared as well: only two

TABLE 1: **Constituency Size**

Period	Number of constituencies	9	8	7	6	5	4	3
		9	*8*	*7*	*6*	*5*	*4*	*3*
1921–1923	28	—	2	1	2	4	16	3
1923–1937	30	1	3	5	—	9	4	8
1937–1948	34	—	—	3	—	8	8	15
1948–1961	40	—	—	—	—	9	9	22
1961–1969	38	—	—	—	—	9	12	17
1969–	42	—	—	—	—	2	14	26

(header spanning: "Number of members per constituency")

were left after the last redistribution. Three- and four-member constituencies are distributed much as the axioms would lead one to expect: in those regions where *Fianna Fáil* is strongest three-member constituencies are the rule, and *Fianna Fáil* generally picks up two seats out of three; in those regions where *Fianna Fáil* is weaker four-member constituencies are the rule, and *Fianna Fáil* generally wins two seats out of four. The last redistribution, which took effect at the general election of 1969, was a particularly skillful piece of work. *Fianna Fáil* dropped by 2 percent in first-preference votes, as compared with the general election of 1965, yet managed to increase its strength in seats from seventy-two to seventy-five.

The legal arrangements for voting follow closely the British pattern. Elections are administered by civil servants in the Department of Local Government, working in conjunction with local government officials. Voting is on a single weekday, for any twelve hours between 8:30 A.M. and 10:30 P.M., as decided by the Minister for Local Government. The date is not a legal holiday. Polling stations are numerous and widely dispersed, and there are few complaints that electors find difficulty in recording their votes. Postal voting is not permitted, except for members of the police and defense forces. In the general election of 1969 11,721 postal votes were cast, less than 1 percent of the total.

The concept of a "normal election" is difficult to apply in Ireland. The last two general elections have produced an artistically pleasing symmetry in party strengths. The three main parties divided the support of the electorate almost in the proportions 3:2:1. *Fianna Fáil* gained 48 percent of the first-preference votes in 1965 and 46 percent in 1969; *Fine Gael* gained 34 percent in both 1965 and 1969; Labour gained 15 percent in 1965 and 17 percent in 1969. However, an extension backward in time of the investigation shows that this 3:2:1 division between the main parties has two components, one of long standing and the other of recent development. The long-established factor is that *Fianna Fáil* is comparable in strength to all other groups combined. This has been true for forty years: the percentage of first-preference votes won by *Fianna Fáil* at general elections since 1932 has averaged 46. The more recent factor is that the non-*Fianna Fáil* forces divide two-to-one between *Fine Gael* and Labour. Before the last two general elections the non-*Fianna Fáil* forces had usually been divided between a larger number of parties and independents. Since its formation in 1933 *Fine Gael* has always been the next strongest party after *Fianna Fáil*, although its support has fluctuated considerably, from 35 percent of the first-preference votes in 1937 to 20 percent in 1948. The Labour party has usually ranked third in strength, but in 1944 more first-preference votes were won by *Clann na Talmhan*, and in 1948 by *Clann na Poblachta*.

III. Data for Analysis

Sample surveys of interest to the student of Irish politics are a recent development and still few in number. The earliest was a poll of attitudes to the Common Market, reported in the *Irish Press* of July 12 and 18, 1961. Next came two surveys of attitudes to the Irish language, one confined to the Tralee area of County Kerry, the other nationwide, reported in the *Irish Times* of February 19 and 21, 1964. In 1966 and 1967 students of the School of Public Administration interviewed a small sample of the Dublin electorate, using questionnaires based in part on that developed by Almond and Verba for their *Civic Culture* study (Chubb, 1970, pp. 144, 311; Hart, 1970). More recent surveys of attitudes to particular public issues have been published in the *Irish Press*, April 16–25, 1968; in *This Week*, May 7, 1971; and in *This Week*, June 25-July 9, 1971.

None of the polls so far mentioned, however, contains any detailed breakdown by party affiliation. The bases of party support have so far been explored in only two surveys: one was conducted by Gallup Poll (Dublin) in April, 1969, and extensively reported in the short-lived magazine *Nusight* for October and December, 1969 and April, 1970; the other was conducted by Irish Marketing Surveys in May, 1970, and reported in *This Week* for June 19, 1970, and subsequent issues. The survey unit of the Economic and Social Research Institute in Dublin carried out a study for Stein Larsen of the University of Bergen in 1971; no results are yet available.

Ecological analysis in Ireland suffers from the same drawbacks as in Britain. Official voting figures are not available for any unit smaller than the parliamentary constituency; this is too large and heterogeneous a unit to be entirely satisfactory for analysis. Also, parliamentary constituencies tend not to coincide with the administrative areas for which census material is reported. Nonetheless, interesting results have been obtained from plotting data on maps by Rumpf (1959) and, for the 1920s, by Pyne (1968). They have been able to show how the bases of support for the different parties have evolved.

Moreover, a way around the difficulties of ecological analysis has recently been demonstrated in an important article by Sacks (1970). The author, in a study of the constituency of Donegal Northeast, has used unofficial but reliable voting figures for individual polling districts, obtained from the political parties. At the outset of his article he explains how these figures came to be compiled:

> During the first phase of a count, when the numbers of ballots in each box are checked against the Presiding Officers' report of number of votes cast...party officials, through arrangement with local returning officers, are able to make unofficial "snap" tallys of the number of first preference votes cast for each candidate in each booth. Instead of counting the ballots face downwards, the counting clerks do just the reverse, fleetingly exposing to the local politicians the way each ballot is marked. Usually there is time only to record the first preference marked on each ballot.

Armed with these figures the author has made a detailed analysis of the areas where each candidate gained his greatest support. The main feature to emerge from his account is the extent to which Donegal Northeast, though nominally a three-member constituency, was in fact contested as a federation of single-member seats. On the *Fianna Fáil* side the two sitting deputies, Blaney and Cunningham, divided the constituency between them, Blaney winning the majority of the *Fianna Fáil* vote in every single polling district in the western half of the constituency, and Cunningham

gaining the majority of the party's vote in every single polling district in the eastern
half. These conclusions will come as no surprise to observers of Irish politics: indeed,
they will be able to name many other constituencies where a similar informal division
by party colleagues appears to have been arranged. But what is new about Sacks's
article is that he has been able to demonstrate what hitherto had only been surmised.

Figures for turnout at parliamentary elections are published by constituency in
the annual reports of the Department of Local Government. They show considerable
variations in the absenteeism rate between different parts of the country. The highest
turnouts have usually been found at opposite ends of the state—in Cork and
Tipperary, on the one hand, and Monaghan and Cavan, on the other. The lowest
turnouts are usually found in the city of Dublin and on the western seaboard. Chubb
(1970, p. 156) has suggested reasons for these variations, e.g., that the low turnout in
the west is due to seasonal migration and poor communications, while that in Dublin
is due to greater mobility and volatility in the electorate. No investigation into their
causes has yet been made.

The measurement of party preference might seem to pose difficulties under the
Irish electoral system. The voter marks individual candidates in order of preference,
and there is no obligation on him to rank all the candidates of a given party consecu-
tively. However, election returns indicate that most electors give all their highest
preferences to the candidates of their favored party (Chubb, 1970, p. 157); they can
thus be considered loyal to a party as such. Opinion polls have found no difficulty in
framing a question about party preference, and securing responses to it. The Gallup
Poll in 1969 asked, "If there was a General Election tomorrow, which party would you
vote for?" Irish Marketing Surveys in 1970 asked, "If there was a General Election
here in Ireland tomorrow, which party would you *mainly* give your votes to?"

IV. Social Structure and Voting

This section and the next are based mainly on secondary analysis of the Gallup
survey of April, 1969 (weighted N=1,580; interviewed N=2,135, owing to fuller
sampling of the Dublin area). This was chosen in preference to the Irish Marketing
Surveys poll of May, 1970 (N=1,015), partly because the sample size was larger and
partly because a wider range of questions was put to the respondents. However, the
IMS figures have also been consulted, as a check on the Gallup results. Thanks are
due to the Gallup Poll, Dublin, and to Irish Marketing Surveys for making their data
available.

A. OCCUPATIONAL CLASS

The Gallup Poll used six occupational categories to characterize class:

AB   Upper and middle-class: higher and intermediate managers, administrators
     and proprietors, etc.
C1   Lower-middle-class: clerical staff and junior managers, administrators
     and proprietors, etc.
C2   Skilled manual workers
DE   Unskilled manual workers, labourers, pensioners, etc.
F1   Farmers with more than 30 acres
F2   Farmers with less than 30 acres

An almost identical classification was used by Irish Marketing Surveys, with the exception that farm laborers were coded F2, while they appear to have been coded as manual workers by Gallup.

This sixfold classification, while complicated, has advantages. It distinguishes between the more and less affluent sectors of society, and it also distinguishes between farming and urban groups. This corresponds to realities in Irish life: while differences in economic level are important, the differences of outlook between townsmen and countrymen might also be expected to be influential. The sixfold classification involves no presuppositions about which of these elements matters more. The investigator is left free to make his own assessment of their relative importance.

TABLE 2:   **Class and Party Preference (I), in Percentages**

Total	Class	F.F.	F. G.	Lab.	Other*
7	AB	37	37	10	17
23	C1	48	26	15	11
14	C2	40	21	27	12
33	DE	43	14	28	15
15	F1	38	46	2	14
7	F2	53	26	5	16
100%	all classes	43	25	18	14

*In this and all subsequent tables "other" includes "don't know".

In practice, both elements have some influence (Table 2). In farming groups Labour plays almost no part; *Fianna Fáil* is stronger among the small farmers and *Fine Gael* among the large ones. Among the nonfarm groups *Fine Gael* is relatively strong in the nonmanual groups (AB and to a lesser extent C1), while Labour is relatively strong in the manual groups (C2 and DE). The importance of these biases is offset, however, by the fact that the largest party, *Fianna Fáil*, draws support fairly evenly from all social categories. These features can be brought out more clearly by collapsing the occupational categories into three larger groups: middle-class (AB and C1), working-class (C2 and DE), and farmers (F1 and F2) (Table 3).

In the rest of this section and in the next, data will be analyzed with controls for class, using this threefold classification. This is not because social stratification is

TABLE 3: **Class, and Party Preference (II), in Percentages**

Total	Class	F. F.	F. G.	Lab.	Other
31	Middle (AB, C1)	45	28	14	13
48	Working (C2, DE)	42	16	28	14
21	Farmers (F1, F2)	42	40	3	15

necessarily an important determinant of Irish voting behavior: in fact it appears to matter less than in most western democracies. There are two reasons for selecting it as the controlling factor. First, any other factor would probably be even weaker. Region is the most plausible alternative, but on inspection many regional differences turn out to be class-based: the Dublin region, for instance, has disproportionate numbers of both the working-class and the middle-class, while Munster and Connacht/Ulster have disproportionate numbers of farmers. Second, class is the controlling factor selected for the majority of chapters in this book, so its use here facilitates cross-reference.

B. MEMBERSHIP IN TRADE UNIONS AND IN FARM ORGANIZATIONS

The Gallup Poll provides information on a number of class-related variables. Among these are membership in trade unions and in farm organizations (Table 4).

TABLE 4: **Class, Party, and Membership in Trade Unions and Farm Organizations, in Percentages**

Total		F. F.	F. G.	Lab.	Other
	Middle class				
7	Trade-union member	39	27	23	11
23	nonmember	46	29	12	12
	Working class				
21	Trade-union member	38	12	37	13
26	nonmember	45	19	21	16
	Farmers				
8	Farm organization member	37	47	1	14
13	nonmember	46	35	3	16
100%[a]					

[a] 1.4 percent excluded as divided among three deviant membership categories; farmers in middle-class or in working-class; trade union in farming class.

Trade-union membership makes little differences as between *Fianna Fáil* and *Fine Gael*, but in both the middle- and the working-class it increases the likelihood of an elector supporting the Labour party. The degree of advantage to Labour, however, must not be exaggerated. The preponderance of *Fianna Fáil* in the electorate as a whole is so great that even among trade unionists it has a plurality. Of trade unionists in the sample, 38 percent favoured *Fianna Fáil*, 34 percent Labour, and 16 percent *Fine Gael*.

Members of farm organizations were rather more likely to support *Fine Gael* than *Fianna Fáil*. This is not just because members of such organizations are most likely to be found among large farmers, who tend to support *Fine Gael:* the effect was found among small farmers as well, although sample numbers are small. A possible explanation is that the two principal farm organizations, the National Farmers Association and the Irish Creamery Milk Suppliers Association, have both had fierce disputes with *Fianna Fáil* Ministers for Agriculture in recent years, and their members have therefore tended to become alienated from *Fianna Fáil*.

C. HOME OWNERSHIP

The Gallup Poll collected information on the tenure by which respondents occupied their homes. The two largest categories are those who owned or were buying their homes (66 percent) and those who rented from a local authority (22 percent). There were four smaller categories: those renting from private landlords; lodgers; those living in hostels; and those provided with accommodation by their employers. These together came to only 11 percent of the sample and are collapsed into one category here (Table 5). The table shows that in both the

TABLE 5:   **Class, Party, and Tenancy, in Percentages**

Total		F. F.	F. G.	Lab.	Other
	Middle class				
22	Owns or is buying house	45	30	12	13
3	Rents from council (N=50)	45	17	29	9
5	Other (N=73)	42	30	14	14
	Working class				
24	Owns or is buying house	46	17	25	11
18	Rents from council	35	16	33	16
6	Other (N=89)	45	13	25	17
	Farmers				
20	Owns or is buying house	43	40	3	15
(0.2)	Rents from council	*	*	*	*
1	Other	*	*	*	*
100%					

In this and subsequent tables an asterisk (*) indicates that numbers in the row are too small for classification by party to be profitable.

middle- and working-classes council tenants were disproportionately likely to vote
Labour. As in the case of trade-union membership, however, the advantage to
Labour must not be exaggerated: among council tenants in the sample, 36 percent
supported *Fianna Fáil*, 33 percent Labour, and 16 percent *Fine Gael*. There is no
marked difference between *Fianna Fáil* and *Fine Gael* supporters in any class.
Among farmers, the fact that nearly all owned or were buying their own houses
made it impossible to make comparisons.

D. SUBJECTIVE SOCIAL CLASS

The Gallup Poll asked respondents to place themselves in one of five class
categories: upper, upper-middle, middle, lower-middle, or working. The results, when
those describing themselves as upper class (N=31) are merged with those describing
themselves as upper-middle (N=105), are displayed in Table 6. Here again the figures
show little difference between *Fianna Fáil* and *Fine Gael* supporters, but they do show

TABLE 6: Class, Party, and Subjective Social Class, in Percentages

Total		F. F.	F. G.	Lab.	Other
	Middle class				
5	Upper / Upper-middle } (N=85)	47	28	9	15
15	Middle	44	31	12	13
4	Lower-middle (N=68)	54	25	13	8
4	Working (N=61)	40	20	32	8
1	Don't know	*	*	*	*
	Working class				
1	Upper, upper-middle	*	*	*	*
8	Middle	46	20	24	10
6	Lower-middle (N=100)	47	16	24	13
29	Working	40	14	31	14
1	Don't know	*	*	*	*
	Farming				
2	Upper, upper-middle	*	*	*	*
11	Middle	41	44	1	14
4	Lower-middle (N=56)	43	32	5	20
3	Working (N=49)	59	16	7	18
1	Don't know	*	*	*	*
100%					

a difference between supporters of these two parties, on the one hand, and Labour
supporters on the other. In all classes those who consider themselves working-class
are more likely to vote Labour. The effect, however, appears to be less marked than
that of trade-union membership or council tenancy. Of all those describing them-

selves as working-class, 41 percent supported *Fianna Fáil*, 29 percent Labour, and 15 percent *Fine Gael*.

An interesting feature of the table is how few respondents in any category think of themselves as working-class: only 36 percent of the sample, as against 56 percent who classified themselves as some kind of middle-class. The dominance of middle-class identification in Ireland arises because of the large numbers of farmers in the country, and the fact that only one-seventh of farmers identify with the working-class.

E. EDUCATION

The Gallup Poll collected information on the age at which respondents completed full-time education, grouping respondents in four categories: those who finished their education at age twelve years or less; at age thirteen or fourteen; at age fifteen or sixteen; and at age seventeen or later. Education to age fourteen has been compulsory in Ireland since the School Attendance Act of 1926, so it is not surprising that the first of these categories was the smallest, 4 percent of the sample. It is here assimilated with the next group, those whose education ended at thirteen or fourteen, to form a category composed of those with no more than the legal minimum of education (Table 7).

TABLE 7: **Class, Party, and Age When Education Completed, in Percentages**

Total		F. F.	F. G.	Lab.	Other
	Middle class				
4	Age 14 or less (N=58)	48	19	24	9
9	Age 15–16	49	27	17	7
18	Age 17 or more	43	31	10	16
	Working class				
27	Age 14 or less	41	15	30	14
15	Age 15–16	41	18	27	13
5	Age 17 or more (N=81)	48	19	17	16
	Farmers				
10	Age 14 or less	45	35	2	17
7	Age 15–16	45	41	3	10
5	Age 17 or more (N=71)	33	46	3	18
100%					

Once again the figures show no marked difference between *Fianna Fáil* and *Fine Gael* supporters, although among the best educated middle class and farmers there is greater support for *Fine Gael*. Labour supporters both in the middle- and working-classes are slightly more likely to have minimum education. The influence is less marked than that of trade-union membership, council tenancy, or subjective social class. Of those in the sample with the minimum level of education, 43 percent supported *Fianna Fáil*, 23 percent supported Labour, and 20 percent *Fine Gael*.

It is possible that if respondents had been asked the kind of school they had attended, not the age at which they finished their education, more significant results might have been obtained. There are three possible school careers for an Irish child: he may have only a primary education; he may go from primary school to vocational school; or he may go from primary school to secondary school. Primary schools are all under denominational control, though largely staffed by lay teachers; vocational schools are run by local authorities, are formally nondenominational, and stress practical subjects; secondary schools are practically all denominational, are largely run by religious orders, and provide an academic education.[1] It would be especially interesting to know whether those trained by different religious orders tend to have different voting patterns. Some orders—e.g., the Irish Christian Brothers and the various orders of friars—are reputed to impart a more "nationalist" bias to their education than some others, and this might be expected to have some effect on the voting preferences of their past pupils. (*Fianna Fáil*, as the most self-consciously nationalist of the parties, would be the most likely gainers.) It would be important here, however, to control for parental influence. The chances are that a parent who sends his child to a school with a "nationalist" reputation already possesses nationalist sympathies himself.

F. CAR OWNERSHIP

The Gallup Poll found that 50 percent of its respondents belonged to a car-owning household (Table 7). In the middle-class *Fianna Fáil* supporters were most likely to

TABLE 8: Class, Party, and Car Ownership, in Percentages

Total		F. F.	F. G.	Lab.	Other
	Middle class				
20	Has car	49	27	11	14
10	No car	38	31	20	10
	Working class				
16	Has car	40	20	27	13
31	No car	43	14	29	15
	Farmers				
13	Has car	37	44	2	16
8	No car	52	32	3	12
100%					

have a car, and Labour supporters least likely; in the working class *Fine Gael* supporters were most likely to have a car, and *Fianna Fáil* and Labour supporters about equally unlikely to have one. Among farmers, *Fianna Fáil* supporters were less likely to have a car: this was partly because *Fianna Fáil* is stronger among small farmers, who are less likely to be car-owners, but the relationship was also found among large and small farmers taken separately. None of the differences is marked: car ownership appears the weakest of the class-linked variables in discriminating between parties.

G. COMPOSITE SOCIOECONOMIC INDEX

An index of socioeconomic status can be found by dichotomizing the following characteristics:

minimum education (age 14 or less) vs. more than minimum education
membership in a trade union vs. nonmembership
tenancy of a council house vs. other forms of house tenancy
occupational working-class vs. occupational middle-class or farming
subjective working-class identification vs. subjective identification with another class.

In each case the working-class characteristic is on the left-hand side; those respondents with all five characteristics on the left-hand side score 5 and are ideal-type workers; other respondents score 4 to 0, according to the number of working-class characteristics they possess (Table 9). The table shows that the nearer an elector approaches to

TABLE 9: **Party and Composite Socioeconomic Index, in Percentages**

Total	Composite Socioeconomic Index		F. F.	F. G.	Lab.	Other
24	Highest:	0	45	33	8	14
25		1	43	36	9	13
18		2	48	17	20	14
16		3	42	17	25	16
11		4	35	16	36	12
6	Lowest:	5 (N=89)	35	10	42	13
100%						

being an ideal-type worker, the more likely he is to vote Labour. The advantage to Labour must not be overstated, however: even in the highest category it receives the support of less than half the electors. *Fine Gael* emerges as almost the mirror-image of Labour, strongest in those categories with fewest working-class characteristics, and weaker as working-class characteristics increase. *Fianna Fáil*, although less strong among those with four or five working-class characteristics, has substantial support among all sections: it is much the most broad-based of the parties. The median

Fine Gael supporter has one working-class characteristic, the median *Fianna Fáil* supporter two, and the median Labour supporter four.

H. REGION

Class-related factors are not the only possible influences on voting behavior. Another potential influence is region. Surveys recognize regions derived from the four historic provinces of Ireland. Dublin city and county are separated from the rest of the province of Leinster; Munster is unaltered and Connacht includes three counties of Ulster. Six of Ulster's nine counties are in Northern Ireland. The Dublin region is almost wholly urbanized; the rest of Leinster, in the east and southeast, is a relatively prosperous area of large farms and market towns; Connacht/Ulster, in the northwest, is the poorest region, with small farms and few towns. The most heterogeneous region is Munster, in the southwest: parts resemble the small-farmer countryside of Connacht/ Ulster, while other parts are more reminiscent of Leinster.

The Gallup data show (Table 10) that, when controlled for class, region is a factor of limited importance. Its influence is most obvious in Connacht/Ulster. The poor

TABLE 10: Class, Party and Region, in Percentages

Total		F. F.	F. G.	Lab.	Other
	Middle class				
11	Dublin	35	30	20	15
6	Rest of Leinster (N=98)	50	34	10	6
7	Munster	50	20	14	16
6	Connacht/Ulster	49	30	9	12
	Working class				
17	Dublin	37	14	31	18
12	Rest of Leinster	39	19	33	9
12	Munster	50	12	26	12
7	Connacht/Ulster	45	22	14	19
	Farmers				
(0.3)	Dublin	*	*	*	*
5	Rest of Leinster (N=84)	42	40	0	18
9	Munster	39	46	4	12
7	Connacht/Ulster	47	33	3	17
100%					

showing of the Labour party is not due simply to the weakness of the working-class in that region: even within what working-class exists, Labour has less support than elsewhere.

Among farmers, a fairly even balance between the two main parties in Leinster and Munster is replaced in Connacht/Ulster by a *Fianna Fáil* lead. This reflects the preponderance in Connacht/Ulster of small farmers, among whom *Fianna Fáil* is relatively strong.

I. SEX

Sex appears to be of slight importance. The Gallup data summarized in Table 11 suggest that, when controlled for class, differences between parties by sex are small; and most of such difference as it does indicate is not confirmed by the I.M.S. data.

TABLE 11: **Class, Party and Sex, in Percentages**

Total		F. F.	F. G.	Lab.	Other
	Middle class				
15	Men	48	26	14	12
16	Women	42	32	14	13
	Working class				
23	Men	40	16	31	13
24	Women	43	16	25	16
	Farmers				
11	Men	40	40	3	17
10	Women	46	40	2	12
100%					

Both polls agree however, that in the working class Labour has more attraction for men than for women.

J. AGE GROUP

The Gallup Poll classified respondents in six age groups: 21–24, 25–34, 35–44, 45–54, 55–64, 65+. When control is made by class, however, the numbers in many rows are too small for reliability. In the construction of Table 12 these age groups have been collapsed into three: 21–34, 35–54, 55+. The figures show that in both the middle-and the working-classes Labour is strongest in the youngest age group, a finding confirmed by the I.M.S. poll. The age groups, however, are large and mask differences. This is particularly true of the oldest group, 55+. The more detailed figures show that voters aged 65 and over gave most support to *Fine Gael*, while those between 55 and 64 gave most support to *Fianna Fáil*. The I.M.S. poll confirmed the support for *Fianna Fáil* in the 55–64 range; while it found *Fine Gael*'s greatest strength in the 21–34 age range, it agreed that the party was relatively strong among those over 65. This pattern supports the theory, developed by Butler and Stokes (1969) and others,

TABLE 12:   **Class, Party and Age Group, in Percentages**

Total		F. F.	F. G.	Lab.	Other
	Middle class				
11	21–34	47	24	18	11
11	35–54	46	27	12	15
8	55+	40	37	11	12
	Working class				
12	21–34	32	17	37	14
18	35–54	39	16	31	14
18	55+	51	16	19	15
	Farmers				
5	21–34 (N=78)	41	38	6	17
10	35–54	40	43	3	15
7	55+	47	36	1	16
100%					

that voters tend to retain a lifelong allegiance to the party they adopted in early adulthood. Those electors aged 65 and over first voted when the leading force in Irish politics was *Cumann na nGaedheal* or even the old Irish Nationalist party. It is not surprising that relatively few of them were attracted by *Fianna Fáil*. Electors in the age range 55–64, on the other hand, started voting when *Fianna Fáil* was riding the crest of the wave.

K.   RELIGION

The religious factor hardly comes into a discussion of politics in Ireland today. The designers of survey questionnaires do not bother, as a rule, to collect information on the point. The reason is that the country is religiously homogeneous to almost a unique degree. The overwhelming majority of the people, over 95 percent at the census of 1966, profess allegiance to Roman Catholicism. This in itself might not mean unity of outlook, for the experience of many nominally Catholic countries in Europe shows that a large proportion of the population may be effectively out of contact with the Church. Ireland is exceptional in that the great majority of the people are not nominal but practicing Catholics. Such investigations as there have been suggest that the practice of religion among the Catholic population is of the order of 90 percent (Blanchard, 1963, p. 31; Ward, 1964, p. 26).

Only in a handful of constituencies, where the Protestant minority is large enough to have some influence, may the religious factor be of some importance. So far the only investigation of such a constituency has been Sacks's study (1970) of Donegal Northeast. It shows a considerable degree of cohesion among the Protestant electorate. In this constituency, where, the author states, two-thirds of the Protestant vote was reckoned to go to *Fianna Fáil*, the nomination by *Fine Gáel* of a Protestant candidate had the effect of swinging over to *Fine Gael* a substantial proportion of the Protestant voters; unfortunately the author does not present his figures in such a way as to show precisely what the proportion was.

V. Social Psychological Influences

The most interesting research under this heading has been done by students of the School of Public Administration in Dublin, who surveyed a sample of the city's electorate in 1966 and 1967, using a questionnaire based on that developed for Almond and Verba's survey, *The Civic Culture* (1963). Their findings indicate that Dubliners combine a high degree of interest in politics with a low sense of political efficacy (Hart, 1970). However, since they obtained no breakdown of the sample by party affiliation, their work cannot be employed here.

A. INTEREST IN POLITICS AND ATTITUDES TO PARTIES

The Gallup Poll asked respondents to say whether they were "very interested," "moderately interested," or "only a little interested" in the result of the next general election. On this point there was practically no difference between parties or, indeed, between classes, roughly one-third of the electors putting themselves in each category. Slightly greater divergences were revealed by the question, "Do you think there is any really important difference between the political parties, or are they all much of a muchness?" (Table 13). The data show that in all classes *Fine Gael* supporters were

TABLE 13: **Class, Party, and Attitude to Parties, in Percentages**

Total		F. F.	F. G.	Lab.	Other
	Middle class				
13	Is a difference	49	25	18	7
16	Much the same	41	31	11	16
2	Don't know	*	*	*	*
	Working class				
14	Is a difference	53	14	26	7
27	Much the same	38	18	28	16
6	Don't know	33	12	33	22
	Farmers				
6	Is a difference	45	36	4	15
13	Much the same	43	42	3	12
3	Don't know (N=41)	35	35	2	27
100%					

slightly less likely to see a difference between parties than *Fianna Fáil* or Labour voters. The difference was not marked, however, and a majority in all parties agreed that parties were much the same: 52 percent of *Fianna Fáil*, 53 percent of Labour, and 61 percent of *Fine Gael* supporters.

B.   ATTITUDES TO POLICY

One issue of long-standing interest in Irish politics has been the revival of the Irish language. By the time British rule came to an end in 1921 English had become the main language of the people, and the only Irish-speaking areas left were a few patches along the western seaboard. Since then successive governments have sought to encourage the revival of the Irish language. Irish is a compulsory subject in schools, and posts in teaching or the civil service are generally open only to those qualified in the language. There has been much discussion in Ireland about the wisdom of this policy. The Gallup Poll probed attitudes by asking "Do you think it is a good idea or a bad idea to revive the Irish language as the main spoken language of Ireland?" The question will not distinguish perfectly between pro- and anti-revivalists, because not all those who favour the revival go so far as to wish Irish to replace English as the main language of the country. However, it should provide a rough picture of the distribution of attitudes. The figures (Table 14) show that in all three classes *Fianna Fáil* supporters are the most likely to support the idea of an Irish-speaking Ireland, and

TABLE 14:   **Class, Party, and Attitude to Irish Language, in Percentages**

Total		F. F.	F. G.	Lab.	Other
	Middle class				
9	For an Irish-speaking Ireland	56	20	13	10
19	Against	41	32	14	13
2	Don't know	*	*	*	*
	Working class				
15	For an Irish-speaking Ireland	50	13	27	10
28	Against	37	19	29	15
5	Don't know (N=81)	42	11	24	23
	Farmers				
7	For an Irish–speaking Ireland	58	23	3	16
12	Against	32	51	3	13
2	Don't know	*	*	*	*

Fine Gael supporters least likely, with Labour supporters in an intermediate position. Among farmers, the issue provides an especially good discriminator between the two main parties. It fits the assumption that *Fianna Fáil* supporters are more nationalist in outlook than *Fine Gael* ones. However, this conclusion cannot be pressed too far.

Since 1961 *Fine Gael* has been opposed to the compulsory Irish policy, while *Fianna Fáil* (and Labour) continue to uphold it. One cannot know, therefore, whether *Fine Gael* supporters are less enthusiastic about the language revival because it is party policy, or whether they selected *Fine Gael* as their party because it was less enthusiastic about the language revival. Furthermore, the figures show that the ideal of an Irish-speaking Ireland is not widely popular in any section of the community. In the sample as a whole 31 percent favored the idea, while 59 percent opposed. The only difference between *Fianna Fáil* and the rest was that the majority opposed was less marked (*Fianna Fáil* supporters, 51 percent against; Labour supporters, 61 percent against; *Fine Gael* supporters, 70 percent against).

C. INTER GENERATIONAL INFLUENCE

This seems likely to be an important influence in Ireland, especially in regard to the two main parties. At present policy differences between them are slight, and it would hardly be possible for a voter to choose one rather than the other on grounds either of ideology or of class interest. Yet they each have a large and fairly stable following. The most likely explanation is that this is the result of family tradition: for very many Irishmen today, their choice of party is likely to be the product of the choice their parents or grandparents made at a time when differences between the two main parties were real and deeply felt. The civil war trauma, in particular, may have done as much to shape party allegiances today as any contemporary factor. No work has yet been done on this subject.

VI. A Tree Analysis of Irish Electoral Behavior

Irish electoral behavior is not ideally suited to tree analysis. The technique requires that partisan preferences be dichotomized, a rather artificial proceeding in a country with three parties all competing against each other. However, in practice one dichotomy seems less unnatural than the other possible ones. It is conceded on all sides that the only practicable alternative to a *Fianna Fáil* government is a *Fine Gael*–Labour coalition. This has been recognized even by the Labour party, which after some years of disenchantment with the idea of coalition, empowered its parliamentarians, at a special party conference in December, 1970 to negotiate participation in a government if the occasion arose. In the following analysis (Figure 1) the dichotomy employed has been between *Fianna Fáil* supporters on the one hand and *Fine Gael* and Labour supporters on the other.

The following variables were used: membership in trade union or farm organization; car ownership; nature of house tenancy; level of education; age group; region; occupational class; sex; and attitude to language revival. In classifying age groups, nature of tenancy, and occupational classes the original categories employed by the Gallup Poll (six in each case) were used, rather than the collapsed categories (three in each case) used elsewhere in this chapter.

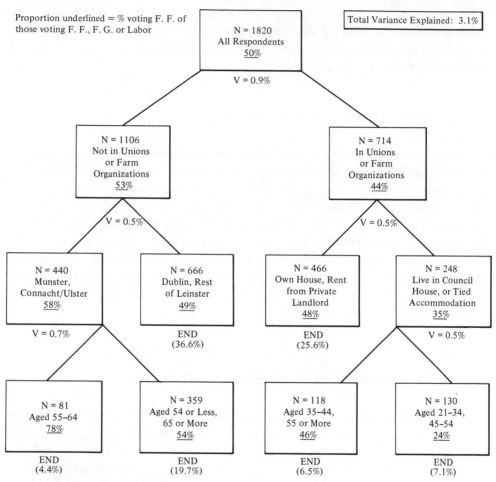

The Ns given represent actual totals of respondents in each group. In calculating variance explained, the effect of weighting for Dublin has been taken into account.
Percent figures in parenthesis beneath end groups give proportion of total sample.

Figure 1: A Tree Analysis of Irish Electoral Behavior

The influences that appear in the analysis are reasonable. Organizational membership appears in the first split because Labour is relatively strong among trade unionists and *Fine Gael* among members of farm organizations. Among the unorganized, the next split occurs by region: this illustrates the relative strength of *Fianna Fáil* in the West, i.e., Munster and Connacht/Ulster. Among the organized, the next split occurs on housing, with those who own their own houses or who rent from a private landlord being more likely to support opposition parties than those who live in council houses or other tenancies. On both sides of the tree the final split is made by age. This reflects the strength of *Fianna Fáil* in the fifty-five to sixty-four age group and of Labour in the twenty-one to thirty-four age group, as well as a lead to *Fine Gael* and Labour combined in the forty-five to fifty-four age group.

What is demonstrated most strikingly by the tree, however, is the low degree to which Irish electoral behavior is structured at all. The total variation explained is only 3.1 percent—the lowest for any country for which tree analysis is available in this volume. Occupational class, which in most countries is an important factor, does not even appear in the tree. Homogeneity is also emphasized by the fact that the two largest of the end groups, containing 62 percent of all respondents, divide almost equally between the two main party alternatives.

It might be objected that the importance of class factors is masked by taking the dichotomy between *Fianna Fáil* and the other two parties as the basis of the analysis, since both the other parties have a more overt class basis. To check on this, two further tree analysis were calculated, one dichotomizing *Fine Gael* versus *Fianna Fáil* and Labour, and the other Labour versus *Fine Gael* and *Fianna Fáil*. When this was done, the salience of class factors did indeed increase. With *Fine Gael* opposed to the rest, the first split took place on the basis of occupational class, with upper- and middle-class and large farmers being more likely to vote *Fine Gael* than lower-middle-class, working-class, and small farmers: the degree of variance explained was 6.1 percent. But only two more splits occurred, one distinguishing lower-middle class from workers and small farmers and the other distinguishing by age groups. Total variance explained was 8.1 percent.

The greatest degree of variance explained emerged when Labour was run against *Fianna Fáil* and *Fine Gael*: 14.8 percent. The first split occurred on class, with working-class being opposed to all others. Within the working class a split first occurred between trade unionists and non-trade unionists, while on the non-working-class side the first split occurred between farmers and nonfarmers. Thereafter other splits occurred on both sides, with age groups, council tenants and non-council-tenants, and eastern and western regions all appearing in the tree. The pattern is not unlike that found in Britain or Australia.

The difference, however, is that the Labour party is much weaker than its counterparts in Britain or Australia: Labour parties gained the support of 44 percent of respondents in the Australian sample and 44 percent in the British sample, but only 21 percent in the Irish one. In only one of nine end groups did Irish Labour receive the support of as much as 50 percent of the respondents. This was a small group, about 6 percent of the total, consisting of trade unionists, chiefly in the younger age groups, living in council houses.

Tree analysis reinforces the conclusion, evident throughout this chapter, that Irish electoral behavior is exceptionally unstructured. What it cannot do is explain why this should be so. One possibility is that, because the principal division in Irish politics dates from the civil war split on a political, not an economic issue, it is only natural that economic divisions should have less influence in Ireland than in many countries. The objection to this explanation is that ecological studies of voting in the 1920s (Rumpf, 1959, Pyne, 1968) indicate that Irish politics were then class-based to a greater extent than they have since become. *Cumann na nGaedheal* was to a considerable extent the party of the haves, and *Fianna Fáil* of the have-nots. An alternative explanation seems more likely: the extension of support for *Fianna Fáil* in the 1930s and the erosion of support for *Fine Gael* at the same period, blurred class lines that had originally been more visible.

VII. Conclusions

A. Ireland is overwhelmingly a Catholic country, with only very small minorities adhering to other faiths. In this it is comparable to Italy, Austria, Belgium, and France. There is, however, an imporant difference in that these four countries, though nominally Catholic, have substantial populations estranged from the Church and supporting anticlerical parties. The clerical/anticlerical dimension is one of the most important—perhaps the most important—division in these countries. In Ireland, on the other hand, the overwhelming majority of the population are practicing Catholics. There is no electoral advantage to be gained from anticlericalism; while close inspection suggests that *Fianna Fáil* is a little more independent of the Church than *Fine Gael* or Labour, what stands out most in the record of all three parties is how closely they mirror the Church's attitudes (Whyte, 1971).

B. A feature that might better facilitate comparison is, not that Ireland is a Catholic country, but that it is a religiously homogeneous country. This opens up comparisons with the Nordic countries, which are overwhelmingly Lutheran, and, though active Church membership appears low, share with Ireland the distinction of having largely avoided the clerical/anticlerical controversies that have so beset continental Catholic countries. The parallel, however, cannot be pushed far. Nordic politics are much more class-based than Irish politics. Lijphart (1971, pp. 8-9) reports indices of class voting of 44 in Denmark, 46 in Norway, 53 in Sweden, and 59 in Finland, higher than those found in any of the other democracies he discusses. In Ireland, on the other hand, the Gallup data produce a figure (taking *Fianna Fáil* and Labour together as Left parties, and including small farmers with manual workers) of 15. Furthermore, despite the apparent indifference to religion of most Scandinavians, differences in religious attitudes have had somewhat more impact on politics than in Ireland. Parties exist in some Scandinavian countries (Christian People's party in Norway and Liberals in Sweden) that have links with particular religious groupings. No such parties can be found in Ireland.

C. A more promising comparison might seem to be with the United States. There also the two main parties can be considered unique products of the country's history, having been founded, or transformed, at a time of civil war. Democrats and Republicans, like *Fianna Fáil* and *Fine Gael*, have no exact equivalents elsewhere. They are not socialists or anticlericals, conservatives or Christian democrats. Again, the normal majority party in each country (Democrats in the U.S.A., *Fianna Fáil* in Ireland) appeals more than its rival to the less well-off sections of the community, while the normal minority party (Republicans or *Fine Gael*) finds its greatest strength in the higher socioeconomic levels. That, however, seems to be as far as the comparison can usefully be taken. Relative party strengths are not closely parallel. The Republicans are proportionately a good deal stronger than *Fine Gael*—they have, after all, won three out of the six postwar presidential elections—and there is no third party in the United States with the proportionate strength or permanence of the Irish Labour party. Moreover, the regional, economic, and ethnic diversity of the United States makes party loyalties much more complex than in a homogeneous country like Ireland.

D. Perhaps Ireland is of most interest in cross-national comparisons precisely because it is such a deviant case. Its uniqueness raises the question: why should it be so different from everywhere else? The answer may be approached by applying the categories worked out by Lipset and Rokkan in their magisterial work on party systems and voter alignments (1967). Lipset and Rokkan point out that the development of party systems in European democracies has been shaped by the way in which four different types of conflict have been handled: those between church and state, between dominant and subject (or peripheral) cultures, between landowners and industrialists, and between employers and workers. Now it can be argued that Ireland has handled all these conflicts to varying extents in exceptional ways:

1. In every other European country, apart from those of Greek or Russian Orthodox obedience, church-state tensions led either to the country breaking away altogether from the Roman Catholic Church in the sixteenth-century, or, if the country remained nominally Catholic, to fierce tensions between clerical and anticlerical in more recent times. Ireland has been unique in meeting tensions in a third way: by remaining solidly Roman Catholic.

2. The centre/periphery crisis was also resolved in Ireland in an unusually absolute way: Ireland is a former part of the United Kingdom periphery that simply broke off. In no country studied by Lipset and Rokkan was such a clean cut made: even Norway, Finland, and Iceland, though subject to foreign overlordship until the twentieth-century, had their own parliaments and an autonomous political life in the nineteenth-century: in other words, the center/periphery crisis occurred between groups within these countries as well as between them and their overlords. One would have to go to the various new states established after 1918 in Eastern Europe, to find parallels to Ireland.

3. The tension between agrarian and industrial interests had less independent strength in Ireland than in many countries. In the nineteenth century it was largely subsumed in the center/periphery tension: the Irish Nationalist party represented not just a subject culture against a dominant one, but also an agrarian interest in a state (the United Kingdom) where the industrial interests of Great Britain came to be

dominant. Here again the crisis was resolved in an unusually absolute way: the agrarian sector broke off to found its own state.

4. Only when we examine the class cleavage do we find some similarity between Ireland and other European democracies. Class tensions do exist in Ireland, and the country has developed, like other European states, a Labour or socialist party. This party is, however, weaker than any of its counterparts elsewhere in Europe. Its weakness cannot be explained as due to the small size of the country's industrial sector: there are other European countries where socialist or even communist parties have made great inroads into the rural electorate; indeed, the main strength of the Irish Labour party, such as it was, lay until recently in rural areas. Lipset and Rokkan suggest part of the explanation themselves. They point out (p. 49) that "the working-class movement tended to be much more divided in the countries where the "nation-builders" and the Church were openly or latently opposed to each other... than in the countries where the Courch had, at least initially, sided with the nation-builders against some common enemy outside." In other words, in a country like Ireland—as in Flanders or parts of Austria—the church had not alienated the workers but was looked on as one of the guardians of the group's values. As a result there was less likelihood of a strong independent socialist movement springing up, and working-class support was more likely to go to catch-all parties in good standing with the Church. There may be some truth in this, but a more important factor seems to be that the Irish Labour party was founded at a time when the independence movement was coming to a head and attention was distracted from social to national issues. Indeed, it stood aside altogether at the general elections of 1918 and 1921, and thus lost crucial ground that it is only now, perhaps, beginning to recover (Farrell, 1970). In no other European democracy did an independence struggle cut across the development of a working-class movement in this way: either the working-class movement was already well established, as in Finland, or the country was already independent, as was true of nearly every other country in the western half of Europe.

It is, then, perhaps a comfort to comparative political analysis that Irish party politics should be sui generis: the context from which they spring is sui generis also.

Postscript

The most important event since this chapter was completed in October 1971 has been the general election of February 1973. The results were as follows: *Fianna Fáil* 69 seats (46 percent of first preference votes); *Fine Gael* 54 (35 percent): Labour 19 (14 percent): others 2 (5 percent). Thus, although there was no redistricting since the previous election in 1969, *Fianna Fáil*, with the same proportion of the first-preference vote, gained six fewer seats. This was largely due to its much reduced success in picking up lower preferences from other parties. This in turn was due to the fact that *Fine Gael* and Labour formed a coalition when the election was announced, and the supporters of each showed great fidelity in casting their lower preferences for the other. Following the election, *Fine Gael* and Labour formed a government.

Note

1. A fourth type of education has appeared since 1966: the comprehensive school, which combines the characteristics of secondary and vocational schools. Such schools are still rare, however, and hardly any of their alumni will yet have reached the electorate.

References

(A few titles not mentioned in the text have been added, in order to make this as complete a bibliography as possible on Irish elections.)

ALMOND, G. A., and VERBA, S. *The Civic Culture.* Princeton: Princeton Univ. Press, 1963.

AYEARST, MORLEY. *The Republic of Ireland: Its Government and Politics.* London: Univ. of London Press, 1971.

BAX, MART. "Patronage Irish Style: Irish Politicians as Brokers." *Sociologische Gids* XVII: 3 (1970).

BELL, J. BOWYER. *The Secret Army. A History of the I.R.A., 1916-1970.* London: Anthony Blond, 1970.

BLANCHARD, JEAN. *The Church in Contemporary Ireland.* Dublin: Clonmore and Reynolds, 1963.

BLANSHARD, PAUL. *The Irish and Catholic Power.* London: Verschoyle, 1954.

BUSTEED, M. A., and MASON, H. "Irish Labour in the 1969 Election." *Political Studies* XVIII: 3 (1970).

BUTLER, DAVID, and STOKES, DONALD. *Political Change in Britain.* London: Macmillan, 1969.

CHUBB, BASIL. "Vocational Representation and the Irish Senate." *Political Studies* II: 2 (1954).

_____. "The Independent Member in Ireland," *Political Studies* V: 2 (1957).

_____. " 'Going About Persecuting Civil Servants': The Role of the Irish Parliamentary Representative," *Political Studies* XI: 3 (1963).

_____. "The Republic of Ireland," In S. Henig and J. Pinder, eds. *European Political Parties.* London: Allen & Unwin, 1969.

_____. *The Government and Politics of Ireland.* Stanford: Stanford Univ. Press, 1970.

COOGAN, TIM PAT. *The I.R.A.* London: Pall Mall Press, 1970.

FARRELL, BRIAN. "Labour and the Irish Political System: a suggested approach to analysis." *Economic and Social Review* I: 4 (1970).

_____. "Dáil Deputies: 'The 1969 Generation.' " *Economic and Social Review* II:3 (1971).

FIANNA FÀIL. *The Story of Fianna Fáil: First Phase.* Dublin: Fianna Fáil, 1960. (Appendix gives election statistics, 1927-1959.)

GARVIN, THOMAS. *The Irish Senate.* Dublin: Institute of Public Administration, 1969.

HART, IAN. "Public Opinion on Civil Servants and the Role and Power of the Individual in the Local Community." *Administration* (1970).

LAKEMAN, ENID. *How Democracies Vote. A Study of Majority and Proportional Electoral Systems.* London: Faber, 1970.

LIJPHART, AREND. *Class Voting and Religious Voting in the European Democracies.* Occasional paper no. 8, Survey Research Centre. Glasgow: University of Strathclyde, 1971.

LIPSET, S. M., and ROKKAN, S. *Party Systems and Voter Alignments: Cross-National Perspectives.* New York: Free Press, 1967.

MCCRACKEN, J. L. *Representative Government in Ireland. A Study of Dáil Eireann, 1919–1948.* London: Oxford Univ. Press, 1958.

MANNING, MAURICE. *Irish Political Parties. An Introduction.* Dublin: Gill and Macmillan, 1972.

MANSERGH, NICHOLAS. *The Irish Free State, Its Government and Politics.* London: Allen & Unwin, 1934.

MOSS, WARNER. *Political Parties in the Free State.* New York: Columbia Univ. Press, 1933.

MURPHY, JOHN A. "The Irish Party System, 1938-1951." In Kevin B. Nowlan and T. Desmond Williams, eds. *Ireland in the War Years and After, 1939–1951.* Dublin: Gill and Macmillan, 1969.

O'CONNOR LYSAGHT, D. R. *The Irish Republic.* Cork: Mercier Press, 1970.

O'LEARY, CORNELIUS, *The Irish Republic and Its Experiment with Proportional Representation.* South Bend: Univ. of Notre Dame Press, 1961.

O'SULLIVAN, DONAL. *The Irish Free State and Its Senate.* London: Faber, 1940.

PYNE, PETER P. "The Third Sinn Fein Party, 1923-1926." Master's thesis, University College, Dublin, 1968.

———. "The Third Sinn Fein Party, 1923–1926." Economic and Social Review I:1–2 (1969-1970). (This is a summary of Pyne 1968, including some of the statistics but none of the maps.)

ROSE, RICHARD. *Class and Party Divisions: Britain as a Test Case.* Occasional paper no. 1, Survey Research Centre, Glasgow: University of Strathclyde, 1968.

ROSS, J. F. S. "Ireland." In S. Rokkan and J. Meyriat, eds. *International Guide to Electoral Statistics.* vol. 1, *Western Europe.* Paris: Mouton, 1970.

———. *The Irish Election System: What It Is and How It Works.* London: Pall Mall Press, 1959.

RUMPF, ERHARD. *Nationalismus und Sozialismus in Ireland.* Meisenheim am Glan: Anton Hain, 1959.

SACKS, PAUL M. "Bailiwicks, Locality, and Religion: Three Elements in an Irish Dáil Constituency Election." *Economic and Social Review.* I:4 (1970).

SMYTH, J. McG. *The Theory and Practice of the Irish Senate*. Dublin: Institute of Public Administration, 1972.

WARD, C. K. "Socioreligious Research in Ireland." *Social Compass* XI.3/4 (1964).

WHYTE, JOHN. *Dáil Deputies: Their Work, Its Difficulties, Possible Remedies*. Dublin: Tuairim Pamphlet no. 15, 1966.

WHYTE, J. H. *Church and State in Modern Ireland, 1923–1970*. Dublin: Gill and Macmillan, 1971.

13. THE UNITED STATES:
The Politics of Heterogeneity

WALTER DEAN BURNHAM

...The wider the area of agreement on political fundamentals, the more heterogeneous the society (or community), the larger the proportion of its members who
have high levels of personal aspirations, and the less centralized the constitutional
system, then the greater the number and variety of factors that operate as determinants of voting behavior.

Applied specifically to the United States, this proposition leads us to claim that
all American history is reflected in past and present voting behavior...(I)n the
United States, unlike other countries, almost every social conflict, tension and
disagreement may function potentially as a significant determinant of voting
behavior.

(Benson, 1961, p. 276)

I. Historical Background

A. SOCIAL STRUCTURE, PRIMARILY SINCE 1900

The United States occupies a territory of imperial size: even without Alaska and
Hawaii, it covers an area equivalent to that of Europe including the USSR west of the
Urals. All comparative analysis involving American electoral politics must keep this
extraordinary extensiveness at the center of its focus, for the country's vast size is a
major determinant of one of its most important political characteristics, that of coalitional heterogeneity.

While a short overview necessarily loses much crucial detail, it is possible to some
extent to reduce the great complexity of American social development to a few salient
and well-known points. The first of these is that the country was settled predominantly
by a single "founding race"—largely from the Protestant portions of the United
Kingdom—and that this settlement occurred long after the Reformation and the
dissolution of the medieval cosmos. Since that time, what is now the United States has
been truly a refuge of peoples from all over the European continent, but the cultural
impress of the original settlers has remained and has been furthered by the dominant
melting-pot ideology particularly prevalent in the first third of this century.

The original founders were preindustrial but not prebourgeois. While many
efforts were made in the Colonial period to establish land-tenure arrangements com-

653

parable with those then existing in people-rich, and land-poor England, such attempts were doomed to a failure that stretches from the collapse of the Carolina Charter drafted by John Locke in the late seventeenth-century through the rent wars involving the Hudson Valley manors in the 1840s. In a real sense it can be suggested that for most Americans most of the time their country and its people were "born free"; in other words, no intractable remnants of feudal social relationships and no recognizably similar church-state conflicts have seriously inhibited the individual's quest for personal enrichment and fulfillment. Many explanations for this state of affairs have been advanced by observers from Tocqueville to the present day. One chief explanation has involved the early anti-Malthusian imbalance between an immensity of land and other natural resources available for the taking, or more generally, a very high level of plenty for white Americans relative to Europe, for as far back as comparative economic series can be traced (Potter, 1954). A variant of this is a stress on the specific influence of the frontier as such in dissolving traditional social patterns and reconstructing them on a highly individualized basis (Webb, 1952).

The other major explanations—and the two are, of course, closely interrelated— lies in the domain of political culture and emphasizes broad consensus among multifarious groups and regional subcultures about the basics of socioeconomic organization. This consensus has been historically liberal-bourgeois or Lockean, and has emphasized the primacy of individual political and social rights, the freedom of economic enterprise from central control, and a deep suspicion of positive government, coupled with what is by European standards a low tolerance for the emergence of the state as a state, i.e., incomprehension of or hostility to the establishment of rationalized internal sovereignty (Hartz, 1955). Such ideas have been commonplace enough in European liberalism, but here they have dominated the culture, the two major political parties, and the practical workings of the constitution. Other cultural fragments of a much broader European spectrum that have been planted elsewhere (e.g., Australia) have shown similar propensities to dominate peripheral, late-settled areas, and have prompted Louis Hartz to develop a more general theory of fragment cultures of which the United States forms a leading example (Hartz, 1964, pp. 1-122). It is clear enough that this middle-class consensus has been of prime importance—for example, in the remarkable failure of any socialist (not to mention Marxist) mass party to take firm root on American soil during or after the industrial revolution. Recent studies of the working-class white American make very clear how utterly outside his individualist and largely privatized experience a Marxist weltanschauung would be (Lane, 1962, pp. 413–435).

A second major aspect of American social development is that American society is extremely heterogeneous and in more or less constant motion. This might be expected in a nation of continental size, one peopled by successive waves of immigrants with the most diverse backgrounds. At no period since the 1840s at the latest can a general analysis of American electoral coalitions fail to place ethnocultural antagonisms at its center; as recent articles have shown, it is at least as likely as not that electoral politics actually sustains and reinforces ethnic-group identities and hostilities (Wolfinger,

1965; Parenti, 1967). It is estimated that in 1790 more than nine-tenths of the white population of the then United States (excluding Pennsylvania) was of white Anglo-Saxon Protestant derivation. By 1910, however, the population breakdown was 54.2 percent native white of native parents, 20.6 per cent native white of foreign or mixed parentage, 14.5 per cent foreign-born white, and 10.7 per cent nonwhite.

Of fundamental significance for the creation and maintenance of American major-party coalitions is the fact that immigrant groups have not settled at random throughout the country. Thus, American Jews constitute about 3 percent of the country's population but about one-quarter of the population of New York City. This asymmetric population distribution has much to do with the major differences that exist between the electoral politics of New York state and politics in the rest of the United States. While Jewish populations are exceptionally concentrated in a few large metropolitan areas, the same phenomenon of local concentration of ethnic groups can be easily detected in every part of the country. If nothing else, Kevin Phillips' recent *The Emerging Republican Majority* is an admirable and quite detailed atlas of politically significant ethnic and subcultural concentrations within the imperial territory of the United States (Phillips, 1969). Two generalizations may be made about the significance of ethnic and regional polarizations for the structure of American major-party coalitions. First, these two variables alone were of transcendent importance from at least the formation of the Republican party in 1854 down through the depression of 1929. Second, they have retained profound significance both for analysis and political action down to the present day, despite the post-1932 intrusion of class cleavages. If American major parties tend to be preoccupied with problems of subcoalition integration to the near-exclusion of problems involving policy integration or articulation, ethnic heterogeneity is one root cause of this condition.

The important point of all this for our purposes is that—impressive as the data on racial and ethnic heterogeneity are for the United States as a whole—it is at the level of state and city politics that groups which seem of a limited importance nationally emerge as profoundly significant forces in electoral politics. It goes without saying that a crazy-quilt ethnic patterning of this kind profoundly inhibits by itself a structuring of national politics along *any* durable and overriding cleavage line, and most especially those related to class conflict. But of all examples of local concentrations of discrete groups that are rather small minorities on the national level, that which has had the most fateful importance for the history of American politics has been the historically conditioned concentration of the Negro in the states of the South, particularly the Deep South. When it is recalled that in 1870 blacks constituted only one-tenth of the national population, but absolute majorities in the states of Louisiana, Mississippi, and South Carolina and more than two-fifths of the populations of Alabama, Florida, and Georgia, much of the peculiarly violent and repressive political style we associate with Southern politics becomes easier to comprehend. There is every reason to believe that the more recent concentration of blacks in the central cities of the nation's metropolitan areas is also producing political leverage—both positive and negative—out of all proportion to the percentage of blacks in the total state or national population. The capacity of locally concentrated racial conflict at the polls to suppress other cleavages, particularly those that might be organized along class lines, has been notoriously great from the Populist era in the 1890s to George Wallace's campaign of 1968 (Key, 1949).

At least as significant a historical contribution to American political heterogeneity as ethnic and racial pluralism is the existence of well-marked and often antagonistic regionalism. It can be argued that the phenomenon of sectionalism dominated national electoral and policy coalition-formation from the 1850s through the 1930s; the results of the 1964 and 1968 elections clearly reveal its enduring significance down to the present.

Politically significant regionalism in the United States rests very broadly on two grounds. The first of these is cultural. As Daniel Elazar has suggested, there are at least three distinct subcultural variants within the American political culture: the moralist, the individualist, and the traditionalist. These have historically been strongly concentrated by geographical latitude, with an original concentration in New England, the Middle Atlantic states, and the South, respectively; and they have spread westward with the settlement of the country (Elazar, 1966, pp. 79-149).

Clearly the most significant political-subculture fault line has been that which has arrayed the traditionalist subculture of the South against the rest of the country, most conspicuously against the moralist subculture that was (and is) concentrated north of the 41st parallel. The bases of the South's deviance from the rest of the country are well known. This region, originally socially organized around a slave-labor system, has been preoccupied for the last century with managing relationships between two races that, in many of the region's states, were initially about equal in numbers. Its people, alone among white Americans, have undergone the experience of total defeat, military occupation, and impoverishment. A century after Appomattox the burden of the Civil War and its aftermath remains massive (Cash, 1941).

The political effects of this center-periphery hostility have been of overwhelming significance for the structure and development of American politics. From the 1880s through the 1960s the South for the most part had a one-party system—hence, a no-party system. It worked out its regional-defense program at the center chiefly through its predominant weight in the congressional Democratic party. The result was the creation of an immense centrifugal force in the party system, a force that served for decades as protection for the region's policy of Negro subordination and electoral disfranchisement. One looks, perhaps, to the Liberal hegemony in Québec after the conscription crisis of 1917, or to the Irish Natonalists in the pre-1922 United Kingdom, for comparable examples.

But the first, or cultural, ground of political regionalism was greatly reinforced by the chief broad consequence of the industrialization that followed the Civil War: the creation in a continent-sized nation of an industrialized, or industrializing, prosperous metropole extending from Boston westward to Chicago; and in counterpoise two economic colonies, the defeated and devastated South and the vast primary-economy spaces of the trans-Mississippi West. It was not until World War II that—urged on at least in part by the fear that the densely concentrated industrial complex in the northeast could become vulnerable to enemy air attack—the government moved through contract procurement and challenges in the courts to overthrow the preferential pricing structure on which the northeast's economic hegemony had been based, and to permit the dispersal of industry. Thus much of American political history and electoral development can be seen not only as a product of ethnocultural antagonisms and a Southern periphery's defense of its way of life against the possibility of a renewed attack from the center. It can also be seen, particularly in the period extending roughly from 1890 to 1940, as involving a succession of colonial insurrections against the metropole's ruling elites, both nationally and locally.

It is important to stress the economic aspects of American political regionalism, for they require us to pay attention to the reality that industrializaton in the United States proceeded quite rapidly in a chronological sense, but extremely unevenly in a geographic or territorial sense. Thus one can suggest that farmers had ceased to be a very significant political force in most of the northeast as early as 1890. But they remained of transcendent importance in the politics of the South and of the trans-Mississippi western states until the great post-1945 wave of urbanization and industrialization, a wave that is changing particularly rapidly the face of the Southern ex-colony. Put another way, Massachusetts and Rhode Island had become predominantly industrial states as early as 1850; Mississippi and North Dakota have yet to pass this threshold.

Viewed in both cultural and economic development terms, the United States ought to be regarded not as a uniformly developed society but rather as a nation that has had all stages from the most advanced to the markedly underdeveloped within its own borders. In this sense it may be analogous to a degree with Italy, which also has a North-South cleavage that involves extremely uneven levels of economic development; it may also be compared with Canada, in which Québec tended to lag for some years behind Ontario and other parts of the country. But the sheer size and national political importance of the chief American underdeveloped country, the South, along with the race problem at the core of its politics, finds new parallels. It may be justly said that the career of a Southern demagogue such as Huey Long has far more contextual parallels, say, with that of a Fidel Castro than with the insurgent non-Southern politicians of his day, such as George Norris or Robert LaFollette. (Williams, 1970). It is even more evidently the case that many of the most serious national integration problems facing the United States have to do directly or indirectly with the legacy of Southern underdevelopment and its central importance to a country that is usually regarded as an exemplar of completed industrialization. It is of more than passing interest to observe that a reworking of the Almond-Verba study reveals attitudes toward political life among inhabitants of the Southern region of the United States that are much more similar to those encountered in Italy or Mexico than to those encountered in the rest of the United States or in the United Kingdom (Jacob and Vines, 1965, p. 13). This is also indicated for the South as a whole in a 1964 survey

(Table 1). The region has a disproportionate share both of low-efficacy voters and of low-efficacy individuals within the entire sample; likewise, at all levels it has a considerably larger share of nonvoters.

Nationally, both urbanization and industrialization begin to describe a clearly ascending curve in the decade between 1840 and 1850, though the predominant rurality of the country in the latter year is recalled by the data that 64 percent of the labor force was then still in agricultural pursuits; only 15 percent lived in urban places. In the employment sector the turning point occurs close to 1880, when the share of the labor force in agriculture drops to 49 percent of the total. But if the Census Bureau's broad definition of "urban", including all places of at least, 2,500 people, is regarded as a criterion, a majority of the population (51 percent) does not appear in such places until 1920. By 1960 the United States had become overwhelmingly industrial, with only 6.5 percent of its labor force employed in agricultural occupations, and with 69.9 percent of its population living in urban places. At the same time, however, only a minority of Americans live today in cities with 100,000 or more persons: 18.7 percent in 1900, 25.9 percent in 1920, 28.9 percent in 1940, and 27.9 percent in 1960.

TABLE 1: **Regional Differentials in Sense of Political Efficacy and Participation: the South as Deviant Region, 1964**

I. POLITICAL EFFICACY

Political Efficacy Index		Whole Sample			Major-Party Voters		
Code	Description	South	Non-South	USA	South	Non-South	USA
0	Very low	20	15	16	16	13	14
1	Low	29	21	23	26	20	21
2	Medium	29	27	27	32	26	27
3	High	16	26	24	19	28	26
4	Very high	6	12	10	6	14	12
	Total	100	101	100	99	101	100

II. PARTICIPATION*

Political Efficacy Index		Voting Democratic or Republican			
Code	Description	South	Non-South	Difference	USA
0	Very low	49	64	−15	59
1	Low	53	73	−20	67
2	Medium	65	72	− 7	70
3	High	69	79	−10	77
4	Very high	64	87	−23	84
	Total	59	75	−16	71

Source : 1964 Survey Research Center study; courtesy of Inter-University Consortium for Political Research. The political efficacy index was constructed by SRC from responses to a number of propositional statements such as, "Sometimes government and politics seem so complicated that a person like me can't understand what's going on."

*Part I, political efficacy, is to be read *down*; Part II, participation, is to be read *across*.

Another way of examining this point is to partition the population of the country into metropolitan/nonmetropolitan segments, with further subdivision of metropolitan areas according to size (Table 2). By these criteria the metropolitan population as a whole constituted only 62 percent of the total in 1960. But a great many of the smaller, detached metropolitan areas in the United States are anything but urbane in their political behavior or subcultural attitudes, however urban or even metropolitan they may be by census definitions. If we assume that a more reasonable definition of metropolitanism should exclude areas of less than half a million people, than the metropolitan share of the American population falls to about 45 percent. Thus despite the impressive gross indices of urbanization in the United States, it is reasonable to suggest that more than half of the American population lies outside of the cosmopolitan social and political influences associated with conurbations. If one were to argue further that suburbanization is a concrete manifestation of Americans' persistent dislike of their cities, the "urbane" residue that is left becomes small indeed. In any event small cities and towns retain a political significance in the United States that is far larger than might be suspected at first glance—not least in the composition of American legislative bodies.

There have been two other profound changes in American political demorgraphy since the end of the World War II. The first, barely suggested by the data of Table 2, is the tremendous growth of suburbanization; and this has also been associated in time with a heavy migration of (mostly white) Americans toward the southwestern and southern peripheries of the country. The former trend in particular was strongly accelerated between 1960 and 1970. To the extent that this suburbanization movement can be associated with growing affluence, flight from blacks and other urban problems, and with a reaffirmation of the virtues of individualist living under superindustrialized conditions, it can be regarded as having profoundly conservative political implications.

TABLE 2 : **Population Distribution, United States, 1960**

SIZE OF AREA	N OF AREAS	POPULATION	PERCENTAGE OF TOTAL
Metropolitan areas :			
1,000,00 and over	24	61,582,070	34.3
500,000-999,999	29	19,214,817	10.7
100,000-499,999	137	30,390,884	16.9
Total Metropolitan Areas	190	111,187,771	62.0
Total Nonmetropolitan Population		68,135,404	38.0
Total 1960 Population		179,323,175	100.0

The second postwar movement has been the mass migration of both black and white Southerners—a migration almost of *Völkerwanderung* proportions—from the countryside to the cities, and particularly to the cities of the north and the west. As late as 1940, for example, about 34 percent of the Southern labor force was employed in agriculture, compared with a national figure of 16.9 percent. By 1960 the agricultural sector of the southern labor force had fallen to 11 percent, compared with 6.5 percent for the country as a whole. Both blacks and whites from such depressed rural areas have problems of acculturation to urban living that are common to underdeveloped peoples everywhere, which are complicated for the blacks in all sorts of ways by their racial distinctiveness. Push and pull have operated on the former Southern rural proletariat and upon the middle-class white city dweller alike to produce urban decay, flight, and violent social tensions, and thus a major part of the sociopolitical crisis in which the United States now finds itself. Thus in 1900, 90 percent of the Negro population resided in the former slave states excluding Missouri; in 1920, 85 percent; in 1940, 77 percent; in 1960, 60 percent. This population, overwhelmingly rural in 1900, has rapidly become concentrated in central cities in and beyond the frontiers of the greater South.

Religion is also an important correlate of political behavior in the United States, but its impact on politics is both diffuse and extremely complex. In contradistinction to the case in many European nations, the United States has several hundred distinct religious denominations. Some of them, like the Church of Jesus Christ of the Latter-day Saints, are of infinitesimal national importance but exert profound influence in the states and regions where their membership is concentrated. Even in the broadest sense no single grouping comes close to a national hegemony. If one reworks the summary data found in the 1971 *World Almanac*, for example, it can be estimated that as of 1970 about 37 percent of the country's population is formally affiliated to some branch of Protestantism, about 23 percent are Roman Catholic, and about 3 percent are Jewish, while 36 percent are not affiliated to any religious denomination.

Since the 1930s the most conspicuous example of religioethnic identity that cross-cuts class-stratification patterns has been associated with the voting behavior of American Jews, who at all income levels have tended to be quasimonolithically Democratic (Fuchs, 1956). Probably the most important religious cleavage of the industrial era, however, has been between native-stock Protestants—especially fundamentalists concentrated in the South and Midwest—and Catholics, a large proportion of whom are of relatively recent immigrant origin. The latter have themselves frequently been divided internally along nationality lines, particularly in the northeast. An earlier and once extremely important ethno-religious cleavage seems to have involved a conflict within Protestantism between adherents of liturgically oriented and evangelically oriented denominations—or between "right belief" and "right behavior"—with major partisan salience extending back to the beginnings of the modern party system (Benson, 1961, pp. 165-207; Kleppner, 1970, pp. 35-91).

There is much evidence to support the proposition that religious influences as such on American voting behavior—particularly the Protestant–Catholic polarization —are undergoing a secular decline in this century. But as the 1960 election clearly revealed, they are still capable of ad hoc reactivation in the contemporary period (Campbell et al., 1966, pp. 78-124; Havard et al., 1963). As is so often the case in contemporary American electoral politics, religious polarizations now compete in a pluralist mixture with racial hostilities, class antagonisms, and political regionalism; they have tended to be of decreasing significance except when Catholics are nominated for high office.

B. ELECTORAL SYSTEMS

In discussing the nature of electoral institutions in the United States, it is of prime importance to stress a determinant that has affected American electoral politics at all times. The United States is a federal state in which even today very broad sectors of autonomy are reserved to its fifty component parts. This has until very recently been conspicuously true in policy areas such as education; if anything, it is even more true of electoral and party politics. With the exception of the federal corrupt practices acts, the entire period from about 1890 until 1965 was one in which the states were left almost totally free to regulate political parties, elections, and suffrage.

The electoral institutions of the United States are both immensely complex and quite simple. Since 1828 the President has been elected substantially by popular vote in each state, with the winning candidate securing all of the state's electoral votes and with a majority of electoral votes (presently 535) necessary to elect. In addition, since 1913 U.S. Senators have been elected by popular vote, with the state at large as the constituency; since 1842 the normal practice has been for members of the House of Representatives to be elected from single-member districts created by the state legislatures. In addition there are a very large number of elective state and local offices. During the past century the uniform mode of securing election has been through the *simple (or relative) majority with a single ballot*. There have been only two significant and durable exceptions to this rule: the use of a crude variety of proportional representation in the lower house of the Illinois legislature, based on three-member districts; and, in most Southern Democratic party primaries, the requirement of an absolute majority on the first ballot, failing which a runoff between the two leading candidates automatically assures such a majority on the second. The complexity inheres in the very wide array of offices for which Americans are expected to cast ballots, not to mention a more or less wide range of referendum questions on which they are also expected to vote. This phenomenon is essentially the artifact of a presidential-congressional, separation-of-powers constitutional regime that is carried to especially great lengths at the state level (Key, 1956, pp. 52-84). The simplicity is found in the universality of this regime—for example, every state except Nebraska has a bicameral legislature, and no state has a cabinet form of government—and in the concomitant universality of the simple-majority mode of election.

Until recently it had been supposed that action of the state legislatures, either through ratification of federal constitutional amendments or through legislative action for the state, was necessary to bring about changes in the franchise. In general, extension of the franchise was not a disturbing force in American politics in the

1820—1830 democratizing era. It was accomplished with remarkably little political conflict very early in the nation's history. By 1860 white male suffrage was virtually universal throughout the United States (Williamson, 1960). The extension of franchise to women was a more gradual and resisted process, beginning in Wyoming in 1869 and terminating with the ratification of the Nineteenth Amendment to the Constitution in 1920. This, however, was also an issue that cut across rather than between parties.

The one case in which bitter and generally successful resistance to the enfranchisement of a discrete social group occurred was that of the American Negro. Prior to the Civil War, blacks could vote on the same basis as whites in only a small minority of the free states. The Fourteenth and Fifteenth amendments to the Constitution (1868, 1870) were part of the price for readmission to the union that was imposed on the defeated South by the Republican victors. Both of these amendments moved a giant step toward providing the constitutional basis for a central political authority with attributes of domestic sovereignty, but both were nullified by Southern whites working through the Democratic party. The counterrevolution was consumated in a series of state constitutional conventions, referenda, and legislative acts between 1890 and 1904, and was legitimated by the Supreme Court in 1896 (*Plessy v. Ferguson*, 163 U. S. 537). As a result virtually the entire black population of the ex-Confederate states was disfranchised, and this in turn created the conditions for monolithic Democratic party supremacy throughout the region.

After the 1930s renewed demands for the use of central power were associated with the left wing of the New Deal coalition and with changing population patterns. In Southern cities, to which blacks increasingly moved, exclusionist practices by local officials were increasingly abandoned. But it was not until the Civil Rights Act of 1965 that the central government reasserted its power to intervene in order to open the polls to the Negro in the rural South; by this time Negroes had largely moved outside the rural South and into cities where their formal right to vote was unchallenged.

A more detailed discussion of suffrage problems is contained below. It is enough to say here that American electoral institutions have assumed their present characteristics largely as a by-product of federalism, separation of powers, and the fragmentation of political authority that both these institutional factors and the hegemonic liberal-bourgeois political culture have mandated.

C. THE DYNAMICS OF THE AMERICAN PARTY SYSTEM

The American party system contains major components that are the oldest large-scale partisan organizations in the world. The Democratic party can be traced in a direct line back to the pro-Jackson coalition of the 1828–1836 period; some would project it—on much more dubious grounds—back to the organization of the Jeffersonian coalition in the 1790s. The Republican party emerged in the northern states, largely on the ruins of the Whig party, in 1854–1856. It was in its earlier years the carrier of an authentically revolutionary, even quasi-Jacobin set of public-policy news that cleared the way for the unchallenged ascendancy of industrial capitalism throughout the national territory.

The candidate name lists of the Inter-University Consortium's historical data archive yield a total of approximately 1,050 party names in the period 1824–1968, a useful reminder that minor parties have always accompanied and been associated with the American two-party system. At the same time the overwhelming majority of these party names represent political organizations that were either temporary secessions from one of the two major parties of the period or were of limited local and virtually no national political significance. Throughout the electoral history of the United States since the beginning of modern politics in the 1830s only eleven of these nonmajor parties (1 percent of them) have polled 5 percent or more of the total vote in a national election. These parties were the Anti-Masonic (1832), Free Soil (1848), American (1856), Southern Democratic (1860), Constitutional Union (1860), Greenback (1878), Populist (1894–1894), Socialist (1912), Progressive (1912), Progressive (1924), and American Independent (1968). Moreover, of these eleven parties four can be classified as the product of major-party ruptures: the three associated with the 1856–1860 realignment that preceded the Civil War, and Theodore Roosevelt's 1912 insurgency. The remaining seven parties that had some national electoral significance form a small residue indeed from more than a thousand names. But as we shall see, they appear to have been of cardinal importance in the recurrent processes of critical realignment in the United States.

One may summarize the currently "normal" state of affairs by noting that seven parties entered the 1968 contest in addition to the Democrats, Republicans, and Wallaceites. These seven, taken together, won 0.3 percent of the total vote. Similarly, of 7,830 seats contested in congressional elections between 1932 and 1968, only 47 (0.6 percent) were won by third-party candidates. This is a tribute not only to the usual insignificance of third parties at the polls but also to the efficacy of the extremely high threshold of representation that is imposed by the simple-majority electoral system (Lipset & Rokkan, 1967, pp. 27–30). It is, moreover, accurate to say that one of the significant long-term trends in American politics (at least until 1968) has been the secular decline of nonmajor parties and an associated tendency toward their organizational decomposition, e.g., contesting only the presidency or a few other key offices (Table 3).

Granted two-party hegemony in the American political system, certain consequences for the shape of electoral politics follow. In the absence of a sufficient sociocultural base for the development of socialist mass parties as a by-product of industrialization, the hegemonic parties will be closely similar in their organization to the classic European bourgeois *Honoriatorenparteien*—modified and, if anything, weakened by the uniquely American direct-primary mode of nomination. Such a party structure is erected on a coalitional base that is necessarily and at all times heterogeneous in the extreme (Rose and Urwin, 1970). It thus tends not to correspond to Michels' "iron law of oligarchy" but to a "stratarchy" that has very weak vertical linkages and is based, in S. J. Eldersveld's phrase, on "alliances of subcoalitions" (Eldersveld, 1964, pp. 73–117).

TABLE 3:   Third-Party Percentages of the Total Presidential Vote by Period, 1876-1968

Period	Mean Third-Party Percentages	
	Excluding Major-Party Bolts	*Including Major-Party Bolts*
1876-1892	4.5	4.5
1896-1912	4.8	10.3*
1916-1928	6.8	6.8
1932-1948	1.5	2.4**
1952-1968	3.3	3.3

Major-party bolts : Progressive, 1912 (from Republicans); Progressive and States' rights (Dixiecrat), 1948 (from Democrats).

It follows from this, as from the heavily dispersive and pluralist behavioral and structural factors emphasized here, that American political parties as organizations normally have only weak policy orientations: a reality that has occasioned controversy among American political scientists (APSA Report, 1950). Such parties may more appropriately be considered as constituent than as policy-making in their chief functions and orientations, they tend to contribute (particularly through realignment sequences and their consequences) to definitions of the "constitution," of the broad agendas of politics, rather more than to specific policies (Lowi, 1967, pp. 238–76). This corresponds, finally, to an ultimate reality of American electoral politics. In the absence of a definitive nationalization of politics around a single dominant cleavage structure it is usually difficult if not impossible to define the partisan outcomes of American elections as involving popular mandates in favor of specific positive policies or programs. While the older view of liberal-democratic ideology that elections produce policy majorities may seem to have greater empirical plausibility in other western political systems, it has normally had very little credibility as applied to the United States, particularly since survey data has become widely available.

It would, however, be singularly inappropriate to conclude that the American electoral system has no longitudinal dynamism of its own, or that pure coalitional chaos reigns. While it is true that the conditions discussed above make the analysis of American electoral politics a remarkably complex enterprise, it still remains possible to detect broad longitudinal patterns in the development of American voting behavior and electoral coalitions. The range of possibilities for temporarily dominant national coalitions is exceptionally large but it is not unlimited (Schattschneider, 1960, pp. 62–77).

There has recently been a good deal of work on typologies of American election sequences (Pomper, 1968, pp. 99–125; Campbell et al., 1966, pp. 63–77; Burnham,

1970). Changes across time in the partisan components and outcomes of election constitute one of the two major dynamic processes that characterize the American electoral system as it is viewed across time. Some agreement among analysis now exists that there have been three major categories of presidential elections: maintaining, deviating, and realigning. To these a variant of the second—the counterdeviating or "reinstating" election—may also be added. A *maintaining* election, as the name indicates, is one in which the dominant coalitional structure hitherto in existence continues its dominance with only limited or marginal changes. A *deviating* election may temporarily appear to supersede the currently normal alignment pattern; in it, short-term influences associated with particular candidacies produce an outcome significantly different from the norm of the period in question—for example, the victory of a minority party, or a landslide. Such elections, however, are temporary disruptions of normal patterns and are followed, after the end of the short-term stimulus, by a more or less complete return to the status quo ante, accomplished in a counterdeviating or reinstating election. A *realigning* election, on the other hand, is a phenomenon of a different order of magnitude. In general it tends to be characterized by (a) massive and durable reshuffles of coalitional elements at the mass base; (b) effects visible not only at the presidential level but in congressional and state electoral patterns as well; (c) abnormal issue-intensity associated with sharp polarizations which, inter alia, normally involve the heavy mobilization of hitherto nonvoting strata in the population; (d) significant consequences for the subsequent shape of public policy and the roles of policy-making and institutions at the center (Key, 1955; Burnham, 1970; MacRae, 1970, pp. 200–207).

A crude array of presidential elections in the 1844–1968 period is provided in Table 4. It should be emphasized, however, that such schematization is at best an abstraction from reality, and that the reality—particularly since about 1916—has become ever more complex and problematic. Thus the 1920 election, for example, could be regarded as both reinstating and deviating in its own right, if 1908–1912 were considered a normal benchmark. Similarly, the classification of elections such as 1928 is especially problematic: in the South it was deviating, in states such as California there were no major effects, and in areas of heavy Catholic and urban populations from Chicago east to Boston it was part of a realignment sequence. Furthermore, the increasing disaggregation of elected coalitions at different levels of election makes the post-1960 voting structure particularly difficult to analyze within the traditional rubrics of such typologies: in some respects there has been no national voting norm to which to refer since 1950. Finally, it should be noted that longitudinal election patterns—particularly those involving realignments—should be viewed as closely spaced sequences rather than as discrete one-election events.

Nevertheless, it can broadly be said that American electoral history has been dominated by two major types of election sequences: the vast majority of maintaining, deviating, and reinstating elections in which the currently dominant status quo is not fundamentally disturbed, and the much more infrequent but periodically recurring incidence of nationwide *critical-realignment sequences*. These realignments form more

or less sharp disjunctive points in a temporal continuum. They are thus capable of
rather precise measurement involving time, geographical space, and the social-structure of given areas. Such measurement, thus far, has included factor-analysis of
residuals (MacRae and Meldrum, 1960; MacRae and Meldrum, 1969) and auto-
correlations of successive pairs of elections (Burnham, 1968; Pomper, 1968). Table 5
presents an autocorrelation of the Democratic percentage of the vote by state for

TABLE 4: **Typology of American Presidential
Elections, 1844-1968**

Maintaining	Reinstating	Deviating	Realigning
1844	1852	1848	1856
1864	1876	1872	1860
1868	1920	1892	1896
1880	1960	1904	1928
1884		1916	1932
1888		1924	1936
1900		1952	1964 (?)
1908		1956	1968 (?)
1912*			
1940			
1944			
1948			
N = 12	5	8	8
% = 37.5	12.5	25	25

* The year 1912, while leading to a Democratic victory atypical
for the period, is behaviorally very similar to 1908, the different net
result arising from the fracture of the Republican coalition into two
parts.

contiguous elections from 1880 through 1968. The scope and limitations of this
measurement technique are clearly visible. For example, because the 1896 realignment
heavily reinforced a sectional structuring of politics already clearly in evidence, its
importance is not very clearly manifested in this array. Similarly, the downward
decay of the correlations after 1948 reflects the growing fluidity of American politics
at this gross level—particularly the post-1948 end of Democratic one-party hegemony
is Southern presidential elections. Even at that the 1964/1968 correlation suggests that
if we view the present era as one dominated by a realignment sequence, one should
look to 1964 rather than to 1968 as the point of origin.

Similarly, more microscopic analysis of the state level confirms both the existence
of sharp breaking points associated with realignment in the 1856–1860 and 1894–1896
and 1928–1936 periods, and the reorganization of electoral coalitions that was
involved (MacRae and Meldrum, 1969; Burnham, 1970). Each was accompanied or
closely preceded by temporary disruption of two-party hegemony and the emergence
of major third-party movements, and each was accompanied and followed by mea-

surable changes in the coalitional structure. In the case of Pennsylvania, for example, strong positive partial correlations at the county level between "urban-industrial" variables (such as percentage of the labor force employed in manufacturing) first appear in conjunction with the LaFollette Progressive movement of 1924. By 1940 they emerge as of salient importance in the Democratic coalition, but prior to 1928 they are of very low significance.

TABLE 5: **Correlations of Contiguous Pairs of Major-Party Percentages of the Total Vote by State, 1880-1968**

Election Pair	DEM. $r=$	REP. $r=$
1880/1884	+0.90	+0.88
1884/1888	+0.93	+0.94
1888/1892	+0.77	+0.79
1892/1896	+0.08	+0.77
1896/1900	+0.78	+0.83
1900/1904	+0.86	+0.92
1904/1908	+0.94	+0.96
1908/1912	+0.95	+0.67
1912/1916	+0.92	+0.64
1916/1920	+0.90	+0.89
1920/1924	+0.97	+0.88
1924/1928	+0.76	+0.80
1928/1932	+0.78	+0.79
1932/1936	+0.93	+0.95
1936/1940	+0.93	+0.89
1940/1944	+0.99	+0.98
1944/1948	−0.27	+0.95
1948/1952	+0.05	+0.79
1952/1956	+0.84	+0.78
1956/1960	+0.38	+0.60
1960/1964	−0.19	−0.32
1964/1968	+0.82	−0.42
1968/1972	+0.89	−0.25

Overall, the normal state of American politics across time is marked by long-term continuity in individual party identification and both individual and aggregate voting patterns. Critical realignments can thus be said to form virtually a dialectical opposite to this norm, and they form an integral part of a characteristic dynamic structure of voting behavior and partisan coalitions across time. At least several different aspects of these dynamic processes should be emphasized here.

1. There have been three nationwide critical-realignment sequences since the mid-1850s. The first of these can be identified broadly as the Civil War realignment of 1854–1860, in which the most important mass polarization appears to have been

ethnocultural on two levels, the first a frontal value-and-interest confrontation between old-stock Americans of New England ancestry and moralist subculture on one hand and white Southerners who increasingly elaborated a traditionalist subculture on the other; and the second (in the northern states) between ethnocultural groups with discordant religious values. (Holt, 1969.) To a significant degree, the victorious Republican coalition was in this period a centralizing or modernizing coalition that was willing and able to use state power as fully as seemed required to overcome agrarian and slaveholding opposition to industrial capitalism.

The second critical realignment, that of the 1893–1896 period, clearly established the Republican party as an ascendant if not hegemonic coalition, as it had not been during the third-party system of 1854–1892. This realignment grew out of two primary sets of conflict that had been exacerbated by socioeconomic development during the preceding period: an agricultural-industrial opposition that found its clearest expression in the Populist movement of 1890–1896, and an overlapping center-periphery opposition involving the South's successful struggle to liberate itself from the last vestiges of central control over its politics, and thus to exclude its large black population from *le pays légal*. As a consequence the Democratic party became even more explicitly than before the party of Southern territorial defense, the party of declining native-stock agrarian sectors that resisted absorption in and domination by the imperatives of high industrial capitalism. Conversely, the Republican party, the political vehicle of industrial capitalism, achieved a commanding position throughout the north and west, and a virtual one-party hegemony in many of its most important and economically developed areas.

The third critical realignment was clearly prefigured by the LaFollette movement of 1924 and by Al Smith's candidacy in 1928, as the second had been prefigured by the emergence of the Populists in 1890. But it was launched—like the second—by a catastrophic collapse in an essentially unregulated industrial-capitalist economy. In a sense it can be said of the 1894–1896 realignment and its aftermath that its overwhelming sectionalism entailed to a significant extent the dissolution of much of the motley local ethnocultural discord that had been so conspicuously reflected in American voting behavior before that time, and hence, by creating a larger regionalism based on colony-metropole antagonism, it made a significant step toward the nationalization of American electoral politics at the mass base. It is clear that realignment of the 1928–1936 period brought much more regional uniformity to American voting behavior than had existed hitherto, largely by introducing for the first time a significant *class* cleavage into American politics. While the transition remained incomplete for many years—largely because the matrix of Southern politics that was formed in the 1890s was not shattered until the 1960s—the Democratic party became for the first time a "left" party in its coalitional structure and policies (Alford, 1963).

It is very possible that the elections beginning in 1964 constitute a fourth critical-realignment sequence. If so, however, this sequence must be regarded as having a number of features that make it quite novel by comparison with its historical precedents. The combination of profound domestic social dislocations with the political effects of the Vietnam War has produced a large number of issue polarizations whose intensity is matched by their lack of coalitional reinforcement or congruence. It is not easy to see, as the mixed results of the 1970 election rather clearly reveal, what single political formula could be used to array most of these issue clusters into a neat two-party cleavage structure. Moreover, extreme fluidity of voting behavior is a chief feature of contemporary American electoral politics. Since decomposition of party linkages with voting behavior and critical realignment are both analytically and behaviorally inversely related to one another, it is scarcely surprising that there is much disagreement and confusion as to whether the post-1963 era has or has not been one of fundamental, durable electoral transformation (Burnham, 1970, pp. 91–174). The only likely prospect for critical realignment that could definitively supplant the broad structure laid down during the New Deal era would entail a kulturkampf leading to a combined cultural, racial, and regional polarization of a profoundly conservative sort—a kind of restoration of the "system of 1896," Republican majority and all. Whether this prospect materializes and comes to dominate American electoral politics during the last quarter of the twentieth century will, as usual, be disclosed by the infallibility of hindsight.

2. The phenomenon of recurrent critical realignment, involving abnormally intense electoral polarization and mass movements of exceptional size and quasi-permanence, interacts longitudinally with much longer stable phases marked by considerable inertia at the mass base and party organizations unable or unwilling to absorb emergent socioeconomic demands until they reach crisis proportions. Nothing less than a generalized, intense, and relatively sudden socioeconomic crisis appears sufficient to produce national critical realignments. It is characteristic of the relationship between politics and economics in the United States that both of the last two realignments grew out of profound economic depressions, and that only the second produced credible evidence of a major class polarization in the electorate. But such is the pluralism of American society, and so various are the possible points of intense, antagonistic mobilizations in it, that it would be most unwise to conclude that only economic crisis can still produce critical realignments under even highly industrialized conditions. It is in any event increasingly clear that *long-term inertia punctuated by short, intense bursts of critical realignment has been the predominant rhythm of partisan politics in the United States over the past century.*

3. It follows from this that the two major-party coalitions have undergone sweeping changes about every generation for at least the last century. A fairly clear impression of these changes emerges from a regional stratification of the mean major-party differential as a percentage of the total vote for president for four time periods—1876–1892, 1896–1928, 1932–1948, and 1952–1968. It should be noted that each of the first three periods is separated from the others by a critical-realignment sequence, but the fourth is not separated from the third by a similar sequence. With its huge longitudinal standard deviations, the data for the 1952–1968 period still come as close as any measure of presidential-election results to a rough definition of a normal vote for the contemporary period.

While Table 6 represents a somewhat crude precipitate of change in the American socioeconomic system and the structure of major-party coalitions, it arrestingly captures several crucial dimensions of long-term conditions. In the first place the economic data reveal the tremendous regional skew in manufacturing: throughout most of the history of the country since industrial takeoff occurred in the 1860s, well over two-thirds of the country's manufacturing population has been concentrated in the greater northeast. Only since World War II has this concentration tended to decline. There is a corresponding regional skew to underdevelopment again most conspicuous to about 1940 while the southern and border states heavily dependent upon agriculture, having very low levels of urbanization and markedly low indicators of literacy, per capita income, and other measures of socioeconomic development. In terms of these crude measures the Pacific region, increasingly dominated by California, is of all areas outside the northeastern industrial metropole the one that most closely resembles it. The Mountain region, with relatively low shares of its labor force in agriculture or manufacturing, was the seat of extractive primary industry and, along with the South and the west-north-central breadbasket regions, tended to fall into economically quasi-colonial relationships with the industrial metropole until quite far into the present century. Particularly conspicuous, finally, is the virtual disappearance of the agricultural sector as a mass economic base during the past generation, especially in its former southern heartland. The contemporary United States has one of the very smallest agrarian economic sectors of any Western nation (Russett et al., 1964, p. 179).

If there is any one variable that Table 6 captures—perhaps to excess it is that of regional differentation in major-party coalitions. As one might anticipate, the regional standard deviations reach a peak in the 1896–1928 period. Moreover, as the table of transitions in Part IV reveals, the industrialist transformation associated with the realignment of the 1890s propelled the South in a pro-Democratic direction, while the maximum anti-Democratic shift was achieved by the group of eight states that were most intensely industrialized or developed. Two regional transformations stand out with particular clarity during this 1896–1928 period. First, the transition from the 1876–1892 to the 1896–1928 periods reveals a massive colonial-metropole regional antagonism, with the greater northeast the Pacific region pitted (in relative terms) against the heartlands of ore mining and cash-crop agriculture. Second, there was a profound collapse of two-party competition throughout most of the country. While in the 1876–1892 period only two of seven regions (the South and the west-north-central regions) were largely noncompetitive, during the 1896–1928 period only two regions remained competitive: the border region, thrust toward the Republicans from a predominantly Democratic position, and the Mountain region, showing very little net change from the preceding period.

Subsequent regional transformations and structures are also of interest in evaluating coalitional patterns. We know on post-1936 survey evidence that the New Deal realignment for the first time brought a major class cleavage into national existence. But the very large standard deviation of regions for the 1932–1948 period serves as a reminder, as do other data in this table, that the effect of this realignment was to make the Solid South more solidly Democratic still; this underdeveloped region not only preserved its asymmetric relationship to the rest of the country but, by virtue of a new nationwide Democratic majority, was able to play an exceptionally important role in national politics. This is particularly evident in the predominant Southern control of committee chairmanships in Congress, a control of the legislative power structures that is still very much a reality in the 1970s.

TABLE 6: **United States: Broad Political and Economic Regions, 1876-1968**

	I. Distribution of Population					
Regional Category	Percentage of Total Population			Percentage of Labor Force Engaged in :		
	Total	*Manufacturing*	*Agricultural*	*Manufacturing*	*Agriculture*	*Other*
1890						
Manufacturing I	25.6	41.7	15.1	36.4	23.4	40.2
Manufacturing II	26.1	33.0	20.0	29.4	31.3	39.3
(Manufacturing)	(51.7)	(74.7)	(35.1)	(32.9)	(27.4)	(39.7)
W. N. Central	9.7	5.9	12.1	15.3	53.6	31.1
Mountain	2.2	2.1	1.6	16.2	31.4	52.4
Pacific	2.5	2.7	2.1	22.3	29.9	47.8
Border	11.1	6.4	13.6	15.5	55.6	28.9
South	22.8	8.2	35.5	9.5	67.8	22.7
United States	100.0	100.0	100.0	24.3	40.6	35.1
1910						
Manufacturing I	25.1	38.3	10.7	41.8	15.5	42.7
Manufacturing II	25.7	32.3	14.6	34.9	19.0	46.1
(Manufacturing)	(50.8)	(70.6)	(25.3)	(38.3)	(16.5)	(45.2)
W. N. Central	9.4	5.5	11.0	18.3	43.5	38.2
Mountain	3.2	2.0	2.8	20.6	34.8	44.6
Pacific	3.2	3.5	2.4	26.6	20.6	52.8
Border	11.7	7.0	15.2	18.3	43.1	38.6
South	21.7	11.4	43.3	13.7	60.5	25.8
United States	100.0	100.0	100.0	27.9	32.5	39.6
1940*						
Manufacturing I	25.5	39.9	9.3	33.2	7.0	59.8
Manufacturing II	25.1	30.9	14.2	25.3	9.3	65.4
(Manufacturing)	(50.6)	(70.8)	(23.5)	(29.3)	(7.7)	(63.0)
W. N. Central	7.1	2.9	13.5	9.1	32.6	58.3
Mountain	3.7	1.0	4.0	7.4	23.8	68.5
Pacific	6.2	4.6	4.2	15.2	10.9	73.9
Border	10.6	6.2	14.8	14.2	26.6	54.2
South	21.8	14.5	40.0	14.1	32.5	52.4
United States	100.0	100.0	100.0	21.7	16.9	61.4
1960						
Manufacturing I	24.6	34.3	9.8	37.0	2.6	60.4
Manufacturing II	24.1	28.1	15.6	30.0	4.1	65.9
(Manufacturing)	(48.7)	(62.4)	(25.4)	(33.5)	(2.8)	(63.7)
W. N. Central	6.2	4.3	17.7	15.8	19.1	65.1
Mountain	3.9	1.7	5.3	12.3	9.9	78.8
Pacific	9.7	8.8	7.2	24.0	4.8	71.2
Border	8.5	6.5	12.1	22.3	10.0	67.7
South	23.0	16.3	32.3	21.3	9.9	68.8
United States	100.0	100.0	100.0	25.7	6.2	68.1

TABLE 6—*Contd.*

II. MEAN MAJOR-PARTY PRESIDENTIAL PLURALITIES BY FOUR TIME PERIODS

Category of States	1876–1892	1896–1928	1932–1948	1952–1968
Manufacturing I	4.6 R	24.5 R	5.4 D	1.9 D
Manufacturing II	1.8 R	17.6 R	8.4 D	0.9 R
(Manufacturing)	(3.6 R)	(21.0 R)	(6.9 D)	(1.3 D)
W. N. Central	20.8 R	22.6 R	5.6 D	7.8 R
Mountain	6.5 R	6.7 R	14.5 D	6.9 R
Pacific	3.8 R	21.4 R	16.7 D	1.8 R

Category of States	1876–1892	1896–1928	1932–1948	1952–1968
Border	11.0 D	0.5 R	19.9 D	3.8 D
South	28.9 D	42.3 D	55.6 D	5.3 D
United States : National Mean	1.3 D	12.4 R	12.8 D	0
Standard Deviations of Seven Regions :	15.65	23.60	17.49	5.05

III. RANKINGS OF REGIONS BY PERIOD, MAXIMUM DEMOCRATIC TO MAXIMUM REPUBLICAN

1876–1892		1896–1928	
South	28.9 D	South	42.3 D
Border	11.0 D	Border	0.5 R
United States	1.3 D	Mountain	6.7 R
Manufacturing II	1.8 R	United States	12.4 R
Pacific	3.8 R	Manufacturing II	17.6 R
Manufacturing I	4.6 R	Pacific	21.4 R
Mountain	6.5 R	W. N. Central	22.6 R
W. N. Central	20.8 R	Manufacturing I	24.5 R

1932–1948		1952-1968	
South	55.6 D	South	5.3 D
Border	19.9 D	Border	3.8 D
Pacific	16.7 D	Manufacturing I	1.9 D
Mountain	14.5 D	United States	0
United States	12.8 D	Manufacturing II	0.9 R
Manufacturing II	8.4 D	Pacific	1.8 R
W. N. Central	5.6 D	Mountain	6.9 R
Manufacturing I	5.4 D	W. N. Central	7.8 R

IV. TRANSITIONS BY REGION AND PERIOD, RANKED FROM MAXIMUM PRO-DEMOCRATIC TO MAXIMUM PRO-REPUBLICAN

Periods 1-2		Periods 2-3		Periods 3-4	
South	+13.4	Pacific	+38.1	Manufacturing I	−3.5
Mountain	−0.2	Manufacturing I	+29.9	Manufacturing II	−9.3
W. N. Central	−1.8	W. N. Central	+28.2	United States	−12.8
Border	−10.5	Manufacturing II	+26.0	W. N. Central	−13.4
United States	−11.1	United States	+25.2	Border	−16.1
Manufacturing II	−15.8	Mountain	+21.2	Pacific	−18.5
Pacific	−17.6	Border	+20.4	Mountain	−21.4
Manufacturing I	−19.9	South	+13.3	South	−50.3
Standard Deviations of seven regional transitions :	11.95		7.94		15.05

The regions used here are as follows :

Manufacturing I (states in which 40.0 percent and over of the 1920 labor force was engaged in manufacturing): Connecticut, Massachusetts, Michigan, New Hampshire, New Jersey, Ohio, Pennsylvania, Rhode Island.

Similarly, the most conspicuous feature of the 1952–1968 period is the steep reduction in the size of the regional standard deviation and the restoration of competitive party conditions to all regions of the country. The regional shifts are also at least as impressive: as an examination of Part IV of Table 6 reveals, the regional shifts from 1932–1948 to 1952–1968 come close to being a mirror-image inverse of the shifts from period 1 (1876–1892) to period 2 (1896–1928). The two manufacturing regions— among the most heavily anti-Democratic in the transition from period 1 to period 2— show much the least anti-Democratic shift from period 3 to period 4. The inverse is true of Southern and Mountain regions. Moreover, an examination of the regional standard deviations of these transitions reminds us that the disappearance of sectionalism that seems to exist for the static data of 1952–1968 masks a sharp increase in regionally differentiated movement from the 1932–1948 to the 1952–1968 periods. The nationalization of politics that is often cited as a major creation of the New Deal realignment seems verified by the decline in the transitional standard deviation to 7.94 for this period; but its increase again for period 4 (1952–1968) to 15.05—even higher than the transitional standard deviation associated with the system of 1896—suggests the resurgence of sectionalism in American politics that was so conspicuous a feature of the 1964 and 1968 presidential elections.

Manufacturing II (states in which 30.0-39.9 percent of the 1920 labor force was engaged in manufacturing): Delaware, Illionois, Indiana, Maine, Maryland, New York, Vermont, Washington, and Wisconsin.

Except for Washington, Delaware, and Maryland, these states are found in the New England, Middle Atlantic, and East North Central regions; and the latter two exceptions are contiguous to the Middle Atlantic census region.

West North Central: Iowa, Kansas, Minnesota, Nebraska, North Dakota, South Dakota.
Mountain: The eight states of the Mountain census region.
Pacific: California and Oregon.
Border: Kentucky, Missouri, Oklahoma, Tennessee, and West Virginia.
South: All of the ex-Confederate states except for Tennessee.

The census definitions of occupational category were radically changed between 1920 and 1940.

Source for 1890, 1910, and 1940 (based on 1930 occupational classification): Harvey S. Perloff et al., *Regions, Resources and Economic Growth* (Baltimore: Johns Hopkins Press, 1960), Appendix Table A-5. The political data in Part II are expressed in terms of differences for each period and state between the mean percentage of the total vote cast for the Democratic and Republican parties. In effect, this presents a concise statement of the strength of party competition.

Approximations to the mean partisan distribution of the two-party vote are as follows :

Partisan Plurality	Democratic Percentage of Two-Party Vote	Status
20.0 % D (and over)	60.0% D (and over)	One-party Dem.
10.0-19.9% D	55.0-50.9%	Modified one-party Dem.
5.0-9.9% D	52.5-54.9%	Leaning Dem.
0-4.9% D	50.0-52.4%	Competitive
0-4.9% R	47.5-50.0%	Competitive
5.0-9.9% R	45.0-47.4%	Leaning Rep.
10.0-19.9% R	40.0-44.9%	Modified One-Party Rep.
20.0% R (and over)	39.9% (and less)	One-party Rep.

Both the regional economic and political data are weighted for the relative size of populations of the states in each region. The national political figures for each time period are derived from the total national vote in presidential elections in each time period.

Such a necessarily cursory review of a mountain of electoral data emphasizes that the structure of American major-party coalitions has undergone massive transformations across time, transformations that at least in the past have been intimately associated with critical-realignment sequences and their aftermath. The Democratic coalition, sharply pushed after 1896 toward the colonial-underdeveloped end of the political spectrum, has retained many of these elements almost to the present time. They were supplemented but not supplanted by the accretion of working-class and ethnic support after 1928 that made the industrial heartland once more competitive between the parties. This coalition produced a national majority, but the result was greatly to increase the control over policy exercised by the coalition's most backward elements. The Democratic coalition has been one of polar opposites among sub-coalitions to a degree never realized among Republicans, even during the period of their national hegemony. Not surprisingly, it has become increasingly incoherent and fissiparous.

Lower-class, ethnic, black, and—increasingly—academic–professional groups were thus added onto the Democratic party's primitive base during and after the New Deal era. One major consequence of this has been the emergence of a functional three-party system under the forms of two-party domination of American electoral politics. Much of the recent fluidity in American voting behavior can be traced to this functional three-party system, and ultimately to the failure of the post-1932 Democratic coalition to integrate industrial politics outside the South with that region's traditionalist, centrifugal, and racist political style and interests. It seems clear enough in any event that at the level of national politics the Democratic parties of 1912, 1936, and 1968 turn out on closer inspection to have much less in common with each other, coalitionally or in policy terms, than the historical continuity of the proper name implies.

4. Significant third parties in the American electoral system have tended to develop at points of major transitional stress in the socioeconomic system. Broadly, these parties have been of two types: those clearly produced by organizational disruption of one of the major parties, and mass movements arising outside of, and against, the leadership structures of both major parties. All of the latter category down until 1968—the Greenbackers of 1878–1880, the Populists of 1890–1896, the Socialists of 1910–1914, and the LaFollette Progressives of 1924—have alike been farmer-labor protest movements in which the agrarian element, while losing in the present century some of the relative weight it had in the last, was of considerable importance. Except for the Socialists of 1910–1914, each of these earlier third-party movements was closely associated with social stress accompanying severe agricultural depression, and all of them reflected major political tensions concomitant with the transition of the United States from a rural republic to an industrial empire. As Lipset and Raab, among others, have pointed out (1970) the Wallace movement of 1968 shared many of the same features of regional concentration and agrarian-working-class support with earlier mass movements. If so, it must be noted that this movement stands on the extreme right, while all preceding ones were leftist for their time as well as anticapitalist to a greater or lesser extent. This transformation provides another clear warning that

fundamental changes have been taking place in American politics since the end of World War II.

The protest movements with the largest mass base have tended historically to be immediate precursors of critical realignments. The two-party structure of American electoral alignments has normally been so heavily favored by institutions, culture, and behavior that such third-party movements must be regarded as particularly significant indicators of stress. Such stress arises from the differential social impact of a capitalist economic development largely free from feudal or traditionalist barriers to modernization, hence free from very many substantive political constraints (Huntington, 1968, pp. 93-139). The critical-realignment sequence arises from the dialectical interplay between socioeconomic dynamism and political stasis in the United States; it has historically been, among other things, a tension-management mechanism through which politics has been brought back into phase with economics and society. On such a view it might be expected that the protest movements that are the harbingers of critical realignment would tend more or less promptly to disappear as one of the major parties absorbs their mass base and some of their policy demands; such has hitherto been the case. Similarly, were significant third-party candidacies frequently to recur in the near future, such a development would imply the probability that the party system has eroded to the point that capacity for critical realignment has been lost. In any event, major third-party protests have been and remain particularly sensitive and important indicators of system stress in American politics.

In addition to these characteristic patterns of major-party voting coalitions across time, there has been a second major dynamic element of change during the present century. If one takes as a benchmark the gross shape of American voting behavior prior to the great industrialist realignment of 1896, a decay both in the comprehensiveness and in the tightness of major-party coverage of the American electorate has been a conspicuous part of electoral history during this century. The first of these, comprehensiveness, can be roughly measured by the analysis of rates of participation in elections across time. The tightness of coverage is measured by indicators of the relative influence of the partisan variable in voter choices across time, as distinguished from the influence of candidate charisma or other components of short-term deviations (Campbell et al., 1966, pp. 40-62). This variable can be measured in a number of ways, e.g., by analysis of the net rate of ticket-splitting in the electorate, or of the relative amplitude of partisan swing over time. Both have been discussed in some detail elsewhere. (Burnham, 1965; Burnham, 1970).

Table 7 yields some indication of the basic changes that have occurred in our period of analysis: there has been a persistent tendency for the amplitude of partisan swing to increase since about 1900—particularly in presidential elections—and for the rate of participation to decline severely between about 1900 and 1930, then to increase somewhat to its contemporary, mediocre level. The results of studies on this point are quite unambiguous, and stand out in particularly bold relief when the analysis descends to the state level or below. The question of causes, and of the relative weights to be assigned to them, remains very much in controversy at the moment.

TABLE 7 :   Presidential and Congressional Results, 1876-1968

1. Percentages of Votes Cast

Year	President				Congress			
	D	R	Other	% D, 2-Party	D	R	Other	% D, 2-Party
1876	50.9	47.9	1.2	51.5	51.8	47.4	0.8	52.3
1878					44.3	39.5	16.2	52.9
1880	48.2	48.3	3.5	49.9	48.3	46.3	5.4	51.1
1882					50.5	45.1	4.4	52.8
1884	48.5	48.3	3.2	50.1	50.2	47.7	2.1	51.3
1886					50.2	45.2	4.6	52.6
1888	48.6	47.8	3.6	50.4	49.8	47.0	3.2	51.4
1890					51.9	41.8	6.3	55.4
1892	46.0	43.0	11.0	51.7	47.5	41.0	11.5	53.7
1894					38.7	48.3	13.0	44.5
1896	46.7	51.0	2.3	47.8	45.1	50.2	4.7	47.3
1898					46.7	45.6	7.7	50.5
1900	45.5	51.7	2.8	46.8	44.7	51.1	4.2	46.6
1902					46.7	49.3	4.0	48.7
1904	37.6	56.4	6.0	40.0	41.7	53.8	4.4	43.7
1906					44.2	50.7	5.1	46.5
1908	43.1	51.6	5.3	45.5	46.1	49.7	4.2	48.1
1910					47.4	46.5	6.1	50.5
1912	41.9	23.2	34.9	64.4	45.3	34.0	20.6	57.1
1914					43.1	42.6	14.3	50.3
1916	49.3	46.1	4.6	51.6	46.3	48.4	5.3	49.2
1918					43.1	52.5	4.4	45.1
1920	34.2	60.3	5.5	36.2	35.9	58.6	5.5	38.0
1922					44.7	51.7	3.6	46.4
1924	28.8	54.0	17.2	34.8	40.4	55.5	4.1	42.1
1926					40.5	57.0	2.5	41.6
1928	40.8	58.2	1.0	41.2	42.4	56.5	1.1	42.8
1930					44.6	52.6	2.8	45.9
1932	57.4	39.7	2.9	59.1	54.5	41.4	4.1	56.9
1934					53.9	42.0	4.1	56.2
1936	60.8	36.5	2.7	62.5	55.8	39.6	4.5	58.5
1938					48.6	47.0	4.4	50.8
1940	54.7	44.8	0.5	55.0	51.3	45.6	3.1	53.3
1942					46.1	50.6	3.3	47.7
1944	53.4	45.9	0.7	53.8	50.6	47.2	2.2	51.7
1946					44.2	53.5	2.3	45.3
1948	49.5	45.1	5.4	52.3	51.9	45.5	2.6	53.2
1950					49.0	49.0	2.0	50.0+
1952	44.4	55.1	0.5	44.6	49.2	49.3	1.5	49.9
1954					52.1	47.1	0.8	52.5
1956	42.0	57.4	0.6	42.1	50.7	48.7	0.6	51.0
1958					56.1	43.5	0.4	56.4
1960	49.7	49.6	0.7	50.1	54.7	44.8	0.5	55.0
1962					52.1	47.2	0.7	52.5
1964	61.1	38.5	0.4	61.3	57.2	42.3	0.5	57.5
1966					50.9	48.3	0.8	51.3
1968	42.7	43.4	13.9	49.6	50.0	48.2	1.8	50.9

TABLE 7—*Contd.*

Year	President					Congress				
	Voting	Non-voting	D	R	Other	Voting	Non-voting	D	R	Other

II. PERCENTAGES OF THE POTENTIAL ELECTORATE

Year	Voting	Non-voting	D	R	Other	Voting	Non-voting	D	R	Other
1876	81.8	18.2	41.6	39.2	1.0	79.9	20.1	41.4	37.9	0.3
1878						63.7	36.3	28.2	25.2	10.3
1880	79.4	20.6	38.3	38.4	2.7	78.0	22.0	37.7	36.1	4.2
1882						65.3	34.7	33.0	29.5	2.8
1884	77.5	22.5	37.6	37.4	2.5	75.2	24.8	37.8	35.9	1.5
1886						65.7	34.3	33.0	29.7	3.0
1888	79.3	20.1	38.5	37.9	2.9	79.8	20.2	39.7	37.5	2.6
1890						65.3	34.7	33.9	27.3	4.1
1892	74.7	25.3	34.4	32.1	8.2	74.3	25.7	35.3	30.5	8.3
1894						66.8	33.2	25.9	32.3	8.6
1896	79.3	20.7	37.0	40.4	1.9	76.8	23.2	34.6	38.6	3.6
1898						62.9	37.1	29.4	28.6	4.8
1900	73.2	26.8	33.3	37.8	2.0	71.5	28.5	32.0	36.5	3.0
1902						53.6	46.4	25.0	26.4	2.1
1904	65.2	34.8	24.5	36.8	3.9	61.3	38.7	27.2	35.1	2.9
1906						48.9	51.1	21.6	24.8	2.5
1908	65.4	34.6	28.2	33.7	3.5	61.6	38.4	28.4	30.6	2.6
1910						49.5	50.5	23.5	23.0	3.0
1912	58.8	41.2	24.6	13.6	20.5	52.8	47.2	24.0	18.0	10.9
1914						49.4	50.6	21.3	21.1	7.1
1916	61.6	38.4	30.4	28.4	2.8	53.6	46.4	24.8	26.0	2.8
1918						38.2	61.8	16.5	20.1	1.7
1920	49.2	50.8	16.8	29.7	2.7	46.3	53.7	16.6	27.2	2.5
1922						35.9	64.1	16.0	18.5	1.3
1924	48.9	51.1	14.1	26.4	8.4	45.2	54.8	18.3	25.1	1.9
1926						32.9	67.1	13.3	18.8	0.8
1928	56.9	43.1	25.2	33.1	0.6	52.4	47.6	22.2	29.6	0.6
1930						36.8	63.2	16.4	19.4	1.0
1932	56.9	43.1	32.7	22.6	1.7	53.9	46.1	29.4	22.3	2.2
1934						44.6	55.4	24.0	18.7	1.8
1936	61.0	39.0	37.1	22.3	1.6	57.3	42.7	32.0	22.7	2.6
1938						46.8	53.2	22.8	22.0	2.1
1940	62.5	37.5	34.2	28.0	0.3	58.8	41.2	30.2	26.8	1.8
1942						33.9	66.1	15.6	17.1	1.1
1944	55.9	44.1	29.9	25.7	0.4	52.5	47.5	26.6	24.8	1.2
1946						38.7	61.3	17.1	20.7	0.9
1948	53.0	47.0	26.2	23.9	2.9	50.0	50.0	25.9	22.7	1.3
1950						42.5	57.5	20.8	20.8	0.9
1952	63.3	36.7	28.1	34.9	0.3	59.1	40.9	29.1	29.1	0.9
1954						42.6	57.4	22.2	20.1	0.3
1956	60.5	39.5	25.4	34.7	0.4	57.0	43.0	28.9	27.8	0.3
1958						43.6	56.4	24.5	19.0	0.2
1960	64.0	36.0	31.8	31.8	0.4	59.7	40.3	32.6	26.7	0.3
1962						46.5	53.5	24.2	21.9	0.3
1964	62.5	37.5	38.2	24.1	0.3	58.3	41.7	33.4	24.7	0.3
1966						45.7	54.3	23.3	22.1	0.4
1968	61.8	38.2	26.4	26.8	8.6	55.8	44.2	27.9	26.9	1.0

We may begin by noting that the post-1900 decay in voter turnout, even outside the Southern states, was well underway before the general enfranchisement of women in 1920. Of course, there can be little doubt that this expansion of the eligible electorate itself contributed significantly to further declines in turnout rates in and after the year of enfranchisement, but it did not initiate the process. Less easy to dismiss as a causal variable is the significant change in the rules of the game around 1900–1910, involving the introduction of personal-registration statutes. There is no question that this requirement by itself has contributed significantly both to reduction in participation and to the creation of the heavy class bias in participation that has existed in the United States throughout the present century (Kelley et al., 1967; Rusk, 1970; Converse, 1971). But subsequent detailed analysis by the author, while not complete as yet, already suggests very strongly that even this significant intervening variable cannot explain by itself more than a part of the decline in turnout between 1900 and 1918. Furthermore, the imposition of personal registration requirements, which place the burden of access to the polls on the individual, is without parallel in contemporary Western nations. Its introduction at the beginning of the industrial-capitalist party-system era was perhaps associated with the elite dominance and management of electoral politics characteristic of that period.

Thus to a significant degree the change in the structure of party competition—or more accurately, its near-disappearance after 1896—was itself of crucial importance in shaping many features that have come to be considered a part of the characteristic structure of modern American electoral politics. The post-1900 decay in electoral participation, the development of markedly antipartisan behavioral norms in the remaining active electorate, the detailed legal regulation of party operations and organization, all point to a remarkably severe erosion during this period of the role of the citizenry as a whole in the American political system. It is as though survival of this extraordinarily nondeveloped polity during the industrialist transformation of society and economy required both the partial liquidation of preindustrial structures of mass mobilization and decisive resistance to the creation of new structures more appropriate to industrial-urban sociological contexts. Heterogeneity of voting coalitions, the political consequences of uneven economic development, and the survival of the bourgeois *consensus rei publicae* seem more plausible as determinants of this remarkable outcome than elite conspiracies.

Table 8 provides a suggestive, if panoramic, view of the long-term trend toward the decomposition of stability of partisan outcomes in American presidential elections. The immense post-1896 increase in longitudinal standard deviations is suggestive of a particularly striking break with typical 19th-century patterns. Similarly, Table 8 captures the reversal of this trend associated with the New Deal realignment and its aftermath, as well as the massive postwar increase of longitudinal volatility of election outcomes. Indeed, contemporary volatility is at a level without parallel even during the 1896-1928 period of dissolution. States containing fully one-third of the country's population now show standard deviations of 10.0 or more, among the very largest to be found in the Western world (Rose & Urwin, 1970). It need only be added here that the

TABLE 8:   **Standard Deviations of Party Vote by Period and
Percentage of Population by State, 1876-1968**

STANDARD DEVIATION	PERIOD AND PERCENTAGE OF TOTAL POPULATION			
	1876-1892	1896-1928	1932-1948	1948-1968
0–2.4	40.6	0	7.6	0
2.5–4.9	35.9	23.4	46.0	0.2
5.0–7.4	9.7	45.5	23.0	24.8
7.5–9.9	5.0	20.9	13.8	41.0
10.0–14.9	6.7	8.7	2.8	27.8
15.0 and Over	2.1	1.4	6.8	6.2

Based on standard deviations of party vote by state and period and, for
population, on the 1890 census for 1876-1892; the 1910 census for 1896-1928;
the 1940 census for 1932-1948; and the 1960 census for 1948-1968. For the
United States as a whole the standard deviations by period are: 1876-1892, 2.08;
1896-1928, 5.25; 1932-1948, 4.13; 1948-1968, 7.11.

massive, uniform increase in partisan swing since 1948 constitutes one major bit of
evidence for the proportion that a normal vote of the sort once found in the United
States and now existing in most developed countries is becoming increasingly difficult
to define. The longitudinal standard deviation for either major American party for the
period since 1948 exceeds by far similar movements in Western Europe, except for the
special case of the Gaullist party in France and, perhaps, certain parties in Luxembourg. It corresponds, interestingly enough, to the very high amplitude of partisan
movements in Canada. Moreover, because of the heavy regionalism in voting both in
1964 and in 1968, a majority of American states reveal higher major-party standard
deviations in the 1948-1968 period than the national figure of 7.06 for the Democrats
and 7.23 for the Republicans. When other indicators such as the relative magnitude of
split-ticket voting are also considered, the conclusion seems not unwarranted that
American politics is increasingly becoming no-party politics.

From a comparative point of view it is of particular significance that the post-1900
American electoral demobilization and the erosion of partisan linkages in voting
behavior occurred at precisely the time when Western European electoral dynamics
involved both electoral mobilization and the emergence of large mass parties, especially
socialist parties. It seems probable that there is a close relationship between the
failure of working-class parties to develop in the United States and the decomposition
of electoral linkages discussed here. The American response to the challenge of
industrialization and urbanization involved a particularly marked demobilization of
the lower classes, a demobilization that approached totality so far as Southern blacks
were concerned. Such a response seems ultimately to have been possible precisely
because a working-class weltanschauung never materialized as a cultural or political
force in the United States. The large decline in participation after 1900 and the
exceptional working-class abstention rate today very much resemble a gap in the active
American electorate that was filled elsewhere by socialist parties. There is thus a
remarkably large pool of nonvoters in this country who, under conditions of acute

stress affecting their daily lives, might well become available for mobilization by some political formation (McPhee and Ferguson, 1962). It is not likely that in the foreseeable future such mobilization would occur within either of the traditional American major parties.

II. The Act of Voting Today

A. ELECTIONS AND BALLOTS

As we have noted earlier, the United States has what is probably the world's largest array of elective offices. This complexity extends to the level of national political institutions, thanks to the separation of powers prescribed by the constitutional structure. Only the presidential election, held every four years, can functionally be regarded as a national election. Of course, members of the national House of Representatives are elected in single-member constituencies every two years, but the influence of local factors on the outcome of congressional elections is immense, including such elements as the large number of uncontested seats (fifty-five in 1970, forty-six of which were held by Southern Democrats) and the increasing invulnerability of incumbents from electoral attack (in 1970 95 percent of the sitting congressmen who sought renomination and reelection were returned for a new term). It is thus problematic whether American congressional elections can be regarded as national in the sense in which one can so regard European parliamentary elections. When the focus of attention shifts to elections for state office, the absence of national issues, while relative rather than absolute, is most striking.

There is no referendum procedure at the national level to correspond to contemporary French practice. This is more than compensated for, however, by the extremely widespread use of referenda at the state level. In Georgia, for example, the voter was called upon to vote in 1968 for President, United States Senator, Congressman, one nonjudicial state official, eleven judicial offices, and, by referendum, twenty-three separate amendments to the state constitution. This is by no means an exceptional case.

The structure of the American ballot differs widely from state to state. In states such as Georgia it is extremely long, but in states with no referendum procedure or very few elective offices—New Hampshire or New Jersey, for example—it is much shorter. Even at its shortest, however, an American ballot will inevitably be more complicated than in a British setting, where the voter's choice is limited to a single set of candidates for a single legislative seat.

In contrast with European practice the American ballot has always included both the names of the candidates and the party to which each adheres. While there is much variation in format, two basic types predominate.

1. The *party-column* ballot—simply a consolidation of the party "tickets" that were in universal use before the Australian ballot reform of ca. 1890—in which all

offices are grouped by party and it is normally possible and simple for the voter to cast a single "straight-ticket" vote. Connecticut, Michigan, and Indiana are examples of states with party-column ballots.

2. The *office-block* ballot, in which candidates for office are grouped by each individual office; as a rule, a voter desiring to vote a straight party ticket must make a separate mark for each of his party's candidates. Massachusetts adopted this form in 1889 with the Australian ballot, and has used it ever since.

There is no question that the form of ballot can make a significant difference in voting behavior (Rusk, 1970). In general it seems to be the case that states with conspicuously strong party organizations have party-column ballots, while electoral fragmentation and weakness of party structure are more likely to accompany office-block formats. It is also worth noting that the form of ballot has occasionally become a political issue in recent years. The two most striking examples of this—Ohio in the early 1950s and Michigan in the mid-1960s—do not offer a broad basis for generalization, but it is suggestive that in both cases conservatives favoured the introduction of the office-block format and liberals and organized labor opposed it; it thus became a partisan issue between Republicans and Democrats.

B. THE LEGAL FACILITATION OF VOTING?

One of many ambiguities in the American political tradition, as we have already observed, is whether the exercise of the elective franchise is a right, an attribute of adult-citizen status, or a privilege for which the individual must demonstrate his worthiness (Burnham, 1971). By contrast with the historical situation in some European countries, question involving access to the polls have rarely risen to the level of explicit conflict between social collectivities in the United States.

There is, of course, one crucial exception to this generalization: the century-long controversy about the legal position of the Negro as voter and citizen. Indeed, it can be more generally asserted that racism, broadly defined, played a most significant role in the creation after 1890 of a variety of effective barriers to the admission of certain categories of adult citizens to the ballot. Nor was this true only in the South. In a number of northern states the post-1890 period was marked by the development of literacy and other qualifying tests. Moreover, the most industrialized states developed a common pattern of personal-registration requirements that were initially directed against the ethnically polyglot populations of large cities. But these changes, unlike the Southern counterrevolution, encountered astonishingly little resistance. As universal white male suffrage came to the United States with comparatively little resistance from the established orders between 1820 and 1850, so qualification requirements that fell disproportionately on the lower classes came to be levied on the suffrage after 1980 with even less opposition.

Until very recent years the accepted legal doctrine was that the state governments had very broad powers to regulate both suffrage and elections. There were constraints in the Constitution. The Fifteenth Amendment as interpreted by the Supreme Court imposed a few limitations on Southern drives to disfranchise blacks after 1890, though these were notoriously ineffective in implementing the intent of the amendment. Similarly, after 1920 states could not prohibit women from voting, nor was any attempt made by them to set up discriminatory practices along lines of sex. But for the rest— literacy tests, payment of poll taxes as a prerequisite to voting, registration statutes, residence requirements, and the like—the result of this very wide autonomy was the creation of "the American suffrage medley" (McGovney, 1949). It is not inaccurate to assert that until the 1960s the basic juridical doctrine concerning voting and apportion-ment of legislative seats—which determined the relative weighting of votes actually cast—was that it was a right heavily qualified by state regulations, and that state inte-rests as defined in their legislation were normally to be regarded as paramount. In many if not most states this abdication by the central government meant in effect that voting was regarded as a privilege for which the individual had to demonstrate qua-lification, while apportionment was entirely determined by the states.

In 1962 the Supreme Court dramatically moved into the apportionment field (*Baker v. Carr*, 369 U. S. 186 (1962)). Since then a veritable egalitarian revolution through judicial decision, constitutional amendment, and congressional legislation has swept the field of voting rights (Claude, 1970). This revolution finds its origins in the preceding legal and political movement toward racial equality. The leading develop-ments to 1971 have been federal supervision of Southern elections, the elimination of poll-tax qualifications for voting, and in the 1970 Civil Rights Act the sweeping extension of congressional power over the suffrage in three areas: (1) a uniform national minimum residence requirement of 30 days; (2) abolishing all literacy tests as prerequisites for voting ; (3) establishing a uniform minimum age of eighteen for voting in all federal and state elections.

This exercise of congressional power was promptly brought under constitutional challenge in the courts. In December, 1970, the Supreme Court—by a five-to-four vote in each instance—invalidated the part of the 1970 statute that attempted to set a uni-form age limit for state and local elections but upheld the part that applied to federal elections (*Oregon v. Mitchell*, 400 U. S. 000). The other provisions of the 1970 Act were sustained by the court without serious division. One result of this peculiarly American ruling has been to create acute ambiguity in electoral law. Henceforth the states will be required either to set an eighteen-year age limit in their elections as three have, or to maintain entirely separate registration and voting facilities for the eighteen to twenty age group.

One may very approximately define the quantitative changes in the American electorate that have resulted (Table 9).The partisan consequences of this increase in the eligible electorate will be mixed, perhaps to the point of invisibility. There is little doubt that both young and illiterate voters tend to be more Democratic (or less Republican) in their voting inclinations than the existing electorate; but both groups tend to have extremely high abstention rates. Thus in 1968 only about 33 percent of the eighteen to

TABLE 9: **Estimated Components of the 1972 Presidential Electorate**

Category of Voters	Number	Percent
Eligible to vote before December 1970	116,000,000	84
Added: 18-20 age group (federal only)	11,500,000	8
30-day residence (presidential only)	10,000,000	7
Abolition of literacy tests (all)	1,000,000	1
Total :	138,500,000	100

Source: *Congressional Quarterly Weekly Report*, Dec. 25, 1970, pp. 3093-94.

twenty age group voted in the three states where they were eligible (U.S. Census, 1969). On the other hand, an indeterminate but large fraction of the 10 million hitherto barred by residence requirements from voting in presidential elections are mobile middle-class and professional people. Such individuals can be expected not only to have much higher participation rates than the first two categories but—at least nationally—to give substantial support to Republican candidates. This expansion of the electorate creates a new set of ambiguities for politicians, and the latter may well respond with more explicit appeals both to young and to mobile voters.

Thus there has been a very strong trend in recent years toward the establishment of uniform, egalitarian standards for voting in American federal elections. Achievement of such standards is, however, by no means completed. Residence requirements remain quite variable from state to state in all but presidential elections, ranging from a minimum of three months to a maximum of two years. Age qualifications have been made uniform by ratification of the 26th Amendment (1971).

The most significant remaining area of diversity in the legal facilitation of voting and the area in which the most disfranchisement of voters now exists is that of registration procedures. These may broadly be classified under three headings : (1) In South Dakota and Idaho procedures for automatic enrollment of eligible voters by state officials somewhat approximate normal European procedures. (2) In the overwhelming majority of states personal registration is required. It is up to the individual who wishes to vote to prove that he is a legally qualified elector, and to present himself at a registry bureau prior to the last legal date. The latter can vary from a time very shortly before the date of the election—the practice in most states—to as much as nine months before, as in Texas. The burdens of personal registration are increased if the procedure is also periodic, i.e., if the individual is required to reregister every year or every several years. Such periodic registration was required in New York City (though not in the state as a whole) before 1957, and was required in Texas until 1971. In the overwhelming majority of states personal registration is permanent, albeit subject to cancellation if the individual has failed to vote within a specified period. (3) In a number of rural areas in states such as Kansas, Missouri, and Ohio no personal-registration procedure of any kind exists. As was nearly universally the case in nineteenth-century America, the voter in such places appears at the polls and votes without further ado. Sometimes lists of voters are prepared by election officials in such areas, and sometimes not. Voting participation in such areas, not surprisingly, tends closely to correspond with the very high levels set in the country as a whole before 1900.

Public law pertaining to personal-registration requirements that are not obviously racially discriminatory is very much in its infancy. It seems probable that the egalitarian trend found in other areas of voting-rights doctrine will begin to make itself felt in this area as well. There is one recent case in point: the invalidation of the 1966 Texas registration statute in early 1971 by a federal district court as in violation of the equal-protection clause of the Fourteenth Amendment. The court relied heavily on the quantitative testimony of political scientists in its determination that the combination of the law's requirements—that registration be accomplished by January 31 and that it be repeated annually—disfranchised well over a million Texans who were otherwise qualified to vote (Burnham, 1971).

The near universality of personal-registration statutes in the United States, and the absence until recently of any serious examination of their class bias in either the professional literature of political science or in public consciousness, reflect very well the congeniality of such laws with the traditional liberal-individualist political culture. American election law has not placed facilitation of voting high in its scale of values. This is now changing, and the effects of the change on the shape of American electoral politics during the last quarter of the twentieth-century should be closely studied by students of voting behavior.

C. TODAY'S POLITICAL PARTIES

Earlier discussion has stressed two major features of the contemporary period: first, the overwhelming dominance of two major-party coalitions in the electoral arena, those of the *Democratic* and *Republican* parties; but second, the accelerating *decline* in party-focussed voting behavior in the current period. Thus despite the apparent hegemony of the major parties there has rarely been a time in the recent history of the country when two-party dominance of electoral politics appeared as problematic as it does today. One must distinguish, of course: American political parties are incomparably more diffuse than the majority of their European counterparts. Their organization ranges by state from the rather clearly defined to the nearly nonexistent. Moreover, the failure of collectivist parties of a new type to develop as significant electoral forces in American politics has been paralleled by the nonemergence of dues-paying or other organizational patterns that could permit a clear identification of party adherents. Thus the triune model of party support suggested by Duverger (1954)—elites, activists, and electoral supporters in a diminishing range of partisan intensity—is largely inapplicable to American major-party structures, as in much of the rest of his discussion. In a certain comparative sense the American political party—even the major party—is something of an optical illusion. It corresponds in some ways to what might have happened to European party organization if collectivist mass parties of the Left had somehow never come into existence. Indeed, the closest comparative parallel to the evanescent American party is probably the kaleidoscopic structure of coalitional politics in France under the Third Republic; though characteristically the *logique* of the situation is easier to follow in the latter case through repeated changes in formal names, if not of *tendances*.

We may turn to a brief review at this point of the fringes of American electoral politics, the third parties of recent decades. The failure to penetrate, or to stay the course if penetration is momentarily achieved, is the most conspicuous feature of such movements. Examples of low penetration with long life include the Prohibition party, which has contested elections since 1872, and the Marxist parties, which have been in being since 1892. The first of these, the Prohibition party, may be regarded as a party of moralist cultural defense; it reached its electoral apogee during the secularist transition to urbanism and industrialism, indeed as early as 1892 (2.3 percent of the total vote). It had a not insignificant influence on Republican coalitional politics before 1900, and temporarily achieved its basic policy goal—through both of the major parties, it should be noted—when nationwide prohibition of the sale of alcoholic beverages was enacted (1920-1933) (Kleppner, 1970). In 1968 its presidential candidate won 15,123 votes, or 0.02 percent of the total.

The Marxist parties have had several representatives in the electoral arena. One of these, the Socialist party, contested presidential elections from 1900 through 1956. For a time immediately prior to the First World War it seemed possible that this party might become an electorally significant movement: its presidential candidate in 1912, Eugene V. Debs, won 6.0 percent of the total vote. There is little doubt that some aspects of social democracy were subsequently represented in the LaFollette movement of 1924 and in the New Deal coalition after 1932, but the party itself declined and disappeared as an electoral force after 1920. Other Marxist parties have included the Socialist Workers, Socialist Labor, and Communist parties, the latter of which has received attention both from officialdom and from scholars out of all proportion to its significance either as an electoral or as an underground party. In 1968 the Communist candidates secured a scattering of votes in a few states, while the Socialist Labor and Socialist Workers parties together won 93,977 votes, 0.13 percent of the total. Both this figure and the failure of all Marxist parties together to win more than 2.6 percent of the vote in the depression election of 1932 suggest how extremely uncongenial the American electoral environment is for organized socialism of any description.

There have been two major kinds of third parties or movements that have made quantitatively significant penetrations in elections; up to the present both types have been "prairie fires," significant for a day or a year but subject to rapid loss of their mass base followed by organizational extinction. The first group, discussed earlier, consists of the farmer-labor movements that have sprung up in periods of exceptional crisis in society and economy, particularly crisis in agricultural economics, and have often prefigured critical realignments. Down to 1968 the last example of such a movement was the LaFollette Progressive party of 1924. The second group of short-lived but regionally or nationally significant third parties has resulted from clear-cut schisms within one of the major parties, as a result of which locally established or nationally prominent major-party elites who have been defeated within their party launch a secessionist movement in the general election. Classic examples of this are the Theodore Roosevelt Progressives of 1912-1914 and the two 1948 movements, the Wallace Progressives bolting from the left wing of the Democratic party and the Dixiecrats, a Southern movement of regional-territorial defense.

The severe internal tension that became manifest in American politics in the 1960s was particularly reflected in the emergence of George Wallace as leader of the American Independent party in the 1968 election. This movement, unlike the Dixiecrat party of 1948, was truly national in scope. Both in the South and conspicuously elsewhere Wallace tapped a magnitude of popular support that had been quite beyond the reach of Storm Thurmond twenty years earlier. Indeed, with just under 10 million votes, or 13.5 percent of the vote, the Wallace candidacy was the third largest insurgency to occur since the Civil War. In some respect this 1968 movement can be regarded essentially as another in a long series of recent Southern periphery-oriented insurrections against the center. Yet, regionally biased though his showing was, Wallace's racist and extreme-right campaign clearly had a universalism in its appeal that is quite at variance with the Deep South Dixiecrat bolt of 1948. This requires us to distinguish quite sharply between the two—perhaps by the formula that if the civil-rights revolution and industrial-urban development have worked to nationalize Southern politics, white reaction to the mass migration of blacks to metropolitan centers outside the South has contributed, along with other things, to the Southernization of national politics.

In any event the evanescent quality of American party life in the contemporary period is also reflected in such protest movements, not only by their usual failure to stay the course but by a marked twentieth-century tendency for them to be concentrated in a single person at a single, highly visible level of election—usually the presidency. Without exception nineteenth-century protest parties, such as the Greenback and Populist parties, fielded complete slates of candidates at all levels, and significantly contested off-year as well as presidential elections. Indeed, they normally won their maximum national followings in such nonpresidential years (Benson, 1961). As late as 1912 both Progressives and Socialists likewise ran candidates at most if not all levels of election. The LaFollette movement of 1924, however, inaugurated a pattern from which later insurgencies have not deviated; that movement was a presidential movement only. For all practical purposes the same can be said of the Dixiecrats and Progressives of 1948 and the Wallace "party" (characteristically known under a number of labels such as American Independent, George Wallace, American, Independent, and Courage) in 1968.

It is thus quite symptomatic that in 1968 American Independent candidates contested only eighteen out of 435 congressional seats; that, while Wallace himself won 440,425 votes in these districts (13.3 per cent of the total), his party's congressional candidates won only 64,772 (2.0 percent of the total); that Wallace himself should win renomination and reelection to the Alabama governorship in 1970 as a Democrat; and finally, that the fall-off in this insurgent vote from Wallace's 1968 level to the 1970 total for American Independent candidates for governor and senator should approach 90 percent in both Southern and non-Southern states. All of this should not be interpreted as predicting either that candidacies of this sort will or will not recur. Whatever the future of Wallaceite or related politics may be, contemporary electoral insurgents must be regarded as organizationally tenuous in the extreme.

One prominently publicized development of the post-1964 period has been the development, under the stimulus of the Vietnam War, of a variety of new-politics movements, some of which have been explicitly oriented towards electoral politics and others of which, such as John Gardner's citizen's movement, *Common Cause*, are not. These movements share one thing in common, if little else—a profound dissatisfaction with the existing structure of action both within the major parties and within the government itself. A peak in this dissatisfaction was reached in the 1968 nomination politics of the Democratic party, when a new-politics challenge to the party's established leadership contributed to President Johnson's decision to retire; it did not in the end displace the regulars' control over either platform or nomination. Only minute traces of this movement could be found in the general election: a scattering of write-in votes for Eugene McCarthy and the Peace and Freedom party. All of these splinters together won 62,938 votes, 0.09 percent of the total.

One attribute of American politics that is associated with its porosity and the more or less exiguous organizational strength of its party organizations is that significant impact on policy, both of the short- and long-run varieties, has repeatedly been exercised by aroused minorities whose electoral focus has been limited or nonexistent. While the movement centering around Senator Joseph McCarthy in the early 1950s had certain correlates with previous electoral coalitions and was actively employed by the Republican establishment in its campaign to break the Democratic monopoly on the presidency, it arose and eventually vanished outside the structure of party coalitions (Rogin, 1967). Yet its temporary influence on American political life was profound; similar are the great Red scare movement of 1918-1920 and—at the other end of the spectrum—the peace movement that flourished after 1965. Such movements, which also arise directly from crises of transition affecting the political system, parallel in an even more shadowy way the "prairie-fire" rise and fall of the great protest parties. They serve as an important reminder that American policy structures can be extremely sensitive to such diffuse and often unorganized *levées en masse*, and that the latter are also quite significant, recurrent phenomena in what might be called the frontiers of electoral politics. It is thus essential for analysts of political behavior in the United States to realize that the effective influence of a popular movement on policy is by no means necessarily related to the extent to which its candidates penetrate into electoral politics, assuming that they even make such an attempt. This consideration applies with considerable force both to the extreme right and to the new-politics groups of the post-1965 period.

A discussion of contemporary American electoral politics would be incomplete without an examination of the nomination systems of the major party organizations. These systems are of very great importance: the normal outcome of an election, even under conditions of massive ticket-splitting and other nonpartisan voting behavior, still remains victory for a Democrat or a Republican. The nomination process is a key gatekeeping function that is exercised to a greater or lesser extent by party activists, and it shows no visible signs of attenuation in the current period. At least as important as the determination of who gets elected is the screening out of potential candidates who lack favor with established party leadership, or who lack the large financial resources to compete in direct primaries (Heard, 1960). Elected legislative bodies in all political systems are skewed more or less heavily toward the top of the socioeconomic system compared with the adult population at large. In the United States the proportion of working-class or dependent white-collar persons elected to Congress is markedly lower than in any European political system. This can be attributed both to the absence of political socialism and to the peculiarities of major-party nomination processes (Matthews, 1954; Matthews, 1960).

The American nomination structure can be described as a pluralist mixture of the party convention, surviving from the nineteenth-century, and the direct primary, which is now the mode of nomination in most but not all states. The nomination of the presidential candidate is effected through a party convention that meets every four years. Before nominating a candidate this convention also drafts a party platform; the proposals therein are by no means necessarily translated into policy if the party wins (Pomper, 1968).

The first of these conventions was that of the Anti-Masonic party in 1831; the first major-party convention was that held by the Jacksonian Democrats in 1832. While there have been significant changes in some aspects of convention rules, and particularly in behavioral norms and modes of delegate selection, they remain today quite visibly the lineal descendants of these first organized in the 1830s. By a set of apportionment formulas that have varied from party to party and across time, each state is entitled to cast a fixed number of votes for nominees at the convention. It has been universally the practice until the 1960s that state party organizations were left entirely free by the national party authorities to elaborate their procedures for choosing delegates to the convention. These state organizations, however, tend to be closely governed in their organization and procedures by detailed laws enacted by the state legislatures, a legal control over party that is also a peculiarly American phenomenon.

The most significant formal changes in American presidential conventions have been the abolition in the Democratic convention of the rule requiring a two-thirds vote for nomination in 1936, which eliminated a Southern veto over convention choice, and the establishment in many states of presidential primaries and popular-vote selection of delegates, largely in the period 1910-1920. The presidential primaries exist in a constantly fluctuating minority of the states, and vary widely even there in binding delegate choice on the first and succeeding ballots. In most of the states there are no presidential primaries; delegate selection—even where nominally a matter of popular vote—is effectively in the hands of the currently dominant group in the state party organization. But the appearance of the presidential primary has greatly affected (and complicated) the procedure by which presidential candidates are nominated. In 1960, for example, it seems clear that John Kennedy secured the nomination because he was able to demonstrate a consistent pattern of victory in presidential primaries. Similarly, it may be the case that in 1968 President Johnson's near loss to Senator McCarthy in New Hampshire's primary influenced his decision to retire. The 1968 Democratic case makes clear, however, that insurgent victories in presidential primaries are not sufficient to wrest control of presidential nominations from old-guard state organizations and major affiliated interest groups such as organized labor, when these latter believe their vital interests to be at stake. The fact that about 80% of the presidential-primary vote was cast either for Kennedy or McCarthy insurgent slates was not sufficient to prevent the nomination of Vice President Humphrey and the rejection by the convention of the peace plank, though the uproar at Chicago may have decisively contributed to Richard Nixon's vcitory in November. The presidential nominating process is extremely complex. As the importance of mass media to political campaigning grows, it is also becoming enormously costly to candidates (Alexander, 1966). This process cannot be further discussed here. For a detailed and definitive exposition through 1956 see David et al., 1960, and Bain, 1960.

At the state level the most significant historical change in party nomination processes occurred in the period 1903-1920, when the direct primary was adopted in the large majority of states. This uniquely American nominating device involves a choice of major-party nominees by all persons claiming adherence to the party in question. It emerged for a number of reasons, not least of which was a turn-of-the-century reaction against corruption and manipulation of the older state nominating convention system (Ostrogorski, 1902, vol II). But a major reason for its appearance seems to have been the collapse of two-party competition, in the South and elsewhere, which followed the critical realignment of the 1890s. This collapse effectively deprived the general election of decisive significance in a very large part of the country, and thus created widespread popular demand for a substitute where it mattered, at the level of choosing the nominees of the locally dominant party (Key, 1956, pp. 87-96). From the turn of the century until the 1960s the Democratic nomination was tantamount to election in the Southern states. The Republican nomination was similarly decisive between 1896 and 1932 in such major northern states as California, Michigan, Pennsylvania, and Wisconsin.

The electoral effects of the direct primary have been discussed widely in the American literature, with the seminal work being done by the late V. O. Key, Jr. (Key, 1956, pp. 85-196). They can be generally summarized as follows :

1. The direct primary is quintessentially oriented to ad hoc candidacies of individuals and away from party voting of any kind. This gave Southern politics before about 1960 much of its peculiar flavor, and in a number of states conspicuous control over policy was exercised for extended periods of time by a small politicoeconomic

oligarchy. During the pre-1960 era, the only Southern state to develop rigorous bifactional competition based substantially on class and on durable political opposition was Lousiana (Sindler, 1956; Howard, 1957).

2. Under conditions of imperfect party competition direct primaries evidently work to reinforce one-party dominance in general elections by stripping the minority party of its major resource, the monopoly of opposition. Ambitious and able young men interested in a political career will tend under such circumstances to declare themselves members of the hegemonic party and seek success through its primary elections. For this and other reasons a tendency exists for the minority major party to undergo secular decline both in the quality of its leadership and in the size of its mass following in general elections. The same considerations apply, *mutatis mutandis*, to minor or third parties, and with even greater force.

3. Participation in direct primaries under conditions of substantial two-party competition in general elections draws a fraction of the electorate that is both relatively very small and biased toward the hard core of mass party support. In states where ethnocultural antagonisms within a major-party following are exceptionally intense—for example, in Massachusetts—primary elections frequently result in the nomination of a slate of candidates that is skewed sufficiently to deny them wider acceptability to the larger electorate in the general election. This has contributed conspicuously to the extreme fragmentation of the Massachusetts Democratic party, among others. (Key, 1956, pp. 154–163; Levin, 1963; Litt, 1965.) In such cases, and they are quite numerous, direct primaries contribute to a loss of control over central functions by party organizations and thus to a fragmentation of electoral politics, which tends to work particularly to the disadvantage of the Democratic party.

4. The expense of campaigns is greatly increased by this double appeal to a mass electorate. Expense becomes crucially important as a screening device at the primary stage, since the resources of the party are normally not available to any primary candidate. This reinforces the growing tendency for all but the wealthy or their friends to be excluded from serious candidacies for major office (Heard, 1960).

In only a few states has the older convention system of nominating for major office survived, as in Indiana or Connecticut. Such states tend to be among those with the strongest central party organizations. But there is continuing pressure for adoption of the direct primary. New York yielded to this pressure in 1967, and the coherence of the extremely heterogeneous Democratic party coalition has evidently already suffered severe erosion as a result.

To summarize, we can make three broad generalizations about contemporary American major parties. First, the two major parties can very broadly be described as comparatively left liberal (Democrats) and right liberal (Republicans). They continue to dominate the electoral system, particularly by gatekeeping control of nominations for major office. They are organizationally decentralized, with extreme local variations in the strength or cohesiveness of party organization below the national level.

Second, the cleavage bases on which these parties rest are extremely heterogeneous. It is entirely possible, for example, to find cases in which—as in Massachusetts in 1966—one Democratic candidate for statewide office wins 37 percent of the two-party vote, while another in the same election wins 71 percent. On the whole, as class cleavages in the United States have decayed in recent years, the Democratic party has shown significant gains among managerial, technical, and academic strata, particularly in the northeastern states. It remains in the ascendant in most American large cities. Thus in 1968 Humphrey carried nineteen of twenty-one cities with a 1960 population of 500,000 or more, with Nixon winning only Dallas (fourteenth in size) and San Diego (eighteenth in size). Democratic candidates usually enjoy nearly monolithic support among blacks and Spanish-speaking Americans. The Republican party, on the other hand, is enjoying swift secular growth in the ex-Democratic South, especially at the presidential level. It remains ascendant in the suburbs of metropolitan areas outside New England, and may be achieving ascendancy as well in the areas of South and West where 1960-1970 population growth was most rapid. It is clear that the two most problematic coalitional elements in the currently fluid electoral picture are the white working-class and the white Southerner, both of which were key components of the New Deal coalition (Phillips, 1969; Burnham, 1970).

Third, the hegemony of the two major parties over voting behavior is threatened at present along at least two fronts. The first is that represented by the Wallace movement of 1968, a movement that can be subsumed under the comparative label, "radicalism of the middle" (Lipset, 1960, pp. 131-76). But a second possibility cannot be overlooked. Movements against the existing order from the left may well arise during the 1970s, particularly if the Democratic party remains as resistant to change as it was in 1968. Since instability of voting coalitions has characterized the 1960s, it is particularly difficult to describe the coalitional structure of either major party. The possible number of winning coalitions available to politicians has markedly grown, conspicuously in states such as New York; the uncertainty of electoral outcomes has grown *pari passu* with this increase in coalitional volatility. The Democratic party seems to be moving away from its New Dealish class-ethnic base and toward a coalition of what David Apter has called the "technologically competent" and "technologically superfluous" strata at the top and bottom of postindustrial society. The Republican party is moving rather clearly toward a position of defense of a "silent majority" that has many similarities to Apter's "technologically obsolescent" stratum at the center of his paradigm (Apter, 1964, pp. 15-43). A strong element of political regionalism has also become clearly defined at the presidential level during the 1960s, though this is much more difficult to define in legislative and state elections.

D. NORMAL ELECTIONS SINCE WORLD WAR II

This discussion has emphasized the growing disappearance of normal benchmarks in American electoral outcomes. It is possible to speak of "normal elections" in the United States during the period 1940-1950, a period in which a very high stability in the outcome of elections could be measured, except for the heavily Republican deviating election of 1946. To be sure, in 1948 locally important segments of the dominant New Deal coalition were drawn off into the Progressive and States' Rights (Dixiecrat) parties, but this election can righly be viewed on the national level as a maintaining election, the last of its type down through the early 1970s.

Similarly, one may view the two Eisenhower presidential elections of 1952 and 1956 as "deviating" at the presidential level, a tribute to Eisenhower's very considerable crosspartisan appeal. But they were not by any means as conspicuously so below the presidential level, particularly in 1956 when Eisenhower's personal landslide proved insufficient to produce a Republican majority in either house of Congress. In turn, the 1960 election was clearly influenced by religious polarizations that prompted normally Democratic Protestant voters to vote Republican and normally Republican Catholics to vote Democratic. Even so, the similarities between 1960 voting patterns and earlier variants were great enough to justify its characterization by the Survey Research Center team as a "reinstating election" (Campbell et al., 1966, pp. 78-95).

There was one major secular trend, however, that sharply differentiated the election sequence beginning in 1952 from earlier contests; the emergence of durable presidential Republicanism in the Southern states, and the consequent restoration there of two-party competition in presidential elections. But in an important sense this regional realignment tended merely to reinforce the national class polarization by extending it to a region where it had hitherto been largely absent. Much of Eisenhower's Southern support came from middle- and upper-class elements in the South's metropolitan areas, as well as from transplanted northern middle-class Republicans in rapidly growing states such as Florida (Strong, 1960).

The first profound rupture of these coalitional patterns occurred as a consequence of Barry Goldwater's capture of the Republican presidential nomination in 1964 (Kessel, 1968). The outcome of the general election in November, 1964, revealed voter swings without precedent in twentieth-century American electoral history. The Republicans lost—and by landslide margins—states such as Vermont, which had remained faithful to the party since its first presidential campaign in 1856; conversely, the Republicans captured—also by landslide majorities—five Deep South states that had not supported a Republican candidate since the end of Reconstruction in 1877. Black voters had hitherto normally given about three-quarters of their votes to Democratic candidates; in 1964 the black vote rose to 97% Democratic, a level of extraordinary monolithic support that has tended to endure. In the Northeast, where class polarization between the parties before 1964 had tended to be about as intense as in the rest of the country, this polarization nearly vanished in the Goldwater election, the product of a huge surge of middle-class and native-stock Protestant voters toward the Democrats not equaled by pro-Democratic movement among working-class and Catholic white voters (Burnham, 1968). The results of the 1968 election indicate that part of this 1964 realignment in the Northeast also seems in the process of becoming durable.

Since 1964 the American party system has evidently moved loose from its moorings to a considerable extent. As a consequence it can be said that American elections in the past decade have tended to lose whatever characteristics of normality they may have once possessed, a phenomenon that makes more difficult than ever the statement of generalizations concerning the determinants of American voting behavior in the present period. There is as yet no immediately visible prospect that the 1972 elections will be normal, or what the defining characteristics of normality will be when the present era of transition comes to an end. It is enough to make a comparative note of considerable importance: if one measures gross transitions in partisan percentages and swing between a set of contiguous pairs of elections, the United States has much the highest shifts for either major party—and consequently much the highest level of mean partisan swing—of any Western nation since World War II. It is approached in this respect only by Canada (Table 10). Viewed longitudinally by employing "moving averages" of five sets of transitions across time, we find that the current mean magnitudes of partisan shifts and swings have been exceeded in our electoral history only during the highly volatile era that commenced with the deviating election of 1916 and ended with the advent of the New Deal in 1932 (Table 11).

III. Data for Analysis

SAMPLE SURVEYS

Modern, scientific sample surveys of voting behavior were initially developed in the United States, arising out of the experiences and refinements of techniques employed in market research sampling of consumer preferences. Stimulus was undoubtedly increased by the conspicuous failure of a major nonrandom poll, that of the *Literary Digest*, to predict the outcome of the class-polarized 1936 election successfully. The most important of the polling organizations in the Gallup (American Institute of Public Opinion) poll, which began operations in 1935. More refined and intensive panel studies emerged first at the local level: the 1940 survey of Erie county, Ohio (Lazarsfeld et al., 1944), and the 1948 survey of Elmira, New York (Berelson et al., 1954). Since 1948 the Survey Research Center at the University of Michigan has become preeminent in the construction and execution of highly refined and complex national surveys of public opinion and voting behavior.

The first complete, essentially contemporary national survey was carried out by the S.R.C. in 1952 (Campbell et al, 1954). The series has continued since then, with at much more comprehensive set of interview protocols for presidential than for off year election years (Campbell et al., 1960; Campbell et al., 1966). Students of American voting behavior are thus particularly fortunate in having an extended series of first-rate survey data at their disposal. This now provides opportunities for secondary

TABLE 10 :   **Variations in Partisan Percentages of the Total Vote and in Major-Party Swing: The United States and Selected Western Nations, 1945-1969**

Country and Party	Period	Mean % of Total	S. D.	Partisan Shifts between Elections	
				Mean	S. D.
United States	1948-1968				
Democratic		48.3	7.06	9.0	6.09
Republican		48.2	7.23	7.2	3.64
Partisan Swing				8.1	3.64
Canada	1945-1968				
Liberal		42.0	5.17	4.9	2.92
Prog. Conservative		34.9	7.85	5.9	6.14
Partisan Swing				6.3	3.90
Australia	1946-1966				
Australian Labour		46.1	3.24	3.5	1.49
Liberal-Country		47.0	2.87	3.0	2.15
Partisan Swing				3.1	1.81
New Zealand	1946-1966				
Labour		45.7	3.16	2.7	1.75
National		47.6	3.76	3.3	3.18
Partisan Swing				2.4	1.61
United Kingdom	1945-1966				
Labour		46.4	1.99	2.3	1.14
Conservative		45.1	3.93	3.0	2.11
Partisan Swing				2.2	0.88
Austria	1949-1966				
SPÖ		42.5	2.12	2.7	2.72
ÖVP		44.9	2.34	3.2	1.75
Partisan Swing				2.6	1.71
Germany (West)	1953-1969				
SPD		35.8	5.59	3.3	1.98
CDU/CSU		46.8	1.87	3.5	0.64
Partisan Swing				2.1	1.88
France (5th Rep.)	1958-1968				
UNR (Gaullist)		35.5	10.79	8.5	6.70
Ireland	1948-1965				
Fianna Fàil		45.2	2.57	4.1	0.77
Italy	1946-1968				
DC		40.6	4.52	5.7	5.10
Norway	1945-1965				
Labor		45.3	2.69	2.5	1.59
Sweden	1948-1968				
Social Democrat		46.9	1.74	1.3	0.98

Source: Derek W. Urwin ed., *Elections in Western Nations, 1945-1968* (Glasgow: University of Strathclyde, Occasional Papers Nos. 4/5, n.d.).

A complete reporting of major party swings and partisan swing is given for two-party systems, here defined as those in which the two leading parties won a mean of 75 percent or more of the total vote in the 1945-1968 period. "Hegemonic" parties in multiparty systems are also presented alone. Except for the Gaullist UNR in France—included here for its suggestiveness and its present hegemonic position in French electoral politics—these are parties with means of at least 40 percent or more of the total vote during the 1945-1968 period.

analysis of the data in any one survey as well as longitudinally. Such secondary analyses now abound in the literature; they are now commonly found in textbooks for undergraduates as well as in monographs and articles of all kinds (See, e.g., Alford, 1963; Flanigan, 1968; Greenstein, 1963; Key, 1961; Pomper, 1968).

TABLE 11: **Longitudinal Aspects of Variability in Partisanship and Partisan Swing in American Presidential Elections, 1876-1968**

Election Transition Period	Democratic Shift (*Mean*)	Republican Shift (*Mean*)	Partisan Swing (*Mean*)
1876/80-1892/96	1.3	2.8	1.4
1880/84-1896/1900	1.0	2.9	1.4
1884/88-1900/04	2.5	3.7	2.5
1888/92-1904/08	3.6	4.6	3.4
1892/96-1908/12	3.3	3.8	3.2
1896/1900-1912/16	4.7	3.1	3.6
1900/04-1916/20	5.6	5.8	6.2
1904/08-1920/24	6.9	6.2	5.2
1908/12-1924/28	8.2	6.0	4.9
1912/16-1928/32	11.3	9.6	8.4
1916/20-1932/36	10.5	9.3	8.0
1920/24-1936/40	8.7	8.1	6.6
1924/28-1940/44	7.9	7.1	6.6
1928/32-1944/48	6.3	6.4	6.2
1932/36-1948/52	3.9	4.7	4.1
1936/40-1952/56	3.8	4.5	4.0
1940/44-1956/60	4.1	4.4	4.1
1944/48-1960/64	6.1	6.4	6.1
1948/52-1964/68	9.0	7.2	8.1

Based throughout on the means across time for five transitional sequences.

B. ECOLOGICAL AND SYSTEMIC ANALYSIS

Survey analyses of electoral behavior have more completely dominated the mainstream of voting research in the United States than in any other country. There are a number of reasons for this development. One such reason has been the absence until very recently of any effective central collection of machine-readable aggregate election data and cognate census materials. This barrier is in the process of being overcome through the development of archives at the Inter-University Consortium for Political Research. A second factor is associated with the possibly greater suitability of survey research as a tool for the study of voting in densely populated conurbations. A third, which has its own historical and cultural roots, has been the overwhelming preoccupation with analysis at the individual level by American researchers, to the near exclusion of analysis at the system level. This is in all probability a reflection in itself of the normal lack of close relationship between electoral politics and questions of socioeconomic or state power in the United States. A final contribution to the ascendancy of survey over aggregate analysis may well have been an academic overreaction to the dangers of the ecological fallacy in social research (Robinson, 1950).

Thus ecological analysis in the United States has, with few if notable exceptions, been conducted on the periphery of voting-behavior research. It is also fair to say that to this day such studies have tended to remain less methodologically sophisticated than European, and notably Scandinavian, research efforts (Katz and Valen, 1964; Rokkan and Valen, 1964; Rokkan, 1966). In particular, no national ecological study has yet been performed at the county level, in part at least because of the formidable technical complexities of data collection and processing. A number of regional studies involving ecological analysis have been performed for the South (Key, 1949), the border states (Fenton, 1957), New England (Lockard, 1959), and the Midwest (Fenton, 1966). A number of state studies involving ecological analysis have also been carried out (Wisconsin: Epstein, 1958; Ohio: Flinn, 1962; Florida: Price, 1955; Louisiana: Sindler, 1956, Howard, 1957, Havard et al., 1963; Pennsylvania: Burnham and Sprague, 1970). Of these studies the one that can perhaps lay most claim to methodological sophistication in the analysis of ecological data is that of Pennsylvania, because of its use of parallel, theoretically grounded multivariate models. Nevertheless, the Louisiana studies have proved exceptionally illuminating because the state's social structure and the voting behavior of its inhabitants lend themselves exceptionally well to ecological analysis. Certain national studies have also been performed in recent years, with states as the primary unit of analysis. These have cast genuine light on the structure of American politics, including electoral politics, but most of them have emphasized the study of differentials in state policy outputs, especially social-welfare outputs more than the study of voting behavior as such (Dawson and Robinson, 1965; Dawson, 1967; Dye, 1966).

At the same time a word should be said about an emergent range of analysis based on aggregates but not immediately oriented to ecological correlates of voting. This may be said to be the study of aggregate data as system indicators, of a kind no-dissimilar to some of the indicators set forth in the pioneering *World Handbook of Political and Social Indicators* (Russett et al., 1964). The primary concern of this mode of analysis is the identification of common and discrete properties, continuities and changes in whole systems of electoral politics. This may then form the basis for fruitful comparative statements and theoretical generalizations. Such work, of course, bypasses methodological and conceptual problems associated with possible ecological fallacies, since no individual-level statements arise from it. But it also calls with increasing urgency for the construction of adequate bridges between macro- and micro-levels of analysis. Recent examples of explicitly comparative work in this area include Rose and Urwin (1969, 1970) and—for the United States alone but with clear comparative implications—Burnham (1970).

It seems virtually certain that greater emphasis will be placed on aggregate analysis in the future study of American voting behavior than has been the case thus far. There are several reasons for this. First, "quantitative revolution" that developed among American political historians during the 1960s, has already produced illuminating, if on the whole still methodologically primitive, studies of the American past (e.g., Holt, 1969; Kleppner, 1970; Rogin, 1967). Second, in an era of crisis affecting the political system as a whole system-level analysis becomes more salient as a scholarly concern than was once the case, and ecological analysis becomes a major tool of research in such analysis (Rogin, 1967; Key, 1955; Burnham, 1970). Third, for many system-level questions, most notably those involving critical-realignment sequences and their ecological correlates, survey research has been of dubious utility. This has been so because of methodological difficulties—for example, the problem of response distortion associated with the interview situation itself (Clausen, 1969), and the difficulty that arises when heavy regional and urban-rural polarizations suddenly appear, as in 1964 (Burnham, 1968). Moreover, and most importantly, its time-span is too short for the exploration of certain long-term processes. In this regard two scholarly convergences seem to be particularly likely to emerge during the 1970s: a convergence between survey and aggregate analysis of the sort already pioneered in Norway, and a convergence between political scientists and quantitatively oriented political historians with complementary longitudinal research interests.

C. NONVOTING AND ITS MEASUREMENT

The problem of nonparticipation is particularly salient for the study of American electoral politics. The United States has consistently had the highest abstention rate to be found in any Western political system during the past fifty years. During the period beginning about 1890 and ending shortly after 1960 nonvoting was of no official concern for all intents and purposes; it is dealt with only rarely in the scholarly literature of the time. In recent years the Survey Research Center has dealt systematically with the correlates of nonvoting at the individual level (Campbell et al., 1954; Campbell et al., 1960, pp. 89–115). Since 1964 the Census Bureau has also conducted very large surveys of nonvoting as part of its *Current Population Reports* series (Census Bureau, 1969).

The 1960 SRC study concentrates heavily on the intensity of individual preference, sense of efficacy (cf. Table 1), and involvement, but says very little about the class correlates of turnout. The evidence that nonvoting in the United States is heavily concentrated among lower-status people is, however, overwhelming. Both the SRC 1964 election surveys and the 1968 Census Bureau survey reveal this (Table 12), as does aggregate data for cities at the precinct level. Moreover, American surveys—whether SRC or Census—report far higher rates of participation among their respondents than the actual figure that can be closely estimated from aggregate data. Thus the 1964 survey revealed a 79 percent turnout, compared with 62 percent based on voting returns, an overreporting of 17 percent that may be a function of stimulus among penelists arising from the interview situation itself (Clausen, 1969). The much more broadly based Census Bureau survey of 1968 indicated a turnout rate about 10 percent higher than the actual level of adult-citizen participation. In view of the recently analyzed problems associated with substantial underenumeration of the poor— especially the black poor—in both censuses and surveys, it is reasonable to suppose that the actual class differential in voting participation is even more extreme than the data of Table 12 would indicate (Heer, 1967).

Partly because of the emergence of the civil-rights movement and the consequent pressure for federal action in the voting-rights field, nonparticipation has recently been subjected to much more extensive analysis. Recent studies have demonstrated that American electoral participation declined heavily throughout the country after 1900 (Burnham, 1965), that personal-registration barriers very probably have much to do with that historical change and are major contributors to the depression of turnout today (Kelley et al., 1967), and that the post-1900 decline was the result of both rules-of-game and behavioral changes, probably with a heavy class skew (Burnham, 1970, ch. 4). In a political system that has no Socialist party or political labor movement, and in which much of the working-class shares bourgeois political and cultural values, one would anticipate finding a profound lack of political interest among lower social strata that closely parallels the limited crystallization of the social infrastructure. Analysis of the 1968 Census survey reveals that of those citizens not registered to vote, 61.5 percent of those with a grade-school education gave "lack of interest" as the reason for failure to register. This compares with 61.5 percent of high-school dropouts, 59.0 percent of high-school graduates, 46.8 percent of those with some college education, and only 32.7 percent of those with at least four years of education beyond high school.

TABLE 12 : **Participation in American Elections, 1964-1968**

Category	SRC, 1964	Census, 1968
White-Collar Workers:	(87)	(80)
Professional, technical, etc.	89	83
Managers, proprietors	86	80
Clerical, sales, etc.	87	77
Manual Workers:	(75)	(62)
Skilled (craftsmen, etc.)	83	69
Semi-skilled (operatives, etc.)	74	59
Unskilled (laborers, etc.)	50	55
Service Workers:	69	63
Farmers:	(80)	(70)
Farm Managers, farmers		82
Farm Laborers		51
Total	79	71

In addition to social class, American voting participation is also significantly influenced by sex and by age. When the two variables are examined together for the 1968 election, it appears that (1) women vote about as often as men in the twenty-one to thirty-four age brackets but increasingly fall behind male participation in the age classifications above thirty-five, with an overall participation rate of 70 percent for men and 66 percent for women; and (2) a steep, age-related curvilinear pattern of participation is evident for both sexes: estimated turnout in 1968 was 51 percent for the twenty-one to twenty-four age group, rising to 75 percent for the forty-five to fifty-four age group, declining to 71.5 percent for the sixty-five to seventy-four age group and to 56 percent for those seventy-five years of age and older (Census Bureau, 1969, p. 10). Both age and sex differentials of similar types are encountered in other Western political systems (Tingsten, 1937; Lipset, 1960, pp. 179–219).

In the United States there are also conspicuous differentials in electoral participation along racial and regional lines. In 1968 an estimated 69 percent of the national white population voted, compared with 58 percent for Negroes. Similarly, in the North and West the overall turnout level was 71 percent, compared with 60 percent in the South. The relative differentials in the voting rate by race were somewhat different in the two broad regions: 72 percent for whites and 65 percent for blacks in the North and West, 62 percent for whites and 52 percent for blacks in the South. The differential along racial lines is probably considerably greater than this because of the acute problem of underenumeration and undersurveying of young Negro men, but there seems considerable evidence that this differential is rapidly declining, in part because of the imposition of nondiscriminatory registration and voting controls in parts of the South by the federal government since 1965 (U.S. Commission on Civil Rights, 1968). Indeed, in some cases—such as the Cleveland and Gary mayoral elections of 1967, in which black candidates ran for office and won—black turnout rates have considerably exceeded those for whites. Currently available census surveys suggest that participation rates among middle-class blacks are comparable with those for middle-class whites; it is among working-class blacks—who are relatively a much larger component of that population than are their working-class white counterparts—that the differential is most pronounced.

The regional differential in participation has undergone a particularly sharp decline in the past twenty years; since 1960, moreover, a striking remobilization of Southern electorates, both white and black, has been matched by a moderate decline in participation in non-Southern areas. Thus in 1948 turnout in the ex-Confederate states was only 25 percent, compared with 62 percent elsewhere in the country. By 1968 aggregate estimates indicate a Southern turnout of 52 percent, while non-Southern turnout increased but 3 percent to 65.

The measurement of nonvoting from American aggregate data is complicated by the absence of any universal enrollment system for the eligible adult population. This is a consequence of the personal-registration system commonly found in the United States; analysis are thus required to compute turnout percentages, particularly those before 1960, on the basis of estimates of the total adult citizen population. Consequently, to an indeterminate extent—perhaps between 3 and 5 percent—such bases of estimate include institutional populations and other categories of adults who would also be excluded from voting in Europe or Canada. Even when problems associated with old registers are taken into account in the latter case, American turnout estimates are a shade too broadly inclusive for complete comparability of participation rates. Nevertheless, it has remained the case that the "party of nonvoters" in the United States has usually been larger than the percentage of the potential electorate supporting either major party during the past fifty years: only 1936 and 1964 are exceptions

(Table 7). Moreover, the "party of nonvoters" has always been larger than the active electorate in off-year congressional elections during the same period.

IV. Social Structure and Voting

Detailed exposition of survey findings regarding the contemporary American voter is beyond the scope of this chapter. A number of excellent general studies exist of which *The American Voter* (Campbell et al., 1960) may justly be regarded as a classic. What we shall attempt primarily to do here is to provide some secondary analysis of certain parts of the 1964 SRC study and a limited discussion of certain recent transformations in voting behavior that show up especially clearly far below the national level.

A. SOCIAL CLASS

Social class is one significant determinant of American major-party preference and voting. Social class can, of course, be measured in a variety of ways: income, education, and occupation tend to be heavily intercorrelated in the United States. Moreover, the respondent may also be asked for his subjective evaluation of his class position, as in the Michigan survey studies. Whatever the measurement, since the 1930s the Republican party has tended to be favored by members of the middle- and upper-classes, while the Democratic party has tended to be heavily favored by the working-classes. Even in 1964, an election in which the competition of regional and racial with class polarization was exceptionally intense, the relationship held both in terms of party identification and voting at the national level and was, moreover, virtually monotonic.

While class correlates with both party identification and party voting, there has evidently been a long-term decline in Republican party identification among all strata since the early 1940s. There is some reason to think that the decline in Republican identification has been relatively greatest among the middle-classes, although these still remain bastions of Republican strength at the polls. The 1964 voting array is, of course, associated with one of the two greatest Democratic landslides in our electoral history.

At the same time it seems evident—especially in recent elections, both at the national and state levels—that class correlation with voting is undergoing a massive transformation from the classical New Deal model. This becomes particularly conspicuous at the microscopic precinct level in elections where racial and/or sectional polarizations have become particularly intense. For example, an examination of the movement of white precincts in Baltimore for the 1960-1968 period yields the following generalizations: (1) The pro-Democratic shift between 1960 and 1964 is almost wholly confined in these areas to middle-class precincts, and is positively correlated with a given area's indicators of socioeconomic status, i.e., the more wealthy the area, the

TABLE 13: **Correlates of Class with Partisan Identification and Voting, 1964**

OCCUPATIONAL CATEGORY	PARTISAN IDENTIFICATION*						
	Strong Dem.	Weak Dem.	Ind.	Weak Rep.	Strong Rep.	Dem.	Rep.
Professional-technical	17	23	31	11	17	40	28
Managerial	22	20	28	14	15	42	29
Clerical-Sales	24	25	23	16	11	49	27
Skilled workers	30	25	29	6	10	55	16
Semiskilled workers	30	23	25	13	6	53	19
Service workers	34	31	22	9	2	65	11
Unskilled workers	57	15	17	3	3	72	6
Farmers	30	30	9	15	11	60	26
Total	27	25	22	13	11	52	24

OCCUPATIONAL CATEGORY	REPORTED VOTE, 1964	
	Democratic	Republican
Professional-technical	53	47
Managerial	56	44
Clerical-sales	68	32
Skilled,Semiskilled workers	81	19
Service workers	87	13
Unskilled workers	87	13
Nonmanual	60	40
Manual	80	20
Farmers	60	40
Total	67.5	32.5

Source: Data from 1964 Survey Research Center election study. Courtesy of Inter-University Consortium for Political Research.
*Excludes "apolitical" and other residual categories (about 2 percent).

heavier the swing to Johnson in 1964. (2) The percentage Democratic of the total presidential vote in 1968 was appreciably higher in the upper-class precincts than in the two-party contest of 1960. (3) The steep decline in the Democratic percentage of the total vote between 1964 and 1968 broke two ways. Among middle-to-upper-class white precincts the movement was overwhelmingly toward the Republican candidate, with George Wallace receiving a tiny proportion—uniformly less than 10 percent, sometimes less than 5 percent—of the total vote. The Democratic relative defection, extraordinarily uniform across class lines, was heavily associated with massive support for Wallace in proletarian precincts, and with heavy 1964–1968 defections to the Republicans in middle-to-upper-class areas.

Similar patterns are to be found elsewhere. They include—as in the New York City elections for mayor in 1969 and senator in 1970—a peculiar "curvilinear" alignment structure in which liberal candidates win large majorities in both upper-class and black or Puerto Rican poverty areas, but lose heavily to their opponents in lower-middle-class communities (Burnham, 1970, pp. 146–70). It is characteristic of this

702

Anglo-America

emergent pattern that the highest-status area in New York City and one of the wealthiest areas in the United States, the "silk-stocking" Assembly District 66 (Central Park East), gave 59.2 percent of its 1968 to Humphrey, 38.0 percent to Nixon, and 1.9 percent to Wallace.

The relatively heavy penetration of the white working-class by the Wallace movement appears in national survey data almost as clearly as in precinct-level aggregate data.

TABLE 14:   **Class Correlates of 1968 Voting**

Occupational Category	Humphrey (D)	Nixon (R)	Wallace (AIP)
Professional	36	57	7
Business (managerial)	37	55	9
Clerical-sales	38	50	12
Skilled, Semi-skilled workers	43	43	15
Service workers	33	44	23
Unskilled workers	47	35	19
Nonmanual	37	54	9
Manual	43	40	17

Source: AIPO 771-d, November 7, 1968; Lipset & Raab, 1970, pp. 380–81.

Among other things Table 14 reveals that, nationally, the Alford index of class voting dropped to 11 as between the major parties in 1968, the lowest on record. The siphoning off of normally Democratic working-class votes by the Wallace movement largely accounts for this.

A detailed discussion of this propensity for the American white working-class to support candidates of the extreme Right must lie beyond the scope of this chapter. It is one of the most significant changes of the post-1960 era in American politics that such support has materialized, and it should be noted that disproportionate working-class voting for candidates of the Right is a distinctly unusual phenomenon in the politics of industrialized western nations.

A major factor that conduces to this peculiarity is perhaps the absence of a separate working-class *conscience politique* in the United States, and the parallel failure of socialism or laborism to develop as the characteristic vehicle for working-class political expression. Here, as elsewhere, we may suggest that American electoral politics is a kind of *ceteris paribus* politics. If all other things were equal elsewhere, a politically "unchurched" working-class might as a rule have high abstention rates and be available for capture by a certain kind of mass rightist movement. Such conditions may indeed have been approximated in some European countries during the last half of the nineteenth-century; something like these conditions in Germany formed the context of the epic struggle between Lassalle and Marx. This would by itself form a most fruitful area for comparative study; nor is it the only point at which American electoral politics in the present era seems to resemble European models of the last century more closely than any of the present era. In such a context the suspicion would arise a priori that American working-class behavior under stress conditions would most closely approximate that of the lowest politically unorganized (or "non-confessional") strata in European nations under roughly analogous kinds of stresses, i.e., predominantly the petite bourgeoisie and parts of the peasantry. That large parts of the white American working-class are in fact thoroughly petit bourgeois in outlook has been repeatedly demonstrated in recent research (e.g., Lane, 1962).

The notion that much of this class may thus be a kind of sociological analog to the pre-1933 German lower-middle-classes and their role in politics may seem farfetched or, at the least, operationally relevant only to a remote contingency. At the same time the American system of electoral politics is marked to a surprising degree by lack of "political immunization" among individual voters, i.e., such voters tend not to become insulated from extremist movements by cumulative sociopolitical learning through participation in electoral politics across time (McPhee and Ferguson, 1962, pp. 155-79; Burnham, IPSA, 1970). To be sure, one of the leading properties of American politics has been its failure to develop the kinds of hard political oppositions that have been so commonplace in European politics. This may precisely make it both unnecessary and unfeasible to organize a durable extreme-right *Bewegung* along German lines in order to achieve certain right-wing objectives in American politics. In any event, the results of both the 1968 and 1970 elections make it clear that the traditional class alignment laid down during the New Deal, while weakened, is far from dead.

B. RACE AND ETHNICITY

One may distinguish at least three types of ethnocultural polarizations in the United States today: (1) racial antagonism based on skin color, mostly black vs. white but also including locally salient cleavages involving American Indians and Chicanos (Mexican-Americans); (2) ethnic antagonisms involving conflicts among populations of the" newer immigration" and between them and older immigrants, including white Anglo-Saxons; and (3) religious antagonisms which, in twentieth-century politics, have been structured along Protestant, Catholic, and Jewish cleavage points. In actual fact ethnic and religious antagonisms have tended heavily to overlap, particularly at the level of national politics. Difficulties of classification thus arise: for example, are American Jews a religious or an ethinic group? Fortunately, for purposes of classification it is possible to assert that American Jews are a distinctive ethnocultural group that has in the main behaved quite distinctively in American politics. Religious Jews do not seem to behave very differently in politics than those who do not attend a synagogue or profess Judaism as such, but who continue to have ethnocultural identification with the group (Fuchs, 1956).

Jewish voters constitute one of the most distinctive and left-liberal groups in American politics. The origins of this particular ethnic asymmetry can be traced not only to a certain subcultural congeniality to the New Deal—a very substantial part of the New York Jewish electorate supported Socialist candidates between 1910 and 1922 and LaFollette in 1924, for example—but also to Franklin Roosevelt's status as leader of the anti-Nazi coalition in World War II (Lubell, 1952). Jewish voting behavior has tended thus to be heavily pro-Democratic at all income levels down to the present, unlike the class-stratified pattern that predominates elsewhere in the white electorate. Thus in 1968 identifiable Jewish areas in Baltimore more than half of whose adult male populations were in professional and managerial occupations cast 78.8 percent of their total vote for Humphrey, compared with 30.6 percent in similar areas elsewhere.

While Jewish voting behavior constitutes one of the most striking examples of ethnocultural-group influence in contemporary American politics, other conflicts involving religious and ethnic groups remain of high if generally declining salience. The Protestant-Catholic division was of especially great salience in 1960, as it had been in 1928 (Campbell et al., 1966, pp. 78-124): about 7.5 million out of nearly 69 million voters were affected more or less directly by the "religious issue." Similarly, some sense of ethnic differentials in fairly recent times comes from the 1952 SRC study. Of those voting for major-party candidates that year, Eisenhower won 74 percent among Germans, 71 percent among Scandinavians, 69 percent among those of English and Scottish background, 51 percent among Poles, 44 percent among Italians, and 41 percent among Irish. It is clear that this array also measures a religious dimension: except for the Germans, divided largely between Catholics and Lutherans, the first three groups are overwhelmingly Protestant, while the latter three are overwhelmingly Roman Catholic (Campbell et al., 1954, p. 77). Moreover—a point to be remembered when one attempts to disentangle class as an autonomous political variable—historical patterns of immigration have been such that both ethnicity and religion tend to be strongly correlated with social-class, particularly in the metropolitan areas of the greater Northeast.

The recent literature of American politics from Lubell (1952) through Phillips (1969) is replete with analyses of ethnocultural hostilities as major determinants of coalitional structure and shifts in voting behavior. It is also worth noting that in the local politics of the more industrial states, and particularly in New England, acute rivalry among large ethnic groups of recent (and Catholic) immigrant origin has tended to supplant the older conflicts between Yankee Protestants and immigrants (Lockard, 1959, pp. 196-203). These conflicts—conspicuously those involving Irish and Italian groups—have contributed significantly to the improved fortunes of Republican candidates in such states.

There is some reason for believing, however, that these ethnocultural conflicts that have such a rich tradition in American political history are being eroded away. One chief factor in this erosion has been emergence of intense racial polarizations outside the South. Black voting behavior, where permitted, has normally tended toward the monolithic—overwhelmingly Republican until 1932, increasingly lopsidedly Democratic since the New Deal realignment. But as late as 1960 black support for the Democratic party was often not much greater than that given by the lower strata of the white working-class. Indeed, there was a clear regional polarization in 1956 between Southern and non-Southern blacks. The Goldwater candidacy of 1964, however, produced a heavy pro-Democratic realignment among blacks; since then support for Democrats has normally been nearly universal among that community.

In some cities during the 1960s the size of the black population increased to the point where black candidates ran as Democrats against white Republicans. These cases provide among the most extreme examples of racial polarization that can be found in the data of electoral politics; they rival even the political cleavage in Ireland before 1918, or at least the nonviolent side of Northern Ireland electoral politics today. Thus in Cleveland (1965, 1967, 1969) examination of five class, ethnic, and racial variables at the ward level yields partial correlations of percentage Democratic with percentage nonwhite ranging from $+.95$ to $+.99$. Such contents produce nearly dichotomous results: 80 to 90 percent of working-class whites voting Republican, 95 to 99 percent of the blacks voting Democratic.

Racism and racial polarization have had an immense significance, both latent and overt, for American electoral politics over the last century. The tremendous electoral deviation between the Solid South and the rest of the country, visible as early as 1880 and definitively established by 1904, was solidly rooted in the region's successful effort to expel blacks from the active electorate and to define for them a legal status halfway between that of slavery and full citizenship. This regional thrust toward political separateness, especially concentrated in the Deep South, was the motive force behind the Dixiecrat revolt of 1948, the massive 1964 shift toward Goldwater's Republicanism at the region's core, and above all the Wallace movement of 1968. The South is very far from monolithic, of course, and there is excellent reason to support that the effects of the region's recent urbanization will include the development of "moderate" political leadership styles of a blandness increasingly similar to those found in other parts of the country. But the effects of this regional political asymmetry on the course of national politics during this century have been profoundly conservative. They still are, and are likely to remain so for some time to come, so long as the Democratic party enjoys a nominal ascendancy in Congress and the seniority system continues to determine congressional chairmanships.

The massive inflow of blacks from the rural South to the central cities of the nation's largest metropolitan areas has served to multiply the points of racial friction and polarization of throughout the country. This racial conflict in the urban setting is patently most acute at the point where blacks and lower-class whites who cannot readily flee to the suburbs are in closest contact with each other. Two results of this unplanned demographic transformation, as we have suggested, have been the development of a Wallaceite and "hard-hat" movement among working-class whites and a parallel coalitional structure that, at the local level, pits the bottom (mostly black) and top (well-to-do white liberals and moderates) against the middle, immobile, and economically vulnerable working-class and white-collar whites.

It is quite probable that a crucial reason for the original failure of a separate working-class politics to develop in the United States lies in the close intercorrelation between class and ethnoracial structure. In the most heavily industrialized parts of the country before 1932 new-immigrant whites and blacks were both heavily concentrated in the working-class, while the middle and especially the propertied classes were heavily native-stock Protestant in social origin. Indeed, one is tempted to speculate that the salience of Roman Catholicism to immigrant-group social identity contributed not a little to the failure of working-class parties to develop effectively in the United States. Today ethnoracial cleavages within working-class populations remain, but they have tended to undergo radical simplication along black-white lines. The antagonism thus engendered is profound; it is also a prime breeder of conservative, if not of radical-right, politics.

C. RELIGIOUS PATTERNS

Mass politics in nineteenth-century America was heavily polarized from the beginning by social cleavages based on divergent religious perspectives and church membership (Benson, 1961, pp. 165-207; Kleppner, 1970, pp. 35-91). The secularization of society that has accompanied the urban-industrial transformation has not led to explicit de-Christianization or to virtual disappearance of churchgoing in the United States, as it has tended to do in Scandinavia. But it has neverthless led to a progressive decay in explicit intergroup religious conflict in electoral politics, even along the primordial Protestant-Catholic fault line (Campbell et al., 1966, pp. 78-124). Such cleavages, as Converse has shown, are capable of sudden, unexpected reactivation, as in 1960. But such data tend on the whole to support the view that religious cleavages in contemporary American electoral politics are like many others that involve discrete groups. They tend to be especially salient only when the group feels specifically attacked by others, or when a symbolic office of the highest importance—the Presidency, for example—is being contested by one of the group's members but has not yet been won. The long-term decay in Catholic influence that Converse pinpoints is probably expressive of a true longitudinal trend toward disappearance. The emergence of racial polarization involving Catholics—but as members of economically insecure strata rather than as Catholics—reinforces the suspicion that the old Catholic-Protestant tension that reached its peak in the 1920s is undergoing secular decline.

The 1964 survey does reveal some significant differences along religious lines within Protestant denominations, particularly by comparison with the recalled 1960 vote by those interviewed. Persons belonging to denominations founded in the Reformation era tend systematically to have voted more Republican both in 1960 and 1964 (59 percent and 47 percent, respectively) than any other religious group; the pro-Democratic swing from the recalled 1960 vote to 1964 was also larger among members of such denominations than among any others of significant size (+12 percent Democratic compared with — 5 percent for Catholics). But it is a well-known fact of American social life that membership in such denomination as the Presbyterian, Episcopalian, and Congregationalist churches tends to be strongly correlated with superior socioeconomic status. The relative Republicanism of such groups in this sample tends to confirm this, as does the exceptional pro-Democratic movement of 1960-1964. These two characteristics are commonly found in geographical areas with large concentrations of *both* native-stock elements of New England origin and among upper-status areas as well, particularly in the Northeastern states. One is inclined to think, therefore, that regional, subcultural, and social-status factors explain more of this pattern than does religious preference per se. This is particularly suggested by the fact that in 1964 there was no statistically significant difference in the level of Democratic support by frequency of church attendance: the range is between 66 and 59 percent Democratic, with no progression along lines of frequency of attendance.

D. URBAN-SUBURBAN-RURAL RESIDENCE

1. RURAL POLITICAL BEHAVIOR

In the post-World War II period agriculture has occupied a small and rapidly diminishing part of the labor force. The United States now shares with Great Britain the distinction of having the smallest rural-farm population component of any Western nation. Thus it will no doubt be said by future historians that 1948 was the last election in which partisan shifts in the "farm vote" contributed significantly to the general outcome. At the same time a very large portion of the American population, especially in the South, is still of recent rural origin. A significant proportion—not less than one-quarter—continues to live in nonurban areas.

During this century the relative volatility of the farm vote has been very high, particularly under conditions of economic stress (Campbell et al., 1960, pp. 402-40). This volatility is largely the result of the acute vulnerability of cash-crop producers to adverse changes in market conditions. During 1870-1930 the period of transition to mature industrial capitalism, agrarian insurgent movements formed a significant part of American electoral politics. At least two of them—the Populists of 1890-1896 and the LaFollette Progressives of 1924—were clear precursors of subsequent national critical realignments. Within the American political spectrum all of these movements could be defined a falling at the left-liberal end. Moreover, support by both Southern and Midwestern-Western agrarians for the New Deal was extremely massive in both 1932 and 1936.

In recent years the farm vote has become more conservative or rightist than the country as a whole, and its electoral response has become sharply differentiated along sectional lines. Following the Republican National Committee's selection of 762 counties whose populations were at least one-third rural farm and extending the series for the 1960-1968 period, it can be noted first that while 24.6 percent of the nation's counties are included in this grouping, only 4.3 percent of the total 1968 vote was cast in these counties (RNC, 1969, pp. 223-27).

TABLE 15: **Behavior of 762 Most Rural Farm Counties,
1960-1968, by Region**

	SOUTH			NON-SOUTH		
Year	Dem.	Rep.	Other incl. Wallace	Dem.	Rep.	Other incl. Wallace
1960	53.0	39.5	7.5	42.9	57.1	
1964	46.9	53.1		56.2	43.8	
1968	29.0	27.1	43.9	36.1	55.2	8.6

Using this aggregate array as a benchmark, the recent political behavior of heavily rural areas in the United States can be summarized as follows: The first and most conspicuous point is the intense sectionalism displayed both by the contrary 1960-1964 electoral movement in the two areas and most especially by the relative difference in Wallace's 1968 showing. Second, both areas are markedly less liberal than the nation as whole throughout this period, if voting for Democratic candidates is used as a standard. This represents a major inversion of historical experience involving rural areas and is, of course, most conspicuous in the Southern rural-farm counties. Third, a pattern of regional differentiation in the 1964-1968 Democratic collapse emerges that is strikingly similar to that already identified within the urban white class structure: the non-Southern farm areas, predominantly old-stock and traditionally Republican, returned to a traditionally large Republican majority in 1968, while the Southern areas—until 1952 overwhelmingly Democratic—reveal a massive break to Wallace. Indeed, in the latter instance, the break clearly involves Wallace's capture not only of 1960 and 1964 Democratic voters, but of Nixon and Goldwater voters as well. There is reason to suppose that what little is left of the farm vote has become rightist in its voting behavior relative to the rest of the country in response to the abnormally intense cultural or way-of-life polarizations found in contemporary American electoral politics.

One further aspect of rural-urban cleavage should be noted. In the South the transition to industrialization and urbanization occurred later than elsewhere; it is very largely a post-1945 phenomenon. A very large share of its population continues to reside in small towns and rural jurisdictions, even though most Southerners now derive their income from nonagricultural occupations. If one examines the Wallace vote within the region, it becomes crystal clear that—controlling for the subregional dichotomy between "Upper South" and "Deep South"—the more rural a given jurisdiction is, the larger the Wallace share of the total vote except in "black belt" counties of heavy Negro population. Conversely, the more urbanized the area, the lower Wallace's relative share of the vote. For the one-half of Wallace's total vote that was cast in the ex-Confederacy, it is evident that rurality and race were the two most significant determinants (Table 16). Indeed, in the case of Louisiana a two-variable multiple correlation of the Wallace vote with percentage urban and percentage Negro registrants in 1967 by parish yields a partial r of -.575 with the first variable and -.454 with the second, with an R^2 of .604 for the two predictors. Thus in this state the urban-rural variable was, if anything, more important even than the racial variable in estimating the proportion of the vote cast for Wallace. This tendency of a rural *Landvolk* to develop monolithic surges toward extremist movements has been well documented in the case of differentials in the Nazi vote in Germany during the 1928-1933 period (Heberle, 1963). The behavior patterns of rural Southern whites in the past two presidential elections bear some similarity to this earlier development.

TABLE 16: **The Structure of Wallace Support in the South, 1968**

Area:	%D	%R	% Wallace
*Deep South:**			
Counties 33 percent and over rural-farm	22.0	17.3	60.7
Other nonmetropolitan	23.2	20.0	56.8
Metropolitan areas, less than 300,000	26.5	31.3	42.2
Metropolitan areas, 300,000 and over	32.7	28.9	38.4
*Upper South:***			
Counties 33 percent and over rural-farm	29.5	34.5	36.0
Other nonmentropolitan	30.5	37.9	31.6
Metropolitan areas, less than 300,000	32.3	43.8	23.9
Metropolitan areas, 300,000 and over	38.8	40.3	20.9
Deep South Total:	25.3	24.0	50.8
Upper South Total:	33.6	39.6	26.7
Non-South Total:	45.9	45.8	8.3
United States Total:	42.9	43.6	13.6

*Deep South: Alabama, Georgia, Louisiana, Mississippi, South Carolina.
**Upper South: Arkansas, Florida, North Carolina, Tennessee, Texas, Virginia.

2. SUBURBS AND CITIES

Of far greater and ever-increasing relative weight in American electoral politics is the central city-suburban cleavage within the major metropolitan areas: 41 percent of the total national vote was cast in such areas in 1968. In these thirty-five metropolitan areas with populations greater than 835,000, Democratic candidates for the presidency won pluralities from 1960 through 1968. In terms of only the two-party vote, there was a Republican suburban gain from 52.7 percent in 1960 to 53.7 percent in 1968, a larger Republican loss in the cities (from 41.1 percent in 1960 to 37.7 percent in 1968), and very little net change for the metropolitan areas as a whole (46.5 percent Republi, can in 1960, 46.9 percent Republican of the two-party vote in 1968).

Such gross figures cover up at least as much as they reveal. The accelerating white flight to the suburbs resulted in these areas casting more votes than their central cities for the first time in 1968. The net Republican decline in the central cities accurately reflects that they are both poorer and blacker in 1970 than they were in 1960. Moreover, the Republican suburban plurality, while durable except for the special case of 1964, is not conspicuously large. The vast movement into the suburbs, one of the chief changes in American social structure of the past twenty years, has involved whites of all except perhaps the poorest classes and of all ethnic backgrounds. Indeed, since the mid-1960s it has also increasingly involved blacks as well. As a consequence suburban voting behavior rather faithfully reflects metropolitan voting behavior as a whole, for the suburbs themselves are becoming increasingly socially heterogeneous. Thus analysis at a minute level will reveal that for suburbs as for cities voting behavior is still very largely a function of social status, ethnicity, and race. In the suburbs as in the cities Wallace's greatest strength in 1968 was to be found in areas with large concentrations of white blue-collar workers; conversely, his lowest share of the white vote was located in solidly upper-class areas.

Suburban-urban polarization tends to be particularly acute when local referenda involving proposals for consolidation of local governments or services are on the ballot. The administrative structure of most American metropolitan areas involve a fairly large and unified central-city territory on one side and a welter of suburban *Kleinstadten* on the other; each of the latter tends jealously to guard its autonomy against all comers, from metropolitan-government advocates to its own neighbors. Thus in 1960 the range in the St. Louis metropolitan area lay between St. Louis City (750,026) and the tiny village of Champ in St. Louis county, with a population of fifty. Such fragmentation of local suburban governments corresponds to the perceived interests of their inhabitants, who seek above all to enjoy the amenities of metropolitan life while walling out its accompanying social pathologies.

A form of metropolitan sectionalism has emerged from all this since the end of World War II, and it is growing as population transfers within the metropolitan areas accelerate. American suburbs as a whole tend in all major metropolitan areas to be much more Republican than the center cities, and this is determined by the concentration there of white middle-class populations. Correspondingly, secular trends toward increasing Democratic strength in the central cities are largely the product of middle-class flight from them and the resultant and growing concentration of racial minorities and the very poor within their limits. As these population transfers continue, polarization seems certain to increase along these geographical boundaries both in intensity and in national electoral importance.

It should also be noted, however, that other variants of suburban voting behavior exist. Usually it is the case that there is a strong correlation between class stratification among suburban communities and their voting behavior, paralleling and reflecting the continuing importance of class politics in America since the New Deal (Burnham, 1970, pp. 145-52). Secondly, old-fashioned political sectionalism or regionalism is very much in evidence in presidential elections of the 1960s. To take two relatively extreme cases: the suburbs of Boston in 1968 cast 63.3 percent of their vote for Humphrey and only 33.6 percent for Nixon, while the suburban areas of Southern California cast 38.1 percent for Humphrey and 54.8 percent for Nixon (RNC, 1969, pp. 197, 200). Nor is this difference simply the result of demographic differences between the two areas. The pro-Democratic presidential realignment from 1960 through 1968 has been exceptionally large in upper-income, mostly native-stock suburbs in the Northeast, reflecting the broader pattern of regionalism that surfaced in the 1964 election.

E. POLITICAL REGIONALISM IN THE UNITED STATES

So immensely salient are regional polarities in American electoral behavior that it is virtually impossible not to mention them, even when the primary focus of discussion has been placed on some other determinant of voting. In the party-system era of 1896-1932 sectional polarization dominated. A solid Democratic South faced a Northeast that was nearly as solidly Republican, particularly in presidential elections. Nationwide class cleavages were virtually nonexistent. The policy structure, as one might anticipate, was overwhelmingly conservative in both one-party areas and at the center. This sectionalism was destroyed after 1932 in the Northern and Western states by the effects of a critical realignment polarized largely along class and ethnic lines. But in the South one-party Democratic hegemony endured virtually unchanged at the presidential level until 1952 and at the state level until the mid-1960s. Examination of standard deviations of presidential percentage by state for the period 1896–1968 reveals that the highest peaks of sectionalism were reached in 1904 and 1896. From 1932 to 1960 there was a downward trend in standard deviations, with an acceleration of the trend between 1944 and 1948 and again between 1956 and 1960. The latter election must qualify as the least sectionally polarized at least since the demise of the Whig party in 1854. It seemed reasonable to many observers in the early 1960s that

TABLE 17: **Standard Deviations of Republican Presidential Percentages by State, 1876-1968**

Year	Standard Deviation	Year	Standard Deviation
1876	8.9	1928	13.5
1880	9.7	1932	14.0
1884	8.3	1936	12.6
1888	10.7	1940	13.4
1892	12.8	1944	12.3
1896	17.5	1948	9.8
1900	14.0	1952	8.5
1904	18.8	1956	8.3
1908	14.9	1960	5.8
1912*	14.8	1964	10.3
1916	13.4	1968 – Dem.	9.6
1920	16.1	1968 – Rep.	9.9
1924	16.0	1968 – Wallace	15.0

Source for 1896–1964 (except 1912): Sorauf, 1968, p. 49. Standard deviations are based on the Republican percentage of the total vote, except in 1912 (where the combined Republican-Progressive total was used) and in 1968 (in which the standard deviations are included for all three parties).

* Based on combined Republican-Progressive percentage of total vote by state.

the nationalisation of American electoral politics, steadily progressing during the New Deal and post-New Deal eras, was now reaching its culmination.

This vision of a nationalized politics has been shattered by the post-1960 disruption of voting coalitions. The sectional skewing of the Wallace vote in 1968, fully comparable to the major-party standard deviations of the pre-1928 era, speaks for itself. But prior to the Wallace revolution of 1968 stands the Goldwater revolution of 1964. Goldwater's candidacy marked the first time in American history that a major-party presidential nomination was captured by an ideological rightist. In addition to producing the largest landslide since 1936, this election generated an regionally concentrated pattern of deviations from the normal American electoral pattern. These deviations were most heavily concentrated in the Deep South on one hand and New England and upstate New York on the other. Both Goldwater in 1964 and Nixon in 1968 pursued quite self-conscious sectional strategies, the basic purpose of which was to establish a rightwing electoral majority based upon "middle America" i.e., the South, parts of the Midwest and the West, and to isolate a Northeast that was the bastion of liberal Republicanism and of cosmopolitanism generally. The differences between the two campaigns—and in particular the parts of the South to which appeal was made—were shaped more by tactical considerations than by any basic divergence between the 1964 and 1968 Republican campaigns in the kind of coalition the party's leadership wished to construct (Phillips, 1969). The intent is to produce a decisive conservative majority based upon the heartland's defence of the traditional American way from unsettling change, and cutting regionally athwart the class-based New Deal coalition that kept the American right out of power for so many years.

The regional consequences of the 1964 Goldwater candidacy are brought into sharp relief by a geographical partition of the 1964 Survey Research Center sample (Table 18). A heavy sectional component of the Northeastern vote is seen not only in its aggregate pro-Democratic bias compared with the rest of the country but particularly by the massive difference between the voting behavior of middle-class, well-educated voters in this region and in the rest of the country. This compression of normal class and other socioeconomic differentials among discrete categories of voters is peculiarly a characteristic of sectional polarization in the United States, as in different ways it is characteristic of Catholic or nationalist movements in countries with multiparty systems. Thus, using Alford's crude index of class voting, we discover that it is only 4 in the Northeast compared with 27 for the rest of the country. Aggregate data also disclose the same pattern: the Democratic candidate in 1964 won sixty-six of the sixty-seven counties in New England (including thirty- five rural counties of largely native-stock ethnic composition which had not deserted the Republican party at any time during the preceding 108 years). The polarization worked as severely in the Deep South, but in favor of Goldwater Republicanism (Burnham, 1968, 1970).

In its pure form political regionalism is one of a range of phenomena that, by virtue of their tendency to gather all members of a categoric group into a single political movement irrespective of class cleavages, can be called horizontal cleavages.

At one time it appeared that the nationalization of American politics during and after the depression would work across time to eliminate regional polarities and that

TABLE 18: **Selected Social Characteristics and the 1964 Vote: the Northeast as Deviant Region**

Social Category	Northeast %D	Rest of U.S. %D	Difference
Occupation			
Professional-managerial	62	52	+10
Clerical-sales	81	63	+18
Skilled workers	72	74	− 2
Semi-and Unskilled	76	87	−11
Retired	72	62	+10
Housewife, etc.	79	60	+19
Non manual strata	70	56	+14
Manual strata	74	83	− 9
Education			
College graduate	77	38	+39
Some college	66	56	+10
High school graduate	73	64	+ 9
Some high school	71	74	− 3
Grade school, none	84	79	+ 5
Perceived Social Class			
Self-Identified			
Middle class	69	49	+20
Working class	82	77	+ 5
Not Self-Identified			
Middle class	67	53	+14
Working class	80	79	+ 1
Total middle class	68	51	+17
Total working class	81	77	+ 4
Total	74	65	+ 9

complementary economic interests would keep working-class people of both major races in the same political coalition. But despite all superficial evidences of cultural homogenization Americans remain deeply divided along horizontal fault lines, many of which find geographical expression. It may even be that the supposedly homogenizing influence of television and other mass media, by making people of starkly contrasting political and social values aware of each other's existence and the extent of their differences, has contributed to the massive upsurge of horizontal cleavages in American electoral politics during the 1960s. It is certain that the influence of sectionalism and other horizontal cleavage patterns on the outcome of national elections has been restored to a position of significance unparalleled since before the great depression. The absence of any mass-based working-class *conscience politique* in the United States implies that class polarizations always remain subject to cross-cutting by sectionalism, racial antagonisms, and other horizontal cleavages.

V. Recent Changes in the American Electorate

In a sense the whole of this chapter is a discussion of an electorate that—always quite labile in its voting behavior compared with other nations—is particularly fluid at present. A summary of these changes in one place focuses upon the cumulative implications of these trends.

A. CHANGES IN PARTY IDENTIFICATION AND IN PARTISANSHIP

Party identification has typically been regarded by American scholars as one of the most durable attributes of voters, and also the single most powerful predictor of American voting behavior (Campbell et al., 1960; Campbell et al., 1966, pp. 245-68). Viewed across time, it has tended until recently to be a characteristic that has shown only very slow aggregate change, in general favoring the Democrats. In particular, the balance between the proportion of strong and weak party identifiers on one hand and independents on the other tended toward great stability through the entire 1952-1964 period, despite the massive shifts in actual voting behavior that characterized the period. The first inkling of a loosening up of these relationships came in 1964, when the proportion of Democratic party identifiers reached an absolute majority of 53 percent for the first time and Republican identifiers shrank to one-quarter of the total electorate. But the most dramatic change occurred in 1966, with a drastic decline in strong party identifiers (particularly on the Democratic side), coupled with an almost equally steep and sudden increase in the proportion of independent identifiers. The latter, from a stable plateau of about 23 per cent during the first half of the 1960s, has now stabilized at about 30 percent of the electorate. While some counter-movement is evident in the 1968 data, the time of domestic and international stress for the United States has been clearly associated with a loosening of partisan ties within the electorate. There is also some reason to suppose that this drift toward political independence is particularly heavily concentrated among the better-educated, those with higher occupational status, and those with higher incomes (Burnham, 1970, ch. 5).

Similar longitudinal findings apply to the question of split-ticket voting at the individual level: from 1952 through 1966 (excluding the three-party 1968 contest) the proportion of those voting a straight (or entirely partisan) ticket declined from 74 percent to 50 percent, and the proportion of voters who voted for the same party's presidential candidate in two or more elections declined in the same period from 68 percent to 46 percent. Aggregate data analysis abundantly confirms the latter trend in particular: in states like Massachusetts and Rhode Island the variance and standard deviation among partisan percentages for all state offices rose geometrically between 1960 and 1966. In Milwaukee official statistics from 1960 include a separation of straight and split ballots. Examination of the proportion of straight voting to the total vote across the 1960-1968 period indicates a massive decline: 68 percent in 1960, 53 percent in 1962, 61 percent in 1964, 51 percent in 1966, and 37 percent in 1968.

Such accelerated tendencies toward the sloughing off of partisan commitments have been particularly conspicuous among young voters (under thirty), and most especially among college and university students. The Gallup postelection survey of 1968 reveals, for example, that 66 percent of the voters in the twenty-one to twenty-nine age bracket split their ballots among candidates of different parties, compared with 59 percent of voters between thirty and forty-nine years of age, and only 46 percent of those fifty and over (RNC, 1969, p. 262). Among college students the movement toward political independence is still more visible; according to Gallup data the proportion of independents among such students increased from 44 percent to 53 percent within the single year of 1969. Such movements, which have given the party of independents an absolute majority among college students, reflect the much larger student protest movement of the contemporary period, a movement that does not work primarily through the instruments of electoral politics.

B. CHANGES IN AMERICAN VOTING PATTERNS

One can summarize the leading changes of the 1960s as follows.

1. A movement that shares classic similarities with other forms of radicalism of the center has emerged as a major force in the late 1960s. The coalitional structure of the Wallace movement can be summarized as being predominantly Southern, small-town or rural outside the industrial centers, Protestant, male, working-class, and, above all, white. This movement made an exceptionally deep penetration into the presidential electorates of both parties, especially the Democratic party. Survey evidence down through the end of 1970 also reveals that the movement's adherents have remained remarkably faithful to George Wallance: a postelection support that is also quite exceptional by ordinary twentieth-century standards for American third parties.

2. As a consequence of the Democratic presidential party's espousal of civil rights and the re-enfranchisement of rural Southern blacks after 1965, the party's Southern base of support in presidential elections has been severely undermined. As late as 1944 this region could be expected to produce a solid Democratic vote in the electoral college; in 1956, except for Missouri, it gave Adlai Stevenson his only electoral votes. In 1968, in contrast, Hubert Humphrey ran behind both Nixon and Wallace in the states of the ex-Confederacy, winning a shade under 30 percent of their total vote.

This development has transformed the geography of American electoral politics. Among other things it frees Republican candidates from the necessity of competing as intensely as was once the case for the electoral votes of the highly urbanized Northeast. During the New Deal era—and indeed down through 1960—the political geography of the United States was such that the states with the largest metropolitan areas became crucial battlegrounds in presidential elections. But were the South to become heavily anti-Democratic, the electoral-vote strategies of politicians would undergo the most profound change, for the geographical center of presidential politics would shift away from the metropolitan conurbations and toward the smaller cities and towns of middle America. As Phillips (1969) has pointed out, the structure of Nixon's 1968 victory closely reflects such a shift.

3. The Democratic party, on the other hand, has won both absolute and relative accretions from middle-class and native-stock Northeasterners, blacks, academics and certain parts of the technical-professional social superstructure.

4. Voting behavior in all parts of the country has become less and less clearly related to partisan labels—whether measured across time, as with indices of partisan swing, or across a number of candidates within the same election. As this happens the concept of party in the United States is growing more evanescent than ever. It is worth noting in this regard that of all the Northern and Northeastern states Humphrey carried in 1968, Democrats won gubernatorial elections in 1966 or in 1968 in only two—Connecticut and Rhode Island. Similarly, Democratic congressmen from the eleven Southern states continue to outnumber Republicans by nearly four to one, despite the Democratic presidential ticket's dismal 1968 showing in that region. The decadence of party as an instrumentality of public policy in the United States has become more pronounced as coalitional incoherence—especially among Democratics —has rapidly increased.

An overview of these major recent changes in the shape of American electoral politics suggests two competing alternative descriptions: partisan realignment with a markedly conservative bias, or a far-reaching dissolution of party-related voting behavior. Beyond a certain undefined point, critical realignment in the classic sense and the dissolution of party-related voting behavior are mutually exclusive. One cardinal attribute of critical realignment is durability of electoral consequences, and it is just such durability that these erosive tendencies directly question. Such tendencies reached a maximum once before, in the golden age of business rule during the 1920s; it took the brutal, nationwide shock of collapse in the market economy to create the conditions for vast political realignment.

As Maurice Duverger argues, the historical development of newer and tighter party-linkage structures in the European political context has been largely a matter of contagion from the Left: the Right or the bourgeois element in politics, has tended not to organize beyond the loose structures of cadre-notability parties unless required to do so in self-defense (Duverger, 1954, pp. 422-27). But as this discussion has repeatedly emphasized, there is no stable sociocultural basis in the United States for a Left of anything approaching even a laborite European type. There is, consequently, no secure social basis for strong party organizations or for strong partisan commitments within the American electorate as a whole.

From the developmental patterns discussed here one may even speculate that, under American conditions, the dominant systemic response to the sociopolitical pressures arising from industrialization and urbanization in the United States has been *the liquidation of the political party as an action intermediary between the voter and the candidate*. Such a view, if accurate, would place the New Deal countertrend in a very different perspective from that which is commonly found in the literature of American politics. It would suggest that while the political consequences of collapse in the country's capitalist market economy were intense, they were temporary. Even at that, they were conspicuously associated with the personal charisma of an outstanding political entrepreneur, Franklin D. Roosevelt. Such coherence as he was able to provide his unwieldy coalition—and at the congressional level it was never very great even at its best—grew out of his institutionalized charisma. While this has survived his death, the party that Roosevelt virtually re-created has been at most indifferently successful at the polls since that time. As the social conditions that gave Roosevelt his immense entrepreneurial opportunity recede ever further into the mists of history, such partisan hold on voting behavior as was restored by the New Deal has receded with them. So far as the emergent trend toward no-party politics is concerned, a reading of national political history during the 1920s or of Key's classic *Southern Politics* (1949) alike make it clear how congenial such a trend is to the preservation of an oligarchic status quo.

VI. Conclusions

A. VARIABLES OF COMPARATIVE SIGNIFICANCE

A considerable amount of informative comparative work using American survey data has been done in recent years (Alford, 1963; Campbell et al., 1966, pp. 243–345). It is not the purpose of this chapter to recapitulate the findings of such studies. We may begin this brief summary by noting, with Alford, that social-class differentials, of considerable importance in American electoral politics since about 1934, have been severely circumscribed by other behavioral determinants. This is a political system in which the "politics of diversity," to use Alford's phrase, prevails at all levels. While the United States has a class-stratification structure that is similar to those in other industrial countries, it diverges sharply from most of the others in the frequency with which resultant class-determined political cleavages are crosscut by others.

The politics of regionalism forms a particularly important comparative variable, one that is exceptionally accessible to study by ecological-aggregate analysis. It is the opinion of the author that this variable has been inadequately presented in the survey-research literature, especially in the most recent period. It appears that the design of nationwide probability samples has suffered from inadequate recognition of the salience of this regional factor (Burnham, 1968). Political regionalism in the United States exists on a scale probably greater than in any other political system in the West except for Canada, where it is if anything of even greater electoral importance (Meisel 1964, pp. 272–88).

Racial polarization is becoming a variable of ever-increasing electoral importance in American politics. In some cases since 1960 it has been much the most important single determinant of voting behavior. No other Western nation has so large a nonwhite minority in its population, and in no other country has a deprived nonwhite minority moved en masse so close to the nerve centers of the socioeconomic system. It is thus to be expected that political cleavages based on racial hostilities exist on a scale—and with a potential and actual significance—that is not to be found elsewhere.

But if the analytical focus is broadened somewhat to include political conflicts rooted in the social antagonisms of sharply discrete ethnocultural groups, comparative similarities come at once to mind. Canada, with its conflicts between the two "founding races," is a leading example; so is Northern Ireland. In both cases the power of intense group-centered antagonisms to override class cleavages is particularly conspicuous. Indeed, the asymmetric position of Québec in the Canadian Confederation or of Northern Ireland in the United Kingdom seem clearly comparable to that of the South in the American union. So far as black voting behavior is concerned, on the other hand, it has come in recent years to resemble nothing so much as a functional equivalent of a solidary nationalist movement which, in a multiparty system, would lead to an extremely stable and *verzuilt* pattern of voting behavior.

B. AMERICAN PARTIES AND VOTING BEHAVIOR IN COMPARATIVE PERSPECTIVE

"No feudalism, no socialism": with these four words one can summarize the basic sociocultural realities that underlie American electoral politics in the industrial era (Hartz, 1955; Hartz, 1964, pp. 1–122). It has always been a vexed point in the professional literature whether appropriate comparisons can thus be made at all between the politics of the United States and those of other industrial societies. There may well be much to support a theory of "American exceptionalism," a theory that emphasizes the uniqueness of the historical and cultural factors that have gone into the making of the United States. While the socioeconomic system changes and evolves with immense rapidity, the political system—including the electoral-politics system— tends to remain inert unless confronted by a social crisis of system-wide proportions. This is related in turn to a central power whose sovereignty at home is extremely problematic except in the most intense crisis conditions.

Yet there is one political system of the present day with which the United States may be fruitfully compared: that of its continental-sized, pluralistic neighbor to the north, Canada. In that country also one finds two old and loosely articulated bourgeois parties that are hegemonic in the electoral system, if not as much as the Democrats and Republicans in the United States. In that country also—and by all evidence, in even more marked degree—political regionalism and intense antagonisms between highly discrete ethocultural groups tend to dominate the mainstream of electoral politics, CCF/NDP efforts to the contrary notwithstanding. While no comparisons can ever be exact, it seems fair to say that the historical, economic, geographical, and ethnocultural factors that have dominated American politics down to the present find their closest parallels in Canada. If one accepts Leon D. Epstein's argument that most of the important political differences between the two nations can be traced to a single *institutional* difference—the Canadian adoption of the British parliamentary system in a North American context—the comparison becomes neat indeed (Epstein, 1964).

The electoral disruptions of the 1960s were clearly symptomatic of a profound transitional crisis in the United States. This crisis is ultimately rooted in the emergence of a technological socioeconomic system so complex and so demanding of sustained interdependence among its constituent units that the primordial Lockean negative-government consensus has manifestly achieved bankruptcy as a principle of social and political organization. The need for a sustained and capable internal sovereignty at the center has grown step by step with the growth of density, complexity, and interdependence in socioeconomic life. Moreover, the debate over the American adventure in Vietnam has tended to crystallize in at least one conclusion about the behavior of executive decision-makers: though such leaders are elected by the people, they are not—at least not adequately—responsible to them. One by-product of this war has also been the emergence of a genuine constitutional crisis involving the president and congress. This crisis itself is the fruit of the separation of governmental powers that has been celebrated for so long in the annals of Lockean politics.

The events of 1968, from the New Hampshire primary to the Democratic convention and then through the election in November, bear particularly vivid witness to the role of the major parties as key institutions of Lockean politics-as-usual. They also suggest forcefully the basic incompatibility of the newer forms of issue-oriented, activity dissent with the existing order of party politics. For these dissenters—whether blacks, students, those intensely opposed to the Vietnam war, or those concerned by the looming shadow of urban and ecological disasters—tend to share one thing in common that separates them from the mainstream. At a bare minimum their objectives require the establishment of something approximating responsible government in the United States. They almost certainly require the development of stable sovereign authority at the center as well.

And yet, how can one expect this to happen in the foreseeable future? Neither the perceived interests nor the ideology of the American middle classes are in any way compatible with such institutional transformation. One cannot impose a political community by fiat, unless one is also prepared to abandon political democracy in the process. Such a community does not now exist: with a missing feudalism and a missing socialism, there has also been a missing social solidarity. This absence of political or social community, one may suspect, has always been real, if masked by Lockean consensus. The heavy strains that swamped American politics during the late 1960s suggest that the political effects of this noncommunity have begun to pass from latency to overtness.

Thus, if Lockean liberalism is indeed in bankruptcy, it is probably pointless to look to either of the major parties to undertake the immense risk of saying so openly. Still less can we expect either of them to suggest the appointment of a receiver. We should perhaps rather take a cue from one of the architects of the Third Republic in France, Adolphe Thiers: "This Republic will be conservative or it will not be at all."

Postscript on the 1972 Election

From beginning to end, the 1972 election bore the marks of a critical turning point in American electoral history. Because the election fits so well into the foregoing discussion, comment can be brief. President Nixon, with 60.7% of the total vote to George McGovern's 37.5%, won by a great landslide. The character of this landslide was remarkable. First, McGovern's victory at the Democratic convention—a victory for moral opposition to the Vietnam war, and for the liberal, managerial-academic wing of the party—decisively accelerated the breakup of the New Deal coalition. Second, the removal of George Wallace from the scene freed the Alabaman's supporters for a merger with Nixon's following. The overwhelming majority of Wallace supporters cast a Republican presidential vote in November. Third, this landslide was accompanied by the lowest participation rate outside the ex-Confederate states since the all-time lows of 1920 and 1924. Fourth, the white working class gave a clear-cut and large majority to a Republican candidate for the first time since 1928 (the Alford class-voting index, already at a low of 11 in 1968, declined to 7 in 1972). Fifth, Nixon's landslide was reflected in almost no other office. The proportion of split-ticket voters and of split partisan outcomes jumped to their highest points in American electoral history.

The significance of this election can be suggested by seven proportions: (1) American electoral politics appears to have become *decisively* restructured along office-specific lines, with significantly different coalitions appearing at each level of election and in each succeeding election. (2) Such drastic reorganization of voting behavior reflects a "critical realignment" which works *against* rather than *through* the traditional mechanisms of two-party competition. *It involves the de-alignment of the American electorate.* (3) This change has very probably developed because the number, intensity and diversity of politically significant polarizations in society have become too great to be successfully integrated within the traditional two-party structure. The parties are bursting asunder under the strain. (4) The emergence of diverse office-specific electoral coalitions greatly reinforces the centrifugal, fragmenting policy effects of the American constitutional structure. (5) An American equivalent to a multiparty system is being created on the ruins of the older major parties. (6) For at least the short run this critical reorganization of American electoral politics represents a very great victory for the political Right. Among other things, the nationalization of Southern politics has marched hand in hand with the Southernization of national politics. (7) Accordingly, it is becoming increasingly pointless for electoral analysts to speak of "Republican" or "Democratic" coalitions unless candidates, offices (or levels of election) and times are also specified.

Many of these remarkable developments can be traced, proximately or ultimately, to a fact of basic change which Louis Hartz foresaw nearly twenty years ago: after a century and a half of splendid isolation from many of the common problems afflicting mankind, the United States has been forced to rejoin world history. The traditional party system, created and developed in those decades of isolation, has necessarily become one of the most visible casualties of this process.

References

ALEXANDER, HERBERT E. *Financing the 1964 Election.* Princeton: Citizens' Research Foundation, 1966.

ALFORD, ROBERT R. *Party and Society.* Chicago: Rand McNally, 1963.

American Political Science Association. Committee on Political Parties, *Toward a More Responsible Two-Party System*, Supplement to 44 *American Political Science Review* (September, 1950).

APTER, DAVID E., ed., *Ideology and Discontent.* New York: Free Press, 1964.

BAIN, RICHARD C. *Convention Decisions and Voting Records.* Washington: Brookings, 1960.

BENSON, LEE. *The Concept of Jacksonian Democracy.* Princeton: Princeton Univ. Press, 1961.

BERELSON, BERNARD, et al. *Voting.* Chicago: Univ. of Chicago Press, 1954.

BURNHAM, WALTER DEAN. "American Voting Behavior and the 1964 Election." *Midwest Journal of Political Science* 12 (1968): 1–40.

———. "The Changing Shape of the American Political Universe." *American Political Science Review* 59 (1965): 7–28.

———. (IPSA) "Political Immunization and Political Confessionalism: Some Comparative Inquiries." Munich: IPSA, 1970. Journal of Interdisciplinary History (1972): 1–30.

———. *Critical Elections and the Mainsprings of American Politics.* New York: Norton, 1970.

———. "A Political Scientist and Voting-Rights Litigation: The Case of the 1966 Texas Registration Statute." *Washington University Law Quarterly* (Spring, 1971).

———, and Chambers, William N., eds., *The American Party Systems.* New York: Oxford Univ. Press, 1967.

———, and Sprague, John D. "Additive and Multiplicative Models of the Voting Universe," *American Political Science Review* 64 (1970): 471–90.

CAMPBELL, ANGUS, et al. *The Voter Decides.* Evanston: Row, Peterson, 1954.

———. *The American Voter.* New York: Wiley, 1960.

———. *Elections and the Political Order.* New York: Wiley, 1966.

CASH, W. J. *The Mind of the South.* New York: Knopf, 1941.

CLAUDE, RICHARD. *The Supreme Court and the Electoral Process.* Baltimore: Johns Hopkins Univ. Press, 1970.

CLAUSEN, AAGE. "Response Validity: Vote Report." *Public Opinion Quarterly* 32 (1969): 588–606.

CONVERSE, PHILIP E. "Change in the American Electorate." Ch. 8 of Angus Campbell and Philip E. Converse, eds., *The Human Meaning of Social Change*. New York: Russell Sage Foundation, 1972.

DAVID, PAUL T., et al. *The Politics of National Party Conventions*. Washington: Brookings, 1960.

DAWSON, RICHARD E. "Social Development, Party Competition, and Policy." In William N. Chambers and W. D. Burnham, eds., *The American Party Systems* (vide Supra), pp. 203–37.

————, and ROBINSON, JAMES A. "The Politics of Welfare." In Herbert Jacob and Kenneth N. Vines, eds. *Politics in the American States*. Boston: Little, Brown, 1965, pp. 371–410.

DUVERGER, MAURICE. *Political Parties*. New York: Wiley, 1954.

DYE, THOMAS R. *Politics, Economics and the Public*. Chicago: Rand McNally, 1966.

ELAZAR, DANIEL J. *American Federalism: A View from the States*. New York: Crowell, 1966.

ELDERSVELD, SAMUEL J. *Political Parties: A Behavioral Analysis*. Chicago: Rand McNally, 1964.

EPSTEIN, LEON D. *Politics in Wisconsin*. Madison: Univ. of Wisconsin Press, 1958.

————. "A Comparative Study of Canadian Parties." *American Political Science Review* 58 (1964): 46–59.

FENTON, JOHN H. *Midwest Politics*. New York: Holt, Rinehart & Winston, 1966.

————. *Politics in the Border States*. New Orleans: Hauser, 1957.

FLANIGAN, WILLIAM. *Political Behavior of the American Electorate*. Boston: Allyn & Bacon, 1968.

FLINN, THOMAS A. "Continuity and Change in Ohio Politics." *Journal of Politics* 24 (1962): 521–44.

FUCHS, LAWRENCE. *The Political Behavior of American Jews*. Glencoe: Free Press, 1956.

GREENSTEIN, FRED I. *The American Party System and the American People*. Englewood Cliffs, N. J.: Prentice-Hall, 1963, 1968.

HARTZ, LOUIS. *The Liberal Tradition in America*. New York: Harcourt, Brace, 1955.

————, ed. *The Founding of New Societies*. New York: Harcourt, Brace, 1964.

HAVARD, WILLIAM C., et al. *The Louisiana Elections of 1960*. Baton Rouge: Louisiana State Univ. Press, 1963.

HEARD, ALEXANDER. *The Costs of Democracy*. Chapel Hill, N. C.: Univ. of North Carolina Press, 1960.

HEBERLE, RUDOLF. *Landbevölkerung und Nationalsozalismus*. Stuttgart: Deutsche Verlags-Anstalt, 1963.

HEER, DAVID M., ed. *Social Statistics and the City*. Cambridge, Mass.: Joint Center for Urban Studies, 1967.

HOLT, MICHAEL F. *Forging a Majority*. New Haven: Yale Univ. Press, 1969.

HOWARD, PERRY. *Political Tendencies in Louisiana, 1812-1952*. Baton Rouge: Louisiana State Univ. Press, 1957.

HUNTINGTON, SAMUEL P. *Political Order in Changing Societies.* New Haven: Yale Univ. Press, 1968.

KATZ, DANIEL, and VALEN, HENRY. *Political Parties in Norway.* Oslo: Universitets-forlaget, 1964.

KELLEY, STANLEY, Jr., et al. "Registration and Voting: Putting First Things First." *American Political Science Review* 61 (1967): 359–79.

KESSEL, JOHN H. *The Goldwater Coalition.* Indianapolis: Bobbs-Merrill, 1968.

KEY, V. O., Jr. *Southern Politics.* New York: Knopf, 1949.

———, "A Theory of Critical Elections." 17 *Journal of Politics* 17 (1955): 3–18.

———. *American State Politics.* New York: Knopf, 1956.

———. *Public Opinion and American Democracy.* New York: Knopf, 1961.

KLEPPNER, PAUL J. *The Cross of Culture.* New York: Free Press, 1970.

LANE, ROBERT E. *Political Ideology.* New York: Free Press, 1962.

LAZARSFELD, PAUL, et al. *The People's Choice.* New York: Duell, Sloan and Pearce, 1944.

LEVIN, MURRAY B. *The Compleat Politician.* Indianapolis: Bobbs-Merrill, 1963.

LIPSET, SEYMOUR M. *Political Man.* New York: Doubleday, 1960.

———, and ROKKAN, STEIN, eds. *Party Systems and Voter Alignments.* New York: Free Press, 1967.

———, and RAAB, EARL. *The Politics of Unreason.* New York: Harper & Row, 1970.

LITT, EDGAR. *The Political Cultures of Massachusetts.* Cambridge: M.I.T. Press, 1965.

LOCKARD, DUANE. *New England State Politics.* Princeton: Princeton Univ. Press, 1959.

LOWI, THEODORE J. "Party, Policy and Constitution." In W. N. Chambers and W. D. Burnham, eds. *The American Party Systems* (vide supra), pp. 238–76.

LUBELL, SAMUEL. *The Future of American Politics.* New York: Harper, 1952.

MACRAE, DUNCAN, Jr., and MELDRUM, J.A. "Critical Elections in Illinois, 1888–1958." *American Political Science Review* 54 (1960): 669–83.

———. "Factor Analysis of Aggregate Voting Statistics." In Mattei Dogan and Stein Rokkan, eds. *Quantitative Ecological Analysis in the Social Sciences.* Cambridge: M.I.T. Press, 1969.

MACRAE, DUNCAN, Jr. *Issues and Parties in Legislative Voting.* New York: Harper & Row, 1970.

MATTHEWS, DONALD R. *The Social Background of Political Decision-Makers.* New York: Doubleday, 1954.

———. *U.S. Senators and Their World.* Chapel Hill: University of North Carolina Press, 1960.

MCGOVNEY, DUDLEY O. *The American Suffrage Medley.* Chicago: University of Chicago Press, 1949.

MCPHEE, WILLIAM, and FERGUSON, JACK. "Political Immunization." In William McPhee and William Glaser, eds. *Public Opinion and Congressional Elections.* New York: Free Press, 1962, pp. 155–79.

MEISEL, JOHN H., ed. *Papers on the 1962 Election.* Toronto: University of Toronto Press, 1964.

OSTROGORSKI, MOISEI. *Democracy and the Organization of Political Parties,* Vol. II, The United States. New York: Macmillan, 1902.

PARENTI, MICHAEL. "Ethnic Politics and the Persistence of Ethnic Identification." *American Political Science Review* 61 (1967): 717–26.

PHILLIPS, KEVIN H. *The Emerging Republican Majority.* New York: Arlington House, 1969.

POMPER, GERALD. *Elections in America.* New York: Dodd, Mead, 1968.

POTTER, DAVID. *People of Plenty.* Chicago: Univ. of Chicago Press, 1954.

PRICE, H. DOUGLAS. "The Negro and Florida Politics, 1944–1954." 17 *Journal of Politics* 17 (1955): 198–220.

Republican National Committee (RNC). *The 1968 Elections.* Washington: 1969.

ROBINSON, W. S. "Ecological Correlations and the Behavior of Individuals." 15 *American Sociological Review* 15 (1950): 341–57.

ROGIN, MICHAEL. *The Intellectuals and McCarthy: The Radical Specter.* Cambridge: M.I.T. Press, 1967.

ROKKAN, STEIN, "Norway: Numerical Democracy and Corporate Pluralism." In Robert A. Dahl, ed. *Political Oppositions in Western Democracies.* New Haven: Yale University Press, 1966, pp. 70–115.

————, and VALEN, HENRY. "Regional Contrasts in Norwegian Politics." In Erik Allardt and Yrjo Littunen, eds. *Cleavages, Ideologies and Party Systems.* Helsinki: Academic Bookstore, 1964.

ROSE, RICHARD, and URWIN, DEREK. "Social Cohesion, Political Parties and Strains in Regimes." *Comparative Political Studies* 2 (1969): 7–67.

————. "Persistence and Change in Western Party Systems since 1945," *Political Studies* 18 (1970): 287–319.

RUSK, JERROLD G. "The Effect of the Australian Ballot Reform on Split-Ticket Voting: 1876–1908." *American Political Science Review* 64 (1970), 1220–38.

RUSSETT, BRUCE, et al. *World Handbook of Political and Social Indicators.* New Haven: Yale University Press, 1964.

SCHATTSCHNEIDER, E. E. *The Semi-Sovereign People.* New York: Holt, Rinehart & Winston, 1960.

SINDLER, ALLAN P. *Huey Long's Louisiana.* Baltimore: Johns Hopkins University Press, 1956.

STRONG, DONALD S. *Urban Republicanism in the South.* University, Ala.: Bureau of Public Administration, Univ. of Alabama, 1960.

TINGSTEN, HERBERT L. A. *Political Behavior.* Stockholm: 1937.

U. S. Bureau of the Census, Current Population Reports, Population Characteristics. *Voting and Registration in the Election of November 1968,* Series P-20, No. 192 (December, 1969).

U. S. Commission on Civil Rights. *Political Participation.* Washington: Government Printing Office, 1968.

WILLIAMS, T. HARRY. *Huey Long.* New York: Knopf, 1970.

WEBB, WALTER P. *The Great Frontier.* Boston: Houghton Mifflin, 1952.

WILLIAMSON, CHILTON. *American Suffrage from Property to Democracy, 1760–1860.*
Princeton: Princeton Univ. Press, 1960.

WOLFINGER, RAYMOND E. "The Development and Persistence of Ethnic Voting."
American Political Science Review 59 (1965): 896–908.

14. SOME PRIORITY VARIABLES IN COMPARATIVE ELECTORAL RESEARCH
PHILIP E. CONVERSE

My commission for this working paper has been to provide a discussion of those variables in voting behavior "which seem to have the greatest explanatory power for comparative research and which therefore should become standard items in all social surveys." The mandate includes both psychological and sociological variables.

I intend to tackle this assignment in good cheer in a moment, but it is difficult to get underway without some initial trimming and shaping. At first glance the commission is overwhelming in its breadth, especially for a short working paper. At second glance it may be less difficult, for a priority ordering of independent variables is being summoned, and one can stop abruptly almost anywhere in such an ordering without esthetic calamity. Moreover, what appears to be a very crisp criterion of priority—explanatory power—is provided.

Yet it is here the troubles begin. Variables do not have explanatory power as some self-contained property. They only have explanatory power vis-a-vis other variables, and these relationships radiating from any given independent variable are likely to be rather various in strength. An independent variable that might be indispensable on the face of it for one specific type of comparative electoral inquiry might be quite irrelevant for another. In short, the question "Explanatory power with respect of what?" needs a more specific answer than "Voting behavior."

Furthermore, there is some question as to how closely one should hew to "explanatory power" as a criterion of importance. No one will doubt its importance, yet cases arise frequently in which another good criterion, that of theoretical significance, accords rather poorly with explanatory power. And I shall later mention at least one variable that is totally unexciting from a theoretical point of a view, that at any given point in time accounts for precious little variance in much of anything that interests us, yet may represent one of the more important parameters for the long run that election surveys can help to estimate.

This working paper was prepared for an International Conference of the Committee on Political Sociology of the International Sociological Association at the Free University of Berlin, January 16–20, 1968. It was circulated in a pre-publication form as Occasional Paper No. 3 of the Survey Research Center of the University of Strathclyde.

With these problems and anomalies in view, then, let me suggest the more limited way in which I intend to approach the subject. I expect to be influenced, and quite willingly, by what I take to be the ongoing interests of the participants at this gathering. Thus, for example, I will tend to place emphasis on variables that tie voting behavior into social structure, reflecting the specific concerns of political sociology. This certainly does not mean any doctrinaire avoidance of so-called "psychological variables," but it does imply a principle of selection from that very large pool of possibilities.

Similarly, it seems useful to accept some limitation in the general type of dependent variable being presumed where the explanatory power of independent variables is concerned. That is, within the study of voting behavior there is a major watershed between the set of dependent variables relevant to choice among political alternatives (ideological positions, policy alternatives, and political parties), and those dependent variables bearing on political interest, participation, and "mobilization." A book like *The Civic Culture*[1] focuses almost exclusively on the second bundle of concerns; a book like *Party Systems and Voter Alignments*[2] gives primary attention to the first. While it would be natural for us to give unusual priority to independent variables that tend to discriminate with some power on both sides of this divide, the fact remains that such variables are few. It is most often the case that variables predicting well to one class of concerns have little or spurious discriminating power on the other. We shall try to keep this divide in mind during our discussion, but given limits of space we shall tend to emphasize variables relevant to voter alignments rather than problems of political mobilization.

Within this general framework we shall try to keep our discussion as future-oriented as possible. By this we mean to recognize the fact that the research environment for comparative research on electoral problems is changing, and perhaps more rapidly than the survey instruments we use. Whereas ten years ago a researcher might account himself lucky to have access to more than one national political survey for his own country or for another particular country of comparative interest with his own, it is now quite common in North America and Western Europe to have ready access to a multiplicity of surveys within a very narrow time period for a number of countries. Computer capacities for manipulating larger files of data in more intricate ways have thrust forward, and statistical sophistication is at least struggling to keep up with the horizons of possibilities. Increasingly formal models of the voting process are being proposed, and the parameter needs of these models should influence as rapidly as possible the ways in which even old and familiar types of information are elicited and coded. We would hope to keep our remarks sensitive to these changes in our research environments.

It is perhaps useful to restate the emphases we propose for our discussion in a slightly different and more concrete way. We take the general concerns with socio-political cleavages represented so well by *Party Systems and Voter Alignments* as a boundary-setting device for our discussion, without in any sense implying (as we would not) that this circle of concerns—already very large—exhausts the set of serious scholarly interests in the electoral process. From this point of departure we shall ask what choices need to be made in the selection of items for national-level electoral surveys in order that subsequent generations of researchers may have a more detailed and incisive view of these processes in our time than is available commonly today or certainly for the deeper past.[3] There are three subquestions hidden in this general query:

(1) What have we already learned about sociopolitical cleavages that would help to establish new priorities among old, familiar items?

(2) Are there new ways in which old items should be treated or expanded as a routine matter in our surveys?

(3) Are there "forgotten" variables that deserve to be brought, or brought back, into view?

I. The Face Sheet and Beyond

It might be a delightful game to take a devil's-advocate position here and propose that all or most of the common face-sheet items used in virtually all surveys—age, sex, education, occupation, and so on—are not worth the candle and should be replaced by some fresh set of new items. It would, however, tax my ingenuity unduly to defend such a position. While I am as interested as anyone in ferreting out other new variables concerning social position and experience, I would immediately want to know how such further variables interrelate with these most common bread-and-butter items. Therefore, given limited space and need for stringent priorities, the conventional face sheet would have to take a place at the head of the list of sociostructural independent variables.

Indeed, it is charming to reflect that if one were to take the first chapter of *Party Systems and Voter Alignments* and ask what four simple items would be most necessary to maintain in any monitoring of sociopolitical cleavages, they would not only be common face sheet items, but three of the four—*social status*, *religion*, and *urban-rural* residence—were enshrined by Lazarsfeld and his collaborators twenty-five years ago in an "Index of Political Predisposition," which more or less purported to answer the question, "What sociostructural items (or, more crudely, face sheet items) are the best joint predictors of party choice?" And assuming that the fourth item would be "region of residence," then its absence on the Lazarsfeld Index is readily understood in view of the fact that the Erie County study was on a local, not transregional base.

Although it is tempting to take the face sheet for granted and pass to less mundane concerns, I have decided to invest much of my time at just this point. In the first place, even across the ten most common face-sheet items there remain interesting questions or priority. It is not true, for example, that the four critical variables of the preceding paragraph turn up in every survey. Religion is missed with great frequency. Sometimes urban-rural residence is not apparent. "Social status" can be assessed in a variety of ways, with the tactical dilemmas this state of affairs entails. In the second place, and much more important to my mind, we need to go well beyond these as crude single variables. The conventional ways in which they are assessed and coded is reasonable enough as a first approximation, but the current need to explore beyond them taken in their conventional form is obvious enough. They need not be counted off as single variables—they are clusters of variables, with parts and extensions that deserve much more systematic tracing in the future.

I must admit that I have little new to say about either the importance of sex, how it should be elicited in the future, or new, more differentiated ways in which it needs to be coded. Perhaps this tokens a certain lack of imagination in the hippie era, but I would like to pass by sex with a nod and explore the rest of the face-sheet in greater detail.

1. EDUCATION

If there is anything like a universal solvent across conventional face-sheet items, there is no question to me but that education claims the role. It is almost unique in that while it is a prime predictor, and probably *the* prime predictor for the whole class of dependent variables reflecting political interest, participation, and mobilization, it also shows remarkable discriminating power as a status measure in predicting to variables on the other side of the watershed—ideology and party position. Moreover, unlike a number of the other conventional face-sheet items, it recommends itself unusually for cross-national comparisons, for the simple reason that societies of interest to us show much greater absolute variation in education distributions than they do in age, sex composition, or perhaps even occupational structure. It is no idiosyncracy that Almond and Verba in *The Civic Culture* wore their IBM cards thin running this particular column. And it is for this cluster of reasons that I feel obliged to place it at the head of a priority list.

I would feel moreover that this position accorded education is not entirely an obvious one. Certainly the sociological training I received before working with voting materials had led me to assume that whatever correlations might emerge between education and other dependent variables surrounding political activity and choice would tend to be spurious, in the sense that some predictors reflecting structural location with respect to the means of production (i.e., various dimensions of "occupation" as a variable) could be expected to be the prime "causes" in such instances, with education showing a correlation only because it in turn is quite positively correlated with occupational measures of status. Yet in a very surprising number of cases (primarily within the United States) I have discovered just the opposite to be the case: using education and occupation as competing status indicators, the occupation relationship washes out when education is controlled, but a residual relation with education remains when occupation is controlled. This certainly suggests the primacy of education as the true predictor in the situation. I do not say that this pattern is always present, nor do I intend to cast any doubt on the great value of measures of occupational location for their variety of more intricate analytic uses. But I have become convinced that the role of education is basic in many of the affairs that interest us, and that its effects are still only poorly assimilated in our broader sociopolitical theories, and were ridiculously underestimated fifteen years ago.

THE OPERATIONAL TREATMENT OF EDUCATION

Most common surveys that include education as a face-sheet variable provide four to seven gross levels reflecting the "discharge points" that are standard for the educational institutions of the country being studied. This is reasonable as a crude approximation, but numerous improvements, particularly for cross-national relevance, can be made.

Treating education first as a single variable, I think it would be beneficial to code the basic information as "number of years of formal education." Here, as in so many other places, the issue is one of virtually nothing to lose and something to gain by capturing the fuller information. That is, even a foreigner who knows nothing of the educational system can see the institutionalized "discharge points" very clearly in such a distribution, and can collapse the information back around those points if he so desires. But the fuller information has a number of other analytic advantages. Thus, as one small example, it is usually the case that "nonfinishers" (people who emerge from the educational system at some noninstitutionalized point) show weaker political participation than people who have less education but who at least have completed some more standard level of education, an effect that is minor but totally obscured by the classic way of coding the variable. Also, the more nearly quantitative variable has at least some advantages in correlational analysis. More important still are some of the advantages for cross-national comparisons, as well as cross-time comparisons within the same country over periods when educational expectations are undergoing change, as they usually are. Now it is a commonplace in this regard that the same number of years of formal education may mean quite different things from country to country, and I have no doubt that this is true. On the other hand, I have been surprised in the past at the cross-national "fits" than can be found if this commonplace is ignored. They are certainly more impressive (though admittedly rough) than what will be found if one respects the commonplace and fears to look at all. And generally one is in a much better position for such a consideration than in attempting to match obscure and disparate batches of qualitatively denoted levels.

Many of the inadequacies that remain, however, could be remedied at least in part if we stop considering "education"as a single variable and begin to regard it as a cluster of dimension. Such treatment would permit us to indicate, for example, what portion of the last years of formal education were in relatively nonacademic tracks such as secretarial or vocational training, a source of some of the discomfort at direct cross-national comparison of the simpler "year of education" variable.

But if we are to differentiate the education variable further, then I am convinced that the main "payoff" for political studies lies in much greater differentiation at the upper, quasi-elite end of the education continuum. Little attention has been given to this problem in mass surveys because case numbers tend to be discouragingly small in any single survey. Assuming, however, the new environment where surveys in increasing numbers can be pyramided to provide sturdy Ns, I think we can approach a much fuller understanding of lines of sociopolitical conflict by this focus for attention than is currently appreciated.

I cannot speak as firmly from cross-national experience here as I would like, in part because the education area is almost never given this more differentiated treatment in studies I have seen abroad. In the United States, however, we have increasingly expanded our examination in this area, collecting information that permits us to know not only that a certain amalgam of our respondents is "college-educated," but how far the education progressed, what degrees were received, and, most important for our immediate discussion, what colleges or universities were attended.

The importance of this information has now been well substantiated by the remarkable heterogeneity, at analytic point after analytic point, shown by these college-educated respondents invariably thrown together as a single ensemble in more conventional treatments. Indeed, where ideologies are concerned, one can almost feel that these materials capture more firmly than any mass data I have seen the true "blood-and-guts" of political differentiation and conflict as it stands in the United States, and that they make something of a mockery of the "college-educated" category presented by the newspapers in summarizing public opinion poll materials.

I cannot report in any detail on this work here, in part because the additional information collected concerning education permits a variety of analyses. As one quick example, no few of American college-educated were trained in regions other than those in which they now reside, and sometimes regions different from those in which they grew up as well, a matter that helps to blur and confound many regional analyses based on cruder data. Most important, however, is the kind of differentiation that emerges between the small portion of those educated at large and leading institutions and the much larger proportion whose degrees were received at one or another of the hundreds of small, provincial, and often sectarian colleges scattered in all sorts of unlikely places across the United States. Here the differences in ideology and, one can suppose, in contextual information about the modern world become profound. Having experienced pregraduate training myself at one of the reasonably respectable provincial institutions, it was my subsequent observation that the intellectual frontiers purveyed by the faculty had been anywhere from fifteen to forty years out of date, according to the age of the specific professor involved and the epoch at which he last experienced close contact with a more major institution of learning. A bit of cynical extrapolation thus suggests that for the "college-educated" man of fifty-five or sixty in 1968 residing in a moderate-sized community in Missouri, any systematic exposure (as opposed to subsequent informal experience) to the dynamics of social, economic, and political systems rests on a social science—if any—as it stood in major institutions of higher learning in the United States about 1900. Thus it does not seem at all surprising that his world-view differs substantially from that of the new graduate of a major institution —this is certainly the flavor purveyed by the empirical materials.

Naturally some of these findings flow from peculiarities in the American educational system. However, I suspect there are numerous counterparts abroad that would well repay closer investigation. It goes without saying that the education variable, differentiated in these directions, is not only relevant to status conflict but is also beginning to bite deeply into the kind of "center-periphery" cleavage dimensions emphasized in the *Party Systems* volume.

2. RELIGION

If party location alone was at stake as a dependent variable, we might move religion into the front rank of determinants. This is true despite the fact that numerous polities fail to present the religious heterogeneity that encourages cleavage along this dimension. Wherever such heterogeneity exists, political polarization along religious lines seems much more intense than earlier theories with less empirical base would have led us to suppose; even in monoreligious systems controversy over religious matters seems to pervade the mass public and affect its partisan alignments in surprising degree.

In a setting of marked religious pluralism such as the United States recent historical reconstructions by S. M. Lipset and Lee Benson have indicated that while religious animosities have never generally been thought of as primary sources of partisan differentiation, it can be argued convincingly that as a sort of "hidden agenda" they have affected the main trends in party alignments more deeply and persistently than any other types of social differentiation. A book such as Lenski's helps to show that these effects have not died away.[4] Indeed, any simple cross-tabulation of major creeds by party choice shows the current effect of religion quite convincingly. However, in an unpublished exercise I have tried to push the matter further by organizing a much more differentiated religious continuum, taking into account not only main creeds but differentiation within the population with respect to religious fidelity, and also certain interesting interaction effects between religion and region that can blur analyses. A second "status" variable was then commissioned, with exactly the same end in view of squeezing the maximal accounting for partisan variance that the whole set of status measures could yield. Then these two "maximal-discrimination" versions of religion and status were paired against each other in a regression analysis predicting to party identification, again as a proliferated "degree" measure. And the result were quite unequivocal in favoring religion as the more potent determinant of partisanship.

The *Party Systems* volume provides considerable witness as to the potency of religious creed as a current predictor in the polyreligious societies along the frontier in Europe where the advance of the Protestant Reformation was finally stabilized. This is of course further documentation of the current vitality of religious differentiation in popular political life. I am as greatly impressed, however, by the signs of religious intrusion in countries to the north and south of this frontier despite the fact that religious heterogeneity in many of these countries, superficially speaking, is slight.

Numerous independent inquiries in France, for example, seem to have brought to the surface the same finding: that religious attitudes (here, clericalism vs. anti-clericalism) appear to predict party or so-called "Left-Right" locations more efficiently than status. Thus the religious factor emerged very clearly in independent aggregate ecological analyses by Dogan and MacRae. In sample survey work done with Dupeux in 1958 questions on personal religious practice were excluded from the questionnaire on grounds that they would be resented and spoil the interviews. However, it was noted that policy-attitude questions on clerical-anticlerical issues predicted more successfully to Left-Right location than did either measures of social status or attitudes on a conventional set of socioeconomic Left-Right issues. I have been told—although I have been unable to locate them—that IFOP has recently released results from much more extended probings of religious practice and shown again the remarkable links with political preferences. Or to the north of the Reformation line, in work on dimensions of party-preference perceptions in Norway, another society with essentially a single religion, a dimension reflecting religious fidelity and concern over public morality seems second only to the conventional Left-Right dimension in explanatory power. Thus the general rule seems to be that religious differentiation intrudes on partisan political alignments in unexpectedly powerful degree wherever it conceivably can.

The Operational Treatment of Religion

In societies involving multiple religions standard face-sheet information simply locates the respondent in one or another of the nominal religious categories. Possibilities for amplifying this information are several, however, and not uncommon. Frequency of church attendance or other indicators of strictness of religious practice help to divide coreligionists along a "more-less" continuum that almost invariably show, if religious cleavages between parties are abroad, the expected differences in partisan homogeneity within the same creed. Lenski in *The Religious Factor* entitles such measures "associational involvement," and deals as well with a competing measure of "communal involvement": the degree to which one's close friends and relatives are limited to the same religious group. The two types of religious involvement are often only loosely correlated, and tend to show additive effects with respect to partisan homogeneity. Within societies dominated by a single religion religious information is often sadly lacking on the face sheet. When such information is gathered, it usually involves some indicator of fidelity of religious practice.

Since these intensifier variables give rather predictable results that fit sociological theory in simple and obvious ways, a question might be raised as to the priority to be accorded such variables. It can be argued that there is little point in replicating the same results and nauseam, when the same questionnaire space could be given over to more novel phenomena. However, as we look across wider ranges of time and polities, the strong possibility of significant variations and secular trends with respect to population distributions on these intensifier variables salvages some sense of importance in continuing to monitor them over time and in various countries. This importance would be comparatively slight if religion itself were not such a central discriminator; but the role it appears to play argues for a more extended and continuing measurement investment.

Perhaps the most striking deficiency for our purposes in all standard treatments of religion, including those that register "intensifier" indications within each religion, is that they fail to provide any further information as to degrees of negative feeling on the part of members of a particular creed toward another creed. In general one expects to find—and does find, within my experience—that the more devout adherents of a particular creed tend on the average to look more hostilely toward a neighboring creed than their less devout coreligionists. But it is only a tendency, of course, and the question of negative as well as positive reference groups is so obviously vital to the study of social cleavages that efforts to improve measurement in this regard seem necessary. This is true even in societies where a single religion dominates: feeble or non-existent religious practice may token very low salience of religion and general non-passionate disinterest or sense of irrelevance; or it may token very high salience along with bitter antagonism and supercharged alienation. In other words most survey items in this cleavage area give us, so to speak, only half of the distribution that should interest us. We shall postpone a constructive suggestion in this regard to a later point in the paper.

2a-b. RACE AND ETHNIC DIFFERENTIATION

We shall take the liberty to subordinate mention of race and ethnic differentiation to the discussion of religion, in part because of space limitations and the fact that many of the same things may be said of racial and ethnic subcultures as for religious ones; and in part because major ethnic and racial heterogeneity is somewhat less frequent than religious heterogeneity in the polities of salience to us. Where it occurs, however, it seems to become expressed in partisan cleavages as persistently and vigorously as religious differentiation and would deserve equal priority for investigation. There is room for a good deal of systematic comparative work in contrasting situations where racial and ethnic boundaries coincide more or less well with religious, regional, and/or status differentiation, as is so frequently the case. And it is as important in these situations as with religion to establish something of the character of cross-group attitudes, as we shall discuss later.

3. OCCUPATION

Although education alone can provide a reasonable general measure of status, there is no question but that some measure of occupation is equally indispensable, not only to add depth and reliability to any generalized status index, but also because of the numerous special effects that have been demonstrated in sociologically peculiar pockets of the array of occupations (such as the political behavior of domestic servants, fishermen, or members of the military).

In addition, a variety of simple extensions from the assessment of occupation per se have been frequently used and heavily worked. These relate to the individual's work situation and include such variables as the industry within which the occupation is located, whether the respondent is employed by the government, by private enterprise, or is self-employed, recent unemployment history, occupational mobility, size of work place, and membership in work-related organizations (whether trade unions or professional associations). This list does not purport to be complete, nor have I attempted any preference ordering across items. Indeed, it is my impression that various of these aspects of work-life show rather different effects in different national settings and vis-à-vis different aspects of voting behavior. The important point is that some good prior assessment of occupation is to be presumed for virtually every one of these items, and it is here we shall focus our attention for the moment.

The hard fact of the matter is that occupation is difficult to elicit and code reliably. I suspect it could be demonstrated that of all of the face-sheet items we are covering here, its assessment is markedly the least reliable. One- or two-word occupational tags given the interviewer are frequently ambiguous and sometimes systematically misleading. Almost a minimal precaution is to require the interviewer to probe, after the occupational tag has been stated, in some such manner as, "And exactly what is it that you do?" except in cases where the occupational tag leaves no shred of ambiguity. This procedure helps to reduce ambiguities for the coder, and might be called a "careful" assessment of occupation, as opposed to the casual assessment that would characterize most hurried or nonacademic surveys. The unreliability that remains even after such a careful assessment is likely to be sobering. We once used the "careful" method in successive waves of a national panel survey at two-year intervals. We deliberately did not compare the second and third interview protocol with the first in the coding process, but let the coders handle the new wave of material exactly as they would a fresh survey. The interwave correlation between occupational location for the same people (where occupations were arrayed in a standard 8-9 category status ordering) was only .72 (rank-order coefficient). A graduate student subsequently interested in short-term occupational mobility spent a good deal of time comparing the verbal responses on the interview protocols given by people whose status location had "changed" between waves. He concluded that perhaps a majority of the apparent changers were in fact still working at the same job. Some few of these discrepancies could be attributed to inevitable mechanical errors in coding, but the bulk of them represented differences in vocabulary employed by the respondent to describe his work at the two visits, which were sufficient to mislead coders not permitted to compare the two responses.

Since occupational-mobility measures rest on the formation of some difference in occupation description, and since the formation of such differences tends to compound error (rather than internally compensate for it), the amount of "noise" present in such mobility assessments—unless carried out with extraordinary time investment—must be embarrassing indeed, and may help to explain why mobility indices laid against political variables so frequently show such indifferent results relative to theoretical expectations.

All of these problems are compounded, of course, when cross-national comparisons are to be made. In no other area is the need to urgent for concerted activity among relevant scholars toward standardization or at least the establishment of functional equivalences and the detailed description of nonequivalences (i.e., work roles that are clustered in unusual ways in particular countries, giving rise to intrinsically noncomparable occupational classes). Any such guide should also organize information as to the most reasonable location in a national occupational-status hierarchy of some of its more idiosyncratic occupational classes.

Perhaps one of the most obvious improvements on the way in which simple occupational codes are conventionally organized in surveys is to ask the further probes necessary to establish gross rural status differentiations as well as urban ones. Various conditions of land tenure, size of holding, nature of crop, and the like are obviously important to get within the usual gross categories "peasant" or "farmer".

The growing potential for pyramiding multiple surveys signifies that finer and finer occupational types can be examined meaningfully; hence occupation codes that do not proceed beyond eight or nine categories, while adequate for some uses, are likely to become increasingly frustrating. Certainly the capacity to look at various well-populated professional occupations would be illuminating.

This is obviously too cursory a set of remarks about the care and nurture of occupation as a variable in our surveys. Undoubtedly a substantial monograph could be devoted to the attendant problems, but space does not permit further treatment here.

Nor do we have time to discuss at any length some of the more specific work- or occupation-related variables cataloged in the second paragraph of this section. Two such variables that seem particularly potent discriminators in country after country do, however, need at least brief attention. These are labor union membership and subjective social-class identification. Both compete closely with religion, for example, in the "tree" analyses generated by Liepelt and others for a number of countries in the West.

It is usually effective to find out not only whether the respondent is or is not himself a union member, but also whether anyone in his household is unionized. In some situations, as in the United States where there is a multiplicity of independent or semi-independent large unions some of which are politically inert and others of which actually tend to support Republican candidates, getting information on the actual union of membership helps to further clarify the effects of membership. Another obvious "intensifier" variable is some measure of degree of sympathetic identification with the union on the part of the member. This becomes particularly important in situations where membership can be resented as involuntary, or at least taken as much more routine or accidental than is membership in, say, religious associations.

Subjective social-class identification is interesting from several points of view. First, it seems to predict to status cleavages in partisanship fully as successfully as objective measures do. It remains independent enough from the objective measures so that, coupled with them, it increases prediction visibly. Moreover, being a relatively "soft" variable, there is reason to believe that it may register significant variations, both between nations at comparable points in time and across "political generations" within nations as status cleavages wax and wane in intensity. Therefore it may have some interest not shared by the objective measures, which are more inert in these regards.

As a minimal investment it is customary to ask the respondent whether he considers himself to be in the middle or working class (sometimes the alternatives "upper" and "lower class" are appended as well). As a more extended investment, the respondent may first be asked whether he ever thinks of himself as being in one or another social class, the responses here showing some value again as intensifier variables, and having a clear cross-national interest as well. Then he may be posed the fixed alternatives, or first asked to describe in a more open-ended fashion his class location, and only then asked to choose between middle and working class if he fails to volunteer either answer.

4. URBAN-RURAL RESIDENCE

5. REGION OF RESIDENCE

Both of these variables reflect a territorial base, and are simply and directly relevant to the variants on territorial cleavages treated in *Party Systems and Voter Alignments*. Both are likely to appear in some form in sample-survey data, since they usually play a role in sample design. And although slightly different things need be said about coding problems with each, the most useful extension can be discussed in common.

One of the main defects characteristic of crude codes treating size of population of place of residence is the failure, for smaller communes or rural places, to indicate even rough ecological relationships with larger population centers. Thus residence in the rural fringes of a large metropolis or in the green interstices of a megalopolitan sprawl may be classified in the same code with rural hamlets or open places deep in the national hinterlands. Somewhat comparable ambiguities are built into crude codes with respect to moderate-sized suburbs adjoining large population centers. A little care and expansion of the code can permit some useful purification of categories. Pressure on sample survey agencies to code the inadvertently available information on actual identity of sampling points (communes by name, for example), would permit subsequent investigators to take into account a number of more subtle or originally unforeseen ecological effects.

A somewhat parallel difficulty lies in gross regional codes, where regions may sometimes be defined in such a manner that traditional political differentiations are poorly represented or unreconstructible. Since political studies are likely to be but a minor part of an agency's work, and regional definitions necessary for stratification in sample design depend in some measure on readily accessible census aggregations, some of the lack of fit with "political" regions is inevitable. Once again, however, pressure toward somewhat finer regional codes (even though the subdivided regions may not have played a role in the original sample design and may not be, strictly speaking, "self-weighting") or, better yet, the precise identification of sampling points as before, preserves a much more satisfactory flexibility for secondary analyses.

Perhaps the most important extension of both of these residential variables seems to be available in remarkably few sample surveys. This is some reflection of geographic mobility: whether the respondent is a lifetime resident of this region and type of place or may have more or less recently arrived after having spent his formative years or even much of his life in a totally different region and type of place. Ideally, of course, the whole history of geographic mobility (if any) should be traced out. Such a procedure, however, can be prohibitively cumbersome both for interview time and for subsequent analyses. At a minimum, however, two simple questions ascertaining where (region and size of place) the respondent "mainly" lived "while he was growing up" can provide invaluable further territorial information.

It is our impression on the basis of data in the United States, for example and we have seen too little comparable data available in political surveys in other countries), that a surprising portion of the partisan variability within our large urban centers, and particularly within the working-class cores of those centers, derives from the continuing admixture of migrants from rural areas who frequently fail to take on at any rapid rate (if at all) the political coloring of their new milieu. Indeed, certain forms of center-periphery conflict may take place entirely within the arena of the city. We are reminded of a recent interview study of a sample drawn from urban member-ship lists of a "radical-right" organization attempting to pin down some of the social and psychological correlates of such membership. While many standard socio-structural variables showed indifferent results, one finding stood out: people attracted to the organization were disproportionately of rural backgrounds within their own lifetime. The standard coding lumps all such people as "city-dwellers," of course, and misses a key dynamic that links political affairs with broad phenomena of urbanization and territorial exchanges of population, while blurring some of the true strength of center-periphery and regional cleavages.

The above completes our consideration of the clusters of variables covering the most basic and obvious cleavages. And with one exception, to be treated immediately below, it completes our consideration of the bread-and-butter face-sheet items, as well as extension thereon that strike us as particularly fruitful. We should note here that there are two further status variables that are quite familiar, although we have ignored them up to this point. These are income and the frequent interviewer assessment of status (by the observed gestalt of life-style). Both may well be collected, and undoubtedly ought to be in any study putting particular stress on status differentiation. Nevertheless, whatever other researcher's experience may be, ours would suggest that neither of these items rate first priority consideration.

At least in the United States income is a notably poorer predictor of partisanship than either occupation or education. Detailed methodological studies with external bases for validation as to the accuracy of income reports in sample surveys would lead us to feel that the weakness of income as a predictor is less a problem of dishonest reporting than of the numerous sources of slippage between status in a full-blown experiential sense and the details of current income. Noncomparabilities abound here, in the relative incomes of respondents in different stages of the life-cycle (young adults, middle-age, postretirement); of urban and rural people; of double-income families as opposed to the single breadwinner; persons driven to "moonlighting" by large families, and the like.

Interviewers' subjective assessments may add a further useful element to a conglomeration of status measures. However, problems of unreliability between interviewers, and even deeper problems of cross-national comparability, combine to relegate such measures to a secondary role.

6. AGE

The age of the respondent is the last variable that belongs within the top priority level for face-sheet items. This is so despite the fact that in a strict sense it tends to predict rather poorly in any simple linear way to partisanship variables, and only somewhat better to participation variables. It is instead a critical "sorting" variable for locating respondents in a temporal process, both with respect to irregular features of the life-cycle and equally irregular impressions that history may have left on particular "political generations." Historical effects, when they can be disengaged from life-cycle effects, are of unusual interest for they often permit one to foresee, given the inexorable population turnover processes, trends that can be expected to diminish or accentuate in the future. Furthermore, in any systematic modeling of temporal processes in an electorate of the type that I believe will be done increasingly, age is the most critical "working variable," even though it may not play much of an explicit role in a prediction system.

The fascination of age as this kind of working variable grows for the investigator as surveys become available to him covering longer and longer periods of time, in no small part because the added data make it increasingly possible to disentangle historical from life-cycle effects, so that there is a clearer sense of the significance of various irregularities that it may turn up in age distributions. At the same time any such investigator rapidly comes to realize that there is one and only one way to capture and code age, and that is in its natural two-digit form. Otherwise analysis is likely to be a series of frustrations trying to match grosser age cohorts across samples that one knows in advance cannot purport to represent the same pool of people, since the bracketing years do not in fact fit each other. At one time the argument for coding age in gross classes (often as few as three categories) was to have enough cases in each class for internal analysis. Yet now, pyramiding samples, I am able to work with over 200 cases of people reporting birth years, for example, in 1916. This may sound a little precious, and indeed it is, but some historical effects appear most clearly when precision very close to this, such as three-year-cohorts, is used.

Because of a personal interest in temporal process, there is a whole class of variables to which I would give unusual priority. These are reports by respondents of important parental characteristics or characteristics of their families of origin. Once again, I am pleased to note that an argument can be made in some degree as well on the basis of objective data: some parental or family characteristics emerge at fairly early levels in the Liepelt et al. tree analyses focused on partisanship, suggesting predictive power deserving of attention as well.

As for the choice of important characteristics, it seems reasonable to let the selection run along the lines that show themselves to be important in ego's own generation. These items would include parental partisanship (if any); political interest; religious affiliation (in societies where there is any transition in or out of sects at all); degree of religious interest; father's occupation; level of parental education; subjectively estimated class status for family of origin; urban-rural and regional background of parents prior to the time when the respondent was growing up, etc. Since we have already called for data relevant to the respondent at an earlier period of life with respect to some reliably recalled information (region and type of place in which he grew up, for example), getting comparable information for the parental generation gives at least a three-ply (or "three-state") view of important transitions or stabilities leading to the respondent as a current political actor. Such data are excellent for capturing evidence on the relevance of some of the broadest historical trends of our era to current voting behavior, including such things as urbanization, the upgrading of education, and the new roles of women in politics. Through such efforts we come as close as remains possible to establishing some contact with the wider historical concerns expressed in the *Party Systems* volume.

7. OTHER SOCIOSTRUCTURAL INFORMATION

Although the priorities up to this point already represent quite a load on an average interview schedule that has other goals to fulfill as well, there are naturally many items we have failed to mention that warrant interest, especially in particular research contexts. Among the more generally interesting of these, perhaps, is the number of memberships in voluntary associations (in addition to labor union and religious associations mentioned above). Military experience, home-ownership, or the possession of other major durable goods that may provide some indication of life-style also can be valuable, although perhaps of less cross-national interest.

One variable that is almost invariably ignored is the number of children per family unit. On the face of it, this is a rather drab variable that could rarely be expected to show more than a trace relationship with partisanship. However, even a slight difference in birthrate between adherents of different parties, if sufficiently persistent over an extended period of time, can have significant effect in generating secular trends in balance of strength between parties if other things remain equal. A canvass of the number of children under twenty-one reared in the household of the interview that registers their ages as well can produce some suggestive simulations of such trends.

II. Party Location

Although our commission was limited to independent variables with high explanatory power, a number of worthwhile remarks may be made about the sample survey treatment of one of the key dependent variables, or what we conceptualize generally as "party location." Strategies of measurement here can be quite various.

The conventional measure available from most surveys has to do with a particular vote, either intended, hypothetical, or one just cast. Whereas an item like this is almost certain to be posed, it has several deficiencies as a general measure of party location. Some fraction of the sample at least is likely to go unclassified, representing people who don't know how they would handle a hypothetical vote at the moment, or who were nonvoters in the election of reference. Moreover, because of attractive (local) personalities or momentary shifts in party fortune, the party chosen for a specific vote need not coincide with a more generalized party preference that has been stable over a longer period of time.

Therefore there is some advantage in posing, beyond a vote question itself, some item that attempts to measure a more enduring sense of attachment or commitment to one of the available parties, along the lines of the "party identification" measure we have always used.[5] Such a question also paves the way quite naturally for further probes to establish the relative strength of this sense of commitment, an interesting variable in its own right both as an index of partisan mobilization of the individual and, more collectively speaking, the partisan inertia of the system.

Systems involving a multiplicity of parties, while posing certain analytic problems, also offer exciting potentials for enriching the measurement of partisan location while amplifying the diagnostic view of the investigator. Whereas it may remain important to secure a separate estimate of strength of attachment to the party most favored, it is then extremely worthwhile to go on and establish whatever further hierarchy of preferences the respondent may entertain with respect to the other parties in the system.

This fuller information has a variety of advantages. It can readily be shown to discriminate ideological "wings" of the larger parties, which are meaningful in terms of intra-party differences on further independent items tapping attitudes on relevant policy issues. More important, perhaps, is the fact that multidimensional analyses of the Coombsian "unfolding" type[6] can be employed on the total set of preference orders to establish (1) the primary dimensions along which the public organizes its view of party competition; (2) the relative strength of those dimensions in generating the aggregation of rank orders; (3) some sense of relative distances between parties in such a space. The latter information should be particularly helpful in estimating the lines along which interparty shifts of support are more or less likely to occur, and of course any more objective evidence as to cleavage dimensions perceived in the constellation of national parties gears in perfectly with the concerns of the *Party Systems* volume.

Operationally, the necessary preference orders can be established rather painlessly, even where parties are quite numerous. In a system involving six parties, for example, the question on own party identification can be followed by items like ——"What other party would be your next preference (if you could not vote for)? And your next preference after that? What party would you be least likely to vote for under any circumstance? What party would you most want to avoid after that one?" If a list of parties is offered to the respondent in such a sequence, care should be taken to randomize the order so that no familiar dimensionality (e.g., Left to Right) is artificially stimulated. It may generally be preferable not to offer such a list, for while the respondent may be unable to recall all of the parties and hence fail to provide a complete order, such a procedure yields further information as to what parties are naturally salient for him. In the most complete procedure the respondent might be reminded of other parties he is forgetting after salience is established and registered on the questionnaire, in order to provide the fuller rank order for analytic uses where this is desirable.

III. Cross-Group Attitudes

Conceptually, the establishment of full party-preference orders rather than leaving the problem of party location at a single "preferred" party is but another special instance of our recommendation, made several times earlier, that in the study of cleavages it is important not only to locate the individual in one of the competing groups as is conventionally done, but also to assess the degree of hostility or indifference he feels toward what are, for him, the "outgroups." The latter information is rarely provided in conventional surveys.

Often these cross-group attitudes are left to be inferred quite indirectly through the use of other relevant material in the questionnaire. Thus, for example, in the American system where Catholics are the main beneficiaries of any public funds that can be diverted from public education for one or another type of aid to private education, resistance to such policies on the part of mainstream Protestants can be loosely taken as some indication of anti-Catholic feeling. On the other hand, it is quite apparent that such indirect inferences leave a great deal to be desired, for there is no reason to believe that a good measure of anti-Catholic feeling would show more than moderate correlations with reactions to such an educational policy. Obviously a whole cluster of unrelated attitudes toward education and the role of government also help to influence these policy attitudes. Therefore we have recently been experimenting with more direct ways to assess cross-group attitudes efficiently in our electoral surveys.

One format we have tested seems successful enough on the basis of preliminary work to be worth reporting here.[7] Among its virtues is its extreme simplicity, although the initial explanation to the respondent tends to be more elaborate than usual. The interviewer presents the respondent with a card showing a scale running from 0 to 100. He explains the scale as follows:

There are many groups in America that try to get the government or the American people to see things more their way. We would like to get your feelings toward some of these groups. On this card is something that looks like a thermometer. We call it a "feeling thermometer" because it measures your feeling toward groups. Here's how it works. If you don't know too much about a group, or don't feel particularly warm or cold toward them, then you should place them in the middle, at the 50-degree mark.

If you have a warm feeling toward a group, or feel favorably toward it, you would give it a score somewhere between 50 and 100 depending on how warm your feeling is toward the group. On the other hand, if you don't feel very favorably toward some of these groups—if there are some you don't care for too much—then you would place them somewhere between 0 and 50.

Our first group is the. . . . Where would you put them on the thermometer?

Respondents seem to have no trouble with the idea, and in more recent uses we have abbreviated the instructions considerably. Then ratings for a sequence of groups can be elicited. In one use, for example, we covered fifteen groups: farmers, liberals, Southerners, Catholics, big business, Democrats, military, Jews, whites, labor unions, Republicans, Easterners, Protestants, Negroes, and conservatives. In another use we have applied the scheme to relatively radical political organizations of the Left and the Right. In a study of the 1967 elections in France twenty-two objects were assessed in these terms, including: six prominent political leaders; six major political parties; four nations (*les Américains, les Anglais, les Allemands et les Russes*); and a variety of interest groups: *les syndicats, le clergé, les petits commerçants, le grand patronat, les fonctionnaires et l'armée*.[8]

While work has not yet begun with the French materials and only a limited amount is finished with the American version, enough ground has been covered in the latter case to indicate an apparent success of the measurement. When ratings on two naturally polar groups are elicited, it is reasonable to form the difference in the two ratings as an index of feeling (which we have tended to "norm" again between 0 and 100). The fit of such measures with other more qualitative measures whose behavior we know in great detail is excellent. Thus, for example, the average values of the Democratic-Republican difference scores for the set of people who elsewhere in the questionnaire insist that they are "independents" where party identification is concerned, is 50.04, or exactly in the middle of the scale. More impressive still, the absolute distances between the means for the rest of party identification categories reflect beautifully a good deal of information we have concerning apparent relative distances (assessed by criterion variables) between the ordered classes of identifiers. Or again, about 40 percent of the electorate fails to give any differential rating to the terms "conservative" and "liberal," a figure matching other "recognition" tests we have given. And among Republican partisans in 1964, for example, impressive correlations between conservative-liberal difference scores and preference for Goldwater over more liberal candidates were apparent. These are but a few of the internal validation checks that have been most reassuring.

Although it may seem somewhat risky to ask for reactions to groups without providing any more context than the question gives, such a measurement of relatively pure effect becomes a strength, once given some outside evidence that the item does draw meaningful responses. In fact, we were looking for some measure that could be posed intelligibly in exactly the same form three and four decades hence, and it is hard to see why this would not be true of the pure-affect measure. More detailed contexts for the measurement would of course tend to obsolesce with the passage of events over long periods of time. Moreover, the pure-affect measure promotes somewhat greater confidence in comparisons if intensity of cross-group hostilities across varying cleavage lines at the same point in time within a country than one would feel for measures burdened with group-specific contextual detail.

And, of course, it is just this property we tend to seek in cross-national measurement, so that while comparative experimentation has not yet been completed, we are optimistic that the measure may show unusual value for these kinds of comparisons as well. With such increasingly sensitive tools the study of these cleavages, and their expression in party politics, may be progressively expanded.

Notes

1. G. Almond and S. Verba, *The Civic Culture* (Princeton: Princeton University Press, 1963).

2. S. Lipset and S. Rokkan, eds., *Party Systems and Voter Alignments* (New York: Free Press, 1967).

3. We feel that the *Party Systems* book, even in its most past-oriented parts (such as the opening chapter), is quite congenial to a future-oriented discussion. This is true most notably because the more intensive exploitation of history puts an emphasis on time-change or temporal process, which fits the needs of future modeling admirably. It also fits the change in data resources from the single cross-section survey to trend series that now stretch over a decade or two, which certainly should affect the way we construct our questionnaires.

4. G. Lenski, *The Religious Factor* (New York: Doubleday, 1961).

5. The standard question we have used in our two-party system is, "Generally speaking, do you usually think of yourself as a Republican, a Democrat, an Independent, or what? [*If Republican or Democrat*] Would you call yourself a strong——or a not very strong——? [*If Independent*]. Do you think of yourself as closer to the Republican or Democratic party?" The use of major party names in the root question is of course awkward in a system of multiple parties, requiring some revision of the question structure, although the essential features of the item—habitual self-identification—can be preserved.

6. C. Coombs, *A Theory of Data* (New York: John Wiley, 1964).

7. This format was worked out by Dr. Aage Clausen.

8. The French instructions provide a sample of an abbreviated form:

> Il y a des personnes et des groupes qui influencent le Gouvernement ou l'opinion publique. Nous aimerions savoir quels sont vos sentiments à leur égard. Voulez-vous mettre une note de 0 à 100 aux personnes ou groupes que je vais vous citer en fonction de la sympathie que vous éprouviez pour eux: (*Tendre la liste avec l'échelle de sympathie*)
>
> 100 signifie que vous avez beaucoup de sympathie;
>   0 signifie que vous ne les aimez pas du tout;
> 50 signifie soit que vous n'êtes ni pour ni contre eux, ou
>   soit que vous ne connaissez pas grand chose sur eux.

Index